ENCYCLOPEDIA *of*
Recreation *and* Leisure
in AMERICA

Editorial Board

ENCYCLOPEDIA *of*
Recreation *and* Leisure
in AMERICA

Gary S. Cross
EDITOR IN CHIEF

Volume

2

Magazines – Zoos
Index

CHARLES SCRIBNER'S SONS
An imprint of Thomson Gale, a part of The Thomson Corporation

Detroit • New York • San Francisco • San Diego • New Haven, Conn. • Waterville, Maine • London • Munich

Encyclopedia of Recreation and Leisure in America

Gary S. Cross, Editor in Chief

Permissions Department
The Gale Group, Inc.
27500 Drake Rd.
Farmington Hills, MI 48331-3535
Permissions Hotline:
248-699-8006 or 800-877-4253, ext. 8006
Fax: 248-699-8074 or 800-762-4058

Library of Congress Cataloging-in-Publication Data

Encyclopedia of recreation and leisure in America / Gary S. Cross, editor in chief.
   v. cm. — (The Scribner American civilization series)
   Includes bibliographical references and index.
   ISBN 0-684-31265-4 (set hardcover : alk. paper) — ISBN 0-684-31266-2 (v. 1) — ISBN 0-684-31267-0 (v. 2)
   1. Leisure—United States—Encyclopedias. 2. Recreation—United States—Encyclopedias. I. Cross, Gary S. II. Series.
   GV53.E53 2004
   790'.0973'03—dc22

                                                            2004004617

This title is also available as an e-book.
ISBN 0-684-31450-9

Contact your Gale sales representative for ordering information

Printed in the United States of America
10 9 8 7 6 5 4 3 2

ENCYCLOPEDIA *of* Recreation *and* Leisure *in* AMERICA

MAGAZINES, MEN'S

Men's magazines are, and have been throughout American history, a varied lot. Girlie magazines, business periodicals, sports reviews, physique pictorials, veterans' newsletters, scientific journals, gay-themed publications, science-fiction "fanzines," and certain professional and alumni magazines have been aimed at a male readership. Even the *Saturday Evening Post,* which is justly remembered as the quintessential family magazine, was, in the late nineteenth century and early twentieth century, a men's magazine. Moreover, family and non–gender-specific magazines promote and reflect certain cultural notions of masculinity. Rather than exhaustively covering the history of magazines with a male readership, this review outlines changing representations of masculinity in American magazines aimed at men. It situates this discussion in histories of gender and magazine publishing within the United States.

The Development of the American Magazine Industry

American magazines before the Revolution were, in general, poor imitations of successful London magazines such as *Gentlemen*'s and the *London Magazine.* The *Boston Weekly* and the *American Magazine and Monthly Chronicle* directly mimicked the established style of these magazines by placing political articles, commentary on manners, plays, and sermons side by side. In many cases, the articles for early American magazines were copied directly out of English publications. Although men wrote (and presumably read) the bulk of the material, many pre-Revolutionary magazines also included verse written by and for women. The magazines, then, provided for a gendered, but not homosocial, middle-class and elite readership.

During the late eighteenth and early nineteenth centuries, three changes in American magazine publishing occurred: (1) many magazines became Americanized in content rather than imitations of British publications; (2) separate magazines for women and men emerged; (3) increasingly, periodicals were aimed at specialized audiences. In keeping with the ideals of the Revolution, magazines such as *Royal American* and *United States Magazine* sought to textually demonstrate independence by printing articles that examined American politics, manners, and fashion. The emergence of an ideology of republican motherhood and the concomitant emphasis upon separate masculine and feminine spheres resulted in the establishment of publications for women. Conversely, a greater number of editors at "general" magazines began to assume an exclusively male readership.

The masculine ideal promulgated by these magazines was a man of responsibility and independence: a self-reliant American who filled his station with dignity. M. L. Weems's portrayal of a virtuous George Washington, who was unable to tell a lie, epitomized this representation of republican manhood. Selections from his *Life of George Washington,* particularly the famous story of the cherry tree, appeared in numerous post-Revolutionary publications.

The early nineteenth century marked the development of market segmentation within the American magazine industry, a process begun by religious communities seeking to communicate with the faithful. By 1825, there were magazines focusing upon such diverse topics as child rearing, agriculture, antislavery, colleges, the theater, travel, and partisan politics. In part, this segmentation reflected (and produced) the greater social prominence of the male scientific expert. Magazines such as *The Medical Repository* (1791–1824) created and supported homosocial communities that developed in scientific fields such as medicine and mineralogy. Most of these scientific publications were circulated to interested amateurs and gentlemen scholars, although they were the precursors of modern professional journals. Laurel Thatcher Ulrich's work examining the life of midwife Martha Ballard aptly demonstrates one of the consequences of this discursive production of the masculine expert: the discrediting of women's (and non-bourgeois men's) forms of knowledge in areas increasingly deemed to be under the purview of science.

However one should not think of the magazine industry during this "golden age" as solely the purview of the privileged classes. The market diversification also allowed for the emergence of publications written for the common reader, albeit a literate one. "Miscellanies" flourished throughout the country, circulating information within farming communities and sometimes purveying national news. "Pornographic" circulars (with depictions of scantily clad women) seem to have been distributed relatively widely in mid-century working-class saloons and among Civil War soldiers. These publications circulated in a "sporting male" culture that emerged in northern urban areas in the 1830s and 1840s, reflected in *The Spirit of the Times,* a newspaper dedicated to reporting on sports such as horse racing, rowing, and especially baseball. Additionally, two publications aimed at African Americans emerged in 1838, *The Mirror of Liberty* and *The National Reformer.* Although both publications proved to be short-lived, they set the stage for later magazines with a predominantly black readership.

The Rise of Mass Circulation Magazines

Immediately following the Civil War, the magazine industry expanded in step with the rapidly developing American economy. There were 700 magazines at the close of the war; twenty years later, in 1885, there were approximately 3,300 magazines. Fully a quarter of these magazines were published in New York City, indicating the extent to which the developing industry was tied to the urbanization and commercialization endemic to the

period. The rural "miscellanies" did not disappear. Many professional journals also emerged in the late nineteenth century—to name but one example, the *Journal of the American Medical Association* was founded in 1883. But neither the professional journals nor rural publications formed the basis of the development of the magazine industry in the second half of the nineteenth century.

Magazines that served as accompaniments to middle-class leisure activity and consumerism drove the increase in the number of publications and their circulation figures. This was the case prior to 1893, but especially after this date magazines were to become a central medium of consumerism in the emerging modern, mass culture. Within a few months of one another in 1893, *Munsey's, McClure's,* and *Cosmopolitan* slashed their newsstand prices and relied upon advertising revenue to reach audiences that would soon number in the hundreds of thousands. *Munsey's* and *McClure's* are justly remembered for their sensationalistic, muckraking articles, but it was as cornucopias of marketing that they changed the face of the industry. By 1898, *Munsey's* contained roughly eighty pages of advertisements in each issue. Other publications soon followed suit, and these newly commercialized magazines became staples at newsstands around the country. Although advertisements in these magazines were aimed at both men and women, the advertisers made their appeals on different grounds. As Historian Tom Pendergast has written, "While women were being taught the logic of desire, a logic based upon what the product could do for them, men were schooled in the more familiar logic of reason, a logic based upon the intrinsic quality of the merchandise. For women goods could transform; for men goods would perform" (p. 60).

If magazines at the time of the Revolution presented the honorable man of stature as the masculine ideal, by the late nineteenth century the "cult" of the self-made man was increasingly central to the rhetoric of magazines. This is true of *Munsey's* and *McClure's*—both publishers were veritable Horatio Algers themselves—but, given the lack of editorial vision in both publications, their representation of masculinity necessarily lacked consistency. A more constant vision of masculinity was to be found in another magazine that developed a mass circulation in the wake of the transformations of 1893: the *Saturday Evening Post.* Although it had nominally been in circulation for many years, the modern *Post* was expressly developed as a men's magazine in the late nineteenth century. The masculine ideal represented in the magazine was that of a self-made, successful businessman mastering the rapid capitalist expansion of the period. Yet his success was attributable to old-fashioned values that would not have seemed out of place in Revolutionary publications: honesty, diligence, and thrift. This hegemonic representation of masculinity—the *Post* remained one of the widest circulating magazines well into the twentieth century—can be termed the self-made businessman of worth. Largely absent from the pages of the publication were the competition and conflict so central to turn-of-the-century capitalism. Instead, the heroes of the *Saturday Evening Post* were men who (naturally) rose to the top of their chosen profession because of the strength of their character. This traditionalist rhetoric was remarkably successful: long after *Munsey's* and *McClure's* had folded, advertisers and middle-class readers flocked to the *Saturday Evening Post* .

The *National Police Gazette* was another, very different magazine that emerged as a mass circulation publication at the same period. Founded in 1845, by the 1890s its advertising rates and circulation had risen dramatically along with other mass-market publications of the era. The *Police Gazette* had long printed stories covering crime and mayhem, and particularly cases associated with sexuality and urbanity. During the first decades of its run, it managed to maintain a veneer of moral approbation. By the 1880s, this veil had been lifted, and the articles and line drawings reveled in the sensationalism and titillation of urban vice. It also included a host of articles on boxing and other "manly" sports. The *Saturday Evening Post* 's traditionalist man of character would presumably be at odds with the *Police Gazette* 's representation of pugilistic, sexualized manhood. As Howard P. Chudacoff demonstrates, the *Police Gazette* flourished in an urban bachelor subculture; the *Post* was the magazine for the family man. Yet, both publications were popular among middle-class men, and probably attracted many of the same readers, a complication to simplistic accounts of the history of masculinity. What the *Police Gazette* lacked in paid circulation it made up for in informal circuits of exchange: it was ubiquitous in saloons, barbershops, and firehouses.

Consumerist Masculinity and Twentieth-Century Magazines

During the first decades of the twentieth century, a number of mass circulation magazines emerged with a distinctly masculine focus. In addition to the *Saturday Evening Post,* consumers had the option of choosing *Vanity Fair, American Magazine, Collier's, Athletic World,* or *Sporting Life.* Each had a somewhat different readership to match their varying presentations of manhood: *American Magazine* appealed to a more urbane audience than *Collier's,* but was less elitist than *Vanity Fair.* Despite the focus on men in each, none of these

Hugh Hefner. *Playboy* magazine founder Hugh M. Hefner (1926–) sits on a TWA Superjet in January 1962 with Cynthia Maddox, who was featured on the cover of the following month's issue. © *Corbis*

magazines was explicitly a men's magazine, including the *Saturday Evening Post* after 1908. The same was true of the magazines with a predominantly black readership that began publishing during this period, including Booker T. Washington's *Colored American,* J. Max Barber's *The Voice of the Negro,* and W.E.B. DuBois's *Crisis.* Whether advocates of a success ethic for black men (*Colored American*) or critical of racist barriers to success (*The Voice of the Negro, Crisis*), these publications forwarded a vision of idealized masculinity similar to the *Saturday Evening Post* 's hardworking patriarch with moral self-discipline.

The masculine ideal was presented very differently in *Esquire,* launched in 1933. *Esquire* was written for the urbane man-about-town, or at least for a man who so imagined himself. Rather than moral self-discipline, *Esquire* 's man of distinction was noted for his style, wit, and consumption. Line drawings of scantily clad women, the famous Vargas Girls, first appeared in the magazine in 1940, but since Esquire's founding, its attitude toward sexuality (and the masculine gaze) was markedly different from its mainstream predecessors. The period from 1930 to 1960 was central to the transformation of American men's clothing. Style, leisure, and color all became increasingly central to men's wardrobes, and *Esquire* was seen by many contemporaries to have created the trend (though a menswear trade publication begun in 1931, *Apparel Arts,* can best claim that distinction). Through its features on subjects such as clothing, home furnishings, literature, and music, to name but a few, *Esquire* represents the integration of men into the consumerist logic of desire: the man of distinction is increasingly judged by the quality of his tastes, not character.

This forging of masculinity with consumerist desire became even more explicit in *Playboy,* first published in 1951 by former *Esquire* writer and editor Hugh Hefner. By the end of the 1950s, *Playboy* had become by far the most widely circulated men's magazine in the United States, indicating a transformation in masculinity writ large. *Playboy*'s nude pictures of women were the most obvious draw for readers. But the other features of the magazine were more than just window dressing: there were many other, more explicit magazines available with much more limited circulations. The discourse in *Playboy* centered upon the pursuit of pleasure and a "cool" aesthetic based upon urbanity, high culture, and modernity. The *Playboy* bachelor was definitively anti-marriage, yet resoundingly domestic. Above all, he was a consumer. The magazine served as an etiquette manual of sorts to guide the self-made man to independence and pleasure through consumption. *Playboy* mobilized elements of European aristocratic culture and consumerist femininity for middle-class, masculine readers. The result is a rhetoric that is deeply invested both in independence and conformity, sexual rebellion and domesticity. If Hefner depicted himself and his idealized man as something of a rebel, it represented a limited challenge, since *Playboy* commodified rebelliousness itself in the service of the spectacle of consumer capitalism.

Other important magazines emerged mid-century that would forward consumerist masculinity, if in more limited form. *Sports Illustrated* began in 1954 by writing about yachting, cricket and other blue-blood sports, but soon followed the Eisenhower-era spectator sports boom to cover more popular, and marketable, athletics. *Physique Pictorial* literalized consumerist masculinity by placing male, muscular bodies on display as commodities for homosexuals and others. *Ebony,* though not a men's magazine, became the first commercially successful magazine for African Americans after 1945 by depicting images of black success and the baubles that served as rewards for this success. In this new positive spin on the black experience, gone was the Victorian moral code of hard work, thrift, and honesty. Also absent was any substantial discussion of racism. Finally, in the wake of *Playboy*'s success, a slew of ever more sexually explicit

men's magazines were formed, the most notable being *Penthouse* and *Hustler* .

By the 1970s, the connection between masculinity and consumerism was so established that product-driven men's magazines had emerged to match every masculine interest in America: cars, sports, sex, tools, bodybuilding, guns, camping, and many others. This trend has continued since 1990 with the launch of a new crop of men's publications led by *Maxim.* Though little work has been done examining these magazines, this proliferation would seem to provide historians with a way to move beyond unitary conceptions of masculinity and instead map a range of possibility. And certainly as both cause and symptom of mass consumer culture, magazines and print cultures can continue to provide a wealth of information about the historical development of American consumerism.

See also: Comic Book Reading, Comic Magazines, Genre Reading, Magazines, Women's, Men's Leisure Lifestyles

BIBLIOGRAPHY

Chudacoff, Howard P. *The Age of the Bachelor: Creating an American Subculture.* Princeton, N.J.: Princeton University Press, 1999.

Kimmel, Michael. *Manhood in America: A Cultural History.* New York: Free Press, 1996.

Mott, Frank Luther. *A History of American Magazines, 1741–1850.* New York: D. Appleton and Company, 1930.

Osgerby, Bill. *Playboys in Paradise: Masculinity, Youth and Leisure-Style in Modern America.* Oxford, U.K.: Berg, 2001.

Pendergast, Tom. *Creating the Modern Man: American Magazines and Consumer Culture, 1900–1950.* Columbia: University of Missouri Press, 2000.

Tebbel, John, and Mary Ellen Zuckerman. *The Magazine in America, 1741–1990.* New York: Oxford University Press, 1991.

William R. Scott

MAGAZINES, WOMEN'S

Women's magazines, which are enormously popular in the United States, entertain and educate readers, help create and sustain mass markets for consumer goods, and provide a unique glimpse into women's and commercial culture. Hundreds of women's magazines have been short-lived; several, however, have lasted over a century.

From the *Ladies' Magazine and Repository of Entertaining Knowledge*, founded in 1792, to *More*, founded in 1998, women's magazines have defined as well as responded to women's needs and aspirations. They address women as they are and as they hope to be. As Margaret Beetham argues, the woman reader is a real entity, but she is also an ideal, something the magazine hopes to construct in its pages and through its influence. As they promise to meet women readers' needs, magazines must also always leave enough unsaid to justify the following month's edition. Ephemeral, attractive, and timely, women's magazines have both a fascinating history and a promising future.

The Early History

Although the earliest magazines in the United States targeted men, they discussed and debated women's roles and laid the groundwork for periodicals aimed primarily or exclusively at women. Eighteenth-century publications discussed the role of women in the colonial context, debating the degree to which "woman" could be equated with "citizen." In the postrevolutionary period, women discussed these issues and a range of others in their own female publications. Patricia Okker explored the career of Sarah Josepha Hale, the first successful woman editor, who edited the *Ladies' Magazine* from 1828 until 1836, and then *Godey's Lady's Book* from 1837 to 1877. Not only did Hale carve out a space for herself and other women in the periodicals industry, but she also influenced the development of nineteenth-century literary culture. Hale promoted the notion of separate spheres, an essentialist argument about the differences between women and men that located women's sphere in the home, men's sphere in the public world. Nevertheless, many of *Godey's Lady's Book*'s features, including its signature fashion, poetry, and sentimental fiction, helped to define and encourage a female world that found expression, at least in part, in the commercial culture of magazines, advertising, and shopping.

The "Big Six," the Seven Sisters, and More

The commercial world that *Godey's Lady's Book* tentatively promoted found greater expression in the late nineteenth century with the founding of the "big six" women's magazines: *Ladies' Home Journal, Woman's Home Companion, Good Housekeeping, Delineator, Pictorial Review,* and *McCall's*. With the simultaneous development of national advertising, these publications, whether directed at women's home lives or fashion pursuits, flourished. They also shifted the editorial focus of women's magazines even further from literary to commercial culture. Technolog-

ical improvements in printing facilitated the production of magazines, while the introduction of rural free delivery, increased urbanization, advances in literacy, and the spread of electricity combined to enlarge potential target audiences. The rise of nationally branded consumer goods and national advertising further supported publishers' efforts to reach the reading public. Advertising served as the intermediary between consumers and American industry, magazines as the intermediary between advertisers and consumers. Because women were thought to purchase over 80 percent of household goods, the middle-class white woman became the darling of manufacturers, advertisers, and magazines.

In *Inarticulate Longing* Jennifer Scanlon explores the significance of the most successful of the "big six," the *Ladies' Home Journal,* whose circulation reached 1 million in January 1904. The *Journal,* particularly under the influence of its most famous editor, Edward Bok, defined twentieth-century womanhood primarily through consumer culture. Known as the "monthly Bible of the American home," the *Ladies' Home Journal* promoted what Bok called "the simple life," a world in which simple fashions, small homes, and community life forged women's identities. At the same time, Bok's relationships with advertisers fostered the movement of advertising from the back of women's magazines to the front, from a position of marginality to one of centrality in the magazines' presentation, editorial position, and mission. The *Ladies' Home Journal*'s conservative agenda regarding women's education, suffrage, and paid employment was influenced at least in part by advertising: the woman at home acted out her consumer role more fully than did women with outside interests. At the same time, images of consumer culture offered promises about the excitement of worlds outside the home. In the face of conflicting messages, women readers actively read and responded to the *Journal* and other magazines, negotiating womanhood and consumer culture in an era of change. As Scanlon puts it, women found not only instruction but also a voice for their "inarticulate longings" in the pages of the *Journal.*

The *Ladies' Home Journal* and its contemporaries proved slow to address the needs of women outside their limited target audience. Editors lamented the choices of middle-class married women who worked by choice and pitied those women who worked by necessity, but neither of those groups of women found themselves courted by women's service magazines and their advertisers. African American women found themselves in the magazines as the butt of jokes in editorial pages or as service providers to white consumers in the ads; otherwise, they remained absent. Scanlon argues that advertising agencies and women's magazines ignored African American women

Oprah Winfrey. In April 2000 the premiere issue of *O* magazine is introduced at a press conference in New York City by its creator Oprah Winfrey (1954–). Published by Hearst Magazines, the monthly publication focused on items of interest to women. © *AP/Wide World Photos*

even when industry research demonstrated that this group of women had high literacy rates and consumer spending rates.

In the years following World War I, however, the magazine industry sought out working-class white women with new genres: the movie fan magazine, the detective magazine, and, most significantly, the confessional magazine. Publisher Bernarr MacFadden, reading letters from readers of *Physical Culture,* his popular men's magazine, realized that readers, including women, desired frank discussions of sexual and marital issues. His first confessional publication, *True Story,* debuted in 1919 and quickly came to rival even the *Ladies' Home Journal* in national circulation. By 1927, it reached newsstand sales of over 2 million per issue. As economic conditions improved, working-class readers of the 1920s also purchased middle-class magazines in increasing numbers. Advertisers and magazine publishers did not seriously consider African American women as a specific target audience,

however, until 1970, when *Essence* hit the newsstands. *Essence* stands out because, in addition to beauty, fashion, and fitness features, the magazine has focused on black women's struggles in contemporary American society. It also proved influential in opening up the modeling profession to women of color.

Grocery store magazines arrived on the scene in the 1930s, offering depression-era tips for low-cost meals and inviting women to shop in supermarkets rather than corner stores. *Family Circle,* founded in 1932, typifies the genre. A tabloid weekly, offered free until 1946, it quickly made its way into thousands of chain grocery stores and then into the homes of female consumers. Supermarket magazines continue to hold a significant share of the magazine market—and continue to place food purchasing and preparation responsibilities with women. At the same time, they, too, changed to recognize women's broader roles by featuring women who "made a difference" in their communities.

Seventeen magazine premiered in 1944 and introduced a new market: the teenager. Advertisers took notice, particularly advertisers for cosmetics, fashion, and toiletries. As in other women's magazines, editorial matter complements advertising in teen magazines, and girls receive strong messages to participate in and cultivate identities through consumer culture. In recent years, beauty magazines for teens and for women have incorporated more socially relevant editorial matter, focusing on women's finances, relationship violence, and sexual harassment and discrimination. Nevertheless, women's service magazines retain a significant share of the women's magazine market, although the "big six" list has been replaced by the "seven sisters": *Family Circle, Woman's Day, Good Housekeeping, Ladies' Home Journal, McCall's, Redbook,* and *Better Homes and Gardens.* These publications retain a focus on women's homemaking roles, but each has in its own way responded to changes in women's lives and aspirations by addressing the competing interests of individual women, work, and families. Despite the ups and downs in that process of accommodation, the seven sisters alone had a readership of almost 34 million consumers at the end of the twentieth century. Newer magazines focused specifically on women's complicated work and family lives. In addition to their role as aide to women who negotiated the double day, as Ellen McCracken notes, magazines such as *Working Woman* and *Working Mother* attempted to solve the problem that advertising agencies identified early in the twentieth century: working women were too busy to shop. These magazines served as a kind of consumer clearinghouse for the woman whose double-duty day could not easily accommodate the triple duty of committed consumption.

Competing Interests

Virtually all magazines face the dilemma of pleasing readers and advertisers both, despite the competing interests of the two audiences. As early as 1920, Upton Sinclair bemoaned advertising's influence in his muckraking study *The Brass Check: A Study of American Journalism.* Sinclair argued about magazines, essentially, as many have argued more recently about television, that editorial matter existed simply to fill the space between the advertisements. In 1973, Herbert Schiller argued in *The Mind Managers* that advertising's reach discourages editors from addressing controversial topics. In *The Lady Persuaders* (1960), Helen Woodward argued that women's magazines claim to be public-service tools but primarily function to serve the needs of advertisers. Women's magazines have faced more aggressive attempts at editorial control by advertisers than have other types of magazines. Feminist journalist and activist Gloria Steinem provided a thorough exposé of the control advertisers held over women's magazines in a *Ms.* magazine article in 1990. Founded in 1972, *Ms.* magazine operated with the dual goals of inviting women into the women's liberation movement and persuading the advertising industry to treat female consumers with a great deal more respect. More successful in the first goal than in the second, *Ms.* ran ad-free for a number of years and in 2004 still included advertisements for nonprofit organizations and feminist publications.

The Future of Women's Magazines

A new form of new magazine emerged in the 1990s: the zine. These do-it-yourself grassroots publications, amateur in production and often more political in content than commercial magazines, come in print and cyber formats. As Karen Green and Tristan Taormino demonstrate in *A Girl's Guide to Taking Over the World,* zines provide a more direct means of communication among girls and women. Operating arguably outside the commercial culture, zines demonstrate the diversity of girls' and women's voices and allow for some of the woman-to-woman identification women's magazines promise but often fail to provide. They often mock the invitations to beauty offered in traditional magazines or, alternately, expose the dangers of subscribing to mainstream ideals of beauty through personal accounts of eating disorders, androgynous rather than feminine coding in dress and appearance, and resistance to dominant heterosexuality. It remains to be seen, however, whether zines will prove ephemeral or remain a strong part of the magazine scene in the twenty-first century.

In the meantime, new commercial magazines for women and girls continued to emerge, and the new and old alike vied for readers and advertising. Specialized publications targeted women in terms of ethnicity, class, and status: One could purchase a magazine that was aimed at single women, mothers, working women, Latinas, homemakers, women over forty, brides, and so forth. Other magazines targeted women in terms of interest: fitness, beauty, health, decorating. Women's service magazines struggled to maintain an identity in the face of social change. *House and Garden,* in response to changes in women's lives, changed its name to *HG* and began to feature people as often as it did homes. Other service magazines developed online editions to reach women as they stole a few minutes of alone time at work or at home. Feminist magazines like *Bust* attempted to reach young women and bridge the competing and often conflicting needs of feminist readers and consumer culture. Researchers debate the degree to which women's magazines have changed with the times, reliant as those magazines are on the dictates of consumer culture. Ahmed Belkaoui and Janice Belkaoui argue that, as the portrayal of women in domestic roles decreases, their portrayal as sexual objects increases. Nevertheless, the world of women's magazines was an exciting and financially lucrative one in the early twenty-first century. New publications alternately highlighted or collapsed differences among women as they attempted to make it in the vibrant, culturally complex, and highly competitive environment.

See also: Genre Reading, Magazines, Men's, Women's Leisure Lifestyles

BIBLIOGRAPHY

Beetham, Margaret. *A Magazine of Her Own? Domesticity and Desire in the Woman's Magazine, 1800–1914.* London: Routledge, 1996.

Belkaoui, Ahmed, and Janice M. Belkaoui. "A Comparative Analysis of the Roles Portrayed by Women in Print Advertisements." *Journal of Marketing Research* 13 (1976): 168–172.

Endres, Kathleen L., and Therese L. Lueck. *Women's Periodicals in the United States: Consumer Magazines.* Westport, Conn.: Greenwood Press, 1995.

Garvey, Ellen Gruber. *The Adman in the Parlor: Magazines and the Gendering of Consumer Culture, 1880s to 1910s.* New York: Oxford University Press, 1996.

Green, Karen, and Tristan Taormino, eds. *A Girl's Guide to Taking Over the World: Writings from the Girl Zine Revolution.* New York: St. Martin's Press, 1997.

McCracken, Ellen. *Decoding Women's Magazines: From Mademoiselle to Ms.* New York: St. Martin's Press, 1993.

Okker, Patricia. *Our Sister Editors: Sarah J. Hale and the Tradition of Nineteenth-Century American Women Editors.* Athens: University of Georgia Press, 1995.

Scanlon, Jennifer. *Inarticulate Longings: The Ladies' Home Journal, Gender, and the Promises of Consumer Culture.* New York: Routledge, 1995.

Schiller, Herbert. *The Mind Managers.* Boston: Beacon Press, 1973.

Sinclair, Upton. *The Brass Check: A Study of American Journalism.* Pasadena, Calif.: Upton Sinclair, 1920.

Steinem, Gloria. "Sex, Lies, and Advertising," *Ms* (July/August 1990): 18–28.

Thom, Mary. *Inside Ms.: Twenty-five Years of the Magazine and the Feminist Movement.* New York: Henry Holt and Company, 1997.

Woodward, Helen. *The Lady Persuaders.* New York: Obolensky, 1960.

Zuckerman, Mary E. *A History of Popular Women's Magazines in the United States, 1792–1995.* Westport, Conn.: Greenwood Press, 1998.

Jennifer Scanlon

MANUSCRIPTS

See *Books and Manuscripts*

MARATHONS

The marathon footrace of 26.2 miles emerged from the modern Olympics, but has evolved into city festivals fed by commerce, competitiveness, and individualism. Although talented athletes run marathons for prize money or as Olympic qualifiers, marathons also serve as popular recreation and spectacles. Unlike most other athletic contests, in the marathon, professionals and amateurs compete in the same event. Tracing its roots to the nation's early years, the marathon progressed along with industrialization from class-based and ethnic rivalry to mass and segmented markets. Over time, the marathon's meaning as an athletic event has shifted along with technology, social change, and leisure trends.

In the antebellum era, long-distance footraces of varying distances proved to be one of the most popular spectator sports. Featuring prize money, tippling, and betting, the races drew large crowds and often focused on interracial or international competition (and sometimes included interspecies competition, including men versus horses). Traditional Highland games sponsored by the nation's Caledonian Clubs charged admission and offered purses for long-distance footraces. Caledonian Clubs not only inspired the first collegiate track competition in the 1860s, but also the exclusive New York Athletic Club's founding. A venue for cross country, track, and field competition among middle and upper-class men, the club spawned many other status-conscious athletic clubs that sought to regain a sense of manliness lost in white-collar work.

Until the late nineteenth century, competitive long-distance runs varied in length and did not use the term "marathon." The first modern Olympics in 1896 instituted the marathon as a symbolic link between the ancient and modern Olympics. Initially set at 24.8 miles (40 kilometers), the modern footrace recalled an incident in 490 B.C. when an Athenian ran to Sparta with news of victory at Marathon. The Olympic marathon, publicized by an aggressive modern press corps, gave long-distance running value and legitimacy as both an athletic and spectator event. A prestigious New York athletic club, the Knickerbocker, sponsored the first United States marathon, a twenty-five-mile run from Stamford, Connecticut, to the Bronx just months after the Olympics ended. As in other early marathons, trained cross-country runners comprised the field. Although the New York run did not resurface for another decade, Boston launched a 24.7-mile marathon the following year that has endured as the oldest continuous American marathon. (Not until 1912 was the official marathon distance of 26 miles, 385 yards established by the International Amateur Athletic Federation [IAAF], which advises the International Olympic Committee.) By 1905 Chicago and St. Louis hosted marathons, and San Francisco and Detroit began marathons during the World War I era. But marathon running continued to be centered in the East, and attempts elsewhere often soon faded, only to be revived again years later.

The Twentieth Century

In its first few decades after the turn of the twentieth century, the American marathon displayed both order and democracy that characterized the sport later. The earliest marathons were controlled by the Amateur Athletic Union (AAU), a New York governing body for athletic clubs founded in 1888, that welcomed all athletic clubs regardless of class or size. Establishing a system of rules and record keeping, the AAU, by 1909, had issued *Marathon Running,* a booklet that included training techniques, rules, and the history of American marathons. Yet despite their AAU influence and absorption in physical vigor, the middle- and upper-classes never dominated marathons. Ethnic groups founded their own athletic

New York City Marathon. About 32,000 people begin the 1998 New York City Marathon on Sunday, 1 November 1998 on the Staten Island section of the Verrazano Narrows Bridge. The annual 26.2 mile race that was established in 1970 proceeds through Brooklyn, Queens, Manhattan, and the Bronx, and finishes at the Tavern on the Green restaurant in Manhattan. *© Richard Drew for AP/Wide World Photos*

clubs in New York and Boston, sometimes within settlement houses or factories, and embraced the marathon as inexpensive but meaningful competition. Entire neighborhoods often turned out to cheer ethnic runners, who metaphorically acted out the immigrant's long journey, struggle, and eventual success in the United States.

A proliferation of marathons in the post-World War I era resulted from surging patriotism as well as a 1925 call by the AAU for a national marathon championship. The 1920s nativist mood generated new patriotic celebrations in many cities, which frequently included marathons. Ironically, while the marathon helped indoctrinate ethnic groups into the American culture of commercialism and competitiveness, it also provided an opportunity for expression of ethnic pride. Indeed, when the Great Depression reduced the number of marathons, ethnic neighborhood track clubs and industrial teams helped sustain the sport.

During the post-World War II era, social change transformed the marathon from working-class athletics to middle-class pastime. Ethnic consciousness faded as ethnic groups melded into the American middle class. At the same time, the Cold War called attention to the physical condition of Americans, and American and Soviet rivalry in the Olympics boosted the marathon's visibility. As Americans moved to the suburbs, they searched for

ways to fulfill President John F. Kennedy's call to undertake vigorous exercise. Bland corporate work, along with an abundance of high-calorie convenience food, contradicted by expectations of a trim physique, drove many Americans to the uncomplicated fitness routine of jogging. Middle- and upper-class women took to the roads in large numbers during the 1970s, prompted not only by cultural standards but by feminism's emphasis on well being and individual effort. Their drive to test the limits of equality, along with American Frank Shorter's 1972 Olympic victory in the marathon, inspired many men and women joggers to advance to marathons.

By the mid-1980s cities across the nation hosted hundreds of marathons driven by both big business and nonprofit organizations. The Road Runner's Club of America (RRCA), founded in 1957, sponsored "fun runs" as well as marathons that gave runners of every ability a feeling of accomplishment. Surveys suggesting that runners were high-income, white-collar professionals encouraged sponsorship from corporate advertisers. As athletic shoe and apparel companies turned out ever more expensive products, corporate advertising turned running togs into vogue fashion, further increasing interest in running. In the mid-1970s, the New York City marathon led the way for luring corporate dollars. Officials hired Olympic medallists who not only drew big sponsors but also upper- and middle-class entrants, media attention, crowds, and hearty support from municipal officials who eyed the marathon as a profitable and unifying city festival.

Participants in the marathon boom no longer reflected talents of the past's trained amateur. Marathons welcomed nonathletic, nontalented individuals who viewed the marathon as an opportunity for achievement and recognition otherwise denied them. Men and women with no athletic potential could now compete with seeded professionals and share in the media glow. Regardless of their finishing time, regardless of whether they combined running with walking to finish, all who crossed the finish line received medals, certificates, and T-shirts that conferred elite status. Among this elite, the marathon provided sociability in spite of its isolating activity and self-absorbing rewards.

The Twenty-First Century

By the turn of the twenty-first century, the number of marathons had decreased compared to the previous decades, in part a reflection of waning interest in exercise. Moreover, when the marathon's popularity reduced its cachet, serious competitors moved up to the triathlon, an endurance event requiring 112 miles of biking and a two-mile swim in addition to the marathon. Yet trends pointed to even greater segmentation of the marathon market. Permutations of the triathlon sprouted, including shorter distances and other, less demanding events such as canoeing. In addition, signs of a second boom of runners prepared to undertake marathons emerged late in the 1990s. Unlike the small group that first launched interest in the marathon, participants in this more recent movement included a broader range of society, which is more reflective of the marathon's history in the United States.

See also: Olympics, Running and Jogging, Triathlons

BIBLIOGRAPHY

Cooper, Pamela. *The American Marathon.* Syracuse, N.Y.: Syracuse University Press, 1998.

Green, Harvey. *Fit for America: Health, Fitness, Sport and American Society.* Baltimore, Md.: Johns Hopkins University Press, 1988.

Rader, Benjamin G. "The Quest for Self-Sufficiency and the New Strenuosity: Reflections on the Strenuous Life of the 1970s and 1980s." *Journal of Sport History* 18, no. 2 (Summer 1991): 255–266.

———. *American Sports: From the Age of Folk Games to the Age of Televised Sports.* 5th ed. Upper Saddle River, N.J.: Prentice Hall, 2004.

James Weeks

MARCHING BANDS
See *Band Playing*

MARDI GRAS

Mardi Gras is French for Fat Tuesday or Shrove Tuesday. In the Christian tradition, the forty days prior to Easter constitute Lent, for many a somber spiritual period of fasting and penance. Lent starts on Ash Wednesday, and, on the Tuesday immediately before Ash Wednesday, Mardi Gras is celebrated. It is a rich and complex psychological, social, and economic phenomenon that takes place in locations all over the Christian world. However, Mardi Gras reaches its zenith in southern Louisiana in February or March.

The concept and the experience of Mardi Gras are part of the larger celebration of carnival. Carnival, loosely translated as "festival of flesh," is actually a season that can last up to two months, whereas Mardi Gras is one day and is usually the apex of the season. While the earliest beginnings of carnival and Mardi Gras remain somewhat murky, it appears that carnival or something like it took place in pagan Rome. Saturnalia, one of several spring rituals, honored Saturn, the god of agriculture. During this seven-day festival, some slaves were granted limited and temporary freedoms and allowed to change roles and clothing with their masters. During this time, it appears they had the privilege to act in ways otherwise unacceptable—even to the point of criticizing their masters. After the seven days of merrymaking, life resumed as before and the social order was once again reestablished.

Carnival's central element of licensed social disruption can be traced through history with the classic example being the riotous fairs and festivals of the seventeenth and eighteenth centuries in Europe, particularly England. Some sociologists and historians—Mikhail Bakhtin, Roger Caillois, Terry Eagleton, Peter Stallybrass, and Allon White, for example—have argued that carnivals act as collective catharses allowing the safe release of pent-up aggression against unequal and unjust social orders. While on the surface these activities seem to seriously challenge the establishment, carnivals are purely licensed affairs carefully limited in time and space.

Given the widespread shedding of inhibitions, purposeful violation of social convention, and reversal of roles, it is not surprising that masking is a common element of carnival and Mardi Gras. The timid may become bold, and plebs rulers. Men may become women and vice versa. Obviously, disguises facilitate these inversions. In addition, these actions involve some risk to participants. The anonymity offered by the creative and elaborate costumes is necessary to protect all but the most unacceptable actions.

Moreover, carnivals serve to establish and maintain individual and community identity. Barry Jean Ancelet has documented the ability of southern Louisiana Mardi Gras to encourage commitment to the community through various Mardi Gras activities. Drawing on Clifford Geertz's theory of deep play, Ancelet contends that what may seem like simply colorful and chaotic frenzy may reflect the community's deep-seated realities and concerns. Carrying out playful rituals and maintaining the traditions of Mardi Gras that are often passed down through several generations may be a marker for differentiating between locals and outsiders.

Carnivals, condoned and even encouraged by the order that they mock, typically involve various leisure activities such as storytelling, singing, dancing, eating, and drinking. As might be expected, the consumption of alcoholic beverages at carnival is customary. Not only does the overconsumption of alcohol contribute to risqué behaviors, it is an example of the relaxed attitude of enforcement of society's laws and regulations.

Mardi Gras in Southern Louisiana

While Mardi Gras is celebrated in countries other than the United States (Spain, England, Brazil, and France) and in states other than Louisiana (Texas, Alabama, and California), it is most famous in the Mississippi River delta.

While Mardi Gras is practiced differently in the early 2000s in rural areas and in urban areas, it has a common, although sometimes sketchy, history. The French settled Louisiana in the seventeenth century. Interestingly, they came from different areas of the world. A handful of French explorers traveled from Canada down the Mississippi River to its end in the Gulf of Mexico. Some stayed in the area that is now Louisiana. Shortly thereafter a large contingent of French Canadians from the Acadian region arrived. These Acadians had been forced to flee the areas of Nova Scotia and New Brunswick by the Seven Years War. In addition, many French from Haiti fled to what had by now become a haven for their countrymen. The new French establishment at the mouth of the Mississippi was soon drawing a large number of brave souls directly from the mother country. Of course the area was already

the homeland of Native American Indians. Over the course of the next century and a half, Africans, as well as a large number of Spanish, arrived in the area. The current population of Louisiana consists largely of Cajuns (historically rural French ancestors) and Creoles (a more inclusive collection of African, American Indian, Spanish, and French).

The French—as well as the other cultures—brought with them their beloved customs, including those related to Mardi Gras. Early Mardi Gras, largely an outdoor festival that included eating, dancing, singing, and drinking, had become increasingly rowdy during its first fifty years. When Spain took control of southern Louisiana for a short period to time, the Spanish attempted to eliminate the festivities, first by mandating revelers to move inside and then by completely banning parties and parades. After the French regained control a couple of years later, Mardi Gras celebrations resumed. With the Louisiana Purchase in 1803 by the United States and subsequent control of the region, plus the increasingly wild parties in the streets, the future of Mardi Gras was once again in doubt.

Recognizing that something had to be done, citizen groups formed around 1850 to loosely plan and oversee the events. The first of these clubs or krewes, the Mystick Krewe of Comus, established contemporary Mardi Gras in Louisiana. In the following years over 100 large and small krewes would become involved in the celebration.

During its development, two types of Mardi Gras emerged—a rural or country celebration and an urban celebration, the largest of which takes place in New Orleans. Country Mardi Gras, the less broadly known of the two types, consists of small groups of men on foot and horseback who visit local farmhouses in the area. Each group of masked participants begs and generally acts up for the farmers and spectators. After some time of frivolity, the leader of the group makes a request for food. In keeping with tradition, the farmers release a live chicken after which the costumed participants chase, much to the delight of the crowd. After the chicken has been captured and stuffed in a bag, the small procession moves on to another farmhouse, where the process is repeated. By midafternoon, the Mardi Gras runners return to a park for a feast that features a large gumbo from the chickens and other foods that were collected. The ensuing party involves music and drinking and lasts well into the night.

The urban version of Mardi Gras consists of several separate parades that wind their way through the New Orleans area. Elaborate floats, bands, and individuals in wild costumes create a wild party atmosphere for participants and spectators. Three colors (purple for justice,

Mardi Gras. People crowd the street as Krewe of Rex floats and court jesters pass by during the Mardi Gras parade in 1993. © *Getty Images*

green for faith, and gold for power) are featured in every parade every year. The tradition of tossing strands of colorful beads to spectators has become a mainstay of the parades. Much has been made of the showing of women's breasts in exchange for the beads, but many contend that this sleazy side of Mardi Gras is limited and receives more attention than is justified.

New Orleans Mardi Gras is billed as the world's largest free party. Neither the state of Louisiana nor the city of New Orleans makes direct financial contributions to the events. There are no corporate sponsorships. Mardi Gras festivities are paid for entirely by the krewes that collect annual membership fees that range from $250 to $850. Local governments do contribute through the provision of law enforcement, crowd control, and refuse collection.

Mardi Gras, in all of its forms in southern Louisiana, has become a famous tourist attraction. The influx of nearly 750,000 visitors generates nearly one-half billion dollars in local spending. In the last few years, New Orleans, its surrounding communities, and the krewes have attempted to offer a balanced event that recognizes the negative impacts on the infrastructures and the less-than-wholesome reputation as well as the positive economic and cultural benefits.

See also: Carnivals, Easter, Mumming

BIBLIOGRAPHY

Ancelet, Barry Jean. "Falling Apart to Stay Together: Deep Play in the Grand Marais Mardi Gras." *Journal of American Folklore* 114, no. 452 (2001): 144–153.

Bakhtin, Mikhail. *Rebelais and His World.* Translated by H. Iswolsky. Cambridge, Mass.: MIT Press, 1968.

Caillois, Roger. *Man, Play, and Games.* Glencoe, Ill.: Free Press, 1961.

Eagleton, Terry. *Walter Benjamin: Towards a Revolutionary Criticism.* London: Verso, 1981.

Geertz, Clifford. *The Interpretation of Cultures: Selected Essays.* New York: Basic Books, 1973.

Stallybrass, Peter, and Allon White. *The Politics and Poetics of Transgression.* Ithaca, N.Y.: Cornell University Press, 1986.

Daniel G. Yoder

MARTIAL ARTS

In the United States, martial arts are mostly defined as fighting skills. However, in ancient and oriental countries, martial artists practiced these skills to condition the mind, body, and soul so they would be better able to defend and to live, even to "stop fighting."

Arts for Peace

The true ideal of martial arts is embodied in the Chinese characters for "martial arts." The symbol, which translates as "martial," is formed by two important elements, "stop" and "fight." Thus, the term "martial arts," from the earliest time, has truly meant "arts for peace."

Most martial arts revolve around a set of principles—such as honesty, persistence, courage, self-expression, self-control, and creativity—to promote individual physical, psychological, social, and spiritual growth. Based on individuals' length of time of practice, mastery of curriculum, success in competition, and contribution to the system, ranks are commonly awarded to form hierarchies. In the late nineteenth century, judo was the first martial art that awarded different colored belts worn with practice uniforms to form the ranking system. Since then, most contemporary martial arts have followed the Japanese lead in indicating rank to motivate learning.

Styles in Martial Arts

According to John Corcoran's *The Martial Arts Sourcebook* (p. 3), there are 1,158 forms and styles of traditional, nontraditional, and contemporary martial arts in the world. Boxing, judo, kung fu, tae kwon do, tai chi chuan, and wrestling are commonly practiced within the United States today.

Tai Chi Chuan and Kung Fu: As Recreational Activities
Tai chi chuan refers to the sequences of movements (chuan) that flow with the power of universe, yin and yang (tai chi). It is considered the most "peaceful" martial art, and this style preserves the original meaning of martial arts. Tai chi, which utilizes soft, slow, low-impact, fluid sequences of movements that emphasize self-control and mental awareness, is primarily practiced for active meditation and health promotion, including circulation, balance, relaxation, and stress relief. Since tai chi has been used therapeutically in China for more than 600 years, and its positive effects were demonstrated in recent research, this form of exercise has become increasingly popular and has been used to rehabilitate and promote health in the area of allied health professions.

Compared to tai chi chuan, kung fu is an aerobic form of exercise that originated from monks' Shaolin-style physical training. It is presumed to emphasize striking over grappling techniques and ultimately develops external and internal strength. Kung fu has become popular in the United States since the 1970s, probably because of its association with Bruce Lee, the late star of several martial arts films.

Boxing, Judo, Tae Kwon Do, and Wrestling: Professional/Spectator Sports
The term "boxing" derives from the Latin word *pugnus,* which means "fist." As an ancient martial art, boxing combines attack and defense by using hand strikes. The earliest evidence of boxing as a sport is found in the Mediterranean area and dates from about 1500 B.C. It reappeared in England in the early eighteenth century. Until nearly the end of the eighteenth century, boxers did not wear gloves and played with no rules. In 1839, the London Prize Ring rules were first introduced; these rules stipulated that bouts be fought within a twenty-four-foot square, enclosed by four ropes. Matches were to be made up of three to fifteen three-minute rounds, with one-minute intervals between the rounds. Kicking, gouging, butting, biting, and blows below the belt were explicitly made fouls. The first great period of boxing popularity began in the 1920s. Boxing has been held in the Olympic Games since 1904.

Judo means the way (do) of gentle (ju). It is a safe and efficient competitive sport in which grappling with effective throws, hold-downs, joint locks, and choking techniques to control opponents are highly evolved. Dr. Jigoro Kano developed judo in 1882, formulating it from styles of jujitsu. In 1904, the American president Theodore Roosevelt started to learn judo and helped ignite this first oriental martial arts boom in the United States. In 1951, the Congress of the European Judo Union established the International Judo Federation. Judo has been an Olympic event since 1964.

Tae kwon do means the way (do) of kicking (tae) and punching (kwon). It is characterized by the extensive use of kicking techniques and is one of the few martial

Bruce Lee. Movie star and martial arts legend Bruce Lee (1940–1973) demonstrates his unique style of fighting during a karate exhibition. Lee's charismatic appeal led many people to take up karate and other martial arts in the 1970s, before Lee died under mysterious circumstances in 1973. © *Corbis*

arts that execute kicks to targets that are notably higher than the head. Tae kwon do comprises hand techniques and six major types of kicks, including front, side, roundhouse, ax, back, and wheel kicks. General Choi Hong Hi developed modern tae kwon do for Korean military training in 1955. The next year, Jhoon Rhee introduced it formally to the United States in San Marcos, Texas. In the 2000 Olympic Games in Sydney, tae kwon do became a full medal sport. By 2003, tae kwon do was practiced in over 60 countries by more than 20 million people.

Wrestling was an integral part of the pentathlon in the Olympic Games of ancient Greece. Modern Greco-Roman wrestling was created to represent this classic Greek and Roman sport in France in the early nineteenth century. In this style of wrestling, the legs may not be used in any way to obtain a fall, and no holds may be taken below the waist. This style of wrestling is practiced in Olympic and international amateur competitions.

Social Uses of Martial Arts

Individuals study martial arts for body sculpting, prevention of bullying, curiosity, personal empowerment, and redemption through pain; and societies use the martial arts similarly. Joseph Svinth listed twenty categories of social uses of martial arts in *Martial Arts of the World*. One of the most common social uses of martial arts at the turn of the twenty-first century was for military and police training. Used in military and police training in China since 1561, martial arts have been used increasingly by police and soldiers elsewhere to restrain the opponent and increase self-confidence and physical aggressiveness. In the United States, Officer S. J. Jorgensen first started a jujitsu program for the Seattle Police Department in 1927. The army began providing martial arts courses in 1985, and the navy and the U.S. Marines followed later. In all cases, the idea of using martial arts was not to create great hand-to-hand fighters, but instead to instill the warrior ethos.

Women in Martial Arts

In 1891, Richard Kyle Fox and the *National Police Gazette* sponsored a women's championship wrestling match in New York City. During the early 1900s, feminists often regarded combative sports such as boxing, wrestling, and judo as tools of women's liberation because these sports were historically associated with prizefighting and saloons. Female boxing became popular throughout the United States after 1989. Since then, martial arts became fashionable for women. In 2002, this trend received a boost again in the United States with the release of the Taiwanese martial art movie *Crouching Tiger, Hidden Dragon.*

See also: Boxing; Recreational Fighting

BIBLIOGRAPHY

Corcoran, John. *The Martial Arts Sourcebook.* 1st ed. New York: HarperPerennial, 1994.

Crider, Duane A., and William R. Klinger. *Stretch Your Mind and Body: Tai Chi as an Adaptive Activity.* State College, Pa.: Venture Publishing, 2001.

Cuevas, Antonio, and Jennifer Lee. *Martial Arts Are Not Just for Kicking Butt: An Anthology of Writings on Martial Arts.* Berkeley, Calif.: North Atlantic Books, 1998.

Green, Thomas A. *Martial Arts of the World: An Encyclopedia.* Santa Barbara, Calif.: ABC-CLIO, 2001.

I-Tsun Chiang

MEDIA, TECHNOLOGY, AND LEISURE

The last decade of the nineteenth century, and the whole of the twentieth century, saw a revolution in the use of time for leisure, from live events to technology-related entertainments. More and more time was devoted first to attending movies and listening to recorded sounds—either on radio broadcasts or on phonograph records—and later to watching television, and, during the final years of the twentieth century, listening to digital-quality recordings and watching telecasts delivered by cable and satellites, along with watching videos and DVDs and playing video games. By the close of the twentieth century, the middle-class American had a plethora of media entertainment options available, and devoted increasing amounts of leisure and recreational time to electronically-based amusement.

Since the 1890s, these mass media technologies have increasingly served as a substitute for live, "in-person" leisure-time activities. Indeed, more people have seen and heard the average prime time television program on one night in one hour than attended the hit play *Oklahoma!* over its then record-breaking Broadway run. Depending upon one's values, this extensive use of technology has had a good or bad impact on live entertainment, expectations of viewers and listeners, and quality of leisure. Yet as people devote more of their time to media technology, one can assume they are voting their preference for this form of leisure and recreation.

Film

While all forms of mass technological media are popular, the top one in terms of its world impact must be the films produced by Hollywood. Before the advent of the cinema, there was a vast array of live entertainment. The reduction of live entertainment did not come instantly, but became discernable with the first showings of films in the late 1890s, and accelerated after World War I when Hollywood coalesced and its productions began to dominate the world market. Hollywood would continue its domination through the rest of the twentieth century.

The production and distribution of cinema since the 1920s has been dominated by eight or fewer giant Hollywood studios. These vast multinational enterprises created films that were presented in virtually every technologically-advanced country in the world, frequently capturing a major share of the business in those countries, despite competition from nationally-made and distributed motion pictures. Almost continuous technological change—led by the Hollywood oligopolists—did not lessen Hollywood's industrial power, and other film industries sought to mimic Hollywood's continuous success. The addition of sound and color, the innovations of cable TV and home video simply extended Hollywood's influence, and increased its profits and presence.

Hollywood's grip on leisure time has not been lessened by world or regional wars, the Great Depression, and the innovation of a variety of television technologies. Indeed, with the explosion of home video during the final fifth of the twentieth century, Hollywood has gained more power, and its films dominate a world culture as no other medium ever has.

The enhancement of sound to movies during the late 1920s solidified control by four studios over the world cinema market, names still familiar as the twentieth century ended: Paramount Pictures, MGM, Twentieth Century Fox, and Warner Bros. Led by Paramount through the 1930s and 1940s, Hollywood perfected its first "Golden Age" based upon control of movie theaters. Paramount represented the most profitable, powerful, and traditional business-like Hollywood company. More than any of the others, Paramount relied on its chain of more than 1,000 theaters to maintain its corporate might. Not surprisingly, it was a former theater operator, Barney Balaban, who stood at the top of this corporate colossus, hiring more lawyers and MBAs than movie stars. MGM ranked second, technically functioning as a successful unit of Loew's, a theater chain. MGM, more than any other studio, relied on the star system, producing films from its massive Culver City, California-based "factory" of twenty-seven sound stages and a 168-acre back lot.

Twentieth Century Fox and Warner Bros. ranked just behind Paramount and MGM. These four tolerated some competition from RKO, Universal Pictures, Columbia Pictures, and United Artists through the 1930s and 1940s. What changed the studio system was the suburbanization of the United States after World War II. Suddenly Hollywood's U.S. customers lived miles from the downtown picture palaces. Later, television enabled Universal, Columbia, and United Artists to prosper. Warner Bros. began its transition into what became AOL Time Warner when in 1956 the founding brothers sold out, and a series of new owners embraced television production. Paramount was re-invented as a part of the conglomerate Gulf and Western Corporation.

Whoever owned these studio colossuses, their management figured ways to accommodate, and even dominate television. The transition saw Hollywood producing fewer films, but most were produced with an eye toward their becoming potential blockbusters. In 1962, NBC-TV's "Saturday Night at the Movies" began the transition to television as the dominant delivery system of Hollywood's feature films. The surprise hits of *Jaws* (1975) and *Star Wars* (1977) moved Universal and Fox to the top of the Hollywood studio hierarchy.

The architect of this re-invention of Hollywood was Universal's longtime president Lew Wasserman. Starting in 1961, Wasserman transformed the former minor studio into a television and film powerhouse. Universal ascended to the top of the Hollywood movie and television studio hierarchy as Wasserman innovated the made-for-TV movie, and released the first true modern film blockbuster, *Jaws*. Wasserman tied Hollywood closely to TV production, and by the 1980s it became clear that Hollywood and television would merge. By 1999, Disney owned the ABC television network, Paramount owned the CBS television network, and Twentieth Century Fox owned the Fox network. Only NBC, owned by General Electric, remained "independent" of the new, even more "golden" Hollywood studio system.

As the twentieth century ended, despite all the social, technological, and industrial changes, the major Hollywood companies alone continued to be able to distribute films around the world. At considerable expense, all maintained offices not only in the United States, but in every region of the world. Owners of theater chains knew the Hollywood majors alone could continuously deliver popular films, and so even theater owners outside the United States preferred Hollywood films to native productions. The Hollywood studios' record at the box office satisfied theater owners—a conservative lot with most of their assets invested in real estate. Economies of scale prevented rivals from building and maintaining equal world distribution networks.

Through the final quarter of the twentieth century, the Hollywood oligopoly learned to generate profits from creations that premiered with blitz TV advertising, which in turn was married to a multi-revenue generating machine to sell musical sound tracks, novelizations of the stories, "action figures" from movie characters, and video. Each movie aspired to become a smash hit, because if it succeeded, the feature turned into a "product line," designed to fill all entertainment needs and desires, from toys to theme park rides to campaigns to sell more McDonald's hamburgers.

The blockbuster strategy, in turn, led to ever-escalating costs of production, so it became more difficult for rivals to compete with the exclusive Hollywood club. By the close of the twentieth century, the average Hollywood feature cost in excess of $50 million to produce, and half again that amount to publicize. *Titanic* doubled those averages, but then earned in excess of $2 billion in revenues. Potential filmmakers knew that if they aspired to ever have a world audience see their creation, and to attain undreamed-of wealth, they needed to be "green lighted" by one of the major Hollywood studios.

Alone, Hollywood could keep the revenues flowing year after year—particularly from home video. While theaters still premiered new films, it was "downstream" on video where the bulk of the profits were generated. The theater functioned as the "voting booth" where hits were made, and necessary publicity generated. But once the film had fully milked the box-office it went into release

Football game. A group of men gathers around a large projection television to watch a football game. Projections systems, such as this one, and even newer plasma-based systems are making television screens bigger and clearer than ever before. © *Leng/Leng/Corbis*

on cable TV and home video, which created more than two-thirds of the average film's total revenues. Hollywood executives carefully planned—in classic price discrimination fashion—to drain all possible revenues from each of these release venues, only releasing it to home video when they calculated that all the monies movies from theatrical and then cable TV had been procured. Each window in this sequence was an exclusive; a new window opened only when all value of the previous window had been captured. This exploitation of video represented Hollywood's newest advantage in the film industry.

Globally, only in the rare nation does Hollywood not capture more than half the business. But other nations did try. During the 1920s, European nation-states—led by the United Kingdom, France and Germany—sought to build their own studio systems, and were successful for short periods of time, until their leading filmmakers left for Hollywood. Meanwhile, the new Soviet Union tried to build an alternative national cinema industry under

Communism. The 1930s saw an end to most of these experiments, though many propaganda films and sentimental stories were made. At the close of the World War II, the focus shifted to state-sponsored television, and in Japan and India, studio systems did succeed, even while conceding to Hollywood a vast share of the monies paid for cinema attendance.

Hollywood has long maintained an influential trade association: the Motion Picture Association of America (MPAA). Best known in the early 2000s for ratings of films, the MPAA has long been far more influential around the world for lobbying to smooth the way for Hollywood's domination of international distribution. The MPAA worked closely with the U.S. State Department to keep cinema trade "free" so as to permit the Hollywood studio oligopoly to continue pulling billions in revenue from the foreign market. While globalization seems like a new concept, Hollywood has been practicing it for three-quarters of the twentieth century.

Recorded Sound and Radio

Since the creation of the phonograph in the last quarter of the nineteenth century, people have been able to listen to recorded sounds—first on cylinders, then on records, then audio cassettes, and, as the twentieth century ended, compact discs (CDs) and MP3 computer files. A library of recorded music is part of many people's possessions. Recordings actually led to an increase in live performances, as stars were discovered on recorded media, and then people wanted to see these stars in person. Technological media reduced live amateur music making, but did little to dampen the desire to see and hear celebrity musicians play in person.

Since about 1920, people have also had the ability to listen to sounds—principally musical—via radio broadcasting. Because of their reliance on music, radio and recorded sound have been closely linked. In times of economic slowdowns, particularly during the Great Depression, people listened to free radio broadcasts as a substitute for purchasing music. It may have been Al Jolson in the 1920s, Benny Goodman in the 1930s, Bing Crosby in the 1940s, Elvis Presley in the 1950s; but whatever the decade, radio broadcasts held a prominent position in developing twentieth-century entertainment. Music listening, whether on radio or through one's one technical apparatus, has become a constant presence, and recordings have made all the difference. As the twentieth century ended, for example, country crossover diva Patsy Cline had been dead for twenty-seven years, but she still "lived" through her recordings and radio play, enabling young listeners to discover her, and older listeners to continue to buy her recordings in numbers measured in the millions.

Since the early 1930s, radio has been a ubiquitous mass medium, in nearly every home and automobile. In the 1990s, the average household—because of the low price of radio receivers—had access to more than five radios. In a typical week, radio broadcasting reached nearly all possible listeners, at least for a few moments. During the 1930s the average person listened three hours per day. That figure dropped as television entered the scene in the 1950s, but radio advertisers targeted a diverse set of listeners—all ethnic groups, age groups, and income classes. Blending together certain musical formats seems to attract certain specific audiences. As the twentieth century ended, listening crested at "drive time," or "rush hour" in major cities. And the choices, particularly in major cities, numbered fifty to a hundred different stations.

Because of radio promotion, music sales were being measured in the billions of dollars as the twentieth century ended. This came in the form of compact discs (CDs), CD singles, audio cassettes, cassette singles, long playing vinyl records, vinyl singles, and music videos. In 1997, the International Federation of the Phonographic Industry (IFPI) pegged world music sales at around $40 billion, of which the United States represented about a third. The key difference between the radio and music recording industries is that music sales are dominated by five companies. As of the commencement of the twenty-first century these were AOL Time Warner (U.S.–based), EMI (British), Universal (French), Bertelsmann (German), and Sony (Japanese). All were among the largest corporations in the media business, indeed in the entire corporate world. Again using Patsy Cline, her recordings are principally controlled by Universal, and help substantiate that company's vast catalog. All Patsy Cline sales flow to the bottom line, as production costs have long been paid off.

As new technology improved, and CDs became pure renditions of music making, and as FM radio replaced AM broadcasting as the dominant medium, the sound could be broadcast in digital quality. As the century ended, direct radio broadcasting via satellite seemed to be the latest technological innovation in radio broadcasting, seeking to reformat the radio industry as the CD had the recorded music industry in the 1980s and 1990s.

Television

Television broadcasts from towers fundamentally changed the use of mass media technologies more than any other medium since the rise of Hollywood after World War I. When TV was introduced in the United States during the late 1940s and early 1950s, people cut back on other leisure time pursuits and began to use television as their principle leisure time activity. Survey after survey demonstrated that once a local station went on the air, the evening hours were nearly always devoted to television watching by the majority of available viewers. By 1960, television became the primary leisure time activity for persons in the United States. By the close of the twentieth century, the average home in the United States had the television on some seven hours per day.

The United States television industry has grown into an economic force generating mass media's greatest revenues, costs, and profits. In the United States, the production, distribution, and broadcasting of television (and later cable casting, and delivery directly by satellite) has long been dominated by a few vertically integrated networks—which produce much of their own programming, and often own broadcast stations, cable systems, and satellite-to-home divisions. While a variety of state-controlled or semi-independent publicly-funded television systems have existed around the world, by the end of the twentieth century more and more TV industries in other countries were deregulated—that is, privatized—and began to look more like the commercial model of the United States.

From its introduction after World War II to the mid-1980s, in the United States three national systems of interconnection or networks dominated the TV business: the American Broadcasting Company (ABC), the Columbia Broadcasting System (CBS), and the National Broadcasting Company (NBC). Then came cable TV's 100-plus networks, and in the 1990s, even more offerings through satellite and digital cable. Yet this seeming plethora of TV choices is actually produced by seven conglomerates, all built around organizations producing programming allied with other parts of the same company. In most cases, the entertainment programs were made in Hollywood, in a deal with a studio such as a Disney or Paramount. These corporations also own TV networks that broadcast, cablecast, or deliver programming via satellite to the home. Executives with the same company make programming decisions either aimed at mass audiences (the so called traditional networks such as Disney's ABC), or, increasingly, to niche networks, such as Disney's growing number of cable channels.

By the close of the twentieth century, all the networks—save NBC—were tied directly to Hollywood-based companies. Broadcast television became a classic case of vertical integration. Except for live sports and news, their Hollywood parents were creating all forms of programming, from comedies to dramas, from reality shows to news magazine programs. They produced the show, distributed it through their own networks, and then much of the nation watched it on one of their networks. The Australian media baron Rupert Murdoch innovated the Hollywood vertically integrated TV network system when in 1985 he bought a studio—Twentieth Century Fox—and then launched the first new TV network in thirty years: the Fox Television Network. During the 1990s, Viacom followed Murdoch's lead and fashioned its United Paramount Network (supplied by its Paramount studio), and the Time Warner corporation created the Warner Bros. network. Disney underscored the importance of this new broadcast network economics when in 1995 it acquired ABC. In 1999 Viacom purchased CBS, and in doing so became the owner of two broadcast networks.

As late as 1980, most viewers in the United States watched solely broadcast TV, but more and more households began to subscribe to cable television. As the twentieth century ended, about two-thirds of Americans paid monthly fees to a local cable monopoly. After the passage of the 1996 Telecommunications Act, which further deregulated the TV and radio industries, cable franchises consolidated, and in 1998 AT&T acquired cable franchises representing about a third of all customers in the United States. AT&T's CEO Michael Armstrong bet his corporation's future on cable, based on three principles. First, cable was a legal monopoly, reminding Armstrong of the old phone company. Second, Armstrong saw that cable's broadband wires could offer not only television, but also Internet access. Finally, through his corporate partner Liberty Media, he controlled the Discovery Channel (in its five variations), The Learning Channel, Black Entertainment Television, and a host of other cable networks. Armstrong then sold this package to the fourth largest cable company, Comcast Cable.

But not all cable networks were controlled by these vertically integrated vast media conglomerates. As an alternative tactic, a few Hollywood moguls reasoned that it was not necessary to spend billions of dollars to wire local cable franchises, but simply produce desirable programming, and TV viewers would find and pay for those channels, regardless who was their local monopoly cable franchise. Disney, Fox, and Viacom executives, for the three leading examples, concentrated in creating programming to feed cable networks such as ESPN, The Family Channel, and Music Television (MTV), respectively. They did not vertically integrate.

In sum, cable networks added no dominant new owners to the list of traditional Hollywood and television corporate powerhouses. Indeed, to think of broadcast TV as distinct from cable TV industries no longer makes sense from an ownership perspective. The longtime Hollywood companies dominate, in partnership with a couple of cable TV giants. So HBO may have been famous for programs such as *The Sopranos* and *Sex in the City* as the twenty-first century commenced, but they were simply small divisions of the AOL Time Warner media megacorporation. The programs were meant to shock, but were directed to an audience who first had to pay for cable access, and then extra for a "premium" channel.

The 1990s saw a whole new means of gaining access to television: satellite-to-home direct delivery. By 2000, one in ten households in the United States had signed up. Paying even higher fees than for cable TV service in some cases, satellite subscribers could access up to twice as many channels, principally pay-per-view movies and sports broadcasts from all regions of the United States and around the world.

As the twenty-first century began, the major TV conglomerates relied more and more on exporting programming around the world. Yet Hollywood-made TV by no means monopolizes the world's television. For example, Brazilian and Mexican TV industries succeeded in exporting TV programming in Latin America. In Europe, French and German companies did the same. Still, overall, Hollywood functioned as the leading maker and exporter of TV entertainment. Its influential trade association the MPAA smoothly paved the way for export by lobbying both the United States Department of State and governments worldwide to keep TV trade open and unrestricted. (Note that Hollywood and the television industries were represented by the same trade association.) Foreign governments resented U.S. pressure, and formally and informally struggled to protect their domestic TV industries.

Social Influence of Media

The impact of the movies was not truly felt until the latter days of the 1910s. With Hollywood, the white establishment took control of media, technology, and leisure time. African Americans, Asian Americans, Hispanics, and Native Americans did not own the means of production, distribution, or presentation. Even in the 1930s and 1940s, movie houses catering only to "Negro" audiences were most often owned by whites, and minority group images were stereotyped. So Native Americans were seen exclusively as fiery "Indian warriors" ever seeking to prevent the "proper" manifest destiny of European settlers taking the west for themselves. African Americans appeared primarily as servants or slaves—for comic relief. In 1930s Hollywood there were a few African American stars, such as Bill "Bojangles" Robinson, Hattie McDaniel, Stepin Fetchit, and Willie Best. Hattie McDaniel won an Oscar for her powerful supporting role in *Gone with the Wind* (1939), but far more popular with white audiences were Stepin Fetchit and Willie Best, playing the role of the "shufflin' lackey coon."

Change commenced during World War II as the federal government pressured Hollywood to fashion films with realistic African American characters. During the 1950s, from motion pictures such as *Carmen Jones, Island in the Sun,* and *Take a Giant Step,* movie audiences finally saw African Americans as leading actors and actresses. In particular Sidney Poitier became a big star and won an Oscar. By the 1970s, there was even a genre with black action heroes—Jim Brown and Richard Roundtree—as well as positive images effected in *Sounder, Claudine,* and *The Wiz.* During the 1980s came independent African American film makers making powerful and widely distributed films. No more famous film maker emerged during this period than Spike Lee, with his *She's Gotta Have It, School Daze, Do The Right Thing,* and *X: The Story of*

Malcolm X, distributed by Time Warner, then the largest media conglomerate in the world.

This same historical cycle—negative stereotyping, followed by slow transformation and acceptance—played out in the images of Hispanics as well. The "Mexican greaser" image was a minor stereotype found in films of the 1920s and 1930s, principally westerns. This only changed after World War II as the U.S. government, seeking better relations with neighbor nations to the south, pressured Hollywood to offer positive images. Momentarily such films as *Jaurez* set positive images. But after the war this pressure abated and it would take many more years until films such as *La Bamba* entered mainstream Hollywood.

Female filmmakers operated under severe constraints as well. Women have always been among the most popular of performers, but precious few have had any power behind the camera or in Hollywood's boardrooms. Only early star Mary Pickford has helped create a major studio—United Artists. But through years, except for their roles as stars and supporting actresses, it was more likely to find a woman as a screenwriter (for example, Frances Marion, Anita Loos, or Bess Meredyth, to name three) or as an editor such as Margaret Booth and Dorothy Arzner.

It was not until the 1980s that one could locate more than the occasional working female Hollywood filmmaker. In 1980 the Directors Guild reported that during the previous thirty years only seven women had directed feature films in Hollywood—Elaine May, Claudia Weill, Martha Coolidge, Joan Miklin Silver, Amy Heckerling, and Susan Seidelman.

Much of the same script was followed by radio and recorded sound. This sector of the U.S. entertainment industry also began at the turn of the century and followed the same stereotypes that were employed in Hollywood. African Americans, Asian Americans, Hispanics and Native Americans did not own the means of production. But at the level of performance minorities could make their way. And none did so more than African Americans. It was during the final decade of the nineteenth century and the first two decades of the twentieth century that jazz as a separate musical form was fashioned. African American jazz defined white "Big Bands," and with soul music, gospel, rhythm and blues, and hip-hop, the popular music of the latter twentieth century was principally of African American origins.

During the 1950s, with the formation of rock and roll, the twin influences of white country music (based on Scottish American and Irish American music makers) and African American merged. But a white man,

Elvis Presley, rather than an African American, Chuck Berry, was able to gain the greatest popularity, fame, and fortune. Indeed African American–inspired rock and roll, has always been primarily marketed to whites, with noted exceptions. African American Berry Gordy's Motown records stood as the rare example of an African American owned recording company. The Supremes and Temptations made Motown famous, and Gordy rich.

With radio tied to recorded music, the same trends were seen. Amos 'n' Andy may have seemed a black show, but its creators and actors were white. From a multicultural perspective there was little impact on radio through the network era of the 1930s and 1940s. Women were performers; Native Americans were invisible; other ethnic groups made rare appearances.

But with the rise of television, the era of network radio being dominated by a handful of stations in each city was soon over. Radio stations turned to different formulas for music and began to identify a "sound." As the twentieth century ended, stations catered to Hispanics, African Americans, Asian Americans, indeed all ethnic cohorts in the United States of America.

The television entertainment industry began with an extension of Hollywood stereotypes. There were precious few minorities (by any definition) behind the cameras. One report issued in 1980 stated that during the previous thirty years (the formative ones for television) only twenty-three women had been employed as directors of prime-time television. It was not until the late 1960s, with Bill Cosby in *I Spy,* that a major prime-time series character was portrayed by an African American. But in 1977, with Alex Haley's mini-series *Roots,* courageously backed by a Jewish American David Wolper, a new era commenced. *Roots* set ratings records and was followed by the 1980s hit *The Cosby Show.* The television era was fundamentally transformed during the late 1970s as cable TV entered millions of homes. By the end of the 1980s multicultural channels on cable TV were in place. In particular, Black Entertainment Television offered an African American owned and operated network of sports, movies, and original shows made and offered for persons of color. For Hispanics the all-Spanish network Univision provided Hispanics with twenty-four-hour Spanish language programs, from game shows to movies to soap operas. For females, Lifetime developed talk shows and movies and selected reruns aimed at female interests.

By 1990 there was a great deal of diversity and multiculturalism in media images on cable TV. However, in the early 2000s, progress still needed to be made. The ownership of these entertainment industry portraits continued to be controlled by whites. Critics on the left have long seen the television industry as an increasingly influential cultural industry no different from other industries in monopoly-driven capitalism. Like Hollywood, they see domination by giant corporations, and the lack of true alternatives that challenge the dominant political-economic structure. Even with the increasing number of cable channels, one strains to find any progressive alternatives to corporate voices that sing largely in unison. The dominant TV powers have continuously increased their influence as they fashion a global media presence. Yet it must be acknowledged that sales and rentals of video in both its forms—VHS and DVD—do offer increasingly diverse choices. There surely is more television than ever before, and more diversity as TV continues to dominate the mass technological media leisure activity.

See also: Movies' Impact on Popular Leisure; Radio Listening, Car and Home; Television's Impact on Popular Leisure

BIBLIOGRAPHY

Bruck, Connie. *Master of the Game: Steve Ross and the Creation of Time Warner.* New York: Simon and Schuster, 1992.

Burnett, Robert. *The Global Jukebox: The International Music Industry.* London and New York: Routledge, 1996.

Compaine, Benjamin, and Douglas Gomery. *Who Owns the Media?* Competition and Concentration in the Mass Media Industry. Mahwah, New Jersey: Lawrence Erlbaum Associates, 2000.

Gomery, Douglas. *The Hollywood Studio System.* New York: St. Martin's Press, 1986.

———. *Shared Pleasures: A History of Movie Presentation in the United States.* Madison: University of Wisconsin Press, 1992.

Herman, Edward, and Robert McChesney. *The Global Media: The New Missionaries of Corporate Capitalism.* London: Cassell, 1997.

Herwig, Godfrey W., and Ashley Page Herwig. *Radio's Niche Marketing Revolution: Futuresell.* Boston: Focal Press, 1997.

Hull, Geoffrey P. *The Recording Industry.* New York: Allyn and Bacon, 2004.

Lardner, James. *Fast Forward: Hollywood, the Japanese, and the Onslaught of the VCR.* New York: W. W. Norton, 1987.

Litman, Barry Russell. *The Motion Picture Mega-Industry.* New York: Allyn and Bacon, New York 1998.

MacDonald, J. Fred. *Don't Touch That Dial! Radio Programming in American Life, 1920–1960.* Chicago: Nelson Hall, 1979.

McFarland, *David T. Future Radio Programming Strategies: Cultivating Listenership in the Digital Age.* 2d ed. Mahwah, New Jersey: Lawrence Erlbaum Publishers, 1997.

Millard, Andre J. *America on Record: A History of Recorded Sound*. New York: Cambridge University Press, 1995.

Morin, Albert, ed. *Film Policy: International, National, and Regional Perspectives*. London and New York: Routledge, 1996.

Neale, Steve, and Martin Smith, eds. *Contemporary Hollywood Cinema*, London and New York: Routledge, London, 1998.

Owen, Bruce, and Steven S. Wildman. *Video Economics*. Cambridge, Mass.: Harvard University Press, 1992.

Parsons, Patrick R, and Robert M. Frieden. *The Cable and Satellite Television Industries*. Boston: Allyn and Bacon, 1998.

Walker, James, and Douglas Ferguson. *The Broadcast Television Industry*. Boston: Allyn and Bacon, 1998.

Whetmore, Edward Jay. *The Magic Medium: An Introduction to Radio in America*. Belmont, Calif.: Wadsworth Publishing, 1981.

Wyatt, Justin. *High Concept: Movies and Marketing in Hollywood*. Austin: University of Texas Press, 1994.

Douglas Gomery

MEMORIAL DAY

Memorial Day's origins lie in the carnage of the Civil War, which demanded some ritual of remembrance, and in the new rural cemetery, which provided the ideal spot for the ritual of grave decoration. Columbus, Georgia; Boalsburg, Pennsylvania; and Waterloo, New York, all claim the first Memorial Day. (Congress recognized Waterloo's claim in 1966.) But the annual holiday began in the South in the spring of 1866, when ladies' memorial associations in Columbus and other southern towns instituted Memorial Days to recognize the Confederate dead by visiting and decorating their graves.

The first official Memorial Day for the Union dead did not occur until 1868. General John Logan, a Republican congressman from Illinois and commander in chief of the Grand Army of the Republic (GAR), a Union veterans organization, designated 30 May as Memorial Day and ordered all GAR posts to decorate the graves of their fallen comrades. Logan's wife later claimed that she had suggested the idea to him after observing southern exercises in Virginia.

The two Memorial Days spread quickly through the efforts of the GAR and the ladies' memorial associations. Congress made 30 May a holiday in 1876, and, by the 1880s, most states outside the former Confederacy had legalized it. The Confederate Memorial Day had no uni-

form date. In the lower South, 26 April, the anniversary of General Joseph E. Johnston's surrender, was common, while other states observed 10 May the date of Stonewall Jackson's death, or 3 June, Jefferson Davis's birthday.

Early Commemorations

The exercises for both holidays were similar in the postwar period, centering on the cemeteries and taking mourning as their main theme. Ladies' memorial associations sponsored the Confederate ceremonies, while GAR posts took charge of the federal exercises. For both Union and Confederate veterans, Memorial Day was a sacred occasion, which generally began with a church service. The exercises then moved to the cemeteries for oratory by distinguished veterans, followed by the grave decoration. The ceremonies concluded with "Taps" and a twenty-one-gun salute.

Despite these similarities, the messages of the early Memorial Days differed. The GAR made clear that the federal holiday honored the Union dead only and celebrated the preservation of the Union and the end of slavery. It made observance of the holiday mandatory for members, and even posted armed soldiers to prevent the decoration of Confederate graves. The ladies' memorial associations decorated Confederate graves only, while Confederate veterans proclaimed that they had fought not for slavery but to defend their liberty. The veterans even fought over the holiday's name; each side contended that its holiday had the most legitimate claim to the designation of Memorial Day. When the federal holiday became popularly known as Decoration Day, the GAR campaigned against the new name, arguing that it did not properly reflect the day's purpose.

Reconciliation

As Reconstruction ended, however, Union and Confederate veterans began to find common cause in keeping their sacrifice before an increasingly indifferent public. They condemned the desecration of Memorial Day with recreation and sports, and instituted military parades to attract crowds. The former foes also turned to each other for recognition of their valor and to recapture the camaraderie of battle. The 1880s saw a spate of blue-gray reunions, often held on Memorial Day. Richmond's Lee Camp of Confederate Veterans even sent a delegation in 1886 to Brooklyn Memorial Day exercises marking the death of General Ulysses S. Grant. On Memorial Day 1895, Chicago's ex-Confederate Association dedicated the first Confederate monument

Brooklyn parade. Gustav Perl, right, was among the many veterans attending what is perhaps the oldest Memorial Day parade in the U.S. in Brooklyn, New York—the 129th annual event was held on 27 May 1996. Mr. Perl fought in World War II in the Normandy Invasion and the Battle of the Bulge. © *Adam Nadel for AP/Wide World Photos*

outside the South to honor Confederates who had died in a prison camp and been buried in Oak Woods Cemetery. The city's leading businessmen welcomed ex-Confederate officers, and tens of thousands of Chicagoans turned out for the dedication.

This reconciliation was clearly for white veterans only. Across Oak Woods from the ceremonies at the Confederate monument, the black John Brown post of the GAR held its annual Memorial Day exercises before a much smaller crowd. It was left to black veterans to remind Americans that they, too, had fought for the Union and for freedom for African Americans, facts increasingly ignored by white veterans. African Americans had to join segregated GAR posts even in the North, and in the South white and black GAR posts held separate ceremonies for the federal holiday.

Diversification of the Holiday

Diverse Americans embraced Memorial Day in the late nineteenth century. Ethnic Americans honored their countrymen who had fought in the Civil War with exercises that combined expressions of ethnic and American patriotism. Many Americans adopted the custom of decorating the graves of relatives on Memorial Day, beginning its transformation into Decoration Day, a more general day of the dead.

The day also served political purposes. It became customary for the president to speak at the GAR's exercises at Arlington National Cemetery. In 1902, President Theodore Roosevelt used his address to justify the American conquest of the Philippines. In 1914, President Woodrow Wilson, a Virginian, caused a national stir by declining the GAR's annual invitation but agreeing to speak at Arlington just five days later at the dedication of a Confederate monument. Wilson ultimately attended both ceremonies, as did the commander in chief of the GAR, in another show of reconciliation.

Both Memorial Days continued to be important throughout the first half of the twentieth century. As the last veterans died, however, the holidays declined in significance, hitting a nadir during U.S. involvement in Vietnam. Congress in 1968 moved Memorial Day to the last Monday in May, paving the way for it to become the kick-off to summer vacation. Most Americans observe the holiday by holding barbecues, traveling, or shopping.

Nevertheless, Memorial Day continues to be meaningful to veterans, who still observe the federal holiday by decorating graves and parading. Likewise, Confederate Memorial Day is still commemorated in some fashion in most southern states. Although an ever smaller number of Americans decorate the graves of their parents and grandparents on Memorial Day, it remains for many the American day of the dead.

See also: Fourth of July, Labor Day, Patriotism and Leisure

BIBLIOGRAPHY

Albanese, Catherine. "Requiem for Memorial Day: Dissent in the Redeemer Nation." *American Quarterly* 26 (October 1974): 386–398.

Blight, David W. *Race and Reunion: The Civil War in American Memory.* Cambridge, Mass.: Harvard University Press, Belknap Press, 2001.

Cherry, Conrad. "Two American Sacred Ceremonies: Their Implications for the Study of Religion in America." *American Quarterly* 21 (Winter 1969): 739–754.

Foster, Gaines M. *Ghosts of the Confederacy: Defeat, the Lost Cause, and the Emergence of the New South, 1865 to 1913.* New York: Oxford University Press, 1987.

Kinney, Martha E. "'If Vanquished I Am Still Victorious': Religious and Cultural Symbolism in Virginia's Confederate Memorial Day Celebrations, 1866–1930." *The Virginia Magazine of History and Biography* 106 (Summer 1998): 237–266.

Litwicki, Ellen M. *America's Public Holidays, 1865–1920.* Washington, D.C.: Smithsonian Institution Press, 2000.

O'Leary, Cecilia Elizabeth. *To Die For: The Paradox of American Patriotism.* Princeton, N.J.: Princeton University Press, 1999.

Warner, W. Lloyd. *American Life: Dream and Reality.* Chicago: University of Chicago Press, 1953.

Ellen M. Litwicki

MEN'S LEISURE LIFESTYLES

American leisure patterns have always been heavily gender-based, providing men with an opportunity to display their manliness, gain recognition, develop a measure of self-worth, and escape from the confinements of domesticity. Leisure opportunities varied in different eras when they were a product of social class, race, ethnicity, residency, prevailing social norms, changing definitions of manliness, and the impact of the processes of urbanization, industrialization, and immigration.

Local governments, especially Puritan Massachusetts, which banned immoral activities like gambling and all pastimes on the Sabbath, and carefully supervised taverns, regulated men's leisure options in colonial America. Puritan leisure had to be moral and recreational, such as teaching useful skills, promoting closer bonds with sons, and enhancing community security. Training Day on the Boston Common provided opportunities to participate in marksmanship, foot races, cricket, and beer drinking. Strong religious opposition to leisure also existed in early Pennsylvania, where the Quakers worried that amusements diverted men from work and God.

Eighteenth-century cities were more secularized and demographically diverse, and had rich elites. These conditions helped create a more cosmopolitan social life. Philadelphians enjoyed a much more entertaining social life centered in its taverns and coffeehouses. New York's elite attended clubs, theater, and sporting events like horse racing, yachting, hunting, and sleighing. Philadelphians played a big role in developing organized sport. They emulated the English gentry by establishing a wide-ranging club life to facilitate sociability and maintain ethnic and class distinctions, and by copying English country pleasures like hunting, riding, and fishing. Philadelphia's first sports club, likely the first in the English-speaking world, was the Schuylkill River Colony, founded in 1732. It promoted conviviality among men who enjoyed fishing, hunting, and good eating, and it became the city's most exclusive club. In 1766, local gentlemen established the Gloucester Foxhunting Club.

The colonial elite copied the English by promoting horse racing. Late-seventeenth-century Virginia planters raced their own mounts across short distances to demonstrate their courage, brawn, intelligence, materialism, and honor. Beginning in 1735 in Charles Town, elite jockey clubs built racetracks and organized meets. Semiannual race weeks became the center of the social season in Charles Town, Williamsburg, and Annapolis, accompanied by elite balls and plebeian social events. The more humble sort could hunt and fish in nearby woods and streams, and patronize taverns, where they enjoyed blood sports like cock fights, bull baiting, and gander pulling. Backcountry folk engaged in rough-and-tumble fighting to prove their courage and honor.

The Nineteenth Century

Most men in 1800 were farmers who worked long hours determined by the seasons. They had their occasional social events like parties celebrating New Year's, the Fourth of July, and Election Days, when they enjoyed socializing, drinking liquor, competing in marksmanship contests, wrestling, running and trotting races, attending orations, and listening to musical entertainment. Rich plantation owners sponsored lavish balls, and slave musicians, singers, or storytellers often entertained the guests. The plantation owners were avid sportsmen who hunted, bet on cock fights, and attended thoroughbred races. Their slaves had free time on Sundays and during Christmas week when they were unsupervised. They sang, danced, listened to folktales in the slave community, and visited other plantations to see women.

Men's leisure in the antebellum era was strongly influenced by the male bachelor subculture that thrived in antebellum cities, especially among workers unaccustomed to timework discipline, and postbellum mining camps. About 30 to 40 percent of nineteenth-century urban male workers were single and lived anonymously in boardinghouses and rooming houses in a convivial homosocial world. They mainly hung out at such nearby male bastions as firehouses, saloons, barbershops, cigar stores, and brothels. These men enjoyed drinking, chasing women, gambling, and participating in the sporting fraternity in such blood sports as pugilism and animal baiting, which demonstrated their manliness, prowess, and honor. They were customers for leisure entrepreneurs who operated saloons, billiard parlors, theaters, music halls, gambling halls, and brothels. The illegal entertainments were mainly located in vice districts like Chicago's Levee District and New Orleans's Storyville, which were broken up in the 1910s.

Working-class men read male-oriented publications. During the antebellum era, there were penny-press publications of lurid adventure accounts and cheap paperbacks and weeklies that focused on sex and crime. There was a lot of interest in the sporting press, like *The Spirit of the Times,* (1831–1902), which covered turf, cricket, rowing, foot racing, yachting, and baseball. The *National Police Gazette* (1845–1916) originally published crime stories, but it became a popular sporting weekly with

Poker game. A man holds three-of-a-kind in his hand during a poker game. Poker, a popular game with males since the days of the Old West, saw a surge in popularity in 2003 thanks to televised tournaments on the Travel Channel and ESPN. © *Michael Prince/Corbis*

many illustrations of sexy women once Richard K. Fox took over in 1877. He sold reduced subscriptions to saloonkeepers, barbers, and hotel managers, which helped the periodical become readily available to American men.

Middle-class Victorians gained their sense of manliness through work, not leisure, made the family the centerpiece of life, and were threatened by the bachelor subculture's anti-Victorian lifestyle. They were more likely to join literary societies, music clubs, evangelical church groups, and fraternal organizations. Reformers created the rational recreation movement that advocated uplifting and moral pleasures, like the new game of baseball as a substitute for vile amusements. The new man would be a muscular Christian, strong in body, soul, and spirit.

Immigrants' low incomes and their cultural baggage, which included a continental Sabbath that permitted Sunday entertainment after church, influenced their leisure. The Irish arrived with their own bachelor subculture, which they re-created at their modestly appointed neighborhood taverns with traditions of treating and drunkenness, while Germans brought their family-

Billiards. Men sit on a bench and relax in front of a billiard parlor in Collins, Iowa, in 1939. Billiards has long been a staple of the working-class male's leisure time activities. © *Arthur Rothstein/Corbis*

oriented *bier gartens.* They organized men's choral societies, German theater companies, and the *turnverein* for gymnastics and a community center. New immigrants from eastern and southern Europe who also maintained their traditional gender-based leisure patterns of saloons (coffeehouses among Greeks and Jews) and social clubs, but not athletics, followed the Irish and German groups.

Working-class leisure was hindered by the expansion of industrial capitalism and the rise of the factory system, which displaced small workshops with their casual pace of work. Poorly paid employees averaged sixty-hour workweeks, allowing little free time. They relied heavily on saloons or "poor man's clubs," where they met friends, made new acquaintances, played billiards and other games, gambled, and drank. Their attendance at spectator sports was curtailed by inaccessibility, ticket costs, and Sunday blue laws.

A bureaucratized and less independent middle class emerged after the Civil War. They worked a five-and-a-half-day week and looked to leisure for self-improvement, reinvigoration, and a sense of accomplishment they were not getting from work. They attended the theater, light opera, lectures, museums, and professional baseball, and avidly joined fraternal organizations to socialize with similar men. They also spent considerable time with their families, playing music and singing at home, attending vaudeville shows, or taking outings like picnics.

Upper-class men in the late nineteenth century employed their leisure time to demonstrate their social status by sponsoring and participating in expensive and exclusive entertainment. They organized downtown clubs that focused on politics, culture, and sports like track and field. These clubs provided an escape from work and family, where elite men dined lavishly, smoked expensive cigars, and drank fine wines. The elite also founded suburban country clubs for golf, tennis, and field sports. Their participation in sports and vacation time spent at western dude ranches enabled them to demonstrate their manliness at a period when WASP (white Anglo-Saxon Protestant) virility was widely questioned.

The Twentieth Century

A 1910 survey of over 1,000 workingmen found that their entertainment included attending movies, art galleries, and libraries, and reading magazines, playing cards, and shooting pool. Married men tended mainly to spend over half their leisure time with family, followed by at social clubs, movies, theater, dance saloons, and pool halls, and with friends. Single men spent most of their time with friends and at commercial amusements. They spent an average of 15 cents a week at the neighborhood nickelodeons. These nickelodeons had cheap, simply furnished rooms with just a few tables; they were often adjuncts of saloons or clubs that were popular social centers. They were considered dangerous hangouts where young men were initiated into a working-class culture of smoking, drinking, and gambling. On the other hand, downtown poolrooms that attracted businessmen and politicians were spacious and elegant, with dozens of tables.

YMCAs, which were racially segregated, began catering to the working class in the early 1900s, though a full membership was a substantial $15. These men also spent time at bathhouses that cities were operating to promote better public health. Chicago had fifty-one public bathhouses by 1917. There were also higher-class private Turkish, Roman, or Electric bathhouses that charged up to 25 cents. Chicago, New York, and San Francisco had facilities that tolerated gays or served only gays. Sexual connections occurred inside dressing rooms (private cubicles) and steam rooms. Gays found bathhouses and YMCA hotels convenient and safe places to organize their own subculture.

Young blue-collar men sought female companionship, although they did not spend a lot on dates. A date with a respectable girl might entail skating, sleigh riding, going on a picnic, or taking a trip to an amusement park or the beach, places where inhibitions were left behind. By the 1910s, men looking for fun with less-reputable girls might pick up unescorted women at amusement parks, dance halls, and cabarets, hoping these "charity girls" might provide them with sexual favors. Dancing became a popular entertainment in the 1910s. Working-class men and women went separately to public dance halls or ethnic dances, while middle-class cabarets and dance resorts regulated relations between the sexes by banning un-

escorted women, suggestive dancing, and sexual contact off the dance floor. Taxi-dance halls, where men paid women to dance with them for a fee (per ticket), opened in the late 1910s, often following the closure of vice districts. Women at these halls sold tickets to men for the privilege of dancing with them. They mainly attracted unmarried immigrants seeking female companionship.

In the 1920s, leisure boomed, thanks to improved wages, shorter working hours, and the decline of Puritanism, including liberalized Sunday blue laws. All men in the 1920s emulated heroes of consumption such as movie stars, athletes, and even gangsters. The hyper male figure was the playboy, a hedonistic, narcissistic fashion plate who dated fast women, socialized at illegal speakeasies, and gambled at the racetracks. Even middle-class courtship became more informal as couples went to movies, restaurants, and nightclubs, where they enjoyed exuberant dances like the Charleston and drove home in enclosed automobiles. While times became tight during the Great Depression, men relied a lot on government-sponsored leisure programs to replace industrial recreation programs. Men who wanted to be urbane and sophisticated emulated role models like Fred Astaire and Clark Gable, and read *Esquire* (1933), the arbiter of good taste, stylish elegance, and refinement. Zoot suiters were the African American and Mexican American sophisticates.

After World War II, social class was losing its significance in demarking manly leisure because of rising standards of living for unionized blue-collar workers. Men who grew up in the depression and fought in World War II devoted more attention to domesticity than ever before, especially other directed and consumer-driven middle-class suburbanites. Men in the 1950s became avid viewers of television—particularly boxing and other spectator sports, and westerns, like the *Rifleman*, a vivid depiction of frontier manhood— and fans of Elvis and rock music. They aspired to the lifestyle of the hyper male, epitomized by the Rat Pack, Las Vegas, and *Playboy*, which idealized the consumptionist bachelor who was obsessed by cars, stereos, wine, and women. The periodical stressed a new hedonism that challenged domesticity and Puritan values.

In the 1950s, gay men focused their social life on the bar scene. In Boston alone, there were over twenty-four gay bars. Homosexuals also congregated at street corners, certain parks, bus stations, and bathhouses. The gay subculture became more open and assertive following the 1969 Stonewall Inn riot in New York City. The Stonewall Inn was a gay bar in Greenwich Village. The riot broke out between patrons and police who raided the bar. The rioting lasted until late into the night. Graffiti calling for "Gay Power" appeared all along Christopher St. where the bar was located. This event marked a critical divide in the politics and consciousness of gay folk. Gay liberation became a large movement. By the late 1970s, a thriving and openly gay culture revolved around social activism, bars, health clubs, travel, and periodicals.

The counterculture of the late 1960s and early 1970s continued to challenge middle-class mores, encouraging men to "let it all hang out." Manliness was less concerned with grooming and expensive clothing than with personal fulfillment. Sport remained a cornerstone of a manly culture, though there was greater interest in participatory athletics, especially jogging, as men embraced physical fitness. The athlete was the hyper masculine male, especially football players with their padded uniforms, as well as lightly clad basketball players. African American ballplayers excelled at a jazzed-up, individualistic style of the game. Basketball became a contest of male "peacocks" in short shorts, who dribbled between their legs, stuffed baskets, and put up shots "in your face."

At the end of the twentieth century and the beginning of the twenty-first, male leisure continued to focus on the traditional themes of sports and sex. Younger men employed extreme sports that required participants to exhibit creative and risky athletic maneuvers to display their manliness. In regards to sexuality, AIDS and other sexually transmitted diseases made men more cautious, but not abstinent. Instead of visiting pick-up bars, men met potential sexual partners at health clubs, through friends, via advertisements in magazines, through dating services, and over the Internet.

See also: Civic Clubs, Men; Gay Men's Leisure Lifestyles; Hunting; "Muscular Christianity" and the YM(W)CA Movements; Teenage Leisure Trends

BIBLIOGRAPHY

Chauncey, George. *Gay New York: Gender Urban Culture and the Making of the Gay Male World, 1890–1940.* New York: Basic Books, 1994.

Chudacoff, Howard P. *The Age of the Bachelor: Creating an American Subculture.* Princeton, N.J.: Princeton University Press, 1999.

Gorn, Elliott. *The Manly Art: Bare Knuckle Prize Fighting in America.* Ithaca, N.Y.: Cornell University Press, 1986.

Kimmel, Michael. *Manhood in America: A Cultural History.* New York: Free Press, 1996.

Nasaw, David. *Going Out: The Rise and Fall of Public Amusements.* New York: Basic Books, 1993.

Osgerby, Bill. *Playboys in Paradise: Masculinity, Youth, and Leisure-Style in Modern America.* Oxford: Berg, 2001.

Rader, Benjamin G. *American Sports: From the Age of Folk Games to the Age of Televised Sports.* 4th ed. Upper Saddle River, N.J.: Prentice-Hall, 1999.

Riess, Steven A. *City Games: The Evolution of American Urban Society and the Rise of Sports.* Champaign: University of Illinois Press, 1989.

Steven A. Riess

MIDDLE-BROW READING

See *Literary Societies and Middle-Brow Reading*

MILITARY BANDS

See *Band Playing*

MINOR LEAGUE BASEBALL

See *Baseball Crowds*

MISS AMERICA

See *Beauty Pageants*

MODELING (AIRPLANES, TRAINS, ETC.)

Models are representations of other things. Many different kinds of models are built and used for a variety of purposes. In particular, model collecting, model building, and other activities with models are important hobbies in the United States.

Models differ from what they represent in three important ways. First, they usually differ in scale: models are often smaller, although sometimes larger, than the real life thing or activity that they characterize. Model airplanes, such as those constructed by hobbyists, are normally much smaller than the originals, while models of molecules, such as those used in teaching chemistry, are much larger than reality. Models differ from what they represent in terms of complexity: some models of ships or trains constructed by hobbyists are exceedingly intricate, with many working parts, while toy ships or trains for children can be very simple. Finally, models differ in terms of verisimilitude, or true-to-lifeness. Plastic scale models of World War II aircraft, for example, may very accurately depict the external appearance of the originals, but represent few, if any, of their internal parts. Powered models are usually less accurate in their external appearance, but actually fly like the originals.

Models have a variety of purposes. For one, they act as information reduction devices. That is, they eliminate needless detail, although what specific detail is needless depends on the purpose served by a model. Maps, for instance, are models, but topographic maps and road maps each eliminate some and emphasize other details. Models also serve as information storage devices. The study and preservation of history is often an important function of models for hobbyists. The original trains, ships, airplanes, or other artifacts modeled may no longer exist, so the models store valuable information about them. Similarly, bow and arrow or black powder arms hunters maintain knowledge of the use of obsolete weaponry, just as paintings, drawings, and photographs preserve scenes, clothing styles, and behavior patterns from the past. Models are also used in teaching and learning, especially where learning with the real thing could pose a danger. One might learn to fly a jet fighter plane by strapping in and taking off, but the potential for disaster in such a situation is overwhelming. A flight simulator offers a far safer learning environment. Similarly, models of aircraft in their design stage are tested in wind tunnels in order to gain information about aspects of their aerodynamic characteristics, and model battlefields are constructed to appraise strategies. These are examples of the information generation function of models wherein they are used to safely simulate conditions that have never before existed.

Models, Miniatures, and Replicas

Models are sometimes referred to as miniatures or replicas. Each of these terms, however, has a slightly different connotation, principally in terms of the three characteristics of models—scale, complexity, and verisimilitude—and each is often used with respect to a certain genre of models. Miniatures are, as the term implies, models that are normally much smaller in scale than the originals, but are usually high in complexity and, especially, in verisimilitude. Models of buildings, such as the White

House, the United States Capitol building, or various houses—especially historical colonial homes, but also houses from American frontier days, such as log houses—are generally referred to as miniatures. In creating miniatures, artisans and hobbyists are meticulous about detail, trying to make their creations as true-to-life as possible.

Replicas are often full-scale working models. That is, they are identical, or nearly so, to the original. While few flying examples of World War I or World War II aircraft remain, enthusiasts have built numerous full and partial scale replicas of Fokker Triplanes, Messerschmidt 109s, and other aircraft for recreational flying, air shows, and the like. Replica World War I aircraft can be seen at the Memorial Flight Association's site at http://memorial .flight.free.fr/indexuk.html.

Static and Dynamic Models

Models can be either static or dynamic. That is, they may be for display only or they may emulate that which they represent to some limited extent. Static models are primarily used for display purposes and, as such, are generally as nearly proportionate as possible to the real objects that they represent. Ships-in-bottles are classic examples of static display. The techniques for constructing ships-in-bottles were developed during the early nineteenth century by sailors on long voyages, who used materials at hand. While techniques differ among builders, basically ships-in-bottles must either be constructed of parts that can be inserted into a bottle and assembled or be constructed so that they collapse for insertion. The masts for model sailing ships, for example, are usually raised after insertion by extra long rigging that is then cut after the masts are up. Static models of cars, trains, ships, airplanes, animals, weapons, soldiers, buildings, terrain, and many other things exist, but those of various kinds of land, sea, and air vehicles are particularly popular. Some are constructed or carved from wood; others are paper, metal, or plastic; and still others are made from a combination of materials. Some are die cast (all of one piece) while others are assembled. Model airplanes provide an illustrative example: static die cast metal or assembled plastic scale models exist for aircraft, ranging from the first Wright Flyer to the Concorde and the latest fighter jet. There are even models of craft that have never existed, such as the USS Enterprise and Klingon battle cruisers of Star Trek fame.

Most static models are built to scale. That is, they are proportioned to match the original as closely as possible, at least in terms of external appearance. Model airplanes, for example, usually come in standard scales such as 1/32, 1/48, 1/72, and 1/144. The scale denotes the proportional

Louisiana Toy Train Museum. A collection of toy trains and working models that date back as early as the 1880s is on exhibit at the Louisiana Toy Train Museum in Kenner, Louisiana (shown here in 1995). © *Robert Holmes/Corbis*

relationship in size between the model and the actual aircraft. In a 1/48 scale model, one unit of measurement (inches usually) on the model represents forty-eight on the real airplane.

Dynamic, or working, models are those that emulate some functions of the original on a small scale. The first models that represented real aircraft were developed around 1930 in the United States. These models were made of wood (usually balsa, spruce, pine, or basswood) and covered with a tissue-like substance called silk span. The silk span was then covered with cellulose acetate nitrate dope (a type of lacquer finish) that, when hardened, provided a firm skin for the model. Working airplane models are of three basic types. "Free flight" models, as the name suggests, are designed to fly on their own, with no guidance from the ground. Very simple model airplanes made of balsa and powered by rubber bands that control a propeller are of this type. "Control line" model airplanes are flown by operators on the ground. Generally, control line models are flown by two wires or cables attached to a hand-held yoke. The pilot can then control up and down movements as the model flies in circles around him or her. "Radio control" models are flown by an operator who uses a transmitter to control servos that move the control surfaces of the craft. The first powered radio control aircraft were developed and flown by Walter and Bill Good in 1937.

The electric train is one of the most popular dynamic models, and it comes in a variety of sizes, usually indicated by gauge and scale. Gauge indicates the distance between the rails of a train. A full-size train track measures 1435.5 mm (4 feet, 8.5 inches between the inner sides of the rails. Gauge 1, the earliest model railroad size developed in the late nineteenth century in Germany by Märklin Bros. and Co., has a track width of 45 mm and a scale of 1/32. O gauge, introduced in the early 1900s, is 1/48 scale (1/43 in Great Britain and France, 1/45 in the rest of Europe). S gauge, introduced by the American Flyer Company in 1946, is 1/64 scale. HO gauge, by far the most common and commercially important, developed in the early 1930s and has a track width of 16.5 mm and a scale of 1/87. OO gauge, the most common size in England, has the same track width as HO, but a scale of 1/78. TT (which stands for table top) gauge has a track width of 9mm and a scale of 1/120. N gauge is somewhat smaller than TT, with a track width of 9 mm and a scale of 1:160. Finally, Z gauge, the smallest commercially available size, has a track width of 6.5 mm and a scale of 1/220.

Lionel, the company founded by Joshua Lionel Cowen, has dominated the model train market in the United States. Lionel began producing model trains in late 1900. After World War I, Cowen had the idea to include toy trains as part of crèche displays in department stores during the Christmas season. This marketing ploy led to a huge rise in the popularity of model trains, and the 1920s are often regarded as the golden age of model trains.

Commercial Aspects of Models

Models and modeling support large industries, as well as major hobby associations in the United States and elsewhere. Revell, Minicraft, Matchbox, and Testor are major producers of models of land, sea, and air craft in the United States. In addition to the models themselves, numerous books and magazines are devoted to building and collecting various kinds of models. Modeling associations include the National Association of Miniature Enthusiasts, founded in 1972 and devoted to the hobby of making and collecting doll houses and furniture; the Academy of Model Aeronautics, the official governing body for model aviation and publisher of *Model Aviation* magazine; and the National Model Railroad Association, founded in 1935, which is the largest model railroading association in the United States. Finally, shows and museums dedicated to model airplanes, trains, ships, and the many other genres of models attract millions of visitors each year.

See also: Hobbies and Crafts; Railroads and Leisure

BIBLIOGRAPHY

ABC Park Flyers. "RC Model Planes: History." Available from http://www.rc-model-planes.com/history.html.

Boyd, Norman Napier. *The Model Ship: Her Role in History.* Woodbridge, U.K.: Antique Collectors' Club, 2000.

Granville Island Museums. "Lionel Trains Museum." Available from http://www.modeltrainsmuseum.bc.ca/.

Munson, Robert S. "Pathways Within Model Aviation and Beyond." 2002. Available from http://www.mindspring.com/∼thayer5/pathways/.

National Association of Miniature Enthusiasts. Home page available at http://www.miniatures.org/.

Ships in Bottles Association of America. "Ships-in-Bottles History." Available from http://www.shipsinbottles.org/history.asp.

Souter, Gerry, and Janet Souter. *Classic Toy Trains.* St. Paul, Minn.: Motorbooks International, 2002.

Wang, L. T. "International Lists of Scale Model Related Web Sites." Available from http://scalemodel.net/.

Zaic, Frank. *Model Airplanes and the American Boy.* Northridge, Calif.: Model Aeronautic Publications, 1982.

Garry Chick

MOUNTAIN CLIMBING

People have climbed mountains for the whole of human history, and they have done so for a variety of reasons—spiritual, strategic, prospecting and hunting, surveying, and probably simple curiosity. Mountains were climbed in biblical and classical times, and even before recorded history: arrowheads have been found at the summits of North American mountains, a bronze spearhead was found at the summit of the Riffelhorn in Switzerland, and "the ice man"—who died some 5,300 years ago—was discovered close to a pass in the Austrian Alps at a height of 3,210 meters. The sport and recreational pastime of mountain climbing began in the European Alps in the mid-nineteenth century. It grew out of a complex combination of exploration, tourism, and scientific fieldwork, all of which were beginning to take larger numbers of people to the summits of mountains.

Mountain climbing, often called "mountaineering" and sometimes "Alpinism," is the activity of attempting to reach the summits of mountains. The activity is distinguished from hiking or backpacking by the difficulty of the ascent. Many mountain summits are achievable by competent walkers—for example, the Appalachian Trail takes hikers over many summits. Mountain climbing usually involves some rock or ice climbing. A distinction that is often made is that mountain climbing involves the use of both feet and hands, and, in more recent times, these have been combined with the use of specialized equipment and the knowledge of specialized techniques.

The activity has both competitive (sporting) and recreational forms, although the informality of the activity and the absence of institutionalization (no governing bodies, no uniforms, no formal rules, no referees or judges) sometimes makes it difficult to distinguish between the two forms. Competition usually takes the form

Mount McKinley. Forty-four-year-old Linda Burdette stands 17,000 feet up on Mount McKinley, the tallest mountain in North America. Located in Denali National Park in Alaska, the 20,320-foot mountain was officially named after President William McKinley (1843–1901) in 1897. The first successful climb occurred by the Sourdough party in 1910 when the shorter North Peak was reached; the Karsten-Stuck expedition achieved the true peak (South Peak) in 1913. In modern times a climbing fee of $150 is required. © *Galen Rowell/Corbis*

of achieving (and recording) a first ascent of both the summit of a mountain, and of a particular route to the summit (for example, North Face, or West Ridge). It should be pointed out that there is a particular form of arrogance associated with recording an ascent and claiming it as a "first." Often, mountain climbers have no way of knowing if a previous ascent has been made. However, the activity emerged out of the same colonial ethos of exploration that allowed Europeans to claim that they had "discovered" already inhabited lands such as the Americas and Australia, and to claim them for their own. Variations of "first ascents," such as first female ascent and first winter ascent, may also be recorded. Competition can also take place with regard to the speed of an ascent, and the style of an ascent (style is usually associated with the amount of equipment used, or the tactics that are used to achieve a summit). The vast majority of mountaineering is recreational, and involves following established routes to summits, routes that are often recorded in guidebooks.

Mountains in the United States

The United States is bracketed by two major mountain ranges. In the East, the Appalachian/Adirondack chain is of less interest to mountain climbers. The summits are, for the most part, accessible to hikers (as are the volcanoes of Hawaii); only in winter are some routes to some summits in the Adirondacks and the White Mountains (New Hampshire) of interest to mountain climbers. In the West, between the prairies and the Pacific Ocean, lie a number of major interconnected mountain regions—specifically, the various ranges of the Rocky Mountains, the Sierra Nevada, the Cascades, and the Olympic Mountains. A large number of the mountains are high enough to have permanent snow cover on the summits, and these and many others are of interest to mountaineers. The western mountain ranges continue northward through Canada and into Alaska, wherein lies the highest mountain in North America—Mount McKinley at 6,194 meters. To the South, the highest mountain in the contiguous United States is Mount Whitney in California (Sierra Nevada) at 4,418 meters.

Mountain Climbing in the United States

Many peaks in the United States were climbed before mountain climbers began to record their ascents. Scouts, prospectors, survey crews, native people on spirit quests or hunting, all found their ways to the summits of mountains, and some even recorded their achievements. For example, Josiah Whitney and his survey crew (William Brewer and Charles Hoffman) were making ascents in the Sierra Nevada in the 1860s. Darby Field's legendary ascent of Mount Washington (New Hampshire) in 1642 is unlikely to have been the first ascent, but it has been recorded as such.

The first American mountain climbers were middle or upper-middle class, educated northeasterners, who climbed in the European Alps. In the mid-nineteenth century, it was easier to travel to Europe from the northeastern United States than to the Rocky Mountains. Some Americans, still at this time looking to Europe for their sport and culture, began to follow the new European fashion of mountain climbing. Perhaps the best known of the early mountain climbers was William Augustus Brevoort Coolidge (1850–1926). As a teenager, he moved to Europe for health reasons, with his aunt, Miss Meta Brevoort, and began a mountain-climbing career (often with his aunt) that made him among the leading mountaineers of his day. Perhaps the best evidence of this eastern U.S.–European academic connection lies in the fact that less than six years after the formation of the very first mountain-climbing club, the Alpine Club (UK) in 1857, the Williamstown Alpine Club was formed in Massachusetts in 1863.

The development of the railroads made the western mountains much more accessible by the latter part of the nineteenth century, and western settlement took many interested in mountain climbing to live in states such as Colorado and Wyoming and to the West Coast. The Canadian Pacific Railroad imported Swiss mountain guides to work at their hotels in the Canadian Rockies in the 1890s, and the developments of mountaineering and tourism brought Canadian, European, and American climbers to this region. Yale professors were particularly active in the Lake Louise area, and the death of a former law student, Phillip Abbot, on Mount Lefroy in 1896, is often identified as the first mountaineering fatality in North America.

The early development of mountain climbing in the United States was sometimes characterized by novelty as-

cents involving local people, and by controversy. When the California survey team in the 1860s declared that the summit of Half Dome (Yosemite Valley) was "inaccessible," it was taken as a challenge completed by George Anderson in 1875—he drilled a series of holes and inserted eyebolts into the smooth rock; his route is close to the modern *via ferrata* that now leads to the summit. Local ranchers Willard Ripley and William Rogers made the first ascent of the "inaccessible" Devil's Tower (Wyoming) by hammering wooden stakes into a crack leading all the way to the summit. A group of "sourdoughs" with no mountaineering experience set out to achieve the first ascent in 1910, but they are now believed to have reached only the lower North Summit. The mountain was finally "claimed" in 1913.

These achievements are, in many ways, characteristic of the development of mountain climbing in the United States. Despite the early European experiences, mountain climbing in the States often took place in isolation from European developments in terms of technique and safety. The Appalachian Mountain Club was founded in 1876, followed by the Sierra Club in 1892 and the American Alpine Club in 1902. The West Coast clubs, the Sierra Club, the Seattle Mountaineers, and Mazamas (Oregon) developed an approach that involved mass ascents of mountains—a technique unknown in Western Europe, but widely adopted in Soviet mountaineering. These lasted until the 1930s. Similarly, European rope techniques were not well known in the West, and many thought that the use of a rope was unsporting.

This began to change in the 1930s with two key moments. The first was the publication in the *Sierra Club Bulletin* (1931) of Robert Underhill's article "On the Use and Management of the Rope in Rock Work." Underhill was a Harvard professor who had climbing experience in the European Alps, and had developed European rope techniques while rock climbing in New England. The second occurred when well-known German climber Fritz Wiessner emigrated to the United States in the 1930s. Underhill and Wiessner spearheaded a period of exploration and advances in technique in the period leading up to World War II.

Until this time, there were few mountain climbers in the United States, and the activity was well below the cultural radar. Changes started with World War II, as some U.S. troops received training in mountain warfare, enjoyed the opportunity of climbing in places such as Europe and Japan, and benefited (as did mountaineers around the world) from technological advances that often were a result of wartime efforts. These included nylon ropes, which were much stronger than the previous hemp ropes, and Vibram (rubber) soles for boots, replacing the nails that had been used previously (Vibram soles still replicate the pattern of climbing boot nails).

There were small increases in participation after the war, resulting from an increasingly democratized population (for example, increased income and leisure time, and rapidly increasing automobile ownership) that had the time, money, and means to travel to mountains, and sometimes the benefit of wartime mountain training. This period saw the start of an extended period of exploration and new ascents by U.S. mountaineers in the United States, Canada, and Alaska, and in other parts of the world. The first U.S. ascent of Chomolungma (Mount Everest—8,848 meters) was made by Tom Hornbein and Willi Unsoeld in 1963. This climb came ten years after the first ascent, but announced U.S. membership in the "Everest club" in grand style by not only ascending what is now derogatorily termed the "yak route" (the South Ridge), but also by making the first ascent of a new route—the West Ridge—and traversing the mountain.

As *National Geographic* magazine and newspapers across the country reported on the ascent, U.S. mountain climbing began to come to public attention, and did so at an interesting time in U.S. culture—just as the counterculture was beginning to emerge. Many young people began to travel to wilderness areas, and to take part in new noncompetitive or less competitive (alternative) activities.

This period saw a significant increase in participation, mostly in rock climbing, but also in mountain climbing. The period was also characterized by significant challenges to traditional ways of climbing, and by the beginning of a period of technological advances (related primarily to increased safety, comfort, and convenience, in addition to enabling more and more difficult ascents) that continued into the early twenty-first century.

New fibers such as GoreTex and Thinsulate, safer equipment (improved ropes, carabiners, crampons and ice axes, descenders, and various belaying devices), and the increasing availability of lightweight clothing, equipment, and freeze-dried foods changed the climbing experience. They have also been associated with a rapid period of commercialization and growth in participation since the 1980s. Although mountain climbing is by no means a mass recreational activity in the United States, it has become well established as a part of U.S. culture. The activity is regularly featured on the Outdoor Life Network, in mass-circulation magazines such as *Outside* and *Climbing*, and in Hollywood movies. The participants are, for the most part, still male, white, middle class and urban, as has been the case for the last 150 years. The only

real change has been the increasing number of female participants since the mid-1980s.

Increasing commercialization resulted in mountain climbing becoming a significant part of the adventure tourism industry. In terms of publicity for the activity, the influence of Jon Krakauer's work for *Outside* and his 1997 book *Into Thin Air* cannot be underestimated. His account of the deaths of members of two adventure tourism groups on Chomolungma in 1996 not only sparked a whole publishing wave in what the *New York Times* has termed "explornography," but also created a new wave of interest in mountain climbing. That interest is also reflected in the corporate world where images of mountain climbing are being used to symbolize achievement and corporate aspiration, and where mountain climbing has become a component of executive leadership and character training courses.

See also: Extreme Sports, Rock Climbing

BIBLIOGRAPHY

Coolidge, W. A. B. *The Alps in Nature and History.* London: Methuen, 1908.

Jones, Chris. *Climbing in North America.* Berkeley: University of California Press, 1976.

Krakauer, Jon. *Into Thin Air.* New York: Villard Books, 1997.

Mellor, Don. *American Rock: Region, Rock and Culture in American Climbing.* Woodstock, Vt.: Countryman Press, 2001.

Mummery, Albert F. *My Climbs in the Alps and Caucasus.* London: Fisher Unwin, 1895.

Pyatt, Edward. *The Guiness Book of Mountains and Mountaineering: Facts and Feats.* London: Guiness Superlatives, 1980.

Unsworth, Walt. *Everest.* Harmondsworth, Eng.: Penguin, 1982.

———. *Encyclopaedia of Mountaineering.* London: Hodder and Stoughton, 1992.

Peter Donnelly

MOVIES' IMPACT ON POPULAR LEISURE

The movies came to America at the beginning of the twentieth century, a time of immense social and technological change. They were part of a bubbling cultural stew that also included the introduction of radio, national magazines, advertising, automobiles, paved roads, prohibition, and enfranchised women. As the country entered two decades of prosperity, and middle- and working-class Americans found that they had money, mobility, and spare time, they began going to the movies. In the years since, the fortunes of studios and producers have varied with the national economy, but audiences have consistently seen feature films as one of their favorite leisure activities. In the first years of the twenty-first century, more Americans were watching more movies in theaters, on video monitors, and on home computers than at any time in the history of the medium.

On the most basic level, moving images fascinate the eye. Early nineteenth-century experiments with various toys and devices created the illusion of motion. Soon after still photography was perfected in the nineteenth century, inventors capitalized on the human eye's "persistence of vision" to recreate fully animate, lifelike motion with a series of still images. The development of celluloid film by George Eastman in 1888 made it possible for Thomas Edison's assistant, William Dickson, to invent the movie camera in 1893.

Movies proved to be so popular that, particularly in America, they evolved quickly, becoming more sophisticated in their efforts to attract more viewers. In those formative decades, Europe and Russia created vibrant motion picture communities, but during World War I many of the chemicals used for photography were also needed for explosives. Movie production suffered, giving American filmmakers an advantage they never surrendered. Lack of governmental control, an abundant source of natural light in Southern California, and political and economic stability were also important factors. The American movie industry developed on two tracks. First, millions of people went to local movie theaters at least once per week; second, much larger audiences attended heavily promoted epics, such as *Ben-Hur* (1925 and 1959). The most successful of those became cultural milestones.

That extraordinary popularity did not arrive without controversy and economic setbacks, but throughout the first half of the twentieth century, the movies were the dominant form of visual entertainment and a major element in American life.

Vaudeville, Peep Shows, and Nickelodeons

Vaudeville variety shows had prepared Americans for movies. At the beginning of the twentieth century, most towns and cities had at least one vaudeville theater that presented two to six shows every day. They were meant to appeal to the largest possible audience; not only men,

but also middle-class women and families. Movie theaters would do the same in later decades.

In America, Thomas Edison's Kinetoscope, or peepshow, was the first method of distribution for movies. Instead of projecting a film onto a screen, these hand-crank devices showed a short movie to one viewer at a time. They became popular in arcades and amusement halls, but, when the film projector was introduced in 1895, exhibitors quickly realized that projecting films on a screen to large audiences was more profitable. Vaudeville halls and other theaters were the first to add movies to their programs.

When vaudeville performers went on strike in 1901, the theater owners filled their schedules with films and bought projectors in record numbers. Equipment manufacturers ramped up production and cranked out as many machines as they could. Then when the strike ended, the manufacturers had to cut their prices drastically to sell the equipment they had on hand. That discount made it economically feasible for ambitious entrepreneurs to rent storefronts; install projectors, screens, and seats; and show nothing but short films. Eventually, the movies eclipsed vaudeville; the last vaudeville palace (the New York Palace) closed in 1932. Many of its stars—Buster Keaton, W. C. Fields, the Marx Brothers—found greater fame on screen.

In 1902, Thomas Talley's Electric Theater became the first permanent movie house in America. Three years later, a Pittsburgh theater opened with a more luxurious interior and a piano to provide musical accompaniment for the films. Admission was five cents; the nickelodeon was born.

In those first years, the motion picture business was an example of unfettered free enterprise. There were virtually no laws governing the production or distribution of movies. Thomas Edison had patented his equipment, but he'd neglected to secure European protection, and so other companies used imported cameras and projectors. Initially, his two biggest competitors were the Biograph and Vitagraph studios, which had set up business in New York. All three companies made films in New York and New Jersey. Edison's gangs intimidated other production crews both legally and physically, though none of them were averse to rough-and-tumble methods when needed. (See Jeffries-Sharkey Championship sidebar.)

Some of the short one-reel films they made were nothing more than shots taken from trains rolling slowly through cities, or subway cars rattling through tunnels, but people were fascinated by any moving image. The nickelodeons flourished. Before the decade was over, there were more than 5,000 of them in operation in

The Jeffries-Sharkey Fight

On the night of 3 November 1899, James J. Jeffries, "the Boilermaker," defended his heavyweight championship against challenger "Sailor" Tom Sharkey at Coney Island. It was, Jeffries later modestly claimed, "perhaps the greatest combat ever waged in a ring between two human beings." Public interest was intense and so the Biograph company arranged to set up special lights to film the fight.

The Biograph camera crew was positioned at ringside. While the bout was going on, they learned that a group from their rivals at Vitagraph had set up a camera several rows farther back. The Biograph crew immediately dispatched Pinkerton detectives to seize the unauthorized camera and film, but the rowdy crowd got into the action and prevented the enforcers from getting to the other crew. The Vitagraph poachers actually managed to capture the fight on film, and hurried away to develop the reels at one of their labs. That night, though, their film stolen from the lab, presumably by someone from the Edison company.

Eventually, both Vitagraph and Edison released movies of the fight while Biograph never made any money from their film. Jeffries retained his title.

America, and 80 percent of the population went to the movies every week. Though European filmmakers had been telling stories in films for years, the first American film to use "creative geography" (editing shots filmed at different places to create a unified scene) was Edwin S. Porter's 1903 *Life of an American Fireman,* a rescue story that combined footage of real fire fighters with fictional characters. It was an immediate success with audiences, as was Porter's next film, *The Great Train Robbery.* In 1908, the movie business made two significant evolutionary leaps. First, The Motion Picture Patents Co., commonly called "The Trust," was formed when Biograph, Edison, Vitagraph, and six other companies merged. They created the basic economic structure of the industry: the producer who created the film; the distributor who arranged the rental agreements; the exhibitor who showed it. The Trust also had an exclusive contract with the Eastman Company for raw film stock. It forced distributors to consolidate as the General Film Company, which would rent only to exhibitors who agreed to handle noth-

ing but Trust films and to pay a $2 weekly licensing fee. The arrangement did not last. Almost immediately, two distributors—William Swanson in Chicago, and Carl Laemmle, who would go on to found Universal Pictures—objected and urged other "Independents" to join them against The Trust. For the next decade, they fought in the courts and sometimes in the streets, until the companies that had formed The Trust died out, and the Independents became the Hollywood studios.

D. W. Griffith and *The Birth of a Nation*

For the decade or so following *Life of an American Fireman,* moviegoers were satisfied with short films. But cinematic storytelling developed steadily during those years, and David Wark Griffith emerged as the pre-eminent director. A failed actor and writer, he found his medium working behind the camera for Biograph. His first one-reel movie was *The Adventures of Dollie,* about a baby kidnapped by gypsies. Griffith took to the job immediately and worked steadily at a rate of about one movie per week. He made more than 400 films during the next six years.

Some have given Griffith credit for inventing many of the basic techniques of narrative filmmaking in those years, including the close up, the fade out, the long shot, and the cross cut. It is wrong to give him sole credit; examples of their use elsewhere are numerous, either earlier or at the same time. But he used those devices so well and he perfected them in so many films that it is not an exaggeration to say that he invented the feature film as audiences came to know it—an extended well-made story that makes use of the malleability of film in editing and camerawork, and is told with attractive actors, easily recognizable characters, and familiar plots. He developed a stock company of actors and technicians who remained loyal to him. He was also one of the first filmmakers to go to California in search of good lighting and authentic Western locations.

Griffith had an excellent eye for casting, particularly for younger actresses who could express the emotion and sentimentality that were central to his work; he discovered and nurtured the talents of Mary Pickford and the Gish sisters. He rehearsed seriously and thoroughly with his cast before the cameras rolled. He created new lighting techniques and helped actors to develop a new more natural, less exaggerated style specifically for film. He was one of the first to realize that an audience's conception of time is changed by the pace of editing, and a moment can be manipulated—either compressed or elongated to fit the needs of the film. Just as importantly, he used the camera to tell the story, not simply to record the story. He was able to combine quiet intimate interiors with

Movie theater. Large playbills cover the front of Havlin's Theatre in St. Louis, Missouri, where moviegoers only had to spend a quarter to see a show in 1910. © *Corbis*

large-scale action scenes involving thousands of extras so that each reinforced the other.

Griffith had already been working with ambitious two-reel (twenty- to forty-minute) projects in 1913 when the full-length (two-hour) *Quo Vadis?* was imported from Italy. Because of its length, the film played only in the larger "legitimate" theaters, and not the nickelodeons. American producers and executives doubted the economic viability of such a long feature, but the film became a commercial success, and it inspired Griffith to strike out on his own to create the epic *The Birth of a Nation*.

Originally titled *The Clansman, The Birth of a Nation* was the first "event" movie. The melodrama revolves around two families during the Civil War and Reconstruction, and ends with the Ku Klux Klan riding to the rescue. The NAACP and other progressive organizations protested the film's most egregious racist elements, but it was embraced by a segregated society and became an unprecedented popular hit. Despite a ticket price of $2, when the standard price was less than 25 cents, the crowds were enormous.

The American movie as an art form was born with Griffith's masterpiece. Before *The Birth of a Nation,* the movies were a diversion, a form of entertainment not really worthy of consideration by serious people. After it, the movies could claim at least a degree of artistic legitimacy. Griffith's success motivated other filmmakers to

The Most Expensive Movies Ever Made

When D. W. Griffith made *The Birth of a Nation* in 1915, nothing approaching that scale or expense had been attempted in the United States. Knowledgeable people within the film business predicted that no matter how popular the picture was, it could never make a profit. They were wrong. It was such a commercial success that, at regular intervals in the years since, ambitious filmmakers have attempted epic productions that cost more than any previous film. These are the 21 most expensive movies ever made and their budgets:

Birth of a Nation (1915) $110,000

Intolerance (1916) $385,906.77

Thief of Baghdad (1924) $2m

Ben-Hur (1925) $3.9m

Hell's Angels (1930-31) $3.95m

Gone With the Wind (1939) $4.25m

Wilson (1944) $5.2m

Duel in the Sun (1946) $8m

Joan of Arc (1948) $8.7m

Ten Commandments (1956) $13.5m

Ben-Hur (1959) $15m

Mutiny on the Bounty (1962) $19m

Cleopatra (1963) $44m

Superman (1978) $55m

Rambo III (1988) $63m

Who Framed Roger Rabbit? (1988) $70m

The Abyss (1989) $69.5m

Terminator 2 (1991) $100m

True Lies (1994) $100m

Waterworld (1995) $175m

Titanic (1997) $200m

undertake similarly gargantuan projects. (See Most Expensive Movies sidebar.)

Then, as now, such productions represented a huge financial risk for an industry that depended on a steady stream of more modest but reliably profitable works. For that, Griffith's one-time partner Thomas Ince paved the way.

Thomas Ince and the Studio System

In many ways, Ince was the opposite of Griffith. While Griffith filmed *The Birth of a Nation* without a written outline or script, Ince believed in managing production costs with careful preparation. At his Culver City studio, called "Inceville," he worked with writers to create solid, fast-moving stories. Those were translated into scripts complete with dialog and directions for action and camera work. That was the beginning of the studio system, essentially a motion picture assembly line that would create a large number of features at a predictable rate to play at a growing number of theaters and to satisfy an ever-increasing public appetite for movies.

For many years, the studios and producers tried to focus audiences' attention on the films themselves, not the actors who were given no credit. But moviegoers came to care for individual actors and wanted to know who they were. Carl Laemmle of Universal argued that by promoting his stars, he could charge higher rates for his films. The others followed suit, and by the end of World War I, Hollywood was producing the most polished movies in the world, familiar melodramas and comedies that were experienced by audiences in the dreamlike setting of a darkened movie theater.

Ince's mass production system worked. The studios were able to create a large number of technically sophisticated films and still charge a relatively modest admission. Moviegoing became an important social activity. By the 1920s, 500-700 features were produced every year and they brought in $2 billion in ticket sales. By the end of the decade, more growth occurred; America had more than 22,500 theaters, half of those in towns with populations of less than 5,000. Seating capacity was 18 million. The motion picture industry was making films that were designed to appeal to audiences of every age and socio-economic level.

It is impossible to separate the importance of movies as a leisure activity from the other social changes that were going on in those years. The "Roaring Twenties" was also a decade obsessed with youthful beauty and that stemmed, at least in part, from Hollywood stars—both the characters they played on screen and the carefully crafted fictions that the studio publicity departments and fan magazines passed off as their real lives. Movies became a common cultural force that cut across all economic divisions. People in every part of the country watched the same films, were attracted to the same actors and, to varying degrees, shared the same fantasies. As Cary Grant so aptly put it, "Everybody wants to be Cary Grant. Even I want to be Cary Grant."

As the country became more prosperous, the idea that people could spend time and money on pleasurable leisure activities filtered down to the middle and working classes. Movie theaters became places for young people to congregate in couples and groups, away from adult supervision, at least for a few hours in the darkness. Some social critics and reformers were outraged. An early study of children in Portland, Oregon, found that 90 percent went to the movies regularly, and of those, 30 percent went at least twice per week. A 1909 Chicago Vice Commission report decried the sexual activity that went on between young people and adults in movie theaters.

Decades later, from the 1930s to the 1950s, when the movies were more respectable, theaters would provide special weekend matinee programs for children. For less than a dollar, a boy or girl could spend an entire afternoon with multiple features, cartoons, serials, and lots of popcorn

Sound and Color

Successful technological advances in American movies have been driven by audiences. Some changes are immediately embraced; others, like 3-D, never become anything more than curiosities.

One of the first major developments was the change from orthochromatic black and white film to panchromatic black and white. "Ortho" film was sensitive to blue and green areas of the spectrum, but did not record reds. Because of that, early silent films lacked gradations of gray, and had a high contrast look that has been called "soot and whitewash." Panchromatic film, developed in 1926, was sensitive to the entire spectrum and so captured a much more detailed image, particularly in the recreation of flesh tones.

That same year, sound was introduced. The Lumière brothers and Thomas Edison had been experimenting with the synchronization of sound and moving images since the 1890s, but difficulties in their coordination stood in the way until the development of the sound track and efficient amplification by 1926. Radio provided the first real competition to movies as a leisure activity, and

made audiences more disposed to the idea of "talking pictures." The first commercial radio broadcast was made by Frank Conrad from his barn in East Pittsburgh, Pennsylvania, in 1920. By 1925 there were 571 radio stations in America and 5 million homes had receivers. As radio became more popular, movie attendance declined, and Warner Bros. was the studio that suffered the most.

Unlike the other major studios, Warner did not own theaters. Brothers Sam, Harry, Albert, and Jack knew they had to do something dramatic. They decided to buy the Vitagraph company, which owned thirty-four theaters in America and Canada, and then to convert them to sound. Their first release was a collection of short films featuring the New York Metropolitan Opera Company and the feature *Don Juan*. In all of them, the use of sound was limited to music. The films were well-received critically, but were only modestly successful at the box office. That was enough, though. The studio took the next step and put *The Jazz Singer* into production in 1927.

It contained only four talking segments, including the famous line, "Wait a minute, you ain't heard nothing yet!" The film was an immediate hit and despite the fact that it could cost as much as $25,000 to retrofit a silent theater for sound, the other studios realized that they had no choice but to follow the Warners' lead. In the years following the introduction of sound, weekly attendance doubled from 50 to 100 million.

The third major change was three-color Technicolor. Limited use of color had been part of films for decades. Griffith and others routinely tinted scenes with primary colors for effect, and a few films contained hand-painted scenes and stenciled effects. The Technicolor company was founded in 1915. It developed several processes for adding selected colors to film, but it did not achieve commercially viable full color until 1932. Disney's animated short *Flowers and Trees* was the first to use the process. The first feature to employ it was 1935's *Becky Sharp*. The Technicolor equipment was expensive: a three-color camera cost $30,000. The company retained control of the equipment and personnel, and charged top dollar for their rental. The studios reserved the process for their most ambitious projects—*Gone With the Wind*, *The Wizard of Oz*, *Fantasia*, and the like. Until the 1950s, most studio films were made in black and white, and the big full-color picture was relatively rare.

The studio system depended on a large number of films being cycled through a large number of theaters. The huge, ornate movie palaces that were built in the largest cities were really an aberration. Almost all theaters built in the suburbs and small towns were on a more modest scale that was appropriate to the presen-

Saturday Night Fever. John Travolta (1954–) starred in the 1977 movie sensation *Saturday Night Fever* as Tony Manero. Dressed in his classic white suit that touched off the national disco music craze, he dances with actress Karen Lynn Gorney, who played Stephanie. © *The Kobal Collection*

tation of smaller films. Construction of theaters increased steadily from 19,409 in 1926 to 20,457 in 1946. It was not unusual for a theater to change programs twice per week. They usually ran double features with short films, newsreels, and trailers along with the main attraction, or an "A" picture and the shorter "B" picture. (Though the term "B-picture" has come to mean any low-budget film, the original B-pictures were made by divisions within the larger studios and by such companies as Monogram and Republic. John Wayne and many other stars learned their craft working in these swiftly-made genre pieces.)

Ticket prices remained less than 25 cents until the beginning of World War II. Attendance declined during the Great Depression, but even in the darkest years, 60 million people went to the movies at least once per week. By then, movies had become an accepted part of American culture.

Hollywood movies were aimed at a broad general audience, though the individual studios established reputations for different types of pictures. MGM had the most famous stars and made polished films with the most lavish production values. Warner Bros. became known for crime films and more socially relevant dramas. Paramount specialized in sophisticated fare, lighter entertainment, and comedy. Universal was the home of horror and Deanna Durbin musicals. Twentieth Century Fox made period pieces and adventures. Columbia had director Frank Capra, B-pictures, and later, more ambitious serious films. Disney made the most advanced animation.

Sex, Scandal and Censorship

Mainstream movies have always traded on a carefully calculated amount of controversy and the perception of their product as something exotic and glamorous with a strong hint of the forbidden. Promotional material for 1924's *Alimony* promised "brilliant men, beautiful jazz babies, champagne baths, midnight revels, petting parties in the purple dawn, all ending in one terrific smashing climax that makes you gasp." Even though films almost never lived up to such hyperbole, various groups objected and worked to prevent their distribution, or to edit their content. Over the decades, the industry has responded with conciliatory words, the appearance of concession, and self-regulation, either lax or strict.

In 1907, the New York clergy complained that movies were promoting immorality and that they were being screened on Sundays. Mayor George B. McClelland then revoked the licenses of 600 theaters. The production

companies answered with the creation of the National Board of Review (NBR) of Motion Pictures. Their efforts came at a time when vaudeville houses were being transformed into movie theaters, and they helped to make movies and moviegoing more acceptable to new audiences. Theaters were cleaned up and made more respectable with ushers who actually enforced standards of behavior. Women became more comfortable in theaters and movies gradually came to be perceived as middle class entertainment.

Then in 1915, the U.S. Supreme Court ruled that movies were a business, not an art form, and therefore were not protected by the First Amendment. That decision opened the door to government censors and to more protests against movies from such organizations as the Women's Christian Temperance Union and the Legion of Decency. Despite the best efforts of the studio publicity departments to present their stars as upstanding model citizens, tales of alcohol and drug abuse and sexual excess in Hollywood led to more protests. In the early 1920s, those protests found focus with two highly-publicized scandals. The first was the unsolved murder of director William Desmond Taylor, who had been linked romantically to two young actresses, one a teen-ager. The second was the death of actress Virginia Rappe following a wild party and the trial of comedian Roscoe "Fatty" Arbuckle for her murder. Arbuckle was eventually acquitted (she died after a botched abortion), but the damage had been done.

In 1922, the industry responded with the creation of the Motion Picture Producers and Distributors of America, which would become the Motion Picture Association of America (MPAA). At its creation, it was more commonly known as the Hays Office after its leader Will Hays. He had been Chairman of the Republican National Committee and Postmaster General in the Harding administration. Given his political connections and reputation for strict morality, Hays was able to hold off censorship on a national level and in all but six states. The studios agreed to submit scripts to his office for editing and films were given a seal of approval before they were released. Hays also demanded that the studios insert a "morals clause" in all contracts with actors, and he was instrumental in the creation of the famous Production Code in 1930. This remarkable document (See Hays Code sidebar) is a lengthy list of forbidden subjects and acts, statements of principle, and guidelines for the treatment of "difficult" stories.

The forces of moral rectitude were particularly strong then. Mae West was a favorite target. Her film *She Done Him Wrong* is said to have caused the creation of the

The Motion Picture Production Code of 1930

"The Hays Code" explicitly stated that it was the duty of motion pictures to promote morality. "No picture shall be produced that will lower the moral standards of those who see it. Hence, the sympathy of the audience should never be thrown to the side of crime, wrongdoing, evil or sin."

Here are some examples of how those high standards were to be met:

"Brutal killings are not to be presented in detail."

"Revenge in modern times shall not be justified."

"The use of firearms should be restricted to the essentials."

"Illegal drug traffic must never be presented."

"In general passion should so be treated that these scenes do not stimulate the lower and baser element."

"Miscegenation (sex relationships between the white and black races) is forbidden."

"Scenes of passion must be treated with an honest acknowledgement of human nature and its normal reactions. Many scenes cannot be presented without arousing dangerous emotions on the part of the immature, the young or the criminal classes."

"Obscenity in word, gesture, reference, song, joke, or by suggestion (even when likely to be understood only by part of the audience) is forbidden."

League of Decency, and she was banned from NBC radio after she participated in a skit about Adam and Eve on the Edgar Bergen Show. Her name was not to be spoken on the network.

As long as movies lacked serious competition and remained profitable, studios—if not filmmakers—were happy enough to abide by the Hays Code. Creativity and experimentation were sacrificed; direct governmental regulation had been prevented, though during World War II, scripts and films were cleared with the War Department. While critics and intellectuals decried the blandness of Hollywood studio productions in those years, movies rose to their highest levels of popularity.

Weekly attendance ranged between 85 and 90 million throughout the 1930s and 1940s. During those same years, movies accounted for about 20 percent of America's total recreational spending, and more than 80 percent of spectator recreational spending. Though it is impossible to quantify precisely, the social aspect of moviegoing was part of the entertainment value for most audiences. Particularly during the war years, the shared experience of escapist musicals, comedies and unashamed propaganda drew people to theaters.

The Paramount Decision and the Arrival of Television

After World War II, the Hollywood studios were at the peak of their power and profitability. That happy state ended abruptly in 1948 when the Supreme Court decided *U.S. v. Paramount et al.* The matter had been brewing since 1921 when the Federal Trade Commission investigated block booking, an arrangement that forced an exhibitor to accept several films in a single package, often sight unseen, from a studio or distributor. In 1930, the major studios were found guilty of monopoly practices. They owned chains of theaters and effectively controlled production, distribution, and exhibition of all films. But the Roosevelt administration worked out a controversial deal with the studios to prevent the ruling from going into effect during the darkest days of the Great Depression.

By 1938, the economy was doing better, and Roosevelt then ordered the Justice Department to take another look at the issue. Again, circumstances (such as World War II) prevented a quick resolution. But in 1948, the Court ordered the studios to eliminate block booking and to sell their theaters. The studio system was over, and independent producers assumed a more important creative role.

Through all of this, people still went to movies. Drive-in theaters, which had been invented in 1931, flourished in the 1950s, which was a decade of relatively inexpensive suburban real estate and large cars with comfortable seats. Drive-in double features appealed primarily to two audiences. One was families with young children who would be entertained by the first movie and would fall asleep before the next (presumably more mature) feature. The second audience was teenagers who found other uses for the partial privacy afforded by a darkened automobile at night.

But neither conventional theaters nor drive-ins could compete with television. Movie ticket sales plummeted as TV set sales rose after World War II. In the 1950s and 1960s, the major networks took over the role that the studios had played, providing different types of low-cost entertainment—primarily comedies and melodramas—to an audience of all ages and economic levels.

The movies tried to compete by becoming bigger with widescreen image formats. Such processes as CinemaScope, VistaVision and Todd-AO were used for biblical epics, period pieces, and westerns. The single-screen theater became a rarity as older movie houses were divided and new theaters were constructed with multiple screens surrounding a concession stand that became an increasingly significant source of revenue. Though moviegoing continued to be a popular leisure activity, the studios never regained their power. Television fundamentally changed the structure of American recreational viewing as a social activity. The audience no longer had to go to the theater to find movies: the movies came to the audience. It took the Hollywood studios about thirty-five years to adapt to the new reality.

In 1953, the RKO studio was bought by the Desilu company. It ceased making movies and started producing TV shows. The others sold off their back lots also, and one by one, the studios themselves were purchased by larger corporations.

The MPAA Ratings System

The Hays Code remained unchallenged until 1952 when the Supreme Court reversed its ruling that movies were a business. It stated that Roberto Rossellini's *Il Miracolo,* in one segment of the film *L'Amore,* could not be censored on religious grounds, and that all films are protected by the First Amendment.

Rossellini's work was part of a wave of European imports that were dealing with more mature subject matter and more explicit content. Those films were competing with studios' productions for the adult marketplace at the same time that television was providing free family entertainment. Movie attendance continued to decline throughout the 1960s, and the studios struggled to regain their audience with more challenging and controversial films. The matter was partially resolved in 1968 when Jack Valenti, president of the MPAA, came up with the ratings system.

In that year of political and social upheaval, he realized that the Hays Code was no longer viable. Valenti's immediate concerns were the language in *Who's Afraid of Virginia Woolf?* and the nudity in *Blow Up.* In April, the

Supreme Court upheld the constitutional power of cities and states to prevent children from being exposed to books and films that could not be denied to adults. On 1 November, Valenti introduced the G-M-R-X ratings system, and said that the MPAA would no longer attempt to forbid the depiction and description of specific acts in films; instead the studios' films would come with a classification letter so that parents could decide whether children should attend.

The system, still in effect in the early 2000s (with the subdivision of M to PG and PG-13 and the addition of NC-17), recognized the fact that Hollywood movies were no longer meant for a universal audience. The MPAA ratings system effectively made theater operators responsible for policing the audience, and after almost forty years under the Hays Code, the movie industry decided that the marketplace, not a governing body, would determine content. Since the mid-1970s, the business has been dependent on escapism—mostly science fiction, fantasy, and adventure—aimed at teen-aged audiences for its biggest profits.

The Home Video Revolution

Industry changes since the 1970s have had little to do with movies themselves and more to do with the medium where they are displayed. As television expanded with the growth of cable broadcasting, and as videocassette recorders became widely popular in the 1980s, people watched films in record numbers. They just didn't go to theaters to see them and the social aspect of movies continued to decline. At first, the studio heads and producers regarded these "secondary markets" as an afterthought, but home video grew quickly. In the 1980s, mom-and-pop video stores appeared in every neighborhood and small town. By the mid 1990s, they faced competition from larger chains, and the video market was earning more money than theatrical releases.

That trend accelerated sharply with the introduction of the DVD (Digital Versatile Disk) in 1997. While the videotape market was primarily a rental medium, with cassettes typically priced at $80-90, DVD was developed as a sales market, with discs at $20. At about the same time that DVD was introduced, the prices of widescreen video monitors and surround-sound systems were lowered dramatically, and even modest home theater systems were able to create a visual and auditory experience comparable to the multiplex.

The massive advertising and promotional campaigns that Hollywood mounts for its most expensive releases continue to be the engine that drives the industry, but the home market is much more important economically. In 2003, the theatrical box office was $9.16 billion, a slight drop from 2002. Home video sales and rentals were $22.2 billion, a 9.3 percent increase from 2002. As ticket prices increase, and as alternate methods of distribution (such as Internet, cable, and satellite) proliferate, home viewing will become even more significant.

See also: Commercialization of Leisure; Expansion of Leisure Time; Media, Technology, and Leisure; Postwar to 1980 Leisure and Recreation; Television's Impact on Popular Leisure; Urbanization of Leisure

BIBLIOGRAPHY

Allen, Frederick Lewis. *Only Yesterday.* New York: Harper, 1931.

Baritz, Loren. *The Culture of the Twenties.* Indianapolis, Ind.: Bobbs-Merrill, 1970.

Basten, Fred E. *Glorious Technicolor.* South Brunswick, N.J.: A.S. Barnes, 1980.

Batchelor, Bob. *The 1900s.* Westport, Conn.: Greenwood Press, 2002.

Bogle, Donald. *Toms, Coons, Mulattoes, Mammies, and Bucks: An Interpretive History of Blacks in American Films.* New York: Viking Press, 1973.

Brownlow, Kevin. *The Parade's Gone By. . .* New York: Knopf, 1968.

Gardner, Gerald. *The Censorship Papers: Movie Censorship Letters from the Hays Office 1934 to 1968.* New York: Dodd, Mead, 1987.

Green, Harvey. *The Uncertainty of Everyday Life 1915–1945.* New York: HarperCollins Publishers, 1992.

Henderson, Robert M. *D. W. Griffith: His Life and Work.* New York: Oxford University Press, 1972.

Knight, Arthur. *The Liveliest Art: A Panoramic History of the Movies.* New York: Macmillan, 1957.

Konigsberg, Ira. *The Complete Film Dictionary.* New York: New American Library, 1987.

Leff, Leonard J., and Jerold L. Simmons. *The Dame in the Kimono: Hollywood, Censorship, and the Production Code from the 1920s to the 1960s.* New York: Grove Weidenfeld, 1990.

Mast, Gerald. *A Short History of the Movies.* Chicago: University of Chicago Press, 1971, 1976, 1981.

Mayo, Mike. *VideoHound's War Movies.* Detroit: Visible Ink Press, 1999.

Miller, Nathan. *New World Coming.* New York: Scribner, 2003.

Norman, Barry. *The Story of Hollywood.* New York: New American Library, 1988.

Robertson, Patrick. *Film Facts.* New York: Billboard Books, 2001.

Schickel, Richard. *D. W. Griffith: An American Life.* New York: Simon and Schuster, 1984.

———. *Good Morning, Mr. Zip Zip Zip.* Chicago: Ivan R. Dee, 2003.

Schoen, Juliet P. *Silents To Sound: A History of the Movies.* New York: Four Winds Press, 1976.

Steinberg, Corbett. *Film Facts.* New York: Facts on File, Inc., 1980.

Valenti, Jack. "The Movie Rating System: How It Began; Its Purpose; How It Works; The Public Reaction." Brochure. Encino, Calif.: Motion Picture Association of America.

West, Elliott. *Growing Up in Twentieth-Century America: A History and Reference Guide.* Westport, Conn.: Greenwood Press, 1996.

Mike Mayo

MUMMING

Ancient folk rituals in Europe celebrating fertility, birth, and renewal during annual festivals such as Halloween, Christmas, New Year's, and Easter preceded mumming in early America, a practice that matured into the modern-day Philadelphia Mummer's Parade and Mardi Gras in New Orleans. Some of the clearest parallels among these festivals are the use of costumes and masks, traveling from house to house, and a salutary chant made by a leader or captain.

The origins of mummery can be traced back to the Roman Saturnalia festivals in 400 B.C. This popular holiday, held in December, was a feast day for the god of agriculture, Saturn. During Saturnalia, the Romans celebrated the new solar year with merrymaking, music, dance, and prayers for their winter crops. Age and rank were forgotten as slaves were waited on and wore their master's clothing. A rex Saturnalitius led the revels making ludicrous commands.

Organized parading developed from masked revelers in seventeenth- and eighteenth-century European villages. The colonial settlers transplanted these traditions to America. Mummers would make noise and wear disguises to protect themselves from being recognized by evil spirits who would bring bad luck. Disguised as trees, wheat stalks, or animals, they transfigured their faces with masks, makeup, or burnt cork. One popular disguise for men was to dress as women. In some cultures it was believed that it was lucky for a male to cross the threshold first and that this good fortune would last for the year to come. The English "mummers' play" of St. George was a major influence on early American mumming. Traditionally, men would travel from house to house, performing and collecting donations and drinks. The chosen leader of the group spoke a prologue and claimed a welcome from the audience. A predecessor of this play is the "sword" or "Morris" dance, which had stock characters called "Tommy," the fool, and "Bessy," who was dressed as a woman. Similarly, in rural Ireland, boys participated in "Hunting the Wren" on St. Stephen's Day. The first group of Wren Boys to visit a house on St. Stephen's Day was believed to bring good luck. Upon arrival, the leader of the crew, the *ceannaire*, danced carrying a holly bush, supposedly containing the wren, while the boys sang a traditional Wren Boys song.

The Swedish settlers' Christmas custom was to travel about visiting friends and having parties. With faces smeared with red wash, burnt cork, and flour, and wearing old and comic clothes, they went from house to house visiting and performing. These groups also appointed a type of captain who would dance and sing rhymes such as:

Here we stand at your door,

As we stood the year before;

Give us whiskey, give us gin,

Open the door and let us in!

German immigrants brought with them the tradition of *belsnickling*, in which adults disguised themselves as half demon, half Santa Claus–type figures. These frightening men visited the village children at Christmas–time and rewarded their good behavior with gifts. There is also evidence of New Year's celebrations in revolutionary America, including parades and disguises on the part of both the American and British troops.

African American holiday parades in early America had elements of mummery as well. These celebrations, rooted in African traditions, had free exchange between spectators and performers, noise in the form of improvised music, and the firing of guns. One such celebration was the Jon Koonering Parade of the southeastern United States. Although there are scattered references to mumming activities in the major cities of Boston and New York, the concentration and consistency of the practices in Philadelphia and New Orleans create the most compelling story of mummery in early America.

Elements of the Philadelphia New Year's Day Parade date back to colonial times, though it was not officially organized until 1901. Court records of 1702 show evidence of men and women wearing masks and cross-dressing. As the popularity of masquerading grew among the lower classes, newspapers reported on the dangerous nature of the crowds and fear among the upper-class residents. These reports prompted a Public Nuisance Law regarding mumming in 1808. The Act to Declare Masquerades and Masqued Balls to be Common Nuisances, and to Punish Those Who Promote Them, made mumming in public or private illegal. However, this law was not strictly enforced, for there were no recorded convictions.

The tradition of visiting homes during the holidays began to move to the streets in the early nineteenth century. In 1839, Swedish settlers celebrating New Year's gathered in the road, disguised as clowns, and shot off their guns like their European ancestors, earning the name "New Years Shooters." The ban on mumming in Philadelphia was lifted after the Civil War and the Public Ledger for 3 January 1876, reported that the "Shooters" celebrated and paraded all of New Year's Day.

By the mid-nineteenth century, all-male social groups were popular in America. In Philadelphia, the clubs began to represent the composition of their neighborhoods' cultural background. Group activities sometimes turned violent, and the revelry turned to intimidation. Disguises aimed at mockery and degradation of rival clubs, and particularly of African Americans, Native Americans, and other ethnic groups.

"Fancy Clubs" began to spring up in the late 1880s. As the Mummers began to compete, music became a much more important aspect of their association. The parade unofficially began to organize once the clubs began to compete for cash prizes and merchandise offered by Philadelphia merchants. The first instance of a club parading up Broad Street was on New Year's Day 1888.

Carnival in New Orleans during Mardi Gras also has roots in ancient mumming. This celebration began in Italy and France and was established in America in the southern United States. The French settlers of New Orleans in the eighteenth century held elaborate masked balls under the direction of the provincial governor the marquis de Vaudreuil. The first evidence of Mardi Gras festivities among Anglican whites came in the early 1830s in Mobile, Alabama, on New Year's Day. This annual celebration eventually moved to New Orleans, where masking was also banned. But, as in Philadelphia, these laws were ignored, and the masked revelry continued.

In 1857, organized carnival clubs produced a controversy in New Orleans with French traditional celebrations, but eventually the disparate ethnicities joined together to celebrate. In 1872, the "Rex" organization marched for the first time during the New Year's Parade, with floats and outrageous costumes, and, in 1873, the tradition moved permanently to the Thursday before Mardi Gras.

See also: Carnivals, Mardi Gras, New Year's

BIBLIOGRAPHY

"The Ancient Custom of Mummery." *Mummer's Magazine* [1950]. Article reprinted online at Quaker City String Band Web site. Available from http://www.quakercitystringband .com/.

Chambers, Edmund K. *The Medieval Stage.* London: Muston Company, 1903.

Davis, Susan G. "'Making Night Hideous': Christmas Revelry and Public Order in Nineteenth-Century Philadelphia." *American Quarterly* 34, no. 2 (Summer 1982): 185–199.

———. *Parades and Power: Street Theatre in Nineteenth-Century Philadelphia.* Philadelphia: Temple University Press, 1986.

Fox, Selena. "Saturnalia." Available from http://www .circlesanctuary.org/pholidays/.

Osbourne, Mitchel L. *Mardi Gras! A Celebration.* New Orleans, La.: Picayune Press, 1981.

Pencak, William, Matthew Dennis, and Simon P. Newman, eds. *Riot and Revelry in Early America.* State College: Pennsylvania State University Press, 2002.

Restad, Penne L. *Christmas in America: A History.* New York: Oxford University Press, 1995.

"St. Stephen's Day in Ireland." Available from http://www. noblenet.org/.

Segal, Erich. *Roman Laughter: The Comedy of Plautus.* New York: Oxford University Press, 1987.

Welch, Jr., Charles E. *Oh! Dem Golden Slippers: The Story of the Philadelphia Mummers.* Camden, N.J.: Thomas Nelson, 1970.

Valerie M. Joyce

"MUSCULAR CHRISTIANITY" AND THE YM(W)CA MOVEMENTS

Neither the Young Men's Christian Association nor the Young Women's Christian Association began as an agency of muscular Christianity, though both moved in that direction before 1900. The first YMCAs took the form of self-improvement societies dedicated to evangelizing young men. A clerk named George Williams founded the first YMCA in London, England, in 1844; similar associations sprang up in major American cities during the 1850s, combining libraries and literary societies with Bible classes and prayer meetings. YMCA evangelizing sought explicit conversion experiences, and, in 1869, North American YMCAs limited their voting membership to men who were in full communion with "evangelical" (i.e., orthodox Protestant) churches.

Varied initiatives to meet the needs of young working women (in New York in 1858 and Boston in 1866) spurred the formation of twenty-eight YWCAs by 1875. Most sponsored prayer meetings; many offered temporary or permanent lodgings and employment bureaus; and some ran Bible or secular classes. Though evangelistic in practice, city YWCAs did not impose a test for full membership like that of the YMCAs until 1906, when they merged with the more dogmatically orthodox student YWCAs.

Early Physical Training and Recreation

Although in 1866 New York City's YMCA expansively declared its object to be "the improvement of the spiritual, mental, social and physical condition of young men" physical exercise entered the YMCA as a peripheral attraction, intended to rival commercial gymnasiums. Beginning in 1869, new association buildings began to include facilities—there were fifty-one YMCA gymnasiums by 1880—but they offered little more than a setting to act out boyhood dreams of circus stardom, with acrobatics, boxing, and weightlifting beckoning the foolhardy. Robert Roberts became the YMCA's first professedly Christian gymnasium superintendent when he took charge at the Boston association in 1876. After falling from a trapeze, he designed easier and much safer dumbbell and medicine ball exercises suited to men of average ability; class enrollments multiplied more than twelvefold in four years, and other YMCAs followed Roberts's lead. Swimming pools first appeared in the 1880s and 1890s, also as recreational diversions. By then, however, YMCA leaders feared more for safety, as novice swimmers took their first strokes secured by overhead lines.

Drawn by these attractions, the majority of young men who enrolled were nonvoting, fee-paying associate members. YMCA secretaries sought, in the words of a YMCA magazine in 1886 "to gain personal influence over them" and secure religious conversions. Formal training for YMCA physical educators began in 1887 at a School for Christian Workers in Springfield, Massachusetts, renamed the International Young Men's Christian Association Training School in 1890 and later Springfield College. Here Luther Gulick, the leading theorist of YMCA physical education, encouraged athletics and team sports in place of routine drills and fostered development of powerful new attractions: In 1891, James Naismith, a Springfield instructor, invented basketball, which swept the associations, men's and women's colleges, and high schools. Four years later William Morgan, just graduated from Springfield, designed volleyball as a less strenuous sport for middle-aged men.

The YWCA followed at a distance, using entertainments and some physical training as enticements for new members. Boston built the first YWCA gymnasium in 1884. By 1893, nine of fifty-two city associations reported gymnasiums (Sims 1936, pp. 40, 42), and others held physical culture classes elsewhere. By 1910, the YWCA handbook considered a gymnasium and swimming pool standard equipment for city associations; 142 of 189 reported physical training classes, though only about 14 percent of total Y membership enrolled (*Handbook,* p. 80).

All-Round Development and Muscular Christianity

As physical culture and sports outdrew other activities, YMCA physical directors sought a rationale that went beyond merely luring young men within reach of evangelizers and emphasized instead the integral role of physical education within the ideal of a balanced development. Gulick expressed this rationale as a symbol, the red triangle, whose three sides signified the symmetrical physical, mental, and spiritual development of young men. Aggressive promotion by Gulick and his fellow physical directors established the red triangle as the YMCA's de facto emblem by the late 1890s, and balanced development of young men and boys as the association's raison d'être.

Their triumph drew upon a fund of gendered anxieties summed up by a gymnasium leader's declared ambition in 1901 to foster "a new conception of manly, muscular Christianity". The phrase "muscular Christianity" had first gained currency in the late 1850s to describe the message of English novelists Charles Kingsley and Thomas Hughes, whose manly heroes' Christian ideals and hardy physiques prepared them to struggle against the evils and evildoers of this world—most famously against bullies in Hughes's *Tom Brown's Schooldays.* Although initially used to disparage mindless strenuosity in both the rhetoric of self-consciously manly evangelists such as Dwight Moody (a good friend of the YMCA) and American gymnasts' conflation of strong muscles with good character, the phrase acquired mostly positive connotations in the United States by the 1890s.

Historians disagree about whether the apparent crisis of American masculinity in the late nineteenth century was particularly novel and about exactly what it was, but cultural tensions were evident among middle-class male Protestants in the growing cities and towns of the North. Nineteenth-century Protestantism's celebration of tender, emotional virtues and the roughly three-to-two majority of women among church members stirred fears that clergymen constituted at best a third sex and Christianity itself was unmanly. Among boys, misbehavior became the touchstone of authenticity. Senator Henry Cabot Lodge endorsed boys' "wholesome dislike" of the "religious prig"; for the "real" boy was Tom Sawyer, not a Sunday school pupil.

Narrowly considered, muscular Christianity offered defensive assurance, in the 1884 words of a YMCA leader, that a "real" boy "need not cease to be a boy because he is a Christian". More broadly, turn-of-the-century alarmists feared "overcivilization". Sedentary lifestyles, excessive brainwork, feminization, and the constraints of living in a highly organized, urbanized society seemingly sapped manly independence, fostering instead nervousness and enfeeblement. Schoolboys spent their weekdays doing book work under female teachers and then went home to their mothers' care. Meanwhile, their absent white-collar fathers sat at desks carrying out the directives of corporate superiors. Vigorous exercise and all-male companionship helped conscientious Christians bolster their sense of masculinity. New team sports such as basketball prepared boys and young men for corporate life by making subordination to the group and obedience to coaches' orders seem manly. Eventually, joining the team became the master metaphor for participating in both business and church life.

YWCA rhetoric reflected similar tensions induced by the urban industrial transformation of traditional roles, although with differently gendered emphases. Turn-of-the-century alarmists presumed that girls and women were weaker than boys and men, less energetic, less resistant to disease, and—even compared to male brain workers—more prone to debilitating nervousness. Since early YWCA leaders saw their primary mission as service to young employed women, they justified calisthenics and later swimming as preparing these working girls to stand the physical and especially the nervous strain of long hours in the shop and office. Whereas the YMCA stressed physical culture for its own sake, YWCAs tended increasingly to subsume it under broader concerns for the health of girls.

Programs for Boys and Girls

Rapid expansion of YMCA junior enrollments (mostly boys aged twelve to sixteen, and later eighteen) from 11,455 in 1890 to 30,675 in 1900, 103,570 in 1910, and 219,876 by early 1921 greatly expanded YMCA emphasis on gymnastics, swimming, and sports, since these were what boys wanted. Whereas exercises in the 1890s had been almost as disciplinary as military drill, by 1920 physical directors suggested that boys twelve to fourteen should have only twenty-five minutes of calisthenics and

Weightlifting. New York City office workers lift dumbbells at their local YMCA in 1922 as part of an exercise regime initiated by Arthur Leslie. At the age of forty-seven, Leslie was an out-of-shape white-collar worker—by age fifty, he had become the leading amateur weightlifter in the world in his age group. © *Bettmann/Corbis*

gymnastic instruction, then twenty-five minutes of basketball or other recreation, and a twenty-minute swim. Y workers struggled to balance the Christian and the muscular. By 1920, 35 percent of juniors enrolled in Bible classes, but 79 percent flocked to gymnastics and sports (Macleod, pp. 78, 120, 252). In reaction, Y men fell back on the ideal of all-round development. A rather ineffective Christian Citizenship Training Program, promulgated in the late 1910s, tried to chart boys' physical, intellectual, religious, and social "efficiency"; on this chart, the perfectly "symmetrical" boy was a square. Summer camps, pioneered by the YMCA in the 1880s, offered manly outdoor rigors, though considerations of comfort and sanitation prevailed sufficiently by the early 1900s that most camps scheduled short hiking or canoeing excursions to give the boys experience roughing it. Camps of one to three or four weeks allowed time for more intensive religious and moral formation; most camp leaders sought campfire conversions and judged success by

numbers, though pressures on campers abated toward 1920. Camp fees, however, limited participants to fewer than one-sixth of YMCA juniors as of 1915 (Macleod, pp. 237–238).

Separate YWCA programs for girls lagged, especially before 1909, when Y secretaries first focused concern on adolescence, and emphasis remained less muscular. In 1910, YWCAs reported 8,829 junior members, of whom just 33 percent enrolled in physical training and 20 percent in Bible classes (*Handbook*, pp. 80–81). Toward 1920, the YWCA designed an elaborate Girl Reserve program with a large health education and recreation component. Although the organizers briefly endorsed sports such as tennis, baseball, basketball, volleyball, and hiking, these were distinctly secondary to concerns about diet and posture and recommendations for simple, unstrenuous physical exercises and social recreation. Similarly, camping instructions emphasized health concerns, focusing on diet rather than strenuous activity as the main means of improvement.

Homosocial and Heterosexual Orientations

In the view of one historian, muscular Christianity weakened the intense homosocial bonds of friendship and religious commitment that inspired the early YMCA. John Gustav-Wrathall laments that, with the 1880s shift "from a purely spiritual mission" to one "that encompassed physical culture and vigilance against sexual immorality, trouble entered paradise," (p. 46). Recruitment of younger boys, emphasis on physical development, and partial nudity in gym and pool increased the danger of sexualized relationships. Scandals in 1887 at the Chicago YMCA and in 1912 in Portland, Oregon, purportedly involved "men and boys" (p. 164), though their ages were uncertain.

By the 1920s, pressure on YMCA secretaries to marry and expanding enrollment of women and girls would undermine the association's single-sex ethos. Indeed, suggests Gustav-Wrathall, the withering of more acceptable emotional and religious commitments at Ys may have helped to foster the gay cruising scene in downtown YMCAs during the decades after World War II. Indirectly, muscular Christianity may thus have motivated the YMCA's counteremphasis on family recreation in suburban facilities. Within the YWCA female solidarity survived, relatively unembarrassed by the pressures to demonstrate one's heterosexual orientation that prevailed among YMCA leaders by the 1920s. Indeed the greater threat to YWCA identity derived from YMCA encroachment through programs for girls and women and YM-YW partnerships in which Y men often arrogated to themselves the senior roles.

Shifting Memberships

Over the course of the twentieth century, the YMCA and YWCA moved away from tightly defined "Christian" standards for membership and cast wider nets in terms of age, sex, and race as well as religious affiliation. During the 1930s, the YMCA redefined itself as a fellowship "united by a common loyalty to Jesus, for the purpose of developing Christian personality and building a Christian society.". At the level of formal commitment, a liberal Social Gospel triumphed. As Clifford Putney describes the result, at a Massachusetts YMCA camp in 1969 the old ritual "wherein boys had taken Jesus to be their personal chum had . . . vanished. In its place was an evening candlelight service, at the height of which boys rose to pledge their commitment to building a just society" (1997, p. 237). As early as 1951 nearly 40 percent of YMCA members were Roman Catholic or Jewish (1997, p. 234); formal church affiliation ceased to matter.

In other ways, membership broadened. The age range expanded during the 1920s, as Friendly Indian programs enrolled boys under age twelve. Women gained full membership by 1933, though they comprised only 22 percent of the total as late as 1959. The YMCA had long maintained a system of separate black YMCAs, with 81,209 members in 1944 (Putney 1997, p. 232; Mjagkij, p. 138). Southern white YMCAs long resisted desegregation. In both the YMCA and YWCA, swimming pools were particular points of contention, as white members feared contamination by water-borne contact. Contention lasted well into the 1960s, when the YMCA's national board finally required promises of nondiscrimination from all associations. By 1995, the YMCA reported some 14 million members, almost half female and fully half under age eighteen (Putney 1997, p. 237; "Putting Demographics," pp. 28–29).

The YWCA in 1920 dropped the requirement of church membership, substituting an individual declaration of Christian purpose, and in 1964 bestowed voting membership on any woman or girl who joined and was seventeen or older. Boys and men participating in coed activities were YWCA associates. Local associations formally desegregated around the 1940s in the North and the 1960s in the South, although the suburbanization of new buildings risked undercutting the cross-class unity of the older black YWCAs. In Charlotte, North Carolina, for instance, African American membership fell sharply. Overall, the YWCA remained smaller than the YMCA, reporting 1.6 million members in 1995 (*World Almanac,* p. 630).

Athletics, Fitness, and Health

Two enthusiasms of the 1920s—commercial sports and employer-sponsored industrial leagues—displaced gymnastics and moved the YMCA toward highly competitive athletics, more or less divorced from the character-building balance of muscular Christianity. City YMCAs organized basketball, softball, and track-and-field competitions, often fielding star YMCA teams against outside competitors, and held national YMCA championship competitions in basketball, swimming, handball, and (in the 1930s) wrestling. Meanwhile, however, basic instruction in swimming and lifesaving certification expanded hugely, with 134,112 white and 3,072 black YMCA members taught to swim in 1925; only seventeen of fifty-one black city associations had pools (Johnson, p. 267; Mjagkli, p. 134). Although the depression of the 1930s and the continuing expansion of school-based sports somewhat curbed competitive athletics, aquatics programs persisted, elaborating a system of multilevel individual certifications and merging into the fitness programs of the 1950s. The YMCA also assiduously spread volleyball as a participant sport during the depression and World War II.

Like its middle-class constituency, the YMCA suburbanized after World War II, building 338 family YMCAs by 1956; these YMCAs furnished recreation to fee payers of all ages. A flurry of social reformism, aided by government grants, fostered programs for inner-city youths in the late 1960s, but, by the late 1970s, family-oriented programs and individual services for the middle class again predominated. Training in aquatic skills, youth soccer, and basketball for both boys and girls flourished in the 1970s. In place of religious proselytizing, the YMCA offered values education through lessons in athletic participation and good sportsmanship and programs in values clarification. As individual fitness became an end in itself, described only half jokingly as a secular religion, YMCAs of the 1980s and 1990s invested heavily in upscale facilities to rival private health clubs. Putney concludes regretfully that "for many Americans the YMCA has come to symbolize nothing but sport" (1997, p. 245).

The YWCA has sought a different image. From early in the twentieth century, when the YWCA provided physical training and sports in summer camps, swimming pools, and gymnasiums, the underlying purpose was to improve young women's health. This health emphasis expanded first to sex education and later included defense of women's access to birth control and abortion. By the 1990s, local YWCAs led in fighting domestic violence and sheltering victims. Women's issues predominated and merged into still-larger concerns for social justice. The declared purposes of the national YWCA emphasized peace, freedom, and dignity for all peoples and the elimination of racism. The liberal ideals of social Christianity prevailed.

See also: Basketball; Civic Clubs, Men's; Civic Clubs, Women's; Gilded Age Leisure and Recreation; Progressive-Era Leisure and Recreation; Swimming; Volleyball

BIBLIOGRAPHY

Gustav-Wrathall, John Donald. *Take the Young Stranger by the Hand: Same-Sex Relations and the YMCA.* Chicago: University of Chicago Press, 1998.

Handbook of the Young Women's Christian Associations of the United States of America. New York: National Board of the Young Women's Christian Associations of the United States of America, 1910.

Hopkins, C. Howard. *History of the YMCA in North America.* New York: Association Press, 1951.

Johnson, Elmer L. *The History of YMCA Physical Education.* Chicago: Association Press and Follett Publishing, 1979.

Macleod, David I. *Building Character in the American Boy: The Boy Scouts, YMCA, and Their Forerunners, 1870–1920.* Madison: University of Wisconsin Press, 1983.

Mjagkij, Nina. *Light in the Darkness: African Americans and the YMCA, 1852–1946.* Lexington: University Press of Kentucky, 1994.

Mjagkij, Nina, and Margaret Spratt, eds. *Men and Women Adrift: The YMCA and the YWCA in the City.* New York: New York University Press, 1997.

National Board, Young Women's Christian Associations. *The Girl Reserve Movement: A Manual for Advisers.* New York: The Womans Press, 1924.

Putney, Clifford. "From Character to Body Building: The YMCA and the Suburban Metropolis, 1950–1980." In *Men and Women Adrift.* Edited by Nina Mjagkij and Margaret Spratt. New York: New York University Press, 1997.

———. *Muscular Christianity: Manhood and Sports in Protestant America, 1880–1920.* Cambridge, Mass.: Harvard University Press, 2001.

"Putting Demographics in the Driver's Seat." *Association Management* 49 (May 1997): 28–29.

Sims, Mary S. *The Natural History of a Social Institution—The Young Women's Christian Association.* New York: The Womans Press, 1936.

———. *The YWCA—An Unfolding Purpose.* New York: The Womans Press, 1950.

———. *The Purpose Widens, 1947–1967.* New York: National Board of the Young Women's Christian Association of the U.S.A., 1969.

Vandenberg-Daves, Jodi. "The Manly Pursuit of a Partnership Between the Sexes: The Debate over YMCA Programs for Women and Girls, 1914–1933." *Journal of American History* 78 (1992): 1324–1346.

World Almanac, 1996. Mahwah, N.J.: Funk & Wagnalls, 1995.

David I. Macleod

MUSEUM MOVEMENTS

The American museum essentially began in the late eighteenth century, a by-product of the Enlightenment and its belief that knowledge could improve society and increase prosperity. Precedents for this movement commenced in Europe. In 1737, Anna Maria Ludovica, sister of the last de'Medici Grand Duke, willed the art-laden Uffizi Gallery to the city of Florence, believing its collections would benefit the public and attract visitors to Florence. It was in England, however, where the seeds of the first national public museum flowered, planted somewhat surreptitiously by London physician Sir Hans Sloane. During his ninety-three years, Sloane collected 71,000 natural history specimens, antiquities, manuscripts, a herbarium, and a library. Believing these collections would increase practical knowledge, Sloan bequeathed his collection to King George II for a national museum, in exchange for 20,000 pounds payable to his daughters. Sloan wanted this museum located in densely populated London, where he believed it would benefit the greatest number of visitors. In 1753, Parliament passed the British Museum Act, accepting and providing support for the collection. Governed by trustees responsible to Parliament, the British Museum opened free of charge to the public in 1759. Average citizens did not freely sail through the museum's doors; rather, visitors were limited to applicants judged to be curious or studious, and the world's first public museum firmly barred children from its portals.

The creation of American public museums was neither so straightforward nor so restrictive. Neither colonial nor the federal governments felt empowered to use public funds for museums, and the lines between public and private sectors blurred. Many museums began as private collections open to the public for minimal fees and gradually garnered public support. The Philadelphia Museum, begun by artist Charles Willson Peale, received rent-free space in public buildings, just as many modern private institutions receive significant support through state and federal grants and deliver significant public services in exchange.

One aspect of the American museum movement, however, that has remained a fixed mark since the creation of the first museum in 1773 through 2004, is a steadfast commitment to public service and education. Museums frequently disagreed on how to meet those goals, but most shared Anna Maria Ludovica's vision—that collections serve the public good.

Natural History Museums

America's earliest museums primarily concerned themselves with natural history collections. Moreover, scholarly and amateur interest in natural history science exploded after Swedish botanist Carolus Linnaeus developed his system for classifying plants. This scientific plan imposed order and clarity upon the plant world, inspiring an unprecedented passion for plant collecting. Nowhere was plant collecting undertaken more enthusiastically than in North America, where a whole unexplored continent teemed with unstudied species of flora and wildlife. Private individuals—generally gentlemen of means with an appetite for knowledge and an eye for profit—laid the groundwork for America's future museums. In 1773, the Charleston Library Society, enlisting public support, appointed a committee to collect every

species of the animal and plant world native to South Carolina, plus minerals, soils, shells, and other materials that would advance knowledge of South Carolina's natural history. Like Sir Hans Sloane, the society believed that practical knowledge gleaned from the collections would provide educational advantages translating into agricultural and industrial progress. Unfortunately, the Revolutionary War and fire destroyed much of the collection, but in 1785, the society revived its museum, and eventually the Charleston Museum, now known as America's first public museum, acquired the collections.

While the Charleston Library Society restocked its shelves, Philadelphia artist Charles Willson Peale announced the formation of his own natural history museum on 18 July 1786 in the *Pennsylvania Packet.* Its purpose, Peale explained to the corporation and citizens of Philadelphia on 18 July 1816, as quoted by Charles Coleman Seller, was "to form a school of useful knowledge, to diffuse its usefulness to every class in our country, to amuse and in the same moment to instruct the adult of each sex and age" (p. 18).

Peale's Museum, also called the Philadelphia Museum, deserves special mention as America's premier museum, which set standards for future institutions. In 1801, Peale organized America's first scientific expedition and excavated a mastodon skeleton, thereby establishing what every museum director has known since: Nothing attracts visitors better than large prehistoric lizards and beasts, or animated facsimiles thereof. Peale acquired significant collections of natural history specimens, aided both by ordinary citizens and by public figures including President Thomas Jefferson, who dispatched specimens gathered by Meriwether Lewis and William Clark to Peale's museum. Peale also engaged sea captains, diplomats, explorers, and learned societies to gather materials from abroad. These he displayed according to the Linnaean system, presenting the public with a three-dimensional "book of nature" that he believed reflected the divine plan. Over his carefully ordered display Peale hung his portraits of Revolutionary War heroes, to inspire patriotism and a sense of history.

With public education at the forefront, Peale conducted guided tours and public lectures, using collections and lantern slide illustrations. He pioneered museum methods still used today, such as the diorama, placing specimens before painted backdrops of native habitat, providing visitors with context. Peale designed cases that controlled light levels dangerous to fragile specimens and provided visitors with magnifying lenses for interactive views of museum collections. Peale also initiated traveling exhibits, published museum catalogs, and opened the museum for public concerts. For the convenience of working-class patrons, Peale's museum offered evening hours.

Peale's museum also attracted serious scientists who used the collections for original research. Despite continual effort, however, Peale failed to secure financial support from either the state or federal government to make his private museum a public institution. His sons Rubens and Rembrandt Peale, and later Titian and Franklin Peale, eventually assumed management, establishing branches in Baltimore, Maryland; New York, New York; and Utica, New York. By 1820, much to Charles Willson Peale's dismay, the Philadelphia Museum featured a one-man band, Signor Hellene, and other "curiosities." Faced with hard financial times during the 1830s and 1840s, the Peale museums leaned heavily toward popular entertainment. Scientists and scholars drifted away, as did the public, when more fashionable forms of entertainment developed. Attempts to revive the museums failed. In the 1840s, showman Phineas T. Barnum purchased the institutions, incorporating them into his American Museum in New York.

Other institutions continued collecting and exhibiting natural history however. In 1799, Salem's East India Marine Society instructed seafaring members to collect specimens for their museum, now the Peabody-Essex Museum. The Massachusetts Historical Society believed that gathering local natural history specimens served as the logical foundation for their collections, as did sister institutions, including the Albany Institute, New-York Historical Society, Brooklyn Museum, Philadelphia's Academy of Natural Sciences, the Franklin Institute, New England Museum, Maryland Academy of Sciences, and the state historical societies of New Hampshire, Rhode Island, Maine, Connecticut, and Michigan. Although Harvard and Yale did not open museums to the public until the 1860s, they actively collected natural history materials, anticipating George Peabody's future support for their museums.

Not all museums had lofty educational goals. Most cities sported museums akin to sideshows, which mixed natural history specimens with fraudulent mummies, sensational waxwork figures, and live entertainment. Perhaps the most famous of these museums was Cincinnati's Western Museum of Cincinnati, founded in 1820. These "museums" eventually faded away, but their very existence indicated the popularity natural history held for average citizens.

State and federal governments fostered the growth of natural history collections through boundary surveys and expeditions, instructing participants to collect artifacts and specimens. New York's Geological and Natural History Survey, begun in 1836, yielded so many specimens that, in 1843, the New York Legislature authorized the formation of the State Cabinet of Natural History, later the New York State Museum, which opened free of charge to the public in 1845.

While states dealt with their burgeoning collections, an unexpected bequest from Englishman James Smithson, forced the U.S. government to become an active museum player. Smithson willed more than $500,000 in 1835 to the U.S. government to form the Smithsonian Institution to increase and diffuse knowledge. After eight years of debate, on 10 August 1846, Congress created the Smithsonian Institution, America's first public national museum, with the proviso that the institution be accessible to all. Though initially focused on scientific research, the Smithsonian opened its Apparatus Room to the public in 1854. Part exhibit gallery, part demonstration lab and lecture hall, the Smithsonian's first venture into public education, was welcomes enthusiastically by visitors.

The post–Civil War years brought tremendous growth for American museums. The enormous wealth generated by industrialization in an income-tax-free era provided financial support while new scientific developments challenged the accepted understanding of natural history collections. An improved and expanded rail system allowed museums to haul boxcars of dinosaur bones and Native American artifacts from western states, while westward-bound trains bore precious cargoes of European artwork to the coast. Just as London's Crystal Palace Exposition of 1850 led to the formation of the South Kensington Museum, now the Victoria and Albert, as a repository for industrial art previously exhibited at the Crystal Palace, American expositions also spawned new museums and expanded older ones. Numerous countries and firms that exhibited at Philadelphia's Centennial Exposition (1876) donated their displays to the Smithsonian Institute, mandating the construction of the Arts and Industries to house the materials. In other cities, local governments recycled grand and stately buildings built for expositions into public museums.

Natural history museums such as the Smithsonian and Philadelphia's Academy of Natural Sciences grew even larger and more popular as curators displayed the impressive skeletons of dinosaurs and other prehistoric animals discovered in the West. As Steven Conn noted in *Museums and American Intellectual Life, 1875–1926,* so many people flocked to the Academy of Science in 1869 to view the fifteen-foot skeleton of the reptilian Hadrosaurus that museum officials charged 10 cents admission to discourage visitors. Further north in Connecticut and Massachusetts, Yale's Peabody Museum and Harvard's Peabody Museum of Archaeology and Ethnology opened in 1866.. The real tour de force, however, was New York's American Museum of Natural History, which opened to the public in 1877. This museum was especially significant because it represented a partnership between New York and its citizens. The city provided the land, building, and building maintenance. Citizens and patrons contributed funds and collections. The American Museum established a tradition of public education that continues into the new millennium; its early lecture program, illustrated by lantern slides, reached over 1 million persons in a relatively short time.

According to Steven Conn,, natural history museums themselves were forced to adapt once scientists recognized the implication of *Origins of the Species* (1859), by naturalist Charles Darwin. Natural history museums had touted themselves as mirrors of God's benevolent creation, reflecting divine order. Darwin's observations about extinction, evolution, natural selection, and survival pointed to a less kindly, more random scheme, raising troublesome questions about biblical events. Many scientists gradually shifted from natural science museums to laboratories, where microscopic research yielded advances in biological sciences. As the scientific community looked toward the university and laboratory for original research, natural history museums strengthened their efforts to educate average visitors. While these institutions continued to conduct collecting and research expeditions, many museums such as Chicago's Field Museum (1894) and Denver's Museum of Natural History (1897) emphasized engaging displays rather than technical research.

The broader cultural trend toward specialization, which characterized late-nineteenth-century America, influenced natural science museums. Museums were formed that were devoted to specific branches of science, represented by Harvard's Peabody Museum of Archaeology and Ethnology (1866) and the University of Pennsylvania Museum (1889). Science and technology museums, along with herbariums, arboretums, and planetariums, developed during in the first half of the twentieth century.

Art Museums

Public art museums lagged behind natural history museums. Certainly art education did not promise financial and technological gains the way many assumed natural history studies might. There was also an undeniably democratic aspect to natural science—anyone could collect and appreciate natural history, but only the elite could afford art. Some museums included the odd canvas or two, but few museums dedicated themselves exclusively to art by 1860. These included the Pennsylvania Academy of Fine Arts (1805), the Wadsworth Athenaeum (1842), and the New York Historical Society, which in 1858 received the Luman Reed collection, a private art collection, formerly the New York Gallery of Fine Arts.

The study of natural sciences and mechanics indeed produced the money that sent wealthy Americans to Europe on Grand Tours that cultivated the taste for museums and art. In 1870, New York businessmen, financiers, artists, and concerned citizens created a museum to bring art and art education to New York. Like the American Museum of Natural History, they sought public support, successfully petitioning the New York State legislature to raise and use public funds for an art museum constructed on city land. Two years later, the Metropolitan Museum opened, and in 1880 the Met moved to its Central Park location. The Met collected aggressively, aided by wealthy patrons who developed the Met into a colossus among museums. The Met also inspired other cities to work out their own civic partnerships. In Boston, Massachusetts, the Museum of Fine Art (1870) chose to rely on citizen contributions alone. By the late nineteenth century, a city's museums became the measure of its sophistication and prosperity, and an impressive roll call of art museums played across America, with a new institution joining the fold almost every year (see Table 1).

TABLE 1

Formation of art museums

Institution	Founding date
Metropolitan Museum of Art	1870
Museum of Fine Arts	1870
Smith College Art Gallery	1875
Philadelphis Museum of Art	1876
The Art Institute of Chicago	1879
The Walker Art Center	1879
The Rhode Island School of Design Museum of Art	1880
The St. Louis Art Museum	1881
The Princeton Art Museum	1882
The Indianapolis Museum of Art	1883
The Detroit Institute of Art	1885
The Cincinnati Art Museum	1886
The Portland Art Museum	1892
The Fogg Museum	1895
The Carnegie Museum of Art	1897
The Cooper-Hewitt,	1897
The Worcester Art Museum	1898
The Isabelle Garner Museum	1900
The Museum of Fine Arts, Houston	1900

Metropolitan Museum of Art. Founded in 1870 the Metropolitan Museum of Art was moved to its current site in Central Park in 1880. The museum was a cooperative effort of the state government in New York, artists, and concerned citizens and led to museums in other eastern cities. © *The Library of Congress*

Large exhibitions and department stores that astonished Americans with vast displays of objects created visual experiences that influenced museum exhibits. Some museums chose comprehensive visible storage techniques used by England's South Kensington Museum, displaying complete collections by material or type, such as glass and ceramics, and then by chronology or pattern. Other curators followed the Boston plan, developed by the Museum of Fine Arts in the late nineteenth century, which displayed the highlights of a collection on one floor for casual visitors promenading by, while study collections exhibited on a lower level attracted serious museum goers.

This continual concern about display techniques that made collections intelligible reflected the deepening commitment to education shared by public museums in the twentieth century as they endeavored to reach working-class visitors while retaining wealthy patrons. Many museums offered classes, workshops, lectures, guided tours, and museum clubs for the young, as well as the museum field trip, which became a universal experience for American schoolchildren. A few museums, such as the Newark Museum, saw museums as community centers. Under John Cotton Dana's direction during the 1910s and 1920s, the Newark Museum used temporary exhibits to include minority groups within Newark by exhibiting the contemporary crafts of Newark's immigrants. Newark's educational programs interfaced readily with school curriculum and placed artifacts in the classroom.

On the eve of the Great Depression, another type of art museum devoted to contemporary art appeared. The Museum of Modern Art opened in 1929, followed by the Whitney Museum of American Art in 1930, and the Guggenheim Museum in 1937, making New York a leading art center and awakening American interest in contemporary art.

History Museums

Like art museums, history museums were initially sparse, but as citizens gained awareness of their own history and its passing, towns and counties established local history museums. The Pilgrim Society, for example, formed in 1820 to commemorate the bicentennial of the 1620 landing at Plymouth. The society gathered objects of historical significance, and in 1824 Plymouth Hall Museum opened to the public. On the north shore, citizens established the Essex Historical Society in Salem, later renamed the Essex Institute, and incorporated into the Peabody Essex Museum in 1992. State historical societies began forming in the late eighteenth century and that growth continued throughout the nineteenth and twentieth centuries as territories gained statehood. Along with the requisite natural history specimens, historical societies collected documents and artifacts of historical significance, developing impressive collections related to state history, such as those in the Minnesota Historical Society.

By 1850, the historic house museum emerged, partly because of developing tourism facilitated by steamboats, railroads, and turnpikes. As Patricia West observes, "Advocates for the preservation of historic houses as museums argued that [they] would meet the recreational and inspirational needs of nineteenth century tourists, while exerting a much-needed refining and uplifting influence" (pp. 3–4).

Uplifting influences were indeed needed in those days foreshadowing civil war. One subject that easily united all Americans was patriotic pride in America's first president, George Washington. On 4 July 1850, New York State opened the Jonathan Hasbrouck house in Newburgh, New York, Washington's headquarters during the Revolutionary War. Not long after, the Mount Vernon Ladies' Association of the Union rescued Washington's deteriorating home; They received their charter in 1856. Though the Civil War interrupted the restoration, Mount Vernon became a model for the preservation of other historic houses later in the century.

As America's 100th birthday approached, many citizens took a new interest in America's past. The number of historical societies more than doubled between 1870 and 1890; by the 1890s, two house museums opened each year. The Daughters of the American Revolution (DAR) contributed to the movement by collecting historic houses in the 1890s, as did the Association for the Preservation of Virginia Antiquities (APVA). Other museums joined the effort, including the Essex Institute; in 1910, the Society for the Preservation of New England Antiquities formed to preserve New England's historical home and buildings. By 1920, the Philadelphia Museum of Art assumed responsibility for the Fairmount Park mansions, and in 1931 the National Park Service gathered historical houses under its protective aegis.

The "New History" promoted this movement. In the 1890s, some historians exchanged the study of political and military events for that of the daily lives of average people. In 1912, historian James Harvey Robinson published his classic work, *The New History*. As the study of everyday life, with its spinning wheels and craftsman's tools, became acceptable, many historic houses became classrooms for this new school of thought. But historical houses conveyed political messages, too, usually championing a sanitized version of Anglo-American history as immigration from Eastern Europe, the Middle East, and Asia increased.

The popularity of historical houses was not lost on art museums. Period rooms were hardly new, but rather were a staple of fairs and expositions. In 1863, the Brooklyn and Long Island Sanitary Fair re-created an old colonial New England kitchen, one of its most popular attractions. In 1876, the Centennial's installation of a colonial New England kitchen drew enthusiastic crowds to this display that placed objects into context—even if that context was more initially quaint than correct. It wasn't until 1924 that the Met installed its period rooms, followed by the Philadelphia Museum of Art. Popular interest in history and a contextual framework that made learning easy are two factors that made period rooms popular. Motion pictures may have been another. As Americans gained a new visual experience and format watching the lavish sets shown in early-twentieth-century movies, museums began presenting artifacts within a big picture format. While art museums used period rooms to help visitors experience the past, natural history museums installed large, life-sized dioramas that unfolded the story of natural history like the scenes of a film.

The popularity of historical homes led to the outdoor or "living history" museums. Although Swedish historian Artur Hazelius developed the first outdoor museum at Skansen in the 1890s, America's first outdoor museum formed in 1926 when millionaire John Rockefeller, aided by Reverend D. A. R. Goodwin, began preservation and reconstruction efforts at Colonial Williamsburg. Industrialist Henry Ford, compelled to preserve the preindustrial past the automobile ironically helped to destroy, founded an outdoor museum of his own in Dearborn, Michigan—Greenfield Village, which opened in 1929. On the Connecticut coast, historians and citizens pondered Connecticut's disappearing marine industry and created Mystic Seaport, also opened in 1929.

Outdoor museums were particularly appealing because they offered visitors a hands-on experience of the past. Costumed interpreters engaged visitors by demonstrating crafts, farming techniques, and the daily chores

TABLE 2

Formation of outdoor museums

Institution	Founding date
Sturbridge Village	1946
Shelburne Museum	1946
Plimouth Plantation	1947
Old Salem	1950
Shaker Village, Old Chatham	1950
Historic Deerfield	1952
Pioneer Village, Nebraska	1953
Strawberry Banke	1958
Hancock Shaker Museum	1960
Shaker Village at Pleasant Hill	1961

of past eras, and sometimes involved the visitors directly in these activities. The typical outdoor museum also explored subjects not easily treated by other museums, such as landscape, agriculture, weather, and animal husbandry. While the depression and World War II curtailed their growth temporarily, outdoor museums flourished after 1944, starting with the organization of the Farmer's Museum, in Cooperstown, New York. More outdoor museums followed close behind (see Table 2). Like historical houses, outdoor museums often romanticized history, ignoring social issues such as slavery and ethnic diversity, a concern addressed after the 1960s.

Change and Persistence Since 1960

Momentum to establish new museums accelerated in the 1960s and 1970s, buoyed partly by postwar prosperity and the foundation of federal granting agencies such as the National Endowment for the Arts (NEA), the National Endowment for the Humanities (NEH), both founded in 1965, and the Institute for Museum Services (IMS), now the Institute for Library and Museum Services, founded in 1977. By 1965, the Statistical Survey by the American Association of Museums (AAM) reported that a new museum was founded every 3.3 days between 1960 and 1963 alone. America's national museum, the Smithsonian Institute, underwent considerable expansion itself during this time, adding what is now the National Museum of American History in 1964, followed by the Renwick Gallery, dedicated to American crafts, in 1965, the Anacostia Neighborhood Museum in 1967, the National Portrait Gallery in 1968, the Hirshhorn Museum and Sculpture Garden in 1974, the National Air and Space Museum in 1976, the Cooper-Hewitt in 1976, and the East Wing of the National Gallery in 1978. The growth of these and other museums reflected America's plural-

istic society that sought to express their diverse and highly specialized interests through museums.

Perhaps the most profound changes resulted from the civil rights movement, which heightened awareness of communities typically underrepresented and underserved by museums. Organizations representing African American, Hispanic American, Native Americans, Jewish American, and Asian American citizens, as well as many women's groups, angrily pointed out that their communities' art, history, and stories were either absent from museum exhibitions and collections or misrepresented. In some cases, communities formed their own neighborhood-based museums, such as New York's El Museo del Barrio, founded in 1969. This museum organized initially to highlight Puerto Rican culture, though it subsequently expanded to include Latino culture in general. In response to the needs of the African American community, the Smithsonian worked with an interested group of citizens that included a youth advisory board to open the Anacostia Neighborhood Museum in 1967 in a predominately black slum area in D.C. This museum, known today as the Anacostia Museum and Center for African American History and Culture, enlisted the help and support of residents to focus on topics of community concern.

While providing important services to their constituents, however, special interest museums, because they were apart and separate from established institutions, sometimes accentuated the gap between museums and their communities. The need for museums to be more inclusive and sensitive to their diverse constituencies became evident, motivating some institutions to launch new collecting initiatives to make museums and their collections more reflective of the people they served. Those museums that were most successful in those efforts enlisted community advisory groups and established outreach programs, which in turn informed and guided museum exhibits and programs.

Along with pluralism came a renewed and redefined commitment to public service. That commitment had existed from the beginning of the American museum movement, although the success rate in meeting those goals often varied. After the 1960s, however, that commitment gradually grew stronger, more inclusive, and more democratic, not though that evolution did not come easily for all museums. Controversy dogged some museums, particularly because Americans had become more vocal about their own input into their public museums, proof in itself that the public believed it had a right to shape public museum programming. In 1969, the Metropolitan Museum of Art, for example, mounted a show entitled "Harlem on My Mind," which managed to offend African Americans, Jewish Americans, and Irish Americans due to miscommunication and a lack of what president emeritus of the Ford Museum Harold Skramstad, called "connectiveness," which he defined as "the process of a close, continuous, long-term connection between an organization and its audience" (p. 126). The National Air and Space Museum experienced similar problems in 1995 over the Enola Gay exhibit, which initially appeared to sympathize with the Japanese, a controversial matter at best, and particularly in 1995 when thousands of World War II veterans streamed into Washington for the fiftieth-year commemoration of the end of World War II.

Museums have also stepped into the role of social instrument, mounting exhibits addressing pressing social concerns, such as drug use, alcoholism, venereal disease, and AIDS. As public concern regarding environmental damage grew, natural history museums found new relevance by focusing exhibit and educational programming on ecological concerns. Other museums saw themselves as civic centers and public forums, theaters and music halls, job-training centers, as well as keepers of community memories. More recently, many museums experimented with schools and early childhood learning and day-care centers in response to changing community needs.

Emphasis on education increased across the board, and in 1992 the American Association of Museums further defined the educational role of museums in their landmark report, "Excellence and Equity: Education and the Public Dimension of Museums." This study guided museums toward making public programs more inclusive and diverse while making educational programs a central part of the museum's public service program. Following such initiatives, the American Museum of Natural History launched a $35 million program to educate children and adults about science, while the Henry Ford Museum and Greenfield Village worked with local educators to open a public high school. The Autry Museum of Western Heritage collaborated with Los Angeles Unified School District to revise school curriculum to include the multicultural resources of the museum.

Staff in many museums explored different educational theories to make exhibits more accessible, such as the constructivist method that encourages visitors to frame their own questions and to create their own meanings. Museum educators experimented with teaching techniques that addressed the multiple learning styles of museum visitors, as well as those with learning or physical disabilities. Museums also grappled with ways in which to evaluate themselves and the success of exhibitions and public programs.

Experimentation marks the post-1960 years as museums constantly have sought to improve museum practices. Seeking a broader vision, many museums adopted an interdisciplinary approach to exhibits and programs, so that various points of view inform and enrich museums projects. At the turn of the century, museums developed new interpretive frameworks for old collections. The High Museum, for example, placed its art collections within a thematic framework rather than by the standard chronological and cultural framework. The Henry Ford Museum and Greenfield Village based a new furniture exhibit on a market study where they studied their visitors and determined what kinds of information visitors typically wanted to know about the collection.

Another major change was the growing professionalism that developed after the 1960s, encouraged by professional organizations such as the Association for American Museums (AAM), the American Association for State and Local History, and the Association of Living History, Farm and Agricultural Museums. A turning point occurred in 1968 when museum professionals, working with the Federal Council of the Arts and Humanities, studied the state of American museums and made recommendations in their report, "America's Museums: The Belmont Report," published in November 1968. This report concluded that museum visitation had increased four times in the years between 1938 and 1968, that museums provided a considerable amount of educational services to America's schoolchildren, and that those museums required federal support to continue their work. The report also recommended that AAM develop a museum accreditation program, a plan adopted by AAM in 1970. The accreditation program raised the bar for museums by establishing minimal standards for a museum's policies, procedures, and practices. Similarly, universities partnered with museums to establish graduate training programs to better prepare workers entering the field.

Just as earlier museums relied on familiar mediums to attract museum goers, museums turned to film, video, computers, digitalization, multimedia kiosks, lasers, holograms, the Internet, and other technological innovations to create a multisensory presentation appealing to a younger, more technologically savvy generation. Object theater, a dramatic sound and light presentation of objects, graphics, commentary, and music, developed during this time, as did interactive exhibits that expanded visitors' experiences by allowing people to touch, discover, manipulate, compare, and evaluate.

The 1990s brought an increased emphasis upon families as market surveys identified museums as prime venues for family outings. To accommodate visitors of all ages, most museums have provided discovery rooms and family centers where grandparents, parents, and children can learn and have fun in a safe environment. While some museums offer special weekend programs, activities, and tours to further the family's experience, the Denver Art Museum and other museums have endeavored to incorporate family spaces and learning centers throughout the entire gallery space.

Although museums have always been in the business of providing experiences for their audiences, museums have found themselves competing more and more for their visitors' time and discretionary income with theme restaurants, parks and malls, and an experience-based market place. Museums borrowed heavily from the experience economy exemplified by Disney World, and in many cases the commercial sector has offered valuable lessons, particularly about marketing techniques and about creating welcoming, family-friendly environments. In order to entice new audiences into exhibits, some museums have opened their doors to commercially produced exhibitions. In 2000, the Museum of Science and Industry in Chicago, for example, hosted the exhibit "Titanic" organized by SFX Entertainment, a theatrical production group.

As emphasis has shifted to providing unique experiences as a museum's main event, some museums have pushed collections to the back burner. This trend has created controversy within the museum field. Many in the museum field see the development of themed museum experience as a positive and meaningful direction for museums of the future. The director of Cranbrook Institute of Science, essayist Elaine Heumann Gurian, suggested that "museums may not need them [objects] any longer to justify their work," and argued that "the essence of a museum is not to be found in its objects," but in "being a place that stores memories and presents and organizes meaning in some sensory form" (p. 165). Others disagree, such as author Hilde S. Hein, who speculated that "glorifying museum experience at the expense of the objects that make it possible will not be economically profitable in the end. Experiences grow stale. Their shelf life is brief and the cost of refreshing them enormous" (p. 147).

In their attempts to appeal to the family purse, museums have also become more commercialized, again borrowing marketing ideas and strategies from the experience-based economy; this change, too, has provoked discussion within the museum community. While acknowledging that museums must be savvy about managing and marketing their resources, some museum professionals worry about the blurring of nonprofit public museums with the for-profit sector, believing that museums may sacrifice their own identity and authority as providers of authentic experiences if perceived by the public as just another contender for the buck. In their attempt to cultivate a new market and to offer a new type of museum experience, for example, the Guggenheim Museum, a privately funded institution, opened a branch museum tucked inside a Las Vegas casino where slot machines gave way to blockbuster exhibits on pop culture and museum shops. Despite a great deal of hype, the Las Vegas Guggenheim failed only fifteen months after it opened, one of the many museum casualties in a down-turning economy. It is this type of venture, however, that the director of the Whitney Museum of American Art, Maxwell L. Anderson, may have envisioned when he wrote, "If we increasingly paint ourselves as destinations indistinguishable from malls, we will be forced to compete with malls, and the absence of a price tag on our paintings, sculptures, and photographs will not always provide us with an advantage" (p. 131).

In 2003, AAM reported that America had roughly 16,000 museums, drawing 850 million visitors a year. Many museums, both private and public, were in the midst of ambitious expansions, such as the Peabody-Essex Museum, the Cleveland Museum of Art, the Indianapolis Museum of Art, and the Albuquerque Museum of Art and History. Yet, at the beginning of the twenty-first century, the future looked bleak for many museums, and financial advisers predicted that more tough years were ahead. Dwindling endowments, shrinking stock portfolios, and shortfalls in state and federal budgets produced what experts call a financial "perfect storm." Consequently, many museums and historical societies were forced to downsize their staffs, close sites, and curtail public services, ironically the very area museums need to offer communities sharing the same financial pain.

See also: Children's Museums, Rational Recreation and Self-Improvement, Zoos

BIBLIOGRAPHY

Alexander, Edward. *Museums in Motion.* Nashville, Tenn.: American Association for State and Local History, 1979.

———. *Museum Masters: Their Museums and Their Influence.* Nashville, Tenn.: Association for State and Local History, 1983.

American Association of Museums. *Mermaids, Mummies and Mastodons: The Emergence of the American Museum.* Edited by William T. Alderson. Washington, D.C.: American Association of Museums, 1992.

———. *Museums Count.* Edited by Ann Hofstra Grogg. Washington, D.C.: American Association of Museums, 1994.

Anderson, Maxwell L. "Museums of the Future: The Impact of Technology on Museum Practices." *Daedalus* 128 (1999).

Conn, Steven. *Museums and American Intellectual Life, 1876–1926.* Chicago: University of Chicago Press. 1998.

Darlington, David. "Facing 'The Perfect Storm.'" *Museum News* 82 (July/August 2003).

Dublin, Steven. *Displays of Power, Memory, and Amnesia in the American Museum.* New York: New York University Press, 1999.

Gurian, Elaine Heumann. "What Is the Object of This Exercise? A Meandering Exploration of the Many Meanings of Objects in Museums." *Daedalus* 128 (1999).

Hein, Hilde S. *The Museum in Transition.* Washington, D.C.: Smithsonian Institution Press, 2000.

Katz, Herbert, and Marjorie Katz. *Museums, U.S.A.* Garden City, N.Y.: Doubleday and Company, 1965.

Peare, Susan M. *Museums, Objects, and Collections: A Cultural Study.* Washington, D.C.: Smithsonian Institution Press, 1992.

Richardson, Edgar P., Brooke Hindle, and Lillian Miller. *Charles Willson Peale and His World.* New York: Harry Abrams, 1983.

Ripley, Dillon. *The Sacred Grove: Essays on Museums.* Washington, D.C.: Smithsonian Institution Press, 1969.

Sellers, Charles Coleman. *Mr. Peale's Museum: Charles Willson Peale and the First Popular Museum of Natural Science and Art.* New York: W. W. Norton and Company, 1980.

Skramstad, Harold. "An Agenda for American Museums in the Twenty-First Century." *Daedalus* 128 (1999).

Weil, Stephen. *A Cabinet of Curiosities: Inquiries into Museums and Their Prospects.* Washington, D.C.: Smithsonian Institution Press, 1995.

———. "From Being *About* Something to Being *for* Somebody: The Ongoing Transformation of the American Museum." *Daedalus* 128 (1999).

West, Patricia. *Domesticating History: The Political Origins of America's House Museums.* Washington, D.C.: Smithsonian Institution Press, 1999.

Wittlin, Alma S. *Museum: In Search of a Usable Future.* Cambridge, Mass.: MIT Press, 1970.

Patricia M. Tice

MUSIC

See *Barbershop Quartets; Choral Singing; Country Music Audiences; Performing Arts Audiences; Piano Playing; Radio Listening, Car and Home; Rap Music Audiences; Rock Concert Audiences; Slave Singing/Music Making; Traditional Folk Music Festivals*

MUSICAL THEATER
See *Theater, Live*

MUSLIM AMERICAN LEISURE LIFESTYLES

Although certain aspects of immigrant Muslim American society resemble the

process by which non-Muslim immigrant society undergoes assimilation and adaptation as it settles in North America, certain characteristics need to be recognized as paramount. Among these distinctions are the tenacity with which Muslims preserve their religious practices and beliefs, their identity with the Islamic Nation, and the hospitality that they invariably show to guests. Some understanding of Islamic principles is necessary to understand recreation and leisure as Muslim North Americans engage in it. "Islam" is the name of the monotheistic faith that the Prophet Muhammad founded in Makkah (modern-day Saudi Arabia) in the six and seventh centuries after the Common Era. The term "Muslim" normally refers to a follower of the Islamic religion or the community of Muslims. "Islamic" is the adjective used when making reference to nonhuman aspects of the faith.

Socioeconomic Categories and Ethnicity

The Muslim community in North America may be divided into the following categories:

1. Students and professionals here for a limited period of time. Spouses and children who accompany them should be classified in this group.

2. Immigrants and holders of permanent residency, as well as their descendants.

3. American-born converts to Islam. A significant number of those belonging to this category are of African American descent. Accordingly, the leisure lifestyle is essentially that of their non-Muslim family members, unless it has changed to accommodate their Muslim friends or spouses of Middle Eastern origin.

Figures from the early 2000s indicate that about one-third (32 percent) of Muslims in the United States are of South Asian origin, with Arabs constituting roughly one-quarter (26 percent) and African-Americans holding the third position, at 20 percent. The rest are of either sub-Saharan origin, or presumably of European ancestry, including Hispanic, American, and Asian Muslims not originally from the Indian subcontinent.

The Muslim immigrant and permanent resident community of the Detroit, Michigan, metropolitan area is a microcosm of the larger permanent United States Muslim community. Together with Ann Arbor, which lies about thirty miles west of Detroit proper, and Windsor, Ontario, which lies south of Detroit, being separated by the Detroit River, it is home to approximately 125,000 Muslims. Although precise figures are impossible to obtain, a reasonable estimate of the total Muslim population in the United States is between 4 and 6 million, with projections for growth to continue into the indefinite future.

Only a minority of Muslims worldwide are Arabs, in other words, speakers of the Arabic language. Many nations with significant Muslim majorities, including Iran, Turkey, Pakistan, Afghanistan, Bangladesh, Indonesia, and Malaysia, are not Arabic-speaking. Furthermore, in the Arab world, significant and productive Christian communities live side by side with Muslims, particularly in Egypt and the Fertile Crescent. Christian Arabs are virtually indistinguishable from their Muslim neighbors in all aspects save religious belief.

The Leisure Patterns of Immigrant Muslim Americans

Unlike lifestyles and religious faiths followed by many other citizens of North America, Muslims live according to the requirements of their religion without separating sports, food, entertainment, and other aspects of their personal and professional lives into a separate category for secular activities. This overt religious aspect of Islamic life appears pervasive to the observer from outside the Muslim community. On the other hand, most Muslims pursue various sports and hobbies according to their education and socioeconomic status in a manner superficially similar to their non-Muslim counterparts and neighbors.

Team and Individual Sports Passing familiarity with sports is useful for conversation over coffee in the workplace, especially for recent arrivals. Most Muslim immigrants are familiar with soccer, tennis, volleyball, and basketball. Since primary and secondary schools emphasize these team sports, most Muslim immigrants under the age of fifty have participated in them at some point in their lives. Naturally, most Muslims of South Asian origin are also familiar with cricket. On the other hand, most

Muslims are acquainted with U.S. football and baseball, at the spectator level at least.

The degree of involvement varies widely for individual sports, such as swimming, backpacking, hiking, fishing, hunting, and golf. Factors such as socioeconomic status determine how interested an individual is in any specific activity. For instance, Muslim professionals and sales personnel are far more likely to engage in sports and activities related to business, such as golf, than are other Muslims. This involvement is similar to that of American communities in general.

In terms of winter sports, many Muslim American immigrants hail from countries with developed Alpine ski resorts (Lebanon, Morocco, Turkey, Iran, and Iraq). Obviously, those with the ability and desire to ski pursue skiing after having settled in North America, particularly in regions blessed with adequate snowfall and terrain.

Verbal discussion Most Muslims are interested in verbal discussions about philosophy, religion, politics, and related topics considered somewhat controversial in the West. The ability to engage in verbal sparring is encouraged by the Islamic faith, which views intellectual interaction as a part of its dialectic. Generally speaking, North American Muslims are not personally offended by an individual whose views, if presented eloquently and courteously, differ from Islamic doctrine. As a result, Muslim Americans are able to enter into political discourse without the difficulty facing some other immigrant communities, and display a keen sense of patriotism reflected in their love for their adopted country.

This proclivity to engage in verbal discussion with friends and acquaintances actually approaches that of a hobby, but it depends on the speaker's facility to express himself or herself in English. Many inside the immigrant community have limited skills in formal English.

Because only a working knowledge of English is needed to survive within the community, many second- and even third-generation members of the community also have not yet attained the level of linguistic and social assimilation prevalent in certain other immigrant groups. At the same time, many of them have only limited adeptness in their ancestral languages while retaining a certain familiarity with their ancestors' customs. The widespread belief held among Muslims in North America that outsiders have no interest in things Islamic, unless there is an (insidious) ulterior motive for this interest sets up a barrier between those with limited skills in English and their non-Muslim neighbors. This barrier, in time, both reinforces the sense of community held among its members and isolates and ghettoizes them.

Farida M. Ali. Farida M. Ali sings Arab classical and folk songs with the Iraqi Maqam Ensemble (Wisam Ayyoub playing the santur, left, and Abdellatif Saad playing the dumbek) in her American debut during a World Music Institute concert at Symphony Space, New York City on 5 May 2001. © *Jack Vartoogian*

Television and Radio The role of television in the life of Muslims living in the twenty-first century cannot be overstated. Because television is a great leveling factor in the formation of popular tastes and concepts, popular programs and news broadcasts serve to homogenize the tastes and sensibilities of virtually everybody in the United States. Despite the fact that all significant immigrant communities watch dish networks in their ancestral tongue, including many Muslim Americans, most children of Muslim immigrants watch the majority of programming in English, not, for example, in Arabic, Turkish, Farsi, or Urdu. In addition to cable TV and satellite broadcasts, countless videos are available for both pleasure (films, music, video clips) and religious instruction.

For music and news, the medium of radio is still extremely popular, with several variety broadcasts combining news, music, and community service announcements broadcast daily in the Detroit area. Based upon listening to Arabic music broadcast from Detroit, it is quite apparent that the tastes of the Arabic-speaking community in the New World are sentimental and old-fashioned. Famous singers, including Umm Kalthoum, Muhammad Abd ul-Wahhaab, and Fariid al-Atrash, who were most popular when Frank Sinatra was at the peak of his popularity, still attract Muslim audiences in North America in the early 2000s. Arabic satellite networks in the Middle East, being largely imitative of MTV and its offshoots, are beginning to shake this conservatism.

Religious programming (Christian as well as Islamic) constitutes a significant proportion of Arabic-language broadcasts. Many Muslims listen to Koranic broadcasts on the radio, in Arabic, Urdu, Farsi, and English.

Other Interests and Hobbies Chess, checkers, backgammon, and various card games either originated in the Middle East or became popular in the region centuries ago. Although religious sentiment may restrict many Muslims from engaging in these activities, that sentiment has not driven leisure games out of existence among the Muslim community. In fact, in the Middle East, a great deal of leisure time is passed over coffee and tea, either at home, or in cafés and teahouses. During this time, many indulge in chess, checkers, and backgammon, as well as &dquo;balluut," a card game resembling bridge. This custom, together with the related custom of entertaining guests at home and fostering the art of eloquent conversation, has survived intact and indeed flourishes in the Muslim American community. Since an optimal location for these games is a cafe, individuals living in communities sufficiently large to support such a locale would typically participate in board games. In Islamic belief, gambling is specifically restricted.

As is common with men of other backgrounds, many Muslim American men lavish care on their cars and spend much time and money on maintenance and customization. A similar pattern obtains for televisions, VCRs, and audio systems, as well as computers and ancillary equipment.

Community Activities and Volunteer Organizations

Muslims in North America take pride in their participation in relief efforts, whether under religious auspices or not, as well as in school-oriented programs and clubs. Muslim professionals serve actively in organizations related to their practice, as do members of trade unions.

Cultural activities also enjoy widespread support in the Muslim community, particularly when it relates to ethnic identity.

Contributory Factors

Since many Muslim immigrants are pursuing careers and raising families simultaneously, the untrained observer may imagine incorrectly that conservative Muslim Americans are indifferent to sports. It is true that many female Muslim American immigrants move to North America for the express purpose of marriage and having children. Naturally, this factor temporarily precludes their rapid assimilation into typical American leisure and sports activities. But like American-born couples with babies, who typically forgo certain of their favorite leisure activities until their children can engage in them as a family activity, such a situation need not last indefinitely. As long as time and finances permit, educated and professional Muslim immigrants normally continue to engage in their favorite sports and hobbies after moving to North America.

Since the Muslim American community is tightly knit, group pressure to engage in community service activities as well in charitable organizations may take precedence over sports and leisure.

Religious Aspects

Since a high majority (79 percent) of Muslim Americans hold that religion is very important to their lives, the effect of Islam is pervasive and comprehensive.

Practice of one's repertoire in the culinary arts takes a decidedly religious cast. Elaborate dishes and pastries are expected on Islamic holidays, such as Eid Al-Fitr (at the end of Ramadhaan) and Eid Al-Adha (at the end of the Pilgrimage to Makkah). Those who do not cook may contribute by slaughtering livestock or poultry according to Islamic law, either on an ad hoc or commercial basis. As a reflection on this reality, halal (i.e., in conformance to Islamic dietary law) abattoirs are no longer an unusual sight in most metropolitan areas.

Religiously inspired sewing and clothes making is also popular among Muslim immigrants, particularly in the regions where Islamically appropriate attire is difficult to obtain. In the Detroit area, women in traditional Muslim families frequently wear the hijaab (head shawl) in public areas, including school, particularly in Dearborn, the city with the highest concentration of Muslims. Not all Muslim women observe this practice, however, even in the Middle East. The issue of separation of the sexes is also variously observed, and depends on the norms of the community, the socioeconomic level, and the inclination of the individual.

Mosque-sponsored and affiliated schools normally offer courses in the Arabic language to disseminate the teachings of the Koran, the Islamic scriptures. This activity serves a double function, as it also connects the younger generation with the religious training their parents received.

Cuisine and Dietary Habits

Food Ethnic cooking is naturally a popular practice in virtually all ethnic enclaves, enabling one to state that enjoying Middle Eastern cuisine is perhaps the most durable aspect of culture among Muslims in North America. Islam specifically prohibits the consumption of sausage, bacon, and other pork by-products. This practice may not loom as an obstacle where the Muslim community in North America is significant, as in virtually all large metropolitan areas and in college towns. Under these circumstances, such products as "halal" (Islamically slaughtered, hence permissible) beef sausage, beef bacon, and chicken are readily available. Furthermore, many Muslims avail themselves of meat or sausage labeled "kosher" when it is available; "kosher" foods are normally acceptable for Sunni Muslims at least. In this regard, both the Koran and the Hadiith, the compilation of the normative sayings of the Prophet Muhammad, refer to the issue of food specifically. "O ye who believe! Eat of the good things that We have provided for you, and be grateful to God if it is Him ye worship" (Koran 2:172).

Since Muslim immigrants generally prefer lamb or goat meat for ethnic cooking, Islamic butchers specialize in such offerings. Christians of Middle Eastern origin frequent such abattoirs because of the reputation they maintain for offering high-quality meat at reasonable prices. Middle Eastern Christians purchase their ethnic foods at the same shops as do their Muslim brethren.

Beverages and Refreshments Muslims in North America observe the Koranic prohibition of inebriating beverages, but they may drink alcohol-free beer or wine if so inclined. On the other hand, many strict Muslims avoid the appearance of consuming prohibited liquids no matter what the situation.

Traditionally, Muslims drink coffee or tea as their main refreshment, and will offer sweets or cakes to guests accompanied by one, the other, or both. They enjoy as well juices, milk, yogurt drink (a savory, herbal buttermilk), and other traditional beverages.

With meals, North American Muslims also drink soft drinks, particularly cola drinks. This practice clearly parallels other religious communities. Cola, with its complex flavor, complements spicy foods particularly well because it cleans the palate.

Fasting in the Muslim Community Muslims in North America strictly observe Ramadhaan, the Islamic holy month of fasting. They will eat only after sundown and before sunrise during this month, unless mitigating factors (pregnancy, childhood, illness, or traveling) occur. Being based on the Islamic lunar calendar, Ramadhaan arrives eleven days earlier on the Gregorian calendar each year. Muslims enjoy special dishes during Ramadhaan, including regional specialties. In accordance with Prophetic custom, the fast is normally broken by eating the fruit of the date palm, with the first meal, known as "'IfTaar," following soon after the dates are eaten.

Conclusion

Leisure lifestyles and their related activities, including spectator and participant sports, as they are pursued by the Muslim community in metropolitan Detroit, resemble the patterns exhibited by non-Muslims. This should come as no surprise. What may be more surprising is that the tenacity of Muslims in terms of religious practice and cohesion, so apparent to anyone who has spent time in the Middle East, has taken root in Detroit as well.

Where no conflict between religious practice and leisure occurs, Muslim Americans feel no compunction to pursue leisure habits common to their neighbors. That being said, the influx of new Muslim immigrants to the Detroit area has a history of at least five decades, and exhibits no signs of abating. This continued immigration has allowed the community to flourish, while it has prevented complete assimilation of many uslim Americans until at least the third generation.

See also: Coffee Houses and Café Society

BIBLIOGRAPHY

Al-Askari, Sulaiman I. "Our Arab Culture and Their Western Culture." *Al-Arabi* (Safat, Kuwait) no. 522 (May 2002).

Ali, A. Yusuf. *The Holy Qur'an: Text, Translation, and Commentary.* Brentwood, Md.: Amana Corporation, 1983.

Esposito, John L. *Islam: The Straight Path.* New York: Oxford University Press, 1998.

Gibb, Hamilton A. R. *Studies on the Civilization of Islam.* Princeton, N.J.: Princeton University Press, 1962.

Hayyani, Ibrahim. "Recognizable Attempts in Émigré Lands: An Effective Role Which Is Crystallizing Quietly." *Al-Arabi* (Safat, Kuwait), no. 523 (June 2002).

Hoffiz, Benjamin T., III. Questionnaire on Leisure Activities. Fall 2002.

Ibrahim, Ezzeddin, and Denys Johnson-Davies. *An-Nawawi's Forty Hadith.* Damascus, Syria: Holy Koran Publishing House, 1976.

Lerner, Robert E., et al. *Western Civilizations.* 13th edition. Volume 1. New York: W. W. Norton and Company, 1998.

Mansfield, Peter. *History of the Middle East.* London: Penguin Books, 1991.

Piamenta, M. *Islam in Everyday Arabic Speech.* Leiden, Netherlands: E. J. Brill, 1979.

Rahman, Fazlur. *Islam.* 2nd edition. Chicago: University of Chicago Press, 1979.

Sabbagh, Isa Khalil. *As the Arabs Say . . .* Washington, D.C.: Sabbagh Management Corporation, 1983.

Spencer, W. *Global Studies: The Middle East.* 9th edition. New York: McGraw-Hill, 2003.

Stiles, T. J. *The Colonizers: Early European Settlers and the Shaping of North America.* New York: Berkley Publishing Group, 1998.

U.S. Department of State. International Education Programs. "Muslim Life in America." Available from http//:www .usinfo.state.gov.

Zacharias, Ravi. *Light in the Shadow of Jihad.* Sisters, Oreg.: Multnomah Publishers, 2002.

Zogby, John. American Muslim Poll. November/December 2001. Available from http://www.projectmaps.com.

Benjamin T. Hoffiz

NASCAR

See *Auto Racing; Stock Car Racing*

NATIONAL PARKS

While Yellowstone National Park is regarded as the first National Park, it was not the first area to be set aside or reserved. Military commemoration, one of the areas forming today's National Park System, began on 29 October 1781, when the Continental Congress, inspired by the news of the surrender at Yorktown, authorized the erection of "a marble column, adorned with emblems of the alliance between the United States and His Most Christian Majesty; and inscribed with a succinct narrative of the surrender." Not actually erected until nearly a century had passed, it was the initial authorized form of battlefield commemoration that evolved into the National Military Park System, which became part of the National Park System in 1933.

In 1790, Congress authorized the founding of the District of Columbia. Although the plan for the city developed by Pierre Charles L'Enfant was only partially implemented, the commissioners purchased seventeen public reservations. These areas, now known as the National Capital Park System, were placed under the Department of the Interior in 1849; transferred to the Chief Engineer of the U.S. Army in 1867; placed under the Office of Public Buildings and Public Works of the National Capital in 1925; and finally placed with the National Park Service in 1933.

In 1832, forty years prior to the establishment of the first National Park, the federal government set aside public lands in the Ouachita Mountains of Arkansas for future use by the government The Hot Springs Reservation was deemed to be of significant medicinal value to the entire nation, and, in 1921, it was designated a National Park. Although recreation was not the reason for the creation of the reservation, the action was recognition of the fact that certain unique land features could be of greater public benefit if not given to private development and exploitation.

In 1833, George Catlin, an explorer and artist, wrote for a New York newspaper that portions of the West should be "preserved in their pristine beauty and wilderness in a magnificent park . . . a Nation's park, containing man and beast, in all the wild and freshness of their nature's beauty"—a policy given partial recognition in wilderness area designations of the following century.

The battlefield memorial movement began with private organizations such as the Bunker Hill Battle Monument Association (founded in 1823) and the Gettysburg Battlefield Memorial Association (founded in 1864). The first national cemeteries were established under the authority of an act signed by President Lincoln on 17 July 1862. These sites, initially administered by the War Department, were also transferred to the National Park System in 1933.

In 1864, Yosemite Valley was entrusted to the state of California to be held for "public use, resort, and recreation"—thus bringing the National Park idea one step closer to realization. In 1870, the Washburn-Langford-Doane Expedition into Yellowstone initiated the series of events that culminated in the act signed by President Grant on 1 March 1872—the creation of the world's first National Park at Yellowstone. This legislation specified that a designated tract of land would be set aside and dedicated for use as a public park for all to enjoy.

The National Park idea—public preservation of an extensive area of wilderness and unique natural resources—was a new concept and a recognition of the recreational values of natural resources. Funding, however, was not immediately forthcoming. In his letter of appointment as the first superintendent of Yellowstone, Nathaniel P. Langford was instructed not to beautify the area being set aside, but rather simply preserve and protect it from mining and other outside interests. It also informed him that his appointment was without pay but that he could apply any money from leases for carrying out the purposes of the act.

However, few government officials and politicians considered National Parks to be worthy of funding, and efforts were made to turn these lands over to the states for administration. The nation's second National Park was designated in 1875—the military property on Mackinac Island—but was ceded to the state of Michigan in 1895. A lack of appropriated funding, coupled with the absence of legal authority to provide the needed protection of the resources, resulted in the National Parks eventually being assigned either to the U.S. Army or to the supervisors of adjacent national forest lands.

Historic Preservation

For the period of 1875 to 1889, the only other acquisitions were the Washington Monument (1876), the Statue of Liberty (1877), Custer's Battlefield National Cemetery (1886), and Casa Grande (1889). A flurry of activity in the 1890s saw the establishment of five National Military Parks (administered by the War Department) as well as the new National Parks of Sequoia, General Grant, Yosemite, and Mount Rainier. Acquisition of the Gettysburg National Military Park was accompanied by a Supreme Court decision in 1896 that upheld the right of the government to condemn private property for the purpose of preserving battlefields and erecting monuments. This decision sanctioned congressional action to acquire such sites for the benefit of the country.

Historical preservation as a legitimate governmental function was formalized in the Antiquities Act of 1906. This legislation ushered in a period of expansion of historical and scientific monuments, including Mesa Verde,

Devil's Tower, El Morro, Montezuma's Castle, and the Petrified Forest, all reserved from the public domain in the six months following passage of the act. Functioning under the authority granted him by the Antiquities Act, President Theodore Roosevelt proclaimed the Grand Canyon National Monument on lands within the Grand Canyon National Forest in Arizona in 1908. This action was prompted by the reported plan to build an electric railway along the canyon rim. Challenged in the courts but sustained by the U.S. Supreme Court, this action created a National Monument of 818,560 acres. The monument remained under the jurisdiction of the Department of Agriculture until Congress placed it under the National Park Service in 1919 as Grand Canyon National Park.

It was the increasingly popular idea of conservation, rather than recreation, that served as the impetus for setting aside lands as either monuments or parks. Public support for some coordinating agency for the parks and other areas led to the formation of the National Park Service in 1916. All of the parks and monuments of the Department of the Interior were placed under the jurisdiction of the National Park Service along with the Hot Springs reservation. In 1933, the monuments and battlefields under the War Department were also made a part of the National Park System.

Philosophy of Park Development

The original language of the Yellowstone act specified the philosophy of National Park development, and this was continued in the legislation that formed the National Park Service. The specific charge was "to conserve the scenery and the natural and historic objects and the wild life therein and to provide for the enjoyment of the same in such manner and by such means as will leave them unimpaired for the enjoyment of future generations." To some, this is an irreconcilable dichotomy because use implies degradation of the resource, and while the differences between conservation and preservation may appear slight to some people, it has been a major point of contention. The Hetch-Hetchy controversy of 1913—the congressionally authorized damming of the Hetch-Hetchy Valley of Yosemite to provide a water supply for the city of San Francisco—brought a major split between John Muir and the preservationists on the one side and the conservationists on the other.

In his 1915 report, Mark Daniels, the general superintendent and landscape engineer of the National Parks, identified three purposes of the National Parks: 1) the stimulating of national patriotism; 2) the furthering of knowledge and health; and 3) the diverting of tourist travel to the scenic areas of the United States. Of these three, he felt that the first two would be an end result of the third.

This report recognized that transportation systems needed to be developed in order to facilitate tourist travel to and within the parks, as well as accommodations and sources of supplies, so that the traveler would not be subjected to serious discomfort or expense. Mark Daniels also noted that parks with inferior scenery but better infrastructure would always outdraw parks that had better scenery but poorer roads and accommodations Larger appropriations would be needed to attract the tourists. Traveling the "Wylie Way," where one had to rent saddle animals, pack horses, a guide, a cook, and all forms of supplies, was no longer affordable to the increasing numbers of visitors.

Despite their grandeur or their historical significance, the National Parks have remained the impoverished stepchild of the federal government since the creation of Yellowstone National Park. Nathaniel Langford, the first superintendent, served for five years without pay, doing his best with the funds available from leases or fees. Since this was insufficient, the park was turned over to the state of Wyoming, but the fiscal problems were equally bad. Eventually, the park was turned over to the jurisdiction of the U.S. Army, and a cavalry unit was assigned to protect the park, build the roads, and provide whatever assistance they could.

The funding that Mark Daniels identified as needed for proper development did not come as national resources went into the war effort in Europe. The Great Depression of the 1930s actually benefited the Park Service, as various Civilian Conservation Corps and "make-work" projects were conducted in the parks and funded by the federal government. However, with the advent of World War II and rationing, visitation dropped along with funding. The postwar situation was no better. With no increase in funding or personnel, and with a growing number of visitors, the situation became critical. In the *Harper's Magazine* of October 1953, Bernard DeVoto detailed some of the problems faced by the service.

Since postwar funding did not keep pace with increasing visitor pressures, the National Park System embarked on a program named Mission 66 to better define the needs for increased funding for maintenance and development. This ten-year program did result in a greater awareness of the needs and resulted in increased congressional appropriations. However, these funds were still inadequate to meet the needs created by vastly increased visitation; in the early 2000s, many observers still charged that funding is inadequate to preserve these national treasures in their natural state.

Controversy in Park Management

The National Park Service, like most federal land management agencies, is subject to intense scrutiny by environmental groups, adjacent landowners, user groups, and other interested parties. Over the years, Yellowstone National Park has been at the heart of various disputes over management practices dealing with the bear population; the reintroduction of wolves to the park; the use of snowmobiles; fire control; and attempts to ameliorate the parking, transportation, and crowding problems. Court injunctions and lawsuits sometimes appear to be a constant drain on resources and personnel of the service; groups with vested interests in the park operations oppose even accepted management practices.

The need for control burning to reduce the likelihood of disastrous wildfires was recognized in the 1950s. As Bernard DeVoto stated, " high plateaus covered with lodgepole pine are natural fire-traps which some day will be burned out because the budget will not permit adequate fire-protection" (p. 52). The fire protection problem has surfaced several times since that 1953 article, and the results can be described as disastrous at several of the western parks.

From the Hetch-Hetchy controversy at Yosemite, which pitted Stephen Mather against John Muir, to the early-2000s discussions about limiting the use of snowmobiles at Yellowstone and other National Parks, the controversies will, without doubt, continue.

See also: City Parks, Park Movements, State Parks

BIBLIOGRAPHY

Albright, Horace M. *The Birth of the National Park Service: The Founding Years, 1913–33.* Chicago: Howe Brothers, 1985.

Albright, Horace M., and Frank J. Taylor. *"Oh, Ranger!" A Book About the National Parks.* New York: Dodd, Mead, and Company, 1947.

Department of the Interior. *The Mesa Verde National Park.* Washington, D.C.: U.S. Government Printing Office, n.d.

DeVoto, Bernard. "Let's Close the National Parks." *Harper's Magazine* 207, no. 1241 (October 1953): 49–52.

Everts, Truman. *Lost in the Yellowstone.* Edited by Lee H. Whittlesey. Salt Lake City: University of Utah Press, 1995.

Hampton, H. Duane. *How the U.S. Cavalry Saved Our National Parks.* Bloomington: Indiana University Press, 1971.

Melbo, Irving R. *Our Country's National Parks.* Volumes 1 and 2. New York: The Bobbs-Merrill Company, 1941.

Tillotson, M. R., and Frank J. Taylor. *Grand Canyon Country.* Palo Alto, Calif.: Stanford University Press, 1935.

Louis Hodges and Rachelle Toupence

NATIVE AMERICAN LEISURE LIFESTYLES

The Native communities of the North American continent, both historically and today, have extensive, healthy, and complex leisure traditions replete with entertaining yet socially instructive activities: from the rubber ball game of Mesoamerica to the ball races of northern Mexico, the seasonal dances and ceremonies of the Native Southwest, the Sun Dance and festive powwows of the Plains, the potlatches and dances of the Northwest Coast, and the stickball games of the East and Southeast. These activities and others are vital components of the Native experience, heavily imbued with social meaning, replete with symbols that reflect the fundamental norms and values of their particular cultural settings, and critical to social process and adaptation.

Leisure has many forms; the complexity of cultural definitions and understandings of leisure make a definitive listing impossible. However, leisure in Native America covers a wide range of activities that includes, but is not exclusive to, games, dance, sports, outdoor recreation, festive or celebratory ceremony, humor, art, and crafts.

Leisure also has many functions. From an etic, or objective, perspective, one could suggest that some physical games and sports implicitly help participants develop skills that have direct economic importance (for example, archery as practice for the hunt). Other activities, such as team sports and ceremonies, provide community-based activities that reinforce kin networks and solidify relationships and a sense of community. Festivals and dances are sometimes seen as an opportunity for young men and women to meet and ultimately make important marriage decisions.

From an emic, or insider's, perspective, there are many other possibilities, as leisure activities take on the meaning of particular cultures and individuals. For example, a study among the Cree of Northern Manitoba isolated five themes central to that group's understanding of leisure: (1) pursuit of freedom, (2) extrinsic motivation, (3) sense of being close to nature, (4) responding to inner drive to be outdoors, and (5) interactions with other humans or with nature. In another study, a group of Native Canadians suggested with reference to recreation that it was important for reasons of pure joy, relaxation, stress reduction, health, relief from boredom, social development, and cultural expression.

Historical Background

The early archaeological, historic, and ethnographic records are witness to the rich and complex leisure ethic of Native North America. While archaeologists have been limited in their ability to speak to the wide varieties of leisure activities that embellished prehistoric Native American life, they have uncovered and documented such objects and places as gaming devices, ball courts, dance grounds, and musical devices such as drums. As a result of work by archaeologists and prehistorians, much is known about the diffusion of the Mesoamerican ball game into the North American West and Southwest. For example, a large ball court has been unearthed at Snaketown, Arizona, a major Hohokam site, suggesting clearly that somewhere around 2,000 years ago the ball game was an important part of life among Native southwesterners. Historians and ethnographers, however, have had more to work with and thus have been more helpful in painting a picture of Native life in its entirety and documenting the place of leisure activities within that life than have the archaeologists. One of the most important contributions to current understandings of Native leisure by an anthropologist was Stewart Culin's work, most notably his *Games of the North American Indians*. Culin describes the games of 225 Native American tribal groups, dividing those games into two major categories: games of chance and games of dexterity. It is noteworthy that Culin was not aware of any games of strategy that were native to the Indian communities of North America. In his words, "games of pure skill and calculation, such as chess, are entirely absent" (p. 31).

The games of chance include dice games, in which dice were thrown and total points calculated, then recorded with sticks, small stones, or some form of counting board. For example, the Bellacoola of British Columbia made dice from bone, hemispheric in shape and two-sided, with either dots or chevrons carved on one of the sides. Another popular game of chance was a guessing game in which one or more players attempted to determine where an object of some sort had been deliberately concealed. Points were accumulated based on the number of successful guesses. The most common game of this type was the hand game, in which objects would be moved from hand to hand with players being challenged to guess in which hand the object ultimately came to rest. Also popular among some groups was the hidden-ball game. This game, as among the Zuni, involved taking several round objects (beans, pebbles) and placing them in specially prepared baskets or tubes. The players were then expected to guess where the objects had been placed.

The games of dexterity included various forms of archery, sports in which javelins or darts were slid along the hard ground or ice, games of throwing wooden spears at some form of moving target, racing games, and various ball games. One of the most popular sliding games was chunkey. Among the Choctaws of the early nineteenth century, this game involved one contestant rolling a large round stone (chunkey stone) along the path of a specially prepared area (chunkey ground) and others throwing large poles along its path. The object was to have one's pole come to rest as closely as possible to the point at which the chunkey stone came to a stop.

The most popular ball games were the racket games and the ball games. In the racket games, two teams competed by moving a ball up and down a field, using only a racket or rackets to propel the ball, either tossing it through a goal or striking it against a goal to score points. Perhaps the most common of the ball games was shinny, a game in which one struck or slapped the ball with a club or bat; Culin found shinny among 26 percent of the tribes represented in his analysis. Double ball, a game most typically played by women, involved using sticks to sling a contraption made of two balls tethered together up and down a field and scoring points, as in the racket game, by striking a goal. Also common among Native tribal groups were the ball race, running while kicking a ball or stick, and a variety of football games, games in which participants used their feet to kick a ball against or through a goal.

Culin cites many other games of dexterity common to nineteenth-century Native American communities, games he called "minor amusements," including shuttlecock, tipcat, quoits, shuffleboard, jackstraws, tops, bullroarer, popgun, bean shooter, and cat's cradle.

Other anthropologists described some of these games in much greater detail than Culin, and documented the way in which these and other leisure activities were so thoroughly integrated into Native American life. For example, James Mooney wrote an entire monograph on the racket game of the Cherokee, describing the extensive preparation, the elaborate rituals and religious meanings surrounding the formal ball game, and the heavy wagering.

Importance of Gambling Gambling seems to have been a ubiquitous complement to games and other leisure events among nineteenth-century Native American groups. For example, at most formal ball games, the spectators wagered on the outcomes. In most cases, there were no odds, one bet only on one's own team, and the winner took all. For example, among the Choctaws the formal racket game, the parent game of lacrosse, was the locus of heaving gambling. Members of the competing communities brought to the game large amounts of food, blankets, household goods, animals, and weapons. Everyone got into the act. Betting seemed to be more of a moral obligation than an effort to better one's economic circumstances. These accumulated goods were piled at opposite ends or sides of the playing field. At the end of the game, immediately upon the outcome being determined, the winners and their supporters swooped down on and claimed the items wagered by their opponents. This is not unlike a pattern that is common across traditional Native America and a phenomenon that served both social and economic function. For example, it can be argued that the distribution of surplus goods in this fashion served as a leveling device, ensuring the even allocation of limited goods across an entire population, militating against the possibility that a tribal population would be split into have and have-not communities. This process would have ensured maximal efficiency in the distribution of resources as well as lowering the likelihood of conflict sparked by economic inequity.

Ritual and Religion Also common to the games and leisure activities of traditional Native America were a variety of ritual activities designed ostensibly to affect outcomes. It was normal practice among most tribes for competitors to enlist the help of shamans, sorcerers, medicine people, witches, and other religious practitioners to facilitate winning and ensure against losing. Spells were put on opponents, players were "treated" so as to enhance their skills, game equipment was "treated," and the weather was manipulated so as to affect game outcomes. At least that is the way it appeared on the surface. In reality, there is evidence that much of the ritual surrounding Native American sport activity was not so much an effort to manipulate game outcomes as it was a statement about the forces of fate and one's obligation to recognize and resign to that fate. This approach to ritual as it relates to games and sports can be viewed as an illustration of a broader pattern of environmental adaptation common to Native America, a world in which one works with rather than attempts to control the forces of nature. If this is the case, it is no wonder that games of chance are so common and games of strategy so rare among traditional Native American societies.

Ceremonies and Dances Other activities helping to define the leisure lifestyles of Native America include the ceremonies, dances, singing, and other festivals important to community life in many ways besides recreation. For this reason, it is difficult to distinguish between what is leisure and what is not in these societies. It is clear, however, that the participants viewed these activities, although designed for specific purposes other than recreation, as leisure.

For example, the dances of Native American tribal groups were often associated with elements of the natural environment and were viewed as appeals to the cooperative sentiments of nature. Consider the Buffalo Dance of the Mandan; it was a form of communal entertainment but was also designed to coax the buffalo to return each year to the Mandan hunting grounds. The dance ceremonies of Native America were consistently colorful and complex. However, they varied immensely in their motion, associated singing, and seriousness. Perhaps the most serious of Native American dances was the Sun Dance of the Plains Indians, involving as it did bodily mutilation, pain, and bravado that put one's physical well-being at risk. The so-called fancy dancing of the Plains was at the same time perhaps the most colorful, both in the dress of participants and in the intensity and tempo of the dances themselves.

One of the best known and thoroughly documented of nineteenth-century Native American dances is the Ghost Dance. The brainchild of a Paiute shaman named Wovoka, the Ghost Dance was designed to facilitate the revitalization of Native America. In sum, it was a ritual that if properly performed would bring back the ghosts of Native ancestors and simultaneously drive the white man away, leaving the Indians of America once again in control of their native lands, their communities, and their destinies. In the dance itself, participants, both men and women, lined up in a large circle, usually around a large fire, and shuffled slowly, following the course of the sun, singing the songs of the Ghost Dance. The Ghost Dance virtually died in 1890 at the Battle of Wounded Knee as almost 200 Lakota men, women, and children lost their lives in a bloody battle with the U.S. Cavalry. Many of the warriors went into that battle with the assumption that their Ghost Shirts would protect them from the white men's weapons.

The relationship between leisure and the Ghost Dance is best illustrated in anthropologist Alexander Lesser's classic monograph "The Pawnee Ghost Dance Hand Game." The Pawnee hand game was a guessing game involving two special bones or dice that were pitched from hand to hand so as to make it difficult for one to determine where the pieces were located at any point in time. Successful guesses were recorded, participants wagered on the outcomes, and the game was taken quite seriously. With the advent of the Ghost Dance among the Pawnee, the hand game became much more stylized and highly ritualized, in many ways becoming a virtual component of the Ghost Dance itself.

Other Ceremonies Other traditional Native American ceremonies can also be viewed as leisure. For example, one of the most complex repertoires of ceremonial activities belongs to the Navajos of the American Southwest. These ceremonies include Blessingway, In-da (once inappropriately referred to as the "Squaw Dance"), the Night Chant, Yeibichai, and others. Most of these ceremonies involve extensive singing and chanting, some include sand painting, and most go on for long periods of time. Yeibichai, for example, is a nine-day ceremony. All Navajo ceremonies are designed for healing, are focused on individual patients, and frequently involve sweating and induced vomiting on the part of the patients. These ceremonies function to bring the patients into harmony with the rest of the world and in this way actuate healing. They bring together many Navajo families, clans, and outfits, who eat, dance, sing, and mingle. While the ceremonies have a clear medicinal and ritual purpose, they are also important to the leisure culture of the Navajos. This situation is not unusual among Native American groups and illustrates the integration of leisure and other types of activities in Native American life.

Humor was also an important part of Native American ceremony. The role of the clown was of particular importance in this context. For example, among the Hopi of the American Southeast, most of the major ceremonies (for example, the kachina dances) and special performances involved ritual humor (Hieb). Clowns were critical to providing this humor and in contexts that can be defined as elements of leisure culture.

Arts and crafts also are significant as components of Native American leisure lifestyle. In many ways, it is difficult to draw a clear line between what is art and what is craft in the artifacts of Native culture in North America. The designs of baskets, the painting on pottery, and the drawings left on canyon walls (petroglyphs) are just some of the evidence speaking to the rich aesthetic of prehistoric Native American life.

With the advent of European contact and the integration of Native America into the history of the Western world, the nature of its arts and their relationship to community life in general and leisure in particular becomes more obvious. Even though these arts are in some cases important sources of income, they remain products of leisurely pursuit. For example, the rug weaving of Navajo women up until recent decades was largely a labor of love. It is estimated that even as late as the mid-1900s, Navajo women who spent untold hours carding wool, spinning thread, coloring the thread, and actually weaving the rug sold their creations for a mere pittance. The net effect was that the weaver's compensation often amounted to less than five cents an hour for the time invested in her creation. However, this economic injustice was often dismissed by the weavers themselves who contended that the rug weaving was a leisurely pursuit, an end in itself, and not work. Similar attitudes surround the craft-making industries of many other tribes: the jewelry of the Pueblo peoples, the beadwork of the Plains groups, the carvings of the Native Northwest, the stone carvings of the Arctic Natives, the basketry of the Native Southeast. In short, the visual arts of traditional Native America can be viewed as products of a complex, multifaceted, and highly integrated culture of leisure.

Native Leisure Culture Today

Many of the leisure traditions of Native America survived into the twentieth and twenty-first centuries. But many were lost as tribal and linguistic groups became virtually extinct or lost their identity through assimilation. Also, many were altered as a result of westernization, contact with European values, and the adaptation of Anglo-American leisure activities and ethics. However, the fundamentals of a distinctively Native American lifestyle remained intact.

During the nineteenth and early twentieth centuries, there were a variety of efforts on the part of American authorities to ban or significantly reshape those components of Native leisure life that were perceived as "savage," irreverent, or excessively violent. For example, in 1904, the federal government outlawed the Sun Dance, although benign forms survived that were still performed in some Native communities, typically on the Fourth of July. Missionaries and government personnel condemned many traditional ceremonies because they seemed to condone if not encourage sexual behaviors deemed inappropriate by fundamentalist Christians. Kiowa dancing was prohibited by law in the period between 1889 and 1934. Also, in 1898, the state of Mississippi passed a law banning gambling at Indian ball games, assuming that if there were no wagering the Choctaw ball game would die. In fact, the formal ball game faded into the shadows, but not because of the new law. Rather, the Choctaw Removal of 1903 took such a toll on the size of the Choctaw population in Mississippi that the demographics necessary to support the formal matches were decimated. The game itself stayed alive, but on a much reduced scale.

Ironically, many elements of Native leisure culture to which white authorities objected resulted from European contact. For example, perhaps the single most significant cause of violence, social problems, and abuse in the Native American community has been alcohol, which came to be a part of Native American leisure life despite efforts by tribal leaders and others to curb drinking and preserve a tradition independent of white man's liquor. Many of the incidents of violence or the sexual abuse of women that occurred in conjunction with Native American leisure activities could be attributed directly to white men who invited themselves to those events, drunk themselves into stupors, insulted their hosts, and harassed the women.

At the same time, Native American leisure traditions have in many ways been enriched by the adoption of Euro-American sports and games. The rodeo, an original creation of the Spanish, became important to many Native societies, particularly in the West. Among the Navajo, for example, the rodeo became an important community event, a wholesome activity for young men and a favorite spectator sport for many. In addition, basketball, softball, baseball, and American football became important to community life among many Native American groups. The schools, particularly Bureau of Indian Affairs (BIA) schools, played a key role in that development, as Native young people were taught non-Indian sports and games as a part of the physical education curriculum. However, as a variety of social scientists pointed out, when Native peoples adopted those sports, they tended to redefine them in ways that reflected Native culture. For example, among the Navajos, basketball, though learned as a result of contact with Anglo-Mormons, quickly took on a significantly Navajo flavor, becoming in time a distinctively Navajo game. This change was reflected in the goals of the game, style of play, game strategy, intra-team play, attitudes toward coaches and officials, and approach to the rules. In all cases, the distinctive nature of the game could be understood as a manifestation of traditional Navajo culture and values. This same phenomenon was documented in many Native communities, with both basketball and other so-called modern sports.

As a result of the emphasis placed on leisure activities in general and sports in particular, the Native American community produced many great athletes, such as Jim Thorpe. Many written accounts of those individuals, their lives and athletic accomplishments, appeared during the past two decades.

Another leisure-related phenomenon of the mid-twentieth century was a resurgence of interest in Native leisure traditions, in most cases as a direct result of the new interest tribal peoples in America took in their own respective heritages. The revival of traditional ceremonies, dances, and sports, in conjunction with the development of new pan-Indian activities, not only enriched the leisure life of Native America, it also helped to bring a new sense of pride, community, and identity to particular tribes or nations and to Natives in general. For example, among the Mississippi Choctaws, the formal stickball game was revived in the late 1940s as a part of a newly developed celebration, the annual Choctaw Fair. The competition continued to grow in outreach, magnitude, and media attention, and in many ways it came to symbolize the growing economic and political power of the Choctaws in the state of Mississippi. Thanks to the success of its industrial park, its gaming enterprises, and tourist business, the Choctaw Nation became one of the largest employers and taxpayers in the state.

The pan-Indian movement also affected Native leisure culture. As tribal groups from across the continent found and celebrated their commonality, they invented new activities that functioned to symbolize, reinforce, and solidify that common ground. The powwow was perhaps the most visible of these activities. While some suggest that powwow attendance was a way to "express tribal identity," it was just as likely to be viewed as a pan-Indian celebration (Eschbach and Applbaum, p. 69). The powwow was seen by some as a forum for the debate of the powwow experience itself as well as tribal issues. Out of those discussions that occured within the leisurely character of the dance itself "emerges a set of beliefs, commitments, and practices that partially determine the identity of Indian communities" (Mattern, p. 198).

One modern development in the Native American community that had a direct impact on its leisure culture is commercial gaming. While its positive economic impact has been documented repeatedly, no conclusions have yet been drawn on its effect on the lives of individuals in that community. Clearly, within those tribes with casinos, employment rates improved, per capita income increased, and the community infrastructure was enhanced. However, they may also have exacerbated problem drinking and gambling addiction. One of the few studies that looked specifically at that issue was conducted in Minnesota in the mid-1990s (Cozzetto, p. 127). The results suggested that legalized gambling in the state increased the number of persons exhibiting signs of problematic gambling and those who were pathological gamblers. However, pathological gambling seemed to be more prevalent among Indians than non-Indians.

Conclusion

Native American leisure lifestyles reflect the fundamental values of Native culture, its mode of environmental adaptation, and the nature of its social life. It is rich with a plethora of games, sports, festivals, ceremonies, dances, arts, and crafts, all of which serve a variety of functions that both enrich and strengthen community life. While European contact, economic development, and the forces of modernity had a profound impact on the nature of Native American leisure styles, they retained their distinctive identities, social importance, and cultural significance.

See also: Western America Leisure Lifestyles

BIBLIOGRAPHY

Ager, L. "The Reflection of Cultural Values in Eskimo Children's Games." In *The Study of Play: Problems and Prospects.* Edited by David Lancy and Allan Tindall. West Point, N.Y.: Leisure Press, 1977.

Blanchard, Kendall. "Basketball and the Culture-Change Process: The Rimrock Navajo Case." *Council on Anthropology and Education Quarterly* 5, no. 4 (1974): 8–13.

———. *The Mississippi Choctaws at Play: The Serious Side of Leisure.* Urbana: University of Illinois Press, 1981.

Boyd, Susan. "Stick Games/Hand Games: The Great Divide." In *Forms of Play of Native North Americans.* Edited by Edward Norbeck and Claire Farrer. St. Paul, Minn.: West Publishing Company, 1979.

Cheska, Alyce Taylor. "Games of the Native North Americans." In *Handbook of Social Science of Sport.* Edited by R. F. Gunther Luschen and George H. Sage. Champaign, Ill.: Stipes Publishing Company, 1981.

Cliff, Janet M. "Navajo Games." *American Indian Culture and Research Journal* 14, no. 3 (1990): 1–81.

Cole, D. "Recreation Practices of the Stoney of Alberta and Mohawk of the Six-Nation Confederacy." *Journal of Applied Recreational Research* 18, no. 2 (1993): 103–114.

Colton, Larry. *Counting Coup: A True Story of Basketball and Honor on the Little Big Horn.* New York: Warner Books, 2000.

Cozzetto, Don A. "The Economic and Social Implications of Indian Gaming: The Case of Minnesota." *American Indian Culture and Research Journal* 19, no. 1 (1995): 119–131.

Culin, Stewart. "Games of the North American Indians." *Twenty-fourth Annual Report of the Bureau of American Ethnology.* Washington, D.C.: Government Printing Office, 1907.

Dorsey, J. O. "Games of Teton Dakota Children." *American Anthropologist* 4 (1891): 329–345.

Eschbach, Karl, and Kalman Applbaum. "Who Goes to Powwows? Evidence from the Survey of American Indians and Alaska Natives." *American Indian Culture and Research Journal* 24, no. 2 (2000): 65–68.

Fox, J. R. "Pueblo Baseball: A New Use for Old Witchcraft." *Journal of American Folklore* 74 (1961): 9–16.

Gems, Gerald R. "The Construction, Negotiation, and Transformation of Racial Identity in American Football." *American Indian Culture and Research Journal* 23, no. 2 (1999): 127–132.

Hieb, Louis A. "The Ritual Clown: Humor and Ethics." In *Forms of Play of Native North Americans.* Edited by Edward Norbeck and Claire Farrer. St. Paul, Minn.: West Publishing Company, 1979.

Keith, Susan. "Native American Women in Sport." *The Journal of Physical Education, Recreation and Dance* 70 (April 1999).

Kennedy, John G. "Contemporary Tarahumara Foot Racing and Its Significance." In *The Tarahumara.* Edited by Ralph Beals. Los Angeles: University of California, n.d.

Kracht, Benjamin R. "Kiowa Powwows: Continuity in Ritual Practice." *American Indian Quarterly* 18, no. 3 (1994): 321–348.

Lesser, Alexander. "The Pawnee Ghost Dance Hand Game: A Study of Cultural Change." In *Columbia University Contributions to Anthropology 16.* New York: Columbia University Press, 1933.

McDonald, Daniel, and Leo McAvoy. "Native Americans and Leisure: State of the Research and Future." *Journal of Leisure Research* 29, no. 2 (1997): 145–167.

Mattern, Mark. "The Powwow as a Public Arena for Negotiating Unity and Diversity in American Indian Life." *American Indian Culture and Research Journal* 21, no. 2 (1999): 43–60.

Mooney, James. "The Cherokee Ball Play." *American Anthropologist* 3 (1890): 105–132.

Nabokov, Peter. *Indian Running: Native American History and Tradition.* Santa Fe, N.M.: Ancient City Press, 1981.

Opler, Morris K. "The Jicarilla Apache Ceremonial Relay Race." *American Anthropologist* 46, no. 1 (1944): 75–97.

Oxendine, Joseph. *American Indian Sport Heritage.* 2d edition. Lincoln: University of Nebraska Press, 1995.

Paraschak, Vicky. "Native Sport History: Pitfalls and Promises." *Canadian Journal of History of Sport* 20, no. 1 (1989): 58.

———. "Sport Festivals and Race Relations in the Northwest Territories of Canada." In *Sport, Racism, and Ethnicity.* Edited by Grant Jarvie. London: Falmer Press, 1991.

Salter, Michael. "The North American Indigenous Games." *Native Journal* (August/September 1993): 26.

Smith, Jerald C. "The Native American Ball Games." In *Sport in the Sociocultural Process.* Edited by M. Marie Hart. Dubuque, Iowa: William C. Brown, 1972.

Spencer, Robert F. "Play, Power, and Politics in Native North Alaska." In *Forms of Play of Native North Americans.* Edited by Edward Norbeck and Claire Farrer. St. Paul, Minn.: West Publishing Company, 1979

Vennum, Thomas, Jr. *American Indian Lacrosse: Little Brother of War.* Washington, D.C.: Smithsonian Institution Press, 1994.

Walker, J. R. "Sioux Games." *Journal of American Folklore* 18 (1905): 71.

Whitney, A. *Sports and Games the Indians Gave Us.* New York: David McKay, 1977.

Wissler, Clark. "Societies and Dance Associations of the Blackfoot Indians." In *American Museum of Natural History, Anthropological Papers XI* (1913): 359–460.

Woodward, J., and V. Woodward. "A Leisure Time Activity of the Plains Cree." *Anthropological Journal of Canada* 8, no. 4 (1970): 29–31.

Kendall Blanchard

NEEDLEWORK

See *Quilting Parties; Women's Leisure Lifestyles*

NEW YEAR'S

Celebrated as 1 January according to the Gregorian calendar, both New Year's Eve (31 December) and New Year's Day are widely celebrated throughout the world, wherever Western standards of time are followed. Often, traditional calendars are also maintained, so that various national and ethnic new year celebrations occur at other times, such as the Asian new year, based on a lunar calendar, or Rosh Hashanah, the Jewish new year, which is celebrated in the autumn in the United States. The first day of January became the first day of the year in the Roman calendar initiated by Julius Caesar, ca. 46 B.C. Caesar set the new year as beginning after the end of the two-week period of festivities known as the Saturnalia, which corresponded to the shortest day of the year, the winter solstice. Later, the Roman Catholic Church assigned the feast of the nativity of Christ to this same period, 25 December. Many pre-Christian customs such as decorating with evergreens and giving gifts at the new year have been inherited by later generations. In this way New Year's has an organic relationship with the solar year, and retains a strong relationship with other celebrations of the season to form a period of festivity unmatched at any other time of the year.

Throughout the nineteenth century in the United States, New Year's Day overshadowed Christmas as a major holiday, although this would change by the end of the century. Until then, New Year's cards were much more commonly exchanged than Christmas cards, and gifts were commonly exchanged on New Year's as well.

Periods of transition are frequently ritualized. In the life cycle, examples include annual recognition of birthdays, or the name day celebrations of the feast day of the saint for whom one is named, in Greek and other Orthodox religions. New Year's is a social, calendrical festival that marks the annual turning of the year. The exact point of transition, the betwixt and between moment of midnight (which belongs neither to one day or the next, but is shared by both) is the occasion for carnivalesque, disruptive activities such as kissing friends and strangers, popping champagne bottles (as much for the noise as for the intoxicating drink), and exploding fireworks. Midnight is highlighted by a countdown. In Spain, couples customarily feed each other twelve grapes, very quickly, one for each month of the year as they count down from twelve to the instant of transition. In rural areas of the United States, people frequently "shoot in" the new year with firearms; this has long been a tradition in rural Pennsylvania among other areas. Equally traditional is the banging of pots and pans at midnight to produce a "rough music." In all of these traditions, noise is paramount. Sometimes it is said that this noise frightens away demons and thus ensures a good year, as in Hawaii, where fireworks are exploded. More generally, the disruptive noise is a sign that at that transitional moment, people are in a "time out of time," and the regular rules of society do not apply.

Large, public New Year's Eve gatherings are found in many cities in the United States and abroad, with New York's Times Square probably the most famous. There, hundreds of thousands of revelers gather to witness the descent of a ball down a pole at midnight. Boston initiated a citywide arts and performance festival known as First Night in a successful attempt to create a family-friendly atmosphere. Since the late 1970s First Night has spread to other cities throughout the country. The city of Philadelphia is known for the annual Mummers and Shooters Parade held every 1 January. The name of the parade derives from earlier eighteenth and nineteenth century traditions of shooting in the New Year, and the practice of wearing odd and outlandish costumes, going from home to home, and performing a song or a skit in return for a "gift" of food or drink. This latter custom is known as "mumming," meaning to masquerade, and is performed during the midwinter holidays as well as at other times of the year in both Europe and North America. In Philadelphia the customs became more formalized in the twentieth century, so that in the early 2000s the parade was a highly elaborate affair reminiscent of New Orleans' Mardi Gras processions. It retained its folk roots, however, as various clubs of largely Italian-Americans in South Philadelphia prepared their troops, planned themes and performances, and sewed costumes for the big event throughout the preceding year.

Certainly not all New Year's observances are raucous or carnivalesque. Many Christian churches hold New Year Watches to allow people to enjoy a spiritual and reverent ushering in of the new year. In the Roman Catholic Church, New Year's Day, 1 January, is a Holy Day of Obligation, one of six days other than Sundays when observant Catholics are required to attend mass. Conversely, when the Soviet Union existed, the country was officially atheist. The Christmas tree became identified as a New Year's tree, Santa Claus was transformed into Father Frost, and any other customs that might be traced to a religious background were secularized. Many Russians, including Jews and other non-Christians, continue to use the decorated evergreen tree as a symbol of New Year's.

Widely recognized symbols of New Year's are the baby representing the new year and the old man—Father Time—representing the old year. This old man–baby duality parallels in the secular sphere the old man–baby duality of Santa Claus and the baby Jesus at Christmas a week earlier. In both cases, the figures point to the opportunity for rebirth and renewal at the darkest time of the year, but when the light is beginning to grow strong again, that these holidays represent.

Also related to the transitional nature of the celebration is the belief that one can influence the fortunes of the coming year on New Year's Eve or New Year's Day. For instance, the practice of "first footing" is found throughout Great Britain, Ireland, and much of Europe. The belief is that it is good luck if the first person to cross one's threshold in the new year is of a certain type—tall and dark, usually. As a result, people in these countries often send a friend outside at midnight to fulfill the requirements immediately upon return. A more serious, and more sacred, example is that of Rosh Hashanah, a period of ten days that culminates in the Yom Kippur, the Day of Atonement. Throughout Rosh Hashanah, Jews are encouraged to apologize to friends and acquaintances for any slights they may have caused during the year. On Yom Kippur, one's name may be inscribed by God in his sacred book, if the individual is deserving. In some ways, the secular American practice of making New Year's resolutions is also related to the ideas of rebirth and renewal that are implicit in the ending of one year and the beginning of another.

Certain foods are customarily eaten on New Year's Day, often for good luck. Throughout the southern United States, "Hoppin' John," a dish made of black-eyed peas, is a New Year standard. In areas of the country influenced by German and middle-European settlement, such as the Midwest, sauerkraut is the New Year food. New Year's customs vary internationally, but also within nations. In the United States traditions differ by region and by one's national or ethnic background, one's religion, and even one's occupation. For instance, it is a tradition in the U.S. Navy and the U.S. Coast Guard to write the first entry of the new year in the ship's log in verse.

The poems are often satirical in nature, and the practice is well known and practiced among seagoers.

In this brief overview, one can see certain themes repeat: as a time of transition, New Year's is important, possibly dangerous, and is marked with rituals and celebrations to acknowledge and ease the transitions. Actions are taken, traditional dishes prepared, wishes and resolutions are made, however seriously or frivolously, to ensure good fortune during the coming year. Ultimately New Year's, despite its excesses, is an opportunity for celebrants to re-imagine themselves and hope for a better world.

See also: Christmas, Mardi Gras, Mumming

BIBLIOGRAPHY

Alford, Violet. "Rough Music." *Folklore* 70 (December 1959): 505–518.

Bakhtin, Mikhail. *Rabelais and His World.* Translated by Helene Iswolsky. Cambridge, Mass: M.I.T Press, 1968.

Falassi, Alessandro, ed. *Time Out of Time: Essays on the Festival.* Albuquerque: University of New Mexico Press, 1987.

Santino, Jack. *All Around the Years: Holidays and Celebrations in American Life.* Urbana: University of Illinois Press, 1994.

Thompson, Edward Palmer. *Customs in Common.* New York: The New Press, 1991.

Jack Santino

NIAGARA FALLS

Niagara Falls, the great cataract on the Niagara River between Lakes Erie and Ontario, is one of the world's most spectacular natural phenomena. Since the late 1600s, Niagara Falls has been the one spot in the American landscape that travelers felt they had to see. A source of awe, terror, and reverence, the cataract defied description, though almost everyone took a turn at describing it. Throughout the first half of the nineteenth century, Niagara Falls topped a list of favorite artists' subjects. For landscape painters looking to supply a missing national tradition, nature and Niagara Falls represented American antiquity, God's blessing for the new nation, and the infinite potential and resources of the United States. Niagara Falls became an icon of the American sublime and a symbol of the United States. Although the more impressive Horseshoe Falls and viewing prospects are on the Canadian side, the United States appropriated Niagara Falls as its own.

Tourism at Niagara Falls

Thanks to the emerging fame of the cataract, as well improvements that increasingly domesticated nature there and throughout North America, tourism flourished at Niagara Falls. By the early 1800s the land around the cataract was private property. Local landowners and entrepreneurs erected hotels, built staircases down the gorge-side to the base of the falls, and also established other visitor-friendly conveniences. The transportation revolution, from the Erie Canal in 1825 to the railroad, rendered Niagara Falls increasingly accessible and permitted women as well as men to visit in large numbers. Niagara was the culminating stop of the American Grand Tour or Fashionable Tour. Elite visitors came for the summer season and, by the 1830s, newly married couples made Niagara Falls the focus of their wedding journeys.

Curiosity about such a wondrous natural phenomena may have brought visitors to Niagara, but once there, those visitors found that delight in nature was seldom a sufficient attraction on its own. Tourists wanted comfort and diversions, and local entrepreneurs happily set up souvenir shops and built walkways and towers to the edge of the falls, through the Cave of the Winds, and behind the tumbling water torrent. They also added numerous other tolled attractions. By the mid-1840s, tourists could ride the *Maid of the Mist* steamboat, which approached the base of the falls and doused them with spray from the torrent. Guidebooks helped visitors "do" the falls by highlighting each attraction and interpreting Niagara's meaning and history. As Niagara Falls became a commodity, it also invited outlandish stunts that attracted national attention. Beginning with Sam Patch, who jumped into the gorge below the falls in 1829, and continuing with tightrope walkers and the barrel craze, Niagara's popular history encompassed death-defying feats.

Technology and Tourism

Tourism and technology have always been inextricably intertwined at Niagara Falls. Transportation advances enabled more and more visitors to come to Niagara to delight in the spectacle. Yet even as Niagara inspired reverence for nature, to a nation more accustomed to romantic conquests of nature, the technological accomplishments at Niagara Falls became fascinating attractions and added a new realm to visitors' experience. In 1855, John Roebling's Niagara Railway Suspension Bridge established the falls as a bridge-building site. Railroad lines competed to erect their own bridges—each new construction representing an advance in technology—in front of the falls. Similarly, Niagara became the highly publicized hydroelectric power center of the world in the 1890s, as engineers did the unthinkable: they conquered Niagara Falls by harnessing the cataract. World's fairs at Chicago in 1893, and especially Buffalo in 1901, dramatically revealed Niagara's contributions to American progress and spawned public interest in the technological wonders at Niagara Falls. Also in 1901, the Natural Company, later the Shredded Wheat Company and still later Nabisco, built a showplace factory that lured visitors to see the latest "wonder of Niagara Falls." The technological improvements at Niagara offered a visible counterpoint to nature and ensured that the Falls would remain at the forefront of the national consciousness.

The Preservation of Niagara

Almost as soon as tourist facilities and commercial development began dotting the Niagara landscape, visitors and commentators lamented the loss of Niagara's natural purity and beauty. Unsightly and polluting mills, tacky tourist facilities, and endless fee charges eventually led many tourists to bypass Niagara for more pristine and peaceful resorts, even as the railroad brought more short-term visitors to the Falls. Publicity about Niagara's "disgraceful" appearance spurred appeals to serve the greater public good by securing Niagara from private control and creating a free park that would restore the landscape to its natural appearance. In the 1860s and 1870s, outrage over conditions at Niagara Falls also contributed to the creation of the nation's first national parks at Yosemite and Yellowstone, to safeguard the United States' most beloved places of nature. At Niagara itself, the Niagara Preservation Movement finally succeeded, in 1885, with the formation of government parks on the lands adjacent to the Falls on both the American and Canadian sides of the border.

On the American side, the New York State Reservation at Niagara ensured that visitors could see the Falls for free by eliminating tolls and removing artificial attractions. Frederick Law Olmsted and Calvert Vaux drew up the blueprint for the State Reservation, which resembled their urban parks in its high-minded Victorian order and emphasis on the quieter, picturesque aspects of the surroundings. The New York Sate Reservation established a 430-acre sanctuary of nature amidst rampant industrial and technological development and unabated commercial tourism immediately beyond the preserved grounds. In fact, early in the twentieth century preservationists waged a second battle to prevent hydropower companies from diminishing the appearance of the cataract by diverting too much water from above the falls.

Niagara in the Era of the Automobile

By the twentieth century, power plants and attending industries had transformed a once sleepy tourist hamlet into a world-renowned power production center. Tourists, especially railroad excursionists, continued to flock to Niagara, but as the automobile displaced the railroad as the nation's leading mode of transportation, the average duration of visits to Niagara decreased even further. While wealthy tourists bypassed Niagara for more exotic, pristine, and exclusive resorts, the automobile and roadside motels further democratized Niagara's popularity as a honeymoon capital. Under such conditions, tourism fared far better on the more visually spectacular and vibrant Canadian side of the Falls.

Niagara Falls continues to lures tourists from all over the world who come so see the great cataract, but Niagara is anything but the embodiment of wild, untamed nature. Instead, while power companies regulate the flow of the tumbling waters, kitschy tourism prevails. In the early 2000s, though the *Maid of the Mist* and the Cave of the Winds remained prime attractions at Niagara, most visitors stayed in the area just a few hours, took cursory glances at the cataract, and spent very little money. Niagara is seldom spoken of as a resort, and economic decline hit the communities on both sides of the falls hard in the late twentieth and early twenty-first centuries. While the introduction of casino gambling lured more people to Niagara Falls and buoyed hopes for the tourist trade in the early 2000s, it was telling that these visitors were not coming to see the Falls of Niagara.

See also: Honeymooning, National Parks; Tourism

BIBLIOGRAPHY

Adamson, Jeremy. *Niagara: Two Centuries of Changing Attitudes, 1697–1901.* Washington, D.C.: Corcoran Gallery of Art, 1985.

Berton, Pierre. *Niagara: A History of the Falls.* New York: Kodansha International, 1997.

Greenhill, Ralph. *Spanning Niagara: The International Bridges, 1848–1962.* Niagara Falls, N.Y.: Niagara University, 1984.

Irwin, William. *The New Niagara: Tourism, Technology, and the Landscape of Niagara Falls, 1976–1917.* University Park: Pennsylvania State University Press, 1996.

McKinsey, Elizabeth. *Niagara Falls: Icon of the American Sublime.* New York: Cambridge University Press, 1985.

Sears, John F. *Sacred Places: American Tourist Attractions in the Nineteenth Century.* Amherst, Mass.: University of Massachusetts Press, 1998.

William Irwin

OLYMPICS

In 1895, the Ging government of China received through the French Embassy in Peking an invitation to send athletes to compete in history's first modern Olympic Games, planned for Athens, Greece, in the spring of 1896. Chinese officials knew nothing about a phenomenon referred to as modern Olympic Games. They ignored the invitation.

Thousands of miles to the east, Americans were similarly ignorant of such games, except for one individual, William Milligan Sloane, professor of history at Princeton. In June 1894, Sloane, also faculty adviser to Princeton's intercollegiate athletics program, attended a conference in Paris; two agenda items were directed toward defining international rules for amateurism, and the prospect of reestablishing in modern times the noted ancient Greek phenomenon of Olympic Games. A young Frenchman, energetic Pierre de Coubertin, organized the conference. The conference proceedings never resolved common rules of amateur competition, but under Coubertin's leadership the concept of Olympic Games in modern times was approved, the International Olympic Committee (IOC) struck, and the first edition of such Games planned for Athens less than two years hence. Sloane, by 1894 a fast friend of Coubertin's, was named as one of the original members of the IOC.

Charged with the primary responsibility of organizing an American team for the Athens Games, Sloane was only moderately successful. Only a few Princeton athletes went, joined by a small cadre of college boys and amateurs from Boston. Sloane did not accompany them. None were among the more prominent track and field athletes in the United States; nevertheless, in Athens they performed in magnificent fashion, winning eight of the eleven track and field events. Fifteen countries sent some 300 athletes. Women competitors were prohibited. Back home in America, hardly a ripple of media reaction greeted their exploits. A century or so later, in Sydney, Australia, over 10,000 athletes competed in various Olympic competitions, about 45 percent of them women. Some 3.7 billion people the world over watched the Games on television. Such had become the growth, appeal, and exposure of the modern Olympic Games by the turn of the millennium.

The rise of an American awareness of the Olympic Games occurred in 1904 commensurate with the Games of the Third Olympiad. Though awarded the Games originally, Chicago could not raise the necessary civic financial support and the festival was sent to St. Louis, where it was ultimately immersed in the program of the Louisiana Purchase Exposition. This, of course, was long before the advent of television, corporate sponsorship, and other grand fund-raising initiatives that now underwrite much of the costs associated with putting on the festival. The St. Louis Games were largely a flop because of limited foreign participation, but newspaper coverage of the controversy surrounding their transfer to St. Louis, together with first-rate achievement by American athletes, served to extend knowledge of the modern Olympic movement to every nook and cranny of America. From then on, American effort to do better than any other country at the Olympic Games was pursued with missionary zeal by American sports authorities. After all, hadn't Americans always been endowed with a competitive spirit? The rambunctious and confrontational Jim Sullivan, founder and longtime secretary of the Amateur Athletic Union, prodded this zeal. Under his leadership, the United States encountered few equals in the blue ribbon track and field Olympic competitions of the 1908 London and 1912 Stockholm Games. Jim Thorpe, a Native American athlete who later was voted by sports scribes as the athlete of the first half century, won both the pentathlon and decathlon in Stockholm. Though later disqualified for minor breeches of "Sullivan's amateur code" in America, he nevertheless remained in the American mind as the nation's first and most enduring Olympic hero.

Olympic Games scheduled for Berlin in 1916 were canceled; but in the war-devastated Belgian city of Antwerp the Games of 1920 were celebrated, thus restoring the interrupted Olympic cycle. Again, American athletes did well, but the ominous specter of European progress in all athletics, including track and field, began to evolve. More Europeans and fewer Americans than previously began to share in Olympic medal harvests, beginning with the Games in Paris, Amsterdam, and Los Angeles in 1924, 1928, and 1932, respectively. In effect, the rest of the world was beginning to catch up to the United States, known before World War II as the world's preeminent athletic nation.

Commencing in 1924, Olympic Winter Games evolved, the first in Chamonix (France), the second, third, and fourth in San Mortiz (Switzerland), Lake Placid (United States), and Garmisch-Partenkirchen (Germany). American competitors, usually outshone by athletes from Scandinavian countries, nevertheless acquitted themselves well, signaling promise for the future. Four gold medals in speed skating at Lake Placid in 1932 by Jack Shea in the sprints and Irving Jaffee in the distance events confirmed American progress.

By the 1936 Games in Berlin, the Olympics had grown to the extent that forty-nine countries were represented by some 4,700 athletes in the Summer Games, including almost 338 women; the Winter Games had grown to include twenty-eight nations and 756 competitors, 76 of them women. The United States had not at first embraced women's competition in the Games, but once European influence confirmed their opportunity to compete, the United States became a genuine champion of their inclusion. The 1936 Olympics in Nazified Berlin concluded the pre–World War II festivals. Much of the

world reacted with concern over Nazi government policy, particularly toward Jews; indeed, in the United States, ethnic, educational, religious, and labor organizations mounted a campaign to keep American athletes at home in a form of boycott protest. In the end, however, no countries stayed away, including the United States. The Games, a triumph for Jesse Owens, the great black American sprinter, unfolded with all the Germanic pomp, ceremony, and impressive athletic performance that the Third Reich could muster. It won more medals than any other country, including the United States. Lost somewhat in the Berlin proceedings was the beginning of the most critical technological event in the entire Olympic history to date—the advent of television.

Though modest in its evolutionary form during the 1930s, in just five short decades the medium of television would expose the Olympic Games to almost three-fifths of the world's population. Such exposure, combined with its public images of youth, excellence in performance, health, fair play, and sportsmanship, would transform the modern Olympic movement toward becoming a corporatized organization of extraordinary wealth, almost all of it gained from the sale of exclusive television rights to the Games and the linking of consumer product advertising to the five-ring Olympic symbol.

The Games of both the Twelfth and Thirteenth Olympiads in 1940 and 1944 were canceled due to World War II, as were their respective winter editions; the Olympics resumed in 1948 in London and St. Moritz, respectively. Beginning with the Summer Games of 1952 in Helsinki and ending with the disintegration of communism and the fragmentation of the Soviet Republic in 1991, the Olympic stage in both summer and winter context was dominated by the two great "Cold War" superpowers, the United States and the U.S.S.R. The U.S.S.R. replaced the United States as the world's preeminently successful Olympic-performance nation.

The Olympics, celebrated in the 1960s, 1970s, 1980s, and 1990s under the leadership of a trio of IOC presidents—the American Avery Brundage, the Irishman Lord Killanin, and the Spanish marquis Juan Antonio Samaranch—rode the crest of startling escalation in television rights sales, spurred on by the development of satellite television in the mid-1960s. By the end of Samaranch's presidency in 2001, many questioned whether the Games were a competition for athletes, or an arena for showcasing the products and services of multinational corporations.

The gathering snowball of IOC wealth ushered in the professionalization of the Games, a product of Sama-

1984 Summer Olympics. Los Angeles played host to the games of the XXIII Olympiad in the summer of 1984, when 140 nations participated. The event was notable for nations that did *not* participate, however, as the Soviet Union and thirteen other Soviet allies boycotted the Games in reaction to the American-led boycott of the 1980 Summer Olympics in Moscow. The closing ceremonies, shown here, were held at the Los Angeles Coliseum on 12 August and featured singer Lionel Richie, breakdancers, and fireworks. © *Corbis*

ranch's quest to serve the interest of the American television and advertising market. In carrying this banner, Samaranch preserved the IOC's financial underpinning, roughly 75 percent of which is derived from American business sources. There are other negative social ramifications attached to massive Olympic wealth: (1) the immensity of the Games, often leaving huge public debt for organizing them, (2) growing incidences of drug-related issues in the face of what may be at stake for a winning Olympic athlete in the commercial marketplace, (3) the erosion of the generally pristine image of the Olympics, and (4) the susceptibility toward corruption, internally and externally, as well as lack of accountability.

On the other hand, there continued to be extraordinary interest in and appeal for the Olympic Games. The Baron Pierre de Coubertin set out to construct a sporting phenomenon enveloped with cultivation of peace and tolerance, physical and mental health, both high and pop culture, and above all, a better world for tomorrow. There are many who feel that the Olympics

have made a substantial contribution to the baron's original goals; others would argue that those designed qualities have not been attained.

See also: Professionalization of Sport; Skiing, Alpine; Skiing, Nordic

BIBLIOGRAPHY

Baker, William J. *Jesse Owens: An American Life*. New York: The Free Press, 1986.

Barney, Robert K., Stephen R. Wenn, and Scott G. Martyn. *Selling the Five Rings: The International Olympic Committee and the Rise of Olympic Commercialism*. Salt Lake City: University of Utah Press, 2002.

Guttmann, Allen. *The Games Must Go On: Avery Brundage and the Olympic Movement*. New York: Columbia University Press, 1984.

Lucas, John A. *Future of the Olympic Games*. Champaign, Illinois: Human Kinetics, 1992.

Preuss, Holger. *Economics of the Olympic Games*. Sydney: University of New South Wales, 2000.

Seagrave, Jeffrey and Donald Chu. *The Olympic Games in Transition.* Champaign, Illinois: Human Kinetics, 1988.

Senn, Alfred E. *Power, Politics, and the Olympic Games.* Champaign, Illinois: Human Kinetics, 1999.

Tomlinson, Alan and Garry Whannel. *Five Ring Circus: Money, Power and Politics at the Olympic Games.* Sydney: Pluto Press, 1984.

Robert K. Barney

OPEN WHEEL RACING

Open wheel racing involves vehicles that have their tires and wheels exposed, rather than enclosed under fenders as with sports cars or stock cars. The first racecars were open wheeled, and open wheeled vehicles dominated the racing scene in the United States for the first half of the twentieth century. The most sophisticated open wheel racecars of the twenty-first century are technological wonders with a one-piece chassis and a carbon fiber body that fits over the chassis. The driver sits in a highly protected cockpit known as the "tub." With car speeds of nearly 250 miles per hour attainable, the tub must be an ultimate protective cocoon for the drivers. Surrounding the tub, the chassis and body are designed to dispel energy by breaking away in pieces in the case of a crash, making these among the safest cars in the world.

The *Chicago Times Herald* sponsored the first automobile race in North America in 1895. Only two cars finished the 54.36-mile race between Chicago and Evanston, Illinois, with Frank Duryea winning at an average speed of 7.5 miles per hour. The nation's initial closed track auto race took place in Narragansett Park, Rhode Island, in 1896. The winning car more than tripled the average speed of the previous year's race, averaging twenty-seven miles per hour. By 1905, open wheel racecar drivers were averaging more than seventy miles per hour in the Vanderbilt Cup races, an early international race run on Long Island, New York, designed to inspire competition between American and European auto manufacturers. By 1909, the Indianapolis Motor Speedway was completed and featured a stone and tar track. In 1910, the track was paved with bricks (leading to the track's famous nickname, "the Brickyard"), complete with corners that were able to withstand the punishment from cars traveling at seventy miles per hour. The prize money for the 1911 Indianapolis 500 was $25,000, an amazingly high amount for that time. Although there was a great deal of negative

publicity from the nation's press because of gory newspaper reports of high-speed automobile accidents, the sport of open wheel racing had come of age.

Sanctioning Bodies

Two sanctioning bodies, the American Automobile Association (AAA) and the Automobile Club of America (ACA), fought for control of American automobile racing in the early 1900s. In 1910, these two organizations created the Motor Cup Holding Company, with the purpose to organize the American Grand Prix and the Vanderbilt Cup races. These races were held together until the outbreak of World War I. After the war, oval track racing dominated in the United States, and grand prix racing was not revived until 1959. The United States Auto Club (USAC) replaced the AAA as the new sanctioning body for auto racing in 1956. Because of a variety of grievances with USAC, a group of drivers and car owners formed the Championship Auto Racing Teams, Inc., (CART) in 1978. CART's first season in 1979 included the Indianapolis 500, and the series achieved instant popularity. Initially, CART sponsored thirteen races, eventually expanding to sixteen races in five countries. Trouble, however, was on the horizon.

The CART-IRL Split

In 1994, Tony George, the owner of the Indianapolis Motor Speedway, announced plans for an all oval track racing series, the Indy Racing League, to compete with CART in three races, including the Indianapolis 500, beginning in 1996. George felt that American open wheel racing was being diluted by too many foreign drivers, too many international races, and too many events on road courses. While CART was the more-established series, the IRL had one huge bargaining chip with which to lure drivers and fans to its series—the Indianapolis 500. At first only IRL teams were allowed to race in the 500, the most famous open wheel race in the United States. Eventually, the IRL did allow CART drivers to compete in the 500, but the technical restrictions and animosity between the rival owners and organizations effectively eliminated CART teams from participating. As of early 2004, the split between CART and the IRL was still in place. It was likely, however, that only one of these groups would survive, and the IRL was the leading candidate. In fact, CART, having failed to pay millions of winnings from the 2003 season, filed for bankruptcy in December 2003; the organization was purchased by a holding group and renamed the Champ Car Series. Sixteen races were scheduled for 2004, although teams continued to desert the Champ Car Series for the Indy Racing League. Racing fans continued to hope that the turmoil between the two groups would come to an end as the division of drivers, teams, and resources between them has led to a noticeable decrease in the quality of open wheel racing in the United States.

In addition to USAC, CART, and the IRL, the Sports Car Club of America (SCCA), founded in 1944, sponsors open wheel as well as stock and sports car racing. SCCA has six open wheel "formula" classes of racecars, ranging from the Formula Atlantic, which has a 1,600-cubic-centimeter engine with about 240 horsepower, to Formula 500, powered by motors derived from snowmobiles. While the SCCA sponsors professional racing, amateur road racing is its mainstay.

Types of Open Wheel Racecars

Several varieties of open wheel cars were raced in the United States in the early 2000s. These included cars in the six SCCA classes, CART championship cars, IRL cars, Formula 1 cars, and sprint and midget cars designed for racing on short dirt or paved oval tracks. Until 1961, all open wheel racing cars used in the United States had engines in front of the drivers. Then, in the 1961 Indianapolis 500, veteran Australian Formula 1 driver Jack Brabham finished ninth in a rear-engine Cooper. Twelve of the thirty-three cars that started the 1964 Indianapolis 500 were rear-engine and, since the late 1960s, only a few attempts have been made to qualify traditional front-engine "roadsters." In the early twenty-first century, all of the SCCA, CART, IRL, and Formula 1 cars raced in the United States had rear engines. Only USAC sponsored sprint and midget series cars retain the traditional front-engine, rear-wheel drive configuration.

The average speed of winners at the Indianapolis 500 over the years illustrates the immense changes in technology and driving skills that have taken place. Ray Harroun won the inaugural Indianapolis 500 in 1911 with an average speed of 74.6 miles per hour. Ten years later, in 1921, Ralph DePalma won the pole position with a speed of 100.75 miles per hour, while Tommy Milton won the race, averaging 89.6 miles per hour. By 1941, Mauri Rose won the pole position with a speed of 128.1 mph and combined with Floyd Davis to win the race at an average speed of 115.1 mph. In 1978, Al Unser won the pole position with the first speed of more than 200 miles per hour, 202.156 to be exact. Although organizing bodies have attempted to slow cars down from time to time via rule changes, advances in aerodynamics and tire technology have largely negated those efforts. Buddy Lazier

recorded the fastest ever qualifying speed of 233.1 mph in 1996, while Arie Luyendyk holds the fastest race average at 185.981 mph in 1990.

Formula 1 cars, all of which are constructed in Europe with engines supplied by manufacturers such as Ferrari, Honda, BMW, Mercedes, Cosworth, and Renault, are designed and raced only on road courses. While Formula 1 racecars represent the epitome in both technology and cost, their smaller engines mean that they are slightly slower than CART or IRL racecars in straightaway speed. SCCA formula cars are much less powerful—and therefore considerably slower—than Formula 1, CART, or IRL racecars. Finally, USAC sprint and midget cars have engines derived from stock American passenger cars and, although sprint cars have plenty of power, their speeds are restricted by the nature of the tracks on which they are raced, which is often wet dirt.

The Spectacle that Is the Indy 500

Regardless of the outcome of the CART-IRL rift, open wheel racing will remain synonymous with one word: *Indy,* which all racing fans know refers to both the Indianapolis Motor Speedway (the crown jewel of auto racing) and the Indianapolis 500 race. With seating for nearly one-half million fans, the speedway remains the famous host of the "greatest spectacle in racing."

The race is held each Memorial Day weekend (with the exception of war-related hiatuses), with the entire month of May serving as a massive buildup to the major event. Terms such as "time trials" "sitting on the bubble," and "carburetion day" (the last day that the race cars are allowed on the track before the actual race) become normal, every day language in Indianapolis during the month of May. Hotels, motels, and restaurants fill as the month's activities progress, making the race the greatest economic boon to Indianapolis each year. While for many years the Indianapolis 500 was the only race held at the famous track, in the early 2000s the Brickyard 400, for stock cars, and the United States Grand Prix (USGP), for Formula 1 cars, also began to race there (an infield road course, used in conjunction with part of the oval track, was constructed for the 2000 USGP).

Open Wheel Racing and the Future

Open wheel racing dominated motor sports in the United States for most of the twentieth century. It remained popular as of 2003, with more than three million fans attending events each year and many more watching on TV worldwide. Stock car racing, however, with its meteoric rise in track attendance and television coverage since the mid-1980s, abetted by the decade-long dispute between CART and IRL, had surpassed open wheel racing in popularity by the early twenty-first century. Nevertheless, the United States Formula 1 Grand Prix at Indianapolis continued to draw crowds approaching 300,000, and sprint and midget races were enjoyed by millions more each year. Finally, open wheel racing, with cars that have no pretense of street use, continued to remain the purest of motor sport forms.

See also: Auto Racing, Drag Racing, Hot Rodding, Sports Car Racing, Stock Car Racing

BIBLIOGRAPHY

David, Dennis. "American Grand Prize." Available from http://www.ddavid.com/formula1/.

Fuller, Michael J. "A Brief History of Sports Car Racing." Available from http://www.mulsannescorner.com/history.htm.

Ross, Frank Xavier. *Racing Cars and Great Races.* New York: Lee and Shepard, 1972.

OPERA

See *Performing Arts Audiences*

ORCHESTRAS

See *Performing Arts Audiences*

ORIENTEERING

The term "orienteering" has two common meanings within the vernacular of outdoor recreation. The more general definition refers to way finding or land navigation utilizing a map and compass. The second definition is more specific and refers to a competitive sport where participants walk or run a course consisting of a series of points to be found utilizing topographic maps and a compass. The sport is similar in some ways to cross-country running, with the notable exception that the actual course is not prescribed as it is in most running events, but instead is variable and subject to the participants' best judgment as to how to navigate from point to point.

The most prominent early authority on the sport of orienteering is Björn Kjellström, who wrote the seminal book on the subject, *Be Expert with Map & Compass: The Complete Orienteering Handbook.* This text was originally released in 1955 and has gone into its fifth edition. Kjellström's book consists mainly of introductory exercises to learn map and compass skills, but it also provides a section that helped introduce the competitive sport to the world outside of its native Scandinavia. Throughout the years, different editions have also included study aids, including foldout topographic maps and compass templates.

Kjellström's book was written in a style that is technically accurate yet accessible to a wide range of audiences. A half century after its initial release, it is still widely available and serves needs as diverse as leisure reading, a valuable youth programming guide, and a basic college textbook.

While land navigation has been an essential skill for centuries, and some precursor events may have been organized earlier, Kjellström cites 1919 as the year that competitive orienteering got its start in a race organized just outside of Stockholm, Sweden. Kjellström also notes that the sport's development was slow at first, but the development of the Silva protractor compass helped accelerate the popularity of competitive orienteering.

While orienteering's original growth was greatest in Europe and North America, particularly in more northerly latitudes such as Scandinavia and Canada, over the subsequent seventy years the sport has become popular across the world. It is governed by the International Orienteering Federation (IOF), which has sixty-two member nations and supervises the World Championships and World Cup Series. Within the United States, it is represented by the United States Orienteering Federation (USOF) and is most prominent in areas with large population centers, particularly New England, Philadelphia, San Francisco, and Atlanta.

Topographic, or contour, maps are most typically utilized, although occasionally street maps or other forms may be utilized in variations of traditional orienteering. The original orienteering compass features a specialized design that typically includes a movable housing, measured straight edge, and template cutouts that permit a number of field calculations and map markings by the user. In the early 2000s, these compasses and other orienteering gear, such as map cases and specialized clothing and shoes, were manufactured by a number of companies, including Silva, Suunto, and Brunton.

In its most basic form, point-to-point orienteering, participants are either given a premarked map or instructed to run to a map control station where they are permitted to mark their own maps while they view a master map. Participants are often given staggered starts to prevent crowding or following. In some events, the points are numbered and meant to be found in a specific sequence, while in others the participants are free to find the points in any order.

Participants seek out preset points called "controls," which are identified by red circles on the map, prism-shaped orange and white markers, flags, or pylons in the field. Orienteers use specially designed "punches" or other instruments to prove that they reached the controls. The participant completing the course in the shortest elapsed time is declared the winner. Courses differ in length and number of control points, with some events offering as many as seven separate courses for participants, ranging in ability from basic-beginner to advanced.

Participants utilize skill by locating the points using their primary two resources of map and compass. The ability to move rapidly and efficiently through the environment is obviously an advantage, as is the ability to "read" the landscape (that is, the ability to visualize map features in the real environment). Strategy is exercised in a number of ways, with the most important being skillful route selection. GPS (global positioning system) units are permitted in many races, although their use does not necessarily provide a competitive advantage.

Competition styles utilizing variations on the basic rules are numerous. "Night orienteering" courses add a level of excitement and limit participants' reliance on obvious visual cues along the course. "Score orienteering" resembles an Easter egg hunt, where a large number of points are set out and the winner has a limited time to find as many as possible. Orienteering can also involve mountain bikes, snowshoes, or cross-country skis, and can be done as a team or relay competition. A form called "trail orienteering" is gaining popularity and is highly accessible to participants utilizing wheelchairs.

One variant of orienteering evolved into a sport called "rogaining." Rogaining is a form of long-distance cross-country navigation utilizing compasses and a vari-

ety of map types. The standard competition features a twenty-four-hour course and team participation. The International Rogaining Federation (IRF) is the governing body of this emerging sport. Other sports with connections to orienteering include "geocaching," a form of treasure hunt utilizing GPS units, and "letterboxing," which utilizes written clues for navigation ("Think Inside the Box").

In addition to aiding in the development of navigational, gross motor, and spatial development skills, orienteering can be a valuable teaching tool for addressing a number of other educational topics. Some orienteering courses incorporate lessons about earth science, ecology, or even poetry into control points along the course.

Orienteering enthusiasts consider it a lifelong sport and a family activity in which participants of all ages and backgrounds can compete. Robin Shannonhouse, executive director of the USOF, says that orienteering continues to grow in the United States and the rest of the world, and that one of the most salient recent trends is participant retention and return to the sport because of its universal appeal and strong sense of community.

See also: Scouting Movements

BIBLIOGRAPHY

Jenkins, Mark. "The Tools, the Rules, and the Hunch." *Backpacker* (August 1992): 52–57.

Kjellström, Björn. *Be Expert with Map & Compass.* 5th ed. New York: Macmillan, 1994.

McNeill, Carol, Jean Cory-Wright, and Tom Renfrew. *Teaching Orienteering.* Doune, Perthshire, U.K.: Human Kinetics, 1998.

Muir, Sharon Pray, and Helen Neely Cheek. "Assessing Spatial Development: Implications for Map Skill Development." *Social Education* (September 1991): 316–319.

Shannonhouse, Robin. Personal interview. April 2003.

Tawrell, Paul. *Camping & Wilderness Survival.* 13th ed. Shelburne, Vt.: Paul Tawrell, 2002.

"Think Inside the Box." *Backpacker* (May 2003): 20.

Watters, Ron. "Navigating from the Classroom to the Outdoors." *Journal of Physical Education, Recreation, and Dance* 67, no. 5 (May/June 1996): 55–56.

David Matthew Zuefle

PARADES

Parading may be one of humankind's oldest social customs. American colonists brought ancient European traditions with them to the North American continent, itself the site of festive processions among its indigenous peoples for centuries. Americans continued to developed new parade rituals and traditions over the 400 years of their colonial and national history.

Etymologically, the word "parade" comes from the Latin and French root *parer,* meaning to prepare, adorn, garnish. With the attached suffix *ade,* indicating act or action, *parade* suggests the act of adorning social life. An early sense of the word was: a boasting appearance or show of bravado. "Parade" continued to connote ostentatious or garish display, but, by at least the seventeenth century, the word had taken on the specific meaning of an assembly or muster of troops for inspection or display. Its meaning expanded to embrace not only the ceremonial formation of a body of troops but any formal or informal march or procession, particularly the movement of any body of people or things marshaled in something resembling military order in public. "Parade" can signify the participants, the promenaders themselves, and/or the grounds where they assemble and march. Not merely a noun, parade is also a verb—a classic action word, expressing the showy act of marching in public, to promenade flamboyantly, sometimes to masquerade.

These meanings begin to suggest the variability and complexity of parades and parading, and their history in America. Parades can be celebratory, but they can also express mourning. They can affirm social and political order, yet they can criticize, protest, or transgress that order. They can include, as well as exclude, members of the communities through which they meander, constructing broad allegiance, building ethnic, racial, class, or religious solidarity, or, on the other hand, aggravating social animosity. They can express deep truths and fundamental principles, and they can lampoon such verities, provide relief, entertainment, and promote commerce. They are a popular mode of communication, through movement, words, music, and signs; they are public dramas, expressing social and political relations, performed for audiences, which include the marchers themselves. Parades are extraordinary events that punctuate ordinary life—acts and moments of leisure in which fun and games, pomp and circumstance, are filled with social, political, religious, and economic potency.

Native American Traditions

Before the arrival of Europeans in America, and continuing through the colonial era and beyond, Native Americans incorporated parading into their cultural life. Formal processions played critical roles in various social, religious, political, and diplomatic ceremonies. The ostentation of such pageantry among some southeastern tribes, such as the Natchez of the lower Mississippi, particularly impressed European colonial observers, who could compare such practices to the grand courtly and religious processions of Europe dating from the Renaissance. In most cases, however, the small-scale and perplexing rituals of Native parading, combined with the condescension of colonial Europeans, allowed outside spectators to devalue Indian processions and leave them unrecorded.

The Natchez were among the surviving peoples of the Mississippian mound-building civilization, which had emerged by A.D. 1000. Their rich ceremonial life, set amid large towns arranged with numerous dwellings, fields, extensive plazas, mounds, and temples, caught the newcomers' attention. The Natchez, like other Native people, paraded to honor each other; to welcome and cultivate diplomatic ties with Europeans, as extensions of, or melding into, ceremonial dance, and to honor and mourn their dead and restore political order. Among the most dramatic parade events recorded by European observers was the funeral ceremony following the death of The Tattooed Serpent, the great chief and god of the Natchez, in 1725. In an elaborately patterned, circular movement, mourners ascended a great mound, carrying the deceased chieftain to the temple where he would be interred along with some sacrificial members of the procession itself. The naturalist William Bartram witnessed similar funeral processions and festivals—feasts of the dead—among the Choctaws and other Native people in his travels throughout the southeast in the 1770s.

Across Native North America, Indian people also paraded, not only in connection with various funeral rites but to display their power and bravery to themselves and others, and in conjunction with diplomatic efforts. The Five (later Six) Nations of the Iroquois, for example, developed an elaborate condolence ceremony, designed to mourn passing leaders, assuage the grief of kinspeople, and restore the social and political world through the installation of new chiefs. A fire was kindled outside the village for those in mourning, and Iroquois brethren charged with condoling them assembled nearby and sent a message of their imminent appearance. Following a preliminary rite of condolence, they proceeded together, the bereaved in the lead, into the village and the longhouse. The evolving parade traditions of plains Indians, beginning in the nineteenth century, are particularly striking. As plains people adopted the horse and spread onto the Great Plains, they became highly mobile societies, moving considerable distances as they followed buffalo herds and sought forage for their livestock and shelter for themselves. Parading, in a sense, became a way of life, particularly when they joined together in communal buffalo hunts and traveled to meet kinspeople and allies to trade, socialize, and perform religious ceremonies (such as the Sun Dance) each summer. These summer encampments offered the occasion for grand entries, astride or leading their horses, their bodies adorned and dressed in their finest clothes. During the reservation era, Native people continued to parade. In some instances, while traditional dances were proscribed by white authorities, Indians were permitted to stage parades, often in conjunction with U.S. national holidays—Washington's Birthday, Memorial Day, or the Fourth of July for example. The cover of such holidays enabled Indians to celebrate Native feasts surreptitiously, while they increasingly reflected a particular sort of Native American patriotism, a result of Indians' increasing and disproportional service in the United States military in the twentieth century.

Some Native Americans became prominent participants in classic American parades through their performance with Buffalo Bill's Wild West show, beginning in the 1880s. These wildly popular shows, which toured the United States and Europe, rehearsed the "Old Glory Blowout" parades typical of William Cody's hometown of Platte, Nebraska, on Independence Day. Building on this prototype, Cody made the grand parade the opening act of his nightly commercial spectacles. Indians played a key role as actors—playing a white-scripted version of themselves—and they would continue this new tradition on their own terms in their own communities. In the early 2000s such traditions continue in Indian powwows and rodeos—often scheduled for the Fourth of July—which feature as their most stately and spectacular event the Grand Entry, a parade of dance performers, wearing war bonnets, dancing regalia, and often military uniforms, amid American flags, state banners, and Indian staffs.

Colonial and Early National Traditions

In America, colonists did not initially imitate the grand Elizabethan circumambulations, entries, or royal progresses of Britain and Europe. They did sometimes march in salute to monarchs on their birthdays or coronation days, form funeral processions, and import folk dramas that incorporated elements of parading, often festive revelry, masquerades, or burlesques, and "rough music." Generally, even after the emergence of the United States in 1776, when parades grew to celebrate the new American nation, these traditions emerged less through official efforts than *laissez-faire* processes. As Susan G. Davis has shown, they were the work of voluntary militia companies, elite clubs, political parties, and ethnic communities, as well as the exuberant expressions of plebian culture, and they generally assumed one of two styles—respectable or rowdy.

The very first parades in the new nation, which exhibited both styles, appeared almost spontaneously after 4 July 1776 to declare and celebrate American independence. The popular acclamation of the Declaration of Independence occurred in boisterous demonstrations throughout the thirteen colonies, as revolutionary supporters surged through narrow urban streets, sometimes committing acts of violence and destroying property, as in the patriots' demolition of the statue of King George III on the Bowling Green in lower Manhattan. John Adams wrote from Philadelphia predicting that the publication of the Declaration would in later years become a "great Anniversary Festival," commemorated "by solemn acts of devotion to God Almighty, solemnized with pomp and parades, shows, games, sports, guns, bells, bonfires, and illuminations" (Dennis, 2002, p. 16). Adams's words proved prophetic, though not with regard to the solemnity of Independence Day parades.

During the ratification process of the United State Constitution in 1788, American Federalists employed parades as a festive means of political communication and persuasion. The greatest of these parades was Philadelphia's Grand Federal Procession of 4 July 1788, then the largest spectacle in the city's history. Some 5,000 marchers participated and took three hours to pass along the three-mile parade route. Soldiers on foot and horse, dignitaries, bands, carriages, and great floats thrilled the multitudes, and city artisans and mechanics marched in units to represent the trades. The procession was itself a carefully crafted play, beginning with a chronological pageant of American history from 1776 to the present, featuring local leaders and elites, and offering as its climax a Constitution float crowned with a thirteen-foot high eagle, and the Carpenters' Company float, "The Grand Federal Edifice," featuring a dome supported by thirteen Corinthian columns, ten columns complete and three left unfinished. At the parade's terminus, in Union Green, some 17,000 people sat down to a mammoth banquet.

Building on this festive experience, Americans applied the formula to other patriotic events, marshalling troops and trades, officials and professionals, masters and working men, in ranks amid banners, floats, tableaux, and bands of music. These parades sometimes marked the visits of honored guests, such as George Washington, who embarked on a grand tour of the young nation when he journeyed north from Mount Vernon to New York City to assume the presidency in 1789, or the returning hero the Marquis de Lafayette, who spectacularly toured the country in 1824 and 1825. In both cases may be seen republican versions of the classic European royal progress, when a newly-crowned monarch traversed his realm.

In contrast to the celebration of great men, the patriotic parade formula could be used more democratically (if less frequently) to honor humble, often anonymous, Americans, as it was on 26 May 1808 by the New York Tammany Society in a great parade through lower Manhattan, across the East River, and through Brooklyn to ceremoniously re-inter the mortal remains of soldiers and sailors who had perished on prison ships in New York harbor during the Revolution and whose bones continued to wash up in Brooklyn's Wallabout Bay. Tammany Society officials, hundreds of marchers, symbolic figures, and horse-drawn floats escorted thirteen coffins containing the revolutionary martyrs' sacred remains.

Amid these unusual spectacles, more common, regular musters of private military clubs and public militia came to define and refine the conventions of respectable parades of the early republic and antebellum America. These events grew out of training days, common throughout colonial America when all eligible white males mustered and drilled as local militia in the interest of public defense. After the Revolution, elite volunteer companies, composed of the most affluent residents, increasingly distinguished themselves from public militia, in which working-class men were compelled to serve. An array of occasions—Washington's Birthday, May Musters, Independence Day, and Christmas—provided opportunities for militia parades, in which a city's most privileged young men, splendidly dressed with elaborate accoutrements and equipage, and amplified by hired brass bands, drew public attention and cast themselves as the guardians of order. By the 1820s, these volunteer companies sometimes took their shows on the road, marching to join other cities' elite militia for combined performances and conviviality, especially on the Fourth of July. When dignitaries arrived, typically it was the city's volunteer military companies who met and escorted the honored guests through the streets to their ceremonial destinations and paraded in their honor.

In a variation on these practices, ethnic societies began to celebrate their mythic patrons, often with parades. Societies of St. Patrick emerged before the Revolution, for example, initially as nonsectarian benevolent associations to aid poor or unfortunate countrymen. Similar fraternities developed among other groups, a St. Andrew Society among Scotsmen, for example, and an English St. George Society. As early as 1779, New York City witnessed a St. Patrick's Day parade, organized by Irish soldiers—both Protestants and Catholics—among the occupying British troops. By the 1820s and increasingly in the 1830s, St. Patrick's Day became a more aggressively working-class Irish-American occasion to fend off discrimination and assert ethnic solidarity, worth, and respectability. By the 1850s, the St. Patrick's Day celebration had become massive in New York. St. Patrick's Day parades were less about devotion to a Catholic saint than a statement of the legitimacy of Irish-American identity and a defiant if festive demonstration of Irish social and political power.

In a similar fashion, Columbus Day parades, first organized in 1792 by the Tammany Society and Columbian Order in New York City on the occasion of the 300th anniversary of Columbus's 1492 voyage, came to represent religious and ethnic pride and strength. Beginning in the 1880s, Irish-American founders of the Knights of Columbus (first in New Haven, Connecticut) marched in celebration of Columbus as a non-Anglo, non-Protestant, Catholic "American." Quickly, Columbus became the political patron saint for Italian Americans, who paraded on his "discovery" day in cities across the United States to proclaim their legitimacy as hyphenated-Americans. African American parades, conducted often at great peril, given the hostility of whites and their unwillingness to share the streets with blacks on occasions such as the Fourth of July, similarly promoted the worth and protested the continuing discrimination of people of color. Such marches (sometimes forced to the Fifth of July) called America's attention to the unfulfilled promises of the Declaration of Independence. Despite the order and dignity of their processions, African Americans were often derided in the antebellum press and sometimes attacked by white mobs. Although some were more successful than others, these various ethnic parades sought to shape the social and political landscape of America, promoting pluralism and courting respectability for their sponsoring communities.

Topsy-Turvy Parade Traditions

Other parade traditions in the United States historically showed little concern for respectability. Indeed, some actively contested the very standards of respectability or the pretensions of those exemplars of respectability—the rich and powerful, social and political elites, or the emerging middle class in the first half of the nineteenth century and its new sensibilities and behavioral expectations. Urban poor and working people continued to celebrate folk dramas in the streets, parading in the context of festivity, such as Christmas and New Year's, processing boisterously while enforcing community moral standards though rites of skimmington, charivari, or rough music (a crowd action, often noisy, comical, and sometimes violent, to mock or punish those the crowd deemed guilty of moral turpitude), or marching in consciously ridiculous fashion to lampoon the high and mighty.

Such activity could be rowdy, even riotous; it could express a worthy democratic critique of social, political,

and economic authorities; it could sometimes be vicious and unjust, when it targeted the weak and vulnerable or enforced community standards that were nativist (anti-immigrant), racist, or misogynist. Increasingly, self-conscious social superiors drew back from this plebian festivity, deemed it hideous and barbaric, and sought to control or eliminate it. Common people nonetheless continued such practices, adjusted them to accommodate changing realities, and found new support for their playfully unruly, mobile festivity in the increasingly vibrant commercial theatre and print media that began to flourish in the nineteenth century.

Carnival and the carnivalesque came to America early, though it is not certain exactly when, carried not only by European colonists and immigrants, but also by Africans, often by way of the Caribbean. In Christian Europe, Carnival was a latter-day version of the pre-Christian, pagan Saturnalia—a season or festival of merrymaking before Lent, characterized particularly by feasting and masquerading in the streets. In America as well as Europe, plebian carnivalesque parades represented common peoples' festivity, which offered release from the daily strictures of life and its social order, an order that often confined them at the bottom. Carnival and its parades temporarily produced a topsy-turvy world, with inversion of normal rules and ranks and the crossing of boundaries, of class and status, even of race and sex.

This temporarily authorized violation of social order could occur not only in pre-Lenten festivity but at other seasonal moments as well, during Christmastime, in mumming (masked merrymaking in outlandish disguise) or the carousing of Belsnickles (an aggressive, mischievous version of St. Nicholas impersonation, among Pennsylvania Germans), or during Pinkster, a celebration of Whitsuntide (Pentecost) among Dutch Americans, which became largely a black holiday in the nineteenth century.

Pinkster in New York and New Jersey, and "Negro Election Day" in New England, featured, for a few days, African Americans in the role of rulers rather than the enslaved or oppressed. These fêtes drew large numbers of blacks from the countryside into towns and cities; there they dressed in elaborate finery or costume, listened to fiddling, drumming, and banjo music, indulged in merrymaking, song, and dance, and paraded in the streets. The festival's centerpiece was often the election and inauguration of black kings, governors, or judges, who then led, in mock splendor, parades of black militia and bands of music, which parodied whites and offered momentary fun, while cultivating self-worth and offering the opportunity for blacks to honor their own notables.

Such burlesque emerged simultaneously in working-class white militia parades, which mocked the self-important spectacles of elite volunteer military companies. In these irreverent, ludicrous musters, or on ceremonial occasions such as the Fourth of July, plebeian men marched through the streets in outrageous regalia, in fake wigs and whisker, sometimes in blackface, carrying canes and cornstalks instead of arms, keeping time with loud brass "callithumpian" bands.

The grandest expression of an American carnivalesque flowered in New Orleans in its Mardi Gras. There, at least as early as the 1830s, semi-organized parades grew out of street masking by young French Creole men, with minimal organization. By the end of the decade these parades had grown into "grand cavalcades." A lavish parade along Royal Street in 1839 featured discordant music, banners, fishing poles, men on Arabian horses and donkeys, "heathen and Christian, Turks and kangaroos, ancient Greeks and modern Choctaws; friars and beggars; knights and princesses, … polar bears and chicken cocks" (Mitchell, p. 22).

Exclusive French control of these festivities ended in the 1840s, as Anglo-American men adopted the tradition of informal processions, added new themes, pageantry, and tableaux, and sought to impose greater order, insisting on distinguishing between the parade and its audience, which had been promiscuously mixed. And amid this inter-ethnic contest, another tradition—African American Carnival—infused New Orleans's Mardi Gras parades. As early as 1827, a northern observer had witnessed a black Saturnalia, most likely a Mardi Gras festival, that featured "the great Congo-dance," in which "some hundred of Negroes, male and female, follow the king of the wake." (Mitchell, pp. 29–30). Later, African American Mardi Gras parading would lampoon white parades. During the Civil War and early in Reconstruction, parades ceased or were banned in New Orleans; parades returned in 1872. The Krewe of Rex (the fraternal organization that would continue to stage parades and balls annually for Mardi Gras), along with other such clubs, increasingly transformed the more individualistic, wanton, chaotic masking of Mardi Gras into an ordered, hierarchical, respectable civic ritual. Mardi Gras parades and festivity could also degenerate into violence, sometimes expressing virulent racism. But as more krewes emerged to stage parades, representing a broader array of Orleanians—"Mardi Gras Indians" (actually blacks dressed as such), other African Americans (for example, the Zulus, founded in 1909), gay men (such as the Mystic Krewe of Apollo, founded in 1969), and women (such as the Krewe of Venus, founded in 1941)—the grandeur of Mardi Gras grew. Simultaneously it became a more commercialized event, national in appeal, with its parades helping to attract tourists and to advertise New Orleans as an enterprising city of the New South by the early twentieth century.

The Twentieth Century: Patriotism, Civics, Commerce

Meanwhile, mercantile interests, in partnership with civic elites, increasingly transformed other disorderly parades into more respectable, controlled, civic events, boosting cities and promoting merchants' products. Philadelphia in 1900 staged its first official New Year's Mummers Parade, along a prescribed route with licensed performers and prizes supplied by merchants. This trend in regulation and authorization by city officials would grow. Department stores parades, to encourage shopping, began to appear in increasing numbers; Gimbel's Department Store sponsored a Thanksgiving parade as early as 1921, while Macy's Thanksgiving Day Parade originated in 1924 in New York City and became the premier event of its type in the United States. Though staged on Thanksgiving, the parade inaugurated the Christmas shopping season, encouraging purchases at Macy's in particular and more general rites of consumption. In Pasadena, California, in 1890, boosters initiated a parade that quickly evolved into the Tournament of Roses, a celebration of southern California as a healthy, sun-kissed paradise. Some 2,000 spectators watched flower-covered carriages roll by on the first parade, which soon expanded to include marching bands and ever-more-elaborate horse-drawn and eventually motorized floats. In the early 2000s, nearly a million people lined the streets on New Year's Day for the parade, and hundreds of millions watched on television.

Such festivities built on an older tradition of commercial and promotional parades and exhibitions, dating to the early nineteenth century—circus parades promenading into American towns, entertaining in their own right, but designed to entice viewers to become paying customers; grand processions inaugurating canals, railroads, and bridges; mobile spectacles advertising new commercial or industrial endeavors. In the twentieth century, however, these commercialized parades reflected an unprecedented mass culture, built through new commercial networks, advertising, and innovative media—particularly radio and television—which separated paraders from audiences and encouraged self-indulgent leisure and consumption; such commercial extravaganzas often reflected a new emphasis on youth, insulated or distracted viewers from the harsher realities, and in general invoked the wonder and delight of a child in a toy store.

Tournament of Roses Parade. Sponsored by Thai Airways International the "Getting to Know You" float won the Craftsman Trophy for "Outstanding Showmanship and Dramatic Impact Over 55 Feet" in the 112th Tournament of Roses Parade in Pasadena, California, on 1 January 2001. Raul Rodriguez designed what was the parade's longest float at sixty-seven feet long, eighteen feet wide, and thirty-two feet high and based the theme on the heritage of Thailand. Made of some 50,000 orchids, onion and millet seeds, beans, and rice grains (all fresh materials as was required of participants), it comprised three parts. © *Reed Saxon for AP/Wide World Photos*

The new mercantile-sponsored and city-boosting parades of the twentieth century cooperated with civic elite in their efforts to control the streets and public culture. As they rationalized fêtes and made them more spectacular, they sought to render them "safe and sane," used them to instruct and inform citizens and consumers about proper behavior, and set them in opposition to the disorderly or anti-authoritarian use of the streets by immigrants, organized labor, and political radicals. A massive New York City parade celebrating the centennial of Washington's inauguration in 1889, for example, was designed didactically to use the mythic Washington to model order, hierarchy, stability and control, in contrast to the labor walk-outs, parades, and strikes that troubled business and political leaders in the late nineteenth and early twentieth centuries.

A series of festivals and parades in Cleveland, Ohio, during the twentieth century similarly exemplified these trends, expressing a mixed agenda of patriotism, civic order, local and ethnic pride, and anti-radicalism, as well as

entertainment and commerce. Cleveland leaders grappled especially with the challenge of integrating a large immigrant population and dealing with United States participation in two world wars. The city's Americanization parade of 4 July 1918, for example, featured 75,000 immigrants and their children, who demonstrated their loyalty to "America First," but often managed to display ethnic pride simultaneously through traditional costumes and floats extolling homelands. Subsequent parades wavered between expressions of civic and ethnic harmony, particularly during peacetime (Cleveland's sesquicentennial parade in 1946, for example), and a more dogmatic and conformist patriotism during periods of greater perceived peril.

Meanwhile, beginning in the 1880s and gathering steam in the twentieth century, labor activists and liberal authorities invented Labor Day—characteristically marked by enthusiastic parades of working people—and ensconced it in the American calendar in early September.

Labor Day and parades are anomalous. From their origins in the early republic, as celebrations of the strength, solidarity, and determination of workingmen's associations, or as actual strikes, labor processions represented respectability and defiance, working-class order, and (for some) social disorder. By the early twentieth century, however, Labor Day and its parades were institutionalized and conventional if nonetheless spectacular, in contrast to working-class marches on May Day, which carried more radical implications. Although Labor Day continued to celebrate organized labor in America, the holiday and its elaborate parades increasingly signaled a day of leisure rather than one of protest, in the end perhaps a fitting tribute to organized labor's long struggle to shorten workdays and carve out weekends as periods of rest.

Military parades provide another example of the complexity of modern American parading. Military marchers figure most prominently in parades designed to memorialize veterans and war dead, as on Memorial Day and Veterans Day, occasions that can simultaneously express appreciation to soldiers, valorize the military, and condemn war. The most joyous of twentieth-century military parades were those celebrating the returning troops following the World War II. But no such parades marked the dénouement of the Korean or Vietnam conflicts. The "Welcome Home" parade of 10 June 1991 in New York City, following the Persian Gulf war, seemed to reverse this trend, attracting nearly 5 million viewers, and dumping eighty-seven tons of paper shavings on Broadway's "Canyon of Heroes." But when the United States endured a devastating terrorist attack on 11 September 2001 and embarked on two wars, in Afghanistan and Iraq, and New York offered to host another such parade during the summer of 2003, none materialized. Americans remained unsure about the future and sought greater solace in conventional, more diverting and less political parades.

By the late twentieth century and into the twenty-first, parades continued to play an important role in American leisure and celebration, occasionally conveying partisan political messages or civic seriousness, but more often functioning as light, festive expressions of community. In small towns across the United States, as well as in large metropolitan areas, communities stage parades to coincide with an array of national, state, or local holidays or other commemorative occasions. New York City streets host some 270 parades annually, while small towns may struggle to stage a single parade each year. Such festive processions offer inhabitants the chance to celebrate themselves and their institutions—schools, civic organizations, local businesses, government agencies, community youth, notables, and political leaders. School marching bands remain a fixture in these events, as they do at high school and college football games, where they perform parades each half-time. Whether processing on the football field, or through the public streets along with floats, equestrian troops, beauty queens, ambitious politicians, fire engines and slow-moving municipal equipment, marching bands exemplify community values—teamwork and the individual and collective pursuit of excellence—while they provide entertainment and fun.

Parades have evolved substantially throughout United States history, as the country itself has been transformed socially, economically, politically, and geographically. Earlier parading styles, both rowdy and respectable, continue nonetheless, amid the changed urbanized and suburbanized landscapes, mass culture, and the technological complexity of contemporary America. In the early 2000s, women as well as men, and diverse groups of Americans, representing various ethnicities and races, classes, and sexualities marched legitimately (though not necessarily without controversy) in U. S. parades. In small towns and urban neighborhoods, parades could still be home-made and intimate, though planning was more often handled by public and private officials, and such events competed with (or could be overwhelmed by) larger festivities available nearby or via television. In urban streets, marchers and audiences could still mix in helter-skelter revelry, in New Orleans's Mardi Gras, in New York's Greenwich Village Halloween Parade, and elsewhere. But modern urban landscapes, with parkways and boulevards designed to promote automobile traffic, not foot traffic and sociability, and with workplaces and living spaces widely separated, had more often isolated parades from their constituencies, made them more performances than vernacular expressions of communities. Civic parades could still command respect, even while they entertained; and they could entertain respectably and offer political messages, even through controlled burlesque, as in Pasadena's self-consciously informal Doo Dah Parade (first held in 1978), countering and lampooning the city's more famous Rose Parade. Parades remained complicated and diverse events in the United States, protean affairs that could instruct, persuade, distract, intimidate, amaze, amuse, delight, and entertain. They demonstrated both the seriousness and the playfulness of leisure in America.

See also: Fourth of July, Labor Day, Mardi Gras, Memorial Day, Mumming, Native American Leisure Lifestyles, Patriotism and Leisure

BIBLIOGRAPHY

Bodnar, John. *Remaking America: Public Memory, Commemoration, and Patriotism in the Twentieth Century.* Princeton, N.J.: Princeton University Press, 1992.

Davis, Susan G. *Parades and Power: Street Theatre in Nineteenth-Century Philadelphia.* Philadelphia: Temple University Press, 1986.

Dennis, Matthew. *Red, White, and Blue Letter Days: An American Calendar.* Ithaca, N.Y.: Cornell University Press, 2002.

———. "Patriotic Remains: Bones of Contention in the Early Republic." In *Mortal Remains: Death in Early America.* Edited by Nancy Isenberg and Andrew Burstein. Philadelphia: University of Pennsylvania Press, 2003.

Falassi, Alessandro, ed. *Time Out of Time: Essays on the Festival.* Albuquerque: University of New Mexico Press, 1987.

Glassberg, David. *American Historical Pageantry: The Uses of Tradition in the Early Twentieth Century.* Chapel Hill: University of North Carolina Press, 1990.

Hoxie, Frederick E. *Parading through History: The Making of the Crow Nation in America, 1805–1935.* Cambridge and New York: Cambridge University Press, 1995.

Kammen, Michael G. *Mystic Chords of Memory: The Transformation of Tradition in American Culture.* New York: Alfred A. Knopf, 1991.

Kugelmass, Jack. "Wishes Come True: Designing the Greenwich Village Halloween Parade." In *Halloween and other Festivals of Death and Life.* Edited by Jack Santino. Knoxville: University of Tennessee Press, 1994.

Lawrence, Denise L. "Rules of Misrule: Notes on the Doo Dah Parade in Pasadena." In *Time Out of Time: Essays on the Festival.* Edited by Alessandro Falassi. Albuquerque: University of New Mexico Press, 1987.

Litwicki, Ellen M. *America's Public Holidays, 1865–1920.* Washington, D.C.: Smithsonian Institution Press, 2000.

Mitchell, Reid. *All on a Mardi Gras Day: Episodes in the History of New Orleans Carnival.* Cambridge, Mass.: Harvard University Press, 1995.

Newman, Simon P. *Parades and the Politics of the Street: Festive Culture in the Early American Republic.* Philadelphia: University of Pennsylvania Press, 1997.

Nissenbaum, Stephen. *The Battle for Christmas: A Cultural History of America's Most Cherished Holiday.* New York: Alfred A. Knopf, 1996.

Pencak, William, Matthew Dennis, and Simon P. Newman, eds. *Riot and Revelry in Early America.* University Park: Pennsylvania State University Press, 2002.

Pleck, Elizabeth Hafkin. *Celebrating the Family: Ethnicity, Consumer Culture, and Family Rituals.* Cambridge, Mass.: Harvard University Press, 2000.

Schmidt, Leigh Eric. *Consumer Rites: The Buying and Selling of American Holidays.* Princeton, N.J.: Princeton University Press, 1995.

Schultz, April R. *Ethnicity on Parade: Inventing the Norwegian American through Celebration.* Amherst: University of Massachusetts Press, 1994.

Waldstreicher, David. *In the Midst of Perpetual Fetes: The Making of American Nationalism, 1776–1820.* Chapel Hill: University of North Carolina Press, 1997.

White, Shane. "'It Was a Proud Day': African Americans, Festivals, and Parades in the North, 1741–1834." *Journal of American History* 81, no. 1 (June 1994): 13–50.

Matthew Dennis

PARK MOVEMENTS

The Boston Common was the first designated public space in America. When it was created in 1634, it was a multiple-use space on which cows grazed, witches were executed, women branded with scarlet letters, and Indians and British troops fought. New York City, however, would soon take the lead in designating open spaces and developing public and private parks.

New York

Around 1675, when Fort James (lower Manhattan) was being restored, "the Plaine afore the Forte" was designated. This was a multiple-use open space used for parades and fairs. It was turned into a park in 1733, and renamed Bowling Green. During the nineteenth century, however, many public open spaces were monopolized by the wealthy. In the 1820s, the rich started to build their homes around existing public green spaces like Bowling Green and the Battery—effectively privatizing them. The Battery, renovated in the 1820s, had sculptured lawns, shade trees, and ornamental iron railing. As the rich sought more exclusivity, they built private parks such as St. John's Park. In 1827, wealthy buyers flocked to the neighborhood, and only landowners whose property surrounded the park had access to it. They built a tall iron fence around the park and landscaped it. The square was soon surrounded for blocks around with the homes owned by the most prominent families. By the 1850s, similar projects like Union Square Park and Gramercy Park were developed.

Philadelphia

When William Penn acquired the charter to build a city on the Delaware River, he decided to build Philadelphia—a "greene Country Towne." Penn included five public squares in his 1682 city plan. He did not include more public open space because he expected each home to have a yard and garden. During the 1750s and 1760s, however, more provisions were made for the public open space, and some private pleasure gardens, such as Springettsbury, were opened to the public. Cherry Garden, a public garden, was extended from Front Street to the Delaware River. In 1755, two small plots of land were set aside as a campground for Native Americans. Just beyond the city limits was a forested area known as Governor's Woods. As was the case in New York City, by the early nineteenth century, wealthy Philadelphians had begun to cluster around the available open space .

Boston

Like their counterparts in New York City and Philadelphia, wealthy Bostonians also lived around the city's open spaces. Pemberton Square, designed in the 1830s, had a small park surrounded by elegant homes. Wealthy Bostonians also settled in homes surrounding the park on Bunker Hill. The fashionable residences of Park and Beacon Streets overlooked the Boston Common. Cattle grazing was banned in the common in the early 1830s. Built in the 1830s and 1840s, the Louisburg Square neighborhood was another elite residential enclave, with homes overlooking a private park. More homes of the wealthy flanked the Public Garden.

Baltimore

Baltimore's elite built elegant homes around its squares. In the 1830s, the Canton Company began developing squares similar to those in Manhattan. The wealthy lived in large dwellings that flanked Waverly Terrace, Franklin Square, Mount Vernon, Charles Street and Madison Avenue, Bolton, Hoffman, Preston, Lexington, and Pearl Streets. By 1860, Baltimore had developed six new squares on hilltops.

Early Park Advocacy

In 1785, a park advocate writing under the pseudonym "Veritas" suggested that the Battery and the Fields (later converted into City Hall Park) in New York City, be reclaimed and turned into public parks. Shortly thereafter, a planner suggested constructing a park around the Collect, a freshwater pond, but that park was never built.

Though large urban parks were not a part of the American landscape until the mid-1800s, wealthy Americans had access to private parks and gardens long before that time. Notwithstanding, it was wealthy, urban elites who campaigned for public parks during the middle of the nineteenth century. Though there were many reasons why these activists supported park development, one significant factor was cultural nationalism. American elites,

feeling that the country's civility and cultural attainment lagged behind that of Europe, began searching for ways to enhance the prestige of American culture at home and abroad. Thus they set their sights on developing and promoting art; supporting national cultural and educational institutions; identifying natural wonders that had no counterparts in Europe; and building elegantly landscaped urban parks (see Nash for a discussion of elites and cultural nationalism).

As elites campaigned for parks, they developed some consensus on the meanings of the urban park and the range of functions they served. Urban parks functioned as mechanisms of social control, providing moral upliftment and "tranquilizing" recreation and freedom. They were considered to improve gentility and civility, and aid in socializing the masses to middle-class norms, values, and tastes, as well as to educate the public and induce better attitudes toward work. Additionally, the parks served as a place for acceptable expression of manliness and were also seen as repositories for works of art and sources of cultural enlightenment wherein people were exposed to beauty in pastoral settings. Moreover, the parks were expected to improve health; ease overcrowding—literally provide a breathing space in congested cities—act as urban resorts for people with no access to the countryside; function as the commons or social nerve center of the city; structure the plan and growth of the city (parks acted as a form of zoning to control commercial development, housing patterns, and unwanted land uses); protect the urban water supply; increase property values; mute class conflicts; provide jobs; and function as a mechanism for dispensing political favors. As these ideas were propagated in elite circles, public parks were included in official city-planning documents. In 1811, New York became the first city to include public parks in its city plan. Park advocates relied heavily on some or all of the above arguments to advance their cause.

Despite these efforts, even as late as 1857, no American city had a major, completed landscaped park. Thus anyone wanting to experience pastoral landscapes had to go the countryside or to the cemetery. As the first planned open spaces close to urban centers, cemeteries like Grove Street (New Haven, Connecticut), Mount Auburn (Cambridge, Massachusetts), Laurel Hill (Philadelphia, Pennsylvania) and Greenwood (Brooklyn, New York) were enormously popular.

The Campaigning for Urban Parks Intensifies

Noting the popularity of the rural cemeteries and the general lack of open space in the cities, park advocates such as poet and newspaper owner William Cullen Bryant and horticulturalist Andrew Jackson Downing campaigned to get cities to build public parks in the 1840s. At about the same time, Americans traveling to Europe began urging city leaders to build parks in the United States. At the time, London had devoted about 13,000 acres of land to park space, and many Americans, seeing this, were impressed. Bryant promoted the idea of a planned park system in New York. Writer Walt Whitman, then editor of the *Eagle,* also campaigned in favor of parks. Whitman, who lived in Brooklyn, led the campaign to create a park in the working-class section of the city. The campaign led to the choice of the Fort Greene site for a park.

Other luminaries, such as Henry David Thoreau, also supported the creation of public parks. Despite the efforts of these early advocates, no coordinated park movement emerged to implement plans to build the parks. This is due, in part, to the fact that during the early 1840s, the country was just recovering from the financial Panic of 1837 and it was not feasible to embark on large park-building projects. In the early 1850s, however, New York was booming economically, and the city's business class grew interested in the park movement. Other cities soon followed New York's lead.

In 1851, a group of wealthy businessmen gathered for a dinner meeting to discuss the possibility of building a park in Manhattan. The group picked Jones Wood, on the East River, for the site of the proposed park and set out to acquire the property. In May 1851, the Common Council was asked to approve the proposed park. At the time of this proposal, it was unheard of for public funds to be used to pay for large landscaped parks. Though the 1811 city plan set aside 450 acres for open space, that amount had dwindled to 144 acres. Soon after the Common Council approved the park proposal and it became public, Bryant's *Post* and Horace Greeley's *Tribune* began promoting it. In July, a bill authorizing the city to build a large public park passed the state assembly.

Not everyone, however, was enthused about developing Jones Wood Park; some questioned the motives of the park supporters. Critics argued that there was no need for a park, and that land speculators wanted to enrich themselves from it (some of the businessmen choosing the Jones Wood site owned country estates close by). Some argued that the park would remove valuable real estate from the market and that the poor would have no access to it. Others opposed the creation of Jones Wood Park by alleging that the chosen site was not big enough.

Benefits Assessments

Prior to the Jones Wood proposal, large property owners were taxed for land improvements (streets, lights, sewers,

development of squares) adjacent to their property. As the cost of these benefits assessments mounted, the landowners began organizing themselves. They argued that instead of charging them for improvements, the cost should be borne by the general public. Jones Wood supporters, aware of the growing aversion of the wealthy to benefits assessments, proposed a general public tax to pay for the park. This was an important break with tradition that would set a new precedent for financing public works projects. Some reformers, however, objected to funding the park through general taxes.

Aldermen from working-class districts used the Jones Wood proposal to negotiate more open space in poor neighborhoods; they voted in favor of Jones Wood on the condition that the Battery would be enlarged to almost twice its size. Meanwhile, other park advocates developed an alternative proposal to Jones Wood. Arguing that the Jones Wood site would be too inaccessible to many New Yorkers and that it was too small, West Side landowners lobbied for a larger, more centrally located park, funded under a different tax structure. They proposed that the public pay about two-thirds of the cost of the park and private landowners adjacent to the park pay the remainder. In the summer of 1853, the proposal to build Central Park was approved. Several months later, it was decided that Jones Wood Park would not be built. The 778-acre Central Park (expanded to 843 acres in 1863) would be almost five times as large as all existing parks and squares in the city combined.

Pastoral Scenery and Tranquilizing Recreation

Frederick Law Olmsted and Calvert Vaux were the landscape architects chosen to build a landscaped park that would serve the dual purposes of meeting the needs of the wealthy while uplifting the masses. In the process, both of these men elevated landscape architecture to a new level. They saw Central Park as a cultural institution that served important social functions.

Olmsted believed that scenery, nature, and parks countered the "severe and excessive exercise of the mind," and put one in a contemplative mood. Throughout his career, Olmsted sought to foster or induce that state of mind through the designs of his park. He used subtle designs in his parks to create this mood and believed that pastoral landscapes made the ideal park scenery. Together, Olmsted and Vaux incorporated pastoral scenery by building their parks with broad stretches of gently rolling greensward, edged by irregular borders of trees and shrubs to create a sense of space and distance. This technique was used to induce a setting of unconscious recreation in which the park-goer is absorbed in the park experience without being fully conscious of the process by which it occurs. Olmsted described this process as the "unconscious influence," of "tranquilizing" recreation. Olmsted recognized that the demands of urban life left people with the need to unwind, to stimulate the brain in ways that compensated for work-related stress without over-stimulating..

Olmsted and Vaux also wanted to include picturesque elements in the parks they built; they were largely responsible for much of the spread of picturesque landscapes in the United States. Rejecting the symmetrical, geometric designs of European gardens such as those at Versailles, France, which were laid out in the gardenesque style (that is, dominated by floral arrangements and specimen plantings), they opted to contrast wilderness vistas with more subtle arrangements to express their visions. To create picturesque scenery, Olmsted and Vaux used a wide variety of densely planted and contrasting native foliage to create a complex picture of light and shadow near the eye. They also thought that people would find "unrestricted movement" and a "sense of enlarged freedom" in the broad open lawns (the pastoral parts of the park).

Drawing on Romantic and Transcendental beliefs that wilderness provided the sharpest contrast with civilization, Olmsted and Vaux also sought to work with wilderness themes. Recognizing, however, that pure wilderness would be very difficult to re-create in an urban environment, they opted for a compromise the author calls pastoral Transcendentalism—creating landscapes that combined rural, pastoral, and picturesque effects. Pastoral Transcendental scenery combined the open, gently sloping, manicured, and domesticated spaces of the pastoral style with the wilder, untamed, more irregular look of the picturesque. This kind of composition is described in Olmsted and Vaux's discussions of Brooklyn's Prospect Park (Olmsted, "Preliminary Report Upon Yosemite"; Olmsted, Vaux and Company, "Preliminary Report to the Commissioners").

Parks and Social Order

Soon after Central Park received final approval for development, the United States slipped into a recession that lasted till 1857. There were daily demonstrations in Philadelphia, Chicago, and other cities around the country. Parks and public squares became the sites of numerous protests. In New York, mass demonstrations were held at City Hall Park, Washington Square, and Tompkins Square. The unemployed demanded that the government expand work opportunities in Central Park; however, some politicians questioned the wisdom of spending large sums of money to construct a park in the face of a recession. Some park opponents suggested reducing the size of the park. Realizing that the park could provide thousands of jobs, however, Mayor Fernando Wood vetoed a bill that would have reduced the size of the park.

Because of the unrest, park commissioners moved quickly to limit public gatherings in the parks. Rallies, public meetings, and religious services were excluded from park programming. Boston park commissioners did not allow any public meetings in its parks; Philadelphia allowed only religious meetings; and the Chicago South Parks forbade public meetings that would lead to speech making and crowds; Brooklyn permitted only the parades of Sunday school children. Despite these restrictions, the parks were built with military parade grounds, and military exercises were conducted in them. While public gatherings were considered to have the potential to spin out of control, military exercises were seen as a show of law, order, civility, and national unity. Thus, the high visibility of the military personnel in the parks could be considered as another dimension of social control.

Park designers believed in enforcing social order by a variety of means. They used indirect and subtle techniques imposed through park design. In addition, rules and regulations were drafted for the parks. In Central Park, regulations prohibited visitors from walking on the grass, picking plants, defacing structures, throwing stones, annoying birds, selling merchandise, behaving in a lewd manner, entering or exiting in unauthorized places, being in the park after closing, having firearms, playing musical instruments, gambling, making speeches, or displaying flags and banners. Violation of these rules could result in fines or imprisonment. Law enforcement officers (park keepers) patrolled Central Park and Prospect Park. Regulations prohibiting walking on the grass were also found in Chicago's parks, but not in San Francisco's. These restriction signs were finally banned in Central Park in 1897.

Central Park was used as a model for the development of hundreds of municipal parks across the country. Its organization, policing policies, regulations, funding structure, and design were copied. Even before Central Park was completed, residents in Brooklyn, San Francisco, Baltimore, Boston, Buffalo, Philadelphia, and Chicago began lobbying for or building parks of their own.

The Rising Demand for Active Recreation Spaces

As the public demand for active recreational spaces grew, landscape architects began to make provisions for active recreation in the parks they designed. For instance, school children who attended school regularly and had good grades were allowed to play ball and croquet in Central Park. By 1868, Olmsted began to design parts of some parks for active recreation. He designed a park with a baseball lot in Buffalo and placed some of the city's parks to be close to working-class neighborhoods.

Olmsted and Vaux experimented with ways to permit use and relax restrictions of people's movements in parks, while still maintaining its turf in good condition for a reasonable price. In the design of New Britain's Walnut Hill Park in Connecticut, they opened up most of the grounds to the public. Moreover, in planning Chicago's South Park in 1871, they made room for sports such as baseball, cricket, football, and running games. Olmsted designed the Boston park system, the "Emerald Necklace", from 1878 through the 1880s. He included opportunities for active recreation in parts of Franklin Park and Charlesbank. Olmsted also placed developed, active recreation space in South Park in Buffalo in 1888. In general, by 1895, more active and unstructured recreation was common in parks across the country.

The Rise of the Recreation Movement

The need for parks—both as a source of employment and for recreation—was strong, but most cities found it difficult to fund elaborate landscaped parks. For instance, in 1867, Newark, New Jersey, balked at paying more than $1 million to build a city park. It was also becoming clear that in addition to large parks, there was a need for the smaller neighborhood parks and playgrounds, designed for the more active recreational use advocated by the working class in the 1850s. Consequently, a new breed of park advocates arose in the 1880s to respond to this need. While the landscape architects and early park advocates made general claims about the therapeutic nature of parks, they did not make any direct interventions to change the actual health status of urban residents. Once the parks were built, the health improvements heralded by the park builders were left to chance. As living conditions in the cities worsened, however, middle-class reformers sought to more deliberately link the goals of the sanitary reform movement to the goals of the parks and recreation movement. They combined their desire to provide park access to the poor with efforts to improve health and hygiene. Reformers believed that, in addition to vis-iting parks, other steps had to be taken to improve the health of urban residents.

This resulted in a shift from wealthy businessmen controlling the park discourse and agenda to women and working-class people being more active in the discussions. Instead of building parks that primarily catered to the needs of native-born, upper- and middle-class adults, the reformers focused on poor, immigrant children. These parks were not intended for middle-class use; instead, they were part of a package of charitable acts directed at working-class clients. The socialization role of the parks was not left to chance; it was taught as part of the playground experience. These newer parks were built not with an eye toward the picturesque or for the purpose of tranquilizing recreation, they were built for active recreation. The reformers took this approach because they believed that changing environmental conditions was critical to improving people's lives.

Thus, the recreation movement activists augmented the work of the landscape architects by encouraging cities and small towns to build parks and playgrounds. The movement activists were also responding to the spread of diseases, lack of public open space, the popularity and overuse of existing parks, and the severe overcrowding in working-class communities. Public concern grew when it became evident that city dwellers had no place to play, rest, or relax. Therefore, the quest for recreation space became intimately connected to the campaign to improve public health, environmental conditions, and the rapid assimilation of new immigrants.

Sand Gardens and Neighborhood Playgrounds

Many of the activists were upper- and middle-class members of the women's clubs and settlement houses, who were concerned with what children and adults did in their spare time. While the landscape architects were males working on grand designs supported by large allocations of public and private funds, the Progressive Era reformers were dominated by women undertaking smaller, underfunded local (neighborhood) projects. The Massachusetts Emergency and Hygiene Association (MEHA), one group involved in the early phases of the development of playgrounds in the United States, typifies the goals and posture of these groups as they tried to establish playgrounds and parks. Children were the favorite targets of the reformers because they were deemed more controllable, and reformers believed that if they were converted in their youth, there would be no need to reform them in adulthood. MEHA placed the first pile of sand in the yard of the Parmenter Street Chapel, a mission in Boston's North End slum, in 1885. MEHA volunteers used the structured environment of the sand garden to give the children lessons in morals, manners, hygiene, and social skills.

In 1886, Bostonians set aside a portion of the Charles River embankment as a children's play area. The city also dumped piles of sand at various sites in working-class neighborhoods. By 1888, however, MEHA abandoned its practice of placing sand gardens in missions and convinced Boston city officials to place them in public school yards because the group lacked the resources to develop and maintain the sand gardens. This happened in New York as well; by 1910, playgrounds were being built and operated by the city. Building on the MEHA model, sand gardens and playgrounds were quickly established in many cities.

Competing Definitions of Leisure Behavior

Though the working class built the urban parks, they were not free to use these parks as they pleased. For instance, tensions between the wealthy and the poor grew so high in Central Park that German immigrant children threw stones at wealthy families as they paraded through in their fine carriages. By the 1880s, however, the working class was primed and ready to be more assertive about its recreational needs. Henry George helped to galvanize working-class support for increased leisure time. George wrote, ". . .give all the classes leisure, and comfort, and independence, the decencies of life, [and] the opportunities of mental and moral development." As he campaigned for mayor in working-class neighborhoods of New York, George argued that, "the children of the rich can go up to Central Park, or out of the country in the summer time; but the children of the poor, for them there is no playground in the city but the streets" (Rosenzweig and Blackmar, p. 223; George).

Similarly, in Worcester, Massachusetts, in the late 1800s, the city's working class began campaigning for greater access to parks. In 1870, the city had two parks: the first was a scruffy eight-acre common and the second, the twenty-eight-acre Elm Park, was being used as the city dump. Like wealthy New Yorkers before them, Worcester elites wanted to use an elegant landscaped park to transform their neighborhood into an exclusive residential enclave. They landscaped the park and banned active leisure pursuits. "Keep off the Grass" signs were also posted.

The tensions around leisure space in Worcester brought to the fore two distinct and conflicting defini-

tions and perceptions of the park. While the upper class emphasized passive leisure pursuits, cultural improvement, and refined manners, the working class sought active recreation in such places. While industrialists urged the city to develop parklands on the West Side for the purposes of fire protection, health, civic pride, stabilizing real estate values, and social control, working-class residents demanded leisure space for more active, play-oriented activities. The need for recreation space was so great in the burgeoning working-class communities that children resorted to playing in the streets, even though they were sometimes arrested for doing so. By 1880, East Siders began to demand their own parks, plus better maintenance of the common. In 1882, a petition drive netted the signatures of 140 workers who were requesting a "few acres of land" for "the less favored children." Petitioners declared, "There is no public ground in that vicinity [Fifth Ward—East Side] where children or young men can resort, either for health or amusement" (Rosenzweig, 1987, pp. 217–218, 220; 1983, p. 132).

Editorials in the local newspapers accused the city of siding with the West Siders and neglecting the working-class residents of the East Side. The editorials noted that open sewers ran through the neighborhoods and that cholera and diphtheria were common in the cramped quarters of the East Side. As time passed, the East Siders became more strident in their demands for a park. The lack of access to outdoor space spawned a movement of Irish working-class activists who demanded public playgrounds. They also embarked on a letter-writing campaign in the newspapers, where they complained about Elm Park. They charged that they had to stand when they visited the common because the "people's seats" had been removed from the common and placed in Elm Park, which they described as a "desolate spot where nobody will use them excepting the crows" (Rosenzweig, 1983, p. 30).

Exasperated by the stalling tactics of the city government, in 1884, the East Side representatives on the City Council used a tactic pioneered during the New York City park battles. Working-class supporters withheld their votes for park improvements in upper-class neighborhoods until parks were approved in working-class communities. The threat to block the purchase of additional parkland for the West Side worked. In 1884, a Park Act was passed, and a comprehensive park plan was developed in 1886.

The plan, however, sanctioned a scheme of dual-tract recreational development. Worcester, Massachusetts, built scenic parks on the West Side and two playgrounds on the East Side. Most of the money was spent on the parks in well-to-do neighborhoods, and people soon noted that Worcester had created a separate and unequal system of "class parks." Two playgrounds did little to ease the overcrowding in working-class neighborhoods. Demand for park space was so great that people wanting to use the baseball diamond in Crompton Park had to camp on the field overnight to secure it. By the time the second wave of ethnic groups in Worcester started to demand parks, they got minimally landscaped, barely adequate ball fields. In the late 1890s, the Swedish wireworkers of Quinsigamond Village campaigned for a playground in their village. The city finally acquiesced and purchased Greenwood Park in 1905; it was proclaimed a "park for sport," in which no special attention was paid to flowers or shrubbery. Other ethnic groups campaigned for parks as well. In 1901, the English carpet weavers petitioned for a park on College Hill.

Ironically, this discriminatory approach to park development, whereby the working class had access to fewer, poorly equipped and maintained parks, increased the level of discontent and ensured that working-class people continued to seek out and use parks in middle-class neighborhoods. Consequently, when Worcester East Siders used parks outside of their neighborhoods, the battle over proper park behavior raged unabated. In the East Side parks, working-class park behavior was, for the most part, understood, condoned, or ignored. Because of continuing class conflicts, the workers' fight for parks, and the obvious need for more open space in the city, by 1907, the parks commissioners gradually began to endorse the petitions for more public recreation space throughout the city. In 1908, voters helped to pass the Massachusetts Playground Act, which mandated that cities provide at least one playground for every 20,000 residents.

Neighborhood Park Campaigns Elsewhere

In the 1880s, merchants in the Bronx opposed what they saw as unwarranted park development, as wealthy residents campaigned for parks to anchor upscale residential development. Bronx park advocates, however, prevailed by stressing that the park would improve property values. By this time, politicians realized that they also had to pay attention to working-class demands for parks. Thus, Mayor Hewitt argued that it was the "city's duty to provide at least as many facilities for the poor as it does for the rich." Cognizant of the fact that Henry George garnered working-class support by campaigning for parks in immigrant neighborhoods, Hewitt supported plans to build parks in poor neighborhoods. Hewitt endorsed an 1887 law authorizing a million-dollar annual appropriation to build small parks in poor neighborhoods.

The campaigns in New York and Worcester influenced other cities to develop park systems. In 1890, Kansas City, Missouri, hired George Kessler to develop a complete park system. After Kessler presented the city with his report in 1893, the city began acquiring land and developing the system. Also, in 1892, the Massachusetts legislature created the Metropolitan Park Commission to develop the Greater Boston park system. By 1897, Philadelphia had constructed thirty-one playgrounds in the city. As late as 1900, however, Chicago had a woefully inadequate park infrastructure. The City Homes Association report claims that there were no parks in the tenement districts and very few in the city overall. A few vacant lots existed in working-class neighborhoods, but they were low-lying swamps filled with rubbish. In 1900, Chicago, following New York's lead, passed a resolution that all future schools had to be built with a playground.

Race and the Parks

When one analyzes park use, class and ethnic conflicts among whites were prominent from the seventeenth century to the early twentieth century. This is the case because African Americans and other minorities were not allowed to use the parks or could use them only under very restricted circumstances. During the early 1900s, however, racial conflicts erupted in parks as African Americans began demanding access to recreational spaces and using park facilities. For instance, race riots in Chicago originated when African Americans tried to use sections of beaches from which they were banned. During the 1940s and 1950s African Americans in northern cities like Gary, Indiana, linked their struggles for civil rights with efforts to integrate parks and beaches.

Conclusion

For the past 200 years Americans have invested in an extensive network of urban parks that people from a range of backgrounds can use and enjoy. These parks have emerged from the efforts of elites as well as that of the working class. The parks have evolved as park builders and users have developed mechanisms to collaborate on design, functions, and uses. Though some urban parks still struggled with issues related to funding, competing park uses, crime, and racial and ethnic conflicts, the legacy of the past two centuries of park development offered hope that those problems could be resolved and provided models to help do that.

See also: Central Park, City Parks, Leisure and Civil Society, Progressive-Era Leisure and Recreation

BIBLIOGRAPHY

Anbinder, Tyler. *Five Points: The 19th-Century New York City Neighborhood That Invented Tap Dance, Stole Elections, and Became the World's Most Notorious Slum*. New York: Free Press, 2001.

Beveridge, Charles E., and Carolyn Hoffman, eds. *The Papers of Frederick Law Olmsted, Supplementary Series, Volume 1. Writings on Public Parks, Parkways, and Park Systems*. Baltimore: Johns Hopkins University Press, 1997.

Beveridge, Charles E., and David Schuyler, eds. *The Papers of Frederick Law Olmsted, Volume 3. Creating Central Park, 1857–1961*. Baltimore: Johns Hopkins University Press, 1983.

Boyer, Paul. *Urban Masses and Moral Order in America, 1820–1920*. Cambridge, Mass.: Harvard University Press, 1978.

Bryant, William Cullen. "A New Park." *New York Evening Post*, 3 July 1844.

Burrows, Edwin G., and Mike Wallace. *Gotham: A History of New York City to 1898*. New York: Oxford University Press, 1999.

City Homes Association. *Tenement Conditions in Chicago*. Chicago: City Homes Association, 1901.

Cranz, Galen. *The Politics of Park Design: A History of Urban Parks in America*. Cambridge, Mass.: MIT Press, 1982.

Davis, Allen F. *Spearheads for Reform: The Social Settlements and the Progressive Movement: 1890–1914*. New York: Oxford University Press, 1967.

Dickason, Jerry G. "The Origin of the Playground: The Role of Boston Women's Clubs, 1885–1890." *Leisure Sciences* 8, no. 1 (1983): 83–98.

Downing, Andrew Jackson. "A Talk About Public Parks and Gardens." *Rural Essays* (October 1848): 138–146.

———. "The New York Park." *Rural Essays* (August 1851): 147–153.

Dunn, Mary Maples, and Richard S. Dunn. "The Founding, 1681–1701." In *Philadelphia: A 300-Year History*. Edited by Russell F. Weigley. New York: W. W. Norton and Company, 1982.

"The East River Park." *Journal of Commerce* (1851).

Fee, Elizabeth, Linda Shopes, and Linda Zeidman. *The Baltimore Book*. Philadelphia: Temple University Press, 1991.

George, Henry. *Progress and Poverty: An Inquiry into the Cause of Industrial Depression and of Increase of Want with the Increase of Wealth*. San Francisco: W. M. Hinton and Company, 1879. Reprint, New York: Modern Library, 1938.

Hurley, Andrew. *Environmental Inequalities: Class, Race, and Industrial Pollution in Gary, Indiana, 1945–1980*. Chapel Hill, N.C.: University of North Carolina, 1995.

McNulty, Elizabeth. *Boston Then & Now*. San Diego, Calif.: Thunder Bay Press, 1999.

Nash, Roderick. *Wilderness and the American Mind*. 3d ed. New Haven, Conn.: Yale University Press, 1982.

Olmsted, Frederick Law. "Rules and Conditions of Service of the Central Park Keepers." *Frederick Law Olmsted Papers*. Washington, D.C.: Library of Congress, 1859.

———. "Preliminary Report Upon the Yosemite and Big Tree Grove." *Frederic Law Olmsted Papers*. Washington, D.C.: Library of Congress, 1865.

———. "Preliminary Report to the Commissioners for Laying Out a Park in Brooklyn, New York: Being a Consideration of Circumstances and Site and Other Conditions Affecting the Design of Public Pleasure Grounds." *Frederick Law Olmsted Papers*. Brooklyn, N.Y.: Board of Commissioners of Prospect Park, 1866.

———. "Report on the Proposed City Park." *Frederick Law Olmsted Papers*. Washington, D.C.: Library of Congress, 1868.

———. "Letter to the Board of Park Commissioners of the Borough of New Britain, Conn." *Frederick Law Olmsted Papers*. Washington, D.C.: Library of Congress, 23 March 1870.

———. "Report Accompanying Plan for Laying Out the South Park, Chicago South Park Commission." *Frederick Law Olmsted Papers*. Washington, D.C.: Library of Congress, 1871.

Olson, Sherry H. *Baltimore: The Building of an American City*. Baltimore: Johns Hopkins University Press, 1997.

"The Proposed Great Park." *Journal of Commerce* (1851).

Roper, Laura Wood. *FLO: A Biography of Frederick Law Olmsted*. Baltimore: Johns Hopkins University Press, 1973.

Rosenzweig, Roy. *Eight Hours for What We Will: Workers and Leisure in an Industrial City, 1870–1920*. Cambridge, U.K.: Cambridge University Press, 1983.

———. "Middle-Class Parks and Working-Class Play: The Struggle Over Recreational Space in Worcester, Massachusetts, 1870–1910." In *The New England Working Class and the New Labor History*. Edited by Herbert G. Gutman and Donald H. Bell. Urbana: University of Illinois Press, 1987.

Rosenzweig, Roy, and Elizabeth Blackmar. *The Park and the People: A History of Central Park*. Ithaca, N.Y.: Cornell University Press, 1992.

Schuyler, David. *The New Urban Landscape: The Redefinition of City Form in Nineteenth-Century America*. Baltimore: Johns Hopkins University Press, 1986.

Schuyler, David, and Jane Turner Censer. *The Papers of Frederick Law Olmsted: The Years of Olmsted, Vaux and Company*. Volume 6. Baltimore: Johns Hopkins University Press, 1992.

Shand-Tucci, Douglass. *Built in Boston: City and Suburb, 1800–2000*. Cambridge, Mass.: MIT Press, 1999.

Spann, Edward K. *The New Metropolis: New York City, 1840–1857*. New York: Columbia University Press, 1981.

Taylor, Dorceta E. "Central Park as a Model for Social Control: Urban Parks, Social Class and Leisure Behavior in Nineteenth-Century America." *Journal of Leisure Research* 31, no. 4 (1999): 420–477.

———. "The Urban Environment: The Intersection of White Middle Class and White Working Class Environmentalism, 1820–1950s." *Advances in Human Ecology* 7 (1998): 207–292.

Thayer, Theodore. "Town into City, 1746–1765." In *Philadelphia: A 300-Year History*. Edited by Russell F. Weigley. New York: W. W. Norton and Company, 1982.

Tuttle, William M. *Race Riot: Chicago in the Red Summer of 1919*. New York: Atheneum, 1980.

Dorceta E. Taylor

PARKS

See *Central Park; City Parks; National Parks; Parks Movement; State Parks*

PATRIOTISM AND LEISURE

Patriotism and leisure have deep connections in the United States. John Adams, exhilarated by the passage of the Declaration of Independence in 1776, wrote to his wife Abigail that the new nation would henceforth commemorate Independence Day (which Adams regarded as 2 July but quickly became 4 July) with a "Great Anniversary Festival." Adams ruminated that Independence Day "ought to be solemnized with pomp and parade, with shows, games, sports, guns, bells, bonfires, and illuminations, from one end of this continent to the other from this time forward evermore" (p. 2–30). The original Fourth of July rites were based on the slightly older revolutionary customs that developed during the colonial Stamp Act protests, which were in turn part of a Western tradition of festivals with deep cultural and political meanings that dated to the Middle Ages.

Crafting a Patriotic Calendar

Fourth of July became the original national holiday celebrated in the new United States. As Adams wished, Independence Days were filled with tolling liberty bells, flamboyant orations, ornate parades, enormous bonfires, sparkling fireworks, crackling gunfire, and, increasingly, sports and games. These practices laid the groundwork for the creation of a national calendar of pageants and pastimes that cemented the links between patriotism and leisure in American culture. Holidays such as Independence Day, Thanksgiving Day, Memorial Day, and Labor Day have blended with leisure practices, from summer picnics to autumn football seasons to winter feasts to springtime renewals of baseball, providing Americans

with annual rituals for celebrating and contesting the meanings of nationhood and citizenship.

The patriotic leisure calendar offers Americans opportunities to share collective memories and occasions to express national, regional, and local identities. Sometimes these annual rituals express unity and solidarity. At other times they highlight conflicting ideas of nationalism. Born as a symbol of rebellion against an established political order, Fourth of July has been used to defy as well as to glorify. Partisan bickering, sectional hostilities, and eruptions of violence frequently marked Independence Day carnivals. In 1903, the *Journal of the American Medical Association* began to keep Fourth of July casualty counts. In 1909, middle-class reformers in the Playground Association of America developed a "Safe and Sane" Independence Day campaign that pushed the urban masses to celebrate the Fourth through sports or commercial recreations rather than with gunfire, bonfires, and alcohol. Working-class communities resisted the sanitized Fourth of July rites and continued to use Independence Day festivities to express dissatisfactions with the political economy.

Patriotic Shows and Tours

Like the Fourth of July, patriotic holidays and leisure practices frequently reflect class, ethnic, and religious differences in American society. Social tensions invade not only holiday parades but also the other entertainments that John Adams had predicted would become the core of patriotic leisure practices. Historical reenactments of famous battles, particularly Civil War engagements, often provide competing regional interpretations of national histories. Wild West shows, rodeos, heritage pageants, carnivals, local and state fairs, and other festivals reflect both national and regional patterns in American patriotic leisure customs. Among the most nationalistic of American shows were world's fairs and international expositions. During the heyday of international expositions, from the 1876 World's Fair in Philadelphia celebrating the centennial of the Declaration of Independence through the 1939 World's Fair in New York City, fairs offered the United States venues for competing against the rest of the world's nations. Beginning in 1896, the modern Olympic Games, modeled in part on the exposition format, provided the United States with an additional opportunity for national measurements. Expositions in this era garnered enormous media attention and drew millions of visitors. American displays at fairs were frequently financed and controlled by the federal government in an effort to present a unified national culture. Still, regionalism sometimes shaped American fairs. Urban boosters in Chicago in 1893 and St. Louis in 1904 staged competing world's fairs that were in part designed to convince the nation that their respective metropolis was the leading city in the booming Middle West. As an added attraction in its battle against Chicago, the St. Louis Exposition staged the first Olympic Games held in the United States.

In the second half of the nineteenth century and the first half of the twentieth century, expositions drew large numbers of American tourists to patriotic displays. During the same period, first the railroad and then the automobile made pilgrimages to historic sites a significant part of patriotic leisure. George Washington's home at Mount Vernon, Virginia, was the first national tourist magnet, drawing large numbers of visitors beginning in the 1850s. Other historic sites developed quickly thereafter, including Philadelphia's Independence Hall, Abraham Lincoln's tomb in Illinois, Thomas Jefferson's estate in Monticello, Virginia, and Revolutionary War and Civil War battlefields. In the late nineteenth and twentieth centuries, Washington, D.C., developed the world's largest collection of national monuments, museums, and galleries, transforming the nation's capital into the most important stop on the patriotic travel circuit. In spite of the memorial-building boom in Washington, the United States generally lacked the traditional European architectural monuments to high culture. The nation turned to natural landscapes to highlight American exceptionalism. The dramatic vistas of the American West especially captured patriotic fancy. The federal government set aside some of the nation's most spectacular terrain as national monuments, beginning with Yellowstone in 1872 and Yosemite in 1890. Most Americans imbibed landscapes from a distance until the 1920s, when outdoor recreation boomed as the automobile opened the nation's vast spaces to common folk. American vistas have always rivaled historic monuments as sites for patriotic leisure.

Patriotic Consumption of Alcohol and Sport

Americans reveled in nationhood through the consumption of both liquor and tourist experiences. In the early republic, patriotic celebrations were frequently fueled by alcohol. A republican drinking culture, committed to egalitarian quaffing and characterized by numerous patriotic toasts to health of the new nation, flourished in antebellum taverns. All men, according to dictums of these drinking practices, were truly equal when they were besotted in saloons. For many Americans, Fourth of July carnivals and other national holidays became bacchanals devoted to drunken revelry.

Alcohol soaked other patriotic leisure-time activities. In saloons and other male hangouts, a sporting fraternity, as the contemporaries labeled it, gathered to imbibe, gamble, and consume sports such as billiards, darts, cards, rat baits (a gambling spectacle that pitted dogs, and occasionally humans, in contests to determine how quickly they could dispatch rodents), pedestrianism (a professional form of foot racing), rowing, horse racing, and, especially, prizefighting. The games of the sporting fraternity were part of a thriving international commerce in spectator sports in the Anglo-American world. For the sporting fraternity's loyal members, sports served as fulcrum for the smelting of class, ethnic, regional, and national identities. Prize-ring battles highlighted the class, ethnic, and national tensions roiling the rapidly urbanizing and industrializing Great Britain and the United States. Early bare-knuckle champions embodied the complexities of national identity in the era. An Irish immigrant brawler who took the ring name Yankee Sullivan personified both his new American loyalties and his ties to his old homeland. Yankee Sullivan was the first of many American sporting celebrities who symbolically mixed both Americanism and immigrant pride.

In the late nineteenth and twentieth centuries, as prizefighting was homogenized from a folk rite into a mass spectacle, it continued to serve as both a patriotic tableau and an arena for showcasing conflicting loyalties. On the Fourth of July in 1910, African American champion Jack Johnson whipped "great white hope" challenger James J. Jeffries in a highly publicized fight. Several days of race riots and lynchings ensued as white Americans reacted to Johnson's symbolic threat to their supremacy. Throughout the twentieth century, the prize ring continued to offer pugilistic dramas of racial and national identities. During the 1930s, Joe Louis became a national hero for black and white Americans in his epic bouts against Nazi Germany's Max Schmeling. In the 1960s and 1970s, Muhammad Ali became a polarizing national figure, beloved by some and reviled by others, for his role in the Vietnam War, racial relations, and other national issues.

Constructing a National Pastime

While prizefighting for two centuries illuminated struggles to define American identities, it never garnered the broad social acceptance necessary to rank as a truly national pastime. As a popular countercultural rejection of mainstream bourgeois values, prizefighting remained beyond the pale of middle-class sensibilities. Americans adopted other leisure pursuits as their national pastimes, first and foremost baseball. Baseball developed during the 1840s and 1850s in the nation's industrial and urban heartlands, especially in New York City. Early boosters promoted the provincial game as a patriotic force. The Civil War and the nationalizing processes it unleashed transformed baseball. Spreading rapidly to the West and the South, baseball served as an important postwar symbol of national reconciliation. The game quickly evolved from a regional recreation into a cultural force that merited its self-proclaimed label as the national pastime.

Baseball became a mainstay of Fourth of July celebrations in postwar North and South, in small towns and big cities. Patriotic passions infused the game throughout the rest of the season as well. In 1876, the centennial year of American independence, entrepreneurs founded the National League, and major league baseball cemented its position at the center of patriotic American leisure. Quickly thereafter, baseball's boosters engaged in a nationalistic crusade to make the game entirely American and distance it from the British folk-sporting traditions that actually spawned it. Beginning in the 1880s, Americans started to claim that baseball had no British lineage whatsoever. In 1907, a commission sponsored by the leading promoter of American baseball, Albert Goodwill Spalding, created an origin myth that freed the game from any British connections. However dubious the evidence and fabricated the history, Americans cherished the tale. In 1939, for baseball's alleged centennial, major league magnates built a national shrine to the game in its mythical hometown of Cooperstown, New York. The Hall of Fame, filled with the diamond's American heroes, draws hordes of pilgrims who venerate the legends of the nation's original national pastime.

From the end of the nineteenth century through the middle of the twentieth century, baseball enjoyed an unchallenged position as America's national pastime. Patriotism regularly infused the spectacle. Singing the national anthem before games was a common practice that was institutionalized in the second decade of the twentieth century. Since 1910, when William Howard Taft began the tradition, American presidents have opened the season by throwing out the first ball. During world wars and economic depressions, presidents urged the major leagues to keep playing in order to bolster national morale. The World Series, begun in 1903, became a season-ending national event in the patriotic calendar, complete with stadiums wrapped in red, white, and blue bunting. American folklore even claimed that exciting World Series delayed the deliberations of the U.S. Supreme Court. In the musings of foreign observers of the national condition and native crafters of popular culture, baseball became synonymous with Americanness.

As baseball wrapped itself in patriotic iconography and became the nation's favorite amusement, it swamped older ethnic and regional pastimes. For new immigrants, playing and watching baseball became a path for joining the American mainstream. In the nineteenth century, some ethnic groups used leisure practices to maintain older traditions. English cricket clubs, Scottish Caledonian clubs, Irish Hibernian societies, German *Turnverein* (clubs dedicated to promoting German gymnastics and national pride), and other ethnic sport clubs dotted the American landscape. They were eventually swallowed by baseball and other native sports as immigrants, by choice or coercion, adopted American recreational habits.

Inventing New National Pastimes

By the twentieth century, sports were embedded in celebrations of national holidays. Memorial Day, originally devised to remember those who had given their lives in the nation's bloodiest conflict, provided a holiday weekend centered on sporting events. Since 1911, the Indianapolis 500 automobile race has been a Memorial Day weekend institution. Tennis matches, golf tournaments, triathlon races, rodeos, and every manner of sports sprout on days that were originally devoted to the veneration of national memories. Sports have also become a staple feature of the American patriotic calendar, creating an annual athletic cycle that supplements holiday traditions.

One of the key events in the sporting calendar occurred quadrennially rather than annually. The creation of the modern Olympic Games in 1896 provided Americans with an international stage to tout American exceptionalism. Patriotic trappings—flags; anthems; red, white, and blue uniforms; Uncle Sam caricatures—have adorned American teams. Beginning in 1908, when the U.S. flag bearer at the opening ceremonies in London ignored international protocol and refused to dip the stars and stripes to the English king, jingoistic displays have been a regular feature of American Olympic performances. The tradition of refusing to dip the flag in the Olympic parade of nations, initially an irregular practice that generated foreign condemnations of American manners, became firmly entrenched at the 1936 "Nazi" Olympics in Berlin. Thereafter, American teams have paraded before the world with their patriotism on full display.

At home, two games developed in the late nineteenth century emerged by the mid-twentieth century as baseball's partners in an American trinity of patriotic national sports. The American version of football, adapted from English rugby in the 1870s and Americanized, as baseball had been, to remove the taint of British origins, became a thriving national spectacle. By the end of the nineteenth

Dearborn, Michigan, Memorial Day parade. On 26 May, 2003 the seventy-ninth annual Dearborn Memorial Day parade drew a large crowd proudly waving American flags in commemoration of those lost to war. The event is the longest-running in the state of Michigan and actually was established five years prior to the creation of the city. © *Paul Warner for AP/Wide World Photos*

century intercollegiate and interscholastic football were enmeshed in the patriotic pageantry of Thanksgiving Day. Thanksgiving tilts in New York City between Yale and Princeton drew such large crowds that churches moved services from afternoons to mornings to accommodate the big game craze. "Thanksgiving Day is no longer a solemn festival to God for mercies given," observed the *New York Herald Tribune* in 1893; "it is a holiday granted by the state and the nation to see a game of football." The late-autumn harvest rite that dated to New England's Pilgrims would never be the same after it was swallowed by patriotic leisure.

The American South initially resisted the celebration of Thanksgiving, a holiday nationalized in 1863 by Abraham Lincoln to solemnize the sacrifices required to preserve the Union. Southerners, however, quickly adopted intercollegiate football. By the early twentieth century southern teams played hugely popular intersectional contests against northern and western squads that the south-

ern press and fans viewed as chances to redeem southern honor from the miasma of the "Lost Cause." College football served as a popular spectacle that allowed American cities, towns, and regions to compete for prestige on a national stage. If baseball was the original national pastime, then football was a new venue that allowed regions to assert their own identities in a national contest for prestige. Football became the autumnal counterpart of spring and summer baseball in the seasonal fabric of patriotic American leisure.

After World War II, television transformed the American leisure landscape. In the television era, baseball declined in relative popularity. Football's hold on the national imagination has grown. Professional football has boomed since the 1950s, rivaling the college and high school variants for public attention. Baseball's World Series remains a nostalgic fortnight of patriotic display, but college football's season-concluding bowl games and professional football's climactic Super Bowl draw much larger television audiences. Indeed Super Bowl Sunday has become in American popular culture an unofficial national holiday wrapped in patriotic rites that rival those of Memorial Day, Thanksgiving, and even Independence Day.

Basketball formed the third component of the American trinity of national games. Unlike baseball or football, basketball can honestly claim a wholly American birth, coming to life at the YMCA's Springfield College in 1891—although a Canadian, James Naismith, crafted the original set of rules. The U.S. branch of the YMCA initially promoted the game as a missionary tool to spread the gospels of evangelical Christianity and Americanism at home and abroad. Boosters pitched basketball as the perfect vehicle for teaching efficient teamwork and good citizenship in modern societies. By the mid-twentieth century basketball had joined baseball and football, filling the winter months in the national calendar of patriotic pastimes.

Of the three major American national pastimes, basketball spread the most widely throughout the world. By the end of the twentieth century, basketball was in terms of both participation and spectatorship the world's second most popular sport—behind only soccer. The game's biggest star, Michael Jordan, reigned as the most recognizable person on the planet and served as a major commercial force hawking Nike shoes and other products in a thriving global consumer culture. Jordan, who Chinese school children in a poll during the 1990s ranked as the second most important historical figure in world history behind revolutionary leader Zhou Enlai, symbolized the dominance of American culture and leisure goods in this new world system.

Jordan's global profile sprang from a combination of marketing strategies and patriotic zeal. After a U.S. basketball team consisting of collegians lost to the Soviets and finished third in the 1988 Olympics in Seoul—only the second loss in Olympic history for an American team—public demands to reclaim American pride merged with corporate desires to acquire bigger market shares and paved the way for Jordan and his professional "Dream Team" comrades to dominate future Olympic competitions. The "Dream Team" debuted at the 1992 Olympics in Barcelona, launching the U.S.-based National Basketball Association into global markets. On the victory stand to receive their gold medals after dispatching their overmatched rivals, Jordan and fellow Nike pitchman Charles Barkley used American flags to hide the Reebok (a major competitor of Nike in international sporting goods wars) labels on their warm-ups.

By the end of the twentieth century, as Michael Jordan's global fame highlighted, American-style consumption of leisure had spread throughout the world. Patriotic leisure in American society had evolved from the consumption of folk cultural practices to modern cultural products, as the department store–sponsored parades, furniture sales, and television-produced sports that littered patriotic holiday landscapes testified. The consumption of leisure, in either folk or mass form, links past and present in the history of American patriotic leisure. American patriotic leisure practices had from the beginnings of the republic been intertwined with patterns of consumption. Indeed John Adams's original cry in 1776 for a "great annual festival" of patriotism commanded citizens to consume folk leisure traditions as certainly as Fourth of July automobile sales in the early twenty-first century beckon Americans to make patriotic purchases. Leisure, consumption, and patriotism remain firmly entwined in the United States.

See also: Fourth of July; Memorial Day; Labor Day; Olympics; Thanksgiving; Tourism

BIBLIOGRAPHY

Adams, John. *The Adams Family Correspondence.* 6 volumes. Edited by L. H. Butterfield, Wendell D. Garrett, and Marjorie E. Sprague. Cambridge, Mass.: Harvard University Press, 1963–1993.

Daniels, Matthew. *Red, White, and Blue Letter Days: An American Calendar.* Ithaca, N.Y.: Cornell University Press, 2002.

Dyreson, Mark. *Making the American Team: Sport, Culture, and the Olympic Experience.* Urbana: University of Illinois Press, 1998.

Gorn, Elliott J. *The Manly Art, Bare-Knuckle Prize Fighting in America.* Ithaca, N.Y.: Cornell University Press, 1986.

LaFeber, Walter. *Michael Jordan and the New Global Capitalism.* New York: W. W. Norton and Company, 1999.

Levine, Peter. *A.G. Spalding and the Rise of Baseball: The Promise of American Sport.* New York: Oxford University Press, 1985.

Oriard, Michael. *King Football: Sport and Spectacle in the Golden Age of Radio and Newsreels, Movies and Magazines, the Weekly and Daily Press.* Chapel Hill: University of North Carolina Press, 2001.

"Princeton's Great Victory." *New York Herald* (1 December 1893): p. 3.

Pope, S. W. *Patriotic Games: Sporting Traditions in the American Imagination, 1876–1926.* New York: Oxford University Press, 1997.

Rader, Benjamin. *American Sports: From the Age of Folk Games to the Age of Televised Sports,* 5th edition. Englewood Cliffs, N.J.: Prentice-Hall, 2001.

Roberts, Randy. *Papa Jack: Jack Johnson and the Era of White Hope.* New York: Free Press, 1983.

Rorabaugh, W. J. *The Alcoholic Republic: An American Tradition.* New York: Oxford University Press, 1979.

Rydell, Robert. *All the World's a Fair: Visions of Empire at American International Expositions, 1876–1916.* Chicago: University of Chicago Press, 1984.

Smith, Ronald A. *Sports and Freedom: The Rise of Big-Time College Athletics.* New York: Oxford University Press, 1988.

Travers, Len. *Celebrating the Fourth: Independence Day and the Rites of Nationalism in the Early Republic.* Amherst: University of Massachusetts Press, 1997.

Zelinsky, Wilbur. *Nation into State: The Shifting Symbolic Foundations of American Nationalism.* Chapel Hill: University of North Carolina Press, 1988.

Mark Dyreson

PERFORMING ARTS AUDIENCES

Following the American Revolution, performing arts audiences fell under the worried eye of American elites. The elites feared social disorder from active "degenerate" and unruly people, and, consequently, felt the need to control audiences. Audience prerogatives included the right to call for tunes, chastise performers and managers, hiss, shout, and throw things. Rowdiness in the past had turned to violence when audiences felt insulted or protested against English performers. During the Jacksonian era in the 1830s and 1840s, the upper classes feared that working-class audience sovereignty—rowdyism—might be applied to larger economic and political issues.

Profitability led some performing arts entrepreneurs to cater to middle-class clientele and respectability. This meant quiet, polite, passive audiences, and measures to attract women to their theaters. Marginalized "small time" entertainment sought the patronage of rowdy audiences. The minstrelsy variety show, with unrelated acts of whites portraying black song and dance, and low-brow comedy became respectable in vaudeville in 1880. At the turn of the century, "ten-twenty-thirty" theaters charging ten, twenty, or thirty cents admission, featured melodrama for the working class. Managers prohibited vocal and rowdy behavior by such tactics as bolting chairs to the floor and darkening theaters. Segmented markets served different social classes and purposes. Performing arts events were places for the elite to be seen, and they exhibited only intermittent attention to the entertainment.

Twentieth-century critics feared audience passivity—unquestioning acceptance of the entertainment's message. Proscenium stages held sway until the avant-garde developed theater in the round, and productions in which the boundaries between performer and spectator dissolved. For example, in one production of "Mother Courage" by the Performance Group in New York in the mid-1970s, spectators followed performers through the theater space and actually ate soup with them.

Attending performing arts events (such as plays, classical music, opera, musicals, jazz, ballet, striptease, other forms of dance, pantomime, and figure ice skating) is usually a person's recreational choice. Venues vary from theaters and opera houses, universities and colleges, and churches, to nightclubs and town squares, and to holiday camps, hospitals, and prisons. In the nonprofit arena, educational institutions in the late twentieth and early twenty-first centuries were the most prevalent performing arts venues. The 1997 Survey of Public Participation in the Arts demonstrated that the arts were very popular in the United States: 442,300,000 visits were made during that year. The Rand Corporation's 2001 studies support the survey.

Performing arts participation is not only an individual's decision driven by personal attributes and experiences; one's social situation also plays a role. In a marital relationship, men are likely to attend performing arts activities if their wives do, although women also attend without their husbands. Sometimes young people are brought to performing arts activities for educational purposes, and people occasionally attend the performing arts because of social expectation or pressure. There are performing arts programs for different ages, genders, sexual orientations, and ethnic groups, although most programs have a wide appeal that crosses these distinctions.

The role of the audience in performing arts productions is to keep these arts alive through attendance and support. There are special festival and subscription series, as well as one-time packages, of which audience members can take advantage while simultaneously generating financial and community support for the arts. Some audience members become patrons, contributing significant monetary support that is essential for the noncommercial performing arts. More than money, however, is involved in supporting the arts. Some spectators volunteer their help (working as a ticket taker, for example) for specific performing arts groups or venues. Arts groups also perform in schools to build audiences and to attract potential performers.

Audiences may support professionals and nonprofessional amateurs in the performing arts. Amateur dancers are estimated to outnumber professionals by a factor of twenty or thirty to one, and their performances attract audiences comprised of family and friends, as well as the interested public.

Ethnic and national groups perform for their own members, as well as others, as a way to mark identity, preserve their heritage, and promote the collectivity. Authentic folk dances may be free of theatrical staging. Audiences for professional ethnic and national dance companies, such as the Moiseyev Dance Company, attract a wider population among outsiders.

Audiences have antecedent and contextual factors. Over the years, studies report that higher education, family, camp, or school support of attendance or classes in the performing arts as a child, understanding, and motivation (affected by cost, availability, access, and scheduling) promote participation in the performing arts. The performing arts for children are learning experiences that stimulate imagination and provide entertainment. Those who had more arts education were more likely to attend arts performances, a relationship that is about four times stronger than that of any other factor considered. To find out what promotes participation in the arts, researchers use phone and mail surveys, focus groups, panels, and census data. For the National Endowment for the Arts 1997 Survey of Public Participation in the Arts, 12,349 telephone interviews of a nationally representative sample were conducted.

The central issue that arts organizations face in designing audience engagement strategies is deciding which available tactics are appropriate for different target populations and when they should be used. Most respondents to the National Endowment for the Arts survey learned about a particular art event from a friend, neighbor, relative or co-worker. Newspapers were the next most common source.

Women attended arts events at higher rates and had higher distributions among arts audiences than men did. Whites generally had the highest arts participation rates. There were, nonetheless, exceptions to this pattern. At 15.6 percent, African Americans, for instance, had the highest attendance for live jazz musical performances. Opera was most popular among Asians (6.9 percent), and Hispanics attended dance performances other than ballet at the highest rates (14.6 percent). Adults who have had some college education comprised the largest percentage of every live arts event.

Of the ten most populated states (California, Florida, Illinois, Massachusetts, Michigan, New Jersey, New York, Ohio, Pennsylvania, and Texas), New York, Massachusetts, and New Jersey had comparatively higher performing arts audience participation rates.

Ballet is relatively more likely to be presented in small cities and rural areas than other dance genres, whereas wider opportunities are available in cities. Urban areas have more activities because there is the critical population mass to support them. Yet audiences flock to warhorses such as the staples *The Nutcracker, Riverdance,* and *Tango Argentina* in dance.

Classical music and opera are underrepresented among the youngest adults. Younger performing arts audiences are more likely to be found at ballet performances, jazz, and plays.

Although many people participate in both the "high art" and "popular culture" performing arts, there are some distinct audiences. Interviewed attendees felt the high arts, including ballet, opera, and symphony, were elevated, influential, and inspiring. Non-attendees, by contrast, felt that these arts were too formal, stuffy, difficult, heavy, expensive, and arty. Popular arts were felt by their attendees to be fun, stimulating, laid-back, informal, fashionable, and approved. Non-attendees felt that they were crowded, superficial, and expensive. Popular arts stand for modernity, however, and are borrowed and transformed into part of high culture performing arts. Popular arts should even be seen to include the approximately 3,000 exotic dance (striptease, nude) adult nightclubs in the United States. They attract about 1.5 million visitors per day, who spend a total of $550 million per year. The average guest at exotic dance locales is a male, between twenty-one and forty-five years of age, who spends about $150 per visit.

The number of Americans attending live performances has been growing over the years. Nonetheless, the most dramatic growth has been in the market for recorded performances—television and videotapes/DVDs. Deterrents to being a live audience member include formal and forbidding buildings that are difficult to navigate or are located in high-crime areas; travel and transportation (distance, cost of parking); lack of information; culturally-specific language; cost; lack of time; availability of an art form; cramped seating and distractions caused by coughing or other audience noises; and fear of not understanding the performance. Despite these obstacles, it is certain that the performing arts will continue to find an audience—be it for a live or a recorded performance—for many years to come.

See also: Amateur Theatrics; Choral Singing; Country Music Audiences; Leisure Class; Rap Music Audiences; Rock Concert Audiences; Theater, Live

BIBLIOGRAPHY

Butsch, Richard. *The Making of American Audiences: From Stage to Television, 1750–1990.* New York: Cambridge University Press, 2000.

McCarthy, Kevin, Arthur Brooks, Julia Lowell, and Laura Zakaras. *The Performing Arts in a New Era.* Santa Monica, Calif.: Rand Corporation, 2001.

McCarthy, Kevin, and Kimberly Jinnett. *A New Framework for Building Participation in the Arts.* Santa Monica, Calif.: Rand Corporation, 2001.

Millman, Ann, and Steve Wolff. "Arts Unbound." Presentation at the International Society for the Performing Arts Foundation. Annual Conference, New York, 1996.

National Endowment for the Arts Research Division, Report #36. *Effects of Arts Education on Participation in the Arts,* Washington, D.C.: National Endowment for the Arts, 1996.

National Endowment for the Arts Research Division, Report #39. *1997 Survey of Public Participation in the Arts* (Summary Report). Washington, D.C.: National Endowment for the Arts,1998.

National Endowment for the Arts Research Division, Note #71. *Demographic Characteristics of Arts Attendance: 1997.* Washington, D.C.: National Endowment for the Arts, January 1999.

Judith Lynne Hanna

PET CARE

In its survey for 2003–2004, the American Pet Products Association found that more than 60 percent of American households kept animals as pets or had recently done so. More Americans keep pets than play golf, fish, garden, or go to church. Yet until the 1970s, little was known about either the history or the impact of pet keeping.

What is a "pet," anyway? Despite the efforts of animal-welfare organizations to replace the word with "companion animal," pet is the word most people use. Rooted in the French *petit,* the word "pet" is ambiguous, like the status of the animals themselves, for pets are not simply companions. Some pets are living objects of art ornamenting their owners' living spaces; others are ambulatory status symbols, or hobbies, or child substitutes—or some combination of all of the above. Social critics have argued that pet keeping is confined to prosperous Western, industrial societies, but in fact pets turn up repeatedly in the world historical record, in both complex and simple societies, from ancient China to the indigenous peoples of North and South America. Pet keeping in America is distinctive from these examples, however,

because it is the only kind of routine, hands-on contact almost all Americans have with living animals. Pet animals are the mirrors and the beneficiaries, or sometimes victims, of people's ideas about themselves and each other.

The history of pet keeping is an important part of the larger history of everyday life. It is connected to changing ideas about human nature and evolving conceptions of individual responsibility and the obligations of stewardship to all kinds of dependent beings, including people. Pet keeping is part of the history of family life in America, and it speaks to the history of social class and changing understandings of gender roles. It is linked to the industrial and commercial development of the United States and its evolution into a nation of consumers. It is even an aspect of urban history with the development of municipal animal-control and anti-cruelty law enforcement.

Although most animals were raised for their muscle power or the materials their bodies provided, some colonists kept dogs, cage birds, cats, and other animals for the purposes of delight and companionship. Cage birds were the most popular and coveted pets, since their songs provided company and cheer in silent rooms. Not everyone who kept a pet was wealthy or white, however. Indigenous peoples had long used dogs as pack animals and hunters but they also valued them as companions. In 1790s Philadelphia, both the well-to-do family of Elizabeth Sandwith Drinker and her free African American neighbor across the alley were both "fond" of pets.

While no statistics are available, pet keeping seems to have become more popular by the early nineteenth century, a trend that continued to the early 2000s. By around 1800, pets were associated with the extended childhood enjoyed by increasing numbers of children. Adults also sought the companionship and diversion of canaries (sold along the Erie Canal by the late 1820s), goldfish, and family cats and dogs; by the 1840s, thousands were involved with "fancy breeding" of ornamental birds; by the 1870s, the purebred dog craze of England had arrived in the United States. Different definitions of appropriate pet care sometimes led to class conflict. This was the case when elite New Yorkers prevailed upon the city government in the 1820s to use dogcatchers in working-class neighborhoods where pets were routinely allowed to wander, in part because they could scare up their own food in the streets. "Dog cart riots" were the result, as working-class residents attacked the dog catchers and freed their animals.

By the mid-nineteenth century, having multiple pets, caring for them intensively by providing special food and

Westminster Kennel Club. A judge presides over the first day of the two-day Westminster Kennel Club dog show (held annually since 1877) on 10 February 2003 in New York City's Madison Square Garden. He is evaluating Shiba Inu dogs held by handlers as part of the four groups of dogs (working, terrier, toy, and nonsporting) that competed for the "Best of Group" title that day. Sporting, hound, and herding dogs follow on the second day. © *Teru Iwasaki for AP/Wide World Photos*

medicines, and "civilizing" them through training became another characteristic of respectable family life. What changed? Some Americans had long been drawn to pets simply as sources of delight and did not link their presence to ethical or social questions, and this certainly remained the case. But society did not actively encourage the practice until a distinctive middle-class culture coalesced in the United States during the first half of the nineteenth century. With that development, kindness to animals began to be generally accepted as an important attribute of good character. Especially in the northeastern United States, popular understanding of the place of animals in the household reflected changing ideas about the nature of good family relationships and the importance of family life as a medium for creating good citizens. Animals became "dependents," grouped with children, the aged, and family servants; like people, their value could not be defined either solely or primarily in economic terms. Some parents used pets as one medium for socializing children into the stewardship of responsible adulthood. Further, sensitized people were increasingly disposed to see selected animals as emotional, and even moral, beings, entitled not only to an absence of pain and suffering but to actual well-being. These ideas laid the groundwork for the rise of organized animal welfare work in the late 1860s, but they also led to a broadly accepted ethic of kindness to animals that remains in place in the early 2000s.

Yet this new pet keeping coexisted with longstanding and highly visible uses of animals as workers and the source of both food and raw materials in towns and cities. People were accustomed to negotiating what may appear as contradictions in their relationships with animals as part of the common sense of everyday life. For example, many families named and cared for dairy cows with kindness and even affection, but this did not prevent them from selling off or killing the calves born each spring. The new domestic ethic of kindness to animals that encouraged pet keeping grafted changing ideas about human relations to animals onto this existing set of understandings. In fact, through its emphasis on the individual animal, the individual household, and the individual heart as the frontline for creating a good society, nineteenth-century understanding of the dynamics of animal-human bonds may have inhibited the development of a more comprehensive critique of animal treatment in a rough-and-tumble industrializing society. Even the treatment of animals commonly kept as pets, particularly cats and dogs, was marked by contradictory behavior. The status of the pet was granted by people, and it could be taken away as creatures were neglected or abandoned, or the decision made to euthanize "nuisance" animals.

As with many other parts of American life, sentiment and status concerns were bound together with commerce in the development of a market for purebred animals, the development of specialized supplies and equipment, and the rise of a "pet industry" by the end of the nineteenth century. The European "dog fancy" arrived in the 1870s, although American Kennel Club (1884) registrations for purebred did not top 10,000 until 1906. (Registrations in 2002 numbered 958,503.) The experience of pet keeping was elaborated as pet owners with spending money were encouraged to buy animal novelties such as white mice and tropical fish, to feed their pets special foods, to treat their ailments with medicines designed for the purpose, and to foster play and exercise. Commercial cage-bird foods were the first pet foods in the 1840s; dog food arrived in the United States from England in the 1870s, although it did not capture the majority of pet owners until the 1940s. After 1945, buoyed by new prosperity but underpinned by what were, in essence, nineteenth century arguments for its beneficial qualities, Americans became increasingly involved with pet keeping and spent more of their discretionary income on it, leading to an annual expenditure of $33 billion-plus commerce in animals, products, and services in the early twenty-first century. By 2001, 13,353 veterinary practices were devoted to small animals exclusively, and "high-tech" medicine for pets includes many of the techniques used people, from diagnostic MRIs to joint replacement surgery.

Most other uses of animals have become invisible in everyday life, and pet keeping has become the emblematic relationship between modern Americans and animals. Since the early 1980s, research has suggested that contact with pet animals is good for people; a cat resting on one's lap can reduce blood pressure, and live-in or visiting pets are used as one way to combat the boredom or depression of nursing home residents. A large professional organization, the Delta Society (founded 1978) is dedicated exclusively to all forms of "animal-assisted therapies," most of which involve the species of animals commonly kept as pets. The show *The Planet's Funniest Animals*, on the cable station "Animal Planet," depicts the pleasure pet owners take from their animal companions.

Contact with humans may not be equally good for them, however: abuse and neglect of pets is strongly associated with other forms of family dysfunction and violence. Even purebred dogs and cats are the victims of human carelessness, as poor breeding practices have resulted in increasing rates of genetic disease, the most common of which is the familiar problem of large dogs, hip displasia. The Humane Society of the United States estimates that, each year, 6 to 8 million dogs and cats are turned over to shelters; half are euthanized after failing to be adopted. Exotic pets, including reptiles and parrots, are still sometimes smuggled from their native habitats, or they are bred for sale in less-than-ideal conditions. Like the life trajectories of ordinary Americans, the life stories of America's pets are marked by the increasing importance of consumer goods, the increasing complexity and expense of medical care, and by the successes and failures of modern family life.

See also: Zoos

BIBLIOGRAPHY

Arluke, Arnold. *Brute Force: Policing Animal Cruelty.* West Lafayette, Ind.: Purdue University Press, 2004.

Arluke, Arnold, and Clinton R. Sanders. *Regarding Animals.* Philadelphia: Temple University Press, 1996.

Grier, Katherine C. *Pets in America: A History.* Chapel Hill: University of North Carolina Press, forthcoming.

Jones, Susan. *Valuing Animals: Veterinarians and Their Patients in Modern America.* Baltimore: The Johns Hopkins University Press, 2003.

Mullin, Molly. "Mirrors and Windows: Sociocultural Studies of Human-Animal Relationships." *Annual Review of Anthropology* 28 (1999): 201–224.

Myers, Gene. *Children and Animals: Social Development and Our Connections to Other Species.* Boulder, Colo.: Westview Press, 1998.

O'Neill, Charles, ed. *The American Kennel Club 1884–1984: A Source Book.* New York: Howell House Books, 1985.

Ritvo, Harriet. *The Animal Estate: The English and Other Creatures in the Victorian Age.* Cambridge, Mass: Harvard University Press, 1987.

Rowan, Andrew J., ed. *Animals and People Sharing the World.* Hanover, N.H.: University Press of New England, 1988.

Salem, Deborah J., and Andrew Rowan, eds. *The State of the Animals 2001.* Public Policy Series, Washington, D.C.: Humane Society Press, 2001.

———. *The State of the Animals II, 2003.* Public Policy Series, Washington, D.C.: Humane Society Press, 2003.

Serpell, James, ed. *The Domestic Dog: Its Evolution, Behaviour, and Interactions with People.* Cambridge and New York: Cambridge University Press, 1995.

———. *In the Company of Animals: A Study of Human-Animal Relationships.* Cambridge and New York: Cambridge University Press, 1996.

Unti, Bernard Oreste. "The Quality of Mercy: Organized Animal Protection in the United States, 1865-1930." Ph.D. dissertation, American University, 2002.

———. "*Protecting All Animals*". *A Fifty Year History of The Humane Society of the United States, 1954–2004.* Washington, D.C.: The Humane Press, 2004.

Katherine C. Grier

PHILANTHROPY

Alexis de Tocqueville once commented that the ability to propose a project to numerous individuals and ultimately convince them to voluntarily pursue the project is particularly American. Philanthropy, an integral part of American culture, and traceable back to preliterate times, can be described in two ways. The first broadly describes philanthropy as promoting well-being through a love of humankind. In particular, philanthropy includes functions such as voluntary work and the donation of services, gifts, and/or blood. A second description of philanthropy refers solely to the financial contributions by individuals to charitable organizations, in other words, charitable giving. Both types of philanthropy can occur simultaneously and represent a classic example of social exchange theory. Both types have influenced the evolution of recreation and leisure service delivery. The period from the 1800s and onward coincides with the formative years of most organized recreation and leisure opportunities.

Philanthropic Origins—Nineteenth Century

During the 1800s, affluent women were involved in philanthropy through voluntary work using a hands-on approach in asylums, hospitals, and the slums of downtown cities for reasons related to "noblesse oblige." More than half of New York's richest 1 percent were involved in voluntary associations prior to the Civil War (1861–1865), and there is evidence that many used a major portion of their leisure time to fulfill civic activities. Rational recreation, a movement intended to instil the values of domesticity, self-control, and respectability among working-class individuals through recreation activity, swept the nation between the years 1870 and 1880. While the outcomes of this noble movement were limited, it did influence the role that private individuals were willing to play in the allocation of recreation and leisure in society. The success

of the playground movement (and subsequent recreation movement) has been linked with the voluntary efforts of individuals.

Charitable Giving Emerges

At the same time, charitable giving began to emerge. Increased personal wealth was one factor that prompted this shift in philanthropic orientation because individuals were now able to support charitable organizations with financial gifts rather than with time and effort. For some, charitable giving replaced voluntary work. For instance, after the Chicago fire in 1871, individuals in New York raised $500,000 in thirty hours and $2 million in three weeks (McCarthy, 1982). Previously, individuals would not have had the financial resources to support charitable organizations at that level.

In addition to increased personal wealth, the nature of charitable work changed. Grand fundraising galas, which emphasized financial contributions, replaced "hands-on" voluntary work In particular, individuals came to the realization that attending a fundraising gala yielded greater "social value" than volunteering in a hospital. The status (an egotistical motive) linked with attending a gala replaced or at least supplemented altruistic motives. Even in 2004, social value is considered an important motive underlying philanthropic behavior. Charitable organizations now recognize that galas provide donors with social status/value and in turn often exploit individuals aspiring to be recognized as donors.

The Boston Sand Garden

The effects of this philanthropic shift between the years 1870 and 1880 impacted the development of recreation and leisure. For instance, the establishment of the Boston Sand Garden in 1885 by public citizens marked the beginning of the recreation movement. The goal of the sand garden was to provide a supervised play area for children. Prompted by the "moral effect" seen on the children in the sand garden, the Boston playground movement soon followed. In an effort to address youth delinquency and crime in large cities, Joseph Lee and the Boston Park Commission created a model playground to be implemented in 1889. By the turn of the century, Boston had twenty-one playgrounds.

Elsewhere, settlement houses were established, which had a significant effect on recreation and leisure. The first settlement house was built in 1886 in New York City, followed three years later by Hull House in Chicago, opened by Jane Addams and Ellen Gates. Settlement houses pro-

Hull House Founded in 1889 by social reformer Jane Addams (1860–1935) and Ellen Gates Starr, Hull House, shown here in 1905, served as a neighborhood center for children and adults in Chicago. It offered day care facilities, an employment bureau, art gallery, English and citizenship classes, and a library. Addams went on to win the 1931 Nobel Peace Prize as a result of her international peacekeeping work. © *AP/Wide World Photos*

vided educational classes, civil rights advocacy, and recreational services (sports, social clubs, and cultural arts), primarily to urban poor and uneducated individuals. All across the country, affluent individuals began to organize recreation and leisure activities for others based on anticipated societal benefits. In turn, there was an expectation that the government would assume responsibility for some of these projects once initiated. In "Philanthropy and the Boston Playground Movement," Gerald Marsden mentions that the experimentation by private individuals frequently results in new social techniques that then become accepted as the function of public agencies.

Evolution of Philanthropy—Twentieth Century

Government involvement not withstanding, the work of Addams and others set a precedent for the twentieth cen-

tury. In the same way, the early twentieth century saw individuals making substantial charitable donations. By 1929, thirty-one families in Chicago had donated million-dollar gifts to various nonprofit organizations including culture (nine), health (three), and the YMCA (one). A few families were able to sustain the charitable sector and, as a result, help shape society. However, the mid-twentieth century presented charitable organizations with a challenge because too many organizations required support from too few families. Therefore, a decision was made by charitable organizations to encourage more individuals, in particular the middle class, to engage in philanthropic activity, while still concentrating on elite philanthropic activity. Hence, mass fundraising was born. In modern times, even though approximately 10 percent of individuals are responsible for 90 percent of all charitable donations (Mixer), 44 percent of all American households engaged in voluntary work and 89 percent made charitable donations in 2000 (Wiener et al.).

Philanthropy, from its early roots, similar to recreation and leisure, continues to evolve. In the early 2000s, there are an increasing number of researchers and professionals dedicated to understanding the complex study of philanthropic behavior. As well, in part due to mass fundraising, philanthropy is once again expanding its focus, and individuals are paying deliberate attention to the creation of community and special interest foundations. The funds available to a foundation are derived from many donors and held in an endowment that is independently administered and then used to award grants.

Consequently, the end of the twentieth century and the beginning of the twenty-first century could be characterized as a time during which all in society were encouraged to engage in philanthropic behavior. In view of this widespread philanthropic activity, the field of recreation and leisure saw more parks, monuments, recreational centers, symphonies, libraries, and arts programs established across the country that served a broad population.

In the future, voluntary work and/or charitable giving will likely continue to influence the growth of recreation and leisure. With the abundant number of recreation and leisure opportunities that have been established by the philanthropic efforts of individuals, one cannot begin to quantify the impact that philanthropy has had on recreation and leisure.

See also: City Parks; Museum Movements

BIBLIOGRAPHY

Blau, Peter. *Exchange and Power in Social Life.* New York: John Wiley and Sons, 1964.

Crompton, John. *Financing and Acquiring Park and Recreation Resources.* Champaign, Ill.: Human Kinetics, 1999.

Cross, Gary. *A Social History of Leisure Since 1600.* State College, Pa.: Venture Publishing, 1990.

de Tocqueville, Alexis. *Democracy in America, 1835.* Edited by Richard Heffner. New York: New American Library, 1956.

McCarthy, Katherine. *Noblesse Oblige: Charity and Cultural Philanthropy in Chicago, 1849–1929.* Chicago: University of Chicago Press, 1982.

———. "American Cultural Philanthropy: Past, Present and Future." *The Annals of the Academy of the American Academy of Political and Social Science* 471 (1984): 13–26.

———. *Women's Culture.* Chicago: University of Chicago Press, 1991.

Marsden, Gerald, K. "Philanthropy and the Boston Playground Movement." *Social Service Review* 35 (1961): 48–58.

Mixer, Joseph. *Principles of Professional Fundraising.* San Francisco: Jossey-Bass, 1993.

Ostrower, Francie. *Why the Wealthy Give.* Princeton, N.J.: Princeton University Press, 1995.

Poe, Donald. B. Jr. "The Giving of Gifts: Anthropological Data and Social Psychological Theory." *Cornell Journal of Social Relations* 12 (1977): 47–63.

Reddy, R. "Individual Philanthropy and Giving Behavior." In *Participation in Social and Political Activities.* Edited by David Horton-Smith, Jacqueline Macaulay and Associates. San Francisco: Jossey-Bass, 1980.

Russell, Ruth. Pastimes: *The Context of Contemporary Leisure.* Dubuque, Iowa: Brown and Benchmark, 1996.

Wiener, S., C. Toppe, N. Jalandoni, A. Kirsch, and M. Weitzman. *Giving and Volunteering in the United States: Findings from a National Survey.* Washington, D.C.: Independent Sector, 2002.

Martha L. Barnes

PHILATELY

See *Stamp Collecting*

PHOTOGRAPHY

Although credit for photography's invention cannot go to the United States, America did pioneer, and has continued to shape, the transformation of photography into a leisure activity. Once difficult, messy, and even dangerous, photography metamorphosed into one of the simplest and most accessible of all leisurely activities by the end of the nineteenth century, requiring neither skill nor great expense from the American consumer.

Even though early photos show subjects looking stiff and grim, many people in the United States responded to photography with wonder and delight. Photography's invention is typically attributed to England, where an amateur scientist named William Fox Talbot invented the paper-based "talbotype" process, and to France, where professional illusionist Louis Jacques Daguerre invented the copper-based "daguerreotype" process. But it was in the United States that photography, particularly daguerreotype, met with its most enthusiastic and widespread reception. Indeed, there were more daguerreotype galleries in New York City than in all of England in 1853, and more on Broadway alone than in London. Broadway was the favored location of daguerrean artists not only because it was the center of business but because it was fashionable to promenade along the thoroughfare when the week's work was done. A popular diversion while walking down Broadway, in fact, was to drop into a daguerrean gallery either to have one's portrait taken or to view the ones hanging on display.

A survey of the history of photography from 1839 to 2004 reveals that every major advance in the popularization of the medium originated in the United States. Four of these phenomena are especially noteworthy: (a) the development of the Kodak camera and roll film in 1888, and the opening up of a new mass market for amateur photography; (b) the emergence of amateur film in the 1920s as the new informal chronicler of domestic life; (c) the digital camera's reinvigoration of popular interest in photography since the early 1990s; and (d) the rise of the "memory book" industry.

The Invention of the Kodak Camera and Roll Film

Even though many Americans enjoyed having their portraits taken for the relatively low cost of $2, few of them practiced photography as a recreational activity before 1888. This comes as no surprise when one considers the extreme difficulties involved in the practice prior to Kodak's invention. For example, bringing a camera along on an outdoor excursion involved lugging heavy and cumbersome equipment (cameras in the 1850s could weigh as much as fifty pounds), a tent in which to develop the photographs, lenses, tripods, collodion, silver nitrate, alcohol, iron sulfate, filters, nitric acid, developing and fixing trays, scales and weights, glass plates, and bottles of various sizes. As a practice, photography could not be called "leisure"; it was work! Consequently, most of those who practiced photography in the United States were professionals, not amateurs.

In 1888, however, an American businessman by the name of George Eastman patented his box camera and roll film and revolutionized photography by simplifying it to such a degree that, as the original ads claimed, even children could use it. To begin with, Eastman eliminated the darkroom component of photography by assuring customers that the Kodak Company would handle all development of the photos. At approximately two pounds, the original Kodak camera was also small and lightweight and thus easy to carry. Moreover, the camera was designed to produce acceptable-quality images with no need for focusing or light adjustment. Operating a camera had indeed become, in the words of one of the most famous advertising slogans in history, as easy as pressing a button.

By simplifying photography to such an extent, Eastman was capitalizing on a new and distinctly American breed of amateur. Unlike the "gentleman amateur" of early Victorian England, the late-nineteenth-century amateur in America was not committed to erudition but amusement. With increased leisure time available, the new amateur wished to engage in hobbies that required little or no technical expertise or intellectual effort. In 1839, photography had been born into a much different climate, where a rhetoric of industry and a seriousness of purpose circumscribed the scope of amateurism. Kodak, on the other hand, aimed at making photography into an effortless pastime. Indeed, during the first twenty years of its advertising campaign, the sheer pleasure and adventure of taking photographs were the main subject: the delight of handling a diminutive camera, of not worrying about developing or printing, of capturing subjects in candid moments, of recording travel to exotic places. Concomitantly, Kodak marketing enticed consumers to view photography as a form of outdoor recreation—an activity to accompany and enhance cycling, playing tennis, camping, sailing, or going for motor rides. The representative of this new amateur was the Kodak Girl. Young and beautiful, she was always depicted in ads as traveling or otherwise engaged in recreational activities.

In 1900, Kodak marketed a camera specifically designed for children, effectively reinforcing this association between photography and recreation. Although children never took to photography the way Eastman hoped they would, the inexpensiveness of the Brownie camera (it originally sold for $1) truly made photography accessible to most Americans. Whereas the relatively high cost of earlier cameras necessitated that only the upper and upper-middle classes could enjoy photography as a form of leisure, the Brownie camera transformed photography into a cheap means of entertainment.

Amateur Films and Videos

By the time of World War I, due partially to improvements in indoor film, photography had moved into the home. Its central function now became the recording of familial and domestic activities rather than the recording, for example, of trips abroad. Reinforcing this trend was the development of the "home movie" phenomenon in the 1920s. In 1923, Kodak and another company, Bell and Howell, issued 16mm film available for amateur use. Almost immediately, home movie production emerged as an important national hobby, propelled by the scientific interest in "good parenting" during the 1920s. Home movies from the late 1920s to 1960s are remarkably consistent. They show children engaged in such activities as riding horses, sunbathing, swimming, dressing in cowboy costumes, and playing in the snow.

This equation of amateur movies with the home and family persisted until the 1960s, effectively overshadowing all other functions for amateur filmmaking. By the 1970s, video had emerged as the latest technology for recording family and domestic life. Originally considered an avant-garde art form, video by the 1980s had replaced home movies as the new medium for chronicling family life. Increasingly automated and lightweight, the camcorder obliterated what soon came to be seen as the cumbersome, intrusive, and much too complicated home-movie camera; by 1981, in fact, Kodak had stopped marketing home-movie cameras altogether.

Digital Photography

There are presently three distinct ways to produce digital images: (a) by using a kind of sensor array or scanning device able to transport preexisting images into the computer; (b) by using an interactive computer graphics program that electronically "paints" an image on the screen; or (c) by designing a computer program that assigns certain features (such as hue and color) to the digital geometric of an object or scene. Regardless of the specific differences, all three forms of digitization have emerged as highly popular forms of recreation within the past decade. Now that digital cameras have gone down radically in price, many middle- and upper-class Americans have begun using them instead of regular cameras, which means that they have also taken to using computer discs instead of film and to using computers and software rather than darkrooms or the nearest developing lab. Part of the pleasure located in this use is the ability, developed in the early 2000s, to send photos electronically to family and friends.

The Rise of the Memory Book Industry

Since the early 1990s, creating "memory books" has emerged as one of the fastest-growing hobbies in the United States. In any craft store in the country, one can find entire sections of the store dedicated to the hobby. Resembling scrapbooks, but with a much greater emphasis on photographs, memory books consist mainly of personal photos coupled with standardized stationery and other decorative materials. Each page is regarded as a potential site for personal and creative expression. Memory books are not marketed simply as places to store photographs; instead, consumers are encouraged to see these books as opportunities to transform their photographs into works of art and as crucial parts of an im-

portant narrative. Creating these books has become so popular that "memory book clubs" now exist all over the United States, populated mainly by women who are also mothers of small children. Magazines such as *Memory Makers* are also in abundance, offering readers tips and suggestions on how to make these books.

Surveying the history of photography, one can find many other ways in which the medium has been appropriated for leisure and recreation—including the advent of the Polaroid camera and the pleasure it delivered of instant pictorial gratification—but these four phenomena represent the most noteworthy. With each, as with the rest, one can see not only how much photography's popularity has depended on the promise of fun and adventure, one can also see how photography has been used to prolong leisure, allowing consumers to "relive" vacations and other pleasurable moments through their snapshots.

See also: Commercialization of Leisure; Hobbies and Crafts

BIBLIOGRAPHY

Lister, Martin, ed. *The Photographic Image in Digital Culture.* London: Routledge, 1995.

Seiberling, Grace, with Carolyn Bloore. *Amateurs, Photography, and the Mid-Victorian Imagination.* Chicago: University of Chicago Press, 1986.

Sontag, Susan. *On Photography.* New York: Farrar, Straus, and Giroux, 1973.

Spence, Jo, and Patricia Holland, eds. *Family Snaps: The Meaning of Domestic Photography.* London: Virago, 1991.

West, Nancy Martha. *Kodak and the Lens of Nostalgia.* Charlottesville: University Press of Virginia, 2000.

Zimmermann, Patricia R. *Reel Families: A Social History of Amateur Film.* Bloomington: Indiana University Press, 1995.

Nancy Martha West

PHYSICAL CULTURE

See *Body Culture and Physical Culture*

PIANO PLAYING

"They Laughed When I Sat Down at the Piano—But When I Started to Play!" The promise inherent in John Caples's 1925 advertisement for mail-order piano lessons from the U.S. School of Music, which *Advertising Age* calls "arguably, the 20th century's most successful such ad," underscores the natural appeal of amateur piano playing—self-expression, self-esteem, popularity, and the power of music to transform life. Once a passionate symbol of Victorian virtue, the upright piano in the home was associated with affluence and respectability, being marketed as such even as instruments became more affordable through mass production, payment plans, and a lively used-piano trade. The labor of learning to play reflected a devotion to the work ethic; traditional piano lessons stressed classical music, scales, exercises, and perseverance. Moreover, playing the piano imparted the merits attributed to music as "medicine for the soul," offering therapeutic if not spiritual rejuvenation ("Music hath charms to soothe a savage breast"), and popularized in music periodicals like *The Etude*. Current university research proves that piano playing does indeed reduce anxiety, depression, and loneliness, even improving cognitive development.

As the primary musical instrument once so symbolically rich that a home was considered "incomplete" without one, the piano was especially associated with women and domestic culture. Talented males might become virtuosi, but boy players were teased as "sissies." Girls and women primarily provided music in home, school, and church circles, where the piano was a supremely social instrument, crucial in family life and romantic courtship. Victorian postcards popularly portrayed mothers and girls playing piano, or even daring lovers embracing *appassionata* at the keyboard. In a far-too-often repressive existence, piano playing allowed women freedom of expression, as portrayed in Louisa May Alcott's *Little Women* (1868) and in Jane Campion's film *The Piano* (1993).

As seemingly endless product choices defined the twentieth-century consumer culture, as Americans embraced Tin Pan Alley songs, ragtime, and jazz, piano playing took on a notably different character—for recreation rather than for cultural or moral uplift. Greatly accommodating this change were player pianos, which manufacturers marketed as the means to a musical democracy in which the untrained, less-talented, or even males could "play," for what could be "unmanly" about operating a machine? But the high-fidelity phonograph and improved radio offered the same passive musical experience at a much cheaper price, leading to the collapse of the player-piano market in the 1920s.

Piano manufacturers responded by utilizing radio to promote music appreciation and sponsoring a revolution in piano lessons, especially in public schools, which em-

phasized learning to play "for the fun of it." Adults were also encouraged (the subject of John Caples's renowned ad is conspicuously male). Then, in the midst of the Great Depression, manufacturers introduced the first new piano design in half a century, the console model. Sales increased steadily after World War II until the 1980s, when competition from so many alternative entertainments again sent the piano trade into a slump (a trend from which it is still suffering). Nevertheless, a new amateur market arose playing jazz, gospel, and rock 'n' roll on electronic keyboards, synthesizers, and digital pianos—instruments now composing 40 percent of all beginning piano sales.

As of 2003, there were about 17 million pianos in the United States, with about 100,000 new pianos of all types purchased each year, most commonly for children to take lessons. Yet the fastest-growing group among aspiring pianists was adults aged twenty-five to fifty-five years. Modern piano lessons continue to emphasize music for enjoyment. The National Guild of Piano Teachers sponsors the Annual National Piano Playing Auditions, the largest piano-playing event in the world. The National Piano Foundation (the educational outreach of the Piano Manufacturers Association International) promotes amateur piano playing, designating September as "National Piano Month." The public's fascination with the piano was underscored with the Smithsonian Institution's celebration of the instrument's 300th anniversary in 2000 to 2001. The "Piano 300" Exhibit received over 250,000 visitors, one of the most successful the Smithsonian ever presented.

See also: Band Playing, Home Decoration

BIBLIOGRAPHY

American Music Conference. Home page at http://www.amc-music.org.

American Music Therapy Association. Home page at http://www.namt.com.

International Association of Electronic Keyboard Manufacturers. Home page at http://www.iaekm.org.

Loesser, Arthur. *Men, Women, and Pianos: A Social History.* New York: Dover Publications, 1991.

National Guild of Piano Teachers. Home page at http://www.pianoguild.com.

National Piano Foundation "PianoNet." Home page at http://www.pianonet.com.

Palmieri, Robert, ed. *Encyclopedia of the Piano.* 2d ed. New York: Routledge, 2003.

Piano 300. Home page at http://www.piano300.org.

Piano Education Page. Home page at http://pianoeducation.org.

PianoWorld.com. Home page at http://www.pianoworld .com.

Roell, Craig H. *The Piano in America, 1890–1940.* Chapel Hill: University of North Carolina Press, 1989.

———. "The Rise of Tin Pan Alley, 1890–1940." In *America's Musical Pulse: Issues and Aspects of 20th Century Popular Music.* Edited by Kenneth J. Bindas. Westport, Conn.: Greenwood Press, 1992.

———. "The Piano in the American Home." In *The Arts and the American Home, 1890–1930.* Edited by Jessica H. Foy and Karal Ann Marling. Knoxville: University of Tennessee Press, 1994.

Craig H. Roell

PIERCINGS

See *Body Culture*

PLANTATION ENTERTAINING

Southern planters were renowned for their hospitality and entertainments. From the late seventeenth through the eighteenth century, the plantation was the center of entertainment in the world of elite Southerners. Suppers, balls, picnics, barbecues, and other celebrations were more than mere amusements, however. These events intertwined genteel sociability, fashionable display, and fierce competitions for communal status.

Plantation parties were generally large and inclusive affairs, involving not only family and friends, but also many whites from the surrounding neighborhood. The entertainments generally combined feasting (a supper, picnic, or the famous barbecue) and dancing (sometimes a formal ball, sometimes merely spontaneous jigs). The hosts provided enormous quantities of food and drink. Tables groaned under the weight of meats, fowl, seafood, and desserts. Guests sipped copious amounts of wine and champagne. The dancing occasionally started the festivities, but usually it followed the supper. For formal balls, dancers came arrayed in their finest attire. At times, plantation entertainments were sex-segregated, with the women joining the men after their own suppers for dancing or card playing. Many parties lasted all day and long into the night. Two- or three-day parties were not unusual, especially for wedding celebrations.

Hosting a plantation entertainment was one of the main ways for a planter to display his wealth for peers and his entire community. Throwing such a large entertainment conferred local status upon him. His wife or daughter usually oversaw the affair, making sure the food or drink never ran out and that everyone had a good time. Though the parties included guests from various social and economic levels, social distinctions were never erased. Non-elites clearly understood that the unstated price of admission was deference to their hosts. For the colonial elite, plantation entertainments served as one of the primary vehicles for distinction. They competed against one another through parties. Though many planters grumbled about the expense, they used the vast outlays of food and drink, their sumptuous dress, and their knowledge of fashionable dances to vie with one other.

Plantation entertainments served another important function for white Southerners, strengthening the community even as they affirmed the host's place in that community. The events were special community gatherings that relieved the monotony and isolation of day-to-day life. At these suppers, barbecues, and balls, neighbors came together to gossip and exchange business and political news. Young men and women found the opportunity to court. Guests took pleasure in simply being together. Such events also may have promoted community in slave society by bringing together slaves from various areas as they accompanied their masters. Even in the absence of white parties, slaves participated in their own forms of plantation entertainments in their quarters or elsewhere, far from the supervision of whites. These amusements usually blended elements of African and American culture. Like whites, slaves held dance for special occasions, such as weddings, and gathered together for storytelling and the playing of musical instruments. Their religious ceremonies combined spirituality and entertainment with sermons, dancing, and singing.

By the beginning of the nineteenth century, the plantation no longer stood as the main place of planters' entertainments. With improved transportation and the rise of fashionable travel, Southern elites expanded their spaces of sociability and status competition to new venues, often wintering in cities and summering at resorts, particularly the fashionable and exclusive Virginia Springs.

See also: Colonial-Era Leisure and Recreation, Frolics, Slave Singing/Music Making, Southern America Leisure Lifestyles

BIBLIOGRAPHY

Isaac, Rhys. *The Transformation of Virginia, 1740–1790.* Chapel Hill: University of North Carolina Press, 1982.

Kierner, Cynthia A. *Beyond the Household: Women's Place in the Early South, 1700–1835*. Ithaca, N.Y.: Cornell University Press, 1998.

Kulikoff, Allan. *Tobacco and Slaves: The Development of Southern Cultures in the Chesapeake, 1680–1800*. Chapel Hill: University of North Carolina Press, 1986.

Wyatt-Brown, Bertram. *Southern Honor: Ethics and Behavior in the Old South*. New York: Oxford University Press, 1982.

Charlene Boyer Lewis

PLASTIC SURGERY

See *Beauty Culture*

PLAYGROUNDS

Contrary to common thought about play and playgrounds, the formal playground movement in America originated well before the beginning of the twentieth century. The roots of America's formal playgrounds can be traced to early nineteenth century Germany where Johann GutsMuth, influenced by Jean-Jacques Rousseau, introduced outdoor play and exercise training in Schnepfenthal. In 1812, his ideas were extended in the Jahn Gymnastic Association and the first system of school play. The emphasis of this system on physical exercise reflected the traditional physical fitness values of the German people.

Early Playgrounds

A crude outdoor gymnasium without supervisor or instructor was established in 1821 at the Latin School in Salem, Massachusetts. Everett Mero credited this playground to New England physical training sources, but two events suggest German influences. These were the chronological proximity of the development of German and American outdoor gymnasia and the use of German-type apparatus to form a second Massachusetts playground in 1825 in Northampton, Massachusetts. Dr. Charles Beck, a former student of Friedrich Jahn in Germany, supervised this playground. The outdoor gymnasia, consisting initially of indoor exercise apparatus transported to the outdoors, influenced the design of manufacturers' commercial playground equipment, which was to be distributed widely during the first decades of the twentieth century.

The outdoor gymnasia were reserved primarily for older boys. The first organized American playgrounds for girls and younger boys were piles of sand patterned after those placed in the public parks of Berlin, Germany, during the 1880s. Marie Zakerzewska, an American visitor to Berlin who observed the "sandgartens," influenced their development in the yards of the Children's Mission on Parmeter Street in Boston in 1886. The sandgartens represented the first organized playgrounds for young children in America, and, together with the outdoor gymnasia, were developed throughout America's major cities during the early twentieth century. This development characterized the first serious playground movement in America.

The American Playground Movement

The early twentieth-century American playground movement was a multifaceted phenomenon with respect to motives, values, and locales. Motives for the early outdoor gymnasia were linked to providing sedentary older boys in cities opportunities to exercise muscles in danger of atrophy and focused on physical development. Other motives included protecting children and youth from the hazards of traffic-filled city streets and the criminal influences of slum districts. While physical and moral motives were valued for playgrounds in city parks and schools, broader social, intellectual, and educational motives and values were to be realized in early-twentieth-century American nursery schools and kindergartens with philosophical roots dating to John Comenius, Jean-Jacques Rousseau, Johann Pestalozzi, and Frederick Froebel.

The organization of the Playground Association of America in 1906 and the publication of their journal, *The Playground,* were perhaps the most influential factors in casting playgrounds into the conscience of the American public and resulting in their unprecedented growth. In 1906, fewer than twenty cities in the United States maintained playgrounds, some unsupervised, but, by 1913, 342 cities had playgrounds under regular paid workers. Coinciding with the rapid growth of city playgrounds, manufacturers designed and manufactured a growing array of steel equipment, including merry-go-rounds, jungle gyms, slides, giant strides, and swings. Yet, even in this early period, the secretary of the Playground Association of America, Henry Curtis, and other professionals wrote of the need to train and provide play leaders, provide playgrounds for "little children," and to provide living things in the playground environment. "Various living things are almost as essential to it (the playground) as play equipment, and there should by all means be flowers in abundance," (Curtis, p. 42).

Playground Facts

- Motives for early playgrounds were primarily to protect children from the hazards of city streets and the influences of delinquent older boys.

- Early twentieth-century playgrounds were remarkably different in the country and in the city, with playgrounds of large cities featuring manufactured equipment, while country schools continued to rely on natural materials and traditional games.

- Adventure playgrounds, popular in Europe, had only limited impact on American playgrounds.

- Contemporary children are at greater risk than children in past decades because not only have they lost the traditional recess period, but they are also suffering from growing health problems resulting from the unhealthy mix of sedentary lifestyle, junk food, television, video games, and computer play.

- The best modern playgrounds combine manufactured equipment intended for motor development with natural play materials providing broad developmental benefits for children.

The Many Faces of the Playground Movement

The multifaceted nature of the playground movement was seen in the striking differences in city versus country locales. While cities rapidly built mammoth steel structures designed primarily for physical development and trained supervisors to oversee them, children in rural areas, including country schools, had only limited access to manufactured apparatus and relied on locally fabricated equipment and the natural environment for their play. Autobiographies and personal accounts are rich sources of printed information about the differences in city and country playgrounds.

The writers of personal accounts of early-twentieth-century playgrounds tend to speak more positively of the creative, inventive, natural play environments than of the "manufactured" playgrounds. Writing about his Philadelphia boyhood, Paul Hogan spoke of vacant lots as city playgrounds; of hills and valleys for digging, sledding in the winter, sliding on cardboard boxes, and building tree houses; and of close relationships with neighbors, the iceman, and the organ grinder. In their neighborhood playground—a large empty lot with hills and valleys—the

children dug tunnels, built fire pits, and cooked meals. Teenagers engaged in sports while adults enjoyed picnics. Soon, the city developed the site into an official playground. The empty lot was leveled by horse-drawn graders, a high fence was installed, a foot of sharp cinders buried the entire site, steel equipment was installed, and "My neighbors stayed away in droves," (Hogan, p. 151).

Other writers told similar tales to tell about growing up and playing in country schools. Joe Frost spoke of children's school play in the Depression-era Ouachita Mountains of Arkansas and the creativity and ingenuity of constructing one's own playground—but the context and playthings were different from those of city contexts. Country kids had virtually unfettered access to hills, streams, animals, and wild places, and they created their own playthings from scrap and natural materials. The school followed the lead of city schools in installing swings and climbers, fabricated by the local blacksmith, but after a few weeks of exploration, both boys and girls returned to their contrived games and the apparatus stood empty most of the time. The stream that ran swiftly through the school grounds after a rain and the pine-covered hillside offered infinitely more challenges and excitement. When the play moved high on the hill away from the school, a guard was posted to listen for the bell and alert the players. Teachers usually stayed indoors during extended play periods, which included periods before school, recesses, and lunch break. By the 1950s, three recesses a day were the norm

"Most (country) schools had no designated playground or fences. Children could wander as far as they wished as long as they still could hear the bell," (Gulliford, p. 50). Children were not isolated from adult work and play. Younger children learned from older and older children from adults. Some games were tightly segregated, with boys engaging in traditional games of marbles, top spinning, leapfrog, mumblepeg, and inventive games of dam building and war games, and girls playing traditional games of house, four-square, skip rope, and drop the handkerchief. Boys and girls joined together to play antyover, chase, crack the whip, dodge ball, hide-and-seek, and occasional ball and bat games organized by teachers or the children themselves. Gender preferences in play continue to the present time, with boys engaging in more superhero and adventure scenarios and girls in more domestic play.

Limitations of the Playground Movement

By 1910, the catalogs of manufacturers featured iron, steel, and wood equipment, and the Playground Association of America's *Report of the Committee on Equipment*

Aquarium of the Pacific. Children can crawl through a replica of a whale skeleton that is part of a playground at the Aquarium of the Pacific in Long Beach, California. Opened in 1998 the 156,735-square foot structure houses over 12,500 ocean animals in fifty exhibits and uses 1 million gallons of seawater. The playground is one of the more popular attractions at the Aquarium. © *Kristi J. Black/Corbis*

published recommendations for supervised public playgrounds. Soon playground specialists recognized that American playgrounds were in a miserable state, ". . . a disgrace to the systems to which they belong. The school trustees apparently finish the building and forget all about the playground," (Curtis, p. 1211). Public park and elementary school playgrounds continued to reflect the emphasis on physical fitness, but the sponsors of nursery schools and kindergartens recognized the value of free, creative play for social and intellectual development and focused on a broader array of play materials to accommodate various forms of play. Sand, water, portable materials, building materials, tools, and downsized equipment were available.

The World War II years (1941–1945) saw limited manufacture of playground equipment because steel was diverted to the war effort. Consequently, equipment aged and deteriorated, and play in schools and parks focused on traditional and invented games. Following the war, the earlier "manufactured appliance era" was complemented by the "novelty era." Artists, architects, recreation spe-

cialists, educators, and child-development specialists influenced play environments. Novelty and fantasy structures, spray pools, miniature trains and cars, animal figures, and play sculptures were designed to ostensibly reflect aesthetic qualities and enhance play value and interest. However, these designs were frequently more appealing to adults than to children.

The Reemergence of the Playground Movement

Adventure playgrounds, originating in Denmark during World War II, allow children to form and structure their own play with the support of trained play leaders rather than having it imposed by an unmalleable environment. Adventure playgrounds spread throughout several European countries and remain viable there in 2004. Lady Allen of Hurtwood introduced adventure playgrounds in London in 1968 and spoke of the "ironmongery" and "prison" periods of playground development as "an administrator's heaven and a child's hell."

Although the adventure concept continues to influence American playgrounds, the impact has been minimal. Play specialists believe this to result from Americans' lack of appreciation for free, unstructured play for healthy child development. Perhaps of greater concern has been the belief that playgrounds built by children are unduly hazardous, a notion not supported by experience. The American Adventure Playground Association (AAPA) was formed in 1976. By May 1977, sixteen adventure playgrounds were identified in the United States, but the AAPA was short lived. A number of designers and associations—for example, American Association for the Child's Right to Play and the Community Built Association—continue to promote adventure play concepts and free, unfettered outdoor play.

During the 1970s and 1980s, space age plastics and metals were increasingly used in playground equipment, and mammoth, modular structures linking play events or challenges began to dominate the playground equipment industry. The growing concern about children's injuries on playgrounds—revealed by National Electronic Injury Survey System data (U.S. Consumer Product Safety Commission 1975), and resulting in a proliferation of lawsuits—paralleled the development of national safety guidelines (U.S. Consumer Product Safety Commission 1981) and standards (American Society for Testing and Materials). By 1990, as a result of industry efforts to meet growing specificity in safety guidelines and standards and the corresponding dearth of research on play value of play materials and equipment, American playgrounds increasingly took on an aura of sameness, and a "standardized era" of playgrounds emerged.

Contemporary Play and Playgrounds

Perhaps the most pronounced factors influencing play and playgrounds during the last decade of the twentieth century were the lack of understanding of the value of free, unfettered, creative play and a growing array of competitive entertainment devices and venues. Computer play, television, video games, theme parks, and other technological tools and entertainment increasingly replaced free, creative play and resulted in reduced time on playgrounds. A growing national emphasis on academics led to deletion of recess and physical education in many schools. Parental fear about child molesters, crime, and terrorism, and the absence of working parents to supervise outdoor play further reduced time on playgrounds. The resulting sedentary activity coupled with excessive junk-food consumption contributed to a growing pattern of obesity and a related "epidemic" of health problems among children and youth.

The conferences and journals of some professional organizations are among the counters to the above trends. These organizations include the Association for Childhood Education International, the National Association for the Education for Young Children, the International Association for the Child's Right to Play, and the Association for the Study of Play. Their work with respect to outdoor play focuses on its developmental benefits and the virtues of free, creative play and traditional games. The National Recreation and Park Association and the National Program for Playground Safety sponsor a range of activities for enhancing safety during outdoor play.

Although the basic playground equipment designed primarily for physical development—slides, swings, climbers, and overhead equipment—continues to be popular, some designers and manufacturers are slowly turning to research to guide playground and playground equipment design. Consequently, the most exciting playgrounds and equipment accommodate varied forms of play intended to promote social and cognitive development as well as motor development. Such playgrounds focus on natural features—dirt, sand, water, woodlands, flowers, streams, hills, small animals and insects, rocks, logs, and gardens—and essentially bring the countryside to the city.

See also: City Parks; Park Movements

BIBLIOGRAPHY

Allen, Lady of Hurtwood. *Planning for Play.* Cambridge, Mass.: M.I.T. Press, 1968.

American Society for Testing and Materials. "Standard Consumer Safety Performance Specification for Playground Equipment for Public Use." Philadelphia: American Society for Testing and Materials, 1981.

Cavallo, Dominick J. *The Child in American Reform: A Psychohistory of the Movement to Organize Children's Play, 1880–1920.* Ann Arbor, Mich.: University Microfilms International, 1976.

Curtis, Henry. S. *The Practical Conduct of Play.* New York: Macmillan Publishers, 1925.

Frost, Joe L. *Children and Injuries.* Tucson, Ariz.: Lawyers and Judges Publishing Company, 2001.

Frost, Joe L., Sue C. Wortham, and Stuart Reifel. *Play and Child Development.* Columbus, Ohio: Merrill Prentice-Hall, 2001.

Frost, Joe L., and Theodore B. Sweeney. *Cause and Prevention of Playground Injuries and Litigation.* Olney, Md.: Association for Childhood Education International, 1996.

Gulliford, Andrew. *America's Country Schools.* Niwot: University Press of Colorado, 1984.

Hogan, Paul. *Philadelphia Boyhood: Growing Up in the 1930s.* Vienna, Va.: Holbrook and Kellogg, 1995.

Koch, K. "Folk and Child Play: Report of the Central Committee on Folk and Child Play in Germany." Translated by A. Osten. *American Physical Education Review* 13 (1908): 325–334.

Mero, Everett B. *American Playgrounds: Their Construction, Equipment, Maintenance and Utility.* Boston: American Gymnasia Company, 1908.

Moore, Robin C., and Herb H. Wong. *Natural Learning: Creating Environments for Rediscovering Nature's Way of Teaching.* Berkeley: MIG Communications, 1997.

Nabhan, Gary P., and Stephen Trimble. *The Geography of Childhood: Why Children Need Wild Places.* Boston: Beacon Press, 1994.

U.S. Consumer Product Safety Commission. *Hazard Analysis: Playground Equipment.* Washington, D.C.: 1975.

———. *Handbook for Public Playground Safety,* Volumes 1 and 2. Washington, D.C: 1981.

Joe L. Frost

POKER

See *Atlantic City, Card Games, Gambling, Las Vegas*

POOL

See *Billiards/Pool*

PORNOGRAPHY

In contrast to other forms of leisure pursuit, both makers and users of pornography frequently deny the nature of their activity. Material that might be clearly pornographic to one observer might be better classified as literature, art, erotica, instructional material, or any one of a number of other categories to another. These issues of definition are so significant because, through much of American history, the term *pornography* implied criminal activity, inviting serious penal sanctions. So contorted did debates over the nature of pornography become that many have resorted in despair to the famous assertion of subjectivity by Supreme Court Justice Potter Stewart, who wrote in 1964: "I know it when I see it."

The lack of strict definition raises problems because historically many of the items used for purposes of prurient sexuality were not avowedly pornographic. In colonial Massachusetts, Jonathan Edwards denounced a clique of local boys and young men who were deriving sexual excitement from a "bad book," namely a serious manual of midwifery. Through the nineteenth century, some of the best-selling works of erotica and sexual perversion were ostensibly serious exposés of sexual misdeeds by religious minorities, including Catholics and Mormons. Arguably, the best-selling pornographic work in nineteenth-century America was the convent exposé, *The Awful Adventures of Maria Monk.* In the twentieth century, the label of pornography was applied to works of literature like *The Well of Loneliness* and *Ulysses* .

American cities have, at least since the early nineteenth century, had substantial black markets in explicitly pornographic materials, erotic books and prints, and, from the 1870s, photographs. The illegal nature of the trade raises serious difficulties about tracing its history, and much evidence stems from morality campaigners with a strong vested interest in making the smut trade seem as vast and threatening as possible. Still, when such campaigns were waged, as in the 1870s or the 1890s, activists never found much difficulty in uncovering many thousands of pornographic publications and visual items in major cities. These items circulated in the wider "sporting" culture that appealed to young urban men, and that overlapped with the worlds of sports, gambling, saloons, and prostitution. Like these other industries, the smut trade operated with the acquiescence of law enforcement, whose toleration was purchased with bribes. The circulation of sexual images apparently reached new heights with the Civil War era, in which millions of young men were mobilized, and the postwar period witnessed yet another morality crusade. The Comstock Law of 1873 provided for the fine and imprisonment of any person mailing or receiving "obscene," "lewd," or "lascivious" items, a definition that was taken to cover any material describing or promoting contraception or abortion.

Much of the knowledge of the pornography trade comes from the first half of the twentieth century, not because the business necessarily reached new heights, but because so much evidence was produced by the religious pressure groups active during this period, above all by the fiercely motivated Legion of Decency. Also, censorship standards had relaxed enough to allow serious mainstream authors at least to refer to the topic of pornography. Raymond Chandler's *The Big Sleep* (1939) depicts a California vice ring active in selling pornographic books and nude photography, with a sideline in

Times Square. Pedestrians walk past some of the adult entertainment shops on 42nd St. in New York's Times Square in 1995. In the early 2000s, then-mayor Rudolph Guliani led a successful campaign to remove much of the pornography available in Times Square. © *AP/Wide World Photos*

blackmail. Typical of many real-life operations in mid-century, Chandler depicts urban crime syndicates as well represented in the production and marketing of pornography. Apart from books, photographs, and playing cards, there were cheap comics, the legendary "Tijuana Bibles," which often used contemporary celebrities as their protagonists. In addition, pornographic movies were a well-known part of the repertoire no later than the 1920s. Often, these seem to have been made by companies and actors on the fringes of the legal cinema world, and a lively folklore still claims that many later stars began their career in this netherworld. Though all these materials were technically illegal, an abundance of literary and journalistic references suggests that they were widely accessible to anyone with an interest in procuring, for example, a stag film for a party.

In the second half of the twentieth century, pornography left its criminal ghetto and largely entered the social mainstream. Partly, this move reflected much greater public awareness of sexuality and tolerance for open discussion. Milestones in this process included the publication of the Kinsey Report in 1948—*Sexual Behavior in the Human Male*—and the appearance of *Playboy* magazine in 1953. By the early 1960s, demographic factors came into play, as the baby boom generation began to enter their late teens, and sexual mores changed swiftly.

Meanwhile, the federal courts began a gradual liberalization of the old-established censorship laws. In 1957, in *Roth v. the United States,* the U.S. Supreme Court revised the definition of obscenity to give much more latitude to publishers and filmmakers, and contributed to a substantial change in social and cultural attitudes. The *Roth* test asked "whether, to the average person, applying contemporary community standards, the dominant theme of the material taken as a whole appeals to prurient interest." In other words, a book could no longer be suppressed because one pressure group found some portion of it smutty. In 1966, moreover, the Supreme Court, in a ruling on the book *Fanny Hill,* declared a work pornographic only if it was "utterly without redeeming social value." In *Miller v. California* (1973), obscenity was defined as material that depicted sex in a "patently offensive way," lacking in literary, artistic, scientific, and political merit, and appealing to an average person's "prurient interest," as determined by the local standards of each community. That definition gave accused "pornographers" a great many legal loopholes, and most police and prosecutors soon found that pursuing smut was just not worth the effort. Some states went still further; a 1988 case effectively decriminalized the making of pornography in California.

By the late 1960s, the availability and openness of pornography had reached levels that would have staggered and probably appalled previous generations. Most cities of any size had adult bookstores, often in areas offering an array of other sexual services, and the range of materials on display was broadening year by year. By the 1970s, many such stores were openly selling films and magazines that depicted not just hard core sex (intercourse) but also perverse material such as bestiality, and sadomasochism.

Moreover, the cornucopia of semilegal smut was affecting the standards prevailing in the mainstream market. By the early 1970s, magazines like *Playboy* took the once unthinkable step of depicting women with pubic hair, and *Playboy* was conservative compared to other widely available magazines. The ostentatiously shocking *Hustler* published its first issue in 1974. Regular newsstands were now offering over-the-counter books and magazines with content that in the 1930s would have been available only in the darkest recesses of the vice subculture. Equally unthinkable to previous generations, the growing assertiveness of gay rights movements permitted the expansion of gay-themed pornography.

Technology played a major role in mainstreaming pornography, whether heterosexual or homosexual. Pornographic films enjoyed a massive upsurge with the liberalization of sexual mores during the late 1960s, and a few productions enjoyed crossover success with mainstream audiences. *Deep Throat* (1972) was perhaps the best known, while *Debbie Does Dallas* was also immensely profitable. However, the industry found its natural medium with the popularization of the videocassette recorder. Following the introduction of the pioneering Betamax in 1975, JVC introduced its VHS format in 1978, and from the early 1980s, video recorders began a near-total penetration of the U.S. market. This development allowed pornographic films to be enjoyed in the privacy

of the home. The ensuing boom offered a massive boost to the manufacture of pornography, which became a substantial industry centered in parts of southern California.

The rise of the Internet contributed further to the spread of pornographic films and images. One revolutionary effect collapse of prices, since images that would once have cost a substantial investment in films and magazines were now available gratis, if connection charges and subscription to service providers are set aside. It also encouraged the democratization of porn, since so much of the content was "amateur" imagery posted by ordinary citizens, usually not for profit. The result was a substantial extension of the concept of sexual attractiveness, since so many Web sites offered images of people who by traditional standards were overweight or plain, not to mention middle-aged or old. Though the social effects of these changes have not been well studied, the mainstreaming of pornography probably contributed to the wide diffusion among the average population of erotic practices and fetishes once the preserve of sex workers and aristocratic libertines.

Nevertheless, it is not true that over the last three decades American attitudes to pornography have been entirely laissez-faire. Since the late 1970s, courts and legislatures enforced strict laws against child pornography, a category that includes any individual under the age of eighteen, and this prohibition received the support of a wide social consensus.

See also: Brothels; Computer's Impact on Leisure; Internet; Magazines, Men's; Prostitution

BIBLIOGRAPHY

Downs, Donald A. *The New Politics of Pornography.* Chicago: University of Chicago Press, 1989.

Gertzman, Jay A. *Bookleggers and Smuthounds: The Trade in Erotica, 1920–1940.* Philadelphia: University of Pennsylvania Press, 1999.

Jenkins, Philip. *Beyond Tolerance: Child Pornography on the Internet.* New York: New York University Press, 2001.

Lane, Frederick S. *Obscene Profits: The Entrepreneurs of Pornography in the Cyber Age.* New York: Routledge, 2000.

Rembar, Charles. *The End of Obscenity: The Trials of Lady Chatterley, Tropic of Cancer, and Fanny Hill.* New York: Harper and Row, 1986.

Stoller, Robert J., and I. S. Levine. *Coming Attractions: The Making Of An X-Rated Video.* New Haven: Yale University Press, 1993.

Philip Jenkins

POSTWAR TO 1980 LEISURE AND RECREATION

Nearly three years after World War II ended with the 1945 Japanese surrender to the Allies, *Life* magazine convened eighteen prominent Americans for a roundtable discussion of the nation's "Third Freedom"—the "pursuit of happiness," as named in the Declaration of Independence. In summer 1948, *Life*'s editors and their guests, mostly high-ranking figures in business, media, education, and the clergy (plus the nation's Mother of the Year), worried particularly about the "Problem of Leisure." In a suburban, upper-middle-class, country-club setting designed exclusively for golf, tennis, swimming, dining, and social drinking, the magazine asked, "Are Americans using their leisure time to good advantage?" (Davenport, p. 99).

The question was momentous for a nation long defined by its work ethic. America's major nineteenth-century poet, Walt Whitman, had created a persona who loafs at his ease, and leisure and recreational gear, from bicycles to ice skates, had been mass-marketed for decades. In the United States, nonetheless, leisure often had been viewed as synonymous with sloth, an invitation to dissipation and social decline.

Yet the postwar years seemed uniquely poised to transform America's longtime work ethic into one of leisure and recreation. True, the atomic bomb, as one roundtable participant said, now hung like the "sword of Damocles" over America and the world as the Cold War years began (*Life*, 2 January 1950, p. 98). But a new age of unprecedented factory automation seemed imminent. This meant that the manufacture and distribution of products, which historian Allen Nevins called "the bone and sinew of democracy," would soon require only token human effort (*Life*, p. 85). Office tasks, too, would be carried out by new mechanized systems.

According to such prominent mid-twentieth-century social analysts as David Reisman, C. Wright Mills, and Herbert Marcuse, legions of manufacturing and clerical workers throughout the country could soon expect a much shorter workweek and liberation from repetitious, dull, dangerous toil. They would enjoy an exponential expansion of hours available for leisure and recreation in a context of material bounty, which had been envisioned in the late nineteenth century in Edward Bellamy's popular utopian novel *Looking Backward* (1887). Mills, a sociologist, proclaimed that the gospel of work would be replaced by one of leisure, and by 1958 *Life* published a special issue entitled "The Good Life," its lead editorial

cautiously asserting that "Leisure Could Mean a Better Civilization."

It could—but only if it served the advance of civilization, according to the social theorists and the *Life* roundtable, who represented the American business and intellectual elite. They feared that the mass of Americans too readily squandered their recreational leisure hours in pursuit of trivial diversions, "passive" enjoyments, cheap thrills, and "canned" entertainment.

Their angst was characteristic of the ambivalence and class-based anxiety repeatedly expressed in postwar decades. The envisioned era of work-free leisure did not actually arrive, but postwar (white) Americans enjoyed a level of material prosperity that made them, according to historian David C. Potter, "people of plenty." Americans enthusiastically embraced such varied forms of leisure and recreation as backyard barbecues, fast-food meals, hot rods and muscle cars, basement "rec" rooms, beach-blanket movies, billiards, bowling, popular music, motoring, surfing, spas, yoga, cooking, camping, cruises, and sports from football and soccer to NASCAR to hot-air ballooning and snowmobiles. The decades from the mid-1940s to 1980 would see ever-evolving forms of American recreation based on gender, on youth (and age), on race, on suburban or urban demographics, on concerns about health and fitness, and on disposable income and easy access to installment-plan credit and credit cards.

The period would also show class status as a taxonomic index of leisure and recreation. Certain social critics, notably the prominent arbiter of taste Dwight Macdonald, reinforced earlier eugenics-based twentieth-century ideas on social division by sectioning the U.S. population into three top-down groups: highbrow or high culture, midcult or middlebrow, and masscult or lowbrow. Macdonald's 1960 landmark essay, "Masscult & Midcult," critiqued the popular masses as mindless and the middle as creatures of an anesthetizing capitalist system that debased or flattened authentic good taste and dulled powers of discernment.

The appetites of the majority of Americans, warned Macdonald and his supporters, must be ignored by those of discriminating taste—meaning those, in effect, responsible for upholding the highest standards of the arts. These class divisions were extended to leisure and recreation. Those of high culture, for example, would distinguish themselves by appreciation of vintage wines, high-order complex literature, and subtitled foreign films shown in art houses, such as the 1961 Alain Renais film, *Last Year at Marienbad*. Outdoors, they might ski or play tennis.

The midcult, meanwhile, would consume mixed drinks (highballs or rum and Coke) and sate themselves on melodramatic best-seller novels and Hollywood epics with specious claims to intellectual content. These might include the 1958 Leon Uris novel, *Exodus,* based on European Jews' twentieth-century struggle to establish the state of Israel, together with the 1960 Otto Preminger movie version starring Paul Newman and Eva Marie Saint. Their outdoor recreation could be golf.

For their part, the working-class masses would listen to country and western tunes over beer at honky-tonks and go to outdoor drive-in movies to see "spaghetti Westerns," which minimized dialogue but maximized violent action—perhaps the 1964 Sergio Leone film *A Fistful of Dollars.* Their favorite sport would be bowling. Although these caste-based categories persisted well into the 1970s, Americans' eclectic recreational choices continuously exposed these strata as procrustean and simplistic. As popular culture burgeoned, it permeated leisure and recreation at all levels.

Leisure did not displace the notion of work in the postwar era. Instead, the national work ethic was newly configured for peacetime recreation. Advertisers and marketers promoted ethnically white American lifestyles as a blend both of leisure and labor, especially when the G.I. Bill provided returning veterans the opportunity for home ownership in the new suburban tracts under construction nationwide. Citizens' wartime savings of some $150 billion were about to be spent as the economy of tanks, warships, and munitions shifted to production of automobiles, home furnishings, and appliances (and such recreational items as underwater swim fins and portable radios).

Suburban Life

New homeowners were encouraged to undertake do-it-yourself home-improvement projects for creative recreation as well as thrift. Through the 1950s and beyond, advertisements for paints and flooring in such mass magazines as *Collier's* and *The Saturday Evening Post* typically showed a smiling, coiffed, and manicured white housewife in sportswear expressing personal taste by rollering paint on interior walls or laying linoleum floor tiles in the family's kitchen ("Lay the Tile Yourself That's Worth Your While"). Appliances were marketed as a gateway to the good life—for instance, the new clothes dryer meant to turn "irksome labor into new-found leisure." Household products from brushes to detergents promised to make tasks easy and fun, including the Velvet latex paint that "glides on by itself."

From the mid-1950s to the 1970s and beyond, entrepreneurial suburban at-home women masked their business initiatives as recreational events, selling cosmetics, giftware, and plastic Tupperware food containers in women's neighborhood gatherings known as home parties. These were held at morning coffee klatches or evening gatherings where guests wore makeup and stylish clothing. The hostess served light refreshments (perhaps a "last-minute" Pillsbury boxed cake "glamorized" with aerosol whipped cream). She earned a percentage on the sales of items ranging from bowls to Jell-O molds. The event was always a party, never a sales transaction.

The home party might take place in the "rec" or recreation room, formerly a suburban basement now converted by do-it-yourself weekend effort to recreational space with a Ping-Pong or pool table, or a wet bar and newly tiled floor for dancing. (The dances indicated a generational split in recreation, with the rhumba or cha-cha taught to adults by the nationwide franchised Fred Astaire or Arthur Murray Dance Studios and promoted by the Murrays' 1950s TV show—while the new rock-and-roll dances such as the twist, the chicken, or the frug were demonstrated for teens on TV on Dick Clark's *American Bandstand.*)

Any member of a household became a personal disc jockey from the 1950s to the 1980s, when commercial radio and TV served as marketing engines for the new 45 and 33 1/3 r.p.m. durable and affordable vinyl recordings. These could be stacked for hours of turntable play on high-fidelity (hi-fi) and stereo home equipment, followed by the audiocassette tapes and tape-deck players of the 1960s and 1970s, all purchased over months on "easy-payment" credit plans or charged on the newly widespread Visa or Mastercard, which joined Diners' Club and American Express cards in wallets and purses.

Popular Music Recreational popular music, a prewar staple of American leisure, flourished to an unprecedented degree through a succession of superstar artists and distinct musical styles, the listener's personal spaces (automobile, bedroom, or rec room) filling with the sound of black artists such as Chuck Berry and Bo Diddley, in addition to the phenomenal Elvis and rock-blues singer Janis Joplin, plus the Broadway ballads of Barbra Streisand and folk songs of Joan Baez and Bob Dylan, advocates for peace and critics of the Vietnam War. The Beatles, Rolling Stones, and Jefferson Airplane widened the parameters of rock and roll, and in the 1970s the psychologically reflective Carole King and Joni Mitchell rode high on the *Billboard* charts, as did disco's Donna Summer and southern-rock bands the Allman Brothers and Lynyrd Skynyrd. High-quality FM radio frequencies in these years enhanced tonal quality. Popular styles ranged from rockabilly and rhythm-and-blues to the ballad, psychedelic, and disco, and to acid and punk rock and heavy metal.

By the late 1960s, the rec room might be outfitted with psychedelic-effect strobe-lighting, which was featured at huge dance halls coast to coast (just as club venues of the 1970s disco era glinted with revolving mirror-ball lighting, which for some patrons intensified the effects of mind-altering recreational drugs in wide use since the 1960s, including marijuana, barbiturates, amphetamines, hashish, cocaine, and LSD, none of them legal for recreational use). Quieter forms of recreation also underwent major change. By midcentury, canasta competed in popularity with bridge, and new board games, notably Scrabble and Trivial Pursuit (1970s and 1980s, respectively), gained loyalists, the latter based largely on data from American popular culture. Needlecraft, which in prewar years had served a family's sewing and mending needs, now became a hobby, the sewing machine a recreational device. Home crafts flourished, too, as well as paint-by-numbers, which produced finished oil portraits and landscapes by simply filling in numbered spaces on a prepared canvas with designated paints packaged in a kit.

Leisure reading expanded in the postwar decades with paperback production of "pulps," named for the cheap paper on which popular fiction was printed. Sold for under fifty cents at tobacconists, drugstores, bus stations, airports, and discounters from the five-and-tens to the newer big-box retailers, the books included Mickey Spillane's 1950s hardboiled detective, Mike Hammer; the cowboy heroes of Louis L'Amour; female-focused novels such as Valerie Taylor's (pseudonym of Velma Young) proto-feminist 1959 *The Girls in 3-B;* and bodice-ripping romance fiction, notably Harlequin romances.

The 1950s was also the beginning of the blockbuster popular novel (and its inevitable movie and TV versions), from Grace Metalious's exposé of small-town sex, *Peyton Place* (1956), which sold more than 10 million copies, through Jacqueline Susann's *Valley of the Dolls* (1966) and Stephen King's psychological thrillers *Carrie* (1974), *The Shining* (1977), and *The Dead Zone* (1979). Literary fiction, too, appeared in paperback—the Pocket Book imprint with its kangaroo logo indicating portability, just as Doubleday's Anchor editions connoted the stability and endurance of tasteful literature. Literary paperbacks reprinted such established authors as D. H. Lawrence and Virginia Woolf, and the format became a staple of college courses and leisure reading, especially the trade paperbacks printed in hard-finish paper and a larger trim size than the pulps—the size difference indicative of the class divisions set forth by the Dwight Macdonald group.

Outdoors, the suburban manicured lawn and yard mixed obligation with leisure as the wartime Victory gardens gave way to flower and vegetable beds—the vegeta-

bles now a hobby in the new era of supermarkets. At home on weekends, the husband-father (assisted by his son, at least in ad images) maintained the family grounds with a power mower that evolved in the 1970s into the small lawn tractor. Swimming pools, both in-ground and above-ground, appeared in backyards (as did whirlpool hot tubs on home decks in the 1970s, beginning in California). Marketed in the 1960s as affordable family and neighborhood entertainment, pools were repositioned for the managerial-professional classes as exercise equipment in the physical fitness craze of the 1970s, when hot tubs were presented to this same group as sensual antidotes to workplace stress and combined with quasi-recreational transcendental meditation and other New Age therapeutics.

Outdoor patio barbecue grills from the 1950s were gendered male, with outsize utensils (and chef's aprons) signifying the masculinity appropriate to grilling meat on weekends for family and friends. These occasions sometimes reflected fashion trends tinted by the exotic. For instance, the growth of Caribbean recreational travel and the admission of Hawaii to statehood in 1959 (together with such movies as 1958's *South Pacific*) prompted "Island" parties or Polynesian patio luaus with fertility god tiki mugs containing mixed drinks accented with tropical fruit, and each man encouraged to wear a floral-patterned "aloha" shirt. (This "South Seas" moment anticipated the recreational, though somewhat competitive, regimen of gourmet cooking fostered by Julia Child, the "French Chef," in public-television programs of the 1970s and favored by the new class of careerist Americans dubbed Yuppies, short for young urban professionals.)

The most prized—and ubiquitous—home entertainment item in all these postwar decades was television. TV sets multiplied from the 9,000 black-and-white sets of 1948 to the 50 million (or one TV in nine of ten U.S. households) in 1960 and a color set in 38 percent of U.S. homes by 1970. Marketed in the postwar moment in part as an educational tool and "window on the world," TV was also ready to provide American families nonstop recreational pleasure. Sold initially in elaborate wood cabinetry as fine furniture for the living room, TV went portable in the 1960s with units for the kitchen, family room or den, bedrooms, even the bath. The 1950s quasi-hearthside gathering of the whole family for certain scheduled evening programs thus gave way to the personal TV for individual tastes.

Distinct TV program formats proved enduring over decades—for instance, comedy variety shows, from the early (1948) success of the sober Ed Sullivan and "Mr. Television," Milton Berle, to comedians Jackie Gleason, Carol

Burnett, Dan Rowan, and Dick Martin (*Laugh-In*) and *Saturday Night Live,* which debuted in 1975. Game shows also proved their recreational popularity, from the early 1950s *Queen for a Day* through *The Sixty-Four Thousand Dollar Question* and *Twenty-One* (the latter the casualty of a contestant cheating scandal), to the long-running *The Price Is Right* and *Wheel of Fortune* through *Jeopardy.*

Dramatic series also endured in different genres, including daytime serials (soap operas), which migrated from radio (*The Guiding Light, As the World Turns*) to entertain housewives at their ironing boards. Mixed audiences enjoyed evening broadcasts of Westerns (e.g., *Gunsmoke, The Virginian, Bonanza*) and police dramas (*Dragnet, The Untouchables, Hawaii Five-0, The Rockford Files, Kojak*), not to mention Cold War spy concepts (*The Man from U.N.C.L.E*) and medical dramas (*Doctor Kildare; Marcus Welby, M.D.*).

TV dramas reflected new social norms and nostalgic yearnings. The white nuclear family was reinforced in its pioneer formulation in *Little House on the Prairie* (1974–1980), based on Laura Ingalls Wilder's *Little House* novels, while viewers took nostalgic comfort in the small southern town of Mayberry in *The Andy Griffith* (1960–1968). The Korean War prompted the long-running antiwar dark comedy *M*A*S*H* (short for Mobile Army Surgical Hospital), which ran from 1972 to 1983, while sci-fi fans of *Star Trek,* which debuted in 1966, drew a cult following of Trekkies to TV and film through the 1970s and beyond. By the later 1970s, the videocassette brought Hollywood movies to the home TV screen, enabling home viewers to rent or build film libraries, just as the videocassette recorder (VCR) let viewers tape scheduled TV programs to watch at their convenience.

Sitcoms (short for situation comedy series) became a recreational TV staple, starting with Lucille Ball and Desi Arnez's early 1950s *I Love Lucy* and then reflecting changing mores and social issues, from the nuclear-family-centered *Leave It to Beaver, Ozzie and Harriet,* and *Father Knows Best* to the broad satiric critique of bigotry, racism, and class division (*All in the Family,* 1971–1983). The civil rights movement brought African Americans into prime time (*Sanford and Son, The Jeffersons*), just as the women's movement from the late 1960s brought the highly popular *Mary Tyler Moore Show* (1970–1977), its protagonist a female TV journalist, and *Laverne & Shirley* (1976–1983), featuring two wisecracking working-class women workers at a Milwaukee brewery.

Televised sports broadcasts became a staple of weekend leisure hours, from the blurry black-and-white small-screen broadcasts of roller derbies, wrestling, and baseball of the late 1940s and early 1950s to the crisp lines and vivid color close-ups and replay images of major league baseball, boxing, wrestling, football, basketball, golf, tennis, hockey, and special events such as the Olympics and Kentucky Derby. Sports advertisers often promoted leisure-based products, notably beer and tobacco, to a largely male audience (who were often seated in TV recliner lounge chairs, enjoying chips and other processed snack foods promoted for recreational eating). It is noteworthy that the popularity of thoroughbred horse racing declined when the sport refused to be broadcast regularly on network TV, its officials fearing that fans would not come to the racetrack.

Children's Television Children's TV was on the scene from the early to mid-1940s, with *The Howdy-Doody Show* centered on a title-character marionette, an avuncular emcee, Buffalo Bob, and a mixed cast of live actors and puppets. A science-fiction adventure of the 1950s, *Captain Video and His Video Rangers,* included the hero and sidekick in space-age adventures bolstered with futuristic technology. *The Lone Ranger,* a successful radio series adapted for TV (1949–1957), joined *Hopalong Cassidy* as long-running TV Westerns. Cartoons and other children's programming tied to products, notably sugared breakfast cereals, became morning and weekend fare for children. Hanna-Barbera cartoon series such as *Josie and the Pussycats* and *Scooby-Doo* ran from the late 1960s into the 1970s and later were broadcast in syndication, as were such programs as *I Love Lucy,* so that generations of children watched some of the same programs their parents had watched as children.

Over decades, the quality of U.S. TV-based leisure was hotly debated. In 1951, social critic Paul Goodman foresaw a nation afflicted with "spectatoritis," while others charged the nation with narcotic addiction to the small screen. In 1961, Federal Communications Commission (FCC) chairman Newton Minnow accused the nation's broadcasters with creating a TV "vast wasteland," an image drawn from T. S. Eliot's classic poem and resonant of the qualms of the mid-twentieth-century American social theorists. At times this debate focused on children, with TV accused of fostering passivity, of inciting violent behavior, of wasting time better spent in creative play, and of stimulating consumerist cravings in those too young to exercise proper judgment. Programming designed to educate children via recreation drew much public support, notably public television's *Sesame Street,* which premiered in 1969, and *The Electric Company.*

Americans' recreation was at moments guided by political leaders. The 1957 launch of the Soviet satellite *Sputnik* shocked many into belief that the nation had become complacently "soft," falling behind its Cold War adversary in science and technology—and physical fitness. Elected president in 1960, John F. Kennedy projected an image of physical vigor maintained through outdoor sports and games, from sailing to backyard touch football with family and friends. JFK popularized physical exercise and, in 1960 and 1961, promoted the fifty-mile hike.

The Fitness Boom

That fad faded, but fitness thereafter became a major recreational preoccupation, especially of the managerial-professional class. Jogging and running were favored from the 1970s as James Fixx and others promoted their efficacy in fending off cardiac disease and maintaining mental agility. Boston's venerable, 26.2-mile annual marathon became a model for other cities' marathon footraces, from New York to Chicago to San Francisco. Women and men ran, just as both joined indoor gyms and health clubs and spent after-work hours on treadmills and lifting and bench-pressing weights.

By the late 1970s and the 1980, deskbound business executives boasted that they played as hard as they worked, and hotels installed gyms and health clubs for business travelers, even as affluent women were lured to spa resorts (such as the Elizabeth Arden Golden Door) for a combination of leisured personal care and health-fitness regimen. Executives and professionals were said to be entitled to R&R (rest and relaxation), a term originating in the Vietnam War years when armed service personnel were flown to Hawaii for relief from combat. The post-Kennedy presidency shifted but did not end the emphasis on fitness in leisure hours, as exemplified by the chief executive. President Lyndon B. Johnson was shown on horseback at his Texas ranch, while Gerald Ford golfed (Ford had also played football in college). President Jimmy Carter was shown relaxing on the softball diamond in his hometown of Plains, Georgia, while Ronald Reagan rode horses and cleared brush at his ranch near Santa Barbara, California.

California Culture California, indeed, became the mythic domain of the American leisured life defined by youthfulness. Leisure itself was mythologized geographically in the Golden State and promoted in the mid-1960s music and lyrics of the Beach Boys, who sang of "California Girls" and muscle cars. Here was a Lotus Land image of a beachfront surfing life never interrupted by work or school or even harsh weather. This California ideal, notably of ethnically white (if sunbronzed) males, was projected nationally as a utopia of perpetual youth (and challenged only in the late 1960s by race riots in the L.A.

section of Watts and by the anti–Vietnam War protests largely of student-age Americans). The mythic California implied nonetheless that all America was a Golden State.

Rise of the Automobile The automobile became central as a recreational vehicle, and driving a pleasure in itself, even on near-to-home recreational jaunts, which included sporting events, sometimes to cheer children participating on school or organized league teams (Little League baseball, Pop Warner football). Those within reach of pro sports stadiums or arenas drove (or took public transportation) to major league games, and families or groups of friends sometimes shared the cost of season tickets. Tailgate parties—picnic-style pregame meals named for the station-wagon rear dropgate on which the food and drinks were spread—became popular at autumn football games.

Automobile road travel furthered the long-term American romance with the road, which was celebrated in Walt Whitman's *Song of the Open Road*, in Jack Kerouac's *On the Road,* and in Bobby Troupe's pop song about getting kicks on "Route 66." The theme song of vocalist Dinah Shore on her weekly NBC network TV show struck a chord: "See the USA in Your Chevrolet." The jingle (1956–1963) coincided with low-cost fuel and the construction of the U.S. interstate highway system, begun in 1958, which permitted coast-to-coast, high-speed (sixty to seventy-five miles per hour) motoring on multilane, limited-access roadways. The American family vacation was newly defined with the 1955 opening of Disneyland, a 100-acre park near Los Angeles that combined amusement park rides with movie-set environments (e.g., "Tomorrowland," "Frontierland").

By 1965, 50 million Disneyland visitors had proved the viability of recreational theme parks, and others, such as Knott's Berry Farm, SeaWorld, Busch Gardens, Dollywood, and Opryland, became automotive destinations rivaling the National Parks in attraction (and sometimes paralleling them—Silver Dollar City, which became Dolly Parton's Dollywood, was developed nearly adjacent to the entrance of the Great Smoky Mountain National Park in Tennessee).

Kindred to the theme parks, America's historic or cultural sites also became prime destinations for auto vacationers. These included cities of historic interest (such as Paul Revere's Boston, Massachusetts, and the Liberty Bell of Philadelphia, Pennsylvania). They also included American mansions, such as Hearst Castle, William Randolph Hearst's estate from the 1910s to the 1940s on the California coast, and the late-nineteenth-century palatial summer "cottages" of the Astors and Vanderbilts in Newport, Rhode Island. Following the death of Elvis Presley in 1977, his Memphis home, Graceland, also became a tourist mecca with the customary gift shop and snack bar.

In the 1970s, the notion of educational—or cultural—tourism gained momentum, promising self-improvement combined with entertainment. Vacationers might take a road journey in Wisconsin, for instance, to seek out the houses of master architect Frank Lloyd Wright. In 1975, a cultural tourism enterprise for Americans over fifty-five years old, Elderhostel, was founded to offer older adults, especially retirees, national and international travel-and-learning opportunities, many based on college and university campuses and focused on topics from music to Klondike gold mining.

Leisure tourism in the 1970s also meant stays at deluxe gambling casinos now luring middle-class vacationers by air or auto (including vacation rental cars) to gaming resorts with spectacular stage shows featuring such acts as Elvis, Frank Sinatra and his "Rat Pack," or 1970s vocalists Wayne Newton or Englebert Humperdink in Las Vegas or Atlantic City.

By the late 1960s, young Americans motored to days-long music festivals, notably 1969's legendary Woodstock (New York) "Three Days of Love and Peace," featuring performances by the Jefferson Airplane and Jimi Hendrix, among others. The concertgoer's festival experience was not solely to enjoy but to bear witness or pay homage to revered artists in a communal campground setting, the concert sometimes a quasi-religious recreational event.

Outdoor Life Outdoor hobbies took on larger importance for millions of Americans from the late 1960s, including traditional sports such as tennis and golf (whose popularity waxed and waned according to the performance on TV of star players such as tennis pro Billie Jean King and golf champions Jack Nicklaus and Arnold Palmer). Other traditional outdoor recreational activities included camping and hiking, a longtime cornerstone of the scouting movement, and bird-watching, hunting, and fishing.

The environmental movement of the late 1960s, hastened by the success of Rachel Carson's *Silent Spring* (1962) and annual Earth Day festivities (beginning in 1970), spurred newly rigorous outdoorsmanship, including rock climbing, mountain biking, and white-water canoeing, which gained impetus from the production of gear and equipment made of new, lightweight materials. Maine outfitter L.L. Bean now stood for a year-round outdoor recreational way of life in the United States and a protective, pro-environmental "green" stance.

Motorized recreationists, however, found themselves in turf battles with hikers and preservationists. Motor-

boating, motorcycling (from street to dirt bikes), to snowmobiles and off-road or all terrain vehicles (ATVs) marked what some call America's love of the internal combustion engine. By the mid-1970s, however, Congress moved to regulate the degree to which off-road motor vehicles could crisscross National Parks, forests, wilderness, and other public lands, as these activities damaged pristine conditions and caused noise pollution.

Shopping Malls Motor vehicles also shuttled Americans in ever-larger numbers to malls, which represented the postwar American demographic shift of retail and leisure centers from the downtown to the burgeoning suburbs. In the postwar years, Austrian-born mall designer, architect Victor Gruen, designed malls as new centers for cultural and community activity throughout the United States. In 1954, Gruen's Northland Mall outside Detroit became the model for a "shoppers' paradise," with open spaces called terraces, courts, lanes, colonnaded walks, sculptures, fountains, and landscaping, together with such urban touches as kiosks, cafés, and benches. The signature Gruen mall was nothing less than a new downtown, and it appeared in major urban area suburbs from Houston, Texas, to Minneapolis, Minnesota. Malls became the antitheses of cities, which were now thought by many to be dangerous, dirty, and chaotic. Enclosed malls soon freed shoppers from inclement weather and became mini-vacation spots for shopping, strolling, snacking (on American and ethnic franchised foods at the food courts), even ice skating and amusement park rides, as the mall took on characteristics of the theme park.

Changes at the Movies Not surprisingly, movie theaters also relocated to the suburbs, the single-screen theater evolving into a new identity, the multiplex, in which multiple theaters showed several movies concurrently. Film entertainment included musicals and romantic comedy (such as Doris Day in *Pillow Talk;* 1959). The postwar decades reflected ongoing American values, aspirations, and fears. Frank Capra's postwar *It's a Wonderful Life* (1946), starring Jimmy Stewart, reaffirmed traditional American small-town virtues (the film gradually becoming an annual December holiday-season TV staple). The first two *Godfather* films (1972, 1974) arguably centered on family values even as they set a new standard in graphic violence in Hollywood movies. Decades of escapist action-adventure films were launched with the 1975 release of the smash hit *Jaws,* in which a killer white shark, a pop Moby Dick, menaces a vacation fishing village.

Americans' social conformity, as noted by postwar critics, was challenged in a series of films, including Marlon

Brando as a Hell's Angels–like biker in *The Wild One* (1954); *Blackboard Jungle* (1955), which critiqued high school as a prison; and *Rebel without a Cause* (1955), in which the male lead, played by James Dean, embodies alienation from parents and other authorities. This stance was reprised in *The Graduate* (1967), which critiqued U.S. material success.

The nuclear threat in a Cold War context, furthermore, prompted such movies as Alfred Hitchcock's spy thriller *North by Northwest* (1959) and the apocalyptic dark comedy *Dr. Strangelove, or How I Learned to Stop Worrying and Love the Bomb* (1964). Cold War fears were indirectly expressed in certain Westerns, notably John Ford's *The Man Who Shot Liberty Valence* (1964), plus science-fiction films such as *Invasion of the Body Snatchers* (1956; remake 1978).

Social movements of the late 1960s and 1970s (e.g., Vietnam antiwar activism, civil rights, feminism) were reflected onscreen in *Easy Rider* (1968) and *Alice's Restaurant*, both celebrations of the 1960s counterculture, together with the antiwar *The Deer Hunter* (1978) and *Apocalypse Now* (1979). Backlash movies were also popular, notably *Straw Dogs* (1971), which tried to legitimize macho violence against women. So-called blaxploitation films appeared from Melvin Van Peebles, notably *Shaft* (1971), featuring a sexy, tough, stylish black private eye. Sylvester Stallone's *Rocky* (1976) showed the triumph of a long-shot, underdog boxer who defies the odds to win a championship, a film affirming American spirit against a background of gasoline shortages, the Watergate scandal, and Vietnam.

Movies of personal choice and intimate relationships were also box-office hits, especially in the 1970s, sometimes called the "Me Decade." *Love Story* became the top-grossing movie of 1970, a complement to *Jonathan Livingston Seagull* (1973), based on an allegorical tale of existential individualism. It is noteworthy that Americans spent leisure time willingly in movie theaters (and in front of TV) whose screens were filled with images of contemporary social conflict and Cold War threats. Some of the most successful of these movies (such as *The Graduate*) critiqued the materialism of the very moviegoers relaxing in the theater with popcorn and soft drinks.

One successful Cold War–era Hollywood series featured a dashing British secret agent, James Bond (007), played by Sean Connery, who combined debonair sophistication with erotica and astounding feats of physical courage in such films as *Goldfinger* (1964) and *Diamonds Are Forever* (1971). The James Bond character mirrored the urban American male who had emerged in Hugh Hefner's Chicago-based *Playboy* magazine (and who patronized Hefner's key-clubs in major cities). First pub-

lished in 1953, *Playboy* was immediately successful, sexualizing recreation to an unprecedented degree as it promoted the image of the single male consumer of sports cars, liquor, deluxe travel, sophisticated clothing, home furnishings, and, above all, women.

Through its rabbit mascot, *Playboy* advanced a philosophy of hedonistic male bachelorhood, with Hefner himself representing the prototypical playboy in silk lounging pajamas and robe, ever surrounded by nearly nude, young, nubile women. The playboy signaled the totally leisured life in an American-style harem. In part, his mystique was one social consequence of the development of the oral contraceptive—"the Pill," as it became known in the 1960s—which virtually detached reproduction from heterosexual sexual relations, thus fostering the idea of sex acts as risk-free play (perhaps enjoyed on the new waterbed, which was promoted as sexually enhancing in the popular book *The Joy of Sex*). The ambivalence many women experienced about this new situation was captured in Erica Jong's 1973 best-selling novel, *Fear of Flying*.

Looking back from 1980, the American good life seems substantially validated by its myriad forms of recreation. Yet the trepidation and anguish of the 1948 *Life* roundtable group had not entirely disappeared over the postwar decades. Anxiety lingered in some quarters that leisure and recreation were Americans' escape routes from life's serious purpose. In 1984, critic-author Neil Postman, in a well-received book, renewed the charge that the nation had become one vast televisual amusement park. In a larger sense, his book title, *Amusing Ourselves to Death*, implied that leisure and recreation were the nation's fatal flaws, that democracy was imperiled by the seduction of nonstop entertainment. The Cold War was concluding officially, but Postman spoke for critics who warned that Americans had their fun on borrowed time.

See also: Automobiles and Leisure; Baseball, Amateur; Baseball Crowds; Basketball; Contemporary Leisure Patterns; Disneyland; Football; Movies' Impact on Popular Leisure; Teenage Leisure Trends; Television's Impact on Popular Leisure; Theme and Amusement Parks; Walt Disney World

BIBLIOGRAPHY

Clark, Alison J. *Tupperware: The Promise of Plastic in 1950s America.* Washington, D.C.: Smithsonian Institution Press, 1999.

Davenport, Russell W. "A Life Round Table on the Pursuit of Happiness." *Life.* (12 July 1948): 94–99

Edelstein, Andrew J., and Kevin McDonough. *The Seventies: From Hot Pants to Hot Tubs.* New York: Dutton, 1990.

Halberstam, David. *The Fifties.* New York: Fawcett Books, 1993.

Hardwick, M. Jeffrey. *Mall Maker: Victor Gruen, Architect of an American Dream.* Philadelphia: University of Pennsylvania Press, 2004.

Inge, M. Thomas, ed. *Handbook of American Popular Culture.* 2d ed. New York: Greenwood Press, 1989.

Jenkins, Virginia Scott. *The Lawn: A History of an American Obsession.* Washington D.C.: Smithsonian Institution Press, 1994.

Marcuse, Herbert. *One-Dimensional Man.* Boston: Beacon Press, 1964.

May, Kirse Granat. *Golden State, Golden Youth: The California Image in Popular Culture, 1955–1966.* Chapel Hill: University of North Carolina Press, 2002.

Mills, C. Wright. 1951. *White Collar: The American Middle Classes.* Reprint, New York: Oxford University Press, 1977.

Mintz, Stephen, and Randy Roberts, eds. *Hollywood's America: United States History through Its Films.* St. James and New York: Brandywine Press, 1993.

Nye, Russel B. *The Unembarrassed Muse: The Popular Arts in America.* New York: Dial Press, 1970.

Osgerby, Bill. *Playboys in Paradise: Masculinity, Youth, and Leisure-style in Modern America.* New York: Berg Publishers, 2001.

Postman, Neil. *Amusing Ourselves to Death: Public Discourse in the Age of Show Business.* New York: Penguin Books, 1986.

Potter, David M. 1955. *People of Plenty: Economic Abundance and the American Character.* Reprint, Chicago: University of Chicago Press, 1999.

Riesman, David, with Nathan Glazer and Reul Denny. 1950. *The Lonely Crowd.* Reprint: New Haven, Conn.: Yale University Press, 1969.

Rosenberg, Bernard, and David Manning White, eds. *Mass Culture: The Popular Arts in America.* Glencoe, Ill.: Free Press, 1957.

Schulman, Bruce J. *The Seventies: The Great Shift in American Culture, Society, and Politics.* New York: Free Press, 2001.

Tichi, Cecelia. *Electronic Hearth: Creating an American Television Culture.* New York: Oxford University Press, 1991.

Tindall, George Brown, and David E. Shi. *American: A Narrative History.* 3d ed. New York: W. W. Norton and Company, 1993.

Winship, Michael. *Television.* New York: Random House, 1988.

Cecelia Tichi

PRIVATIZATION OF LEISURE

Traditionally, leisure activities have been shared in public rituals that expressed and affirmed communal values. This was no less true in American history. Gradually, more private and familial recreational customs emerged with the full development of market and middle-class society across the nineteenth and twentieth centuries.

On the eve of the colonization, Europeans experienced leisure primarily in groups, either as part of the daily life of long workdays or in communal festivals and fairs. Leisure built around workmates was enjoyed in periodic breaks in the day's labor when drink, wagering, and other activities broke the monotony and created bonds between boss and worker and especially between laborers of differing ages and statuses (such as apprentices and journeymen). The work year was punctuated with festivals, often coinciding with seasonal downturns in agricultural or craft work. Many were held in winter (from All-Saint's Day on 1 November through Christmas, New Year's, Mardi Gras, Easter, and May Day). Most had religious origins, but all involved secular activities. While summertime leisure was rarer due to the press of farmwork, celebrations like the midsummer English wakes' week and Midsummer or St. John's Eve (in late June) were communal diversions of sport, drinking, and dancing. Leisure breaks were also linked to annual fairs—the traditional marketing of farm and craft goods and the annual hiring of servants. Moreover, because most people lived and worked in the confines of one- or two-room rural cottages or quarters connected to their shops, communal space (like public squares and taverns) rather than the home dominated leisure moments, especially of men. Women's leisure was more confined to domestic and work situations (such as in the many variations of the work bee). Poverty may have dictated these collective pleasures. Yet even for the rich there was no privacy, and thus dining, drinking, sports, games, and other leisure activities were performed in large groups.

Festivals established bonds between unequals through shared rituals and feasts as well as gift exchanges. The powerful and wealthy were expected to share in their bounty, and they recognized that drinking and even temporary assaults on authority were necessary "safety valves. In mumming, meandering youths and laborers sometimes intimidated the rich into "gifts" of food and drink on holidays. Perhaps the most unique feature of traditional popular leisure culture was its principle of saturnalia. Like the ancient Roman custom of a week of drinking in early December, from which this term gets its name, Europeans who migrated to America enjoyed lengthy breaks from the daily drudgery of manual work. The "binge"—the unrestrained indulgence in food and drink, so often noted by anthropologists studying "primitive" village culture—was common during holiday periods. Finally, in annual festivals like Mardi Gras and May Day, the common people indulged in a variety of games, plays, and songs that expressed many subtle forms of protest against the rich and powerful. Still, the elite—be it the church, local lord, or king—seldom attempted to repress these popular enjoyments. Even though they were often chaotic and crude, even violent and critical of the status quo, they were often patronized by the powerful, who contributed land for games or food and drink.

Many European communal holidays did not travel with the colonists or later immigrants, in many cases because European farming and village life, around which festival leisure was organized, was not reestablished in the colonies. Still, communitarian leisure did not disappear, but often was expressed in different ways than in Europe (for example, group hunting expeditions, plantation house parties, work frolics, parades, and celebrations around election days). Older collective traditions imported from Europe also survived, like cock fighting, horse racing, and rowdy holiday traditions formed around Christmas mumming and partying, especially outside Puritan-dominated areas.

Challenges to Traditional Community-Based Leisure, 1500–1800

The trend toward more privatized forms of leisure was part of a set of complex economic, social, and cultural changes that interacted and reinforced one another as they emerged during the long process of modernization. A major trend was the withdrawal of the patronage of the wealthy and powerful from traditional forms of popular leisure and their attempt to impose new, more family-oriented recreations on the collectivity. The Renaissance of northern Italy of the fifteenth century began the long process of separating elite from popular leisure in Europe in the development of a unique urban culture that eventually spread to many European cities. These societies were characterized by their quest for individual expression and their openness to—even obsession with—change or fashion as opposed to the traditional and slow-changing character of festival culture. It sparked the development of clothing industries in Italy and the European Low Lands and led to a virtual revolution in home furnishings (with the development of upholstered chairs, wallpaper, carpets, paintings, and even miniatures). These trends created new standards of domestic comfort and led elites to focus their free time and income on private interests. They also led to a rejection of the rough and often chaotic pleasures of the peasant and street festival for the cultivation of refined arts and pleasures away from the crowd. In 1516, Baldesar Castiglione set the standard for a new genteel leisure culture when he insisted that one should "shun the vulgar herd," for refined pleasures that followed a "decorous mean" (pp. 104, 139).

Religious reformers of the sixteenth and seventeenth century (especially in the radical form of Puritanism that migrated from England to the colonies in 1620) aggressively resisted communitarian festivals and crude sports like bull running and animal baiting as godless or as corruptions of biblical religion. Reformers attempted to ban and later restrict saints days and public holidays. Puritan Protestants in England especially condemned theater and public drinking, but they embraced more private recreations such as moderate exercise as well as reading and singing (at first only for devotional purposes). This venting of emotional needs in song and literature provided the foundation for new sedate and often individualized pleasures. The new markets for the novel and magazine in the eighteenth century were indirectly due to the Puritans. Still, even in the more traditional, non-Puritan regions of Europe and colonial America, religious leaders including Catholics, especially the Jesuits, also condemned the "excesses" of carnival and other feast days that seemed to undermine the sanctity of holy days and efforts to increase the output of workers.

Both the religious animosity toward saturnalia and the elite quest for privacy and refinement contributed to the decline of communitarian leisure in colonial America. Members of the southern colonial gentry like George Washington cultivated an exclusive culture of Sunday afternoon rounds of visits with occasional treks to Annapolis, Williamsburg, or Charleston for balls or plays. Plantation house parties brought the elite together for bowling, boat and horse racing, dancing, and even cock fights and fox hunts. The emergence of an urban culture in colonial New York emulated London society with exclusive balls, card parties, and especially the theater in the eighteenth century. Seventeenth-century New England Puritans attempted to restrict communal festivals, famously banning May pole celebrations in 1620 and Christmas celebrations in 1659.

Increasing social distance between the rich and poor in cities in the 1700s and the early 1800s was compounded by the appearance of social disorder. For example, between 1834 and 1844, there were more than 200 gang wars in New York City, and throughout the 1840s and 1850s, Saint Louis was continually disrupted by fistfights between rival voluntary fire companies. Many conservatives believed that the democratic "excesses" of the American and French Revolutions had led to an increase in a lack of discipline among the masses. When the vote was extended in America to the poorer males in the 1820s, elites feared that politicians would look the other way when confronted with the threats of drink, gambling, and prostitution. One solution to these perceived threats was to restrict public

132

leisure activities—especially by restricting or banning drinking and gambling. Despite the fact that Sunday was the only day in the week available for amusement, powerful religious elites attempted to prohibit access to public leisure (theater, travel, and spectator sports) on the Sabbath so as to promote religious study and honor God.

Another solution was to promote new leisure customs that would compensate for the withdrawal of the industrial and propertied elite from popular culture. Leisure was perhaps the best place to inculcate the important virtues for success in a growing commercial economy—self-control, familialism, and "respectability." This effort took many forms, all of which reinforced a trend toward private leisure. Instead of the boisterous celebrations of the Fourth of July, temperance and other reformers advocated family picnics. New institutions like the YMCA (appearing first in Boston and New York in 1851) were subsidized by merchants and bankers who wanted to create a substitute home for lonely single men who were new to the city and to provide an alternative to the theater and tavern. These facilities reached mostly middle-class transients and only a generation later would the YMCA transform into a center of physical fitness. Other alternatives to traditional crowd leisure were city parks (especially from the 1850s), which encouraged family or individual strolls rather than team games, and public libraries notably from the late 1890s when hundreds of Neo-Roman structures were erected to house the libraries built by the philanthropist Andrew Carnegie.

Affluence and Expansion of Domestic Space in the Nineteenth Century

The most important form of the privatization of leisure took place in the home. In the nineteenth century, the middle class sought refuge from the crowd in new residences, often suburban or isolated from both wage earners and entertainment districts that, in turn, became a site of familial and private leisure. Industrialization and the commercial office had led to the separation of work and leisure. With increased affluence and the quest of all for increased privacy, the billeting of clerks, wage workers, and apprentices in or near their masters' houses declined and eventually nearly disappeared, and, with it, most forms of cross-class leisure. Except in some retail shops, where long hours made this separation of work and leisure impossible, the home was increasingly a retreat from the market, not its center. The home became a "haven" for a small circle of family members, opened on special events to a few friends and distant relatives. In the domestic space, new family recreational "traditions" were created to reinforce family, no longer communal, bonds.

Women became the principle innovators in family/private recreation, tasks essential to new definitions of the homemaker. Industrialization meant the removal of, at least, affluent married women from the workforce; and changes in household and childrearing work of wives cleared the way for female leadership in creating a new domestic leisure.

By the 1850s, affluent American families were beginning to flee the crowded city streets of row houses (even in rich neighborhoods) for the detached suburban homes with their surrounding yards. A park-like feel was cultivated in neighborhoods that featured winding lanes and green spaces. Mid-nineteenth-century model suburbs like New Jersey's Llewellyn Park and Chicago's Riverside set the pace. Wealthy districts in Westchester County, New York, and Chestnut Hill near Philadelphia, for example, radiated from train stations, because they were surrounded by open country, they were isolated from business and manufacturing districts as well as poorer neighborhoods. They were supplied with elite amenities like country clubs and small parks surrounded by mainline Protestant churches.

The Victorian suburban home, now totally bereft of economic purpose, was transformed into a multipurpose private retreats. Homes of increased size and specialization were designed to reflect a clear separation between the formal and private, male and female, adult and child space. Often replacing the simple layout of two rooms to a floor was the formal parlor and family sitting room on one side of the entry and a dining room and kitchen on the other. The entryway was also broadened by the creation of a hall for receiving guests. A well-appointed parlor was thought to have a positive influence on the character of those who entered it. In it were displays of female accomplishment in handicrafts, the performance of amateur singing and piano playing, the playing of "uplifting" parlor games (educational card and board games), and demonstrations of "magic lanterns" and other precursors of movies, for example. This room was the site for the custom of paying calls. On the second floor, the nursery allowed for not only the separation of the very young from the relaxation of parents but also an environment that could be devoted especially to children's needs, including toys and play space. Even the respectable working class devoted a large share of scarce living space to dining room and parlor, often never used except for the formal visit of guests, on Sunday evenings especially. In the middle classes, the family and its celebration of itself on weekends and holidays challenged the boisterous and bizarre festival and became an effective alternative to the unwelcome crowd.

Technology and commercial enterprise combined to provide for rich and diverse home-based leisure activities. Steam presses and more efficient distribution led to a revolution in publishing. If in 1825 there were no more than 100 magazines in the United States, by 1850 there were about 600. From midcentury, piano and sheet music became widely available. The late Victorian suburb used its lawns to play croquet and its front- and backyard gardens to cultivate the hobby of horticulture. A vast market emerged for domestic-centered leisure goods from the camera (from 1888 with the marketing of the easy-to-use Kodak) to the table settings for the increasingly more elegant dinner parties of the middle class.

The familial trend was evident also in a reorganization of holidays. Christmas, until the 1830s an often boisterous holiday, celebrated with parties and even street rituals, gradually became a more subdued domestic celebration. The idea of the family Christmas with Yule log, tree, songs, and the exchange of gifts was promoted by middle-class magazines and books. Gradually, the day became a celebration of childhood and domestic values when gift giving shifted from exchanges across social classes to the indulgence of children in the name of the largesse of Santa Claus. By the end of the nineteenth century, the American Thanksgiving became a tradition of family reunion.

Impact of Transportation and Markets on the Privatization of Leisure

Increased impersonal economic and technological forces of industrialization in the nineteenth century also facilitated the breakdown of traditional communal leisure. The revolution in transportation and communications resulted in both new leisure opportunities, but also an uprooting of traditional pleasures. From the 1830s, the railroad made distant travel accessible to the middle class and, with the gradual reduction in prices, to time-starved workers. The steam tram (or streetcar) was developed first in America and improved in the mid-1880s with electrification. This development vastly eased the movement of people of often-modest means around the now-sprawling urban centers like New York. The tram freed them from exclusive reliance on the neighborhood café, tavern, or ethnic fraternal society for the mass leisure of baseball games, amusement parks, and dance halls, theaters, and department store. The streetcar dominated urban travel and in some places suburban and regional travel until it was replaced by the bus and car after about 1920.

In the nineteenth century, the railroad led to the decline of smaller local fairs and festivals when it became possible for rural people to travel to regional urban cen-

ters for the larger and more diverse entertainment. The train (and steamboat) also facilitated larger, more commercialized amusements that could spread costs over a wider regional and national market. For example, after the Civil War, large train circuses reached relatively large audiences. Performers traveling by train increasingly relied on agents, impresarios, and owners of chains of theaters and music halls to find bookings. Audiences enjoyed more diverse and probably superior entertainment, but local traditions began to die out as local sports figures and other performers could not compete with regional or national talent.

Capitalist business practices—especially profit maximization based on the mass market and unfettered competition—transformed and uprooted communal leisure practices. The key was in broadening the appeal of a leisure activity or entertainment by introducing it to a new market. This process took many forms. For example, popular amusements like in the circus were reformed to appeal to a middle-class audience with claims of sentimental or educational value. By contrast, an originally middle-class leisure, like the railroad excursion to uplifting sites such as Niagara Falls, appealed to wider, more popular markets on a strictly commercial basis with circus-type shows. All these changes created mass audiences but also undermined community-based leisure.

Relatively few nationally dominant corporations attracted mass audiences by adopting new technologies. In the 1890s, investors in established leisure industries—like music halls or vaudeville—were the first to feature films in their houses and to abandon the old entertainment when the market warranted it. This change had the effect of rapidly transforming leisure practices and encouraging continuous innovation. In the 1890s, for example, entertainment districts like Times Square and Coney Island in or near New York City embraced the potential of electric lighting and power to attract thousands of visitors from local neighborhoods. Bright night lighting and electric-powered Ferris wheels and roller coasters drew people away from traditional communal leisure and into the anonymous crowds. While these new throngs seemed to be anything but "private," they consisted of relatively passive individuals responding to general and often novel appeals rather than communities sharing a festival tradition. For example, Coney Island in the 1890s and 1900s provided young urban immigrants with an alternative to the ethnic and neighborhood dances, dinners, and socializing dominated by their elders in a crowd where they could break from expectations of accustomed social roles and values. Traditional pleasures were undermined and leisure delocalized, creating the atomized crowd at new specialized places of play.

The Middle-Class Quest for Privacy in the Twentieth Century

While the wealthy and political elites had long feared crowds as a threat to the political order, susceptible to demigods and professional revolutionaries, the twentieth century brought a new kind of anxiety—fear of amassed consumers of popular recreation and entertainment. American elites lamented that mass production created a culture of the lowest common denominator, with neither the depth and unique quality of folk culture nor the refinement of high culture. The popular "habit of being amused" had created a mass market for an unscrupulous entertainment industry for whom "the lust for profit has picked open the bud" of insatiable desire, especially among vulnerable youth. (Edwards, p. 133). Middle-class critics complained that crowds at amusement parks and dance halls lacked the restraint of family, ethnic, and religious tradition. Behind this belief in the presumed impulsive and suggestive behavior of people in crowds was the conviction that cultivated, constrained, and uplifting leisure could be realized only in private and domestic life.

In the twentieth century, the middle-class quest for escape from the crowd along with new technologies contributed to new meanings of individualized leisure. By the early 1900s, the automobile was already providing the upper-middle class with alternatives to the crowds of pleasure seekers in city centers and amusement parks (who remained dependent on trains and other public transportation). Automobiles made possible individualized touring and reinforced the goal of making the family the focus of holidays. Not only were families traveling by car liberated from the timetables and routes of the streetcar and train, they were freed from having to share space with anyone but household members. The parkway (first built in New York in 1911) was designed to be aesthetically pleasing as well as useful, encouraging private travel. Newly built or refurbished county, state, and national parks, accessible only by car, freed car travelers from the crush of tourist sites like seaside resorts and amusement parks reached by the less affluent via public transportation. The Interstate Highway System (begun in 1956) made the vast expanses of America accessible to millions of vacationers who could bypass small towns and metropolitan congestion.

The car culture produced a plethora of new privatized pleasures. The drive-in restaurant that appeared in the South and West in the early 1920s not only was fast and convenient, but allowed diners to avoid social contact with strangers. From the 1940s, these drive-ins often provided "carhop" waitresses that let customers remain in their cars. Later, "drive-through" ordering eliminated

even the social contact between parked cars. In the 1950s and 1960s, the automobile began to displace the downtown business district because lack of parking and traffic forced major retailers to build large stores in suburban districts with good-sized free parking lots. The drive-in movie theater (appearing first in New Jersey in 1933) provided an alternative to the close contact and lack of privacy in regular theaters. By the 1950s, 4,000 of the big screens dotted rural and suburban roads, providing teenagers privacy and offering parents a way of taking children to the movies with minimal frustration. The car privatized not only shopping, dining, and entertainment but even homes. Beginning in the 1920s, the large front porch, which had so long served as a place from where to greet and socialize with neighbors, was gradually eliminated from new houses and replaced with the attached garage, which eliminated face-to-face contact with neighbors.

More generally, the car intensified the suburbanization process and gradually broke the symbiosis between city and suburb that had made cities centers of entertainment and leisure in the early twentieth century. In the long run, suburbanites both worked and played on the periphery of the city along commercial strips, industrial parks, and shopping malls. By the 1980s, even the traditional annual ritual in December of visiting downtown shopping districts to see giant Christmas tree displays, store windows, toy shop attractions, and Christmas parades had declined. This change, critics argued, weakened urban cultural centers. Residential neighborhoods became small, private islands accessible only by car, with backyards that were private and reclusive places. The disappearance of sidewalks from suburban streets is testimony to the decline of social interaction between neighbors.

Private access to entertainment media accelerated these trends, beginning with the phonograph (invented in 1876, but marketed only after 1887) and culminating with the radio (accessible for domestic use from the 1910s) and television after World War II. Recorded music and speech played on the phonograph (along with domestic appliances like the player piano) allowed individuals to experience high and popular arts from the sanctuary of the home. The radio began to supplant the phonograph when in the early 1920s commercial broadcasts began to offer regional and national entertainment to individual listeners. The emergence of network radio in 1926 (and with it a full day of regular programs) led to a fundamental transformation of Americans' leisure time when passive listening began to supplant more social forms of leisure. As early as 1938, 40 percent of households on a typical winter evening had the radio turned on.

Radio became an appliance well adapted to combining private household activities (and driving) with entertainment. Since the 1920s, radio relieved the isolation of homemakers and provided the sick, immobile, and lonely with a form of companionship. This development was particularly important because the number of relatives and children at home all day was declining due to mass education and the increase in the role of the wage economy on all households. The radio offered a viable alternative to going out to movies, concerts, and even visiting friends by providing national programs through the networks that reached nearly everyone with a twist of the dial. By the early 1930s, the networks had developed a schedule of programs that appealed to different age and gender interests in the family: quiz, advice, and "soap operas" during the day, children's adventure in late afternoon, and comedy, variety, and drama programs in the evening, all appealing to different combinations of men and women. What may have contributed to families' congregating around the radio also led to new interests separating families by age and gender. From the mid-1920s, radio was mobile; in the late 1930s it became common in cars, allowing small groups or individuals to find entertainment that formerly had required joining an audience in a theater or around a bandstand. The radio allowed listeners to avoid the crowd while enjoying a national, even global entertainment in private.

Television was an extension of radio and emerged from the same companies that had marketed radio (especially NBC). While in 1950 only 9 percent of American homes had TVs, four years later the figure was 55 percent, and by 1967, virtually all households (95 percent) contained at least one set. That year Americans watched an average of five hours of television per day. It reinforced the trend established by radio of home-bound leisure. Even more than radio in the 1930s, television expressed the personal power to experience the world without having to join a crowd. In the 1950s, radio programming shifted to news and music, adapting itself especially to youth on the go with rock music. At the same time, television took over radio's family format, reaching each age and gender segment over the course of a day's programming. The TV reduced conversation in the living room and required new family rules over control of the knobs. The TV became a family member—a babysitter, a welcomed guest for the bored or lonely, and sometimes even an annoying relative. The development of the home computer in the 1980s and the Internet in the 1990s only reinforced the privatization of leisure, replacing social games with video games and face-to-face communications with socializing through e-mails, electronic chat groups, and Web surfing.

More broadly, increased affluence has reinforced the privatization of leisure since 1960. While the car had promised to bring the family together, gradually increasing disposable income made it possible for many American households to possess two or more cars. If there were 3.74 Americans for every car in 1950, that figure dropped to 2.9 in 1960 and 1.86 by 1980. This development facilitated the pursuit of individualized recreation, especially in families with older children. The same process is evident in the cheapening of electronic entertainment from the mid-1950s with the replacement of tubes with transistors and later integrated circuits. When families could possess two or more radios, TVs, and other entertainment devices, members no longer had to share time or space together. While early TV was an electronic hearth in American living rooms, the possession of several sets and Internet-accessible computers, located in bedrooms, kitchens, and "family" rooms, made the home into a "multiplex theater," with each family member finding a private refuge to enjoy his or her own entertainment without the need to share or compromise. The general tendency for the average American home to increase in size (with the median square footage of new homes increasing from 1,385 square feet in 1970 to 1,950 by 1998) reinforced this trend. Even more important, with the development of specialized radio (beginning with FM stations in the 1960s), cable TV (in the 1970s), and the Internet (in the 1990s), increasingly narrow and segmented leisure communities emerged (even if sometimes on a global scale). The growth of consumerism with affluence made it possible for each family member to have an increasingly large array of personal leisure "tools," be they a child's own toy box or a basement hobby shop full of father's tools, or a kitchen equipped with exotic cookbooks and appliances. In addition, personal vacations and separate activities on family vacations have appeared, even if they remain mostly of interest to the two-income professional classes.

Implications

These private forms of leisure, creations of technology, and a penchant of a dominant middle-class culture to avoid crowds led not only to cultural uplift or even family togetherness as early promoters of the car, radio, and TV had hoped, but also to a new kind of mass leisure. Instead of physical interaction within communal or crowd settings, modern Americans have become private recipients of mass-produced leisure. Americans desired the mechanized entertainment of radio and television because it privatized the site of leisure, but they still wanted to share the same information and entertainment with other Americans. Thus, a relatively crowdless, but still mass, culture emerged in the twentieth century. The individualized mobility of the car privatized the space for pleasure while creating new congestion on roads. Even when entertainment became increasingly individualized and segmented, quasi-monopolies dominated their production on a national and global scale. The result was a mass leisure but also a decline of recreation built around the social interaction of communities, neighbors, and in the early 2000s even families. By the 1950s, mass (but privatized) leisure built around mass media, automobility, and the suburb seemed to have displaced much local, ethnic, class, and even family tradition.

These changes often liberated the young from the culture and control of their elders and have, in some cases, given minority and regional cultures a voice that was formerly ignored and suppressed. But it also has the potential to fragment American culture, reducing the ability of citizens to share common aspirations and values. When taken to extremes, the primacy of individual leisure and pleasure has resulted in the decline of Americans' willingness and skill in working through civic and social organizations that have been an essential part of American democracy for two centuries.

See also: Crowds at Leisure; Radio Listening, Car and Home; Suburbanization of Leisure; Television's Impact on Popular Leisure; Urbanization of Leisure

BIBLIOGRAPHY

Boyer, Paul. *Urban Masses and Moral Order in America, 1820–1920.* Cambridge, Mass.: Harvard University Press, 1978.

Burke, Peter. *Popular Culture in Early Modern Europe.* New York: Harper and Row, 1978.

Carson, Jane. *Colonial Virginians at Play.* Williamsburg, Va.: Colonial Williamsburg, 1965.

Castiglione, Baldesar. *The Book of the Courtier.* Translated by Charles S. Singleton. Garden City, N.Y.: Doubleday and Company, 1959. The original edition was published in 1527.

Cross, Gary. *A Social History of Leisure.* State College, Pa.: Venture Publishing, 1990.

———. *An All-Consuming Century: Why Commercialism Won in Modern America.* New York: Columbia University Press, 2000.

Daniels, Bruce. *Puritans at Play: Leisure and Recreation in Colonial New England.* New York: St. Martin's Press, 1995.

Dulles, Rhea Foster. *A History of Recreation: America Learns to Play.* New York: Appleton-Century, 1965.

Edwards, Richard. *Popular Amusements.* New York: Association Press, 1915.

Flink, James. *The Automobile Age.* Cambridge, Mass.: MIT Press, 1993.

Grier, Katherine. *Culture and Comfort: People, Parlors, and Upholstery, 1850–1930.* Madison: University of Wisconsin Press, 1988.

Kasson, John. *Amusing the Millions.* New York: Hill and Wang, 1978.

Lasch, Christopher. *Haven in a Heartless World.* New York: W. W. Norton and Company, 1977.

Leach, William. *Land of Desire: Merchants, Power, and the Rise of a New American Culture.* New York: Vintage Books, 1993.

Lynd, Robert, and Helen Lynd. *Middletown: A Study in American Culture.* New York: Harcourt, Brace, 1959. The original edition was published in 1929.

McDannel, Colleen. *The Christian Home in Victorian America.* Bloomington: Indiana University Press, 1986.

Putnam, Robert. *Bowling Alone: The Collapse and Revival of American Community.* New York: Simon and Schuster, 2000.

Rorabaugh, W. J. *The Alcoholic Republic: An American Tradition.* New York: Oxford University Press, 1979.

Smulyan, Susan. *Selling Radio: The Commercialization of American Broadcasting, 1920–1934.* Washington, D.C.: Smithsonian Institution Press, 1994.

Tichi, Cecelia. *The Electronic Hearth Creating An American Television Culture.* New York: Oxford University Press, 1991.

Turow, Joseph. *Breaking Up America: Advertisers and the New Media World.* Chicago: University of Chicago Press, 1998.

Gary Cross

PROFESSIONALIZATION OF SPORT

The history of professionalism in American sports could well be written in terms of the class-biased ideologies concerning policies about amateurism, "shamateurism," and professionalism. It should be recognized, however, that such distinctions are quite modern and had little meaning in pre-modern sporting contests. As Steven Pope observes:

Sport historians have demonstrated that as far back as ancient Greece, sports promoted gambling, cheating, profiteering, privilege, and exclusivity. Neither the ancient Greeks nor their Western European descendants had any conception of "amateur" sports. Professionalism—

featuring money prizes, cash payments, and wagers—was the norm for most athletic competitions of public note (p. 19).

By focusing briefly on Greece, one can locate the roots of an "invented tradition"—symbolic responses to novel situations that take the form of references to old situations (Hobsbawm, p. 6). The concept of amateurism fits the notion of an invented tradition. It was not until the emergence of the Victorian gentleman with all of his status anxieties that the appellation "amateur" came to serve as a form of status protectionism and as a mechanism of social exclusion. The first recorded definition of the sporting amateur by Edwin D. Brickwood in 1866 captures this exclusionary process:

> Amateurs must be officers of Her Majesty's Army, Navy, or Civil Service, Members of the Clerical, Medical, or Legal professions, of the Universities of Oxford, Cambridge, St. Andrew's, or Aberdeen, and the Queen's Colleges in Ireland, Or Eton, Radley, Westminster, and other Public Schools, or of any established Club not composed of tradesmen or working mechanics, which would be allowed by the stewards of the Henley-on-Thames Regatta to compete for their Grand Challenge Cup, Silver Goblets, or Diamond Sculls (Glader, p. 100).

By 1881, the Amateur Athletic Association had developed a less-cluttered definition of an amateur and had dropped the clause concerning mechanics, artisans, and laborers, and it was this definition that seems to have caught the attention of amateur cultists elsewhere. For example, the Canadian Amateur Athletic Association, on its formation in 1884, stated that:

> An amateur is one who has never competed for a money prize, or staked bet or with or against any professional for any prize, or who has never taught, pursued, or assisted in the practice of athletic exercises as a means of obtaining a livelihood. (The Minute Book, AAAC, cited in Metcalfe, p. 47).

In the United States, the journalists William B. Curtis and John Watson similarly defined the amateur, and their position was quickly institutionalized with the creation of the Amateur Athletic Union (AAU). Thus, as McIntosh noted: "Between 1870 and 1890 the amateur came to be defined no longer in terms of social status but in terms of rewards and payments" [the absence thereof] (p. 181). The Victorian gentleman, then, "invented" professionalism, too: It was the negation of the amateur ideal.

McIntosh argued that the nineteenth-century sport legislators saw three dangers and had three corresponding fears. "These fears were coloured by their social attitudes and prejudices but the dangers were not unreal" (pp. 180–182). The first was that money corrupts. Here, the argument was that payments would lead to the poaching of players (what in the United States was called "revolving"), where athletes would sell their labor power to the highest bidder. Moreover, concerns were raised about the bribery of competitors and the arranging of results in advance. The second danger, argued McIntosh, was that performers who made sport their livelihood would outclass their amateur counterparts and that amateurs would be discouraged and drop out of competitions where professionals were also involved. Glader adds that the initial exclusion of manual laborers also rested on the idea of unfair advantage. Because of the nature of their work, they were perceived to be physically stronger than the amateur gentleman. The third danger was subtle and was framed around cultivation. The gentleman, having attended the private academies and the elite universities, tacitly understood the conventions and etiquette required on the playing fields. Thus, in addition to the codified rules, the gentleman understood the meanings of gentlemanly conduct and upheld its virtues. In contrast, the working-class professional could guarantee no such assurances. The "spirit" of the law would be abandoned for the "letter" of the law in the pursuit of the professional's quest for a livelihood and "victory."

Amateurs/Shamateurs/Professionals

Although focused on the sports of cricket, soccer, and rugby, and their development in England, Dunning provides an informative typology of forms of professionalism. The American examples of each specific type give some indication of the many forms of professionalism characteristic of sports in the United States since the 1870s.

Shamateurism

Dunning argues: "Broadly speaking, the term 'professional sport' can be said to refer to any kind of ludic activity from which people obtain financial gain" (p. 114). Using this broad definition, Dunning suggests that there are nine types of sports professionalism. The first four fall under the heading "Covert, non-legitimate types of sports professionalism," or what is known as shamateurism. They include the following:

1. A type in which nominally amateur sport persons are supported by the state via sinecures in the military, police, or civil service. This type was most

138

pronounced in "Iron Curtain" countries during the Cold War. But examples of such types have occurred in the United States. For instance, the late General George Patton competed in the modern pentathlon at the 1912 Olympic Games in Stockholm, and for the past century participants in the modern pentathlon have typically been recruited and sponsored by America's armed forces.

2. A type where support is provided through jobs in private and industrial firms or through administrative/organizational jobs in the sport per se. In the United States, this type of professionalism was evident in the National Industrial Basketball League of the 1940s. Players were nominally employed by a corporation in some kind of formal position, but were being largely paid to practice and compete in basketball. Paradoxically, these industrial teams received official endorsement by the AAU. Bud Browning, of the Phillips 66ers, served as the head coach of the victorious U.S. Olympic Team in the 1948 Games.

3. A type in which sport persons are subsidized by means of university scholarships or athletic grants-in-aid. This is a uniquely North American phenomenon. American colleges and universities offer National Collegiate Athletic Association (NCAA)–approved athletic scholarships that, as Sperber notes, "come in a variety of sizes and shapes":

> The most expensive are "full rides": the athletic program pays all tuition and fees, books required for courses, room and board, and miscellaneous expenses such as tutoring. The least expensive are "partial grants" where only a percentage—usually between 33 and 50 percent—of an athlete's costs is paid. Most big-time programs have at least two hundred athletes on full scholarship and an even higher number on partial grants. . . . (p. 101).

In short, student-athletes receive benefits for playing college sports. Thus, from an amateur purist's perspective, these payments for services rendered must seem like shamateurism. From a realistic perspective, some might argue that student-athletes do not receive sufficient compensation for the symbolic and economic values they produce. Many college athletes may sympathize with the latter position and this may lead to the final type of professionalism.

4. A type in which nominally amateur sport persons gain financially by being given clandestine payments from the gate or from funds provided by rich patrons, commercial sponsors, and so on.

Professionalism

Under the heading "Overt, legitimate types of sports professionalism," Dunning includes a fifth type: (5) a type in which wealthy individual patrons provide financial support. This kind of support has been more prevalent in premodern rather than modern sports. A parallel example to that of cricket in eighteenth-century England might be found in the boat races of coastal Georgia. It was initially the case that the slaves who manned the water transports were no more valuable to their masters than those working in the fields. As Coulter notes, boat clubs developed and boat races became sporting events, honor became attached to what was originally menial labor. Indeed, menial labor was elevated to an athletic and manly sport.

While it may be stretching the category five definition, individuals often sponsor Little League–type sports by providing uniforms bearing the names/logos of their businesses. Obviously, such sponsorship does not include direct payments to the athletes. And the further an athlete goes up the feeder system of sport, the more likely that such kinds of sponsorship transfer from individual businesses to more corporate capital levels. For example, in collegiate level sports coaches receive perks for the assurance that their players will wear a company's equipment.

Dunning's other categories include: (6) a type where financial support is provided from money taken at the gate; (7) a type where financial support is provided by the fund-raising activities of supporters or members; (8) a type where financial support is provided by commercial and industrial advertisers and sponsors, and (9) a type where financial support is provided by the media in payments for the broadcasting and telecasting of matches and events are ideal types and, in the economic realities of professional sport, they often overlap. A professional athlete's salary is dependent upon most of these sources of revenue.

Phases of Professionalism: The Case of Baseball

By modern definitions, baseball was the first professional team sport in the United States. Originating in the game of "rounders," baseball began to replace cricket in popularity after the Civil War. The first organized baseball team about which something is known was the Knickerbocker Base Ball Club of New York, established in 1842. This was primarily a social club and as Seymour points out: [Its members] "were more expert with a knife and fork at post-game banquets than with a bat and ball on the diamond" (p. 15). The rivalry between the Knickerbockers and the Gothams inspired others to form clubs of their own. In 1858, twenty-two metropolitan New York clubs were represented at a convention, and they formed themselves into a permanent body, the National Association of Base Ball Players. A committee was set up to codify the rules. In terms of the players, no one was eligible to play who received compensation at any time and no one directly involved in the game was allowed to bet on a game. The NABBP ruled for thirteen years. During this period, it would appear that backers of a club footed the bills for various tournaments and single-game events (Dunning's category seven).

> The very success of the amateur Association contained the ingredients of its downfall. Baseball was now accessible to the masses . . . . A game can remain amateur only as long as a privileged minority plays it as an aristocratic diversion. Once those who must also earn a living to devote themselves to a game, it ceases to be a pleasurable pastime, and becomes instead a serious affair. (Seymour, p. 47).

Baseball was passing from this twilight stage from amateurism to professionalism under the very nose of the amateur association . Under-the-table payments (Dunning's category four) began at least as early as the 1860s. According to Seymour, "gifts" were offered to lure players, and some were provided with jobs and salaries ostensibly for their work, but in reality for their ball-playing skills (Dunning's category two). Clubs began playing for a share of the gate receipts (a mixture of Dunning's categories—six if it were legitimate professionalism; four if it wasn't). All in all, the association proved to be powerless in stopping the march of professionalism and, inevitably, came to conclude that there were two classes of players.

On the professional side of things, the success of the Cincinnati Red Stockings was not lost on other cities. Many tried to emulate it. Emulation brought its own problems—too many clubs, uneven competition, uneven revenues from gate receipts, and too many problems trying to play in the geographically distant regions. The game and the players needed to be disciplined! Enter William Hulbert, an officer of the Chicago Baseball Club.

It is important to spend some time with Hulbert's initiatives, because they would set a pattern for all of American professional sports. With Hulbert and his cronies, there would be only one major league, and, therefore, three words became significant—cartel, monopoly,

and monopsony. Since there would be only one major league, all clubs "invited" to become members formed a single, collusive economic unit. Thus, the league (the cartel) is the dominant authority, and members of the league become its franchises. The league would and still does determine where franchises are to be located or relocated. The league guarantees to the franchise exclusive rights to the market in which it is situated (monopoly). And the league guarantees to the franchise the rights to player contracts which, until recently, would be known as the reserve clause (monopsony)—a clause that enabled the franchises to retain player services for the player's entire career should a franchise choose to do so.

In the beginning, the reservation system was limited to five players. The number of players placed on reserve increased over the years until the reserve clause was written into every standard player's contract in 1887, where it remained until 1975. It was the Curt Flood case—*Flood v. Kuhn*—that set the stage for its abolition. It ran from January 1970 to June 1972 and ended in defeat for Flood (see Flood's *The Way It Is* for his account of his moral and legal objections to the reserve system). In retrospect, Flood probably was ill advised to challenge baseball through the antitrust process and would have been better served by the "Rule of Reason" argument that monopsony constituted unfair labor practices that restricted the movement of athletes in the marketplace. But the *Flood* case ultimately led to a victory for the players because the owners made a tactical error. They argued that the reserve clause should not be a matter for the courts, but one that should be settled through collective bargaining. Moreover, binding arbitration for salary and other contract disputes became a feature in major league baseball in 1974. In December 1975, Peter Seitz made an assault on the reserve clause in an arbitration case involving Andy Messersmith of the Los Angeles Dodgers and Dave McNally of the Baltimore Orioles. Both had played the 1975 season without signing a contract, and they argued that they were entitled to free agency because the reserve clause could no longer apply to them. Peter Seitz, the arbitrator, agreed. The owners unsuccessfully challenged his decision in the courts. In 1976, as a result of collective bargaining between the owners in major league baseball and the Major League Baseball Players Association (MLBPA), a new basic agreement was signed, freeing players from the reserve clause after six years of their contract (later reduced to the actual term of the contract only). This marked the end of nearly 100 years of involuntary servitude and the beginning of true professionalism—the ability of players to seek their true labor-market value. Much of the credit for the improved conditions for the athletes should go to Marvin Miller—the use of grievance arbitration, salary arbitration, and other collective bargaining agreements were his brainchildren—and to Donald Fehr, Miller's successor as the leader of the MLBPA.

Other Capital/Labor Relations

Professional basketball, football, and hockey all once had reserve clauses similar to that of baseball. None of these sports, however, had baseball's exemption from antitrust litigation, and it was this lack of exemption that eventually led to the abolition of the reserve clause in each of the sports. Before 1976, professional football players entered into the game through drafting by single teams (monopsony). Players signed standard player contracts that bound them to their teams for their careers unless they were traded, sold, or put on waivers. Challenges to this system began in 1957 when William Radovich contended that he had been blacklisted by the National Football League (NFL) and prevented from earning a living in his profession. He charged the league with conspiracy to monopolize and control professional football in violation of the Sherman Act of 1890. The U.S. Supreme Court did not award damages to Radovich, but it did establish the principle that professional football did involve interstate commerce and was not exempt from the Sherman Act. This decision was a step in turning the reserve clause into an option clause. The option clause entailed that a player had to play one more year beyond the stated contract (often at reduced pay) before becoming a free agent. While this may have seemed like a victory for the players, the option clause was essentially nullified by what would be called the Rozelle Rule. Under this rule, the NFL commissioner, Pete Rozelle, was allowed to determine compensation (players, draft picks, money) to a player's former club when he signed a new contract with another team. Thus, the team willing to sign a free agent really had no idea how much compensation they would have to give to the player's former team and this discouraged teams from acquiring the free agent's services.

Joe Kapp, a quarterback for the Minnesota Vikings, and John Mackey, a tight end for the Baltimore Colts and president of the NFLPA, challenged the Roselle Rule. The Kapp ruling argued that the Rozelle Rule was too severe and caused unnecessary hardship to the players. The Mackey ruling found that the Rozelle Rule was an unreasonable restraint of trade because it acted as a prohibitive deterrent to player movement in the NFL. What really broke the back of the Rozelle Rule was the emergence of a new league: the United States Football League (USFL). A new league does not have to abide by the rules

Dream Team. David Robinson pulls down the rebound as Earvin "Magic" Johnson (left) and Michael Jordan (right) look on during the semifinal game with Lithuania at the XXV Summer Olympics in Barcelona, Spain. The so-called Dream Team, which easily won the gold medal, was comprised of the leading players from the National Basketball Association (NBA). Using NBA players in the Olympics for the first time permanently blurred the line between professional and amateur in the Games. © *AP/Wide World Photos*

of the existing leagues, and players can jump from the old to the new.

The "right of first refusal" clause replaced the option clause in basketball and ice hockey. What this means is that when a club bids for a free agent, the club for whom the athlete once played has the right to counter the offer within thirty days. If the counteroffer is made, then the free agent stays with the old club. This is also a deterrent to player movement; why should a club enter into the extensive contract negotiations with a free agent only to have the old club take advantage of its work and resign the free agent? Much will depend on how much the new club really wants the free agent.

The college draft and the option clause have also been tied together. The draft awards the most-talented player to the least-talented club. While the league maintains that the draft is an attempt to preserve equity or competitive balance in the league, the players suffered in that the least-competitive club usually did not have the financial resources to provide the kind of compensation that a first round draft choice deserved. The U.S. Court of Appeals found that the draft reduced competition by taking away opportunities for college players to sell their talents to the highest bidder. In the NFL, the draft also restricted when a player could enter into a professional contract. That is, it required that the athlete complete four years of college eligibility before being drafted. Other sports such as basketball, hockey, and baseball have the opportunities to draft players out of high school and during their "tenure" as collegiate players. In a sense, the NFL can and does use the colleges to prepare its talent and, as a result, does not have to pay a professional contract even to the most talented players until they are twenty-two or twenty-three years of age. To mollify the courts, the NFL modified the draft: there were fewer rounds by the early 2000s, and if an athlete refused to go to the drafting team, he was permitted to enter a reentry draft a year later. Given the short career span of professional athletes (much depends upon position), sitting out a year is a costly option that few take.

The developments in football influenced the capital-labor relations in basketball. Given the Kapp and Mackey decisions, basketball quickly assumed that it would lose the 1975 Oscar Robertson versus the NBA court decision. It moved from a reserve to an option clause and to the "right of first refusal." In the case of hockey, the National Hockey League (NHL) used a reserve clause similar to that of baseball. However, once the league found out that the courts would not support the use of this clause to stop players from jumping from the NHL to the World Hockey Association (WHA), they abandoned it in favor of the option clause used by the NFL and the NBA.

Women in a Masculinist Cultural Formation

Modern sports were created by men for would-be [gentle] men. Modern sports have developed within the hegemony of masculinity, and sponsors, media channels, and all other sources that generate revenue continue to undervalue women's sports. This has always been a vicious cycle. Without revenues, women's sports cannot really prosper, and without the resources to secure talented athletes, the product suffers. While the talent pool was strong, financing was not; so the women's professional soccer league (WUSA) that had formed after the heady days of the first women's World Cup to be held in the United States folded.

Women have had to compete against the men for economic and symbolic recognition. In a masculinist cultural formation such as sport, even individual sports played by men seem to be devalued by the physical contact, team sport orientation (the exception being the Olympic Games). Hegemonic masculinity and its complement, hegemonic femininity, have always tried to place limitations on what women can and should do. Thus, women's gains in the professionalization process have to be seen in this light. The sports that have received economic and symbolic endorsements are typically those that have the femininity restriction—golf, tennis, aquatics, gymnastics, figure skating, and so on. Other sports of a more physically contested team orientation are broadcast with reference to the sexualities of the athletes. The media have insisted on a heterosexual spin to pacify an audience that they (the media) define unproblematically as following the norms of compulsory heterosexuality.

When it came to professionalism, it was the individual sports that first attracted attention. This attention, just like the men's, concerned the amateur (closed) and open (professionalized) problematic. The professionalization of women's sport has progressed from the individual to include the team sports.

For most of the history of women's collegiate sports, women themselves resisted the male orientation to sport. They engaged in intercollegiate play on days in which teams did not have a representational function. Representational identities were devalued so that a quality competitive experience could be provided to all. Women created separate governing bodies, the most notable recent two of which are the Division for Girls and Women's Sport (DGWS), founded in 1957, that operated under the umbrella of the American Association for Health, Physical Education, and Recreation, and the Association for Intercollegiate Athletics for Women (AIAW) founded in 1971.

However, the AIAW—an organization governed by women—went out of business in 1982 because the NCAA—an organization governed by men—started to offer women's championships. The AIAW rules were different from the NCAA especially in the areas of financial aid, recruiting, and the transfer of an athlete from one institution to another. And for several years, the AIAW did not permit schools to offer athletic scholarships. This stance changed in the 1980s as the AIAW grew to 971 institutions, and it created forty-one national championships in nineteen sports. Moreover, the AIAW had signed contracts with NBC and ESPN for the coverage of women's athletics. The NCAA did not offer women's championships for the first seventy-five years of its existence. But on the advice of its legal counsel and with reference to Title IX, the NCAA, in 1973, rescinded its rule that had prohibited female student-athletes from competing in NCAA championships. This set the stage for discussions within the NCAA to adopt a full governance plan for intercollegiate athletics, both male and female. In 1980, the NCAA began to incorporate women's championships into its program starting with Division 2 and 3 schools. Schools in Division 1 were incorporated in 1981. This marked the death knell for the AIAW. The AIAW membership dwindled, and NBC canceled its television contract. The AIAW closed its doors and filed suit against the NCAA in 1982, stating that the NCAA had violated the Sherman Antitrust Act by attempting to create an athletics monopoly. The AIAW lost, and many of its prominent supporters found themselves on NCAA committees a few years later.

Despite the dissolution of the AIAW, a contradiction remains: the reality of distributive growth and recognition for women's sports, the difference in values and ethics between men and women, and the subjugation of the latter by the former within patriarchal relations of power. Illustrations of such power relations are clearly evident within the two primary women's professional team sport leagues, the Women's National Basketball Association (WNBA) and the WUSA.

The WNBA had its origins with the NBA. In 1996, the NBA board of governors approved the concept of the WNBA. It was to begin play in June 1997. The WNBA signed deals with NBC, ESPN, and Lifetime. It would not compete with the NBA for consumers because the WNBA games would be played in the summer. During its successful inaugural season, the WNBA had 50 million viewers, and in 1999 the WNBA games were broadcast in more than 125 countries. In the audience gender breakdown, 70 percent women attend at the arenas (primary consumers) and 50 percent watch the WBNA on television (secondary consumers) with a strong percentage falling into the nonadult category. Established in 1997, there were sixteen franchises. In 2004, there were thirteen franchises, and this included two franchise relocations and two franchise name changes. There is little doubt that the success of the WNBA was derived from the incorporation of women's basketball into the NCAA into its national championships. Its success as a professional sport probably should be linked with its close association with the NBA in terms of marketing strategy and the sale of WNBA marks and logos. The NBA is a global phenomenon, and it has incorporated the WNBA into its globalization strategies. As with the incorporation of women's sports into the NCAA, the NBA/WNBA coalition raises

the question of dependency. In 1999, the WNBA and the Women's National Basketball Players Association (WNBPA) entered into a collective bargaining agreement—a first of its kind in women's team sports. But this collective agreement was a within the female sport framework of negotiations. It left the patriarchal dominance of the NBA untouched.

As with the incorporation of women's sports into the NCAA, the NBA/WNBA coalition raises the question of dependency. Is the WNBA separate, but equal? Have there been any changes in the male/female relations of power? Is it the NBA that determines the fate of the WNBA? This may seem a trifle, but why do women's professional team sports have "women" in their titles? If women are separate but equal, why should the NBA not be the MNBA? The appellation "Women's" suggests a lesser status in the prestige hierarchy. If parity with the men is to be achieved only through the men, is there any sense of resistance or equality in this accommodation? Other women's professional leagues are in the "offing." The Women's Professional Football League (WPFL) finished its fourth season in 2003. However, the economic formula for success was missing. Progress was being made to establish a professional softball league, the National Pro Fastpitch, in 2004. To succeed, does it need the MLB to endorse and sponsor it?

Summary

On the entrepreneurial side, professionalization has been transformed from the original capital-labor relation where capital assumed that anyone interested in making a career in sport would be ever so grateful for employing them under conditions of total monopsonistic control— the reservation system—and viewing athletes as chattel to a capital-labor relation in which more power in the configuration has been usurped by the athletes in order to obtain a true market value for their labor power. Television revenues, from over-the-air and cable, luxury boxes, and personal seat licenses, have increased revenues to the leagues and players seek more of the pie since it is they who actually produce the events. Here, player associations and player agents have assumed quite dominant roles. The point again is that professionalism was not an evolving process. It was a process that involved struggle over the last 120 years as athletes sought to achieve, through "free agency," a return to themselves from the surplus values (profits) they produced for their owners. Sport in the "modern" period has always been a business despite the reactionary practices of an amateur few. With the commercialization of sport, the amateurs and shamateurs may have been the most exploited of all athletes in an incipient capital-labor relation. They played for little or nothing in economic terms, and they still do.

See also: Baseball, Amateur; Basketball; Football; Football, Collegiate; Ice Hockey; Skiing, Alpine; Tennis

BIBLIOGRAPHY

Bourdieu, Pierre. *Distinction: A Social Critique of the Judgement of Taste.* Translated by Richard Nice. Cambridge, Mass.: Harvard University Press, 1984.

Christopherson, Neal, Michelle Y. Janning, and Eileen Diaz McConnell. "Two Kicks Forward, One Kick Back: A Content Analysis of Media Discourses on the 1999 Women's World Cup Soccer Championship." *International Review for the Sociology of Sport* 38 (2003): 387–396.

Coulter, E. Merton. "Boating as a Sport in the Old South." *Georgia Historical Quarterly,* 27, no. 3 (September 1943): 231–247.

Daddario, Gina. "Chilly Scenes of the 1992 Winter Games: The Mass Media and the Marginalization of Female Athletes." *Sociology of Sport Journal* 11, no. 3 (September 1994): 275–288.

Dunning, Eric. *Sport Matters: Sociological Studies of Sport, Violence, and Civilization.* London and New York: Routledge, 1999.

Dunning, Eric, and Kenneth Sheard. *Barbarians, Gentlemen and Players: A Sociological Study of the Development of Rugby Football.* New York: New York University Press, 1979.

Finley, Moses I., and H. W. Plecket. *The Olympic Games: The First Thousand Years.* London: Chattus and Windus, 1976.

Flood, Curt, with Richard Carter. *The Way It Is.* New York: Trident Press, 1971.

Glader, Eugene A. *Amateurism and Athletics.* West Point, N.Y.: Leisure Press, 1978.

Hawes, Kay. "Voice for Change: Donna Lopiano Has Delivered a Constant Message for the Expansion of Women's Sports Opportunities." *NCAA News* (6 December 1999). Available from http://www.ncaa.org/news/1999/.

Henderson, Robert. *Ball, Bat and Bishop: The Origin of Ball Games.* New York: Rockport Press, 1947.

Hobsbawm, Eric. "Introduction: Inventing Traditions." In *The Invention of Tradition.* Edited by Eric Hobsbawm and Terence Porter. Cambridge and New York: Cambridge University Press, 1983.

Ingham, Alan, Bryan Blissmer, and Kristen Davidson. "The Expendable Prolympic Self: Going Beyond the Boundaries of the Sociology and Psychology of Sport." *Sociology of Sport Journal* 16 (1999): 236–268.

Ingham, Alan, Jeremy Howell, and Todd Schilperoort. "Professional Sport and Community: A Review and Exegesis." *Exercise and Sport Sciences Reviews* 15 (1987): 427–465.

Lucas, John and Ron Smith. *Saga of American Sport.* Philadelphia: Lea and Febiger, 1978.

Lumpkin, Angela. "The Contributions of Women to the History of Professional Tennis in the United States in the Twentieth Century." In *Her Story in Sport: A Historical Anthology of Women in Sports.* Edited by Reet Howell. West Point, N.Y.: Leisure Press, 1982.

McIntosh, Peter C. *Sport in Society.* London: C. A. Watts, 1963.

Metcalfe, Alan. "The Growth of Organized Sport and the Development of Amateurism in Canada, 1807–1914." In *Not Just a Game: Essays in Canadian Sport Sociology.* Edited by Jean Harvey and Hart Cantelon. Ottawa: Ottawa University Press, 1988.

Miller, Toby, David Rowe, Jim McKay, and Geoffrey Lawrence. "The Over-Production of U.S. Sports and the New International Division of Cultural Labor." *International Review for the Sociology of Sport* 38, no. 4 (December 2003): 427–439.

Morford, Robert, and Martha McIntosh. "Sport and the Victorian Gentleman." In *Sport in Social Development: Traditions, Transitions, and Transformations.* Edited by Alan Ingham and John W. Loy. Champaign, Ill: Human Kinetics Publishers, 1993.

Pope, Steven. *Patriotic Games: Sporting Traditions in the American Imagination, 1876–1926.* New York: Oxford University Press, 1997.

Sack, Allen. The Underground Economy of College Football. *Sociology of Sport Journal* 8 (March 1991): 1–15.

Seymour, Harold. *Baseball.* New York: Oxford University Press, 1960.

Sperber, Murray. *College Sports Inc.: The Athletic Department vs the University.* New York: Henry Holt and Co., 1990.

Staudohar, Paul. *The Sports Industry and Collective Bargaining.* Ithaca, N.Y.: ILR Press, 1986.

Wensing, E. H, and T. Bruce. "Bending the Rules: Media Representations of Gender During an International Sporting Event." *International Review for the Sociology of Sport* 38, no. 4 (December 2003): 387–396.

Alan G. Ingham

PROGRESSIVE-ERA LEISURE AND RECREATION

Leisure and recreation can be defined broadly as nonwork, but recreation, since the nineteenth century, has had a more specific connotation: It strengthens participants' bodies and uplifts their morals. Historians have argued that there was a leisure and recreation revolution in the Progressive Era, from approximately 1890 to 1914. The opportunities for leisure and recreation expanded, leisure became a commodity sold by national industries, and the audience for leisure grew dramatically. In addition, new leisure technology, such as motion pictures, pioneered a standardized mass culture in the United States. As leisure and recreation grew during this period, they also became the subject of debate between reformers, wageworkers, and immigrants; between parents and children; and between men and women. Changes in nature of recreation and leisure and struggles to control free time were thus central to the Progressive Era.

Around the turn of the century, more Americans than ever before began to participate in organized sports and outdoor recreation as well as to patronize commercial leisure venues in American cities. By 1900, for example, there were 10 million bicycles in use, as opposed to 1 million in 1893. Women joined equally in the cycling fad, promoting the image of the athletic "new woman" and undermining the ideal of the frail Victorian lady (Gorn and Goldstein, pp. 169–170). San Francisco had one opera house and two playhouses in 1870, but in 1912, the city had five playhouses along with many new entertainment venues, including eleven vaudeville theaters and sixty-nine movie theaters. The growth in baseball parks, amusement parks, dance halls, and world's fairs was also staggering. While there were no amusement and baseball parks in 1870, by the early 1900s, these attractions were in every city and town in the country. Whereas leisure in the 1870s and 1880s was divided between highbrow and lowbrow venues—between elite pursuits like opera and "sporting" activities like the smoky, bawdy concert saloons—twenty years later leisure was popular for a much larger, diverse audience.

Causes of the Leisure and Recreation Revolution

What caused this leisure and recreation revolution? Most of the new leisure in this period emerged in rapidly growing American cities between 1870 and 1920. Several processes account for the urbanization of America during this period. People's movement from country to city, particularly the migration of southern blacks, was one cause, but immigration was even more significant. By 1890, most of the population of the major urban areas consisted of immigrants: 87 percent of the population in Chicago, 80 percent in New York (Brinkley, pp. 488–489). Immigrants created their own urban enclaves that included theaters in their native languages. Several technological advances, including electric streetlights, made the city safer, and better transportation made cities more accessible for evening recreation. The first electric trolley line was completed in Richmond, Virginia, in 1888, and the first American subway opened in Boston, Massachusetts, in 1897.

In the early twentieth century, the number of work hours decreased, due to union campaigns and public concerns about work safety. Unions achieved the fifty-four-hour workweek in six industries by 1900 and the eight-hour day by 1914. Furthermore, many states passed laws that limited the working hours for women. In 1908, the Supreme Court upheld Oregon's restriction of women's work to ten hours per day (*Muller v. Oregon*); social reformers Florence Kelly and Josephine Goldmark—along with attorney Louis Brandeis—supported the legislation with a legal brief outlining the moral and physical benefits of shorter working hours.

Along with working less, most Americans became more prosperous during this period. The growth of salaried workers such as government employees and managers helped expand and consolidate a middle class that first emerged in the early nineteenth century. Composing 2.4 percent of the workforce in 1870, clerical and sales positions increased to 11 percent by 1920 (Nasaw, p. 5). It was this group of white-collar workers who, with more vacation time and usually more money than blue-collar employees, contributed heavily to the rise of commercial amusements around the turn of the twentieth century. The salaries of these white-collar workers rose by approximately one-third between 1890 and 1910, and there were also increases in the salaries of professionals and some wage workers, such as those in the iron and steel industries. Robert Chapin's surveys of workers' budgets in 1909 found that 25 percent of families earning between $600 and $700 a year (including janitors, waiters, and teamsters) spent money on the theater, but 51 percent of families earning between $900 and $1,000 (including tailors and city railroad operators) bought theater tickets.

The increase in wealth helped lay the foundation for the consumer culture, including leisure, which emerged in this period. After approximately 1880, leisure oligopolies replaced family businesses and mass markets superseded local markets. It is not surprising then that "leisure became consumption" during this period (Butsch, 1990, p. 14). In the 1890s, for example, massive department stores (some with as many as twelve departments) began to replace small, neighborhood stores. In 1896, in New York City, Henry Siegel opened Siegel-Cooper's, a six-story department store, and by the early twentieth century, he established a circuit of retail houses from Manhattan to Chicago. Similarly, professional baseball expanded and became consolidated in the second half of the nineteenth century. After the establishment of the

National League in 1876, baseball owners drove out rival clubs, brought players under tighter control, and developed a bureaucracy to oversee the growth of the game. These developments in sports, entertainment, and retail contributed to a new urban consumer culture around the turn of the twentieth century.

Finally, religious and intellectual developments, dating back to the mid-nineteenth century, supported the proliferation of leisure in the United States in the Progressive Era. Protestant clergy pointed to the dangers of "intemperance at work" because it suggested an unhealthy attachment to worldly objects. Thus, along with the values of thrift and industriousness, they also added the "duty to play." Herbert Spencer, a leading proponent of Social Darwinism, argued that overwork threatened the health of Americans; his answer was the "gospel of recreation" (Grover, p. 23). For these thinkers, and many middle-class Americans of this period, recreation could counter stifling work regimes. Yet religious leaders remained concerned about leisure, which they believed drained rather than rejuvenated the body's energy. Protestant leaders condemned drinking, gambling, and dancing in the late nineteenth century, and argued that religion and recreation must go hand in hand for a healthy mind, body, morals, and Christian nation. Despite these misgivings, the Christian moral framework loosened to sanction an increasing amount of amusement in the Progressive Era.

The Spread of Leisure

Leisure became available to more people in the United States around the turn of the century. Wealthy Americans traveled to Europe or spent vacations at the beach in the early nineteenth century, but in the early twentieth century, vacations were enjoyed by people of diverse classes. The growing number of white-collar employees began to take unpaid week-long holidays. With the encouragement of reformers who worried about the health of the poor and employers interested in a refreshed workforce, the vacation was thus "democratized" (Aron, p. 4). And, though they often sought a break from city life by escaping to the country or the seaside, many vacationers were attracted to the new urban recreations, which were cheaper than resorts.

Worlds' fairs, amusement parks, and baseball parks helped make American cities popular places for leisure in the summer. For example, the World's Columbian Exposition in Chicago in 1893 included a "Midway"—a long stretch of restaurants, stage shows, and rides—in contrast with the "White City"—the main exhibit area at the fair. The chaotic pleasures of the Midway contrasted with the

White City's emphasis on orderly displays of art, technology, and education. Subsequent worlds fairs expanded Chicago's successful Midway. The alleged education offered by worlds fairs thus helped patrons feel comfortable in an arena in which amusement was the primary goal. Worlds' fairs promoters were thus pivotal in drawing Americans out for fun in the city.

Most of the new leisure opportunities were public sites like the world's fairs, which drew consumers away from home and work. But some home-based pastimes were also part of the expansion of leisure during this period. Hobbies, once considered a harmful obsession became an uplifting, useful endeavor after approximately 1885. Collecting, gardening, and crafts became popular hobbies in this period. Hobbies had dual roles in relation to work, according to Steve Gelber's *Hobbies* (p. 30). Performed under the control of the enthusiasts in their free time, hobbies were a respite from industrialization. But the underlying values of hobbies, such as the marketplace and work ethic, supported business and industry, and brought these values into the home.

The leisure revolution affected men and women of various class, ethnic, and racial backgrounds differently. The pursuit of leisure as a distinct segment of time has been easier for the elite to enjoy, as the idea of leisure itself implied that one was not overburdened with labor, and the enjoyment of leisure in public spaces had long been a male prerogative. Progressive Era leisure broke down many of these different traditions: the new audience for public urban amusements included white men and women of different classes and ethnic groups, but it did not blur the color line. Blacks were still excluded from "white" leisure crowds.

Leisure Differences by Class, Ethnicity, and Gender

In the Progressive Era, leisure was particularly important to elites, as the amount of leisure activity increased and the competition for high social status became more intense. Leisure activity for American elites consisted of attendance at art galleries and opera theaters, as well as formal socializing. Thorstein Veblen's *The Theory of the Leisure Class* (1899) argued that leisure was a spectacle that conveyed refinement, family connections, and erudition to others. Women of the leisure class, he claimed, had a prominent role in displaying this class status.

Prior to 1870, the elite woman was supposed to pursue leisure in private (such as reading or entertaining small groups) or in carefully circumscribed public spaces (such as taking a carriage ride in Central Park). But in the late nineteenth century, women's leisure became more public and required lavish purchases of commodities and services. Balls and tableaux vivants, the silent recreation of famous paintings, scenes, or statues by a person or groups of people in costume, offered women a chance to show off a wide array of fashion, and women were more often on display in restaurants and opera boxes. In addition, their leisure became the topic of society columns in major newspapers. Women of the leisure class came under careful public scrutiny, but they also found enjoyment and attention in their new leisure pursuits. As opposed to work or reform activity, leisure was elite women's primary route into the public realm of the turn-of-the-century city.

Most nineteenth-century commercial leisure was dominated by men. Variety theaters and dime museums catered primarily to men with alcohol and attractive showgirls as drawing cards. Saloons, which reached their peak in popularity around the turn of the twentieth century, offered sociability and social services (such as employment and banking services) to working-class men. They reinforced public expressions of masculinity—rough language, bellicose behavior, and gambling. Women, on the other hand, had different patterns of leisure in the nineteenth century. Middle-class women, discouraged from attending public, commercial amusements, sought amusement within their families, churches, and clubs. Working-class women confronted less strict divisions of public and private space and often socialized on the streets, but scarce financial resources prevented their participation in commercial leisure. Commercial entertainment entrepreneurs confronted these patriarchal gender relations as they tried to expand their audiences in the early twentieth century.

To attract female consumers, entrepreneurs had to break down the ideological and economic barriers that discouraged women from participating in public leisure. Promoters of popular entertainment argued that their theaters were safe and educational for women and tried to convince patrons that their establishments complemented women's family obligations. In the process, they had to transform the masculine identity of their leisure enterprises. Leisure entrepreneurs barred prostitutes, limited the consumption of alcohol, and tried to curtail obscene performances.

The emergence of vaudeville in the late nineteenth century is a vivid example of the many ways that the leaders of this commercial leisure recruited women into their public spaces. Vaudeville, a variety show for "respectable" audiences, emerged in the 1880s from several working-class men's venues, such as concert saloons and variety theaters (terms often used interchangeably), which com-

bined bars with cheap or free amusements in connected rooms. They were smoky, noisy, and crowded; patrons were likely to be drunk, and waitresses were often willing to sell sex along with liquor. Another source of vaudeville was the dime museum, a combination of pseudoscientific displays and variety shows on stage, which was housed in storefronts in inexpensive urban areas and usually attracted men only. Vaudeville entrepreneurs sought to bring the variety show out of these male enclaves to a mass audience, including respectable women. The uplift of variety into vaudeville and the transition from a fragmented to a diverse audience depended on the recruitment of female patrons. Vaudeville administrators such as B. F. Keith advertised their clean and educational attractions, their safe and comfortable theaters, and their family-oriented fare. They claimed that the rowdy, intrusive variety audience became polite and passive for vaudeville. Keith's circuit gained a reputation for being the "Sunday School Circuit." But this is only one part of the story. Many vaudeville acts continued to mock the pretensions of Victorian elites, celebrate a masculine combativeness, and use the sexual display of women to appeal to men. The cheapest seats in vaudeville theaters—the gallery—continued to interrupt acts, sing along, and express their displeasure by stomping and hissing.

In these ways, amusements such as vaudeville were actually on the cutting edge of the dramatic changes in women's lives around the turn of the century. The nineteenth-century doctrine of domesticity, passivity, and passionlessness for white women was crumbling. Women pursued higher education and employment in greater numbers, the movement for women's suffrage gained momentum, and women expressed sensuality and assertiveness in the new heterogeneous institutions of mass culture.

Nevertheless, popular amusements did not liberate women because the female consumer, usually not economically independent, had to rely on men in many ways for access to this world, and women's patronage was often encouraged not as part of individual autonomy but as part of a family or romantic partnership with a man. As women became part of the collective audiences of commercial leisure, they were also increasingly silenced as objects on stages and screens. Did working women's leisure prevent women from being serious workers and politically astute union activists? Union leaders saw consumer culture in a negative light, but recent historians have noted that the emergence of women as patrons of commercial leisure coincides with large numbers of striking women in the early twentieth century. Popular leisure was perhaps one resource for working-class women's political resistance.

The processes of homogenization, standardization, and consolidation of American mass culture were uneven and incomplete in the Progressive Era. Historians have demonstrated that racial, ethnic, and working-class communities were "filters" through which consumers encountered mass produced brands, chain stores, and movies. A Victrola, for example, could actually help keep immigrant culture alive, as ethnic workers often bought foreign-language records and used the record player as a focal point for traditional dances and discussions of the old country. Mass-produced commodities did not necessarily draw consumers away from their indigenous cultures into mainstream, bourgeois culture.

While most commercial leisure ventures were seeking a mixed-sex crowd around the turn of the century, baseball emerged as a male-dominated alternative during the same period. Baseball stadiums, accessible by trolley or subway lines, were situated beside central business districts. Between 1903 and 1908, big-league admissions doubled, even though the prices were not as low as other commercial leisure fees. Whereas amusement parks in Kansas City charged an average of 10 cents for admission 1911, baseball spectators paid between $1 and $1.50 for tickets to big-league stadiums. Many contemporary observers noted that businessmen seemed to make up the majority of the crowds. Baseball parks also featured segregated seating, separating cheap and expensive sections and restricting African Americans to the least desirable parts of the stadium. Baseball filled a particular niche in commercial leisure: It was a male preserve that sanctioned yelling, smoking, and swearing, yet the ballparks were not associated with vice or disrepute. Though baseball did not live up to its flaunted democratic reputation, it did offer spectators from different ethnic groups and classes the opportunity to develop masculine camaraderie.

Immigrants brought distinct leisure patterns with them to the United States. Germans, for example, drank and sang with their families in beer gardens; Italians celebrated saints' days with parades and fireworks; and the Irish enjoyed St. Patrick's Day with parades and picnics, often interspersed with fisticuffs and drinking. With weddings and parties in their homes, immigrants experienced leisure as an integral part of family life. American commercial leisure was thus a novelty for immigrants; they were not accustomed to buying leisure as a separate aspect of daily life.

Second-generation immigrants spent more money than their foreign-born parents at commercial leisure. Old and new worlds of leisure often mixed together. One historian noted that some Italians celebrated saints' days, but then visited Coney Island in the summer. There were

significant generational tensions over American commercial leisure, as immigrant parents often wanted to preserve their traditional cultures, but sons and daughters sought the individual freedoms promised by cheap amusements. The daughters of immigrant parents created more controversy than their brothers when they tried to enjoy themselves with men in public places. Italian parents often forbade their daughters from going out, or arranged chaperones for their dates. Jewish parents, less strict than Italians, still sought some control over their daughters' leisure time and money. For immigrant women, going to amusement parks, movies, or dance halls was often an act of rebellion against their parents and an attempt to find their own way in a modern, heterosocial world of commercial leisure.

Progressive Attempts to Reform Leisure

Progressive reformers attacked the new regime of commercial leisure, and they also tried to develop health recreation programs. Reformers were upset by the sexual liberalism of contemporary amusements—the intensified focus on women's bodies, women's assertion of sexual desire, and the portrayal of sexual diversity (or the inclusion of gay and lesbian sexuality). They also hoped to improve a variety of urban problems, including crime and disease and, more broadly, working-class immigrant disorder. The Woman's Christian Temperance Union (WTCU), for example, launched a department for the Suppression of Impure Literature (later the Department for the Promotion of Purity in Literature and Art) in 1883. They promoted programs to keep children out of dance halls as well as vaudeville and movie theaters. In *Spirit of Youth* (1909), Jane Addams, leading reformer and settlement house founder, discussed her alarm at children's addiction to motion pictures. She noted the daughters of a shopkeeper who would steal from their parents to pay for their movie tickets, and she warned that movies caused boys to imitate the crimes they saw on screen.

Censorship received widespread support from reformers in the early twentieth century. Chicago passed the first movie censorship regulations in 1907, and by 1913, many cities and states enacted laws against children attending movies without adults at night. The WCTU, like many other women's groups, supported federal legislation to regulate the motion picture industry. In 1914, the first bill to authorize federal oversight of motion pictures was introduced in Congress, and statewide boards were active in the pre-exhibition censorship of movies. Anti-vice crusaders also wanted movie houses closed on Sundays, and expressed some concern over the fire safety of theaters. After New York City mayor George McClellan closed all movie theaters because of complaints about their indecency, elite, Protestant reformers in New York formed the National Board of Censorship in 1909. With no legal standing, the board tried to communicate its moral vision to movie producers, but they found it difficult to agree on a single standard of decency. The Motion Picture Producers and Distributors of America was established in 1921, following the formation of New York's board of movie censorship. This new organization promoted industry self-regulation as an alternative to legal censorship.

But Progressive reformers did more than try to suppress the overstimulating commercial amusements. Various reform groups, including settlement houses and the Young Men's Christian Association (YMCA), pioneered a broad "recreation movement." The playground movement was one of the most vigorous of these campaigns. The theories of psychologist G. Stanley Hall and others provided the intellectual basis for the playground movement. He argued that children went through all the earlier phases of human evolution in their individual development. The savage stage, in particular, was dangerous for children of the city, for they could be easily lured into gangs and crime. Indeed, the play instinct, according to leaders of the playground movement, contained basic human instincts—to fight, to join a pack, and to hunt. The playground, with its organized games and team participation, would provide an outlet for these natural drives, and adult playground supervisors would also mold them into more civilized behavior.

According to these reformers, playgrounds could deter crime, Americanize immigrants, decrease class tensions and ultimately help create a "cohesive urban moral order," according to historian Paul Boyer. Playground advocates in Pittsburgh, for example, argued that these new recreational facilities would improve the "moral nature" of children and offer "social training and discipline" to immigrants (p. 243). Reformers wanted to get children off the streets and into new recreational spaces where they would instruct youth on legitimate athletics. The Playground Association of America (PAA), founded in 1906 by Joseph Lee, Dr. Luther H. Gulick (head of physical training in New York City public schools), and others, urged cities to build playgrounds for urban youth and publicized their idea through conferences and its magazine, *Playground*. Playground funding increased in cities, and between 1911 and 1917 the number of playgrounds in cities more than doubled, according to PAA statistics.

Playground advocates often criticized other aspects of Progressive reform, arguing that their ideas were more effective than Sunday School or the YMCA programs. One writer noted that the playground movement, unlike the YMCA, had no sectarian boundaries. Catholic, Protestant, and Jewish children were all beneficiaries of playgrounds. Despite these debates, the playground movement found widespread popularity. Jacob Riis, a journalist, photographer, and reformer, noted that the playground was one of the "wholesome counterinfluences to the saloon, street gang, and similar evils" (Boyer, p. 245), and Jane Addams believed that playgrounds could counteract the dangerous commercial leisure of the metropolitan areas.

The playground movement illustrates several key themes of progressivism. First, these reformers believed in the power of the environment to shape individuals. In this case, a new environment for play could change the most malleable individuals—children. Second, they believed in the authority of experts to guide play. They hired trained supervisors to manage playgrounds and supervise play. Thus, they introduced another cadre of professionals into American urban life. Third, playground advocates shared a class bias—a desire to control what they perceived as working-class disorder.

Working-class communities, however, did not simply follow reformers' "social control" agenda. While park advocates believed that this new recreation space would encourage temperance, workers and their families often used public parks for drinking, perhaps because of the proximity of their neighborhood parks and saloons and because of the lack of privacy in their cramped housing. In addition, parks often supported immigrant leisure pursuits, rather than the Americanization of immigrants, as reformers often claimed. Immigrant fraternal and church groups used public parks for their own picnics, rallies, and celebrations. In *Eight Hours for What We Will*, historian Roy Rosenzweig contends that "parks provided a leisure space in which workers expressed and preserved their distinct ethnic cultures" (p. 140).

More than the expansion of playgrounds, the invention of basketball at the YMCA training school in Springfield, Massachusetts, had a lasting impact on American recreation and leisure. Trained as a Presbyterian minister but drawn to the new field of physical education, James Naismith created the new game of basketball when he was faced with a wintertime gap in organized sports (after football ended and before baseball began). Basketball spread rapidly through YMCA channels, settlement houses, and colleges (where it proved particularly attractive to college women). Basketball was well suited to urban recreation because it did not need the large space required by football or baseball. In the early years of the sport, basketball was most often played in supervised settings. Though Naismith had invented basketball only to address a gap in wintertime athletics, his innovation enabled the broad expansion of "organized, supervised play" in the first decades of the twentieth century (Gorn and Goldsmith).

Leisure Meets Technology

Technological innovation was at the heart of the expanded world of leisure in the Progressive Era. By the early twentieth century, "automatic" amusements began to compete with live entertainment. The phonograph, pioneered by Thomas Alva Edison in 1877 as a dictation machine, and Alexander Graham Bell's graphophone became singing machines popular in two types of outlets: They were side attractions at fairs, vacation spots, and hotel lobbies and they also became, by the 1890s, the main attraction in phonograph parlors, often in the main business districts of cities. The artificial reproduction of sound was soon joined, in 1893, by the first moving picture machine, the kinetoscope, which revealed moving images through a peephole and was operated by a switch. These machines were popular mainly as novelties and technological marvels. They transformed leisure by offering a few minutes of entertainment; for the first time, consumers could find cheap, quick diversions in railroad terminals and theater lobbies.

Inventors soon succeeded in bringing the moving pictures out of separate boxes and onto a screen—a shift that made it more economical for businessmen to cater to a large audience. The vitascope was invented by Thomas Armat and C. Francis Jenkins, but marketed with Edison's name and produced by his company. The vitascope projected everyday events and exciting spectacles, such as speeding trains and fire drills. It became part of traveling, illustrated lectures that often had temperance themes or political debates. Such edifying entertainment in the 1890s and early 1900s further expanded the public appetite for commercial leisure.

At the same time, vitascope films also became attractions on vaudeville bills. In fact, prior to approximately 1910, film historians argue, there was no film spectator. Rather than being immersed in the action on screen in a dark theater, consumers in this transitional period quickly shifted their attention to diverse attractions and interruptions—live acts and short films. By the turn of the century, movies emerged as an independent entertainment industry, while the kinetoscope and other early innovations faded away quickly as novelties. First, picture shows became the main attraction at penny arcades and then arcade owners (and other businessmen, particular saloon keepers) began to open up storefront theaters to project movies on a screen. Needing only chairs, a projector, window coverings, and a canvas screen, many entrepreneurs quickly opened "nickelodeons," so named for the nickel admission fee.

Italian, Greek, and Irish, but particularly Jewish immigrants, were active in the nickelodeon business. The theaters were most often located in immigrant and working-class neighborhoods but some were also in central business districts, where the brash hawking of new shows disrupted surrounding merchants. Nickelodeons were identified as the "workingman's college" or a "poor men's entertainment" because the price allowed workingmen to take their families to the shows, but movies were also the favorite entertainment of young single women. Children, too, were primary component of the early movie audience.

The term "nickelodeon" has long been equated with immigrant working-class audiences, but recent histories have uncovered several different outlets for movies during the nickelodeon period. In large cities middle-class Americans could stop into a nickelodeon during shopping trips in New York City. Some movie theaters, in fact, were built next to prestigious department stores. Movie theaters in small towns also contrast with the image of movies as a refuge for poor immigrants. Requiring broad support to succeed, small-town movie houses worked to attract the "best people" along with other strata of these communities, according to historian Richard Butsch. Thus, the class composition of the nickelodeon audience varies in three venues: neighborhood nickelodeons, larger theaters in commercial districts, and the small-town theaters.

Some historians have argued that immigrant movie patrons were a new audience for commercial leisure. But immigrant filmgoers had patronized their own ethnic theaters in the nineteenth century. Eastern European Jews were enthusiastic supporters of Yiddish theater and Sicilians were fans of puppet shows. These theatergoers became avid movie fans. The significance of the film audience, therefore, is that movies saturated these markets to a greater degree than live theater did. More people, particularly children, attended nickelodeons than had gone to live stage entertainments, and movies reached more parts of the country than live theater or vaudeville ever had.

African Americans, Mexicans, and Asians were segregated in galleries or excluded from nickelodeons and from the renovated movie theaters entirely. There were, however, black-owned theaters on the south side of

Chicago that cultivated a distinctive entertainment. The movies were usually the same as the ones featured in white-owned theaters, but African American performers, often blues singers, offered the live performances before and after the films, and the performers and audience joined in a call-and-response participation that differed from other theaters. Black audiences were not monolithic. Middle-class African Americans condemned rowdy behavior and criticized some forms of commercial leisure, namely dance halls, as unrefined.

The owners of nickelodeons sought ways to increase their profits: To reach a middle-class audience they renovated their dank storefronts into elegant theaters. Nickelodeons expanded to include live vaudeville acts along with movies, or solely devoted their larger spaces to movies alone. Boston had two movie palaces by 1910, including the Scenic Temple with 1,444 seats. Similar to the grand vaudeville houses, these movie theaters often had art galleries and rest rooms with attendants. These new theaters offered elegance to patrons at reasonable prices, and audiences, largely middle class, were well behaved. Uniformed ushers ensured silence, and the darkened theater further decreased the sociability of the nickelodeon. As the movies became more formal and respectable, the casual sociability of the ethnic working-class nickelodeon diminished. Once boisterous and assertive, the audience for commercial leisure was now largely passive and polite.

Conclusion

In the Progressive Era leisure became legitimate; it also became a commodity—something to be purchased or watched. The significant debates about leisure in this period remind us that free time, including its relationships to work, is a political issue. Struggles over leisure addressed not only the physical, mental, and spiritual health of leisure participants and spectators; deep convictions about social order and progress were at stake also. The history of leisure and recreation around the turn of the twentieth century illustrates a growing, albeit conflicted, acceptance of leisure, as well as a fundamental transformation of leisure into entertainment and mass media.

See also: Automobiles and Leisure; Baseball, Amateur; Baseball Crowds; Basketball; Coney Island; Football; Gilded Age Leisure and Recreation; Impresarios of Leisure, Rise of; Media, Technology, and Leisure; Movies' Impact on Popular Leisure; Prohibition and Temperance; Railroads and Leisure; Theater, Live; Tourism

BIBLIOGRAPHY

Aron, Cindy. *Working at Play: A History of Vacations in the United States.* New York: Oxford University Press, 1999.

Boyer, Paul. *Urban Masses and Moral Order in America, 1820–1920.* Cambridge, Mass.: Harvard University Press, 1978.

Butsch, Richard, ed. *For Fun and Profit: The Transformation of Leisure into Consumption.* Philadelphia: Temple University Press, 1990.

———. *The Making of American Audiences: From Stage to Television, 1750–1990.* Cambridge, U.K.: Cambridge University Press, 2000.

Cohen, Lizabeth. "Encountering Mass Culture at the Grassroots: The Experience of Chicago Workers in the 1920s." *American Quarterly* 41 (March 1989): 6–33.

Cross, Gary. *An All-Consuming Century: Why Commercialism Won in Modern America.* New York: Columbia University Press, 2000.

Enstad, Nan. *Ladies of Labor, Girls of Adventure: Working Women, Popular Culture, and Labor Politics at the Turn of the Twentieth Century.* New York: Columbia University Press, 1999.

Gelber, Steve. *Hobbies: Leisure and the Culture of Work in America.* New York: Columbia University Press, 1999.

Gorn, Elliott, and Warren Goldstein. *A Brief History of American Sports.* New York: Hill and Wang, 1993.

Grover, Kathryn. *Hard at Play: Leisure in America, 1840–1940.* Amherst: University of Massachusetts Press, 1992.

Hunnicutt, Benjamin. *Work Without End: Abandoning Shorter Hours for the Right to Work.* Philadelphia: Temple University Press, 1988.

Kibler, M. Alison. *Rank Ladies: Gender and Cultural Hierarchy in American Vaudeville.* Chapel Hill: University of North Carolina Press, 1999.

Montgomery, Maureen. *Displaying Women: Spectacles of Leisure in Edith Wharton's New York.* New York: Routledge, 1998.

Nasaw, David. *Going Out: The Rise and Fall of Public Amusements.* New York: Basic Books, 1999.

Peiss, Kathy. *Cheap Amusements: Working Women and Leisure in Turn-of-the-Century New York.* Philadelphia: Temple University Press, 1986.

Powers, Madelon. *Faces Along the Bar: Lore and Order in the Workingman's Saloon, 1870–1920.* Chicago: University of Chicago Press, 1998.

Rosenzweig, Roy. *Eight Hours for What We Will: Workers and Leisure in an Industrial City, 1870–1920.* Cambridge, U.K.: Cambridge University Press, 1983.

Somers, Dale. "The Leisure Revolution: Recreation in the American City, 1820-1920." *Journal of Popular Culture* 5 (1971): 125–147.

M. Alison Kibler

PROHIBITION AND TEMPERANCE

America has long maintained a reputation as a nation of drinkers. In colonial America, beer and cider were common table beverages, and nearly every social occasion and ceremony—from communion to Election Day—became the occasion for the consumption of alcohol. Both farm labor and city labor were punctuated by frequent breaks for a drink. In New England towns, shops and businesses closed down every day at eleven and four as employees repaired to taverns for "'leven o'clock bitters," and farmers brought liquor into the fields for their hired hands. No social class abstained from this considerable alcohol use, with the result that Americans before the Revolution probably drank about twice as much as Americans do today. But while drinking was ubiquitous, authorities from an early date were aware of the potentially destabilizing impact of liquor on society. Increase Mather's famous dictum that "the wine is from God, but the Drunkard is from the Devil" was codified in colonial New England laws against drunkenness, with penalties that included fines, jailings, the stocks, and corporal punishment.

Taverns had become centers of community life in America by the early eighteenth century, and one way that authorities tried to limit drinking was by limiting the numbers of taverns through strict licensing. But upper-class control of taverns began to erode after 1720 when rum became cheaper and more plentiful, and unlicensed taverns began to proliferate. In the years preceding the Revolution, taverns gained a reputation as centers of resistance to the British, and the success of the Revolution only increased the status of taverns.

By the 1790s, Americans had switched their loyalties from rum to whiskey. Indeed, the production of whiskey had become such an integral part of America's rural economies that Alexander Hamilton's attempts to tax whiskey created the first great crisis of the new American republic: the Whiskey Rebellion of 1794. Farmers in western Pennsylvania refused to pay the tax, and they roughed up revenue officials. Order was not restored until a large federal army marched into the state. The hated whiskey tax was repealed in 1802, and, as American consumption of this liquor steadily increased, the whiskey-scented American male assumed the proportions of a national stereotype. Frances Trollope, the famously sour critic of the young republic, observed that "the near approach of the gentlemen was always redolent of whiskey and tobacco." The American "love of spirits," in Trollope's opinion, "savours a little of savage life." But despite the heavy alcohol consumption of Americans, the use of liquor was generally not considered to be a serious social problem during the colonial era and the early years of the new republic.

The Temperance Movement

Complacency soon turned to alarm as Americans in the first thirty years of the nineteenth century went on an alcoholic binge the likes of which had never been seen before, or since. By 1830, Americans of drinking age were consuming over seven gallons of pure alcohol per year—a staggering quantity in a quite literal sense. Why this particular era witnessed so much alcohol consumption is a matter of some debate, but it was both a rural and an urban phenomenon. Whatever the cause, the impact was ubiquitous; with many fearing that intemperance might topple the young republic, concerned Americans began to create temperance organizations to counter this threat. The first of these groups to achieve national prominence was the American Temperance Society. Created in 1826, this group was blunt in its assessment of the impact of alcohol use, comparing America's drinking problem to a "fearful plague" carrying "death and havoc."

The various threads of the temperance movement had a number of sources. Business interests increasingly viewed a temperate workforce as essential to maintaining efficient operations. Indeed, so many workers returned to their jobs at the start of the workweek still reeling from the wretched excess of the previous weekend that businesses were forced to recognize the institution of "blue Monday"—a day on which virtually nothing could be accomplished. With the competitive pressures of a national market forcing American businessmen to "rationalize" and mechanize their shops to make them more efficient, the liquor issue now became part of the business productivity equation. The on-the-job conviviality of the old local retail shop, which had included frequent breaks for beer, became a luxury that a business owner felt he could no longer afford.

With liquor now banished from the shop floor, drinking became weighted with symbolic significance, and temperance became a signifier of class. The working class increasingly saw alcohol as an emblem of their independent social life, while the middle class was beginning to see alcohol use both as a detriment to its own self-image and as an impediment to its aspirations. Intemperance became a sure path to economic ruin, while abstinence put one on the road to economic advancement and respectability. While there was some interest in temperance among the working class (most notably in the Washingtonian movement) and some temperance activism among Catholics (the Catholic Total Abstinence Union enjoyed a degree of success among Irish Americans), it was generally the case that temperance reform was a middle-class Protestant activity. Leading the way were American women, and in an era in which women had few legal rights, it is not difficult to discern why. The consequences for a woman married to a drunken, abusive husband were especially grim. While the degree to which women were able to participate in public forums was greatly restricted in antebellum years, women could have a huge impact on their own domestic realms. Here the idea of "home protectionism" (that women bore the chief responsibility for protecting their homes from evil) dovetailed neatly with the notion that the banishment of liquor was essential to such a goal.

As women used their "moral suasion" to drive liquor from the home, temperance reformers working in the larger political realm were trying to enact state prohibition laws. To a remarkable degree they were successful, with thirteen states during the 1850s adopting such laws. While problems associated with state prohibition laws included a chronic lack of funding for enforcement, the open hostility of city residents, and a tendency to run afoul of state constitutions (eight of these laws would be struck down as unconstitutional), they did mark a new stage in the temperance movement. The original meaning of "temperance," that there was nothing wrong with drinking per se but that alcohol should be consumed temperately, had gradually given way to "abstinence," that temperate drinking was not possible and that individuals should abstain totally from alcohol consumption. By midcentury, the temperance movement began to edge into its last, most coercive stage, "prohibition." Temperance "ultraists" now argued that the impact of alcohol on the individual and on society was so dire that the manufacture of alcohol must be prohibited altogether. Although increasing concern with the slavery issue drained away a great deal of temperance activism, the end of the Civil War would mark the return of a reinvigorated movement.

The Saloon and Prohibition

It is no coincidence that the post–Civil War prohibition movement coincided with a huge influx of immigrants. Increasingly coming from southern and eastern Europe (rather than northern and western Europe) and dominated by Catholics rather than Protestants, these new arrivals would settle in American cities, establish their own communities, and continue the recreational and ritual drinking that had always been part of their cultures. As immigrant populations overwhelmed American cities, there was an explosive growth in the number of saloons.

Prohibition. The era of Prohibition lasted from 1919 to 1931 in the United States, making the manufacture and distribution of liquor illegal. Here, a government agent destroys a barrel of illegal beer after stopping a smuggler's delivery. © *The Library of Congress*

Saloons per capita in America increased from one for every 400 persons in 1870, to one for every 250 persons by 1900. American cities had especially impressive saloon concentrations: Boston had one saloon for every ninety-seven people, San Francisco one for every ninety-six people. The dramatic growth in these public drinking venues, and the middle-class perception of them as symbols of filth, vice and, depravity, added more recruits to the prohibition movement than any other single factor.

Often lost in the critique of saloons was that patrons frequented them for a variety of reasons, and for immigrant working-class men especially, the saloon could serve the social functions of hiring hall, political headquarters, and bank (one Milwaukee coal handling firm reported that 64 percent of its German employees, and 100 percent of its Hungarian and Polish employees, cashed their paychecks at saloons). Most important, the saloon was not strictly a venue for drunkenness, but a place where those living in humble quarters could meet to socialize with their friends. Whatever useful community role the saloon may have served was lost on temperance reformers, however, even though they tried, and for the most part failed, to find a viable alternative.

The saloon was targeted by the Woman's Crusade of 1873, when thousands of women took to the streets and attempted to shut down drinking establishments and wholesale liquor outlets by praying in front of them. Their partial success led to the formation of the Woman's Christian Temperance Union (WCTU) in 1874. More women would be attracted to the temperance cause than any other reform in the nineteenth century; by 1892, the WCTU boasted a membership of 200,000, dwarfing the numbers of every other women's organization.

Guiding the WCTU during its most important years was Frances Willard, who was able to unite the organization's moral suasionist, conservative wing and the liberal, suffragist wing under the rubric of home protectionism. Willard posited a universalist woman, whose natural instincts toward preserving her home from the scourge of alcohol had been ordained by God himself: "God has indicated woman, who is the born conservator of home, to be the Nemesis of home's arch enemy, King Alcohol." Willard then expanded the idea of home, claiming that women "must make the world itself, a larger home," and that banishing King Alcohol from "home" could be best accomplished by women having the vote. Without devaluing the considerable energy and resources that the WCTU poured into temperance campaigns, the most important accomplishment of Willard and the WCTU may have been the creation of the idea of woman's natural opposition to alcohol. Both proponents and opponents of antialcohol measures would accept this premise as a political article of faith until the late 1920s, when another women's group would begin to undermine this notion.

The other major temperance organization created after the Civil War was the Anti-Saloon League (ASL), which began as a national organization in 1895. As its name indicates, the ASL focused on the elimination of the saloon, an approach that it knew would resonate with the middle class. Because those who were doing most of the public drinking in saloons—working-class immigrant males—lived lives very far removed from the ambit of temperance reformers, it was often the case that below the surface of temperance activism in the United States lurked a vicious class and nativist critique. For instance, the WCTU's first president, Annie Wittenmyer, claimed that a majority of the liquor business in the country was "in the hands of a low class of foreigners," and the ASL's "Americanization movement" was a transparent attempt to strip immigrants of whatever cultural values might be at a variance with prohibitionist WASPS. It should thus come as no great surprise that mainstream temperance organizations failed to attract many immigrant members; because temperance societies were unstinting in their condemnations of "Popery" and depended heavily on the support of Protestant churches, the lack of appeal to Catholics is also no mystery.

The creation of the Prohibition Party in 1869 made prohibition a third-party issue. But despite the endorsement of Frances Willard and the WCTU, the Prohibition Party was a consistent loser at the polls; upon Willard's death in 1898, the WCTU disencumbered itself from this alliance and give its full support to the ASL. Now operating in an era of Progressive reformism, the combined force of these two organizations would prove to be irresistible. On the eve of America's entry into World War I, momentum was gathering for a national prohibition amendment, and twenty-six states had adopted statewide prohibition laws. While these numbers are impressive on the surface, they reveal problems when examined more closely. Only two industrial states had adopted state prohibition laws; it was undeniably the case that almost all the support for state prohibition came from the less-populated states of the West and the South (even here, urban centers opposed such laws). Urban constituencies were underrepresented at both the state and national levels in the 1910s, but the House of Representatives would be reapportioned after the 1920 census. With a greater urban voice in the House looming in the near future, and with the unlikelihood that such a House would approve a prohibition amendment, those who harbored hopes for national prohibition understood that it was now or never.

World War I was exactly the catalyst needed to put prohibition over the top. The anti-German propaganda whipped up by the government was considerable; because German Americans dominated the brewing industry, prohibition forces were able to link "Hun" atrocities with the brewing industry, and American patriotism with prohibition. Congress approved a national prohibition amendment in 1917 and sent it to the states. Less than two years later, in early 1919, Nebraska's ratification of the amendment provided the last state needed to approve the Eighteenth Amendment and national prohibition. It went into effect one year later, on 20 January 1920.

Prohibition and Its Discontents

Prohibitionists had promised that nothing less than a millennium would follow approval of the Eighteenth Amendment (the ASL's Purley Baker rhapsodized about a "a saloonless and drunkless world"). The hoped-for dry uptopia never materialized, however, and much of the trouble that prohibition forces had in the coming years was related to promising much more than they could deliver. While reliable consumption figures on an illegal substance are difficult to obtain, most likely there was a slight downward trend in drinking among the working class, while everybody else consumed about as much as before. Voters and legislators had been assured that prohibition would be so popular that no great expenditures would be needed to enforce it. Instead, federal prohibition violations were so numerous that they threatened to paralyze court systems in many areas, and expenditures for enforcement doubled between 1924 and 1932. Resistance to prohibition was especially entrenched in urban areas, to the point that enforcement in many American cities became virtually impossible.

The promise that prohibition would protect the home and community from the "liquor traffic" also received a blow when organized crime moved into the liquor business. The vast sums of money to be made from liquor frequently sparked violence among competing gang lords, the most spectacular example being Al Capone's "beer war" in Chicago. But shootouts resulting from liquor violence occurred even in respectable neighborhoods with no major gang influence. The development of a youth culture devoted to the hip flask, the proliferation of "speakeasies" (the illegal replacement for saloons), and the advent of the cocktail party as a naughty-but-nice institution of the middle class further undercut the notion of prohibition as a home protectionist measure.

Even the combined weight of these negative factors may not have been enough to dismantle prohibition had it not been for two additional elements: the arrival of the Great Depression and the formation of the Women's Organization for National Prohibition Reform (WONPR), a group of prominent women dedicated to repeal. As the nation's economy worsened, business leaders began to gravitate toward the antiprohibition camp. A group of mainly Republican businessmen created the Association Against the Prohibition Amendment, and argued that the repeal of prohibition and the relegalization of the liquor industry would create jobs, provide the government with a reliable source of tax revenue, and reduce the tax burden on everyone else. These businessmen joined the rising chorus of anti-prohibitionists that included intellectuals, who saw prohibition as a blue-nosed affront to their personal liberties, and trade unionists, who condemned prohibition as sumptuary legislation aimed at the working class.

The opposition to prohibition from intellectuals, trade unionists, and even business elites is not greatly surprising. But when large numbers of women took up the mantle of prohibition repeal, the result was a considerable political stir because of the pervasive notion that women would "always" support prohibition. Pauline Sabin, a prominent New York socialite who had been active in the Republican Party, created the WONPR in 1929, and promoted the repeal of prohibition on grounds that she knew would resonate with women—as essential to home protection. This turned the prohibition equation on its head, with Sabin arguing that it was prohibition itself that had spawned increased lawlessness, licentiousness, and drinking among teenagers. The situation had become so dire, according to Sabin, that "the mothers of the country feel something must be done to protect their children." That something was prohibition repeal, and it is a great irony that the home protection argument that had played such a pivotal role in the passage of the Eighteenth Amendment now became a compelling factor in its repeal. The argument that prohibition posed a threat to home and family was relentlessly promoted by the WONPR in its posters and other campaign materials; this conservative, maternalist appeal, coupled with the large membership claimed by this group (over 1 million) undercut the woman-as-universal-prohibitionist claims of groups such as the WCTU. By 1932, opinion polls showed the public's overwhelming support for prohibition repeal, and part of Franklin Roosevelt's success as a presidential candidate in 1932 (aside from the fact that he was not Herbert Hoover) was his unequivocal endorsement of repeal. Even before Roosevelt took office, support for a repeal amendment had increased to such a point that it sailed through the lame duck Congress in 1933, and less than nine months later it was ratified by the states. The Twenty-first Amendment was approved more quickly than any previous amendment.

In the wake of prohibition's repeal, the control of alcohol by and large returned to the states, creating a patchwork of liquor laws that vary from state to state and even from county to county. There is little doubt that America's prohibition era created a negative legacy, and among the "lessons" of prohibition frequently cited by social critics is that "you can't legislate morality"—a foolish assertion, as this is what legislatures do routinely.

Promarijuana groups, such as the National Organization for Marijuana Legalization (NORML), have also drawn parallels between the prohibition of alcohol and the prohibition of cannabis, claiming that marijuana's illegal status has turned decent citizens into lawbreakers, has fostered violence and a criminal trade, and has denied to the government a potentially lucrative source of tax revenue. While this analogy has some merit, it is also true that alcohol use has been part of Western culture almost from the beginning, while our experience with drug use has been relatively recent and fairly limited. Unfortunately, there is a paucity of research on the effects of marijuana, and it is simply not known what impact this drug would have on the general public if it were legalized and widely available. Still, there seems to be increasing support for bringing marijuana into the mainstream, especially in state laws authorizing medical marijuana. It is highly unlikely that American society will ever again call for the prohibition of alcohol, and the future of the prohibition of marijuana is increasingly an open question.

See also: Drinking; Home Brewing; Wine Tasting

BIBLIOGRAPHY

Blocker, Jack S., Jr. *American Temperance Movements: Cycles of Reform.* Boston: Twayne Publishers, 1989.

Bordin, Ruth. *Woman and Temperance: The Quest for Power and Liberty, 1873–1900.* Philadelphia: Temple University Press, 1981.

Boyer, Paul. *Urban Masses and Moral Order in America, 1820–1920.* Cambridge, Mass.: Harvard University Press, 1978.

Burnham, John C. "New Perspectives on the Prohibition 'Experiment' of the 1920's." *Journal of Social History* 2 (Fall 1968): 51–68.

Clark, Norman H. *Deliver Us from Evil: An Interpretation of American Prohibition.* New York: W. W. Norton and Company, 1976.

Duis, Perry. *The Saloon: Public Drinking in Chicago and Boston, 1880–1920.* Urbana: University of Illinois Press, 1983.

Epstein, Barbara Leslie. *The Politics of Domesticity: Women, Evangelism and Temperance in Nineteenth-Century America.* Middletown, Conn: Wesleyan University Press, 1981.

Gusfield, Joseph R. *Symbolic Crusade: Status Politics and the American Temperance Movement.* Urbana: University of Illinois Press, 1963.

Kerr, K. Austin. *Organized for Prohibition: A New History of the Anti-Saloon League.* New Haven, Conn.: Yale University Press, 1985.

Kyvig, David E. *Repealing National Prohibition.* Chicago: University of Chicago Press, 1976.

Lender, Mark Edward, and James Kirby Martin. *Drinking in America: A History.* New York: Free Press, 1987.

Odegard, Peter H. *Pressure Politics: The Story of the Anti-Saloon League.* New York: Columbia University Press, 1928.

Rorabaugh, W. J. *The Alcoholic Republic: An American Tradition.* New York: Oxford University Press, 1979.

Rose, Kenneth D. *American Women and the Repeal of Prohibition.* New York: New York University Press, 1996.

Timberlake, James H. *Prohibition and the Progressive Movement, 1900–1920.* Cambridge, Mass.: Harvard University Press, 1963.

Tyrell, Ian. *Sobering Up: From Temperance to Prohibition in Antebellum America, 1800–1860.* Westport, Conn.: Greenwood Press, 1979.

Kenneth D. Rose

PROSTITUTION

Prostitution has traditionally been described as the provision of sex, sexually associated, or closely related activity in exchange for money (or something of value). That description is contested, however, because it creates a liminal zone that can easily embrace the giving or receiving of gifts, including money, in a largely social context. Thus, today's discussion of the phenomena usually relies on terms such as "sex professional," implying that the person is self-defined as a service provider. "Prostitute" and "prostitution" still imbue the sex professional or activity with a socially suspect tone.

The work of sex professionals—the process of exchanging intimacy for money—is an ancient undertaking. As did most forms of work, the tasks of the sex professional changed over time. The coming of the Industrial Revolution precipitated particularly rapid and widespread economic, social, and labor changes. Naturally, prostitution changed as well. Because industrial forms of social organization were imported with the relevant waves of immigration patterns, prostitution does not have exactly the historic background of that in Asia, Europe, or elsewhere.

Although the stimulus for individual New World European colonial attempts came from a number of roots, all took place after a protracted and sanguinary series of religious wars in Europe. This experience spawned the notion of "European Liberalism," or the idea that mutual toleration of religion could possibly be a better approach than further ruinous open hostilities. The traditional faith in a "voice of authority" was deeply rattled when the religious wars failed to uncover a clear winner; Church authority remained absolute, but adamantly regional. Toleration and the consideration that human beings could act in a reasoned way—features of the Enlightenment—further contested the previously unquestioned faith in a God-centered universe.

Prostitution in the United States must be examined in the context of this nation. It is vitally important to understand that the legal structure of the United States was being formed in the very early part of the Industrial Revolution and that the founding documents are saturated in the ideas of the Enlightenment: reason and toleration.

The great expansion westward in the United States presented special opportunity for the entrepreneurial facet of prostitution, while at the same time little resistance could be offered by formal or traditional controls. Indeed, when the 1803 Louisiana Purchase doubled the size of the nation, by bringing such a vast watershed into the United States at a time when steam power was developing, the happenstance acted to virtually invent riverboat and rail prostitution.

Regulatory apparatuses do not always involve active suppression of prostitution, or the access to sex professionals, in its broadest sense. For much of human history, prostitution and management mechanisms designed to coordinate provision of that service have coexisted with imposed regulation and the principles of the marketplace. In broad strokes, it was typical for the United Sates to use criminalization, and for Europe to approach the problem as one of regulation, including licensing and policing both professional and client.

Thus, it is possible to think of two categories of prostitute, "industrial" and "craft" (depending on the organization through which service is provided), or to rank individual prostitutes into categories by "motivation" (Is there a strong push into the practice? Is there strong pull into the practice?), or to define prostitution in yet other ways. The reality that prostitution is richly complex, and that participation is almost always dynamic, explains the difficulty in reaching a single, usefully narrow definition.

Soliciting. In New York City a prostitute approaches a car. As of 2004, prostitution was illegal in every state except Nevada. Advocates for legalizing prostitution argued that decriminalizing the act would lead to better healthcare for the women and increased tax earnings for municipalities. © *Brooklyn Production/Corbis*

Prostitution in the Historic Record

Until the end of the nineteenth century, military corps, including those of the United States, frequently included brothel service or access as a means of maintaining order and reducing local disruptions, as well as acknowledging basic human desire. Prostitutes and prostitution, organized through brothels, bordellos, or by other means, were part of the urban fabric of city life in the United States through the 1800s. This even included the nation's capital. Washington, D.C., had, even for those unsettled times, an unusually large transient population, full of soldiers, functionaries, government employees, and other nonresidents. It ably represented the typical cluster of market forces and demography that supports a commercial sex industry.

In the late mid-nineteenth century, a wave of reform activity swept the nation, dealing in very general terms with victimization of workers. The so-called Recreation Reform Movement was quite elastic. Anxiety about pop-

ular conditions near factory areas in urban centers spawned a range of activist groups, from those involved with child labor to the notoriously volatile temperance league champions. If a unifying feature existed, it was a concern, or claimed concern, for the health of the working class. Participants in the activity at this time were not governmental organs, nor vested with regulatory powers. Nor, in the main, was there general agreement about topics such as prostitution or temperance, the distribution of birth-control information, or access to wagering. However, after decades of fairly vigorous national debate, by the end of the First World War, supporters of the criminalization of prostitutes and prostitution seemed to have gained ascendancy by a fair margin. Still, the appropriate method of dealing with sex workers continues to be a richly contested issue in legal discourse.

In the New World, prostitution developed along lines reflecting very local conditions, but still echoing a basic formula. Large towns, ports, and emerging and developed cities hosted both industrial (organized bordello, etc.) and craft prostitution. Free agents, or craft prostitutes, took advantage of economic opportunity at the fringes. Indeed, when the recreation reform movement wrecked worker's leisure warrens at the end of the 1800s, the greatest impact was on largely rural-style commercial sex provision. Workers, drawn into the city for factory employment, also drew in their traditional means of recreation and leisure, including heavy drinking and whoring.

Craft- and cottage-style prostitution was extirpated, reluctantly closed by local police as activists worked to get the idea of commercial sex repositioned in the public mind away from harmless, or even downright useful and necessary, service to unsanitary public health hazard. It took much longer for the bourgeois bordellos to feel the edge of the reform axe. Importantly, class considerations so important at the beginning of the 1900s were reconfigured, in the hands of middle-class and, later, academic activists, into gender considerations by the end of the 1900s. A century and a half ago, prior to the full criminalization of prostitution, madams were wealthy women of substance in New Orleans. A prostitute was paid, or could avail herself of the courts, as could any other legitimate businessperson. Today, while there is no indication of any diminution of activity among commercial sex consumers, providers are generally bereft of legal protection, suffer chronic underprotection in terms of health care, and are routinely victimized, largely as a result of their criminalized status as sex professionals. Repressive law seems unburdened by toleration or a reasoned relationship to the well-understood dynamics of commercial sex provision. Tangible concerns for a fair wage in a safe workplace were replaced by theoretical concerns for resistance to a real or imagined "heterosexualist patriarchy" uttered by a small but vocal minority. San Francisco's Barbary Coast, New Orleans's Storyville, and related urban "zoned" areas of prostitution illustrate the transition from laissez-faire to heavily regulated and repressed commercial sex economies. New Orleans offers a good example.

In about 1897, the New Orleans city council passed a unique ordinance. It was designed to confine and regulate prostitution within a specified district of the city. The special neighborhood came to be nicknamed "Storyville," after alderman Sidney Story, who proposed the now famous legislation. The district was home to legalized prostitution from 1 January 1898 until 12 November 1917. Ernest J. Bellocq, a hydrocephalic photographer, worked in the Crescent City, famously recording daily life. Like Toulouse-Lautrec in Paris, equally famous for his disability, Bellocq frequented brothels, where he was ac-

cepted as a fellow fringe dweller and outsider by some of the more sympathetic prostitutes. Both artists were allowed to move freely within the demimonde setting and record the environment. Each left images showing both the gaiety and the great humanity of these special places.

Because of the intense emotions circulating around the issue of prostitution, Louis Malle was successfully able to base his 1978 film *Pretty Baby* on E. J. Bellocq's Storyville experiences. Keith Carradine played the "deformed" photographer, providing a hint at the movie's zest for accuracy, with Brooke Shields and Susan Sarandon as prostitutes. *Pretty Baby* was thirteen-year-old Shields's first leading role in a major motion picture, and for both content and age issues the film raised a furor. It also joined the popular cultural package of information—or misinformation—available to the otherwise naive viewer. Mass-media portrayal (some could say betrayal) of sex professionals is common in films, novels, and other commercial releases. While markedly good renderings of the life experiences of sex professionals do exist, for the most part prostitutes perform the role of infinitely flexible foils to plot development or mise-en-scène decoration.

Streetwalkers, tarts, prostitutes—when they are other than plot devices in film, their representation ranges from complex to little more than propaganda. They represent the base and the carnal, virtue and human durability, just as traditionally the trade finds a narrative place from Genesis to the Whore of Babylon in Revelation.

Greta Garbo's icy beauty was well used in her first "talkie," *Anna Christie* (1930), based on Eugene O'Neill's play of the same name. Garbo walks the docks of New York, plying her trade, pausing between tricks at a typical tavern with fellow tramp Marty (Marie Dressler). Anna rescues a sailor, but, in keeping with many of O'Neill's characters, she must first display a dark secret.

When the repressive veil of the Production Code fell, this character was for a while virtually lost to Hollywood, if not to screens. The 1940 English film *Waterloo Bridge* tells the story of Vivien Leigh's character, a good woman, "forced" into the life when her husband is slaughtered in the war. Even with the edgy subtheme, it was necessary to have the character die in the end to atone for the sins of earning a living. It took a long time, but stories dealing with prostitution returned to the screen. These include *Moulin Rouge* (1952, later revisited), *East of Eden* (1955), and Shirley Jones's Lulu Bains in *Elmer Gantry* (1960), Jane Fonda in *Walk on the Wild Side* (1962), and, of course, Shirley MacLaine as *Irma la Douce* (1963), with a big step by Elizabeth Taylor in *Butterfield 8* (1960).

Modern Circumstances

By the turn of the twentieth century, both commercial and domestic sex was regulated and criminalized, with little exception. Antiprostitution activists played on class-based, racial, and religious fears, fueled by waves of immigration, in order to enact an increasingly thorough regulatory system. This included legislation such as the Mann Act (1910), which responded to a wave of hysteria about white slavery and whose scope was expanded over the next few decades from preventing nonconsensual sexual commerce to regulating consensual sexuality. Over time, sex workers were stripped of many protections normally offered citizens and, in addition, became increasingly burdened by restrictive law. Predictably, prostitutes became easy prey as prostitution itself was pushed underground.

Beginning in the 1950s, but accelerating in the 1970s (especially with the introduction of sex professionals working in a burgeoning pornography industry), attempts were made to build trade associations or labor unions within sex-worker constituents. Their aim was to lobby for better conditions and relief from the patriarchal legal system seen to be a mechanism to suppress or punish women capitalizing on their sexuality. At the same time, anti–sex industry activists have been struggling for the opposite: increased regulation, more rigorous criminalization, and a general expansion to embrace criminalization of marginal participants—the consumer, the business landlord, technical support industries associated with pornographic production, and even publications.

See also: Brothels, Pornography

BIBLIOGRAPHY

Bourdin, Ruth. *Women and Temperance: The Quest for Power and Liberty, 1873–1900.* New Brunswick, N.J.: Rutgers University Press, 1990.

Cooper, M., and Hanson, J. "Where There Are No Tourists . . . Yet: A Visit to the Slum Brothels in Ho Chi Minh City, Vietnam." In *Sex Tourism and Prostitution: Aspects of Leisure, Recreation, and Work.* Edited by Martin Oppermann. Elmsford, N.Y.: Cognizant Communication Corporation, 1998.

Donlon, Jon G. "A Travel Model in the Runway Setting: Strip-Tease as Exotic Destination." In *Sex Tourism and Prostitution: Aspects of Leisure, Recreation, and Work.* Edited by Martin Oppermann. Elmsford, N.Y.: Cognizant Communication Corporation, 1998.

Gay, Peter. *Pleasure Wars: The Bourgeois Experience—Victoria to Freud.* New York: W. W. Norton and Company, 1998.

Hobson, Barbara Meil. *Uneasy Virtue: The Politics of Prostitution and the American Reform Tradition.* New York: Basic Books, 1987.

MacLeod, David I. *Building Character in the American Boy: The Boy Scouts, YMCA, and Their Forerunners, 1870–1920.* Madison: University of Wisconsin Press, 1983.

Macy, Marianne. *Working Sex.* New York: Carroll and Graf Publishers, 1996.

Odzer, Cleo. *Patpong Sisters.* New York: Blue Moon Publishers, 1994.

Sweetman, David. *Explosive Acts: Toulouse-Lautrec, Oscar Wilde, Félix Fénéon, and the Art & Anarchy of the Fin de Siècle.* New York: Simon and Schuster, 1999.

Wiltz, Christine. *The Last Madam: A Life in the New Orleans Underworld.* New York: Faber and Faber, 2000.

Jon Griffin Donlon

PURITANS AT LEISURE

Puritans and leisure: seldom have two words seemed so antithetical. The word "puritan" conjures up images of a dour, ascetic person who pursues a life dedicated to eliminating leisure rather than enjoying it. From William Shakespeare, a contemporary of English Puritans, to Arthur Miller, a contemporary in the twenty-first century, playwrights, novelists, poets, journalists, and assorted literary gadflies have laughed at the Puritans supposed inability to have fun or relax. Historians have come to know that these morally superior critics were wrong. Puritans did know how to relax, they did endorse leisurely activities by both word and deed, and they did believe that saints had more fun than sinners did. Far from being incompatible with piety, Puritans argued that the right kind of leisure reinforced a good Christian's pursuit of eternal salvation.

Historical Killjoys

If Puritans were not sour misanthropes, why then have they enjoyed such an extraordinary reputation as killjoys? Something about the Puritans must have given rise to such misunderstandings among their contemporaries in Elizabethan England, colonial Virginia and New York, and virtually everywhere else. What about the Puritans' world has called forth this ubiquitous historical misunderstanding?

Plenty. At home in England, they condemned many of the aspects of the Elizabethan world that history has elevated to iconic heights. They hated theater with a vehemence that defies description. Stage plays subverted authority, corrupted morality, rewarded lying, encouraged promiscuity, and embraced homosexuality, they argued. They condemned the art of the Renaissance because it violated the Second Commandment's injunction not to make graven images. They refused to allow poor men, women, and children to play games and enjoy recreations on Sunday, the one day of the week that they did not have to toil from sunup to sundown. Puritans despised most traditional holidays and some pastimes that retrospectively seem idyllic such as dancing around a Maypole. Regarded as holier-than-thou by less pious neighbors, Puritans were quick to find fault in others as well as in themselves.

In the New World when they were given a chance to institutionalize their values in governments, the Puritans whipped young men and women who had sex before marriage, placed harmless gossips in the stocks to be ridiculed by passersby, cropped the ears of those who dared challenge religious orthodoxy, and passed laws that rebellious children could be put to death for dishonoring their parents. Puritan New England produced a steady supply of educated writers and scholars—John Cotton, Michael Wigglesworth, Cotton Mather, and many more—who harnessed their considerable literary talents to the proposition that humanity must constantly be on guard against the temptations to sin that existed everywhere on every day. All told, Puritan culture gushed forth geysers of grim laws and language that would convince any casual reader that leisure, pleasure, and recreation were anathema to a saintly life.

Wary Watchfulness

But these laws and languages were only part of the story—albeit an important part. The Puritans were deeply ambivalent about much of the world about them. They worked hard, pursued their vocations with the same zeal they pursued their afterlife, and believed that God rewarded virtue with success and punished wrongdoing with failure. Yet, they also believed that wealth and success promoted vanity and pride and led to a soul-destroying emphasis on worldliness. Puritans wanted to live in the real society of families, villages, politics, and the workplace unlike monks and nuns, whom they condemned, yet they knew that the profane world was full of sin and temptations. Nowhere was this more true than in the pursuit of leisure and recreation. Puritans believed that all pleasurable diversions contained within them the seeds of sin. Temptations lurked behind every rock and in every cranny to seduce the unwary from a righteous path. The old deluder, Satan, of course, lay behind all

these temptations: innocent pleasures provided the devil with some of his best lures to snare souls for his own kingdom.

Thus, Puritans believed in leisure—they were too mindful of human psychology not to believe in it—but they always approached it with a wary eye. In sermons and published tracts, Puritan ministers often endorsed a wide range of leisurely activities that would include activities that might be found surprising such as sexual intercourse, dancing, and the drinking of alcohol; but almost always these statements of support were accompanied by warnings against excess or variations of the activities. The preaching often took on a give-and-take quality whereby one clause in a sentence would authorize people to indulge in something and another clause would warn of all the problems that might arise from doing so inappropriately. The message was clear and constant—be ever vigilant—because, as a group of ministers warned potential abusers of alcohol, people "often drink down poison in their pleasant cups and perceive it not" (*A Serious Address*, p. 10).

These constant exhortations to beware excess also account for some of the associations made between Puritanism and hatred of leisure. Moreover, these mixed messages made the pursuit of leisure psychologically conflicting for many people who took the warnings seriously and felt more required to keep their guard up than authorized to let their hair down. The warnings often moved from general wariness to specific prohibitions that further hedged the endorsements with restrictions. Among things forbidden: any activities denounced in scriptures or that reflected unfavorably on God or tended to inflict physical injuries or harmed the commonweal. All of the above, of course, were open to interpretation, and some zealous ministers stretched scriptural analysis into a wide variety of prohibitions. Moralists also condemned many activities as guilty by association. If the Roman Catholic Church supported something, Puritans usually did not like it; nor did they tend to like activities associated with the French and Italians, both of whom they felt wallowed in licentious and lascivious conduct. Puritans also denounced leisure that did not genuinely refresh a person and by this they meant leisurely activities that left a practitioner frustrated or upset when the activity was over. They insisted that leisure had to allow a person to return to the serious business of re-creating the soul after recreating the body or mind. One can imagine that many golfers who bemoan their poor putting or errant drives would have a hard time convincing a Puritan minister that golf was a good form of leisure for them.

Productive Leisure

Puritans prized productive leisure above all other forms of relaxation. Thus, the fabled barn or house raisings that are more associated with the pioneer west of the nineteenth century, fit perfectly into the seventeenth-century New England world. Puritans were a congregational people who emphasized group activities over individual ones: in addition to gathering to raise barns and houses, they made community parties out of many activities such as husking corn, aiding an injured neighbor, milling grain, quilting and spinning wool, splitting wood, and so forth. Some of these activities such as barn and house raisings brought men, women, and children together—the men and boys did the heavy lifting and construction, while the women and girls prepared food and drink. Others such as woodcuttings were usually male only; and sewing bees, which sometimes had as many as forty participants, were for women and girls. Young girls from ten to fourteen frequently went on berry outings; corn huskings, which did not become popular until the late seventeenth and early eighteenth centuries, were parties for young adults.

Two special sets of activities, one bucolic and one boisterous, deserve special mention in any discussion of Puritan leisure because they were so prevalent and they so perfectly illustrate the full range of productive parties: fishing and militia training. Virtually all New England men loved fishing, and all of them between the ages of sixteen and sixty took part in militia training usually held once a month. Ubiquity did not, however, indicate similar conduct.

Fishing was New England's favorite sport. It could be done almost anywhere in the region, and, unlike hunting, fishing always provided bounty for the dinner table. Fishing also could be contemplative, and, although not healthy for the fish that were caught, it did not seem violent. Families went on fishing picnics; ministers swapped information with one another on particularly productive sites; diarists recorded their catches with pride; and correspondents bragged to friends in England about the never-ending supply. Harvard, the very serious college for New England's most pious young men, did not allow its students much leisure time but explicitly authorized them to go fishing. At the end of the colonial period, New England formed its first sports association the Shad and Salmon Club of Hartford (1780).

Militia-training day was another story. If Puritan society had a boy's night (day) out, it would be training day. Colonial New England lived in constant war or fear of war, and thus militia-training day had a serious purpose.

Customarily, in the morning, the officers formally drilled men in the tactics needed to defend their communities against attacks from natives or European rivals. The afternoons, however, were devoted to martial arts games: marksmanship contests, wrestling matches, horse and foot races, and other competitive feats that would help men hone the skills they needed to be good soldiers. These games ran the danger of turning a bit rowdy in the early evening as young men sometimes mixed their competitive juices with a beer or glass of flip (a hot, mulled, wine drink immensely popular in New England) at a local tavern on the way home. Militia-training days tended to be extremely serious when genuine outside threats to the peace were perceived, and they tended to be much less serious—"real toots"—when the biggest threats came from the local boys getting out of hand.

Quiet Times

Real toots were the exception, not the rule, in Puritan New England. Puritans placed an enormous emphasis on education as an aid to pursuing eternal salvation *and* earthly success. Ministers were learned men educated in Latin, Greek, classics, logic, and history, and the bulk of the general population of the first generation—perhaps as many as 80 percent of men and 60 percent of women—could read and write. The percentages got even higher in the New World, and Puritan society was one of the most literate in the Atlantic world. Thus reading played a major role in pursuing a life of piety, but it played an equally important role in leisure activities.

Puritans read a version of the Bible, the Geneva edition, which relied heavily on textual notes, sidebars, and pictures to generate interest among all people but particularly the young. Merchants in most large towns imported books from England within a few months of their being published. A printing press began operation in Boston in 1640. Everywhere a New Englander looked in the seventeenth century, he or she saw books. And they read them. They read advice manuals, printed sermons, poetry, and books meant solely to charm. New England produced its own best-selling poets, the lovely Anne Bradstreet, whose sensuous odes to her husband and family remain evocative in the early 2000s, or the thundering Michael Wigglesworth, whose *Day of Doom* (1662) terrorized a generation of adolescents who saw their own sinful souls described. Among the best-selling imports, Henry Preacher's *The Complete Gentlemen* (1622) gave aspiring members of the gentry a lesson in manners, and Izaak Walton's *The Compleat Angler* (1653) soothed the souls of fishermen (and women).

A new genre of sensationalist literature emerged in the second half of the seventeenth century. Captivity tales related the experiences of pious saints—usually women—who had been captured by natives and forced to live among them for extended periods. After being ransomed or escaping, these former prisoners, often assisted by a minister, would tell their tales in print in a curious mixture of anthropology, moral lesson, and horror story.

Nor was all literature meant to be serious. Reading should not be irreverent, but it could be witty. Puritans poked fun at themselves and their world. Five ministers of renowned piety—Samuel Danforth, Edward Johnson, Hugh Peters, Nathaniel Ward, and Thomas Wendle—wrote wonderfully humorous poems and essays. Ward's *The Simple Cobbler of Aggawam* (1647) was said to have given rise to more than 100 clever sayings, many of which presaged the homespun philosophy and curmudgeonly satire of future humorists such as Samuel Clemens and Will Rogers. A recent widower looking unsuccessfully for a wife, Ward wrote, "The World is full of care, much like unto a bubble; women and care, and care and women, and women and care and trouble."

Music, too, afforded some quiet moments of leisure to many Puritans. The role of music in Puritan society has also been much misunderstood. Puritans hated the way Europe's great cathedrals had employed trained choirs and organists to aid in church services. Orchestrated church music, they argued, distracted from the true purpose of worship and stifled individual expression. Thus, they vehemently denounced the use of any musical instruments inside a church and reserved a special contempt for the most ubiquitous church instrument, the pipe organ. They were not against all music in church, however, and from the first days of settlement, Puritan congregations sang psalms at their services. They did not, however, give singers any accompaniment or any direction, so each singer felt free to pursue any tune he or she liked. One can imagine that the result would not be aesthetically pleasing if 300 people all launched into separate, simultaneous interpretations of the same tune.

One result has been that people have wrongly assumed Puritans hated music. Not only did they sing psalms in service, they often sang in their homes, and they did use instruments—particularly violins, citterns, lutes, guitars, harpsichords, spinets, trumpets, and drums. Young men often carried and played Jew's harps. People often entertained on musical instruments in taverns. Even the prohibition on choirs and instruments in church came under attack before the seventeenth century ended as ministers began to realize that God might not be pleased by a cacophony of babble. Early in the eighteenth

century, the supporters of singing "by the new way" triumphed, and New England entered a century sometimes called a "golden age" of choral music.

Gathering Together

The ideal Puritan village consisted of forty or fifty houses closely clustered around a meetinghouse, which would be built on the highest hill in town. The ideal, however, was beleaguered from the start by the abundance of land. In addition to being Puritans, New England's founders were farmers. Their desire for land initiated a relentless assault on the concept of a nucleated Puritan village. As the size of landholdings increased, the village ideal gave way quickly to the reality of the dispersed farm. Nevertheless, the metaphor persisted of the meetinghouse being at the center of Puritan life. It remained central to many of their leisure activities.

New England churches held three meetings per week: two on Sunday—one in the morning and one in the afternoon—and one on Thursday afternoon. The community expected every person to attend and punished those who did not. No one would describe the services as entertainment, but ministers gave original sermons that went beyond mere exhortations to do good: people often took notes on them and met after in groups to discuss them. Germane to the present discussion, however, a host of socializing activities surrounded the meetings. People living distant from the village center streamed into town and often stopped both coming and going at the houses of friends and relatives. Between the two Sunday meetings, parishioners partook of the good fare of brown bread and the gospel. No one played games because the Puritans did, indeed, take Sabbatarianism seriously, but then again, no one worked either. A quietude descended on New England each Sunday as people used the day to renew their ties to family, friends, and community as well as to their search for salvation.

The afternoon meeting held on Thursday—often called "Lecture Day"—afforded a half day of similar activities but without the same restrictions imposed by respect for the Lord's Day. Children could be noisier after meetings and play games, and men and women sometimes went to a tavern for a beer to enliven the conversation. Moreover, the community came together as one congregational entity on a multiple of other episodic occasions. Days of fasting or of feasting were held to mark good or bad events that may have befallen the parish or the wider community of saints. Usually the entire parish attended funerals. The ordination of a new minister provided a parish with its greatest occasion to celebrate. Ministers often served for life and choosing and ordaining a new one marked a great moment in church history. Elaborate preparations preceded the ceremony, which lasted several days and always attracted well-wishers and visiting ministers from surrounding towns. Sometimes local taverns would brew a special "ordination beer," and by the third quarter of the seventeenth century, more urbane churches held ordination balls. The new minister customarily did not dance but would be the recipient of a steady supply of congratulations and statements of respect.

Although the meetinghouse played a central role in congregational socializing, Puritans adamantly refused to acknowledge any of the religious holidays associated with Saint's days in European Catholicism. "If every day be holy, how can there be holy days," constituted the smug Puritan rebuke to the Catholic practice of singling out special days routinely. Thus, although the Plymouth Pilgrims celebrated a day of thanksgiving in the late fall of 1621, which is regarded as the progenitor of modern American Thanksgiving, they did not celebrate one every year and most certainly would not celebrate one if the harvest was bad. Similarly, they tended not to celebrate individual birthdays in the early years of New England settlement, but by the early eighteenth century, birthday good wishes might be expressed from one to another. Puritans reserved a special hatred for Christmas or "foolstide," as they called it. Condemned as ahistorical—Jesus was not born on 25 December, they believed—Christmas was a pagan holiday co-opted by idolatrous Romans and celebrated by drunkenness and hedonism in most parts of Christendom. Plymouth Colony fined some visiting sailors for celebrating Christmas in its first year of settlement, and Massachusetts briefly made celebrating Christmas an illegal activity before being forced by English officials to repeal the law. As late as the era of the American Revolution, however, the respectable sort of New Englanders still associated Christmas celebrations with the lower strata of the social structure.

Ironically, the one holiday celebrated on an annual basis—although never officially sanctioned—was acknowledged to be a celebration of the rougher sort. Guy Fawkes Day, 5 November, commemorated the foiling of the Gunpowder Plot, whereby Catholic terrorists had planned to blow up the houses of Parliament. Puritan leaders tolerated Guy Fawkes celebrations because they solidified the community and all of New England in an anti-Catholic ethos. Young men and especially sailors and servants would make effigies of the pope and burn them over a late-evening bonfire amid outbursts of antipapal rhetoric. Magistrates turned a blind eye unless events became too rowdy. Somewhat akin to Halloween celebrations in the twentieth century in that the community

seemed willing to accept defined quotients of misbehavior, Guy Fawkes Day was perhaps the least "Puritan" day in New England's year because of the rowdiness but perhaps the most "Puritan" in the sense of affirming the region's anti-Catholicism.

Romance and Courtship

Probably nothing is more associated with alleged Puritan asceticism than the relationship between the sexes. For this association many people can be thanked, among whom the most notable may be Nathaniel Hawthorne and Hester Prynne. Choosing a mate, however, and the courting relationship between men and women afforded many opportunities for leisure. Parents arranged marriages, and practical considerations always played a prominent role in the choice. Nevertheless, young men and women acted on personal mutual attractions and usually initiated the process. After a young couple decided they would like to be together, they would approach the two sets of parents who then began the process of negotiating a marital contract.

Everyday contact in a village, religious services, and assorted social occasions gave prospective brides and grooms ample opportunities to size up possibilities and even to flirt. Wedding receptions themselves furnished a favorite place to socialize with the opposite sex. Justices of the peace rather than ministers performed marriage ceremonies because Puritans believed marriage to be a civil contract not a sacrament. Thus, the ceremony took place in the home of the bride and was always followed immediately by a reception. Friends and relatives of the bride and groom and their parents would attend, and people often traveled substantial distances from towns too remote to allow them to go back home on the same night. One wedding reception therefore might lead to another, and invariably it led to a chance for much interaction between young men and women of marrying age who tended to be of similar (and thus acceptable) social status. As the seventeenth century wore on, wedding receptions became more boisterous affairs, and in the final quarter of the century they began to embrace high jinks, mixed dancing, and even kissing games between the unmarried.

Dances afforded other opportunities for young people to socialize in a flirtatious setting as Puritan moralists realized all too well. Ministers always endorsed dancing as a theoretical concept, but they hedged it with so many restrictions that one might be inclined to doubt their sincerity. In the first generation of settlement, "mixed dancing," or "gynecandrical dancing," as ministers termed dancing that involved physical contact between men and women, was proscribed. But since

A New Bundling Song (Boston, 1785)

A bundling couple went to bed

With all their clothes from foot to head

That the defense might seem complete

Each one was wrapped in a sheet

But O! this bundlings such a witch

The man of her did catch the itch

And so provoked was the wretch

That she of him a bastard catch'd

dancing itself was not banned, the leap from same-sex exercise to couple dancing was easily made. By the mid seventeenth century, "country dances," or what would later be called "square dances," made their appearance in the larger towns, and, by 1675, young men and women could go country dancing throughout the region. The advantage of country dancing, of course, was that partners were frequently changed, and they did not hold each other in a close embrace that would create a great *flabella Libidinis* (fanning of sexual desire). By the end of the seventeenth century, large balls were held in over a dozen of the region's major towns and dance schools opened in Boston, Newport, and Portsmouth.

As do many religious peoples, the Puritans often organized social occasions around food. Of all the deadly sins, gluttony inspires the fewest concerns. As they discovered the geography of a New World, New Englanders also discovered the delights of new and tasty foods. Families exchanged dinner invitations frequently with neighbors and relatives. Outdoor parties held on beaches—clambakes and oyster bakes—were wonderfully popular with all New Englanders but young people especially. Clams, oysters, and lobsters, however, could not compete with the excitement offered by a "turtle frolic." Chefs plunged a giant turtle, towed back alive from the Caribbean, into a caldron of boiling water, to the cheers of guests in attendance. Turtle frolics were infrequent and sufficiently well advertised in advance to attract travelers from out of town.

And not only did Puritans like food, they liked drink. After the meetinghouse, the tavern was New England's second most popular public place to gather. All English people—men and women, pious or irreligious—could

usually be counted on to agree that beer promoted digestion and relaxed a weary person. All villages with more than fifty families were required by law to have an inn to house travelers, and all inns served a variety of alcoholic beverages: beer, flip, and fermented juices such as hard cider and perry (from pears). By the late seventeenth century, most taverns also carried wines and made more exotic drinks. Men and women both attended taverns, and children often drank slightly fermented fruit drinks with evening meals. Taverns dotted inter-town highways and often anchored a ferry slip. Not only were taverns functional for travelers and centers of leisure for local residents, they also served as newsstands and forums for political/civic discussions.

Thus, alcohol presented no problem to Puritans who joined the early modern world in being suspicious of drinking too much water and in thinking of moderate amounts of alcohol as being healthful. Drunkenness did bother Puritans, however, as did tavern haunting—wasting time and idling over drink. Puritans punished abuse of alcohol and tavern culture with a severity that probably accounts for the mistaken historical notion that they tended to be prohibitionists. They also carefully regulated taverns and passed dozens of laws specifying how long a person could stay and how much he or she could consume in a single visit. In the early years of Puritan settlement, taverns tended to be fairly quiet and decorous, but as the century neared closing, many tavern owners added music, and young men and women incorporated tavern visits into the burgeoning custom of courting.

No discussion of taverns, travel, romance, and Puritanism can ignore New England's most famous/infamous courting institution—bundling. The subject of much humor among contemporary writers and among satirists ever since, bundling was not invented by the Puritans—the Swiss, Dutch, and Welsh had practiced it in the late Middle Ages—but by the early modern period, "queesting" as the Dutch called it, had died out everywhere until reintroduced briefly by the third generation of New England Puritans in the early eighteenth century.

Bundling made practical sense in two ways. First, if a young man traveled a distance of several miles to court a young woman, it might be dangerous to insist that he return to his home after dark. Second, if he had to stay with the family of the woman he was courting, why not allow him to become more acquainted with the object of his affections by spending the night in her presence? Of course, no one would sanction illicit sexual activity, but bundling proponents thought that they could easily prevent this through any one of a number of physical measures. They could sew the man and the woman into several layers of thick clothing that made any intimate contact impossible. Or they could put a "bundling board" down the middle of the bed that prevented any contact beyond chatting. These bundling arrangements made sense in an early modern world, where travelers staying at inns often had to share beds with strangers, and where most children were raised sharing a bed with siblings or an elderly aunt or uncle.

Bundling first emerged as an expedient for traveling swains and tended to be practiced primarily among the lower orders of society. But well-placed young men and women and local courting couples perceived the social benefits of the bundling bed and often demanded that they, too, be allowed to be bundled together for the night. As bundling became legitimized among some New Englanders in the second quarter of the eighteenth century, it also brought forth an avalanche of attacks by moralists who argued that bundling proponents seriously underestimated the ingenuity of young people confronted by the devil's temptations. A great bundling fight ensued, and by the American Revolution, the anti-bundlers had carried the day. Bundling thus disappeared after having a short life in late Puritan America—but it has had a rich life in the folk culture ever since.

The Edge of Respectability

Bundling brought Puritan New England to the edge of respectability. Several other activities did so also, and some ranged beyond the edge of respectability that Puritan ministers and magistrates were willing to tolerate.

For a variety of reasons, Puritans did not support any ball sports. Football, the most prevalent English ball sport, engendered too much violence. It customarily pitted dozens—hundreds at times—of men from one village against another. Usually the goal required the men of the successful village to carry the ball to the center of the opposing village, and combatants broke many arms, legs, and necks along the way. Puritans condemned tennis by negative reference: they associated it with the French and Italians and also with the cloistered walls of abbeys and monasteries, where it had originally been played. Although not violent and thoroughly English, bowling too readily lent itself to tavern lounging for Puritans to accept it as a legitimate form of recreation. By the end of the seventeenth century, however, a little bowling did take place in New England, and the magistrates tended not to punish it. In general, ball sports did not get played in New England until during the Revolution, when the great grandsons of the Puritan founders started to play them with their southern comrades in arms in the Continental Army.

Card games spread to Europe from Asia in the fourteenth century but remained an elite pastime until the late sixteenth century, when they became popular with all classes of people. By the 1630s, the decade of the "Great Migration" of Puritans to New England, card playing was the most prevalent English indoors game. Puritans did not condemn card games with a broad brush: they recognized the extraordinary potential for genuine relaxation in the wide variety of games that could be squeezed from such a small and easily available source. They recognized, also, something better: cards taught basic skills in numeracy and logic with a rare ease. But, danger lurked in those fifty-two little pieces of paper. They lent themselves very easily to gambling. Thus, Puritans tended to be wary about cards but never condemned them completely. They condemned the specific card games that were most conducive to gambling.

Puritans condemned gambling as many religious people do but not with a great degree of ferocity. Sailors and other single men often played huzzle cap (a form of penny pitching) and hazard (the forerunner of modern craps) and would be warned or fined if caught but not whipped or placed in stocks unless they were frequent offenders. And Puritans occasionally used lotteries to raise money for public purposes, although invariably some of their number opposed doing so and a debate would ensue. They also often assigned strips of land in fields by the drawing of lots, so the idea of random chance was not anathema.

A Hard-Headed People

As their willingness to split hairs on card playing indicates, many factors went into the Puritan assessment of what separated good leisure from bad leisure. Most basically, their sense of scriptures and the history of Christianity informed many of their decisions about appropriate and inappropriate forms of relaxation. So, too, did sociology. Ball sports were not proscribed by scripture and were not inherently violent: but since empirical observation showed that they usually were, ball games were frowned upon. Few things about Puritanism's likes and dislikes should surprise modern Christians, Muslims, or adherents of most of the world's faiths. Perhaps most surprising is not that Puritans had many unusual ideas about leisure—they did not—but that they enforced the ones they had with regularity and with the power of government. Modern society is awash with double standards and huge gaps between stated values and actual behavior. Puritans more consistently practiced what they preached. For the most part they secured compliance with their values about leisure by codifying them in legislation and then by requiring magistrates to make sure that men and women, rich and poor—all people alike—obeyed the law. Posterity has rewarded the Puritans for their consistency, frank legal codes, and unswerving enforcement by branding them as repressive, joyless prudes.

See also: Barn Raising, Colonial-Era Leisure and Recreation, Frolics, Mumming, Parades, Work and Leisure Ethics

BIBLIOGRPAHY

Archer, Richard. *Fissures in the Rock: New England in the Seventeenth Century.* Hanover, N.H.: University Press of New England, 2001.

Conroy, David. *In Public Houses: Drink and the Revolution of Authority in Colonial Massachusetts.* Chapel Hill: University of North Carolina Press, 1995.

Cressy, David. *Coming Over: Migration and Communication Between England and New England in the Seventeenth Century.* New York: Cambridge University Press, 1987.

Daniels, Bruce C. *Puritans at Play: Leisure and Recreation in Colonial New England.* New York: St. Martin's Press, 1995.

Deetz, James, and Patricia Deetz. *The Times of Their Lives: Life, Love, and Death in Plymouth Colony.* New York: W. H. Freeman and Company, 2000.

Durston, Christopher, and Jacqueline Eales, eds. *The Culture of English Puritanism.* New York: St. Martin's Press, 1996.

Erikson, Kai. *Wayward Puritans: A Study of the Sociology of Deviance.* New York: John Wiley and Sons, 1966.

Hall, David D. *Worlds of Wonder, Days of Judgment: Popular Religious Beliefs in Early New England.* Cambridge, Mass.: Harvard University Press, 1990.

Kamensky, Jane. *Governing the Tongue: The Politics of Speech in Early New England.* New York: Oxford University Press, 1977.

Miller, Perry. *The New England Mind in the Seventeenth Century.* Cambridge, Mass.: Harvard University Press, 1939.

Morgan, Edmund S. *The Puritan Family: Religion and Domestic Relations in Seventeenth-Century New England.* New York: Harper and Row, 1966.

Morison, Samuel Eliot. *Builders of the Bay Colony.* Boston: Houghton Mifflin, 1930.

Serious Address to Those Who Unnecessarily Frequent the Tavern, and Often Spend the Evening in Publick Houses, A. Boston: S. Gerrish, 1726.

Solberg, Winston. *Redeem the Time: The Puritan Sabbath in Early America.* Cambridge, Mass.: Harvard University Press, 1977.

Struna, Nancy. *People of Prowess: Sport, Leisure, and Labor in Early Anglo-America.* Urbana: University of Illinois Press, 1996.

Thompson, Roger. *Sex in Middlesex: Popular Mores in a Massachusetts County, 1649–1699.* Amherst, Mass.: University of Massachusetts Press, 1986.

Ulrich, Laurel Thatcher. *The Age of Homespun: Objects and Stories in the Creation of an American Myth.* New York: Alfred A. Knopf, 2001.

Bruce C. Daniels

PUZZLES

See *Crossword Puzzles*

QUILTING PARTIES

A quilting party is an informal gathering of a small group of primarily women who work, collectively or individually, on quilts, the usually three-layered textiles intended for use as warm bed coverings or decorative wall hangings. Quilting parties provide opportunities to share in getting necessary work done more quickly and to socialize with friends and families. Sometimes also referred to as "bees," quilting parties have existed in the United States since colonial times. The practice of mutual aid and exchanging labor was an integral part of the post-contact years of American settlement and has continued to be important as social and economic activities in rural and agricultural communities. Family, religious, ethnic, and occupational traditions also determine the popularity of holding parties.

As of the beginning of the twenty-first century, there were over 20 million quilters in the United States and thousands of organized quilt clubs and quilt guilds that hosted quilt parties. Some groups met as frequently as every week, others only when a special project demands a gathering. Special projects were varied. Some quilt parties were held to make quilts for those with health problems; especially popular was the making of lap quilts for shut-ins and baby quilts for premature HIV-infected infants. Quilts were also made for the temporarily needy, such as disaster victims or women and children living in domestic abuse shelters. Parties were held to make quilts that memorialize those who died of AIDS or those killed in wars and disasters such as 11 September. In some communities, it was traditional to produce friendship or album quilts as presents for the anniversaries, weddings, graduations, baby showers, or going-away parties of loved ones. Others produced quilts to commemorate a special local or national event or to honor the service or achievements of an individual or organization. While some quilt gatherings were formed to produce quilts as a source of income for the quilt makers, more typically they produced quilts to be given away or to be used to sell or raffle off as fund-raisers for a wide array of causes and organizations.

As diary accounts, letters, and oral histories testify, quilting parties have long been important times for building friendships and social relationships through shared work, conversation, news, information, gossip, sometimes music, and—often—food. Favorite or new dishes were shared with friends; the food component of parties proved so popular that quilters' recipes were published in numerous cookbooks. Although by the early 2000s quilting parties were almost strictly for women, in earlier times men sometimes held simultaneous work parties or joined the women for food, dancing, music, and socializing among neighbors and friends after the actual quilting was finished.

Quilting parties also were important occasions during which quilting was learned, as more skilled artists passed on their quilting knowledge to others. Many individuals recall their first introduction to quilting occurred as children at quilting parties, where they played under a quilt stretched on a frame or were allowed to sew a few stitches.

Typically, quilting parties were held in homes, churches, senior centers or retirement homes, fabric stores, and community centers. With the rise of a quilt industry (including professional quilting classes, design and production of fabrics especially for quilts, expansion of new tools developed for quilting, and Internet-based listservs), quilting parties were held on cruise ships, at conferences, and even in cyberspace. Quilting parties, regardless of their venue or the intended outcome of their work, continued to play a vital role in building and sustaining networks of individuals engaged in a shared and valued communal activity.

See also: Colonial-Era Leisure and Recreation; Frolics

BIBLIOGRAPHY

Atkins, Jacqueline Marx. *Shared Threads: Quilting Together— Past and Present.* New York: Viking Studio Books, 1994.

Dewhurst, C. Kurt, Betty MacDowell, and Marsha MacDowell. *Artists in Aprons: Folk Art by American Women,* New York: E. P. Dutton, 1979.

Ice, Joyce, and Linda Norris. *Quilted Together: Women, Quilts, and Communities.* Delhi, N.Y.: Delaware County Historical Association, 1989.

Marsha MacDowell

QUINCEAÑERA
See *Latinos Leisure Lifestyles*

RACIAL DIVERSITY AND LEISURE LIFESTYLES

Racial discrimination and intolerance have been a sad part of our history. Many people believe that, after decades of struggle, race relations have not significantly improved. Despite apparent racial tensions, a large percentage of white Americans remain oblivious to racial issues and continue to endorse the idea that America is a country of equal opportunity. However, based on a long history of bigotry, prejudice, and discrimination, members of racial minority groups commonly believe white Americans are insensitive to racial problems.

American culture is also replete with negative stereotypes about African Americans, Jews, Latinos, and other minorities. Latinos, for instance, are often portrayed as lazy, shiftless, lawless, thieving, immoral, or violent. Their sexuality is viewed as exotic, which is demonstrated by the numerous Web sites offering dates with Latino women. Complaints have been raised that Hollywood does not have enough Latino movie and television stars, and that those they do have are typically associated with crime. Conversely, Asians and Pacific Islanders in the United States have been stereotyped as the "model minority" because the majority are college-educated with middle- or upper-income occupations. Some American institutions of higher education, like Harvard, Brown, Princeton, Yale, and Stanford, have restrictive admissions policies for Asian Americans because too many Asian students overshadow white college students.

Thus, it is not surprising that race relations in the United States in the early twenty-first century were characterized by racial distance and racial distrust. Because the United States is becoming an increasingly diverse society, it is imperative that Americans find ways to foster a climate of mutual tolerance and understanding. Many of the conditions necessary to promote positive interracial attitudes and behaviors can be found in leisure settings. According to the research, to be effective interracial contact should occur under specific conditions. The contact should take place within a cooperative context; it should be sustained rather than episodic; and it should be personal, informal, and one to one. The contact should also grant equal status to all parties rather than duplicate the racial status differential that exists in society. These conditions exist in leisure settings because such settings typically have the important qualities of free choice and self-determination. However, leisure settings are some of the most segregated spaces in society. While laws have integrated schools and other formal settings, no similar laws have been enacted to integrate leisure spaces. Moreover, even when different racial groups do share a leisure setting, the setting is likely to have some kind of implicit racial boundary. These issues have a direct impact on the leisure lifestyles and leisure spaces of racial minorities.

Theories of Racial Integration

The investigation of the distinct leisure behaviors of different racial groups has been the subject of research for many decades. Early studies examined differences between African Americans and white Americans in selected leisure activities. Later research expanded the range of studies to include other racial groups, including Hispanic, Asian, Native American, and mixed-race populations. In general, these studies concluded that, although there is a set of leisure activities that is common among most groups (including reading, watching television, spending time with family and friends), there are also many differences in how racial groups spend their leisure time and in which activities they choose to participate during that time. Ruth Russell stated that the leisure interests and participation patterns of racial groups help to explain who they are and provide them with the means to express their unique identities.

Early theories of the nineteenth and early twentieth centuries, such as the Anglo-conformity and melting pot theories, predicted the disappearance of important racial differences. Society was expected to merge into a culturally homogenous family, with the premise of this anticipated collectivity being the belief that racially distinct groups would assimilate into their host cultures. Some assimilation this did occur, but widespread assimilation has not taken place. Rather, minority groups have sought to maintain some measure of their own racial identity, and their leisure behavior often contributes to this identity formation process. For instance, university campuses often have racially specific fraternities and sororities, and community festivals that highlight distinct racial groups are common. Therefore, perhaps a more relevant paradigm is a cultural pluralism ideology that is based on the accommodation of racial group differences within a single social system.

Particularly relevant to leisure is a variation of the cultural pluralism paradigm that has been labeled "selective acculturation", in which minority group members adopt certain strategic traits of the dominant culture, while maintaining other traditional cultural values. In other words, a form of "ethnic boundary maintenance" occurs in which racial groups find ways to build and emphasize racial and cultural differences between themselves and outgroup members, while promoting racial and cultural solidarity within their own group. Leisure behavior can be a major contributor to the selective acculturation process. Susan Shaull and James Gramann argued that leisure has two characteristics that enable it to facilitate the expression of traditional racial and cultural values. First, leisure is often characterized by fewer social limitations than activity at work or school, and therefore it provides a potential for cultural expression that may not be possible in more restricted institutional settings. Second, leisure often occurs in the context of family and friendship groups, and, in the case of many minority groups,

intimate social life within the home and family tends to be racially and ethnically enclosed.

Therefore, while many people may argue that theories such as the melting pot or Anglo-conformity may be antiquated and no longer appropriate for our changing society, they may be particularly inappropriate for understanding racial influences on leisure behavior. Leisure is an important social space where racial and cultural values can be expressed and maintained. Thus, leisure can play a critical role in the persistence of minority group identity, despite trends toward mainstream conformity in the other social arenas such as work and school. During leisure time people have the most freedom to choose what they would like to do and with whom. Therefore, it should not be surprising that people tend to racially segregate during their leisure time. However, because majority-group members are typically accepting and understanding of other racial group members' unique leisure expressions, leisure settings do have the potential to play an important role in fostering a climate of mutual tolerance and understanding, and facilitating positive interracial interactions. Russell referred to leisure as a potential "tool" for helping develop more positive interracial relations, and stated that organized leisure could be used as a means of overcoming some of the hostility and tension that exists in many communities due to the negative stereotyping of minority populations. She suggested that the arts, in particular, offer an opportunity for sharing cultural traditions and increasing racial and ethnic pride and tolerance. Richard Kraus described programs at the YMCA, where one of their primary goals is the elimination of prejudice and discrimination, and some youth camping programs that have been established to promote intercultural friendship and understanding.

What has the research taught us about the leisure behavior of racial minority groups? Much of the research has been built on the work of Randel Washburne and Michael Woodard. Washburne's contrasting explanations for differences in leisure participation patterns between white mainstream and racial and ethnic groups, and Woodard's study regarding the impact of discrimination-related factors on leisure lifestyles both made significant contributions to this line of research and laid the foundation for future studies. However, for several reasons, these paradigms have limited value for advancing social theory, and thus, other frameworks have been offered to help understand the leisure behavior of racially diverse groups. For example, researchers have suggested that examining the constraints of subgroups of the population (that is, racial minorities) might help us better understand their leisure habits. Monika Stodolska commented that it is difficult to study the leisure of racial minorities without understanding the constraints they face, and Eva Tsai and Denis Coleman noted that, through leisure, racial minorities are exposed to constraints that affect their leisure preferences and enjoyment and their desire to undertake new activities. The concepts of selective acculturation and assimilation have also provided insight into the leisure choices of racial minorities. The following discussion provides an overview of some of the research that has built on these concepts and has led to a better understanding of racial minorities' leisure lifestyles.

Previous Research on the Leisure of Racial Minorities

Washburne presented two explanations to describe racial minorities' limited participation in wildland recreation. His two frameworks, the marginality and ethnicity perspectives, then became the basis for understanding racial differences in leisure behavior. The marginality perspective suggests that minorities do not participate in certain leisure activities, such as sailing, snow skiing, and scuba diving, due to socioeconomic discrimination. In other words, underparticipation in some activities by minority populations is a function of their marginal position in society, which reduces their opportunity to take part in desired forms of recreation. Further, differences in participation reflect not only differences in current socioeconomic status, but also a history of inequitable access to resources and opportunities. The alternative explanation, ethnicity, contends that the leisure choices of minorities are based on their subcultural style and that leisure is a reflection of their own unique culture. In other words, racial differences in participation are explained by culturally based value systems, norms, and socialization patterns. This perspective assumes that racial groups preserve distinct cultural identities and beliefs that they then carry into their leisure interests and behaviors. For example, African Americans may value the natural environment differently than their white counterparts because nature and open space may hold more negative connotations for African Americans (white domination of land ownership). Similarly, Carolyn Dragan found distinct cultural differences between Native Americans and white Americans in the meanings attached to the use of National Parks, and Susan Tirone and Susan Shaw found that Canadian women of Indian origin did not view private time, which is typically associated with the opportunity for leisure, as positive or desirable. Rather, they referred to being lonely and even depressed when they were on their own without children, husbands, or extended family members.

Woodard highlighted the impact of discrimination on leisure participation. More specifically, he examined "fear of race prejudice" (feeling safe from racial prejudice when recreating within one's own neighborhood), "discrimination" (experiencing some form of racial discrimination the proceeding year), "coracialism" (interacting socially with other African Americans), and "criticism" (receiving peer or family criticism for interracial social interaction) and their influence on leisure participation. His findings indicated that many of these factors affected African Americans' participation in leisure activities, suggesting the importance of discrimination as a constraint. Since then, it has become widely accepted that racial groups experience a significant degree of discrimination in leisure settings. Patrick West observed that expectation of negative treatment caused African Americans to avoid parks in predominantly white neighborhoods in Detroit. West stated that neither marginality nor ethnicity adequately explained his findings and concluded that interracial relations among different racial groups most greatly affected respondents' park use. African Americans felt more unwelcome and uneasy because of interracial factors.

Over the last several years, numerous research studies have reported on minorities' experiences with discrimination in leisure settings such as parks, campgrounds, recreation areas, pools, beaches, golf courses and forests. Discrimination has been shown to affect the quality of recreation experiences, to prevent people from frequenting leisure places of their choosing, and to force people to isolate themselves during their leisure engagements For example, Cassandra Johnson, S. M. Bowker, Donald English, and Dreamal Worthen examined factors in relation to wildland visitation patterns among rural African and white Americans. They found that African Americans were more than three times as likely as whites to report that they were unaware of nearby wildland areas (marginality), but that ethnicity factors were not significantly different between the two groups. They concluded that an alternative explanation for nonvisitation was racial antagonism or discrimination. One of the authors of the study had several conversations with African Americans, and concluded that many believed there were racially demarcated recreation areas in the study area because African Americans and whites tended to use different spaces in the forest. Moreover, many indicated they would not feel comfortable camping in the forest because they were concerned about being "hassled" by whites. Gobster's 2002 study of a popular urban park in Chicago also found that racial discrimination was a problem for some park users. In his study, park users were asked if there were any times or situations where they felt discriminated against because of their race or ethnic background. Reports of racial discrimination were highest among African Americans, and somewhat less for Latinos and Asians. Gobster concluded that discrimination might lead to feelings of discomfort among users and lower their enjoyment of the leisure experience. In more severe cases it can lead to feelings of anger and physical violence, which may ultimately lead to user displacement or nonuse.

Jennifer Livengood and Monika Stodolska conducted a study that examined the treatment of American Muslims over a one-year period following the events of the 11 September 2001, terrorist attack. They examined how these discriminatory experiences affected their leisure behavior, and analyzed strategies they used to overcome adversities and to deal with obstacles to their leisure participation. Individuals included in the study were from Palestine, Jordan, Lebanon, Iraq, Egypt, Tunisia, Algeria, Turkey, Pakistan, India, Mexico, and Korea. Results indicated that most of the negative treatment had been of a nonviolent nature, such as bad looks, verbal abuse, being watched, and social isolation; however, more serious experiences such as threats, physical attacks, and vandalism were also reported. These experiences led to feelings of fear, insecurity, anxiety, guilt, shame, and depression. Muslims experienced restrictions on movement; they could not travel at a desired time and to their desired destinations, and they could not engage in certain leisure activities. They employed negotiation strategies to adapt to their new environment, such as being vigilant and conscious about their surroundings, walking in groups, blending in, restricting travel, or modifying travel patterns.

Studies regarding the leisure lifestyles of Chinese Americans have used some of these same frameworks to explain their findings. Maria Allison and Charles Geiger employed the ethnicity perspective to identify and analyze leisure patterns among Chinese American elderly. They found that these individuals were involved in a wide range of leisure activities, some of which were based on cultural traditions and habits, such as tai chi, mah-jongg, sewing traditional clothing, and cooking native dishes, while other activities were used to educate them about the language and ways of the American culture, such as reading English and watching American television. Tsai and Coleman employed more of a constraint framework to understand the leisure lifestyles and constraints perceived by Chinese immigrants in Australia. These researchers examined the constraints connected with various leisure participation decisions, including those that intervened in their desire to begin new leisure activ-

ities and those that caused them to reduce or discontinue leisure participation. Their findings suggested that the most important leisure constraint for Chinese immigrants were resource constraints and interpersonal constraints. They concluded that understanding the meanings and values of leisure to different racial groups and gaining insight into the contexts in which constraints are experienced or perceived will help develop a greater understanding of the leisure perspectives of racial and ethnic minorities.

A study by Cassandra Johnson, J. M. Bowker, and H. Ken Cordell highlighted the importance of examining within-groups differences. They found that African Americans who did not participate in outdoor recreational activities had concerns about safety that were not shared by participating African Americans. The authors noted, therefore, that this difference suggests that constraints for minority groups may not be uniform, and applied William Wilson's diverging class structure argument as support. Likewise, constraints experienced by minorities may also vary by sex. Karla Henderson and Barbara Ainsworth conducted a study that focused specifically on constraints for physical activity among women of two racial minority groups: American Indian and African American women. The women indicated that finding time and space for physical activity was problematic, and concluded that several specific constraints (including job demands, physical tiredness, physical illnesses and ailments, expectations and needs of the family and others in the community) limited their participation. Further, many of the women believed opportunities for physical activity had not always existed for them due to historical, marginality, cultural, and daily living issues.

The connection between several frameworks, including marginality, discrimination, and constraints, is depicted in two studies conducted by Steven Philipp (1995, 1999). Philipp's first study examined the relationship between race and two measures related to leisure constraints, appeal and comfort. His findings indicated that African Americans and whites rated the appeal of many of the activities differently, and that African Americans felt significantly less comfortable in approximately half of the leisure activities examined. To explain his findings he applied the marginality and prejudice-discrimination frameworks and stated that many of the leisure activities that take place outside the home and local community are associated with lower appeal and comfort, which may be related to perceptions of present or historical patterns of discrimination. He concluded that it is difficult to discount centuries of discrimination

Crowd stands and cheers. Sporting events and other situations where large crowds gather for a common goal provide opportunities for different racial groups to experience leisure activities together. © *Herb Watson/ Corbis*

against African Americans when considering leisure constraints. In his second study Philipp examined the perceived "welcomeness" of several leisure pursuits by asking African Americans and white Americans how welcome African Americans would feel in a variety of activities. Results indicated that African Americans reportedly felt unwelcome in a number of leisure pursuits, whereas whites reported that they thought African Americans would feel welcome in these same activities, thus indicating that they failed to appreciate or recognize these feelings among African Americans.

The levels of assimilation and selective acculturation have also been used as frameworks for studying the leisure patterns of racial minorities. For example, Myron Floyd and James Gramann examined the effects of Mexican Americans' acculturation and assimilation on outdoor recreation pursuits. Their findings indicated that the recreation behavior of highly assimilated Mexican Americans was more similar to white Americans than to less-assimilated Mexican respondents.

Other studies that have examined recreation participation among Mexican Americans often focus on between-group differences, primarily comparing Mexican Americans to white Americans. Many of these studies have suggested Mexican Americans have significantly lower levels of involvement in outdoor recreation and active sports. Ray Hutchison and Keith Fidel (1984) and Hutchison (1987) showed that in Chicago parks Mexican Americans and other Hispanic groups did not participate in sports activities at the same rates as white Americans and African Americans. Peter Cunningham, Stella Leivada, and Yioros Apostolopoulos examined participation in sports and fitness activities and concluded that Hispanics and African Americans were less likely to participate in sports such as golf, skiing, aerobics, and swimming. This finding is consistent with a 1990 study by Steven Murdock, Kenneth Backman, E. N. Colberg, Hoque, and Rita Hamm, who found Mexican Americans participated less frequently in expensive activities such as golf and horseback riding (marginality theory). Some activities in which participation by Mexican Americans was found to be higher than that of white Americans were more sedentary family activities such as picnicking, visiting with others, relaxing, and playing with children.

A Critique of the Theoretical Frameworks Used in Leisure Research

A number of issues regarding the relationship between race and leisure lifestyles have not been examined. As mentioned, many of the studies on race and leisure have used one of three theories to guide their research: the marginality hypothesis, ethnicity hypothesis, and perceived discrimination. Myron Floyd presented some of the limitations of the marginality and ethnicity theories, and contended that discrimination, as an explanatory concept, needs further theoretical development. In particular, he noted that more work is needed on the types and range of discrimination and how they impact leisure choices and constraints.

Others have also noted the lack of frameworks to guide the research. For example, Tsai and Coleman called for conceptual frameworks that incorporate the social and cultural perspectives of specific subgroups of the population in order to better understand their leisure attitudes, behaviors, and constraints. For instance, studies regarding the constraints women often face have highlighted ethic of care, sense of entitlement, body image, and violence as constraint issues that may impact women more often than men. Further, researchers have raised questions about how multiple identities such as gender, social class, education, and residence interact and influence leisure lifestyles, as well as how the level of assimilation and selective acculturation impact leisure, thereby suggesting that multiple factors should also be taken into account in a model reflecting the leisure lifestyles of racial minorities.

Thus, if we apply all of these concepts to a framework that examines the leisure lifestyles of racial minorities, then we should take into consideration the importance of race, the multiple identities within racial minorities, and the need to include constraints that are most salient to racial minorities (such as lower levels of enjoyment, feeling unwelcome, fear of personal safety). Perhaps one useful method for considering the leisure lifestyles of racial minorities is to examine whether they are resisting or reproducing the leisure lifestyles emphasized in white mainstream society.

Leisure as Resistance or Reproduction

The conceptualization of leisure as resistance is based on the notion that leisure choices and activities are linked to hegemonic power and power relations in the social world. Leisure is seen as a space in which people, either individually or collectively, can challenge power distributions and the ways in which power is distributed within society. Leisure becomes an arena where power can be gained or reinforced, or conversely an arena where power can be diminished or lost. Shaw explored the notion of women's leisure as a form of resistance, but stated that leisure could also be a context for resistance to racism.

Resistance can be approached from different theoretical standpoints, and thus it can take on different meanings. From a structuralist position, resistance is conceptualized as acts that can challenge the structured power relations of class, race, disability, ethnicity, gender, sexual orientation, or other forms of societal stratifications that exist, such as levels of assimilation. Resistance in this case typically focuses on disadvantaged groups or individuals who are seeking to challenge power structures and gain individual or collective empowerment, such as ethnic boundary maintenance. However, a structuralist approach also recognizes leisure can be a site that reinforces or reproduces inequalities. In other words, hegemony may be perpetuated through leisure because it can also be a site for the reproduction or legitimization of unequal access to power and resources. An example might be the weakening of racial and ethnic leisure identity by white mainstream power forces. However, given that hegemony is a continuous process and never complete, resistance is also plausible and might be considered the "flip side" of reproduction. Further, according to Shaw, those who adopt a structuralist perspective view the outcomes of resistance as both individual and collective. She posited that individual empowerment has the potential to empower others in similar situations, thereby reducing systemic inequalities.

A poststructuralist or postmodern approach conceptualizes resistance as linked to personal power, and the freedom to develop new identities and new freedoms that are not subject to someone else's control. The concept of ethnic boundary maintenance fits under this approach as well. Poststructuralist or postmodern leisure researchers focus more on personal empowerment and individual resistance. Power is seen as having multiple sources, which suggests there are also many possibilities for resistance. Diversity is emphasized in this approach, and thus it is not assumed that racial minorities share a "common world" or common repression. This perspective focuses more on individual resistance as opposed to collective resistance, with the outcome being individual empowerment rather than broad social change.

A third approach used to conceptualize resistance is the interactionist perspective. This perspective focuses on the subjective experiences of leisure in different social and interactional contexts. This approach attempts to combine aspects of the structuralist and poststructuralist or postmodern perspectives and reflects both individual and collective outcomes of resistance. Leisure reflects resistance from the interactionist perspective when racial minorities make choices that provide them with personal empowerment while simultaneously challenging traditional and constrictive views. For example, if a racial minority chooses activities that are nontraditional for his or her race, such as downhill skiing, that choice is considered an individual act of resistance that may also have broader implications in its ability to create social change.

Whether approached from a structuralist, poststructuralist/postmodernist, or interactionist perspective, the notion of resistance emerges when racial minorities use their leisure or gain from their leisure a sense of empowerment and sense of identity. However, as suggested by Shaw, resistance is not always in the form of a conscious deliberation or intent. For example, some acts may not be motivated by a desire to challenge hegemony, whereas other acts may clearly have that as their goal. Furthermore, resistance can be both individual and collective, and thus intentions may relate to one or both levels. These issues notwithstanding, leisure's link with resistance to hegemonic forces suggests its potential to play a pivotal role in the leisure lives of racial minorities Through leisure experiences racial minorities may gain a sense of autonomy, personal control, and sense of entitlement and identity that may be lacking in other aspects of their lives.

With these different theoretical perspectives in mind, resistance can take several forms. One type of resistance could be what Washburne referred to as participating as "pioneers," those individuals or collectives who participate in leisure activities despite constraints and despite being an extreme minority. Such individuals resist conformity and sanctions associated with their particular group and break through the barriers that exclude their participation. This type of resistance could be viewed as intentional resistance, with the outcome being individual or collective empowerment. Another type of resistance can be seen through participation in "parallel" or corresponding activities, yet doing so exclusively within one's own race. For example, this could be in the form of racially exclusive ski clubs and scuba clubs for the more affluent, or in the form of street cultural activities for those who are less affluent. In this type of resistance, the focus is intentional resistance, with the goal being to create one's own sphere of influence and control. "Abstention" among racial groups who deliberately choose not to participate in certain leisure activities as a form of protest might also be a demonstration of resistance. Racial minorities who intentionally and freely choose not to participate in stereotypical white leisure pursuits suggests an individual form of resistance and "self-determination." In other words, this type of resistance could be taken to indicate that they do not feel the need to "conform." Or rather they "resist" participation in what might be considered white-mainstream activities (such as nature-based activities, certain fitness activities), thereby consciously choosing pursuits that are more attractive to them and also reinforce their own unique racial subculture. This concept is similar to ethnic boundary maintenance, when a group finds ways to emphasize differences between themselves and outgroup members. Similarly, Washburne and Wall suggested leisure choices might be made to confirm traditions valued by the group, and to avoid those activities that are inconsistent with racial and ethnic norms, values, or tradition. Further, they concluded that some leisure activities may have white identities associated with them, and consequently be "across the boundary" for some racial groups. Corliss Outley's study of leisure socialization among African American youth illustrates this point. She found that young boys criticized their peers who participated in middle-class activities like golf or tennis. In their neighborhoods and in their school, such activities were labeled as "white activities," and those who participated in such activities were "acting white." By rejecting these white middle-class activities and supporting the activities of their neighborhood, they perpetuate a perceived boundary between themselves and the white majority. This can be related back to "abstention" as a form of resistance that was described earlier.

Clearly, however, leisure is also connected to the reproduction of white mainstream society. Previous research has demonstrated that one's level of assimilation is positively related to Anglo activities and value systems, and that as social class and interracial interaction increases, the leisure behavior of different racial groups becomes more similar. These findings notwithstanding, leisure offers a unique environment for racial minorities to express their distinct identities, as well as an environment in which leisure can serve as a vehicle for helping develop more positive interracial interactions and increasing racial and ethnic pride and tolerance.

See also: African American Leisure Lifestyles, Asian American Leisure Lifestyles, Jewish American Leisure Lifestyles, Muslim American Leisure Lifestyles

BIBLIOGRAPHY

Allison, Maria T., and Charles W. Geiger. "Nature of Leisure Activities Among the Chinese-American Elderly." *Leisure Sciences* 15 (1993): 309–319.

Barth, F. *Ethnic Groups and Boundaries: The Social Organization of Culture.* London: Allen and Unwin, 1969.

Cunningham, Peter H., Stella Leivadi, and Yiorgos Apostolopoulos. "Race, Class, Economic Status, and Participation in Sport and Fitness." Proceedings of the 1994 NRPA Leisure Research Symposium. Minneapolis, Mn.: National Recreation And Park Association, 1994.

Dragan, Carolyn. "Native American Under-Representation in National Parks: Tests of Marginality and Ethnicity Hypotheses." Master's thesis, University of Idaho, 1986.

Emerson, Michael O., Rachel T. Kimbro, and George Yancey. "Contact Theory Extended: The Effects of Prior Racial Contact on Current Social Ties. *Social Science Quarterly* 83 (2002): 745–761.

Floyd, Myron. F. "Getting Beyond Marginality and Ethnicity: The Challenge for Race and Ethnic Studies in Leisure Research." *Journal of Leisure Research* 30 (1998): 3–22.

Floyd, Myron F., and James H. Gramann. "Effects of Acculturation and Structural Assimilation in Resource-Based Recreation: The Case of Mexican Americans." *Journal of Leisure Research* 25 (1993): 6–21.

Floyd, Myron. F., and Kimberly J. Shinew. "Convergence and Divergences in Leisure Style among Whites and African-Americans: Towards an Interracial Contact Hypothesis." *Journal of Leisure Research* 31 (1999): 359–384.

Gobster, Paul H. "Managing Urban Parks for a Racially and Ethnically Diverse Clientele." *Leisure Sciences* 24 (2002): 143–159.

Gordon, Milton. *Assimilation in American life: The Role of Race, Religious, and National Origins.* New York: Oxford University Press, 1964.

Henderson, Karla. A., and Barbara E. Ainsworth. "Researching Leisure and Physical Activity with Women of Color: Issues and Emerging Questions." *Leisure Sciences* 23 (2001): 21–34.

Henderson, Karla. A., M. Deborah Bialeschki, Susan M. Shaw, and Valeria Freysinger. *Both Gains and Gaps: Feminist Perspectives on Women's Leisure.* State College, Pa.: Venture Publishing, 1996.

Hutchison, Ray. "Ethnicity and Urban Recreation: Whites, Blacks, and Hispanics in Chicago's Public Parks." *Journal of Leisure Research* 19 (1987): 205–222.

Hutchison, Ray, and Keith Fidel. "Mexican-American Recreation Activities: A Reply to McMillen." *Journal of Leisure Research* 16 (1984): 344–349.

Jackman, Mary R., and Marie Crane. "Some of My Best Friends are Black: Interracial Friendships and Whites' Racial Attitudes." *Public Option Quarterly* 50 (1986): 459–486.

Jackson, Edgar. L., and David Scott. "Constraints to Leisure." In *Leisure Studies: Prospects for the Twenty-first Century.* Edited by Edgar L. Jackson and Thomas L. Burton. State College, Pa.: Venture Publishing, 1999.

Johnson, Cassandra, J. M. Bowker, Donald B. K. English, and Dreamal Worthen. "Wildland Recreation in the Rural South: An Examination of Marginality and Ethnicity Theory." *Journal of Leisure Research* 30 (1998): 101–120.

Johnson, Cassandra, J. M. Bowker, and H. Ken Cordell. "Outdoor Recreation Constraints: An Examination of Race, Gender, and Rural Dwelling." *Southern Rural Sociology* 17 (2001): 111–133.

Keefe, Susan, and Amado Padilla. *Chicano Ethnicity.* Albuquerque: University of New Mexico Press, 1987.

Kraus, Richard. *Recreation and Leisure in Modern Society.* 6th edition. Boston: Jones and Bartlett, 2001.

Livengood, Jennifer S., and Monika Stodolska. "The Effects of Discrimination and Constraints Negotiation on Everyday Life and Leisure Behavior of American Muslims in the Post-September 11 America." *Journal of Leisure Research* 36 (2004).

McLemore, S. Dale. *Racial and Ethnic Relations in America.* Boston: Allyn and Bacon, 1991.

Mueller, E., and G. Gurin. "Participation in Outdoor Recreation Behavior: Factors Affecting Demand Among American Adults." *Outdoor Recreation Resources Review Commission Study Report* 20. Washington, D.C.: U.S. Government Printing Office, 1962.

Murdock, Steven H., Kenneth Backman, E. Colberg, N. Hoque, and R. Hamm. "Modeling Demographic Change and Characteristics in the Analysis of Future Demand for Leisure Services." *Leisure Sciences* 12 (1990): 79–102.

Outley, Corliss W. "Kickin' It: An Investigation of Leisure Behavior Among Inner-City African American Children." Ph.D. dissertation, Texas A&M University, 2002.

Philipp, Steven F. "Race and Leisure Constraints." *Leisure Sciences* 17 (1995): 109–120.

———. "Are We Welcome? African-American Racial Acceptance in Leisure Activities and the Importance Given to Children's Leisure." *Journal of Leisure Research* 31 (1999): 385–403.

Russell, Ruth V. *Pastimes: The Context of Contemporary Leisure.* Champaign, Ill.: Sagamore Publishing, 2002.

Shaull, Sandra L., and James H. Gramann. "The Effects of Cultural Assimilation on the Importance of Family-Related and Nature-Related Recreation Among Hispanic Americans." *Journal of Leisure Research* 30 (1998): 47–63.

Shaw, Susan M. "Conceptualizing Resistance: Women's Leisure as Political Practice." *Journal of Leisure Research* 33 (2001): 186–201.

Stodolska, Monika. "Assimilation and Leisure Constraints: Dynamics of Constraint on Leisure in Immigrant Populations." *Journal of Leisure Research* 30 (1998): 521–551.

Tirone, Susan, C., and Susan M. Shaw. "At the Center of Their Lives: Indo Canadian Women, Their Families and Leisure." *Journal of Leisure Research* 29 (1997): 225–244.

Tsai, Eva H., and Denis J. Coleman. "Leisure Constraints of Chinese Immigrants: An Exploratory Study." *Society and Leisure* 22 (1999): 243–264.

Washburne, Randel F. "Black Under-Participation in Wild-land Recreation: Alternative Explanations." *Leisure Sciences* 1 (1978): 175–189.

Washburne, Randel, and P. Wall. "Black-White Ethnic Differences in Outdoor Recreation." USDA Forest Service Research Paper. INT-249. Ogden, Utah: Intermountain Forest and Range Experiment Station, 1980.

West, Patrick C. "Urban Region Parks and Black Minorities: Subculture, Marginality, and Interracial Relations in Park Use in the Detroit Metropolitan Area." *Leisure Sciences* 11 (1989): 11–28.

Wilson, William J. *The Declining Significance of Race.* Chicago: University of Chicago Press, 1978.

Woodard, Michael D. "Class, Regionality, and Leisure Among Urban Black Americans: The Post-Civil Rights Era." *Journal of Leisure Research* 20 (1988): 87–105.

Kimberly J. Shinew

RACING

See *Auto Racing; Drag Racing; Hot Rodding; Open Wheel Racing; Sports Car Racing; Stock Car Racing*

RACQUETBALL

Racquetball derives from several sports: tennis, paddle tennis, squash, paddleball, and handball. The roots of modern racquetball date back to the 1920s when Earl Riskey of the University of Michigan developed a new game called paddleball. He watched tennis players use the university handball courts for practice, and began his new game by adapting paddle tennis and its wooden paddle to a sponge rubber ball on a handball court.

A player scores points only when serving, and can win a game by only one point. After serving, each player may hit the ball to the front wall using any combination of walls, striking the ball in the air or after one bounce. A player may only take a court position that affords an opponent the ability to make an unobstructed straight-in or cross-court shot. Matches are typically played in a best-of-three-games format, with the first two games to fifteen points and a tie-breaker game (if needed) to eleven. Professional matches are typically best-of-five games, each to eleven points.

Evolution of a Sport: Developing and Disseminating Enjoyment

Joe Sobek, a tennis and squash pro, wanted a faster, more enjoyable indoor court sport. He felt that handball was too hard on the hands, and that paddleball and squash were too slow and the rackets too cumbersome. In 1950, he began designing a lighter wood-frame racket using nylon strings and a lively ball. At the Greenwich, Connecticut, YMCA, employing the existing rules from handball, Sobek promoted a game called "paddle rackets" that soon evolved into modern racquetball.

The next twenty years saw paddle rackets and paddleball spread quickly via outdoor one-wall, three-wall, and indoor courts at mostly YMCAs and Jewish Community Centers (where most handball courts had already been built), and to a lesser degree at universities, municipal recreation sites, and the armed forces. Along with Sobek, Larry Lederman, director of the Jewish Community Center of Milwaukee, did a great deal to promote paddle rackets. In 1968, he led the organization of the first National Paddle Rackets Tournament in Milwaukee. By this time, paddleball and paddle rackets had established centers in New England, in and around New York City, in the Midwest, and in southern California (mostly San Diego).

By the late 1960s, the game of paddle rackets was superceding paddleball in popularity. Both new players and players from other sports found that paddle rackets was easier to play and more enjoyable. Sobek's vision had gained rapid and wide acceptance because the challenge level of the game was adaptable to a wide range of ability levels, from beginners to advanced players. Because play allowed for large margins of error compared to other ball games, new players to racquetball could achieve successful results quickly. With more first-time players and an influx of former handball, squash, tennis, and paddleball players across the country, paddle rackets had reached a "take-off" stage of development, poised to evolve from a recreational game into a bona fide sport.

Two major developments were responsible for racquetball's transformation into sport. First, the name was changed from paddle rackets to racketball, and finally to racquetball (a French derivative fulminated by Robert McInerny, a San Diego–based tennis pro). This name segue created a more distinct and therefore recognizable entity. It also paved the way for more autonomous control and a separate identity, as evidenced by its own magazine, *Racquetball,* in 1972. Second, formal organizational attempts culminated in 1969 with the International Racquetball Association (IRA) under the guidance of Bob Kendler, a wealthy seventy-two-year-old entrepreneur from Chicago.

Kendler, who was also the president of the United States Handball Association, played a pivotal role in shaping the early days of organized racquetball. Against pressure from handball players, who for the most part did not want racquetball players competing for time on "their" courts, Kendler fought for years to have the two sports share facilities, organization, and a common promotional effort within one magazine. He quickly brought together many splinter groups and was the president of the IRA for its first five years, attempting to shepherd the direction and growth of both racquetball and handball.

Expansion: Rapid Rise, Slump, and Steady Growth

With a solid organization and unique name of its own, the first official International Racquetball Association Championships were held in 1969 at the Jewish Community Center in St. Louis, won by a San Diego dentist "Bud" Muehleisen. By 1972, with its own magazine, racquetball was breaking away from handball. Women players quickly entered the sport and became part of the national championships in 1970, though men had dominated the sport's leadership. In 1973, Kendler broke with the IRA and formed the U.S. Racquetball Association (USRA) for amateur play, and the National Racquetball Club (NRC) to promote a pro tour. The NRC eventually gave way to the International Racquetball Tour and the Women's International Racquetball Tour, while the USRA became the national governing body.

From the early 1970s to the mid-1980s, thousands of private court clubs and other racquetball facilities sprouted across the country as racquetball grew steadily in popularity. Americans, becoming more conscious of their sedentary and stressful lifestyle, sought fitness and game alternatives like racquetball that could achieve optimum health benefits within a short time frame. Equipment advances, which have paralleled those of tennis and golf, with larger frames, high-tech designs, and more expensive materials (graphite, titanium, and composites), along with faster, more durable balls, have doubled the speed at which the game can be played—in excess of 180 miles per hour.

The demand for racquetball slumped in the mid-1980s. Over time, as with players in many sports, the enjoyment of steady improvement diminished and the game's novelty wore thin, so many players left racquetball. In tandem, many facilities reduced the number of racquetball courts, also realizing that converted court space could increase revenues through other profit centers like aerobics, fitness/weight rooms, and other recreational classes. By 1987, participation leveled off, and growth proceeded at a slower, steadier rate. From a small group of hard-core players in the 1960s, racquetball participation has grown to around 6 million, most of whom are recreational players.

Racquetball's "Olympic Dream," inclusion as a full-medal sport, has been a persistent goal of the sport's leadership. The principal figure in the drive for Olympic inclusion has been Luke St. Onge, secretary general of the International Racquetball Federation from its inception in 1979. After the USRA successfully staged the first World Championships in 1981, the United States Olympic Committee (USOC) granted the USRA "Group C" Olympic status, followed in 1989 by USOC "Full Member" status—the youngest sport ever to achieve such status.

Current Status and Demographics

Racquetball is played in over ninety countries worldwide, with a biannual World Championship drawing teams from thirty nations on six continents. Americans continue domination of the sport at both the amateur and pro levels. While 60 percent of the players are in the twelve to thirty-four age category, young children and seniors represent a significant portion of the participants. Glass walls and portable courts have increased the viewability and spectatorship of top-level racquetball. Most USRA-sanctioned tournaments, including the two major U.S championships (National Racquetball Championships and U.S. Open), feature a wide range of both age and skill divisions. Participants who are mostly young (twenty-five to forty-four) and middle-income earners (household incomes of $50,000+ in mostly professional occupations) place racquetball fourth in sport popularity for their demographic group (behind downhill skiing, golf, and bicycling).

Because it is enjoyable and sufficiently challenges players at all levels, racquetball has a steady, growing base of participants; through its relative convenience, affordability, and continued efforts at marketing through sports broadcasting, it is poised for future success. Racquetball represents an American sport success story by virtue of its meteoric rise in popularity among all ages and abilities, its focused mission with steps realized toward internationalization and full-medal Olympic status, and its nature as a professional and top amateur game that is colorful in fashion and personality. At the advanced level, racquetball has evolved into a lightning-fast, intensely played sport that requires advanced strategies, spectacular shot making, and keen mental focus, as well as extreme athleticism. Racquetball has become a safe, expedient, and enjoyable game of choice for achieving rapid gains in overall fitness.

See also: Handball

BIBLIOGRAPHY

Fleming, A. William, and Joel A. Bloom. *Paddleball and Racquetball.* Santa Monica, Calif.: Goodyear Publishing, 1975.

Hiser, Jim. *Racquetball: Winning Edge.* New York: McGraw-Hill, 1999.

"It Had to Start Somewhere." *Racquetball* (Summer 1974): 30.

Keeley, Steve. *The Complete Book of Racquetball.* Chicago: Follett Publishing, 1976.

Spear, Victor I. *Sports Illustrated Racquetball.* New York: J. B. Lippencott Company, 1979.

United States Racquetball Association. "USRA Demographics." Available from http://www.usra.org.

James A. Therrell

RADIO LISTENING, CAR AND HOME

Radio listening has been a popular entertainment form for more than 100 years. During the twentieth century, patterns of listening and styles of programming underwent dramatic changes. Located inside the home and out, consisting of music, news, drama, and comedy, the sounds of radio broadcasting have provided entertainment to millions of Americans.

Early Amateurs

During the first two decades of the twentieth century, amateur radio operators were the most significant group of popular radio listeners. Known as "hams," these men and boys captured the public imagination. From locations in garages and attics, these amateurs listened intently for stations located in far-flung locales, a practice call DXing. They exchanged elaborate and ornamental station cards that provided tangible evidence of contact with a fellow operator. Their efforts were largely responsible for the development of the technology and craft of radio during this period. These operators formed a national organization, the American Radio Relay League, in 1915. In 1916, on the eve of American entrance into World War I, more than 8,500 licensed operators transmitted speech, music, and Morse code. During the war, however, the government closed down all amateur stations. Although amateurs returned in bulk after the cessation of hostilities, the

growth of broadcasting caused congestion and interference on the air. The Radio Act of 1912 had consigned amateur operators to 200 meters or lower in bandwidth, but DXing continued in earnest through the first half of the 1920s. However, the practice largely ended shortly after the passage of the Communications Act of 1927. This act established the Federal Radio Commission, which promptly reorganized the broadcast spectrum and established minimum technical standards for broadcast stations. The combination effectively drove many amateurs off the air and gave preference to large, professional broadcasters.

Domestic Listening During the Golden Age

During the "radio craze" of the 1920s, radio listening exploded in popularity, and the radio receiver ceased being an exotic instrument and became an everyday domestic appliance. In 1922, there were only 60,000 radio homes. Two years later the number had grown to 1.25 million. By the end of the decade, there were more than 10 million. It took the better part of the decade for radio-receiver technology to catch up to the demands of listeners. Early 1920s radios were bulky, temperamental, and battery operated. Only in 1926 did receivers completely powered by household current become readily available, easing radio's transition to household appliance. Radios still represented a significant financial investment: the average radio cost $83 in 1925, and they were second only to the car as an installment purchase during the decade.

Unlike the point-to-point communication of ham operators, radio had become a broadcasting medium. Soon radio networks and powerful stations would begin beaming programming from metropolitan areas across the country. Radio brought entertainment into the home. Its popularity was so strong that it threatened earlier forms of domestic entertainment such as piano playing, phonograph listening, and singing as well as affecting public entertainments like film and vaudeville. Radio listening was part of a desire, for some, especially the middle classes, for domestic rather than public entertainment.

The formation of national networks in the second half of the decade established radio-listening patterns that would continue until the 1950s. The period between 1926 and 1956 is often referred to as the "Golden Age" of network broadcasting. Networks relied on programming personalities and genres that they perceived to have widespread appeal. Music and talk dominated 1920s radio programming, but the spectacular success of *Amos 'n' Andy* in 1929 demonstrated to networks and advertisers that dramatic programming had widespread popular appeal. Borrowing from vaudeville and serial fiction, radio dramas, comedy, and variety programs like *Fibber McGee and Molly, The Jack Benny Show,* and *The Lone Ranger,* to name just a few, created national audiences for their sponsors.

Radio split its broadcast day along gendered lines, with daytime programming oriented toward women and evening programs oriented toward men or "all-family" tastes. Daytime radio consisted of soap operas and home economics programs. Programs like *The Romance of Helen Trent* and *Guiding Light* developed large and devoted audiences. In contrast, the radio networks offered higher prestige dramatic and musical programming during evening hours. They used such programming to demonstrate that they programmed "in the public interest, convenience, or necessity."

Radio continued to grow in popularity throughout the 1930s. On the eve of World War II, the radio had grown to 28.5 million homes, or 81 percent of American households. This was a 100 percent increase from just ten years earlier. Four-fifths of the domestic radios produced were inexpensive table models. Price cutting drove radio purchase prices downward. Although the average radio cost nearly $40, there were also models that cost under $10. Families of all income levels owned radios. Ubiquitous in upper-class homes, even the majority of families that earned less than $1,000 per year had a radio by the end of the 1930s. Although production for civilian use ceased during the war, Americans grew to depend on radio for up-to-the minute news reports.

Postwar Changes in Listening Patterns and Locations

After World War II, there was a massive increase in the number of multiple-radio homes. Supported by industrial campaigns that promoted "a radio for every room" and inexpensive sets, especially clock radios, the majority of American homes soon had several sets. The increase in the number of receivers was complemented by an increase in the number of stations broadcasting. Between 1946 and 1950, the number of AM radio stations more than doubled. Radio listening was becoming more individualized and more specialized.

The widespread introduction of television in the late 1940s caused significant changes to radio-listening patterns. Television quickly replaced radio as the primary domestic entertainment medium as evening network radio listening plummeted. The dramatic and variety formats and star personalities that had dominated network radio for twenty-five years migrated to the new visual medium, leaving holes in network schedules. Yet radio was not dead. Daytime listening remained relatively stable through the end of the 1950s. The rise of the disk jockey and the growth of "block programming" that mixed music and news in the late 1940s filled the void. Advertisers' "discovery" of new consumer markets, especially the teenage market, created outlets for targeted radio programming. Entrepreneurs such as Gordon McLendon and Todd Storz rationalized the trends toward disk-jockey personalities and musical programming and combined them with heavy station promotion and on-air jingles, giving birth to the Top 40 format.

Throughout this period, car radio listening was gradually increasing. As with home receivers, amateurs paved the way. Although experiments were common throughout the 1920s, commercial production of car radios began only at the end of the decade. Also like their domestic counterparts, early car radios proved technically troublesome. They required careful installation and shielding from the vehicle's electrical system to avoid severe interference to the broadcast signal.

But the appeal of car radio listening was undeniable. In the 1940s, stations began offering "drive-time" programming for commuters. In 1940, 7.5 million cars, slightly more than one-quarter of the total, had radio receivers installed. By 1951, the majority of American automobiles were equipped with one of 21 million car radio receivers. After the widespread introduction of television, morning and evening composed the largest radio audience segments.

The invention of the transistor in 1948 accelerated the trend toward out-of-home listening. By the middle of the 1950s, small transistor radios allowed true portability for the first time. Though expensive at first, transistor prices rapidly declined. By the middle of the decade, the average cost of a radio had fallen to $20. In the late 1950s and early 1960s, new low-cost imports allowed people to take their transistor radios with them.

The Rise of FM and the Future of Radio Broadcasting

While AM radio ruled the airwaves in the early 1960s, this soon changed. In 1963, the Federal Communications Commission (FCC) ruled that AM and FM stations in the same area with the same owners could not broadcast the same programming. This nonduplication rule created the opportunity for new programming formats. The markedly superior sound quality of FM lent itself to musical fare, and FM stations soon appropriated the narrowly conceived program formats that dominated AM stations. In the last quarter of the twentieth century, radio formats became more and more specialized. Middle-of-the-Road (MOR), Country and Western, and Adult-Album-Alternative, for example, all conceived of markets and programmed to what the industry felt that audience wanted.

Despite inroads by new entertainment forms such as television, DVDs, and the Internet, radio remained a popular and viable entertainment medium in the early twenty-first century. Increases in average commute time functioned to ensure a continued audience for radio. The rise of political talk radio in the late 1980s ushered in a new era for AM radio that competed with FM's heavily formatted music programming. The 1996 Telecommunications Act eased ownership restrictions and ushered in a new era of consolidation. The practices of companies such as Clear Channel Communications and Infinity Broadcasting represented the return of nationally based programming. At the same time, new technologies, such as satellite radio, offered more programming choices to listeners. However, critics charged that those resurgent national institutions threatened stations' local orientation, leaving the future of radio broadcasting an open question.

See also: Amateur Radio; Television's Impact on Popular Leisure

BIBLIOGRAPHY

Butsch, Richard. *The Making of American Audiences: From Stage to Television, 1750–1990.* New York: Cambridge University Press, 2000.

Douglas, Susan J. *Listening In: Radio and the American Imagination.* New York: Times Books, 1999.

Hilmes, Michele. *Only Connect: A Cultural History of Broadcasting in the United States.* Belmont, Calif.: Wadsworth, 2002.

Hilmes, Michele, and Jason Loviglio. *The Radio Reader: Essays in the Cultural History of Radio.* New York: Routledge, 2002.

Kitross, John, and Christopher Sterling. *Stay Tuned: A History of American Broadcasting.* 3d edition. Mahwah, N.J.: Lawrence Erlbaum Associates, 2001.

Squire, Susan Merrill, ed. *Communities of the Air: Radio Century, Radio Culture.* Durham, N.C.: Duke University Press, 2003.

Smulyan, Susan. *Selling Radio: The Commercialization of American Broadcasting, 1920–1934.* Washington, D.C.: Smithsonian Institution Press, 1994.

Alexander Russo

RAILROADS AND LEISURE

Railroad tourism, especially seen from the vantage point of the early twenty-first century, is often coupled with the notion of romance, luxury, and opulence, a view fueled by the indeed wonderful accoutrements found in coaches and stations of the past. Prior even to entering one's railcar, the stately terminal of the metropolis prepared the traveler for his or her long-awaited trip. These portals were almost always architectural gems that not only welcomed the traveler into an exciting realm but also proclaimed to the world a sort of national optimism and company pride. Between 1896 and 1916, the heyday of train travel, these terminals and many others, large and small, would see a tripling of passenger ridership. Nineteen hundred twenty-eight saw 20,000 different scheduled passenger trains in the United States, including short commuter hops and long-haul interstate and intercompany trains; by 1968, a mere 600 were left (Goddard, pp. 19, 215; see Table 1).

To speak of luxury train travel is to speak of the Pullman Company, which grew to be a monopoly the railroad companies tolerated, mostly because of the firm's ability to supply large numbers of cars with standardized service. In most cases, the Pullman Company supplied cars and staff, while the railroad company provided heat and light. In addition to the well-known sleeping cars, the Pullman Company operated parlor, lounge, and club cars, some with open-air observation vestibules at one end. John Stilgoe writes of stewards serving drinks to first-class passengers in the rarefied atmosphere of the club car; tea, books, magazines, the latest newspapers, postcards, and company stationery supplied by car attendants; and the comfortable, revolving chairs allowing passengers to gaze straight through plate-glass windows at the passing scene. Sleeping car porters—almost exclusively African American and thus helping make luxury train travel a sort of microcosm of American society—still enjoy one of the best reputations for polite and reliable service of any group of employees in American history.

Pullman interiors reminded travelers that they were indeed in another "place," a luxurious and protected linear realm that separated passenger from the ruggedness, foreignness, or emptiness of the landscapes outside. Paneling, tables, and furniture were constructed of the finest hardwoods; upholstery and carpeting were plush and attractive; and the various fittings were often of polished brass. Technological improvements saw candles give way to various gas lamps and then to electric lighting; electric fans were soon augmented by air cooled by ice

Tom Thumb Locomotive. Peter Cooper constructed the first locomotive that could pull a load of passengers in 1829. It was built near Baltimore, Maryland, and ran on the Baltimore and Ohio Railroad. © *Corbis*

carried beneath the car's floor; showers became standard in larger compartments. In most cases, these were gendered environments—sleeping berths were often advertised as being the epitome of domestic space and thus the best way for a woman to travel, whereas the various versions of the club or lounge car were for years a male realm, a place where traveling salesmen and other businessmen drank and smoked in plush armchairs, telling tall tales to whoever would listen. Important to most stories concerning the "romance" of rail travel is the food served onboard. In almost all cases, companies lost money on their splendid dining services, but it was an integral part of their attempt to win customers. The dining car was a fine restaurant on wheels with a well-trained staff and was often situated next to a club or lounge car, allowing patrons to engage in pre- and postmeal drinking and conversation.

Traveling Coach

It tends to be forgotten that the "golden age of rail travel" was only so gilded for a lucky few. Even for those who

were able occasionally to afford a regular Pullman berth (not a larger private room, "drawing room," or "roomette"), much has been written about how the cramped quarters and fairly flimsy separation between travelers—oftentimes nothing more than a heavy curtain—led to a mingling of sounds and smells of sleep that one had not necessarily expected. For those who could not afford sleeping accommodations, there was "coach." Such a journey, across distances short and long, saw paying passengers in their own seats, whether benches or separate chairs. Traveling coach often entailed riding in an older car with a less-than-smooth ride and a nonexistent air-cooling or ventilation system. In many cases, soot from the locomotive soiled clothes of passengers, hence the popularity in the early part of the nineteenth century of the famous advertising jingle of the Lackawanna's poster girl, Phoebe Snow, who claimed that "my dress stays white though I ride all night, when I take the road of anthracite" (quoted in Goddard, p. 19).

The worn wood of the aisle may not have even led toward a dining car for many coach passengers, either because there was no such car on their train or because prices made such a meal impossible. Dining cars were not a standard element of many passenger trains until 1945; it had been common for trains to stop at regular intervals to allow passengers to detrain and purchase snacks or meals from vendors. Perhaps the most famous examples of such establishments were the Harvey Houses; the Santa Fe granted Fred Harvey a contract in the 1880s to operate a chain of restaurants along its lines in the Southwest to service its passengers. Harvey's organization became famous for its unmarried, young women employees, known as "Harvey Girls"—who also received free room and board near the restaurant—and for its standardization, profitability, and popular food.

Fellow Passengers and the Passing Scene

Given that for many years train travel was the only way to cover long distances, it necessarily brought all kinds of people together. In the coaches, passengers from all walks of life, oftentimes dressed in their finest clothes, mingled and shared stories; in the case of long-distance train trips, travelers were often together for a handful of days. In order to fill the seats in a dining car most efficiently, stewards seated people across from complete strangers; conversation, argument, or flirting naturally followed. However, the idea of the rolling melting pot is only partially accurate. There were indeed different classes of coach, and the aforementioned lounge cars might have been available only to select passengers. As the narrator learns in the opening passages of Willa Cather's *My Ántonia* (1954), which takes place beginning about 1880, there was sometimes an "immigrant car." Although African Americans were well represented in the corridors and compartments of the Pullman cars as porters, as passengers they often traveled in one or two crowded coaches while whites spread themselves comfortably among several.

Although some passengers paid little attention to the almost cinematic scene that passed before them, many did indeed spend hours gazing sideways at the farms, factories, and forests that flashed past. The rail corridor allowed travelers an interesting and perhaps even rare glimpse of the iron, steel, brick, and concrete of the country's infrastructure. Often mentioned by travelers was the "ugliness" of the city as seen from the rails, with its ubiquitous billboards and trash-strewn rights-of-way. The backsides of buildings were on display, a more blue-collar world than many passengers were accustomed to seeing. Indeed, rail travel also opened an interesting window on the fascinating technology of the railroad itself. Views were obstructed on either side, sometimes for

miles, as passengers strained to look through the gaps between the cars of other trains. Telegraph poles carrying numerous crossbars and dozens of wires invited the eye to follow an undulating and mesmerizing course. The tourist's view from the tracks made visible the "jungles"— vegetated areas near rail yards, where hoboes tended to camp, convene, and wait to hop the right freight. Rail travel was a trip through space—not over or past it—and was therefore quite different from what its successor transport modes would become.

Railroads played a major role in the success of many resorts and parks. In the east, locales such as Newport, Rhode Island, and, especially, Saratoga Springs, New York, were removed from their seasonal clientele but served well by railroads. The converse was also true: heavy demand for service between Philadelphia and Atlantic City or Cape May led to ruinous competition between the Pennsylvania and the Reading, which in turn led to a merger of their operations in this corridor. The Camden–Jersey Shore service was profitable enough to be kept alive until 1982, well past the 1971 creation of Amtrak. As in the railcars in which the tourists traveled, most resorts were subdivided by class. The National Parks in the West, whose creation often coincided with the expansion of particular railroad companies, were marketed to the public as scenic and "wild" destinations, but also as exclusive retreats where the wealthy, safely ensconced in their chateaus and lodges, could feel protected not only from animals and the vagaries of weather but also from the masses of the large cities they sought to escape. In its advertisements, the Northern Pacific assured its upper-class, eastern, potential customers that the people visiting Yellowstone National Park would be the same people riding the trains, thus ensuring a feeling of security for those contemplating such a trip. Using many of the same strategies, and appealing to an ever-more-mobile and wealthy population at the end of the nineteenth century, railroad companies helped to open and increase the popularity of places like the Grand Canyon (Atchison, Topeka & Santa Fe), Yosemite (Southern Pacific), and Glacier National Park (Great Northern, whose symbol was for years the mountain goat, one of Glacier's most popular mammals).

Contributing both to the glamour of rail travel and to new streams of revenue, many railroads built and managed their own terminal hotels, among them architectural gems such as Le Château Frontenac in Québec City, the Royal York in Toronto, the Banff Springs Hotel (all three built by the Canadian Pacific), and the El Tovar Hotel on the South Rim of the Grand Canyon (built by the Atchison, Topeka & Santa Fe). Many railroad companies made

TABLE 1

The rise and decline of passenger rail travel in the U.S., 1890–1970

Period	Avg. Passengers per Year (1,000)	% Change	Avg. Total Passenger-Miles per Year (1,000,000)	% Change
1890	492,431		11,848	
1891–1895	546,762	11.0%	13,383	13.0%
1896–1900	520,459	−4.8%	13,863	3.6%
1901–1905	681,261	30.9%	20,737	49.6%
1906–1910	885,003	29.9%	28,683	38.3%
1911–1915	1,018,804	15.1%	33,768	17.7%
1916–1920	1,152,566	13.1%	42,548	26.0%
1921–1925	982,320	−14.8%	36,869	−13.3%
1926–1930	801,503	−18.4%	31,846	−13.6%
1931–1935	483,006	−39.7%	18,375	−42.3%
1936–1940	471,362	−2.4%	23,068	25.5%
1941–1945	772,393	63.9%	71,713	210.9%
1946–1950	638,334	−17.4%	43,775	−39.0%
1951–1955	457,755	−28.3%	31,642	−27.7%
1956–1960	381,012	−16.8%	24,157	−23.7%
1961–1965	312,530	−18.0%	18,896	−21.8%
1966–1970	300,814	23.7%	13,718	−27.4%

These data reveal the defined boom and bust in passenger rail traffic from 1890 to 1970, on the eve of the creation of the National Rail Passenger Corporation (Amtrak). Note that the First World War represents the apex of passenger rail travel in the United States. World War II brought a short period of relative prosperity to many of the country's railroad companies, but the decline resumed shortly thereafter. Note that passenger-miles (a unit that represents one passenger being transported one mile) show much more pronounced swings. Especially in the case of WWII, these data show that the jump in the number of passengers was compounded by the distance they traveled—soldiers from all over the country were being transported to both coasts for deployment in multiple theaters. Note that the steady drop in total passengers since WWII is complemented by a drastic drop in passenger miles. Because the number of commuters tended to stay relatively constant through this period, this represents the fact that many trains were being cancelled and that many travelers were turning to cars and airplanes for long-distance travel.

SOURCE: U.S. Bureau of the Census. *Historical Statistics of the United States: Colonial Times to 1970. Bicentennial Edition, Part 2.* Washington, D.C.: U.S. Department of Commerce, 1975, pp. 729–730.

profitable real estate deals with other hoteliers, as in the cases of the Waldorf–Astoria and Biltmore near Grand Central Terminal in Manhattan, elements of the New York Central's "Terminal City" concept.

The End of the Line and the Coming of Amtrak

Even in the heyday of rail travel, many companies lost money on passenger rail service. Beginning in 1929, except for two positive years during World War II, the country's railroads ran deficits in passenger service every year. Although the automobile is often referred to as the culprit—due especially to the support of the federal government for road building—airlines also took away a large chunk of the customer base, in part due to their ability to offer speedy and luxurious service. In the 1930s, the lightweight, sleek, cinder-less, and futuristic designs of the aluminum-alloy "Streamliners" did indeed fascinate the public, but they only briefly slowed the decline already occurring (Table 1). Washington, in response to the alleged abuses of railroad managers and presidents over the years, was notoriously unwilling to listen to the industry's complaints regarding (over)regulation. As a result, companies were forced to continue offering passenger service on many lines where it made absolutely no sense to do so. Some railroad companies actually let the quality of their service slide precipitously in an effort to get people to stop taking the train, thereby making abandonment of the service inevitable. In 1971, the federal government decided to save what remained of the country's passenger routes by forming Amtrak, a subsidized, quasi-private company to take over most existing passenger services. Amtrak exists into the 2000s, although it continually operates in the red and politicians opposed to its survival often threaten its annual financial support.

Even though Amtrak's service is a far cry from that of the New York Central's Twentieth-Century Limited, it still offers the enthusiast—and the passenger who does not want to drive or fly for various reasons—the chance to see the country from an interesting vantage point. As opposed to driving on interstates and, especially, flying, Amtrak still integrates the passenger into the surroundings, whether through the stops at stations small and large, the accents and local knowledge of the crews, or the stoppage of alcohol sales while the train rolls through a dry county. Although food tends to be prepackaged where there is no dining car, and service is rarely on time due to the priority given to freight trains, Amtrak still has loyal customers who value the uniqueness and comfort of rail travel. Dinner trains and other tourist trains still do offer the enthusiast and the well-to-do traveler a chance to ride the rails in style, and to see a corridor not often seen by many. Amtrak is often a travel option chosen by less-wealthy individuals and families, thus revealing the importance of preserving this now "old-fashioned" mode of transport.

See also: Automobiles and Leisure; Tourism

BIBLIOGRAPHY

Cather, Willa. *My Ántonia.* Introduction by Walter Havighurst. Boston: Houghton Mifflin Company, 1954. The original edition was published in 1918.

Cofone, Albin J. "The Harvey Girls: Women Who Opened the West." *The History Teacher* 28, no. 1 (1994): 115-116.

Drury, George H. *The Historical Guide to North American Railroads.* Waukesha, Wis.: Kalmbach Publishing Company, 1985.

Goddard, Stephen B. *Getting There: The Epic Struggle Between Road and Rail in the American Century.* Chicago: University of Chicago Press, 1994.

Jakle, John A. *The Tourist: Travel in Twentieth-Century North America.* Lincoln: University of Nebraska Press, 1985.

Martin, Albro. *Enterprise Denied: Origins of the Decline of American Railroads, 1897–1917.* New York: Columbia University Press, 1971.

Schlichting, Kurt C. *Grand Central Terminal: Railroads, Engineering, and Architecture in New York City.* Baltimore: Johns Hopkins University Press, 2001.

Stilgoe, John. *Metropolitan Corridor: Railroads and the American Scene.* New Haven, Conn.: Yale University Press, 1983.

Stover, John F. *American Railroads.* Chicago: University of Chicago Press, 1997.

Vance, James E., Jr. *The North American Railroad: Its Origin, Evolution, and Geography.* Baltimore: Johns Hopkins University Press, 1992.

Henry J. Rademacher

RAP MUSIC AUDIENCES

Rap music audiences have changed over time in important ways in both form and function. Over the past twenty years, rap has moved from a local, party-oriented art form to one driven by mass mediation. The majority of rap is produced today in a studio and is received in solitary settings, such as in cars and through Walkmans. While many more people are exposed to rap in such settings, the art itself is increasingly a part of a global recording industry. Audiences are more and more dispersed, heterogeneous, and unpredictable today.

Hip-hop began as a local artistic practice, one dependent on a whole series of artistic activities, including dance, music, and graffiti. Events took place in parks, basements, gyms, and clubs like Harlem World, Club 371, Disco Fever, and the Funhouse in New York City areas such as the South Bronx and Harlem (Rose). Rap's connection with live performance can be seen on early rap singles as well as on bootleg tapes from early shows, from groups like the Fantastic Five and artists such as Busy Bee. This sense of the event is evidenced in the use of "call-and-response" routines. For example, on the 1979 single "Rapper's Delight," by the Sugarhill Gang, the group raps, "Go Hotel, Motel, What ch'a gonna do today?" and the in-studio audience responds, "Say what?" to which the rapper answers, "Say I'm gonna get a fly girl, gonna get

some spank, and drive off in a def O.J." These routines were ever-present in live hip-hop shows and were also featured on nearly all the earliest rap singles, showing how hip-hop was a local face-to-face art form.

These call-and-response routines disappeared from hip-hop during the early to mid-1980s, a period marked by the rise of Run-D.M.C. and related artists. Run-D.M.C. was the first mega-successful rap group, earning rap's first gold, platinum, and multiplatinum album awards (for *Run-D.M.C.* [1984], *King of Rock* [1985], and *Raising Hell* [1986]). They were the first rappers to appear on MTV, the first to grace the cover of *Rolling Stone,* and the first to have a major endorsement deal with an athletic wear company (Adidas). Rap became a popular American music with the ascent of Run-D.M.C., one that circulated widely in traditional commodity form, attracting broader and more dispersed audiences.

This move into the studio enabled the art's base of production to expand. During the early to mid-1980s, the outlying areas of New York City such as Hollis, Queens (the home of Run-D.M.C.), became increasingly important, as did areas around the country like Los Angeles (the home of Uncle Jam's Army and the World Class Wreckin' Crew). The so-called suburbanization of hip-hop began during this period, as a much wider group of performers and audiences began to have access to the art.

The widening reach of rap music opened the art up to new possibilities around this time. Specifically, a kind of black nationalist identity politics became apparent in rap during the late 1980s, especially on the East Coast, as its community and audience stretched beyond local boundaries. For example, Public Enemy's second album, *It Takes a Nation of Millions to Hold Us Back* is structured as a fifty-eight-minute, self-contained radio broadcast, its individual songs linked together conceptually. Tracks are interspersed with portions of a concert, static, the sound of a radio dial turning, and bits and pieces of radio shows. Communication itself became most important as Public Enemy envisioned an African American community and audience that could be linked together through media technology.

In addition, "gangsta rap" emerged at almost exactly the same time on the West Coast that Public Enemy and other nationalist rappers did on the East. While there are important differences between the lyric content of "positive pro-black" artists such as Public Enemy and "negative gangsta rap" artists such as NWA, these groups share some key characteristics. In particular, both groups engaged hip-hop as a mass-mediated art form—one no longer continually linked to live practice and performance. The now familiar "rap as ghetto reporter" equation entered West

Coast parlance during this period as Chuck D's oft-quoted "rap as black America's CNN" entered the East's. As a concurrent phenomena, the video became a much more prevalent part of rap during the late 1980s and early 1990s, primarily through the influence of MTV's *Yo! MTV Raps*. The video medium reinforced prevailing currents in hip-hop music during this period, dispersing its stories on a mass scale. Audiences were linked across the country and globe to this more informational medium.

The gangster narrative has become a big part of the art form, fostering an entire musical genre. Its wild financial success has helped to shape the contours of rap's present landscape. Most artists of the early twenty-first century acknowledge the genre either implicitly or explicitly, as values such as "hardness" and "realness" dominate. "Hardcore" artists of the 1990s and early 2000s such as Method Man, Nas, Redman, 50 Cent, and Jay-Z all embraced the violently impenetrable outlaw stance on some level, though they all proclaimed a love for rap as an art form as well. They all employed performance tools, though they are all operating on a popularly determined landscape, both in medium and message.

In conclusion, rap music audiences have grown and dispersed in complex ways. Accordingly, more attention was being given to the ways young people were using these texts both in the United States and globally. In the early 2000s, rap music was a global media. Young people from around the world were using its complex cultural markers to help them navigate their own particular concerns and needs. These young people were appropriating the work of U.S. artists in specific ways, conjuring up their own local circumstances. This is a move made clear by paying attention to the changing role and nature of rap music audiences.

See also: Radio Listening, Car and Home; Record, CD, Tape Collecting and Listening; Rock Concert Audiences

BIBLIOGRAPHY

Dimitriadis, Greg. *Performing Identity/Performing Culture: Hip-Hop as Text, Pedagogy, and Lived Practice.* New York: Peter Lang, 2001.

Dolby, Nadine. *Constructing Race: Youth, Identity, and Popular Culture in South Africa.* Albany: State University of New York Press, 2001.

Mitchell, Tony, ed. *Global Noise: Rap and Hip-Hop Outside the USA.* Middletown, Conn.: Wesleyan University Press, 2002.

Rose, Tricia. *Black Noise: Rap Music and Black Culture in Contemporary America.* Hanover, N.H.: University Press of New England, 1994.

Greg Dimitriadis

RATIONAL RECREATION AND SELF-IMPROVEMENT

"Rational recreation" was the ideal that nineteenth-century middle-class reformers hoped to impose on the urban working class of their day. They believed that "leisure activities should be controlled, ordered, and improving" (Cunningham, p. 90), qualities not typically found in the free-time behavior of laboring men. More particularly, recreation was viewed as rational when it fosters personal acquisitions like self-improvement and self-enrichment and, as a result, enhanced self-expression and personal and social identity. Pursuing excellence in, say, amateur tennis, hobbyist stamp collecting, or volunteer work with youth exemplifies such recreation; whereas nonrational recreation—leisure that leads to no such acquisitions but, rather, is done for pure pleasure—is the classificatory home of activities like napping, strolling in the park, and, of course, watching television (primarily for entertainment).

In the past, leisure theory has treated rational recreation under a variety of headings, of which that of "serious leisure" has gained widest currency. One advantage of this perspective is that it incorporates "casual leisure," the theoretical label for nonrational recreation. Both terms were coined by Robert Stebbins (1982), following the way people he interviewed and observed defined in daily life the relative importance of these two kinds of activity. Serious leisure is systematic pursuit of an amateur, hobbyist, or volunteer activity that participants find so substantial and interesting that they may launch themselves on careers centered on acquiring and expressing its special skills, knowledge, and experience. The adjective "serious" (often used by participants) embodies such qualities as earnestness, sincerity, importance, and carefulness, rather than distress, gravity, solemnity, and joylessness. Although the second set of terms occasionally describe serious leisure events, they are uncharacteristic of them and fail to nullify or dilute the overall deep satisfaction gained by participants. The idea of "career" in this definition follows sociological tradition, where careers are seen as available in all substantial, complex roles, including those in leisure. By contrast, casual leisure is immediately rewarding, relatively short-lived pleasurable activity requiring little or no special training. It is fundamentally hedonic, pursued for its appealing measure of pure enjoyment.

Amateurs are found in art, science, sport, and entertainment, where they are invariably linked in a variety of ways with professional counterparts. The two can be distinguished descriptively in that the activity in question constitutes a livelihood for professionals but not amateurs. Furthermore, professionals work full-time at the activity whereas amateurs pursue it part-time. The part-time professionals in art and entertainment complicate this picture; although they work part-time, their work is judged by other professionals and by the amateurs as of professional quality. Amateurs and professionals are locked in and therefore defined by a three-way professional-amateur-public system of relations, known as the P-A-P system. Hobbyists lack this professional alter ego, suggesting that all amateurs were hobbyists before their fields professionalized. Both types are drawn to their leisure pursuits significantly more by self-interest than by altruism, whereas volunteers engage in noncoerced helping of others that requires a more or less equal blend of these two motives.

Six Qualities

The rational nature of serious leisure is evident in the six qualities that distinguish it from casual leisure, qualities uniformly found among its amateurs, hobbyists, and volunteers. One is the occasional need to persevere. Participants who want to continue experiencing the same level of satisfaction in the activity have to meet certain challenges from time to time. It happens in all three types of serious leisure that deepest satisfaction sometimes comes at the end of the activity rather than during it, from conquering adversity along the way.

A second quality distinguishing serious leisure is the opportunity to follow a career in the endeavor, as shaped by its own special contingencies, turning points, and stages of achievement and involvement. Nevertheless, in some fields, notably certain arts and sports, this career can include decline. Moreover, most, if not all, careers here owe their existence to a third quality: Serious leisure participants make significant personal effort based on specially acquired knowledge, training, and skill.

Fourth, serious leisure is further distinguished by several durable benefits, or tangible, salutary outcomes of such activity for participants. They are self-actualization, self-enrichment, self-expression, regeneration or renewal of self, feelings of accomplishment, enhancement of self-image, social interaction and sense of belonging, and lasting physical products of the activity (for example, a painting, a scientific paper, a piece of furniture). A further benefit—self-gratification, or pure fun, which is by far the most evanescent benefit in this list—is also enjoyed by casual leisure participants. The possibility of realizing such benefits constitutes a powerful goal in serious leisure.

Fifth, serious leisure is distinguished by a unique ethos that emerges in each expression of it. At the core of this ethos is the special social world that evolves when enthusiasts in a particular field pursue over many years substantial shared interests. According to David Unruh every social world has its characteristic groups, events, routines, practices, and organizations. In the typical case, the social worlds of serous leisure participants are neither heavily bureaucratized nor substantially organized through intense face-to-face interaction. Rather, communication is commonly mediated by newsletters, posted notices, telephone messages, mass mailings, radio and television announcements, and similar means.

The sixth quality—participants in serious leisure tend to identify strongly with their chosen pursuits—springs from the preceding five. In contrast, most casual leisure, though not usually humiliating or despicable, is for most people too fleeting, mundane, and commonplace to generate distinctive identities.

The Emergence of Rational Recreation

Gary Cross notes that, during much of the nineteenth century, employers and upwardly mobile employees looked on "idleness" as threatening industrial development and social stability. The reformers in their midst sought to eliminate this menace by, among other approaches, attempting to build bridges to the "dangerous classes" in the new cities in order to transform them in the image of the middle class. This approach led to efforts to impose (largely rural) middle-class values on this group, while trying to instill a desire to engage in rational recreation—in modern terms, serious leisure—and consequently to undertake less casual leisure.

Part of this reform revolved around attempts to get the working classes to embrace an ethic of self-control, individualism, and respectability, an approach that did not meet with great success. More central to the rational recreation movement were projects that facilitated serious leisure, such as establishing museums, opening reading rooms, and providing spaces for athletic and performing arts activities. Some of these activities were organized by working men's social clubs, established in part for this reason, and some were organized by their employers. Many of today's urban parks and museums owe their existence to this movement.

Cross concluded, "It is doubtful whether workers' leisure became more respectable in precisely the ways endorsed by reformist patrons" (p. 99). He noted that the social classes may have walked the bridges that the patrons built, but no new understanding resulted. Yet, even if most wage earners failed to replace traditional casual pleasures with rational satisfactions, many added aspects of the reformers' program to their leisure repertory. "The result was in part a more privatized, more sedate, and more universal recreational culture. For some individuals, rational recreation may have helped to create a personality suitable to the competitive upwardly mobile society of the Victorian city" (p. 100).

The Rise of Modern Amateurism

As professionalization spreads from one occupation to another, what was once considered play in some of these spheres is evolving quietly but inevitably into a new form— one best named "modern amateurism." Modern amateurism has been rising alongside those occupations where some participants in the occupation are now able to make a substantial living from it and, consequently, to devote themselves to it as a vocation rather than an avocation. Although there are possibly others, we know that science, entertainment, sport and games, and fine arts are major occupational areas where work was once purely play and where modern amateurism is now a parallel development.

What has been happening is this: Those who play at the activities constituting the core of these occupations are being overrun in significance, if not in numbers, by professionals and amateurs. It is a process that seems to unfold as follows. As opportunities for full-time pursuit of a skill or activity gradually appear, people with even an average aptitude for such skills are able to develop them to a level observably higher than that of the typical part-time participant. With today's mass availability of professional performances (or products), whatever the field, new standards of excellence soon confront all participants, professional or not. Although the performances of professionals are frequently impressive, no category of participant is more impressed than that of the nonprofessionals who, through direct experience, know the activity intimately. Indeed, once they become aware of professional standards, all they have accomplished seems mediocre by comparison. For example, amateur basketball and hockey players are frequently in awe of the abilities of those who play in the National Basketball Association and the National Hockey League, as are amateur classical musicians of the way their counterparts perform in the New York Philharmonic Orchestra or the Juilliard String Quartet. They are thus faced with a critical choice in their careers as participants: Either they restrict identification with the activity so as to remain largely unaffected by such invidious comparisons, or they identify sufficiently with it to attempt to meet those standards.

With the first choice, which is still common, the part-time participant remains a player, dabbler, or dilettante. Following Johan Huizinga, we can say that leisure of that type lacks necessity, obligation, and utility, and will be produced with a disinterestedness that sets it, as an activity, apart from the participants' ordinary, real lives. The second, increasingly common choice impels part-time participants away from play toward the pursuit of durable benefits. The road to these benefits, however, passes through necessity, seriousness, commitment, and agreeable obligation as expressed by regimentation (such as rehearsals and practice) and systematization (through schedules and organization), and progresses on to the status of modern amateur for some and professional for others. Jacques Godbout has noted this trend in what he calls the "professionnalisation des loisirs" (professionalization of leisure), basically its regimentation or systematization. As evidence of all this note the emphasis on perfection of play in the Olympic Games, in college sports, and even in high school athletics, as well as the standards held up to civic orchestras and community theaters, amateur writers and Sunday painters.

Players in the nineteenth and early twentieth centuries in sport and music, and quite possibly other fields, were referred to as "gentlemen" (few were women). But first Johan Huizinga and then Gregory Stone commented on the gradual disappearance of such players from sport. Indeed, it is an ongoing process. Jacques Barzun discusses this transformation in music.

Furthermore, in the nineteenth and early twentieth centuries, players and amateurs (probably differences existed between them even then) were alone in their activities, without the existence of professionals. In fact, during this period many contemporary professions (for example, astronomy, music, soccer) were made up exclusively of amateurs. In effect, these endeavors were too new, too little in demand, or too underdeveloped to be pursued as livelihoods. Thus, when their fields began, a number of astronomers, archaeologists, teachers, musicians, painters, jugglers, bowlers, soccer players, and so forth earned their living through other means; clearly, however, they were experts, by standards of the day, in their respective areas of leisure.

In some fields amateurism was an honorable tradition, and attempts at full-time employment and professionalization were met with derision. It was considered despicable to make money that way. But, as the two categories of participant began to diverge in these fields, amateurs often could be distinguished from professionals by social class. Garry Whannel notes that, in the nineteenth century, those who played sport for money belonged to the lower class, whereas those who played purely for enjoyment belonged to the upper class. For many years, informal or formal arrangements prevented the different classes of teams and individuals from competing with one another. Today, however, all but the poorest classes participate in amateur activities, even if a few activities disproportionately attract the rich (polo, for example) or the working classes (dirt bike racing).

As professionals began to dominate a field pioneered by amateurs a transformation in the meaning of "amateur" seems to have occurred. During this period, which, depending on the field, ran anywhere from the late nineteenth to mid-twentieth century, old definitions clung tenaciously, merging in common discourse with new ones springing up to describe modern amateurism. From a research standpoint, the result was emergence of the idea of amateur, now an everyday term, though one defined with annoying imprecision in contemporary dictionaries.

The entries in *Merriam-Webster's Unabridged Dictionary* exemplify the problem. Amateurs, for instance, are defined, in one sense, as devotees who love a particular activity; in another sense as dilettantes or dabblers. Dilettantes, on the other hand, are defined, in the first sense, as lovers of the arts and, in the second, as people with discrimination or taste. Consider, also, the logical difficulties posed by yet another sense of "amateur" —that is, the inexperienced person (or player)—and the fact that devotees of an activity quite naturally put in much time at it, thereby achieving remarkable competence (that is, modern amateurs).

Leisure Education

However important rational recreation is for self-improvement and, in the case of volunteering, for community development, such activity has always been pursued by only a minority of the population. Casual leisure is far more popular. The central problem, then, is how to reach a more evenly balanced ratio of participation in the two. One way to tackle this problem is through routine, easily accessible leisure education for youth and adults. This way includes instructional programs in schools and adult-education focused on the nature of serious and casual leisure and their interrelationship, general rewards (and costs) of both types, possibility of finding a (serious) leisure career there, and variety of social and psychological advantages people can gain by pursuing a given amateur, hobbyist, or volunteer activity. Among these advantages is acquisition of a special identity, routine, lifestyle, organizational belonging, central life interest, and membership in a social world.

Although a huge variety of activities courses for youth and adults were offered everywhere in North America as of 2004 (such as those for dance, golfing, ceramics, and woodworking), rare are those expressly designed to educate about leisure and rational recreation. In the interest of enhanced personal and collective well-being, this deficiency should be eliminated.

See also: Hobbies and Crafts, Leisure Education, Literary Societies and Middlebrow Reading, Museum Movements

BIBLIOGRAPHY

Barzun, Jacques. *Music in American Life.* Bloomington: Indiana University Press, 1956.

Cross, Gary. *A Social History of Leisure Since 1600.* State College, Pa.: Venture Publishing, 1990.

Cunningham, Hugh. *Leisure in the Industrial Revolution.* London: Croom Helm, 1980.

Godbout, Jacques. "La Participation: Instrument de Professionnalisation des Loisirs." *Loisir et Société/Society and Leisure* 9 (1990): 33–40.

Huizinga, Johan. *Homo Ludens: A Study of the Play Element in Culture.* Boston: Beacon, 1955.

Stebbins, Robert A. "Serious Leisure: A Conceptual Statement." *Pacific Sociological Review* 25 (1982): 251–272.

———. *Amateurs, Professionals, and Serious Leisure.* Montreal; Kingston, Ontario: McGill-Queen's University Press, 1992.

———. *New Directions in the Theory and Research of Serious Leisure.* Mellen Studies in Sociology, volume 28. Lewiston, N.Y.: Edwin Mellen, 2001.

Stone, Gregory P. "American Sports: Play and Display." In *Sport.* Edited by Eric Dunning. Toronto: University of Toronto Press, 1972.

Unruh, David R. "Characteristics and Types of Participation in Social Worlds." *Symbolic Interaction* 2 (1979): 115–130.

———. "The Nature of Social Worlds." *Pacific Sociological Review* 23 (1980): 71–296.

Whannel, Garry. *Blowing the Whistle: The Politics of Sport.* London: Pluto Press, 1983.

Robert A. Stebbins

RAVES/RAVING

Raves originated in England during the late 1980s as acid house parties (that is, parties that featured the form of dance music known as "acid house" and related forms) held in clandestine venues, such as warehouses, aircraft hangars, and barns. The parties fused live, deejay-mixed techno music with all-night dancing, and they were often associated with drug use, particularly the use of Ecstasy, a drug referred to more formally as 3,4-methylenedioxyamphetamine (MDMA). By the early 1990s, the phenomenon arrived in the United States fueled by the desire of many American deejays to bring the sounds and experience of rave to an American audience. Initially arriving in California, the rave scene expanded quickly to the East Coast, where Frankie Bones, credited as one of the founders of the rave movement in the United States, began throwing a series of large underground parties called "storm raves" at which many renowned rave deejays made their debuts. Rave events have since been organized in every state across the country.

The Rave Culture

While a broad examination of rave culture reveals anything but a homogeneous crowd, U.S. ravers at the beginning of the twenty-first century were generally Caucasian youth of middle-class backgrounds between the ages of fifteen and twenty-five. Content to live a middle-class existence during the week, ravers viewed their participation in raves as "mini vacations," during which they challenged their parents' norms of behavior. As part of their resistance to adult norms, ravers forsook discipline, the staple of productivity, in favor of abandonment.

Ravers typically wore androgynous clothing, including baggy pants, baseball hats, and T-shirts emblazoned with cartoon characters. Children's toys, plastic chains, lollipops, and pacifiers were typical accessories, too. All told, infantilism is symbolic of ravers regaining their innocence and escaping from their adolescent problems. The androgynous clothing also implies ravers prided themselves on their lack of pretension. Rave clothing became increasingly provocative, however, largely because of the introduction of new members into the rave community, particularly the regular denizens of dance clubs, and the fashion trends they bring with them. In the early 2000s, a club crowd frequently joined in attendance at raves, although their presence was generally unappreciated by serious ravers. As with any subculture, the community orientation associated with rave is confined only to those who "belong" to the group, not to outsiders. Nevertheless, increasing outsider attendance demonstrated its expanding appeal.

Rave Environments

The venues at which raves took place were usually announced the day prior to their occurrence, presumably to evade police surveillance. Amazingly, the communication networks of rave culture could organize thousands of people in only a matter of days. First-time participants accessed a rave if an active participant in the scene took them to it. The only way to continue participation was to attend the parties; inactivity resulted in exclusion. By 2004 it became more common for raves to be held at a variety of public venues or other "legal spaces," venues that have safety features such as emergency exits, event security, and drinking water. The increasing number of raves that took place in legal spaces was indicative of the expanding popularity of these events.

With respect to music, techno was the original music of choice of the rave scene during its earliest stages of development, but other related genres soon developed. The choice of music acted as a filter to determine who was attracted to the events. Irrespective of the genre, the music had a high level of bass and tended to be fast-paced, playing anywhere between 115 and 300 beats per minute. Computers, samplers, synthesizers, and sequencers produced the music, with few or no vocals. The chief purpose of the music was to inspire dance. Given the importance of the music, disc jockeys played a salient role by "spinning," the art of mixing songs together by using different pitches and tempos to create a seamless flow of music. Surprisingly, rave music lacks an established star system, presumably because the focus is on the rave, not the artist. Most musical releases are left unlabeled, a practice referred to as "white labeling."

Alcohol was often unavailable at raves because of its tendency to incite aggression and violence, which are counter to the ideals that underpin rave culture. Drugs, by contrast, played a significant role. Much of the bonding that occurred at raves happened while ravers were under the influence of Ecstasy, whose users reported feelings of empathy and well-being. Known as the "hug drug," Ecstasy allowed users to overcome social barriers. Because Ecstasy was known for inhibiting the sexual drive of its users, social interaction found at raves was largely affectionate, not sexual. Female participants have commented appreciatively about the lack of sexual tension at the events they have attended. Ravers' heightened sense of empathy prompted participants to embrace and touch each other affectionately. The crowd's behavior reflected a sense of community, even tribalism, among participants.

The four pillars of the rave scene—peace, love, unity, and respect (PLUR)—embodied the inclusive nature of raves. Ostensibly, the "vibe" encountered at raves was not replicated at other parties or clubs. Ravers frequently reported the absence of "attitude," fear of violence, and crowd aggressiveness, unlike at other similar events. The

Groove Jet. A crowd fills the dance club "Groove Jet" in South Beach, Miami, in September 1999. At parties like this one and at all-night "raves," partygoers often take Ecstasy and other illegal drugs to heighten the euphoric feelings generated by the music and the crowd. © *AP/Wide World Photos*

participants encountered at raves were generally welcoming, and claimed not to judge others on their clothing, physical appearance, sexual orientation, race, gender, or dancing ability. Of course, the presence of such accepting attitudes changed as new participants entered the scene; like any community, only those who fail to subscribe to the values that underpin the activity are marginalized.

Ecstasy

The recreational drug use associated with the activity was disconcerting to many people, however. Moral objections aside, the use of Ecstasy and other rave-related drugs could pose potentially harmful consequences to those who partook. Ecstasy increases water retention in its users, disturbing the balance of water and sodium levels. Urinating less and keeping more water in the body causes sodium levels to drop, which can result in seizures and cerebral edema, though such outcomes are exceedingly

rare. Ecstasy can also produce severe toxicity, if overdosed, and hyperthermia, both of which can result in death. High environmental and core-body temperatures and muscular exertion from long-drawn-out dancing are believed to lower the risk of serious Ecstasy-related adverse effects, however. Moreover, active cooling measures (such as drinking water) and the use of the muscle relaxants, anticonvulsants, and sedative medications are believed to decrease mortality from the toxic ingestion of Ecstasy. Adequate facilities, such as drinking fountains, however, were often unavailable at the "underground" venues at which many raves were held. Consequently, venues ill equipped to respond to emergencies could jeopardize the safety of participants.

Complications following Ecstasy ingestion are unpredictable and surprisingly do not appear to be dose-dependent. In response to the unpredictable nature of the consumption of Ecstasy, the rave community launched awareness programs to educate ravers about pills. Nonetheless, the dangers associated with Ecstasy use were extended to rave culture, most notably by the press and municipal policy makers. Consequently, active discussions regarding the prohibition of raves were taking place across the United States by 2004.

See also: Drinking, Recreational Drug Use, Teenage Leisure Trends

BIBLIOGRAPHY

Critcher, C. "'Still Raving': Social Reaction to Ecstasy." *Leisure Studies* 19 (2000): 145–162.

Glover, T. D. "Regulating the Rave Scene: Policy Alternatives of Government." *Leisure Sciences* 25 (2003).

Linder, M. J. "The Agony of the Ecstasy: Raving Youth." *Red Feather Journal of Graduate Sociology* 4 (2001).

Martin, D. "Power Play and Party Politics: The Significance of Raving." *Journal of Popular Culture* 32 (1999): 77–99.

Reynolds, S. "Rave Culture: Living Dream or Living Death?" In *The Clubcultures Reader: Readings in Popular Cultural Studies.* Edited by S. Redhead. Malden, Mass.: Blackwell, 1997.

Tomlinson, L. "'This Ain't No Disco'. . . Or Is It? Youth Culture and the Rave Phenomenon." In *Youth Culture: Identity in a Post-Modern World.* Edited by E. S. Epstein. Malden, Mass.: Blackwell, 1998.

Weber, T. R. "Raving in Toronto: Peace. Love, Unity and Respect in Transition." *Journal of Youth Studies* 2 (1999): 317–336.

Weir, E. "Raves: A Review of the Culture, the Drugs and the Prevention of Harm." *Canadian Medical Association Journal* 162 (2000): 1843–1848.

Troy D. Glover

READING

See *Books and Manuscripts; Literary Societies and Middle-Brow Reading; Magazines, Men's; Magazines, Women's*

RECORD, CD, TAPE COLLECTING AND LISTENING

In 1877, inventor Thomas Edison revolutionized modern-day leisure when he recorded the first human voice on his phonograph. Edison originally created records using a metal cylinder wrapped in tinfoil and sold in cardboard tubes. As technology infiltrated society, other, more sophisticated sources of listening to music were developed, including shellac 78-rpm discs, introduced in the early 1900s, and in 1925 the use of electrical recording vastly improved the quality of recorded sound. In the modern era, the first and longest-lasting medium for prerecorded music was the long-playing (LP) vinyl record, introduced by Columbia Records in 1948; the American and world standards for stereo records were established in 1958.

The phonograph, the earliest device on which to play prerecorded sounds, served as a vehicle for the explosion of popular recorded music and album collecting. It is difficult to pinpoint when people actually started "collecting" recordings. Although the very first records created were not strictly for music, it is plausible to assume that as long as "collectible" music has existed, so have "collectors" of this music. Record collecting remained popular in the 2000s, although few artists still released versions of their albums on vinyl records; these items were more for purists and collectors.

The next major development occurred five years after mass stereo standardization, when the audio cassette "tape" was created, followed three years later in 1966 with the introduction of the 8-track tape, which offered the ability to skip more easily to other tracks on the album than did the cassette. However, the mechanically cumbersome 8-track package, with its continuous-loop tape that often jammed and broke, soon lost its appeal, and the cassette quickly became America's preferred standard. It was not until 1988 that a new format, the compact disc (CD), became the most popular selling format, a mere six years after it was first introduced. Collectors enjoyed enhanced digital sound, convenient size, and increased ability to quickly skip tracks. Several other formats, including the mini-disc, were introduced but quickly disappeared; CDs became so popular that in the early twenty-first century, records and tapes were available only in specialty shops. In 1999, the super-audio CD and DVD-audio were also introduced and found success in niche markets; it is plausible, because they both offer improved sound capabilities and protection against digital copying, that their popularity will continue to grow.

Collecting

Official While musical formats have come and gone, the collection of albums (each containing a number of songs, usually—but not always—by a single artist or group) as a leisure activity has grown in popularity and has become big business in the twenty-first century. In America, strict regulations govern the official release of albums. There is a "street" date decided upon by labels (but always a Tuesday in America) that is the first date that one can legally acquire the album. Two interesting variations for hardcore collectors are unofficial releases and purchasing products in foreign countries. In Canada, for example, one can often get a copy of an album well before it is legally available in America. Additionally, many European countries offer products with enhanced features (special packaging, bonus tracks) at higher cost, but available earlier than in America. Often, albums become highly collectible because they were originally reproduced in such small numbers and/or production stopped due to decreased demand, making them rare or out of print. In some cases, albums become rare and immediately collectible because of events that are outside the control of record companies, retailers, and artists. Online auction sites, the most popular being eBay.com, have become acceptable means of buying and selling recordings, especially rare, out-of-print albums in various formats.

Unofficial Unofficial releases, those not approved or produced by the artist or the record company, can be either studio recordings or live recordings. These illegal releases are commonly referred to as "bootlegs," and neither the artist nor the record company receives any money from the sale of these items. Although it is hard to trace when bootlegging first became vogue, Bob Dylan's now-legendary live concert performance in Manchester, England, on 17 May 1966 is often credited as the first rock and roll bootleg, and is now available domestically. Over successive decades, bootlegging became more and more popular; some bands, such as the Grateful Dead, Dave Matthews Band, and Phish, actually encouraged taping and sharing of their live concerts. Pearl Jam officially released every live show from its 2001 tour, starting a trend that found artists finally cashing in on a market segment that previously was untapped—those fans, referred to as "completists," who collect everything ever produced by a band.

The Future of Collecting

Formats for prerecorded music will continue to progress. Currently, both DVD-audios and super-audio CDs are flooding the market, although neither format is playable on standard CD players, and it is unknown whether consumers will adopt these formats. An even more intriguing advancement is the MP3, a compressed digital file format that has come under fire because of copyright laws. The popularity of MP3 trading, via online communities (like the defunct free version of Napster), has come under fire because of issues related to copyright protection, royalties, and impact on retail sales.

See also: Country Music Audiences; Radio Listening, Car and Home; Rap Music Audiences; Rock Concert Audiences; Teenage Leisure Trends

BIBLIOGRAPHY

Clarke, Donald. *The Penguin Encyclopedia of Popular Music.* London: Penguin Books, 1989.

Hendler, Herb. *Year by Year in the Rock Era.* New York: Praeger Publishers, 1987.

Smith, Joe. *Off the Record: An Oral History of Popular Music.* New York: Warner Books, 1988.

Strunk, William, Jr. *The Elements of Style.* New York: Macmillan Publishers, 1959.

Ward, Ed, Geoffrey Stokes, and Ken Tucker. *Rock of Ages: The Rolling Stone History of Rock & Roll.* New York: Summit Books, 1986.

Joshua Shuart

RECREATIONAL DRUG USE

The widespread use of illicit drugs for recreational purposes is not unprecedented in the early twenty-first century. In the absence of any federal regulation in the nineteenth century (state regulatory drug laws were not adopted until the 1890s), drug use was so prevalent Edward M. Brecher observes that America could have been described as a "dope fiend's paradise" (p. 3). Technology contributed to some drug use. The introduction of the hypodermic needle in the 1850s made it easier to administer morphine, and its use to treat wounded and ill soldiers during the Civil War confirmed its legitimacy as an extraordinarily effective pain reliever. Named for the Greek god Morpheus, the drug remained popular through the latter half of the century.

Physicians dispensed opiates directly to patients in their offices or wrote prescriptions for the drug. Even without a visit to the family doctor it was possible to purchase opiates over the counter at the local pharmacy, where they were sold without a prescription. Opiates were available just about everywhere, it seemed, including grocery markets and general stores. Countless patent medicines such as "Mrs. Winslow's Soothing Syrup,"

"Dover's Powder," and "McMunn's Elixir of Opium" were widely advertised in newspapers, magazines, and billboards as "pain-killers," "cough mixtures," "women's friends," and "consumption cures."

If users were unable to buy opiates in person, they could order them through the mail. At late as 1897 Sears Roebuck advertised a hypodermic kit, which included a syringe, two needles, two vials, and a carrying case for $1.50. Extra needles cost 25 cents each or $2.75 for a dozen. Drug paraphernalia was not always required, however; the popular new soft drink Coca-Cola contained cocaine until 1903. In 1906, however, Congress passed the first piece of drug-related legislation, which inaugurated the federal government's century-long war on drugs that has continued into the early 2000s.

Analysis of Users and Their Motivations Over Time

Although drugs were freely available in the nineteenth century, opiate use was regarded as a vice similar to dancing, smoking, gambling, or sexual promiscuity. Although considered immoral, the use of opiates was not subject to moral or legal sanctions as it was by late in the twentieth century. Employees were not fired for addiction, drug use was not recognized as a legal cause for divorce, and addicts functioned as normal members of the community while sustaining their drug habits. Demographically and socioeconomically, the drug-using population also differed dramatically from that of the early 2000s, when it was composed mostly of young, urban males. At the beginning of the twentieth century, most drug users were white, middle-class women who consumed morphine or opium—what physicians referred to as "G.O.M.," or "God's Own Medicine"—to alleviate diarrhea, dysentery, menstrual cramps, menopausal discomfort, and a host of other maladies.

Drug addicts in the 1880s were older than they were in the early 2000s, according to a Chicago study that showed an average age of about forty. In the late nineteenth century, like in the early twenty-first century, drug use filtered through every social strata, but in the nineteenth century opiate use was more extensive among the wealthy and educated classes. Also significant, and contrary to popular notions, there was no disproportionate use of opiates among black Americans; in fact, two surveys conducted in the South confirmed a lower proportion of black drug users than white drug users (Courtwright, pp. 37–38; Morgan, p. 34).

By the 1920s, the perception of the drug user began to change from that of a white, middle-class person to a foreigner, a criminal element, a racial minority, or a member of some other socially marginal group. Nearly a century later, the image of an illicit drug user remained essentially unchanged. One area of commonality for people who consume illegal drugs is the stigma still associated with the behavior. "Typical" drug users also share demographic characteristics: in 2003, white males between the ages of twenty-six and thirty-four were more likely to use drugs than any other segment of the population; as they aged, most of these users tended to "grow out" of the practice.

Researchers have offered numerous explanations for why people take drugs. Some people use drugs to avoid reality, however brief their escape might be. Others use drugs as an act of rebellion against society or parental authority, or as a response to peer pressure. A smaller group of people may be susceptible to an addictive personality. Sociologist and widely published author Andrew Weil argues in "Why People Take Drugs" that people use drugs out of a normal, innate drive to alter their consciousness, and that individuals take drugs much like they endeavor to fulfill hunger or sex drives. Using drugs may not be an aberrant behavior if Weil is correct that "the ubiquity of drug use is so striking that it must represent a basic human appetite," (p. 3). Whatever the motive for using drugs, we can safely assume people do so because drugs make them feel better.

Efforts to Ban Drugs in the Twentieth Century

Manufacturers of patent medicines were still not legally required to indicate the specific ingredients in their products until muckraking journalists began crusading for social reforms in the beginning of the twentieth century. Responding to their demands for regulatory legislation, Congress in 1906 passed the Pure Food and Drug Act, which required the label on a bottle of patent medicine to indicate the ingredients. The new law did not criminalize the use of any drugs, nor did it contain any enforcement provisions, but it was a major step in the control of opiate addiction.

In 1914, less than a decade after the Pure Food and Drug Act took effect, Congress passed the Harrison Anti-Narcotic Act, which required anyone who handled cocaine and opiate derivatives such as morphine and heroin—manufacturers, importers, pharmacists, and physicians—to register with the Treasury Department, pay a special annual $1 tax, and maintain records of all transactions. Anyone who did not register faced a $2,000 fine and a five-year prison sentence. On the surface the new law was essentially a revenue measure that merely regulated the distribution of certain drugs. Over the next

Rally for drug law reform. Supporters of the effort to legalize drugs such as marijuana attend a rally in Albuquerque, New Mexico. As of 2004, only marijuana used for medicinal purposes was legal in the United States, and even then only in a limited number of states. © *AP/Wide World Photos*

several years the Treasury Department, charged with enforcing the law, interpreted it to mean that a doctor could not prescribe opiates to a patient-addict to maintain the patient's addiction, a position Supreme Court decisions upheld.

In the 1920s, the United States expanded control of the use and distribution of illegal substances. To better enable the federal government to monitor the use of legitimate narcotics and to more effectively reduce the volume of illicit drug traffic, Congress passed the Jones-Miller Act, officially known as the Narcotic Drugs Import and Export Act of 1922, which also established a Federal Narcotics Board.

Congress took another step in drug enforcement in the 1930s by creating a separate, autonomous Federal Bureau of Narcotics (FBN), which almost immediately began receiving reports from public officials and private citizens detailing the dangerous effects of a "new" drug that was especially popular in southwestern states. Marijuana, or what FBN Commissioner Harry J. Anslinger

called the "assassin of youth," had not been included in the Harrison Act. In response to exaggerated and sometimes graphic accounts about the violent effects of marijuana, and predictions that marijuana smoking would rapidly spread beyond the Southwest, President Franklin D. Roosevelt signed the Marijuana Tax Act into law in August 1937. Modeled after the Harrison Act, the new legislation permitted the medical use of marijuana, but mandated a transfer tax of $1 per ounce if the person was registered and $100 per ounce if the person had not purchased a transfer tax stamp. The first violator of the law, fifty-eight-year-old peddler Samuel R. Caldwell, received a four-year sentence in Leavenworth Penitentiary and was fined $1,000.

World War II effectively disrupted international narcotics distribution, which resulted in a general decline of drug use in the United States. By the early 1950s, however, Cold War anxieties about Soviet aggression and media reports alleging that communist China was trafficking in heroin—a claim repeatedly confirmed by Anslinger in the media and before numerous congressional hearings—prompted Congress to adopt a more punitive response to illicit drug use in the form of the 1951 Boggs Act. Mandatory minimum sentences were stipulated for all marijuana and other drug offenses. First-time offenders received sentences of two to five years, second-time violators were sentenced to five to ten years, and third-time offenders faced mandatory prison sentences of twenty years with no probation. All offenses also carried fines up to $2,000. In 1956, concern about a communist plot to flood the West with heroin, and reports of a rise in the number of teenage drug addicts, sparked a renewed concern about drug use. Again, at Commissioner Anslinger's urging, Congress passed the Narcotic Control Act, which doubled the Boggs penalties and added the death penalty for anyone who gave or sold heroin to a person under eighteen years old.

Drug use did not decline in the 1960s, but a decrease in the media coverage and a transition from punitive legislation to a gradual relaxation in the public's attitude toward drug use resulted in an ideological shift in drug control policy. In 1970, Congress passed the Comprehensive Drug Abuse Prevention and Control Act, which abolished mandatory minimum sentences and reduced the penalties for simple possession of marijuana. The legislation also classified all drugs according to their medical use, and their potential for abuse and addiction. A Schedule I substance, such as heroin or LSD, was considered to have no accepted medical use and a high potential for abuse and addiction. Codeine in cough syrup is an example of a Schedule V drug with a low potential for abuse. In 1973, soon after the act took effect, President Richard M. Nixon's specially appointed Commission on Marijuana and Drug Abuse recommended that marijuana possession be decriminalized. Although the commission's findings indicated a rejection of the "get-tough" approach to drug use, Congress has not significantly reduced the penalties for marijuana offenses.

In the mid-1980s the appearance of "crack," a smokable form of cocaine, created a wave of fear similar to that of marijuana in the 1930s and heroin in the 1950s. The government's response to the crack "epidemic" also was similar to that of the earlier drug scares. In the Anti-Drug Abuse Act of 1986, Congress authorized nearly $4 billion for an intensified war on drugs and restored mandatory minimum sentences. Two years later the Anti-Drug Abuse Act of 1988 added the death penalty for anyone who kills a law enforcement officer during the commission of a drug-related crime. Because policymakers considered crack to be more dangerous than powder cocaine, the law differentiated between the two substances: a person who

sells 500 grams of powder cocaine receives a mandatory five-year minimum sentence; a person who sells only five grams of crack cocaine receives a five-year sentence. The 1988 legislation is also notable for announcing the government's objective "to create a Drug-Free America by 1995." No significant piece of drug control was passed during President Bill Clinton's tenure, or during the George W. Bush administration through 2002.

Linkages of Drug Use to Ethnic Culture and Cultural Protest

As early as the nineteenth century drug addicts were identified with racial minorities. Chinese laborers, originally encouraged to emigrate to America to help build railroads, brought with them the custom of smoking opium. In the South cocaine use among blacks fueled white fears that under the drug's influence, black users were induced to commit crimes and sexually assault white women. No evidence existed to confirm such an effect, but it reinforced white insecurities about race relations. Unconfirmed allegations that cocaine empowered black users with extraordinary human strength also circulated among the white citizenry, and even local law enforcement officers were concerned about blacks acquiring superhuman powers. Convinced that .32-caliber bullets were not sufficiently powerful to bring down a "cocaine-crazed Negro," David F. Musto notes, some police switched to .38-caliber bullets (p. 7).

Morphine was not associated with an ethnic minority, according to drug historian David F. Musto, because it was used for medicinal purposes and therefore accepted by mainstream society. He does note, though, that when opiates began to be perceived as addictive, morphine was linked with "lower classes" and the "underworld."

A major factor in the enactment of the Marijuana Tax Act in 1937 was an increasing volume of complaints about Mexicans bringing marijuana across the border into the United States. Commissioner Anslinger also claimed that many jazz musicians were regular marijuana users, and he was convinced that provocative song titles such as "Sweet Marijuana Brown," "Reefer Song," and "The Funny Reefer Man" confirmed marijuana use within a jazz subculture. Later, in the 1960s, marijuana and a recently discovered hallucinogen called lysergic acid diethylamide, more popularly known as LSD, were closely identified as counterculture drugs. Marijuana and LSD in particular were used predominantly by hippie types, usually young people who protested conventional values and lifestyles. In the 1980s, blacks were again associated with cocaine in the form of crack, rather than powder cocaine.

Contemporary Patterns of Recreational Drug Use

Drug use is frequently determined by geography and the users' socioeconomic status. In the 1980s, crack cocaine use was more prevalent among inner-city black Americans because it was sold in smaller, cheaper quantities than powder cocaine. "Ice," a freebase form of methamphetamine, has been more popular in Hawaii and on the West Coast than in other regions, while "huffing," or glue sniffing, is more likely to occur among younger adolescents in rural areas where access to cocaine and heroin is more limited than in urban areas. Cocaine, which stimulates the central nervous system, is popular because it enhances alertness and produces euphoria, or a sense of well-being. In the late 1990s the hallucinogen MDMA (methylenedioxymethamphetamine), called Ecstasy or "X" on the street, gained popularity among young people who used it at "raves" because at low levels the potentially fatal drug was mildly intoxicating.

In spite of more severe state and federal penalties, educational programs such as Drug Abuse Resistance Education (D.A.R.E), the adoption of a zero-tolerance policy by many schools, and a $19 billion federal drug budget for fiscal year 2003, illicit drugs remained immensely popular in the early twenty-first century. Some indicators suggested that drug use generally appeared to be leveling off, but it was still a critical social problem. Estimates tend to vary according to research methodology, but in 2000 the Office of National Drug Control Policy (ONDCP) reported that millions of Americans used drugs, including an estimated 5.74 million who were chronic or occasional users of cocaine; 1.2 million who were chronic or occasional users of heroin; approximately 600,000 who used methamphetamines; and perhaps 12 million who smoked marijuana at least once a month. According to ONDCP figures, users spent an estimated $64 billion annually to consume 13 metric tons (1 metric ton is about 2,200 pounds) of heroin, 20 metric tons of methamphetamines, 259 metric tons of cocaine, and 1,047 metric tons of marijuana.

Illicit drug use is a complex phenomenon that should not be viewed as a one-dimensional problem. The ONDCP reported that nationwide in 2000 there were nearly 4 million persons over age twelve who needed but did not receive treatment for an illicit drug problem. One-fifth (21 percent) of state prison inmates and three-fifths (61 percent) of federal prison inmates are drug offenders. Health care costs, productivity losses, and other drug use–related expenses totaled more than $160 billion.

Research on drug use completed in the late 1990s and early 2000s provided mixed results. A 2001 National Household Survey on Drug Abuse found that the use of marijuana, cocaine, and other illegal drugs increased sharply among young Americans during the previous year. Perhaps more disturbing is that fewer young people regarded drug use as risky behavior. According to the University of Michigan's Monitoring the Future (MTF) survey of eighth, tenth, and twelfth graders, in 2001, fewer respondents in all three grades perceived using marijuana once or twice a week to be harmful than the same grades ten years earlier in 1991.

Drugs were everywhere. At least it seemed so. According to an August 2002 survey conducted by the National Center on Addiction and Substance Abuse (CASA), teenagers said marijuana was easier to buy than cigarettes or beer. More than one-quarter (27 percent) of the 1,000 teenagers polled said they could find it in an hour or less. For the first time since CASA began the survey in 1996, marijuana was the easiest of the "major" drugs to access.

However, there was reason for optimism. The 2002 MTF survey indicated that illicit drug use among eighth, tenth, and twelfth graders "remained stable or decreased in some cases." This finding was confirmed when 63 percent of the respondents felt their schools were drug-free, suggesting that educational programs were having a positive impact.

See also: Drinking, Prohibition and Temperance, Raves/Raving, Smoking, Teenage Leisure Trends

BIBLIOGRAPHY

Brecher, Edward M. *Licit and Illicit Drugs: The Consumers Union Report on Narcotics, Stimulants, Depressants, Inhalants, Hallucinogens, and Marijuana—Including Caffeine, Nicotine, and Alcohol.* Boston: Little, Brown and Company, 1972.

Chatterjee, Sumana. "More Young People Using Illegal Drugs, Survey Finds." *Philadelphia Inquirer* (13 September 2002): A3.

Courtwright, David T. *Dark Paradise: Opiate Addiction in America Before 1940.* Cambridge, Mass.: Harvard University Press, 1982.

"Drug Use Trends Fact Sheet." Office of National Drug Control Policy, NCJ 190780. Washington, D.C., 2000.

"High School and Youth Trends." National Institute of Drug Abuse. Washington, D.C.: United States Department of Health and Human Services. Available from http://www.nida.nib.gov/.

Inciardi, James A. *The War on Drugs: Heroin, Cocaine, Crime, and Public Policy.* Palo Alto, Calif.: Mayfield Publishing Company, 1986.

McWilliams, John C. *The Protectors: Harry J. Anslinger and the Federal Bureau of Narcotics.* Newark: University of Delaware Press, 1990.

Morgan, H. Wayne. *Drugs in America: A Social History, 1800–1980.* Syracuse, N.Y.: Syracuse University Press, 1981.

Musto, David F. *The American Disease: Origins of Narcotic Control.* New York: Oxford University Press, 1973.

"National Drug Control Strategy," Washington, D.C.: U.S. Government Printing Office, 2002.

Toppo, Greg. "Teens: Marijuana Easy to Get." *Philadelphia Inquirer* (21 August 2002): A3.

Weil, Andrew. "Why People Take Drugs." In *The American Drug Scene: An Anthology.* Edited by James A. Inciardi and Karen McElrath. Los Angeles: Roxbury Publishing Company, 1995.

John C. McWilliams

RECREATIONAL FIGHTING

"Recreational fighting" (RF) designates group battles fought with fists, stones, or sticks, and prohibiting more lethal weapons. As with organized sports, RF has rules of "fairness." Here men fight for "fun" or for "honor" rather than for material gain; this article compares instances of RF in Ireland, the American frontier, and two other societies. Although it is not known why RF arose in these societies and not in others, one notices a similarity of motivation in these groups of fighters. It is left to sociologists to determine how much RF contributes to battles that continue to rage between rival street gangs.

Faction Fights in Rural Ireland in the Nineteenth Century

These public fights were common in Ireland from 1800 to 1880, despite strong disapproval of civil and religious authorities. Unlike contemporary gang fights, older men joined in these contests with the same enthusiasm as their sons. The group battles reflected rivalries between extended families, towns, or parishes. Yet the only reasons for these men to fight were that it was traditional and they enjoyed it. The emphasis on "fighting for fun" is clear in accounts of witnesses recorded in court records, where fighting had led to charges of homicide. In reviewing records of 800 rural homicide trials, Carolyn Conley noted that while judges urged juries to prosecute those who killed a neighbor (usually with a stout oak club called a *shillelagh*), the juries argued that because combatants had entered freely into the battles, none should be punished for the unfortunate accidents.

Fights began at public events—parties, weddings, wakes—but most often at seasonal fairs. At the notorious "Donnybrook Fair" faction fights were expected events. After preliminary combat with shillelaghs by captains of two factions, all-out battles between dozens or even hundreds of combatants would last all afternoon. As drinking induced a convivial mood within one faction, the bonding among friends enhanced their readiness to battle with the other faction. Yet their mood was not one of anger. The fight is seen as a kind of play, with rules of restraint: a larger group does not attack a much smaller group; weapons are meant to be sticks and stones; knives and scythes are expressly forbidden. The problem was that when a family member was injured before one's eyes, the urge to retaliate created a new and angry mood. It is likely that preparation for fighting by drinking whiskey dissolved the fear of such injuries.

The American Frontier: More Recreational Fighting

RF was also prominent among loggers on the northern frontier during the nineteenth century. Drinking and fighting by loggers was associated with end-of-season sprees in towns whose sleazy entertainment was geared up for the sudden invasion of men with pent-up emotions and money to spend. One writer recalls:

> The jacks swaggered along the wooden sidewalks, marching, singing and shouting from one saloon to the next. When one brigade confronted another there was a moment's hesitation, after which there might be either a joyous reunion or a pitched battle. Even the reunions quickly degenerated into the all-too-common "free fights" in which twenty or more shanty boys would have at it in a so-called "friendly" battle. After the dust had settled, they all became buddies. (Kilar)

J. C. Frolicher tells of a battle at a party between two groups of loggers who respond to intervention in the same manner described of faction fighters: when local farmers try to break up the brawl, both groups turn on them, heaving them through windows. Afterwards, they escort their dates home like perfect gentlemen.

Football Hooliganism as Recreational Fighting

While there was no faction fighting in England or Ireland, what we have to compare in the twentieth century is football-related gang violence. In the early 2000s, it was English (rather than Irish) footfall fans that had a reputation for fighting for fun. An "anthropological" study by

Armstrong (1998) that reported on a working-class gang in Sheffield called "the Blades." From his account, the rivalry between the Blades and their city rivals, the Owls, didn't involve issues of race, class difference, money, or drugs (as do many U.S. gang rivalries). As with faction fighting, these confrontations were "for fun." In addition, Armstrong noted that women expected and rewarded this violence—they were prominent among the onlookers for whom the fighting "dramas" were staged.

Like faction fights, these gang battles were meant to be "fair:" the use of knives and guns was prohibited, as was having many combatants gang up on just one (or a few) opponents. While posturing with verbal insults and gestures occurred when gangs met, such encounters were usually free of violence, since police were on the watch whenever large groups gathered. Leaders of the two gangs had to confer in order to designate a battleground that was free from police surveillance. When such fights happened, a gang leader was likely to intervene if one of his own disciples attacked a younger or smaller opponent. Before a battle could even happen, it had to be agreed upon by both parties, and it stopped when one side gave up. Armstrong's long list of rituals involved in selecting targets and in escalating aggression stressed the game-like context of those fights and the inhibition of pure impulsiveness or anger.

Brawling Venetians During the Renaissance

Another cultural institution that bore resemblance to Irish faction fighting is described by Robert Davis in *The War of the Fists* (1994). By the fifteenth century, two major factions in Venice battled routinely throughout the year for control of certain bridges over the canals. Those bridges (rather than fairgrounds or bleachers) became public stages on which young men engaged in vigorous battles for the sake of "honor," public approbation, and raucous fun. The battles at first included some nobles (and even priests), who fought with sharp sticks and wore armor as added protection. After 1570, the use of sticks was abandoned in favor of fistic combat. The doffing of armor made the fights affordable to a large variety of working men (sailors, fishermen, gondoliers) and artisans, who joined neighborhood brigades under the banner of one major faction or the other.

Like Irish faction fights, emotions escalated during preliminary one-on-one matches between representatives of each faction held in the middle of a bridge. Those preliminary fist fights provided some comic relief, as one or more fighters were usually tripped or butted into the canal—a defeat that was much worse than being bloodied while standing one's ground. Like the Irish fights,

group fights in Venice included a great deal of stone throwing. Despite the mad, headlong rushes over the bridges by the two sides, Venetians prohibited the use of knives and other weapons to strictly enforce "fairness."

Large crowds, including nobles and government officials, rewarded these fighters with wild approval. The honor accruing to group captains (*padrin*) could elevate the status of a working man and allow him entrance into a higher social echelon (as a guest). That increased prestige apparently was an effective reward for accepting such battering. On the other hand, fear of being shamed—even from one's own family—motivated young men to accept hard punishment. Davis quoted a contemporary:

> "The losers . . . are so humiliated that there are those who do not even dare to return to their houses, because their women folk will sometimes close their doors to them and drive them away, reproaching them for their cowardice with such terms as 'Away from here, dishonorable, ignominious pig! '"

The Psychology of Fighting for Fun

In the above examples of RF, social bonding is stressed as a basis for aggression, rather than a breakdown of social rules by hot-headed individuals. The motives of these fighters are relatively pure: they *enjoy* fighting. They are rewarded by the excitement of onlookers and by the inherent pleasure of executing physical skills. Although a keen rivalry with similar groups is often felt, RF does not depend upon hatred of the rival, or even anger amidst the fray. If one proposes that adult fighting can be a form of play, one must ask how fighting can be enjoyable—as a quotation from one British hooligan dramatically affirms:

> "Most people can't understand how it could possibly be fun to be punched, booted and battered and to have bottles and stones thrown at you, but, believe me, I've experienced it and when you're in the thick of the action, even sex doesn't come close to the feeling of being hyped up." (Guilianotti)

It is common knowledge that participants in rough sports (as well as other risky activities) experience a so-called "adrenaline rush" during their confrontations with danger. There is much evidence implicating the release in the braneurotransmitter dopamine (DA) during activities that are intrinsically rewarding. Moreover, Van Erps and Miczek report a release of DA in the brains of rats who have attacked an intruder rat. Thus, DA release may produce this rewarding adrenaline rush during fighting. (In fact, to take that one step further, it can be suggested that since DA release provides a "pleasurable high," frequent fighting may in fact lead to an actual addiction in the same manner that—as psychiatrists have proposed—gambling and sexual activity can be addictive.)

See also: Blood Sports; Boxing

BIBLIOGRAPHY

Armstrong, Gary. *Football Hooligans: Knowing the Score.* Oxford and New York: Berg Press, 1998.

Conley, Carolyn. "The Agreeable Recreation of Fighting." *Journal of Social History* 33 (Fall 1999): 57–72.

Davis, Robert C. *The War of the Fists: Popular Culture and Public Violence in Late Renaissance Venice.* New York: Oxford University Press, 1994.

Frolicher, J. C. "Lumberjack Fights." *Four L Lumber News* 10, no. 43 (1928).

Guilianotti, Richard. "Ungentlemanly Conduct: Football Hooligans, the Media and the Construction of Notoriety." *Football Studies.* 1, no. 2 (August 1998).

Kilar, Jeremy W.. "Great Lakes Timber Towns and Frontier Violence: A Comparative Study." *Journal of Forest History* 31 (April 1987): 71–85.

Panskepp, Jaak. *Affective Neuroscience: The Foundations of Human and Animal Emotions.* New York: Oxford University Press, 1998.

Pellis, Sergio M., and Andrew N. Iwaniuk "Adult-Adult Play in Primates: Comparative Analyses of Its Origin, Distribution and Evolution." *Ethology* 106 (2000): 1083–1104.

David Ingle

RECREATIONAL VEHICLES

The recreational vehicle (RV) is so familiar to travelers on America's highways that few people pay attention to them. But its taken-for-granted state masks fascinating cultural phenomena. An RV on the road may contain a family on vacation, or a family with children who live on the road full-time. It could be the only residence of a retired couple who are visiting their children, or a vehicle rented by European tourists out to "see" North America. It may be the home of an itinerant worker headed for a pipeline, or the temporary "house" of volunteers headed to a Habitat for Humanity work site.

Recreational Vehicles: What They Are

While sizes and shapes vary enormously, recreational vehicles can all be towed, hauled, or driven, generally without a special license. Further, they are all designed to be on the move and to require no specialized equipment to make them mobile. Most recreational vehicles are "self-contained," meaning that they carry supplies of water, have holding tanks for sewage and waste water, and have integral systems for electric power, heat, cooking, and sanitation. These features distinguish RVs from other vehicles and structures, such as "mobile homes" (once called "house trailers," but now called "manufactured houses"), which are not, except in the narrowest sense, "trailers" at all, and are not "mobile" once they are delivered. The point of *recreational* vehicles, after all, is that they can be used to take their occupants to places where they can have recreation. The places where this happens and the ways that Americans use their RVs are what make them worthy of comment.

There are more than 9 million RVs in North America. They are on the roads, parked in driveways, or hooked up to facilities in RV parks. They are also found parked with no facilities in the desert or on roadside pullouts—RVers call this "boondocking." The category RV includes vehicles of various shapes and sizes: campers that slide onto the beds of pickup trucks; motor homes of all sizes; trailers of all types, including pull trailers, fifth-wheels, and the pop-up trailer. Many RVers see themselves as heirs of those who crossed North America in covered wagons. Indeed, one of the first commercially built travel trailers was named the "Covered Wagon" and looked a bit like a small Conestoga wagon on rubber tires. A contemporary fifth-wheel trailer bears the name "Prairie Schooner."

Modern RVers think of themselves, too, as the embodiment of freedom and independence, and many play with pioneer images as they travel. Caravans of RVs are often led by a "wagon-master," for instance, and folks at rallies of the Wally Byam Caravan Club (Airstream owners) may dress in period costume and park in a circle — circling the wagons. This practice allows them to enclose their social space and form a temporary community that keeps out others.

Any adult who has ever taken a long automobile road trip with small children can understand the attraction of an RV. They have comfortable seats, tables at which games can be played, onboard toilet facilities, and entertainment facilities that may include a TV and VCR. Families can pull off the road at will for a snack, a rest, or just to explore an interesting path or trail. All these factors help to account for the popularity of owning or renting recreational vehicles for family vacations. Those who use RVs this way argue that the vehicle makes traveling an enjoyable part of the trip, recreation in itself, and that the

Early RV Enthusiasts. In 1959 a family camps in Carson National Forest's Santa Barbara Campground with an early-model camper. Trailers such as this one were one of the earliest types of RV and made it easier for the average family to take up camping. © *Bluford W. Muir/Corbis*

cost of buying or renting the vehicle and fueling it is off-set by the lowered cost of accommodation and meals.

Retirement and Full-Time Recreation

The second half of the twentieth century witnessed the emergence of a new social form—retirement—whose possibilities were still being explored. Increasing numbers of people in good health, with twenty or more years of healthy life expectancy and adequate financial resources, are excluded from traditional paid employment. Nothing in history has prepared either the people experiencing retirement or the society in which they live for this development. Many of these people must literally re-create themselves. Some accomplish this through volunteering in their communities, through continuing education, or through part-time paid work. Some have found that full-time life on the road in a recreational vehicle provides them

with a satisfying way to "be retired." While there are no hard figures, there are estimates that as many as 2 million people in North America—most of them retired—live as "full-timers." That is, their motor homes or trailers are their only homes—many refer to their RVs as "my house." While they may have a "home base" for mail delivery and legal residence, these individuals are essentially nomads, staying nowhere more than a few months before moving on. While these people, like their more sedentary fellow retirees, may give additional meaning to their lives through volunteering or part-time work, they do it as part of a floating community largely invisible to ordinary mainstream society. The full-timer's RV is not only his or her home, it is a passport to re-creation in the broadest sense.

If they are a couple whose children and grandchildren are scattered from coast to coast or north to south, the RV is their temporary apartment in the children's community. They can be neighbors for a month, take the grandchildren fishing, or camping, or to the zoo. And they will not be house guests. They will awake each morning in their own beds, follow their own morning rituals, and retire to bed when they choose.

If they are interested in continuing education, there are Elderhostel programs that make space available for participants with their own accommodation on wheels. Alternatively, their recreation in retirement may involve traveling to trace their genealogies, or to find where their ancestors are buried, or to visit all the states within the United States or all the provinces of Canada. They may want to experience hands-on history in Revolutionary or Civil War battlefields, or in national parks and monuments.

They may spend a winter on a guided caravan to Baja California with other RVers, or they may simply join a community of friends met on the road and "boondock" for the winter in the Arizona desert on lands set aside for the purpose by the U.S. Bureau of Land Management. In such places they will participate with their neighbors in potluck suppers, learn crafts, go on hikes, visit casinos, go fishing, or even become vendors in flea markets. In summer, they may volunteer as hosts in a National Forest or provincial campground and do their own traveling when there are not so many tourists on the road.

Some full-time RVers organize their lives by whim, moving from place to place as fancy strikes—mountains in the summer, desert in the winter. Some are free spirits who make no plans until they arrive at a crossroads, where they then decide in which direction to travel next. Others make more formal arrangements, and enhance their recreation with memberships in RV clubs that provide structured rallies and other services (such as voice mail and mail forwarding) or even parks that are exclusively for the use of their members.

Whether they are re-creating themselves or only seeking temporary recreation at some destination, the people who use RVs have created a new cultural form combining travel, recreation, and home—even if only temporary—that is particularly appropriate to North America, with its vast distances, and a quintessential product of the twentieth century.

See also: Automobiles and Leisure; Tourism

BIBLIOGRAPHY

Bernhagen, Stephanie. *Take Back Your Life! Travel Full-Time in an RV.* Livingston, Tex.: Bernham-Collins, 2000.

Counts, Dorothy Ayers, and David R. Counts. *Over the Next Hill: An Ethnography of RVing Seniors in North America.* 2d ed. Peterborough, Ontario: Broadview Press, 2001.

Hall, Jamie, and Alice Zyetz, eds. *RV Traveling Tales: Women's Journeys on the Open Road.* Livingston, Tex.: Pine Country Publishing, 2002.

Hofmeister, Ron, and Barb Hofmeister. *Move'n On: Living and Traveling Full-Time in a Recreational Vehicle.* 3d ed. Livingston, Tex.: R and B Publications, 1999.

Peterson, Kay. *Home Is Where You Park It.* Revised ed. Livingston, Tex.: RoVers Press, 1982.

Thornburg, David A. *Galloping Bungalows: The Rise and Demise of the American House Trailer.* Hamden, Conn.: Archon Books, 1991.

David R. Counts and Dorothy Ayers Counts

REGIONAL LEISURE LIFESTYLES

See *Southern Leisure Lifestyles; Western Leisure Lifestyles*

REGULATION AND SOCIAL CONTROL OF LEISURE

All societies attempt some regulation of recreation and leisure, often through a combination of legislation and community pressure. In Western Europe, for example, attempts to limit popular participation in rough ball games—the forerunners of later football—go back to the Middle Ages, where royal decrees lamented frequent injury and even loss of life (without, however, much effect in restraining the pastime). Concerns about safety or morality frequently join with other motives. Regulating leisure may be a matter of social class, with one group attempting to discipline its inferiors; or a question of generation, with rules designed to keep youth in check. Gender factors, particularly in terms of restricting women's recreations, also exist. Larger anxieties about preserving public order, especially in those forms of leisure that involve crowds and high emotion, and about maintaining capacity for work frequently underlie the patterns of social control.

American history has gone through three main periods in terms of the regulation of recreation and leisure. During the two centuries of colonial settlement, when community controls predominated, moral concerns most obviously shaped efforts to restrain certain forms of leisure activity. But there was considerable regional variation because religious affiliations varied from Puritan New England to the more latitudinarian southern colonies; and disciplining slaves and Indians also created concerns. A high moralistic content did not disappear with the advent of a new nation and the stirrings of industrialization and urbanization. Indeed, many analysts would argue that a moralistic impulse defines a distinctive American approach to leisure even to the present day. But the leisure regulations of the nineteenth century, the period often called "Victorian," did move away from colonial patterns, attempting some important new limitations but also accepting certain new latitudes. The key leisure problems changed with the advent of industrial cities and growing immigrant populations. The Victorian period began to yield, in turn, during the decades between 1920 and the 1950s. The effort at Prohibition was at once a last gasp of extreme Victorianism and an opening to new approaches. A third pattern of social control emerged fairly clearly by the second half of the twentieth century.

The Colonial Period

The American colonists who attempted to set rules for recreation came from a Europe that was tightening its approaches to popular leisure. There are many indications, in sixteenth- and seventeenth-century Europe, of growing upper-class disapproval of many popular pastimes, which seemed to threaten the appropriate social hierarchy and good manners alike. European gentry, who had once participated actively in popular festivals, enjoying the coarseness of rough games and bawdy dances and even tolerating symbolic mockings of the powerful, began to pull away. Protestantism was in a sense part of this process, introducing a new note of seriousness, for example, into the keeping of the Sabbath and often attempting to curtail dancing and other frivolities. But there were similar attempts in Catholic regions, partly in response to the Protestant threat.

Many American colonial leaders participated, or sought to participate, in this broad early modern process of greater social control. But they also had to contend with weak governments, whose reach was frequently challenged by frontier communities, and with unusual racial diversity. The combination resulted in some distinctive American themes and in the unusual regional variation.

Puritan New England was particularly active in attempts to limit leisure through legal means along with strong community pressures. A variety of laws and religious sanctions sought to outlaw gambling, card playing, dancing, and other amusements deemed dangerous to morality. Enforcement of the Sabbath as a day of worship

and rest was particularly strict. Puritan zeal should be not exaggerated. Puritans were quite tolerant of certain forms of enjoyment, such as drinking. Overall, however, the moral criteria were rigorous. Some would outlast the colonial period, picking up backing from other groups (including, in some regulatory areas, Irish American Catholics). Sabbath restrictions, for example, continued in many states into the mid-twentieth century.

Other regions in colonial America contrasted with the Puritan approach. The South, particularly, saw much greater tolerance of roughhousing and gambling, and a number of violent games persisted well into the nineteenth century. Moral concerns did emerge. By the later eighteenth century, many upper-class southerners were withdrawing their support from popular violence, setting up standards of respectability (though, on the whole, fewer outright laws) not dissimilar to those of New England. Groups in some of the middle colonies, such as Philadelphia Quakers, were also active in the moral regulation of leisure, again including constraints on Sabbath activities. Specific laws and a more general sense of the validity of moral controls over leisure activities constituted a colonial legacy to later periods in American history.

The Industrial Age

Developments in the nineteenth century did not totally unseat colonial forms of leisure regulation. The strong moralistic current continued to inform many American reactions, and this preserved some contact with earlier Puritan strictures. On the whole, however, both motives and forms of leisure regulation changed in the nineteenth century. For example, popular drinking came in for anguished comment, and a great deal of newfound moralism, in ways Puritans had not imagined. A battle between forces of order and respectability, and popular leisure interests, became more acute at this point than either before or after.

A number of innovations spurred new concerns, and they were intertwined. In the first place, the gradual surge of industrialization forced a reconsideration of various popular recreations that seemed to interfere with regular and intensified work. This new attitude was a standard part of the industrialization process wherever it occurred. It happened at roughly the same time in Britain and Western Europe, and would happen again later in Japan and Soviet Russia. Factory labor required punctuality and group coordination. It required assiduous attention to the operations and regularities of machines. Habits of wandering around, chatting, and even singing on the job were now seen as anathema, strenuously opposed by shop rules and fines. Of course, irregular leisure habits that encroached on regular starting times, or that threatened consistent operation of expensive commitment for the sake of occasional festivals, had to be combated. Factory owners set out to discipline the labor force in new ways, and many older leisure habits were among the first victims of the process.

In reaction to the forces of control, many early industrial workers quit their jobs; others went home to the countryside during harvest periods, in part to find a bit of respite from industrial discipline and to recover some personal leisure time. Precisely because some group leisure forms were regulated, many workers clung all the more vigorously to personal escape; drinking, for instance, loomed larger in popular leisure during the industrialization period in part because other options were scaled back.

Along with industrialization, urban growth spurred concerns about certain popular leisure traditions. Crowds that might seem innocuous in the countryside, because they were small and isolated, took on a different air in cities, where popular rioting might threaten. Newly formed urban police forces spent an immense amount of time seeking to regulate popular leisure and enforce restrictions, mainly in protection of real or imagined threats to public order.

Urban pressures were another standard feature of the industrialization process, but in the United States they received additional impetus from the patterns of immigration that, by the 1840s, were bringing new numbers of Irish, Germans, and French Canadians and that, later on, would involve massive numbers from Eastern and Southern Europe. Immigrant leisure habits easily seemed more menacing or vulgar than popular leisure habits in general.

Finally, partly in reaction to new aversions to urban crowds and immigrant masses, a growing American middle class held itself up as a beacon of respectability defined in part in terms of restrained leisure tastes. Even as political democracy spread, as least for free males, the democracy of manners was increasingly challenged. From the late eighteenth century onward, middle-class children were schooled in the importance of being able to avoid unseemly display, to discipline body movements, and to engage in worthy forms of leisure such as piano playing for girls and uplifting reading for both genders. Respectable leisure, in this image, should contribute to the family's social standing, to the cohesion of the family itself, and to the promotion of good work habits. Leisure that smacked of vulgarity or merely letting off steam was roundly condemned. Part of this respectability current

merely reinforced broader efforts to encourage more diligent and regular work or to provide a more vigorous basis for criticizing immigrant groups.

But there were other components as well. Leisure that involved cruelty to animals, for example, was now reproved, for it seemed wrong on its face and also risked rousing animal passions in onlookers. New regulations sought to outlaw cock fighting and other traditional pastimes—though often the result was merely to drive these activities underground. There was new appreciation of European refinement as well, in an American middle class that was increasingly wealthy but unsure of its social graces. Here, particularly, was a reason to scorn rural and frontier leisure as uncouth.

Industrialization, urbanism, and the push for immigrant respectability provided powerful incentives for a variety of specific contests about leisure during the nineteenth century. The workplace itself was one. By the second generation of industrial workers, employers reported growing success in instilling a modern time sense and a reduction of older recreational combinations with work—like group singing. Attempts to prevent workers from drinking on the job were tougher. Certain work contexts—like office work—made attempts to limit chatting more difficult than others. On the whole, however, a clear separation between work and leisure was a key result of nineteenth-century regulatory efforts, and the distinction was new.

Attacks on gambling particularly illustrated the hold of middle-class beliefs on the social control effort. Most states and localities sought to bar gambling, on grounds that it offered dreams of rewards for no effort and drained the pockets of the poor. A good bit of police time was devoted to gambling prevention, often in poor and immigrant neighborhoods and with incomplete results.

Urban space was another contest area. Conflicts arose over the use of the new public parks, for example. Many working-class and immigrant groups, including German Americans, saw parks as a chance for group gatherings that might generate considerable noise, some roughhousing, and opportunities for beer consumption—in other words, they sought to transpose traditional recreational elements into new space. Middle-class opposition was fierce, on grounds that parks should provide opportunities for safe and sedate leisure and contacts with nature. Rules for park use usually represented the middle-class view. In another case, new ideas about juvenile delinquency typically criminalized minor acts of vandalism that had traditionally been seen as recreational expressions on the part of young men.

Control of urban leisure space was not just a matter of rules and laws. Respectability codes greatly influenced the kinds of public leisure in which "good" women could participate, keeping taverns but also many sports venues beyond their reach. Long, constraining dress styles also inhibited leisure activities for middle-class women.

The growing interest in sports provided opportunities for direct regulation and also outlets that might facilitate the wider interest in disciplining leisure. Many middle-class leaders, for example in schools and settlement houses, believed that sports could help distract urban youth from other, more destructive leisure habits, including vandalism. At the same time, sports themselves became more structured. Fixed rules and refereeing were applied to many sports that had previously been more casual and sporadically violent. Sports in this way came to resemble the features of modern work. Spontaneity and roughhousing were discouraged. Some whole sports hung on the edge of acceptability; boxing drew great interest, including from middle-class audiences, but it was also fiercely debated because of its violence, and stricter rules were recurrently introduced to limit the sport.

In the later nineteenth century, many middle-class leaders faced increased concerns because of new waves of immigrants and sheer urban growth. The interest that some middle-class people took in participating in working-class leisure, for its liveliness and earthiness, seemed to threaten the social control effort. A key response (and not only in the United States) was the creation of "red light" districts in cities, generally for workers and men. In these districts, bars, prostitution, and gambling were allowed fairly free expression, with minimal police interference. The hope was that other city neighborhoods could remain free of these activities. This was a major compromise, seeking control but now recognizing that some people—like certain immigrants—could not be prevented from recreational excess.

There were also new successes to record in the battle for leisure respectability. By the early twentieth century, middle-class rules of decorum increasingly prevailed in the new movie houses. Early movie audiences were often loud and raucous, but house rules increasingly disciplined spectators to passive silence—an achievement that has largely persisted to the present day.

The long war against working-class drinking also came to a head. Temperance campaigns had formed one of the recurrent battlegrounds in nineteenth-century social control efforts since the 1830s, pitting middle-class reformers (including, by the 1860s, many women eager to curb male recreational success) against many workers, immigrants, and brewery interests. Regulation of tavern hours and some statewide prohibitions had dotted the campaign, and, by 1916, nineteen states had passed prohibition laws, but the impact was modest. Amid growing fears of popular excess, Congress in 1917 passed a constitutional amendment requiring nationwide prohibition; the amendment was fully ratified two years later, taking effect in 1920. This triumph of social control has often been judged a failure, because widespread liquor smuggling combined with more open middle-class and women's drinking during the 1920s, until in 1933 Prohibition was repealed. In fact, however, Prohibition, along with the larger measures of industrial discipline, did significantly alter working-class leisure patterns. The ubiquity of neighborhood bars was never revived. Other aspects of tavern-based leisure, including frequent brawls, also declined dramatically. The industrial age ended with substantial success for the forces of respectability, clouded by the inability to sustain the explicit regulatory thrust.

The Twentieth Century

On the whole, the nineteenth-century approach to leisure regulation extended into the 1930s, and then for another two decades depression and war distracted from major new commitments to leisure pursuits. Gradually, however, and then decisively during the 1950s, a new climate developed, in which many previous efforts at social and legal control fell by the wayside. To many observers, the idea of social control over American leisure seemed a contradiction in terms. This was not, in fact, the case, but it was true that control efforts for the most part moved toward more subtle mechanisms.

Three major developments, again intertwined, changed the regulatory climate. First, the pursuit of leisure and pleasure became increasingly open and approved. In 1951, sociologist Martha Wolfenstein wrote a perceptive article on the leisure ethic, arguing that from early childhood onward, Americans were being pushed toward a search for enjoyment. Employment and school applications began to include sections on leisure interests, with the clear implication that a person lacking some defendable recreational interests was deficient. In this climate, blatant efforts to control leisure on grounds, for example, that it might interfere with work became less plausible. Gender-specific leisure rules also declined in this context.

Commercial interests supporting a variety of leisure activities also became increasingly powerful, easily surpassing the powers of saloon and brewery interests that had attempted to block Prohibition. Giant media, music, and movie companies, in particular, steadily pressed against regulations of public taste that might inhibit the commercial appeal of radio shows, films, and later television. They were not always successful, but their impact was undeniably vigorous.

Finally, landmark court rulings in the 1950s made it clear that constitutional freedom of speech provisions applied to consumer leisure, blocking most attempts at censorship except to an extent where child audiences were involved. One historian has aptly termed the new legal climate the "repeal of reticence." More generally, the widespread (if, in fact, overlysimple) belief that Prohibition had not only failed but proved counterproductive in encouraging new drinking habits made legislators wary of attempting to regulate public morality in many of the ways that had been standard during the nineteenth century. With leisure, many Americans came to believe—whether in praise or in blame—that they had entered a period in which anything goes. From the 1950s onward, each new decade seemed to bring new latitudes in the lyrics permitted in popular music, the amount of flesh that could be exposed in movies or on television, and the language that could be used in the same media. By the century's end, the advent of violent computer games and pornographic uses of the Internet added new technological venues to what had become an established trend.

Yet the theme of social control did not disappear. In fact, by the end of the twentieth century, Americans had considerably more restricted leisure lives than did Western Europeans or Japanese, their colleagues in advanced industrial societies. Topless beaches for women, standard in Europe, were severely limited in the United States. Sexually explicit television and the use of nudity in advertising were similarly less restrained in Europe. The availability of leisure time, expanding in Europe and even work-oriented Japan, may actually have been diminishing for many Americans. Whatever the common impression, and despite undeniably significant relaxations in standards, various social controls persisted or were newly introduced.

Some staple regulations, introduced in the nineteenth century, simply remained, often with some intensification. Prohibitions against mistreatment of animals for entertainment purposes were extended, with growing protests, for example, against some standard circus routines. Some of the same thinking now applied to humans with particular misfortunes. A combination of legislation and changes in public taste gradually wiped out the freak shows that had bedecked circuses and county fairs into the early twentieth century, for people with disabilities or deformities were no longer appropriate game for the entertainment industry.

Effors to Regulate Children's Leisure

In a climate of growing leisure permissiveness, efforts to regulate children's leisure gained increasing salience in the twentieth century. Here was a clear new response to the changing leisure trends. The most ambitious efforts characteristically failed, but they revealed a strong social control impulse that did restrain commercial vendors and that did feed a more successful attempt to instill internal controls in many children as they were socialized for adulthood.

The early twentieth century saw a growing interest in controlling children's access to city streets at night, to protect them against overstimulation and irregular leisure habits. The idea of applying curfews specifically to children was new, and it spread from the 1880s onward. Cities like Chicago joined the parade in the 1920s. By 2001, 80 percent of all American cities with populations over 30,000 had juvenile curfew restrictions.

In the same period, from 1900 onward, a seemingly endless sequence of efforts to regulate the media available to children took shape. Middle-class magazines and various experts took up a crusade against comic strips, on grounds they promoted violence and hostility to authority. By the 1920s, radio and the movies drew anguished attention from parent and school groups. Attempts to boycott sponsors of radio shows that presumably played on children's emotions made little headway, as did outright regulatory proposals, though radio networks periodically promised to clean up their shows. Movies seemed still more dangerous to children's character, and a host of scientific studies by the 1920s purported to demonstrate their contribution to juvenile delinquency and excessive nervousness. The 1950s saw a renewed crusade against comic books, because of their appeals to violence and sensuality, again with claims of direct links to juvenile crime. Television violence drew attacks by the 1950s also, with parents urged to regulate children's viewing habits. Rock music was the menace of choice in the 1980s, with appeals for industry self-regulation or possible legislation. Video games were another 1980s target, while the spread of the Internet drew concern in the 1990s.

None of the various crusades rolled back the clock on explicit images available to child audiences, at least more than temporarily. Concerns about movies did generate a new Hollywood code in which the industry did pull back on sexual imagery while regulating scenes of violence such that, for example, a shooter or a victim could be shown, but never both in the same scene and never with blood. The code was progressively abandoned after the mid-1950s. Other campaigns generated the movie ratings system, in which children were presumably barred from some films outright and allowed into some others only with adult accompaniment. Sexually explicit magazines were pulled from grocery and convenience store shelves, thanks to a 1980s campaign, and available only in concealing wrappers elsewhere. By the 1990s, Internet and cable TV access could be regulated by parents through use of control devices on the equipment that would block certain forms of access. These regulations, however, were modest at best and were not always enforced.

The more important impact of the regulatory efforts involved the many parents who followed up the warnings with efforts at their own regulations in the home. They involved the children who, as a result, learned at least some distinctions between "good" and "bad" leisure, distinctions that could carry over into adult self-control in the leisure field. They involved some constraints on the leisure industry, both to limit certain kinds of fare that might draw more pronounced regulation, and to provide leisure alternatives that would avoid the regulatory brickbats altogether. Leisure companies like Walt Disney made much of their fortune by providing entertainments that parents could count on as healthy and uplifting.

For the availability of dubious leisure outlets, and the many hortatory campaigns against them, produced a growing effort by experts, adults, and many vendors to produce recreational activities for children that would help them in school, later work, and general character development while, of course, keeping them away from excessive exposure to the lures of violence and sex. The idea of training children for leisure gained ground rapidly after World War I. A new interest in hobbies followed from this impulse in the 1920s and 1930s. Children or adults who collected stamps or built model radios were using leisure to good effect, honing skills that might look good on applications or that could carry directly onto constructive adult leisure.

Sponsorship of music or sports lessons was another outlet, and many parents and schools joined in the wider effort to provide guided leisure experiences for children. A host of camps arose to teach children these skills and at the same time keep them away from the dreaded alternatives that might lead to delinquency during potentially idle summers. Parents whose children did not show healthy leisure interests or talents were easily made to feel deficient. From the 1920s onward, reports of overprogrammed middle-class children surfaced recurrently. These were children for whom leisure was a task (though possibly also enjoyable) and for whom spontaneity was largely excluded, as well as children who were simply too busy for TV or other less-regulated outlets. By the 1990s,

parental efforts, including that new breed called soccer moms, had actually succeeded in reducing TV watching by middle-class children. Correspondingly, American educators and government authorities placed great reliance on character-building campaigns to get children to "just say no" to leisure activities that might cause trouble, including drink, drugs, and sexual activity.

Beyond childhood, leisure regulation in the later twentieth century was more limited or subtle, partly, of course, because of the hope that children properly raised would carry self-control into adult choices. There were, however, several areas in which explicit regulation continued or even expanded. Safety was one. It was perfectly legitimate, in twentieth-century culture, to regulate leisure on safety grounds. Compared to counterparts in other countries, American parks were filled with railings and other restraints, as well as warning signs. Aided by increasingly expensive equipment, but also more stringent rules and referees, sports activities were regulated with safety in mind. Some of this applied particularly to children. After an exaggerated scare in 1981, spontaneous trick or treating was largely eliminated from Halloween, in favor of careful adult chaperonage lest children receive poisoned candy. Dodge ball, once a rough playground sport, was increasingly regulated to prevent bruising. But adult leisure habits could be regulated on grounds of safety concerns as well. The most noteworthy instance was the active campaign against drinking and driving organized from the 1980s onward, which did play a role in reducing adult alcohol consumption.

Health was another legitimate target. After great debate, complicated by huge pressures from tobacco companies, smoking became a recreational habit that could be heavily regulated, from the 1980s onward. In this and other areas, the concept of addiction, which had gained attention and range of application from the 1930s onward, promoted both educational campaigns and outright regulation. The idea was that a minority of adults might fixate so intensely on some substance or pastime that they would lose the capacity for rational control and therefore they needed some combination of warning and regulation. Addiction concepts were applied to substances like nicotine and alcohol, but also to recreations like gambling. The result was great debate about restricting certain kinds of access and a series of warnings about symptoms of addiction that could serve social control purposes directly for some worried adults.

In a climate of increasing political conservatism, concerns about children, health, and safety led to growing regulation of leisure by colleges in the 1980s and 1990s.

Fraternity hazing was widely controlled, and a variety of festival days that had traditionally involved drinking were curbed or eliminated. Pennsylvania State University, for example, in the 1990s outlawed a Phi Psi race (jogging from bar to bar in bizarre costumes) and "gentle Thursday" (a spring event with free beer).

The wide-ranging regulatory campaign against drug taking, a twentieth-century innovation, drew together many of the social-control themes in an even more extensive fashion: the concern about vulnerable children, the commitment to health and safety, and the commitment to maintaining rational control over recreational activities. Medical regulation of drug access was introduced in the early twentieth century (the Harrison Anti-Narcotic Act of 1914 was fundamental, regulating the distribution of opiates), in marked contrast to nineteenth-century permissiveness; but it was in the 1930s that legal attacks on recreational drugs began to gain ground. While many of the attacks sought to protect children and guard against addiction, the attacks on drugs also expressed concerns about other recreations associated with drug use (such as jazz and later rock music) and—in ways that recalled the nineteenth-century—fears about the recreational habits of certain groups, such as inner-city African Americans.

Legal attacks on recreational drug use began under Harry Anslinger, who served as commissioner of the Federal Bureau of Narcotics from 1930 to 1962. Anslinger particularly attacked the legality of marijuana and hashish, through the Marijuana Tax Act of 1937. Penalties for recreational drug use were stiffened during the 1950s, and most states did the same during the 1960s, producing mandatory minimum jail sentences for drug possession. Prison populations swelled as a result, amid accusations that sentences for drugs widely used by African Americans were stiffer than those for drugs popular with whites. In the 1970s, new federal legislation attacked drug use, in what was now termed the "war" on drugs under the newly created Drug Enforcement Administration (DEA). By this point, American regulatory zeal was becoming unusual among industrial countries, producing a genuine battleground where leisure was concerned.

The focus on guiding children, and hopefully instilling permanently sound character, plus wider regulations over health and safety, defined the most explicit twentieth-century investments in social control over recreation. Two more diffuse facets deserve mention as well. The interest in providing all-embracing leisure experiences that limited spontaneity, choice, and exposure to objectionable fare was an innovation of the 1950s, launched by the first Disney theme park near Los Angeles. Such experiences became the most popular leisure destinations in the United States. Vigorous appeals to the work ethic constituted the second general constraint in twentieth-century leisure culture, limiting the commitment to recreational time and warning against leisure indulgences that might harm the work capacity. Emphasis on the virtues of work was revived in the 1920s and then, after some debate over excessive work devotion in the 1960s, again in the 1980s and 1990s, when the time committed to work actually began to rise.

By the end of the twentieth century, even as the United States generated leisure styles and media offerings spread around the world, the cumulative effect of several successive approaches to monitoring recreation had distinctive impact. An unusually strong moral component, in evaluating leisure, maintained clear traces of Puritan concern; the taming of popular recreation on grounds of respectability and the work ethic maintained some of the flavor of the industrial age; and the twentieth century, while loosening some specific regulatory approaches of the past, added important ingredients as well, particularly in the area of child training. The American leisure ethic was real, but it was shadowed by a variety of constraints.

See also: Boxing, City Parks, Crowds at Leisure, Drinking, Prohibition and Temperance, Rational Recreation and Self-Improvement, Sabbatarianism

BIBLIOGRAPHY

Burnham, John C. *Bad Habits: Drinking, Smoking, Taking Drugs, Gambling, Sexual Misbehavior, and Swearing in American History.* New York: New York University Press, 1993.

Rodgers, Daniel T. The *Work Ethic in Industrial America, 1850–1920.* Chicago: University of Chicago Press, 1978.

Rosenzweig, Roy. *Eight Hours For What We Will: Workers and Leisure in an Industrial City, 1870–1920.* New York: Cambridge University Press, 1983.

Starker, Steven. *Evil Influences: Crusades Against the Mass Media.* New Brunswick, N.J.: Transaction Publishers, 1989.

Stearns, Peter N. *Battleground of Desire: The Struggle for Self-Control in Modern America.* New York: New York University Press, 1999.

Peter N. Stearns

RELIGION

See *Church Socials, Easter, Muscular Christianity and the YM(W)CA Movements, Puritans at Leisure, Sabbatarianism*

RESORTS

See *Summer Resorts*

RESTAURANTS

See *Diners, Dining Out, Fast Food*

RETIREMENT LEISURE

See *Senior Leisure Lifestyles*

REUNIONS

Reunions have become a mainstay of American life, bridging the growing geographic distance between family members and friends. While family reunions center around a shared past and heritage, school and military reunions offer attendees the chance to catch up with and compare themselves to peers.

Family Reunions

Although many families have a reunion tradition dating to the 1930s or earlier, reunions became widespread in early twenty-first century American culture because of an increased interest in genealogy and family heritage and the greater ease of travel. Each year, Americans celebrate an estimated 200,000 family reunions, many of them lasting three or more days and including more than 100 family members. Reunions are often organized months in advance: Older women commonly take on the task of contacting family members and planning activities, but large families may form planning committees that include younger generations.

Most reunions are held in summer, both to accommodate children's school schedules and to provide an alternative to gatherings during winter holidays. While smaller groups may meet at a relative's home, most families opt to gather at public sites such as hotels, campgrounds, and resorts. Wealthier families may splurge on a cruise vacation or convene at tourist sites such as Walt Disney World. The location of a reunion will often change

from year to year to accommodate family members' interests and travel needs. Large families may hold a full reunion every few years, with smaller, regional gatherings in between.

Family reunions have a particularly rich history in African American culture and have historically served as a means to reunite northern blacks with relatives in the southern United States. Alex Haley's *Roots* —which became a popular TV miniseries in 1977—spurred Americans' interests in genealogy and may have contributed to a rise in black family reunions in the late twentieth century. Nearly half of African American travel each year is associated with a family reunion, according to *Ebony* magazine. Family members may convene at an ancestral home or meet in cities that contain black historical sites. One reunion expert recommended Atlanta's "Freedom Walk" as a meaningful family activity. Reunions have also become more common in Hispanic families—a recent reunion of a multigenerational family in Texas drew 2,500 people from six countries. European immigrants have also held prominent reunions in New York that connect relatives from both sides of the Altantic.

Many families reunite at campgrounds and resorts, engaging in shared outdoor leisure and sports activities. However, families also use reunions as a targeted time to explore family heritage, often emerging from the events with written histories, family trees, scrapbooks, recipe collections, photos, and videos. The Internet has encouraged the growth of family reunions, making it possible to both locate and invite far-flung family members, as well as create reunion web sites that enable others to share in the event. Many families use technology to connect with family members who can't attend, making conference calls or gathering around the computer to communicate in real time online.

Class Reunions

Some family members approach reunions with dread, but still feel an obligation to attend. High school and college reunions, in contrast, are generally voluntary events held at less regular intervals. Americans hold an estimated 150,000 high school reunions each year, with events becoming larger and more prominent since the baby boom generation celebrated its milestone anniversaries. Americans are most likely to attend their ten-year high school reunion: One-third of alumni attend their ten-year reunion, compared to one-fifth of alumni at the twenty-year event. Alumni are more likely to attend reunions if they considered themselves successful in high school, participated in extracurricular activities, or have kept in touch with old friends, who may well invite and encourage them to attend. Alumni who attend reunions are also more likely than non-attendees to have met perceived standards of success, such as holding a professional job or having a spouse and children. As is often the case with family reunions, alumni who live far from the school are more likely to attend than those who live nearby, as they consider the event a rare opportunity to reunite with classmates.

Because a graduating class represents a cross-section of one's peers—people of the same age, geographic and often economic background—school reunions have become a means for alumni to compare themselves to others. Alumni who attend reunions often work to improve their physical appearance—beginning a weight-loss regimen months in advance, or even undergoing minor plastic surgery. Award-giving is a common reunion custom, as classmates assess each other based on categories such as Most Gray Hair, Most Well-Kept Figure, and Most Times Married.

For private high schools, as well as colleges and universities, reunions have become a means to maintain contact with alumni who may contribute financially to the school. Because college alumni are more likely to attend twenty- and thirty-year reunions than earlier ones, organizers are increasingly trying to appeal to young alumni by planning family-friendly activities. Reunions have a long history at prominent universities such as Princeton. Beginning in the 1800s, alumni would return to the university the week before commencement to socialize over dinner and drinks and to cheer Princeton on in its annual baseball game against Yale. Old traditions run strong—reunions in the 1990s drew more than 9,000 alumni to march in the annual "P-rade" across campus.

Military Reunions

For Americans who have served in the military, reunions provide a way to honor shared experiences. Military reunions number in the thousands each year, many of them for World War II veterans, who are retired and have freedom to travel. Popular commemoration of World War II events in the mid-1990s also spurred a growth of such reunions. Most military reunions are held in the fall, often near a military base or at a resort with a golf course. According to *American Demographics* magazine, the service that reunites most often is the Navy, perhaps due to the close social networks that develop between officers on ships. Vietnam veterans are the least likely to celebrate reunions, both because of negative associations with the war

and because they lack the structure and group cohesion of World War II veterans.

Negative experiences, however, are quickly giving rise to a new type of reunion: Meetings of retired and laid-off corporate and government employees who commiserate and network with each other, remembering the joys and frustrations of their work.

See also: Birthdays, Christmas, Weddings

BIBLIOGRAPHY

Christmas, Rachel Jackson. "Gathering the Clan." *Essence* (August 1992): 92–95.

Holmstrom, David. "Family Reunions: Don't Wait for the Next Wedding." *Christian Science Monitor* 24 (June 1998): B1.

"How to Plan the Best Family Reunion." *Ebony* (April 2002): 118–23.

Ikeda, Keiko. *A Room Full of Mirrors: High School Reunions in Middle America.* Stanford: Stanford University Press, 1998.

Machado, Melinda. "Uniting Generations." *Hispanic* (March 1994): 25.

Mergenhagen, Paula. "The Reunion Market." *American Demographics,* April 1996: 30–35.

Mulrine, Anna. "In Praise of Black Family Reunions." *U.S. News and World Report* (28 July 1997).

Vinitzky-Seroussi, Vered. *After Pomp and Circumstance: High School Reunion as an Autobiographical Occasion.* Chicago: University of Chicago, 1998.

White, Dan. "Looking Back at Going Back." *The Princeton Alumni Weekly,* June 1994. Available from http://www.princeton.edu/.

Katherine Lehman

RITES OF PASSAGE

Rites of passage are rituals and ceremonies that celebrate the transition from one stage of life to another. The recognition of many of these, especially birth and death, is universal, in all known cultures, both past and present. Additionally, one or more important points between birth and death, such as the transition from childhood to adulthood, marriage, and retirement, are marked with ceremonies. Sometimes these rites demark a biological change, such as a girl's first menstruation, while many others commemorate purely cultural events, such as religious affirmations and confirmations (for example, baptism and confirmation in Christianity, bar and bat mitzvahs in Judaism), or secular events such as getting a driver's license, graduating from high school, or retirement may also be associated with rituals and ceremonies that are largely expressive.

The concept of rites of passage was first explicated in 1909 by Arnold van Gennep (1873–1957) in his book *Les Rites de Passage.* While the title of van Gennep's book is usually translated into English as "The Rites of Passage," it might be better translated as "The Rites of Transition" as his study dealt with the ceremonies that accompany the transitions individuals make between various life stages. In addition to the rituals and ceremonies associated with life transitions, van Gennep identified a second category of rites of passage, those that mark particular points in the passage of time, especially as indicated by celestial events. These include, for example, the coming of the new year, the new moon, the summer and winter solstices and the vernal and autumnal equinoxes. Van Gennep then distinguished three sequential stages of rites of passage: rites of separation (*séparation*), rites of transition (*marge*), and rites of incorporation (*aggrégation*). Taken together, he called these the *schéma* of the *rites de passage.* While the three stages characterize all rites of passage, van Gennep claimed that they are not equally emphasized in all ceremonies or by all cultural groups. For example, the element of separation is accentuated in funerary rituals while transition, which marks the period when an individual is removed from one status but not yet admitted to another, is most prominent in initiation ceremonies. Rites of incorporation are emphasized in marriage.

Van Gennep showed that rites of passage involve symbolism such as simulated birth and death or death and resurrection. Sometimes rites involve a ritual passing through a door or archway, symbolizing an individual's "death" and "rebirth" into a new status. In the incorporation stage of rites of passage, the individual is often given a new name or title, as has traditionally been the case in Western culture when women marry or when one receives an advanced academic degree (such as Mr. to Dr.).

The anthropologist Victor Turner (1967) characterized the transitional phase as particularly sacred or troublesome. This "liminal" (from the Latin *limen,* meaning "threshold") period is one where the individual is between one status and another. During the liminal phase, initiates often feel a sense of separation from the everyday but also a feeling of togetherness with other initiates. Turner (1969) referred to this sense of togetherness as

communitas. He also emphasized the importance of rituals, such as those that demark life transitions. Mary Douglas, another anthropologist, argued that all social transitions are perceived as dangerous. Moreover, because people in the transitional phase between life stages exist in a temporarily undefined status, their place in society is itself undefined.

While van Gennep focused primarily on rituals directed at life transitions for individuals, in their 1942 text, *Principles of Anthropology,* Eliot D. Chapple and Carleton S. Coon distinguished between individual-oriented rites of passage and group-oriented rituals that they termed "rites of intensification." Chapple and Coon claimed that events such as birth, marriage, and death alter normal social interaction and that rites of passage are mechanisms that serve to restore social equilibrium. Rites of intensification, such as planting and harvest ceremonies, in contrast to rites of passage, are community, rather than individual, events and create and maintain identity and cohesion in social groups.

Rites of Passage in America

The development of rites of passage in America parallels the populating of the continent as well as the social change that has taken place since colonial times. Native Americans had, and continue to maintain in many cases, their own rites of birth, transition to adulthood, marriage, and death, while the first settlers from Europe, and later from other parts of the world, brought their particular rites of passage with them. The forms and functions of rites of passage have changed over time as culture has changed, as well. In the American colonial period, for example, children were often regarded as small adults who should transition to fully adult behavior and responsibilities as rapidly as possible. Adolescence, as the social category acknowledged in the early twenty-first century, was either nonexistent as it seems to be in many other cultures, or very brief. This meant that life transitions not only took place at different times than they do now but that their meaning was often different from today's, as well. Moreover, some of the rites of passage that may have been important in the past are no longer significant while others that integrate with modern society and culture have been introduced in relatively recent times.

Examples of Rites of Passage in America

Since there are many different cultural and ethnic groups in America, the examples of rites of passage that follow are necessarily both selective and brief. They are arranged to approximate chronological order over the lifespan, although some, such as marriage and death, do not necessarily occur when individuals reach specific ages.

Birth Rites Although van Gennep claimed that birth constitutes one of the primary transitions in human life there are relatively few true birth rites, either in America or elsewhere. Several explanations for this are possible. For one, until very recently in human history, infant mortality was so common that expending ritual effort on births, or the newborn, may have been regarded as premature. Or, babies may have not been thought to be fully human until certain rites, such as naming, took place. Rites that take place either before the birthing and soon after are common, however.

Giving small gifts to newborns or new parents dates, at least, to Roman times in Europe. However, the modern form of such gift giving, the "baby shower," appeared in the late nineteenth century in the form of "teas" for new mothers. These took place after the baby was born because pregnant women, and especially those of social standing, did not appear in public. In the early twentieth century, these teas became "showers." The "showering" of gifts on expectant mothers is largely a post-World War II phenomenon. Showers involve gifts for the baby, often accompanied by advice for the parents-to-be, a meal, and, commonly, party games. Showers are generally held for first children only. Similar events for second or later children, if held, are sometimes called "sprinkles." Traditionally, men were excluded from baby showers although that rule has become relaxed since the 1970s.

Rites of Passage for the Young While rites of passage for birthing and for newborns are rare in America, religious rituals for infants and children are important.

Baptism Baptism is the closest thing to a birth rite in Christianity. The modern form of baptism is descended from ancient Judaism wherein non-Jews were baptized as part of a conversion rite. Baptism, derived from the Greek word "baptizein," meaning "to immerse," involved immersion in early Christianity. While immersion continues to be practiced in some Christian denominations, the more common practice of sprinkling water on the foreheads of infants developed later. For early Christians, baptism, normally held during the Easter vigil, served to initiate neophytes into the Christian community, usually after an extended period of study. Because baptism was a rite of conversion, it was not a rite of birth in early Christianity. However, with the Christianization of Europe, it evolved into a rite to be held within eight days of birth. As such, baptism resolved the child's ambiguous

status of being incapable of committing a sin yet tainted by original sin. Because the rite publicly initiated a Christian, baptisms became known unofficially as "christenings." Social gatherings, similar to the receptions held after weddings and funerals, also frequently follow christenings. Many Christian denominations now either disregard baptism entirely or, at minimum, no longer hold it as essential for salvation.

Circumcision Jewish fathers are prescribed to circumcise their sons on the eighth day after their birth. This practice is based on the belief that when God chose Abram (eventually known as Abraham) to be the founder of Judaism, he commanded him to circumcise himself and his sons. The ritual of circumcision is termed a *brit* or *bris milah,* meaning "the covenant of circumcision." Normally, fathers do not do the circumcision themselves but, instead, call on a *mohel,* or ritual circumciser. The two main parts of a bris milah are the circumcision and the naming of the baby. In addition, a religious feast, the *seudat mitzvah,* follows the ceremony. A similar rite for baby girls, called a *bris bat,* involves no medical procedure, and is primarily a naming ceremony. In addition to the bris, the Hebrew naming, and the banquet, godparents are usually designated at these events.

Rites of Passage to Adulthood Ceremonial markers of the transition from childhood to adulthood are, worldwide, the most common form of rites of passage. In traditional societies, such ceremonies, often known as initiation rites, may involve tests of physical stamina, ordeals that include pain and/or mutilation, periods of seclusion, and instruction in esoteric or secret information.

In Western culture, including the United States, individuals have an extended transitional period—adolescence that is largely absent in traditional societies. Hence, for the most part, American society lacks definitive markers of the child-adult transition. For most young Americans, there is a series of events that, in effect, string out the child-adult transition. These include such secular events as moving from grade school to high school (perhaps with middle or junior high school in between), getting a driver's license, registering to vote, graduating from high school or college, and achieving the age at which consumption of alcoholic beverages is legal. Since boys and girls alike share these events, their substitution for traditional ceremonies, that were usually religious in nature, reflects the weakening of traditional gender roles. However, some rituals involve entrance into society, most often for young women, that announce adult status and, hence, eligibility for marriage and child rearing. The "sweet sixteen" party and the debutante ball, described below, are two examples of such rituals. Although both have faded somewhat in popularity, they served to announce that initiates had attained adult status and, thus, could now engage in dating and, eventually, marriage. The quinceañera, traditionally celebrated on the fifteenth birthday, is a similar event for girls of Hispanic descent.

Unlike boys, the transition from childhood to adulthood for girls has more significant physiological markers. While a public announcement of their first menstruation would be embarrassing and humiliating for most American girls, this was not the case in many Native American cultures. Among the Apache, for example, the Sunrise Ceremony is a rite of passage for girls to women and is held during the summer following a girl's first menstruation.

In the United States, the confirmation, practiced by Catholics and some Protestant denominations, and the bar and bit mitzvah for Jews are rites of passage that demarcate childhood and adulthood in a religious sense, although not necessarily with respect to life in general.

Confirmation The evolution of baptism from a rite of initiation into Christendom to a birth rite left behind a ritual vacuum. That is, baptism no longer functioned as a transitional rite between childhood and adulthood. Hence, confirmation, initially a part of the baptism rite, eventually replaced baptism as an adolescent rite of passage into adulthood. Although some sects, such as the Anabaptists, rejected the validity of infant baptism and hence required rebaptism, for Catholics and some Protestant denominations confirmation serves to reaffirm the grace bestowed in infant baptism.

Bar and Bat Mitzvah Jewish boys become full participants in community religious life at age thirteen when they become bar mitzvah. The bar mitzvah ceremony, while common, is not a requirement for becoming bar mitzvah and is a relatively recent innovation. The ceremony commonly consists of the initiate being called on to recite a blessing over the weekly reading from the Torah. The initiate usually makes a speech, beginning with the phrase "Today, I am a man," as well. The bat mitzvah, first celebrated in 1922, is a similar ceremony for Jewish girls and it takes place when they are twelve years of age, although the ceremony can be postponed until they are thirteen, as with boys. In some Jewish sects, the bat mitzvah is similar to the bar mitzvah while, in orthodox orders, females cannot participate in certain religious rituals and, hence, the bat mitzvah is essentially a party.

A rite of passage from childhood to adulthood at age twelve or thirteen may seem early and, indeed, those who become bar and bat mitzvah rarely assume fully adult roles. However, in strictly Orthodox eastern European Jewish communities, boys of thirteen did experience a fundamental life change: they left their families for study at schools known as *yeshivas* for religious study. Except for holiday visits, many never returned to their families. Among modern Jewish communities, this practice is retained only among strictly Orthodox groups such as the Hasidim.

Bar and bat mitzvahs usually involve elaborate receptions that follow the ceremony itself, much as is the case with weddings. The ceremonies and the receptions are important social events for members of local Jewish communities and also reunite family members who may live far apart.

Graduation Graduation is the culmination of a student's high school or college career. Traditionally, graduations consisted of two parts, the commencement and the baccalaureate. Commencement is the part of the graduation ceremony where graduates receive their degrees and, traditionally, flip the tassels on their hats from one side to the other to show their changed status. The baccalaureate, which dates to a 1432 statute at Oxford University, required the graduate to deliver a sermon in Latin. The tradition has continued in America although the sermons are no longer in Latin, no longer religious in nature in public institutions, and are delivered either by school officials or an invited guest. The class valedictorian, the student who has graduated first academically in his or her class, delivers the *valediction* at the ceremony. The valediction usually involves a recollection of the classes' past and exhortations for the future.

Like many other rites of passage, graduation involves symbolic clothing. These involve caps, gowns, and, depending on the degree being received, hoods. Because early university education in Europe was in the hands of clerics and was largely religious in nature, students and teachers alike wore robes. Hoods may have served to protect tonsured clerical heads until the introduction of the skullcap. Oxford and Cambridge standardized university dress in the sixteenth century and these traditions were exported with the founding of the first American universities beginning with Harvard College in 1636.

An intercollegiate commission met at Columbia University in 1895 in order to establish a system for academic dress. The commission prescribed the materials and styles for gowns, including the colors that designated different fields of study. Although some minor changes have been made since, the regulations adopted by the American Council on Education in 1932 remain in place for academic costumes. While black is the prescribed color for gowns, in the 1950s, graduates from high schools, colleges, and universities began to wear gowns in their school colors.

Diplomas, class rings, and yearbooks are common markers of graduation. Early diplomas were of sheepskin Parchment began to replace sheepskin around 1900 although diplomas are still often referred to as "sheepskins." The first class ring was developed in 1835 at the United States Military Academy at West Point but rings for high schools and colleges did not become fashionable until the turn of the twentieth century. The high school and college yearbook developed from school newspapers and literary magazines. Yearbooks, which may date to the 1600s in the United States, were initially scrapbooks that contained various school memorabilia. The Yale Banner, the oldest college yearbook in the United States, dates to 1842 and originally published enrollment statistics and memberships in societies. Waterville Academy in Waterville, New York, began publishing *The Evergreen,* the first high school yearbook, in 1845.

Graduations at all levels are commonly celebrated with graduation parties. These celebrate the changed status of the graduates. While most high school graduates in the early 2000s went on to higher education of some kind, those who did not were expected to become employed and assume fully adult roles in society. The same was true of college graduates.

Other "Coming of Age" Rites

The Debutante Ball The debutante ball is a traditional means of introducing young women, aged sixteen to eighteen, to society. The ball is a format for their "debut" into the adult world. The American debut tradition is rooted in English custom and is based on the idea that mates for daughters of aristocratic families were to be of similar social standing. While there is no formal aristocracy in America, debutante balls are most often for the daughters of well-to-do families.

Balls begin with the formal introduction of young women and their partners to guests in the form of a promenade across the ballroom. Masters of ceremonies, who introduce the debutantes, often comment on their gowns and some of their activities. Normally a cohort of young women debut at the same time. The introductions are followed by several formal dances. A formal meal and more dancing follow.

The tradition of the debutante ball began in American in 1748 in Philadelphia but the best-known event for debutantes is the Mayflower Ball, held in New York City. The New York branch of the Society of Mayflower Descendents was organized in 1894. They held their first annual meeting at the Waldorf Hotel in 1895 and, thereafter, held dinner banquets each November in celebration of the signing of the Mayflower Compact. The first Society of Mayflower Descendants in the State of New York Annual Debutante Ball was held on 29 October 1959 in the Grand Ballroom of the Plaza Hotel and was received by then Governor and Mrs. W. Rice Brewster. The balls, traditionally held in October or November, involve a gourmet meal, orchestral music, and presentation of the Plymouth Awards to recognize individuals for their efforts in philanthropy and education. The ball is regarded as one of the highlights of the New York social season.

Getting a Driver's License and Turning Twenty-One The automobile is just over a century old but has established itself as one of America's most useful, and cherished, commodities. In response to accidents by unskilled motorists, states demanded licenses and drivers' tests in the decade after 1908. In the early 2000s, most states licensed drivers at age sixteen. For young people, this is a momentous event. The ability to drive affords new opportunities in terms of getting a job and driving to work, driving to sporting events or other recreational destinations, dating, or simply cruising. Moreover, cars are major status markers for adolescents. In terms of van Gennep's stages of rites of passage, getting and driving with a drivers permit can be regarded as a rite of separation while the drivers test is the rite of transition. Acquiring a license is a rite of incorporation.

Attaining legal drinking age, now twenty-one in all states, is a second secular rite of passage to adulthood. While many, and perhaps most, young people in the United States consume alcoholic beverages before turning twenty-one, the ability to do so legally and openly is important as it also permits access to establishments, such as bars and nightclubs, that were previously off limits. While there are no standardized or socially sanctioned rituals for either getting a drivers license or turning twenty-one, these are typically events to be celebrated, the former by driving and the latter by drinking, usually with peers. Both males and females share these particular coming-of-age events, reflecting the breakdown of traditional adult gender roles in modern America.

Marriage Marriage is, by far, the most ceremonial of American rites of passage. In terms of rites of passage, it probably also has the most explicitly formulated stages in terms of van Gennep's typology with the engagement, the marriage ceremony, and the honeymoon.

The marriage ceremony itself is often both preceded and followed by expressive events directed at both the prospective bride and the groom. "Bridal showers" are parties wherein friends and relatives "shower" the bride-to-be with gifts. Bridal showers are probably a legacy of the practice of the dowry, the goods that a bride brings with her upon marriage. Dowries often included both items of value, such as jewelry and money, as well as household items, and helped in establishing a new household. Traditionally, the maid or matron of honor or the bridesmaids host the bridal shower but if they cannot, other family members or friends may do so. Early bridal showers involved only very close friends or family member and were restricted to female participation. "Couples" showers wherein both the bride and groom attend, along with their female and male friends and relatives, are becoming popular.

Males who are about to be married are commonly the honored guests at bachelor parties, also known as "stag" parties. Soldiers in ancient Sparta reputedly held the first bachelor parties on the night before the groom's wedding. At the feast, the groom said goodbye to his previous life of freedom and pledged loyalty to his colleagues. Modern bachelor parties are held either at a bar or night club or at the residence of one of the groom's friends. Such parties may involve a great deal of drinking, sometimes accompanied by pornographic films and/or the participation of female strippers or prostitutes. In the early twenty-first century, golf outings or weekend trips to destinations such as Las Vegas have become more common forms of bachelor parties. Bachelorette parties for prospective brides, although of more recent origin, are common and similar to those for males.

Joining Voluntary Organizations Most Americans are members of one or more voluntary organizations such as clubs, churches, sports teams, college fraternities and sororities, and even secret societies. Many of these, particularly those that involve secret information and signals of recognition, such as handshakes, involve rites of passage for initiates. The Freemasons provide an illustrative example. While the exact origin of Freemasonry is not known, it most probably grew out of medieval stonemason guilds. When apprentice masons became master stonemasons, they were provided with secret passwords that permitted them to work anywhere in Europe. By the 1600s, membership in guilds was opened and individuals joined the secret societies as a display of status. The governing body of Freemasonry, the Grand Lodge of England, was established in 1717 and Masonic lodges opened in the United States by the 1780s. In America, such lu-

minaries as Benjamin Franklin, George Washington, and Paul Revere were Freemasons.

Initiation into the Freemasons and similar societies requires a secretive rite of passage laden with symbols. Initiates are blindfolded and a noose is placed around their necks with the rope hanging down their backs. A dagger is held to the left side of their chest. One pants leg is rolled up and initiates wear one shoe and one slipper. In this condition, they are led around the lodge. As the initiates make their oaths of allegiance, the noose and the dagger are removed. They are then told that had they attempted to escape they would have either been stabbed by the dagger or choked by the noose. Like other rites of passage, this liminal stage exhibits disorientation and possible danger. The rite of passage is complete when the newly initiated freemason is awarded a lambskin apron and white gloves by the master of the lodge. The initiation is followed by a communal meal.

Freemasonry in the early 2000s was devoted to social improvement via self-development and philanthropy, as was the case with many of the other social organizations, such as the Shriners and Odd Fellows. For example, Masons founded orphanages, homes for widows, and homes for the elderly in the nineteenth and early twentieth centuries, prior to government provision of such social safety nets. These societies also provide camaraderie, social support, and recreational programs and resources for members.

Hazing On 4 February 1978, Charles Stenzel, a Klan Alpine Fraternity pledge at Alfred University, died after drinking a pint of bourbon and a mixture of wine and beer and being forced into the trunk of a car with two other pledges. For some years, students at Glenbrook North High School in Northbrook, Illinois, held a "powder puff" football game each spring between seniors and juniors as a rite of passage for the juniors to their senior year. On 4 May 2003, the event got out of hand with junior girls being beaten, covered with paint, and having mud and feces thrown in their faces. Five of the girls had to be hospitalized as a result of the hazing.

According to a study conducted by Nadine Hoover and Norman Pollard of Alfred University hazing, like the examples above, is extremely common in American high schools. They found that 48 percent of students who belong to groups report that they were subjected to hazing and that 43 percent indicated that their hazing involved humiliating acts. Moreover, 56 percent of those who were subjected to humiliating activities during hazing were expected to engage in illegal or potentially illegal behavior, typically involving substance abuse, sexual activities, or vandalism. Hoover and Pollard reported that 81 percent of college athletes who experienced humiliating acts during hazing were expected to engage in potentially illegal activities. While both male and female high school students are at risk of being hazed, males appear to be most at risk, especially in terms of dangerous activities. Forty-two states in the United States had anti-hazing laws by 2004.

Retirement Americans often face retirement with varying degrees of anticipation and dread. The anticipation is for a future free of work while the dread is based on the massive lifestyle change that will follow, the possible loss of friends and colleagues from work, and the questions about what one is to do with all of the newly found time and freedom. This was not always so, however. Retirement is largely a development of the twentieth century. In agrarian American, people continued to work so long as they were physically able to do so. With migration to cities and the rise of factory labor, however, youth became an asset and age a liability so changeover in the workforce became a necessity. In 1935, the Social Security Administration was created to provide older workers with income should they retire, allowing younger workers to take their place. While social security initially provided meager income, Congress increased benefits by 77 percent in 1950 and again by 20 percent in 1972 along with yearly cost of living increases. Employer retirement programs covered approximately half of all workers by the 1960s and the average retirement age fell from 70 in 1930 to 62 in the early 2000s. Poverty rates among the elderly of nearly 35 percent in 1960 declined to under 10 percent by 2004.

Dora Costa illustrates that income has become a less significant constraint on retirement than once was the case because of retirement plans. Moreover, she points out that leisure had become cheaper than it had ever been. Television was the major source of leisure for Americans and public leisure facilities that were once available only to the wealthy, such as golf courses and parks, were now assessable to the public. The automobile and relatively inexpensive air travel made that leisure travel affordable.

The act of retirement itself typically involves a celebration. These can take on a variety of forms but usually involve a dinner, speeches, and gifts. Retirement speeches often are in the form of "roasts" wherein retirees undergo mild ridicule for their exploits during their working years. The gold watch is a traditional retirement gift but has come to be regarded as somewhat of a joke.

Death Funerals are big business in America but they were not always so. In pre-Civil War times, death was a family affair. The great majority of deaths occurred at home and preparation of the deceased for burial took place there, as well. Female relatives usually prepared corpses by washing and dressing in a sack or winding cloth. The deceased was then placed in a pine coffin. After a one or two day vigil over the body by family and friends, the deceased was transported to the burial site. For urban dwellers, burials took place in cemeteries but rural residents were often buried on their own land.

Prior to the Civil War, embalming was practiced only for preserving corpses for dissection in medical schools. With the massive war casualties, and the need for transporting the dead home for burial, embalming became a necessity. The National Funeral Director's Association was founded in 1882 and members immediately began campaigns to convince the public of the need for embalming and professional funeral services. Funeral "homes" were established in order to move the business of dealing with the dead from their real homes. While pre Civil War mourners occasionally viewed the deceased either at home or during the funeral procession, viewing became an integral part of the death rite in funeral homes.

While a great deal of research has been directed at attitudes toward death and dying, funerals in America have undergone remarkably little academic study. There seem to be some commonalities, however. Ronald Grimes lists several of what he calls "gestures" rather than rites, *per se,* that surround death in America. These include:

1. Anticipating death through stories, contemplation, and rationalization.

2. Observing taboos such as wearing special clothing, often of symbolic colors and not saying anything bad about the deceased.

3. Mourning, which may involve weeping, wailing, appearing to be sad, refusing to eat, or avoiding laughter.

4. Marking an end to mourning by holding a ceremony after a specified period of time or remarrying.

5. Protecting survivors from the dead through rituals and behaviors that send the soul or spirit toward its destination or dealing with remains in symbolic ways.

6. Announcing deaths via notices and obituaries.

7. Congregating and comforting the bereaved through visitation, religious ceremonies, or parties.

8. Either dramatizing death's finality by displaying the corpse and then disposing of it by burial or cremation or denying its finality by embalming or otherwise preserving the body and referring to the deceased with circumlocutions such as "being at rest."

9. Commemorating the dead by making donations in their memory, naming children after them, retaining keepsakes, maintaining grave sites or memorials, and visiting graves.

American ethnic groups, as well as individual families, emphasize these "gestures" to varying and different degrees. Culture and individual attitudes prescribe and proscribe which of these are emphasized. In many ethnic groups, funerals and interments are followed by feasting, music, drinking, and revelry while, in others, mourners simply go home.

Other Rites of Passage

Numerous other rites of passage and/or intensification exist in contemporary America. Some of these are celebrated on national holidays, such as Memorial Day, the Fourth of July, Labor Day, and Veteran's Day. W. Lloyd Warner described Memorial Day rituals as follows:

> The Memorial Day rite is a cult of the dead, but not just of the dead as such, since by symbolically elaborating sacrifice of human life for the country through, or identifying it with, the Christian church's sacred sacrifice of their god, the deaths of such men also become powerful sacred symbols which organize, direct, and constantly revive the collective ideals of the community and the nation. (p. 236)

Others rites are religious, such as Easter and Christmas for Christians or Chanukah and Yom Kippur for Jews. Pilgrimages to quasi-sacred sites, such as Disney World for families with young children or Graceland for devotees of Elvis Presley, may constitute rites of passage for some. Joining and leaving the military often involves rites of passage, sometimes including hazing.

Chapple and Coon suggested that some events, such as the coronation of a king, involve both rites of passage and rites of intensification. While America has no king, presidential elections seem to function as rites of passage and intensification. The campaign period, including the primaries, is characteristically a time for candidates to separate themselves from the rest of the citizenry and from each other. The inauguration, a betwixt and between period when the candidate has been elected but is not yet president, is a time of transition. Actually taking office, appointing a cabinet and other officials, and beginning the task of governing is a period of incorporation. While presidential elections are the most dramatic of political rites of passage and intensification, the election of other officials, from governors and mayors to school board members, exhibit similar traits.

See also: Birthdays, Automobiles and Leisure, Honeymooning, Weddings

BIBLIOGRAPHY

Costa, Dora L. *The Evolution of Retirement: An American Economic History, 1880–1990.* Chicago: University of Chicago Press, 1998.

Davis-Floyd, Robbie E. *Birth as an American Rite of Passage.* Berkeley: University of California Press, 2003.

Douglas, Mary. *Purity and Danger.* New York: Routledge, 2002.

Grimes, Ronald L. *Deeply into the Bone: Re-inventing Rites of Passage.* Berkeley: University of California Press, 2000.

"History of Graduation: The Ceremony, the Ring, the Yearbook, the Diploma, the Music, the Cap & Gown, Valedictorian and Baccalaureate." Available from http://www.brownielocks.com/graduation.html.

Hoover, Nadine C., and Norman J. Pollard. *Initiation Rites in American High Schools: A National Survey.* New York: Alfred University, 2000. Available from http://www.alfred.edu/news/html/hazing_study.html.

Laderman, Gary. *The Sacred Remains: American Attitudes toward Death, 1799–1883.* New Haven, Conn.: Yale University Press, 1996.

Mintz, Steven, and Susan Kellogg. *Domestic Revolutions: A Social History of American Family Life.* New York: The Free Press.

Moore, Robert L., and Havlick, Max J., Jr., ed. *The Archetype of Initiation: Sacred Space, Ritual Process, and Personal Transformation: Lectures and Essays.* Philadelphia: Xlibris Corporation, 2001.

Nuwer, Hank *Wrongs of Passage: Fraternities, Sororities, Hazing, and Binge Drinking.* Bloomington: Indiana University Press, 1999.

Sullivan, Eugene. *An Academic Costume Code and an Academic Ceremony Guide.* Reprinted from American Universities and Colleges, 15th ed. Walter de Gruyter, Inc. Available from http://www.acenet.edu/.

Turner, Victor. *The Forest of Symbols: Aspects of Ndembu Ritual.* Ithaca, N.Y.: Cornell University Press, 1967.

———. *The Ritual Process: Structure and Anti-Structure.* Ithaca, N.Y.: Cornell University Press, 1977.

Tyler May, Elaine. *Homeward Bound: American Families in the Cold War Era.* New York: Basic Books, 1988.

van Gennep, Arnold. *The Rites of Passage.* Translated by M. B. Vizedom and G. B. Caffee. Chicago: University of

Chicago Press, 1960. (The original edition was published in 1908).

Warner, W. Lloyd. *Structure of American Life.* Edinburgh: The Edinburgh University Press, 1952.

Garry Chick

ROCK CLIMBING

Rock climbing is the sport and recreation activity of climbing cliffs; it is closely related to ice climbing—climbing steep snow and ice and frozen waterfalls. Both activities developed in Europe, particularly the United Kingdom, in the second half of the nineteenth century. They were seen as off-season practice by alpinists for the summer season of mountain climbing—especially in the European Alps. Rock and ice climbing skills were necessary for the more difficult peaks, and the more difficult routes to the summits. The mountain cliffs, and occasionally the sea cliffs of Britain provided off-season recreation as well as valuable training.

These activities began to become recreational and sporting activities in their own right by the end of the nineteenth century. However, there were more practical precedents for such pursuits. Historically, cliffs were climbed to reach birds' eggs for food, to seek refuge from pursuers, and as part of the process of prospecting for minerals. Scientific endeavors led to more systematic rock climbing in the eighteenth and nineteenth centuries as naturalists searched for botanical life, birds' eggs, and insect specimens, and geologists searched for rock samples and fossils. Some of these pre-recreational ascents were recorded. For example, in 1850 two prospectors, Robert Clarke and Alexander Ralph, climbed what is now known as Trap Dike Route on Mount Colden in the Adirondacks.

As with mountain climbing, those engaged in rock climbing in the United States drew originally on European precedent, but the activity developed mostly in isolation. Thus, while techniques for using the rope as a safety device were evolving in Europe, U.S. climbers tended to regard using a rope as a liability, or as unsporting, or they would attempt to figure out its use while engaged in a climb. Guy and Laura Waterman discovered, and in *Yankee Rock and Ice* reproduced, George Flagg's cartoons of a 1910 ascent of the Pinnacle in Huntington Ravine (White Mountains, New Hampshire). They show Flagg with Paul Bradley, Mayo Tollman, and

a Mr. Dennis, in "scenes of two men hauling a less able companion up a steep section and of one man holding his partner roped on the edge of a platform, heaving boulders into the abyss" (Mellor, p. 25).

Climbing Games

Rock climbing and ice climbing are clearly dangerous activities. Without safety measures, the possibility of a fall leading to serious injury or death is ever-present. In order to understand the development of rock climbing in the United States, it is important to understand how a climb occurs, and how a rope is used. Using the rope for safety in climbing involves a system known as belaying, of which there are two types: the fixed belay, and the running belay. Although there are variations on this, a roped climb (on rock or ice) occurs with two climbers, one attached to each end of a rope, moving one at a time. The first climber sets off, reaches a point where it is possible to make an attachment to the rock or ice (a fixed belay), and takes in the slack rope (keeping the rope relatively tight) between the two climbers as the second person climbs. The safety of the second climber is assured in the case of a fall because the first climber is able to hold the second without being pulled off, and before the second falls any distance.

If a climb is longer than the length of a rope (normally about fifty meters), the process continues as the second climber then takes a fixed belay, and pays out the rope to the leader climbing the next "pitch". Although the second climber is usually relatively safe, a fall by the lead climber is much more serious. On the first pitch the leader could hit the ground; on subsequent pitches the leader is likely to fall at least as far below the second as had been climbed above. To prevent this, the leading climber may be protected from a long fall by a series of running belays or "protection"—snap links (karabiners) are attached to the rock or ice by a variety of means, and the moving rope runs through them. Proper belaying techniques by the second climber will ensure that a leader will only fall as far below a running belay as had been climbed above it.

If protection is only used for safety, the technique is known as "free" or "clean" climbing. When protection is actually used by the climber to assist progress, the technique is known as "aid" or "artificial" climbing. Between these two extremes there are numerous micro-variations and various meanings associated with particular styles of climbing. The informal, often local, and continually modified (by rock climbers themselves) sets of rules that govern how rock climbs are to be accomplished are known as "ethics."

In Lito Tejada-Flores' 1967 article, "Games Climbers Play," he points out that "climbing is not a homogeneous sport, but rather a collection of differing (though related) activities [games], each with its own adepts, distinctive terrain, problems and satisfactions, and perhaps most important, its own rules" (p. 23). In his hierarchical typology of climbing games, the first four relate specifically to rock climbing—the bouldering game, the crag climbing game, the continuous rock climbing game, and the big wall game (the first three also apply to ice climbing).

The games are characterized by increasing height and danger, and by the increasing use of equipment. In addition to these games, there has evolved a major distinction between two styles of rock climbing—the more traditional "adventure" climbing and the more modern "sport" climbing.

Climbing Areas in the United States

As might be expected, most rock climbing in the United States occurs where there are mountains. Thus, in the east, there are climbing cliffs ranging northwards from West Virginia along the Appalachian and Adirondack mountains. There are also outlying, and perhaps unlikely, areas such as cliffs along the Potomac River, Ragged Mountain in Connecticut, Quincy Quarries outside Boston, and the sea cliffs around Mount Desert Island in Maine. The best-known rock climbing areas in the east are the Shawangunks and Adirondacks in New York State, and the White Mountains in New Hampshire. In the west, rock climbing areas are far too numerous to mention, although special note should be made of Yosemite and Joshua Tree in California, the climbing areas around Colorado Springs and Boulder in Colorado, and the canyon and desert climbing areas of the southwest. However, it is also possible to rock climb in some places in the United States where there are no mountains, such as Minnesota, Wisconsin, Alabama, and Texas.

History of Rock Climbing in the United States

As with mountain climbing, rock climbing in the United States really started to develop in the 1930s, particularly under the influence of such individuals as Harvard professor Robert Underhill and German immigrant Fritz Wiessner. Their widespread introduction of European rope techniques made more difficult ascents possible. Although there had been earlier developments in rock climbing by climbers with European Alpine experience (for example, John Case's climbs in the Adirondacks from 1916; Willard Helburn's ascent of Chimney Route on Mount Katahdin, Maine, in 1919), European rope tech-

Indoor Rock Climbing. In the Field House building at New York's Chelsea Piers Sports & Entertainment Complex, a woman navigates the forty-foot-tall rock climbing wall. The eighty-six-year-old Chelsea Piers was revitalized in 1995 and turned into the sports and entertainment facility. Thanks to the popularity of the extreme sports X Games on the ESPN television network, rock climbing on man-made, indoor surfaces such as this one continued to increase in popularity in 2004. © *Mark Lennihan for AP/Wide World Photos*

niques first became widely used in the U.S. rock climbing community in the 1930s.

The technological (nylon rope and Vibram soles) and experiential developments (mountain warfare and cliff assault training) of World War II, and the post-war increase in income, leisure time, and automobile ownership, all led to a slowly-growing population of rock climbers in the U.S., and the start of a conflict between traditional and new approaches. These conflicts came to a head in California (Tahquitz Rocks and Yosemite) and New York (the Shawangunks) in the 1950s and 1960s. Because of the lack of strength in hemp ropes (strong enough to hold a falling second, but unlikely to hold a falling leader), and limited knowledge of running belays or pitons, a tradition had emerged among established climbing clubs—such as the Sierra Club and the Appalachian Mountain Club—that involved a long apprenticeship as a second climber with an experienced leader, and to strictures such as "the leader must not fall," and "don't climb up anything that you can't climb back down." These traditions imposed clear limits on progress.

However, the availability of the much stronger and safer nylon ropes, and the increasing use of pitons and other means of attaching running belays, meant that younger and more ambitious and able rock climbers were more likely to take the chance of a fall. Royal Robbins's 1952 ascent of the route called Open Book at Tahquitz signaled this shift, and represented a whole new standard of difficulty in U.S. rock climbing. In the United States, the difficulty of climbs is represented by the so-called Yosemite Decimal System (YDS); free climbing is number 5 on the scale, and a climb rated 5.1 is relatively easy. Robbins's climb was the first to be rated 5.9. Given the rapid increase in standards in recent years, early twenty-first century American rock climbers were waiting for the first climb rated 5.15.

The clash between traditional and new approaches came to a head during the countercultural 1960s. While similar conflicts were occurring in Europe, Canada, and other parts of the United States, the "war" between the "Appies" (more traditional Appalachian Mountain Club members) and the "Vulgarians" (an informal club devoted to hedonism and hard climbing) became legendary. Risks were being taken to accomplish first ascents of more difficult routes, and in Yosemite, rock climbers were embarking on multiday routes on 1,000-meter cliffs that were previously considered impossible. Climbers such as Yvon Chouinard began to develop specialized equipment (such as pitons) specifically for the hard granite of Yosemite. The developments in Yosemite brought U.S. rock climbing to the attention of the international climbing community for the first time, and for a while, California climbers were considered to be world leaders in the sport.

The development of relatively affordable jet travel in the 1960s brought international rock climbers to the United States, and took U.S. climbers to other parts of the world. This led to the exchange of ideas, techniques, equipment, and growing concerns for U.S. climbers. In particular the Yosemite style of hard steel piton was causing permanent damage to rock faces, and environmental conservation concerns led to a search for new safety equipment. The development of chocks, new camming devices, and the increasing use of fixed expansion bolts in some areas, generally replaced the use of pitons. New techniques also emerged, particularly the "French style" of climbing developed on the cliffs of the Verdon Gorge.

As with mountain climbing, competition in rock climbing also involves achieving the first (recorded) ascent of a route on a cliff or ice face, as well as other variations such as first solo or first female ascent. There is also competition for the style or quality of an ascent, which may refer to the speed of an ascent, and to technique and limitations on the use of equipment. However, unlike mountain climbing, formal competition emerged in rock climbing, first in the Soviet Union (speed climbing), later (in the 1980s) in Italy, where climbers attempted to reach the greatest height on routes of increasing difficulty. The first Italian competitions took place on natural cliff faces, but the environmental damage caused to the rock, and by the spectators, led to a rapid shift in many countries to competitions on artificial, usually indoor climbing walls.

These walls had first been developed in the 1960s for instructing novices in safe environments, and for evening and winter training for more experienced climbers. New, more sophisticated walls, with moveable holds to create varying difficulties of ascent, became ideal for competitions, and a Grand Prix professional circuit was established, as well as numerous amateur competitions. A combination of competition ethics with French climbing techniques led to a new style of climbing known as "sport" climbing (as opposed to the more traditional "adventure" climbing). The differences are related to how and when protection is attached to the rock, how the protection is used, and how the ascent is accomplished. These two styles co-existed in the United States in the early 2000s, not always happily, and there was usually local agreement about which style prevailed on local cliffs.

All of these changes were accompanied by rapid commercialization and increasing numbers of participants. Rock climbing continues to predominantly involve white, male, middle-class participants, although there is a rapidly increasing number of female climbers. Although rock climbing is a much older activity than many of the other so-called extreme sports, its inclusion at some extreme sports competitions, and in adventure racing, has added to the public recognition of the activity. Also, the use of rock climbing in advertisements for a variety of products and services, its appearance in popular films ranging from *The Eiger Sanction* to *Mission Impossible*, and its association with mountain climbing and the growing interest in that sport occasioned by various ascents of Mount Everest, has generated a great deal of publicity that has attracted new participants. These participants are often from the same social categories (young, middle class, white, predominantly male) found in other so-called extreme sports.

With the growth of indoor climbing gyms in urban areas, there are large numbers of rock climbers who have reportedly never climbed outdoors. The gyms have become a part of the fitness industry, and even some mainstream fitness clubs have introduced climbing walls. Portable climbing walls may be seen at street festivals and fairgrounds, and there are walls on cruise ships and in outdoor equipment stores. The activity is still practiced in various forms, but its recognition as one of the so-called "extreme" sports has brought it to more mainstream attention in the United States.

See also: Extreme Sports, Mountain Climbing

BIBLIOGRAPHY

Donnelly, P. "The Great Divide: Sport Climbing vs. Adventure Climbing." In *To the Extreme: Alternative Sports Inside and Out.* Edited by Robert E. Rinehart and Synthia Sydnor. Albany: State University of New York Press, 2002.

Harding, Warren. *Downward Bound: A Mad Guide to Rock Climbing.* Englewood Cliffs, N.J.: Prentice Hall, 1975.

Jones, Chris. *Climbing in North America.* Berkeley: University of California Press, 1976.

Mellor, Don. *American Rock: Region, Rock, and Culture in American Climbing.* Woodstock, Vt: The Countryman Press, 2001.

Roper, Steve. *Camp 4: Recollections of a Yosemite Rockclimber.* Seattle: The Mountaineers, 1994.

Scott, D. *Big Wall Climbing.* New York: Oxford University Press, 1974.

Tejada-Flores, Lito. "Games Climbers Play." *Ascent* 1 (1967): 23–25.

Unsworth, Walt. *Encyclopaedia of Mountaineering.* New York: St. Martin's Press, 1975.

Waterman, Guy, and Laura Waterman. *Yankee Rock and Ice: A History of Climbing in the Northeastern United States.* Mechanicsburg, Pa: Stackpole Books, 2002.

Peter Donnelly

ROCK CONCERT AUDIENCES

Compared with other genres of music, rock glorifies its audience. As the cliché goes, rock and roll is "for the fans." Think of an audience at a classical music performance or jazz club. The performers play and await applause. Rock-and-roll performers want more—cheers, song requests, and, as so many stars claim, the energy of their fans. For instance, remembering the Beatles, people recall not only the four performers but also the screaming girls who attended concerts—that is, the "Beatlemania" that transcended the band.

Sociologists in cultural studies confirm this conclusion. Contrary to those who scorn rock audiences as passive recipients of hyped-up trends concocted by big business, many writers today believe audiences imbue music with meaning. People are told that performers and promoters might intend one outcome, but audiences can create another outcome with any cultural "text" (a song or performance). Still, documenting the history of rock audiences is difficult. Audiences are ephemeral; as the sociologist David Riesman once commented, it is hard to tell what is happening when someone says they like something (Frith and Goodwin, p. 12).

Much of our knowledge about rock audiences is of styles—clothing, dance, and drugs, all of which typically correlate with genres of music. Rock audiences of the 1950s consisted of boys with sideburns and tapered hair (a "duck's ass") and girls wearing pedal pushers. By 1960, these adolescents were dancing "the twist" while turning to longer hair and miniskirts. As the 1960s progressed, the hippie became a mainstay of rock listeners—with body paints, beads, bells, flowers, as well as marijuana and the hallucinogenic drug LSD (also known as acid). During the 1970s, marijuana and long hair remained, but there were also hot pants and enormous collars on polyester shirts (especially among disco fans). With punk rock, audiences exhibited safety pins, chains, and spiky and colorful hair as they collided off one another in local clubs where they "slam danced" and "pogoed." Rap audiences wore gold chains and break-danced while listening to DJs spinning records and "rapping" over them. In whole, rock audiences and genres reflected the ever-changing nature of postmodern culture.

Of course, style tells only so much about rock audiences. Delving deeper reveals more interesting lessons about the nature of mass culture. For instance, it is known that the original audience for rock and roll (a mix of country and blues during the 1940s and 1950s) was predominantly working class, urban, and often African American. Early record producers were small businessmen from working-class neighborhoods. Rock's most famous breakthrough performer, Elvis Presley, was from a working-class background. Nonetheless, when he played on the *Ed Sullivan Show* in 1956, infamously shot from the waist up, he became a mass commodity, widening rock's audience to include middle-class consumers who

Woodstock. Nearly half a million people attended the Woodstock Music and Art Fair in Bethel, New York. Held on a 600-acre dairy farm in the Catskill Mountains, the event was dubbed "Three Days of Peace and Music" and kicked off on 15 August 1969. The mainly youthful audience enjoyed musicians such as Joan Baez, Jimi Hendrix, the Grateful Dead, and The Who, and neither heavy rains nor huge traffic jams could dampen the crowd's enthusiasm. © *AP/Wide World Photos*

had the purchasing power of postwar prosperity. This new audience discovered numerous forums for music: jukeboxes in restaurants and soda fountains, "record hops" at dance halls, radios in cars, 45 rpm records, and television at home.

Some feared this mass audience, while others embraced it. Fear grew out of historical coincidence—rock correlated with growing concern about juvenile delinquency during the 1950s. In the wake of World War II, sociologists discovered a "youth culture" made up solely of peers. As it became more autonomous, some believed young people got out of control—citing vandalism and unruly schools. In 1955, *Blackboard Jungle* was released in American theaters; the movie depicted rowdy adolescents getting out of hand at a public school (trying to rape a teacher) and, for the first time ever, featured rock mu-

sic (Bill Haley's "Rock around the Clock"). The film hinted at an underlying perception that rock music and young audiences were inducing social breakdown in America.

Two years after *Blackboard Jungle* was released, Dick Clark started his famous television show *American Bandstand.* Building on his prior experience as a local Philadelphia disc jockey, Clark displayed to national audiences young people dancing. People who watched the show reported watching the audience more than the rock performers. Clark had strict rules about behavior and dress: Boys wore ties; girls wore skirts (and no tight sweaters). He made clear something that many DJs and record promoters had already learned: that the rock audience was not something to be feared but plumbed for its consumer potential.

By the 1960s, more marketers caught on. What's known as the "British Invasion"—the success of bands like the Beatles, the Rolling Stones, and the Who—relied upon marketing. Before 1964, when the Beatles arrived in the United States, Capitol Records had launched a successful and unprecedented blitz of publicity. The band's performances became well known for screams from middle-class adolescent girls, with the Beatles winking and nodding at audience members. Though pushed by marketing, audiences still tried to assert control. For instance, when the Beatles came to Milwaukee, Wisconsin, teenage girls tried to get jobs at the hotel where the band stayed and broke through the police cordon where the band landed. Here was a central tension in rock audience history: Audiences were managed props for big acts, signifiers of success, and autonomous entities pressing their own desires.

It was not until later in the 1960s that a more reciprocal relation between audience and performer emerged. By the mid-1960s, America's "counterculture" blossomed, centered in the Haight-Ashbury neighborhood of San Francisco. Young people "dropped out" by using marijuana and LSD, living communally, and resisting materialism. Two major bands—Jefferson Airplane and the Grateful Dead—played local venues for this new counterculture. The Dead participated in a series of "Acid Tests," organized by Ken Kesey, where audiences dropped acid (which was still legal) and danced to music and light shows, trying to build off the energy of the bands. Films of these events depict the audience and performers evenly, showing that both mattered. This relationship between performer and audience became a trademark for the Grateful Dead, who continued to tour up into the 1990s. The Dead performed audience requests and reported a spiritual connection with their audiences, who performed a variety of rituals, including gathering in parking lots before shows, trading tapes of performances, and tripping on acid.

The role of the countercultural rock audience culminated in the Woodstock Music Festival of 1969. Here again a central tension emerged: a corporate desire for control versus audience autonomy. Promoters who organized the festival hoped to gross profits by hiring Jimi Hendrix, Jefferson Airplane, and other key countercultural acts, but the event spun out of control. Half a million young people showed up, many without tickets. Soon they were scrambling over fences and making the event their own. Any viewer of the film *Woodstock* remembers audiences swimming in lakes, feasting on communally prepared food, helping one another through bad acid trips, and sliding through mud during torrential rain-

storms. Many report that the event belonged to the audience and not the performers.

During the 1970s, the grander hopes of the counterculture faded. After all, dropping out had not transformed society. Rock audiences during this time still donned long hair and smoked marijuana, but there were no more Woodstocks. Nor was rock just about youth anymore. Indeed, during the 1970s, "youth" signified lifestyle more than age, as baby boomers continued to listen to rock. Rock audiences also became more suburban, less urban. In the process, audiences became bigger, as record companies consolidated during the 1970s, forming the "Big Six" of Warner, Columbia, Polygram, RCA, Capitol-EMI, and MCA, and rock acts played in large arenas and stadiums, supported by massive promotions. Rock musicians became icons consumed by large, faceless audiences.

During the late 1970s and early 1980s, some young people hoped to make popular music more local and participatory, thus creating more decentralized audiences. Hip-hop music and rap started in the basements of South Bronx homes ("house parties"), where kids break-danced and socialized. Punk rock encouraged participation in local "scenes" via shows at smaller venues (bowling alleys and recreation centers), "fanzines," and independent record companies. By 1981, MTV (the music television network) hit the air and eventually started to promote rap and the first inklings of "alternative" music. In the late 1980s and early 1990s, one local "scene" in Seattle known for "grunge music" managed to break big, thanks to the pioneering work of Subpop Records (who, in their promotional materials, used pictures of local audiences as much as bands) and the hype created by the national media. By the 1990s, the corporate-culture industry seemed to swallow up local music scenes.

It is impossible to predict the future of the rock audience. It will probably be segmented, made up of diverse "taste publics" (see Kotarba). Needless to say, rock's rebelliousness seems a thing of the past. Almost any trend, no matter how out of the ordinary, can be marketed. On the other hand, rock audiences still try to assert control. Recall Napster, a free Internet downloading service for rock music fans. Though shut down in 2000, it illustrates that audiences always manage to find ways to take back control from big record companies and their promotional infrastructure. The rock audience's future is up for grabs, but its past highlights a clear pattern of pushing and being pulled.

See also: Country Music Audiences; Rap Music Audiences; Record, CD, Tape Collecting and Listening; Traditional Folk Music Festivals

BIBLIOGRAPHY

Du Noyer, Paul, ed. *The Story of Rock 'n' Roll: The Year-by-Year Illustrated Chronicle.* New York: Schirmer Books, 1995.

Epstein, Jonathan, ed. *Adolescents and Their Music: If It's Too Loud, You're Too Old.* New York: Garland Publishing, 1994.

Friedlander, Paul. *Rock and Roll: A Social History.* Boulder, Colo.: Westview Press, 1996.

Frith, Simon, and Andrew Goodwin, eds. *On Record: Rock, Pop, and the Written Word.* New York: Pantheon Books, 1990.

Jackson, John. *American Bandstand: Dick Clark and the Making of a Rock 'n' Roll Empire.* New York: Oxford University Press, 1997.

Kasparek, Jonathan. "A Day in the Life: The Beatles Descend on Milwaukee." *Wisconsin Magazine of History* 84 (2000–2001): 14–23.

Kotarba, Joseph. "Styles of Adolescent Participation in an All-Ages, Rock 'n' Roll Nightclub: An Ethnographic Analysis." *Youth and Society* 18 (1987): 398–417.

Lipsitz, George. *Time Passages: Collective Memory and American Popular Culture.* Minneapolis: University of Minnesota Press, 1990.

Mattson, Kevin. "Did Punk Matter? Analyzing the Practices of a Youth Subculture during the 1980s." *American Studies* 42 (2001): 69–97.

Miller, James. *Flowers in the Dustbin: The Rise of Rock and Roll, 1947–1977.* New York: Simon and Schuster, 1999.

Pearson, Anthony. "The Grateful Dead Phenomenon: An Ethnomethodological Approach." *Youth and Society* 18 (1987): 418–432.

Kevin Mattson

ROCKHOUNDING

Popular American rockhounding began in the 1930s. Native Americans and other amateur geologists had collected, carved, and polished stones of various sorts, but electrification and automobility pushed a new mass of rock-hungry hobbyists into the mountains and deserts of the American West, where myriad varieties of agate, jasper, petrified wood, and other precious stones were waiting to be picked up. Rock and gem clubs were eventually established throughout the country, publishing news of "agate rushes" and other geoevents in newsletters with such names as *Tourma Lines, Chert Chatter, Alaska Pebble Patter,* and *Rockhound's Bark.*

Social and natural forces converged to foster the hobby. The rise of the westward family vacation was important, as was road building and other heavy construc-

tion, which exposed new kinds of rock to human eyes. The Great Depression played an interesting role, as people fleeing unemployment ended up wandering the canyons, quarries, and ploughed fields of California and other areas of the west looking for whatever gems they could turn into jewelry and an extra buck. Many of these early rock hounds set up rock shops along popular desert highways where vacationers might stop in.

After World War II, some of these first-generation rock hounds began to share their knowledge in popular "how-to" gem-cutting guides, giving simple instructions on rock tumbling, metal craft, and the use of the diamond saw and silicon carbide grinding wheels for gem cutting. "Gem trail" field manuals were also published—at least fourteen in the 1950s alone—usually with crudely drawn maps to appeal to the treasure hunter. Rockhounding came to be regarded as a wholesome, instructive, and to some extent patriotic activity, as when amateurs were urged to prospect for radioactive rocks for sale to the Atomic Energy Commission.

In 1963, there were an estimated 3,000 rock shops and 900 gem and mineral clubs in the United States, many of which were listed in the *Rockhound Buyer's Guide,* published annually by the *Lapidary Journal* (founded in 1947). Ready-made saws, laps, tumblers, and templates were available from companies like Covington, Frantom, and Highland Park. Whereas rock hounds were, prior to about 1940, primarily adults who had built their own equipment, postwar rock hounds were often teens or even preteens who could now purchase equipment on a modest budget. Lelande Quick, in his 1963 *The Book of Agates and Other Quartz Gems,* proclaimed rockhounding "a great leveler of people" (pp. 84–85).

America's rock hound romance peaked in the early 1960s, when the Bureau of Land Management estimated there were 3 million American rock hounds in the country. A 1972 pamphlet declared there to be at least one rock shop for every western town with a population above a thousand, though by this time the hobby was already showing signs of decline. Television was taking its toll, and people were beginning to wonder whether grinding a lot of rocks in their garage or basement was a healthy way to spend their time. Many of the early "easy" rock-gathering sites were becoming exhausted, and military expansion and privatization were closing access to other sites. Commercial and urban development also destroyed many sites. The coastal towns of Redondo Beach and Hermosa Beach in southern California, for example, used to be popular spots for collecting; both sites became barren, since the building of breakwaters and boat harbors altered the tidal action that once tossed stones onto the shore. Mining laws and machines also limited many sites. Liability laws made mine owners reluctant to allow gem hunters onto their property, and new kinds of mining techniques—such as the crushers that break up Lake Superior gravel—destroy many gems before they are ever seen. Many once-beloved rockhounding sites have been bought up by ranchers or retirees who frown upon collecting: tire tycoon Les Schwab, for example, purchased the Teeter Ranch of central Oregon, home to Teeter Plume Agate, and permitted no mining. Many interesting rocks were out of reach within areas protected by the Wilderness Protection or Wild Rivers Acts, both of which barred collecting.

One positive sign for rock hounds was the establishment of rock hound state parks (for example, at Deming in New Mexico), where collectors were guaranteed the right to dig in perpetuity (using only hand tools). Rock hounds were also still able to use their "silver picks" at gem shows and rock hound gatherings in places such as Quartzsite and Tucson, and in virtual commercial spaces such as eBay. The idea of rockhounding as some kind of familial glue or escape from the mundane now seems quaintly archaic, judging from the (interestingly apocalyptic) paean to the hobby authored by Ellis Wilhite of Deep River, Iowa, in 1965:

> Will there still be any people in a thousand years or so,
>
> To be strictly on the level, I'll admit that I don't know,
>
> But if there's one survivor, and he's a rockhound tried and true,
>
> He will burst if he finds something, and [has] no one to show it to.

See also: Collecting, Hobbies and Crafts

BIBLIOGRPAHY

Fry, Paul. *Meanderings of a Montana Rockhound.* Miles City, Mont.: Paul Fry, 1972.

Proctor, Robert N. "Anti-Agate: The Great Diamond Hoax and the Semiprecious Stone Scam." *Configurations* 9 (2001): 381–412.

Quick, Lelande. *The Book of Agates and Other Quartz Gems.* Philadelphia: Chilton Books, 1963.

Wilhite, Ellis. "Out of the Dinosaur's Gizzard." *Rocks and Minerals* (August 1965): 593.

Zeitner, June Culp. *Midwest Gem Trails.* Portland, Or.: Mineralogist Publishing Company, 1956.

Robert Proctor

RODEOS

Since the first attempts to domesticate animals, humans have been pitted against them. Civilizations throughout time and across the world have a history of providing spectacles of man versus beast. Rodeos of today reflect elements from each of these cultures.

The rodeo of North America is different, however, from all other events involving humans and animals due to the presence of one character: the cowboy. The beginnings of rodeo are tied to the men who worked cattle from the back of a horse. Cowboys were hired as laborers by cattlemen to drive feral cattle (longhorns) across the plains from Texas to Kansas and Missouri, where they were put on railroad cars and shipped to eastern markets. Cattle drives across the open plains lasted only thirty years, with the peak from 1870 through the 1880s. By the close of the 1880s, the long cattle drives were losing their usefulness and importance. The decline was due to the completion of the Transcontinental Railroad at Promontory Point, Utah, in 1869 as well as the change from herding wild longhorn cattle across open plains to the raising of docile Herefords, imported from England, in fenced-in range land.

Though cattle drives had ended, the life and romantic image of the western cowboy did not. Working cowboys still had to round up cattle off the range, to count and brand spring calves, and to attend to the sick ones. The roundups were a relished time for cowboys; it was a time to see people and hear all the local news. It was a time for drinking, gambling, running footraces, and having "cowboy fun"—roping and bronc-riding contests and horse racing. The term *bronc* is a colloquialism for bronco, which is a partially-tamed or wild horse. The cowboy fun of the late 1800s and early 1900s closely resembles what is called rodeo today, which is no accident. As Michael Allen notes, "Rodeo is derived from the Spanish verb *rodear*, meaning 'to encircle' or 'to round up,' and American rodeo is a direct descendant of the work festivals of early North American cowboys," (p. 16).

The Pro Rodeo Hall of Fame indicates that the first recorded rodeo contest was held in eastern Colorado near a town called Deer Trail in 1869; the event was bronc riding. The contest involved cowboys from two rival ranches, and each group bet on their best rough rider. There were no rules, no spectators, and no entry fees, and the cowboys were the judges. The winner, Emilnie Gradenshire, an Englishman, received no cash reward, but the cowhands from his ranch gave him a new suit of clothes.

National Finals Rodeo. Las Vegas has been the home for the National Rodeo Finals since 1985; the event debuted in Dallas in 1959. Established by the Rodeo Cowboys Association (now called the Professional Rodeo Cowboys Association), the National Finals features competitors who rank among the top fifteen money-winners in their event. Events include calf roping and steer wrestling. Here, Terry West wins a round in bull riding on 10 December 1995, although he fell just short of defeating Jerome Davis for the national title. © *Jack Dempsey for AP/Wide World Photos*

In the 1880s, rodeo contests became commonplace in western towns. At typical organized events, spectators paid admission, officials judged the events, and winners received cash prizes. The events at the rodeo were also becoming standardized.

Standard Events in Rodeo

In modern rodeo, there are four timed events and three roughstock events. The timed events include steer wrestling, calf roping, team roping, and barrel racing. The roughstock events are bareback, saddle bronc, and bull riding. While women are not barred from competing in any of these events by the Professional Rodeo Cowboy Association (PRCA), large numbers of women have not competed in any of the events except for barrel racing.

Timed Events In the steer wrestling event, the cowboy jumps from a running horse and wrestles a steer to the ground. The "bulldogger" (the cowboy wrestling the steer) is assisted by another cowboy called a hazer. The hazer rides on another horse alongside the steer to keep the steer running straight. With the steer between the hazer and the bulldogger, the bulldogger leans from his horse, grabs the

steer's horns, then jumps from his horse and, using his momentum, drops with the steer to the ground.

The objective of the cowboy in the calf-roping event is to rope and tie a running calf. Both horse and calf start running from chutes—small holding areas in the arena—with the calf getting a head start. As the roper approaches the calf, he swings the loop of his rope over his head and then casts it toward the calf. Once the calf is caught in the rope (the most common catch is around the head) the roper quickly pulls the slack out of the rope as the horse slides to a stop. As the roper dismounts the horse to run to the calf, the horse keeps the line taut. Grabbing the flank of the calf, the roper throws the calf to the ground. Using a six-foot rope called a "pigging string," the roper ties three of the calf's legs together.

The team-roping event involves two cowboys, a header and a heeler, and a steer. Both cowboys and steer leave the chutes with the steer between the cowboys. The header, riding in the lead, ropes the steer's horns and moves to the side so the heeler can move into position to cast his rope. The heeler is aiming to catch both back legs. If only one is caught, a five-second penalty is added to the team's time. After the heeler tightens his rope, both cowboys must face each other with the steer between them.

In professional rodeos, barrel racing is the only all-female event. Most PRCA rodeos have barrel racing, but in American rodeos it is considered an optional event and is governed by the Women's Professional Rodeo Association (WRPA). In this event, the horse and rider enter the arena, and the cowgirl directs her horse into a sprint. The clock starts when the horse crosses an electronic timing signal. The rider guides the horse through a cloverleaf pattern around three barrels crisscrossing the arena. After the horse has circled the last barrel, it runs full speed back to the starting line. While technically considered an optional event, barrel racing is the most popular and exciting event in the rodeo next to bull riding.

Roughstock Events While the goal of timed events is speed, roughstock events capitalize on the style of the cowboy.

In bareback riding the cowboy mounts the horse in a chute. The horse does not have a saddle but a strap running around its girth. The cowboy holds on to a rawhide "suitcase" handle that is attached to the strap. The event starts by the chute door opening and the cowboy leaning back and spurring the horse. The cowboy must "mark" or spur the horse on the first jump. If a rider doesn't mark the horse he is disqualified. The rider has eight seconds to perform the best style of bucking on the back of the horse and is judged on his style and ability to spur the horse.

Of the three roughstock events, saddle bronc riding is the only one whose roots are in ranch life. The event is similar to bareback riding, but the horse is saddled. The rider is again judged on his style and ability to spur the horse; failure to mark the horse on the first jump results in the rider being disqualified.

Compared to most other cowboys, bull riders are small, averaging 150 pounds. The bulls they attempt to ride can weigh ten times that weight. The event starts in a chute with the rider mounting the bull's back. The only handhold is a specially plaited rope that encircles the bull just behind its front legs. In order to successfully ride such a massive animal that is capable of jumping five feet in the air, the bull rider relies on his sense of balance, timing, and anticipation of the bull's moves. The bull rider is not expected to mark the bull as in bareback and saddle bronc riding; rather he is judged on his showmanship and riding skills. The bull wants the rider off his back and tries to do this by bucking, jumping, spinning, and cranking his head from side to side to get at the cowboy. After the bull rider either falls off or dismounts following a successful ride, bull fighters (not rodeo clowns) distract the bull to keep the rider safe.

Varieties of American Rodeo

The most common and highly publicized rodeos are the PRCA-sponsored events with men competing in all of the events except barrel racing. There are variations to PRCA events, however, that receive less media coverage and mass appeal yet serve specific cultural and ethnic groups. Several rodeo associations have formed to represent these specific groups and allow riders to participate without facing prejudice or discrimination. Specialty rodeos include Mexican American or Hispanic rodeo; Native American rodeo; Hawaiian rodeo; Black American rodeo; gay rodeo; celebrity rodeo; prison rodeo; police, firefighter, and military rodeo; senior rodeo; and women's rodeo.

See also: Western America Leisure Lifestyles, Wild West Shows

BIBLIOGRAPHY

Allen, Michael. *Rodeo Cowboys in the North American Imagination.* Reno: University of Nevada Press, 1998.

Fredriksson, Kristine. *American Rodeo, from Buffalo Bill to Big Business.* College Station: Texas A&M University Press, 1985.

LeCompte, Mary Lou. *Cowgirls of the Rodeo: Pioneer Professional Athletes.* Urbana: University of Illinois Press, 1993.

Wooden, Wayne S., and Gavin Ehring. *Rodeo in America: Wranglers, Roughstock and Paydirt.* Lawrence: University Press of Kansas, 1996.

Patti A. Freeman

ROLLER SKATING AND BLADING

Since the late nineteenth century, roller skating has played an important role in the history of American leisure. Through a series of "skating booms," from high-society clubs in the 1860s to the popular roller derbies of the 1930s, and the inline skate craze of the 1990s, roller skating has taken a variety of forms and meanings: professional sport and popular past-time, upper-class fad and commercialized mass entertainment.

First invented in eighteenth-century Europe, roller skating overcame a series of technical problems before it became suitable for any sort of mass leisure. Early models, such as Londoner John Tyer's 1823 inline skate

"Volito," allowed for only limited direction and glide, and generally made for a bumpy ride. By the middle of the nineteenth century, roller skating had reached the United States. Joseph Gidman patented the first American skate in 1852, soon to be followed by the Woodward skate and a series of other models. Massachusetts businessman James Plimpton's 1863 invention of the "rocking skate", however, presented a real technological breakthrough. His skate allowed skaters to take curves easily through the addition of a compressible rubber pad that enabled the skate to lean in the direction of the turn. The invention of the "toe stop" (1876) and friction reducing ball bearings (1884) paved the way for the mass proliferation of roller skates by the 1880s. Samuel Winslow and Micajah Henley were among the first mass producers of skates. Sales of Winslow's successful model (the "Vinyard" skate) soon reached 260,000 pairs per year, but encountered competition in the national market such as the popular "Chicago Skates."

By the 1880s, the roller skate had technically developed into its modern form, though the utilization of polyurethane wheels since the 1970s made skating even easier. Most skates were equipped with four wheels attached in two pairs (so-called "quads"). Inline skates did not prove economically successful throughout much of the twentieth century. Only after existing models were modified in the early 1980s and equipped with better wheels and a heel brake, did the "quads" loose their dominant position. Successfully marketed to a young, fitness oriented consumer segment by companies such as Rollerblade, (often used synonymously with inline skate), the inline skate has virtually eclipsed the classic roller skate in the popular imagination since the mid 1990s.

As a Spectator Sport: Roller Polo, Roller Derbies, Roller Dancing

Since the mid-nineteenth century, a variety of roller sports from roller hockey to roller derby and roller dancing has emerged. While never wholly successful in gaining wide-spread recognition as competitive sports (unlike ice skating), roller sports have seen the development of professional associations and, at times, managed to draw considerable crowds of spectators.

Roller polo and figure skating appeared as early as the 1870s, as upper class leisure activities. As skating became more widespread, commercial roller rink operators encouraged competitions, races, and roller polo or hockey. In 1885, one of the first six-day race meets was held in New York's Madison Square Garden. By the beginning of the twentieth century several roller hockey teams were playing in the United States; a first World Championship was played out in 1936. A professional roller hockey league was established in the 1930s, but proved short-lived. From then on, roller hockey's most important popular outlet was the informal street hockey, played on the increasingly-paved roads of twentieth-century America.

The 1930s also witnessed the roller derby craze. In many ways a spin-off of the six-day bicycle races during the Great Depression, the derby race on oval tracks grew into a popular spectator sport. The 1935 Transcontinental Roller Derby, lasting more than 57,000 laps (equidistant to a trip from New York to Los Angeles), drew 20,000 spectators. By the 1940s, artistic roller skating and roller dancing drew increasing audiences, especially among youths. A first World Championship was hosted in Washington, D.C., and competitions were broadcast on television well into the 1950s. While several roller sports (such as roller hockey and speed skating) appeared as "demonstration sports" at Olympic Games, none has managed to acquire official recognition as an Olympic sport. In the late twentieth and early twenty-first centuries, roller sports have played only a marginal role as spectator sports in America. Still, USA Roller Sports, located in Lincoln, Nebraska, functions as a governing body for roller sports in the United States and provides an organizational framework for various disciplines, as well as maintaining the National Museum of Roller Skating.

As a Popular Pastime: From Roller Parlor to Roller Rink and Roller Disco

More important for roller skating's place in the history of American leisure has been its role as a popular pastime. Plimpton was the first to open a skating club for gentlemen in New York. To skate on the parlor's maplewood floor, guests had to apply and prove "good social character." Roller skating then became a leisure activity for the "educated and refined classes."

With the increasing availability of affordable skates and the proliferation of commercial roller rinks charging between twenty-five and fifty cents, however, the roller skating audience quickly widened by the 1880s. The Casino roller rink in Chicago, for example, could accommodate up to 1,000 skaters by 1884, and was equipped with a modern lighting system from the Siemens corporation. Special dances such as the "Richmond Roll" contributed to the roller skate craze of the 1880s and 1890s. Around the turn of the century, the popularity of adult roller skating subsided somewhat. While children continued to skate on wooden sidewalks and elsewhere, sales of skates declined and upper-class patrons increasingly shunned the roller rinks.

Still, roller rinks continued to exist, and the 1902 opening of the Chicago Coliseum drew an astounding 7,000 skaters. The leisure activity, however, was increasingly associated with a "gutsier culture": teenagers, dusky skating rinks and an "other-side-of-the-tracks" atmosphere. Cheap, mass-produced, steerable skates, and roller rink tents allowed for another boom in roller skating as an affordable pastime during the Great Depression. The Roller Skating Rink Operator Association (now Roller Skating Association International) was formed in 1937 to ensure a minimum of standards among members, and rinks in the 1940s and 1950s attracted patrons with popular "roller bowls." Rink operators in the postwar era attempted to market their venues towards family leisure, but roller derbies and other events associated with "tough crowds" often continued to taint the image of roller skating. The association of roller rinks with working class and minority youth has led to a decline in recreational rink skating among middle-class families.

The 1970s saw another skating boom following the invention of plastic wheels, and the transformation of roller rinks into roller discos. The (once again) successful combination of wheels, lights, and music during the disco-era even helped adult roller skating to leave the confines of the rink and to enter public life. Commuting to work or shopping on skates became a fad, and in the 1980s roller skates once again returned to the stage in the popular musical "Star Light Express." A decade later, in-line skates succeeded in penetrating public life even further, drawing on their appeal to a growing number of "fitness-enthusiasts," and a slightly more upscale, modern image. Most skating rinks have since adapted to the inline skate. What began as the upscale roller parlors of the 1860s, and proliferated as commercial skating rinks for a mass audience, had, at the close of the twentieth century, largely evolved into "family entertainment centers" that combine roller skating with video games, laser tag, and other activities.

See also: Fads, Postwar to 1980 Leisure and Recreation, Skateboarding

BIBLIOGRAPHY

Dulles, Foster R. *A History of Recreation: America Learns to Play.* New York: Appleton-Century-Crofts, 1965.

Harwood, J. A. *Rinks and Rollers.* London and New York: Routledge, 1876.

Lewis, David. *Roller Skating for Gold.* Lanham, Md.: Scarecrow Press, 1997.

Roller Skating Association International. Available from http://www.rollerskating.org.

Traub, Morris, ed. *Roller Skating through the Years: The Story of Roller Skates, Rinks, and Skaters.* New York: William-Frederick Press, 1944.

Turner, James, and Michael Zaidman. *The History of Roller Skating.* Lincoln, Neb.: National Museum of Roller Skating, 1997.

USA Roller Sports. Available from http://www.usaroller-sports.org.

Jan Logemann

ROTISSERIE LEAGUES

See *Fantasy Sports*

RUNNING AND JOGGING

From the earliest times, running has been a natural part of humans' existence, whether to pursue food or to escape enemies. However, for centuries people also ran for pleasure, and competed against one another over set distances. This eventually led to the desire in many to improve their speed and their ability to run longer—the basic premise of running and jogging in the twenty-first century.

Modern Running

In 1850, the first rules to govern running, racing, and record keeping were established in London. Here, set distances such as the half mile, mile, and three mile were established as the core events of the sport. The first official modern track-and-field contest was held in 1860 between the university teams of Oxford and Cambridge. In 1894, the first modern international track meet was staged between Oxford and Yale.

In the United States, the development of running as an official sport followed the English, with the formation of the Amateur Athletic Union of America in 1876. Shortly thereafter, in 1896, the first modern Olympics were held in Athens, thanks to the dedicated efforts of Frenchman Baron Pierre de Coubertin. From this point onward, running became an accepted and highly popular sport.

Not just exercise. Jogging can also be a social activity as seen by these two couples who talk and smile during their run. © *Ariel Skelley/Corbis*

The Science of Running

At the beginning of the twentieth century, those who took part in competitive running races were generally fit and strong due to the demands of their vigorous lifestyles—farming, forestry, labor. Specific training, therefore, was rarely undertaken. Any training that did take place consisted of two to three moderate sessions per week, never totalling more than four to five miles. But with the growth of international competition, particularly following World War II, running became more serious. Paavo Nurmi of Finland, who won nine Olympic gold medals in the 1920s, was one of the earliest runners to train full time. Following, Nurmi, the German coach Werner Gerschler devised a system of conditioning athletes known as interval training that was still widely used as of the early 2000s.

Interval training consists of mixing hard bursts of running over short distances with a prescribed period of rest. As the distance and frequency of these bursts increases over the course of a season, the recovery period should decrease. Using this method, the athlete's fitness improves greatly.

The Running Revolution

With the publication of his acclaimed text *Aerobics* (1968), the Texas physician Kenneth Cooper popularized health and fitness, and soon Americans everywhere were concerned with their diet and daily exercise. Capitalizing on this fitness trend, and people's growing awareness of the importance of exercise, a number of lifetime runners wrote easy-to-read training manuals and charismatic personalities that captured the public's attention, and running become an everyday routine for millions of Americans. Bill Bowerman, the long-time University of Oregon track coach, along with Jim Fixx, released books titled *Jogging* (1967) and *The Complete Book of Running* (1977), respectively, which provided Americans with a clear route to an improved quality of life. Also adding inspiration to the running boom sweeping America was Frank Shorter's gold medal–winning performance in the marathon at the 1972 Munich Olympic Games.

Along with the growth in the number of runners across the United States came specialty running magazines such as *The Runner* and *Runner's World*. In addition, there was an increase in the number of annual road races that ranged anywhere in distance from three miles to the full marathon of 26.2 miles. Road running also became fun and fashionable as numerous cottage industries around footwear and running clothes burst onto the scene. Runners came in all shapes, sizes, and ages. It was a sport considered to have no limits or barriers to entry as exercise soon became part of many people's everyday routine.

A survey conducted by the United States Track and Field association showed that in 2002, 450,000 Americans ran a marathon (60 percent men, 40 percent women), and 40 percent of those were first-timers. Furthermore, according to American Sports Data, 10.5 million Americans ran 100 days or more in 2002, and spent a record $2.7 billion on running shoes. Such a large number of runners also contributed to the ongoing establishment of safe and well-designed running surfaces such as tracks and forest and park paths across the country, not to mention the increasing affordability and availability of running equipment, such as shoes and apparel.

Running and Racing in the Early Twenty-First Century

Running's popularity, at both the participation and spectator levels, showed no sign of decreasing. In fact, big-city marathons in New York and Chicago regularly attracted more than 30,000 contestants, including an elite section where prize money in the hundreds of thousands of dollars was available to both men and women. Runners from northern and eastern Africa dominated the sport, holding almost every men's and women's world record, from 800 meters up to the marathon. In addition, while the act of running remained simple, various new technologies—doping, genetic engineering, altitude houses—raised debates within the sport over the naturalness of running. While largely an ethical debate, it did shed light on the increasing growth of the sport of running as a full-time occupation for many athletes that could bring prestige and wealth both to the individual athlete and his or her nation.

See also: Marathons; Triathlons

BIBLIOGRAPHY

Bresnahan, George, and William Tuttle. *Track and Field Athletics.* London: Henry Kimpton, 1948.

Encyclopedia of Athletics. Twickenham, U.K.: Hamlyn, 1985.

Henderson, Joe. *The Complete Runner.* Mountain View, Calif.: World Publications, 1974.

Newsholme, Eric, Tony Leech, and Glenda Duester. *Keep on Running.* Chichester, U.K.: John Wiley and Sons, 1994.

Noakes, Tim. *Lore of Running.* Champaign, Ill.: Human Kinetics, 1991.

Jim Denison

SABBATARIANISM

Sabbatarianism, a movement devoted to preserving the sanctity of the Sunday Sabbath, emerged in the Anglo-American world in the seventeenth-century, but it gained force in the nineteenth century. Although multifaceted, Sabbatarians primarily focused their efforts on preventing the tumultuous and burgeoning worlds of recreation and leisure from interfering with the observance of Sunday in what they considered to be a biblically mandated manner, that is, as a day of rest. No single Protestant denomination accounted for all Sabbatarians. Rather, liberal Protestants tended to shy away from placing heavy restrictions on Sunday activity, a tendency that stood in striking contrast to traditionalists' (or orthodox) emphasis on prohibitions of all sorts. Sabbatarians dominated American religious and political approaches to Sunday through the nineteenth century, but with each decade of the twentieth century their power waned.

After the American Revolution, politicians wrote into state constitutions an array of Sunday laws that grew out of the Sabbatarian orientation that Puritan and Anglican colonists brought to North America; more important, however, a Sabbatarian bias against Sunday activity of any sort other than the religious had become customary by 1800. In the early decades of the nineteenth century, the Sabbatarian movement took institutional form, largely around the issue of transporting and delivering mail on Sunday. After the failure of their efforts to prevent the United States Post Office from functioning on Sunday, Sabbatarians turned to other depredations, mainly the unwillingness of many Americans to observe Sunday in such a manner that rest would be distinguished from work. They formed various organizations, sent petitions to elected officials, and published tracts urging the strict observance of Sunday as a day of rest. It is here that the pertinence of Sabbatarianism to the history of leisure and recreation comes into focus, for it was the inability of Americans to agree on what differentiated work from rest that animated controversies about not only Sunday observance but leisure and recreation in general.

Until the second half of the nineteenth century, dominant meanings for rest (that is, the meanings written into law and shaping custom) precluded all activity outside the home on Sunday except for attending divine services. It was believed that rest could be obtained only through prayer, church attendance, and meditation upon religious themes. But throughout the century, new theories about how to rest were developing. Unitarians and liberal Protestants embraced natural and man-made delights on all days of the week, and they argued that what refreshed the body and spirit at once provided rest and created opportunities for uplift that could lead to spiritual awakening. Additionally, German immigrants brought with them an expansive view of rest, as did other immigrants steeped in Catholic and European traditions. Within cities, churches, and homes, debates were waged over what was restful, with German Americans arguing that Sunday afternoons at beer gardens were in keeping with the spirit of the day of rest, ministers urging congregants to bicycle Sunday afternoons, and mothers admonishing children to put away their weekday playthings and devote their energies to biblical toys and games. But Sabbatarians resisted the creep of these views: in insisting on the closing of saloons, public libraries, and museums on Sundays, in petitioning in favor of stilling world's fairs each Sunday, or in lobbying behind the scenes to prevent Sunday afternoon baseball games—just to name a few instances of their work—they hewed closely to a circumscribed meaning for rest.

Additionally, Sabbatarians pointed to the incontestable fact that most recreation and leisure activities depended on the labor of railroad men, ticket takers, stage performers, star athletes, concession operators, and many others. To be sure, numerous Americans also toiled on Sundays, as well as the other six days of the week. Work without rest was nearly as troubling as rest without work, and with boom-and-bust characterizing the American economy none could be assured of steady work, but unemployment was hardly restful. Few Sabbatarian organizations took on the industrial giants of the period who ran their plants continuously. Instead, they focused their energies on reforming amusements and recreations.

In the meantime, the development of networks of commercial amusements and recreations further challenged the prohibition against Sunday work; picnic grounds, beer halls, saloons, beach resorts, amusement parks, concert halls, theaters, world's fairs, and such relied on the labor of many to operate. The vast majority of Americans were able to patronize these venues only on Sunday, for they were either working the other days of the week or broke. Indeed, attendance figures support such a contention: Sunday business exceeded that of all the other days of the week put together. And increasingly, as Americans argued that such diversions were restful, a concept of leisure developed that pivoted on commercialized opportunities for rest. Sunday soon became a day for leisure rather than a day of rest; by the 1920s, when this transformation was irreversible, Sabbatarianism lost its valence.

Despite the diminished political and theological potency of Sabbatarianism in the twentieth century, many Sunday laws remained on the books and many customs associated with proscribing the sphere of Sunday activity continued to hold sway. One of the first set of Sunday laws to disappear were those that banned theatrical shows. Oregon and California led the way in the nineteenth century and, by 1910, most states allowed certain kinds of theaters to open on Sunday, though the content of the spectacles was censored so as to showcase material in keeping with the sanctity of the day. World War I was a turning point in the diminution of Sunday laws, in part because entrepreneurs opportunistically linked Sunday opening with patriotic fund-raisers and morale

boosters. Before the war, all but six states prohibited the screening of movies on Sundays, but a campaign led by the National Association of the Motion Picture Industry led to the granting of local option for movie palaces to open on Sundays. By the mid-1920s, all large cities, with a few exceptions such as Knoxville, Tennessee, allowed movie theaters, dance halls, roller-skating rinks, bowling alleys, and other commercialized recreation venues to open Sunday afternoons and evenings. It was only in the 1970s that prohibitions against Sunday morning openings dissipated, and then it was because the Sabbatarian impulse was vestigial at best.

Sunday as a widespread day of rest helped to shape professional baseball and football during their formative periods. Self-imposed Sabbatarian regulations helped baseball become the sport of the middle classes. In banning Sunday contests and the sale of beer in 1878, the National League sought to foster a family-oriented, respectable image. By the 1890s, it was no longer necessary to avoid play on Sunday. In order to appease the sensibilities of Sabbatarians, however, baseball's managers sponsored sacred concerts and other such exercises before the first pitch. Some states where Sabbatarians held significant political power, notably Massachusetts and Pennsylvania, banned Sunday games; during World War I, owners of teams in these states held exhibition games to raise monies for the war effort. Still, through the 1930s, Sunday baseball was illegal in Boston, Philadelphia, Pittsburgh, and most southern cities. In the 1920s, semiprofessional football games were held on Sundays, mostly because players were not available at other times. As the sport took shape, a distinct calendar solidified, whereby high schools played on Fridays, colleges on Saturdays, and the pros on Sunday. Ironically, until the 1990s, Sunday— a day idealized as separate from the quest for profit—was solely the province of professional sporting contests, with amateur contests held at other times.

Although Sabbatarianism as a movement was on the wane during the first third of the twentieth century, the commercial aspect of theater and sports bothered enough Americans that Sunday laws remained on the books. While Americans had accepted the existence of multiple and conflicting styles of rest, and sought to accommodate them, the majority was uncomfortable about making Sunday into a day of gain, or in the words of one critic, in "putting the dollar mark on it." However, by the 1960s, most Americans were no longer discomfited with the rampant commercialization of every day life, and thus Sunday laws came to seem antiquated and anachronistic. Although the Supreme Court upheld the constitutionality of Sunday laws in 1961, state legislatures began to repeal such laws. Americans wanted to be able to shop, play, and even work according to the dictates of their own consciences and the demands of their schedules. Today, the only proscriptions that remain in effect across the nation are against the sale of alcohol on Sundays. And so, a long period of Sabbatarian hegemony over Sunday recreation and leisure gave way to an age when only private sentiment regulates Sunday observance.

See also: Church Socials, Regulation and Social Control of Leisure

BIBLIOGRAPHY

Evenson, Bruce J. "'Saving the City's Reputation': Philadelphia's Struggle over Self-Identity, Sabbath-Breaking, and Boxing in America's Sesquicentennial Year." *Pennsylvania History* 60 (1993): 6–34.

John, Richard R. "Taking Sabbatarianism Seriously." *Journal of the Early Republic* 10 (1990): 517–567.

McCrossen, Alexis. *Holy Day, Holiday: The American Sunday.* Ithaca, N.Y.: Cornell University Press, 2000.

Marion, Forrest L. "Blue Laws, Knoxville, and the Second World War." *Journal of East Tennessee History* 68 (1996): 41–62.

Raucher, Alan. "Sunday Business and the Decline of Sunday Closing Laws: A Historical Overview." *Journal of Church and State* 36 (1994): 13–33.

Solberg, Winton. *Redeem the Time: The Puritan Sabbath in Early America.* Cambridge, Mass.: Harvard University Press, 1977.

Alexis McCrossen

SAILING AND YACHTING

Sailing refers to the pastime of cruising for pleasure in vessels powered by sail only; a combination of sail and steam, diesel, or gas power; or engine propulsion only. Yachting is the sport of racing in yachts with sails for money or plate (the terminology used for a plaque or trophy). While there is no single "yacht type" of boat, there are many types of vessels used for yachting and sailing, including sloops, cutters, brigantines, shallops, yawls, catamarans, schooners, and ketches.

History of Sport Sailing

With their focus on exploration and trade, early explorers would have thought of sailing for pleasure as a ridiculous notion. By the 1600s, however, scouting craft, or

"jaghts," used by the seafaring Dutch served a dual purpose. As warships suited to sheltered waters, they were also well matched for pleasure sailing by affluent Dutch burghers. In the early seventeenth century, Dutch settlers then introduced both the sport and the pastime to the American colonies. It was not until the nineteenth century, however, that yachting and sailing took firm hold in the New World. Different in shape and design from commercial and naval vessels of the time, the *Onkabye,* a ninety-foot schooner built in 1840, is generally credited as the first American sailing yacht.

During the period from the early 1800s to the early 1900s, several technological advances in ship design and construction formed a crucible for three key pioneers— George Crowninshield Jr., Cornelius Vanderbilt, and James Gordon Bennett Jr.—to foster growth and popularity in this leisure activity.

Key Pioneers

Historians generally credit as the first American luxury or pleasure yacht *Cleopatra's Barge,* a schooner-type powered by sail and launched in 1816 at Salem, Massachusetts, for her independently wealthy owner, George Crowninshield Jr. (1766–1817). Conceiving it as a floating home, not only did Crowninshield raise the bar at the intersection of speed, seaworthiness, capacity, and comfort, but his outgoing personality was also instrumental in fostering a new level of public awareness of sailing. With paneled walls, gilt-edged ceilings, a fireplace, and fine appointments, the bill for this ship was $50,000 (in 1815 dollars), approximately three times the cost of a similar-sized merchant ship. Furnishings added another $50,000. Once launched, it became a source of curiosity wherever it went. When it docked in Barcelona, Spain, on its maiden voyage, it attracted 20,000 visitors over a five-day period. After the death of its owner, this piece of art was sold for a mere $15,400.

Although the onset of the Civil War and the resulting need for speed would further push development of steam vessels, individuals like Cornelius Vanderbilt (1821–1885) played important roles in attracting international attention to the advantages of steam yachts. First in a long line of Vanderbilts associated with yachting and sailing, Cornelius amassed a merchant fleet of sixty-six vessels over a fifty-year period. By 1853, he was the richest individual in America. To enjoy his wealth, he ordered not just a luxury yacht but also the first luxury steam-motor yacht. A massive hybrid paddle wheeler, *North Star* was 270 feet long with thirty-four-foot wheels grafted onto the traditional clipper hull in addition to two masts for auxiliary sails. With many of the crew on the maiden

Sailing. Off the coast of St. Thomas sailboats cruise in the Caribbean Sea. © *Corbis*

voyage volunteers from affluent families, the yacht was large enough to accommodate the Vanderbilt family in style. Yet, the purpose of the ship was much the same as *Cleopatra's Barge*: to voyage to Europe and show the Old World the New World's achievements and to attract the attention of royalty.

The Vanderbilts' maiden four-month trip to Europe —a trip that would have taken over a year by sailing yacht—not only succeeded in attracting public attention to the speed of steam-motor yachts, but also acted as a harbinger for what was to become an annual migratory pattern for scores of wealthy American yachtsmen and yachtswomen. These young people sailed to the French Riviera in spring, the Baltic in summer, and royal regattas at Cowes, England, and Kiel, Germany, in August. (A regatta is a short event held over a weekend or a week. Cruisers and yachters gather to compete and socialize. Generally held by a yacht club, these events are an annual tradition for many clubs in coastal inland waterways. Regattas contrast with ocean racing, which is a long-term, long-distance event.) Following a winter spent cruising the Caribbean, yachtsmen would then bring their vessels back to the United States, refurbish them, and then start the cycle over again.

James Gordon Bennett Jr. (1841–1918), a newspaperman in his own right, inherited his wealth from his Scottish immigrant father's tabloid paper the *New York Herald*. As the owner of the racing schooners *Dauntless* and *Henrietta* (one of only two sailing yachts accepted by the Union navy during the Civil War; the other seventy-nine were steam-powered vessels) and steam-motor yachts *Polynima*, *Namouna*, and *Lysistrata*, his wealth enabled him to pursue his dual passions of competition yachting and cruising. Not only did this two-time commodore of the oldest, most prestigious yacht club in America, the New York Yacht Club (founded in 1844), attract international publicity, his penchant for excess fostered the development of several technological and aesthetic advances in yachts—such as welding instead of riveting, the introduction of stabilizers and double-hulled vessels, and the development of stunning, unique interior designs—as he strived to push the intersection of speed, seaworthiness, and comfort. His newspaper offices located in both New York and Paris coupled with his involvement in the New York Yacht Club honed his interest in reducing time to cross the Atlantic Ocean. Indeed, the New York Yacht Club had only four steam yachts in its fleet in 1870. By 1890, it had seventy-one, in part due to Bennett's enthusiasm for steam-motor yachts.

Women, Sailing, and Yachting

Dominated by affluent families with names like Astor, Roosevelt, Vanderbilt, and Whitney, yachting and sailing were historically considered spectator sports for women. However, many notable American yachtswomen also played central roles in broadening women's participation in sailing and competitive yachting. Lucy Carnegie, owner of the 135-foot steel-hulled *Dungeness* and a successful yachtswoman, challenged male supremacy at the New York Yacht Club in 1894. When she petitioned to be the first female member of the all-male club, members convened a special committee to consider this embarrassing matter. After deliberation, the club admitted women as "Flag Members." Allowing yachtswomen to fly the club's flag and to use various mail stations established along the eastern coast of the United States, the club did not permit women to enter its New York headquarters. Fifty years later, the New York Yacht Club finally admitted women as full members.

Throughout the twentieth century, women have continued to take more active roles in sailing and yachting. The first direct challenge between two women members of opposing teams—Phyllis Sopwith, a timekeeper, representing Great Britain and Gertrude Vanderbilt, a crewmember, representing the United States—took place in 1934 in the prestigious yachting race called America's Cup. It was not until 1995 that American Dawn Riley, a veteran of competitive yacht races, including the grueling 32,000-mile Whitbread Round-the-World Race, became captain of the first all-women's team to enter the race for America's Cup.

America's Cup

Considered by many to be the pinnacle of competitive yachting, the America's Cup race has a long, tumultuous history. With centuries of control over the high seas, Great Britain sought to test that supremacy during the Great Exposition of 1851 by challenging the United States to a yacht race. The United States accepted, and the New York Yacht Club commissioned the building of a ninety-foot sail-powered schooner *America*. Not only did *America* break the record for a transatlantic crossing en route to the race, covering the distance in twenty-one days, but also this schooner went on to beat the British in a competitive race against fifteen other yachts around the Isle of Wight. In recognition, a trophy known as America's Cup was commissioned and deeded in 1857 for safe-keeping between races to the New York Yacht Club. Despite numerous international challenges, America's Cup remained in the hands of the United States for a period of 132 years. Only in 1983 did Australia succeed in its challenge for the cup. The United States regained the cup in 1987, lost it to New Zealand in 1995, and lost again to New Zealand in 2000.

During the 1980s and 1990s, fierce competition and all-out efforts to push design and technology limits shrouded many of the teams challenging for America's Cup in controversy and scandal. In an effort to create a uniform set of rules and measurement standards—an ongoing problem since the early 1800s, when yacht racing first became an organized sport in the harbors of New York, Boston, Chicago, and San Francisco and each yacht club operated under its own set of rules and regulations—the International Sailing Federation (ISAF) specified that challenging yachts must follow specific guidelines for dimensions and design. Thus, since 1992, a new class of longer, lighter boats, the seventy-foot International America's Cup Class—carrying 40 percent more sail on a higher mast—have been used in cup races. Since Australia's victory in 1983, extensive media coverage of the event has meant that millions of Americans who had never heard of the America's Cup race now take an interest in the sport of yachting.

With yachting being traditionally a sport of the wealthy, original sailboats and yachts had wooden hulls and canvas sails. Nowadays synthetic materials predominate for hulls and sails. The introduction of plywood and fiberglass has been ideal for development of lighter, stronger hulls and more powerful rigs (which are composed of the mast, a boom, and the sails).

The advent of synthetic sail fabrics, improved electronic instrumentation, and mass production has opened up the pursuit of sailing to thousands of individuals. From light, maneuverable one-person dinghies to larger vessels requiring trained crew, from cruising for pleasure to ocean racing for competitive purposes, from cruising with friends on inland waters to sailing across oceans single-handedly, from belonging to the Midget Racing Club of America to being sponsored to compete by corporations, cruising and yachting have undergone remarkable democratic transformations in the last fifty years. In the United States alone, there are now over 40,000 registered yachters, yet unlike many other leisure activities, cruising and yachting are accessible to individuals with physical, visual, auditory, and learning impairments. Indeed, in 1998, Geoffrey Hutton-Barber became the first visually impaired individual to sail single-handedly across an ocean.

See also: Boating, Power; Fishing, Freshwater; Fishing, Saltwater/Deep Sea

BIBLIOGRAPHY

Bond, Bob. *The Handbook of Sailing.* New York: Alfred A Knopf, 2001.

Chappelle, Howard. *History of American Sailing Ships.* New York: Bonanza Books, 1935.

International Sailing Federation. Home page at http://www.sailing.org.

MacTaggart, Ross. *The Golden Century: Classic Motor Yachts.* New York: W. W. Norton and Company, 2001.

Rousmaniere, John. *The Seafarers: The Luxury Yachts.* Chicago: Time-Life Books, 1981.

Sleight, Steve. *Complete Sailing Manual.* New York: DK Publishing, 1999.

Careen Yarnal

SALOONS

See *Bars*

SATELLITE RADIO

See *Radio Listening, Car and Home*

SCOUTING MOVEMENTS

Scouting is a worldwide organized youth movement for boys and girls, usually aimed at children and adolescents in the six- to seventeen-year-old age range. Scouting is one of the oldest such movements, and the two organizations based in the United States have served a large number of youth. On 4 April 2000, the Boy Scouts of America (BSA) registered its one-hundred-millionth member since its founding in 1910. The Girl Scouts of America (GSA) has had over 50 million members since its 1912 founding. As of December 2001, the BSA reported having 3.3 million boys and young men registered in its seven programs across the age groups; the GSA reported 2.8 million girls registered in its age-graded programs.

The Boy Scouts

Although there were precursor youth movements in the nineteenth century, including the Young Men's Christian Association (YMCA), the movement known as scouting began with the founding of the Boy Scouts in England in 1908 by Lord Robert Baden-Powell, a military hero of the Boer War (1899–1902). Disturbed by the poor physical condition of the young men in the army he led, Baden-Powell established the Boy Scouts to revitalize British manhood through an organized program teaching campcraft and other skills meant to improve the mental and physical condition of these young men. From the start, the Boy Scouts embraced a military-style uniform, earned badges and ranks, and possessed a patriotic fervor. The term *scouting* came from the figure of the military scout, who could live off the land and move about without detection. Baden-Powell's first handbook (*Scouting for Boys*) for the movement instructed boys in these skills and others, often using games as a means of teaching certain skills.

The ideas evident in the founding documents of the movement reflect a number of currents in late-nineteenth-century England and the United States. Social Darwinism was the dominant thought system, and the creators of youth movements (such as the YMCA and the Boy Scouts) saw no incompatibility between the Darwinian and religious—primarily Protestant Christian—worldviews. In fact, there emerged in this period a coherent theory of "muscular Christianity" that linked physical activity like team sports with moral development and the building of character. The social Darwinism of Herbert Spencer in England and of figures like William Graham Sumner in the United States accepted the view that the human race evolved through distinct, developmental stages, and, with the rise of Darwinian scientific psychology in the 1880s, those reformers interested in revitalizing English and American youth had a full theory of youth instincts and developmental stages to provide a confident, scientific basis for the movements they were creating. The psychology of G. Stanley Hall (1844–1924) in the United States, especially, provided a developmental scheme for understanding how the child's own physical and mental growth "recapitulated" the history of the human race. The publication of Hall's massive work, *Adolescence*, in 1904 helped create a whole new period in the life course, a period requiring its own, new institutions of socialization and development. Scouting and other movements designed their activities to take advantage of youthful instincts and developmental stages rather than work against this powerful, biological, evolutionary foundation for childhood and adolescence.

Boy Scouts. A troop of Boy Scouts sits and listens to its Scout leader. The Boy Scouts were originally founded in Great Britain and then established in the U.S. in 1910. © *Getty Images*

Social changes in both England and the United States also provided impetus for the creation of movements that would revitalize the society by revitalizing young people's minds and bodies. Historians agree that there was a crisis in white masculinity felt in the middle classes in the closing decades of the nineteenth century. Economic volatility created uncertainty for the breadwinners in those classes, and increasing numbers of immigrants (especially into the United States) threatened to disrupt the white man's sense that he had matters under control. Although England had a history as the colonizer and the Boer War was merely one of a string of conflicts necessary to maintain the empire, the United States began its own twentieth-century empire with the Spanish American War of 1898, another symptom of the masculinity crisis and response.

The creation of the Boy Scouts by Lord Baden-Powell, therefore, drew the attention of Americans who

were experiencing the same ideas, forces, and anxieties as their English cousins. The founding story of the Boy Scouts in America traces its origins to an English Boy Scout who did a "good turn" helping American publisher William D. Boyce, who was lost in the London fog. Refusing a tip and declaring himself to be a Boy Scout, the young man's gesture so impressed Boyce that he inquired into the movement and returned to the United States determined to found a similar organization for American boys. Boyce and a number of men already active in youth work gathered in New York City in 1910 to create the Boy Scouts of America. This group included Ernest Thompson Seton, the naturalist, artist, and author, who was experimenting with his own youth movement based on American Indian lore, the "Woodcraft Indians" (founded 1903); Daniel Carter Beard, creator of the Sons of Daniel Boone (founded 1905); and three men—Edgar M. Robinson, John L. Alexander, and James E. West—who brought considerable programmatic and organizational experience from their work with the YMCA. The BSA sought and obtained a charter from Congress in 1916, cementing its claim to the name and protecting its developing commercial interests, which included designating a range of commodities—from camping equipment to rifles to novels—as "official Boy Scout" products.

The first major task of the founders of the BSA in 1910 was to "Americanize" the English movement, which included making changes in the uniform, revising the Scout Oath and Scout Law, and writing the *American Handbook for Boys* (1911). Seton wrote large portions of the first *Handbook*. The program described in those pages reflects the founders' ideas that boys' minds and bodies could be trained together through a number of outdoor activities, including games. Seton was a great advocate of using games to teach physical skills and mental ability, but he also believed that games taught character-related values, such as teamwork, sportsmanship, and pride in accomplishment. Seton admired Native Americans as the model for American youth, and he incorporated a number of Native American games in the *Handbook,* along with traditional games from the United Kingdom (e.g., capture the flag has its roots in an old English game about the border wars between England and Scotland). A harsh critic of the commercialism and competitive individualism of modern American society, Seton promoted the idea of "honor by standards," an approach that favored boys' competing against objective standards tailored to their age and physical characteristics, rather than traditional competitions that required winners and losers.

In 1912, the BSA acquired a magazine, *Boys' Life,* and made it the official monthly of the organization. Still published, *Boys' Life* stands alongside the BSA's official publications (the *Handbook,* the *Field Guide,* the *Scoutmaster's Handbook,* the *Patrol Leader's Handbook,* and numerous merit badge pamphlets and booklets) as a chronicle of the activities the organization promotes for boys. What the organization calls "campcraft"—the various skills associated with living in the outdoors—is central to the program reflected in these publications, as are games and sports (as reflected, for example, in the merit badge for "Sports"). A central consideration in designing all Scout activities is that the boys experience them as "fun."

Across the decades, the American public has come to see the Boy Scouts as the model organization for creating wholesome young men, sound in body, mind, and character. The Boy Scout approach is based on the "patrol idea," which makes the boy's patrol of eight (within a larger troop supervised by a Scoutmaster) the primary group within which the boy, aged eleven to seventeen, engages in the activities that constitute the Boy Scout program.

While a great many of the activities in the BSA program would be pursued in the weekly troop and patrol meetings, hiking and camping required weekends and summers. From the informal patrol campout to the elaborate, formal Boy Scout Council summer camp, boys aged eleven through seventeen have been able to enjoy the full range of Scout activities, including hiking, cooking, crafting, archery, shooting, canoeing, rowing, swimming, and sports. Some of these activities are purely recreational, while others are part of official requirements for earning badges and ranks in the organization. The highest rank in the organization is Eagle Scout. Campfire programs are a staple of Boy Scout camps, and these programs include singing and storytelling, especially of scary stories or local legends.

Thanks largely to Ernest Thompson Seton's initial influence, "Indian lore" has been a staple of the BSA program since its founding, especially through the activities of the Order of the Arrow, the elite service fraternity within the BSA. Making "authentic" Native American costumes and reenacting Native American ceremonies and dances, Boy Scouts were among the larger set of hobbyists who have pursued Indian lore, arts, and crafts as a leisure-time activity. Some Scout troops—notably the Koshare Indians of La Junta, Colorado—have built their programs entirely around Indian lore.

In 1930, the BSA created the Cub Scouts for boys aged eight through ten, with a program geared more for that age group and led by "den mothers," an acknowledged role for adult women in the organization. Alarmed at the large numbers of boys whose interests shift by middle adolescence and responding to the criticism that girls do not have access to the BSA program, the organization has tried various coeducational programs (e.g., Explorers, Varsity Scouting, and Venturing) for teen boys and girls aged fourteen through seventeen, but these have had mixed success.

The huge baby boom generation born in the wake of World War II flocked to Scouting as a wholesome activity that combined physical recreation with the generalized patriotic fervor of the Cold War 1950s. This linking of physical fitness and moral strength with patriotism was not new; the nineteenth-century notion of "muscular Christianity" had a patriotic dimension as well. But the increased public concern about youth's physical fitness in the 1950s and 1960s served well the BSA's highly visible program for linking physical, mental, and moral "fitness," all desirable traits for a strong America in the Cold War.

The Girl Scouts

At the request of young women in England, Lord Baden-Powell enlisted the help of his sister, Agnes, in creating a movement for girls to parallel his own Boy Scouts. This Girl Guides movement was founded in 1910. Juliette Gordon Low (1860–1927), called "Daisy" by her friends and family, was an American friend of Robert and Agnes Baden-Powell. While visiting England, Low expressed interest in this movement created by Agnes. Low helped found Girl Guides groups in Scotland and London, and upon her return to the United States in 1912, she began an American Girl Guide troop in her native Savannah, Georgia. In 1913, the name was changed to the Girl Scouts; Walter John Hoxie, a naturalist, worked with Low in writing the first handbook for the movement.

In 1916, Low wrote a revised handbook (*Scouting for Girls*) that reflected the full program of the movement, a program that taught girls outdoor skills and self-reliance in addition to the domestic skills that were considered a proper upbringing for girls on the eve of World War I. Low wanted girls to be prepared to enter professional lives and to be skillful citizens (women did not win the vote until 1920, with the ratification of the Nineteenth Amendment to the Constitution). The first official Girl Scout uniform was blue, but, in 1928, it changed to the green now so closely identified with the GSA (colors now differ by program for four distinct age groups, created in 1963). The GSA published a popular magazine, *The American Girl,* from 1917 to 1979; like *Boy's Life,* this magazine recorded the broad range of activities Girl Scouts were expected to undertake. Unlike the BSA, which established early a powerful national office and a hierarchy of organizational levels (council, district, troop, patrol), Low preferred to keep the Girl Scouts decentralized, giving most organizational power to the local troop. She also worked in the 1920s to create a healthy World Association of Girl Guides and Girl Scouts (WAGGGS), which still existed in 2004.

Related Organizations

The Scouting movement was the dominant movement for young men and women in the twentieth century, but other organizations have served young men and women. Dr. Luther Gulick and his wife, Charlotte Vetter Gulick, founded the Camp Fire Girls in 1910; that organization and its programs (now coeducational and called Camp Fire USA) reports over 700,000 registered members as of 2002. After a falling-out with BSA leaders in 1915, Ernest Thomson Seton returned to his Woodcraft Indians idea and rebuilt a decentralized, coeducational organization

that lasted into the 1940s. The Young Men's Christian Association (YMCA), in addition to its usual recreational activities, also built a movement based on Native American lore. The decentralized "Indian Guides" program began as a strategy for fathers and sons to work together on costumes, rituals, and related projects, all taking advantage of the "romance," "beauty," and "color" of Native American cultures. The Y-Indian Guides eventually developed programs for fathers and daughters ("Indian Princesses") and then for mothers and sons and mothers and daughters ("Indian Braves and Indian Maidens"). Increasing pressure from Native American groups has influenced the Y-Indian Guides program to move away from Indian lore as the basis for its programs.

Conclusion

Scouting has been the most visible and dominant youth movement of the twentieth century, providing organized recreational and educational experiences for millions of girls and boys, ages five through seventeen. The Boy Scout and Girl Scout programs stress the connection between strong bodies and moral character, so the activities of the organizations are designed to strengthen minds, bodies, and morals. While the Boy Scouts became embroiled in controversy in the 1990s as various people sued the BSA for excluding atheists, gay men and boys, and younger girls, the GSA has managed to avoid these controversies by adopting inclusive policies. The exclusionary policies of the Boy Scouts remain controversial in the opening years of the new century, and the long-range effects of these controversies are hard to predict. The controversies do confirm that for the BSA, recreational programs are not simply about physical fitness. In linking physical fitness to mental and moral fitness, the BSA hearkens back to its late-nineteenth-century roots in a crisis in masculinity.

See also: Camping, Childhood and Play, "Muscular Christianity" and the YM(W)CA Movements

BIBLIOGRAPHY

Boy Scouts of America. Available from http://www.scouting.org.

Boy Scouts of America. *Boy Scout Handbook.* 11th edition. Irving, Tex.: Boy Scouts of America, 1998.

Choate, Anne H. *Juliette Low and the Girl Scouts: The Story of an American Woman, 1860–1927.* Garden City, N.Y.: Doubleday, Doran, and Company, 1928.

Deloria, Philip J. *Playing Indian.* New Haven, Conn.: Yale University Press, 1998.

Girl Scouts of America. Available from http://www.girlscouts
.org.

Jeal, Tim. *The Boy-Man: The Life of Lord Baden-Powell.* New York: William Morrow and Company, 1990.

Macleod, David I. *Building Character in the American Boy: The Boy Scouts, YMCA, and Their Forerunners, 1870–1920.* Madison: University of Wisconsin Press, 1983.

Mechling, Jay. *On My Honor: Boy Scouts and the Making of American Youth.* Chicago: University of Chicago Press, 2001.

Murray, W. D. *The History of the Boy Scouts of America.* New York: Boy Scouts of America, 1937.

Rosenthal, Michael. *The Character Factory: Baden-Powell and the Origins of the Boy Scout Movement.* New York: Pantheon Books, 1986.

Shultz, Gladys D., and Daisy Gordon Lawrence. *Lady from Savannah: The Life of Juliette Low.* Philadelphia: Lippincott, 1958.

Jay Mechling

SCUBA DIVING/SNORKELING

Humans have long sought ways to extend the time they could spend underwater and the depth to which they could descend. Accounts of using long hollow reeds as snorkels, or breathing tubes, date to the first century A.D. Breathing tubes were ineffective at depths of more than three feet because of the force needed to exchange the air in the tube. It was not until 1535 that Guglielmo de Loreno found a way to provide a source of air at greater depth. He developed the diving bell that, when lowered into the water, trapped air inside of it. The diver was able to breathe underwater by keeping his head inside the bell.

Over the next 400 years, diving equipment evolved slowly. Developments included air pumps that could force air into diving bells, air tanks filled with compressed air delivered from a surface hose, and self-contained diving rigs that used compressed oxygen. Diving was of great interest to naval forces, and the Royal Navy established the first diving school in 1843. As experimentation with diving continued, risks associated with time submerged and depth were better understood. Decompression sickness, or the bends, was first reported in 1843, but no explanation for its cause, or how to avoid it, was presented until 1878.

Snorkeling equipment—consisting of face mask, fins, and snorkel—was in common use by the mid-1930s. The snorkel is a curved tube hollow tube that when placed in the mouth allows a swimmer to breath while facedown

in the water. True scuba (self-contained underwater breathing apparatus) was developed in 1943 by Jacques-Yves Cousteau and Emile Gagnan. They designed the Aqua Lung by piecing together a demand-valve regulator, hoses, a mouthpiece, and a pair of portable tanks filled with compressed air. This development opened the door for recreational, or sport, diving.

Scuba diving began to gain popularity as a recreational activity in the United States in the 1950s. The Web site for the National Association of Underwater Instructors (NAUI) reports that in the early years of scuba diving, the Aqua Lung was sold to anyone who could afford it. Often the extent of training was a warning "not to hold your breath." There were few formal training opportunities available to recreational divers. Books such as *The Silent World* by Jacques Cousteau, and the television series *Sea Hunt*, added to the popularity of scuba diving. As participation increased, concerns grew over safety. NAUI was formed in 1960, and the Professional Association of Diving Instructors (PADI) was formed in 1966, both with the purpose of training and certifying recreational divers.

Advances in equipment, such as buoyancy-control devices and dive computers, have made diving much safer, and its popularity continues to grow. The Sports Business Research Network Web site reports an estimated 500,000 new divers are certified in the United States each year, with about 2 million people participating in diving each year. Divers are primarily between the ages of twenty-five and forty-five, and male divers outnumber females by about two to one. The proliferation of dive magazines, dive computers, dive vacations, and dive equipment has created a multibillion dollar industry.

Snorkeling is enjoyed by people of all ages because it provides a glimpse of the underwater world without requiring participants to undergo training or purchase expensive equipment. Over 5 million people engage in snorkeling each year. As with scuba diving, snorkeling is most popular with individuals aged twenty-five to forty-five, however, male participants only slightly outnumber females.

What Is Recreational Diving?

Recreational diving is defined as diving that uses only compressed air as the breathing mixture, is never done solo, does not exceed a depth of 130 feet, has a depth-time profile not requiring decompression, and does not require training beyond the basic open-water courses. However, increasing numbers of recreational divers are engaging in what has been defined as technical diving: in caves, under ice, at depths greater than 130 feet, using

Underwater life. Exploring marine life in the Caribbean Sea, a woman scuba dives in 1986 near Grand Cayman Island. © *Corbis*

various gas mixtures (for example, nitrox), wreck diving, and so on. As a result, the distinction between recreational diving and technical diving is blurring.

Where People Dive and Snorkel

Scuba divers may be found in almost any place where there is water. Saltwater divers explore shipwrecks, caves, fish life, and reefs; spearfish, catch lobster, and take underwater photographs all along the coastline of the United States from Maine to the Florida Keys, throughout the Gulf of Mexico, from Baja California to Washington, Hawaii, and Alaska. These environments differ greatly in water temperature, visibility, currents, marine life, and objects of interest. Freshwater divers can be found in lakes, rivers, flooded quarries and mines, grottos, and springs, from Florida to Alaska, in the Great Lakes, and in the Dakotas. As with saltwater diving, environmental conditions vary greatly from setting to setting. Divers in salt and fresh waters encounter

water temperatures from just above freezing to over eighty degrees Fahrenheit, and visibility from a few inches to over one hundred feet. In contrast, snorkelers tend to gravitate to clear warm waters with marine life to be seen at depths of less than thirty feet. Although Florida and Hawaii attract the greatest numbers of snorkelers, they may also be found in a variety of aquatic settings.

Environmental Issues

Protection of underwater areas Until the 1970s, there was little awareness of the damage divers and snorkelers were doing to coral by touching it and removing pieces as mementos. John Pennekamp Coral Reef State Park in Key Largo, Florida, established in 1960, was the first underwater park in the United States. The park was established to protect a portion of the coral reef in the Florida Keys. Snorkelers and divers, who were collecting excessive amounts of coral, conch, and tropical fish, were damaging the natural conditions. The purpose of Coral Reef State Park is to provide public outdoor recreation. Park managers seek to maintain a balance between preserving natural conditions and providing recreation opportunities.

In 1975, the first National Marine Sanctuary was established to protect marine areas. Some sanctuary activities are regulated or controlled, however, multiple uses, including recreation, are encouraged. Since 1975, twelve other sites have been designated as marine sanctuaries.

Numerous underwater parks, at state and national levels, have been established to preserve and protect reefs and other marine life. Efforts are resulting in the resurgence of some species, better-educated divers, and less removal of marine life and artifacts from shipwrecks and other sites.

Dive clubs often team with agencies such as the National Park Service for the underwater cleanup of lakes, rivers, and other underwater sites. These efforts benefit the agency and environment while offering divers a different diving experience, sometimes providing access to areas that are usually off limits.

Artificial reefs Artificial reefs, which are made of concrete, rock, obsolete military aircraft, oil rigs, cars, and other hard surface materials, are being created along coastlines to provide habitat for marine life. They have been criticized as being little more than ocean landfills, as there are no established guidelines for what constitutes an artificial reef. Many artificial reefs are unstable and may be pushed by storms onto living reefs or beaches. Sport fishers and divers support the development of artificial reefs because they attract fish. Environmentalists have not been convinced that the reefs actually increase fish populations rather than relocating them from other sites. However, recent research indicates that properly constructed reefs comprised of concrete do increase fish populations, according to Vernon Minton, director of the Marine Resources Division of the Alabama Department of Conservation and Natural Resources. Placement of concrete artificial reefs can create dive sites in areas where none now exist.

See also: Beaches, Swimming, Tourism

BIBLIOGRAPHY

Bailey, Ronald. "Reef Madness: How Alabama Fishermen Are Repopulating the Sea." *Reason* (October 2001): 42–45.

Cousteau, Jacques Yves. *The Silent World.* New York: Harper 1953.

John Pennekamp Coral Reef State Park. Available from http://www.floridastateparks.org/pennekamp.

Martin, Lawrence. *Scuba Diving Explained: Questions and Answers on Physiology and Medical Aspects.* Flagstaff, Ariz.: Best Publishing Company, 1997.

National Association of Underwater Instructors. "A Short History of NAUI." Available from http://www.naui.com.

National Marine Sanctuary. Available from http://www.sanctuaries.nos.noaa.gov

"Scuba History." Available from http://www.aboutscubadiving.com/.

Kim L. Siegenthaler

SEA TRAVEL AND LEISURE

In 1867, the paddle steamer *Quaker City* embarked on the first American-origin cruise tour. Mark Twain, who later wrote of his trip in *The Innocent's Abroad* (1869), was one of several wealthy passengers on this round-trip journey from America to the Holy Land, Egypt, the Crimea, and Greece. At the time, merchant ships like *Quaker City* were occasionally outfitted for leisure voyages in addition to their regular commercial activities. From this modest beginning, cruising—or taking a vacation trip by ship—evolved into a vigorous and diversified segment of the tourism industry.

During the late nineteenth to early twentieth centuries, ocean liners such as the *Deutschland, Lusitania, Acquitania,* and *Titanic,* built in Europe and designed for speed, transported mail, cargo, and passengers across the Atlantic. Not only did immigrants form the bulk of these one-way passengers, but also the dominant flow of traffic was from Europe to America. Segregated into first class, tourist or second class, and steerage or third class, there would often be 100 passengers in first class, 200 in second, and 2,000 in third. Conditions for first-class passengers paralleled fine European hotels with exquisite interiors, exceptional foods, and attentive service. In contrast, immigrants slept in crowded, unsanitary conditions, ate poor food, and entertained one another. Although immigrants formed the foundation of their profitability, early ship companies like Cunard, Holland America, Peninsular and Oriental Steam Navigation Company (P&O), and the United States Line actively sought wealthy first- and second-class passengers to fill the empty space aboard their vessels on the return trip from America to Europe.

In this era before stabilizers, regardless of whether travel was first class or steerage, seasickness was common.

As a result, ocean liners developed public image problems. Promoters of this type of travel realized a solution lay in creating diversions to shield affluent passengers from the realities of being at sea. With this pivotal realization, the era of luxury cruise travel was born. Functional Atlantic crossings metamorphosed into fashionable leisure pursuits of considerable social standing. Gambling, drinking, dining, dancing, seeing, and being seen were hallmarks of cruising during the heydays of the early to mid-1900s. Not only did society columns and newspapers publish the cruising itineraries and onboard activities of the elite, powerful, and famous, but the Prohibition period in America during the 1920s and early 1930s further solidified the image of cruising as an extravagant type of travel. By sailing out to sea three miles, a ship would be in international waters and hence beyond U.S. jurisdiction. Clever entrepreneurs took advantage of this loophole and "cruises to nowhere" became important sources of Prohibition gambling and alcohol consumption.

Yet, media focus on cruising as an elite, class-based lifestyle led to the perception that this type of tourism was only for the wealthy. This problem persisted for many years until clever marketing and technological advances—such as the introduction of stabilizers, the abolition of segregated travel, and the partnering of cruise companies with airline companies—slowly softened the rigid class hierarchy. For example, the introduction of air travel across the Atlantic in the early 1930s is generally linked with the demise of transatlantic liner travel. However, the role of airlines has evolved from that of a competitor to that of a partner. Airlines now play a fundamental role in transporting cruise passengers to their departure ports. The phenomenal success of the American television show *The Love Boat,* produced from 1977 to 1986, was also pivotal in reshaping the American public's image of cruising and transforming it into a specialized market with broad appeal and widespread household recognition. No longer did the Blue Ribband—the award given to the fastest ocean liner to cross the Atlantic during the early to mid-1900s—reverberate with consumers. Floating resorts like *The Love Boat* and cruising for fun and entertainment did.

From 1990 to 2000 cruise tourists expanded in number from 3.5 million to over 8 million per year, with Americans accounting for 80 percent of cruise passengers worldwide. In this same period, the number of cruise ships plying international waters increased from 97 to 170, and the number of cruise ship berths almost doubled from 68,474 to 127,943. Nineteen new cruise vessels were delivered in 2002, to be followed by another twenty-one new vessels by 2004 (CLIA, 2000; McDowell). Although some ocean liners were built in the United States in the late 1800s and early 1900s, most cruise ships have been and continue to be built in Europe and Japan. With their history of government subsidies, Europe and Japan have been able to underbid most American shipbuilders.

Types of Cruising Experience

There are many different types of cruising, ranging from small-scale, intimate, expensive "yachtlike" experiences to cruise lines that specialize in mass-market trips affordable by the majority of Americans. Evaluated on ship facilities, decor, accommodation, entertainment, and cuisine, cruisers can select from a diversity of cruise experiences including contemporary, destination/niche, luxury, and premium.

Contemporary Cruise lines include Carnival, Costa, Disney, Norwegian, and Royal Caribbean International. During the 1970s, cruise ships underwent a design revolution. Because speed was no longer a central issue, the streamlined profile of the ocean liner yielded to passenger demands for more space and greater diversity of activities. Wide, square vessels built to make use of economies of scale replaced tapered hulls and sleek profiles. For example, the largest ship to sail the seas at the beginning of the 2000s is more than twenty stories high, longer than three football fields; and at twice the tonnage (142,000 GRT) of the ocean liner *Titanic,* it is capable of carrying almost 4,000 passengers and 1,200 crew. (GRT—gross registered tonnage—refers to the volume of public space available to passengers). This megaship is so large it cannot sail through the Panama Canal, and yet because of onboard satellite technology it does not require an anchor. Passenger diversions include an ice skating rink, a rock climbing wall, a full-sized basketball court, the world's largest roulette wheel, and a shopping mall.

Destination/niche. Cruise lines in this category include Club Med Cruises, Norwegian Coastal Voyage, Royal Olympic Cruises, Windjammer Barefoot Cruises, and Windstar Cruises. Confined to smaller ships such as oversized yachts, barges, riverboats, and masted sailing ships, these companies offer intimate experiences themed around education, soft adventure, or a voyage to particular destinations. In the case of Delta Queen Steamboat Company, for example, passengers can experience what it was like to sail onpaddle steamers that plied the Mississippi River during the nineteenth century. Windstar Cruises and Windjammer Barefoot Cruises offer passengers the opportunity to sail on masted sailing ships.

Luxury. Cruise lines in this category include Crystal Cruises, Cunard Line, Radisson Seven Seas, Seabourn Cruise Line, and Silversea Cruises. Ranging in size from small, luxury yachts like the 4,250-ton, 116-passenger *Sea Goddess 1* to the 50,000-ton, 960-passenger *Crystal Symphony,* the emphasis in this category is on an exceptionally lavish vacation experience, as characterized by attentive staff, flawless service, high staff-to-passengers ratios, exceptional artwork, elaborate dining, well-appointed public areas, and larger-than-average state rooms fused with unusual itineraries. This group includes classic ocean liners such as *Queen Elizabeth II* (*QEII*). Launched in 1969 and regularly refitted and refurbished to reflect changing tastes, this ship continues to make transatlantic voyages and around-the-world cruises.

Premium. Cruise lines in this category include Celebrity Cruises, Holland America Line, and Princess Cruises. In between luxury and contemporary, several cruise lines have sought to capitalize on consumers' preferences for an upscale experience at a realistic price. Well below the per diem of luxury cruises, premium cruises are nonetheless more expensive than contemporary experiences. By offering higher staff-to-passenger ratios, more refined dining, and greater emphasis on attentive service combined with interesting destinations and shore excursions, the ships in this 50,000- to 75,000-ton range target cruisers who want upscale alternatives to the mass-market experience of contemporary cruising.

Ship Size

Ship size is measured in a number of different ways, including number of passengers, number of cabins, staff ratio, space ratio, and GRT. Although there are no definitive rules, generally ships can be divided into five groups.

- Small: Under 10,000 GRT, with under 200 passengers

- Small to medium: 10,001 to 20,000 GRT, carrying 200 to 500 passengers

- Medium: 20,001 to 50,000 GRT, carrying 500 to 1,200 passengers

- Large: 50,001 to 90,000 GRT, carrying 1,200 to 2,000 passengers

- Megaship: 90,001 to 150,000 GRT, carrying 2,000 to 4,000 passengers

With small portholes and windows, circular promenade decks, and varied sizes and shapes of cabins, some cruisers prefer older, classic ships because of their traditional lines and nostalgic feel. Others prefer newer vessels because of their large, light-filled public areas, logical pedestrian flow, and variety of activities. Some cruisers prefer smaller ships; others prefer larger. Space ratio, determined by dividing GRT by passenger capacity, plays a role in the perception of ship size. For example, if a vessel has a GRT of 100,000 and a passenger capacity of 3,000 the space ratio would be 33. The higher the space ratio, the greater the sense of spaciousness. Averaging twenty-five to thirty, some ships have space ratios as high as sixty, others as low as ten. The size of the ship (GRT) does not necessarily correlate with space ratio; a small luxury cruise line may have a high space ratio because few passengers are carried, whereas a megaship that carries many passengers may have a low space ratio despite a high GRT. In general, higher per diems correlate with higher space ratios.

Ship Facilities

Facilities aboard ship vary greatly. In essence, they can be divided into three categories: public, cabin, and private crew space. Public spaces include reception areas (central spaces patterned after hotel lobbies that include front, hotel, information, and shore excursion desks), dining facilities, entertainment spaces (showroom, movie theater, casino, children's play area, health club, shopping area), and medical facilities. Cabin space for passengers equates with "miniature" hotel guest rooms. Most cabins are less than 200 square feet, whereas the average hotel room is 350 to 450 square feet. Cabins are priced according to location on the ship (lower decks equate with lower price), size of cabin (greater square footage equates with higher price), and access to windows and verandas (interior cabins have no windows; suites have sliding glass doors and verandas). A typical cabin will sleep two and will provide a vanity, bedside tables, a closet, a TV, and a small bathroom. Suites have all the features of a cabin plus a sizable living area, a separate bedroom, and a large bathroom with a tub and shower. Private crew space includes the bridge (control center for the vessel), food preparation area, crew cabins, and mechanical and engine rooms.

The Cruise Experience

Although there are myriad variations on the cruise experience, in essence it can be broken into three segments:

planning and purchasing a cruise, the shipboard experience, and traveling to and from the ship.

Planning and purchasing a cruise. The main sources of information for planning and purchasing a cruise are friends and relatives, travel agencies, cruise lines, and the Internet. Because only 15 percent of the North American population has taken a cruise and planning and purchasing is a complex task, especially for first-time cruisers, travel agencies and cruise lines play a central role in the decision-making process. Considered an "all-inclusive" vacation, up-front purchase price includes cabin accommodations, meals, selected beverages, onboard entertainment and activities, children's programs, and access to exercise facilities.

Shipboard experience. Arriving on board—or embarking—most passengers begin by finding their cabins, unpacking luggage, checking on seating assignments for dinner, and exploring the ship. Mock lifeboat drill is compulsory for all passengers and crew and must take place within twenty-four hours of departure. Departure is a lively time for passengers and a feverish time for crew. The first dinner at sea is one of the most important events of the entire experience. At the first dinner aboard ship, passengers meet their dinner companions and wait staff, and, most important, get to taste the food. Passengers select their dinner seating preferences and the number of individuals with whom they would like to be seated when they purchase their cruise. Most cruise lines use two "seatings" to accommodate all passengers aboard. Early in the evening, "First seating" is often used by older people and families with young children. "Second seating" is later and is used by individuals with teenage children and those who enjoy the late-night entertainment—such as a stage show, gambling, dancing, and shopping—that follows dinner.

Subsequent cruise days can be broken into days at sea and days in port. Days at sea provide passengers with the opportunity to engage in or ignore the various activities on the ship, from sleeping to reading, gambling to taking classes, having a massage to playing bridge, attending a religious service to having an onboard wedding. The last night at sea is punctuated by packing, preparing documents for disembarkation, and leaving gratuities for various crew members who contributed to the vacation experience. Days at port provide passengers with the opportunity to sample the variety of destinations included in the cruise. During a weeklong cruise, for example, passengers may have two days at sea and four ports of call. Time spent in port ranges anywhere from three to fourteen hours. Many passengers select shore excursions as a way to explore destinations. Through these excursions—including basic walking tours, snorkeling trips, kayaking, golf, beach outings, helicopter tours, and shopping expeditions—cruise lines offer passengers a wide selection of activities at an additional charge.

Traveling to and from the ship. Although some cruisers extend the cruise experience with pre- and post-cruise packages at the port of departure, most cruisers travel to the departure port on the day of the cruise. Arriving by car, bus, and plane from various origins throughout the United States and beyond, passengers assemble in specially designed dockside facilities. Similar to checking in at a hotel, it is here that passengers show necessary documentation and fill in a variety of forms, including those indicating how they will pay for onboard expenses such as shore excursions, gratuities, alcohol, shopping, gambling, and personal incidentals. Most cruise lines use keyless entry systems that double as onboard credit cards, security checks, and room keys. Passengers then make their way up the gangway to the ship. Most cruises set sail between four and eleven P.M. Departing from the ship follows a similar format. Ships dock between six and eight A.M. The crew has six to twelve hours to ready the ship before the cycle starts again.

Who Cruises, Why, and Where They Cruise

Sixty-three percent of Americans travel (business and pleasure). Of that percentage 42 percent travel for pleasure, yet only 2.6 percent of Americans have taken a cruise. Visiting friends and relatives and resort vacations dominate travel itineraries. Furthermore, only 15 percent of Americans who could afford a vacation and who travel for pleasure have taken a cruise (CLIA, 2000, 2003; NFO Plog).

Cruisers average fifty-six years of age, have above-average incomes ($64,000), and travel more in general. Ten percent travel with children, and 1 percent travel alone. More than one-third are retired. Typically married (74 percent), they have college educations (49 percent) and still work (56 percent). On a typical cruise, 40 percent will be first-time cruisers. Those who cruise once come back again, once every three years; the average number of cruises is five. Those who take luxury cruises average ten. Cruisers spend almost twice as much per person per week ($1,319) as noncruise vacationers ($721) and tend to be more satisfied with their experience (43 percent) than other forms of pleasure travel (28 percent) (NFO Plog). The reasons for cruising are almost as varied as the cruising experience itself. They include pampering, getting away from it all, enjoying a safe, hassle-free, relaxing experience with a wide range of activities, having a chance to make friends, partaking of a learning experience, spending time with family, and receiving good value for the money.

Most cruises (67 percent) occur around North America. Alaska, the Caribbean Islands and Mexican coast, the Mississippi River, and the northeastern United States form the backbone of the cruising itineraries. Europe is the second most popular choice for American cruisers, with South America, the South Pacific, Asia, and Africa distant thirds. However, the search for new markets coupled with consumer demand for more "exotic" ports of call has led to an increase in the demand for more distant itineraries. Attracting cruise ships to a port can be lucrative. For example, 600,000 cruise passengers visited Alaska during the annual season from May to September 1999. Three hundred thousand of these passengers visited the port of Anchorage. Direct expenditures by the cruise industry were $103 million; expenditures by passengers added a further $28 million. In addition, the industry paid $2 million in local, state, and federal taxes and fees for services in the port of Anchorage (Pounds).

See also: Prohibition and Temperance; Sailing and Yachting, Tourism, Vacations

BIBLIOGRAPHY

CLIA, Cruise Lines International Association. (2000). "CLIA Reports Record 5.9 Million North Americans Cruised in 1999; Nine Percent Increase Forecast for 2000." Available from http://www.cruising.org/.

———. (2003). "Kids at Sea; Cruise Lines Create Quality Time for Families." Cruise Lines International Association. Available from http://www.cruising.org/.

Dawson, Philip. *Cruise Ships.* London: Conway Maritime Press, 2000.

Dickinson, Robert H., and Andrew Vladimir. *Selling the Sea: An Inside Look at the Cruise Industry.* New York: John Wiley and Sons, 1996.

Emmons, Frederick. *American Passenger Ships: The Ocean Lines and Liners, 1873–1983.* Cranbury, N.J.: Associated University Press, 1985.

Mancini, Marc. *Cruising: A Guide to the Cruise Line Industry.* Albany, N.Y.: Delmar Thomson Learning, 2000.

Maxtone-Graham, John. *Liners to the Sun.* New York: Macmillan, 1985.

———. *Crossing and Cruising.* New York: Macmillan, 1992.

McDowell, E. "Aboard for the Shorter Haul." *New York Times.* Available from http://www.nytimes.com/.

NFO Plog Research. *Cruise Market Profile Study.* Washington, D.C.: Cruise Lines International Association, 2002.

Peisley, Tony. *The World Cruise Ship Industry to 2000.* New York: Travel and Tourism Intelligence, 1996.

Pounds, Nancy. "Cruise Lines Tout Economic Impact, Growth, Environmental Care." Available from http://www.alaskajournal.com/.

Wood, Robert. "Caribbean Cruise Tourism. Globalization at Sea." *Annals of Tourism Research* 27, no. 2 (2000): 345–370.

Careen Yarnal

SEA WORLD

Sea World Adventure Parks compose the largest chain of marine parks in the United States. Located in San Diego, Orlando, and San Antonio, Sea World merges the modern amusement park with elements of the aquarium and the animal spectacular. Combining entertainment with a claim to inculcate visitors with knowledge and appreciation of nature, the parks successfully aim at the upper segment of the amusement park market and yet consistently rank among the biggest venues in terms of crowd attendance.

A 2002 company press release locates the origins of Sea World in "four fraternity [brothers'] . . . dreams of an underwater restaurant on San Diego's Mission Bay in the early 1960s" realized in 1964 with the opening of "a full-scale marine zoological park." Looking more closely, however, Sea World was from the outset a large, capital-intensive undertaking when compared to most amusement parks of the earlier half of the twentieth century. Thus, it nicely fits into the category of theme parks backed by corporate capital that emerged in the wake of what historian Judith Adams has termed the "Disney Transformation." A group of area investors had responded to San Diego's planning department's solicitation of ideas for a marine park. The growth of Sea World was (at least indirectly) fueled by public funding and a city attempting to establish itself as a magnet for tourism in southern California. The park that in 1965 had introduced a show featuring Shamu, the killer whale, quickly grew during the 1960s and 1970s, outpacing local competitors such as Marineland of the Pacific and expanding through spin-off parks in Orlando, Florida, and Aurora, Ohio (which was sold to Six Flags Inc. in 2001). In 1977, publishing giant Harcourt Brace Jovanovich acquired the chain, which in 1988 opened a fourth park in San Antonio, Texas. The following year Anheuser-Busch's entertainment subsidiary (whose holdings already included such parks as Busch Gardens in Florida and Virginia) became

Shamu. Crowds gather in September 1984 at the Sea World in San Diego, California, to see their famous killer whale Shamu. The trained mammal was one of about 3,000 creatures on exhibit. © *Kelly-Mooney Photography/Corbis*

the new corporate owner of Sea World, now a part of North America's second largest conglomerate of amusement parks.

Like most modern theme parks, Sea World features a highly controlled environment. It organizes attractions in an artificially designed landscape themed around ocean and marine life. Mechanical "thrill rides" so prominent in other modern theme parks were for a long time absent from Sea World. Instead, the park's main attractions consist of animal displays such as aquariums or penguin lagoons and—most prominently—animal shows that feature dolphins, sea lions, and Shamu the "killer whale."

In this, Sea World owes just as much to the traditions of the zoological garden and the circus as it does to that of amusement parks. The parks attempt to deliver conflict-free and universally appealing family entertainment, suggesting that all visitors may find the "child" within themselves in an innate ability to relate to animals. However, as thoroughly commercialized space (admission to the parks ranges between $40 and $50 for adults) Sea World not only promotes its own corporate brand,

but that of other corporate sponsors and of its parent company, Anheuser-Busch, as reflected, for example, in a Clydesdale horse exhibit and an "Anheuser-Busch Hospitality Center."

Education and Entertainment

Two aspects of Sea World that set the parks apart from most other theme parks of its era merit further elaboration. One is the peculiar relationship between education and entertainment and the other is its commercialized representation of nature and the environment. Both topics have received insightful treatment in Susan Davis's history of Sea World California, *Spectacular Nature.*

The park prides itself on being committed to education, promoting stewardship for the environment, and developing interest in marine study and nature appreciation. The focus on education came at least partially out of a provision in the land lease and out of the 1972 Marine Mammal Protection Act that limited the display of marine mammals to educational purposes. Sea World reaches out to elementary schools, provides educational resources for students and teachers, and organizes camps. The park furthermore is involved in marine research and has links to such institutions as the Bronx Zoo and the U.S. Fish and Wildlife Service. Educational programs (*Shamu TV*) were introduced in the 1990s. Field trips from schools or junior areas open up the park to a demographic that would otherwise have no access.

The educational angle that ties Sea World to the instructional and uplifting tradition of zoological gardens strongly appeals to the parks' main customer base, which is largely white, middle class, and college educated. But education at Sea World stands in an uneasy relationship to the entertainment landscape, the mall atmosphere, the rides, and the animal shows. Not only does much of the education bear the mark of corporate control and promotion, but, as Davis observes, the educational content often remains superficial and focuses on the sensational or on animal behavior and training, much in tune with Sea World's main attractions. Such education, then, often takes the form of "infotainment" popular in many areas of commercial culture.

Commercial Representation of Nature and the Environment

In many ways Sea World's icon, Shamu, captures the tension between environmental consciousness and the commercialization inherent in the parks' concept. On the one hand, the killer whale serves as a cultural symbol for the emerging concern over animal protection and the environment since the 1960s. On the other hand, Shamu, both "cute" and appealing *and* a fierce predator, has become a highly recognizable corporate logo and a registered trademark.

In part to deflect criticism regarding the training of animals in captivity, Sea World has become ever more environmentally conscious in its park design. What began during the 1960s as a show celebrating the modern (benign) domination of man over nature and indulging in pacific fantasies (complete with sea maids) adopted an increasingly scientific tone over the following decades. During the 1990s, Sea World cooperated with a number of environmental organizations, such as the World Wildlife Fund, and—backed by Anheuser-Busch funding—supported various environmental projects.

Such engagement, again, appeals to Sea World's key customer demographics. As Davis puts it, a visit to Sea World by itself is construed as an "act of caring." Environmental consciousness becomes consumable. Visiting Sea World is a suburban nature vacation, a contemporary form of nature tourism. Ironically, the "natural land-scape" encountered at the park is highly standardized and artificially controlled. The experience of nature is designed so as to make visitors' encounters with the animals and their environment as predictable as possible. Still, the perceived authenticity and reality of the Sea World experience in the minds of its customers sets it apart from the fantasy world of amusement parks like Disney World.

See also: Disneyland, Park Movements, Theme and Amusement Parks, Tourism, Walt Disney World

BIBLIOGRAPHY

Adams, Judith A. *The American Amusement Park Industry: A History of Technology and Thrills.* Boston: Twayne Publishers, 1991.

Davis, Susan G. *Spectacular Nature: Corporate Culture and the Sea World Experience.* Berkeley: University of California Press, 1997.

Sea World. Home page at http://www.seaworld.org.

Sea World Press Release. 11 November 2002.

Ulmer, Jeff. *Amusement Parks of America: A Comprehensive Guide.* New York: Dial Press, 1980.

Jan Logemann

SELF-IMPROVEMENT

See *Rational Recreation and Self-Improvement*

SENIOR LEISURE LIFESTYLES

In the early decades of the twentieth century, the life course was conceptualized into three distinct, age-segregated stages: education during childhood and adolescence; work during early and middle adulthood; leisure during later life following retirement. The irony of this perspective about the life course was that many individuals never retired unless forced to because of declining health, and average life expectancy was only about seventy years of age. Hence, many older persons never experienced a leisure state, and if they did, a short life expectancy meant they had only a few years to experience leisure in good health.

Today, the life course is conceptualized as an age-integrated structure, wherein education, work, and leisure are possible, and desirable, at all stages as people strive for a more balanced lifestyle across the life course. Thus, just as adolescents attend school, often hold part-time jobs, and engage in a variety of leisure pursuits, so do older adults participate in a variety of leisure activities, perhaps hold part-time jobs or volunteer positions, and pursue formal or informal education.

Social Change: From Work to Leisure in Later Life

In postindustrial societies, leisure has become a lifelong expressive domain that is an integral part of our social, cultural, economic, and political institutions. For each birth cohort that reaches later life, leisure has become a more significant component of lifestyles, and an element of daily life that provides meaning and an identity for older adults. Leisure is no longer viewed as a way to "kill time," or the alternative to work. Rather, it is an integral factor in contributing to successful aging, and to life satisfaction, well-being, personal identity, and a higher quality of life in the future. How and why did this shift in the importance of leisure in later life occur since the mid-1900s? In general, the change resulted from a combination of population aging, social change, and personal agency.

Population aging Because of declining birth rates since the 1960s (about 1.5 children per female), and an increasing life expectancy (about seventy-six years for men and eighty-two for women), adults over sixty-five years of age represented about 13 percent of the total population in North America in 2003. It is projected that this percentage will increase to about 15 percent by 2011, when the first wave of the baby boom generation (born between 1946 and 1966) begins to retire, to 21 percent by 2026, and to 25 percent by 2031, when the last of the boomers will be retired. Clearly, the population is aging. And among this rapidly growing segment of the population, those in the eighty-and-over category are growing the fastest. By 2030, it is projected that those eighty years of age and older will compose 5 to 8 percent of the total population, and about 25 percent of the population sixty-five and over.

These demographic facts are no longer surprising. However, there are a number of lesser-known demographic facts that have implications for leisure lifestyles, policies, and programs for older adults. First, aging is primarily a woman's issue. The sex ratio at age sixty-five is about seventy-five males for every hundred females; this ratio decreases to about twenty-five males per hundred females by ninety years of age. Whereas most older men

are married and thereby have a leisure partner and a potential caregiver, most older women are widowed, divorced, or never married. More older women live alone, more are institutionalized, and older women have less economic security. And, until recent decades, women have had fewer opportunities to engage in leisure throughout the life course beyond the family context, primarily due to the lack of a work career and personal discretionary income.

A second important demographic fact is that as life expectancy has increased, health status has improved, and there has been an increase in the number of disability-free years in later life. Thus, older adults are not only reaching the later years having been more physically and cognitively active during leisure throughout the work years, they have a greater capacity and potential to pursue active lifestyles well into the later years of life. At the start of the twenty-first century, a longer life meant that leisure would serve as a primary social activity for a longer period of time.

A third demographic fact is that the older population is increasingly mobile due to increased economic resources and improved health status. This is reflected in migration rates to a second place of residence to pursue a leisure lifestyle during the winter and/or summer seasons, and by increased travel and tourism within North America and abroad by older adults. The economic potential of this "gray" travel, tourism, and leisure market has yet to be tapped fully, but it will be when the baby boom generation enters retirement with large economic resources and a generational history of expenditures on leisure and consumer products.

Social change Leisure opportunities are related to one's position in the social structure across the life course. Inequities in access to leisure are based on gender, class background, race, ethnicity, and rural or urban residency. Chronological age as well can be a barrier to certain types of leisure through age grading, wherein stereotypes or age discrimination emerge—individuals are perceived to be too old to participate in a specific activity, and therefore facilities or programs are not provided for older adults. This type of ageism, when combined with racism or sexism, means that some segments of society never have an opportunity to pursue some types of leisure—unless social change and democratization occurs.

Leisure lifestyles are influenced by work and family parameters. Harold Wilensky noted that "work routine places a hand on leisure routine" (p. 545). Over time, however, work routines and demands have changed. The workweek is shorter, vacation entitlements have in-

Afternoon outing. Two seniors play cards while out picnicking. © *Michael Keller/Corbis*

creased, more women are employed full-time, there is more "flex time," and wages have increased. By the end of the twentieth century, a knowledge-based economy emerged wherein higher education and lifelong learning were essential for entry to, and success in, the labor force. These trends created new types and meanings for leisure. More recently, careers were shortened as people sought or were forced into early retirement by restructuring or downsizing. Consequently, fewer people over sixty-five work, and more individuals enter retirement in their late fifties. To illustrate, in 1950, about 46 percent of older men in the United States were still in the labor force, but by 2000, only 17 percent of men in this age group were still working (Cutler and Hendricks, p. 463). As the time devoted to work has decreased, leisure has become a more important milieu to create and maintain a self-identity.

In the family domain, more never-married and divorced persons, more childless couples or couples with fewer children, and more dual-career families have changed the nature of leisure during middle and late adulthood. With more discretionary time and income for leisure, and more public and private facilities available,

more leisure occurs outside the home and with nonfamily members, especially among those in higher socioeconomic strata. These trends are especially prevalent among the baby boom generation. Spending and pursuing leisure has been a major characteristic of this generation. Benefiting from high employment and wage rates through most of their working life, and benefiting from large inheritances from parents and grandparents who saved their earnings, this generation will enter the retirement years with a new perspective on leisure, and an ability to pay for their leisure needs. Consequently, leisure for seniors will become "big" business in the mid-twenty-first century, especially for clothing, equipment, facilities, and tourism.

Although it is beyond the scope of this article to develop the following ideas in depth, they have had a significant impact on the changing nature of leisure in later life. First, as higher education became both more important for career success, and more accessible to diverse segments of society, leisure opportunities expanded in terms of diversity, accessibility, meaning, and frequency. Each cohort of retirees is better educated and has a larger leisure repertoire. Second, the feminist movement created expanded opportunities for women in the leisure domain. Women gained more education, entered careers, saved money, and pursued their own leisure interests beyond the family domain. Third, as society evolved over the twentieth century, voluntary behavior became more common during increased leisure time. Many of those entering the retirement years represent an untapped source of experienced volunteer labor that should be utilized, both for the benefit of society and for individuals to feel that they are contributing to society. Finally, while some older persons feel more comfortable in age-segregated environments (such as a retirement homes or communities), many seek intergenerational contact and involvement. Leisure settings present an ideal milieu for age-integrated social interaction.

Human agency People do not age in a vacuum, nor are they passive puppets manipulated by social forces as they move across their personal life course. Rather, people have the capacity to make choices and decisions, and to shift their priorities and seek new opportunities. As active agents, people have the potential and ability, within reason, to use human and social capital in the pursuit of leisure activities. One's place in the social structure, by virtue of gender, class, race, or ethnic background, can facilitate or constrain the opportunities and resources available for leisure. But, with increased education and wealth, and with new social networks, one's leisure world can be changed. Thus, within each cohort that reaches retirement age, there is considerable diversity in terms of leisure experiences, interests, needs, and meanings. Older-age cohorts are the most heterogeneous cohorts in society, and this diversity presents a challenge to policy makers and program personnel who strive to meet the needs of an ever-changing older population. To illustrate, the meaning of everyday activities such as learning, cooking, gardening, and shopping is perceived by some older adults to be a burden; to others these activities are a source of pleasure and a hobby, as well as a necessity.

Leisure in Later Life

The onset of retirement or premature unemployment forces individuals to cope with unstructured time after a lifetime wherein most of daily life was structured around work requirements. Suddenly, large blocks of unstructured time are available (up to thirty or fifty hours per week). As Jiri Zuzanek and S. Box stated, "Having more free time does not automatically translate into greater happiness. Being able to fill this time with activities and to structure it in a meaningful and diversified way does" (p.

Sidebar 1: Barriers to Leisure in Later Life

Individual Constraints

- Declining health and energy, or onset of a disability

- Loss of interest in specific activities

- Loss of a partner due to widowhood or divorce

- Decreased economic resources

- Inability to drive or use public transportation, if available

- Caregiving requirements for a partner

Societal Constraints

- Facilities and programs are not provided or are not accessible for seniors

- Information about leisure opportunities is not disseminated

- Public transportation is not available

- Public subsidies for low-income seniors are not provided

- Stereotypes and myths discourage involvement by seniors in some types of activities (sports, computers, formal education)

---

179). In the later years of life, time can be perceived to pass quickly or slowly. If time is abused or not used in a meaningful way, it drags and boredom results. Boredom is a self-induced state that occurs when there is an excess of discretionary time or an inability to manage time. For those who perceive time to fly quickly, it is usually the case that they are more socially involved and their daily calendars are full with meaningful and satisfying activities.

Patterns of leisure across the life course. Throughout the life course, we acquire a repertoire of leisure skills, interests, and activities. New interests and skills can be acquired and developed at any age, but consistency in the leisure repertoire persists into later life, although the frequency or form might change. A lifetime opera fan may attend fewer live performances in later life but still pursue this interest by listening to opera on radio or CD. Figure 1 illustrates possible patterns of leisure involvement across the life course. The curves can represent different patterns of general leisure involvement for six different individuals; they can represent the degree of involvement in a specific type of leisure (such as reading fiction) across

FIGURE 1

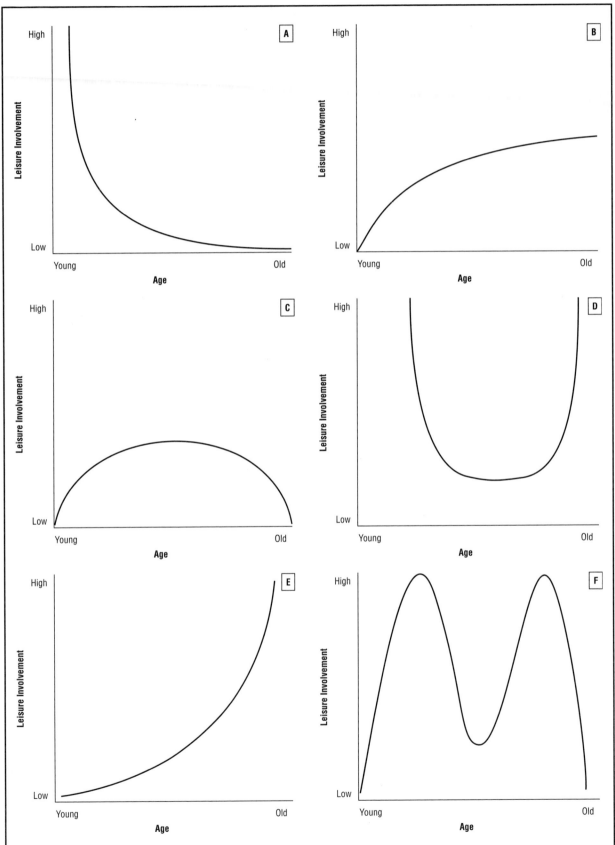

the life course for six different individuals; they can represent, for one individual, patterns of leisure involvement or the degree of importance or meaning for six different activities: A = team sport; B = movie attendance; C = membership in a political party; D = reading for pleasure; E = golf; F = travel. The key point is that among a diverse group of older persons, and within any one individual, many types, patterns, and meanings of leisure can prevail across the life course, and in later life.

Leisure constraints in later life There is continuity between work and retirement leisure lifestyles, although the number of activities and the frequency of involvement may increase or decrease in retirement. Opportunities to engage in leisure in later life can be restricted or prevented by individual and societal constraints, many of which result from one's place in the social structure—female or male; black, Hispanic, white, or Asian; well educated or poorly educated; upper or lower class; rural or urban residents? Sidebar 1 illustrates some individual and societal barriers that can prevent equal access to leisure in later life.

Leisure opportunities in later life Sidebar 2 illustrates some emerging trends and patterns in many leisure pursuits of older adults.

Aging involves both continuity and change across the life course. Most older adults continue to pursue leisure interests initiated earlier in life. But for those who wish to learn and acquire new leisure skills in later life, the capacity to learn is high, if opportunities are provided. In later life, if leisure is to contribute to well-being, life satisfaction, and a high quality of life, activities must be meaningful, and most should involve interaction with others, especially with those who are younger. If older adults are to reach their full leisure potential, constraints on leisure in later life should be eliminated by the individual, and by the public and private sectors. Public policies must allocate more resources to the leisure needs of a growing aging population. No longer is one set or type of leisure activity deemed "ideal" for older adults. Rather, with expanding opportunities and increased health and economic status, most activities available to other age groups can and should be pursued by older adults. Even when institutionalized late in life, appropriate leisure activities are an important resource to enhance the quality of life of residents.

See also: Civic Clubs, Men; Civic Clubs, Women; Leisure and Civil Society

---

Sidebar 2: Leisure Patterns and Trends in Later Life

- Increased involvement in age-integrated or intergenerational activities with those in younger age cohorts

- Increased voluntary association involvement, especially following early retirement, in activities related to lifelong job-related skills or leisure interests

- Increased political participation ("gray power") as voters, candidates, demonstrators, and lobbyists (especially concerning health and pension matters)

- Increased involvement in formal and informal education—lifelong learning persists into the later years if opportunities are provided (for example, reduced fees at universities, Elderhostel programs, computer courses)

- Increased physical activity (for both health and social benefits), especially those in the baby boom generation who were influenced by the fitness and health promotion movements earlier in life; in the sport domain, masters, veterans, and senior competitions held locally, nationally, and internationally

- Greater involvement in activities heretofore seldom, if ever, socially sanctioned for older adults—dating, cohabiting, and remarriage, including the use of the "personal" columns; gambling, especially by women, at casinos; tourism, including adventure tours and visits to exotic locations; starting a business; or moving to a new community to initiate a new lifestyle and a new social network

---

BIBLIOGRAPHY

Cutler, Stephen, and Jon Hendricks. "Emerging Social Trends." In *Handbook of Aging and the Social Sciences.* Edited by Robert Binstock and Linda George. San Diego, Calif.: Academic Press, 2001.

Hendricks, Jon, and Stephen Cutler. "Leisure in Life-Course Perspective." In *Invitation to the Life Course: Toward New Understandings of Later Life.* Edited by Richard Settersten. Amityville, N.Y.: Baywood Publishing, 2003.

Kelly, John Robert. *Peoria Winters: Styles and Resources in Later Life.* Lexington, Mass.: Lexington Books, 1987.

McPherson, Barry. "Aging and Leisure Benefits: A Life Cycle Perspective." In *Benefits of Leisure.* Edited by B. L. Driver, et al. State College, Pa.: Venture Publishing, 1991.

———. "Aging and Social Participation," In *Aging as a Social Process: An Introduction to Individual and Population Aging.* 4th edition. Edited by Barry McPherson. Toronto: Oxford University Press, 2003.

Wilensky, Harold. "Work, Careers and Social Integration," *International Social Science Journal* 12, no. 4 (1960): 543–560.

Zuzanek, Jiri, and S. Box. "Life Course and the Daily Lives of Older Adults in Canada." In *Daily Life in Later Life: Comparative Perspectives.* Edited by Karen Altergott. Newbury Park, Calif.: Sage, 1988.

Barry D. McPherson

SEWING BEES

See *Frolics, Quilting Parties*

SHOOTING

See *Target Shooting*

SHOPPING

People shop for a variety of reasons. Most people buy the products found in shops, supermarkets, grocery stores, department stores, and malls because they need them. Since 90 percent of persons living in the United States or one of the other developed nations no longer farm, they must buy their food and beverages from stores. They also buy an endless quantity of products to furnish or repair their homes, to heal themselves from illness, or to transport themselves from place to place. But people also shop for reasons that have nothing to do with keeping themselves alive, sheltered, or well. People make purchases that allow them to distinguish themselves from neighbors. Shopping provides a psychological uplift: there is a sheer enjoyment in going into a shop and making a purchase that provides a release from mundane activities. In fact, consumerism is one of the largest recreational activities in America and the most important base upon which the economy rests.

It is obvious from the examination of artifacts from antiquity that acquiring material goods has always been a major human activity, especially among the elite. Stalls or later stores for the sale of goods seem to be characteristic of every urban society. In colonial America in each of the seaboard cities, master artisans created and sold jewelry, furniture, silverware, and other items from the

first floor of their homes. The streets of these cities contained a constant parade of people buying and selling from these artisan shops or from street vendors. Shopping was a major part of life in these cities. At times, the sheer pleasure of buying became addictive. In correspondence, husbands and wives complained that their mates' buying habits were causing financial problems. Benjamin Franklin, for example, criticized his wife, Debra, for spending too much money on clothes and furnishings they did not need.

Early American Shops

By the early nineteenth century, each of the urban centers had developed fashionable streets where the elite and the upper middle class shopped. In New York City, which became the largest and most commercial city, a few special shops located on Broadway became centers for shoppers and landmark institutions. Tiffany was the jeweler for the wealthy; Brooks Brothers was a high-fashion custom men's tailor; while Alexander T. Stewart built the leading women's shop, selling yard goods, material for hats, and a sundry of other sewing supplies. Founded in 1846, Stewart's Marble Palace was the perfect shopping place. Women ran their hands over the material, talked to the clerks, sat down, viewed themselves in large mirrors, and enjoyed the aesthetics of one of the grandest public buildings in the city. Smaller, less grand imitators appeared in other cities, including Boston, Philadelphia, and Baltimore. What made shopping in these businesses so attractive to middle-class women was the welcome they received. Prices were generally fixed and clearly noted on the merchandise, and they did not have to haggle. The goods were generally guaranteed for a certain period of time, so customers did not have to fear that they had been cheated on the purchase. For lower-class women, shopping was generally confined to local neighborhoods, where merchants were less scrupulous and women frequently had to bargain over the price.

Golden Age of Shopping

The shifting patterns of retailing after the Civil War led to an era that could easily be called the golden age of shopping in American history. Lasting from the 1870s until after World War II, large department stores were built in every major city in the United States and in many smaller ones. By the time of World War I, these stores came to dominate the skylines of the central business districts. In fact, department stores, often built by leading architects such as David Burnham of Chicago, largely defined the existence of a central business district in cities both large

Rodeo Drive. The rich and famous shop at the world-renowned Rodeo Drive in Beverly Hills, California. The three blocks that house upscale boutiques and designer shops are a favorite of celebrities and the fans trying to catch a glimpse of them. © *M. L. Sinibaldi/Corbis*

and small. Constructed between 1900 and 1920 and often standing ten to fourteen stories high, these department store buildings were the creation of some of the most famous names in retailing, such as John Wanamaker, Marshall Field, Oscar Straus, Bernard Gimbel, and Edward Filene. Their philosophy, as expressed by Marshall Field of Chicago, was to "give the lady what she wants."

John Wanamaker of Philadelphia called his store a "Land of Desire." Department stores drew customers by their sheer beauty and by the vast amounts of merchandise available for purchase. Not only were the stores grand emporiums where someone could freely walk around, looking at and testing the merchandise, but they were also safe havens. Clerks were always available, but they were unobtrusive. To further put the customer at ease, these clerks were often female, allowing many shoppers to develop friendships with the store personnel. Prices and quality of the merchandise were clearly stated, and no bargaining was allowed. Items could be returned if necessary, no questions asked. Customers were thus given the thrill of bringing home a new dress, trying it on, and returning it on the next shopping trip.

Once inside, the store's ambience cast a magical spell over the shopper. Merchandise was displayed on beautifully arranged counters. Imported silks competed for attention with fine linens. Cloth and scarves were displayed in every imaginable color. Crafts from all parts of the world were arranged in innovative ways. The scent of imported and domestic perfumes charged the atmosphere. In the ready-made departments, women could find copies of the latest French dresses. A shopper could purchase a sewing machine, which reduced the drudgery of making and repairing clothes. Stores carried bicycles and sports equipment, artist supplies, and pianos. Some early-twentieth-century stores even sold automobiles.

Not only were many of the newest technical advances on sale, these department stores were also gateways into the future. They were lit by electricity before many of their customers had it in their homes; they had escalators and elevators to move people from one floor to another. In the winter they had central heating, and in the summer a cooling system made life more bearable. At a time when even middle-class families needed an escape from homes that were dark, cold, or hot, the stores provided escape.

These Victorian stores also were great centers of amusement: they held art exhibitions, concerts, and carnivals. John Wanamaker had the largest organ in the world in his Philadelphia store, and he brought in the Philadelphia Orchestra to play. Perhaps the highlights of the year for many shoppers were Easter and Christmas, when large and imaginative displays opened wide the eyes of both adults and children. Is it any wonder that when a reporter for the *New York Times* asked the question as to why women shop, he received the answer, "Why, my dear, it's a cheap entertainment" (Abelson, p. 22)? A person could view the entertainment, enjoy the Christmas displays, and listen to the music for free. But few could view the merchandise on display without making a purchase.

Many women made a trip to the early-twentieth-century emporium a central part of their weekly activities and made two or more trips to shop. Earlier in the nineteenth century, middle-class women were often fearful about walking around city streets. But the new shopping centers gave them a safe destination where they could escape their suburban households. In these stores, women were pampered and catered to. Because the stores provided safety and were located near train terminals, women would come and meet friends and make a day of it. Before entering the store itself, shoppers or strollers would stop to look at the store's windows, which had creative and beautiful displays. One historian has speculated that the museum movement, which developed at about this time, borrowed many ideas from these department store displays.

Shopping Expeditions

To add to the excitement of a day of shopping, the department store provided services such as elegant dining rooms, which gave women a gracious place in which to meet friends. Since the stores were centrally located, a person could comparison shop at more than one emporium. And they were often next to other types of entertainment attractive to the middle class. In Philadelphia, Wanamaker's was situated a few blocks from the Academy of Music, which held special afternoon concerts. When the shopping trip was over, consumers did not have to worry about carrying a large number of packages home because the stores delivered. In every way these stores made a trip downtown a memorable and joyous occasion. Most people who lived in metropolitan areas have fond memories of visiting Santa Claus; of being inundated with the sights, smells, and sounds of the season; and of being surrounded by exhibitions of toys. Particularly during the holiday season, families often made shopping trips to New York City from other parts of the country.

Upper-class families often took trips to Europe on one of the great luxury liners to see the sights and also to shop for clothes in French boutiques or go hunting for antiques in quaint English stores. But people also made "shopping expeditions" to exotic parts of the world such as the Fiji Islands or India. Mary Davis Wallis, when told that it was unsafe for a woman to shop in Fiji, exclaimed, "Not go a shopping! A lady not go a shopping!" But not only women were affected by the lure of foreign purchases. Harriet Bailey Blaine, traveling in 1888 with her husband James J. Blaine, a former presidential candidate, wrote, "He bought and bought and bought." Consuming foreign goods was often not a side aspect of these trips but the centerpiece.

The centerpiece of shopping was the satisfaction that came from bringing home an object of a desire. In the social atmosphere of the early twentieth century this meant acquiring the clothing, furniture, rug, or piano that allowed consumers to show that they had the purchasing power to keep up with their neighbors or compete with a higher class. One female store executive described the effects of clothing on a woman's psyche, "The right clothes mean an added zip to life, a heightening of the woman's belief in herself—youth and gaiety and happiness" (Matt, p. 21). A piano allowed someone to be truly part of the middle class; it turned a house into a center of culture and promised social advancement for the children. Just having the right rug could make a home appear to belong to people of a higher social class. By 1900, factories were turning out imitations of higher-priced materials, so, for example, consumers could purchase an oriental rug that looked as if it had been made in India but had actually been manufactured in the United States. Just by making the right purchase, consumers were able to raise their families' social standing. Besides allowing buyers to rise in importance beyond their class, acquiring enduring household objects gave female shoppers a sense of power that they often lacked in a male-oriented society.

Often the pleasures and recreational nature of shopping would become addictive. The lure of goods and the displays often became too much for consumers. Although credit was often restricted to persons in the highest social class, many families found themselves unable to make the payments on what they had purchased. When credit became more widely available in the mid-twentieth century, addiction became more of a problem in the same way that a casual recreational gambler soon found the debts accumulating. There was another problem as well: girls and women often found the lure of new merchandise so tempting that they began to leave the store with goods they had not paid for. Shoplifting, according to historian Elaine

S. Abelson, became a serious problem both for the stores and for the middle-class women caught by store detectives.

Changes in the late nineteenth century had an impact upon the working class as well. Although these individuals did not shop in the great center-city department stores, they had access to a wide variety of goods because of the Industrial Revolution. Local shops sold cheap ready-made clothes even the poorest workers could afford. As part of this new culture, working girls delighted in shopping for cheap copies of middle-class dresses to wear during off hours. It was an interesting phenomenon as all classes began to acquire numerous changes of dress for different occasions. No longer did people simply own one set of clothes, shoes, and hats for everyday use and another set for Sunday. By the 1920s, with relatively cheap transportation available and with a shortening of the workday, working-class women and men often shopped downtown. To accommodate them, merchants developed a new class of lower-priced department stores. Stores such as Wanamaker's in Philadelphia and Filene's in Boston, which catered to the upper middle class, developed bargain basements that contained clothes and merchandise remaindered from the upper floors. To encourage these shoppers, many of the department stores developed credit cards specifically for the less affluent.

Post–World War II

After World War II, the department store gradually declined in the United States until only a few old-style examples remained. For example, Gimbel's in New York City closed in the mid-1980s while Wanamaker's in Philadelphia shut it doors in the late 1990s. Macy's in New York City is the largest store in America, although it has rivals in Tokyo, London, and Paris. The cause for the decline of the department store ties into the disintegration of the city and the rise of the suburbs and to the shift to automobile in place of mass transportation. With rising crime many people feared going into the city, and a visit to a store became less entertaining and more threatening. Parking was also difficult and expensive and mass transportation deteriorated, making it harder to get into the central business district. Although it took time for the big department stores to disappear, by the year 2000 most were gone. Since much of the middle class now lived in the suburbs, shopping malls became the substitute for the large department stores. As the shopping environment changed, many of the old-name stores built chains in the affluent suburbs, so that soon every major mall in the New York metropolitan area had a Macy's.

Since the largest cities continued to have middle-class residents, they continued to have elite shopping districts that also attracted buyers from the suburbs. Consumers from around the country still had a few destinations. New York's Fifth Avenue from Thirty-fourth Street to Central Park remains the most famous shopping street in the United States, but Walnut Street in Philadelphia and Michigan Boulevard in Chicago also attracted shoppers. With the introduction of cheap transatlantic flights, middle-class consumers began making buying trips to Europe; people wanted to possess goods that no one else in their neighborhood had.

Even without the great department stores and the amusements they provided, shopping is more a leisure activity in the early twenty-first century than it was in the early twentieth century. With the increase in disposable income after World War II, a greater percentage of the population could afford to engage in shopping. Shaken by the Great Depression, governments have since 1945 urged consumers to spend money to help the economy recover from economic downturns. Women, who have less time since most are working, and men, who have more time at their disposal since the advent of the forty-hour week and paid vacations, continue to spend time shopping as a leisure pastime. Large malls, sometimes containing hundreds of shops, are the primary shopping centers, but increasingly discount centers, either standing alone or attached to a dozen or more similar stores, have become a shopping alternative. Malls make an attempt to duplicate on a sparer scale the old department stores by providing decorations at Christmas and by bringing in entertainment.

Class and gender sometimes provide dividing lines in how people spend shopping time. A few upscale shopping areas appeal to the elite shopper. Rodeo Drive in Beverly Hills, California, is only three blocks long, but it contains branches of the most prestigious European and American retailers such as Gucci, Coco Chanel, Valentino, Cartier, Neiman Marcus, and Tiffany. On a smaller scale, upper-class consumer enclaves are found near most of the suburbs. Although most of the malls appeal to women, men are usually there in large numbers. But men with greater free time also visit in greater numbers home repair stores, sporting goods shops, and automobile dealers. With greater independent incomes, women often are found in similar retailers. In fact, there seems to be a greater convergence across wealth and gender than ever before.

Perhaps the one group left out of the consumer revolution has been the poor. Not only do they not have the means to engage in shopping as leisure, but often they do not have any place to shop. Many poor neighborhoods have lost the stores that were prominent there at the beginning of the twentieth century. Transportation to shopping malls from the city is often unreliable and costly.

Whether done in a department store or a suburban mall, shopping is often a transforming experience. People buy for the excitement of the product acquired. Though not the fantasy lands that department stores were, malls continue to be the destinations at which many American choose to spend their weekends and holidays. This leisure-time activity has an enormous impact on the economy. Analysts devote a great deal of time to understanding how much shoppers have spent in the previous month compared to the same period a year before. The stock market has been known to rise and fall on the basis of the consumer confidence index. Few leisure-time activities have this kind of national impact.

See also: Commercialization of Leisure, Shopping Malls, Teenage Leisure Trends

BIBLIOGRAPHY

Abelson, Elaine S. *When Women Go A-Thieving: Middle-Class Shoplifters in the American Department Store.* New York: Oxford University Press, 1989.

Bowlby, Rachel. *Carried Away: The Invention of Modern Shopping.* New York: Columbia University Press, 2001.

Cohen, Lizabeth. *A Consumers' Republic: The Politics of Mass Consumption in Postwar America.* New York: Alfred A. Knopf, 2003.

Ershkowitz, Herbert. *John Wanamaker, Philadelphia Merchant.* Conshohocken, Pa.: Combined Publishing, 1999.

Hine, Thomas. *I Want That! How We All Became Shoppers: A Cultural History.* New York: HarperCollins Publishers, 2002.

Horowitz, Daniel. *The Morality of Spending: Attitudes Toward the Consumer Society in America, 1876–1930.* Baltimore: Johns Hopkins University Press, 1985.

Leach, William, *Land of Desire: Merchants, Power, and the Rise of a New American Culture.* New York: Vintage Books, 1993.

Lears, Jackson. *Fables of Abundance: A Cultural History of Advertising in America.* New York: Basic Books, 1994.

Matt, Susan J. *Keeping Up with the Joneses: Envy in American Consumer Society, 1890–1930.* Philadelphia: University of Pennsylvania Press, 2003.

Peiss, Kathy. *Cheap Amusements: Working Women and Leisure in Turn-of-the-Century New York.* Philadelphia: Temple University Press, 1986.

Herbert B. Ershkowitz

SHOPPING MALLS

"Shopping mall" and "mall" are terms used in common parlance to refer to just about any kind of sizable shopping center, but more precisely they identify a comprehensively planned and fully integrated retail development planned, operated, and generally owned by a single business entity that employs a system of pedestrian ways as its principal circulation spine. Most shopping malls contain at least fifty stores; they are usually anchored by one or more department stores and are intended to draw customers on a regular basis from a large surrounding area. Well before a mall became a key component of such complexes, shopping centers were conceived as alternative retail environments that would attract shoppers because of their amenities as well as the goods and services they purveyed. The foremost pioneer of this concept, Kansas City real estate developer J. C. Nichols, enjoyed nationwide influence through the example of his Country Club Plaza, constructed incrementally over several decades beginning in 1922. Abundant free parking, wide sidewalks, outdoor sculpture, ornate buildings, fashion shows, parades, and holiday pageants were among the features that attracted widespread attention and helped set the tone for shopping centers over the next generation.

The idea of having a pedestrian mall as a spine for shopping centers originated in the 1930s among advocates of reform in the design of residential areas who believed that this inward-looking configuration, which separated shoppers from the parking lot, would reinvigorate social intercourse and a sense of community that purportedly was lost on Main Streets with the widespread use of motor vehicles. In these early plans, the mall was, in fact, a large open green space surrounded by sidewalks and conducive to informal play by children as well as perambulation by adults.

Not until the late 1940s, however, did the reformers' ideal become successfully fused with the retail developers' imperatives to gain an edge in the new and highly competitive market at the rapidly expanding urban periphery. Among the foremost reasons why pragmatic businessmen began to embrace the mall was that a controlled and ostensibly leisurely setting fostered longer visits, greater circulation, and thus greater sales. At a time when the traditional urban environment was losing its appeal among a new generation of consumers, the neat, but relaxed, landscaped outdoor environment of the mall seemed a conspicuous improvement.

By the mid-1950s, the leading advocate of the shopping mall was the Los Angeles–based architect Victor

Mall of America. Located in Bloomington, Minnesota, the Mall of America claims to be the most visited attraction in the United States. It has 525 specialty stores, 4 national department stores, over 50 restaurants, 7 nightclubs, and 14 movie theaters. Opened in August 1992, there is also an 18-hole miniature golf course and a rollercoaster ride. © *Owaki-Kulla/Corbis*

Gruen. Gruen painted an engaging picture of the mall as possessing the vibrancy of street life he had known in his native Austria. The mall proper could support vendors whose wares complement that of the enclosed stores. The mall should be a gathering place of many kinds. Like Nichols a quarter century earlier, he envisioned the shopping center as a place for special events as well as impromptu exchange. Arguably Gruen's greatest contribution to the design vocabulary of such complexes was a fully enclosed mall, where the ensemble was structured and serviced as a single building, the storefronts functioning merely as partitions, rather than a cluster of buildings around an open space. This configuration proved efficient to heat and cool as well as to maintain and protect. The enclosed mall was first realized at Southdale (1953–1956), outside Minneapolis, Minnesota, in response to the region's climatic extremes. While Southdale

attracted widespread attention, the concept was slow to gain acceptance among developers and retailers alike. Once its economic strengths were demonstrated, however, the enclosed mall gained increasing favor, becoming the industry standard by the mid-1960s in virtually all parts of the country.

With a climate-controlled environment, the mall proper could be more fully exploited for the array of uses Gruen promoted. The space outside the stores was hospitable irrespective of heat, cold, or inclement weather. Consuming food and beverages, talking with friends, sitting to rest or read a newspaper, window shopping, or performing any other outdoor activity associated with a retail district in ideal conditions became part of the year-round regime. Cart vendors could more readily peddle their wares. Events associated with holidays could be easily staged, as could raffles and other endeavors organized for charitable purposes. Shoppers could linger and take in the scene. They also could circulate easily throughout the premises and, more often than not, make additional purchases.

The multiplication of shopping malls from the mid-1950s through the 1960s occurred in direct response to continued population growth on the metropolitan periphery. Swelling consumer demand abated previous fears that regions would become oversaturated with these expansive complexes; again and again new shopping malls were constructed in places that had been largely undeveloped only a few years before. By 1960, the largest urban areas had two and frequently more examples; over the next decade, new shopping malls were realized to a much greater extent; collectively they now formed a ring around major U.S. cities. The 1960s were indeed the pivotal period of change when, despite concerted efforts to counter the trend, retailing in the city center became clearly subordinate to, even marginalized by, comparable activity near the perimeter. The mall became a surrogate for downtown—the principal destination for the majority of upper-to-middle-income households.

The shopping mall also began to proliferate beyond the metropolis during the next decade. Increasingly, malls were developed on the edge of small cities and even towns to serve a network of concentrated settlements and rural areas in between. Many of these examples lacked the size and array of leading stores found in major metropolitan areas, but were nonetheless embraced by consumers as a preferable alternative to established retail centers in their respective communities. As a result, shopping in the mall became a widespread American experience.

Concurrently, significant changes occurred in the design of shopping malls serving major cities. Following the example of the Galleria in the Post Oak district of Houston (1968–1970), malls contained two or three levels, with circulation ringing open, skylit wells. This configuration allowed many more retail units to occupy a given ground area, responding to still rising consumer demand and escalating land prices. The multilevel arrangement was acceptable, even appreciated by consumers because of the dramatic, airy ambience afforded by abundant vistas and glazed, arched ceilings. Opening the interior to natural light also greatly reduced electricity costs, a factor that became decisive following the first oil embargo in 1971. As the name of the prototypical Houston complex implied, the model for this form of shopping mall was the grand shopping arcade, or galleria, that became a hallmark of many European city centers during the second half of the nineteenth century. For the first time, the mall began to

evoke urban density and with it the potential for greater sensorial stimulation. Few sequels included anything comparable to the Houston Galleria's ice skating rink, but many designs were crafted to further a sense of visual excitement in the course of moving through the various parts of these enormous retail settings.

Perhaps even more than its proponents intended, the shopping mall evolved into an important social center. Its draw stemmed not so much from special events as from the fact that probably no other place on the metropolitan periphery was so conducive to interaction among numerous groups of people. Adolescents found the mall to be an incomparable place to sample the goods advertising so aggressively portrayed, but also to see and be seen by their peers. Parents tended to regard the mall as a safe haven for offspring too restless to stay at home. Elderly men and women also found the mall an agreeable place to rendezvous with friends and to make new acquaintances without spending much money or making advanced commitments. Many ages in between still came to the mall primarily to shop but found the scene appealing. Aside from sports arenas, houses of worship, and amusement parks, the shopping mall became one of the few places where sizable numbers of people congregated on a regular basis. Unlike those other places, going to the mall required neither an admission fee nor participation in a prescribed ritual. The mall offered complete freedom —to socialize or remain anonymous, to indulge or abstain, to circulate extensively or proceed to a single destination.

From a management perspective, the mall as a social center was normally conducive to greater sales, but it could also be a source of conflict. Demonstrations, solicitations, and disorderly activities of all kinds have always been cast as unacceptable behavior. Mall owners see their premises much like a store, in which the scope of acceptable conduct is quite limited. Others have countered, with some concurrence from the courts, that the mall is in effect a public place and that legitimate forms of expression not related to business are warranted. But irrespective of legality, the mall has never become an important staging ground for public events or public disruptions. The mall's enduring appeal is as a place for unstructured human interaction—in the purchase of goods and in the pursuit of socializing. In the modern consumer world, both are mutually reinforcing forms of recreation and leisure.

See also: Commercialization of Leisure, Shopping, Teenage Leisure Trends

BIBLIOGRAPHY

Cohen, Lizabeth. "From Town Center to Shopping Center: The Reconfiguration of Community Marketplaces in Postwar America." *American Historical Review* 101 (October 1996): 1050–1081.

Gillette, Howard. "The Evolution of the Planned Shopping Center in Suburb and City." *Journal of the American Planning Association* 51 (Autumn 1985): 449–460.

Jacobs, Jerry. *The Mall: An Attempted Escape from Everyday Life.* Prospect Heights, Ill.: Waveland Press, 1984.

Kowinski, William Severine. *The Malling of America.* New York: William Monroe and Company, 1985.

Longstreth, Richard. *City Center to Regional Mall: Architecture, the Automobile, and Retailing in Los Angeles, 1920–1950.* Cambridge, Mass.: MIT Press, 1997.

Zepp, Ira G., Jr. *The New Religious Image of Urban America: The Shopping Mall as Ceremonial Center.* Westminster, Md.: Christian Classics, 1986. Revised edition, Niwot, Colo.: University Press of Colorado, 1997.

Richard Longstreth

SHORTAGE OF LEISURE

As the twentieth century began, Americans were in the midst of what the historian Daniel Rodgers called a "long campaign against overwork" (p. 106). Concerns about the "national intoxication with work" began after the Civil War, smoldered through the 1880s, and caught fire as the nineteenth century drew to its close (p. 104). Critics began to characterize the "excessive working" as a "nationwide obsession," a veritable "national feverishness" that was leaving widespread stress, "nervousness," and fatigue in its wake (p. 102).

Prominent individuals raised the alarm. Commenting on the "American character" on his last trip to the United States, Herbert Spencer observed that "the American, eagerly pursuing a future good, ignores what good the passing day offers. . . ." He knew several people who "suffered from nervous collapse . . . ; friends (one of whom was his uncle) who had killed themselves from overwork, or had been permanently incapacitated. . . ." He saw "immense injury . . . being done by the high-pressure life . . .; serious physical mischief caused by overwork. . . ." The consequences were all too evident; a tragic "inability to enjoy life," a new, voluntary slavery "to accumulation," and the "dwindling away of . . . [American] free institutions [such as the family and community]" (pp. 354–359).

Religious leaders and the medical profession took up the cry. Moralists and ministers likened overindulgence in work to drunkenness—a person could be just as addicted to work as whiskey, and the resulting social devastation just as bad. Physicians such as S. Wier Mitchell and George Beard, observing the "epidemic" of stress and overwork, found it necessary to coin a new medical term, "nurasthenia," to describe the peculiar malady.

"Self-help adviser" Annie Payson Call noted that Europeans had long recognized this ailment as "Americanitis," symptomatic of a singular national preoccupation with money and ignorance of all that life offered except work.

Newspapers and magazines seized the issue, publishing "scores of columns . . . indicting overwork and overworry" (Rodgers, p. 105). So much was written that *Scribner's Magazine* complained in 1896 that too much was being made of the story—that the "great deal of advice being given by writers and preachers to professional and businessmen . . . not to work so hard" had become a little hackneyed (p. 253). Still, the avalanche of articles and books grew.

As the new century began, public concern spread from anxiety about overwork among the middle classes to workers. The famous jurists Josephine Goldmark and Louis Brandise asked, "What good to the workers are the higher standards—better food, clothing, and shelter—so long as over-fatigue continues to limit or destroy their capacity of enjoying them?" (Frankfurter, pp. 284, 305, 669; see also Goldmark.) Numerous state labor bureaus, industrial commissions, and scientific studies bolstered Goldmark and Brandise's case. Based on more than ten years' research, the Yale economist Irving Fisher concluded, "The economic waste from undue fatigue is . . . much greater than the waste from [all] serious illness (sic). The number that suffer partial disability through [overwork] certainly constitutes the great majority of the population" (p. 669).

Even so, Goldmark maintained that "the fundamental" damage caused by overwork was to the family: "when both parents are away from home for twelve or thirteen hours . . . a day, the children receive . . . little attention." Study after study done throughout the industrial world had shown her that overwork "demoralizes all family life. When working hours are so long that the evening is invaded by labor, the exhausted worker . . . must unavoidably neglect all family duties, and loose the elevating influence of family life" (pp. 317, 246).

As the twenty-first century began, little seemed to have changed. Americans seemed just as concerned about overwork as ever; the press and electronic media just as full of stories about the damage done by long hours. If anything, complaints had increased.

Spencer's nineteenth-century warnings find echoes a century later in one of the longest-running mass media stories to come out of Japan. In 2004, American journalists were covering the "Karoshi syndrome," the sudden-death-from-overwork phenomenon that appeared to be sweeping that nation, writing the story as a cautionary tale for the United States. "Workaholic" entered the language in the 1970s and flourished subsequently in the media and among academics, giving a modern-sounding name to the churchmen's nineteenth-century moral concerns.

A myriad of reporters continue to write about the "time famine," enough so that Scribner's' 1886 complaint still seems fair. Adding to the media overkill, the major networks produce dozens of television specials, detailing how Americans are "running out of time," pressed to the wall by the excessive time demands of their jobs.

The Family Institute of American continues to do what Goldmark and Brandise did ninety years ago, documenting the damage done to the family, and concluding with Goldmark that the "fundamental harm caused by overwork is to the American family."

Like Annie Payson Call, journalists still cover the story in depth, coming up with some striking images. For instance, Amy Saltzman uses the "empty front porch" as a metaphor to represents the loss of family and community time to work. Witold Rybczynski sounded another nostalgic note, wondering what ever happened to the weekend—now people all seem to be waiting for the weekend that never comes.

Things appear to have gotten even worse since the early twentieth century; at least then people seemed to have had time for front porches and weekends. Up-to-date twists have been added to the story. Reporters describe how new kinds of electronic communication extend the "long arm of the job" so that few places remain safe from work. They imagine more of us living "above the store," on permanent call by cell phone and e-mail, even on "vacations" that are getting shorter because of the press of work.

Just as the state and national labor bureaus did at the turn of the twentieth century, academics are now trying to gauge the extent of the distress, falling to quibbling in the process. Harvard economist Juliet Schor argued in 1992 in her popular book, The Overworked American, that as a result of a combination of factors—the increase in the percentage of the population working (primarily women), increases in the number of hours worked each week, and reductions in paid time off—the average Joe or Jill works about a month more now than in the mid-

1970s. Her findings seem to support the series of Harris polls that showed the average American working 20 percent more in the early 1990s than in 1973 (up from 40.6 hours to 48.8 hours) and having 32 percent less free time per week (down from 17.7 hours per week to 8.5). In addition to more women working, Harris explained that increasing numbers of retired people are returning to work (see also Hunnicutt).

The President's Council of Economic Advisors' 1999 report "Families and the Labor Market, 1969–1999: Analyzing the 'Time Crunch'" bolstered these claims, showing that American parents had twenty-two fewer hours per week to spend at home compared with the average in 1969. The President's Council accounted for most of the decrease by the entrance of women into the labor force. Still the council concluded that all who worked for pay were increasing their average hours, and that U.S. workers spent more time on the job than workers in any other developed country.

The most widely used measure, the Department of Labor and Bureau of Census joint publication the March Current Population Survey (CPS), shows only a small increase in working hours from 1970 to 2000, ranging from a low of just over forty-two hours per week to a high near forty-four hours for full-time male workers (adjusted for part-time work, self-employed workers, and multiple job holdings). Women average around thirty-seven hours per week on their paid jobs. The Bureau of Labor Statistics also reports that the labor force participation rate (the proportion of the civilian noninstitutional population sixteen years of age and older either at work or actively seeking work) increased to an all-time high, from 60.4 percent to 66.4 percent between 1970 and 1990 (Fullerton, pp. 3–12).

However, studies done by John Robinson, Geoffrey Godbey, and Ann Bostrom using time diary data seemed to show that leisure was increasing, that by the mid-1980s working Americans had about five more hours of leisure per week than in the mid-1960s. They explained that when answering survey questions (such as those use by the CPS), most people overestimated how long they worked, and that the difference between the reported and the "actual" workweek increased each year until by the 1980s men were saying they worked ten to eleven more hours each week than they really did; women, about six. The "myth of the overworked American" was widely touted in the media, contradicting earlier stories about overwork (passim).

However, the time diary studies have also been questioned. Jerry Jacobs found that the discrepancy between the survey data and the time diary measures could be no more than a statistical anomaly, the result of random measurement error, and that "independent measures of working time largely corroborate the self-reported measures relied on by the standard surveys, such as the census and the *CPS*" that show weekly averages to be around 42.6 in 1997 (pp. 42–53). Moreover, the President's Council and Juliet Schor's conclusions about the expanding percentage of the population entering the workforce, expanding the total number of hours worked, are not rebutted by the time diary studies, nor is the fact that working women face a "second shift" when they return home. At this point, it seems prudent to rely on CPS figures, combined with the census data on increasing labor force participation.

Reality vs. Perception

Nevertheless, all observers do agree on a fundamental fact—that the perception of being overworked is widespread. Whether work hours have increased a little or a lot since the 1960s, the feeling of being overwhelmed remains and seems to be ubiquitous. It appears, then, that "Americanitis" has endured as something of a national character trait. Americans' preoccupation with work seems, on the surface, to be one of the few stable features of American life, and that the "work ethic" has endured as a foundation of American values, even to a fault.

But the similarities are more apparent than real. Attitudes and beliefs about work that lay just beneath the surface of the overwork stories were very different at the beginning of the twentieth century, and careful comparison of the two sets of discourses reveal historical changes of the first order of importance.

At the turn of the twentieth century, those who wrote about overwork were generally optimistic—overwork was widely seen as a temporary phenomenon that might be mitigated by enlightened business practices and by feasible social reforms in the short run; but, in all cases, bound vanish before the onrush of history.

Industrial scientists demonstrated that fatigue hindered production, proving to their satisfaction that after eight hours, workers' productivity decreased dramatically. Fatigue was bad business. The eight-hour day swept the nation after 1910. Reformers pressed for new laws, among the most important of the Progressive Era, limiting child labor and overly long hours in hazardous occupations and for children and women. Important parts of the discourse surrounding these events were about protecting the family from the excessive demands of industry, and were predicated on a widespread agreement that overwork was bad for the health of everyone and should be remedied by state regulation.

Moreover such practical reforms were set in the context of a larger optimism and broader vision. For decades before and after the turn of the century, writers defined progress in terms of higher wages and shorter hours—industry's increasing productivity was providing more of the material goods of life, nearing the time when everyone would have enough to live on. But just as important, industrial progress was offering more time to live. Of course, problems such as overwork remained, but the machine promised and was delivering a "golden age" of abundance, humane as well as material.

Fully expecting "necessity's obsolescence," utopian books flooded the market after the 1888 publication of Bellamy's *Looking Backward,* many employing the traditional utopian themes of the four- or six-hour workday. Bellamy set the tone, imagining a twenty-first-century world blessed by technology that freed humans from work and "necessity" for the best part of their lives. The inhabitants of Bellamy's "perfect society," realizing that "it is not our labor, but the higher and larger activities . . . the intellectual and spiritual enjoyments and pursuits . . . that are . . . the main business of life," retired at forty-five (chapter 18).

Such a vision permeated the age. But for the practical-minded, increasing liberation from work was not about some distant utopia but was an achievable goal, as realistic as higher wages. For more than a century, organized labor and workers succeeded in reducing their working hours, and they fully expected their victories to continue. By 1887, George Gunton was calling labor's repeated claims that "if twelve hours' labor a day is better than fourteen, then six must be better than twelve, three better than six . . ." stale. However "stale" this project may have appeared at the time to Gunton, in the event, it turned out rather to be the well-worn road map for progress in the labor movement, as working hours were being cut virtually in half over the century of shorter hours. The coming of the age of leisure was hardly utopian speculation (Horowitz).

Economists, aware of the century-long work-reduction phenomena around the turn of the twentieth century, confidently forecast that work's long-term decline would continue—there was no reason to expect its ending. Indeed, this was arguably the longest and most influential social and economic movement in modern times.

American scientists and engineers prided themselves in leading the way, confident that their chief contribution to society was the new range of "labor saving-devices" they were delivering. Perhaps their paramount contribution to human betterment was the lifting of the six-hour day out of the realm of utopian speculation into the everyday calculation of practical-minded business-people.

Prominent individuals and journalists wrote dozens of books and articles predicting that work would soon become a subordinate part of life—that two hours of work per day would be an established norm by the year 2000. This view of progress spread even to conservative businesspeople who put the six-hour day into operation in cities such as Battle Creek, Michigan, and Akron, Ohio, during the 1930s.

Overwork in this context was doubly condemned, not only for damaging family and health, but also for impeding the opening of a fuller, freer life for the masses. Overwork, as working longer than "necessary," could even make the transition from work/necessity to freedom impossible. As work and the marketplace encroached on the realms of human freedom, gradually obscuring them, people might well forget that there was something to life other than economic concerns and perpetual working.

Given the widespread optimism about continuing work's reduction, the one-hundred-year tradition of shorter hours, and the vigorous state regulation of work hours that started the twentieth century, it is strange that Americans are just as concerned with overwork a hundred years later.

It is significant that as the new millennium began, the discussion about overwork was taking place in a very different cultural context. The "scientific" discoveries about fatigue that supported the reduction of the work-day at the turn of the century were generally ignored. Little or no attention was given to what was once understood as a scientific "fact"—that concentration and dexterity decline significantly after eight hours of work. In the early 2000s people working in the most fatigue-sensitive kinds of occupations seemed to take pride in working virtually all the time. Physicians, for example, were notorious for advertising their need to work exceptionally long hours, but they were somehow oblivious to the needs of patients to be treated by someone who was not intoxicated by fatigue. Corporate culture put a premium on "face time"; salaried employees were expected to be on the job or on call day and night. Hourly workers came to depend on overtime, at record levels in the 1990s, as the only way to make ends meet. (From 1991 to 1997, average weekly overtime in manufacturing increased by 1.6 hours, reaching its highest level—4.9 hours—since Bureau of Labor Statistics began publishing the series in 1956.) John Stuart Mill's fear that workers might continue to be "exploited" by "overwork" seems to have come true (Hetrick pp. 30–33).

Meaningful reform of excessive work hours by state regulation is virtually dead in the United States. The solutions now offered for overwork are generally piecemeal, based largely on the "self-help" approach Annie Payson Call espoused in the 1890s. Instead of new and effective state or federal regulation of work hours, in the place of the hundreds of state and national laws limiting work hours that dominated the political landscape in the first part of the twentieth century, Congress offered "Band-Aid" remedies in the 1990s. During Clinton's second term, for example, Democrats attempted to address the national concerns about overwork by making business more "family friendly," proposing regulations that require bosses to give their employees occasional time off for the needs of the family. Republicans, fearful of such government intrusions, pushed instead for a "comp-time" bill, i.e., amendments to existing legislation that would allow employers to compensate workers for over-time by time and a half off work instead of time and a half pay—for example, if a person puts in ten hours of overtime this week, he or she could take off fifteen hours sometime in the future. Even these timid initiatives failed, dying in congressional committees, leaving the sixty-year-long stretch of governmental inaction unbroken. Many criticized the Republican plan as opening the door to the Right's real agenda, the rollback of all hours regulation. Some feared that the sixty-year-old Fair Labor Standards Act was in jeopardy. The few scholars and activists who advocate effective new hours regulation, such as double-time payment for overtime or an overtime tax, are ignored for the most part, consigned to the backwaters of the political terrain.

A Shift in the Popular Thinking

But the most important historical change has been in beliefs about work. Overwork is no longer seen as a mean-while problem, bound to disappear as the economy progresses. Very little remains in the public discourse of the once prominent understanding of work as a means to an end. Discussion about work has shifted dramatically, dominated now by an opposing belief, work as an end in itself.

As the new millennium began, few economists remained who expected the satisfaction of "basic" economic needs to be an immediate, or even a distant likelihood. "Obsolete necessity," once understood as one of progress's givens, seemed more the fond hope of yesterday's benighted dreamers.

The expectation of "abundance" so prominent at the turn of the twentieth century—the widespread belief that it was possible to get enough of the material goods of life and then move on to better things as industry advanced—has been replaced by hopes for an eternally expanding economy, ever higher standards of living, and, ironically, the perpetual advance of necessity.

Instead of hope for expanding freedom, need now springs eternal in American hearts. Intellectuals and politicians, with few exceptions, have ceased dreaming of further work reduction, pining instead for a world full of enough work for everyone or brooding about the "work famine" to come. Instead of viewing progress as transcending work, necessity, and economic concerns, Americans in the early 2000s tended to view work as the ultimate measure of progress and definition of prosperity—the more of it the better. Economists and politicians turned from the notion that human needs for industrial products were finite (and that "economic abundance" was a meaningful term) to embrace the rival faith that economic needs were infinite.

Modern presidents evaluated their administrations by how much work expanded during their term—how many new jobs were created. Academics have concluded that "the disappearance of work is not an opportunity but a tragedy" (Wolf).

Work is no longer the road to finite destinations. Instead work is now widely perceived as a need in itself—not the subordinated, perfected work of the two-hour day Julian Huxley expected, or the fifteen-hour week John Maynard Keynes predicted, but the life-centering, "full-time" job of at least forty hours for an expanding portion of the population.

During the twentieth century, for the first time, "full-time" work was defined as a stable norm (at forty hours or better per week), and valued in and for itself. The "need" of an ever larger portion of the population for this "full-time" work is perhaps the only candidate that might satisfy Keynes's definition of an unchangeable economic need today—a turn of events that doubtless would have shocked the economist.

With the rise of the faith in work as an end in itself, the industrial nations have embarked on what may well be the most fantastic project ever conceived in human history, apart from the Tantalus fable—the eternal replacement of existing work, perpetually being taken away by new technology and capitalism, by new work.

Whereas at the turn of the century, the time that was freed by new machines and efficient business techniques promised the opening up of human life in realms outside work and the market, signaling the advent of a "golden age," in the early 2000s that same process had been largely redefined—economists and politicians hoped that the newly freed time could continually be reemployed by the market or state, transformed into the new work necessary to undergird everlasting economic growth and "full employment."

Whereas American scientists and engineers once rallied round the slogan "labor-saving device," they have turned to proclaiming long and loud the exact opposite, "science makes jobs," defending new technologies such as the computer and the Internet because they will expand "employment opportunities."

Compared to this chimera of work's perpetual regeneration, the utopians' old dreams about "abundance" and necessity's obsolescence seem rather unimaginative. The modern project is made even more wonderful because of the new, widely accepted faith that somehow this newly minted work will become more and more intrinsically satisfying. A new faith in "good jobs" (what Jacques Ellul called "l'idéologie du Travail-Bien") has evolved and largely obscured the old belief that expanding free time was the way to compensate workers for "devitalized" work (pp. 43–48).

Certainly criticism of "deskilled" and dehumanized work has endured—if anything, like concerns about overwork, it has grown stronger since the 1890s. Technology and capitalism continued to produce machine-dominated, highly regulated, specialized, servantlike, and boring jobs. But as the twentieth century unfolded, another solution gained ascendancy—the fond hope that work might be transformed and made the place for community, craftsmanship, personal fulfillment, and cultural expression—the very things that defenders of "progressively shorter hours" once claimed would be fruits of increasing leisure."

Whereas "most critics" of work's degradation at the turn of the century concluded that "if modern industrial work was soulless, then men should do less of it" (Rodgers, p. 90) the dominant myth in the early 2000s was that work would eventually be reengineered and reformed to become the human abode—wonderfully transformed as the place to realize one's full humanity. The fact that few jobs lived up to such expectations is widely rejected as an argument against "l'idéologie du Travail-Bien." Alan Wolf represents the dominant view: "The fact that there remain so many jobs that have little self-direction or that fail to contribute to people's moral development is not an argument to reduce our dependence on work, but to encourage precisely those kinds of work that contribute to "'cognitive complexity,' personal competence, and liberal democratic values." (One is reminded of the biblical Job by such a passage, so rich with faith and patient expectation, and of Job's cry to Yahweh, "Though he slay me, yet will I trust him").

As the project of work's eternal regeneration and the myth of "good jobs" gained ground, free time and free realms outside work and the marketplace were increasingly commodified, commercialized, trivialized, and subdued as the handmaidens of work. Instead of providing new opportunities to strengthen families, communities, and the state, instead of opening up democratic vistas in the nonpecuniary, "free realms of life" to the masses, industrial progress has done the very opposite. As the new work beliefs waxed strong, significant inroads were made by work and the marketplace into those domains of life once understood to transcend economic logic and to be "free" and worthwhile for their own sakes.

As "free time" has been steadily commercialized, it has been transformed from a time for the expression of community-based, culture-producing activities, to passive consumption. Instead of employing time outside work and the market in active engagement with others—conversing, storytelling, making music, performing rituals, and simply playing—citizens of the modern age spend the majority of their leisure passively consuming "culture" that is ready-made for them. The fears that Mill, Patten, and others expressed 100 years ago, that unlimited economic expansion and continued overwork would obscure and then foreclose the realms of human experience outside the utilitarian, now seem prophetic.

Little now remains of the expectation that work's subordination would open up human existence outside of necessity and the marketplace. As what Jürgen Habermas termed the "colonizing of the Lifeworld" has proceeded apace, the time freed by industrialization has been largely trivialized. Few remain who defend steadily increasingly leisure as the hope for the future—as the harbinger of a "golden age." Few now claim that leisure, rather than work, is the place for realization of human potential. Abundant leisure has become for most a freedom too far; a time "lost from work," fit only for the foolish and lazy who are content to waste their lives in pointless idleness (vol. 1, pp. 183, 239–240; vol. 2, pp. 292–293, 422, 452, 470–487).

One of Habermas's main points is that "communities of discourse" have collapsed, replaced in the modern age by a superculture that is passively consumed by most and produced and performed by an increasingly small elite. Writing about the transformation of "a public that made culture an object of critical debate into one that consumes it," he concluded: "no longer cultivation [Bildung] but rather consumption opens access to culture goods." Instead of publicly doing and performing, transmitting and transforming their culture, citizens of industrial societies have become passive, private consumers of

that which was once the place for the discovery of common humanity and life-meaning for individuals. "Citizens" who once, contending with each other in public about the "good and just life," helped create a public world of symbols and symbolic interchange have now given up and adopted a "general attitude of demand." The "commodification and commercialization of culture" systematically displaces "critical-rational discourse" as agencies and structures "outside the community" co-opt fundamental cultural roles.

From progress's brightest promise, leisure has descended to hobbies, TV, and "pass-times"—or to the marginal existence of outcasts who are unable or unwilling to center their existence in the truly meaningful experience of "full-time" work. Leisure is now defended, if at all, as a way to improve work, or better still provide new avenues for work's expansion.

The 100-year process of work's reduction and the vision of progress beyond the realms of work and necessity that was shared by so many earlier in the twentieth century across the political spectrum, including conservative businesspeople and political moderates such as Elihu Root, are now most often dismissed as an anomaly—as the "radical traditions of reducing [work] hours" (Wolf).

Finally, the 100-year work-reduction process, the "century of shorter hours," ended during the 1940s, followed by more than a half century of stable (or perhaps increasing) work hours up to the present. Workers' and labor's old cause, the "progressive shortening of the hours of labor," now radicalized, has virtually disappeared. The shorter hours trajectory, once seen to be an irresistible historical movement, provided a vocabulary for the work-as-a-means-to-an-end discussion. With the end of shorter hours and with the expansion of work to include larger portions of modern life, the old expectations about "progressively shorter hours" now seem incredible, no longer serving as an historical platform for projecting an alternative to what Joseph Pieper called the "rise of the world of total work" (p. 12).

See also: Expansion of Leisure Time, Work and Leisure Ethics, Working-Class Leisure Lifestyles

BIBLIOGRAPHY

Bellamy, Edward. *Looking Backward from 2000 to 1887.* Project Gutenberg, 1996. E-text #624. Available from http://www.ibiblio.org/gutenberg.

Council of Economic Advisors, with commentary by Brian Robertson. "The Parenting Deficit: Council of Economic

Advisors Analyze the 'Time Crunch.'" May 1999. Available from http://www.whitehouse.gov.

Ellul, Jacques. "L'idéologie du Travail-Bien," *Foi et Vie*. For information about this publication, see *Cross Currents* (Spring 1985): 43–48. Available from http://www.jesusradicals.com.

Frankfurter, Felix. *The Case for the Shorter Work Day*. Franklin O. Bunting, plaintiff in error, vs. the State of Oregon, defendant in error. Brief for defendant in error. Felix Frankfurter, of counsel for the State of Oregon. Assisted by Josephine Goldmark. New York: National Consumer's League, 1916.

Fullerton, Howard N., Jr. "Labor Force Participation: 75 Years of Change, 1950–98 and 1998–2025." *Monthly Labor Review* 122 (December 1999): 3–12.

Goldmark, Josephine Clara. *Fatigue and Efficiency: A Study in Industry*. New York: Charities Publication Committee, 1912.

Habermas, Jürgen. *Theory of Communicative Action*. Translated by Thomas McCarthy. Boston: Beacon Press, 1984–1987.

Hetrick, Ron L. "Analyzing the Recent Upward Surge in Overtime Hours." *Monthly Labor Review* 123 (February 2000): 30–33.

Horowitz, Daniel. "Consumption and Its Discontents: Simon N. Patten, Thorstein Veblen, and George Gunton." *Journal of American History* 67 (September 1980).

Hunnicutt, Benjamin. "Are We All Working Too Hard?: No Time for God or Family," *The Wall Street Journal*. 4 January 1990.

Jacobs, Jerry. "Measuring Time at Work: Are Self-Reports Accurate?" *Monthly Labor Review* 121 (December 1998): 42–53.

Pieper, Joseph. *Leisure: The Basis of Culture*. Translated by Alexander Dru. New York: Pantheon Books, 1952.

Robinson, John R., and G. Godbey. *Time for Life: The Surprising Way Americans Use Their Time*. State College: Pennsylvania State University, 1997.

Rodgers, Daniel. *The Work Ethic in Industrial America*. Chicago: University of Chicago Press, 1978.

Rybczynski, Witold. *Waiting for the Weekend*. New York: Viking, 1991.

Saltzman, Amy. *Downshifting: Reinventing Success on a Slower Track*. New York: HarperCollins Publishers, 1990.

Schor, Juliet. *The Overworked American: The Unexpected Decline of Leisure*. New York: Basic Books, 1991.

Scribner's Magazine 19 (1896): 253.

Spencer, Herbert. "The Gospel of Recreation; Address at His Farewell Banquet." *Popular Science Monthly* 22 (January 1883): 354–359.

Wolf, Alan. "The Moral Meaning of Work." *The American Prospect* (September–October 1997). Available from http://www.prospect.org.

Benjamin Kline Hunnicutt

SINGING

See *Barbershop Quartets; Choral Singing; Slave Singing/Music Making; Traditional Folk Music Festivals*

SKATEBOARDING

A skateboard has three main components: a board, axels, and four wheels. The activity involves riding this wheeled board. Throughout its more than fifty-year history the technology of those three components has evolved, allowing for various types of skateboard techniques and riding styles. Even as technology and styles have changed, skateboarding historically has been an activity dominated by teenagers and associated with an antiestablishment youth culture. For example, skateboarders have been associated with surfing in the 1960s, punk rock music in the late 1970s and 1980s, and grunge and hip-hop in the 1990s. This antiestablishment attitude is reflected in the participants' desire to partake in an activity that does not have formal adult control or formal regulations. Instead, skateboarders are drawn to the activity because it allows for individuality and creativity.

Brief History

Although no exact date can be established for the origins of the sport, it is a twentieth-century invention. It is believed that connecting roller-skate wheels to a board created the first skateboards. Skateboarding has gone through many cycles of popularity, often determined by the legal status of the activity as well as the general economy. The beginnings of its popularity can be identified in the 1960s with the mass marketing of skateboards. There were few publicly sanctioned places to skateboard; therefore, it primarily occurred informally on paved streets, parking lots, playgrounds, and sidewalks. The initial rise of popularity had two responses from nonparticipants. First, many medical associations warned people of the sport's inherent dangers. Second, many proprietors were concerned about legal responsibilities and damage skateboarders might cause to their property. In the wake of these concerns, skateboarding lost widespread support and appeal in the late 1960s and early 1970s.

Another boom in popularity occurred in the early 1970s largely due to the technological innovation of polyurethane wheels, which allowed for a smoother and safer ride. During this time, skateboards were long and skinny, and the most popular riding styles were slalom

Boise City Skateboard Park. Teenager Brian Floreani soars off the six-foot wedge at the Boise City Skateboard Park in Idaho in 2002. © *Matt Cilley for AP/Wide World Photos*

and freestyle. Adding to the popularity was a wave of privately funded skate parks that started in the mid-1970s. Initially, these were cement parks that included gradual variation of terrain and pool-like "bowls." The popularity of these parks declined over the years with the increase in the number of injuries and the cost of liability insurance. By the early 1980s, most of the parks had closed.

The 1970s also saw an increased commercial interest. Skateboard competitions became more common, and sponsorship broadened outside of skateboard industries. For example, soft drink companies sponsored teams during this time period. Just as skateboarding was gaining mainstream appeal, it distanced itself during the 1980s by associating with the punk movement. The style and location of skateboarding changed as well. It went from a suburban freestyle sport of the 1970s to an urban street

sport in the 1980s. A crucial technical invention was the "ollie," a skill that enables the skateboarder to propel the board off the ground. With this technique, skateboarders could "jump" on to a variety of objects. This technique was extended to jumping on and then sliding the board over objects such as handrails. Skateboards changed to accommodate this new style by becoming shorter and wider. Along with street style, ramp skating also grew in popularity. According to the Sporting Goods Manufacturing Association, the late 1980s were a peak in the participation rates for skateboarding, reaching nearly 11 million in the United States.

The economic recession of the early 1990s created another lull in the industry and involvement, during which participation declined to approximately 5 million in 1993. Many factors encouraged another period of rapid growth in the late 1990s. Foremost was the increased growth in the general economy. Two other significant factors were the increased media coverage and the changes in the legal status of skateboarding. In the mid-1990s major television networks created televised competitions of skateboarding. ESPN created the "X Games," a festival of various alternative sports. NBC followed with a similar production called the "Gravity Games." In addition, skateboarding's liability status was changed in some states, placing it in the same category as bicycling. These factors encouraged growth of private and publicly funded skate parks. Participation trends in the early 2000s are estimated at 10 million, and approximately 10 percent of skateboarders are female (Sporting Goods Manufacturing Association). Skateboarding's image is so popular among America's youth that it is used to sell everything from soda and fast food to cars and Band-Aids.

Cultural Import and Social Significance

Skateboarding and many other alternative sports became a symbol of the active, creative, independent, and, ultimately, "cool" teenager in the later 1990s. The significance of skateboarding as a cultural marker of "cool" can be demonstrated by looking at the most famous skateboarder, Tony Hawk. In a poll conducted by a teen marketing research firm in 2002, Hawk was voted the "coolest big-time athlete" ahead of Tiger Woods, Michael Jordan, and Derek Jeter (Layden). Hawk's video game, *Tony Hawk's Pro Skater,* has been one of the most successful games since its release in 1999. He also created a tour of alternative sports called "Tony Hawk's Boom Boom HuckJam." In its first years, this event was ranked in the top twenty most lucrative U.S. concert tours.

The Disney Corporation is aware of skateboarding and, in particular, Hawk's cultural significance among teenagers. Disney owns ESPN, which owns the brand X Games; Hawk has a series on ESPN, *Tony Hawk's Gigantic Skate Park Tour.* In addition, Disney bought the rights to Hawk's autobiography; and Hawk is the principal star of Disney's movie *Ultimate X.*

Skateboarding has historically appealed to a teenage audience, and it has generally been identified as an alternative form of physical activity. With the increased commercialization and use of skateboarding as a symbol of "cool," it will be interesting to see if there is a backlash to this mainstream appeal, or whether skateboarding becomes accepted as a conventional sport.

See also: Extreme Sports, Roller Skating and Blading, Snowboarding, Teenage Leisure Trends.

BIBLIOGRAPHY

Beal, Becky. "Disqualifying the Official: An Exploration of Social Resistance in the Subculture of Skateboarding." *Sociology of Sport Journal* 12 (1995): 252–267.

Borden, Iain. *Skateboarding, Space and the City.* Oxford, U.K.; New York: Berg, 2000.

Brooke, Michael. *The Concrete Wave: The History of Skateboarding.* Toronto: Warwick Publishing, 1999.

Davidson, Ben. *The Skateboard Book.* New York: Grosset and Dunlap, 1976.

Davis, James. *Skateboard Roadmap: History, Tricks, Culture, Global Coverage and Top Skaters.* London: Carlton Books, 1999.

Layden, T. "What Is This 34-Year-Old Man Doing on a Skateboard? Making Millions." *Sports Illustrated* (10 June 2002): 80–92.

Sporting Goods Manufactures Association. "Sports Participation Topline Report, 2000." Available from http://www.sgma.com.

Becky Beal

SKATING

See *Roller Skating and Blading*

SKIING, ALPINE

Alpine skiing, in contrast with Nordic/cross-country, is very much a modern sport, with origins in the early twentieth century. The founding father of alpine skiing is British aristocrat Lord Roberts of Kandahar, who donated the trophy for a first race held at Montana, Switzerland, in 1911. While this was a pure—top of hill to bottom of hill—competition, the first slalom-style race took place at Murren, Switzerland, in 1922.

American skiing owes much to Scandinavian immigrants, who brought skis with them in the middle of the nineteenth century as a critical aid in traversing the goldfield territories. John Rooney and Richard Pillsbury, indeed, note that the first American downhill ski race took place in 1854 in the midst of gold-mining country. In a similar fashion they point to America's first ski club, founded in 1867 at La Porte, California, then a West Coast goldfield hub.

Downhill racing in America in the late nineteenth century was intensely competitive and was frequently

Downhill skiing. A woman kicks up some snow as she skis down a mountain in Summit County, Colorado in 1991. © *Corbis*

buoyed up by "copious amounts of alcohol and large wagers" (Rooney and Pillsbury, p. 121). Technology and science had an impact on the sport. Racers adopted streamlined body positions, early forms of wax were rubbed onto skis to reduce friction, and speeds in excess of sixty miles per hour were reached. Rooney and Pillsbury stress that the diffusion of sport skiing, utilitarian skiing, and recreational skiing was intimately tied up with the rapid expansion of the east-west and north-south railroad: "Loggers soon followed the lumber frontier westward to the northern Rockies and finally the Pacific Northwest, carrying their Scandinavian snow traditions with them" (Rooney and Pillsbury, p. 121).

E. John B. Allen notes that, as with many other aspects of winter sports, alpine skiing is a series of activities hugely impacted by new technologies, manufacturing innovations, and the development/evolution of emerging sport disciplines. So, while the Federation Internationale de Ski (FIS) officially recognized the integrity of downhill and slalom skiing in 1930, subsequent decades have witnessed all manners of radical new ski sports. Among these have been freestyle, speed skiing, and snowboarding. Despite colossal advances made by the United States

in the last quarter century, the inescapable fact is that alpine skiing, by culture, legacy, and education, is rooted in Europe. Allen made a telling observation about an American alpine ski instruction manual published in 1935. It had no alternative to using eight foreign words "necessary for understanding a ski lesson" (Allen, p. 915). Quite simply, American skiing—in all its forms—has been contoured and crafted by a European heritage.

Olympic Involvement

The first Olympic alpine skiing contest took place at Garmisch-Partenkirchen in 1936. It was an alpine combined race, with one downhill run and two slalom races. The United States won no medals in either the men's or women's combined. At the 1948 St. Moritz Olympics, alpine skiing was expanded to include downhill, slalom and alpine combined (men), and downhill, slalom and alpine combined (women). While Austria, France, and Switzerland maintained overall domination, the achievements of Gretchen Fraser of Vancouver, Washington, were extraordinary. She won a gold and a silver medal.

Four years later, at the 1952 Oslo Olympics, Andrea Lawrence-Mead, who took gold in both the slalom and the giant slalom, bettered Fraser's superb performance. In both races, her winning margins were significant. They were 1.2 seconds in the slalom and 2.2 seconds in the giant slalom. The nineteen-year-old from Rutland, Vermont, did the unthinkable by finishing fourth despite falling on her first run. In her second run she decimated the opposition with a winning margin of two seconds.

The next winter Olympics to witness American success was Squaw Valley in 1960. Once again it was the women's division. Penny Pitou won two silvers in the downhill and the giant slalom, while Betsy Snite enjoyed similar success in the slalom.

Four years later, at Innsbruck, female successes continued with a giant slalom and slalom bronze from Jean Saubert. One of the real characters of the Games was American William Kidd. Newspaper reporters liked to tag him as a sporting "Billy the Kid." He and fellow team member James Heuga took silver and bronze medals. Some idea of the closely contested terrain that is alpine skiing can be seen in gold and silver medal time differentials. Kidd missed a gold medal by .14 of a second, with a total race time of 2 minutes, 11 seconds.

The next American bright spot was in 1972 at Sapporo. While there were no male medals, Barbara Cochran won the slalom gold, and Susan Corrock took the bronze in the downhill. Four years later (1976), at Innsbruck, the solitary American medal was Cynthia Nelson's bronze medal in the downhill.

With the 1980 Olympics at Lake Placid, New York, American hopes and aspirations were high. Phil Mahr was favored to win but lost to Swedish multimedallist Ingemar Stenmark. Mahr's magical moment was to come four years later at Sarajevo, where he defeated his twin brother, Steven, to win the slalom.

In Calgary in 1988, alpine skiing extended its parameters to include a super G and a combined event. With the super G there are elements of downhill and slalom. The event is primarily a race down the mountain, with a series of control gates directing the ski racers safely down the steep slopes at very high speeds. Despite more openings and opportunities, the United States was unable to make any impression on the medal standings.

At Albertville in 1992, the alpine skiing umbrella was further enlarged with the addition of men's and women's freestyle events. This is a combination sport with four components. There is an aerial component, a ballet phase, a competition dash across and over snow/ice bumps known as moguls, and an amalgamation of those three subdisciplines called the combined. The men salvaged one bronze medal by Nelson Carmichael in the freestyle moguls, while the women came through with silver medals for Hilary Lindh in the downhill and Diann Roffe in the giant slalom. The American heroine was Donna Weinbrecht, who won the gold medal in the freestyle moguls.

In 1994, at Lillehammer, where aerial freestyle skiing was added to the list of alpine skiing, the most dramatic headline-making performance came from downhill racer Tommy Moe. The one-time enfant terrible of American alpine sports—repeated marijuana violations in his teenage years—was sternly mentored by his father during a draconian term laboring on the Aleutian Islands. Moe saw the light and buckled down to the demands of U.S.A. squad training. Unquestionably, Moe's gold medal was unexpected. Up until Lillehammer, he had never won a World Cup event. Lillehammer was a blue ribbon experience for Moe as he took the silver medal in the super giant slalom.

While Moe's successes made him America's stellar male skier at Lillehammer, Picabo Street's silver medal in the downhill made her, if just temporarily, the golden girl of American sport. Her quirky name, flashing smile, gregarious chatter, and oddly engaging manner made her an advertiser's dream, and the sort of instant celebrity who lights up a tabloid, or an evening TV talk show.

Among the significant American successes in Nagano, Japan, in1998, two contrasting personas typified the nature of very different alpine activities and the audiences with which they connect. Jonny Mosely, winner

of the freestyle moguls, when asked about his returning home reception at San Francisco Airport, remarked, "Hopefully there will be a big crowd at the airport and they'll shove a beer in my hand, and that'll be it" (Rushin, 1998, p.36). For Picabo Street, Nagano became the defining moment of a storied career. She won a gold medal in the super G and was presented with her gold medal by arguably the greatest alpine skier of all time, France's Jean-Claude Killy. In the downhill she missed a bronze medal by just .17 seconds.

With the 2002 Olympics set on an American landscape (Salt Lake City), there were justifiable hopes of significant American successes in alpine skiing. Preparations for these Olympics were exhaustive and painstaking. Nagano aerial skiing gold medallist Eric Bergoust settled in Utah in 1997 with a home only three miles away from the snowboarding site. *Sports Illustrated* felt the United States would win gold medals with Bode Miller in the slalom and Eric Bergoust in aerials. In actual fact, Salt Lake City marked a colossal breakthrough in American alpine skiing. For example, on the men's side, the United States took four of the six medals in the half-pipe, including both golds. Picabo Street, watching as American snowboarders received their medals, was quoted as saying, "That's what the Olympics are about: making childhood dreams come true" (Rushin, 2002, p. 55). Street herself, while not able to duplicate her form, power, and speed from Nagano, ended her career by avoiding serious injury, and finished the downhill in sixteenth place.

American Olympic successes were Bode Miller (silver medals in combined and giant slalom), Joe Pack (silver medal in aerials freestyle skiing), Travis Mayer (silver medal in moguls freestyle skiing), Ross Powers (gold medal in snowboarding half-pipe), Danny Kass (silver medal in snowboarding half-pipe), Jarrett Thomas (bronze medal in snowboarding half-pipe), Shannon Bahrke (silver medal in moguls freestyle skiing), and Kelly Clark (gold medal in snowboard half-pipe).

Popular Culture

Alpine skiing has lent itself wonderfully well to a wide variety of feature and documentary filmmaking. Robert Redford's Hollywood career was launched in the 1969 Paramount movie *Downhill Racer*. The story centers on Redford's bid to get onto the U.S. team and, in a dramatic denouement, his bid to medal in the winter Olympics.

The United States National Ski Hall of Fame and Museum is a major repository for archival material on American alpine skiing. Many American champions are members of the Hall of Fame—for example, Gretchen

Fraser (1960), Andrea Lawrence-Mead (1958), Bill Kidd (1976), Phil Mahr, and Bill Johnson (1984).

The Contemporary Scene

American skiing has witnessed colossal changes over the past century. Recreational skiing moved away from its European roots of being an expensive sport reserved for a social-cultural elite and seemed headed toward being an everyman's leisure pursuit. Rooney and Pillsbury describe skiing as a favorite pastime with access to "king and commoner alike." They also note the proliferation of up-scale American ski resorts and the development of luxurious ski and winter sport complexes at centers in Colorado, California, Utah, and New England. Nevertheless, the picture is a complex one. Rooney and Pillsbury draw attention to the fact that the number of U.S. ski areas went from 1,400 in 1960 to 524 in 1988. Quite simply, skiing in the United States, while economically available to significant numbers of a well-to-do middle class, has failed to capture the larger public interest, mainly because of the low number of facilities and the high cost of getting started.

See also: Extreme Sports; Skiing, Nordic; Snowboarding

BIBLIOGRAPHY

Allen, E. John B. "Alpine Skiing." In *Encyclopedia of World Sport*. Volume 3. Santa Barbara, Calif.: ABC-Clio, 1996.

Cazeneuve, Brian. "Advantage USA." *Sports Illustrated* 96, no. 5 (2002): 105.

———. "Who'll Win." *Sports Illustrated* 96, no. 5 (2002): 140–150.

Conners, Martin, et al. *Video Hound's Golden Movie Retriever*. Detroit, Mich.: Gale Research, 1996.

Kemper, Erich, and Bill Mallon. *The Golden Book of the Olympics*. Milan: Vallerdi and Associati, 1992.

Layden, T. "Street Fighting." *Sports Illustrated* 88, no. 8 (1998): 45.

———. "Worldbeater." *Sports Illustrated* 98, no. 3 (2003): 72.

Reilly, R. "A Whack Start for a Goofy Sport." *Sports Illustrated* 88, no. 8 (1998): 114.

Rooney, John F., Jr., and Richard Pillsbury. *Atlas of American Sport*. New York: Macmillan, 1992.

Rushin, Steve. "Hidden Forces." *Sports Illustrated* 88, no. 8 (1998): 36.

———. "Ticket to Paradise." *Sports Illustrated* 96, no. 8 (2002): 55.

Wallechinsky, David. *The Complete Book of the Winter Olympics*. London: Aurum Press, 1998.

Zucker, Harvey M., and Lawrence J. Babich. *Sports Films: A Complete Reference*. Jefferson, N.C.: McFarland, 1987.

Scott A.G.M. Crawford

SKIING, NORDIC

Nordic skiing has origins that go back to the 1700s and Scandinavia. The sport has three integral components: cross-country skiing, ski jumping, and Nordic combined. The latter is a synthesis with portions of ski jumping and cross-country. Cross-country races range from fifteen to fifty kilometers and may be individual or relay team competitions. With ski jumping, the competitions take place on a seventy- or ninety-meter hill.

The concluding years of World War II led to a potent grassroots movement for growth in U.S. skiing. According to E. M. Swift, the U.S. Army needed to find both local and able volunteers to support the development of a U.S. Mountain Division. Many expert skiers from the National Ski Association eventually saw action in 1945 in the Italian Alps. "After the war many members of the 10th Mountain Division moved back to Colorado where they helped boost a fledgling recreational ski industry" (Swift, p. 50).

Nordic skiing has been typified by its constantly changing landscape. For example, at the 1924 Olympics, only men competed, and the four events were eighteen-kilometer cross-country skiing, fifty-kilometer cross-country skiing, ski jumping, and Nordic combined. At the 1994 Lillehammer Olympics, the picture of Nordic skiing was an eclectic mosaic: a coeducational athletic canvas that included five- and ten-kilometer races (classical), combined pursuit (essentially a timed cross-country race), thirty-kilometer (classical and freestyle), 4 x 5 and 4 x 10 kilometer relay, ski jump (normal hill, individual), ski jump (large hill, individual), ski jump (large hill, team), Nordic combined (individual), and Nordic combined (team).

Olympic Involvement

The Chamonix International Winter sports week of 1924 is generally recognized as the first Winter Olympics. In the Nordic skiing category there were four events; Norway won eleven of the thirteen medals awarded. The United States saw their representative, Anders Haugen, win a bronze medal in the ski-jumping competition. Olympic raconteur David Wallechinsky recounts how in 1974 Toralf Stromstad, the silver medalist in the 1924 Nordic combined, found a mistake in the original scores. As a result, the thirty-six-year-old Norwegian-born Haugen, who had paid his own way to the Olympics, was moved up to third place. The International Olympic Committee honored Haugen at a special medal ceremony in Oslo. Four years later, at St. Moritz, the United States had no medalists. In 1932, the Winter Olympics were hosted at Lake Placid, New York, a regional vacation resort in the Adirondacks. In terms of U.S. Nordic skiing, the competition was a medal drought.

An American absence of success was repeated at Garmish-Partenkirchen (1936), St. Moritz (1948), Oslo (1952), Cortina d'Ampezzo (1956), Squaw Valley (1960), Innsbruck (1964), Grenoble (1968), Sapporo (1972), Lake Placid (1980), Sarajevo (1984), Calgary (1988), Albertville (1992), and Lillehammer (1994). One exception, and an exceptional performance indeed, was that by American Bill Koch at Innsbruck in 1976. The native of Guilford, Vermont, became the only American to win an Olympic Nordic skiing medal. He tenaciously fought Serge Saralyev of the Soviet Union and after one and a half hours of frantic activity, during which time the athletes had to battle incredible muscular fatigue compounded with the buildup of lactic acid, Koch crossed the finish line in second place. David Wallechinsky underscores the Cinderella status of Nordic skiing with the pointed comment that at the thirty-kilometer post-race press conference, not one American reporter was present.

Quite simply, Nordic skiing, within the United States, has always been a minor, indeed a marginalized, group of athletic activities. While huge advances have been made within American winter sports in areas such as alpine skiing and speed skating, the same has not been the case with Nordic skiing. Special note should be made, however, of certain American competitors who, despite not receiving medals, were skiing pioneers willing to train ferociously and take on rivals for whom Nordic skiing was their country's premier *cultural* activity. Examples of this come from performers such as the members of the men's 4 x 10 kilometer relay at the 1976 Olympics (sixth place); Casper Oimoen in the large hill individual ski jump at the 1932 Olympics (fifth); Gordon Wren in the same event—and a similar placing—at the 1948 Olympics, and finally Jeffrey Hasting (same event), who, at the 1984 Olympics, missed a bronze medal by only 1.7 points. In women's Nordic skiing, in the 4 x 5 kilometer relay, America produced Olympic squads in 1980, 1984, and 1988 that had creditable seventh, seventh, and eighth places, respectively, in the Olympic finals.

The Contemporary Scene

With the 1998 Winter Olympics in Nagano, Japan *Sports Illustrated* compiled an intensive and exhaustive speculative list, whereby Anita Verschoth gave her top three picks for Nordic skiing, and then, as a footnote sidebar, dis-

cussed the status of American involvement. Repeatedly Verschoth's observations underscore the picture of an "also-ran" sport, where the possibility of American success was not about medal contention but rather a top-ten finish. For example, in the men's ten-kilometer (classical style) cross-country race, Marcus Nash was mentioned as "headed for the top 25." With the women's ten-kilometer pursuit freestyle cross-country race, Suzanne King was named as being a probable finisher in the top thirty. In the men's (4 x 10 kilometer) and women's (4 x 5 kilometer) relay, the prognostication was that the United States would finish in the top half of the twenty national teams. As for the three ski-jumping competitions, the American selections were not deemed able to break into the top twenty slots. Nevertheless, the Verschoth landscape was not totally devoid of American hopefuls: Todd Lodwick of Colorado had been the World Junior champion, and Verscoth prophesized that Lodwick would win a bronze medal for the United States. Sadly, the United States did not win one Nordic medal, despite a gritty performance from fifth-place finisher Lodwick. Nordic skiing, regardless, established itself as an extraordinary medium for sport as both a dramatic theater and cultural conduit. Japanese ski jumper Masatiiko Harada won a bronze medal with a final jump of 136 meters at "the outer limit of human flight," and the situation was so overwhelming that he, his Japan television interviewer, and the Japanese anchor reporter all broke down and wept (Rushin, 1998).

An important aspect of American Nordic training and preparation going into the various ski-jump competitions at Nagano was recruitment and coaching. The American male jumping members were young—ranging in ages from sixteen to twenty-three—and their new team coach was Finn Kari Ylianttila, who had coached the Finnish national team for nine years.

The 2002 Winter Olympics were staged in Salt Lake City and allowed the United States a wonderful opportunity to showcase Nordic skiing. Richard Hoffer, in a *Sports Illustrated* essay, commented on just such attractions being televised from the United States by NBC and reaching a world audience of more than 100 million people: "There goes another guy off the ramp in the Nordic combined, skis splayed, sailing through miles of sunshine. Millions of viewers around the world gawked: 'My God, that looks like fun.'" Another *Sports Illustrated* writer at Salt Lake City, Steve Rushin, evocatively captured the aesthetic appeal of ski jumping. One competitor with "his skis in chevron—like geese flying in formation backward—looks as though he'll never alight." This is a sport where a soaring body in a space suit magically "captivates the imagination."

At the 2002 Winter Olympics, American Nordic skiers had the additional lure of a United States Olympic Committee cash incentive—for a gold medal, $25,0000; silver, $15,000; and bronze, $10,000. Overall, both the policy and American advances in winter sports in general were spectacular. The United States won ten gold and thirty-four overall, more Winter Olympic medals than it had won before (thirteen in 1994 and 1998). Nevertheless, in the sphere of Nordic skiing, the United States again drew a blank.

The high point for the United States was in the Nordic combined twenty-kilometer relay team event. In the two-day event (first day jumping, second day racing) at the halfway stage, the United States was in third place. However, in the cross-country phase the Americans slipped to fourth place.

Nordic skiing requires, for the most part, highly specialized equipment and calls for technically demanding and exhausting skills. Terrain needs to be specially groomed, and a major problem for the sport's grassroots development is that it continues to be perceived as a fringe or marginal pastime. Very few colleges or schools support programs that focus on Nordic skiing. All of that notwithstanding, the cost of cross-country skis has reached a level where it is increasingly affordable. Since the 1990s, the number of people trying cross-country skiing for the first time has been significant.

Alpine skiing lends itself wonderfully well to both feature and documentary film treatment. Sadly, Nordic skiing has garnered little attention, but the spectacular crash landing by European ski jumper Vinko Bogataj was so visually sensational that it became a key opening sequence to the celebrated ABC television network program *The Wide World of Sport*. Commentator Jim McKay famously described Bogataj's ski-jump spill as "the agony of defeat."

Conclusion

At Salt Lake City the United States won ten ski and snowboard medals and followed that with fifteen medals in the 2003 World Championships. What the sport of Nordic skiing desperately needs is a breakthrough personality in the order of a Bonnie Blair (speed skating) or Michelle Kwan (figure skating). U.S. Ski and Snowboard President and Chief Executive Officer Bill Marolt, as he looks forward to the 2006 games in Torino, has a rallying cry of "Best in the World." Certainly the challenges for U.S. Nordic skiing are considerable.

See also: Skiing, Alpine; Snowboarding; Tobogganing

BIBLIOGRAPHY

Allen, E. John B. "Nordic Skiing." *Encyclopedia of World Sport.* Volume 3. Santa Barbara, Calif.: ABC-Clio, 1996.

Danilov, Victor J. *Hall of Fame Museums.* Westport, Conn.: Greenwood Press, 1997.

Findling, John E., and Kimberley D. Pelle. *Historical Dictionary of the Modern Olympic Movement.* Westport, Conn.: Greenwood Press, 1996.

Hoffer, Richard. 2002. "The Fellowship of the Rings." *Sports Illustrated* 96, no. 7 (2002): 40.

Kamper, Erich, and Bill Mallon. *The Golden Book of the Olympic Games.* Milan: Vallardi and Associati, 1992.

O'Connor, Michael. "Yanks' Best-Ever Relay Finish Bittersweet." *Boston Herald* (18 February 2002).

Rushin, Steve. "Hidden Forces." *Sports Illustrated* 88, no. 8 (1998): 34–36.

———. "Ticket to Paradise." *Sports Illustrated* 96, no. 8 (2002): 56.

Swift, E. M. "Skiers' Paradise." *Sports Illustrated* 99, no. 23 (2003): 48–50.

Verschoth, Anita. "Medal Picks." *Sports Illustrated* 88, no. 5 (1998): 131–32.

Wallechinsky, David. *The Complete Book of the Winter Olympics.* London: Aurum Press, 1998.

Scott Crawford

SLAVE SINGING/MUSIC MAKING

Although slaves entered the mainland colonies in 1619, very little notice was given to their music before the late eighteenth century. Much of the early commentary emphasized the religious nature of black folk song, but in a sense the sacred music traditions of African Americans was not made manifest until the late eighteenth century. Prior to the American Revolution, blacks, although usually assigned to segregated pews, generally worshipped in the same churches and sang the same songs as whites. After the Revolutionary War, some slaves were released for participating in the military action; others escaped. Then, beginning in 1778, Northern states initiated laws that within fifty years effectively confined the "peculiar institution" to the South. These changes resulted in blacks forming their own organizations that were not controlled by whites. By the late eighteenth century, several black churches, some of which became well known for their musical performances, were in existence. European tourists who traveled to the United States in the early nineteenth century made black churches and camp meetings essential stops, where they expected to hear and see exotic singing and dancing.

What was the singing that the tourists would hear? There was a great deal of improvisation with considerable use of call-and-response patterns, both features of much black music, such as jazz, blues, and work songs, even in the early 2000s. Religious songs were often sad and concerned with death. "Shouts," sung while a group shuffled counterclockwise in African fashion, were much more lively, but generally were allowed in churches only during Sunday services for blacks. Religious slave songs were further distinguished by the creation of tunes, themes, and words. Despite frequent mention of black sacred song during the antebellum period, it was not until the post-emancipation years that the first collection, *Slave Songs of the United States*, was published.

Work songs appealed to white planters and visitors to the plantation. The songs assured planters that their slaves were busy, and visitors found the songs picturesque; some even found such singing as evidence that slaves were happy and content with their lot. Even so, work songs existed for other reasons. Emphasizing the call-and-response pattern with the leader outlining the song's theme and the rest of the crew responding, work songs guaranteed a steady rhythm, resulting in the work proceeding at an even pace. Also when axes and hoes were being used, the call-and-response of work songs lessened the possibility of accidents by coordinating movements.

Field hollers were work songs that were sung solo, although they might be echoed by other workers, or passed along from one person to another. Most often associated with cotton culture, field hollers were also utilized in other types of work. They were characterized by a loud, long musical sound, making great use of falsetto. Some hollers were wordless, while others were made up of improvised lines embodying the singer's thoughts, while extensively employing elaborated syllables and melisma. Beginning in the mid 1930s, the first recording of hollers occurred; the impetus for collecting them probably was that they were believed to be a precursor of the blues.

In addition to their singing, slaves played a variety of instruments, including drums, musical bow, quills or panpipes, and a xylophone called a balafo. These African instruments did not have the widespread impact that another African instrument, the banjo, did. In its earliest report, in 1653 in the West Indies, the instrument was called the banza or the strum strum. According to a comment by Thomas Jefferson in *Notes on the State of Virginia* (1784), it was later known as the banjar. Despite a persistent claim that Joel Walker Sweeney (1810–1860) invented the five-string banjo, that, too, probably originated in Africa; at least, existing evidence points in that direction. The most telling is a late-eighteenth-century painting of a scene on a plantation in the South that shows slaves dancing while another one plays a five-string banjo. The instrument became widely popular after the arrival of the minstrel show, which was America's most popular form of entertainment from 1843 to 1883. These blackface programs featured a banjo player performing in a down-stroking style in which the thumb and nail of the index or middle finger strikes downward on the strings. This is in contrast to the "Scruggs style," which has a performer picking up on the strings in a three-fingered syncopated roll. This later development is the style of banjo playing most often heard today.

Slaves also played non-African instruments, the most important of which was fiddle. Indeed, black fiddlers became as commonplace as black banjo players. Slave fiddlers were sometimes used to accompany convoys of slaves on the march to another locale. Most, however, played for dances just like their white counterparts. Often, they took the place of white fiddlers and performed music for white visitors and dancing parties.

See also: African American Leisure Lifestyles, Colonial-Era Leisure and Recreation, Early National Leisure and Recreation

BIBLIOGRPAHY

Allen, William Francis, Charles Pickard Ware, and Lucy McKim Garrison. *Slave Songs of the United States*. New York: A. Simpson and Company, 1867; reprint, Bedford, Mass.: Applewood Books, 1995.

Epstein, Dena J. *Sinful Tunes and Spirituals: Black Folk Music to the Civil War*. Urbana: University of Illinois Press, 1977.

Joyner, Charles. *Down by the Riverside: A South Carolina Slave Community*. Urbana: University of Illinois Press, 1984.

Nathan, Hans. *Dan Emmett and the Rise of Early Negro Minstrelsy*. Norman: University of Oklahoma Press, 1962.

Southern, Eileen. *The Music of Black Americans: A History*. Revised edition. New York: W. W. Norton and Company, 1983.

W. K. McNeil

SLEDDING

See *Tobogganing*

SMOKING

In the current social and political marginalization of the cigarette smoker, Americans may forget how tobacco and its use have shaped American leisure habits. Even in the precolonial period, in Native American culture, tobacco was central to the performance of shamanistic rituals, to religious and spiritual life, and to the social ceremonies of manhood initiation rites. It was linked to the fertility of both the land and of women and, as portrayed in countless Hollywood Westerns, it was at the heart of the calumet ritual, when a pipe was passed around a group to seal an agreement concerning political obligations or the exchange of goods. For European settlers, tobacco was a source of fascination, either because of its alleged properties in treating illnesses or for the individual pleasures it gave the newly initiated smoker. Within just a few decades, colonists had stopped trading directly for tobacco and had learned to cultivate it themselves. In 1612, John Rolfe (made famous through his marriage to Pocahontas) grew the first successful crop of tobacco in Jamestown, Virginia. By 1628, the colony was exporting 370,000 pounds of tobacco, and the seed was being planted all over the surrounding region.

Just as the new colonies were dependent on the export of tobacco, so, too, were its inhabitants on the act of smoking itself. Visitors to Virginia in the seventeenth and eighteenth centuries frequently commented on the sight of whole communities smoking, with the majority following the lead of their northern European counterparts by using pipes. The great exception was the popularity of chewing tobacco, which required no special preparation. Users merely bit off the hard, tightly-pressed manufactured tobaccos of twist and plug, which were sold both for pipes and for grating into snuff. The great transformation in smoking practices would come with the arrival of the "Bright" leaf. Grown in the inland Piedmont region of Virginia and North Carolina, flue-cured Bright tobacco produced a lighter leaf with a less harsh and more pleasant taste, as well as a more aesthetically satisfying golden texture.

Initially, "gold leaf" tobaccos were used in pipe mixtures popular in the new urban centers of the nineteenth century. Paralleling the growth in popularity of the cigar, milder pipe tobaccos saw a resurgence in the literary-cum-philosophical "odes" to the weed led by such figures as Mark Twain. In a Victorian and largely bourgeois culture across the English-speaking world, countless pamphlets, books, poems, and periodical articles taught an expanding middle class about what the tobacco manufacturer Alfred Dunhill called "the gentle art of smoking."

Various anecdotal "whiffs" and "pipefuls" were presented as amusing relief for busy city gentlemen who sought solace in their pipes, favorite armchairs, and metropolitan clubs. Smokers learned of the history, anthropology, ritual, literary heritage, production, manufacture, and pharmacology of tobacco, knowledge necessary if the mere smoker was to be transformed into a true connoisseur or "aficionado" of the "Lady Nicotine" or "Diva Nicotina." A man was said to be somehow lacking in character if he did not practice a particular smoking habit or possess his own "paraphernalia of smokiana," including pipes, cleaners, holders, spills, spittoons, ashtrays, pouches, storage jars, lights, smoking jackets, armchairs, hats, and slippers. Hierarchies of taste were established, which for cigars, stretched from Cuban brands at the very top, to cheap, U.S., mass-produced items associated with the urban "swell."

The Rise of Cigarettes

At the very bottom of this hierarchy in this semi-elite culture stood the new mass-produced cigarette, an item frowned upon by the connoisseur but which was to come to dominate the history of smoking. Handmade, expensive cigarettes had secured a small luxury market within the eastern cities from the 1850s, but cigarette manufacturing was to be revolutionized by the patenting of the Bonsack machine in 1880. The new invention could produce up to three hundred cigarettes a minute and was quickly put into use by the dynamo of the modern cigarette industry, James Buchanan "Buck" Duke, who set about transforming the tobacco industry in the 1880s. Through aggressive sales techniques Duke ruined, took over, and beat most of his rivals. In 1889, the greater portion of the cigarette industry merged to form the American Tobacco Company (ATC) with Duke firmly at its helm. The company was to hold a virtual monopoly on cigarette sales in the United States and enabled Duke to expand into Canada and Great Britain and become one of the pioneers of multinational capitalism when he formed the British American Tobacco with the Imperial Tobacco Company of Britain.

Opposition to the cigarette, though, came not only from a traditional, pipe- and cigar-smoking community, but also from the organized temperance movement. Early opposition came from Frances Willard's Women's Christian Temperance Union and later from such luminaries as Henry Ford and the health advocate and cereal producer Dr. John Harvey Kellogg. Most zealous of all was Lucy Page Gaston, the self-styled "extremist of extremists" (Tate, p. 62). In 1899 she created the Anti-Cigarette League of America, an organization that eschewed the education and reform of the sinful smoker and advocated instead outright prohibition. The Anti-Cigarette League's medico-moral rhetoric, which connected smoking with a whole range of degenerative vices and illnesses, proved popular among Anglo-Saxon Protestants, who associated cigarettes with immigrants and urban delinquent youth. By 1901, the league had 300,000 members and, by the outbreak of World War I, the movement had succeeded in outlawing cigarettes in thirteen states, with bills in six others pending (virtually every state had already banned the sale of cigarettes to minors).

Defeat for the movement began with the American entry into the war in 1917 as the government, the army, and newspapers all patriotically recognized the palliative effects of smoking for soldiers. Even former antitobacco groups such as the YMCA, the Red Cross, and the Salvation Army defected to the other side and distributed cigarettes to the troops on the front lines and in hospitals. The war also enabled other cigarette manufacturers to break into the market, helped by the Supreme Court decision to break up the ATC in 1911 under the provisions of the Sherman Antitrust Act (1890). For instance, R. J. Reynold's Camel brand, introduced in 1913, was able to achieve a sales figure of 20 billion cigarettes in 1920, following a government supply order and a successful marketing campaign. Cigarettes were a comfort to the troops in the trenches but also a far more practical method of smoking on the battlefield than the cumbersome pipe. In recognition of its morale-boosting qualities, a soldier's ballad urged men to smile in the face of death with "a Lucifer to light your fag," while, most famously, General Pershing stated, "You ask me what we need to win this war. I answer tobacco as much as bullets" (Klein, p. 135). The cigarette emerged triumphant from the war, a position that was easily sustained as it became the leading legal narcotic during the Prohibition era. In 1919, cigarettes surpassed pipe tobacco in the actual amount of leaf consumed, and, by 1922, they overtook chewing tobacco as well.

The interwar years witnessed the spread of the cigarette among both sexes and every social group, backed by a popular commercial culture that portrayed smoking as the norm rather than the exception. While those smoking "new women" of the pre–World War I period had to experience such reactions as a 1908 New York law prohibiting female smoking in public, the flappers and college women of the 1920s witnessed much less resistance. By 1929, women were estimated to consume 14 billion cigarettes, or 12 percent of total consumption. Advertisers were quick to take advantage of this new smoking trend, and Philip Morris introduced its Marlboro brand in 1925, to target the emerging female market. However,

James Buchanan Duke. An American industrialist who was a leader in the production of tobacco products, James Buchanan Duke (1856–1925) left a substantial trust fund to Trinity College in his home state of North Carolina; it later changed its name to Duke University in his honor. © *The Advertising Archive Ltd.*

more often, advertisers recognized that women were far more likely to smoke the same brands as men; therefore, Chesterfield, in 1926, urged women "to blow some my way" and Lucky Strike, in 1928, suggested they "Reach for a Lucky instead of a Sweet." Certainly, advertising was of some influence—and manufacturers were prepared to pay around 20 percent and more of the total cost of the product on promotion—but women, men, and youths often just followed the lead offered by peers, parents, and popular culture.

Most spectacular of all was the portrayal of smoking in Hollywood. Films featuring such stars as Clara Bow, Louise Brooks, Tallulah Bankhead, Marlene Dietrich, and Mae West glamorized the cigarette while, later, Edward G Robinson, James Cagney, Spencer Tracy, Gary Cooper, and especially Humphrey Bogart and Lauren Bacall raised the image of the cigarette to iconic status, ensuring it would never lose its sophisticated and loftily independent connotations. And for young couples watching Paul Henreid light two cigarettes at once for himself and Bette Davis in *Now Voyager* (1942), the association with courtship and seduction was clearly established.

Smoking Is Linked to Health Problems

When Ernst L. Wynder first published a link between smoking with lung cancer in 1950, it was clear that his findings would be a shock to both America's smokers and its powerful manufacturers. By this time, between 44 and 47 percent of the nation smoked, with the figure much higher for adult, urban males. Many smokers simply refused to accept the evidence, their arguments bolstered by the refutations offered by the tobacco companies and by advertisements that showed medical doctors endorsing the benefits and pleasures of the cigarette. The 1964 Report of the Surgeon General, however, made the link far more indisputable, and, from then on, an average of 2 million smokers gave up the habit every year. By 1978, the overall smoking rate had fallen to 33 percent. These figures, though, are hardly as great as one might expect, even taking into account the role of physical addiction. While many might have given up smoking, many others have also started, and while smokers have regularly—and unsuccessfully—taken cigarette companies to court since as early as 1954, it is clear that others have simply ignored the evidence against their habit.

Approximately 60 million smoking-related deaths have occurred across the developed world since 1950, and it is estimated that around 400,000 people die from smoking every year in the United States, not only from lung cancer, but also heart disease, bronchitis, emphysema, pneumonia, vascular disease, and cancers of the mouth, throat, bladder, kidneys, pancreas, and stomach. Moreover, of those who have quit, the overwhelming number have been professional, affluent men, making smoking today a health problem increasingly associated with women and poverty. And whereas the average U.S. smoker got through twenty-two cigarettes a day in 1954, this had increased to thirty by 1978 (although rates subsequently fell to around twenty in 2000), suggesting that the quitting rate was higher among those who smoked less and that more cigarettes were being smoked by those who still smoked, most of whom had increasingly moved to lighter or filtered brands.

Of perhaps equal importance, therefore, in changing smoking habits has not been the negative evidence against smoking but the positive images of life being promoted by an increasingly health-conscious society. In addition, the comparatively ready acceptance of the dangers of environmental (or "second-hand") tobacco smoke has resulted in a still ongoing series of legislative efforts against smoking in public. California has led the way, but its proscriptions against smokers are now being followed by other states. This has led many to suggest that the smoker is being portrayed as a hero of resistance to the health

faddists, with his or her marginalization creating a counterculture figure demonized by an affluent, nonsmoking majority. But such romantic narratives are hardly the full story, since powerful images produced by a commercial popular culture ensure that smoking remains as "cool" as it was in the days of Bogart and Bacall. A survey of the most successful Hollywood films found that films in 1995 featured four times as much smoking as in 1990 and that three times as many smoking characters were portrayed as "rebellious." The deep-rooted nature of America's smoking culture, stretching back centuries, implies the current hostility to smoking may only be temporary. There remains a demand for tobacco and cigarettes that is unlikely to be overturned by either regulation or prohibition. In the increasing rates of smoking among today's youth, and in the poor quitting rates among the poor and the disenfranchised, smoking is already witnessing a minor revival.

See also: Prohibition and Temperance; Recreational Drug Use

BIBLIOGRAPHY

Brandt, Allen. "The Cigarette, Risk, and American Culture." *Daedalus* 119 (1990): 155–176.

Goodman, Jordan. *Tobacco in History: Cultures of Dependence.* London: Routledge, 1993.

Hilton, Matthew. *Smoking in British Popular Culture, 1800–2000.* Manchester, U.K.: Manchester University Press, 2000.

Klein, Richard. *Cigarettes Are Sublime.* London: Picador Books, 1995.

Kluger, Richard. *Ashes to Ashes.* New York: Vintage Books, 1997.

Sobel, Robert. *They Satisfy: The Cigarette in American Life.* New York: Anchor Press/Doubleday, 1978.

Tate, Cassandra. *Cigarette Wars: The Triumph of "The Little White Slaver."* New York: Oxford University Press, 1999.

Matthew Hilton

SNORKELING

See *Scuba Diving/Snorkeling*

SNOWBOARDING

Snowboards have become a part of everyday life in America. Snowboarders' aerial acrobatics and high-speed downhill races have impressed spectators and inspired a new generation of winter sport enthusiasts. Members of the sport's elite have become common household names, much like the elite of basketball, baseball, and football. Snowboarding has spawned a new culture that has become a defining element for the upcoming generation, and its skyrocketing participation and increasing acceptance in American society have ensured its continued popularity.

History

Although they seem like such an integral part of today's society, snowboards have had a tumultuous and storied history. Based on their currently resounding popularity, one would never know that snowboards got their start as a children's toy sold in grocery stores. These toys, called Snurfers, were invented in 1965 by an engineer from Muskegon, Michigan, named Sherman Poppen, after he observed one of his daughters standing up on a sled. A Snurfer, or snow surfer, was originally two skis bound together with a rope that acted as a controlling mechanism. Between its inception and 1977, over 500,000 Snurfers were sold, including one to Jake Burton Carpenter.

Jake Burton Carpenter, one of the most influential figures in the sport of snowboarding, first gained notoriety at the Snurfer competitions, winning on boards of his own design. In 1977, after graduating from college, he figured he could make some money commercially producing his snowboards and started Burton Boards. At the same time as Burton was living his dream in New England, a former professional skateboarder, Tom Sims, was doing something similar on the West Coast. Using his capital and resources gained from a relatively lucrative skate and surfboard production business, Sims created his first snowboard.

At first, snowboarders were seen as society's outcasts. Ski resorts banned them; the upper-middle-class ski community looked down upon them; a large portion of American society essentially spurned them. They were relegated to riding up in snow cats that groomed the ski areas at night, or to hiking to the top of mountains. In the 1980s, ski areas accepted the fact that there was lack of growth in the ski industry and, with some stipulations, allowed snowboarders on the slopes. This development, along with a more consumer-oriented society, resulted in a tremendous boom in snowboard popularity. Ski shops started selling snowboards, and the number of ski areas that allowed snowboards increased. By the mid 1990s, only a few resorts were skier-specific.

Technology

The snowboards of the 1960s and 1970s looked very different from modern snowboards. Often curved on the bottom with small metal fins attached to assist in turning the board in deep snow, they resembled the surfboards after which they were first modeled. A rider would stand on top, sometimes holding a string attached to the front. Originally, snowboards were designed with only one upward-turned nose. However, in 2004, nearly all of the boards that were made, with the exception of alpine boards, had both tail and nose turned upward. They had become complex combinations of fiberglass, wood, plastic, and metal.

The technology of the snowboard is not the only element that has changed over the years. When snowboarding first started, tennis shoes and winter boots were the footwear of choice. As the manufacturing processes, materials, and performance demands progressed, so did snowboarding boots. In 2004, a variety of flexibilities, binding systems, and styles were available. The type of boot that a rider used depended on what type of boarding he or she preferred. Softer boots were made predominantly out of fabric and were often used more for freestyle snowboarding, while a stiffer plastic boot was designed for use with an alpine board. There were different types of binding systems, strap in and clip in, that also determined what type of boot a boarder used.

Culture

The culture of snowboarding varies depending on where the snowboarder is from and the type of snowboarding in which the snowboarder participates; however, it is an undisputed fact that snowboarding society has its roots in the skate-and-surf culture of the 1960s and 1970s. The nonconformist, anarchistic beliefs that were so popular with the skate-and-surf communities were a naturally conflicting belief structure for a similar activity, skiing, which represented the affluent, bourgeois culture that was predominant in the winter sports arena at the time.

Surfing started it all. A large percentage of the most devout adherents were scouring the nation's coasts searching for the perfect wave. Their life revolved around surfing, and little else mattered. Then came skateboarding, a sport surfers started when there were no waves. The same nonconformist attitudes surrounded skateboarding, and the rest of America looked upon this sport with the same negative sentiment. Skateboarding migrated to the more urban settings, and surfers and skaters developed snowboarding when they traveled to the mountains during winter months, which again embodied the same antiestablishment attitude, and also received the same drifter status.

This nonconformist, antiestablishment counterculture was actually just the skin covering the body of the snow, skate, and surf society. It was the face that the culture chose to show America. Underneath that skin were the common threads that drove the lifestyle. Creativity, independence, the purity of doing something for the sake of doing it; those reasons were the real purpose behind existence as a boarder.

In the early 2000s, snowboarders kept many of those same basic beliefs. Many veered away from the nonconformist attitude and adopted a more traditional stance, in part because of the increasing popularity of the sport. Snowboarders were no longer the extreme minority at resorts, but that cultural acceptance was also due to the change in American beliefs. The longer snowboarding has been around, the more followers it has gained and the more accepted it has become. Snowboarding is now a popular, middle- to upper-class-winter activity, exactly what the originators were rebelling against in the 1960s and 1970s.

Conclusion

Snowboarding's evolution has amazed even its pioneers. The technological and cultural changes that have occurred in such a short time have been monumental. In just forty years, snowboarding has gone from a select few participants to the fastest-growing winter sport, with more than 5 million participants who spend hundreds of millions of dollars annually. From a child's toy to a recreational phenomenon, snowboarding has become a part of our recreation and leisure society.

See also: Extreme Sports; Skiing, Alpine; Surfing; Teenage Leisure Trends

BIBLIOGRAPHY

Baccigaluppi, John, Sonny Mayugba, and Chris Carnel, eds. *Declaration of Independents: Snowboarding, Skateboarding, and Music: An Intersection of Cultures.* San Francisco: Chronicle Books, 2001.

Bennett, Jeff, Charles Arnell, and Scott Downey. *The Complete Snowboarder.* New York: Ragged Mountain Press, 2000.

Gordon, Dan. "Trail Blazers: Once Shunned, Snowboarders Are Now Leading the Extreme Sports Revolution." *Sport* (October 1999): 89.

Heino, Rebecca. "What Is So Punk About Snowboarding?" *Journal of Sport and Social Issues* 24 (2000): 176–191.

Howe, Susanna. *Sick: A Cultural History of Snowboarding.* New York: St. Martin's Press, 1998.

Humphreys, Duncan. "Snowboarders: Bodies Out of Control and In Conflict." *Sporting Traditions* 13 (1996): 3–23.

———. "'Shredheads Go Mainstream'? Snowboarding and Alternative Youth." *International Review for the Sociology of Sport* 32, no. 2 (1997): 147–160.

Marni Goldenberg and Kellen Sams

SOCCER

Soccer in early forms has been played on the American continent for more than three centuries, providing it with a historical lineage that far surpasses those of sporting pastimes considered to be more essentially American (for example, baseball, football, and basketball). Indeed, one noted commentator has gone so far as to describe it as "the elder statesman of American sport" (Sugden, p. 219). However, as with the premodern versions of the game in America, the British influence on modern soccer's genesis and evolution within the United States is pronounced. Fermented within the social laboratories of the British public school system during the early decades of the nineteenth century, the divergent soccer (kicking) and rugby (handling) football codes were exported to the United States, primarily via the migration of staff and pupils. By the 1860s, soccer had become a discernible feature within many East Coast preparatory schools and universities. Indeed, it is frequently overlooked that the first intercollegiate football game was played between Princeton and Rutgers in 1869 using soccer rules derived from those codified by the English Football Association in 1863.

The American Football Association (AFA) was founded in 1884. It was the first soccer league formed outside of Britain, and evidenced the British influence on American sporting culture during the nineteenth century. As in Britain, soccer in turn-of-the-century America was the site of struggles between amateur and professional constituencies. The AFA increasingly became the representative institution for those interested in professionalizing American soccer, whereas, as its name implied, the American Amateur Football Association (AAFA) concerned itself with governing and promoting the amateur game. This division within American soccer culture was nowhere more apparent than during the conference held by soccer's worldwide governing body, the Fédération Internationale de Football Association (FIFA) in Stockholm, Sweden, in 1912. There, both the AFA and AAFA attended independently in an attempt to secure recognition from FIFA as the primary organizing body for the game in the United States. The cleavage in American soccer politics was subsequently resolved, with the conjoining of the rival groups in the establishment of the United States Football Association in 1913 (the USFA ultimately changed its name to the United States Soccer Association [USSA] in 1974). The USFA emerged as a staunchly amateur institution, and one interested in nurturing the European (and particularly British) provenance of the game; both factors contributed to inhibiting soccer's popularity within an early twentieth-century American sporting culture characterized by a creeping professionalism and search for national differentiation.

American soccer's increasingly foreign demeanor was accentuated through the mass influx of workers to industrializing urban centers in the late nineteenth and early twentieth centuries from, among other places, Poland, Ireland, Russia, Germany, and Britain—all places where soccer had already become ingrained into the rhythms of everyday life. In the name of assimilating into life in the new world, many of these immigrants chose consciously to eschew the cultural symbols and practices of the lands from whence they came. However, many did not. To those who did not, soccer, like other cultural forms, including diet, religion, and folklore, played an important function in providing a sense of continuity in the lives of these new American. This explains the emergence of both soccer teams with explicitly ethnic affiliations (such as First German American S.C. in Philadelphia; Stix, Baer and Fuller F.C. in St. Louis; and Shamrock S.C. in Cleveland), and the multi-accented ethnic composition of U.S. representative sides. All of these factors contributed to soccer's failure to break into the American sporting mainstream

Throughout the twentieth century, soccer was viewed as the game of "hyphenated Americans." However, since the 1970s, the game's stupendous growth as a participant sport among middle-class suburban youth has also provided soccer with a distinctly American countenance. Soccer's growth is attributable to numerous factors, including the legacy of the professional North American Soccer League's grassroots youth soccer programs designed to stimulate interest in the sport; the increased opportunity for female sport participation resulting from the enactment of Title IX of the 1972 Education Amendments Act; and the growing perception among the American middle class of soccer as an appropriate health and fitness nurturing activity for their offspring (especially when compared to the perceived brutality of football). The result has been an explosion in youth soccer participation rates that, at the high school level, grew 127 percent for boys and 618 percent for girls

Soccer fever. The growth of soccer's popularity in the United States is most evident at the youth level, as youth soccer leagues have become the fastest growing sports leagues for young boys and girls. © *Corbis*

between 1980–1981 and 2000–2001 (National Federation of State High School Associations). As of 2002, soccer was played by more than 19 million people annually, and was positioned as the third most popular team sport for twelve to seventeen year olds and the second most popular for six to eleven year olds (Soccer Industry Council of America).

In seeking to conclusively establish the game within the United States, and thereby truly actualize the game's global reach, FIFA chose the United States as the host for the 1994 World Cup, which is soccer's premier tournament and one of the most popular sporting events in the world. As part of the political machinations that secured the World Cup, and to specifically address FIFA's global objectives, Major League Soccer (MLS) debuted in 1996 as the latest attempt to establish a truly national and economically viable professional soccer league in the United States. Like the game in America itself, MLS was consciously structured to engage the divided (along ethnic and class lines) American soccer populace. Similarly, in 2001, the Women's United Soccer Association (WUSA) debuted as an eight-team professional league timed to capitalize upon the phenomenal growth in female soccer participation and the outstanding displays of the U.S. women's national team at World Cup and Olympic tournaments. While the MLS has been able to find a niche in the American sports scene, the WUSA folded in 2003, largely as a result of corporate and media disinterest prompted by the league's failure to generate sufficient broader interest beyond its female fan base. While the attendance and television-viewing figures for the MLS are relatively modest, its continued existence speaks to soccer's newly found position within American culture. While perhaps not threatening the broad-based appeal or resonance of football, baseball, and basketball, soccer has become an acknowledged part of the American sporting landscape.

See also: Globalization of American Leisure, Professionalization of Sport

BIBLIOGRAPHY

Andrews, D. L. "Contextualizing Suburban Soccer: Consumer Culture, Lifestyle Differentiation, and Suburban America." *Culture, Sport, Society* 2, no. 3 (1999): 31–53.

Delgado, F. "Major League Soccer: The Return of the Foreign Sport." *Journal of Sport and Social Issues* 21, no. 3 (1997): 285–297.

———. "Sport and Politics: Major League Soccer, Constitution, and (the) Latino Audiences." *Journal of Sport and Social Issues* 23, no. 1 (1999): 41–54.

Giulianotti, R. *Football: A Sociology of the Global Game.* Cambridge, U.K.: Polity Press, 1999.

Markovits, Andrei S., and Steven L. Hellerman. *Offside: Soccer and American Exceptionalism.* Princeton, N.J.: Princeton University Press, 2001.

National Federation of State High School Associations. *High School Participation Survey.* Indianapolis, Ind.: NFSHSA, 2002.

Soccer Industry Council of America. *National Soccer Participation Survey.* North Palm Beach, Fla.: SICA, 2002.

Sugden, J. "USA and the World Cup: American Nativism and the Rejection of the People's Game." In *Hosts and Champions: Soccer Cultures, National Identities and the USA World Cup.* Edited by J. Sugden and A. Tomlinson. Aldershot, U.K.: Arena, 1994.

Wagg, S. "The Business of America: Reflections on World Cup '94." In *Giving the Game Away: Football, Politics and Culture on Five Continents.* Edited by S. Wagg. Leicester, U.K.: Leicester University Press, 1995.

David L. Andrews

SOCIAL CONTROL OF LEISURE

See *Regulation and Social Control of Leisure*

SOCIAL DANCING

An age-old means of communicating messages that reflect social trends, social dancing is secular partnering between males and females or participation among groups. The secular and sacred combine in some cultures, and a few religions ban dancing. Rooted mainly in Europe, Africa, and Latin America, social dancing in America is as varied and changing as its cultural, age, and geographical groups. Attitudes toward the body and sexuality in public affect attitudes toward social dancing, which came to include sexier and faster-paced dances.

Early History

Seventeenth-century Puritan-dominated New England had laws against dancing and punished violators. Only children were allowed to play; the Protestant ethic held that such behavior was the enemy of work and a diversion from spiritual purposes of life. But most settlers in America danced. As a means to improve a person's social life, itinerant masters taught dance with its attendant etiquette. Recreational dance had taken hold in the colonies by the time of the American Revolution. Indeed, George Washington and Thomas Jefferson were zealous dancers. Formal dances such as the minuet required skill, but country dances were for everyone. John Playford first collected English country dances into a book in 1651, and he published subsequent editions of dance manuals until 1728. Social dances occurred at county fairs, jamborees, log rollings, husking and quilting bees, barn raisings, homes, community centers, religious facilities, town squares, formal assemblies, cotillions, dance halls, fire halls, hotels, nightclubs, and stadiums.

Purpose And Growth

Dancing often marks crucial stages of the life cycle, especially "sweet sixteen" parties and weddings. Encouraging cheerfulness and banishing grief, dance also makes manifest good health, provides healthy physical exercise, and helps to keep people young. An escape from mundane realities of the workaday world, dancing often provides a free-feeling and altered state of consciousness. Dancing is a venue of self-expression as well as a way to try out different roles and fantasies.

An acceptable form of body contact with another person as well as an acceptable form of couple switching, dancing is a way for people to meet and court. Each generation sets itself apart with its own movements (often recycled versions of earlier dances), along with social decorum, dress codes, and music. Some classic dances such as the waltz, rumba, and tango persist through generations, and retro fads also occur.

The vast repertoire of folk dance jamborees, dances of different nations, line, group, circle, couple, threesomes, foursomes, and fivesomes provide face-to-face interaction in an increasingly mechanized and computerized society. Dancers talk about the humanity of contra dancing, the etiquette of eye contact, the opportunity through the folk dance network to find dances in different towns in America, and the uniqueness of dancing as a social activity, in which you touch people the same evening you meet them.

Social dancing is central to the way many people celebrate their heritage and maintain a sense of community. Of anonymous origin, handed down by image of eye, national, ethnic, and folk dances may salve nostalgia for eras past. The pan-Native American powwow has religious, social, and competitive elements to celebrate Indian heritage. Dancing may be an anchor or ballast in a sea of uncertainty for immigrants, as well as for inner-city youth and college students. Some traditional dances are transformed into new hip dances—the bhangra, of Punjabi, India, for example, is popular among South Asians.

Of course, the so-called American "melting pot" evolved new forms such as the Juba, ring shout, cakewalk, and street-corner tap dancing, with its roots in the Irish jig, clog, African rhythms, improvisation, and body fluidity. Square dancing emerged from country dance spirit and ballroom elegance.

Coincident with eroding European monarchical power, the waltz appeared in Germany and Austria in 1830 to revolutionize Western social dancing; for the first time, men and women danced in close, sensual physical contact. But because it required stiff control and agile skill, the waltz was replaced by the polka, spieling (wild spinning), and two-step, and then in the twentieth century by more natural "tough" dances known as rag and animal dances rooted in the black vernacular (derived from the dances of numerous African groups). Dancing positions changed from the woman's hand on the man's shoulder, his on her waist, and their other hands clasped, to partners clinging to each other's necks and shoulders and dancing cheek-to-cheek. On the frontier, dancing was rowdy and vigorous. Fiddlers and callers told dancers what to do, and calling became integral to square dancing.

Twentieth Century

From the 1890s to 1930s, immigrants came from southern and Eastern Europe. Working in a factory culture of silence, their self-expression exploded in "dancing madness." The freer style dancing reflected women's growing independence in society. Between 1880 and 1920, the establishment of dance halls commercialized leisure. Undermining old-world chaperonage, dance halls attracted young men and women who found unprecedented autonomy and their own norms. Women authoritatively passed over certain men for dances, refused invitations to step out, and defied parents' notions that companionship led inexorably to commitment and attempts to arrange marriages. Of different nationalities and social classes, yet equal in terms of dance experience, dancers congregated in dance halls and palaces. By 1910, greater New York had over 500 dance halls, some attached to saloons and associated with drink and immorality.

During the ragtime period (1890–1917), America became known as the land of a thousand dances, including the fox trot, turkey trot, bunny hug, duck waddle, camel walk, kangaroo hop, grizzly bear, monkey glide, chicken scratch, kangaroo dip, bull frog hop, buzz, and Texas Tommy. Also popular were dances with instructions, such as ballin' the jack and Argentina's tempestuous tango. The 1912 advent of afternoon tango teas attracted unescorted women to dance with male partners employed by café owners.

The blacks' substantial contribution to American dance was not always known or acknowledged. Blacks created social dances that were later coopted, "sanitized," made less sexy, and stylized by whites. Beginning in 1916, a mass migration of blacks from the South to Harlem led to new dances driving America's roaring 1920s. An element of cultural identity, black dance encoded messages such as hierarchy, inclusion-exclusion, and exchanges across social boundaries. Covert expression of political challenge occurred with symbolic stylistic rule breaking in dance. So artistic freedom for African Americans during the Harlem Renaissance was a historically meaningful civil right.

Some whites deemed the black dance vocabulary of hip swinging, pelvic rotations and thrusts (known as the Congo grind), torso undulations, and shoulder shimmying to be immoral. Yet other whites frequented Harlem nightclubs, thrilled to partake of a sense of illicit sexuality. By the time whites had adopted black dances as their own, blacks had moved on to new dance invention or reinvention.

The shimmy, big apple, black bottom, and flirtatious Charleston, with limbs tossed and kicked, gained popularity during the 1920s. Then one day in a Savoy Ballroom dance contest, all time champion George "Shorty" Snowden did a breakaway, flinging his partner out in aerial flight and improvising a few solo steps of his own to an eight-beat count; he called the step the "Lindy," after Charles Lindberg, who made the first transatlantic airplane flight in 1927. These new dances became part of the 1930s and 1940s jitterbug and swing big band era.

Between 1920 and 1940, taxi dancing (male patrons paying female dancers a fee for a dance) attracted primarily immigrants. In 1930, New York City had thirty-seven dime-a-dance palaces, 35,000 to 50,000 male customers per week, and 2,500 to 3,000 employed female dancers. Taxi dancers in Latino barrios have been catering primarily to undocumented Mexican immigrants since the late 1970s.

Beginning during the 1920s dance craze, diversionary marathons symbolized survival during the Depression. Contests of stamina, nonstop dancing to set records was an escape from crowded tenements, factory drudgery, patriarchy, and poverty. Unemployed youth suffered for the dream of prize money. Alma Cummings danced nonstop for twenty-seven hours in New York City, waltzing and jitterbugging through six partners.

The 1930s and 1940s were the first golden age of Latino dances such as the rumba danzon, cha-cha, and mambo from Cuba, bolero from Puerto Rico, pasadoble from Mexico, samba from Brazil, and merengue from Haiti. African American line dances, such as the Madison originating in Baltimore, hit in the late 1950s. The shuffle, a few dance steps on the football field performed by a player who made a touchdown, appeared.

Accessibility to TV made new dances rapidly accessible nationwide. Dancers could watch programs such as *American Bandstand* (1956, reaching about 20 million people daily), *Soul Train* (1971), and *Solid Gold* (1979). In 1981, Music Television (MTV), playing music videos twenty-four hours a day, arrived on the scene. Then the Internet began providing dance information on sites such as http://www.salsaeb.com.

The 1960s twist (below the waist) wrested apart couple dancing into an era of rock 'n' roll. Twisting hip movements and nontouch dancing remained in the pantomime jerk, frug, skate, pony, swim monkey, mashed potato, and hully gully. Psychedelic hippies engaged in free expression and trancelike self-absorption on the dance floor.

Discotheques with disc jockeys playing vinyl records through big sound systems began in Europe, a product of World War II austerity, and emerged in America in the early 1970s in casual underground spaces. Homosexual, African American, Hispanic, and working-class communities of large urban centers joined with the "beautiful people" at, for example, Studio 54 and Xenon in New York City. An otherworldly admixture of blinding stroboscopic lights and projected images on walls created Dionysian playgrounds.

Closed-couple touch dancing returned in the 1970s with salsa music and the hustle, birthed in New York City among Puerto Rican blue-collar workers.

"Breaking," featuring competitive, sometimes risky, artistically inventive, pyrotechnic acrobatic and gymnastic dance movements, began in the 1970s in the Bronx, New York, among young African American and Latino males as an alternative to inner-city gang violence, and a way to be number one without "blowing somebody away." The 1980s witnessed the eruption of hip-hop solo or group break dancers spinning on their shoulders, buttocks, or back, freezing in pretzel forms, and popping (segmenting body movements that ripple through the body) on sidewalks and in parks. The hip-hop style crossed racial and ethnic boundaries and spread among young people in America.

About this time in New York City, white punk youths in combat boots, torn jeans, and metal-studded dog collars and bracelets were slam dancing to aggressive harsh music. They collided into one another in the "mosh pit" in front of the stage. At rock concerts during the 1980s and 1990s, the grunge movement, with clusters of males circling and charging each other, knocking and stepping on innocent bystanders, began. Thousands of scantily clad, pierced, and inked bodies participated in body surfing (riding the crowd's shoulders, hand over hand, until diving, falling, or being propelled to the stage and recycled back into the arena dancers by ushers).

Jamaican reggae, first appearing in the 1970s, infused hip-hop dancing and influenced Washington, D.C.'s go-go style. Reggae's "winding" (pelvic rotation) was also common in Cuban dance. In the next twenty years, dancers made popular the butterfly, bogoloo, and skettle.

A surge in country-western couple dances, called "shit-kickers," in Texas, occurred in the 1980s. The Tucson swing, two-step, and line dances for couples appeared in bars and honky-tonks. The films *Dirty Dancing, Saturday Night Fever,* and *Flashdance* influenced social dancing.

During the 1990s, voguing (a dance incorporating modeling poses) was common among gays. A swing dance (an umbrella term for Lindy, hand-dancing, Chicago steppin', Philly bop, North Carolina shag, and Detroit hustle) revival of the 1920s to 1940s invention became popular into the twenty-first century. There was also freestyle funk, reggae, house, club, and rap dance. Held in different places, rave dances developed as part of an underground culture. The attraction was experiencing altered states of consciousness through dancing en masse all night to a throbbing repetitive music beat and hypnotic light show. The line dance known as the electric slide replaced the electric boogie. Mexicans danced the banda with the *quebradita*, a little break in which the man straddles his partner and leans her back parallel to the ground.

By this time, male-female partnering included new configurations in teenage and young adult freestyle, including da butt, freaking, booty dancing, "doggy dancing," "front piggy-backing," and "dirty dancing." Partners twined thighs, touched and rotated pelvises, and tilted upper torsos away from each other. In another pattern, females pressing with back and buttocks, or bending over with hands on the floor, pressed and ground against the front of their male partners' bodies. Some females hiked up their skirts, exposing thong underwear.

Latin dancing (rumba, samba, cha-cha, mambo, pachanga, merengue, bolero, paso doble, cumbia, bachata) flourished with Central and South American immigration. The forward- and backward-hugging bodies with intertwined legs of 1989's Brazilian lambada was short-lived and later banned by Brazil. The macarena line dance from Spain hit in late 1993. Ketsup followed. Latino influence escalated with salsa dancing, a recycling of 1950s mambo and merengue. Hot salsa seen in clubs and on television is similar to freaking.

Musical shows encouraged audience members to dance in the aisles. Such performances included the Gypsy Kings, Salif Keita, "Hairspray," and "Harlem Song."

Throughout the twentieth century, people danced waltzes, fox trot, and tamed versions of many less conservative dances at formal occasions, in small cocktail lounges, and in senior citizen centers. People tend to continue to dance the dances of their youth.

In short, social dancing is a nonverbal form of communication about self, heritage, and interpersonal relations that engages mind, body, and feeling. The persistence of social dancing through history, and the religious, civil, and political attempts to control it, attest to its potency in human life.

See also: African American Leisure Lifestyles, Dance Classes, Dance Halls, Latinos Leisure Lifestyles, Raves/Raving, Square Dancing, Teenage Leisure Lifestyles

BIBLIOGRAPHY

Aldrich, Elizabeth. *From the Ballroom to Hell: Grace and Folly in Nineteenth-Century Dance.* Evanston, Ill.: Northwestern University Press, 1991.

Blake, Dick. *Discotheque Dance.* New York: World Publishing, 1965.

Clark, Sharon Leigh. "Rock Dance in the United States, 1960-1970: Its Origins, Forms and Patterns." Ph.D. dissertation, New York University, 1973.

Cressey, Paul G. *The Taxi-Dance Hall: A Sociological Study of Commercialized Recreation and City Life.* Chicago: University of Chicago Press, 1932.

DeGarmo, William B. *The Dance of Society.* New York: W. A. Pond and Company, 1875.

Erenberg, Lewis A. *Steppin' Out.* Chicago: University of Chicago Press, 1981.

Hanna, Judith Lynne. *Dance and Stress Resistance, Reduction, and Euphoria.* New York: AMS Press, 1988.

———. "Moving Messages: Identity and Desire in Dance." In *Popular Music and Communication.* 2d edition. Edited by James Lull. Newbury Park, Calif.: Sage Publications, 1992.

Hazzard-Donald, Katrina. *Jookin': The Rise of Social Dance Formations in African American Culture.* Philadelphia: Temple University Press, 1990.

Lustgarten, Karen. *The Complete Guide to Disco Dancing.* New York: Warner Books, 1978.

McBee, Randy D. *Dance Hall Days: Intimacy and Leisure Among Working-Class Immigrants in the United States.* New York: New York University Press, 2000.

Malnig, Julie, and Barbara Cohen-Stratyner, eds. "The Social and Popular Dance Issue." *Dance Research Journal* 33, no. 2 (2001).

Martin, Carol. *Dance Marathons: Performing American Culture of the 1920s and 1930s.* Jackson: University Press of Mississippi, 1994.

Nevell, Richard. *A Time to Dance: American Country Dancing from Hornpipes to Hot Hash.* New York: St. Martin's Press, 1977.

Peis, Kathy. *Cheap Amusements. Working Women and Leisure in Turn-of-the-Century New York.* Philadelphia: Temple University Press, 1986.

Ragland, Cathy. "Mexican Deejays and the Transnational Space of Youth Dances in New York and New Jersey." *Ethnomusicology* 47, no. 3 (2003): 338–354.

Stearns, Marshall, and Jean Stearns. *Jazz Dance: The Story of American Vernacular Dance.* New York: Macmillan Publishers, 1968.

Vermey, Ruud. *Latin: Thinking, Sensing and Doing on Latin American Dancing.* Munich: Kastell Verlag, 1994.

Judith Lynne Hanna

SOFTBALL

Once considered merely an indoor version of baseball, softball has developed into America's largest participatory sport, with 40 million amateur players and an additional 20 million players outside the United States (Kneer and McCord, p. 1; USOC, pp. 10–11). In softball, two teams compete to score the highest number of runs around the bases. Games take place in gymnasiums, parks, backyards, and on grassy and hard-surface diamonds; men, women, children, and mixed groups play softball games at both recreational and amateur levels. Softball contests are designated as either fast pitch, slow pitch, or modified pitch.

Early Softball Games

The first softball game developed in 1887 from an unlikely encounter between a boxing glove, a broomstick, and a gathering of football fans. Nearly fifty years after the innovation of modern baseball in America, Harvard and Yale graduates assembled at Chicago's Farragut Boat Club to await the results of the annual football match. At the announcement of Harvard's defeat, an overexcited Yalie hurled a scrunched-up boxing glove at a Harvard alumnus, who whacked the glove with a broomstick. By the next weekend, Chicago Board of Trade reporter George Hancock had drawn up the rules of the new game. Originally termed "indoor baseball," ten players (as opposed to baseball's nine) would play the game on a field small enough to fit into a gymnasium; it would feature underhand pitching delivery, a short and slender bat, and a large ball.

From this inauspicious beginning, softball came to flourish in the early twentieth-century Midwest, with game rules as diverse as the names under which it was played: Indoor-Outdoor, Kitten Ball, Diamond Ball, Bush Ball, Army Ball, Mush Ball, and Playground Ball were all common variants. The original Chicago game migrated outdoors in spring of 1888 and was known thereafter as Indoor-Outdoor, since it spent half a year in each domain. In 1895, the sport thrived in Minneapolis, Minnesota, when fire department lieutenant Lewis Rober organized outdoor Kitten League Ball in an effort to keep his firefighters in shape during their downtime. Many turn-of-the-twentieth-century women defied cultural taboos against female sports participation to compete in early softball leagues. Because the sport initially was perceived as a less-violent, slower version of baseball, females were accepted on both single-sex and coed teams. During the first national softball tournament, held at

Chicago's 1933 World's Columbian Exposition, it became clear to tournament organizers Leo Fischer and M. J. Pauley that the sport could benefit from a uniform set of playing rules and equipment guidelines. In response, they created the Amateur Softball Association (ASA), deemed "softball" the official name of the game, and codified the rules of play. The ASA, which in the early 2000s remained softball's national governing body, then classified teams as slow pitch, fastball, or women's teams, and ruled the ball regulation size to be fourteen inches.

A Grassroots Sport Is Born: Impacts of Early Softball

The lean years of the 1930s marked a turning point in softball's national appeal and impact: players of all levels and backgrounds flooded the ballparks, and the sport created a culture of grassroots leisure in America. As part of President Franklin Delano Roosevelt's New Deal plan, the Works Progress Administration (WPA) designated $1 billion from 1935 through 1940 to build more than 3,000 new athletic fields, most of which featured softball diamonds (Dickson, p. 72). Lacking jobs to fill their afternoon hours, many adults frequented softball fields instead, where low-key community competition provided a cheap and enjoyable way to pass the time.

Moreover, softball proved inclusive to people of varied backgrounds. Although early leagues developed primarily among elite social and athletic clubs, during the Depression years the sport expanded to include working-class players. Softball athletes did not have to be moneyed or talented: equipment was cheap and available, and competitions took place between amateurs who modified the game to meet the level of play. Women, too, were accepted as softball players—a status confirmed by the inclusion of a women's softball division in the 1933 national championships. By the mid-1930s, the Bloomer Girl baseball leagues of the early twentieth century had yielded to women's softball leagues, which were supported by the ASA, YWCA, Catholic Youth Organization, National Recreation Association, and National Softball Association (NSA). The combined result of broad societal participation and accessibility culminated at the end of the decade, when the ASA announced an unprecedented 6 million Americans on the softball diamonds. A new national pastime had arrived.

War, Women, and International Participation

Although the onset of World War II initially checked softball's expansion, eventually it extended the sport across

Community softball. Enjoyed by many as a recreational activity, softball also has professional leagues and high school and college tournaments. © *Ariel Skelley*

boundaries of geography and gender. American soldiers played softball overseas, spreading the game to players and spectators in almost 100 countries. Meanwhile, on the home continent, Chicago Cubs owner Philip Wrigley watched major league baseball (MLB) competition decrease as its players left to serve at war. Recognizing spectators' continuing demand for the game, he founded a professional women's softball league in 1943. The style of play soon evolved to modified baseball: the size of the ball decreased, the distance between bases increased, and pitches were delivered overhand. The league became known as the All-American Girls Professional Baseball League (AAGPBL). League players were expected to attend "Charm School" and maintain a ladylike appearance, lest they recall in spectators' minds the rougher style of play and dress used by earlier Bloomer Girls baseball leagues. Games were geared toward working-class fans, with patriotic themes and late start times that allowed spectators to work evenings, yet still attend games. The AAGPBL lasted for more than ten years, until decreased interest in softball and baseball after the war led to the league's termination in 1954.

Technological Advances in Equipment

From just a stick and a ball, softball equipment has evolved to a $300-million-a-year industry. Bat sales account for more than 40 percent of sales, with new technologies pushing batter performance—and expenditures—to unprecedented levels. In the early 1970s, aluminum bats largely replaced wooden bats; they are favored for their light weight and increased bat speed, large "sweet spots" (hitting zones), and resistance to cracking or breaking. Bat companies differentiate their product through diverse manufacturing processes, including varying the aluminum composition, (to increase durability and strength), employing cryogenics (to reduce residual heat stress), and adding graphite and titanium linings (to reduce vibration and make lighter models). One of the most effective and controversial developments in bat technology was the 1997 creation of a double-walled bat, which distributed the ball's impact to create a much larger sweet spot. The ASA has banned numerous high performance bats, ruling the speed of the ball after contact to be at dangerous levels.

The early softball core of cork and latex has given way to more durable polyurethane. Some sixteen-inch softballs, however, continue to be made from long-fiber kapok, which becomes soft with use, making it more suitable for the slower sixteen-inch game. Manufacturers have developed technologies to harden softballs while enabling them to retain their spring from the bat, prompting the ASA to regulate such processes, again in the interest of fielder safety. Improvements in ball technology allow diverse segments of the population to participate. Some companies produce youth balls with a softer core to reduce the risk of injury in children. Invented in 1964, the beep ball allows blind athletes to play softball by emitting a series of beeps by which the players judge the ball's whereabouts. Softball gloves, meanwhile, have advanced primarily in material quality and diversified design options. Players can choose gloves specific to their fielding position, with features such as water-resistant leather, Coolmax finger lining, or gel insets and palm pads to absorb shock. Some brands even allow customers to design their own gloves.

Softball has become safer not only through regulations on bats and balls, but also through the introduction of new safety equipment. A brightly colored protective guard tops ballpark fences, increasing fence visibility and shielding players from rough metal edges. Breakaway bases release when struck, reducing the risk of ankle and leg injuries that result from sliding into stationary bases. Protective gear, including helmets, sliding pads, batting gloves, and catchers' garb, has become both more advanced and more prevalent over the years.

Amateur, International, and Collegiate Softball Organizations

The ASA is the national governing body of United States softball, with more than 250,000 teams and 4 million members (ASA, "About Us"). In addition to organizing national tournaments on the amateur level, the ASA selects coaches and players for the Pan American Games, Olympic Games, and ISF World Championships. The International Softball Federation (ISF) governs softball on a global level, hosting world championship tournaments and regulating international softball rules. From 1968 to 1997, the United States Slo-Pitch Softball Association (USSSA) existed as an amateur slow-pitch organization separate from the ASA, hosting world championships and publishing rules slightly different from ASA rules; in 1997, the USSSA expanded to include several other national sports and changed its name to the United States Specialty Sports Association. The International Softball Congress (ISC), in turn, organizes men's and boys' fast-pitch

softball tournaments on a national and international level. At the collegiate level, the National Collegiate Athletic Association (NCAA) oversaw 850 women's fast-pitch softball teams as of November 2002. Softball leagues and tournaments are also organized on a recreational level within communities, schools, and companies.

Participation Trends and Demographics Among Fast-, Modified-, and Slow-Pitch Players

Softball is generally divided into three categories: fast-, modified-, and slow-pitch. The three games are played by men's, women's, junior, and coed teams and have different rules and field distances depending on the game variation, skill level, and gender. Fast-pitch softball features windmill and slingshot pitching delivery and is characterized by low scoring games; relative skills of pitchers have great influence over game outcomes. In slow-pitch softball, pitchers deliver arced, slow throws called "rainbows" after the shape of their delivery; games often are high scoring, since the ball is easy to hit. Steals and bunts are not allowed in slow-pitch, as they are in fast-pitch, and teams consist of ten players, rather than nine in fast-pitch. Modified-pitch softball is played at an intermediate speed. All three games currently use an eleven- to twelve-inch ball; a variation of sixteen-inch slow-pitch also exists.

Participation trends in fast- and slow-pitch softball illustrate the changing demographics of the game. Early Chicago softball games resembled the sixteen-inch slow pitch of the early 2000s; the ball's large size prevented it from traveling too far in gyms and small neighborhood parks. As the game expanded to other cities and moved outdoors in the early twentieth century, the ball size decreased, and sixteen-inch softball is now played only in a few city leagues. From 1940 to 1960, men's fast-pitch teams became the dominant breed of softball, boasting 25,000 ASA-registered teams in the early 1960s (Kneer, p. 12). By 1996, however, this number had decreased to 10,000 (Farber and Deutsch). At the beginning of the twenty-first century, 90 percent of softball players instead chose to participate in twelve-inch slow-pitch softball, a game more easily mastered by players of all skill levels. The increased popularity of slow pitch reveals preferences of baby boomers for a more family oriented and social setting than fast pitch provides. Increased coed slow-pitch participation also parallels the rise of corporate recreational culture, with many company players heralding the diamond a fertile ground for developing coworker relationships.

Ironically, the sex thought better suited to play a slower ball game years ago now dominates the fast-pitch scene. In 2002, more than 343,000 girls competed in high school softball, while 17,000 played at the collegiate level (Gola, p. 2). Each year, the ASA registers 1.2 million girls on its fast-pitch teams (Gola, p. 2). Lesbian culture thrives on many women's softball teams, allowing increased recognition of and respect for homosexual athletes, but unfortunately encouraging sexual stereotypes about softball players. Although women's softball participation declined in the years following the 1954 dissolution of the AAGPBL, it rebounded with the 1972 implementation of Title IX, which resulted in increased support and money for women's sports. Perhaps the greatest boon for women's softball participation, viewing, and funding, however, has been its 1996 and 2000 inclusion in the Olympics. In the 2000 Games, television ratings proved softball the fourth most popular women's event, while amateur, college, and international softball organizations have reported overall participation increases since the sport's inclusion in the Olympics. The International Olympic Committee's (IOC) 2002 announcement that the 2008 Games might exclude the sport, however, has led to worries and protests among softball supporters. The IOC, which defends the possible exclusion by citing low popularity of the game outside of Asia and the Americas, postponed their final decision until after the 2004 Games.

Softball's rich history and bedrock of amateur players have enabled it to remain one of America's most-played and best-loved games. The shift to slow-pitch softball in recent years reveals the ever more inclusive nature of the sport: everyone can play—from kids and parents, to women and minorities, to professionals, grandparents, and wheelchair athletes. Advances in bat, ball, and safety technologies have served only to make the game more adaptable to varying levels of play. From backyards to Olympic stadiums, players and spectators worldwide enjoy the energy and ease of playing softball.

See also: Baseball, Amateur; Baseball Crowds; Little League

BIBLIOGRAPHY

Amateur Softball Association (ASA). "About ASA: Press Releases: ASA Adopts New Bat Performance Standard." Available from http://www.softball.org.

———. "About Us." Available from http://www.softball.org.

Babb, Ron. *Etched in Gold: the Story of America's First-Ever Olympic Gold Medal Winning Softball Team.* Indianapolis, Ind.: Masters Press, 1997.

Brill, Marlene Targ. *Winning Women in Baseball and Softball.* Hauppauge, N.Y.: Barron's Educational Services, 2000.

Browne, Lois. *Girls of Summer: In Their Own League.* Toronto: HarperCollins, 1992.

Burns, Marty, Kevin Cook and Mark Mravic. "Rescuing an Endangered Species." *Sports Illustrated* 91, no. 15 (18 October 1999): 36.

Cazeneuve, Brian. "Olympics Calling." *Sports Illustrated* 97, no. 23 (9 December 2002): 29.

Deitsch, Richard and B. J. Schecter. "Softball Questions." *Sports Illustrated* 97, no. 10 (9 September 2002): 24.

Dick's Sporting Goods. "Baseball/Softball Buyers Guides: How to Buy a Softball Bat." Available from http://www.dicksportinggoods.com.

Dickson, Paul. *The Worth Book of Softball.* New York: Facts on File, 1994.

Farber, Michael and Richard Deutsch. "Endangered Species." *Sports Illustrated* 87, no. 13 (29 September 1997): 88.

Fetto, John. "The Great Outdoors." *American Demographics* 25, no. 5 (June 2003): 48.

Gilbert, Bil. "America's Favorite Game Is the One Everybody Can Play." *Smithsonian* 27, no. 1 (April 1996): 70–79.

Gola, Mark. *Winning Softball for Girls.* New York: Checkmark Books, 2002.

Gregorich, Barbara. *Women at Play: The Story of Women in Baseball.* New York: Harcourt Brace, 1993.

"Having a Telecom Ball." *America's Network* 101, no. 12 (15 June 1997): 45.

International Softball Congress. "About the ISC: The President's Message." Available from http://www.iscfastpitch.com.

International Softball Federation (ISF). "About Us." Available from http://www.internationalsoftball.com.

Kneer, Marian E., and Charles L. McCord. *Softball: Slow and Fast Pitch.* Dubuque, Iowa: William C. Brown Communications, 1991.

Lopez, Kathryn Jean. "Leagues of their Own: the Delicate Question of Lesbians and Softball." *National Review* 54, no. 19 (14 October 2002): 54–55.

Meyer, Gladys C. *Softball for Girls and Women.* New York: Charles Scribner's Sons, 1982.

Michaelis, Vicki. "Making a Pitch to Keep Softball." *USA Today* (26 November 2002): 3C.

Nutt, Amy Ellis. "Swinging for the Fences." In *Nike Is a Goddess: The History of Women in Sports.* Edited by Lissa Smith. New York: Atlantic Monthly Press, 1998.

Pagnoni, Mario, and Gerald Robinson. *Softball: Fast and Slow Pitch.* North Palm Beach, Fla.: The Athletic Institute, 1990.

Paul, Marla. "Playing Catch-Up." *Family Life* (August 2001): 45–46.

Russell, Daniel A. "Why Aluminum Bats Perform Better than Wood Bats." Available from http://www.www.kettering.edu.

Senior Softball-USA. "Softball News: Dispelling the Double-wall Myth." Available from http://www.seniorsoftball.com.

Stevens, Kathryn. "Have a Ball!" *Prevention* 55, no. 4 (April 2003): 81.

United States Olympic Committee (USOC). *A Basic Guide to Softball.* Torrance, Calif.: Griffin Publishing Group, 2001.

United States Specialty Sports Association (USSSA). "History of the USSSA: 1968–2001." Available from http://www.info.usssa.com.

USA Softball. "The Official Site of USA Softball." Available from http://www.usasoftball.com.

Worth Sports. "About Worth: Worth History." Available from http://www.worthsports.com.

———. "Technology: Cryogenic Processing of Bats." Available from http://www.worthsports.com.

Abby L. Schlatter

SOUTHERN AMERICA LEISURE LIFESTYLES

Distinguishing elements about how people in the southern United States experience leisure and recreation derive from the defining features of southern life: a historical concentration on agriculture and rural life, the centrality of a racial divide and ideas and practices designed to prove and support white supremacy, and the power of evangelical Protestantism. Some, but far from all, southerners have claimed that leisure is an organic part of their society, and many people outside the region find the South such a fascinating place that their interest helps fuel a range of recreations. The commercialization of leisure in the twentieth century led to an increase in the self-consciously southern features of many recreations.

The Colonial and Antebellum South

In the colonial and antebellum periods, members of the southern upper class, aspiring to English precedents, tried to identify and enjoy themselves in ways that legitimated their status, in part through displays of largesse. The first planters at Jamestown tended to bowl in the streets and display luxury goods, because that is what gentlemen were supposed to do. Recreations of the gentry emphasized competition among planters and forms of display. As a competitive spectacle, horse racing helped dramatize the nature of Anglo-American colonial life. Horse racing seemed to confirm gentry notions that elites rode while commoners walked, that elites bred fine specialty horses while commoners were lucky to have work animals, and that the gentry had responsibilities to sponsor the recreations for the rest of society. Elections were also competitive events in which the gentry sponsored the sport—in this case the drunkenness—of the free male population.

Evangelical religion developed in part by opposing the lifestyle of the gentry, the self-indulgence, the clear divisions between the powerful and the rest of society. In the mid-1700s, Baptists, Presbyterians, and Methodists heaped scorn on the signs of elitism, the drunkenness, and the many recreations sponsored by the gentry. As evangelicalism moved from being a religion of the community of equals who opposed hierarchy to a more broadly accepted religion at the center of southern life, church events developed their own recreations—picnics, singing, and eventually, in the late 1800s, Sunday school events. Church leaders tried hard to make sure that church recreations did not take on the character of secular amusements, and evangelicals also developed a special set of Sunday behaviors designed to keep leisure quiet and located in either the church or the home.

The development of southern identity in the antebellum period involved issues of leisure. Boosters of southern settlement had been portraying the South as a warm and leisurely place, perhaps even a garden, since the 1600s, but the image was not common until an intense series of arguments about southern identity emerged in the 1830s. Abolitionists portrayed free southerners as lazy, with all of white society lolling on porches, resting on the backs of slave labor. As William R. Taylor has argued, however, the issue was far more complex than northern diligence and southern leisure. Northeastern intellectuals, worried about their region's fascination with material gain, helped create the myth of the leisurely planter who cared more for ease and manners than for business. Southern apologists, writing primarily to fight the proslavery argument, loved the image that they were fun-loving aristocrats in the Cavalier tradition. The art and literature of the antebellum South more often portrayed themselves as reclining on porches and portrayed slaves as happy folk eating and playing music.

Images of the leisurely South and the happy, musical slave grew so pervasive that Frederick Douglass had to combat them, asserting in his 1845 *Narrative* that "slaves sing most when they are most unhappy" (p. 58). Leisure was, for slaves, a luxury. Most plantation slaves, male and female, worked in agriculture for most of the year, laboring well into Saturday most weeks and had only Saturday evenings, Sundays, and a few days in the Christmas season free from direct oversight from their owners. Slave music and dance were full of complexities that reveal much about both power relations and continuity with African traditions. Black southerners made music that told stories, praised God, and celebrated major events and romance; they also sang in ways that made work easier by synchronizing certain movements and by slowing down late in the day. At leisure, African Americans made music from a range of instruments, most of them that involved drums and stringed instruments that evolved into the banjo. Slave owners loved most of the music of slaves, both because it was appealing and especially because it seemed to suggest to them that slaves were fun-loving happy folks. The cakewalk, for example, consisted of slaves in fine attire strutting or dancing in a row, while owners awarded the most elaborate or demonstrative or interesting with a prize, usually a cake. While owners saw cakewalks as a sign of slaves' lightheartedness, the slaves were actually enjoying an opportunity to mock the dressed-up foolishness of the dances common among elite white southerners.

Away from the plantations, northern and European observers often characterized small southern farmers as lazy, but those farmers generally did not bother to respond. For many farming people, recreation and production were closely related. Farming women spent many hours on porches, talking with family and friends while sewing, mending, and, above all, preparing food. Visiting was a favorite recreation that united family members, often while they helped one another with essential work. Men hunted and fished, both essential and productive activities that were also physically exciting recreations. The men and women who described sewing and hunting in their diaries made clear the cultural differences between the two activities. Women described sewing as "my work," and believed it virtuous to get to their work every day. By contrast, men detailed the excitement of hunting and the sheer pleasure of the will in overwhelming huge numbers of animals. In the colonial period through much of the nineteenth century, men recounted binge kills of numerous animals, with emphasis on both the pleasure and the excess.

Other favorite recreations that joined work and recreation included shucking corn, threshing wheat, and raising houses. Music accompanied most such events. As Bill Malone has shown, English and Scotch-Irish songs tended to emphasize solo singing or fiddle ballads and dances, but a wide mixture of influences meant that southern music was always changing.

The Postbellum South

Before the rise of industry and a national consumer culture, rural life and divisions based on notions of race determined the nature of much of southern leisure. As in many places, urbanization, industrialization, the growth of wage work and the expansion of education stimulated substantial changes in recreation, both among southern people and among tourists, moviemakers, and music pro-

ducers who looked to the region for exotic images. In the early 1900s, the South came to represent an intriguing and sometimes contradictory array of cultural meanings. While leisure had long been central to the identity some groups of southerners constructed for themselves, organized sports and recreation were slower to take hold than in other American regions. Authors in the Vanderbilt Agrarians' 1930 collection, *I'll Take My Stand,* argued that people in the region, valuing European precedents and loving the easygoing nature of rural life, rejected strenuous work and strenuous play in favor of easy pleasures in a community setting. ""John Crowe Ransom's introduction to that volume made the case that the South's best habits included the "social arts of dress, conversation, manners, the table, the hunt, politics, oratory, the pulpit. These were the arts of living and not the arts of escape; they were also community arts, in which every class of society could participate after its kind. The South took life easy, which is itself a tolerably comprehensive art" (p. 12).

Despite these images of calm and continuity, in the urbanizing South of the late 1800s and early 1900s, recreation became, along with transportation, the focus of numerous new laws about racial segregation. As formerly rural white people tried to sort out the privileges of white supremacy—and as politicians looked for ways to appeal to those whites—lawmakers established rules about whites-only restaurants, theaters, and saloons, whites-only areas in public parks, whites-only entrances to circuses and sporting events, and specific days when blacks were allowed at fairs and carnivals. African Americans responded in part by creating their own spaces for recreation—music, art, and sports. All southern cities and many towns had neighborhoods with African American groceries, saloons, and other places for informal leisure.

The growth of wage work, especially in mines and mills, created something agriculture had rarely allowed—a large group of working people with money in their pockets. Baseball started slowly in the South, partly because it grew as a city game and the region had few cities. Many southerners saw baseball first during the Civil War, and a few offered the sport as a way to develop regional pride. Many towns had loosely organized baseball teams in the late 1800s, but the major leagues and many of the minor leagues were slow in coming. Much of the growth of southern baseball took place in the Carolinas and Georgia, where textile mills encouraged workers to wear company names and enjoy themselves at mill-sponsored events.

Another development in the late 1800s was the dramatic rise in high school and college attendance. Education for teenagers had long been only for a small elite, but expanding school opportunities combined with a national craze for team sports. Football made the contradictory demands of learning complicated skills in a team setting while also being physically aggressive. Coaches and other supporters of football called it a "scientific" game, meaning it had complicated rules. Leaders of several southern colleges, especially religious schools such as Trinity College and Wake Forest in North Carolina, banned the game briefly in the 1890s, fearing both for the lives of the players and for the image of college men blocking and tackling one another before excited and often drunken fans. At African American colleges, football and basketball showed enthusiasm about uplift through learning the rules and overcoming obstacles. At both whites' and blacks' colleges, women's sports developed in ways that, educators hoped, would not tax their bodies. For example, a form of basketball developed in the 1890s at Sophie Newcomb College in New Orleans tried to eliminate both running and physical contact.

To people in more urbanized and heavily populated parts of the country, the South seemed to represent a kind of cultural authenticity rooted in the past that they feared they were losing. Thus, many of the first musical recordings from the South featured apparently exotic folk, such as African Americans in the Deep South or Cajuns in Louisiana; sometimes the archetypal Americans such as Texas cowboys or Appalachian mountain musicians. Leaders of southern life often tried to capitalize on the various images of their region's musical life. Around the beginning of the twentieth century, as historian Gavin Campbell has shown, Atlanta, the self-professed city of the New South, stressed that it was the home of an array of musical opportunities. The city and its elites offered opera to appeal to an urban elite hoping to prove their sophistication, sponsored old-time fiddling conventions to celebrate the apparent purity of the local Appalachian culture, and sponsored spirituals to show their support for the notions of dignity and uplift associated with Victorian revisions of African American religious music.

To people in much of the country, parts of the South also offered particularly attractive images of nature. The region's climate and beauty, most notably on the beaches and in the Appalachian and Ozark Mountains, helped stimulate a tourist industry that had long been only a minor importance. A bit less famous was the lure of the South as hunting land for wealthy sportsmen and, by the 1920s, a home for golfers, especially in Florida, Georgia, and the Carolinas. The twentieth-century South thus became a tourist destination, as first wealthy people and then middle-class car owners hurried into and through the region seeking rest, warmth, game, and physical beauty.

Motion pictures came into southern towns and cities in the 1890s and especially the early 1900s in traveling shows, and, by 1910, motion picture theaters had become common. In part because motion pictures early developed reputations for morally dubious entertainment, southern movie houses repeatedly pursued respectability for whites in towns through efforts to improve safety, to ban alcohol, and to segregate black customers in balconies. Movies brought countless stories, images, and experiences to the South, but it would be a mistake to see them as always bringing the outside world into the region. Hollywood films often celebrated southerners' self-images. One of the first extremely popular films was *Birth of a Nation*, the 1915 movie Kentuckian D. W. Griffith based on Thomas Dixon's popular novel *The Clansman*. Griffith's film combined a commonplace North-South romance with action scenes from the Civil War and Reconstruction periods, portraying carpetbaggers who stole the money of land-owning southerners and encouraged interracial sex. In the climactic action scene, the Ku Klux Klan rides in to restore legitimate authority over both southern households and southern governments. While the NAACP protested the film for its racism and celebration of violence, Virginia-born president Woodrow Wilson called it "history written with lightning." In 1939, Hollywood did it again with *Gone With the Wind*, another hugely popular and only slightly more complicated depiction of the Civil War–era South. While many other films challenged these heroic images of white southerners and their faithful slaves and servants, it is important that these two were by far the most popular films about the South.

The Sunbelt South

An increasingly prosperous, comfortable South has helped turn the region into a center for American recreation. Air conditioning and improved travel have made the region more available and attractive; racial desegregation has made the region less morally offensive; some old religious objections to recreation have receded, although evangelical Protestants still condemn the old sin of drinking alcohol and newer sins available through television and the Internet.

Southern interaction with the tourists has been complicated by desires for both cultural authenticity and economic development. Often southerners choose to play a part tourists want to see—Cherokee dancer, mountaintop Li'l Abner and Daisy Mae, creative and dignified blues musician, isolated folk artist, or New Orleans bacchanalian. Sometimes southerners are happy to play those roles; sometimes they feel they have to play them to overcome poverty. The growth of theme parks—Opryland in Nashville; Dollywood in Pigeon Forge, Tennessee; Louis Armstrong Park in New Orleans; music districts in Branson, Missouri; Beale Street in Memphis; and Bourbon Street in New Orleans—offers depictions of certain forms of southern life. At their best, they make food, material life, and music available to interested people. At their worst, they select a handful of cultural features, remove them from their social and economic situations, and turn tourism into a kind of pleasant drama about the oddities of local life. As the appeal of beaches and mountains bring more people into the region, many tourist attractions, such as Walt Disney World in Florida, offer recreations with no ties to specifically southern images.

People in the South have tended to claim four forms of recreation as helping to identify them as southerners. All have some roots in southern history, and few characters seem more crucial to southern life: the lonely deer hunter, the respected football coach, the man-of-the-people stock car driver, and the popular musician. But there are logical or historical problems in drawing a direct line from the southern past to contemporary forms of hunting, college football, stock car racing, or music, and it is important to note the modern sides of each.

While leisure—not sports—seemed central to southern identity as late as the 1930s and 1940s, sports have moved far beyond small college populations to take on special significance in the modern South. College attendance in the South has grown at a higher rate in the region than in most of the country, and with that growth has come an extraordinary increase in the levels of interest, sizes of stadiums, and money spent on football. Tens of thousands of people identify with their old college and its teams as part of their identity and their way to connect to memories of their earlier days. Coaches, players, and a nearly ubiquitous sports press keep the sport and its various meanings in the public eye. On one hand, people who love football consistently tout football as an intricate sport that requires extraordinary intelligence and study. On the other hand, it is also a clearly physical game, based on physical force and violence. And in the South, dramas about racially inclusive sports have been extremely popular as a way to show a kind of acceptance of desegregation since the 1970s. In a crucial change since the earlier twentieth century, when southern teams only occasionally beat teams from outside the region, in the early 2000s, teams, especially in Florida, expect to win national championships.

Sports and recreation were not often central to the civil rights movement, but Jackie Robinson and several boxers were revered heroes in African American com- munities. Certain types of desegregation have been essential to the growth of the culture of the modern South, with biracial college and professional teams with wildly celebrated regional heroes, such as Hank Aaron, playing in Atlanta, the so-called "city too busy to hate." Having sports teams in professional major leagues has become a sign that Charlotte, Nashville, and Jacksonville have the wealth and people and public-funded facilities to host national events and appear on television without embarrassing their residents. The mania of college or pro sports teams when they succeed certainly belies any mystique of the South as a place of calm and leisure.

The southern sport that attracts the largest and fastest-growing attendance is stock car racing. The story is commonplace of how the first racers were Appalachian moonshiners who turned their skills into a semi-legitimate spectator sport. Ultimately more important are the ways NASCAR (National Association of Stock Car Auto Racing) has been a Sun Belt success story, dramatizing the rise of once-poor rural families and attracting both the money that comes through corporate sponsorship and enormous media attention. The first organized racing in the South was in Florida, and the first race sponsored by NASCAR took place in Charlotte, North Carolina, in 1949. These were scenes of the modern South, defined by change, speed and mobility.

Hunting, meanwhile, continues to be a significant recreation, a way to share experiences between generations, a way to escape town and city life, and for some still a way to supplement family food supplies. Many male southerners see the woods as the part of their region that is untouched by economic and technological change. But hunting has changed so dramatically in the twentieth and twenty-first centuries that it has started to resemble other modern sports. Rules are intricate, with enforcement officials who are significant even if they are not as omnipresent as on football fields or basketball courts. A great deal of hunting in the early 2000s takes place at precise times in clearly defined places, like other modern sports, rather than on common land and with a spirit of leisure that characterized many hunts before the twentieth century. And access to hunt clubs and hunting technology makes hunting a sport reserved more than ever for wealthier people.

Rock and roll, soul, gospel, and country music all have significant southern roots, and Nashville, particularly, thrives on its country industry. Sometimes music dramatizes racial integration; sometimes it does not. But all of these forms of music have outgrown their local connections and audiences to become national and international enterprises. Many musicians have to become "southern" in some senses to appeal to international audiences seeking local appeal.

In many ways, the rise of the Sun Belt South reflects the growing regional self-consciousness that comes from being part of a global culture. The old notion that the South is either lazy or leisurely has given way to a frenzied pursuit of numerous recreations, but some of those seem, to the people who pursue them, more distinctively southern than ever.

See also: African American Leisure Lifestyles; Baseball, Amateur; Basketball; Church Socials; Colonial-Era Leisure and Recreation; Football; Football, Collegiate; Hunting; Plantation Entertaining; Slave Singing/Music Making; Stock Car Racing; Western Leisure Lifestyles

BIBLIOGRAPHY

Ayers, Edward L. *The Promise of the New South: Life After Reconstruction.* New York: Oxford University Press, 1992.

Campbell, Gavin James. *Music and the Making of a New South.* Chapel Hill: University of North Carolina Press, 2004.

Daniel, Pete. *Lost Revolutions: The South in the 1950s.* Chapel Hill: University of North Carolina Press, 2000.

Douglass, Frederick. *Narrative of the Life of Frederick Douglass, An American Slave.* New York: Penguin Classics, 1986.

Genovese, Eugene D. *Roll, Jordan, Roll: The World the Slaves Made.* New York: Pantheon Books, 1972.

Grundy, Pamela. *Learning to Win: Sports, Education, and Social Change in Twentieth-Century North Carolina.* Chapel Hill: University of North Carolina Press, 2001.

Isaac, Rhys. *The Transformation of Virginia, 1740–1790.* Chapel Hill: University of North Carolina Press, 1982.

Kirby, Jack Temple. *Media-Made Dixie: The South in the American Imagination.* Athens: University of Georgia Press, 1986.

Malone, Bill C. *Don't Get Above Your Raisin': Country Music and the Southern Working Class.* Urbana: University of Illinois Press, 2002.

Miller, Patrick B., ed. *The Sporting World of the Modern South.* Urbana: University of Illinois Press, 2002.

Ownby, Ted. *Subduing Satan: Religion, Recreation, and Manhood in the Rural South, 1865–1920.* Chapel Hill: University of North Carolina Press, 1990.

Palmer, Robert. *Deep Blues.* New York: Penguin Books, 1982.

Starnes, Richard, ed. *Southern Journeys: Tourism, History, and Culture in the Modern South.* Tuscaloosa: University of Alabama Press, 2003.

Taylor, William R. *Cavalier and Yankee: The Old South and the American National Character.* Garden City, N.Y.: Anchor Books, 1961.

Twelve Southerners. *I'll Take My Stand: The South and the Agrarian Tradition.* Baton Rouge: Louisiana State University Press, 1978.

Waller, Gregory A. *Main Street Amusements: Movies and Commercial Entertainment in a Southern City, 1896–1930.* Washington, D.C.: Smithsonian Institution Press, 1995.

Ward, Brian. *Just My Soul Responding: Rhythm and Blues, Black Consciousness, and Race Relations.* Berkeley: University of California Press, 1998.

Ted Ownby

SPAS

See *Summer Resorts*

SPELUNKING

See *Caving*

SPORTING HALLS OF FAME

Museums have long been recognized as an effective way of preserving cultural heritage, and also as one of the most popular and traditional of tourist attractions. They can be found in every country and exhibit the range of human experience from A (art, architecture, automobiles, etc.), to Z (Zen, zoology). Given the status of sport as an international social phenomenon, it is not surprising to find sport featured prominently in many of these institutions. In fact, there has been a tremendous increase worldwide in the number of museums specializing in sport in recent years, a development in which the United States has played the most significant part.

Terminology

The term "halls of fame" has been attached, although not exclusively, to most institutions specializing in the preservation and display of sporting heritage, and the term "sports hall of fame" is now commonly used. These "halls" are rightly regarded as a type of museum; indeed, many have deliberately added the phrase "and museum" to their title to more accurately describe their function, as well as in many cases to qualify for cultural grants awarded to museums. However, a clarification and distinction should be made between the two terms. The ultimate raison d'être for a sports hall of fame is the celebration of sporting prowess. The word "fame" is all-important since it honors only those accepted as having been famous enough to qualify. The procedures and rules of eligibility for attaining such recognition are almost as varied as the institutions themselves, but ultimately only elite athletes of exceptional and proven ability are admitted.

A museum as such exists to preserve heritage. Its collection may contain artifacts, documents, and relics pertaining to ordinary mortals, as well as the famous (or even the infamous). A "sports museum," therefore, will display a sporting exhibit simply because of its intrinsic historical interest. Old golf clubs, bicycles, and footballs have their place regardless of pedigree—who wielded them, rode them, or kicked them. Such objects would find their way into a sports hall of fame only if acknowledged sports heroes or heroines had used them. The myriad of depositories of sporting memorabilia includes institutions that are exclusively sports halls of fame, institutions that are sports museums alone, and others that perform both functions in the same building. Together, all represent a collection of tourist attractions that reflect the unique place of sport in history.

Origins

The preservation of sports history for public display may be traced back to ancient times, for since sport began, there have been donors, collectors, and viewers of artifacts related to it. Sport has been described in literature and depicted in art forms, such as paintings, pottery, and sculpture, for centuries, providing continuous and vivid evidence for posterity. It may be argued, in fact, that there were parallels to modern sports halls of fame and museums in the ancient world. Victors at the great Greek Games were allowed to erect statues of themselves at the scene of their triumph, and normally another at their home city. It is clear from Pausanias's Book VI that at Olympia alone these statues, with their inscribed bases, constituted a fairly complete history of the Games for passersby. The same was true at Corinth, Delphi, and Nemea, and the civic centers of other cities that honored their athletic heroes in similar fashion. Visitors customarily dedicated small bronze statuettes of themselves in the temples as offerings to the gods who had brought them renown; sometimes even the athletes' discuses, halteres, or strigils were dedicated in this fashion.

Beginnings of the Modern Concept

In the modern world, where sports museums, per se, are located in many countries, reflecting sport's international history and status, the United States has been both inno-

vator and leader in the "hall of fame" concept. This respect underlines the individualism inherent in American culture, and the conspicuous desire to reward success and acknowledge personal attainment of "the American dream." The term probably originated in 1901, by supreme example, when the Hall of Fame for Great Americans was instituted. Thereafter, the term became customary in American life as it was applied to other institutions, such as the National Hall of Fame for Famous American Indians in Oklahoma, a Country Music Hall of Fame in Nashville, and a Circus Hall of Fame in Florida, among many others.

There is no question, however, but that sports halls of fame outnumber all other kinds combined. The main reason for this, apart from the popularity of sport itself, is the large number of sports, each of which may have one or more institutions devoted to it—not just in the United States, but worldwide. Writing in 1971, Jerry Kirshenbaum pointed out that among the ninety-five inductees to the Hall of Fame for Great Americans were presidents and literary figures, but no athletes, and stated, "It is an oversight for which the sports world has compensated with a vengeance, starting with that glorious June day in 1939 when the Baseball Hall of Fame was dedicated on Cooperstown maple lined Main Street" (p. 65).

Actually, a ski hall of fame had been proposed earlier, in 1928, but no building materialized until the National Ski Hall of Fame at Ishpeming, Michigan, opened in 1954. The Helms Athletic Foundation was formed in Los Angeles, California, in 1936, where the Olympic display in Helms Hall attracted thousands of visitors over the years. While these pioneering efforts deserve acknowledgment, the National Baseball Hall of Fame and Museum, as the first such home for "the grand American game," will always occupy a special place.

Growth and Diversity

A significant expansion of sports halls of fame and museums occurred in the 1950s and 1960s, illustrated by the appearance of such institutions as the Indianapolis Motor Speedway Museum (1956), the San Diego Hall of Champions (1961), the Professional Football Hall of Fame in Canton, Ohio (1963), and the Amateur Trapshooting Hall of Fame and Museum in Vandalia, Ohio (1969), among others. The titles of these four examples alone give a small indication of the diversity involved, as sports halls of fame exist for amateurs and professionals (male and female); for minor as well as major sports; to honor athletes, coaches, and administrators ("builders"), regionally by city or state, or nationally; or by ethnic background. Most colleges and universities have their own

Pro Football Hall of Fame. Located in Canton, Ohio, the Pro Football Hall of Fame is a nonprofit museum established on 7 September 1963 by the induction of 17 inaugural members, which had grown to 221 as of 2004. Visited by thousands every year it chronicles the complete history of the game since professional play began in 1892. The site has expanded to nearly 83,000 square feet from its original size of 19,000. © *Layne Kennedy/Corbis*

such institutions, also. Facilities reflect this diversity, as they range from miniature, perhaps some pictures on an office wall, to the magnificent, in a building costing millions of dollars. Funding also varies, coming from many sources, mainly sports organizations, benefactors and sponsors, civic and government grants, and visitors' fees.

Churches of Modern Sport

If there is a common factor within the American sports halls of fame milieu, Jerry Kirshenbaum probably captured it best after having visited most of them in a journey of 10,000 miles. This he described as "an irreverent pilgrimage" in the subtitle of his satirical account, the second paragraph of which begins, "To illuminate the way to some of these holy places. . ." Like all true satire, his words contain the element of truth, beyond the fact that some sports halls of fame have churchlike spires and/or stained-glass windows, or that they are often used for prayer meetings by the Fellowship of Christian Athletes, and similar groups. Athletes become "immortal" when

elected to these "shrines," where "devoted followers" gaze at their "revered figures" and read inscriptions "graven in marble," before departing "very moved" from the many "hushed rooms, filled with nostalgia" (Kirshenbaum). This may be regarded as the jargon of the churches of modern sport, yet another demonstrable act of faith by the masses of sports fans. If the statement is correct that "tourism is the secular counterpart, and the modern successor in the western world, of the religious pilgrimage" (Macdonald and Alsford, p. 42), then visitors to sports halls of fame qualify as pilgrims of sorts.

The IASMHF and Other Landmarks

Americans led in the formation of the International Association of Sports Museums and Hall of Fame, in 1971, with approximately three-quarters of its member institutions located in the United States. Three years later, two sport historians, Guy Lewis and Gerald Redmond, produced *Sporting Heritage: A Guide to Halls of Fame, Special Collections and Museums in the United States and Canada,*

298

the first such book of its type, giving details of fifty institutions. Another significant development was the production of a video, in 1990, by the IASMHF, entitled "Together in Excellence," stating that sports halls of fame spanned the globe, and referring to the association's 110 member institutions. Four years later, the IASMHF sanctioned *A Guide to Sports Museums, Shrines and Libraries*, published by ReView Publications, with details of 123 institutions worldwide. There are now more than 140 member institutions in the IASMHF, and the association's 2003 annual conference was held in October in Indianapolis, Indiana, cohosted by the NCAA Hall of Champions and the National Art Museum of Sport.

See also: Professionalization of Sport, Sporting Memorabilia, Tourism

BIBLIOGRAPHY

A Guide to Sports Museums, Shrines, and Libraries. Irvine, Calif.: ReView Publications, 1994.

Alexander, E. P. *Museums in Motion: An Introduction to the History and Functions of Museums.* Nashville, Tenn.: American Association for State and Local History, 1979.

Gardiner, E. Norman. *Athletics of the Ancient World.* Oxford: Clarendon Press, 1930.

Harris, H. A. *Greek Athletes and Athletics.* London: Hutchinson and Company, 1964.

Hudson, K., and A. Nicholls, eds. *The Directory of World Museums.* London: Macmillan, 1975.

Kirshenbaum, Jerry. "Bats and Busts, Size 15 Sneakers, and a Dead Bird." *Sports Illustrated* (28 June 1971): 62–74.

Lewis, Guy M., and Gerald Redmond. *Sporting Heritage: A Guide to Halls of Fame, Special Collections, and Museums in the United States and Canada.* South Brunswick, N.J.: A. S. Barnes, 1974.

MacDonald, G. F., and S. Alsford. *A Museum for the Global Village.* Hull, Quebec: Canadian Museum of Civilisation, 1989.

Museums of the World. New York: R. R. Bowker Company, 1973.

Redmond, Gerald. "A Plethora of Shrines: Sport in the Museum and Hall of Fame." *Quest* (January 1973): 41–48.

Gerald Redmond

SPORTING MEMORABILIA

Collecting sporting memorabilia is a popular pastime that provides great pleasure for many people. There is the fun of searching for and finding a new artifact, the pride of possession associated with owning something unique, a genuine admiration for the beauty and craftsmanship of an item, a vicarious connection with a favorite athlete or sports team, a real desire to have ties with the past, and the related feelings of nostalgia for sport in another time and place; or more pragmatically, the personal satisfaction of knowing that what one has acquired is a good financial investment. But pleasure aside, collecting sporting memorabilia is a sporting pastime that is old, social, diverse, and consequential.

History

Collecting sport memorabilia is likely as old as sport itself. However, acquiring sporting memorabilia for personal pleasure was initiated in earnest by sporting gentlemen of Victorian and Edwardian England. The majority of our modern sports were formally developed in England during the nineteenth century, and it was during the Victorian and Edwardian periods when now-famous artists produced what have become classic sporting drawings, paintings, prints, and watercolors; when many of the first sporting books were written, especially those about boxing, field sports, fishing, golf, and horse racing; and when new sporting technology such as cricket bats, golf clubs, fishing rods and reels, tennis racquets, sporting firearms, and new types of sportswear were introduced.

In the world of buying and selling collectibles, it is recognized that what is old is not necessarily an antique; that what is an antique is not necessarily valuable; and that a modern collectible may be worth more than an antique. Among collectors and as legally defined by the U.S. government, an "antique" is any object at least 100 years old. Accordingly, given the historical development of modern sport, most antique sporting memorabilia are from the nineteenth century. To be valuable, an antique collectible—in addition to being at least 100 years old—must be unique, of limited quantity, in mint condition, and of fine quality and craftsmanship.

Social Aspects

The twenty-third annual National Sports Collectors Convention held in Rosemont, Illinois, in August 2002 had 900 dealer booths and attracted 40,000 collectors and perfectly illustrates the social nature of collecting sporting memorabilia. Individuals interested in sporting collections are attracted to art galleries, museums, and sporting halls of fame. Those especially keen on acquiring sporting artifacts are drawn to auctions, estate sales, flea

An Early Tobacco Card. This early baseball card was distributed with packs of cigarettes, which was the most common means of distribution for the cards in the early 1900s. This card features Denton True Young (1867–1955), who earned his famous nickname "Cy" because of his cyclone-like fastball. The right-handed pitcher won 511 games during his 22-year career, a record that still stands. He played his last game in 1911 (the year this card was issued) with the Atlanta Braves. *Courtesy of the Library of Congress*

markets, and major sporting events where memorabilia are sold. There are collector clubs for one and all, whether collectors of duck decoys or sport stamps. In addition, one can actively interact with fellow sport collectors via the Internet, or vicariously identify with fellow sport collectors while watching television shows like the *Antiques Roadshow* (both American and British versions), *Attic Finds*, and *The Incurable Collector*.

Diverse Collections

There is great diversity in specialization among sporting collectors. For example, some collect only one kind of sporting object, others collect a variety of items related to

a single sport, still others collect only memorabilia related to a specific sports team, while yet others collect only memorabilia related to a particular athlete. The following broad categories of sporting memorabilia give an indication of the marked diversity of objects sought by sporting collectors:

1. Sports awards. For example: cups, medals, plaques, plates, ribbons, and trophies.

2. Sporting art and literature. For example: books, catalogs, etchings, paintings, prints, periodicals, photographs, and sculptures; plus related artistic sporting artifacts such as porcelain and silver stirrup cups, duck and fish decoys, and taxidermy displays of a sporting nature.

3. Sporting equipment and technology. For example: bats, clubs, racquets, rods, reels, fishing flies and lures, hunting knives, and sporting firearms; as well as specialized sportswear such as cycling costumes, motoring caps and helmets, sports uniforms, and athletic shoes.

4. Sport stamps. For example: federal and state duck stamp prints, and sporting postage stamps from countries around the world. In terms of the latter, an individual can specialize by country, period, sport, or sporting event (like the Olympic Games).

5. Sporting cards. For example: Victorian playing cards with sporting themes, Edwardian sporting cigarette cards, and contemporary sports cards for American professional basketball, baseball, football, and ice hockey players.

One might also add a category for "worst sports memorabilia." For example, during 2002, the University of Georgia auctioned off 125 old wooden football lockers for $87,730; a Wisconsin man paid $10,000 for a wad of chewing gum discarded by Arizona Diamondbacks professional baseball player Luis Gonzalez; another individual bid $23,600 on eBay for three bone chips removed from the elbow of Seattle Mariners professional baseball pitcher Jeff Nelson. However, these worst-case scenarios shouldn't lessen the consequential nature of sport collecting.

Consequential Collecting

The consequential nature of collecting sporting memorabilia is reflected in the ever growing number of sport collectors across all age, ethnic, and gender groups; the exponential growth of sporting halls of fame; the development of new sporting archives and sporting art galleries; and the enormous prices paid for sporting memorabilia.

Examples of the economic value of sporting memorabilia are given in two articles in the 9 December 2002 issue of *Forbes* magazine. One article notes that Marshall Fogel, a Denver attorney, possesses a sporting collection worth $12 million, including Ty Cobb's passport, costing $16,000, and a baseball signed by Lou Gehrig, costing $40,000. Another article reports that Christie's auction house produced a 150-page catalog of Gary Player's collection of personal golf memorabilia, which was to be auctioned off through a private sale that mandated a minimum bid of $5 million and required that the buyer must buy the entire collection and maintain it intact.

Perhaps the most popular sports collectibles in America are baseball cards. A card from Mickey Mantle's rookie season with the New York Yankees that sold for $1,250 in 1984 was worth $6,000 in 1988. A Ted Williams card made in 1954 sold at a Mastronet sports card and memorabilia auction in January 2003 for $95,338. And the most famous card of all, that of Pittsburgh Pirates star Honus Wagner, was once owned by former hockey superstar Wayne Gretzky and last sold for $1.2 million.

See also: Collecting; Coin Collecting, Sporting Halls of Fame, Stamp Collecting

BIBLIOGRAPHY

Farnham, Alan. "Going Private." *Forbes* (9 December 2002): 222–226.

Hall, Dorothea, ed. *Collecting for Pleasure: Sporting Pastimes.* London: Bracken Books, 1992.

Liu, Allan J. *The American Sporting Collector's Handbook.* New York: Winchester Press, 1976.

Slater, J. Herbert. *Illustrated Sporting Books: A Descriptive Survey of a Collection of English Illustrated Works of a Sporting and Racy Character, with an Appendix of Prints Relating to Sports of the Field.* London: L. Upcott Gill, 1899.

Sullivan, Missy. "Revenge of the Pipsqueaks." *Forbes* (9 December 2002): 228.

Watson, J. N. P., ed. *Collecting Sporting Art.* London: Sportsmen Press, 1988.

John W. Loy

SPORTS

SPORTS CAR RACING

Sports car racing has long been a popular sport in the United States. Although never gaining the fame of NASCAR racing or even open wheel racing in America, sports car racing has filled a niche in the American auto racing scene for the past century. Sports car drivers, both North American and international, are among the best-known drivers in the racing world. Drivers such as Mario Andretti, Dan Gurney, and Bruce McLaren, are included in that group. Although most are not household names (Andretti being the exception), they are all synonymous with hard driving and have thrilled millions of American racing fans over the years.

What Is a Sports Car?

Sport cars are typically cars made up of two seats, often with a closed cockpit and bodywork that covers the wheels. These cars are designed for maximum speed not only on straightaways, but also through a series of corners and S-curves (two turns in a row that together form the shape of a letter S). Sports cars differ from the more popular stock cars in that stock cars are more like the typical American-built sedans and coupes that are seen on the road every day. Sports cars are often exotic looking, usually low-slung with a rounded body style, and they are frequently built outside of North America. Ferrari, Porsche, Lotus, and Jaguar are the best-known sports car automakers and are popular throughout the world. The cars have traditionally featured lightweight, aerodynamically tuned, and smooth-cornered bodies that surround the driver in a cocoon of protective roll bars. In the early years, the engine was placed in the front of the car, but by 2004, most sports cars were either mid-engine or rear-engine models. The new Daytona Prototype that was introduced to the Rolex Sports Car Series featured state-of-the-art sports car design, with a specially built, closed cockpit and, typically, a Ford, Chevrolet, Toyota, Maserati, or BMW engine.

Sports Car Racetracks Sports car races are often run on permanent road courses (tracks that include straightaways and both left-and right-hand turns), on modified oval tracks that feature temporary corners and curves, and on oval tracks. Portland International Raceway (Portland, Oregon) and Watkins Glen, located in the Finger Lakes region of upstate New York, are two examples of permanent road courses. There are many popular oval racetracks in the United States, including Daytona International Speedway (Daytona Beach, Florida) and the California Speedway (Fontana, California). Daytona International Speedway also adds a road course to its permanent oval track; the road course includes numerous left- and right-hand turns.

The History of Sports Car Racing

Early sports car racing traces its roots to Europe in the late nineteenth century. In essence, as soon as the automobiles were invented, people started racing them. Races were run from Paris to outlying towns in open wheeled cars at speeds that are a fraction of the speeds found in modern racing. Sports car racing was brought to America in 1904 with the introduction of the Vanderbilt Cup. Run on Long Island, New York, the Vanderbilt Cup was the leading international auto race of its time, and it sparked competition between U.S. and European auto manufacturers.

After World War II, sports car racing gained in popularity in the United States, as American fans had more free time at their disposal, with the U.S. work week reaching an all-time low of forty hours per week. Additionally, about that same time, the automobile began to be viewed as a nonessential item, one that could be used for leisure instead of just for work. Thus, the privately owned car allowed American families to travel together in a timely manner to participate in a leisure activity, in this case, viewing a sports car race. That new, postwar development is considered to be one of the major influences in the change of American leisure patterns.

Other external forces converged to create the opportunity for expanded sports car racing in the decades following World War II. These included the introduction of television to the mass market, an increase in leisure travel, increased marketing of auto racing events, and an increase in discretionary income. Sports car racing as a spectator sport was a relatively inexpensive, family oriented, leisure activity. Mom and dad could pile the kids into the car, drive to a local racetrack, have a picnic lunch, and enjoy a quality family experience for relatively low cost. As spectatorship grew, so did the potential for marketing to that family demographic, both on the racetrack and on television.

Sponsoring Organizations

The Sports Club Car of America (SCCA) is perhaps the most important—and one of the earliest—sanctioning body for sports car racing in the United States. The SCCA was founded in 1944 under the leadership of president Theodore F. Robertson. The idea of professional sports car racing was considered in the late 1950s, but the SCCA didn't sponsor its first professional race until 1963, when it held the United States Road Racing Championship at Daytona International Speedway. When John Bishop took over as SCCA president, he created the very popular and influential Can-Am and Trans-Am racing series.

The first Trans-Am race was held in March 1966 at Sebring, Florida, while the Can-Am (Canadian-American) series debuted in September 1966 at Mon Tremblant-St. Jovite, Canada. The Can-Am series became one of the more popular road course sports car series, and it held regular races from the mid 1960s until the mid 1980s, when the series was discontinued (there was a two-year hiatus from 1975 until 1977 due to the international energy crisis). The Can-Am series was run on road courses throughout Canada and the United States. Can-Am cars were open cockpit, closed body cars with two seats and two doors. Some of the greatest names in racing at that time—including Bruce McLaren, participated in the Can-Am series.

Amateur Racing In addition to its professional racing series, the SCCA also launched amateur club racing, which it continues to organize and promote. As of 2004, more than 8,000 licensed amateurs competed in approximately 300 road racing events annually. Drivers competed in twenty-four different vehicle classes, ranging from Showroom Stock—late model street cars with only minor modifications, primarily to improve safety—to pure racing vehicles, such as single-seat, open wheel formula cars and composite bodied road racing cars that ran in the Sports Racer Category. Major club racing events included the June Sprints, held at Road America in Wisconsin, the Rose Cup, held at Portland International Speedway in Oregon, and the Double National, held at Pocono Raceway in Pennsylvania. The championship event for club racers in 2004 was known as the SCCA Valvoline Runoffs, That event, held annually in late September at Mid-Ohio Sports Car Course, attracted some 600 drivers competing in the twenty-four classes.

Beyond the SCCA In 2004, there were at least two other groups sponsoring popular road racing series—the Grand American Road Racing Association and the American Le Mans Series. Both organizations held several races annually. The Grand American Road Racing Association races were endurance races, with races that lasted twelve to twenty-four hours. Teams of two to three drivers took turns driving during a race, which increased the excitement for fans by providing more drivers and teams to support.

American Le Mans Series (ALMS) events were also endurance races, with some races lasting 1000 miles. The series features four classes of cars, all of which are on the track together competing in the same race. Legions of fans set up campers and tents in the infields and around the courses at ALMS races to watch their teams' cars as day turns to dusk and finally darkness falls. At night, the sports cars seem to take on an entirely new persona as sparks fly from the undersides of the cars and hot brake rotors glow in the dark.

The Future of Sports Car Racing

Two things guarantee that there will be regular changes to sports car racing. First, the technology used in the sports cars and developed by the organizing bodies and teams continues to evolve as market forces change. Technology is always evolving, and teams are constantly seeking any technological edge to make their sports car go faster and hug the turns more tightly. However, because of safety concerns, those same teams are forced to reduce the speed that their race cars carry down the straightaways and into the curves of American sports car racetracks. Thus, since maximum safe speeds may have been reached, teams may turn to using technology to improve gas mileage, meaning fewer stops for gas and thus better overall race times. Second, the organizations that hold the races continue to evolve as well. The companies that sponsor professional race cars must pay attention to market forces, which means they can pressure the sponsoring organizations and influence where and when sports car races are held. The globalization of major corporations has been felt as much in the world of sports car racing as in any leisure business.

See also: Auto Racing, Automobiles and Leisure, Drag Racing, Hot Rodding, Open Wheel Racing, Stock Car Racing

BIBLIOGRAPHY

Kelly, J. R. and V. J. Freysinger. *21st Century Leisure: Current Issues.* Boston: Allyn and Bacon Boston, 2000.

Fuller, M. J. *A Brief History of Sports Car Racing.* Available from http://www.mulsannescorner.com/history.htm.

Bamsey, I. *The Anatomy and Development of the Sports Prototype Racing Car.* Osceola, Wis: Motorbooks International, 1991.

Sports Car Club of America, Inc. "What Is the SCCA?" Available from http://www.scca.org/whatis.html.

Robert Burns

SPRING BREAKS

A contemporary ritual with reminiscences in classic celebrations of the rites of spring, spring break offers North American students the self-declared right to a one-week vacation, typically in warm and sunny locales. With ramifications in the areas of tourism, law enforcement, and social problems, spring break is the annual media-enhanced migration of mostly college students to the sun-and-fun hot spots. In fact, like migrating birds, students uniformly flock to the same places each year. Panama City, Florida; South Padre Island, Texas; Myrtle Beach, South Carolina; and Cancun, Mexico, have become, at least during the month of March, synonymous with a free-spirited mass frolic, chiefly expressed through tiny bikinis, sweaty muscles, and beer.

Throughout its history, spring break has developed under the same influences as other forms of contemporary tourism—the commercialization of leisure, an entitlement-to-play attitude emerging from industrialization, rising discretionary income, and technological advances. Most singularly, perhaps, has been the influence of a "youth" social class established and recognized in the 1940s. As the American sociologist Talcott Parsons put it in his 1962 *Essays in Sociological Theory*, the term "youth culture" described a juvenile fixation on consumption and a hedonistic denial of responsibility, an inversion of the adult roles of routinized work and family duties. Thus, the youth culture has been both a rebellion against received culture and authority from parents, and an affirmation of the consumerist values of parents. All this is reflected in the contemporary expression of spring break.

Student folklore, on the other hand, maintains that spring break originated with the ancient Greeks. As winter would lessen its chilling grip, the thoughts of Athens's youth turned to rejuvenation and regeneration. Endorsed particularly by Socrates, so goes the story, young people were encouraged to welcome spring by venting their

Party time. College students Laura Moritz and Susie Hale dance "The Twist" during spring break in Fort Lauderdale, Florida, in 1962. © *Corbis*

ingrained urges. Later, after enduring the prohibitions of the Middle Ages, Victorian traditions, and the Great Depression, the idea of a serious party in the spring resurfaced with vigor in the 1960s era of the baby boomers. Along with this rebirth was the 1970s rise of Florida—Fort Lauderdale and Daytona Beach in particular—with its warm weather, beautiful beaches, and relatively close proximity to a large number of college students, as the spring break Mecca. By the 1980s, glorification of the overconsumption of sex, sun, and alcohol was firmly established. And in the 1990s, the introduction of super clubs, MTV broadcasts from the beach, and corporate sponsors of concerts, shows, contests, and giveaways had created a mega-industry.

For example, each year approximately 1.5 million U.S. and Canadian students participate in a spring break vacation. In 2001, over 100,000 youths traveled to Cancun over their spring break, and, according to visitor's bureau surveys, spring break lures about 115,000 people to South Padre (in spite of a moratorium on advertising itself as a spring break destination) and 175,000 to Daytona Beach annually. Perhaps the single best example of

age-cohort marketing, today's college campuses are deluged with e-mails, advertisements, and direct mailings showing photos of scantily clad women and wild partying—seducing students with "30 hours of free drinks."

Spring break is good business, translating into a significant boost for local economies—an estimated $60 million in direct expenditures in the case of South Padre, and $70 million for Daytona Beach. Yet, this mega-industry also has mega-costs. Panama City Beach must annually handle the expense of collecting and disposing 206,000 extra pounds of garbage. Traffic along State Road A1A in Daytona Beach moves at four miles per hour for weeks. As well, the American Academy of Dermatology estimates that overexposure to the sun by spring breakers results in 44,200 new cases of melanoma each year.

The most significant cost associated with the spring break ritual, however, is without a doubt injuries and deaths associated with the consumption of harmful substances. For example, "Scoop"—an Ecstasy-like and potentially lethal rave drink of choice—has made inroads into the spring break culture. However, alcohol—particularly beer—is the most widely consumed substance. Annually, college students spend about $5.5 billion on alcoholic beverages—about $446 per student. *The Journal of American College Health* in 1998 reported that during spring break the average man consumes eighteen drinks per day, and the average woman consumes ten drinks per day. To help maintain these figures, brewers target spring break locales with sponsored parties and free clothing. Indeed, one of the attractions of Mexican locations, such as Cancun, is the tolerance for underage drinking.

Spring break behavior is fenced into just this immediate time. Students feel they are in a place far from campus and home where they don't know a lot of people and, even better, won't ever have to see them again. According to a 2002 survey by the American Medical Association, a majority of parents are completely unaware of the activities of their children during spring break.

Yet, these students readily admit the drinking and revelry often get out of hand, occasionally with disastrous consequences. The resulting drunkenness, alcohol poisoning, accidents, sexual assault, and unprotected casual sex can result in fatal forms of fun. Across North American college campuses there has been a swell of programs whose goal is reducing underage and binge drinking among students. For example, the twenty-three-campus California State University has a system-wide alcohol policy focusing on education and restriction of alcohol advertisements on campus. Colleges and universities have also increasingly attempted to counterbalance spring break specific problems by promoting "alternative" spring breaks for their students. For example, some students use their spring break for community service, special courses, or back-road adventures. For example, Stanford University's Alternative Spring Break Program offers students a weeklong vacation of volunteering and learning about other communities. Students from Southern Methodist University in Texas are fanning out to cities across the country to do community service during their spring break. As well, some spring break students travel northward for the week and focus on snow skiing and snowboarding instead of sun and sand.

See also: Beaches, Hook-Ups, Raves/Raving, Teenage Leisure Trends, Vacations, Wilding

BIBLIOGRPAHY

Amada, Gerald. *Mental Health and Student Conduct Issues on the College Campus: A Reading.* Asheville, N.C.: College Administration Publications, 2001.

Aron, Cindy S. *Working at Play: A History of Vacations in the United States.* New York: Oxford University Press, 1999.

Cross, Gary. *A Social History of Leisure Since 1600.* State College, Pa.: Venture Publishing, 1990.

Russell, Ruth V. *Pastimes: The Context of Contemporary Leisure.* 2d edition. Champaign, Ill.: Sagamore, 2002.

Ruth V. Russell

SQUARE DANCING

The phrase "square dancing" refers to a group of four couples, generally four females and four males, dancing in a square-like pattern. Each couple forms one of the four walls of the square, the basic position from which all square dances begin. Dancers move from one place within the square to another, based on figures directed by the caller. The caller is the individual who sings, directs dancers, and generally decides the difficulty of the movements of the dance. In the past, dancers memorized dances as the organizers of the dance took part in the actual dancing. Now, however, most dances include impromptu calls known only to the caller until the moment the call is sung or said as part of the dance. Some of the more well-known calls include the promenade, grand right and left, allemande left, and dosado.

Square-dance calls have been placed in categories based on difficulty and include mainstream calls, plus calls, advanced calls, and challenge calls. Dancers take lessons starting with the mainstream level and may advance, if they wish, to other levels. Most square-dance clubs across the United States and around the world have dances that include mainstream and plus dances. Some clubs include advanced and challenge calls during dances, but most save these types of dances for the national convention held every year.

The exact beginning of square dancing is unknown, but it likely has its roots in European folk dances. Portions of American square dancing have been traced to dances such as the English morris, Scotch reels, Irish jigs, mazurka quadrilles, the polka, and the waltz. One of the most popular early forms of American square dancing was the Virginia reel. This dance includes lines of facing dancers with early forms of moves (calls) now used in modern square dancing. Several moves would be done as couples. Then the head couple would "reel the set," meaning they would dance all the way down the lines and lead the group to a "new" formation, with the lead couple going to the end of the lines and allowing the next couple in line the chance to show off. In the early stages of this dance, wealthy couples or guests were allowed to go first

Ready to dance. Although it does not have the pervasive presence as in its early history, square dancing—which features four couples—remains a popular recreational activity particularly among the older U.S. population. © *Bettmann/Corbis*

as a way of separating the people based on social class. Over time these dances became less about wealth and prestige and more about socializing. Western square dancing, or cowboy dances, also had some influence in modern square dancing. As the industrial era hit the United States and people moved from the farm to the city, these two influences—the European dances and cowboy dances—came together to form the beginnings of modern square dancing.

In the early 2000s, nearly every city in the United States has at least one square-dance club. Larger cities have two or more clubs, and some clubs will be organized for specific groups of people (singles or gays, for example). These clubs generally dance two nights each month on Friday or Saturday. Club dances are open to the public, but there is a charge to pay for callers, the building where they dance, and other expenses associated with the club. These clubs also sponsor classes for those interested in learning to dance or to learn another level of calls. Classes help to recruit new members and involve a new generation of dancers. Square dancers are stereotypically middle-aged and seniors, and have been dancing for many years. A new generation of square dancers is slow in coming, and threatens the existence

of what many states have made their state folk dance. 29As of 1995, twenty-two states had made square dancing the state folk dance, and several others were considering such a move. A bill introduced in the United States Congress to make square dancing the national folk dance was defeated in 1991.

Many state and regional square-dance associations began in the 1950s. State associations promote square dancing through state conventions. Square dancers from a state come together to dance and socialize for one weekend each year. Some go to dance all weekend, while others go to learn how to make their local club more successful in recruiting new members. Whatever the reason for attending, most leave having enjoyed dancing with a variety of people. Modern square dancing lends itself to socialization through the movements in the dance that allow couples to trade partners for periods of time during the dance.

Two other large gatherings of square dancers include the National Square Dance Convention, held in a different location each year, and the other is the Mid-America Square Dance Jamboree, held every October in Louisville, Kentucky. Dr. Lloyd Shaw, of Colorado Springs, Colorado, was instrumental in getting larger groups of square dancers together. The first national convention was held in Riverside, California, in 1952, with around 3,000 dancers in attendance. The national convention was held in Baltimore, Maryland, in 1999; then in Indianapolis, Indiana, in 2000; Anaheim, California, in 2001; and in St. Paul, Minnesota, in 2002. Anaheim saw the largest number of dancers (just under 20,000); St, Paul hosted the fewest (just under 8,900 dancers). The jamboree's high attendance came in 2000, with about 4,000 dancers. The jamboree's final year was 2004.

Square dancing has two major challenges to its existence in the future. One is that the population of square dancers is much older than the average population of the United States. The music at square dances is typically country western in nature, and much of the rising generation has gone to alternative styles of music. This country western type of music, overall, is less popular, making square dancing less popular as well among the younger generation. Current square dancers must find ways of promoting what they love to the next generation while keeping the activity relatively the same, so as not to create problems for the older, current square dancers. Another related challenge is that nearly all of the square dancers are Caucasian. Square-dance clubs would do well to target other populations as they seek to enroll new dancers.

The second challenge is related to travel distance and attractions. National conventions are held at various locations across the United States, drawing people from all over the world. However, only areas with popular attractions draw large numbers of square dancers. For example, the national convention held in Anaheim, California, drew many more dancers than the one in St. Paul, Minnesota. This was due, largely, to the proximity of Disneyland to the convention. This puts pressure on organizers to find locations with popular attractions, while knowing that doing so will lead would-be dancers to "skip-out" and play somewhere besides the dance floor. With the events related to the terrorist attacks in New York City and Washington, D.C., on 11 September 2001, travelers have proven to be less willing to travel long distances and have a tendency to stay closer to home. Even though some types of travel are approaching pre–11 September levels, many people are hesitant to travel by air, and traveling to a convention on the other side of the United States by automobile may be less than appealing. Moving the national convention around means that individuals may choose to attend the convention once every three or four years, instead of making the trip every year.

One significant positive note related to square dancing is an organization called Callerlab. In 1971, Bob Osgood brought together eleven callers to establish standardized calls and to provide training for square-dance callers. This nonprofit organization, formally organized in 1974, provides training, literature, and other information for current and potential callers. Clinics and schools offer hands-on opportunities to learn to call or to learn different levels of calls. Callerlab provides scholarships for their training and publications, both at the national conventions and also at other regional locations throughout the year. This provides individuals with the opportunity to learn how to call square dances, and also teaches lessons to new dancers to help clubs and square dancing overall grow.

See also: Dance Classes, Dance Halls, Social Dancing

BIBLIOGRAPHY

Callerlab: International Association of Square Dance Callers. Home page at http://www.callerlab.org.

Damon, S. Foster. *The History of Square Dancing.* Barre, Mass.: Barre Gazette, 1957.

Jensen, Clayne R., and Mary Bee Jensen. *Beginning Square Dance.* Belmont, Calif.: Wadsworth Publishing Company, 1966.

Kevin Nelson

STADIUMS

Stadiums are enclosed outdoor arenas with large seating capacities used for sports and other entertainments. The term comes from the Greek *stade,* the length of the athletic field at ancient Greek sports sites, which was approximately 202 yards. The first enclosed outdoor sports complexes in North America were racetracks, dating back to the 1730s. In 1858, spectators were charged admission for the first time to see a baseball game, an all-star match between Brooklyn and New York at Long Island's Fashion Race Course. Then in 1862, William Cammeyer built the first enclosed baseball field, the 1,500-seat Union Grounds, in Williamsburg, Brooklyn, New York. He rented the $1,200 site for free to prominent teams, and charged spectators 10 cents. Five years later, ticket prices were increased to 25 cents to improve facilities, compensate players and promoters, and discourage the presence of rowdy lower-class fans.

Baseball Parks

Late nineteenth-century ballparks were privately constructed for about $30,000, and they seated about 10,000 spectators. They were located at the outskirts of town in middle-class neighborhoods, near inexpensive mass transit (horse-drawn street cars or electric trolleys). These wooden structures were dangerous; there were twenty-five fires at ballparks in the 1890s. Teams frequently moved their locations if they found better transportation elsewhere, especially if the surrounding neighborhoods were on the decline or the fields were dilapidated. Major league tickets cost as little as 25 cents in the bleachers and 50 cents in the roofed grandstand where spectators were shielded from the elements.

The modern era of fully fireproof major league ballparks began in 1909 with the construction of Pittsburgh's million-dollar 25,000-seat Forbes Field and Philadelphia's $450,000, 23,000-seat Shibe Park for the Philadelphia Athletics. By 1915, only the Philadelphia Phillies were not playing in a fully fireproof field. The new period began because baseball's enormous popularity encouraged owners to build larger facilities, taking advantage of the available technology employing structural steel and reinforced concrete, cheaper material and labor costs, and new building codes. Furthermore, competition from rival entertainments encouraged owners to provide customers with comfortable and beautiful classically designed facilities. These edifices were known as "fields," "grounds," and "parks," terms that reflected the rustic atmosphere base-

Wrigley Field. The crowd enjoys a baseball game between the Chicago Cubs and Colorado Rockies at historic Wrigley Field. Originally known as Weeghman Park, the park was built in 1914. © *Corbis*

ball tried to promote with green fields and green-painted outfield walls.

In 1923, major league baseball took a big jump forward with the construction of Yankee Stadium in the Bronx. Yankee Stadium was the first ballpark to be known as a stadium, a term first used in the United States for the 12,000-seat athletic field at the 1901 Buffalo Pan American Exhibition. The term represented a more urbane, sophisticated technology, and modern perspective that boldly proclaimed the awesome character of the triple-deck park (seating 63,000) as well as its massive playing size (460 feet to center field).

College Stadiums

Most large outdoor facilities were actually built for college football. In the late nineteenth century, elite college teams often played their big Thanksgiving Day games in New York at a major league site like Manhattan Field. Then in 1903, Harvard's 30,000-seat Soldier Field (also referred to as Harvard Stadium) was built on the campus as a war memorial, designed in a horseshoe shape. In 1914, the 70,000-seat Yale Bowl was built, employing an

elliptical shape, with a U-shaped section at both ends. In the 1920s, state universities built large football fields where spectators could root for their state's team and take pride in their state's progressive character. By 1930, seven college fields had over 70,000 seats, including the University of Michigan's, built in 1927 with a seating capacity of 79,000. By 1956, the capacity had been increased to 101,000; it has since grown to 107,501.

Public Stadiums

These trends encouraged municipalities to construct public sports stadiums to promote amateur athletics and publicize their cities. In 1914, San Diego built a $150,000, 30,000-seat concrete, oval facility, paid for by a bond issue funded by revenues from taxes and admission fees. Next were Pasadena's $325,000, 52,000-seat Rose Bowl, built in 1922 as a joint project with the Tournament of Roses Association; the Los Angeles Coliseum in 1923; Chicago's Soldier Field and Baltimore's $500,000, 80,000-seat Memorial Stadium in 1924; and Philadelphia's Municipal Stadium in 1926. The Coliseum was built by a powerful political elite comprised of white, Anglo-Saxon,

Protestant bankers, realtors, and publishers operating behind the scenes to promote the reputation and wealth of Los Angeles by securing the 1932 Olympic Games. The final cost when fully completed in 1931 with 101,574 seats was $1.9 million. The city and county that gained control of the facility after the Olympics shared the cost.

Soldier Field was an even grander project, costing $8.5 million. It was located at the approximate site where Daniel Burnham's Chicago Plan of 1909 had proposed such a facility. The field was used for many great events, such as the 1926 International Eucharistic Congress, which attracted over 200,000; the Army–Navy football game, which drew 100,000; and the 1927 Dempsey–Tunney "long-count" heavyweight boxing championship rematch, which was attended by 104,000 who paid a record gate of $2.6 million. The largest sporting crowd was 115,000 for the 1937 Austin-Leo high school football championship game. The home of the Chicago Bears since 1971, the field was rebuilt in 2003 at a cost of nearly $600 million.

The municipally publicly financed stadiums of the 1920s provided models for Cleveland, Miami, Dallas, New Orleans, and El Paso, which built public stadiums during the depression, all but Cleveland to facilitate postseason football bowl games to promote tourism. Cleveland's Municipal Stadium was a multipurpose $2.5-million structure that opened in 1931. Its main tenant was the Cleveland Indians, whose first game there on 31 July 1932 against the Philadelphia Athletics was seen by 80,184, the largest crowd that had ever attended a major league game. However, the Depression kept the total attendance down to 387,936. The Indians used Municipal Stadium throughout the 1933 season, the first full use of a city-owned field by a major league team, but only on Sundays and holidays in 1934. Twelve years later Bill Veeck bought the Indians, improved the quality of the team, and moved them back to the stadium, nearly tripling attendance from 1945 to 1947. In 1948, the Indians won the World Series, and set a major league attendance record of 2.6 million.

Municipal Sponsorship of Major League and Football Stadiums

In the 1950s, boosters in cities without professional sports teams made special efforts to attract major league franchises that included subsidizing ball fields. They believed sports teams would promote economic development and community pride. In 1953, the Boston Braves, the "second" team in that city (that is, the second most popular team in a city with two teams), moved to Milwaukee, a city that had been without major league baseball for fifty-two years, lured by a publicly financed ballpark. This move was the first relocation of a major league team since 1903. Political leaders in Milwaukee made available County Stadium, which originally had been built for a minor league club, and expanded it to meet the needs of a major league team. In 1954, the St. Louis Browns moved to Baltimore as the Orioles, and played in the recently completed Memorial Stadium, built to attract a major league team. The Philadelphia Athletics moved in 1955 to Kansas City (and later to Oakland), playing at Municipal Stadium, a minor league park refurbished by the city.

Then in 1958, the Dodgers and Giants brought major league ball to the West Coast. Walter O'Malley's highly profitable Brooklyn Dodgers were playing in the 35,000-seat Ebbets Field, whose neighborhood was becoming unsafe and less accessible to automobile commuters. When the city did not help him secure a site in downtown Brooklyn, he moved to Los Angeles, where the politicians and businessmen wanted major league baseball to certify their city's first-class status. O'Malley built Dodger Stadium with his own funds in 1962 at municipally owned Chavez Ravine, the only large vacant sector near downtown. It was the last privately built baseball park for over fifty years.

Between 1964 and 1970, several cities built blandly designed multisport stadiums in downtown areas near interstate traffic interchanges, including Atlanta (Fulton County Stadium), St. Louis (Busch Stadium), Philadelphia (Veteran's Stadium), Pittsburgh (Three Rivers Stadium), and Cincinnati (Riverfront Stadium). Atlanta sought to secure a major league team, while the others wanted to keep their teams from leaving declining cities. They all sought to promote urban development, especially in their respective central business districts. Previous parks were not built downtown because of exorbitant property costs and accessibility problems, but municipal subsidization of land purchases (often obtained through eminent domain) and the decline of mass transit and its replacement by automobiles changed that scenario. Cities did improve their public image, but they were saddled with large financial losses, underused facilities, and few if any long-term improvements.

New parks were also constructed in suburbia. Between 1965 and 1970, suburban towns like Bloomington, Minnesota, and Arlington, Texas, built one-fifth of the new baseball and football stadiums for prestige and an enhanced tax base, but operating expenses ate up any financial benefits.

The cost of the ballparks rose from $19 million for Fulton County Stadium, to $45 million for Riverfront and $50 million for Three Rivers and Veterans Stadiums. In 1971, New York City took over Yankee Stadium and refurbished the structure at a cost of $106 million. At that time, just 30.4 percent of baseball stadiums and 22.6 percent of football stadiums were privately owned. By 1988, only 20.8 percent of baseball fields and 7.1 percent of football fields were privately owned.

Economists have demonstrated that municipal subsidization of ballparks, which included constructing the fields, improving roads, and underpricing rents and other fees, have been economic mistakes. The cities lost money on the deal, and the ballparks failed to promote urban development. Yet cities have continued to subsidize sports teams. Since 1989, half of the American cities with major league teams have built publicly financed stadiums. The only exceptions were the modest $7.21 million Foxboro Stadium, which opened in a Boston suburb in 1971, and Joe Robbie's $115 million 75,000-seat Dolphins Stadium in Miami (now Pro Players' Stadium), built in 1987.

Contemporary Stadiums

The model for current ballparks is Baltimore's $110 million Oriole Park at Camden Yards, an intimate park designed in the style of early twentieth-century fields that blend in well with downtown. It has been a great success with local fans and tourists, averaging 45,034 in its first five years, a 50 percent increase over the old park. Its success encouraged other cities to build retro ballparks, like Cleveland's Jacobs Field in Cleveland and Comerica Park in Detroit.

Another trend is the construction of domed stadiums, starting in 1965 with the $41-million weatherproof Houston Astrodome, which had a constant temperature of 74 degrees F and introduced the use of artificial turf. Thirteen domed grounds were subsequently built in the United States for major sports teams, including a few that can open their roofs in twenty minutes. They are used year-round for conventions, concerts, religious assemblies, and other activities.

The newest stadiums house football or baseball, but not both. They are financed by a combination of municipal and private funding with costs often in excess of $300 million. The exception was San Francisco's $255-million Pacific Bell, the first privately funded ballpark since 1962, paid for by a private bond issue and $90 million from the sale of the stadium's name, luxury suites, personal seat licenses (PSL) for 15,000 seats, and advertising and concession rights. The New England Patriots' $425-million Gillette Stadium, built in 2002, has about 68,000 seats, mostly on the sidelines, all angled toward the fifty-yard line, plus 80 luxury suites and 6,000 club seats, and two massive video/scoreboards. Luxury boxes can cost as much as $300,000. They provide an environment for business entertaining with theater style, climate-controlled comfort, and such amenities as wet bar, refrigerator, TV monitors, and private rest rooms. These new edifices, and many older ones, have been renamed for the international conglomerates that pay millions for the rights, such as Qualcomm (San Diego), Alltel (Jacksonville), and Federal Express (Washington). Ticket prices are expensive for these facilities, limiting attendance to mainly middle-class fans. An average National Football League ticket in 1999 was $42, while in 2002 the average baseball ticket cost $18, though the top was nearly $40 for Boston. By comparison, in 1973, a Chicago fan could buy a bleacher seat for $1 or a box seat for $4.

See also: Baseball Crowds; Football; Football, Collegiate; Olympics; Soccer

BIBLIOGRAPHY

Danielson, Michael N. *Home Team: Professional Spots and the American Metropolis.* Princeton, N.J.: Princeton University Press, 1997.

Euchner, Charles C. *Playing the Field: Why Sports Team Move and Cities Fight to Keep Them.* Baltimore: Johns Hopkins University Press, 1993.

Gershman, Michael. *Diamonds: The Evolution of the Ballpark.* Boston: Houghton Mifflin, 1993.

Koch, Wilber C., ed. *The Economics and Politics of Sports Facilities.* Westport, Conn.: Quorum Books, 2000.

Kuklick, Bruce. *To Everything a Season: Shibe Park and Urban Philadelphia, 1909–1976.* Princeton, N.J.: Princeton University Press, 1991.

Noll, Roger, and Andrew Zimbalist. *The Economic Impact of Sports Teams and Stadiums.* Washington, D.C.: The Brookings Institution, 1997.

Riess, Steven A. *City Games: The Evolution of American Urban Society and the Rise of Sports.* Champaign: University of Illinois Press, 1989.

———. *Touching Base: Professional Baseball and American Culture in the Progressive Era.* Champaign, Ill.: University of Illinois Press, 1999.

Steven A. Riess

STAMP COLLECTING

In both common sense and the leisure sciences, stamp collecting (philately) is considered a hobby, a systematic, enduring pursuit of a reasonably evolved and specialized free-time activity having no professional counterpart.

Hobbies are also regarded as a type of serious leisure, which contrasts with hedonic, or casual leisure. Thus, hobbyist stamp collecting is more than the mere accumulation of stamps. It is the active, selective, and long-term acquisition, possession, and disposition of these collectables. To do this well requires extensive knowledge of stamps and perseverance in finding them.

The Origins of Stamp Collecting

The first government postage stamp appeared in England in 1840, an idea that quickly caught on in other countries. Robert Obojski ("Stamps and Stamp Collecting") observes that "the idea for the adhesive postage stamp was first suggested by the English schoolmaster and civil servant Rowland Hill as one of the many postal reforms in Britain in 1837. Hill's conception, for which he was later knighted, was derived from similar labels that had been issued almost a century earlier in many parts of Europe to collect a tax on newspapers." The first stamp in the United States was printed in 1847. By 1860, most nations were using postage stamps, at first imitating British design by portraying heads of state or symbols or artistic designs of national significance. Today, according to Obojski, nearly all countries issue large colorful pictorials, mainly to gain revenue through sales to collectors.

Steven Gelber writes that, in the United States, stamp collecting and industrial capitalism arose simultaneously, for the minting of stamps began at about this time. He goes on to say: "Stamp collectors transferred to the leisure sphere the discourse that defined the meaning of industrial capitalism and used the language and images of the marketplace to legitimize both work and leisure. By making their leisure like work, they could bring to it all the honor accorded productive activity in a work-oriented society," (p. 743). But in the middle of the nineteenth century, though men dominated the paid labor force, women and children were nonetheless the first to collect stamps, expressing principally an aesthetic rather than an economic interest in them. More than twenty years elapsed before men began to take an interest in philately, stimulated in good part by the fact that stamps were becoming differentiated according to monetary value as an expression of their age and rarity. So, in the late nineteenth century, the number of men in this hobby began to surpass the number of women, creating an imbalance in stamp collecting that, according to a rare survey of collectors, persists to this day. Surveys by Allan Olmsted and the American Stamp Dealers Association suggest that only between 5 and 7 percent of North American stamp collectors are female.

Although the male vision that old and rare stamps offered a good investment tended to obscure their appreciation of them as beautiful, many men nevertheless claimed to see educational benefits springing from philately. Moreover, besides being educational, such collecting was believed to enrich social life and promote positive personal values. These special practical benefits from leisure were held to enhance the work ethic and make the hobbyist more successful on the job. Gelber cites a handful of studies that support the claim of educational benefit.

Stamp Collecting in 2004

Once in full swing, the hobby of stamp collecting generated a familiar set of specialties. Modern collectors strive to fill albums on whose pages are found printed representations of each stamp issued over the years by national postal services (though some are worldwide collectors, most stick to one or a few countries). Other collectors, however, prefer to acquire first-day covers (envelops franked with newly issued stamps and postmarked on day of issue at city of issue) or specialize in commemorative stamps. The latter has led to topical collecting—amassing stamps that feature certain themes or subjects (such as art, sports, birds, flowers, aviation, famous people). Missing stamps in a collection may be sought by trading with other collectors or by purchasing them directly from dealers or indirectly through catalogues. In all this, "scientific" collectors have always looked for authenticity and absence of repair and artificial enhancement.

Although the hobby is an individualistic undertaking, many collectors are also organized. The American Topical Association (established in 1949) exists for collectors interested in commemorative stamps; its 6,000 members receive a bimonthly periodical and enjoy access to specialized handbooks. The more sweeping American Philatelic Society (established in 1886) is, with over 50,000 members from 110 countries, one of the largest hobbiest groups in the world. It, too, publishes a monthly journal, *The American Philatelist*. Individual trading of stamps is normally a local practice, however, which is facilitated by easily accessible school and community collectors clubs. *Linn's Stamp News*, a weekly periodical, provides a wide range of practical information, including lists of local stamp clubs, glossaries of philatelic terms, guides to foreign exchange, tables of stamp grades, and lists of stamp-issuing entities. The Internet offers extensive electronic contact with the various stamp-collecting organizations as well as with sites offering information on getting started in the hobby, dealing with certain collectors' problems, and finding reading material on stamp collecting.

Scientifically, far more is known about the history of philately than about its status in 2003. Contemporary sociology and psychology—the two disciplines most likely to take an interest in it—have all but neglected this hobby. Allan Olmsted's study of readers of the catalogue mailed out by the Saskatoon Stamp Centre and a somewhat earlier interview study conducted by the American Stamp Dealers Association (discussed by Olmsted) account for most of the research in this area. Olmsted said the findings of both studies were very similar. His study revealed that philatelists tend to be city dwellers, predominantly male, and significantly older and more highly educated than the general population. Over 30 percent of his sample had postgraduate education. In harmony with these findings was the observation that collectors, unless retired, are disproportionately employed in professional, managerial, and technical occupations.

Olmsted found that 75 percent of his respondents spent more than three hours per week with their collections, and in 1986 (the year of his survey), nearly two-thirds spent more than $500 per year pursuing their hobby. Moreover, 78 percent of the sample had started collecting stamps by age fifteen, supporting, thereby, the proposition that people can find a substantial nonwork career in serious leisure.

According to Olmsted's study, people collect because they enjoy the beauty of stamps and value the education they gain from them. Respondents said collecting stamps is like traveling to another country, where they learned about its heroes, cities, and geography, and got to glimpse its culture. Moreover, to collect stamps was to feel the challenge and excitement of hunting for missing items, obtaining them at a good price or fair exchange, and building something personal: one's very own collection. Indeed, a nagging fear was completing the collection, thus leaving the poor collector with nothing further to do. A beloved hobby brought to fruition. But most of all, the respondents said they collected stamps because it was relaxing. As for the investment motive, this sample by and large scorned the idea.

The Future

As of 2003, the future of stamp collecting, at that time one of the world's best-known hobbies, was unclear. Widespread use of commercial couriers, franking machines, electronic mail, and facsimile transmissions had reduced the need for stamps and, consequently, the revenue that national postal systems gained from selling them. The use of stamps was more and more the exclusive province of individuals and households, where such commercial and electronic devices were still uncommon

(although this was least true for electronic mail). In their private lives, many people still sent letters, parcels, postcards, greeting cards, photographs, and the like by ordinary mail, using stamps to accomplish this.

Thus, at the consumer end, the need for the postage stamp seems likely to continue for some time. It also seems likely to continue for some time at the producer end, as a service to consumers and as a mechanism whereby events, people, and environmental features of national importance can be publicly commemorated in cheap and visible fashion. Obviously, there will be fewer stamps in circulation as the need for them continues to decline, even if the number of different stamps printed each year will probably remain the same, though with smaller runs of each issue. Unless the number of collectors declines—which might happen if stamps become less visible in contemporary life than in the past—the hunt for stamps may become more intense, given that there will likely be fewer stamps per collector to acquire. Which, in turn, could increase overall satisfaction in the hobby, however, for the hunt has always been a significant part of the fun of collecting.

See also: Coin Collecting, Collecting, Hobbies and Crafts

BIBLIOGRAPHY

Gelber, Steven L. "Free Market Metaphor: The Historical Dynamics of Stamp Collecting. *Comparative Studies in Society and History* 34 (1992): 742–767.

Obojski, Robert. "Stamps and Stamp Collecting." *Microsoft Encarta Encyclopedia Standard 2001.*

Olmsted, Allan D. "Stamp Collectors and Stamp Collecting." Paper presented at the Annual Meeting of the Popular Culture Association, Montreal, March 1987.

Robert A. Stebbins

STATE PARKS

State parks are publicly owned lands set aside primarily for the purposes of recreation and environmental protection. As of 2002, 5,655 state parks, comprising more than 13 million acres, were distributed among all fifty states. These attracted nearly 800 million visitors. State park lands are generally intermediate in terms of level of development, opportunities offered, and management orientation. This puts most state park areas somewhere between the typically resource-oriented federal lands and the more user- and facility-oriented opportunities provided by local parks and recreation lands. They also tend to be intermediate in size between the larger federal parks, forests, and refuges and the smaller local parks and recreation areas. Finally and most importantly, state park lands tend to be closer to a majority of users than federal lands, with most U.S. counties containing one or more state park areas. With the majority of federal lands concentrated in the west and Alaska, state parks often offer the only easily accessible outdoor recreation opportunities for many Americans.

History of State Parks

States have been involved in the conservation, preservation, and designation of "public" lands and open space since before the "states" were "united." For example, the Massachusetts Bay Colony set aside more than 90,000 acres of land and water for public hunting and fishing through the Great Ponds Act of 1641. The state park concept also has a long history in the United States. In fact, the first "state park lands" were established by the state of California on a federal land grant in the Yosemite Valley in 1870 prior to the designation of Yellowstone in 1872 as the first National Park. However, the first "state park" did not have a very long history. The land was returned to the federal government in 1884 and was soon included in the third National Park, Yosemite National Park, in 1891.

Soon after Yellowstone National Park was established, a number of states started to address growing natural resource issues by setting aside lands for a variety of purposes, including forest conservation, watershed protection, as wildlife habitat, and for outdoor recreation. California and New Hampshire were among the first states to conserve and manage wildlife through creation of game commissions in 1878. The state of New York was the first to set aside state lands, although these early efforts were to protect forests and provide watershed protection, not for state parks. The designation of the first forest reserves through the Forest Preservation Act of 1885 directed the state purchase of lands to create the Adirondack and the Catskill forest reserves—parts of both later become state parks. Additionally, New York set aside Niagara Falls as a state reservation later designated as a state park. During the same year, Fort Mackinac was granted to the state of Michigan as public land that would eventually become a state park. Other states soon followed this lead. California, Colorado, and Ohio created new state boards of forestry. The first state park "systems," which included an agency designated to managed and develop lands set aside as state parks, were Illinois

Division of Parks and Memorials and Indiana Division of State Parks established in 1919. Not long after, New York and Pennsylvania established park systems.

By 1921, many of the states had designated lands as state parks, and most of these had formed state park "systems." The first national conference for state parks was held that year in Des Moines, Iowa, with the mission of promoting the state park concept. Seven years later, the first professional association of state parks was formed as the National Conference on State Parks (NCSP). The development of the state parks was promoted and supported through a variety of efforts. The first director of the National Parks System, Stephen Mather, supported the formation of the state parks systems and played an important role in the formation of the NCSP. By World War II, most of the states had developed state park systems. By the early twenty-first century, all fifty states had established a state parks system. Most state parks were originally acquired as gifts, tax-delinquent lands, original state land holdings, purchased from private individuals or corporations, or federal lands turned over to the states.

The NCSP continued to provide state park advocates a forum to promote and expand state parks. In 1962, the National Association of State Park Directors (NASPD) was created by the NCSP. Since that time this association, along with the National Recreation and Parks Association, has continued to provide a forum for state park issues.

By 1993, state lands and waters collectively amounted to almost 80 million acres, which is approximately 5 percent of the nation's total. These lands, however, are not distributed evenly throughout the country. Just as most federally managed lands and waters are concentrated in the west, an area with the lowest population density, so are the state lands that include state parks. In fact, although the region accounted for just 18 percent of the U.S. population, it contains 65 percent of state lands. Southern states having almost one-third of the nation's population account for only 6 percent of state lands set aside. The north-central and northeast regions, with 27 percent and 23 percent, respectively, of the total population, have protected only 16 percent and 12 percent of state lands.

State Park Organization and Management

While all of the states have park systems managed by a department or a division of the state government, the focus, size, visitation, level of development, and amenities available within these systems vary widely. Most state park systems are modeled on the National Park system and originally tended to focus on providing passive outdoor recreation and contemplative leisure opportunities.

As use increased, visitors demanded more services and opportunities; many park systems responded by increasing their focus on recreative leisure by expanding facilities and increasing amenities. By the early 2000s, the state parks systems spanned the spectrum from resource-oriented, rustic undeveloped lands, offering opportunities for dispersed recreation with associated facilities and amenities such as developed campsites and trails, to more fully developed user-oriented recreation attractions offering full service resorts, luxury accommodations, lodges, cabins, cottages, restaurants, golf courses, ski areas, swimming pools, and marinas. In fact, there are 115 resorts located in state parks, and just over one-half of the states have resorts in their state parks. Campgrounds, both developed and primitive, are by far the most common type of state park facility, but state parks also provide trails, water resources (including lakes, reservoirs, rivers, streams, and swimming pools), and picnic facilities.

The state park systems are managed by a number of different agencies and departments in the various state governments. Typically, state park systems are housed as a division or bureau in a department of conservation, natural resources, or environmental protection, much the same as the National Park Service is an agency within the U.S. Department of Interior. However, this is not always the case: some are located in tourism or recreation departments, while in a few states they operate as independent cabinet-level departments. Additionally, the management styles vary considerably across the states. Some state parks focus primarily on preservation and offer little in the way of developed amenities, while others offer highly-developed facilities, including a range of recreation opportunities and even full-service resorts. Still others remain primarily undeveloped wildlands focusing on the provision of dispersed outdoor recreation opportunities. Many state park systems have shifted their management focus toward nature-based tourism, heritage tourism, and ecotourism. This alliance with tourism has increased park visitation and helped grow park budgets.

State park systems comprise a variety of units, including state parks, state natural areas, state recreation areas, state historic areas, and state water-use areas (such as lakes, rivers, and beaches). In most systems all units are designated as "state parks." There has been a movement to reorganize the state park systems along the lines of the NPS structure, with the more natural undeveloped parks retaining the designation of "state park" while the more developed areas are classified as "state recreation areas." Units protecting and interpreting historic features are being designated "state historic parks" along with a variety of other terminology. However, some state park systems, Florida for example, are moving away from the various and sometimes confusing multiple terms and returning to designating all of their units as "state parks."

State parks are supported financially through a variety of sources, including state general funds, fees, grants, and gifts. Nationally, $1.8 billion dollars were spent for operating expenses in 2001, with less than one-half of that coming from state general funds. Most state park systems derive some of their income from user fees, including visitor entrance fees. Additionally, many states receive federal funds and matching grants from the Land and Water Conservation Fund (LWCF) to help fund acquisition and construction of new parks, infrastructure, and visitor facilities. Another duty that usually is handled by the individual state park agencies is writing the State Comprehensive Outdoor Recreation Plans. This document is a five-year plan required for states and local outdoor recreation agencies to be eligible for monies from the LWCF.

State Park Statistics

The way states organize and categorize natural resource lands varies widely. This makes a discussion of "state parks" somewhat confusing. Some states separate the management of lands "officially" designated as "state parks," while others manage all state outdoor recreation lands within one agency. These other lands are sometimes designated as state recreation areas, state wildlife-management areas, state forests, state historic sites, state trails, state preserves, state wilderness areas, and so on. Additionally, some state park areas contain sizable holdings of non-state-owned lands. New York's Adirondack Park, for example, covers more than 6 million acres, making it the largest U.S. "state park," but much of this acreage is not state owned. While the "park" is constitutionally protected to remain "forever wild," it is actually a patchwork of public, private, and corporate lands. However, this "state park" is managed by the Adirondack Park Agency, an independent state agency that is not part of the New York State Parks, Recreation and Historic Preservation Commission, the official state agency that manages the other state parks. For this discussion, state park lands are lands that are managed by the agency that is responsible for state parks. The data for this discussion comes mostly from the NASPD's Annual Information Exchange (AIX) and the individual state park agency Internet sites. The NASPD has a limited membership of fifty, each member representing one state, and is organized into six geographic regions.

State park acreage continues to increase, but generally these increases are not keeping pace with state population increases and state park visitation. Between 1975 and 1995, the number of state parks grew from 3,804 to 5,541, an increase of 31 percent. State park acreage also increased during the same period but not as much, going from 9,838 to 11,807 acres, an increase of 17 percent. Visitation, however, increased by 31 percent, from just over one-half million visitors in 1975 to almost three-quarter million in 1995, while the total U.S. population increased only 19 percent, suggesting overall population growth isn't accounting for all of the increases seen in state park visitation. During this time, the number of day visitors increased more (from 465,302 to 686,483, a 32 percent increase) than overnight visitation (which grew by only 13 percent, from 51,488 to 59,121). Staffing has increased, but much slower than visitation, up by only 8 percent, and most of this increase was in part-time staff. State parks' operating budgets increased 73 percent, and operating revenue (income mostly from entrance and user fees) increased by almost 80 percent, while capital expenditures actually shrank by 16 percent.

See also: Botanical Parks, City Parks, National Parks, Park Movements

BIBLIOGRAPHY

Center for State Park Research. Home page at http://naspd.indstate.edu/cspr/.

DeLoney, J. "The State Government Role in Outdoor Recreation." In *Outdoor Recreation in American Life: A National Assessment of Demand and Supply Trends.* Edited by H. Ken Cordell, et al. Champaign, Ill.: Sagamore Publishing, 1999.

Donnelly, Maureen P. "Economic Impacts of State Parks: Effect of Park Visitation, Park Facilities, and County Economic Diversity. *Journal of Park and Recreation Administration* 18 no. 3 (1998): 57–72.

Ibrahim, Hilmi, and Cordes, Kathleen A. *Outdoor Recreation: Enrichment for a Lifetime,* 2d edition. Champaign, Ill: Sagamore Publishing, 2002.

McLean, Daniel D. "State Park Systems in the United States." In *Outdoor Recreation in American Life: A National Assessment of Demand and Supply Trends.* Edited by H. Ken Cordell, et al. Champaign, Ill.: Sagamore Publishing, 1999.

McLean, Daniel D., Amy Hurd, Brent Beggs, and Deborah Chavez. "Trends in State Park Operations: A 10 Year Perspective." Available from http://naspd.indstate.edu.

McLean, Daniel D., and Russell E. Brayley. "State Parks: A Diverse System." Paper presented at the 2000 Social Aspects of Recreation Research Symposium, Tempe, Ariz. February 2000.

National Association of State Park Directors (NAPSD). Home page at http://www.naspd.org.

John Confer

STOCK CAR RACING

Stock car racing evokes many different images—from the "redneck" sport, to one of the most lucrative motor sports industries in the world. One of the most well known stock car racing businesses, NASCAR (the National Association for Stock Car Auto Racing), has become the largest organization within one of the largest spectator sports in America. The history of NASCAR is a storied one with many more twists and turns that can be found on a standard NASCAR oval racetrack.

The History of NASCAR

NASCAR began its storied past in the prohibition era of American history, when the production, distribution, and consumption of alcohol was prohibited. Many industrious individuals began to produce and distribute contraband whiskey, and the infamous bootlegger was born. A bootlegger was an individual who illegally transported and distributed moonshine or other contraband material across the Southeast. In order to outwit and outrun the authorities, often times bootleggers would modify their cars to not only to carry large amounts of contraband, but also to go very fast while maintaining their stock appearance. As more and more bootleggers began the dangerous trade, it became inevitable that some of them would start to races each other. Although racing is nothing new to humans, this new form of racing was new to motorsports. Since bootleggers often had fast cars to outrun the law, egos were on the line as to who among them had the fastest cars. Furthermore, many bootleggers would race on Sunday afternoon, and then use the same car to make illegal distribution runs later that night. Often times, these races would draw large crowds of spectators, so it is difficult to determine when exactly watching stock car racing for recreation really began.

It might be expected that once the Volstead Act of 1933 repealed the whiskey ban, that bootlegging might suffer. This was not the case, since there was a large tax placed on whiskey; this meant that bootlegging continued to thrive, as did the independent races. In the summer of 1938, driver and race organizer Bill France organized what is considered the first NASCAR-type race (although the group itself wouldn't exist for another ten years). The race was held at the famous track on Daytona Beach, Florida, with the winner receiving prizes such as a bottle of rum and a box of cigars. France, through foresight, realized that in order for this fledgling sport to grow, it had to become better organized, with one body maintaining records and a list of champions.

Petty vs. Beauchamp. At the first Daytona 500 in 1959, Lee Petty (1914–2000) in his Thunderbird (42) and Johnny Beauchamp (1923–1981) in an Oldsmobile (73) finished side-by-side with Petty later declared the winner by only two feet after racing officials spent three days reviewing photos and movies from the race. Two years later, both drivers were involved in a serious accident at the same event that caused Petty's immediate retirement. © *AP/Wide World Photos*

Stock car racing was put on hold during World War II. In 1947, France organized the first meeting that formally brought into being present-day NASCAR. At the meeting, France and his associates established the ground rules and the specifications governing the sport. In 1948, France and NASCAR ran a 52-race series of what were known as Modified cars, which were different from true stock cars. Thus, the first official NASCAR stock car race is recognized as the race held at the Charlotte (North Carolina) Fairgrounds on 19 June 1949. To compete in this race, cars had to be "strictly stock," meaning that they had to be full-sized American cars with no body modifications, and parts used in the car had to be listed in the manufacturers catalogue for that model year. This is what is meant when a race car is called a "stock car."

The next evolution in NASCAR came about with the construction of the first superspeedway in Darlington, South Carolina. The superspeedways allowed cars to go faster than they had previously due to their long straightaways and high-banked turns. Many ups and downs were experience by NASCAR during the 1950s and 1960s, but in the 1960s NASCAR changed its rules with respect to the meaning of "stock," and race cars quickly evolved past standard stock automobiles.

Again, NASCAR had difficulties during the late 1960s, but prevailed with the emergence of its first superstar, Richard Petty. Many observers believe that Petty almost single-handedly saved NASCAR, and he would go on to set many NASCAR records during his thirty-year-plus career (including most career victories, 200). New fans were exposed to NASCAR in the 1970s when ABC began to televise auto racing segments that included NASCAR on such programs as the *Wide World of Sports*. In 1979, the entire Daytona 500 was televised by CBS and was watched by nearly 20 million spectators. During the 1980s, corporations began to see that the marketing value in NASCAR, and corporate sponsorship took off.

The Business of NASCAR

NASCAR, along with auto racing in general, is one of the fastest-growing spectator sports in the United States. NASCAR runs about ninety races each year, in twenty-five states, through three racing circuits: the Busch, Craftsman Truck, and its signature Nextel Cup Series (formerly the Winston Cup). The Nextel Cup, featuring popular drivers like Jeff Gordon, Dale Earnhardt Jr., and Dale Jarrett, draws more than 7 million race fans each year. NBC, FOX, and Turner Broadcasting have taken note, paying $2.4 billion for broadcast rights until 2006. Since its founding in 1948, NASCAR has been, and, as of the early 2000s, is still privately owned by the France family. NASCAR claimed to have over 75 million fans, with estimated sales in 2002 of over $3 billion. Sponsorships

Daytona 500. A fish-eye lens photo captures the spectacle that is the Daytona 500, held at the famed Daytona International Speedway in Daytona, Florida. NASCAR attendance is second only to NFL football games. *Courtesy of W. Dennis Winn, Gale Group*

from companies selling everything from engine parts to soft drinks have played a major role in this amazing growth. More than 75 percent of NASCAR fans are in the eighteen to fifty-four age bracket and, according to research data, about 40 percent will switch to a product if it becomes a NASCAR sponsor.

In 2004, NASCAR traded cigarettes for cell phones when wireless communications giant Nextel replaced R.J. Reynolds Tobacco Co. (RJR) as the title sponsor of NASCAR's premier series. A 1998 master settlement of state lawsuits against the tobacco industry had limited RJR in marketing its NASCAR sponsorship. Earlier court rulings forbade RJR from advertising Winston, its top cigarette brand, on radio or television, and the company also could not market to minors. Those limitations, and the uncertain business climate in the tobacco industry, led RJR in early 2003 to give NASCAR permission to look for another title sponsor. RJR had been with NASCAR for thirty-one years, signing on in 1972 to take over what was then called the Grand National Series. Various reports have valued the marketing deal between NASCAR and Nextel at as much as $700 million over ten years. At a minimum, it is the largest sponsorship deal in the history of sports.

NASCAR races are the second-most watched televised sport, behind NFL football. Companies have long sought NASCAR's reach; it has more Fortune 500 company sponsors than any other sport. And when it comes to fans loyal to their sport's sponsors, NASCAR fans are a marketer's dream. NASCAR fans are almost twice as likely as baseball and basketball fans to buy a sponsor's product over a nonsponsor's product. On the television side, ratings of NASCAR broadcasts have tripled since 1990, while other sports like hockey, baseball, and basketball have seen ratings plummet.

Although the Nextel Cup is the premier NASCAR series, it also oversees two additional racing series: the Craftsman Truck Series and the Busch Racing Series. Both are conisdered to be "feeder" series for the Nextel Cup, with the best Busch and Craftsman drivers earning a chance to race in the Nextel series. Together, the three series have allowed NASCAR to broaden its share of the racing market. Many of the drivers achieve incredible popularity, with race fans idolizing them and immortalizing them after death. This was perhaps never as true as it was in 2001, when legendary driver Dale Earnhardt Sr. was killed on the last lap of the Daytona 500 race. Since his death, Earnhardt's ardent fans carry on his memory, and memorabilia featuring his name and likeness is still popular.

Another component of NASCAR is the automobile manufacturers. Although the relationship between

NASCAR and the manufacturers has not always been amenable, there exists, as of 2003, a good relationship between NASCAR and the manufacturers. Chevrolet, Ford, and Dodge, who produce all the Nextel Cup cars, use NASCAR to test new technology, and all three realize that the old adage "race on Sunday, sell on Monday" is still true—if a driver wins the Sunday NASCAR race driving a Chevrolet, Chevy dealers across the country can expect to see a sales bump on Monday (with the same true for Ford and Dodge, or course). In addition, the automakers compete each year for the manufacturers championship, earning points throughout the year based on their brand's race-day performance.

Although to the lay individual, NASCAR racing might seem simple, many rules govern the racing including restrictions on engine size and car weight. The cars also have to maintain the basic shape of production automobiles to qualify to race in a NASCAR event. Without downplaying the complexities of NASCAR racing, the basic premise of each race is that drivers race for a predetermined length, for example 250 miles or 500 miles, and the driver who completes the race the fastest wins.

Conclusion

From its humble beginnings during the prohibition era, stock car racing has changed with the times, while continuing to provide fans with thrilling races and surprises. One of the reasons for NASCAR's continued success has been the consistent manner in which the France family has enforced the rules. They have always believed that close, side-by-side racing is what attracts the fans, and to preserve fair competition, NASCAR has shown no favoritism throughout the years. This is evident in the application of consistent penalties, whether the rule violator was a champion or a rising star. An interesting past full of colorful characters and events, a lucrative television contract, and a willingness to consistently govern and monitor all aspects of current-day operations has positioned NASCAR at the forefront of sport entertainment for the foreseeable future. Additionally, the NASCAR fans are some of the most loyal in the industry, making NASCAR, and stock car racing as a whole, a viable entertainment as well as business venture for the future.

See also: Automobiles and Leisure, Auto Racing, Drag Racing, Open Wheel Racing, Prohibition and Temperance, Sports Car Racing

BIBLIOGRAPHY

Derbeyshire, J. "NASCAR Nation: One Journalist's Journey of Discovery." *National Review.* 10 November 2003. Available from http://www.findarticles.com/.

Hagstrom, R. G. *The NASCAR Way: The Business That Drives the Sport.* Hoboken, N.J.: John Wiley & Sons Inc., 1998.

Hemphill, P. *Wheels.* New York: Simon & Schuster, 1997.

Hoovers Online. *National Association for Stock Car Auto Racing.* Available from http://www.hoovers.com/.

Hunter, J. *Stock Car Racing U.S.A.* New York: Dodd, Mead & Company, 1973.

Nascar.com. Available from http://www.nascar.com.

Patsuris, P. "NASCAR Pulls Into Prime Time." *Forbes.* 7 October 2003. Available from http://www.forbes.com/.

Stambler, I. *Great Moments in Stock Car Racing.* New York: G. P. Putnam's Sons, 1971.

T. Jason Davis and Daniel Hedrick

SUBURBANIZATION OF LEISURE

Nineteenth-century suburbs generated leisure activities that complemented the natural lushness and domestic-oriented residential districts in which they were practiced. Even after 200 years of suburban development, the activities that originally drew city dwellers to the urban edge remain central to suburbia's mass appeal.

Some of the first suburbs, pioneered in the first half of the nineteenth century, emerged directly from leisure activities, as the wealthy traveled to the urban periphery to escape the heat and disease of the increasingly unsanitary industrial city. Hotels, offering access to a cooler and less-polluted climate, enticed urbanites with numerous activities, including socializing, lawn games, and horse racing. In a few cases, religious interests brought urbanites out of the city for camp meetings. Around some of these resort or revival districts sprouted cottage and mansion districts. Railroads, seeing a potential financial opportunity, created local service to make possible daily commuting and shopping in bustling downtowns.

The first waves of wealthy nineteenth-century suburbanites lived on large, often multiacre lots relatively isolated from their neighbors. The creation of social and religious organizations by both residents and developers helped to overcome physical distance while still preserving, and sometimes even enhancing, social

Maureen Orcott. Seven-time winner of the Women's Eastern Golf Association Amateur Championship, Maureen Orcott demonstrates her technique to her twin brothers Benjamin (left) and William in 1925 at the White Beeches Country Club, in New Jersey. In early suburbs, the country club was often the center of leisure activity; in fact, many of the first suburban enclaves were built around a country club that was included in the initial development. © *Hulton Archive/Getty Images*

exclusivity. Although many of the first country clubs developed informally, developers by the late nineteenth century consciously shaped many new suburbs around country clubs they started. In planned suburbs such as Roland Park (Baltimore, 1891) and Country Club District (Kansas City, 1906), for instance, country clubs, and the variety of diversions they offered, became essential parts of the exclusive suburban lifestyle marketed to wealthy homebuyers. Golf, demanding large areas of landscaped open space, emerged as one of the most prestigious forms of suburban leisure, but just as important at these clubs were social events, balls, boating, cricket, and tennis. By 1901, there were 1,000 country clubs in the United States, and by 1939, that number had grown to 4,700. In both elite and more modest communities, churches provided the other important outlet for the organization of leisure time in early suburbs and offered their members a wide range of social and philanthropic activities.

Suburban landscapes shifted and diverged as access to their environs widened. For the very wealthy during the pre–Civil War period of suburban growth, scientific agriculture on gentlemen farms had been popular and included serious experiments in animal husbandry and horticulture. For those with purely aesthetic interests, professional designers, particularly in the second half of the nineteenth century, designed elaborately landscaped grounds often in a picturesque, British country-house manner. Greenhouses, plant rooms, and professional garden staffs provided significant diversions for wealthy families. Some developers of elite planned suburbs such as Llewellyn Park, New Jersey (1852), and Riverside, Illinois (1868), hired professional designers who preserved and enhanced natural features with extensive plantings, walking paths, and carriage drives.

In more modest suburban districts, ornamental plants, flowers, and lawns tended to displace experimental horticulture and extensive public spaces. The expanded, yet still private outdoor spaces of almost all suburbs (compared to city lots) nevertheless created opportunities for informal activities; screened back porches and fenced yards made possible the close family interaction prized by those seeking a strong suburban domestic sphere, under female guidance, that would mitigate the competitive and aggressive male world of business and civic affairs. In general, the interiors of suburban homes in more modest suburbs tended to become less formal than urban town houses and featured common family rooms and hearths. Suburban leisure activities close to home revolved closely around seasonal opportunities: Summer was the time for lawn games such as croquet, biking, ball playing, and porch sitting; winter an ideal time for skating, sledding, and inside activities such as reading, word games, musical performance, and sewing. Prosperous suburbanites maintained a strong connection to central city cultural "seasons" in theater, opera, and club life.

Suburban women of the nineteenth and early twentieth century are normally portrayed as quiescent victims of the "cult of domesticity," but the truth of the matter is more complicated. Many women and men in both elite and middle-class suburban communities participated in village or suburban "improvement" societies. These societies tended to be most important in less comprehensively although still elite suburbs such as Chestnut Hill (Philadelphia) and Brookline (Boston). These suburbs included successful efforts to beautify small, ramshackle commercial districts near train stops, lobbying for the burying of electrical and telephone wires, tree preservation and planting, and preservation of local historic homes and landscapes. Many suburban associations focused upon philanthropic efforts in health and welfare for the poor residents of lower-income sections either within or adjoining elite suburban districts. Women's clubs in suburbs even became leading forces in the women's suffrage movement. Even suburban leisure activities might generate civic action; the cycling mania of the turn of the century generated improvements in street paving in both suburbs and cities. By the 1920s, most of these improvement organizations shifted from Progressive politics and serious reform to more conventional social and cultural activities.

Elite and more moderate suburbs during the nineteenth century did not share an extensive interest in shopping as leisure within the suburbs. Both women and men traveled by streetcar or rail to department or dry goods stores downtown. Trains and wagons delivered packages to the suburbs based upon urban orders, and only a few businesses clustered around the rail and streetcar stops. The limited, albeit affluent, market for merchants slowed the growth and development of suburban shopping districts. Above all, middle- and upper-middle-class suburbanites aimed to preserve the wholesome and natural atmosphere of their neighborhoods by limiting commercial development of all types.

Suburbs of the late nineteenth century were not, however, all elitist. By the end of the nineteenth century, suburbs attracted a much wider constituency that favored new kinds of leisure. The ends of streetcar lines became public picnic points, and promoters built attractions, often in partnership with traction companies and real estate developers, to attract city dwellers to the urban fringe. Beer gardens, amusement parks, and stadiums brought city residents to the edge for more formal leisure opportunities. Once in the suburbs, day-trippers often found themselves buying property or homes in heavily promoted new subdivisions. Many of these streetcar suburbs created around leisure, such as Venice (Los Angeles) and Brighton Beach (New York), have since been annexed to nearby cities and are now considered parts of traditional urban centers.

Streetcar suburbs, unlike their more elite relatives, by the 1890s featured a wider range of more traditional urban amusements including numerous shops, bars, pool halls, dance halls, and theaters. Commercial districts tended to line streetcar routes and could be quite extensive because higher density development allowed for a much more lucrative trade. Few of these working-class suburbs featured preserved open spaces and even fewer boasted preplanned social or religious organizations (although they developed in time). Houses in streetcar suburbs boasted less outdoor space than their elite counterparts and "two flat" or "doubles" made for a more urbanized suburban landscape, but residents still grew flowers and pursued other garden activities. Early twentieth-century working-class suburbs were also notable for a strong tradition of subsistence gardening and small-scale animal husbandry (rabbits, chickens).

Toward a Suburban Century

Although commercial development had been largely ignored in elite communities, during the early twentieth century developers in communities such as Lake Forest (Illinois) and Country Club District (Kansas) began creating purpose-designed shopping and civic centers for elite communities. Tudor and Colonial styles minimized the commercial symbolism and blended smoothly into districts of similar appearance. New shopping districts offered a genuine civic focus to many suburbs, but also grew in step with the increasing popularity of the automobile. Developers at these centers made provisions for the automobile, including lots and garages. Movie theaters, the first supermarkets, and retail shops began to allow a more independent and diverting suburban shopping experience.

With the automobile's growing popularity during the 1920s, suburban leisure began to change on a wider scale. Opportunities for distant journeys made suburban residents regional adventurers and drew some to private campgrounds and new state and national parks. The infilling of formerly natural areas between streetcar and railroad lines removed some of the open natural spaces that suburbanites had used for informal leisure and led to a more crowded suburban landscape, but cars made up for the densification of suburbs by opening new areas to development and allowing access to formerly unvisited natural zones. Picnicking and camping on the side of the road became increasingly popular on these journeys, much to the chagrin of agriculturalists. Racing cars became popular among suburban youth as well, and the adolescent access to the automobile allowed for expanded license in dating. More serious and often illicit leisure, particularly during Prohibition, still concentrated in urban districts with large theater and shopping districts that catered to regional populations.

The creation of national radio programs also proved important in the family-centered suburbs of the 1920s and was an important precursor to television mass culture of the 1950s. In this era before air conditioning, however, sitting on porches remained a major summer activity in many suburbs, a visible legacy that is legible in the great number and ample size of porches (screened and otherwise) from the 1910s and 1920s that created animated street life, strong social networks, and safer outdoor zones of play for children.

Suburban Leisure for the Suburban Majority

After World War II, even more rapid development of the new suburbs subsidized by the government brought ever-larger numbers of suburbanites and increased profit potential for suburban merchants. By 1980, nearly a majority of Americans lived in a defined suburban district; many more lived in areas that were older suburbs annexed to cities or in rural districts not yet redefined as suburban rings. Whereas earlier suburbanites tended to maintain a strong connection to the cultural and social circles of the center city, increasingly suburbanites of all classes found a wider range of activities that eliminated almost any reason to travel downtown.

New strip malls and particularly regional-scale malls with ample parking and protected and enclosed pedestrian areas complemented suburban preferences for well-regulated, family-oriented spaces. These shop-

ping malls, pioneered by designers such as Victor Gruen and developers such as James Rouse, offered "public spaces," programmed cultural activities, social gatherings, and a wide variety of shopping opportunities. By the 1980s, these malls played a central role in suburban social affairs and accounted for nearly two-thirds of all retail sales nationally.

Around the most successful of these regional shopping malls have grown other shopping and leisure opportunities to create what journalist Joel Garreau calls "edge cities," suburban communities offering nearly a full range of urban amenities and activities. His description of the Houston Galleria is particularly famous, a complex that includes not only stores and offices but an ice rink, nightclubs, and fine restaurants. Some older, usually working-class suburbs even have districts devoted to short-term motels and red-light activities. The expansion of chains such as Starbucks and Barnes and Noble has added a further touch of urban sophistication to many suburbs.

Developing suburban areas of the postwar era, both planned and informal, primarily used school fields as alternative park spaces, but increasingly spent large sums on building pools, public golf courses, and new parks with a focus on active leisure such as playgrounds and ball fields. In general, suburban districts felt less need for parks than dense urban places because every house had its own yard. League football, softball and baseball, golf, and swimming nevertheless proved particularly popular in suburbs as facilities expanded. In recent years, many suburbs and state governments have bought undeveloped lands as nature reserves. Some large-scale planned suburbs such as Columbia, Maryland, made extensive provisions for land preservation and include grade separated pathway systems stretching over many miles.

Although city centers maintain strong cultural and educational institutions, many suburbs were also investing in new cultural facilities including concert halls and art and craft centers, often in partnership with a new wave of university and college expansion. The growing interstate highway system allowed suburbanites to gain much faster access to the state and national park systems in their regions, and entrepreneurs built amusement parks such as Disneyland that offered sanitized and updated versions of older urban amusement parks. Many suburbanites still occasionally travel to downtowns for cultural activities, and new highways have shortened their trips. Downtown cultural and sporting institutions have tailored their expansions to suburban audiences with plentiful parking and regulated sports and cultural "districts" that shield suburbanites from urban dangers.

Outdoor living. A family enjoys dinner outdoors in 1997. The fact that most suburban homes had large yards meant that families no longer had to travel to a park to hold a picnic. © *Ariel Skelley/Corbis*

The myth of suburban uniformity in leisure popularized by urban critics is largely a canard. Sociologists, for instance, have noticed important differences in leisure activity between working-class, middle-class, and wealthy suburbs during the postwar era. Middle-class suburbs tend to be abuzz with great numbers of associations and fraternal organizations. Nuclear-family-centered activities remain important, but middle-class families have reduced contact with their extended family members even though their friendships and other interests are distributed widely over vast regions. Many of these suburbs near large cities support art colonies, reading and writing groups, lecture series, concerts, and other highbrow activities. In general, too, suburban libraries in middle-class areas possess strong collections.

Working-class suburbs also feature American Legion and Kiwanis groups, but they tend to place a greater value on taverns, stoop sitting, church activities, informal social interaction, and regular extended family gatherings. Working-class suburbanites also look to gardening for not just pleasure but sustenance. Nearly one-half of

American households had vegetable gardens by 1970. In both working- and middle-class suburbs there tends to be a gender division of outside labor with men handling yard work and women gardening. In addition, working-class inhabitants often use their outdoor spaces and garages for more extensive automotive work that is often frowned upon in wealthier communities. Drag racing and cruising became the expression of the disaffected, particularly working-class, suburban adolescent.

Individual homeowners in both working- and middle-class suburbs have continued to devote attention to their yards and do-it-yourself activities. Improvement of homes became a major issue in the hastily built tract developments of the 1950s and 1960s, and most homes have been extensively rebuilt and improved over the decades.

The backyard, freed from almost all of its functional uses, has taken on some of the symbolic value that once adhered to front yards only. The ranch and split-level style houses of the postwar era minimized the distinction between indoor and outdoor spaces with large plate-glass windows and sliding doors on the back of the house. Introduction of many more household appliances, particularly washers and dryers, minimized the functional role of backyards. Parents enjoyed enlarged patio spaces with chairs, umbrellas, Jacuzzis, and extensive plantings (sometimes professionally maintained). Depending upon a homeowner's means, a family might have an inflatable, above-ground, or in-ground pool. Sandboxes, playhouses, and tree houses in backyards also become important zones for unsupervised children, particularly in middle-class suburbs. Many of the newest suburban districts, particularly gated communities, offer extensive recreational opportunities to residents of an individual community. Community associations that tax residents for a separate fee organize most of this recreation in gated communities and often organize summer camps and day care.

The wealthy in their "noble suburbs" in the postwar era continue to enjoy pools, expansive lawns, tennis courts, and elaborate gardens. Country clubs maintain their cachet in wealthy suburbs, as do garden clubs, cultural activities, and philanthropic organizations. Many wealthy homeowners of the postwar period continued to hire landscape designers, but suburbanites also discovered a new fondness for local environmental activities dedicated to preserving natural spaces in their immediate vicinity. Do-it-yourself activities tend to be less important in elite suburbs and socializing tends to be more formal.

Television is the great leveler in contemporary suburban culture. Television provides access to a democratic, sanitized national mass culture and has generated a growing independence of suburban areas from local cultural producers and further amplified the importance of interior domestic spaces. Television, in combination with air conditioning and the Internet, has diminished some of the seasonal shifts in leisure that characterized prewar suburbs and in many cases has dramatically reduced the number of hours both children and adults engage in active leisure, gardening, and associational life.

After 200 years of development, American suburbs preserve many of the leisure elements pioneered in the nineteenth century. Older elite suburbs have preserved to a remarkable extent the attractive environments that first drew suburban pioneers in the nineteenth century. Even suburbanites in suburbs of more recent vintage find themselves surrounded by private outdoor spaces for gardening and lawn games, diverting forms of indoor domestic entertainment, accessible natural and park spaces, and convenient "urban style" excitement in edge cities or nearby downtowns.

See also: Automobiles and Leisure, Gardening and Lawn Care, Urbanization of Leisure, Working-Class Leisure Lifestyles

BIBLIOGRAPHY

Bloom, Nicholas. *Suburban Alchemy: 1960s New Towns and the Transformation of the American Dream.* Columbus: Ohio State University Press, 2001.

Contosta, David. *Suburb in the City: Chestnut Hill, Philadelphia, 1850–1990.* Columbus: Ohio State University Press, 1996.

Fishman, Robert. *Bourgeois Utopias: The Rise and Fall of the Suburbs.* New York: Basic Books, 1987.

Garreau, Joel. *Edge City: Life on the New Frontier.* New York: Anchor Books, 1996.

Girling, Cynthia. *Yard, Street, Park: The Design of Suburban Open Space.* New York: John Wiley and Sons, 1994.

Jackson, Kenneth T. *Crabgrass Frontier: The Suburbanization of the United States.* New York: Oxford University Press, 1987.

Marsh, Margaret. *Suburban Lives.* New Brunswick, N.J.: Rutgers University Press, 1990.

Mattingly, Paul. *Suburban Landscapes: Culture and Politics in a New York Metropolitan Community.* Baltimore: Johns Hopkins University Press, 2001.

Mayo, James. *The American Country Club: Its Origins and Development.* New Brunswick, N.J.: Rutgers University Press, 1998.

Muller, Peter. *Contemporary Suburban America.* Englewood Cliffs, N.J.: Prentice-Hall, 1981.

Nicolaides, Becky. *My Blue Heaven: Life and Politics in the Working-Class Suburbs of Los Angeles, 1920–1965.* Chicago: University of Chicago Press, 2001.

Stilgoe, John. *Borderland: Origins of the American Suburb, 1820–1939.* New Haven, Conn.: Yale University Press, 1988.

Whyte, William. *The Organization Man.* Philadelphia: University of Pennsylvania Press, 2002.

Nicholas Bloom

SUMMER RESORTS

The first American resorts appeared in the late eighteenth century. Located primarily around springs or by the seashore, these watering places attracted elite folks in search of health-restorative waters or salubrious air. South Carolina planters, for example, traveled to Newport, Rhode Island, in the hopes of escaping the heat and disease of their plantations while politicians left Washington, D.C., for Berkeley Springs, Virginia. The difficulty of

Catskill resort. Often referred to as "America's First Wilderness" the Catskill Mountains are located 100 miles northwest of New York City, making them a popular getaway spot for city residents. As a result, numerous summer resorts call the Catskills home, such as the one where this couple sunbathed in 1953.
© *Bettman/Corbis*

travel limited the number of visitors; the few resorts were generally wanting in the way of luxuries or amenities.

The Rise of Summer Resorts

The first half of the nineteenth century witnessed a significant increase in the size of the vacationing public and, consequently, in the number of vacation resorts. Seashores, springs, and mountains began receiving guests. Wealthy urban northerners came to escape the scourges of cholera and yellow fever that swept through cities in the summer, and rich southern planters came fleeing the heat, humidity, and disease that plagued their plantations.

People were also intent upon seeking to improve their health. Nineteenth-century medical opinion held that drinking mineral waters could cure a vast array of illnesses—gastrointestinal problems, respiratory infections, skin eruptions—and that a change of climate could mitigate or heal diseases as varied as gout, consumption, and rheumatism. Recuperation and restoration, thus, motivated many of those who found their way to the early American resorts—places like Balston Spa and Saratoga Springs in New York, Newport in Rhode Island, Cape May in New Jersey, and White Sulphur Springs in Virginia.

Not all visitors were invalids or ailing, however, and even those in search of health needed amusement during their stay. Since travel was difficult—especially to inland springs—many who made the arduous journey chose to remain for the season. Resort owners learned quickly to cater to clients who hoped to combine recreation with recuperation. Health resorts could and did serve equally well as pleasure spots where guests indulged in a variety of activities—some gender-specific but most available to both women and men. Billiards, for example, quickly became a staple of resort life—but only for men. Men also gambled, often at cards. Women and men both enjoyed bathing in salt or mineral waters (although they usually did so at separate times) and both played together at nine pins—or bowling. During the evenings some guests got up games of charades or tableaux vivants (a game in which participants would dress as historical characters or mythological figures and would pose for an audience, presenting themselves as a painting or piece of art), but evenings were primarily devoted to balls or dances. These events encouraged courting, another important amusement for which watering places quickly became known. Resorts, even those initially renowned for their health-giving possibilities, offered arenas for men and women to meet, socialize, play, and sometimes find mates. The entertainment available at early nineteenth-century resorts befitted the class and status of the clientele. Guests were, for the most part, genteel people pursuing genteel pleasures. Only the elite, after all, had the time and the wherewithal to frequent resorts during the first half of the century.

Beginning in the 1850s and only temporarily interrupted by the Civil War, the growth of summer resorts proceeded especially rapidly in the three decades after 1870. The vacationing public expanded as members of an emerging white-collar and professional middle class found themselves the beneficiaries of a designated period of paid vacation. As these growing numbers of vacationers demanded more resorts, savvy entrepreneurs did what they could to accommodate. Railroads played a critical role in fueling the expansion of summer resorts, feeding this new industry in a variety of ways. First, the railroads offered an efficient means of getting visitors to their resort destinations. Trips that in the antebellum period had taken days could by the 1870s be accomplished in hours. Railroads in many cases also provided the capital to build resorts as well as the advertisements to lure visitors there. Supply and demand worked in tandem, making summer resorts more prevalent and more visible in the American landscape. Along the coasts, in the mountains, near river and lakes—resorts appeared throughout the country. No one region claimed a monopoly.

Postbellum resorts varied widely—in size, cost, location, clientele. Some resorts were small towns that swelled to crowded, mini-metropolises during the summer season—places like Cape May, Atlantic City, and Saratoga Springs. Other resorts, like the Catskill Mountain House

and White Sulphur Springs, presented a rural demeanor. The more fashionable resorts were usually large, pricey, and known to attract a well-to-do, fashionable clientele. Bustling crowds, often promenading in fancy dress, filled the streets and piazzas of fashionable resorts. Visitors to less-celebrated spots reported calmer surroundings and relaxed, easygoing days. Both fashionable and quieter resorts, however, provided some of the same sorts of amusements: Seaside resorts offered swimming; mountain resorts touted the pleasures of country walks, hikes, and rides; inland springs added bathing to the pleasures of strolling or riding either through town or countryside; lakes tendered the possibilities of fishing and sailing. Nearly all vacation spots had facilities for bowling, billiards, and croquet. Guests at most resorts spent time lolling or loitering on the porches of hotels, chatting with friends, making new acquaintances, napping, and eating. By the end of the nineteenth century more visitors were engaging in active sports and games—lawn tennis, golf, swimming matches, bicycle races. Like in the early part of the century, vacationers at resorts looked forward to evenings spent at dances and balls, where flirting and courting were primary forms of entertainment.

Women and Summer Resorts

Summer resorts provided middle-class women with a significantly wider range of amusements and pleasures than normally available to them in the postbellum United States. At a time when middle-class cultural norms dictated a restricted range of activities for women and warned about the dangers of "promiscuous" (meaning mixed gender) entertainment, women at summer resorts participated in a variety of recreational activities, usually in the company of, or even in competition with, men.

Women not only played croquet, nine pins, and tennis, but occasionally even amused themselves at the billiard table; by the turn of the century, they were finding their way onto the golf course. They also fished in lakes and frolicked in the ocean, took strenuous hikes in the mountains, and, perhaps most shockingly, flirted with strangers at dances and balls.

Alternatives to Regular Summer Resorts

As the resort culture grew and expanded, some began to fear that resorts were offering guests an environment too beset with sinful temptations—opportunities for drink, gambling, and sexual encounters. As a result, throughout the last half of the nineteenth century institutions took shape that provided the middle-class vacationing public with alternatives to regular summer resorts. Some began as Protestant (predominantly Methodist) camp meetings and grew to be religious resorts where vacationers could be protected from some of the potential dangers of resort life. Wesleyan Grove on Martha's Vineyard, Ocean Grove in New Jersey, and Rehoboth Beach on the Delaware shore all started as camp meetings and became established summer resorts by the 1870s. Although Methodists controlled most religious resorts, members of other denominations made occasional efforts in the same direction. Christian resorts established rules that differentiated them from other summer vacation sites. Some prohibited dancing and gambling; others banned tobacco and card playing. Uniformly, however, they forbade the drinking of alcohol and did their best to proscribe amusements of any kind on the Sabbath.

While religious resorts primarily focused on preventing immorality, other sorts of resorts adopted a curriculum aimed at self-improvement. Chautauqua, founded in 1874 and located in western New York, offered vacationers a unique resort experience. Guests could indulge in a variety of amusements—fishing, boating, swimming, tennis, croquet, and baseball during the day, fireworks and concerts in the evenings—as well as engaging in serious educational endeavors. Chautauqua hired prominent educators and intellectuals who gave courses and lectures in philosophy, religion, economics, art, and literature. Like Christian resorts, Chautauqua kept a fairly tight reign on its guests, interdicting liquor and refusing people entrance on the Sabbath. Regardless, Chautauqua was enormously popular and spread geographically. Within a decade of its founding there were thirty Chautauquas offering people from California to Maryland and from Minnesota to Texas access to a summer resort where they could mix education and recreation.

Discrimination at Summer Resorts

Most American resorts welcomed only white visitors. By the early twentieth century some vacation sites—Atlantic City, Niagara Falls, Cape May—accommodated African Americans in segregated boarding houses or hotels. But racist incidents often plagued black visitors, motivating some to build and frequent their own, separate vacation communities. Some succeeded better than others. An African American resort built at West Baden, Indiana, in 1908 was, by 1916, suffering. But the early twentieth century witnessed the beginnings of what would become enduring black resort communities. Oak Bluffs on Martha's Vineyard, Highland Beach on the Chesapeake Bay, Sag Harbor on Long Island, American Beach in Florida, and Idlewild in Michigan all survived to serve generations of vacationing African Americans.

Like blacks, Jews also faced exclusion from turn-of-the-century resorts. Some resorts advertised openly that "Hebrews need not apply"; others used more subtle means to discourage Jewish clients. As a result, Jews—again, like blacks—established their own resorts, often in the Catskill Mountains of New York, where they could attract New York City's large Jewish population. Fleischmann's, one of the earliest, was catering to well-to-do Jews by the 1890s.

The Working Class and Summer Resorts

In the decades between World War I and World War II, a growing number of working-class Americans found themselves able to enjoy the pleasures of a short vacation and the resort industry grew and changed to accommodate these new vacationers. Resorts that provided low-cost cottages or campsites sprang up around lakes or near the seashore. At the same time, places like Atlantic City began offering more overnight accommodations to people of limited means. While hotels at these resorts continued to welcome both the rich and the middle class, cheaper boarding houses catered to a socially and ethnically diverse crowd. Thus, the process of democratization that had begun as mid-nineteenth-century resorts began to attract a middle-class clientele continued throughout the twentieth century as more members of the working class made their claim to time spent at a summer resort.

See also: Beaches, Early National Leisure and Recreation, Gilded Age Leisure and Recreation, Leisure Class, Tourism, Vacations

BIBLIOGRAPHY

Aron, Cindy. *Working at Play: A History of Vacations in the United States.* New York: Oxford University Press, 1999.

Brown, Dona. *Inventing New England: Regional Tourism in the Nineteenth Century.* Washington, D.C.: Smithsonian Institution Press, 1995.

Chambers, Thomas A. *Drinking the Waters: Creating an American Leisure Class at Nineteenth-Century Mineral Springs.* Washington, D.C.: Smithsonian Institution Press, 2002.

Irwin, William. *The New Niagara: Tourism, Technology, and the Landscape of Niagara Falls, 1776–1917.* State College: Pennsylvania State University Press, 1996.

Lewis, Charlene Boyer. *Ladies and Gentlemen on Display: Planter Society at the Virginia Springs.* Charlottesville: University Press of Virginia, 2001.

Sterngrass, John. *First Resorts: Pursuing Pleasure at Saratoga Springs, Newport, and Coney Island.* Baltimore: Johns Hopkins University Press, 2001.

Cindy S. Aron

SUN CITY

During the late 1950s, the idea of a city designed exclusively for "active retirement" was not widely accepted by psychologists, geriatric specialists, or consultants specializing in the development of new communities. The general feeling was that one could not successfully separate the elderly from their families. Tom Breen, a Del Webb vice president who was the guiding force behind the development of Sun City, Arizona, disagreed and decided to seek the opinions of people who would be potential residents of such a community. The survey was conducted in Florida, a logical place to look for a concentration of elderly. It revealed that while people loved their families and adored their grandchildren, they were not averse to the idea of establishing an independent lifestyle in a new location. Since Florida was notorious for land scams that included selling underwater lots adjacent to nonexistent golf courses, a primary complaint among the elderly was broken promises. Breen was convinced that Del Webb was a company that could deliver a complete and functioning town and expressed his opinion in a memo to corporate headquarters outlining the importance of activity, economy, and individuality for an adult/retirement community. According to Breen, the recreation center and golf course would provide the activity, and it would be economical since the resources would be owned and used by everyone. Breen's idea of individuality was that the Webb Corporation would step away from management and would allow residents to manage their own facilities.

The Webb Corporation was determined not to break any promises and declared that there would be no "site of the future" signs on their property. The golf course, recreation center, and public buildings had to be in place and the shopping center ready for customers before even one house could be sold. Shops, a golf course, swimming pool, shuffleboard, and other amenities were available, and five carefully appointed model homes were finished before opening day.

The first Sun City development began 1 January 1960 on a 10,000-acre parcel of land located a few miles west of Phoenix, Arizona. Marketing its homes to only approximately 20 percent of the potential housing market (those fifty-five years of age or older), corporate officials were hoping to attract 10,000 visitors during the three-day New Year's Day weekend. To their surprise, the response was overwhelming, with 100,000 potential customers visiting the site. Apparently the time was right for a community that provided affordable housing with varied amenities. The idea or concept promoted by Webb

and his staff was a community based on lifestyle rather than location. Sun City soon became one of the most famous retirement communities in the United States. It was particularly appealing to relatively young retirees because it provided a traditional community that included home ownership, independence, and a lifestyle geared to leisure living.

Building on Success

Apparently the Del Webb Corporation succeeded in carrying out its mission of developing high-quality communities and neighborhoods that are conducive to an active and enriching lifestyle for its customers. Since 1960, Del Webb has sold almost 80,000 homes in the active adult market, most under the famed Sun City brand. The corporation has expanded tremendously and now operates ten master-planned communities in nine markets, including Phoenix and Tucson, Arizona; Las Vegas, Nevada; Palm Desert and Lincoln, California; Hilton Head, South Carolina; Georgetown, Texas; Ocala, Florida; and Chicago, Illinois. In July 2001, Del Webb Corporation merged with Pulte Homes, Inc. The combined companies have become the nation's largest homebuilder, stressing customer satisfaction backed by decades of providing quality homes and lifestyle amenities.

Sun City developers spend a great deal of time and effort on the internal layout and design of their communities. The design provides an inclusive community with a wall, although they are not gated. Even though most of the streets are public, there are security patrols and neighborhood watch programs to help prevent crime. Another important feature of the internal design is the integration of recreation centers into Sun City communities. During the early stages of Sun City growth, the use of recreational facilities created a neighborhood problem. The first complex was designed for a given number of residents. As additional homes were built, a new recreational facility was provided to service the residents of the newly developed area. Soon a kind of exclusivity began to occur, and some residents denied one another access unless they "belonged" to a facility. Joining all the centers together throughout the community under one organization and upgrading some of the older facilities solved the problem. The profusion of recreational possibilities open to all residents was a major selling point for the development. In addition to being extremely popular for sports activities, recreation centers serve as the "town hall" and the social hub of activity. The result has been a great deal of social interaction among residents of Sun City communities centered primarily around the recreation centers.

Sun City residents tend to have a large disposable income, a high sense of pride, a strong sense of patriotism, and a love of their community. They tend to be very active and interested citizens, and it is not surprising that the voter turnout rate and community involvement are very high. Community involvement is a bit unique at Sun City since all residents are fifty-five years of age or older and there are no schools. Important issues at Sun City include maintaining a wide variety of leisure activities, participating in neighborhood watch and crime prevention programs, and promoting and maintaining the aesthetic appeal of the community.

Sun City developments are not assisted living communities, but there are assistance clubs for those who are not as active or need limited assistance. Those requiring nursing homes usually sell their homes and move to places offering more extensive health care.

While the aging process may hamper leisure living to a certain extent, it is not detrimental to the ideal of leisure activity during retirement. In fact, an active retirement is often a healthy retirement, a concept that has been at the forefront of Sun City and its appeal to a retirement population.

See also: Senior Leisure Lifestyles

BIBLIOGRAPHY

Del Webb Corporation. Home page at http://www.del-webb.com.

Findley, John. *Magic Lands: Western Cityscapes and American Culture Since 1940.* Berkeley: University of California Press, 1992.

Finnerty, Margaret, Tara Blanc, and Jessica McCann. *Del Webb: A Man. A Company.* Phoenix, Ariz.: Heritage Publishers, 1991.

Patrick, Shawn. National Director of Public Relations, Pulte Homes, Inc. Personal interview, May 2003.

Stroud, Hubert B., and William Spikowski. "Planning in the Wake of Florida Land Scams." *Journal of Planning Education and Research* 19 (1999): 27–39.

Hubert B. Stroud

SURFING

Surfing—standing upright on a board and guiding it across the face of a breaking wave—exists today as a leisure pursuit with its own distinct culture and as a professional sport. While modern surfing is an international pastime, the roots of its technical form and cultural content lie in Hawaii and California.

Origins

Historians trace the origins of surfing to premodern Hawaii. Hawaiians of both sexes and from all social strata surfed, and early European explorers and travelers praised their skills. American missionaries, however, disapproved of the "constant intermingling, without any restraint" of men and women and banned the pastime in the mid-nineteenth century (Dibble, p. 101).

Surfing underwent a revival concomitant with the development of Hawaii as a tourist destination in the early twentieth century. American writer Jack London and Hawaiian surfers George Freeth and Duke Kahanamoku assisted the subsequent diffusion of the pastime around the Pacific. London published several accounts of surfing in popular American magazines after a visit to Waikiki. Henry Huntington hired Freeth as "the man who walks on water" to help promote his new railway line to Redondo Beach in California. An Olympic swimmer, Kahanamoku gave surfing exhibitions in Los Angeles, California; Sydney, Australia; and Wellington and Christchurch, New Zealand, while on swimming tours.

Surfboard Technology

Primitive technology hindered the popularization of surfing. Kahanamoku's generation rode solid wood boards. They were large (eight to twelve feet long, twenty-four inches wide, three inches thick) and heavy (weighing approximately 100 pounds). Tom Blake attached plywood over crossbeams to produce a lighter (sixty- to seventy-pound) "hollow" board in the 1930s. He also added a single fin under the tail, enabling riders to better steer their craft. In the early 1950s, Joe Quigg began making lighter (twenty- to thirty-pound) malibu boards (named after the California beach where they first became popular) from balsa wood wrapped in fiberglass. Toward the end of that decade, polyurethane replaced balsa. Polyurethane and improved catalysts (to harden fiberglass resin) facilitated mass production of malibus. The so-called shortboard revolution occurred in the mid-1960s. Literally overnight, boards dropped from ten feet to eight feet long, and surfers experimented with new shapes. A major influence on shortboard design was George Greenough, a kneeboard rider from California. Still made from polyurethane and fiberglass, contemporary boards have three fins, are around six feet long, eighteen inches wide, and 1.5 inches thick, and weigh about fifteen pounds. Rails (edges), noses, and tails are shaped by hand to meet specific (usually local) wave types.

Surf Riding Style

Board technology was a major influence on riding styles. Early boards had no fins, thus limiting surfers' ability to maneuver their craft; riders simply pointed the boards shoreward. A relaxed, upright stance was the essence of good style. Malibus revolutionized surfing. They enabled riders to "trim" (travel at the same speed as the breaking wave), "stall" (slow the board to allow the breaking wave to "catch up"), and change direction. Regional variations in style followed the malibu, reflecting distinct philosophies of the ocean and waves. Hawaiians sought to flow in rhythm with the breaking wave. They saw "the wave and the performer as a coordinated unit; the surfer dances with the wave, letting it lead him along its natural direction." Hawaiian style derived from an "innate respect for the waves" (Lopez, pp. 101, 104). Californians turned surfing into "an original American dance, a delightful mixture of ancient Polynesian sport, bullfighting, skiing and sailing." Unlike Hawaiians, who flowed with waves under nature's guidance, Californians sought "to enhance the beauty of a breaking wave" (Parmenter, pp. 117–118). Tinged with notions of cultural superiority, Californians believed that surfers aesthetically enhanced waves. A third, overtly aggressive style of riding emerged in Australia, where surfers sought to "dance on the wave, attacking it from all angles and reducing it to shreds" (Lopez, p. 103). This style emanated from within the Surf Lifesaving Association. A paramilitary-type body that gained hegemonic control of Australia's beaches, the association nurtured the idea that properly trained individuals could conquer waves.

By the mid-1980s, aggressive riding had become the dominant style, facilitated by short, finely tuned boards that freed surfers to move across, around, inside, and over waves at will. Urban development and intense competition for waves, particularly at the epicenters of surfing— North Shore (Oahu, Hawaii), southern California, and east coast Australia—reinforced aggressive surfing. Instead of escaping into nature, contemporary surfers immerse themselves in greasy, foul-smelling waters that assault and jolt their senses, and frequently give them ear, eye, and throat infections. Dulled by toxic wastes and detergents, the oceans now merge with ashen skies, waste-strewn sands, and pallid concrete highways and housing estates. Rather than a place for reflection, contemplation, and relaxation, the beach is another industrial urban site where surfers release aggression and express profanity, nihilism, and general dissatisfaction.

Surfing Culture

Malibus popularized surfing and precipitated a unique American youth culture that combined the relaxed, casual hedonism of Hawaii and the free-spirited beatnik philosophy of the mainland. Surfers communicated through their own language ("like wow," "daddy-o," "strictly squaresville"), humor, rituals, dress (T-shirts, striped Pendleton shirts, narrow white Levi's jeans, Ray-Ban sunglasses), and hair styles (bleached-blond hair and goatee beards). At the heart of surfing culture was the "surfari"—a wanderlust trip in search of perfect waves. Surfing rapidly penetrated the consciousness of baby boomers on the back of Hollywood surf films (romantic beach musicals and comedies: *Gidget* [1959], *Ride the Wild Surf* [1964]), surf music (a thundering guitar-based sound played as single-note riffs: Dick Dale's "Miserlou" [1962], the Chantays' "Pipeline" [1962], the Astronauts' "Baja" [1963]), "pure" surf films ("travelogues," with footage of surfers riding waves: *Trek to Makaha* [1956], *The Big Surf* [1957], *Spinning Boards* [1961]), and specialized surfing magazines (*Surfer, Surfing*).

Public commentators frowned upon the nonconformism of surfing culture. They condemned surfers' antisocial behavior (exemplified by the "brown eye"—exposing the anus to public view from a passing vehicle) and branded them itinerants, nomads, and wanderers. Surfing was seen as an indolent, wasteful, and selfish pastime that lacked an institutional anchor.

A sporting element within surfing organized competitions to counter negative images and win the activity social respectability. In 1953, the Waikiki Surf Club hosted the first International Surfing Championships for men and women at Makaha, Hawaii. Makaha marked the official birth of the sport of surfing. Most surfers rejected competition, unable to reconcile it with their quests for autonomy and freedom. Indeed, during the counterculture of the late 1960s and early 1970s surfing competitions virtually collapsed under the belief that they symbolized excessive materialism. Surfers preferred the creativity and self-expression of "soul-surfing"—riding waves purely for the benefit of communing with nature.

Ironically, the counterculture contributed to the development of professional surfing. The "work-is-play" philosophy of the counterculture encouraged a group of perspicacious (predominantly Hawaiian and Australian) surfers to establish the Association of Surfing Professionals in 1976 to coordinate competitions and financially support the best riders. To attract corporate sponsors, the ASP had to portray surfing as a mainstream sport comprising disciplined athletes. But this strategy merely fueled tensions between professional and ordinary surfers. "We [should] encourage surfing to be publicly damned," railed one surfer recently: "People don't have to fear us—they just have to not want to be us, not want to identify with a label that spells sick, perverted deviant" (Stedman, p. 81).

See also: Beaches, Snowboarding, Swimming

BIBLIOGRAPHY

Booth, Douglas. *Australian Beach Cultures: The History of Sun, Sand, and Surf.* London: Frank Cass, 2001.

Dibble, Sheldon. *A History of the Sandwich Islands.* Honolulu, Hawaii: Thomas G. Thrum, 1909.

Finney, Ben, and James Houston. *Surfing: A History of the Ancient Hawaiian Sport.* San Francisco: Pomegrante Artbooks, 1996.

Kampion, Drew. *Stoked: A History of Surf Culture.* Los Angeles: General Publishing, 1997.

Lopez, Gerry. "Attitude Dancing." *Surfer* (June–July 1976): 101–104.

Parmenter, Dave. "Epoch-alypse Now: Postmodern Surfing in the Age of Reason." *The Surfer's Journal* (Winter 1995): 112–125.

Stedman, Leanne. "From Gidget to Gonad Man: Surfers, Feminists, and Postmodernization." *Australia New Zealand Journal of Sociology* 33 (1997): 75–90.

Young, Nat. *The History of Surfing.* Sydney, Australia: Palm Beach Press, 1983.

Douglas Booth

SWIMMING

Most human locomotive efforts are geared toward movement on land. However, Earth is a largely aqueous planet, and people have found that self-locomotion in water is essential, enjoyable, and enlightening for fundamental, recreational, safety, and competitive activities.

As far back as recorded Egyptian history, swimming was utilized as a device for combative strategy. According to Wolfgang Decker, in *Sports and Games of Ancient Egypt,* Egyptians viewed nonswimmers as inferior persons; the escape of Ramesses II and his Egyptian troops from the Hittites in the Battle of Kadesh is credited to

their superior ability to swim. Hieroglyphics on pottery provide evidence of early swimming efforts—with a form of the crawl stroke a common artistic trope—particularly by those Egyptians who lived in the Nile Valley. The Pharaoh is said to have enjoyed swimming contests.

The ancient Greeks enjoyed swimming and bathing as recreational and leisure activities. They built indoor shrines and saw the use of water as cleansing and eternal. While the Greeks swam in streams and rivers and ponds, the Romans constructed "baths" to immerse themselves in controlled water in less natural, more predictable settings. Such Roman baths have been a model for swimming pools throughout the world.

In the ensuing years, swimming has taken on many forms. Humans swim recreationally for pleasure, enjoying the sensual feel of water and the various games and methods of propulsion in the water; people swim for utilitarian reasons, such as the combat-ready United States Navy SEALS, who perform reconnaissance and offensive and defensive maneuvers in the water. Innovative people have found ways to extend their bodies' abilities through use of technological advances such as scuba (self-contained underwater breathing apparatus) gear and a variety of diving (wet and dry) suits. Finally, humans compete in the water in a variety of ways, from the swimming races exemplified in the modern Olympic Games to extreme contests like underwater breath-control exercises, from marathon swimming and under-ice swimming to water polo, diving, and underwater hockey.

Recreational Swimming

People take pleasure from the enveloping feel of water. Those who cannot swim learn to bathe in small amounts of water, and even little children enjoy the pulsing motion of the waves at the sea, often learning to swim at an early age so they may unravel the mysteries of water. Recreational swimming, of course, accompanies wading, diving, body surfing, surfing, and other recreational activities in and around the water.

But water can be an unsafe place for some. Free and spontaneous recreational swimming, usually in open water, occasionally ends in drowning, and swimmers of the late nineteenth century turned to supervised recreational areas for a safer environment. Swimming schools in Europe in the early 1800s, the Surf Lifesaving Association of Australia, and the American National Red Cross in the early 1900s, among many other national organizations, attempted to standardize safety efforts for swimmers and swimming venues so that swimming recreationally became a safer pursuit. Learn-to-swim programs, lifesaving education, and activities like "drown proofing" all have standardized approaches to learning aquatic activities: For example, the crawl is the fundamental stroke first learned in North America, while the breaststroke is foundational in many Asian countries.

Utilitarian Swimming

Swimming has utilitarian roots. When pursued by enemies, humans have taken to the water for escape: In *A World History of Physical Education,* Deobold Van Dalen and Bruce Bennett also speak of Ramsses II versus the Hittites, of Jonathan the Maccabee swimming the Jordan River to escape pursuers, and of the ancient Greeks teaching swimming, especially for those who were serving in the navy. During the battle of Marathon, the Persians were said to have used swimmers to established a beachhead.

The ability to swim to an enemy's site, to reconnoiter, to establish offensive and defensive strategies upon a hostile enemy, has long been valued by armed forces. In 1941, for example, the Italian Navy used closed-circuit scuba devices to set explosives on British merchant marines ships. In 1942, U.S. Navy "Scouts and Raiders" were trained to clear out obstacles for beach landings and to guide troops: They were forerunners of the U.S. Navy SEALS. Underwater demolition teams began training in June 1943. The U.S. Navy SEALS were established in 1961, and employed aquatic skills for offensive and defensive maneuvers in World War II, Korea, Vietnam, and other conflicts.

Use of Technology

In 1535, Guglielmo de Loreno invented a diving bell of sorts, which was used to extend human immersion underwater. Since then, underwater bells, solid metal diving suits with attached diving helmets, and submarine apparatuses have all extended human immersion. But not until 1865, when Benoit Rouquayrol and Auguste Denayrouse invented an underwater breathing apparatus, could humans extend their time underwater without connection to and total dependence upon the surface. The evolution of the underwater breathing apparatus continued until, in 1925, a self-contained underwater breathing apparatus was refined by Yves Le Prieur; a regulator was designed and later perfected by Jacques-Yves Cousteau and Emile Gagnan—they also designed the Aqua-Lung in 1943. Extending immersion time has long fascinated humans, and technological advances have created more and more extensions: In 2001, John Bennett set a world record

Swimming competition. Helen Wainright, Eileen Riggin, and Ethel McGarry are among the swimmers who raced at Memorial Day events at Brighton Beach Baths in New Jersey in 1922. © *Bettmann/Corbis*

for diving to a depth of 308 meters. In 2003, Tanya Streeter set a world record in the "variable ballast" category while diving to a depth of 122 meters, or 400 feet. In the 1930s, Guy Gilpatric used rubber goggles, which lead to the use of mask, fins, and snorkles, and increased the participation rates of snorkeling.

Competitive Swimming

The Greeks had swim competitions at Hermione; the Japanese competed as early as 36 B.C. But competitive swimming in North America has its roots in the (British) National Swimming Association around 1837. Swimming championships were started in Australia in 1846. Competitions soon flourished in many varieties: Races were divided into distances swum, strokes utilized, and professional or amateur. Many of the distances were initially in open water, but by 1904 the St. Louis Olympics conducted their swimming races in "still water."

However, ultradistance swimming was becoming a contest not only of speed in the water, but of endurance. Swims such as the English Channel, Catalina Island, and Lake Michigan were highly challenging. Lean body mass and specific gravity within the water influenced a more egalitarian ratio between the sexes so that women were successful in comparison to men. Gertrude Ederle, Greta Anderson, Abo-Heif, Florence Chadwick, Guilio Travaglio, Horacio Inlesias, and Judith DeNys are some of the early pioneers of marathon swimming.

Competitive swimming in the United States reached age-group swimming initially through Amateur Athletic Union (AAU) programs. Swim clubs flourished, and four strokes emerged as "competitive" strokes: front crawl, back crawl, breaststroke, and butterfly. These—along with medley and freestyle relays, and the individual medley—are raced in a short-course (in pools with twenty-five-yard lengths) and a long-course format (in pools with fifty-meter lengths). Colleges and universities compete in athletic conferences, typically with dual meet champions and championship meet champions emerging at the season's conclusion. The National Collegiate Athletic Association sanctions both men's and women's swimming and diving teams and contests, with culminating national championships in Divisions I, II, and III.

See also: Beaches, Surfing

BIBLIOGRAPHY

"Amphibious Forces." Available from http://www.globalsecurity.org/military/.

Decker, Wolfgang. *Sports and Games of Ancient Egypt.* Translated by Allen Guttmann. New Haven, Conn.: Yale University Press, 1992.

Oppenheim, Francois. *The History of Swimming.* North Hollywood, Calif.: Swimming World Books, 1970.

"Scuba History." Available from http://www.about-scuba-diving.com.

Sprawson, Charles. *Haunts of the Black Masseur: The Swimmer as Hero.* New York: Pantheon Books, 1992.

Van Dalen, Deobold B., and Bruce L. Bennett. *A World History of Physical Education: Cultural, Philosophical, Comparative.* 2d edition. Englewood Cliffs, N.J.: Prentice Hall, Inc., 1971.

Wennerberg, Conrad. *Wind, Waves, and Sunburn: A Brief History of Marathon Swimming.* New York: Breakaway Books, 1997.

"World War II." Available from http://www.navyseals.com.

Robert E. Rinehart

TAE KWAN DO

See *Martial Arts*

TAILGATING

The origins of tailgating in the United States appear to be centered around football. Some of the first football games (such as Rutgers vs. Princeton in 1869 or Yale vs. Harvard in 1894) included pregame activities such as traveling to the game in rented train cars filled with food and beverages for the trip. People also came to the games in horse-drawn carriages and often were allowed to bring their carriages into the spectator area, where they would bring out their baskets of goodies. Because the horses were still harnessed to the carriage, people naturally congregated near the rear of the carriage.

As football gained popularity, teams traveled greater distances in order to play competitively (for example, the University of Michigan began traveling to games in the East in 1881). However, the logistics of long-distance train or carriage travel was somewhat prohibitive to fans as well as teams, so team support remained limited.

In 1901, Ransom Eli Olds built the first mass-produced automobile. Henry Ford's subsequent innovations allowed him to produce the Ford Model-T even more efficiently, which made it affordable to average-income families. By 1927 over 15 million Model-Ts had been sold and almost

everyone owned one. This meant people could get to football games more easily than in the past, and in a car that provided convenient storage space for picnic supplies and food and beverages.

Since people were now driving their own vehicles, they needed parking places, so more expansive areas were set up near football fields. In the quest to show team solidarity, football fans arrived earlier and stayed longer, decorated the areas around their vehicles, and began to engage in more intricate food preparation. Sandwiches, once the norm, gave way to hot meats on cooking spits, paving the way for the modern barbecue grill.

By the early 2000s, the results of that still-growing tradition were visible by simply visiting any college or professional football game. Fans often spent extensive time and money attending games—traveling hundreds of miles, arriving well before the game, and sometimes staying several days after the game. The most dedicated fans purchased special tailgating equipment such as telescoping flagpoles, helmet-shaped grills, and gas-powered blenders. In addition, the food ranged from the traditional hamburgers and hot dogs to spitted roasted pigs, layered dips, and specialty recipes (such as cheeseburger soup, regional breakfast burritos, deep-fried turkeys). Finally, some of the most exuberant fans could be found engaging in elaborate drinking rituals such as beer pong, ice-luge shots, and keg stands.

As the automobile has evolved, its shape and capabilities continue to influence tailgate parties. Large, open-backed pickup trucks, recreational vehicles (RVs), buses, and motor homes, sometimes custom designed for tailgating, increased the ease with which fans could bring ever more provisions to their tailgate parties. During inclement weather, they could lounge in the warmth and protection of their RVs. Increasingly elaborate tailgating behavior and equipment led some people to attend tailgate parties without actually attending the game. During game time, small groups could be seen gathered around portable televisions, which were hooked to generators or satellite connections. Some groups even listened to the game on the radio while watching the action on the stadium's scoreboard big screen, which could often be seen from the parking lot.

While the preferred tailgate vehicle changed from the original horse and carriage in the late 1800s to RVs, people still tailgated for the same reasons: to support their teams, to socialize, and to enjoy good food and drink. Tailgating occurred at a variety of sporting events, although college and professional football were still the primary venues at which to enjoy this tradition.

See also: Automobiles and Leisure; Camping; Football; Football, Collegiate; Recreational Vehicles; Stadiums

BIBLIOGRAPHY

Batchelor, Ray. *Henry Ford: Mass Production, Modernism and Design.* Manchester, U.K.: Manchester University Press, 1994.

Bernstein, Mark. *Football: The Ivy League Origins of an American Obsession.* Philadelphia: University of Pennsylvania Press, 2001.

Drozda, Joe. *The Tailgater's Handbook.* Indianapolis, Ind.: Masters Press, 1996.

Treat, Roger. *The Encyclopedia of Football.* South Brunswick, N.J.: A. S. Barnes and Company, 1979.

Waterson, John S. *College Football: History, Spectacle, Controversy.* Baltimore: Johns Hopkins University Press, 2000.

Laurlyn K. Harmon

TAPE COLLECTING AND LISTENING

See *Record, CD, and Tape Collecting and Listening*

TARGET SHOOTING

Evidence of target shooting activities involving bows and arrows as well as hand propelled projectiles such as spears can be traced as far back as ancient cultures of Asia and Europe. However, modern target shooting with firearms is a relatively recent phenomenon. In Europe, the formula for black powder, the propellant used in guns of the period, was first written down by an English friar, Roger Bacon, in 1242. By the mid-1300s, black powder artillery pieces were in common use throughout Europe, and hand cannons, the predecessors of modern long guns, had been developed. Hand cannons consisted of a smooth-bore iron barrel and were fired by manually igniting the priming powder with a smoldering wick called a match. These early firearms lacked any mechanical firing or aiming mechanisms, making them too inaccurate and impractical for hunting or sporting use. By the late 1300s, attempts had been made at increasing the portability of firearms, which resulted in the introduction of rudimentary pistols in England and Italy.

The development of target shooting as a sport was to a large extent a reflection of the progress occurring in the firearms technology, including the evolution of firing mechanisms and other inventions that increased the accuracy and reliability of early firearms. A device called the matchlock that allowed guns to be fired by pulling the trigger, but still relied on a smoldering match for ignition, was introduced in the early 1400s. In the early 1500s, wheel-lock muskets came into use in Germany. The flintlock was invented in France in the early 1600s. It consisted of the hammer with a piece of flint attached to it and the flash pan with a metal cover called frizzen. Flintlock revolutionized firearms design as it combined reliability, ease of use, and low cost, and thus it contributed greatly to popularizing shooting sports. Another invention that made target shooting a reality was the rifled barrel. Introduced in the first half of the sixteenth century, it substantially enhanced accuracy and range of guns.

Although shooting matches employing early firearms were held, along with archery competitions, as early as the second half of the fifteenth century, it was not until the sixteenth century when the sport of target shooting gained popularity, initially in Germany and then in other nations of Western and Central Europe. Archery societies evolved into shooting clubs that held regularly scheduled competitions often coinciding with religious holidays. Monetary prizes were sometimes awarded to winners. The European custom of holding shooting matches alongside other festivities was eventually brought to the New World where target practice with firearms was already a common pastime.

During the early 1800s, firearms were further improved by the introduction of the percussion cap ignition mechanism, along with breech-loading rifle designs. By the 1860s, breech-loading firearms using metallic cartridges that integrated the bullet, propellant, and the primer became popular, even though muzzle-loading guns continued to be used through the Civil War. In the 1880s, smokeless powder suitable for use in small arms was invented, making black powder guns obsolete, and marking the birth of modern firearms. Partly as a result of the rapid technological progress in the nineteenth century, target shooting had become not only increasingly popular, but also more formal and more competitive. The first national shooting federation was formed in Switzerland in 1825, followed by a number of other European nations. In 1871, Colonel William C. Church and General George Wingate formed the National Rifle Association (NRA), whose goal was to promote shooting sports and improve the marksmanship skills of the American population. In 1886, "The Great Centennial Rifle Match"—involving teams from Australia, Canada, Ireland, and Scotland—was fired at the Creedmoore range, beginning the tradition of prestigious Palma matches. A decade later, the first modern Olympic Games in Athens, Greece, included five target-shooting events. The following year, the first World Shooting Championships took place in Lyon, France. In the United States, national matches began in 1903, followed by National Smallbore Rifle Championships that were first fired in 1919.

Modern Target Shooting

Modern target shooting sports include a wide array of nationally and internationally recognized disciplines characterized by different shooting techniques, targets, firearms, and accessories. Many disciplines go beyond the tradition of shooting at a stationary target from a fixed position and involve either moving targets or the competitor navigating a course with several firing positions. Firearms used in competitive shooting range from unmodified pistols and traditional bolt-action target rifles to highly accurate custom bench-rest rifles, air guns, and replicas of antique muzzle loaders.

International shooting competitions, including the Olympic Games shooting events, are governed by the International Shooting Sport Federation (ISSF), formerly the International Shooting Union. The ISSF, founded in 1907, is composed of 157 national federations from 137 countries. The Forty-eighth ISSF World Shooting Championships that took place in Lathi, Finland, in 2002 included over seventy individual and team events in center fire and small-bore rifle, pistol, air pistol, air rifle, and shotgun disciplines. Target-shooting events were part of all modern Olympic Games with the exception of 1904 and 1928. As of the 2004 Games, there were seventeen in-

dividual Olympic shooting events, including five rifle events, five pistol events, six clay target events, and one running target event. Moreover, the Olympic sports of modern pentathlon and biathlon involve target-shooting activities. Modern pentathlon combines pistol shooting, epee fencing, swimming, equestrian show jumping, and cross-country running. Biathlon, offered during the Winter Games, involves cross-country skiing combined with small-bore rifle shooting scored based on time and accuracy. Women began competing in Olympic shooting events in 1968, and in 1984 separate shooting events for women were introduced.

Besides international shooting sports sanctioned by the ISSF, there are many other popular shooting sports. The Civilian Marksmanship and Firearms Safety Program oversees the service rifle center-fire national matches, in which historical military rifles and copies of current military rifles are fired. Practical shooting events involving target shooting with pistols, rifles, and shotguns using multiple and moving targets are organized by the International Practical Shooting Confederation (IPSC) and U.S. Practical Shooting Association (USPSA). A number of associations promote precision bench-rest shooting and shotguns sports, such as skeet and trap events. A growing number of organizations promote black powder target shooting, using both modern firearms and replicas of historical guns. American shooting enthusiasts with physical disabilities are served by the National Wheelchair Shooting Federation (NWSF), which provides training opportunities and participates in various national and international competitions, including the Paralympic Games.

The choice of shooting sports and the range of resources available to competitive shooters in the United States steadily increased over the past century. However, target shooting plays a more important role as a recreational activity than as a competitive sport. Although no reliable estimates of the number of recreational shooters were available, informal "plinking" appeared to remain among the nation's favorite pastimes.

See also: Archery, Historical Reenactment Societies, Hunting, Olympics

BIBLIOGRAPHY

Blackmore, Howard L. *Guns and Rifles of the World.* New York: Viking Press, 1965.

Blair, Claude, and Hugh B. C. Pollard. *Pollard's History of Firearms.* London: MacMillan Publishing Company, 1985.

Blair, Wes. *The Complete Book of Target Shooting.* Mechanicsburg, Pa.: Stackpole Books, 1984.

Carter, Ray, and Gary Anderson. *The CMP Youth Shooting Opportunities Guide.* Port Clinton, Ohio: Civilian Marksmanship Program, 2002.

Cooper, Jeff. *Art of the Rifle.* Boulder, Colo.: Paladin Press, 2002.

Farnell, G. C., and M. Farnell. *Target Shooting, Small-Bore Rifles and Air Rifles.* Boston: Charles River Books, 1974.

Morrow, Laurie, and Steve Smith. *Shooting Sports for Women: A Practical Guide to Shotgunning and Riflery for the Outdoorswoman.* New York: St. Martin's Press, 1996.

Monika Stodolska

TATTOOS

See *Body Culture*

TAVERNS

See *Bars*

TEENAGE LEISURE TRENDS

In the twentieth century, American teenagers were often among the first to embrace new innovations in commercialized leisure. Teens found in music, dance, movies, and other recreations opportunities to experiment with new identities, form relationships with peers, and assert their independence from parents. At various times, teenage leisure practices alternately reaffirmed and challenged the values of the dominant culture. Invariably, those challenges to mainstream values, both real and imagined, spurred moral panics over the seemingly corrupting influence of mass culture and made teenagers and entertainment industries targets of reform. Teenage leisure was thus the site of numerous struggles for cultural authority in which teenagers, entertainment industries, parents, reformers, and government officials all jockeyed for position and control. In the process, Americans continually reimagined and renegotiated the boundaries of sexual respectability, personal expression, commercial responsibility, teenage autonomy, and parental authority.

Teenage Youth and Mass Commercial Amusements in the Progressive Era

Around the turn of the twentieth century, teenagers were not yet regarded as a distinct leisure market, but they represented a large portion of the audience at nickelodeons, vaudeville theaters, public dance halls, and amusement parks. Such entertainments proved especially popular with working-class and immigrant youth eager to break away from the confinements of factory work, crowded tenements, and the old-world restrictions of immigrant parents. These affordable mass commercial amusements became the public staging grounds for dating and casual sociability among strangers. There, older traditions of chaperoned courtship gave way to the new practice of treating, in which young men paid for their date's entertainment, often with the expectation of sexual exchange in return. Working-class girls set new limits on the shifting boundaries of sexual respectability—engaging, for example, in physical intimacies only with a steady boyfriend or fiancée—but for many, respectability no longer hinged solely on chastity.

The free-and-easy sexuality that mass amusements seemed to encourage alarmed Progressive Era reformers, who warned that unsuspecting young women might be lured into prostitution by white slave merchants posing as charming escorts. In the minds of anti-vice crusaders, the movies were especially fraught with danger. Not only did the darkened theaters encourage sexual delinquency, but the films themselves—with their scenes of crime, violence, and scantily clad women—offered poor moral guides for vulnerable youth. Reformers adopted varied strategies to combat the allures and debasing effects of commercial recreation. Some, seeking to control mass amusements through government regulation, created state and local movie censorship boards and passed laws banning unaccompanied minors in movie theaters. (In response, the movie industry headed off more stringent regulation by creating its own industry review board in 1909.) Other reformers like Jane Addams, sympathizing with adolescents' cravings for adventure, romance, and mystery, sought to uplift amusements through expert supervision. They called for the construction of playgrounds, community recreation centers, and chaperoned parties as wholesome, adult-supervised alternatives.

Reformers, at best, achieved only modest success in controlling adolescents' encounters with mass culture. Adult-supervised recreations were often too sedate to successfully compete with mass amusements, underage children invariably found their way into movie theaters, and the moral endings added to films as the price for including sexually charged fare and depictions of crime nevertheless could not erase all that came before.

The Origins of a Distinct Teenage Leisure Market

During the 1920s and 1930s, teenage leisure developed more distinctive, age-based contours. For the first time in American history, teenagers of all social classes were spending more time in the company of their peers than with adults. Teens' greater access to automobiles facilitated this development, but more important still was the dramatic expansion of high school attendance. Throughout much of the nineteenth century, only a small elite—those preparing for college and professional schools—went to high school. Attendance rose dramatically during the first three decades of the twentieth century, thanks to compulsory education laws, which raised the age limit for school attendance, child labor laws, which forced more working-class youths into the schools, and the rising corporate demand for high school graduates to staff the new economy's expanding white-collar sector. High school attendance rates climbed to nearly 60 percent by the early 1930s and reached nearly 80 percent by the decade's end, owing to diminished job opportunities for youth during the Great Depression.

During the interwar years, the expansion of extracurricular activities and youth organizations that catered to adolescents' recreational needs afforded more opportunities for peer-centered interactions. Organizations that had originated in the Progressive Era—Girl Scouts, Camp Fire Girls, Boy Scouts, YMCA, and YWCA—continued to enlarge their ranks, though at a slower rate in the 1920s. Athletic boys battled for coveted spots on high school basketball and football teams, which became focal points of school spirit. Others found outlets for self-expression and sociability as members of the debate team, drama club, yearbook staff, choral society, or school band. To a certain extent, adult supervision of these activities circumscribed the influence of peers. Indeed, adults often embraced extracurricular activities, youth organizations, and summer camps as antidotes to the growth of an autonomous youth culture influenced by mass commercial recreation. Even so, the very existence of these activities and the conservative motives that inspired them testify to the increasing importance of adolescent sociability and peer-centered interactions.

As teenage leisure became increasingly segregated from adult leisure, teenagers themselves struggled to adapt to the norms and expectations of their own peer culture. Teenagers' preoccupations with their place in the social pecking order were often exacerbated by the competitive "rating-and-dating" system that measured popularity by the frequency and variety of dates one commanded. Especially during the depression, when many postponed marriage because they could not afford a home of their own, young people valued dating less as a means of choosing a lifelong mate than as a means of validating their social standing. On college campuses, where the rating-and-dating system originated, women college students carefully preserved the facade of popularity by turning down last-minute invitations and by never being caught for too long with the same partner on the dance floor. As these dating conventions filtered down to the high school, some female students, eager to avoid humiliation at school dances, actively campaigned to eliminate stags and permit fixed-partner dates.

Swing Culture

Much of teenage leisure, fashion, and dating during the 1930s and World War II revolved around swing music. Listening and dancing to swing music played on the car radio or soda fountain jukebox gave cash-strapped teens a relatively inexpensive way to enjoy dating. Giant movie theaters, eager to pack the house, charged a mere 25 cents during the depression to hear live big bands, while Harlem's Savoy Ballroom offered discounted admissions to its young Sunday Matinee Club dancers. Among swing's biggest fans, high school students helped to make swing music the nation's first multiracial youth culture. For white youth, participating in a musical culture created by African Americans contributed to its allure; most of the new dances were invented by black youth, as were the clothing and slang that went along with swing musical culture. Immigrant teens embraced swing as an expression of their new American cultural identity. Swing culture nevertheless had its mainstream and hipster counterparts. Mainstream white teenage girls—known as bobby soxers—wore saddle shoes, bobby sox, and full skirts that allowed for unencumbered dancing. Boys wore sport coats without ties. By contrast, the zoot suit, popular among working-class blacks, Mexican Americans, Filipinos, and some working-class whites, represented something more rebellious. Wearing the zoot suit expressed defiance of middle-class norms of respectability—it was a look associated with gangsters—but it also expressed deeper disaffection from a society that provided limited economic opportunities and tolerated racial discrimination. The zoot suit—with its wide-kneed, cuffed trousers and long, wide-shouldered jacket—made an especially dramatic statement of rebellion during World

War II, when fabric shortages led the government to prohibit the manufacture and sale of zoot suits.

Although swing sometimes united adolescents in a multiracial youth culture, it also became the focus of racial tensions. Rumors of racial mixing at swing nightclubs in East Los Angeles partially contributed to the nearly weeklong zoot-suit riots in 1943, when white servicemen assaulted young Mexican American and black zoot-suiters, often by "depantsing" them. For many concerned adults, however, the zoot-suit rebels were but one manifestation of a disturbing trend: the rise in juvenile delinquency. World War II had seriously hampered teen leisure, as gasoline rationing limited the availability of fuel for joy riding, dating, or even transportation to high school athletic meets. To compound matters, with fathers at war and mothers assuming breadwinning duties, unsupervised teenagers created their own excitement, sometimes skipping school, committing petty crimes, or getting drunk. Some girls, looking for an adventurous night on the town, enjoyed picking up soldiers. Thought to trade sexual favors for an evening's entertainment or pair of stockings, "victory girls", as critics called them, were blamed for rising venereal disease rates among teens.

Viewing swing music as a cause of delinquent behavior, some state and local authorities tried to ban jukeboxes and institute curfews to keep teens out of juke joints and dance halls. Rejecting such harsh external controls, Mark McCloskey, recreation director for the Office of Community War Services, instead proposed the creation of teen canteens where adolescents could enjoy swing dancing, playing Ping-Pong, and listening to music from the jukebox. McCloskey recognized that teens had few outlets for fun because many cities had cut funding for swimming pools and community centers. Much like Progressive Era reformers, McCloskey sought to contain excesses by offering wholesome, adult-chaperoned alternatives. Rules prohibiting drinking, gambling, and pick-up dates helped the canteens to win community support. McCloskey, however, also tried to avoid the heavy-handed adult guidance that had limited the effectiveness of Progressive Era efforts to uplift amusements by giving teenagers a greater hand in designing and managing the canteens according to their own tastes.

Teen Markets and Teen Rebellion in the 1950s and 1960s

During the 1950s, the most important development in popular culture—the rise of television—relocated the primary site of leisure from the public realm of urban nightlife to the private realm of the home. But even as

television's growing popularity reinforced that decade's obsession with family togetherness, American teenagers often found more satisfying outlets for self-expression in other realms of leisure. As television ate into the profits and popularity of other mass media, television's competitors, ever more conscious of teenagers' consumer clout, tried to increase their market share by going after teenagers. Hollywood catered to teen interests with films like The Wild One and Rebel Without a Cause that explored juvenile delinquency. Radio stations that played rock 'n' roll appealed to teenagers' disdain for the bland conformity of the suburbs. Much to the dismay of established DJs and singers, teens found in rock music's aggressive beat and sexually charged lyrics a refreshing alternative to the cloying pop music of the day.

Teens' attraction to rock music and movie stars like James Dean, who seemed to glamorize teen alienation, alarmed many adults and fueled the nation's intensifying obsession with juvenile delinquency. Juvenile delinquency was on the rise, but typically involved curfew violations and truancies rather than violent crime. Nevertheless, in 1953, a congressional committee criticized movies, rock music, and comic books for undermining parental authority and encouraging teens to revel in their alienation. Some Americans even viewed rock music as a communist conspiracy to destroy American values and discipline. Much like earlier detractors of swing, critics complained that rock music promoted sexual promiscuity and racial mixing. These fears were especially pronounced in the South, where white citizens' councils viewed rock music as a "plot to mongrelize America." Most southern white teens, however, easily ignored the political implications of crossing the musical color line, and remained committed segregationists.

Despite opposition to rock music, the mass market ultimately prevailed. Major record companies, eager to cash in, made rock music less threatening and more appealing to the larger white-teen market by covering black originals with watered-down versions performed by whites. No one, however, more effectively translated black culture to a mass white audience than Elvis Presley, whose hipster clothes, gyrating hips, and rebel image made him something of a surrogate black man. Television shows like American Bandstand also played a crucial role in legitimizing rock music for white teens. Hosted by the undeniably wholesome Dick Clark, American Bandstand featured white teens dancing (only with other whites) to hits by clean-cut artists singing about the agony and ecstasy of teenage romance. On American Bandstand, rock 'n' roll shed its low-class, outlaw image and was repackaged as harmless teenage fun. With the release of

Gidget and other beach films, Hollywood, too, did its part to promote reassuring images of a wholesome and carefree white, middle-class youth culture.

During the 1950s, beatniks and other marginalized teens represented a tiny undercurrent of overt defiance, but by the mid-1960s a much broader spectrum of teenagers openly defied authority of any kind. Teens found much to disdain: the Vietnam War, the escalating arms race, intransigent racism, rigid gender roles, and society's overinvestment in material comfort. Their disillusionment in turn fueled experimentation with drugs, the folk music revival, and a sexual revolution. Thanks in part to the invention of birth control pills at the beginning of the 1960s, teens increasingly conceived of sexual expression as a matter of personal choice rather than an issue of morality. While going steady in the 1950s had often been a prelude to early marriage, teens in the 1960s were more content to postpone marriage and play the field. Counterculture youth in particular rejected anything that smacked of a preprogrammed life and strove instead to live in the moment. In abandoning college to join a commune or using psychedelics to explore alternative ways of thinking about the world, counterculture teens were embracing the reigning ethos of the 1960s: the right to do your own thing.

Teenage Leisure Trends Since the 1970s

In the last third of the twentieth century, teens' investment in doing their own thing led to the proliferation of youth subcultures defined by race, gender, sexual orientation, musical taste, drug habits, sports interests, hobbies, religious affiliation, and academic inclination. High schools, to a certain extent, facilitated this fragmentation when they abandoned dress codes in the 1970s. On high school campuses, congregations of druggies, surfers, computer nerds, goths, and hip-hop fans became easily recognizable. The mass market, however, was the more important engine of fragmentation. Ever-more refined micro-markets replaced the relatively homogenized, white-teen market of the 1950s. Much to the dismay of teens who defined themselves in opposition to mass-market commercialism, marketers became increasingly expert at discerning and then mainstreaming subcultural styles. Teens resisted commercial cooptation by reinventing the meanings of commodities associated with subcultural styles, as rappers did when they substituted preppy sportswear for the droopy pants they had made fashionable in the suburbs. An increasingly rapid pace of cultural reinvention and commercial exploitation characterized teen leisure in the late twentieth century.

If the cultural revolutions of the 1960s seemed to make schools and parents more tolerant of teenagers' desires to do their own thing, teenage leisure nevertheless continued to incite moral panics. At the congressional hearings on gangsta rap in 1994, black civil rights leaders criticized rappers for glamorizing violence and degrading women: some recommended a parental advisory rating system for popular music; others advocated censorship of offending lyrics. New technologies like video games, MTV videos, and the Internet revived long-standing anxieties that commercialized leisure fostered sexual promiscuity and violence. In 1999, a murderous rampage at Columbine High School in Littleton, Colorado, conducted by two teenage boys who played violent video games, compounded such anxieties. That many teenagers enjoyed new technologies of leisure from the privacy of their bedrooms raised concerns that teenagers were at once overindulged and inadequately supervised by working parents. Long-standing worries about the unhealthy consequences of too much passive spectatorship acquired new resonance in the 1990s as childhood obesity rates soared. Such trends in teenage leisure, however, proved far more contradictory than critics supposed. If the Internet encouraged greater passivity and isolation in some teens, it also provided the building blocks for others to forge new cultural identities and associations with like-minded teens.

See also: Computer/Video Games, Cyber Dating, Cruising, Dance Halls, Extreme Sports, Hook-Ups, Internet, Movies' Impact on Popular Leisure, Progressive-Era Leisure and Recreation, Rap Music Audiences, Raves/Raving, Rock Concert Audiences, Scouting Movments, Skateboarding, Television's Impact on Youth and Children's Leisure, Wilding

BIBLIOGRAPHY

Austin, Joe, and Michael Willard, eds. *Generations of Youth: Youth Cultures and History in Twentieth Century America.* New York: New York University Press, 1998.

Bailey, Beth. *From Front Porch to Back Seat: Courtship in Twentieth-Century America.* Baltimore: Johns Hopkins University Press, 1988.

Daniel, Pete. *Lost Revolutions: The South in the 1950s.* Chapel Hill, N.C.: University of North Carolina Press, 2000.

Doherty, Thomas. *Teenagers and Teenpics: The Juvenilization of American Movies in the 1950s.* Philadelphia: Temple University Press, 2002.

Douglas, Susan. *Where the Girls Are: Growing Up Female with the Mass Media.* New York: Times Books, 1994.

Erenberg, Lewis. *Swingin' the Dream: Big Band Jazz and the Rebirth of American Culture.* Chicago: University of Chicago Press, 1998.

Fass, Paula. *The Damned and the Beautiful: American Youth in the 1920s.* New York: Oxford University Press, 1977.

Gilbert, James. *A Cycle of Outrage: America's Reaction to the Juvenile Delinquent in the 1950s.* New York: Oxford University Press, 1986.

Hine, Thomas. *The Rise and Fall of the American Teenager.* New York: Avon Books, 1999.

Jackson, John. *American Bandstand: Dick Clark and the Making of a Rock 'N' Roll Empire.* New York: Oxford University Press, 1999.

May, Kirse Granat. *Golden State, Golden Youth: The California Image in Popular Culture, 1955–1966.* Chapel Hill: University of North Carolina Press, 2002.

Palladino, Grace. *Teenagers: An American History.* New York: Basic Books, 1996.

Peiss, Kathy. *Cheap Amusements: Working Women and Leisure in Turn-of-the-Century New York.* Philadelphia: Temple University Press, 1986.

Lisa Jacobson

TELEVISION'S IMPACT ON POPULAR LEISURE

One of the most significant social trends during the last half of the twentieth century involved the rise of television (TV) as the dominant leisure time activity for most people in nations where TV was widely available. This trend was especially strong in the United States, where TV occupied about 40 percent of leisure time for most Americans in the early twenty-first century. This translates into an average of three hours of TV viewing per day; although some of this viewing is done while engaging in other activities. Many theorists and researchers have sought to explain how TV has come to dominate leisure time. Others have tried to assess the consequences. This essay reviews their arguments below and has documented in detail how leisure time has come to be dominated by TV.

TV can be regarded as the latest in a series of advances in communications technology that have enabled mediated forms of communication to gradually displace older forms of leisure activity, including many activities that involved face-to-face or group communication. Researchers have argued that these media gradually displaced neighborhood gossip and family story-telling. Urban workers had difficulty fitting traditional communication activities into their regimented lives. Print media came to substitute for conversations with family and friends because they could be used whenever and wherever some free time was available. Also, urban workers had often been displaced from rural communities, were cut off from traditional social groups, and so were forced to find other ways of satisfying communication needs.

This basic formula was repeated again and again with the introduction of media that were capable of simulating an ever greater range and variety of leisure activities. Instead of engaging in amateur sports or games, people became spectators for mass mediated professional sports. In many cases, displacement of older forms of leisure activity took place because these activities became harder to pursue due to structural changes in working and living conditions. In general, media-based leisure activity was more flexible and could be more easily adapted to constraints on time and place.

The appearance of radio, phonographs, and movies in the 1920s and 1930s was accompanied by important changes in leisure time activity. These media had attributes that overcame the limitations of print media. Most importantly, it was no longer necessary to be literate to use these media. In general, print media had to be purchased, but once the radio was paid for, the content was free. Radio and phonographs could be used at home at any time of the day. Movies provided a very attractive medium for story-telling that easily displaced competing media. In the 1930s, the popularity of radio was further enhanced by its ability to quickly deliver news about a very problematic social world beset by widespread economic depression and political conflict.

By the time that TV emerged as a mass medium in the late 1950s and early 1960s, mass media already were an important means of filling leisure time. During the decade after its introduction, TV displaced other mass media from newspapers, movies, and radio to books and magazines. All of the competing media industries had to be reorganized during the 1960s to survive as TV took away their audiences and advertising revenue. Most survived by eliminating content or services that competed directly with TV. Radio stopped broadcasting dramatic content that told stories and shifted its focus to music. In what was for many years a losing battle for a mass audience, the movie industry expanded the size of the viewing screen and improved the sound. Newspapers tried to provide in-depth coverage of news stories introduced on TV. Magazines stopped distributing mass entertainment content and focused on delivering specialized entertainment and information. TV became the dominant mass medium and all other media adapted to fill niches left to them by TV.

By the middle of the 1960s and into the 1970s, research on how Americans spend their leisure time began to document even more profound changes in the way that TV filled spare time. With the introduction of color TV in the 1970s, TV did not merely displace other media, it began to displace a variety of leisure activities that had survived the introduction of older mass media. By the 1980s, TV use peaked in part because it had already absorbed such a large part of leisure time. In the 1980s and 1990s, the spread of cable- and satellite-based TV, and the accompanying expansion in the variety of TV content available, did little to alter the overall amount of TV use. The introduction of computer-based media such as the Internet in the 1990s again expanded the overall amount of time spent with media.

Media researchers developed a variety of theories in an effort to understand the consequences of how TV altered use of leisure time. One of the most important and enduring debates over the consequences of TV use focuses on TV as a medium for mass entertainment. From its introduction, TV has been criticized as providing an inferior form of mass entertainment that had many problematic consequences. Some of the earliest and most devastating criticisms of mass entertainment were offered by Frankfurt School scholars, who moved to the United States from Germany in the 1930s to escape the Nazis. They brought with them a deeply skeptical and pessimistic view of the power of mass media to mislead and deceive mass audiences. Frankfurt School theorists such as Max Horkheimer and Theodor Adorno argued that mass media debased high culture content when they created and distributed inferior reproductions. High culture was transformed into mass culture. Mass culture content had lost its power to enlighten or educate; it could merely entertain. Because this content was so attractive, it served to distract people from seeking out better forms of culture. Harold Mendelsohn offered an early defense of mass entertainment. He argued that the critics of mass entertainment were largely members of an elite that refused to acknowledge the many useful purposes that mass entertainment served for average persons. Average persons can not afford the cost of and do not have easy access to high cultural content. Media such as radio and TV provide a low cost alternative to live theatrical performances, museums, or orchestra concerts. Average persons often seek through entertainment media the opportunity to play and escape from the problems of everyday life, and they are not necessarily looking for high culture offerings that may educate or enlighten. TV provides an ideal way to do this at low cost, without having to leave home.

The debate over mass entertainment continued and intensified as television gained popularity. Mass media in general, and TV in particular, were accused of fostering mass culture in which free time was largely used for escapism and commodity consumption. Cultural historian Christopher Lasch describes how "the appearance in history of an escapist conception of 'leisure' coincides with the organization of leisure as an extension of commodity production." Thus, he sees "the same forces that have organized the factory and the office have organized leisure as well, reducing it to an appendage of industry" (p. 217).

From its introduction, television has been a premier medium for selling commodities, showcasing new kinds of life-styles and leisure activities for millions of Americans. Television programming not only rejected the tragic view of life, but also promoted the notion of the "quick fix," in which problems are solved within the context of a thirty-minute show or remedied through consumption of advertised products. Things happen quickly on television because commercial sponsors want the widest possible audiences, including people with short attention spans who require little complexity. These quick fixes often featured portrayals of violence and sexuality, and it was usually an enterprising, engaging and heroic individual, rather than a group or organization, who solved problems.

Television brought an endless variety of attractive material goods to the attention of viewers through advertising, and success and happiness were equated with the use of these products.

In many ways, television worked against the traditional middle-class values of delayed gratification and the work ethic. Both television commercials and programming taught Americans that they could have what they wanted, *now*. Television is believed to have affected the Baby Boom generation, the first generation raised with TV, in three distinct ways. First, it separated the Baby Boomers from traditional social elders, teaching them lessons without the intervention of parents or teachers. TV was the predominant storyteller for this generation. Second, it presented a world that was remarkably similar from channel to channel, referred to as the Golden Age of network TV by its defenders or as a "vast wasteland" by critics such as Federal Communications Commission chairman Newton Minnow. This generation was the first to share a homogeneous, common mass culture that reached all regions of a diverse nation. Finally, television violence, which was so much more prevalent than the violence in real life, created a sense of fear about the world. Television may have led to Americans "amusing ourselves to death," to use Neil Postman's publication title.

In the 1990s, George F. Gilder provided an assessment of TV that summarizes its major failings as an entertainment medium according to its current critics:

> Television is not vulgar because people are vulgar; it is vulgar because people are similar in their prurient interests and sharply differentiated in their civilized concerns. All of world history is moving increasingly toward more segmented markets. But in a broadcast medium, such a move would be a commercial disaster. In a broadcast medium, artists and writers cannot appeal to the highest aspirations and sensibilities of individuals, manipulative masters rule over huge masses of people. (p.49)

According to contemporary critics such as Gilder, although cable and home video use has allowed more individual choice in programming, most of television remains a "top down" managed medium, providing non-interactive entertainment and other programming on a few channels. Increasingly, cable is organized in terms of alliances between channels owned or co-owned by a handful of large corporations. Similar mass entertainment content is produced and shared (repurposed) across sets of channels. Mass culture is being distributed in new ways but it retains many of its older attributes and functions.

The impact of increased time spent viewing television is reflected in domestic architecture. Consider the savage assessment of architecture scholar James Howard Kunstler:

> The American house has been TV-centered for three generations. It is the focus of family life, and the life of the house correspondingly turns inward, away from whatever occurs beyond its four walls. (TV rooms are called "family rooms" in builders' lingo. A friend who is an architect explained to me: "People don't want to admit that what the family does together is watch TV.") At the same time, the television is the family's chief connection with the outside world. The physical envelope of the house itself no longer connects their lives to the outside in any active way; rather, it seals them off from it. The outside world has become an abstraction filtered through television, just as the weather is an abstraction filtered through air conditioning. (p.167)

Elite criticism of television remains a popular sport for pundits, and as a mass medium television is an easy and obvious scapegoat for almost any problem in society. Harder evidence of the consequences of TV use has come from the social sciences in the past three decades.

From cultivation theory and "mean world" hypothesis, to Robert Kubey and Mihaly Csikszentmihalyi's evidence that television fosters viewer passivity and grumpy moods after viewing, to evidence that television has played a role in reducing The United States' stock of "social capital." All of this research suggests that when television occupies too much time in people's lives, the results can be quite problematic.

George Gerbner provides evidence that when people view TV for more than six hours per day, their views of the social world reflect a growing belief that the social world is like what they see on TV—a world where white males wield power and racial minorities provide comic relief; a world where crime and disease are rampant and must be dealt with by heroic police officers, lawyers, and doctors.

Arguments concerning the role of TV in the loss of social capital are especially troubling. Robert Putnam points out that as TV was coming to dominate leisure time in the 1960s and 1970s, more and more people were abandoning their involvement in many different types of formal and informal social groups. According to Putnam, this trend has important consequences for American democracy. Through much of this nation's national history, social groups have brought together people from different racial, cultural, social, and political backgrounds. From fraternal organizations to amateur athletic associations, these groups enabled people to get to know each other as human beings and to develop friendships that spanned racial or ethnic divisions. These informal relationships provided "social capital" that could later be used as a resource when communities faced difficult or divisive political issues and controversies. People who knew and trusted each other could negotiate solutions and accept compromises. The archetype informal social group, according to Putnam, is the bowling league. Participation in such leagues has been in steady decline. Increasingly, bowlers bowl alone and amateur athletes watch sports on TV.

Putnam's views inspired considerable research and praise, but were also criticized as providing a superficial explanation of complex structural changes in American society. Research in the late twentieth and early twenty-first centuries indicated that when definitive research is done, TV will not be found to be a powerful corrosive force that operated in isolation to undermine U.S. social structure. Rather, it is likely that TV provided an easy and quite attractive way to spend time freed up as informal social groups declined for other reasons. If TV had not been there, that decline might have been more widely noticed. People would have had a harder time finding ways to spend their time.

Television has become an important way in which people experience the world, much as hypothesized. Television coverage boosted public support for the space program and the civil rights movement, reshaped public opinion about Vietnam, and made celebrities of many ordinary people. Russell W. Neuman documented how viewers of popular prime-time programs do become actively involved in the plots of programs and do subject them to critical thinking. His research findings are consistent with a large body of research based on uses and gratifications theory. This research demonstrates that TV use stimulates levels of interest and involvement, but the research has also been unable to link this use to any consistent long-term consequences.

Thus, although television has been widely criticized, it remains immensely popular and does engage its audiences. It is ideally suited to taking up small gains in free time. This, then, is where most of the action in time-use dynamics has occurred—and where it can expected it to occur in the future.

Changes in Daily Life Associated with Television

Accurate measurement of how people spend time is a challenging task. One of the most scientifically reliable and valid techniques for measuring time use is the time diary. Surveys that use time diaries to collect data ask that respondents fill out a detailed listing of their activities during a single day. In addition to reporting the time spent on each activity, respondents also report if other people were involved and where the activity took place.

In 1965, an ambitious, multinational project used time diaries to measure time use in twelve nations. In all, thirty thousand persons in twelve nations in North America, Europe, and Latin America were participated in the time-use survey. In the United States, a cross-section sample of Americans was interviewed. Surveys in some other nations, however, were limited to specific cities. In the United States, subsequent surveys of a cross-section of Americans have been conducted every ten years as part of The Americans' Use of Time Project, housed at the University of Maryland. This ongoing research provided an interesting baseline data in 1965, at a time when TV was still relatively new in some nations. Subsequent surveys in 1975 and 1985 in the United States provided insight into how daily life changed as the popularity of TV increased. When the daily activities of television owners and non-owners in the 1965 multinational time-diary study were compared, remarkable similarities were found in the post-TV behaviors of set owners across the twelve nations in the study. European countries were in earlier stages of television diffusion than the 95 percent saturation levels in the United States at the time. Non-owners of TV were heavily concentrated in eastern European nations. Thus, it was possible to study the impact of television by contrasting how owners and non-owners were spending their time. Ideally, it would have been better to compare the same people before and after television acquisition, as T. E. Coffin did, but the 1965 rates of set ownership did vary between 25 percent in Bulgaria and 80 percent in Germany, providing a broad range of respondents in societies at various stages of the television adoption process.

Table 1 shows results from this owner/non-owner comparison using the international time-diary data. In brief, it shows that television owners in almost all societies were spending less time than non-owners in "functionally equivalent" activities: eight minutes less listening to the radio, six minutes less reading books, three minutes less going to the movies, and three minutes less watching television in other people's homes. But they were also spending less time in the non-media free-time activities of socializing (twelve minutes less), hobbies and other leisure activities (six minutes less), and conversation (five minutes less).

More interesting were the changes in non-free-time activities, because these changes could not be accounted for by simple displacement of functionally equivalent forms of communication. Instead, television owners spent thirteen minutes less time sleeping, six minutes less gardening, and five minutes less on laundry and personal grooming. Such differences were not found in all societies or social groups, but they are not the types of changes in activities one might have predicted would result from the advent of television.

Even larger differences were found for secondary activities: there was a twenty-two-minute decline in radio listening, offset by an almost equivalent rise in secondary TV viewing (that is, watching TV while doing something else). Television owners also spent ten to thirty minutes less time alone, and twenty minutes more time with their spouses and children (thus perhaps inadvertently promoting a new form of family life, as described by John P. Robinson in 1990. In line with the declines in socializing with friends and relatives, contact time with friends and neighbors was also lower for TV owners. Equally impressive differences were found by location, with TV owners spending more than half an hour more time at home indoors than non-owners, mainly at the expense of spending time in the yard, in other people's homes, and on the streets. Television did bring people home, but indoors rather than outdoors.

TABLE 1

1965–85 Differences in activities of TV owners vs. non-owners

(In minutes per day. Data are weighted to ensure equality of days of the week and respondents per household across 13 countries.)

	TV Owners	Non-owners	Difference
1. Main job	254.2	253.2	+1.0
2. Second job	3.7	4.1	−0.4
3. At work other	10.6	10.8	−0.2
4. Travel to job	28.2	28.4	− .2
Total Work			**+ 0.2**
5. Cooking	55.0	56.7	−1.7
6. Home chores	57.9	58.1	−0.2
7. Laundry	27.9	32.9	−5.0
8. Marketing	18.1	18.1	0.0
Total Housework			**−6.9**
9. Animal, garden	11.5	17.6	−6.1
10. Shopping	7.7	6.4	+1.3
11. Other house	19.1	20.8	−1.7
Total Household Care			**−6.5**
12. Child care	17.9	16.8	+1.1
13. Other child	11.5	10.1	+1.4
Total Child Care			**+ 2.5**
14. Personal care	55.0	59.5	−4.5
15. Eating	84.7	84.6	+0.1
16. Sleep	479.3	491.8	−12.5
Total Personal Needs			**−16.9**
17. Personal travel	18.4	19.0	−0.6
18. Leisure travel	16.4	20.5	−4.1
Total Non-Work Travel			**−4.7**
19. Study	15.7	18.1	−2.4
20. Religion	3.5	6.2	−2.7
21. Organizations	5.3	3.6	+1.7
Total Study & Participation			**− 3.4**
22. Radio	5.2	13.2	−8.0
23. TV (home)	86.5	7.3	+79.2
24. TV (away)	1.1	4.0	−2.0
25. Read paper	15.2	15.3	−0.1
26. Read magazine	3.9	5.4	−1.5
27. Read books	8.3	14.1	−5.8
28. Movies	3.1	6.5	−3.4
Total Mass Media			**+57.5**
29. Social (home)	14.6	11.7	+2.9
30. Social (away)	22.4	33.9	−11.5
31. Conversation	14.5	19.5	−5.0
32. Active sports	2.4	2.6	−0.2
33. Outdoors	15.8	17.5	−1.7
34. Entertainment	3.9	3.9	0.0
35. Cultural events	1.0	1.1	−0.1
36. Resting	23.8	24.8	−1.0
37. Other leisure	16.7	21.9	−5.2
Total Leisure			**−21.9**
Total Minutes Per Day	**1440.0**	**1440.0**	**0.0**

When similar comparisons with other household technologies were made, these television differences became even more impressive. For example, no systematic or important differences were found in the time spent traveling by people who owned cars and those who did not, nor were there lower (or higher) travel times in so-cieties with more cars. In much the same way, there was little difference in the housework activities of societies that had greater or lower access to household technology. These appliances may have reduced labor, but not the time doing housework, much as James Morgan, Ismail Sirageldin, and Nancy Baerwaldt found in 1966.

Having a TV set in the home, then, was associated with a virtual doubling of time spent with the media as a primary activity, from 1.1 hours per day to 2.1 hours per day. Differences of a similar magnitude were found in the pre-post television study conducted over a six-month period of peak television diffusion in Fort Wayne, Indiana. T. E. Coffin found that the 160-minute daily gain in viewing time (as a primary or secondary activity) was accompanied by a seventy-minute loss in daily radio-listening and a fourteen-minute loss in reading magazines and newspapers. This suggests that television's impact can be dramatically captured directly in terms of how people spend time.

1975 Differences in Viewing

The 1965 multinational data provided the basis for another conclusion about television time—that American television viewing had apparently reached its peak in the 1960s. At the time, researchers concluded that, while Americans watched more television than residents of other countries, that fact was mainly a function of the higher ownership of sets in the United States. On a per-owner basis, viewers in other countries watched virtually as much as Americans did. Moreover, when Americans were asked if they wanted to watch more television, or would have watched more if there had been better programs available on the diary day, only about 10 percent said they wanted to watch more or would watch more. Thus, there seemed to be little reason to expect that Americans would increase their 10 hours of weekly television viewing. Since 96 percent had television sets in 1965, television seemed to be a "mature" medium with a well-established audience.

The 1975 diary data provided a rude shock. They showed that TV viewing had increased to nearly 15 hours per week, about the same five-hour gain that was found for free time. At first, this was believed to be simply a coding error, so a separate set of new coders recoded both the 1975 and the 1965 diaries. The recoded results, however, matched the original results almost identically. People were now reporting 50 percent more television viewing in their 1975 diaries.

Other explanations were sought: longer broadcast days allowing fringe viewing, more independent stations that were now broadcasting, and the early availability of cable television. While these accounted for some of the difference, the major factor associated with more viewing was the availability of color sets, something that was still a rarity in 1965. Whether it was a side effect of color television per se, or the characteristics of those who bought color sets, is not clear, but it was apparent that television had made dramatic new inroads on people's use of time, beyond its original significant impact.

In 1975, moreover, television's gain did not come mainly at the expense of other free-time activities. The main activities to show a decline between 1965 and 1975 were paid work and housework. How much of a direct trade-off was involved is not clear. It is not known to what extent people were cutting corners on these two productive activities to satisfy their appetites for what was on television. It is possible that once again the availability of an attractive mass medium provided people with an easy way of filling time freed up by a reduced work-week and labor saving household technology. Nevertheless, the two trends in decreased productivity at work and at home and increased television use did occur in the same decade.

One free-time activity—newspaper reading—did decline dramatically between 1965 and 1975, and that decline did seem to be television induced. The decline seemed to be a direct byproduct of the increased popularity of local news programs over the same time. These local news broadcasts did have the advantage over local newspapers, in terms of a trained new army of "news consultants," who relied extensively on audience surveys to put newscasters in touch with potential viewers in ways that traditional newspaper journalists could never imagine. Also during this era, newspapers were seeking to reduce the number of low-income readers so that they could provide advertisers with a higher quality audience. Prices were increased and distribution in low-income areas was reduced. The loss in newspaper-reading time was almost directly mirrored in the increased diary time spent watching local news programs. It is interesting that the losses were greater among older newspaper readers than among younger readers reared on television.

As TV viewing went up, what activities showed decline? There were few positive correlations between most activities and television viewing. Of course, people who watched television more worked less, but they also did less housework, did less shopping, and ate out less—and participated less in almost all away-from-home free-time activities: adult education, religion, cultural events, socializing, and recreation. Ironically, television time did correlate positively with activities that had been identi-

fied as earlier victims of the set: sleeping, resting, and newspaper reading.

In other words, the more people stayed home to watch, the more they did other home-based activities. Conversely, the more people watched, the less they interacted with others outside the home, particularly in the form of "social capital" activities such as socializing and organizational participation. Thus, the time use findings provide strong corroboration for the findings and conclusions offered by Robert Putnam.

1985 Differences in TV Viewing

The 1985 data, on the other hand, followed the initial 1965 expectations of viewing constancy rather well. Television viewing was up by less than one hour from 1975 levels (although mainly among women). Table 2 shows much greater growth of viewing in the 1965–1975 decade, and the greater growth of women s viewing since 1965, to the point that women were watching 92 percent as much as men in 1985 (compared with 82 percent as much in 1965). The seven-hour gain among non-employed

TABLE 2

1965–1996 Diary trends in use of time				
(In hours per week)				
	1965*	**1975**	**1985**	**1994–6**
Men				
TV	11.8	16.1	17.0	19.6
Books/mags	1.3	1.7	2.0	2.0
Newspapers	2.8	1.8	1.1	1.2
Radio/recs	.7	.7	.6	.4
Computer	00	.1	.5	1.7
Hobby/play	1.3	1.9	1.9	1.6
Other Free	14.4	15.4	17.0	17.1
Total free	**32.3**	**37.7**	**40.1**	**43.5**
Education	1.9	2.1	2.3	2.6
Fy/Pd Work	59.9	50.6	50.2	49.8
Pers Care	18.0	19.3	18.8	15.5
Sleep	56.8	58.3	56.3	56.7
Total time	**168***	**168**	**168**	**168**
Women				
TV	9.3	15.0	15.8	18.4
Book/mags	1.2	2.1	2.4	2.5
Newspapers	2.2	1.7	1.1	1.1
Radio/recs	.5	.6	.4	.3
Computer	00	0	.2	1.1
Hobby/play	2.4	3.7	3.1	1.8
Other free	16.3	15.1	16.4	17.0
Total free	**31.9**	**38.2**	**39.4**	**42.2**
Education	1.0	1.4	1.8	1.9
Family/paid	59.6	49.4	50.0	48.6
Pers care	18.7	18.7	19.7	16.8
Sleep	56.8	61.7	57.1	58.4
Total time	**168***	**168**	**168**	**168**

*Aged 18–65, Urban, Employed Sample Only

women was particularly pronounced, since their gain in free time was also seven hours.

The data was analyzed to look at changes in TV use by various subgroups and found above-average gains by those aged 55 to 64 (+7 hours), African Americans (+9 hours), the grade-school educated (± 7 hours), those with forty-hour workweeks (+7 hours), and the divorced-widowed (+7 hours). The lowest gains were reported by the lowest income group (+2 hours) and by those with larger numbers of children (+1–2 hours). These groups already had high levels of use in 1975. The gains were slightly lower on Sunday, but otherwise distributed equally across the week. Not one group showed a decrease or constancy in viewing levels, despite several such entries for free time. Some groups may not have gained free time across the study period, but all groups had experienced an increase in television viewing.

Television Use in 1995 and Beyond

Another cross-section of Americans completed time use diaries in 1995. Overall, this data indicated that the amount of time spent viewing television had not changed much. In some ways, this result was surprising given the radical changes that had taken place in the TV industry from 1985 to 1995. Cable television had expanded across the nation and a myriad of popular cable TV channels were providing easy availability to specialized programming. Also by 1995, computer-based media such as the Internet were beginning to come into wider use. Some researchers expected that the Internet would gradually reduce TV viewing time. Research conducted since 1995 shows that the media landscape has become quite cluttered with many new but functionally equivalent media and services. These media appear to be locked in head to head competition for an audience that is already spending as much free time as possible using media. Despite the predicted long-term "convergence" of media, the era of the early twenty-first century was one of media fragmentation. Media ownership "converged" so that most mass media content was delivered by a handful of large corporations. The delivery vehicles for media content, however, diverged.

Changes in the delivery of music may presage possible changes in other forms of mass entertainment. A stable and gradually increasing market for music delivered by radio and compact discs disintegrated as a growing number of young adults exchanged and downloaded music from the Internet. Compact disc players were challenged by a growing array of MP3 players. Radio was rapidly losing young male listeners as they turned to the Internet for music. One way of interpreting the revolution in music delivery was to take into account the increased user activity and initiative necessary to amass large libraries of music from the Internet and then organize this music for everyday use. Turning on a radio was a much easier way of getting music, but that music was necessarily standardized and programmed for a mass audience.

Does the transformation in the delivery of music mean that in the future people will turn away other forms of mass audience programming in favor of highly specialized programming tailored to specific interests? If so, television use could change as radically as radio use or CD use. Proponents of the Internet made this argument: it is possible to view Internet surfing as a do-it-yourself creation of an audiovisual experience that could rival TV viewing as a leisure activity. On the other hand, the Internet could easily become simply an extension of the TV viewing experience. The television industry was doing what it could to promote this way of using the Internet.

In the early 2000s, it was estimated that people use TV and the Internet simultaneously about 30 percent of the time. People tended to have TV sets in the same room that they used the Internet. As wireless access to the Internet grew, it became easier for more and more people to use the Internet while they watched TV. Does this mean that the two activities will converge so that one simply complements the other, or will one use dominate while the other merely provides background entertainment? Some researchers noted that Internet surfing is more like magazine reading than watching TV, but surprisingly, people who used the Internet more also tended to read more magazines. Apparently, Internet use was not functionally replacing magazine use so much as cultivating it. Will this change as the Internet delivers more and better audiovisual content?

What people do with mass entertainment content in the future should reveal a lot about what this content does for them and their commitment to it. Time use trends suggest that people worldwide find mass media generally, and TV specifically, to be quite important for their daily life. More than half of their leisure time is devoted to the use of mass media—40 percent to TV alone. But is this content so important that they will become more active in collecting, organizing, and distributing it as some young adults use music content in the early 2000s? Could such activities come to occupy an even larger proportion of leisure time? Time use data do suggest that overall use of media and mass entertainment has peaked in relation to other forms of leisure time activities. Unless there are significant changes in social structure, such as a reduction in work hours, time available for mass entertainment is somewhat fixed. The time that has been set aside for these activities, however, is so large and the means of delivering entertainment content is becoming so diverse that people could use media to pursue many different but highly interrelated leisure activities. The very popularity of mass entertainment could bring about its decline as the audience fragments and becomes ever more active in the pursuit of what entertains them most.

See also: Commercialization of Leisure; Computer's Impact on Leisure; Contemporary Leisure Patterns; Early National Leisure and Recreation; Expansion of Leisure Time; Internet; Media, Technology, and Leisure; Movies' Impact on Popular Leisure; Shortage of Leisure; Television's Impact on Youth and Children's Leisure.

BIBLIOGRAPHY

Brown, Robert. J. *Manipulating the Ether: The Power of Broadcast Radio in Thirties America.* Jefferson, N.C.: McFarland and Co., 1998.

Coffin, T. E. "Television's Impact on Society." *American Psychologist* 10, (1955): 630–641.

Fine, Ben. *Social Capital Versus Social Theory: Political Economy and Social Science at the Turn of the Millennium.* London; New York: Routledge, 2001.

Gerbner, George, and Annenberg School of Communications, University of Pennsylvania. *Television's Mean World.* Philadelphia: Annenberg School of Communications, University of Pennsylvania, 1986.

Gerbner, George, and Nancy Signorielli. *Violence and Terror in the Mass Media.* Paris: Unesco, 1988.

Gilder, George F. *Life After Television.* Rev. ed. New York: W. W. Norton, 1994.

Horkheimer, Max, Theodor W. Adorno, and Gunzelin Schmid Noerr. *Dialectic of Enlightenment: Philosophical Fragments.* Stanford, Calif.: Stanford University Press, 2002.

Kubey, Robert William, and Mihaly Csikszentmihalyi. *Television and the Quality of Life: How Viewing Shapes Everyday Experience.* Hillsdale, N.J.: Lawrence Erlbaum Associates, 1990.

Kunstler, James Howard. *Home from Nowhere: Remaking Our Everyday World for the Twenty-First Century.* New York: Simon and Schuster, 1996.

Lasch, Christopher. *The Culture of Narcissism: American Life in an Age of Diminishing Expectations.* New York: Warner Books, 1980.

McLean, Scott L., David A. Schultz, and Manfred B. Steger, eds. *Social Capital: Critical Perspectives on Community and "Bowling Alone."* New York: New York University Press, 2002.

McLuhan, Marshall. *Understanding Media: The Extensions of Man.* London: Sphere Books, 1967.

Mendelsohn, Harold A. *Mass Entertainment.* New Haven, Conn.: College and University Press, 1966.

Morgan, James N., Ismail Sirageldin, and Nancy Baerwaldt. *Productive Americans: A Study of How Individuals Contribute to Economic Progress.* Ann Arbor: University of Michigan Institute for Social Research, 1966.

Moy, Patricia, Dietram A. Scheufele, and R. Lance Holberts. "Television Use and Social Capital: Testing Putnam's Time Displacement Hypothesis." *Mass Communication and Society* 2, no. 1 (1999): 27–45.

Neuman, Russell W. "Televison and American Culture: Multiple Messages and Pluralistic Audiences." *Public Opinion Quarterly* 46 (December 1982): 471–487.

Postman, Neil. *Amusing Ourselves to Death: Public Discourse in the Age of Show Business.* New York: Penguin Books, 1986.

Putnam, Robert D. *Bowling Alone: The Collapse and Revival of American Community.* New York: Simon and Schuster, 2000.

Robinson, John P. "Television and Leisure Time: Yesterday, Today, and (Maybe) Tomorrow." *Public Opinion Quarterly* 33 (Summer 1969): 210–222.

———. "The Impact of Television on Mass Media Usage." In *The Use of Time: Daily Activities of Urban and Suburban Populations in Twelve Countries.* Edited by Alexander Szalai. The Hague: Mouton, 1972.

———. *How Americans Use Time: A Social-Psychological Analysis of Everyday Behavior.* New York: Praeger, 1977.

———. *How Americans Used Time in 1965.* Ann Arbor: Institute for Social Research University of Michigan: distributed by University Microfilms International, 1977.

———. "Television and Leisure Time: A New Scenario." *Journal of Communication* 31, no. 1 (1981): 120–130.

———. "Television's Effect on Families' Use of Time." In *Television and the American Family.* Edited by Jennings Bryant. Hillsdale, N.J.: Erlbaum Associates, 1990.

Robinson, John. P., and Geoffrey Godbey. *Time for Life: The Surprising Ways Americans Use Their Time.* 2d ed. University Park: Pennsylvania State University Press, 1999.

Robinson, John P., and L. Jeffres. "The Great Age-Readership Mystery." *Journalism Quarterly* 58, no. 2 (1981): 219–224.

Robinson, John P., P. Converse, and A. Szalai. "Everyday Life in Twelve Countries." In *The Use of Time: Daily Activities of Urban and Suburban Populations in Twelve Countries.* Edited by Alexander Szalai. The Hague: Mouton, 1972.

Schudson, Michael. *Discovering The News: A Social History of American Newspapers.* New York: Basic Books, 1978.

———. *Advertising, the Uneasy Persuasion: Its Dubious Impact on American Society.* New York: Basic Books, 1984.

Szalai, Alexander, ed. *The Use of Time: Daily Activities of Urban and Suburban Populations in Twelve Countries.* The Hague: Mouton, 1972.

John P. Robinson and Dennis K. Davis

TELEVISION'S IMPACT ON YOUTH AND CHILDREN'S PLAY

Most American children live in a media-rich environment, with leisure-time use of television, movies, music, video games, and computers playing an important role in their daily lives. Young people, especially teenagers, tend to embrace new media, often employing them as tools for exploring and expressing their identity. In contrast, parents, government, and scholars have long been concerned about mass media's potentially negative impact on children's development and well-being and, ultimately, on society as a whole. While research on children and the media has been conducted in the United States since the 1920s, debates about the exact nature of media effects persist. As well, the introduction of each new medium brings with it a range of new research questions.

Following a brief overview of children's access to and use of media (which is often mediated by differences in age, gender, race, and family income level), three areas of particular importance to children's leisure-time use of media are discussed: the trend toward individualization of media use, the commercialization of children's leisure, and the potential for media such as television and computers to displace other, more developmentally beneficial leisure activities.

Children's Media Landscape

Access to media. Based on nationally representative survey data, Emory Woodard and Natalia Gridina report that 98 percent of American households have at least one television, 97 percent of homes with children aged two to seventeen have a VCR, and 68 percent of homes with children have video game equipment. With regards to computer technology, the Corporation for Public Broadcasting found that 83 percent of homes with children have a computer, and 78 percent have access to the Internet.

Income, race, and age are all significant predictors of children's access to media. Children from higher-income families are more likely than lower-income children to own almost all media, with the exception of video game equipment. Video game equipment ownership is not related to income, although it is associated with gender. Homes with at least one boy are significantly more likely to have video game equipment than homes with at least one girl. Age also plays a role in children's media

access. Donald Roberts, Ulla Foehr, Victoria Rideout, and Mollyanne Brodie report that access to music media, video game equipment, computers, and the Internet tends to increase with age.

Race is a strong predictor of access to new media, with Hispanic and African American children being significantly less likely than white children to have home computers and at-home Internet access.

Media Use According to Roberts et. al. and Woodard and Gridina, American children spend close six and a half hours with media every day, on average. Screen-based media (TV, videotapes, video games, and computer) account for approximately 75 percent of daily media use. Once again, income, race, and age are associated with significant differences in media use. Generally, children from lower-income families are exposed to more media than their higher-income counterparts. On average, African American children consume more than two hours per day more of media than white children, and an hour more than Hispanic children. This is partially explained by the fact that African American children tend to live in homes that are more "television-oriented" than those of white or Hispanic children. As a result, African American children are significantly more likely than white or Hispanic children to live in homes with three or more televisions and with premium cable subscriptions.

Age also has a powerful effect on the amount of time children spend with media. Using survey data from a nationally representative sample, Roberts et al. found that leisure time media exposure begins early (two- to four-year-olds spent over four hours per day with media), increases to over eight hours per day by age twelve, and then decreases during the teen years as academic responsibilities and social activities begin to take up more time. Location of media within the home can also impact the amount of time children spend with media. In particular, the presence of bedroom media such as televisions and computers may lead to increased time spent with those items.

Bedroom Media and the Trend Toward Individualization

Sonia Livingstone argues that due to the proliferation of media within the home (which results from the availability of cheaper media products, the rise of mobile media, and media diversification) leisure time use of media is becoming increasingly individualized. Instead of families gathering in communal spaces such as the living room to watch television or listen to the radio, individual family members are now able—and often choose—to consume media on their own. For children, this has translated into the emergence of "bedroom culture" (Livingstone, p. 146).

Over 70 percent of children have books and stereos in their bedrooms, and more than 50 percent of children have bedroom TVs. Approximately 20 percent of children have computers in their rooms, and, of that number, more than half have Internet access. Thirty percent of American children have video game systems in their rooms, although boys are almost twice as likely as girls to have bedroom systems. In general, older children are significantly more likely than younger children to have bedroom media. However, a substantial 26 percent of children aged two to four have televisions in their bedrooms. Other predictors of bedroom media include income and parent education. The higher the family income, and the more education parents have, the less likely children are to have a bedroom TV, VCR, or video game system. As discussed above, African American children tend to live in television-oriented homes; as such, African American children are most likely to have bedroom TVs.

Roberts et al. explain that while young people, especially teenagers, have always been able to consume media relatively independently, the media landscape of 2004 (of which bedroom media was a defining feature) gave children unprecedented opportunity to structure their own media diets and to engage in media use free from parental supervision, comment, and, often, awareness. Studies indicated that children with bedroom televisions spent more time watching television than children without bedroom access, and that their consumption tended to include more adult-oriented programming.

The Commercialization of Leisure

Dale Kunkel estimates that American children are exposed to over 40,000 TV commercials a year. Given young children's level of cognitive development, researchers have sought to understand how this deluge of ads affects kids and, by extension, their families. Up until approximately age five or six, children are unable to distinguish between programming and commercials, and before age seven or eight, most kids cannot understand commercials' persuasive intent. As a result, young children are generally unable to watch commercials skeptically and often cannot separate commercial messages from their own wishes. Not surprisingly, research has shown that commercials targeted to children are generally effective in that they tend to succeed in getting children to request the product advertised. For example, studies show that chil-

dren's food choices are affected by advertising. Since content analyses reveal that a large proportion of commercials targeted to children advertise food that is high in sugar and fat, concerns have been raised about advertising's role in contributing to childhood obesity.

Television programming can also be seen as commercials for program-themed products. Toy-based programming (where shows' debuts coincide with the introduction of related toys) first appeared on TV in the 1980s. Widely criticized for being nothing more than thirty-minute commercials, shows like the *Care Bears* and *He-Man* were developed with direct input—and often funding—from toy manufacturers. It was rare in 2004 to come across a television show that didn't have an accompanying line of toys and games. With children highly susceptible to commercial messages, watching television can influence how—and with what—children spend their non-TV leisure time. Ellen Wartella and Sharon Mazzarella explain, "Television not only provides shows for young children to watch but intrudes into other parts of their leisure time by providing the source and objects of their play" (p. 188). This trend is repeated in the movie industry, and the Internet is increasingly being used as means to supplement the marketing messages found on television and in films (for example, Web sites and online games associated with TV shows).

As children grow up, media not only provide them with the content of their play but also gives them the opportunity to explore and express their nascent identities. Livingstone argues that children's identities have become commodified as a result of their leisure time use of media.

Displacement Theory

One of the longest-standing debates in media effects research is whether (and how) the use of new media affects the amount of time children spend engaging in other leisure activities, especially those deemed to be more valuable to a child's intellectual, emotional, and social development. Referred to generally as the displacement effect, this theory posits that time spent with a new medium leads to decreased time spent with other media and non-media leisure activities. Numerous scholars have studied the displacement effect, most frequently with regard to the impact of television. (A few studies have looked at computers and displacement, which will be discussed below.) The findings, however, are not entirely consistent. In reviewing the work on displacement effects, it is useful to examine separately those studies that assess the impact of television's introduction and those that assess the medium's effect after it has been in place for many years. The introduction of a new medium may result in dramatic changes in children's (and adults') leisure, but once the medium is integrated into children's lifestyles, these "novelty effects" may dissipate.

Displacement Effects: Television

Wilbur Schramm, Jack Lyle, and Edwin Parker's landmark study examined the impact of television on children's use of a range of different media. While TV viewing led to a decrease in radio listening and movie attendance, time devoted to newspapers and books was unaffected. Tannis Williams's analysis of television's introduction in British Columbia, Canada, revealed that TV negatively affected reading by interfering with the acquisition of reading skills. Williams also found that increased TV viewing led to decreased participation in activities outside the home, especially sports. In contrast, John Murray and Susan Kippax found that the introduction of TV in rural Australia led to increases in the amount of time children spent reading.

In a two-year study, Cees Koolstra and Tom van der Voort found that television viewing had a small but significant negative effect on children's leisure-time reading. The authors suggest that this occurs because frequent television viewing led to a less favorable attitude toward book reading. Diana Mutz, Donald Roberts, and D. P. van Vuuren followed children's media habits for eight years following the introduction of TV to parts of South Africa. They found that the presence of TV led to a modest but significant decrease in reading (as well as in radio listening and movie attendance). However, over 60 percent of children's TV viewing time came from marginal activities, suggesting a simple displacement of time did *not* occur. And, while TV viewing began to decrease several years following its introduction, participation in other activities did not return to their pre-TV levels. Mutz et al. conclude that an asymmetric form of displacement had occurred and that TV led to a general restructuring of children's leisure time. In contrast, Susan Neuman argues that television has not displaced children's leisure time book reading, stating that the amount of time children spend reading has remained unchanged over the past fifty years, at approximately fifteen minutes per day. In their cluster analysis, Suzanne Pingree and Robert Hawkins found no evidence of a negative relationship between watching TV and the number of books and newspapers read.

Media "Synergy"

Susan Neuman rejects the displacement theory in favor of a "synergistic" approach that sees interests in one medium reflected in others. "Rather than competition there is a spirited interplay between print and video activities that may spark children's interest and enhance literacy opportunities" (p. xiv). Based on Neuman's theory, certain types of educational programming may encourage children to engage in more leisure time reading. While Neuman was unable to provide any evidence that interests generated by TV cause children to pursue more information through reading, others have found increases in requests for particular books featured on children's programming. More recent research, however, provides support for the idea that media content (and not simple usage) will predict the extent to which TV displaces reading.

While previous displacement studies failed to distinguish between the types of TV programs viewed by children, Aletha Huston, John Wright, Janet Marquis, and Samuel Green examined the effects of both educational and entertainment television on children's leisure. Changes in the amount of time young children spent watching entertainment television were negatively related to changes in time spent reading. There was no evidence that changes in the amount time children spent watching educational television was related (either positively or negatively) to changes in time spent reading. Program content was thus a key factor in displacement, providing at least partial support for Neuman's theory.

Displacement Effects: Introduction of Computers

In their review of the effects of home computer use on children's development, Kaveri Subrahmanyam, Robert Kraut, Patricia Greenfield, and Elisheva Gross note that limited research exists on how children's use of computers may displace other leisure activities. Woodard and Gridina found that children who use computers for purposes other than going online spend an average fourteen minutes less watching TV per day. However, some researchers suggest that because of the connections that exist between the content of various media (for example, TV content associated with Web content and vice versa), computer use may lead to an increase in the amount of time children spend watching TV. Subrahmanyam et al. suggest that as time spent with computers increases, children's total "screen time" (time spent using a computer, watching television, and playing video games) increases as well.

Context and Content

Media, both old and new, occupy a prominent place in children's lives, where it both shapes and is shaped by children. Effects associated with media use aren't simply a function of watching a video or playing a computer game; rather, effects depend upon a number of contextual factors, including the child's age, gender, and race; the family's education and income; the environment where media use occurs (for example, in the child's bedroom); and the content featured in the media. Although arguments that media interfere with children's pursuit of more educational activities have been made, the evidence does not support this contention. Instead, media occupy children's lives according to roles children assign each medium. For instance, children may watch a cartoon or read a comic book because they are bored or wish to be entertained; they may watch a show or visit a Web site with information on animals because they want to learn more about a giraffe. As with most activities in which children participate, media serve multiple functions according to a child's particular needs at any given moment. The most important aspect of children's media use is not that they use media; instead, it is what content they are exposed to while using a particular media device.

See also: Television's Impact on Popular Leisure

BIBLIOGRAPHY

Comstock, G., and H. Paik. *Television and the American Child.* San Diego, Calif.: Academic Press, 1991.

Corporation for Public Broadcasting. "Connected to the Future: A Report on Children's Internet Use from the Corporation for Public Broadcasting." 2003.

Huston A. C., J. C. Wright, J. Marquis, and S. Green. "How Young Children Spend Their Time: Television and Other Activities." *Developmental Psychology* 35 (1999): 912–925.

Koolstra, C. M., and T. H. van der Voort. "Longitudinal Effects of Television on Children's Leisure-Time Reading: A Test of Three Explanatory Models." *Human Communication Research* 23 (1996): 4–35.

Kunkel, Dale. "Children and Television Advertising." In *The Handbook of Children and the Media.* Edited by D. G. Singer and J. L. Singer. Thousand Oaks, Calif.: Sage Publications, 2001.

Livingstone, Sonia. *Young People and New Media: Childhood and the Changing Media Environment.* Thousand Oaks, Calif.: Sage Publications, 2002.

Murray, J. P., and S. Kippax. "Children's Social Behavior in Three Towns with Differing Television Experience" *Journal of Communication* 28, no. 1 (1978): 19–29.

Mutz, D., D. Roberts, and D. van Vuuren. "Reconsidering the Displacement Hypothesis: Television's Influence on Children's Time Use." *Communication Research* 20, no. 1 (1993): 51–76.

Neuman, S. B. *Literacy in the Television Age: The Myth of the TV Effect.* Norwood, N.J.: Ablex Publishing Corporation, 1995.

Pecora, N. *The Business of Children's Entertainment.* New York: Guilford Press, 1997.

Pingree, S., and R. P. Hawkins. "Looking for Patterns in Lifestyle Behavior." In *Media Effects and Beyond: Culture, Socialization, and Lifestyle.* Edited by K. E. Rosengren. London: Routledge, 1994.

Roberts, D. F., U. G. Foehr, V. J. Rideout, and M. Brodie. *Kids and Media @ the New Millennium.* Menlo Park, Calif.: Kaiser Family Foundation, 1999.

Schoenbach, K., and L. B. Becker. "The Audience Copes with Plenty: Patterns of Reactions to Media Changes." In *Audience Responses to Media Diversification: Coping with Plenty.* Edited by L. B. Becker and K. Schoenbach. Hillsdale, N.J.: Lawrence Erlbaum Associates, 1989.

Schramm, W., J. Lyle, and E. Parker. *Television in the Lives of Our Children.* Palo Alto, Calif.: Stanford University Press, 1961.

Subrahmanyam, K., R. E. Kraut, P. M. Greenfield, and E. F. Gross. "The Impact of Home Computer Use on Children's Activities and Development." *The Future of Children* 10, no. 2 (2000): 123–144.

Wartella, E., and S. Mazzarella. "An Historical Comparison of Children's Use of Time with Media: 1920s to 1980s." In *For Fun and Profit.* Edited by R. Butsch. Philadelphia: Temple University Press, 1990.

Williams, Tannis MacBeth. *The Impact of Television: A Natural Experiment in Three Communities.* Orlando, Fla.: Academic Press, 1986.

Woodard, E. H., and N. Gridina. *Media in the Home 2000: The Fifth Annual Survey of Parents and Children.* Philadelphia: Annenberg Public Policy Center of the University of Pennsylvania, 2000.

Ariel R. Chernin and Deborah L. Linebarger

TEMPERANCE

See *Prohibition and Temperance*

TENNIS

Tennis is one of the most popular recreational and sport activities in modern society. With a long and fascinating international history, tennis has retained its popularity through the ages. Although the history of tennis in the United States is relatively short, the popularity of tennis has steadily increased since its introduction to the States in 1874. Historically, only the wealthy members of high society played tennis, usually in a country club–type setting. However, tennis has evolved into a game for all people of a variety of cultures, socioeconomic levels, and ages. Now, tennis courts are available to the public in almost every community.

Tennis is a popular leisure-time activity in modern society, with a host of benefits. Enjoyed as both a participatory and spectator's sport, tennis is a game of complex rules, intense physical play, and psychological strategy making. It may produce serious physical injuries as well as negative psychological reactions.

Tennis as a Popular Leisure Activity

There are many reasons for the popularity of tennis. Tennis can be played by a variety of people:, people with disabilities (wheelchair tennis is a common form of the game), the young and old, professionals and nonprofessionals. Tennis requires only two or four players, and it can be played as both an individual and a team sport.

Easy accessibility to courts also contributes to the popularity of tennis. Beginning in the 1930s, communities and schools began constructing tennis courts to make the game more accessible to the public. Tennis courts can be seen in nearly all public parks, recreation centers, and even some schools grounds. Many communities have tennis clubs and leagues that compete with other community clubs. Both public and private courts are widely available in most communities. In some communities, both outdoor and indoor courts are available. The use of public courts is often free of charge. Although at one time tennis was considered a game of high society and played mostly at country clubs, tennis today is attainable for all people. In addition, equipment costs for tennis are relatively low when compared to other sports, and equipment is often available for rent at tennis facilities.

According to the United States Tennis Association (USTA), the two primary driving forces for participation in tennis are exercise (health) and fun (social aspects). Tennis provides a strenuous physical workout, which can vary depending on the competitiveness and vigor of the players. Tennis requires integrated movement and eye-hand coordination, and it provides a good cardiovascular workout. It can be categorized as a vigorous exercise such as jogging, running, bicycling, swimming, or racquetball. Engagement in vigorous physical activities, including tennis, reduces the risk for developing diverticular diseases and heart and coronary diseases, and reduces the mortality rate.

The social nature of tennis is of equal importance. People can meet new friends or play with their family members for the purpose of relaxation or fun. Tennis also can be an appropriate outlet for pent-up aggression and other emotions; it facilitates sublimation and permits unconscious conflict to be expressed. That is, tennis as a recreational sport can provide a safe opportunity to rid the individual of aggressive energy or other emotions, thereby producing relief from the tension or making a person feel better (a form of cathartic notion).

Tennis may be especially appealing to those who like competitive ball sports. It is a fast-paced and physically demanding activity, requiring integrated movement such as speed, balance, and coordination. Due to the physically compelling nature of tennis, people who are not properly trained may experience injury while playing.

Origin, Development, and Organization of Tennis in the United States

Although the origin of tennis is not clear, the sport has a rich and interesting cultural history. Historians have indicated that a form of tennis was played in the ancient Greek and Roman Empires, as well as in the Orient more than 2,000 years ago. However, a clear history of tennis dates back to the twelfth century in France. During that time tennis was called *jeu de paume* (meaning "game of the hand"). It was first a barehanded game of hitting a stuffed cloth bag over a rope. In the fourteenth century, paddles were added, and the game became popular in England as well as France. It is estimated that there were approximately 1,400 professional players in France in the beginning of the fifteenth century. In 1599, the first standardized written rules of tennis were developed.

In 1873, British army major Walter Clopton Wingfield devised an activity in search of a more vigorous game than croquet for the leisure classes. It was called *sphairistike* ("ball game" in Greek), which was later referred to as "lawn tennis." In 1874, Miss Mary Outbridge, a New Yorker, introduced *sphairistike* to the Staten Island Cricket and Baseball Club in the United States. Within a few years, tennis was played at nearly every major cricket club in the East. In 1881, the United States National Lawn Tennis Association (now USTA) was established.

The first tournament for the first official National Championship of the United States was held in 1881 in Newport, Rhode Island. This tournament is now called the U.S. Open and is one of the four "Grand Slam" events on the professional tours. The other three events are the Australian Open, the French Open, and Wimbledon. Tennis was introduced to the Olympics for the first time in 1924. In 1988, it was adopted as an Olympic game and was open to professional players.

Until the 1960s, major competitions were organized and managed by volunteer wealthy men drawn from the membership of the private clubs that served as the sites for the sport's major competitions. The competitions were open exclusively to amateurs. As early as 1926, a small group of players left amateur tennis and began to earn incomes for their efforts as professionals. With the increased popularity, the United States Professional Tennis Association (USPTA) was founded in 1927. In 1968, Wimbledon would be open to professional players; the other national associations followed the lead of the English, therefore initiating the era of open tennis. In 1972, the Association of Tennis Professionals (ATP) was founded as a union for male professionals, and the Women's Tennis Association (WTA) was founded in 1973 for female professionals. In recent years, tennis professionals have joined the ranks of the highest-paid professional athletes in the world, and tennis is one of the few sports played professionally in virtually every country.

Tennis as a Participant Sport

According to the USTA and the Tennis Industry Association (ITA), approximately 23.5 million Americans played tennis as of 2003 (at least one time in the past twelve months). Of the 23.5 million players, 5.1 million people were identified as new players. This boom in participation is attributed to the increasing interest among young people, women, African Americans, and Hispanics. However, the increase in new players is offset by losses of players who at one time regularly played, but no longer do so.

About 20 percent of tennis players identified themselves as frequent players, playing twenty-one or more times per year (USTA). Many players enjoy their games with their friends, families, and acquaintances, while players who are more interested in skills development and competition may be involved in formal games such as leagues, clubs, and tournaments (available through national or local tennis organizations, clubs, centers, and schools).

Not surprisingly, geographic locations and weather influence participation in tennis. The highest levels of tennis participation are in California, Florida, and Texas, while North and South Dakota, Vermont, Alaska, and Wyoming show the lowest participation in the sport.

Tennis as a Spectator Sport

Tennis is also a popular spectator sport. Most major tennis tournaments are televised and watched by millions of people and are often broadcasted as a prime-time television program. The popularity of tennis is also evident when one sees professional tennis players advertising products on television. Players' showmanship, unique styles, and innovative attire are new factors that attract numerous fans and crowd to the stadium and television. For example, 625,000 fans attended the U.S. Open in 2002, more than 100 million viewers watched the U.S. Open on televisions' CBS Sports and USA Network, and international broadcasts reached 165 countries (USTA). ESPN allocates approximately 300 hours per year for tennis coverage. Some cable companies now provide tennis channels for tennis fans.

Courts, Equipment, and Attire

Although the rules of the game of tennis have remained essentially the same over its history, courts, equipment, and styles of players have changed a great deal. Modern tennis courts are typically hard and made of cement, concrete, or asphalt. Tennis was originally played on a grass surface (the Wimbledon tournament is still played on grass). The French Open is played on a surface made of clay. Both the U.S. Open and the Australian Open are played on hard, synthetic surfaces. The introduction of surfaces other than grass played a role in contributing to the development of tennis as a popular leisure and recreational sport in modern society, finally dispelling the country-club image of lawn tennis.

The equipment required for tennis is a tennis racquet and tennis balls. Until the 1970s, racquets were almost all similar in size, shape, and composition. During the 1970s, synthetic materials such as graphite and fiberglass replaced the laminated wood frames. The International Tennis Federation (ITF) regulates the size of racquets, which range between 90 square inches and 120 square inches. The tennis ball measures two and one-half inches in diameter and weighs about two ounces. The ball is made of two rubber cups molded together and covered with soft felt. The official colors for tennis balls are yellow and white.

Traditionally, tennis players have long been ruled by an all-white dress code: white shirt with collars and sleeves, white pants, white hat or cap, and white shoes. Although some private tennis clubs still strictly apply the white rule, most people wear any comfortable sport outfit to play tennis. Many professional players create their own unique images and styles through fashionably innovative and technologically advanced tennis outfits.

Other Considerations

The primary concerns associated with tennis are physical injuries, including elbow injuries (lateral and medial epicondylitis), impingement syndrome (injuries to the rotator cuff), wrist and hand injuries, back strain, abdominal injury, tennis leg, Achilles tendon injury, and ankle injury. Tennis elbow is the most common affliction occurring in recreational tennis players, and it is caused by improper backhand strokes. Ankle injury and back strain are also quite common in tennis players. To avoid these potential physical injuries, players should warm up and stretch before playing tennis. Proper instruction on swing techniques will also help to prevent injury.

Choosing a good teacher or coach is another essential consideration of tennis. Tennis clubs often offer instruction, and private coaches can be hired for lessons. Community centers may offer courses in learning to play tennis. Many schools now have tennis teams and are staffed with tennis coaches to teach students how to play. Tennis camp is a popular way to spend a summer for a youth who excels in the game of tennis, as the multiple complex rules and nuances of tennis can be overwhelming to a new actor.

Tennis is clearly a valued recreational activity in American culture, and internationally as well. Its popularity can be attributed to its ease of play, access to courts and equipment, affordability, and the social and competitive natures of the game. Playing tennis will surely continue to be a popular recreational endeavor in the years to come.

See also: Leisure Class, Professionalization of Sport, Racquetball

BIBLIOGRAPHY

Association of Tennis Professionals. Home page at http://www.atptour.com.

Bull, R. C., ed. *Handbook of Sports Injuries.* New York: McGraw Hill, 1999.

Levinson, D., and K. Christensen, eds. *Encyclopedia of World Sport.* New York: Oxford University Press, 1999.

Mood, D. P., F. F. Musker, and J. E. Rink. *Sports and Recreational Activities.* 13th ed. Boston: McGraw Hill, 2003.

Tennis Online. Home page at http://www.tenninonline.com.

United States Professional Tennis Association. Home page at http://www.uspta.com.

USA Tennis. Home page at http://www.usatennis.com.

"USTA and TIA Complete Most Comprehensive Research in Sport." Available from http://www.usta.com.

Heewon Yang and Kelly Chandler

THANKSGIVING

Various Spanish, French Huguenot, and English explorers and settlers in North America fell to their knees and gave thanks or proclaimed special days of thanksgiving in the late 1500s or early 1600s. Probably the earliest of these acts of thanksgiving was that of Ponce de Leon when he landed in Florida during Easter of 1513. "The first thanksgiving," as a Pilgrim feast in 1621 subsequently came to be known, was not a religious celebration. Instead, the Pilgrims held a three-day feast to celebrate the success of their first harvest sometime between September and early October in 1621. Their event resembled the English "harvest home" custom, a somewhat raucous, entirely secular harvest festival lacking any prayer services.

Fanciful portraits of Pilgrims seated at tables with their Indian guests have given false impressions about the nature of that first thanksgiving. It did include athletic contests, a military drill, and so many Native American guests that they outnumbered their Pilgrim hosts almost two to one. Roast duck, goose, and venison were served, and these items were probably washed down with beer. Whether the assembled also ate turkey is a matter of dispute. The Pilgrims had no harvest home celebration in 1621 or 1622, and held only sporadic ones after that. Thereafter individuals, churches, or colony-wide governments called for days of thanksgiving, largely on an ad hoc basis. The settlers of Plymouth Colony came to acquire their reputation as the national ancestors only in the 1760s. At that time, a group of Plymouth men formed a small local club to celebrate the day in December when the Pilgrims landed, which they deemed the most important way to commemorate the Pilgrims. Landing Day, also called Forefathers' Day, came to include a public feast, oratory, sermons, and fireworks. But it remained a public holiday and thus never developed the familial appeal of Thanksgiving.

The idea of Thanksgiving as a time for a family feast at first coexisted and then overwhelmed the public definition of the day provided in Forefathers' Day. (There was a brief revival of Forefathers' Day in the 1880s and 1890s, when members of the Society of Mayflower Descendants and other elite groups appropriated the day as an event to demonstrate their Anglo-Protestant/American ancestry.) The ideal of Thanksgiving as a family homecoming emerged in tandem with the cult of domesticity of the early nineteenth century. In this cult, the home became a secular shrine, and living adult children were urged to visit their elderly parents to enjoy a special home-cooked feast. Returning home to one's family in the countryside represented a way for city people to rediscover the simplicity and rural virtue they had left behind.

Never simply a holiday about the ideal of the family, Thanksgiving was also supposed to celebrate charitableness and national unity. New England writer Sarah Josepha Hale sang the praises of the New England Thanksgiving in her 1827 novel, *Northwood*. She became editor of a woman's magazine, *Godey's Lady's Book*, and wrote yearly editorials in favor of a national holiday; she also published holiday recipes. In 1846, Hale began writing to governors, presidents, and missionaries, calling for a national day of Thanksgiving. As sectionalism over the Civil War identified the holiday with the North—abolitionist Protestant ministers even delivered sermons on the day—Hale countered by presenting Thanksgiving as a means of preventing war and a celebration of shared American values.

Presenting Thanksgiving as part of America's shared past was not a new idea, as it had occurred as early as the American Revolution. The Continental Congress had proclaimed thanksgiving days during the Revolutionary War, and three American presidents—George Washington, John Adams, and James Madison—also called for them. However, Presidents John Quincy Adams and Thomas Jefferson considered the Thanksgiving a religious day, which violated constitutional provisions for the separation of church and state. Subsequent presidents (until Abraham Lincoln in 1863) accepted this view. Both sides in the Civil War called for days of thanksgiving to celebrate their military victories. In September 1863, Hale wrote to Lincoln urging him to proclaim a national Thanksgiving Day. The victory at Gettysburg as well as Hale's entreaties encouraged Lincoln to declare a national day of Thanksgiving that November. In l863, Lincoln proclaimed the last Thursday in November a national day of thanksgiving and prayer. Ever since then presidents have issued such proclamations.

While states still had the power to decide their holidays, by the late nineteenth century most states had made Thanksgiving a legal holiday. Even so, Thanksgiving was mainly celebrated among the middle and upper classes, in New England and the mid-Atlantic states, and among Protestants. The Catholic Church opposed the holiday as a Protestant rite as late as the 1880s. African Americans tended to celebrate the holiday as a religious day, often giving thanks for emancipation.

There was a sporting tradition on Thanksgiving, since the English harvest home had been celebrated with sporting contests and hunting. Baseball games were commonly played on Thanksgiving in the 1860s and 1870s. The Thanksgiving Day football game began in the 1870s, as the culminating contest in the Ivy League football season. In 1876, four Ivy League schools established the Intercollegiate Football Association and scheduled the first championship game on Thanksgiving Day. Initially, football played on Thanksgiving was seen as a desecration of the religious and national meanings of the day. Ministers and college presidents failed in their efforts to put a stop to football on Thanksgiving. By the 1920s, football had become a form of home entertainment, mainly for the urban middle class who owned radios. By 1956, football games were televised, reinforcing the association between watching football and a festival celebrated in the home.

There had been parades on Thanksgiving since the late nineteenth century, and department stores sponsored Thanksgiving Day parades as early as 1920. Macy's Thanksgiving parade in Manhattan began in 1924. It was deliberately staged as a means of inaugurating the Christmas shopping season. The Macy's parade, like the introduction of football on Thanksgiving, was initially greeted with some consternation. Some patriotic groups protested because the Macy's parade had no national meaning and was held at the same time as morning church services. Macy's moved the parade to the afternoon, where it conflicted with football games. Organizers then decided to hold the parade in the morning, since they perceived greater conflict with football than with church services. In 1927 a puppeteer created the first giant balloons for the parade, thus adding color and overwhelming size to the pageant. The parade was canceled during World War II because of national rationing of helium and rubber. Hollywood enhanced the visibility of the parade in 1947 with the release of the film *Miracle on 34th Street*. In the film, Macy's parade and the endearing Santa Claus that participates in it contributed to the Dickensian definition of Christmas as a time of magic and goodness. A product placement for the store and its parade, the film opened with footage of the real parade.

The desire to revive the faltering economy during the Great Depression led to an ill-starred attempt to advance the date for Thanksgiving and provoked a lasting congressional response. In 1933, the National Retail Dry Goods Association urged President Franklin D. Roosevelt to proclaim Thanksgiving the third Thursday in November in order lengthen the Christmas shopping season. Roosevelt initially thought the calendric change would prove confusing, but he acceded to these requests in 1939. His proclamation affected only federal employees and the District of Columbia. Many state governors followed Roosevelt's lead, while others kept to tradition and a few

The First Thanksgiving at Plymouth, Massachusetts. An oil on canvas painting by Jennie Augusta Brownscombe (1850–1936) in 1914, *The First Thanksgiving at Plymouth, Massachusetts* depicts the peaceful gathering of the English settlers and Native Americans. © *The Granger Collection Ltd.*

proclaimed two Thanksgivings in November. Roosevelt's decision was highly unpopular, however. In 1941, Congress responded to popular outcry by changing the date for the observance of Thanksgiving to the last Thursday of November and passing legislation making Thanksgiving a national legal holiday. Wartime unity and congressional action during war no doubt contributed to this triumph of federalism.

Thanksgiving is often beloved as America's least commercialized holiday. Actually, Thanksgiving was a minor gift-giving occasion in the early nineteenth century. By the 1850s, advertisers were selling gift books of Thanksgiving. Greeting cards, paper goods, candies, flowers, restaurant meals, and travel packages have been and are now marketed on Thanksgiving. Since the early twentieth century, newspapers and magazines carry Thanksgiving ads. In the Thanksgiving edition of the *Saturday Evening Post* for 1931, an advertisement for Camels touted the holiday as "something to be thankful for." Nonetheless, all of these commercial signs are ignored since the looming presence of Christmas makes the somewhat commercial Thanksgiving appear to be the simple, homespun holiday Hale promoted.

See also: Christmas; Football; Football, Collegiate; Magazines, Women's; Memorial Day; Parades; Patriotism and Leisure; Sabbatarianism

BIBLIOGRAPHY

Adamczyk, Amy. "On Thanksgiving and Collective Memory: Constructing the American Tradition." *Journal of Historical Sociology* 15 (2002): 343–365.

Appelbaum, Diana Karter. *Thanksgiving: An American Holiday,* New York: Facts on File, 1984.

Deetz, James, and Patricia Scott Deetz. *The Times of Their Lives: Life, Love, and Death in Plymouth Colony.* New York: W. H. Freeman and Company, 2000.

Dennis, Matthew. *Red, White, and Blue Letter Days: An American Calendar.* Ithaca, N.Y.: Cornell University Press, 2002.

Nylander, Jane C. *Our Own Snug Fireside: Images of the New England Home, 1760–1860.* New York: Alfred A. Knopf, 1993.

Pleck, Elizabeth H. "The Making of the Domestic Occasion: The History of Thanksgiving in the United States." *Journal of Social History* 32 (1999): 773–790.

——. *Celebrating the Family: Ethnicity, Consumer Culture, and Family Rituals.* Cambridge, Mass.: Harvard University Press, 2000.

Pope, S. W. *Patriotic Games: Sporting Traditions in the American Imagination, 1876–1926.* New York: Oxford University Press, 1977.

Siskind, Janet. "The Invention of Thanksgiving: A Ritual of American Nationality." *Critique of Anthropology* 12 (1992): 167–191.

Elizabeth H. Pleck

THEATER, LIVE

While some scholars have termed American theater a "bastard art" because of its marginalized position in American culture, others have seen in it a means of reading the ever-evolving shape of the nation's imagined community. First brought to the colonies in the years before the American Revolution as a means of sustaining a cultural link with Great Britain, then resurrected after the war as something uniquely American, the nation's theater continued to transform itself throughout the nineteenth century in response to the events sweeping the country—from the Age of Jackson to the Industrial Revolution to the Civil War. By the end of the twentieth century, the United States' theater artists could claim that their art was no longer the illegitimate offspring of imperial Britain, but something that represented the diverse racial, ethnic, and class groups that the country had fostered.

The United States' history of opposition to the theater is almost as long-standing as its history inside the playhouse. Seventeenth-century Quakers and Puritans issued edicts against the theater before any professional players had even set foot on American shores. While citizens of Pennsylvania and Massachusetts struggled to keep the theater at bay, however, colonists in New York, Virginia, and South Carolina actively cultivated their nascent theatrical entertainments. The first recorded (amateur) performance in the colonies occurred on 27 August 1665, when a group of citizens in Accomac County, Virginia, staged a production of *The Bare and the Cubb* at Cowle's Tavern. In 1714, the governor of New York, Robert Hunter, produced the first truly American play, a political satire called *Androboros: A Biographical Farce of Three Acts, viz: The Senate, the Consistory, and the Apotheosis.* Hunter's play marks the beginning of a long American tradition of using plays to comment on political trends in American society.

In 1716, William Levingston of Williamsburg, Virginia, established the first permanent theater in British North America. The rectangular theater building approximated the seating arrangements of pit, box, and gallery customary in British theaters. However, Williamsburg simply could not sustain a professional theater and Levingston's playhouse soon closed.

In 1749, the short-lived Murray-Kean Company traveled to the colonies, staging performances in Virginia, Pennsylvania, and New York. The British Licensing Act of 1737 had restricted the operation of professional theaters in England to those specially licensed by the Crown. As a result, many performers looked to the new world as a source of income. The most successful group of actors to leave England for the colonies was the Hallam family. Lewis Hallam, Sr., brought his wife and son, Lewis Hallam, Jr., to the colonies in 1752.

When Lewis Hallam, Sr., died in 1755, his widow married David Douglass, perhaps the most brilliant theatrical manager of the eighteenth century. Douglass had a genius for building playhouses and developing audiences. Yet one of Douglass's greatest challenges in his management of the company was to overcome the lingering anti-theatrical prejudice that still plagued the colonies. While initially grounded in religious sentiment, the colonists' disintegrating relationship with Great Britain in the 1760s prompted an upsurge of anti-British feeling that spilled over into the colonists' perception of the theater, which was still essentially a British import. In 1774, the Continental Congress passed a resolution banning theatrical entertainments as needless and wasteful diversions.

The war had barely closed before Douglass's players (now renamed the Old American Company), brought its troupe back to the United States and tried to re-establish its former touring circuit. But in the intervening years, many states had passed their own anti-theater legislation, and the once popular pastime was now an unpleasant reminder of the colonies' former dependence on Great Britain. It was not until the ratification of the federal constitution and the debut of Royall Tyler's play, *The Contrast,* that American theater began to find a new direction. Tyler's play, written and performed at New York's John Street playhouse in 1787, is perhaps the best-known early American drama. The play focuses on the "contrast" between American manners, which prize Republican virtue and simplicity, and British manners, which are characterized by their haughtiness and hypocrisy.

Each of the major cities in the new nation, including Philadelphia, Charleston, Richmond, Baltimore, New York, and Boston, competed to build lavish playhouses that would reflect their cultural refinement. The craze for

Early Theater. A poster advertising John Sheridan's late-nineteenth century *Fun on the Bristol*, a musical variety show that featured the humorous exploits of the passengers of the steamship *Bristol*. © *Corbis*

theater-building almost killed the American appetite for playgoing altogether, as multiple companies competed for audience attention; it bankrupted a series of theater managers.

There was little space for women in the early American theater. Some of the best-known female playwrights of the early national period, Mercy Otis Warren (1728–1814) and Judith Sargent Murray (1751–1820), wrote plays as political commentary, yet seldom received either public credit (often writing under a pseudonym), or financial or critical reward. Only Susanna Rowson (1762–1824), enjoyed professional success in the American theater, and her *Slaves in Algiers* (1794) provoked enormous controversy for suggesting that women were entitled to the same political freedoms as men.

Early Politics and the Theater

Theater responded to the rapid political shifts of the early national period. The election of Thomas Jefferson to the presidency in 1800, with his emphasis on the "yeoman farmer," the simple Republican character who valued emotion over intellect, coincided with the theatrical trend towards melodrama, a form characterized by its emphasis on sentiment rather than reason. William Dunlap (1766–1839), playwright, artist, sometime manager of New York's Park Theater, and often called the "Father of American Drama," believed that the theater could teach Americans how to be good citizens.

Perhaps nowhere was the theater's power more evident than in the career of Edwin Forrest (1806–1872), star of the Jacksonian stage. Forrest came to the American theater at a time of tremendous transformation in American culture and politics. The election of President Andrew Jackson in 1828 had ushered in an era of aggressive masculinity that vaunted the triumph of the "common man" over the elite. For the working man in the theater's pit, Forrest's commanding style and daunting physical presence embodied the very essence of Jacksonian manhood. The plays that emerged from this tradition include *The Gladiator, Jack Cade,* and *Metamora.*

Forrest's "Americanness" was both a selling point and a challenge for American audiences, who were still uneasy about their own ability to discern worthy native products. American playwrights in particular, often felt slighted by their native audiences, who still seemed to prefer British fare. This schism between British and American taste in the theater also reflected increasing class tensions both within and outside of the playhouse

The Astor Place Riot Those tensions erupted one fateful night in May 1849, at the most infamous uprising in American theater history: the Astor Place Riot. The "Bowery B'hoys," working class toughs of New York's Bowery district, flocked to the Bowery Theater to see their hero Edwin Forrest play the common man, oppressed by his upper-class rivals. Further uptown, millionaire John Jacob Astor and his wealthy cohorts crowded into the newly built Astor Place Opera House to watch one of Britain's most refined stars, William Charles Macready. For Forrest's supporters, Macready symbolized everything foreign, negative, and elitist that plagued American culture. For Macready's adherents, Forrest's Bowery B'hoys were the reason that their theaters and streets were no longer safe and untroubled. On 10 May 1849, Forrest's supporters rallied outside the Opera House. The city militia, called in to keep the peace, fired into the crowd. Thirty-four people were killed and more than two hundred were wounded. In the wake of the riots, few could imagine what form of entertainment might bring American audiences together again.

The answer came in the person of Phineas Taylor Barnum (1810–1891), perhaps the most famous showman—and some would argue con man—in the history of American popular entertainment. In 1841, P. T. Barnum opened the American Museum on Broadway in New York City. Half lecture hall, half freak show, the museum housed such oddities as the Feejee Mermaid and Joyce Heth (a black woman he claimed had been George Washington's childhood nurse), as well as more serious and educational "moral reform" dramas. The best known of these was William Henry Smith's temperance play *The Drunkard* (1844). Barnum used the play to persuade middle class spectators of the moral efficacy of theater. While Barnum successfully combined highbrow and lowbrow culture in his museum entertainments, other forms of American popular entertainment brought these two elements together, but with widely different results.

Blackface minstrelsy is one of the few uniquely American entertainments that the United States can claim, and also one of the few that combines almost every element of class, racial, ethnic, gender, and political tension that challenged the young country during the nineteenth century. Though scholars differ on the exact point of origin for blackface minstrelsy, many attribute its genesis to Thomas Dartmouth "Daddy" Rice (1806–1860), the American actor who created the character of "Jim Crow" sometime between 1828 and 1831. Rice's success helped to spawn the genre of the minstrel show, a form that combined blackface performance with singing, dancing, and short skits. Among the most famous minstrel troupes were Dan Emmett's Virginia Minstrels (Emmett [1815–1904] was the author of the tune "Dixie") and E. P. Christy's Minstrels. The minstrel show combined both highbrow and lowbrow culture, but in parody (not earnestness, as Barnum had done).

The Debut of *Uncle Tom's Cabin*

Minstrelsy and melodrama remained two of the most popular forms of American entertainment through the Civil War, reaching their apex together in the play destined to become the most widely performed show in American theater history, *Uncle Tom's Cabin*. The stunning success of Harriet Beecher Stowe's 1852 novel prompted theater managers to stage their own versions of the story (most famously George Aiken's 1852 version). *Uncle Tom's Cabin* also gave rise to a genre of stage stories dealing with the character of the "tragic mulatto," most notably in Dion Boucicault's melodrama *The Octoroon* (1859).

By the end of the Civil War, American drama had become even more diversified and, perhaps more importantly, even more divided. The rugged, working class manliness of Edwin Forrest no longer dominated the stage. Instead, Edwin Booth (whose brother, John Wilkes Booth had assassinated President Abraham Lincoln), had become the premiere American actor. Known for his intellectual air and reserved demeanor, Booth (1833–1893) represented the quintessential Hamlet—his most famous role—and the ultimate "thinking man's" hero. While Booth catered to middle-class and elite audiences in New York's lavish uptown theaters, working-class audiences and frontier audiences were seeking new diversions elsewhere.

Women and the Theater

The second half of the nineteenth century found theater managers in search of a new audience—women. Prior to the middle of the century, attending the theater, especially alone, was a hazardous pastime for women. It exposed them to lewd behavior from male audience members and possible sexual propositions if they were mistaken for the prostitutes who regularly haunted the theater's upper galleries. Thus Tony Pastor's vaudeville house, New York's 14th Street Theater, which advertised performances "clean enough for women," came as a blessing. Vaudeville acts consisted largely of comic skits, songs, and specialty numbers, and Pastor offered matinees so that women could attend on their own. He awarded door prizes such as hams or sewing machines to further tempt female and family audiences. Vaudeville also offered a showcase for new forms of immigrant entertainment and fostered the comedy duos Weber and Fields, a German or "Dutch" act; and Harrigan and Hart, an Irish act.

On the flip side of vaudeville lived burlesque—a seamier style of performance that flourished in working-class theaters and on the frontiers. Partly launched by the success of the *Black Crook* (1866)—a five-hour extravaganza that featured a chorus of scantily-clad French ballerinas, and partly fostered by the nationwide tour of performer Lydia Thompson and her British Blondes—burlesque tantalized male audiences with unprecedented glimpses of the female form. The genre became so popular that one outraged American actress, Olive Logan (1839–1909) started an active campaign against what she saw as the degradation of professional women.

Burlesque and vaudeville both appealed to new American audiences—particularly those who spoke little English—as floods of immigrants continued to pour into the country and theaters grew increasingly adept at integrating these new influences onto the stage. The influx of immigrants also supported two other phenomena that contributed to the development of the American theater: the railroad and the factory. The spread of railroads enabled theater productions to travel rapidly across the country; it also meant that any town with a railroad stop could host a touring show.

Railroads also contributed to the development of the Theatrical Syndicate, a management group that controlled bookings for playhouses across the United States and established a virtual monopoly on American entertainments by the end of the century. The Syndicate produced only commercially appealing shows and excluded actors and playwrights who refused to cooperate.

By the end of the nineteenth century, American theater artists had begun to struggle against the power of the Syndicate, just as American businessmen had begun to struggle against the system of trusts. This trend was inspired partly by the Realist movement in Europe, which touted "ordinary" characters and action over melodramatic heroes and spectacle, and by the works of English playwright George Bernard Shaw (1856–1950) and Norwegian playwright Henrik Ibsen (1828–1906). Some American actresses such as Mary Shaw (1854–1929), a noted suffragette, and playwright James A. Herne (1839–1901), often known as the "American Ibsen," introduced American audiences to these new forms. In particular, Herne's 1890 *Margaret Fleming* marked a turning point in American theater, as it jolted American audiences out of their melodrama-induced complacency. Herne believed that drama should "instruct" its audiences, and *Margaret Fleming* challenged viewers to rethink their notions of morality and marriage

Into the Twentieth Century

By the turn of the twentieth century, American theater had reached a turning point with the advent of realism and the beginning of the "Little Theater" movement, a reaction against the commercially driven spectacles of mainstream American theater. The movement produced Eugene O'Neill (1888–1953), one of the nation's first authentic dramatic geniuses, whose works, including *The Hairy Ape, The Iceman Cometh,* and *Long Day's Journey Into Night,* remain in the American theater canon.

The frivolity of the Jazz Age ushered in a similarly lighthearted era in American popular entertainment. While some performers and playwrights (most notably those affiliated with the newly created Theater Guild), labored to introduce more serious drama and formal training techniques into the American theater, many producers on Broadway, conscious of the need to compete with the fledgling film industry, focused on creating entertainment for the "tired businessman." These shows, of which the Ziegfeld Follies were a prime example, featured elegantly (if scantily) clad showgirls, and music, songs, and skits by artists such as Fanny Brice and W. C. Fields, Fred Astaire, George and Ira Gershwin, Irving Berlin, and Will Rogers. Ziegfeld also helped to produce Jerome Kern and Oscar Hammerstein II's *Showboat* (1928), one of the most important musicals in American stage history.

The devastating impact of the Great Depression brought a sudden end to the gaiety of the 1920s. Lavish musical shows became too expensive to produce or to attend, and movies and radio became the most popular forms of entertainment. They had been growing in popularity throughout the 1920s with the rise of stars such as Charlie Chaplin, Clara Bow, and Rudolph Valentino. The advent of sound in the 1927 film "The Jazz Singer" had begun a craze for the "talkies," and by 1930, the nation's 1,500 operational playhouses had dropped to 500. Radio, like film, offered cheap and widely accessible enjoyment—whether it was Roosevelt's heartening "fireside chats" during the darkest days of the Depression, or Orson Welles' electrifying 1938 performance of *The War of the Worlds,* which convinced many listeners that an actual Martian invasion was in progress.

The government did try to revive the country's flagging theatrical system with the 1935 creation of the Federal Theater Project, which sponsored nationwide tours of theatrical productions and gave employment to thousands of out-of-work actors, designers, writers, and technicians. The project was terminated in 1939 because of suspected ties to socialist and communist movements.

The coming of World War II did much to reinvigorate the American theater. As movies became more patriotic (featuring stars such as Spencer Tracy, James Stewart, and Clark Gable marching off to war), many American plays tried to recapture a vanished sense of the

American frontier and American greatness, as in the 1943 production of Richard Rodgers and Oscar Hammerstein's *Oklahoma!*.

The postwar period, while it brought an upsurge in the productivity of American playwrights, also brought a distinct change in tone to the nation's theater. The Depression and World War II had effectively shrunk the country's theatrical center to New York City. Within the span of less than a decade, New York witnessed the debut of Tennessee Williams' *A Streetcar Named Desire* (1947), *Cat on a Hot Tin Roof* (1955), and Arthur Miller's *All My Sons* (1947), *Death of a Salesman* (1949), and *The Crucible* (1953). These plays, recognized as some of the greatest of the twentieth century, reflected a growing frustration with the seeming failure of the "American Dream," and with the increasingly rigid politics of the McCarthy era.

Miller's and Williams's work flourished in part because of a new generation of actors, trained in a style that has become known as "The Method." Popularized at the Actors' Studio by stage director Lee Strasberg "The Method's" most noted disciples included Marlon Brando, Eve Marie Saint, and James Dean.

By the 1950s, producing shows on Broadway had become prohibitively expensive. Thus a new phenomenon, known as "Off-Broadway" evolved. Many of Williams's works were produced in these smaller theaters removed from the heart of New York City's Times Square, as were those of later writers such as Edward Albee (*Who's Afraid of Virginia Woolf?*), Sam Shepard (*Curse of the Starving Class)* and David Mamet (*American Buffalo*).

The age of experimentation accelerated rapidly in the 1960s and 1970s, with an ever-increasing number of groups vying to make their voices heard on the American stage. Broadway became the site of the safe and staid, while regional troupes, including El Teatro Campesino, At the Foot of the Mountain, the Living Theater, the Wooster Group, the San Francisco Mime Troupe, the Bread and Puppet Theater, the Negro Ensemble Company, and the East-West Players, sprang up to express the needs of the Latino, women's, gay and lesbian, African-American, and Asian-American communities. In recognition of this upsurge in regional theater activity, the government founded the National Endowment for the Arts (1965).

Modern-Day Broadway: Musical Theater Dominates

By the 1980s–1990s, Broadway fare consisted largely of musical theater—primarily British imports, including the enormously successful *Cats, Phantom of the Opera,* and *Les Miserables* (maverick Stephen Sondheim's musicals tended to be produced off Broadway). Much of the innovative work of the American theater had moved to regional playhouses, including the American Repertory Theater, the Mark Taper Forum, the Steppenwolf Theater Company, and the Actor's Theater of Louisville. New authors, including Wendy Wasserstein, Terrence McNally, Paula Vogel, Craig Lucas, and Tony Kusher began developing their plays at these regional spaces before a *possible* transfer to Broadway (if the plays proved commercially viable).

Two of the most successful transfers of the 1990s include Tony Kushner's Pulizter Prize-winning *Angels in America,* which began at the Taper before moving to New York, and Jonathan Larson's musical *Rent,* which began as a staged reading at the Off-Broadway New York Theater Workshop. Such successes were rare, however, and the trend on Broadway in the early 2000s was towards revivals of big-name musicals (including *Damn Yankees, Oklahoma!, Showboat, Music Man,* and *Annie Get Your Gun*), or revivals of plays from the American canon with well-known movie stars in the leading roles. Producers have also recognized the lucrative possibilities of transforming successful films or cartoons into Broadway musicals. This began largely with the "Disneyfication" of Times Square: during the 1990s, much of the property was purchased by the Walt Disney Company, which cleaned up the derelict downtown theaters. The Disney-Broadway collaborations include *Beauty and the Beast* and *The Lion King.*

Though many Americans still identify Broadway as the theatrical capitol of the nation, since the 1950s its authority and force have shifted to both regional theater centers, and, increasingly since the mid-1980s, to performing arts centers at universities across the nation, including the University of Illinois, Dartmouth College, and the University of Maryland, to name only a few. These institutions house multimillion dollar arts complexes that present music, theater, and dance performances, and serve as the artistic focal point for their communities. They also represent a shift in the nation's understanding of the function of a playhouse—a shift that, interestingly, carries American theater back to its earliest roots. The new performing arts centers combine not only diverse entertainment, but galleries, restaurants, and other non-theater oriented resources for their audiences. The earliest playhouses of the new nation offered a similar range of options—from saloons, to card rooms, to mini-museums. Although American theater has come a long way from its earliest, contested origins, its

Rent in London. The musical *Rent* ran from May 1998 until October 1999 at the Shaftesbury Theatre in London. First brought to the stage as a staged reading at the Off-Broadway New York Theater Workshop, *Rent* managed to succeed at a time when most successful musicals were simply new versions of old classics, such as *Showboat* or *Oklahoma!*. © *Corbis*

founders might be pleased to recognize in the performing arts centers of the early twenty-first century some of their own impulses to unite and foster the arts in one central space.

See also: Amateur Theatrics, Colonial-Era Leisure and Recreation, Performing Arts Audiences

BIBLIOGRAPHY

Agnew, Jean-Christophe. *Worlds Apart: The Market and the Theater in Anglo-American Thought, 1550–1750.* Cambridge and New York: Cambridge University Press, 1988.

Allen, Robert C. *Horrible Prettiness: Burlesque and American Culture.* Chapel Hill: University of North Carolina Press, 1991.

Bank, Rosemarie K. *Theatre Culture in America, 1825–1860.* Cambridge and New York: Cambridge University Press, 1997.

Brown, Jared. *The Theater in America During the Revolution.* Cambridge and New York: Cambridge University Press, 1995.

Butsch, Richard. *The Making of American Audiences: From Stage to Television, 1750–1990.* Cambridge and New York: Cambridge University Press, 2000.

Cook, David A. *A History of Narrative Film.* 2d ed. New York: W.W. Norton and Company, 1990.

Cullen, Jim. *The Art of Democracy: A Concise History of Popular Culture in the United States.* New York: Monthly Review Press, 2002.

Dennett, Andrea Stulman. *Weird and Wonderful: The Dime Museum in America.* New York: New York University Press, 1997.

Dudden, Faye. *Women in the American Theatre: Actresses and Audiences, 1790–1870.* New Haven, Conn.: Yale University Press, 1994.

Engle, Ron, and Tice L. Miller, eds. *The American Stage: Social and Economic Issues from the Colonial Period to the Present.* Cambridge and New York: Cambridge University Press, 1993.

Grimsted, David. *Melodrama Unveiled: American Theater and Culture 1800–1850.* Chicago: University of Chicago Press, 1968.

Hall, Roger A. *Performing the American Frontier: 1870–1906.* Cambridge and New York: Cambridge University Press, 2001.

Levine, Lawrence W. *Highbrow/Lowbrow: The Emergence of Cultural Hierarchy in America.* Cambridge, Mass.: Harvard University Press, 1986.

Lott, Eric. *Love and Theft: Blackface Minstrelsy and the American Working Class.* New York: Oxford University Press, 1993.

McConachie, Bruce. *Melodramatic Formations: American Theatre and Society, 1820–1870.* Iowa City: University of Iowa Press, 1992.

Mason, Jeffrey D. *Melodrama and the Myth of America.* Bloomington: Indiana University Press, 1993.

Moody, Richard. *America Takes the Stage: Romanticism in American Drama and Theatre, 1750–1900.* Bloomington: Indiana University Press, 1955.

Nathans, Heather S. *Early American Theatre from the Revolution to Thomas Jefferson: Into the Hands of the People.* Cambridge and New York: Cambridge University Press, 2003.

Rankin, Hugh F. *The Theater in Colonial America.* Chapel Hill: University of North Carolina Press, 1965.

Richards, Jeffrey, ed. *Early American Drama.* New York: Penguin Books, 1997.

Smith, Susan Harris. *American Drama: The Bastard Art.* Cambridge and New York: Cambridge University Press, 1997.

Wilmeth, Don B., and Christopher Bigsby, eds. *The Cambridge History of American Theatre. Volume I: Beginnings to 1870.* Cambridge and New York: Cambridge University Press, 1998.

Wilmeth, Don B., and Christopher Bigsby, eds. *The Cambridge History of American Theatre. Volume II: 1870–1945.* Cambridge and New York: Cambridge University Press, 1999.

Heather S. Nathans

THEATRICS

See *Amateur Theatrics; Theater, Live*

THEME AND AMUSEMENT PARKS

"Theme park" can be defined as "a social artwork designed as a four-dimensional symbolic landscape, evoking impressions of places and times, real and imaginary" (King, 2000, pp. 837–839). The term is loosely applied within the industry itself, lumping true themed environments with more traditional, but culturally limited, amusement and thrill parks. But the differences are telling.

Although theme parks are associated with the name Walt Disney and Disneyland, the elements of the mid-twentieth-century theme park as assembled by Disney Imagineering (WED Enterprises in 1952) draw from building, landscaping, and understanding material history of world and art history.

The symbolic power of the theme park draws on the fantasy landscapes built and planted by the nobility of Europe and Asia, such as Bavaria's Neuschwanstein Castle, China's Imperial Summer Palace, and England's Kew Gardens and Hampton Court Palace. European pleasure gardens of the eighteenth and nineteenth centuries, led by Vauxhall in London and Tivoli Gardens in Paris, were followed in the late 1900s by the Prater in Vienna, which offered mechanical rides, then the world's fairs in Europe and America, especially the 1939 New York World's Fair.

Theme vs. Amusement Park

The concept of the "themed" environment, as such, first entered the American popular domain with the opening of Disneyland in 1955; a journalist at the *Los Angeles Times* coined "theme park" after the fact when the terminology of the traditional amusement park proved inadequate to capture the themed experience. In a linguistic turnaround, theme park now designates the entire industry, theme and amusement parks together, with the amusement industry (including thrill parks) taking on the theme label for its greater prestige and drawing power with the paying public.

TABLE 1

Attributes of amusement vs. theme parks

Amusement Parks	Theme Parks
Purpose: challenge physical laws for affective rewards.	Purpose: create imaginary places to produce a psycho-social engagement.
Kinetics	Story
Action	Affect
Motion	Emotion
Challenge	Validation
Physical dynamics	Mental dynamics
Adolescence	Children, coming of age, adult, senior
Events	Values
Ride nodes	Landscape, design nodes
Dramatic motion	Dramatic detail
Motion states	Aesthetic states
Amusement	Entertainment
Curiosity	Culture
Thrill	Engagement
Peer-group bond	National communal ethic

The theme park is as different in origins, design, intent, and effect from the amusement park as Ellis Island from Coney Island (see Table 1). As an indication of this confusion, *Consumer Reports'* first survey of "theme parks" in 2003 covers 450 permanent U.S. parks. Of these, most are thrill or amusement parks, but the standard is set by the top rated, which fit the theme park definition: Epcot and Disney-MGM Studios.

Amusement parks use the immediate physical gratification of the thrill ride: the exhilaration of speed, the loft and drag of gravity, the rush of adrenaline sparked by the mimicked prospect of serious bodily harm. The theme park, on the other hand, is a total-immersion art form built to capture a coherent mind experience, one that owes more to film than physics.

Theme Park Origins

Disney's original motivation for creating the theme park was to present the American public with the anti–Coney Island, although roots of fantasy and symbolism can be traced to Dreamland and Luna Park in their heyday (1904–1910), when "the practice of selling leisure as a commodity was initiated" (Weinstein, p. 132).

In fact, Walt Disney's stated reason for creating a new park model was his dismay and disgust with the carnival ancestry of the amusement park—a visit to Coney Island momentarily discouraged his own park dream. Disney's park was built, in direct opposition to the downscale reputation of Coney Island, expressly for the post–World War II emerging middle-class family-on-wheels. The enduring genius of Disney's invention has set the gold standard in the language, as well as the metropolitan/international art style, of attraction design.

The powerful draw of true themed environments relies more on their ability to reflect core cultural values than on providing amusement in the conventional sense of the circus, carnival, and pleasure park, related thematically to turn-of-the-century trolley parks (such as Lake Compounce in Connecticut, Kennywood in Pennsylvania, and Revere Beach near Boston, Massachusetts). Certainly, Disney's original creation, along with the scores of spin-offs, are recognized as iconic masterworks by the public. The U.S. Disney parks attract upward of 40 million visits a year (in 2003), far exceeding visits to the nation's capital and Philadelphia's Liberty Bell. Over the past five decades, the "Disneyland experience" includes California Adventure in Anaheim (2001); at Walt Disney World in Orlando: The Magic Kingdom (1971), EPCOT Center (1981), Disney-MGM Studios (1989),

Animal Kingdom (1998). Abroad are Disneyland Paris (1992), Tokyo Disneyland (1983), DisneySea (2001), and a Hong Kong park in the planning.

Besides their synergistic marketing of movies and merchandise through the parks while promoting the parks through Disney stores and television ads and programming, the huge success of the parks lies in their intergenerational design, allowing each age stage of development—young children, teens, adults, and seniors—to seek out the highest-meaning aspects of the park for their age stage. From child to adult, theme parks offer the high value-added attraction of emotional bonding across generations, the main engine for repeat visitation over the decades (basic to park advertising as well). The parks were not designed for children, but for families that included them—with shared experience as the valued outcome.

Disneyland became instantly popular for the reason any successful American popular culture finds its audience: because it acts as a tool to resolve the classic cultural conflict between the needs of the individual and those of the group. In a highly individualistic culture, the Disney parks provide a common ground by distilling and reconciling, though stories and archetypes, a set of shared values about freedom, initiative, the spirit of creativity and exploration, and their fit with team, family, and community. Among all social art forms, the theme park is remarkable for its ability to bring about this resolution.

Theme Park Features

As a filmmaker, Disney reinterpreted and retold old-world myths, focused through an American lens in a showcase of American themes—optimism, fair play, resistance to oppression, and faith in the future. This recasting of European motifs into American idiom was an immediate hit because it celebrated those qualities Americans most liked about themselves and the ideals they, and others, most admired in their country.

Theme parks are considered prominent, even central, American cultural icons, not only because they are popular forms that cross age and class, but because they offer an index to national culture. Foreigners (including intellectuals such as Jean Baudrillard) have noted that Disneyland is the real America—the world outside is a mere simulation. The Disney parks are capsule concentrations of American ideals, which is the basis for their long-standing popularity. They do not compete with amusement parks on the quality of their rides, but as a mental and aesthetic experience. As park maps reveal, these are symbolic landscapes built on psychological nar-

Cedar Point. Located in Sandusky, Ohio, on the shores of Lake Erie is the Cedar Point amusement park, which in 2004 held the record for most roller coasters in one park with sixteen. Among them was Top Thrill Dragster, shown here. First open in 2003, the coaster was the tallest in the world (420 feet) and fastest (120 mph) in the world at that time. Established in 1870, Cedar Point is considered the second oldest park in the country and it annually draws mre than three million visitors. © *Paul M. Walsh for AP/Wide World Photos*

ratives, stories to be relived by visitors together to validate shared beliefs.

Rides and other attractions are the multidimensional descendants of the book, film, and epic rather than the offshoot of the roller coaster and tilt-o-whirl. Theme rides are designed to position the visitor much as a camera lens is aligned, to move riders past a series of vignettes to advance the narrative and theme. The narrative experience is expanded with cued physical sensations—speed, sound, lighting, evocative smells, temperature changes—but the purpose is always to advance the storyline. It is the architecture, including public space design, landscaping—in fact, natural landscaping is the prime differentiator between theme parks and other types (see Scheu)—layered detailing, and the use of symbols, archetypes, stagecraft, and icons as the communications medium, not the rides, that determine the essence of theme parks. As symbolic landscapes, Disneyland and its progeny are closer relatives to the Zen garden, stage set, world's fair, and Cypress Gardens than to Palisades, Rocky Glen, Cedar Point, or Riverview.

Formative Models

One antecedent of the Disney theme park was the "improving" educational mission of the world's fair. For example, the 1893 Columbian Exhibition in Chicago celebrated American achievement in terms of the old world, particularly in the almost exclusive use of European-inspired neoclassical architecture at "The White City." The Philadelphia Centennial Exhibition (1876) featured American achievements as a generic type.

Frederic Thompson and Skip Dundy's Luna Park (1903) and William H. Reynolds' Dreamland (1904) were Coney Island's contribution to the theme park genre. Unlike the better-known Steeplechase Park, which featured thrill rides like the Ferris wheel, Luna Park and Dreamland used the "experiential" powers of the theme park medium to re-create other times, places, and worlds. Along with the thrill rides, visitors could take "A Trip to the Moon," voyage "20,000 Leagues Beneath the Sea," toboggan on an air-conditioned "Swiss Alp," or even, literally, go to Hell—complete with fluttering tissue-paper flames and menacing demons. These were the immediate ancestors, in both spirit and technology, of Disneyland's Matterhorn, Disney/MGM Studios' "Catastrophe Canyon" and "Star Tours," and Universal Studios' "Earthquake: The Big One."

Unique Features

Disneyland was the first permanent commercial theme park, made possible by the emergence of a mobile, educated middle class enchanted with the new medium of television, notably the *Disneyland* weekly series. Television, the automobile, college educations (through the GI Bill), and the interstate highway systems were the levers that moved America into the middle class after World War II. Theme parks were the symbolic landscapes that allowed a continent-wide ethnically diverse population to share common values, memories, and cultural benchmarks across state and ethnic lines.

Theme parks use the elements of "show" and "story" as communication united by themes: Fantasy, Adventure, the Future, and Exploration, along with Home and Community. The art of graphic and set design, filmmaking (both live action and animation), music, dance, and theater production put to use the technology of stagecraft as altered scale, forced perspective, color harmonics, texture, lighting, sound, and iconography in three dimensions to produce an effect "more real than real." This hyper-reality springboards off our preconceptions—which come from film, paintings, and books, but rarely from memories of the real thing—to evoke the simulation of actually being in a frontier fort, European castle, or turn-of-the-century small town. Theme parks rely very little on signs for directions, place identification, or instructions to park guests. Themes, icons, and images, not words, carry the message—what senior Imagineer John Hench calls the "art of the show" (see Hench).

Within Disneyland's "lands" (Fantasyland, Adventureland, Frontierland, Tomorrowland, and Main Street USA), "one of the most successfully designed streetscapes in human history" (Francaviglia, p. 148), is a clearly coded text, set in icons and images, easily read by any age and across cultures. Almost no written text intrudes, except as part of the image and symbol landscape of various themes within its borders. The reason is that the artifacts within are self-explanatory, because they resonate within their contextual (themed) landscapes. Icons are the signposts that cue the traversing "readers" to the rich patterns of meaning that surround them. The ability of foreign visitors to read the parks as archetypal American landscapes, and to demand park reincarnations abroad in Tokyo and Paris, is testament to the universal symbolic language in which they are couched.

Cultural Significance

Theme parks should be considered among the most innovative social artworks of the twentieth century, if for no other reason than they are deeply rooted in, and reflective of, American core values. Individual industry, creativity, mobility, and success, based on a faith in the future, innovation of the past, and the self-confidence to believe in one's unique vision of the world to invent what is new and different, recap the character of the life history of the park's inventor, Walt Disney. The original Disneyland park in California was a prototype of a new genre of recombinant art form: part art, part artifact, comprising architecture of every era, crafts of every country, and innovative as well as ancient art technologies. They are the hybrid descendants of world's fairs, museums, and the architectural follies and pleasure gardens formerly reserved for royalty and wealth. Conceived and designed by team intelligence—Walt Disney Imagineering—their "collections" of installations and artifacts are integrated in what John Hench called a "sequence of related experiences" (Goldberger, p. 433).

They are closely related to the film arts, which encompass any and all art forms such as set design, special effects, and digital processing. Like film, these places have the powerful ability to evoke because they bypass the conscious mind to plug directly into our pre-conscious cultural matrix. This matrix is built up over centuries of symbol-making, imagery, and iconography. This is an extraordinarily rich resource made up of the received highlights of civilization focused through the lens of creative symbol-making. As Disney expressed it, this perspective was the guiding genius of the prototype park, setting it apart as a personal vision from the more manufactured and standardized (off-the-shelf) nature of amusement park and carnival: "Disneyland would be a world of Americans, past and present, seen through the eyes of my imagination . . ." (*Walt Disney: Famous Quotes*, p. 29).

These robust forms are nevertheless virtual artscapes in three dimensions that incorporate and reinvent their "real" art sources. These multimedia installations are total-immersion environments, highly interactive in the form of enclosed "dark rides," landscapes both interior and exterior, animation combined with live-action, computer-coordinated effects, and visitor-generated narratives that evoke in the guest a mental journey not only to another place, but often to another time—following the lines of various selective historical narratives.

These are visionary, not "authentic," versions of the past and future, based on archetypes (ideal images) rather than historical record. Disneyland's power, shared with other compelling cultural landscapes, is rooted in culture and shaped as an index of cues that point to our most passionate and deeply felt ideas about who we are and how we think as a people. This gravitational field—of values about America's past, present, and promise of the future embodied in Frontierland, Main Street USA, and Tomorrowland embedded in icons and images—moves visitors through and among the park's sequence of themes.

Beyond direct recreation, the parks' thematic legacy has now converged with every sort of public space, from malls, airports, office buildings, restaurants, and hotels to college campuses, main streets, re-created historic spaces, zoos, and museums. Hardly a place remains—including our own homes—where the telltale imprint of the theme park has not left its emblematic and varied impression. This includes the ubiquitous "shrines" to *Star Wars,* Lego, Nike, Hollywood, Coca-Cola, and their universe of collectibles. Institutions from hospitals to malls to visitor and corporate centers hearken to the Disney approach to customer service as "guest relations." And, as Richard Snow pointed out in *American Heritage,* the Main Street revival movement of the National Trust was incubated at Main Street USA.

Parks Modeled on Disney

The first successful non-Disney theme park, Six Flags Over Texas, in Arlington, opened in 1961. Like Disneyland, Six Flags was organized as a spectrum of theme lands dedicated by theme to each of the nations that ruled the state. Since the principles of communication by thematics, the Imagineering design "DNA" can be universally applied to experiential spaces from pure fantasy to hard science, contemporary theme parks come in a broad spectrum of styles and specialties, from science museums to historic shrines to branded character- or product-centered attractions.

Theming has reinvented older park formats. The "nature parks" of Busch Gardens (an Africa theme in Tampa, Florida, plus a second park in Williamsburg, Virginia) and Sea World (Orlando, Florida; San Antonio, Texas; and San Diego, California), and related commercial water parks (Wet n' Wild), take the concept of zoo/aquarium and "marine park" to new heights. This improvement was accomplished thanks to new set designs and live animal performances that allowed the revitalized parks to vastly raise the bar first set a century ago by parks such as Sea Lion Park at Coney Island.

"National" and "international" themed parks draw on regional or world history and culture, expressed by costume, cuisine, music, and decor. Examples are Fiesta Texas (San Antonio, Texas), Polynesian Culture Center (Laie, Oahu, Hawaii), Great America (Santa Clara, California), and the Old Country at Busch Gardens (Williamsburg, Virginia), and sites like the fundamentalist Christian Heritage USA (Charlotte, North Carolina) and Splendid China (Kissimmee, Florida).

Historic theme parks based on the authenticity model include Colonial Williamsburg (Williamsburg, Virginia), whose founding predates Disney; Historic Jamestown and Yorktown; and Plimoth Plantation (Plymouth, Massachusetts). "Process" or "industry" parks include Opryland in Nashville, Tennessee (country music); Hersheypark in Hershey, Pennsylvania (chocolate), and Knott's Berry Farm in Buena Park, California (frontier farming). Popular entertainers occasionally have their own theme parks; perhaps the best-known are Dolly Parton's Dollywood in Pigeon Forge, Tennessee, and Conway Twitty's Twitty City in Hendersonville, Tennessee, respectively). Other parks recreate an old-time village (or "ethnic exposition" historic concept), such as Old Sturbridge in Sturbridge, Massachusetts, and Greenfield Village in Dearborn, Michigan.

While Circus Circus opened the first theme park casino in Las Vegas in the 1960s, theming took over the city in the 1990s. Confirming the shift in audience from high-rolling gamblers to vacationing families, combination casinos and theme parks opened in the same decade; these included the MGM Grand (movies), Excalibur (medieval), the Luxor (Egypt), and Treasure Island (pirates). These were followed by the tour-de-force architectural style "re-creations" of Paris, New York, and Venice.

From Disney's single 200-acre park in Anaheim, theme parks (and their amusement park cousins) have grown to an industry that takes in over $10 billion a year, surpassing even movie theaters in gross receipts (*Consumer Reports*). At the same time, operating costs, such as capital improvements, training, maintenance, enhancement, and marketing, are also high, including the trend toward constant innovations in attractions to encourage repeat visitation (70 percent at Disney parks).

Six Flags, Great Adventure, Great America, Busch Gardens, and Universal Studios have attempted to copy and enlarge upon the Disney theme formula with varying degrees of success. As these forms begin to consolidate and develop, the two types cross-breed look, behavior, audience, and outcome. So coveted is the "theme" label that the Six Flags Company prefers the term over the more accurate "thrill park," resigning to a perpetual second-class position in the industry after Disney, rather than claim their quite legitimate first place in the "thrill industry." In terms of maintaining the theme, creativity, and richness of detail, the Imagineering approach still sets the design standard by which all other parks are compared. Yet the art of thematics has created experiential places from a basic collection of perceptual cues (music, motifs, icons, architecture, landscapes, and historic touchstones) to become mainstream and metropolitan design for public spaces and reinstated forums of public leisure.

See also: Coney Island, Disneyland, Vacations, Walt Disney World

BIBLIOGRAPHY

Adams, Judith. *The American Amusement Park Industry: A History of Technology and Thrills.* Boston: Twayne Publishers, 1991.

Blake, Peter. "The Lessons of the Parks." *Architectural Forum* (June 1973): 28ff.

Findlay, John M. *Magic Lands.* Seattle, Wash.: University of Washington Press, 1992.

Francaviglia, Richard V. "Main Street USA: A Comparison/Contrast of Streetscapes in Disneyland and Walt Disney World." *Journal of Popular Culture* 15 (1981): 141–156.

Goldberger, Paul. "Mickey Mouse Teaches the Architects." In *The Art of Walt Disney.* Edited by Chrisopher Finch. New York: Harry Abrams, 1973.

Hench, John, with Peggy Van Pelt. *Designing Disney: Imagineering and the Art of the Show.* New York: Disney Editions, 2003.

"It's Mickey v. Shamu." *Consumer Reports* 68 (June 2003): 28–33.

King, Margaret J. "Disneyland and Walt Disney World: Traditional Values in Futuristic Form." *Journal of Popular Culture* 15 (Summer 1981): 114–140.

———. "The Theme Park." In *Guide to United States Popular Culture.* Edited by Ray B. Browne and Pat Browne. Bowling Green, Ohio: Popular Press, 2000.

Nusbaum, Paul. "Crowded House: Fun and Gaming." *Philadelphia Inquirer,* (May 29, 1994): 11ff.

Scheu, Diane. "The Role of Horticulture in Theme Parks." Master's thesis, University of Delaware, 1996.

Snow, Richard. "Disney: Coast to Coast." *American Heritage* 38, no. 2 (February–March 1987): 22–24.

Thomas, Bob. *Walt Disney: An American Original.* New York: Simon and Schuster, 1976.

Walt Disney Corporation. *Walt Disney: Famous Quotes.* Lake Buena Vista, Fla.: Walt Disney Company, 1994.

Weinstein, Raymond M. "Disneyland and Coney Island: Reflections on the Evolution of the Modern Amusement Park." *Journal of Popular Culture* 26 (Summer 1992): 131–164.

Young, Terrance, and Robert Riley, eds. *Theme Park Landscapes: Antecedents and Variations.* Washington, D.C.: Dumbarton Oaks Research Library and Collection, 2002.

Margaret J. King

TOBOGGANING

Tobogganing is a popular winter recreational pursuit in which participants coast on a sled down a snow- or ice-covered slope. The word "toboggan" comes from the North American Algonquian term *odabaggan,* which means sled. The Algonquian Indians used this flat-bottomed wooden sled with a curved up front end to pull game and supplies across the winter landscape of snow or ice or rode upon it going downhill. Aside from using the toboggan as a sled to transport goods, it began to be used for winter recreation in Europe as early as the sixteenth century, and was introduced in Canada, the United States, and Europe in the late nineteenth century as a modern sporting event. Three related winter sports grew out of the original tobogganing activity: 1) Cresta Run, or skeleton tobogganing; 2) luge tobogganing; 3) bobsleigh, or bobsled. The Cresta Run toboggan used a "skeleton" sled with metal runners with a rider in a head-first, prone position on the sled. Luge tobogganing involved a sled with metal runners also, but with a rider in a feet-first position sliding down a track. The bobsleigh, or bobsled, had a rider, or several riders, in an upright position, originally with the riders "bobbing" forward and backward on the sled to induce it to pick up speed while coasting downhill.

Development and Current Status

The modern organized sport of tobogganing has its origins in the villages of Davos and St. Moritz, Switzerland. Visitors sought the recuperative powers of the clean alpine air for their respiratory ailments, and, for a winter pastime, they began to toboggan down the slopes. As the activity became popular, teams were developed from the roster of guests at the village hotels, and races were designed from Davos to Kloster, Switzerland, on the Post Roads. The Davos Toboggan Club was established in 1883, and it hosted races. The success of the Davos Club influenced the founding of the St. Moritz Toboggan Club in 1887, and it sponsored toboggan competitions also. Michael Seth-Smith, in his book *The Cresta Run,* described how people began to seek out St. Moritz in the winter. Apparently in 1864, Johannes Badrutt, the proprietor of the Kulm Hotel, the premier place to go in the summer at St. Moritz, asked four guests from England to spend the entire winter there for free, in order to experience the beautiful weather without need for a hat or coat. By 1884, Kulm Hotel guests in St. Moritz decided they needed a toboggan race like the one for hotel clientele in Davos. Since there were no existing Post Roads on which to plot a toboggan run in St, Moritz, they had to build a racing track. Peter Bonorand from Switzerland was hired to design a banked track with several curves. Since the toboggan sled runners cut into the snow on the curves and slowed the sled, the planners decided to ice the curves. Designed by Major W. H. Bulpetts, this course was named the Cresta Run, after the hamlet at the base of the course. A challenge race was organized on 18 February 1885 between sledders from the Davos and Kulm hotels. The Davos team won since they held back and were careful in descending the run. The Kulm Hotel team risked too much and ultimately fell off the toboggan.

The present style of riding on the skeleton toboggan is attributed to McCormich, who, in 1887, navigated the run in the "Grand National" event by riding prone and headfirst on the sled. Each year the three-quarter mile Cresta Run is rebuilt to follow the shape of the valley it runs through, from St. Moritz, to the hamlet of Cresta, to the village of Celerina. The course drops 514 feet from the top to finish.

Technical Aspects

The Swiss devised alpine *Schlitten,* or sleighs, with curved wooden runners. L. P. Child, an American, improved upon these in 1887 with the introduction of twenty-two millimeter metal runners on the skeleton toboggan. A sliding seat was developed and added to the skeleton in 1902 by Arden Bott, but his design is no longer used. Modern skeleton sleds are made from steel, are no longer than 1.2 meters and 0.4 meters wide and high, have a neoprene rubber covering, and a saddle for the rider to rest upon. The runner blades are stainless steel and cut into the ice to provide lateral stability to the ride. Push handles are located at the back end of the sled, and shoulder guards are designed into the front corners for protection from careening into the sidewalls of the track. There are no brakes or steering mechanisms. To brake, one "rakes" or digs one's spiked shoes into the snow or ice. To steer, one shifts one's body weight. A rider puts a skeleton in motion by sprinting fifty meters in five to six seconds, while carrying the sled, then landing on top of the skeleton and riding it down the run.

In 1928 and 1948, the Cresta Run was included in the Olympic Games at St. Moritz. An American, Jennison Heaton, won the first gold medal for the skeleton race. Skeleton tobogganing experienced a resurgence of interest when the event was reintroduced as an Olympic sport for men and women in 2002 at the Salt Lake City winter games. Women have been active participants in skeleton tobogganing from the beginning of the sport.

Internationally, skeleton tobogganing is governed by the Federation Internationale de Bobsleigh et Tobogganing (FIBT). In the United States, skeleton tobogganing is governed by the United States Bobsled and Skeleton (Toboggan).

See also: Skiing, Alpine; Skiing, Nordic, Snowboarding

BIBLIOGRAPHY

Arlott, John, ed. *The Oxford Companion to World Sports and Games.* New York: Oxford University Press, 1975.

Bernstein, Jeremy. "Raking (Cresta Run in St. Moritz)." *The New Yorker* (28 March 1988): 88–90, 93–98.

Smith, Michael Seth. *The Cresta Run: History of the St. Moritz Tobogganing Club.* New York: Foulsham, 1976.

"Tobogganing." *Canadian Encyclopedia: Year 2000 Edition.* Toronto: McClelland and Stewart, 1999.

Katharine A. Pawelko

TOURISM

Leisure travel is usually defined as voluntary, round-trip, and not related to employment or permanent relocation. Within that broad description lies the story of the American tourist as a mirror of social and economic trends, including the democratization of experience, the contest between artificial and natural environments, and the fragmentation of travel interests into niche specialties. But it is also the story of a 300-year effort to use various sources of information to discover a balance between predictability and serendipity, image and reality, and active and passive forms of enjoyment.

Democracy and Discomfort

Leisure tourism has always been directly shaped by the availability, comfort, and price of transportation. Travelers from colonial times to the mid-nineteenth century lacked control over almost every aspect of the journey, including schedules, routes, and levels of amenity. Geography, the technological limitations of the age, and the whims of those providing the service were the primary determinants of the direction and distance of journeys. The more spacious comfort of ship travel was mainly available between major ports, forcing other travelers to accept the crude conditions of land travel. Native trails had often determined road routes. Even the so-called turnpikes were little more than dirt-surfaced gaps between the trees. Those who lacked their own horses were left to the mercy of unpredictable stagecoach schedules. Limited carrying capacity, crude springing, lack of good ventilation or heat, and seating composed of leather straps guaranteed an uncomfortable journey. Travelers were crammed together in a commingling of strangers of both sexes and all social classes, over which they had no control. Breakdowns, washouts, and wrecks were common.

The lack of choice in overnight accommodations posed another unavoidable problem. Inns were unpredictable extensions of their proprietors' personalities, and they varied in comforts; most were rude affairs. Travelers became temporary family members at smaller places, especially in the South, but even larger hostelries offered little privacy. Patrons slept in large common beds, undressed and dressed in front of strangers, and ate at long tables. Sleeping space and dining were first come, first served, especially the food, which emerged almost entirely from a frying pan filled with fat. The same fare was offered during the day to passengers on coaches that stopped to change horses and drivers. Travelers suffered passively, and even those who possessed one of the rare guidebooks to roads and inns that had begun to appear by the 1730s had no real control over where their coaches stopped. It was not until 1794 that the first structure built as a hotel opened in New York City. Boston's Tremont House (1829), with a lobby, parlor rooms, and private sleeping rooms, is regarded as the first modern hotel.

Besides the physical discomforts, leisure travel before the mid-nineteenth century encountered the constraint of general social disapproval. The religious upbringing of most Calvinists allowed nothing so frivolous. The issue was irrelevant to most Americans who labored under six-day work weeks and strict Sabbath observances. Health reasons provided elites who could get away from the daily grind of earning a living with the justification for travel either to escape the summertime epidemic season back home, or to "take the waters" or the clean air of spas, springs, and seashores for curative purposes. The town of Cape May, New Jersey, was founded in 1621 and began attracting seaside visitors around 1790. It grew as one of the earliest tourist areas because it became accessible by steamboat in the 1820s. By that time, Nahant, Massachusetts; Perth Amboy, New Jersey; and Newport, Rhode Island, all on the Atlantic, drew thousands of guests to large hotels, as did such inland places as Saratoga, New York. Improved turnpikes and stagecoaches also allowed the springs of western Virginia to become tourist destinations by 1830; White Sulphur Springs opened a new hotel in 1858. Gradually, the vigorous social life of parties, fencing lessons, horse racing, shopping, and gambling replaced the pretense of improving health. Saratoga Springs, discovered in 1767, began permitting games in the 1820s and opened a racetrack in 1863. By then, those who advocated leisure travel had begun justifying wholesome recreation as a necessary source of the kind of relaxation that would restore workers to peak efficiency without descending into vice.

The nascent travel industry quickly accepted any innovation and the resultant widening of choice. America's canal-building frenzy extended the range of leisurely sightseeing. The boat was smoother than land travel, but limited by fixed routes, seasonal shutdown, and the walking speed and frequent change of animals. Low bridges interfered with riding on the roof, the only place to escape the stifling heat of summer. Well-to-do leisure travelers often grumbled that the common table forced them to mingle with immigrants, native farmers, criminals in transit, and other travelers. And everyone inhabited a single cabin, sitting by day on cushions that were pulled out or placed on shelves let down from the walls at night. Only a carpet suspended from a cord separated the women's sleeping space from that of the men. Meanwhile, as sail gave way to steam, transportation on lakes and rivers became a quest for speed and luxury that was first enjoyed by elite passengers, who enjoyed the luxury of private stateroom, barbershops, libraries, and fine food.

Image and Destination

After 1850, the railroad not only brought major cities within a day's ride of hundreds of such new destinations as the Catskill Mountains and Cape Cod, but its new comforts changed attitudes about the landscape through which it traveled. The rising importance of images coincided with America's embrace of Romanticism and its emotional quest for beauty. Wilderness areas that had once been considered frightening and uncivilized wastelands attracted travelers in search of the kind of scenery depicted in paintings of the Hudson River School and described by such writers as James Fenimore Cooper. Nationalistic beliefs, which now held that the vast rugged territories were what set America apart from Europe, transformed the landscape to America's mythology and fed the fascination that made a visit to the now-precious wilderness a matter of patriotic pride. For instance, early-nineteenth-century travelers through Franconia Notch, New Hampshire, spotted what seemed to be the profile of the "Old Man in the Mountain." By the 1830s, a New England tourist industry had been born. Some even argued that the wilderness that had once been scorned should now be protected. As early as 1831, painter George Catlin called for "a nation's park containing man and beast, in all the wild and freshness of their nature's beauty" (p. 261). By the 1840s, there were early daguerreotype images of the White Mountains of New Hampshire.

As the volume of tourism increased, aspects of travel became less costly and more diversified. Resort accommodations began to serve a broadening spectrum of classes. Trains and cheaper rooms allowed the middle classes to identify upward in their tastes. In the 1850s, the railroad allowed Atlantic City to become Philadelphia's accessible beach, displacing Cape May as the most popular coast destination. Even day-trippers out from the city could walk the sands once trodden by the very rich, who had already fled the hotels for more private "cottages," which were actually grand summer mansions. Other elites tried new resorts, some of which were built by the railroads. Rail traffic also initiated the earliest forms of urban tourism—to see human, as well as natural, wonders—which had first appeared before the end of the eighteenth century. Tourists not only visited the increasingly venerated patriotic sights of Boston and Philadelphia, but also gazed with wonder at urban waterworks and city parks, where nature had been tamed.

By the second quarter of the nineteenth century, a new and unexpected type of tourist had also emerged. Instead of seeking beautiful vistas, tourists of this type came to observe with macabre fascination the site of military battles or even the locations of tragic fires, steamboat explosions, and other events involving loss of life. After viewing images of these events depicted in popular lithographs or reading about them in a cheap book (part of the disaster genre that had begun to appear), they set out to see for themselves. The site of a deadly 1826 avalanche in New Hampshire's White Mountains became a major regional tourist draw. Visitors wanted to use these hallowed places in an attempt to share the experience of what happened there and to inquire about the larger significance of why it occurred. Even before the Civil War ended, veterans, families, and civilians began to flock to cemeteries and battle sites, transforming such places as the sleepy village of Gettysburg, Pennsylvania, into a major tourist destination.

Western Parks and Eastern Images

The completion of the East-West rail link at Promontory Point, Utah, in 1869 established tourism as a coast-to-coast industry, but it was initially limited to elite travelers who rode the new Pullmans. Rail travel to the West grew primarily after prices became competitive, especially on the part of the trip east of Omaha. By the end of the century, the completion of the Great Northern and Northern Pacific routes also drove down Union Pacific fares and brought the vast West within middle-class budgets. These travelers were also responding to two new sources of information and image. One was the travel agent, who simplified the ticketing process, found the best fares, and influenced the choice of destinations. The other was the mass production of printed and photographic images of the West, which were consumed in eastern population centers. Popular fiction and travel guidebooks provided verbal accounts, while the steel engravings in *Harper's Weekly, Frank Leslie's,* and other magazines fixed visual images. By the 1870s, the mass production of stereopticons gave photographers influence over which scenic spots people would seek to visit. The use of lithography and four-color printing in throwaway brochures helped catalyze a popular fascination with these places that increased the market for tourism. City people thus joined in the concern that the westward expansion of agriculture might bring about the loss of places of natural beauty to development. In 1872, Yellowstone National Park, the first, established the model for the subsequent Sequoia, Yosemite, and Mount Rainier Parks.

As the first owner of the land, the federal government could set aside large preserves at minimal cost, but these spots were isolated from transportation and lacked money for amenities. The answer came, once again, via the railroads. During the last two decades of the nineteenth century, the carriers began building elaborate "railroad realism" palaces, which attracted tourists with a compromise between predictable urban hotel amenities and the surrounding cultural heritage. The Florida East Coast's Ponce de Leon Hotel, built in 1885 in Saint Augustine, reflected the state's colonial past, as did other railroad properties constructed during the 1880s boom. Throughout the Southwest the Santa Fe Railroad featured Native American imagery and the Spanish mission heritage in the architecture of hotels, restaurants, and depots. Thus, when the Great Northern built Old Faithful Inn at Yellowstone in 1902 and Glacier Park Lodge eleven years later, both incorporated huge logs and stones, reflecting their natural surroundings. The visitor's dollar also bought atmosphere as well as shelter in other large non-park resorts, such as the Grand Hotel on Mackinac Island, Michigan, and White Sulphur Springs, West Virginia. Urban luxury became part of the ersatz experience of "roughing it." These hotels coincided with the growing popularity of "outdoor sports," like hunting, fishing, and horseback riding. Vermont's first summer camps for children appeared in the 1890s. The railroads also moved into dude ranching, another artificial encounter with the West. In all parts of the country, the addition of observation towers, handrails, bridges, paved roads, cabins, wells, and other injections of human engineering were acclaimed as "improvements" over nature.

World's Fairs

World's fairs expanded the notion of tourism in new ways. The 1876 Centennial Exposition filled Philadelphia's Fairmont Park with a spectacular building that not only drew 9.9 million to celebrate the nation's emergence as an industrial power, but also advertised the notion of seeing the rest of America. Fast-growing Chicago was itself a tourist attraction when it wrestled the right to host the 1893 World's Columbian Exposition from older cities. Over its six-month run 27 million visitors crowded over 600 new hotels. Both fairs involved rearranging parklands to accommodate dreamlike exhibit buildings. Fair goers saw the trip as an efficient, yet thrilling, substitute for travel, since everything worth seeing from around the globe had been collected, cataloged, and displayed as if in some wondrous department store. Both fairs seemed to be windows into the future. Large natural wonders were reproduced in miniature, while some industrial displays such as the Centennial's Corliss Engine were of overwhelming proportions. Armies of workers kept the fairgrounds clean and safe, while the careful study of guidebooks enabled visitors to prechoose what they wanted most to see.

Souvenirs allowed exposition visitors to carry home physical reminders of a pleasant experience as well as remove all doubt that they had made the trip. It was an old custom. Such items as small stones collected at a scenic site also allowed nontravelers to share the experience by gazing upon or touching a part of the destination. (On a more spectacular scale, that has been the function of moon rocks brought back by astronauts.) Early souvenirs also included guidebooks and luggage tags. Commercialized souvenirs, which began to be produced and sold at the tourist destination in the mid-nineteenth century, not only enhanced profits, but also allowed the manu-facturers, the sellers, and the host city or tourist attraction to control their own image. The 1893 Chicago fair brought a quantum advancement in souvenirs. There were trinkets of every description and huge books filled with the recently invented half-tone images. Visitors could send home the new picture postcards, recently approved by postal authorities. A well placed "X" marked on the card often denoted where someone had stayed or eaten or stood.

One of the most controversial decisions made by directors of the Chicago fair was to demand license fees from amateur as well as professional photographers. Although the policy gave the exposition greater control of its own image, it ran counter to the developing trend of democratizing the tourist experience. When George Eastman decided in 1888 to broaden his market by making the photographic process inexpensive and simple, his portable Kodak camera gave its users the ability to customize their souvenirs and control their lasting visual histories of their trips. By placing themselves in the pictures, they were able to provide absolute proof of travel authenticity. The black box and the demand that everyone stand still for a shot became so ubiquitous that they helped generate the term "Kodakers" as a somewhat derisive term for ill-mannered tourists.

The city also remained the focus of various types of tourism. Rural folk in particular were curious about urban life and were commonly found clutching guidebooks and gawking at skyscrapers. Meanwhile, money, time, and information continued to limit access to leisure travel for the urban working class to summer Sundays. The bicycle, once limited to the wealthy because of its cost, dropped in price during the 1890s; this new affordability gave workers access to local tourism that was not controlled by fares and timetables, a hint of what the automobile would later allow. Those Philadelphians with funds for the railroad ride could visit Atlantic City, which erected a large wooden pier in 1870. For wage-earning New Yorkers, a railroad, ferryboat, or transit ride brought them to Coney Island, a hodgepodge resort, catering to all classes, that had emerged after 1870 and thrived for much of the next century. Enterprising captains transformed older ships into tour boats that circled Manhattan and ran to spots surrounding New York harbor. The Chicago working class crowded commercial beaches and lined up to ride weekend lake excursion steamers to Milwaukee, Wisconsin, and Michigan City, Indiana. It was the Midway of the 1893 fair, in particular, that expanded America's notion of leisure by combining the Ferris wheel and other amusements with anthropological displays that were designed to provide a popular form of fake travel to foreign cultures. They could even find artificial "danger" wandering among the Midway's foreign market stalls or looking out across Chicago from one of the Ferris wheel cars. Later, visitors who had traveled thousands of miles to see the Columbian Midway would be able to patronize the same kinds of passive entertainments at urban amusement parks.

Leisure in Prosperous Times

Prosperous times provide the volume of discretionary spending that invariably ignites growth in the tourism industry. Elites develop travel patterns that are out of reach for mass-market tourism. The 1920s saw the wealthy and upper middle class travel outside the United States in record numbers. Travel abroad on a new generation of luxury steamships allowed many to escape Prohibition in style. Americans in the hundreds of thousands poured over the sights of Europe or traveled around the world on a southern route that opened in 1927. Domestically, the railroads responded to competition from the automobile by increasing the class distinctions of their accommodations, adding premium-fare fast trains of luxury equipment. Pulling against the elitist trend was a combination of democratization and individualization of the domestic mass market to include modest budgets. Larger and more powerful autobuses made it possible to make over-the-road runs profitable. A local company that carried Minnesota iron ore miners to work consolidated its service with others and became Greyhound Lines. Buses became less expensive and geographically more flexible alternatives to rail travel. Moreover, the mass automobile ownership engineered by Henry Ford began to have an impact on leisure travel after World War I that was so great that rail ridership in America, which had peaked in 1920, began to lose passengers to the automobile. A planned auto vacation meant that prosperous working-class families could now afford the luxury of individualized leisure travel, setting their own route and schedule. Campers, tourist cabins, and Kodaks were part of what could be considered a new outdoor economy that altered the identities of whole regions. For instance, although improved railroad access to Cape Cod after the Civil War had resulted in a few scattered resorts, the automobile transformed the area into a unified destination in the 1920s.

Out west not only did the U.S. highway system simplify the process of staying on the right road, but the volume of traffic that these routes generated tended to create a linear tourist economy across states that had previously seen little spending from strangers passing through on trains. Grand Canyon and Zion (1919), as well as Grand Teton (1929) added to the roster of National Parks in the West, but the 1920s saw the concept applied to the East with the creation of Lafayette (1919), Great Smoky Mountains (1926), Shenandoah (1926), and Mammoth Cave (1926). It was also becoming clear that parks were subject to a self-destructive fate. That is, the democratic goal of encouraging all Americans to share the uplifting benefits of visiting the parks would result in crowds so large that they would destroy the natural reasons for creating the parks in the first place. That problem had not been considered during the first few decades of the National Park system and remained manageable in the era of rail tourism. In 1927 Scenic Airways began flying over the Grand Canyon, but the advent of automobile tourism brought the first bitter wrangling over the impact of traffic and the presence of private concessionaires to serve tourist needs in National Parks, a debate that continued into the 2000s.

It was perhaps appropriate that two individuals who had profited most from this new automobile tourism would fund two new tourist destinations that were born in the 1920s. John D. Rockefeller's Standard Oil money paid for the archaeological research and physical rebuilding of the ruins of the colonial capital of Williamsburg, Virginia. Meanwhile, Henry Ford embarked on the creation of Greenfield Village, which consisted of dozens of historic structures from around the world plucked from their context and relocated in a re-created nineteenth-century small-town neighborhood. The adjacent Henry Ford Museum housed a variety of mostly industrial artifacts that rivaled the Smithsonian's collections. Both places were, in a sense, artificial destinations that became immensely popular.

Depression, War, and Travel

The devastating business collapse and soaring unemployment of the Great Depression left many Americans on the road, but only to drift from place to place in search of work. *The Grapes of Wrath* could hardly be called sightseeing. Resorts cut services, seashore cottages sat empty, and several major city hotels went bankrupt. But the decade did lay the groundwork for the future, and travel was intimately connected to selling the idea that industrial design would contribute to an industrial revival. During the 1930s, railroads began to embrace lightweight streamlined equipment that promised not only to slash operating costs, but also to run at higher speeds that would attract Depression-era passengers back to trains. But declining ridership forced reductions in the frequencies of other trains.

Nothing expressed that idea more clearly than the decade's two major world's fairs. The themes of both events were futuristic, and leisure travelers arrived with the expectation of being uplifted, excited, and amused. The first, Chicago's Century of Progress (1933–1934), proved profitable despite the hard times. Corporate sponsorship, which was obvious in the overt commercialization of exhibits, eased funding, while a greater emphasis on amusement instead of enlightenment gave the affair a more escapist flavor than its 1893 counterpart. Hard times may also have enlarged attendance by making Americans believe that if they could afford only one trip it should be to a world's fair. Automobility not only reduced travel expenses, but the whole family was able to sleep in the car or at one of dozens of auto camps. The larger New York World's Fair of 1939 to 1940 drew on the same styles and themes. Visitors came to see what lay ahead for them, including television, superhighways, air travel, and the products of chemistry. As the world was moved toward an explosion in international relations, the 1939 to 1940 fairs also emphasized themes of democracy and government service.

Hard times also forced families on modest budgets to enjoy tourism close to home. The Works Progress Administration's Federal Writers' Project produced new information sources in the form of inexpensive state guidebooks that encouraged city dwellers to visit museums and otherwise act like tourists in their own cities. The guides also suggested automobile touring routes and provided scenic and historical detail about the towns and sites along the way. This type of tourism inspired such communities as Sarasota, Florida, and Taos, New Mexico, to create celebrations designed to draw in the tourist dollars. Finally, in several states the Civilian Conservation Corps literally paved the way for future tourism by cutting roads in undeveloped areas and building log cabins and lodges that grew into state park systems.

World War II gasoline and tire rationing virtually halted discretionary automobile use, while military travelers took priority over civilians on trains and planes. The war also interrupted futuristic ideas that had been displayed at the 1930s fairs and were to impact postwar tourism. One was the superhighway displayed at the 1939 Futurama exhibit. The multilane, divided, and limited-access highway took realistic form in the construction of the Pennsylvania Turnpike, which would be the model for postwar interstate travel. Not only were auto excursions cheaper for families and able to liberate them from timetables, but postwar cars promised new levels of comfort. Even streamlined trains with "vista-domes" for scenic routes, new economy sleepers, and fast all-coach trains could not stem the loss of railway passenger share. The railroads chose the hundredth anniversary of Windy

City railroading to stage the Chicago Railroad Fairs of 1948 to 1949. These events advanced the techniques of creating artificial entertainment environments that attempted to re-create other places and time periods. Animatronic characters talked to crowds, which also filled grandstands for a pageant that celebrated an idealized account of America's history and technological progress. Although the fairs failed to stem the national decline in rail tourism, they were significant as a sign of Chicago's growing interest in attracting urban tourists to supplement its industrial base.

Leisure Travel: Everywhere or Nowhere

During the last half of the twentieth century, the tourist industry was pulled simultaneously in many directions, leaving leisure consumers with a bewildering array of choices. One model, the once-scorned landscape, could be found in the West, where tourism benefited from a broadening definition of the term scenic "destination." Artifacts of the disappearing mining industry took on new life as quaint tourist attractions. Played-out mines and ghost towns were part of Colorado's reinvention as a leisure destination, with a tenfold increase in tourists between 1946 and 1964. The same was true of South Dakota's old mining districts, as well as its desolate Black Hills. The 1941 completion of Mount Rushmore's four sixty-foot-high presidential faces represented the transformation of nature into human-made symbols; the sixteen-year process of carving them had served to advertise the feat. Later, such human creations as the Saint Louis arch were similarly designed to draw tourists.

Meanwhile, those who went west by car passed by hundreds of signs advertising such non-natural attractions as "Pioneer Village" in Minton, Nebraska, a large private museum funded by plastics inventor Harold Warp; "Rock City" in Georgia, which evolved from a private estate on Lookout Mountain, overlooking Chattanooga, Tennessee; and South Dakota's Wall Drugs, which offered free ice water in order to draw Mt. Rushmore traffic to a small-town pharmacy that later expanded into a giant general store. At a time when few people traveled with advanced motel reservations, the local economies of towns along the tourist corridors benefited from impulse stopovers inspired by roadside signs. These smaller attractions have amounted to small-town Chamber of Commerce tourism, a low-key and localized promotion. Gradually, towns and regions began to grasp at anything that might possibly bring in tourist dollars. Other manifestations of this type could be found within a few hours' drive of major cities. These places are characterized by the displacement of the original scenic attraction by fast-paced rides, museums, and shows that depend on shocking rather than stimulating the senses. For instance, in the late 1950s a Chicago radio personality named Tommy Bartlett introduced water-ski shows at the scenic dells of the Wisconsin River. This began the transformation of the adjacent town into a concentration of dozens of family-oriented amusements and eateries reminiscent of a carnival Midway. Similarly, Pigeon Forge, Tennessee, remains better known for its mass of neon signs than for its original attraction, the splendor of the nearby mountains.

The postwar years also saw the principles of mass production, mass marketing, and nationalization combine to create corporate tourism. The rise of franchise food and chain motels during the 1950s was obviously a manifestation of an automobile culture, but it also resulted from what seem to be contradictory demands. Vacationing Americans increasingly sought new destinations each summer instead of repeat visits to the same cabins. But they also demanded greater predictability in getting there, in part because interstate highways, frequent jet departures, and greater media-provided knowledge of once-remote parts of the country created the perception of a shrinking nation. At the same time, lower long-distance telephone rates and the increased use of travel agents resulted in itineraries that were preplanned instead of impulsive. These advancements tended to promote the convenience and predictability of national chains of motels and franchised food.

This quest for predictability also promoted the concentration of a larger share of the tourist industry into a more limited number of highly advertised destinations. Serendipity gave way to theme park tourism, which grew out of the mind of Walt Disney. He understood more than almost any other leisure entrepreneur why American families sought predictability. His travel empire was rooted in several aspects of the World's Columbian Exposition, where his father, Elias Disney, had been employed as a carpenter. The young cartoonist visited the world's fairs of the 1930s, but later revealed that he had been influenced most by the 1948 to 1949 Chicago Railroad Fair. Disneyland, which opened in 1955, and its Florida counterpart (1971) offer a heavily promoted one-stop package that revived the 1893 characteristics of fantasy, ersatz danger, cleanliness, orderliness, family accommodations, and an overwhelming choice of activities. Meanwhile, Six Flags, Great America, and other theme park companies also used the 1893 formula, especially the Midway, as an outdoor department store of rides and attractions.

The rise and evolution of Las Vegas as a leisure destination is a recapitulation of modern tourism history.

The original 1950s transformation of the insignificant railroad town grew out of gambling and the raffish reputation that accompanied a state where divorce was a principal industry. The town was a haven for those who defied the American scorn for gambling and excessive alcohol, but fans were willing to travel thousands of miles to see national celebrities manufactured by the entertainment industry. By the late 1980s, Nevada had lost its gambling monopoly when Atlantic City siphoned off East Coast business. Most states adopted ubiquitous lotteries that were geographically placeless, and many others licensed casinos that were regional draws. The 1990s saw "the Strip" hotels of Las Vegas replaced by Disneyesque resorts that combined gambling with safe, clean, family-oriented fantasy environments that imitated faraway times and places.

Tourism became a new cornerstone of the American economy, but many remained uneasy about it. The tourist endured as the object of scorn for critics who complained that leisure travel was by nature an artificial experience. Despite the jobs created by servicing postwar travelers, their presence also revived the debate over the idea of the self-destructive attraction: Did the crowds in fact overwhelm and alter the very attractions they came to see? The roads and campgrounds in the National Parks clogged, while the new technologies of snowmobiles, off-road vehicles, and hiking and climbing gear prompted some visitors to attempt to personalize their itineraries. Such debates were especially cogent as cutting-edge travelers broadened the variety of travel experiences. Some targeted exotic parts of the world for ethnic or cultural tourism; others based their journeys on the quest for new kinds of eating or even sexual experiences; still others created itineraries based on searching out the fine arts. There is also a continuing popular fascination with visiting the "shadowed ground" scenes of assassinations and disasters. Unexpectedly, something as simple—and artificial—as 100 highly decorated fiberglass cows drew tens of thousands of tourists to Chicago during the summer of 1999. By the end of the twentieth century leisure travel was so broadened in its definition that it was in danger of having no definition at all.

Unpredictability remains the most predictable characteristic of the leisure travel industry. Air-conditioning reduced the importance of climate as a motivation for escape and made the South an attractive summertime destination. The 1960s prognostications that everyone's shortened workweek would lead to long periods of leisure travel have reversed themselves into a trend of longer hours; the cell phone and Internet have begun to make it impossible for some to separate themselves completely from their work. When they can go, the short vacation has often replaced the multiweek family hegira of the 1950s. Moreover, surveys indicate that Americans continue to feel guilty about getting away at all. The slowdown of the national economy and the fear and the security-related inconveniences that followed in the wake of the 11 September 2001 tragedy demonstrated how the tourism industry sat atop a shaky foundation of discretionary spending. Foreign visitors virtually disappeared, and Americans chose to stay near home. Airlines cut fares and cities scrambled to find new lures. Las Vegas began to forsake "family entertainment" for the more adult themes of sex, liquor, and gambling.

Perhaps symbolic of the constant change: In May 2003, the great stone face of the Old Man in the Mountains—one of the oldest tourist attractions in American history and New Hampshire's principal symbol—tumbled off its mountainside. State officials were faced with the choice of accepting nature, trying to reposition the giant boulders, or replacing the formation with a fiberglass reconstruction.

See also: Air Travel and Leisure, Automobiles and Leisure, Niagara Falls, Railroads and Leisure, Summer Resorts, Urbanization of Leisure, Vacations

BIBLIOGRAPHY

Aron, Cindy. *Working at Play: A History of Vacations in the United States.* New York: Oxford University Press, 1999.

Belasco, Warren. *Americans on the Road: From Autocamp to Motel, 1910–1945.* Cambridge, Mass.: The MIT Press, 1979.

Brown, Donna. *Inventing New England: Regional Tourism in the Nineteenth Century.* Washington, D.C.: Smithsonian Institution Press, 1995.

Carson, Barbara G. "Early American Tourists and the Commercialization of Leisure." *Of Consuming Interest: The Styles of Life in the Eighteenth Century.* Edited by Cary Carson. Charlottesville: University Press of Virginia, 1994.

Catlin, George. *Letters and Notes on the Manners, Customs and Conditions of the North American Indians.* New York: Wiley and Putnam, 1841.

Cocks, Catherine. *Doing the Town: The Rise of Urban Tourism in the United States, 1850–1915.* Berkeley: University of California Press, 2001.

De Santis, Hugh. "The Democratization of Travel: The Travel Agent in American History." *Journal of American Culture* 1 (1978): 1–17.

Jakle, John. *The Tourist: Travel in Twentieth Century America.* Lincoln: University of Nebraska Press, 1985.

Judd, Dennis R., and Susan S. Fainstein, eds. *The Tourist City.* New Haven, Conn.: Yale University Press, 1999.

Lofgren, Ovar. *On Holiday: A History of Vacationing.* Berkeley: University of California Press, 1999.

MacCannell, Dean. *The Tourist: A New Theory for the Leisure Class.* New York: Schoken Books, 1976.

Marling, Karal Ann, ed. *Designing Disney Theme Parks: The Architecture of Reassurance.* New York: Flammarion, 1997.

Newman, Harvey K. *Southern Hospitality: Tourism and the Growth of Atlanta.* Tuscaloosa: University of Alabama Press, 1999.

Purchase, Eric. *Out of Nowhere: Disaster and Tourism in the White Mountains.* Baltimore: Johns Hopkins University Press, 1999.

Rothman, Hal. K. *Devil's Bargains: Tourism in the Twentieth Century American West.* Lawrence: University of Kansas Press, 1998.

Runte, Alfred. *National Parks: The American Experience.* Lincoln: University of Nebraska Press, 1979.

Schaffer, Marguerite. *See America First: Tourism and National Identity, 1905–1930.* Washington, D.C.: Smithsonian Institution Press, 2001.

Schmidt, Peter. *Back to Nature: The Arcadian Myth in Urban America.* New York: Oxford University Press, 1969.

Sears, John. *Sacred Places: American Tourist Attractions in the Nineteenth Century.* New York: Oxford University Press, 1989.

Smith, Valerie L., ed. *Hosts and Guests: The Anthropology of Tourism.* 2d ed. Philadelphia: University of Pennsylvania Press, 1989.

Weigle, Marta. "Canyon, Caverns, and Coordinates: From Nature Tourism to Nuclear Tourism in the Southwest." *Journal of the Southwest* 39 (1997): 165–182.

Wrobel, David M., and Patrick T. Long, eds. *Seeing and Being Seen: Tourism in the American West.* Lawrence: University Press of Kansas, 2001.

Perry R. Duis

TRADITIONAL FOLK MUSIC FESTIVALS

Folk festivals in the United States evolved from fiddle contests and ballad singing concerts in the early twentieth century into major public events that symbolized the youth movement of the 1960s and the multicultural celebrations of the 1990s. Most of these festivals were organized around folk music and dance, although later festivals expanded beyond music on the concert stage to craft demonstrations and dramatic performances. The adjective *folk* at these festivals often signified tradition that suggested continuity with an earthy past in the midst of rapid industrial change. It typically suggested a recovery of the connection to community and land threatened by American mass consumer culture. Folk festivals celebrated ordinary people producing art and offered a sense of authenticity in a commercial society. Even as folk festivals gained popularity through the twentieth century as a sign of appreciation, or creation, of American tradition, they also signaled for many social critics American cultural weakening and the manipulation of folk culture.

Folk Festivals Respond to Industrialization and Immigration

Folk festivals defined as an array of performers celebrating American traditions grew out of the movement to recover "old-time" music in the early twentieth century. Early commercial recordings drew attention to fiddlers performing traditional dance tunes that reached back to traditions brought to America by settlers from the British Isles during the colonial period. As nostalgia grew for a passing, preindustrial America, fiddlers and contests drew publicity at state and county fairs, and at organized annual "conventions" at locations such as Galax, Virginia (since 1935), and Union Grove, North Carolina (since 1924). In addition to knowing many dance tunes, fiddlers also performed ballads and songs that bespoke America's "ancestors," or so many advocates of the music claimed. Particularly in isolated regions such as Appalachia and Ozarks, which supposedly preserved the sense of old-time America, festivals were organized to celebrate songs that represented a connection to the British roots of rural America in the midst of mass immigration to cities.

Among the notable examples of these song and ballad festivals were the Mountain Dance and Folk Festival in Asheville, North Carolina, in 1928; the White Top Folk Festival in Marion, Virginia, in 1931; and the American Folk Song Festival in Ashland, Kentucky, in 1932. As the country entered the Great Depression, and the virtue of the "common man" became significant to maintaining confidence in America's foundations, Sarah Gertrude Knott organized the National Folk Festival in St. Louis, Missouri, in 1934. She had a vision of a folk festival showcasing the many cultural legacies in America that together formed a national tradition. Her framework was to present big shows in large cities, often presenting rural and immigrant performers to urban sophisticates. In 1936, the festival was held in Dallas; in 1937, it moved to Chicago; it then spent five years in Washington, D.C., taking on patriotic themes at the start of World War II. The festival spawned many similar "Americans All" festivals, often presenting orchestrated European American immigrant troupes in picturesque costumes. During this period, smaller versions of national festivals were staged in various states, including the Pennsylvania Folk Festival, All-Florida Folk Festival, and the Carolina State Fair Folk Festival.

Folkniks and the Folk Revival Voice Idealism and Protest

During the 1950s, college-educated urban youth began singing the old songs, and groups such as the Weavers and the Kingston Trio became commercial stars. The folk festival movement moved to college campuses and featured young performers composing new music in the folk song style. An undercurrent of protest songs for civil rights, labor struggle, and nuclear disarmament played on acoustic instruments could be heard across college campuses. A large-scale folk festival at the University of California at Berkeley in 1958 spawned other festivals at the University of Chicago and the University of Pennsylvania in 1961 and UCLA in 1963. The Newport Folk Festival, established in 1959, attracted many college students in an expanded concert and workshop format. At its height in the mid-1960s, Newport attracted 80,000 ticket holders and popularized regional forms of ethnic music—such as Cajun and zydeco, bluegrass, Tejano, and blues—to northern urban audiences. The festivals had an egalitarian ethic as black, Latino, and white performers appeared on the same stage in ways they never could at southern festivals. Folklorists concerned for preserving authentic native cultures, however, criticized the concert presentations of traditional performers and the "folknik" stylists such as Bob Dylan and Joan Baez who eclipsed the old-time musicians.

Festivals in a Multicultural Era

As the Newport festival ended in 1969 (it was later restarted), it gave way to the folklife festival conceptualized by folklorists as a contextualized presentation of America's diverse traditions. The model for this kind of festival was the Pennsylvania Dutch Folk Festival organized by Alfred Shoemaker in 1950 and held in Lancaster, Pennsylvania. A trained folklorist, he created an open-air setting where visitors encountered crafts workers and performers in different areas demonstrating in front of traditional buildings and structures. The timing of the festival around American Independence Day had a symbolic value for Pennsylvania Germans able to celebrate their ethnic culture as part of an American celebration. As the festival grew into the Kutztown Folk Festival, it was taken over by commercial developers and it became more of a tourist attraction in the "Dutch Country," eventually becoming America's largest folk festival.

Folk festival. David Wilcox performs at the Newport Folk Festival in Newport, Rhode Island, in 1996. Established in 1959, the three-day event features concerts and music workshops and is known for popularizing numerous forms of ethnic music, such as zydeco abd bluegrass. © *AP/Wide World Photos*

The original folklife concept became most evident in the Festival of American Folklife held on the National Mall in Washington, D.C. beginning in 1967. Sponsored by the Smithsonian Institution, it is held annually around Independence Day. In its early years, the festival featured various American ethnic, working, and age groups showcasing their traditions in areas that integrated music, dance, craft, and customs. From that starting point, it evolved into the Smithsonian Folklife Festival, which had more of a global theme. Imitated in various state and city programs, including Michigan, Ohio, and Massachusetts, the folklife festivals emphasized models of face-to-face community in an increasingly mobile, electronic society. Folk music was one aspect of integrated folk arts that worked to chart ethnic-regional cultures in a global map of difference. In addition to regional festivals that emphasized multicultural persistence, other festivals focused on particular ethnic groups or forms of folk music.. Examples flourishing during the late twentieth and early twenty-first century were mariachi, klezmer, tambu-

ritzan, and Native American festivals. For many visitors, attending such festivals revitalized and reinvigorated their participation in, or appreciation for, the featured group tradition. Some critics complained, however, that the experience reinforced the weakening of traditional ties through an intensive entrance into a staged, manipulated event that allowed a safe return to modern life. The fact that the music or culture needed a "festival" was a sign of its fragile state.

See also: Fine Art Festivals; Southern America Leisure Lifestyles; Western America Leisure Lifestyles.

BIBLIOGRAPHY

Bronner, Simon J. *Following Tradition: Folklore in the Discourse of American Culture.* Logan: Utah State University Press, 1996.

Cantwell, Robert. *Ethnomimeses: Folklife and the Representation of Culture.* Chapel Hill: University of North Carolina Press, 1993.

———. *When We Were Good: The Folk Revival.* Cambridge, Mass.: Harvard University Press, 1996.

Cohen, Norm. *Folk Song America: A Twentieth-Century Revival.* Washington, D.C.: Smithsonian Collection of Recordings, 1991.

Kurin, Richard. *Reflections of a Culture Broker.* Washington, D.C.: Smithsonian Institution Press, 1997.

Peterson, Betsy, ed. *The Changing Faces of Tradition: A Report on the Folk and Traditional Arts in the United States.* Washington, D.C.: National Endowment for the Arts, 1996.

Rosenberg, Neil V., ed. *Transforming Tradition: Folk Music Revivals Examined.* Urbana: University of Illinois Press, 1993.

Simon J. Bronner

TRIATHLONS

The history of the sport of triathlon in America can be traced back to the emergence of the "fitness revolution" of the mid-1970s, a decade marked by a burgeoning of athletic participation among individuals of all ages and walks of life. The "revolution" began very modestly when a number of athletes in the San Diego area of Southern California combined their varied interests in swimming, bicycling, and running into one continuous event. Consequently, the first Mission Bay Triathlon, held on Fiesta Island in September 1974, was born. It was a low-key event and was followed by a number of other multisport events that sprouted up throughout California during the late 1970s and early 1980s.

Two individuals played a pivotal role in the development of the sport—real estate entrepreneur Tom Warren and Navy commander John Collins. While on Oahu, in an argument over who was the fittest athlete, Collins suggested combining the 2.4-mile Waikiki Rough Water swim, the 112-mile Around the Island bicycle race, and the Honolulu Marathon into a single event to settle the argument—and the Hawaiian "Ironman" Triathlon was born.

Warren, winner of the 1979 race, was written up in *Sports Illustrated* by Barry McDermott. As noted by Scott Tinley, a key figure in the history of the triathlon from the very beginning, that article was instrumental in sparking nationwide interest in this new, "eccentric" sport. A year later, in 1980, ABC began its coverage of the Hawaiian Ironman on its *Wide World of Sports* television program. However, it was Julie Moss's historic crawl across the finish line at the 1982 Ironman, captured by *Wide World of Sports,* that galvanized public interest in the sport

and ensured that the sport of triathlon would be indelibly linked to the Hawaiian Ironman.

The Hawaiian Ironman has become the premier event of the sport, with close to 1,500 people from more than 78 countries competing each year. Millions watch this event annually on network television, and in 1998 Timothy Carlson of *Triathlete Magazine* estimated that there were more than two million triathletes around the world, with more than 200,000 in the United States alone. For much of the history of the sport, and to a considerable extent even in the early 2000s, this has meant that triathlon itself has been viewed as an endurance sport, with the ultimate measure of triathlete status marked by participation in the Hawaiian Ironman World Championship.

On the heels of Ironman's success, the early 1980s witnessed an unprecedented proliferation of shorter-distance triathlon events, ranging from sprint-distance triathlons (500 m swim/25 km bike/5 km run) to the popular "Olympic" or International distance (1.5 km swim/40 km bike/10 km run) to the increasingly popular half-Iron distance (2 km swim/90 km bike/21 km run) events. Most of these shorter triathlon races emerged within the United States with the establishment of the U.S. Triathlon Series but quickly spread like wildfire in Europe.

A national governing body for the sport, first known as the U.S. Triathlon Federation and later as USA Triathlon, promulgated standards for participation at its sanctioned events. Such events gave thousands the opportunity to participate in the "every person's sport" without having to compete at the Ironman. This subsequently sparked and reinforced the growth of a triathlon subculture. Key attributes of this subculture focus on the value of cross-training and the overall benefits of participation that extend to all aspects of one's life, along with an emphasis on camaraderie with like-minded individuals. At the same time, the explosive growth and popularity of triathlon in the 1980s was coupled with increasing media coverage, primarily through ABC's (and later NBC's) coverage of triathlon's "Holy Grail," the Hawaiian Ironman, allowing nontriathletes an insider's glimpse into an endorphin-fueled and fascinating triathlon subculture. By the late 1980s, triathlon had come of age. *Triathlete Magazine* estimated that 1 million individuals around the world had competed in triathlons by the end of the decade.

The "typical" triathlete is a married, white-collar professional, white male in his mid-thirties who makes at least $25,000 and, more often, over $50,000 per year. The women who participate in this lifestyle likewise have similar traits. Although there are increasing numbers of women and individuals of diverse ethnic backgrounds also participating in triathlons in the early 2000s, triathlon remains a sport of white, middle-class, male participants. At the October 1982 Ironman race, 11 percent of the 850 competitors were women; by 2000, 328 out of 1,531 competitors (21.4 percent) were women. The average percentage of women competing in the Hawaiian Ironman in more recent years has fluctuated, but has always hovered around 20 percent of the total participants. This statistic is also true for women's overall participation in all triathlon races, regardless of distance.

Nevertheless, such statistics on women triathlon participants is a bit imprecise. When given an option to participate in "women only" triathlon races, women's participation at such races swells. For example, the 2002 Seattle Danskin Race set a record for number of participants at a USA Triathlon–sanctioned event for the year, with a record number of more than 3,500 women competing.

Although primary media attention and emphasis has been historically given to male triathlon competitors, it was Valerie Silk's able leadership as race director for the Hawaiian Ironman from 1981 through 1989 that established the race as a premier world event. Moreover, Julie Moss's crawl across the finish line at the October 1982 Hawaiian Ironman almost single-handedly launched the extreme-fitness makeover of thousands of baby boomers and "couch potatoes" from their sedentary lifestyles to lifestyles of fitness and passion for triathlon.

By 1989, the International Triathlon Union (ITU) was founded in Avignon, France, and the first official world triathlon championships were held. The official International or "Olympic" distance for triathlon was set by the ITU at a 1.5 km swim, a 40 km cycle, and a 10 km run, borrowing from existing events in each discipline already on the Olympic program. In 1994, at the International Olympic Committee (IOC) Congress in Paris, France, triathlon was awarded full medal status on the Olympic program, and the sport made its debut at the 2000 Summer Games in Sydney, Australia, at the "Olympic" distances. The women's event took place on the first day, with the men competing on day two—another fact that women's participation in the sport continues to bring enhanced publicity and media attention.

The 2004 Summer Games in Athens marked the second Olympics for a sport barely thirty years old, with all signs pointing to robust growth. And leading the way to the sport's continued growth will be the primary symbol for triathlon—the Hawaiian Ironman.

See also: Bicycling, Olympics, Running and Jogging, Swimming

BIBLIOGRAPHY

Babbitt, Bob, et al. *25 Years of the Ironman Triathlon World Championship.* Oxford: Meyer and Meyer Sport, 2003.

Carlson, Timothy. "Mainstream." *Triathlete Magazine* (August 1998): 74–80.

Danskin Triathlon. Home page at http://www.danskin.com/triathlon.

Edwards, Sally. *Triathlon: A Triple Fitness Sport: The First Complete Guide to Challenge You to a New Total Fitness.* Chicago: Contemporary Books, 1983.

Granskog, Jane. "Tri-ing Together: An Exploratory Analysis of the Social Networks of Female and Male Triathletes." *Play and Culture* 5, no. 1 (February 1992): 76–91.

———. "In Search of the Ultimate: Ritual Aspects of the Hawaiian Ironman Triathlon." *Journal of Ritual Studies* 7, no. 1 (1993): 1–23.

Hilliard, Dan. "Finishers, Competitors, and Pros: A Description and Speculative Interpretation of the Triathlon Scene." *Play and Culture* 1, no. 4 (November 1988): 300–313.

International Triathlon Union. "Brief Triathlon History." Available from http://www.triathlonusa.org.

McDermott, Barry. "Ironman." *Sports Illustrated* (14 May 1979).

Plant, Mike. *Iron Will,: The Heart and Soul of the Triathlon's Ultimate Challenge.* Chicago: Contemporary Books, 1987.

"The State of the Sport." *Triathlete Magazine* (May 1987): 61–79, 111.

Tinley, Scott. *Triathlon: A Personal History.* Boulder, Colo.: Velo Press, 1998.

Triathlon Federation/USA. "Who Are the Triathletes?" *Triathlon Times* (October 1987): 19.

Triathlon USA. Home page at http://www.triathlonusa.org.

———. Visitor Profile statistics. Available from http://www.triathlon.org/stats.

Jane Granskog

ULTIMATE FRISBEE

The game of Ultimate Frisbee would not exist had it not been for the invention of the flying disc, or "Frisbee," as it is commonly known today. In 1871, William Russell Frisbie moved to Bridgeport, Connecticut, to manage a pie company that he soon took over and named the Frisbie Pie Company. The origin of the earliest Frisbee stems from this baking operation; Yale college students who purchased pies from the nearby company were observed throwing leftover pie tins across campus, shouting "Frisbie" to alert potential receivers and others in close proximity.

While students continued to throw pie tins across Ivy League school campuses, it wasn't until 1948 that Fred Morrison, in an attempt to capitalize on the unidentified flying objects (UFO) craze in the United States at the time, found plastic to be the ideal source for crafting a flying saucer. By the early 1950s, Morrison had vastly improved his model and soon came out with the first mass-produced flying disc, called the "Pluto Platter." Produced by the Wham-O toy company of California, the "Frisbee" became a registered trademark for the company's flying disc products in 1959, after Wham-O discovered that "Frisbie-ing" had existed on Ivy League college campuses for years. Five years later Wham-O introduced the Professional Model Frisbee, designed by Ed Headrick; during the same year, Headrick formed the International Frisbee Association (IFA) in Los Angeles, California, to better coordinate and showcase the fledgling Wham-O's Frisbee-related games and activities to the general public. Frisbee was now on the world map.

A Brief History of Ultimate Frisbee

In 1967, Joel Silver and others invented Ultimate Frisbee, also known as "Ultimate," at Columbia High School in Maplewood, New Jersey. In 1968, the staff of Columbia High's school newspaper and members of the student council played the first known game, and they continued to play the following year. Buzzy Hellring, a Columbia High School student, drew up first and second editions of the official rules. In 1970, Columbia and Milburn High School students competed against one another in the first interscholastic Ultimate Frisbee game. A conference of high school Ultimate Frisbee teams was created in 1971, and, by the following year, Ultimate Frisbee had found its way onto nearby college campuses in New Jersey.

The first intercollegiate game saw Rutgers University defeat Princeton University by a score of 29 to 27 in front of 1,000 fans on November 6, 1972. In 1975, Yale University hosted the first organized Ultimate Frisbee tournament; eight teams took part. That same year, Ultimate was introduced at the World Frisbee Championships; the following year, the Yale tournament was expanded and renamed the National Ultimate Frisbee Championships. During this same time, disc sports began to spread to Europe and Asia; numerous disc associations were founded in the 1970s, including the Ultimate Players Association (UPA) in the United States.

The UPA was the first national governing body for the game of Ultimate Frisbee; prior to the UPA, the International Frisbee Association ran and sponsored Frisbee-related events. In 1979, the UPA sponsored their first National Ultimate Frisbee Championships in State Col-

Ultimate in 10 Simple Rules

Published by the Ultimate Players Association

1. The Field: A rectangular shape with end zones at each end. A regulation field is 70 yards by 40 yards, with end zones 25 yards deep.

2. Initiate Play: Each point begins with both teams lining up on the front of their respective end zone line. The defense throws ("pulls") the disc to the offense. A regulation game has seven players per team.

3. Scoring: Each time the offense completes a pass in the defense's end zone, the offense scores a point. Play is initiated after each score.

4. Movement of the Disc: The disc may be advanced in any direction by completing a pass to a teammate. Players may not run with the disc. The person with the disc ("thrower") has ten seconds to throw the disc. The defender guarding the thrower ("marker") counts out the stall count.

5. Change of possession: When a pass is not completed (e.g. out of bounds, drop, block, interception) the defense immediately takes possession of the disc and becomes the offense.

6. Substitutions: Players not in the game may replace players in the game after a score and during an injury timeout.

7. Noncontact: No physical contact is allowed between players. Picks and screens are also prohibited. A foul occurs when contact is made.

8. Fouls: When a player initiates contact on another player a foul occurs. When a foul disrupts possession, the play resumes as if the possession was retained. If the player committing the foul disagrees with the foul call, the play is redone.

9. Self-Refereeing: Players are responsible for their own foul and line calls. Players resolve their own disputes.

10. Spirit of the Game: Ultimate stresses sportsmanship and fair play. Competitive play is encouraged, but never at the expense of respect between players, adherence to the rules, and the basic joy of play.

Ultimate Players Association College–only National Championships held at Tufts University, where eligibility requirements were imposed to distinguish college players from other club team players around the United States. Another new era in Ultimate Frisbee had begun.

In 1984, the World Flying Disc Federation was founded, a year after the International Frisbee Association disbanded, and it was charged with governing all disc sports throughout the world. By 1989, Ultimate was showcased as an exhibition sport during the World Games in Karlsruhe, West Germany, and, in 2001, Ultimate became an official medal sport at the World Games under the patronage of the International Olympic Committee. By the early twenty-first century, an estimated 100,000 players in over thirty countries played Ultimate, with the UPA registering over 13,000 members. Included in the membership are high school-aged youth, for whom membership provides opportunities to play in "junior-level" national and international competitions.

The Game of Ultimate Frisbee and Its Unique Contribution to Society

According to *Official Rules of Ultimate,* Ultimate is a noncontact disc sport played by two teams of seven players, whose object is to score goals by catching a pass in the end zone that a team is attacking. The game observes many different rules and calls of conduct (see sidebar "Ultimate in Ten Simple Rules") and has similarities to soccer, American football, and basketball, although it is distinctly different from each, with varied types of individual throws and team strategies commonplace. One aspect of the game that is commonly described by participants with great enthusiasm is the notion of getting horizontal or "getting ho." "Getting ho" to make a catch or to fairly deny an opposing player a reception generates excitement much the way a "slam dunk" does in the game of basketball. While players can vary or modify rules pertaining to game length, final score, field dimensions, and number of players, what players refer to as the "Spirit of the Game" cannot be negotiated. The Spirit of the Game places on each player the responsibility of monitoring his or her own and one another's sportsmanship (see sidebar "Spirit of the Game"). This Spirit of the Game is what makes Ultimate unique from other team sports; neither referees nor judges are utilized at any level of play, from simple pickup games in a local park to the World Ultimate Frisbee Championships hosted by the World Flying Disc Federation.

With the Spirit of the Game comes a challenge for those who play to respect calls made by the opposing

lege, Pennsylvania, while the first European Ultimate Frisbee Championships took place in 1980. By 1983, the first World Ultimate Frisbee Championships took place in Gothenburg, Sweden. The following year saw the first

Spirit of the Game

Ultimate relies upon a spirit of sportsmanship which places the responsibility for fair play on the player. Highly competitive play is encouraged, but never at the expense of the mutual respect among players, adherence to the agreed-upon rules of the game, or the basic joy of play. Protection of these vital elements serves to eliminate adverse conduct from the Ultimate field. Such actions as taunting of opposing players, dangerous aggression, belligerent intimidation, intentional fouling, or other "win at all costs" behavior are contrary to the spirit of the game and must be avoided by all players.

From the *Official Rules of Ultimate*, 10th Ed., published by the Ultimate Players Association (UPA).

team. (Note: A call or violation occurs when one player accuses another player of an action that results in unfair advantage.) While the history of Ultimate has seen many changes over the years, from rules to participation to disc of choice for play, the Spirit of the Game has not changed. Indeed it may be the "spirit clause" in the rules that has engendered growth of the game into places as diverse as church and corporate leagues, summer, winter, and fall city leagues, intramural college leagues, and physical education classrooms around the world. While the game continues to have a committed and serious following of players who officially compete in sanctioned tournaments at state, regional, national, and world levels, the untold thousands who play unofficially around the world in parks, on beaches, and in school yards are the ones who quite possibly represent the future of the game.

As evidenced by the 2002 World Ultimate Club Championships in Hawaii, where over 2,300 players and 120 teams from twenty-four countries competed in men's, women's, and mixed (coed) divisions, the sport is alive and well. While spectatorship of the sport is still in its infancy, the large number of teams and countries being represented is testimony to the profound effect the game has had on thousands of people around the world. By the early 2000s, both serious and casual Ultimate Frisbee players and nonplayers alike could benefit from specialized Web sites, newsletters, magazines, and electronic mailing lists. Ultimate Frisbee clothing and accessory retailers and manufacturers were commonplace at tournaments throughout the world as well as over the Internet, selling anything from cleats to jerseys to specially stamped flying discs.

While the economic impact of Ultimate Frisbee is possibly quantifiable, the social implications of the game are less quantifiable but clearly positive, for Ultimate Frisbee has that special quality known as the Spirit of the Game. Players can transfer this "spirit" into their lives off the field. Encouraging participants to place their faith in others to do right or to be fair in the face of adversity may be the greatest contribution of the game.

See also: Extreme Sports

BIBLIOGRAPHY

Caporali, John. "Ultimate's Twenty-Year Chronology." *Ultimate Players Association* 22, no.1 (Spring 2002): 23.

Iacovella, Michael E. "An Abbreviated History of Ultimate." Available from http://www.wfdf.org/ultimate.html.

Johnson, Stancil E. D. *Frisbee: A Practitioner's Manual and Definitive Treatise.* New York: Workman Publishing Company, 1975.

Ultimate Players Association. *Official Rules of Ultimate.* 10th Edition. Colorado Springs, Colo.: Ultimate Players Association, 2002.

World Flying Disc Federation. "Timeline Early History of Flying Disc Play." Available from http://www.wfdf.org.disctime.htm.

———. "Ultimate." Available from http://www.wfdf.org/disculti.htm.

Eric Frauman

URBANIZATION OF LEISURE

The emergence of many, though not all, distinctive forms of urban leisure went hand in hand with the transition from the merchant and artisan society associated with preindustrial cities to an urban lifestyle revolving around offices and factories. In turn, demand for leisure activities drove the development of a landscape of leisure in the built environment. Although taverns, coffeehouses, and dance halls had long offered an alternative to leisure in the streets, cities increasingly offered affordable, first-class venues for a broad range of Americans. By the early twentieth century, institutions of the elite, such as art museums, opera houses, theaters, private clubs and gambling halls, and symphony halls, stood alongside sites of mass leisure like vaudeville houses, ballparks, department stores, picnic groves, billiard parlors, and various inexpensive amusements. Visionary entrepreneurs soon began to make such leisure sites more accessible, safe, clean, and attractive to render them respectable to the middle class. The Great Depression ushered in a time of troubles for many leisure venues in American cities, culminating with the decline of the central city as a social and cultural hub for leisure activities. Although downtown areas continued to draw patrons to a wide variety of leisure places in the middle years of the twentieth century, the perception of cities as run-down, unsafe, and undesirable only grew. White flight and disinvestment wracked large and small cities, especially those older industrial centers of the Northeast and Midwest. The animation of street life that so characterized the late nineteenth and early twentieth century city became confined to morning, lunch, and afternoon rush hours, leaving desolate streets and struggling businesses at other times. The surge of population to suburbia only worsened the situation, leaving many cities grasping for solutions by the 1950s and 1960s. Then, a remarkable thing happened: leisure, especially that for tourists and conventioneers, became entwined with urban revitalization, gentrification, and the growing search for heritage, and it fostered a spatial rearrangement of many American cities. The present-day urban landscape of retro ballparks, entertainment districts, waterfront developments, festival marketplaces, tree-studded brick sidewalks, and smart nightspots and cafés represents the efforts of public and private interests to rekindle the excitement of a trip to the city and thereby ensure its long-term viability.

Despite the longtime existence of a small upper class with the time and resources to pursue cultivated leisure activities in the colonial and early national periods, most Americans enjoyed no such clearly defined leisure time. Rather, their days consisted of a variety of work tasks punctuated by occasional moments of rest and leisure. Often leisure meant socializing while engaging in one's work, whether on dock or ship, in mill or shop, or on farm or plantation. Holidays, feast days, and civic festivals dotted the calendar, affording a rare opportunity to seek leisure apart from the workplace. In some lines of work, inclement weather also provided space for leisure. Until the rise of the industrial city in the nineteenth century, however, specialized forms of urban leisure were rare, in part because the United States had few sizable cities. Indeed, as late as 1840, only three American cities—New York, Baltimore, and New Orleans—counted more than 100,000 inhabitants. With the rise of the industrial city in the second half of the century, leisure became a more important and clearly discernable part of the pattern of daily life.

By the second half of the nineteenth century, the familiar rhythms of work were beginning to yield to the more regimented pace of the urban workplace, especially in mills, mines, and factories. Although workdays remained long, with many industrial workers enjoying only Sunday off, gradually workers won shorter work weeks that opened up larger blocks of time to pursue other interests and activities. For many, the workplace became a venue for planning one's leisure activities rather than simply the place where one tried to seize a moment of recreation here and there. In the midst of rapid urban and industrial expansion in the last few decades of the nineteenth century, leisure activities became important vehicles for coping with the problems of daily life in American cities. They offered escape from the noise, filth, and stress of factory and tenement alike. In the medical profession, physicians increasingly prescribed recreation and play to relieve the anxieties and problems associated with arduous labor. Promoters of seaside resorts in close proximity to major urban centers, especially those from Boston, Massachusetts, to Norfolk, Virginia, played to this concern by touting the salubrious climate. Whether they planned excursions outside the city or partook of the opportunities for recreation within, the inhabitants of American cities were, by the end of the nineteenth century, acutely aware of the possibility for separate realms of work and leisure.

The Social Spheres of Urban Leisure

The Saloon and Working-Class Male Leisure For reform-minded Americans, often drawn from the middle and upper-middle classes, leisure became by the closing years of the nineteenth century an important means of social control through sanctioned events and controlled spaces. Nevertheless, their efforts to promote Americanization of immigrants and a middle-class conception of personal comportment through public events, such as civic celebrations and commemorative events, often floundered when the working classes sought leisure in less-reputable locales outside their purview. Of these, the saloon posed perhaps the greatest consternation for reformers. The saloon emerged as one of the most important leisure institutions of the mid-nineteenth to early twentieth centuries in American cities. Germans, Poles, Czechs, and other immigrants brought beer garden traditions from their homelands, contributing to the popularity of the saloon, which was, until the early twentieth century, primarily a man's world. Married men often carried pails of beer home, where their wives could drink it in a more socially accepted place. Saloons represented a major improvement over congregating in crowded tenements or in the streets and became key meeting places in many immigrant neighborhoods, where they served a multiplicity of functions. In addition to leisure activities like singing, games of chance, and storytelling, one could also cash paychecks, learn the latest news, seek employment opportunities, and discuss politics and union efforts, all in a place that promised cheap food and drink. Saloon leisure provided an important sense of community in a rapidly changing urban environment, especially through the rituals of male bonding through treating and pooling money for drinks. The saloon also harbored both organized crime and an array of social pathologies. Those who frequented saloons squandered their earnings to indulge drinking problems, while bar operators, some of them mobsters, often used slot machines, prostitutes, and B-drinkers—barmaids who coaxed tipsy men to buy them drinks—to separate patrons from their money. Despite the problems associated with it, urban saloon culture remained a powerful draw until the onset of Prohibition in the 1920s, brought about in large part as the culmination of years of reform efforts.

Children's Leisure Much of the leisure that emerged in cities was also divided along lines of age, gender, class, and ethnicity, one of the most persistent obstacles to the advent of a mass culture with larger commercial potential. Children, of course, often spent time engaged in leisure activities with their parents, such as on picnics, excursions to amusement parks, and walks in urban parks, but they also developed a distinctive leisure culture of their own. Scavenging, petty street trade, street and alley games, and visits to penny arcades, candy stores, amusement parks, and nickelodeons separated children from their elders and ultimately made them more receptive to the emerging commercialized culture of leisure that marked the twentieth-century American city. Children played in between shining shoes, selling newspapers, gum, candy, and flowers, and other entrepreneurial activities. Most of these children were boys. Often there was a thin line between these activities and those of gangs. This form of youth culture extended into the twentieth century as well, although increasingly it characterized children born into lives of poverty. Throughout much of the twentieth century, for instance, African American children from impoverished neighborhoods poured into the New Orleans French Quarter to earn scarce money by entertaining or hustling tourists, often with tap-dance routines.

Working Women's Leisure Likewise, women partook in leisure-time activities both within and apart from their husbands or families. While well-to-do women continued to find leisure in the arts, cultural events, social clubs, and religious volunteer activities, working women sought some of the same activities as their wealthier counterparts, notably clubs and religious activities. This was particularly true in many immigrant communities in cities. Sometimes, especially in settlement houses such as Jane Addams's Hull House in Chicago, middle-class and low-income women learned from each other's leisure practices, especially arts and crafts. At least until the late nineteenth century, women shared a general separation from men in many of their leisure activities. As a result of the coalescence of a new urban industrial culture, however, working-class women increasingly found amusements in venues also frequented by men. Extending the boundaries of the socially acceptable, they joined young men of their class in dance halls, amusement parks, saloons, and other places where they could explore their sexuality away from the watchful eyes of their parents. In so doing, they helped pave the way for the rising respectability of urban amusements for women of the middle class as well.

Ethnic Leisure Ethnic neighborhoods, as noted, supported saloons as important meeting places, but they also revolved tightly around the leisure activities that surrounded Catholic parishes, Jewish synagogues, home and family life, and unions and fraternal lodges, not to mention the industrial workplace. Ethnic enclaves clustered around houses of worship and factories, and often, notably on the East Side of Cleveland, Ohio, only these former "anchors" remain as tangible reminders of the lively neighborhoods that once looked to them. As ethnic groups moved in successive waves out of inner-city districts and, importantly, as they gradually embraced a growing commercial culture built on movie houses and other amusements, many of these institutions lost their firm hold on immigrant life.

The Rise of Distinctive Forms of Urban Leisure

The Urban Park Movement A variety of distinctive urban forms of leisure appeared, generally in the second half of the nineteenth century. These included the urban park, the department store, the ballpark, the vaudeville house, the world's exposition, the amusement park, and the lighted commercial street. As American cities expanded, often with quality of life yielding to the relentless pursuit of profit, some Americans began to worry that cities lacked places where they could seek respite and recreation. Although early American cities had set aside public lands, pressure to develop them became so intense that many sold them to real estate speculators, merchants, and industrialists, leaving nothing to relieve the dense grid of

Macy's. Broadway and 34th St. in New York City in 1908 was dominated by Macy's department store. Rowland Hussey Macy launched his store in 1858, then expanded in 1924 to over 1 million square feet, giving Macy's bragging rights as "The World's Largest Store." In that same year, the first Christmas parade was held leading to the annual "Macy's Thanksgiving Day Parade." *Courtesy of The Library of Congress*

streets and buildings. Some urban planners began to work in the nineteenth century to reclaim land in the city or buy land in advance of urban expansion into neighboring rural areas to create large urban parks. For inspiration, they turned to the rural cemeteries such as Mount Auburn near Boston, Massachusetts, and Greenwood Cemetery in Brooklyn, New York. Themselves modeled on romantic English and European pastoral preserves, these "gardens of graves" served both as burial sites and places for urban folk to seek fresh air and scenic overlooks above the city. New York's Central Park, designed in 1858 by Frederick Law Olmsted and Calvert Vaux, sought to harmonize city and countryside in an effort to provide urban dwellers a place for refreshment and renewal. Olmsted's firm led the way in designing parks throughout the United States in the remainder of the nineteenth century, not only pointing the way for City

Beautiful plans but also affording a place where city residents could relax, play sports, stroll, or take carriage rides.

Department Stores The department store, likewise, was widely viewed as having an important social function. Earlier in the nineteenth century, the city was considered unsafe and undesirable for women to pursue leisure alone. Through the development of various venues such as the department store, however, it became respectable and popular for women to spend time downtown, and department stores' all-under-one-roof display and impressive architecture made them major civic landmarks and even visitor destinations as urban tourism began its ascent. Indeed, department stores from Marshall Field's, on Chicago's State Street, to Maison Blanche, on New Orleans's Canal Street, converted these thoroughfares into elegant, woman-centered spaces. Reflective of women's often-acknowledged role as the facilitators of household consumption decisions, department stores promoted a national market for fashion and style. Their use of sidewalk display windows made window-shopping almost as important a leisure activity as shopping itself. They offered a means for women to flee the constraints of household work and socialize outside the home.

Ballparks If the department store was primarily aimed at female consumers, the ballpark pitched its attractions more squarely at men. While organized sporting events such as horse racing, cricket, and baseball had long attracted the well-to-do, the dramatic growth in the number of ballparks in the second half of the nineteenth century increasingly brought in laborers and middle-class spectators. Baseball became the most popular sport by the end of the century and often provided a sense of urban community that crossed class and ethnic lines. Sports coverage in newspapers, notably in Chicago, became highly entertaining through the liberal use of humor, making reading sports pages an important leisure activity.

Vaudeville Houses The vaudeville house, whose performances melded features of earlier entertainment forms like theater and variety shows, became another wildly popular leisure-time activity. Earlier burlesque and variety shows catered primarily to men and women of questionable social acceptability with their seedy, risqué fare, which often included lewd jokes and even nudity. Sometimes they also included minstrel performances with white actors wearing blackface makeup to depict African Americans in stereotypical ways. B. F. Keith's Boston vaudeville houses and Henry Davis's Pittsburgh-based vaudeville empire were among the forces that began to transform such entertainment into something more acceptable for broader audiences. The vaudeville format borrowed the variety and novelty of earlier attractions like circuses and dime museums, focusing the audience's attention on juggling, dancing, skits, songs, gymnastics, and comedy routines, while avoiding anything that could be considered morally debasing. As with spectator sports, the fast tempo became a hallmark of this leisure form. By 1900, every city of even middling rank had at least one vaudeville house, often with beautifully appointed interiors. These buildings were intended to provide affordable entertainment in a comfortable, plush setting that brought the refinement of the symphony hall, opera house, or hotel parlor within the reach of millions of urbanites. Gradually the vaudeville format lost ground as motion pictures gained popularity. Many of the theaters that housed vaudeville acts transformed into movie

palaces by the 1920s and 1930s, which themselves ultimately gave way to the suburban phenomenon of drive-in theaters.

World's Expositions Perhaps one of the most influential forms of urban leisure was one that aimed primarily to educate and attract business investment—the world's exposition. Patterned after the influential New York Crystal Palace Exposition of 1853, headed by entertainment mogul P. T. Barnum, a number of similar events were staged in dozens of American cities. The Philadelphia Centennial Exposition in 1876 featured a garden-like setting of boulevards, fountains, terraces, and vistas, as did the Venice-inspired White City and Midway Plaisance at Chicago's 1893 World's Columbian Exposition. While these extravaganzas, lasting for months, were primarily tools of economic development, they also offered a range of leisure activities. Fairgoers could marvel at new technological innovations, including inventive applications for steam power and electricity; measure American progress favorably against grossly stereotyped and racialized depictions of foreign lands and peoples; and even enjoy midway attractions, sideshows, and thrill rides like Chicago's Ferris wheel, which lent a carnival atmosphere. These attractions included lifelike simulations of famous events such as the eruption of Mount Vesuvius, to the delight of the crowds. Trainloads of exposition patrons filed into these attractions, making them one of the nation's most visible forms of leisure.

Urban Amusement Parks The features of the midways found their counterpart in the many amusement parks that dotted American cities. Between the 1890s and the 1940s, every large city had at least one amusement park. Traction companies operated many of the early parks as enticements to riders of their streetcar lines. Some were even called "trolley parks." Parks like Atlanta's Ponce de Leon Park, St. Louis's Forest Park Highlands, and Cleveland's Euclid Beach gave the masses a place to seek leisure, often prompting frowns from middle-class reformers who disapproved of the sensual possibilities of some rides and attractions. Indeed, rides often placed men and women in close quarters and then launched them into dark caves that invited intimacy or hurled them through twisting, lurching turns that threw them into each other or plunged them into soaking water. Switchback railways, modeled after coal mine trains, converted working-class drudgery into delightful thrills for all. Concession stands, sideshows, and other attractions lent a carnival feel to amusement parks.

Perhaps the most influential amusement park prior to Disneyland was Luna Park, which opened in 1903 at

Coney Island in Brooklyn, New York. Luna Park's proprietor, Frederic Thompson, promised not to offend middle-class notions of morality and refused to allow sideshows and other questionable attractions inside the park. Yet he also cultivated a broad patronage by mimicking a variety of popular attractions such as dance and music halls, beer gardens, vaudeville, and tamer versions of sideshow spectacles. In addition to the typical thrill rides like "Shoot-the-Chutes" and tunnel rides like "Canal of Venice," Luna Park presaged Disney's fantastical journey rides with its "Journey to the Moon," "Trip to the North Pole," and "Eskimo Village." As was true of world's expositions, many amusement parks operated on a permanent basis a venue where the urban masses could sample foreign cultures without leaving the city, much less the country.

Electric Lighting and Nighttime Leisure The dramatic use of electric lighting, while particularly important in extending the workday, also added to the possibilities for nighttime leisure in American cities from the 1890s on. Torches and oil-fired "flambeaux" had long illuminated events such as the night parades of New Orleans's Carnival. Gaslight districts such as New York's Bowery also abounded long before electricity, but they were often associated with illicit pleasures such as prostitution and other vice. The appearance of electric lighting transformed the night sky into a warm glow in which purveyors of amusements and attractions could entice urbanites and visitors with the promise of safe enjoyment. Broadway in New York set the pattern by becoming nationally known as the "Great White Way," the city's first fully lighted street, which catapulted the Times Square area to into a three-decade golden age. Other cities scrambled to create their own Great White Ways. New Year's Eve celebrations began to use such lighting in the early 1900s, and, by 1920, New York's Times Square began its annual lowering of an electric "time ball." Christmas lighting celebrations, such as the lighting of the Rich's department store's Great Tree in Atlanta, appeared later, in the 1930s and 1940s.

The Rise of Urban Tourism

All of these leisure destinations attracted not only local residents but also increasingly tourists as well. The rise of affordable, reliably scheduled passenger train travel as well as first-class hotels in downtown areas facilitated the growth of tourism even in the second half of the nineteenth century. Railroad companies and travel services began to promote the attractions along rail lines, including many in cities. New Orleans's Mardi Gras festivities were featured in railroad brochures as early as the 1870s, and subsequent world's expositions in Philadelphia, New Orleans, Chicago, St. Louis, and elsewhere also owed a debt to railway promotions. Tourist guides also began to render cities into knowable places differentiated by their outstanding landmarks and attractions. The spread of public transit, including elevated rail, streetcar, and interurban lines, was a leading factor in creating a city through which the tourist could move quickly and freely, enabling him or her to focus more on the tourist sites along car stops than on the many often less appealing places between them. "Seeing-the-city cars" went a step further by ensuring that all tourists aboard them saw the same sights in a carefully controlled fashion that left little to chance. By the early twentieth century, whole neighborhoods of cities, including Greenwich Village in New York, Chinatown in San Francisco, and the Storyville red-light district in New Orleans, appeared more and more in tourist itineraries.

Urban Leisure in Decline

By the 1930s, with the Great Depression under way, American urban leisure began to go the way of downtown areas, suffering a period of gradual and then marked decline. The movement of more affluent families to tranquil suburbs like Cleveland's Shaker Heights and New York's Forest Hills Gardens was already well underway and was beginning to have an adverse impact on the inner city. Most urban amusement parks fell into decay and began to close, while many vaudeville houses yielded to "B" movie theaters and burlesque shows. World War II also worked a change in many cities as American servicemen and wartime workers flooded into cities in search of nightlife. New Orleans's Bourbon Street became a neon strip of burlesque clubs, many of which turned to more sexually explicit fare in the immediate postwar years. Likewise, Times Square in New York became a gritty, male-centered area that promised not glamour but both straight and gay prostitution, pornography, peep shows, and X-rated movie parlors. The growing popularity of television also contributed to the decline of older forms of urban amusements by the 1950s. As city leaders scrambled to turn downtown areas around amid growing white flight, crime, racial turmoil, traffic snarls, and enticements to suburbanization in the middle decades of the twentieth century, downtown leisure venues catering to a broad segment of the urban population became fewer and fewer. By the 1960s and 1970s, major sports franchises such as the Cleveland Cavaliers and Detroit Lions fled to suburban locations. Only a few cities like New York, Chicago, San Francisco, and New Orleans maintained vibrant downtown areas, largely on the strength of their business or tourist importance.

The spectacular growth of Las Vegas's fantastical, neon-decked strip of casino halls in the decades after the Great Depression and the development of Walt Disney's city of amusement in Anaheim, California, after 1955 only heightened the larger movement of urban leisure to suburban cinemas, malls, drive-in theaters and restaurants, and country clubs that characterized new American preferences. Malls, touted as new community centers by their developers in the 1950s and 1960s, attracted as anchors department stores whose executives saw the need to follow their customers to the suburbs. They quickly evolved into primarily, if not exclusively, sites of consumption but also provided a new place for youth to congregate on evenings and weekends. Perhaps the drive-in theater offered much of the same excitement that turn-of-the-century amusements did, for it offered yet another place for youths to explore their sexuality in an uncontrolled setting. More recently, the popular Cirque du Soleil, a Montreal-based new-age circus troupe, usually favored pitching its Grand Chapiteau in suburban parking lots or performing in special facilities like Downtown Disney and Las Vegas's Bellagio. Urban centers, meanwhile, seldom enjoyed much pedestrian traffic after six P.M. and became subject to devastating programs of slum clearance, urban renewal, and elevated freeway projects, all designed to stem the flow of life to suburbia.

The Rise of the Entertainment City

Few observers in the 1960s, then, could have predicted that in the ensuing decades, urban leisure would stage a remarkable comeback. While the earlier heyday of urban leisure aimed at a broad cross section of urban dwellers and only secondarily to tourists, new development initiatives focused increasingly on wooing suburbanites to large-scale events at stadiums and arenas and to gentrified historic neighborhoods or warehouse districts. They also devoted more effort to making the city appealing to tourists, adding history- or entertain-oriented attractions to make cities exciting and marketable.

Festival Marketplaces and Waterfront Destinations
"Messiah mayors" such as Boston's Kevin White hoped to redevelop their downtown areas around leisure concepts in ways that would increase the tax base and stimulate economic investment. Such mayors often entered their municipalities into highly visible partnerships with major developers, notably James Rouse, who saw the potential of investing in the central city. In 1976, Rouse,

working closely with Boston's mayor, completed a restoration of the city's old Quincy Market, once a lively public market, into a tourist-oriented venue called Faneuil Hall Marketplace. Rouse subsequently took his trademark design concepts to other cities, reviving New York's old South Street Seaport and creating a new tradition with the development of Harborplace along Baltimore's Inner Harbor in 1981. The festival marketplace concept often fit into larger waterfront redevelopment plans that city leaders hoped would reorient these areas from worn-out, abandoned industrial and shipping uses to magnets for leisure seekers. Such waterfront projects often included festival marketplaces, museums, parks, hotels, convention centers, aquariums, and sports stadiums or arenas.

By the 1990s, such developments were practically ubiquitous. The historic market concept even transferred to smaller cities that hoped to become noted leisure destinations. If one had no illustrious history or architecture, one could simply create it. In Scottsdale, Arizona, a suburb of Phoenix, developers created a reservoir in the desert lined with a European-influenced commercial center called the Scottsdale Waterfront. However, the abject failure of Auto World, an automobile industry museum, and the Rouse-developed Water Street Pavilion festival marketplace to create tourist appeal in ailing Flint, Michigan, pointed to the limits of leisure-based plans to remake cities.

Professional Sports and the City Just as ballparks offered an important space for urban recreation in the closing years of the nineteenth century, professional sports franchises did perhaps as much as any entity to anchor adrift downtown areas as leisure destinations in the latter years of the twentieth century. Even as some teams left behind crumbling cities for sparkling suburbs, notably the Lions football team's exodus from Detroit to Pontiac, other teams recommitted to playing downtown, and new expansion teams erected mammoth concrete stadiums in the heart of cities. Beginning with Baltimore's 1992 completion on its waterfront of Oriole Park at Camden Yards, new stadiums began to fuse with heritage-based, leisure-driven urban redevelopment plans in a number of cities. In city after city, older concrete multipurpose arenas met the wrecking ball and were replaced by new architecturally evocative and sport-specific stadiums such as Jacobs Field in Cleveland, Ohio, and Turner Field in Atlanta, Georgia. As the availability of a state-of-the-art facility increasingly drove professional sports, many cities faced the unwelcome prospect of having to scrape together funds to persuade franchises not to move to rival cities.

Urban Entertainment Districts Just as tourism promoters in late nineteenth and early twentieth century cities presented those cities as collections of leisure destinations, in the closing years of the twentieth century they divided their downtown areas into themed districts that could then be commodified for tourist enjoyment. Along with sports-complex-centered districts, arts, theater, museum, warehouse, and entertainment districts abounded in and after the 1970s. Entertainment districts such as Chicago's Gold Coast, Cleveland's Flats, Richmond, Virginia's Shockoe Bottom, and Tampa, Florida's Ybor City tried to recapture public excitement about going downtown. Although many urban entertainment districts focused on creating leisure opportunities in places that produced historic associations, many others increasingly attracted more placeless, themed attractions such as Hard Rock Cafe, a popular rock-and-roll–themed restaurant; House of Blues, a national chain of concert venues; in Atlanta, Georgia, the World of Coca-Cola, a museum operated by the soft-drink manufacturer near Underground Atlanta, a festival marketplace tucked beneath viaducts on the brick streets below. Walt Disney's direction of Manhattan's Forty-second Street redevelopment project in the late 1990s and its sponsoring of a new Frank Gehry–designed concert hall to anchor the emerging downtown Los Angeles in 2003 epitomized the corporate move to colonize downtown for leisure activities. The entertainment giant, which, aside from its ill-fated efforts in the 1960s to locate a theme park on St. Louis's riverfront, had never shown interest in urban leisure attractions, had by the end of the twentieth century demonstrated a profound turnabout from its founder's small-town Main Street centerpiece nestled in the heart of suburban southern California. Cleveland's Playhouse Square, a cluster of elaborate theaters constructed in the early 1920s and closed in the late 1960s, became the centerpiece of a revitalization effort that led to the designation of Theater District, even adding Times Square touches by the 1990s such as electronic ticker tapes and billboards and a glass-enclosed ticket kiosk in a triangular park on Euclid Avenue.

Although many city leaders learned the limits of leisure-oriented redevelopment schemes' ability to rescue their cities from decades of decline, Americans had rediscovered the city and once again romanticized its sophisticated appeal. Unlike in the nineteenth century, however, by the end of the twentieth century spheres of urban leisure were far more divided by class and race. New museums, aquariums, sports complexes, and other leisure attractions now carried admission prices that only the upwardly mobile could afford. Riverboat and land-based casinos proliferated in struggling cities such as Atlantic City, New Jersey; Peoria, Illinois; Detroit, Michigan; and New Orleans, Louisiana. These gambling places aimed at conventioneers but also attracted many low-income gamblers from nearby. Virtually gone were the days when one could visit a museum for free or spend a few dollars to watch a baseball game. Shiny new multimillion-dollar facilities afforded many of the luxuries of old movie palaces but often failed to make these amenities available to a large segment of the urban population. This left the poor and the working class to seek leisure in the crumbling storefronts that punctuated increasingly tidy, pastel-colored stretches of city streets "reclaimed" for the advantaged, or else retreat to the back streets, where corner bars, pool halls, neighborhood parks, community centers, and lodge halls offered spaces for leisure. Thus, by the end of the twentieth century, cities had seemingly moved a little closer to the socially segregated spheres of leisure that had also predated the rise of commercialized mass leisure that had marked their early twentieth-century counterparts.

See also: Automobiles and Leisure; Coffee Houses and Café Society; Railroads and Leisure; Shopping; Theaters, Live

BIBLIOGRAPHY

Barth, Gunther. *City People: The Rise of Modern City Culture in Nineteenth-Century America.* New York: Oxford University Press, 1982.

Cocks, Catherine. *Doing the Town: The Rise of Urban Tourism in the United States, 1850–1915.* Berkeley: University of California Press, 2001.

Cohen, Lizabeth. *Making a New Deal: Industrial Workers in Chicago, 1919–1939.* New York: Cambridge University Press, 1992.

Duis, Perry R. *The Saloon: Public Drinking in Chicago and Boston, 1880–1920.* Urbana: University of Illinois Press, 1983.

Erenberg, Lewis A. *Steppin' Out: New York Nightlife and the Transformation of American Culture, 1890–1930.* Westport, Conn.: Greenwood Press, 1981.

Fogelson, Robert. *Downtown: Its Rise and Fall, 1880–1950.* New Haven, Conn.: Yale University Press, 2001.

Hannigan, John. *Fantasy City: Pleasure and Profit in the Postmodern Metropolis.* New York: Routledge, 1999.

Jablonsky, Thomas J. *Pride in the Jungle: Community and Everyday Life in Back of the Yards Chicago.* Baltimore: Johns Hopkins University Press, 1993.

Kasson, John F. *Amusing the Million: Coney Island at the Turn of the Century.* New York: Hill and Wang, 1978.

Litwicki, Ellen. *America's Public Holidays, 1865–1920.* Washington, D.C.: Smithsonian Institution Press, 2000.

Nasaw, David. *Children of the City: At Work and at Play.* Garden City, N.Y.: Anchor/Doubleday, 1985.

———. *Going Out: The Rise and Fall of Public Amusements.* New York: Basic Books, 1993.

Peiss, Kathy. *Cheap Amusements: Working Women and Leisure in Turn-of-the-Century New York.* Philadelphia: Temple University Press, 1992.

Powers, Madelon. *Faces Along the Bar: Lore and Order in the Workingman's Saloon, 1870–1920.* Chicago: University of Chicago Press, 1998.

Rosenzweig, Roy. *Eight Hours for What We Will: Workers and Leisure in an Industrial City, 1870–1920.* New York: Cambridge University Press, 1983.

Sorkin, Michael, ed. *Variations on a Theme Park: The New American City and the End of Public Space.* New York: Noonday Press, 1992.

Schuyler, David. *The New Urban Landscape.* Baltimore: Johns Hopkins University Press, 1986.

J. Mark Souther

VACATIONS

Travel is an integral part of most modern vacations. However, the word *travel* was originally identical with *travail,* both deriving from the Middle English *travailen* and Old French *travaillier,* which mean to labor *or toil.* Travailen *and* travailler *(and* trabajo *in Spanish) in their turn may be traced back to the Latin* tripalium, *a three-pronged instrument of torture.*

Before the modern age, travel was a pain. The enjoyment of leisure had to be reconciled with the trouble of travel before vacations as we know them were possible. However, the difficulties of travel were not significantly relieved until the 1850s in the United States. Few good roads, and fewer accommodations, were available from the colonial period through the first part of the nineteenth century to ease travel. For enjoyment and recreation, most people stayed close to home.

The coming of the railroads to the United States was a key to the success and expansion of American vacations. Early on, railroads, and then travel resorts, actively promoted travel during extended personal holidays, influencing modern leisure distribution patterns favoring the purchase of goods and services, beginning a continuing process of the modern commodification of leisure.

Before the Civil War, a variety of Americans—"invalids, members of the northern elite, southern planters and their families" (Aron, 1999, p. 32)—began to leave their regular places of residence and occupation for extended periods of time, usually during the summer months, traveling to escape the diseases, heat, smells, and humdrum of city life, in search of health, social contacts, amusement, or spiritual refreshment, engaging in behaviors that we recognize today as vacationing.

Unlike Europeans, however, Americans resisted using the word *vacation>* to describe what they were doing. Before the mid-nineteenth century, only students and teachers had "vacations"; others described their activities in specific rather than generic ways: "going to the shore," "taking the waters," "attending revivals."

It was not until the 1850s that "vacation" came to be widely used in the United States as a categorical term, applied to a variety of activities, pursued for a variety of purposes. The resistance to accepting an existing general term for an increasingly familiar activity is important as an indication of the ambivalence, even resistance, Americans showed to the advent of this form of concentrated leisure.

"Vacation" as a general, nonspecific activity was defined primarily as an extended break from ordinary occupations. As such, "vacations" troubled a nation emerging from a Puritan past, still adhering to a work ethic with powerful religious sanctions. Just as the physical difficulties of travel had to be relieved before modern vacations were possible, the cultural difficulties of reconciling recreation, play, and pleasure with the nation's prevailing work ethic had to be smoothed. Moreover, the fact that only those at the top of the social ladder were initially able to vacation disturbed American egalitarian sensibilities.

Vacations for the Well-to-Do

Purposes other than escaping work dominated the discourse surrounding extended personal holidays before the 1850s. Mineral springs spas such as Saratoga Springs in New York, Stafford Springs in Connecticut, Berkeley Springs and White Sulfur Springs in Virginia—all of which made extravagant claims about the power of their waters to cure everything from "constipation to sterility, from scrofula to gout, as well as female diseases, sleeplessness, chronic diarrhea, bilious complaints, and hair loss" (Aron, "Vacations and Resorts")—catered to a gentry who justified their abundant leisure as a quest for health or as an escape from disease. Seaside and mountain resorts made similar claims about their environs. Examples include Cape May in southern New Jersey, Nahant in Massachusetts, Newport in Rhode Island, and Catskill Mountain House in New York.

Nevertheless, as more people traveled to these resorts, accompanying the sick or following what had become something of a fad by mid-century, the free time that defined resort presented new challenges: to fill the daily time vacuum, and then to justify activities they were discovering that were hardly health-promoting.

Elites at America's first vacation resorts began an American struggle with a question that had occupied Europeans for millennia, dating back to the classical ages: "What is there to do that is worthwhile in and for itself?" Like the aristocracy in Europe before them, they began experimenting with life beyond the constraints of work and the press of necessity.

At their inception, vacations challenged existing social norms and established cultural values. Whereas the leisure of extended personal holidays provided new opportunities, resorts offered places set apart from normal life to test cultural limits and experiment with alternate forms of social engagement.

Gradually, socializing, amusements, parties and balls, concerts, cotillions, recreation, and sports began filling the leisure vacuum. Vacationers appeared to be enjoying themselves. Social contacts between the sexes, impossible in normal circumstances, opened. Clothing styles and manners altered. Even the mixing of social classes occurred as middle-class Americans gained access to some of the elites' resorts.

Above all, extended personal holidays tested work's cultural hegemony by offering the attractive possibility of life lived beyond work and the press of daily life, of alternative ways to construct human community, transient though it might be, based in freedom and a fuller range of choices. Vacations, like other forms of expanding leisure, were a yeasting time, ripe with potential for social change and cultural experimentation.

Predictably, criticism ensued. Pundits and ministers were alarmed by the gambling, courting, and flirting going on, by the scant bathing costumes worn by swimmers, and by the obvious enjoyment people were having. More importantly, vacationers, the vacation industry, and their apologists felt it necessary to justify vacations to a nation still busy with the problems of making a living and building a nation.

Middle-Class Vacations

The problem of justification intensified as an expanding middle class began to vacation. After the Civil War, the American middle classes continued to grow along with new corporations and professions, and government bureaucracies added white-collar and salaried workers to the list of vacationers with time for extended personal holidays and money to travel.

Going beyond the original justifications—health and escape from disease—vacationers turned increasingly to explaining their vacations in terms of dominant work values. Rest and recuperation during extended personal holidays were deemed important because they improved job performance, at least for the new middle classes and professionals. After vacationing, people retuned to their ordinary lives and occupations with renewed vigor and energized commitments, or so it was claimed. Vacations were less a threat to work when they were justified as a way to improve jobs and strengthen the work ethic.

However, vacations were not completely tamed as the handmaidens of the job. Vacationers and those who provided resorts and administered camps also explained the importance of vacations in terms other than work values, arguing that vacations offered a new way to reinforce and express alternate values Americans held dear.

Vacation apologists began to recommend extended personal holidays as new opportunities for spiritual growth, education, cultural and artistic expression, community-building, healthy contact with the natural world, and creativity. Expressions of such values were important in and for themselves. They did not necessarily have to be subordinated to work to be promoted and developed. Values in their own right, they offered viable alternatives to a nation on the verge of being obsessed by work.

For example, among the dominant American values challenging work's hegemony, concern for the sacred was salient. America's strong support of work as *one* of life's central concerns stemmed from strong religious beliefs that dated back to the founding of the nation. But such beliefs also sanctioned alternate forms of religious expression and activities—the job had never exhausted the spiritual energy of the majority of believers, nor completely filled daily or weekly schedules.

Vacations for Spiritual Refreshment

Rising to the challenge to fill vacations' time vacuum in meaningful ways, American churchmen and -women developed their own brand of resorts: an infrastructure of camps designed to promote religion, spiritual exercise, healthful sports, moral recreations, and religion-based (primarily Christian) communities.

Early in the nineteenth century Methodist churches held massive revival meetings, attracting hundreds of faithful to extended stays in camps away from their work and homes. Their original success prompted organizers to offer revivals at the same place year after year. Such revival meetings as those held at Wesleyan Grove on Martha's Vineyard off the coast of Massachusetts, Ocean Grove on the northern New Jersey shore, and Rehoboth on the Delaware shore grew into yearly resorts by the end of the nineteenth century, complete with hotels, auditoriums, boardinghouses and cottages, and recreation facilities. By the turn of the twentieth century, such camps were annually attracting thousands—35,000 in the case of Rehoboth.

Other religious groups followed suit, establishing camps and resort facilities in places exceptional for their beauty, such as the YMCA camp at Silver Bay, on the shores of Lake George in New York's Adirondacks. Searching for meaningful vacation experiences, religious camps and resorts began to offer adult-education opportunities, community-building, and cultural and artistic activities. Foremost among such experiments was the Chautauqua.

In 1874, John Vincent, a Methodist minister, established a new kind of vacation opportunity in Chautauqua in western New York. Building on the camp meeting model, Vincent and his followers expanded leisure opportunities available for vacationers. Beginning by offering spiritual refreshment and instruction (Vincent's original purpose was to train volunteer Sunday school teachers), Chautauqua expanded its educational mission to include lectures, music and art instruction, and classes in a variety of subjects. A fledgling democratic culture emerged as vacationers began using their leisure to actively engage in drama, the arts and crafts, and nature study rather than depend on "professionals" to do these things for them while they sat and watched. Promoting "physical education," health, fresh air, and vigorous exercise, Chautauqua also began to explore ways the human body could be developed and enjoyed rather than covered and ignored. By 1900, the movement boasted over 200 chapters nationwide.

Historians have tended to dismiss these efforts at personal growth and self-improvement as so much bourgeois moral uplift, as attempts to control the behavior of those not held firmly enough in line by the coils of work. In short, historians have understood nineteenth- and early-twentieth-century vacations as simple extensions of the work ethic: since idle hands were the devil's workshop, vacationers had to be kept busy and distracted from doing what came naturally. The title of Cindy Aron's standard history of American vacations is revealing: *Working at Play.*

An alternate reading of early American vacations, however, may be that vacationers were deliberately exploring freedom's potential. By their own accounts, they were testing possibilities outside working and producing, exploring leisure as a unique opportunity for community and for progress in free expression of the things of the mind, the body, and spirit. America's first vacations may also be understood as challenging work's ascendancy, offering things impossible for people to realize fully at work or in economic and market terms.

Outdoor Vacations

Besides religious camps and elite health resorts, nineteenth- and early-twentieth-century vacationers discovered the outdoors. Camping on their own in the woods, hiking, hunting, boating, birding, fishing, and exploring, Americans found an economical alternative to expensive resorts. They also discovered a more private alternative to religious camps' full schedules, moralizing, and community activities.

Interest in camping began during the last quarter of the nineteenth century. Magazines, newspapers, and medical experts, responding to widespread concerns about overwork and neurasthenia, began to recommend extended holidays in the outdoors. However, since there were not many ways to get to the small number of existing resources, few were able to take such advice.

With the coming of the Model T and better roads, governments began to adapt existing public lands for recreation, responding to the building demand for outdoor facilities and services. Through most of the nineteenth century, the federal government's first priority was to transfer its vast tracts of public lands to private hands—homesteaders, ranchers, and the railroads were among the primary beneficiaries.

However, in the last quarter of the century, a movement began to retain in the public sector at least some of the nation's natural heritage. Abstract, idealistic goals dominated the movement at first. Some saw the need to preserve remnants of the rapidly closing frontier as reminders of the wellsprings of America's primary virtues, such as self-reliance, individualism, and the democratic spirit. Other wanted to preserve particularly beautiful parts of the country, such as the Grand Canyon and Yellowstone, from the blight of "development." Still others, conservationists, wanted to manage public land to prevent the depletion of natural resources and the degradation of the environment.

However, "use" of public lands remained a basic political reality. Setting aside millions of acres of public lands from private economic purposes just for their beauty or abstract historical significance, even for conservation, was a political nonstarter.

Consequently, outdoor recreation and vacationing were all-important political engines driving preservation of public lands and conservation of natural resources through the twentieth century. Recreation allowed Americans to use public lands in a way that did not, necessarily, deplete nature or transfer ownership to private hands. Preservationists and conservationists joined forces, championing the recreational use of public lands.

During the first two decades of the twentieth century, America witnessed a fateful confluence of public interest in outdoor vacations and recreation, and the political will to preserve and conserve the nation's natural heritage.

The national forests were among the first and most important vacation resources. In 1905 President Theodore Roosevelt created the U.S. Forest Service, adding 99 million acres to the system in 1907, and renaming the nation's forest reserves the "National Forests." Opening more of the National Forests to recreational use after 1910, the Forest Service saw the number of visitors increase dramatically, from around 500,000 in 1914 to over 15 million in 1925 to nearly 32 million by 1930.

In 1916, Congress created the National Parks Service to oversee the network of National Parks in existence, particularly their recreational use. Congress created the nation's first park, Yellowstone in the Wyoming and Montana territories, in 1872 as "a public park or pleasuring-ground for the benefit and enjoyment of the people" (Report of the President's Research Committee on Social Trends, p. 920). The Park Service's original charter was to preserve the nation's natural heritage. But from the beginning, recreation, "the enjoyment of the people," was a primary directive.

With better roads, the expanding use of the automobile, and more facilities, attendance at parks also grew rapidly. In 1910, the federal government counted only around 200,000 visitors to its National Parks. In 1920, the newly formed Parks Service counted nearly 2 million visitors, and over 3 million by 1931.

Individual states responded as well. By 1928, the states had set aside 4.5 million acres of forests and parks for public use, with states in the Northeast leading the way; New York State accounted for over half of the total.

Outdoor vacations are one of the best illustrations of the ways that leisure has offered alternatives to work's hegemony. The American love of the nation's parks and forests, the popularity of hunting, fishing, and camping vacations, and the national will to preserve nature are emblematic of a historical resistance to the overexpansion of marketplace into the free realms of time and space.

Workers, Shorter Weekly Hours, and Vacations

The majority of Americans, however, were slow to take vacations of any kind. It was not until 1940, when most workers had jobs that provided them with paid vacations, that the phenomenon of mass vacationing was born.

The most common explanation for workers coming so late to vacations is that they were not able to afford them—middle classes vacationed as soon as they had the money. Why, then, did workers begin vacationing when the nation was experiencing its worst of economic hard times? Moreover, workers and labor fought successfully, on their own, for shorter hours for over a century, cutting work hours virtually in half. If they were thus able to shorten their work hours, why did they neglect vacations?

Before World War II, workers were concerned mainly with reducing daily and weekly work hours, having little interest in vacations. Unions stressed the importance of shorter weekly work hours as a way to combat unemployment and improve wages (reducing the supply of labor increased the price—vacations having little impact). Organized labor was committed to shorter hours as an open-ended, continuous process; as a way to win back more and more of workers' lives from the job and marketplace.

Workers were mainly interested in the kind of leisure distribution that shorter days and weeks provided. Shorter daily hours introduced free time into existing worker culture, strengthening local communities and families and promoting expression and creation of local culture.

For example, during the Depression, Kellogg workers found that working a thirty-hour week allowed more time for daily family activities (reading to the children, taking walks, preparing meals, participating in hobbies and games at home), community engagement and service (drinking at bars and taverns, conversing on the front porch, visiting, doing church work, joining clubs, volunteering), and cultural exchange (indigenous activities such as bowling, softball, table tennis, fishing, hunting, music groups). Such locally integrated leisure activities also tended to be "time-intensive," requiring little spending of money in proportion to time spent doing the activity.

Before the 1930s, what little interest in worker vacations existed came mostly from outside the labor movement and worker communities. A few reformers after the turn of the twentieth century tried to encourage worker vacations for health and "hygiene" reasons, offering camps and other facilities and organizing "fresh air funds" for urban children and working-class women. A few business managers provided employees with paid vacations during the 1920s, reasoning that a vacation's rest and recuperation made for more loyal and productive workers the rest of the year.

However, it was only after 1935 that American companies began to offer vacation to their employees in significant numbers. By 1940, over half the workforce had paid vacations, 70 percent of which began between 1930 and 1937—40 percent in 1937 alone. Paid vacations for workers tripled in the period from 1935 to 1937. Despite the worsening of the Depression in 1937 and 1938, few vacation benefits were rescinded.

By contrast, during the Depression, unions concentrated their efforts on work-sharing to relieve unemployment, promoting the Black-Connery Bill to reduce the workweek to thirty hours by federal legislation. Vacations were notably absent in the union agenda simply because they counted little in the primary battle against unemployment. An indication of union disinterest is the fact that in 1940, when most workers had vacation coverage, only 25 percent of unionized workers had paid vacations.

Workers Turn to Vacations

Unions became interested in vacations only during World War II when the federal government froze wages and prices—when their wage demands were stymied. Trying to find a way around federal wage-stabilization policies, unions convinced the War Labor Board to permit fringe benefits to increase, with the result that by the end of 1944, vacations were one of the most frequently discussed subjects in collective bargaining negotiations. By the end

of 1944, 85 percent of organized workers had vacation benefits and had caught up with national averages. Accepting fringe benefits (the most important being vacations) in lieu of wage increases remained an important union strategy throughout Harry Truman's postwar attempts to control inflation.

Moreover, before the war, workers, agreeing that the main fight was to create jobs by job-sharing, were content to continue their century-long struggle for *continuous* work reduction. *Fortune* magazine conducted a nationwide poll in 1935, asking, "If people could have more leisure, which would be better, a shorter working day or a longer vacation?" Over two-thirds of respondents preferred shorter hours, less than 28 percent vacations. *Fortune* concluded: "It was the prosperous who favored longer vacations, 44.2 percent. But this opinion dwindles steadily as the scale descends, and by occupation, 75 percent of both factory and salaried workers favored the shorter day."

The facts that vacations came after the century-long movement to reduce working hours (vacations became common for workers only after the stabilization of the workweek at forty hours), that they spread most rapidly during a period of economic distress, and that they were promoted by *employers* to employees who had little interest in this form of leisure raise additional historical questions.

Employers generally opposed the shorter hours process. The century of work's reduction was a distinctive working-class movement. Why, then, did managers and owners suddenly offer vacations during the 1930s to workers who were largely disinterested and still fighting the battle for shorter workweeks?

Business Encourages Vacations

Employers' motives were complex. Explicitly they maintained that vacations rested workers, who returned to their jobs with more energy and better attitudes. In short, vacations increased production and improved work.

More importantly, however, employers introduced vacations as a way to control workers' leisure-taking. By making vacations a job benefit, employees effectively linked leisure to the stable and steady holding of a "full-time" job, newly defined during the Depression as forty or more hours a week. Uniformly, managers granted paid vacations as a reward for "steady and loyal service," keying them to a sliding scale based on the number of years of service to the company. "Part-time" employment did not qualify.

Vacations, as a full-time-job "benefit," effectively shifted control of leisure-taking from workers to management, who made vacations contingent on a variety of conditions, prominent among them "steady employment."

Moreover, it was no accident that employers made serious efforts to provide paid vacations only when the threat of legislated thirty hours was imminent. During the two years before business' major vacation push—1935 to 1937—the American press and pundits confidently predicted that the thirty-hour week would soon become law and the next giant step would be taken in labor's campaign for the continuous reduction of labor hours. Much of Roosevelt's New Deal may be understood in terms of his administration and his business supporters delaying and offering alternatives to thirty-hours legislation.

Vacations for workers was a sort of backfire, deliberately set by employers to combat the peril of spreading leisure, a century-long conflagration that was threatening the centrality of work and the marketplace in American life.

Commodifying Vacations

Moreover, business recognized that leisure in the form of vacations was much more easily commodified. Franklin D. Roosevelt joined forces with the business vacation initiative, promoting vacations and the vacation industry as ways to get the economy moving and growing and create more full-time jobs. Responding to the threat of work-sharing, Roosevelt mounted a campaign to create new work by new federal programs and policies. Recognizing that tourism provided more jobs than such vital industries as clothing (11 percent more jobs), printing and publishing (45 percent), and banking (185 percent), Roosevelt actively supported the industry. For example, after the creation of the short-lived U.S. Travel Bureau, formed explicitly to "publicize, promote, and stimulate" travel and tourism, he proclaimed 1940 "Travel America Year."

During the 1920s and 1930s, businessmen and economists concluded that one of the best ways to stabilize work was to commodify leisure. To paraphrase Henry Ford: "If people can be persuaded to spend more during their free time, they will have to work more to pay for it."

Vacations became a primary way to implement this theory. Compared with the forms of weekly leisure that workers traditionally preferred, which were integrated into daily life and tended alarmingly toward the "time-intensive" variety, vacations promised to be much more expensive. Indeed, all such leisure "bunches" (weekends, holidays) have proved to be more conducive to "goods-intensive" kinds of leisure experiences, a mixture requiring more spending in proportion to the time available.

American business discovered that vacations offered a marketing bonanza. Representing the emerging business view, Henry Ford concluded that "leisure is a cold business fact. Where people work less they buy more. [B]usiness is the exchange of goods. Goods are bought only as they meet needs. Needs are filled only as they are felt. They make themselves felt largely in the leisure hours" (Ford, pp. 613–614).

The growth of the tourist industry during the twentieth century steadily encroached upon the cultural openings leisure first offered for free experimentation, nonpecuniary activities, and civic engagement. Vacations, requiring expensive travel and lodging from their beginnings, were increasingly commodified.

The industry was founded on transportation, food services, and accommodations. These three still account for most vacation spending. What has changed is the centrality of these basics. Not only have they become ever more expensive, they have occupied ever more of the vacationers' time, energy, and attention, often excluding opportunities for other activities. "Pleasure driving," motoring for its own sake, became widespread during the 1920s. "Pleasure travel" now accounts for nearly 57 percent of all household trips.

Since World War II, successful entrepreneurs have lured vacationers from the relatively cheap amusements of the early resorts and camps to activities that require spending more money. Clothes and recreational-equipment manufacturers vigorously promoted their wares to vacationers. The entertainment industry followed vacationers to resort areas, famously to the borscht belt in the New York Catskills. Roadside advertising and "attractions" began littering highways, catering to vacationers as they traveled. Coney Island established a precedent for amusement parks that proliferated in the twentieth century, providing passive, mass, and impersonal experiences instead of active and civilly engaged opportunities.

Since World War II, tourism has emerged as one of the most important sectors of the American economy. Paid vacations are the most common job benefit in the United States; 96 percent of workers have them. Now, according to the U.S. Department of Labor, nearly half of all Americans take vacations each year, spending about 7 percent of their incomes during the period of the survey, almost as much as they spend on food at home. Shopping has become one of the most frequent vacation activities.

In 2004, states actively promoted the industry, vying with one another for the vacationers' dollars, developing state vacation sites, and attempting to attract tourist-based businesses. Tax revenues from tourism became a major source of income for states and local governments across the nation.

Researchers now conclude, "Tourism has become the world's largest business enterprise, overtaking defense, manufacturing, oil, and agriculture [accounting for] about 6 percent of the world's gross national product" (Lundberg, Krishnamoorthy, and Stavenga, pp. ix, 14). The economic importance of tourism as a source of employment and government revenue is shown in Table 1.

Vacations after World War II

After World War II, vacations stabilized in the United States at about two weeks a year, unlike in Europe, where vacations grew steadily.

The United States has passed no laws mandating paid vacations. By contrast, the European Union (EU) now requires European employers to offer at least four weeks of paid vacation to employees. France has legislation requiring twenty-five days, Germany twenty days, the Netherlands twenty days, and the United Kingdom (coming into compliance with the EU's "Working Time Directive" in 1996) twenty days. However, the average number of vacation days in Europe is significantly higher than the legislated minimums.

Other than legislation, several reasons for this disparity are most often given: the relative weakness of American labor, American labor's abandonment of shorter hours in favor or wages, and the stronger European vacation tradition.

However, other reasons may be suggested. One of the most important is the extent to which American vacations have been commodified. Being more expensive, vacations are less in demand. Moreover, the American vacation may simply be more unattractive. Unlike European companies that tend to hire additional workers, often students and interns, to take up the slack, American firms generally "work around" those on vacation, leaving work piled on desks for the vacationer's return—a major disincentive for employees.

Becoming more homogeneous and commercial, the American vacation may also be less attractive than the European's more varied and active experiences. Another reason for Americans' short vacations may be the "long arm of the job." New technologies, cell phones, the Internet, and fax machines obscure the boundary between work and leisure, and many are now tethered to their jobs regardless of how far they travel.

TABLE 1

Tourism spending in the United States

(In billions of current dollars)
(domestic trips of more than 25 miles plus foreign visitor spending)

	1988	1990	1995	2000
Total tourism spending in the U.S.	579	671	973	1407
Total taxes generated	68	79	114	165
Federal taxes generated	36	42	60	87
State taxes generated	23	27	39	56
Local taxes generated	9	10	15	21

SOURCE: Need to look at source document

Finally, work's cultural centrality discourages all forms of additional leisure-taking. People in the industrial nations, led by the United States, have come to answer traditional religious questions (Who am I? Where am I going? What should I do today?) more and more by reference to their work/job/profession/career instead of traditional religions. The new work ethic is no longer Protestant; there is little or no God-talk associated with it. It is a distinctively modern and secular work ethic/ religion growing to fill the void left by the retreat of the traditional faiths. It has become, as Max Weber noted, the very "Spirit of Capitalism."

Work has evolved as an ultimate measure of progress and human betterment. The more of it, the better. What is work for in the final analysis? What is work's ultimate justification—its supreme purpose? The modern answer: more work.

With such a cultural focus on the job, little attention is paid to creating interests and enthusiasm for active and engaged leisure pursuits. Leisure and vacations then become a freedom too far, a cultural vacuum that Americans have lost the will to try to fill with meaningful activities. Leisure's autotelic question goes largely unanswered as people escape back to their jobs.

As a result, American vacations now may be contracting. Nearly half of all full-time employees, failing to use all their vacation days, lose them each year.

See also: Beaches, Disneyland, National Parks, Recreational Vehicles, State Parks, Theme and Amusement Parks, Tourism, Walt Disney World, Working-Class Leisure and Recreation

BIBLIOGRAPHY

Allen, Donna. *Fringe Benefits: Wages or Social Obligation? An Analysis with Historical Perspectives from Paid Vacations.* Ithaca, N.Y.: Cornell University Press, 1964.

"American Vacation." *Fortune Magazine* 14 (July 1936): 158–161.

Aron, Cindy S. "Vacations and Resorts." *The Reader's Companion to American History.* Available from http://college.hmco.com/.

———. *Working at Play: A History of Vacations in the United States.* New York: Oxford University Press, 1999.

EBRI Databook on Employee Benefits. 4th ed. Washington, D.C.: Employee Benefit Research Institute, 1997.

Ford, Henry. "Why I Favor Five Days' Work with Six Days' Pay." *Worlds Work* 52 (October 1926): 613–614.

Ford, Henry, and S. Crowther. "The Fear of Overproduction." *Saturday Evening Post* 203 (12 July 1930): 3.

Forest History Society. "National Forests vs. National Parks." Available from http://www.lib.duke.edu/forest.

Hunnicutt, Benjamin. *Work without End.* Philadelphia: Temple University Press, 1989.

———. *Kellogg's Six-Hour Day.* Philadelphia: Temple University Press, 1996.

Leopold, Aldo. 1949. *A Sand County Almanac: With Essays on Conservation from Round River.* Reprint, New York: Oxford University Press, 1990.

Lundberg, Donald, M. Krishnamoorthy, and M. Stavenga. *Tourism Economics.* New York: Wiley, 1995.

"Recreation Industry." *Survey Graphic* 27 (March 1938): 184.

Report of the President's Research Committee on Social Trends. Recent Social Trends. *New York: McGraw-Hill Book Company, 1933.*

"Travel Bureau Issues Bulletin." *The Regional Review* 1, no. 5 (November 1938).

U.S. Department of Labor, Bureau of Labor Statistics. *Employee Benefits in Medium and Large Private Establishments 1995.* Washington, D.C.: U.S. Government Printing Office, 1997.

———. "The Evolution of Compensation in a Changing Economy." Available from http://www.bls.gov/opub.

———. "Issues in Labor Statistics." Summary 99-8. August 1999. Available from http://www.bls.gov/opub.

Benjamin Kline Hunnicutt

VOLLEYBALL

Volleyball is a sport played by two teams on a playing court divided by a net. There are different versions available for specific circumstances and purposes. With half a billion organized players in more than 210 countries, volleyball is one of the most widespread sports the world over, and it has had a positive reception in widely differing cultures. In its origins it has certain similarities with basketball. Both games were developed in the United States in the 1890s; both achieved a rapid global spread by means of the international YMCA system, where they were applied in support of a pragmatic muscular Christianity; both are nowadays internationally recognized, dynamic competitive sports with a certain touch of lifestyle. This last point can be demonstrated not least by the latest shoot off the main branch of volleyball, beach volleyball, which signals sunshine, summer, and sandy beaches. Furthermore beach volleyball's inclusion in the Olympic program in Atlanta in 1996 marked the unique occurrence of two internationally widespread variants of the same branch of a sport.

Standard play in modern volleyball involves two teams with six players each—in beach volleyball, there are, however, only two players on each team—playing on a court measuring 29 feet, 6 inches by 59 feet in indoor play, and 52 feet, 6 inches by 26 feet, 3 inches in beach volleyball. The height of the net is 7 feet, 11 and ⅝–inches for men and 7 feet, 4 and ⅛–inches for women. The ball, which weighs about 9.7 ounces and is about 26 inches in circumference, is put in play with a service from behind the end line. The rally continues until the ball is grounded on the playing court or goes out of bounds, or until it is not returned properly.

The team has three hits to return the ball to the opponents court and a player is not allowed to hit the ball twice consecutively. The team winning the rally scores a point; when the receiving team wins a rally, it also gains right to serve, and its players rotate one position clockwise. (Until 1996, the receiving team only won the right to serve, not a point and the right to serve, when it won a rally.) The first team to reach twenty-five points with a two-point advantage wins the game. Volleyball can be divided up into a number of basic techniques. In a "perfect" rally, they will appear in the following order: service, receiving, setting, attacking, blocking, defense, setting, and so forth, until the point is decided. Since the net prevents any actual physical contact between the teams, perfecting—at enormous expense of time—these individual techniques in a precise team collaboration has taken on ever-increasing significance.

The Inventor and His Time

The inventor of volleyball, William G. Morgan (1870–1942), completed his degree in physical education at Springfield College in Massachusetts. Springfield was a

YMCA college, and one of Morgan's teachers was John Naismith, who had developed the game of basketball in 1891. Another of Springfield's teachers was Amos Alonzo Stagg, whom many consider to be the father of modern American football. Thus, three men who played influential roles in the development of three of the most dynamic games of our times were together at the beginning of the 1890s at a minor college in Massachusetts. Stagg refined an existing sport; Naismith and Morgan invented new ones. Morgan's game became publicized when he became physical education instructor at Holyoke, another YMCA college in Massachusetts, in 1895. He called it "mintonette," but, even by 1896, it was being called volleyball.

Morgan developed his game as a combination of tennis, baseball, and "handball"—a ball game along the lines of the French *jeu de paume*. There already existed a game called "minton," which included elements from baseball and tennis. Some have suggested that this game may—considering its name and its earliest rules—have been the inspiration for mintonette. Others have suggested that the game of badminton, which Morgan knew, provided the source for the name. However, Morgan scarcely knew of the German game of "faustball" (fist ball), whose first written rules—in German—date from 1893. It is therefore unlikely that this game inspired Morgan. Wherever the form and the name of mintonette may have originated, Morgan's major new contribution were that, in the net game he created, the ball could only be played in flight (volley), the rules permitted teamwork, and hands alone and no other implement could be used to keep the ball in play.

Like Naismith and Stagg, Morgan can be seen as part of a pedagogical tradition that, in the United States of the 1890s, sought to invent, redefine, and introduce ball games both inside and outside the educational system. As with another initiative of the period, namely the Playground Movement, which took its inspiration from Germany, the game was educative. However, while Naismith designed basketball as a pedagogical "answer" to football and soccer as regards, for instance, central elements of the game such as body contact, movement with the ball, and scoring, Morgan created volleyball for middle-aged and nonathletic men who could not play more strenuous sports, so it is more of a pedagogical "target group game" Behind volleyball from the start lay an exceptionally simple concept. In July 1896, the American magazine *Physical Education* printed the game's first rules—and there were only ten; they have been altered endlessly ever since. The game was developed for men, but before long women were playing as well.

Volleyball spread by means of the worldwide YMCA system, but World War I gave it a powerful shove forward. American soldiers had, in Europe alone, 16,000 volleyballs, imported by the army. Variants of volleyball were played around the world. In Japan, for instance, a nine-a-side version of the game, with no rotation, was popular until long after World War II. Even in the United States, there were for many years varying rules and interpretations of the rules in volleyball circles. Not until 1917 did sports committees of the YMCA, the colleges, and the universities in the United States agree on a unified set of rules; the world had to wait until 1976 for an official U.S. endorsement of the international volleyball rules, which the rest of the world had agreed upon in 1947 when the International Volleyball Federation (FIVB) was founded.

Trends in the Development of Volleyball

On the one hand, the desire to make the game exciting for the players, friendly for the spectators, and interesting for the media guided the development of volleyball. Therefore, officials and participants attempted to keep the techniques simple, the rules comprehensible, and the breaks in play short. Yet, they wished to preserve the original founding ideas of the game as well—for example, that all players should alternate between defense and offense respectively, and that specialization ought not to take place. The attempt to protect this idea from inventive coaches and teams aiming for specialization led in time to the introduction of the rotation system, the attacking line, and restrictive substitution rules. Another fundamental idea was that in the interest of excitement a balance should exist between defense and attack with regard to strength. Since the attacking game in volleyball is the most advantageous, there has traditionally always been an attempt to strengthen the defense. This practice, for example, led to the easing of the blocking rules, the rule permitting players to step on the center line, the antennas, the decision that blocking does not count as a hit, and new and modified techniques of defense partly inspired by beach volleyball.

The United States may have invented and spread the game, but other countries helped develop the game into the version played in the early 2000s, in part for two reasons: because volleyball in its homeland always stood in the shadow of basketball, baseball, and football; and because the spread of volleyball took place to a large extent in areas that, after World War II, belonged under the Eastern bloc. The United States avoided international tournaments when they were introduced at the end of the 1940s and didn't begin to take part in international events

The Spread of Volleyball and Key Rules' Developments

- 1900, Canada is the first "foreign" country to adopt volleyball. It is followed by Cuba (1906), Japan (1908), China and the Philippines (1910), Central and South America, India, Korea (1910–1917), Western Europe (1914–1920), and Central and Eastern Europe (1920–1925).

- 1913, volleyball on the program for the first Far Eastern Games in Manila. Teams were made up of sixteen players.

- 1916 in the Philippines, an offensive style of passing the ball in a high trajectory to be struck by another player (the set and spike) was introduced.

- 1917, the game was changed from twenty-one to fifteen points.

- 1918, only six players per team on court.

- 1920s, three hits per side and back row attack rules were instituted. Serve and return specialists, set and attack specialists and court defense techniques are developed. Blocking (single player) is introduced.

- 1924, volleyball demonstration game at the Olympics in Paris.

- 1927, the YMCA World Championship for men in Copenhagen. Winner: Estonia.

- 1930, the first two-man beach game was played.

- 1931, international tournament in Paris. Winner: USSR.

- 1938, two-man blocks permitted.

- 1947, the Fédération Internationale de Volley-Ball (FIVB) is founded (in English, the International Volleyball Federation, or IVBF).

- 1948, first European Championship for men. Winner: Czechoslovakia.

- 1949, first World Championships for men. Winner: USSR.

- 1948, first two-man beach tournament held.

- 1949, the initial World Championships are held in Prague, Czechoslovakia.

- 1950s, attacking systems, the swerve serve, and the bagger technique are developed.

- 1964, volleyball is introduced at the Olympic Games in Tokyo. Winner: USSR for men and Japan for women.

- 1965, first World Cup for men. Winner: USSR.

- 1970s, back spikes (a smash from behind the attacking line) are systematized.

- 1973, first World Cup for women. Winner: USSR.

- 1983, 100,000 spectators—a record for an international volleyball game—see the USSR defeat Brazil 3–1 in Rio de Janeiro.

- 1987, FIVB institutes a Beach Volleyball World Championship Series. Winner: USA.

- 1990, the World League is created.

- 1990s, the jump service becomes common and defense techniques from beach volleyball gain a footing. Playing the ball with the feet is allowed.

- 1996, two-person beach volleyball is added to the Olympics. Winner: USA.

- 1998–2000, the "libero" is introduced as a defensive player whose jersey must contrast in color to the other players. The game is changed from fifteen to twenty-five points, each serve ending in a point.

until the World Cup in 1956 and especially the Tokyo Olympics in 1964. Nevertheless, in the 1980s, the United States made a serious comeback on the international scene both with regard to men (Olympic gold medals in 1984 and 1988, World Cup winners in 1985, and World Champions in 1986) and women (Olympic silver medal in 1984). In addition, the United States developed beach volleyball and has always been a dominating force in that game. Throughout the 1990s this variant of volleyball, without losing its original stamp as a recreational activity, simultaneously developed its own competition rules and professional tours with corporate sponsorship. In the development of professional indoor volleyball, too, the United States took an early lead in 1975. A professional coed league, the International Volleyball Association (IVA), with men and women players on the same team, was set up. The basketball legend Wilt Chamberlain showed his commitment by becoming both a player and the owner of the league's southern California franchise. In 1980, however, the IVA had to close for economic reasons. In the early twenty-first century, the big money in volleyball was in Europe, especially in Italy.

See also: Basketball, Beaches, Football, "Muscular Christianity" and the YM(W)CA Movements, Olympics, Playgrounds, Professionalization of Sport

BIBLIOGRAPHY

Brandel, Christian. *Volleyball-Welgeschichte.* München, Germany: Copress Verlag, 1988.

Fédération Internationale de Volleyball. *100 Years of Global Link: Volleyball Centennial, 1895–1995.* Lausanne, Switzerland: FIVB, 1996.

Levinson, David, and Christensen, Karen, eds. *Encyclopedia of World Sport III.* Santa Barbara, Calif.: ABC-CLIO, 1996.

Sherrow, Victoria. *Volleyball.* San Diego, Calif.: Lucent Books, 2002.

Shewman, Byron. *Volleyball Centennial: The First 100 Years.* Indianapolis, Ind.: Masters Press, 1995.

Per Jørgensen

WALT DISNEY WORLD

Walt Disney World, opened in 1971 near Orlando, Florida, was a dramatic extension of the amusement and fantasy theme park of Disneyland, built by animator and moviemaker Walt Disney in Anaheim, California, in 1955. Both parks were radical breaks from the tradition of the early-twentieth-century amusement parks at Coney Island and elsewhere in America. Situated in rural and suburban locations, both Disney sites relied on links to highways and private automobile access instead of streetcars and subways to attract crowds. Further, both Disney parks created entirely artificial fantasy environments, completely independent of natural attractions (like the seashore or forest). Finally, both Disneyland and Walt Disney World promised an experience free from the dirt and danger of the carnival world of freaks, barkers, and thrill rides common in the traditional amusement park. Both attracted a predominately white, middle-class crowd, often in family groups. However, while the original Disney theme park was limited to a site of 160 acres and was quickly hemmed in by cheap hotels and alternative amusements, Walt Disney World was built in central Florida, in the middle of land holdings the size of Manhattan Island, facilitating unimpeded expansion and freedom from outside competitors as well as allowing the Disney Company to develop with legal control over utilities and zoning regulations. Even though Walt Disney died in 1966, five years before his Florida park opened, Walt Disney World became the uncompromised and unfettered expression of the Disney vision.

Disney World became much more than an amusement park. From the beginning, it was conceived as a cluster of resorts that distant visitors would make a destination. Far more than ever was possible at the California site, Disney World was a national, indeed international, destination. Not only was it far from major cities (though Orlando eventually became a boom town), it was isolated from competing leisure sites, especially Florida's beaches and ocean. Thanks to air travel, the Disney Company was able to attract 28.4 million visitors by 1990, easily the biggest tourist draw in the United States, with out-of-town visitors spending an average of nearly a week at the site.

The Four Walt Disney World Theme Parks

Disney World's first project was the Magic Kingdom, basically a double of Disneyland, complete with "Main Street U.S.A.," a fantasy replica of an American small town in 1900, and four themed zones—Fantasyland (based largely on cartoon characters and fairy tales), Adventureland (attractions with a world travel theme), Frontierland (organized around a replica of Mark Twain stories and western themes), and Tomorrowland (with a technology, space, and science fiction motif). Before his death, Disney had intended to use part of his vast Florida real estate to create a model urban utopia: the Experimental Prototype Community of Tomorrow (Epcot). Because of costs and other difficulties, Walt's successors, in 1982, opened instead a permanent World's Fair under the same name. They divided it into a cluster of futuristic exhibits (Future World) sponsored by major corporations, and international exhibits (World Showcase) in a semi-circle of idealized replicas of tourist sites.

The company drew upon Disney's earlier involvement with the New York World's Fair of 1964, building a classic icon to the future in a gigantic geodesic dome (Spaceship Earth). Within it was placed a leisurely ride that passed a series of mechanical figures and displays that told the story of human communications. Nearby were built the pavilions of Future World, which promised to teach the wonders of the imagination (sponsored by Kodak), motion (General Electric), energy (Exxon), and land (Kraft; from 1992, Nestlé) with entertaining stories of the history and future of technology. All of this was classic World's Fair material, harking back to a middle-class genteel tradition of uplifting tourism with no thrill rides. The equally important World Showcase, a semicircular area across an artificial lake from Future World, was a distant relative of the earlier World's Fair foreign villages. Ten, mostly European, countries were included at first. The French site featured a miniature replica of the Eiffel Tower, while an idealized version of an eighth-century pagoda marked the Japanese exhibits. Walking through the World Showcase was to be a quick and painless simulation of the global tour of the middle-class traveler.

In 1989 Disney World opened a third park: Disney-MGM Studios. The concept was borrowed from Universal Studio's park built near Hollywood in 1964, which combined movie-based rides with tours of stage sets for real movie and TV productions. While Main Street U.S.A. had originally been designed to appeal to adults born early in the twentieth century, Disney-MGM drew on somewhat younger Americans with fond memories of 1930s and 1940s Hollywood and the classical movies of that period. Disney MGM romanticized the Golden Age of movies with "charming," scaled-down reproductions of 1930s Hollywood Boulevard, ending at a reproduction of Grauman's Chinese Theater. This classic theater was the home of the park's flagship attraction, the Great Movie Ride, which featured exciting clippings from famous movies, seen from cars shaped like soundstage vehicles. For children, Disney bought the rights to Jim Henson's "Muppets," a collection of puppets that were familiar to American children (and most adults) through more than twenty years of TV and movie appearances. Jim Henson's MuppetVision 3-D was the first of a new wave of three-dimensional movies with in-theater special effects.

The fourth theme park, Animal Kingdom, was a marriage of theme park and zoo. Opened in 1998, this park was built on a site ten times as large as Disneyland. Its focal point, a 145-foot-tall concrete "Tree of Life," with an ancient, rugged look of nature, became the hub for the

"lands" of Africa, Rafiki's Planet Watch (a themed nature and ecology center), Asia, DinoLand, U.S.A., and Camp Minnie Mouse (animated animals). Unique to Animal Kingdom was a stress on "authenticity" and conservation. The African and Asian buildings had purposively weathered walls with cracked and faded paint. The Animal Kingdom's Kilimanjaro Safari copied modern zoo design by creating ecosystems rather than simply displaying animals in cages, and placing gazelles, elands, ostriches, zebras, and many other animals in natural settings close to visitors (though behind hidden trenches). The Safari went further by turning the traditional viewing of animals into a ride and story during which guests travel in "authentic" African safari trucks on a twenty-minute voyage, chasing would-be "poachers." Other attractions, such as It's Tough to Be a Bug!, a 3-D film with special in-theater effects like water jets and moving seats, appealed to children.

Resorts, Shopping, and Themed Hotels at Disney World

Following Walt Disney's plans, executives built a series of hotels, golf courses, campgrounds, and water parks, making Disney World a full-service, enveloping experience of destination tourism that the small California site never could be. In 1971, not only did Disney World open the Magic Kingdom, but also Fort Wilderness (a camping compound) and two hotels, the Polynesian Resort and Contemporary Resort. In the early 1970s, an open-air aviary (Discovery Island) and Lake Buena Vista Village and Community (a themed shopping center and cluster of hotels and a golf course) were opened, and, in 1976, a water park, River Country, was built. In 1986, the Disney Company added to its cluster of full-service hotel-resorts the Grand Floridian Beach Resort, designed to evoke "memory" of the days of the Gilded Age when the rich discovered the south Florida beach. Soon, somewhat less lavish Swan and Dolphin hotel resorts were built near Epcot. Beginning in 1988, a series of new hotels—the Caribbean Beach Resort, Port Orleans, and Coronado Springs—were built around the idea of simulated travel to exotic places and times. In 1994, Disney also opened a string of inexpensive family hotels themed around music, movies, and sports and featuring gigantic statues of cartoon characters, guitars, and sports equipment.

The Transformation of the Disney Concept

Changes in the American family and its culture led Disney World to modify its original focus on family togetherness, nostalgia, and the genteel values of the old World's Fairs. In 1984, when the company was experiencing a

Walt Disney. At the International Pan American Airport in Miami, Florida, in 1941, Walt Disney (1901–1966) is flanked by two of his most famous creations, Mickey Mouse and Donald Duck. Thirty years later, Mickey and Donald were featured characters when Walt Disney World opened near Orlando, Florida. © *AP/Wide World Photos*

serious decline, it turned to Michael Eisner, a successful movie producer, to revamp the old Disney formula. Among other changes, Eisner began to appeal to the demands of older children and teens for more thrill rides, and to accommodate childless visitors and others with age-segmented entertainment. In 1989 Epcot modified its commitment to the genteel tradition of uplift in science and world travel by adding thrill rides such as Body Wars, an exciting simulation of rushing through the bloodstream in pursuit of bacteria. Similarly, Disney-MGM Studios introduced the Tower of Terror in 1994, a very elaborate version of a common vertical lift-and-drop ride built around a movie about a defective elevator in a ghostly hotel. Appealing to the ever-increasing demands of older children for thrill rides, Disney introduced the Indiana Jones Adventure in 1995, and an indoor Rock 'n' Roller Coaster in 1999 that catapulted riders from zero to sixty miles per hour in three seconds while 1950s rock music blared from speakers in each car.

Other indications of a shift toward the thrill ride can be seen in the evolution of Disney water parks. The first, River Country (1976), located in the rustic setting of Fort Wilderness, had a western appeal (featuring a campground, playground, and horseshoe tossing). Its rope swings, barrel bridge, and a water slide appealed to adult nostalgia for the old swimming holes of their youth. In sharp contrast was the modern and intense excitement of the Typhoon Lagoon of 1989, with its ninety-five-foot artificial mountain, nine water slides, snorkeling pool, rain forest, and especially its wave-making machines that overwhelmed fun seekers with waves up to seven feet high in a gigantic pool. The third water park, Blizzard Beach (1995), was both more exciting and more fantastic than the other two. Built on a "story" about a freak snowstorm in Florida that led some overenthusiastic entrepreneurs to construct a ski resort, the park was designed to look like an alpine resort with the snow "melted" into a tropical lagoon. It featured the 120-foot-high Mt. Gushmore, with a number of thrilling water slides. This trend away from appeals to uplifting gentility and nostalgia would continue as those values declined and Disney was forced to compete with the intense thrill rides of a new generation of amusement parks.

Another trend is the shift at Disney World toward accommodating childless visitors and families that seek age-segmented activities. In 1989 the company opened Pleasure Island, a sixteen-acre complex of restaurants and nightclubs, as well as a teen dance center and roller-rink disco for the evening entertainment of visitors who seek to be with their own age group. In 1996, Pleasure Island became part of an expanded Downtown Disney complex. That year, the Disney BoardWalk opened. This enter-

tainment complex was modeled after historic Atlantic City and Coney Island, with a luxury inn and numerous shops and nightclubs. Disney World even provided a Sports Complex in 1997 with facilities for amateur and professional sports of all kinds.

By the end of the 1990s, Disney World had invested fully in the idea of total life-stage entertainment. In 1995 it opened a Wedding Chapel for couples willing to buy one of Disney's wedding packages. The chapel included many Disney touches: a glass-enclosed pavilion on its own island located on the Seven Seas Lagoon, with a backdrop of Magic Kingdom's Castle. Disney World also appealed to thousands as a honeymoon site. In 1996, the Disney Institute opened to offer short recreational-education courses in animation, orchestra conducting, golf, gardening, and sixty other activities. In 1998, Disney World took the concept of age-segmented, life-stage entertainment a step further with the launching of the Disney Magic Cruise Line, which brought families to a special "deserted island," the Castaway Cay. While the ship included a Mickey Mouse–shaped pool, it also featured a pool for adults where Disney music was never played. Staff kept children amused at their own club (featuring storytelling and Captain Hook décor), while teens and adults joined separate clubs for age-appropriate group activities. On the island, a beach designated for families with small children was separated from other beaches for teenagers and adults, all in an effort to accommodate the desire for leisure time with one's own age group.

While Walt Disney World remains the mecca of family tourism and, for many, an almost obligatory destination for children, it has also had to accommodate changing expectations of different age groups.

See also: Carnivals; Coney Island, Disneyland, Honeymooning, Theme and Amusement Parks, World's Fairs

BIBLIOGRAPHY

Bryman, Alan. *Disney and His Worlds.* New York: Routledge, 1995.

Cross, Gary. *The Cute and the Cool: Wondrous Innocence and Modern American Children's Culture.* New York: Oxford University Press, 2004.

Dunlop, Beth. *Art of Disney Architecture.* New York: Harry Abrams, 1996.

Findlay, John. *Magic Lands: Western Cityscapes and American Culture after 1940.* Berkeley: University of California Press, 1992.

Fjellman, Stephen. *Vinyl Leaves: Walt Disney World and America.* Boulder, Colo.: Westview, 1992.

Flower, Joe. *Prince of the Magic Kingdom: Michael Eisner and the Re-making of Disney.* New York: J. Wiley, 1991.

Fogelsong, Richard. *Married to the Mouse: Walt Disney World and Orlando.* New Haven, Conn.: Yale University Press, 2001.

Giroux, Henry. *The Mouse that Roared: Disney and the End of Innocence.* Lanham, Md.: Rowman and Littlefield, 1999.

King, Margaret. "Disneyland and Walt Disney World: Traditional Values in Futuristic Form." *Journal of Popular Culture* 15 (1981): 116–140.

Marling, Karal Ann, ed. *Designing Disney's Theme Parks: The Architecture of Reassurance.* New York: Flammarion, 1998.

Project Florida: A Whole New Disney World. Burbank, Calif.: Walt Disney Productions, 1967.

Project on Disney. *Inside the Mouse: Work and Play at Disney World.* Durham, N.C.: Duke University Press, 1995.

Schickel, Richard. *The Disney Version: The Life, Times, Art, and Commerce of Walt Disney.* New York: Simon and Schuster, 1968.

Smoodin, Eric. *Disney Discourse.* New York: Routledge, 1994.

Wasko, Janet. *Understanding Disney: The Manufacture of Fantasy.* Cambridge, Eng., and Malden, Mass.: Polity, 2001.

Zibart, Eve. *Disney: The Incredible Story of Walt Disney World and the Man behind the Mouse.* Foster City, Calif.: IDG Books, 2000.

Gary Cross

WATCHES

See *Clocks and Watches*

WATER SPORTS

See *Waterskiing; White Water Sports; Windsurfing*

WATERSKIING

Ralph Samuelson invented waterskiing in 1922. An avid snow skier, Samuelson was interested in finding a way to extend his skiing into the warmer months. His attempts to water-ski on snow skis and barrel staves failed. On 2 July, Samuelson succeeded in skiing on two pine boards that he had shaped to curve up in front.

Waterskiing requires a towing device moving at sufficient speed to pull the skier out of the water and enable that person to hydroplane on the surface of the water. The heavier the skier, the greater the speed needed to get the skier up. Some types of waterskiing, such as slalom or barefoot, also require greater speed. Most early recreational boat motors lacked the power to pull skiers, particularly heavier skiers. As boat engines increased in power, skiing options expanded greatly. Instead of a single skier on two skis, a power boat could pull two, three, or even a dozen skiers at once.

Waterskiing grew rapidly in popularity, and, by the 1930s, a large number of people in United States were waterskiing. The first ski shows were held in 1932 in Chicago and Atlantic City. *The International Dictionary of Sports and Games* records that the first waterskiing competition was held in 1935 at Long Island, New York. According the USA Water Ski Web page, the American Water Ski Association was founded in 1939 with a dual mission of promoting the growth and development of recreational waterskiing, and organizing and governing the sport of competitive waterskiing. The first National Championships Tournament was also held in 1939, featuring events such as slalom, tricks, and jumping. In this inaugural competition, the tricks event consisted of a skier removing one ski and holding it over his head. The jump ramp was made of wooden rollers.

Development

Participation in skiing had grown to more than 6 million Americans by the 1960s. As interest in waterskiing grew and technology progressed, the sport became more diverse with ski racing (distances from 1.5 miles to 65 miles), kneeboarding, wakeboarding, hydrofoiling, monoskiing, trick skiing, barefoot skiing, and wake skating. Each of these areas has developed competitive events for participants who are more serious about the sport. Specialized boats, tow ropes, skis, boards, gloves, helmets, and life vests have been developed to enhance performance and increase safety. With specialized equipment, recreational skiers are performing flips, jumps, spins, and other feats undreamed of in earlier years of the sport. Two magazines, *WaterSki Magazine* and *The Water Skier,* are dedicated to the sport and contain articles on gear, technique, and competition results.

One challenge often faced by waterskiers is finding a boat driver and spotter. Cable parks, where skiers can be towed by overhead cable, were developed in Florida, North Carolina, and Texas to address this need. Another recent development is the Personal Ski Machine, a remote-controlled jet ski designed to pull a water-skier. The skier controls the jet ski by buttons on the tow handle.

Participation

The popularity of waterskiing has paralleled the development of recreational boating. Because of cost, the sport tends to attract participants who are well educated and affluent. Waterskiing is a family-oriented activity, with USA Water Ski estimating that 11 million individuals participate in the sport in the United States alone. The Sports Business Research Network reports that about 5.5 million individuals in the United States waterski, with an average age of under forty-five.

See also: Boating, Power; Skiing, Alpine; Skiing, Nordic

BIBLIOGRAPHY

Aquaskier—Water Sports Resources. Available from http://www.aquaskier.com.

Desmond, Kevin. *The Golden Age of Water-Skiing.* St. Paul, Minn.: MBI Publishing, 2001.

Madsen, Joyce Styron. "Skiing with Determination." *Boys' Quest* 5 (August–September 1999): 10–11.

Sports Business Research Network. Available from http://www.sbrnet.com.

USA Water Ski. Available from http://www.usawaterski.org.

Kim L. Siegenthaler

WEDDINGS

The major elements of the modern American wedding originated among members of the urban upper and upper-middle classes in the nineteenth century. Borrowing practices popularized by Queen Victoria and other elite Britons, increasing numbers of Americans of means married in flower-bedecked churches, wore clothing designed specifically for the wedding day, and enjoyed bountiful meals featuring elaborate cakes. Weddings with these accoutrements were termed "white weddings" in honor of the recommended color of the bride's gown. This once-in-a-lifetime garment symbolized a young woman's sexual innocence as she left maidenhood to become a wife.

The nineteenth-century white wedding contrasted significantly with previous customs. Before European colonization, for instance, Native Americans east of the Mississippi River typically celebrated the union of husband and wife in a two-part ceremony. In the first stage, the families of the betrothed couple privately exchanged gifts in recognition of the reciprocal nature of Native American marriage. In the second portion of the ceremony, which served as a public announcement of the young couple's change in status, the bride and groom enjoyed a feast with all their clan members or perhaps even with their entire village.

As the colonizers who effected the greatest influence on what would later become the United States, British Protestants established a number of long-standing rules for nuptial celebrations in the seventeenth and eighteenth centuries. Unlike Catholics, Protestants considered marriage a civil contract rather than a sacrament. At first, New England Puritans even prohibited ministers from performing wedding ceremonies. Instead, couples recited vows in front of a magistrate or justice of the peace. Even after the law allowed clergymen to perform weddings, most colonial couples continued to prefer civil ceremonies, and this practice remained intact after the American Revolution. For example, when Maine midwife Martha Ballard's son and two daughters married in 1792, they did so with little fanfare in civil ceremonies attended only by the few family members who happened to be in the vicinity at the time. After the simple rites, both Ballard daughters continued to live with their parents for several weeks until they accumulated enough necessities to set up independent households with their new husbands.

Changes in the Nineteenth Century

In contrast to the modest marriage rites of their predecessors, Anglo-Americans of the antebellum period generally celebrated their weddings with more flourish. Although weddings still seldom took place in a church, a clergyman now presided more frequently at the ceremony, which usually occurred in front of a few guests at the bride's home. A white gown was not yet the standard costume. Instead brides wore dresses of sedate hues, such as gray or brown. They did not consider their garments one-time-only frocks and typically planned to wear their dresses for subsequent occasions. Unlike their ancestors in the colonial and early republic eras, the antebellum bride and groom either moved to their new home immediately following the wedding ceremony or took a post-wedding trip together before officially setting up housekeeping. If the young couple moved into their new home after the ceremony, they spent the next several weeks receiving visitors there. Couples who embarked on a post-wedding trip visited friends and relatives along the way and frequently invited other family members to join them on the journey. Whether the bride and groom received visitors or made a round of visits themselves, these rituals served to introduce the couple's new marital status to the community.

Wedding day. A bride is walked down the aisle by her father as he prepares to "give her away" to the groom. Both are dressed in traditional American wedding attire. © *AP/Wide World Photos*

These new wedding practices reflected the nation's transition from an agrarian to an increasingly urban and industrial society. In the seventeenth and eighteenth centuries, most Anglo-American husbands, wives, and children worked together on farms and other rural-based enterprises. Home and workplace were one and the same. In the nineteenth century, at least for members of the growing urban middle class, domestic life and paid employment occurred in two discrete locations. While the middle-class husband toiled at a place of employment to secure the family wage, the middle-class wife presided over the household. Housekeeping was her unpaid profession, and expectations for maintaining a proper middle-class home were high. For the urban housewife, her life as a married woman now represented a distinct departure from life as a spinster. More elaborate wedding celebrations demarcated these phases of a woman's life and eased her transition into the role of responsible matron.

Not all antebellum Americans participated in these new wedding practices. For instance, rural Anglo-Amer-

ican brides continued to marry in much the same fashion as their grandmothers. Their weddings were simple affairs witnessed by the few nearby friends and relatives who could attend. In a departure from the colonial and early republic eras, however, clergymen rather than justices or magistrates usually presided over these ceremonies. In contrast, the marriages of enslaved African Americans lacked any legal standing, but slave men and women frequently sought their masters' permission to hold public commitment ceremonies in front of family and friends. At the end of a celebration, the couple joined hands and jumped over a broom—an African symbol of housekeeping.

The trend toward more elaborate wedding celebrations expanded in urban America as the century progressed. By 1850, many a well-to-do and even middle-class brides, flanked by multiple bridal attendants, followed the lead of Queen Victoria and wore a white gown to her wedding. These particular brides typically sent engraved invitations to numerous guests, who were then expected to give the bridal couples expensive gifts. In the second half of the nineteenth century, these weddings increasingly took place in churches and were followed by private honeymoons to specific destinations, such as Niagara Falls, rather than visits to friends and relatives. National celebrities, such as White House brides Nellie Grant Sartoris and Frances Folsom Cleveland, enhanced the popularity of the formal white wedding.

The Twentieth Century

Between 1880 and 1920, 23.5 million immigrants arrived in the United States to meet the labor needs of the industrializing nation. Immigrants from southern and eastern Europe significantly increased the Catholic, Jewish, and Eastern Orthodox populations and the wedding customs unique to those faiths. Even immigrants from predominantly Protestant regions brought wedding rituals that differed from Anglo-American standards. By the time an immigrant family reached its second generation in America, members typically combined old-world customs with at least some elements of the American white wedding. When Nebraskans Sophie BisChoff and Carl Nordhausen married in 1927, for example, the entire local German Lutheran community participated in their wedding reception, dancing to a German oompah band and defying Prohibition by drinking home-brewed beer. But BisChoff wore a white gown that was the height of American flapper fashion.

Cost was a significant factor in the way twentieth-century Americans organized their wedding celebrations. Before World War II, most immigrant and native-born families staged weddings that were a patchwork of home-produced and purchased goods and services. Only upper- and upper-middle-class urbanites could afford to purchase all the elements of a formal white wedding. Not until after the war, with the dramatic rise in average incomes, was the formal wedding affordable to most Americans. Postwar expansion of the synthetic fiber industry enhanced that affordability with the production and sale of reasonably priced white gowns. By 1970, white wedding ceremonies launched approximately 80 percent of first-time marriages.

The final three decades of the twentieth century witnessed tremendous change in American society: development of an influential feminist movement, increased non-European immigration, a burgeoning divorce and remarriage rate, a rise in the average age at first marriage, and the expansion of unmarried cohabitation. Yet none of these factors diminished the popularity of the white wedding. First-time brides more typically married in their middle rather than early twenties and had more education, work, and sexual experience than their predecessors. They often paid at least a portion of their wedding expenses and thus looked at their wedding day as the ultimate opportunity for self-expression. Their choice of gown, cake, and ceremony site often conveyed important information about their lifestyle choices. Many of these brides had cohabited with their grooms in an arrangement that was becoming a precursor to modern marriage. In an era when half of American marriages ended in divorce, many brides choosing formal weddings were not making their first trips down the aisle. In fact, late twentieth-century etiquette books and members of the wedding industry applauded white weddings for the "encore bride." African Americans and Asian Americans frequently incorporated elements of non-Western culture into their white weddings, and gay and lesbian commitment ceremonies often conformed to the general parameters of the traditional formal wedding. Having adapted to a more tolerant and diverse American culture, the formal white wedding headed full strength into the new millennium.

See also: Dating, Honeymooning, Rites of Passage, Women's Leisure Lifestyles

BIBLIOGRAPHY

Axtell, James, ed. *The Indian Peoples of Eastern America: A Documentary History of the Sexes.* New York: Oxford University Press, 1981.

Cross, Wilber, and Ann Novotny. *White House Weddings.* New York: David McKay Company, 1967.

Ingraham, Chrys. *White Weddings: Romancing Heterosexuality in Popular Culture.* New York: Routledge, 1999.

Jellison, Katherine. "From the Farmhouse Parlor to the Pink Barn: The Commercialization of Weddings in the Rural Midwest." *Iowa Heritage Illustrated* 77 (Summer 1996): 50–65.

Leeds-Hurwitz, Wendy. *Wedding as Text: Communicating Cultural Identities Through Ritual.* Mahwah, N.J.: Lawrence Erlbaum Associates, 2002.

Monsarrat, Ann. *And the Bride Wore. . .: The Story of the White Wedding.* London: Gentry Books, 1973.

Otnes, Cele C., and Elizabeth H. Pleck. *Cinderella Dreams: The Allure of the Lavish Wedding.* Berkeley: University of California Press, 2003.

Rothman, Ellen K. *Hands and Hearts: A History of Courtship in America.* Cambridge, Mass.: Harvard University Press, 1987.

Seligson, Marcia. *The Eternal Bliss Machine: America's Way of Wedding.* New York: William Morrow and Company, 1973.

Ulrich, Laurel Thatcher. *A Midwife's Tale: The Life of Martha Ballard, Based on Her Diary, 1785–1812.* New York: Vintage Books, 1991.

Katherine Jellison

WESTERN AMERICA LEISURE LIFESTYLES

The leisure lifestyles of western America are closely linked to the unique natural environment of the west. This region of the country, from the flatlands just east of the Rocky Mountains to the western coastline of North America, provides vast expanses of unoccupied space, varied topography, and spectacular natural wonders. The variety of terrain, the abundance of wildlife, and the vastness of the territory all add up to adventure. For those in search of adventure, the West is a natural playground for discovery.

The Land

The topography of the West is so diverse that it includes the lowest point of the United States (Death Valley, California) as well as its highest point (Mt. McKinley, Alaska). Majestic mountains of several major mountain ranges, including the Rocky Mountains, the Sierra Nevada, and the Cascades, stand as vanguards along the western and eastern edges of this western region. Fertile valleys and grasslands, such as the Napa Valley of California and the Thunder Basin National Grassland in Wyoming, lie between these mountain ranges and provide a source for farming and grazing. The dry deserts of the southwest offer a contrast to the cool dense redwood, spruce, and pine forests of the northern and alpine regions of the West. Several major waterways, such as the Missouri, Platte, Rio Grande, Columbia, and Colorado Rivers, find their origins in the West and flow into the Pacific or Atlantic Oceans. Where the western landmass of America meets the Pacific Ocean, there are over 1,500 miles of spectacular coastline and beaches. This diverse landscape is the setting of western leisure lifestyles.

Western History and Culture

For the early settlers of this region of the United States, the combination of environmental characteristics offered not only adventure but opportunity and hope to anyone who desired changes in life, and who wanted the independence to choose a new lifestyle. The West gave a chance for healing of the scars from the Revolutionary War, and later from the American Civil War. As Hal Rothman states, "The new nation embodied in the West transcended the inherent flaws of the first Republic . . ." and ". . . healed the hole in the heart of the nation born anew after its epic and cataclysmic tragedy" (pp. 14–15). The crowding and urbanization of the eastern regions of the United States also played an influential role in developing the attractiveness to the West. This western territory called out to these individuals through promotions that enticed them with fertile land, precious minerals, abundant natural resources, and wide-open spaces. Some of those who did find their promised land in the West became the images of the tamable frontier. Individuals such as politician Teddy Roosevelt, explorers Meriwether Lewis and William Clark, artist Charles Russell, literary figure Mark Twain, performers Buffalo Bill Cody and Annie Oakley, and mountain man Hugh Glass, became folk heroes, and, in their own way, helped to promote the West.

As more and more people came out west and developed a niche for themselves in this frontier, they found that they could define their own culture without bringing their entire European heritage along, which they felt inferior to anyway. This created an appreciation for what was already developed, such as ranches, forts, outposts, and communities, and for what was discovered, such as natural wonders and landmarks. These cultural icons became points of leisure interest.

The concept of tourism in the West was born out of this interest. As the industrialization of the late nineteenth century took hold in America, life improved economically, and free time was more abundant. This, along with the development of better modes of transportation, allowed for more people to travel and venture farther from their familiar territory to pursue leisure. Tourism opened doors for more exposure to the West, and more economic opportunities for the locals of the West. From the cattle rancher and cowboy who transformed their livelihood into rodeos and dude ranches to the American Indians who contributed the game of lacrosse, the craft of kayaking and canoeing, and their arts and crafts, leisure in the west embraced its own heritage.

Patterns of Western Leisure

An interest in outdoor environments, the desire to explore and discover, the willingness to travel in order to see and do things, and the challenge to survive through it all are the leisure patterns that are an integral part of the West. Outdoor recreation and adventure pursuits, including travel, are not exclusive to the West, but they embrace these patterns of leisure. The West's history of exploring the wilderness and surviving off the land still fascinates people today.

Western Recreational Trends

The following leisure pursuits play an important role in people's lives out West, and their popularity continues to attract others to travel out West.

Backpacking, hiking, and camping These are activities that require access to backcountry environments with, preferably, low-density usage. Since the West tends to offer more opportunities for this type of scenario, the core participation of these activities is found out west. With the exception of a temporary decline in this activity during the 1980s, backpacking and camping have seen a long and steady increase due to better equipment that is lighter, warmer, and more protective. Hiking has increased due to the healthy lifestyles trend that is part of the overall wellness promotion. Camping has benefited from the improvements and availability of easily accessible camping areas and recreational vehicles (RVs) that bring the comforts of home to the outdoors.

Horseback Riding and Rodeos Both of these recreational pursuits have close connections with the West. The image of the western cowboy riding his horse across the land, herding his cattle from grazing land to grazing land is as much a part of the West as its landscape. Even though both activities are stable in number of participants, there is a projection that both will see increases in the future due to higher family incomes that will allow ownership and care of horses, and the television media spending more time showing these activities on cable channels.

Mountain Biking This specialized form of biking was born in the West as a way to get around in remote areas. Trend data indicates that mountain biking is reaching its peak, but its popularity is still going strong in the West. The mountain bike has made remote areas more accessible, especially for those who cannot afford specialized motorized vehicles to get to these same areas. Since most of those types of land are only in the West the mountain bike will continue to be a major part of western leisure.

Climbing The western topography lends itself to this recreational pursuit. With the abundance of mountains and variety of weather, climbing options—for example, alpine and high-altitude expedition climbing in the high mountain ranges, rock climbing where the cliffs stay rel-

atively warm, and ice climbing in frigid cold temperatures on frozen waterfalls—are almost limitless. Climbing also fits the culture of the West because it is all about adventure and interacting with the environment. While there is a growing group of climbers who frequent man-made climbing walls, the western leisure lifestyle is better reflected by the outdoor climbers. Even though the actual number of climbers fell slightly in the 1990s and early 2000s, the participation rate has increased by almost double over that same period of time. Climbing has the image of being high risk, which makes this activity a leading adventure pursuit, a nice fit in western leisure lifestyles.

Fishing and Hunting Both of these activities have strong roots in western culture because, at one time, they were the means of survival. Now, fishing and hunting are ways for people to use the natural resources and a way to stay connected to the land and those old days of adventure. Hunting was the first recognized leisure pursuit of the West. Some sociologists claim that the hunting and fishing activities are primal instincts that are almost a necessity for some, even to the point that they take the place of combative behavior in times of peace. No matter the motive, these pursuits depend on the availability of the resource, and, therefore, the close interaction with the land also extends to a close knowledge and care of its natural resources. Fly-fishing has gained popularity since Hollywood's portrayal of this activity in Robert Redford's *A River Runs Through It*. The West offers an abundance of streams and rivers that allow for the solitude and natural resource depicted in the movie, so the fly-fisherman's destinations tend to lead out West.

Canoeing, Kayaking, and Rafting These water-based activities have seen a growing trend in the West due to the accessibility of whitewater rivers and improved equipment. The West offers a variety of waterways that are in rugged terrain and, therefore, produce exciting rides through rapids and incredibly beautiful scenery. The coastline of the West has also become more accessible due to the increased use of sea kayaks, which are easy to transport and easy to master the skills to use them.

Ocean-Based Activities In this category of western leisure pursuits fall the activities of skin and scuba diving, snorkeling, surfing, and windsurfing. The western culture of adventure and exploration is not limited to the land. Since much of the ocean is unexplored, the sense of adventure extends to the open ocean, even though most leisure pursuits on the ocean are within a mile of shore. Surfing and windsurfing were born in the West and continue to be popular due to the accessibility to the extensive coastline that is conducive to the creation of consistent wave patterns and, sometimes, massive surf.

Skiing, Snowboarding, and Snowmobiling Even though skiing has its origins on the European continent, the West has adopted it as its own. The massive mountain ranges of the West can stall moisture-laden weather fronts heading east from the Pacific Ocean. The results are snow-covered mountains that produce some of the most perfect snow conditions for skiing found anywhere in the world. With the technological advances in equipment design, which has made learning the skills easier, and more ski resorts being built, which allow more accessibility to these areas, the sport has grown.

Snowboarding is an offshoot of surfing and had a rough start on snow due to equipment designs and conflict with skiers on the same hills. But it has caught on to the point where the increased number of ski-resort users is due primarily to snowboarders. Media coverage of competitive events in these activities has also enhanced the growing trend. A stabilizing factor has been the cost, but people will overlook that obstacle by believing that skiing and snowboarding will enhance their feeling of freedom, or they let their sense of exploration lead them to cross-country skiing, which allows skiers to roam and explore for far less money. Either rationale appeals to that western leisure lifestyle.

Along with that sense to roam and explore in the snowy winters of the West, the snowmobile, a motorized snow sled, has had a loyal following since its introduction in the 1970s. Costs, limited access to lands conducive for snowmobiling, and varying yearly snow conditions have made this activity's participation rate fluctuate. But, for winter travel and exploration in areas of the West where roads are not usable or available for other modes of motorized transportation, snowmobiling has become a major activity for western leisure.

Arts, Crafts, and Music The leisure of western arts, crafts, and music has an important place in western leisure lifestyles because they reflect life in the West. Paintings and photos of the scenic West, sculptures of western wildlife and people, pottery and jewelry from the Native Americans living in the West, and the music and poetry of the cowboys are an integral part of western leisure and culture. They have become very popular among visitors to the West due to the idea that a person can take home a piece of the western flavor just visited as a personal reminder. Music and poetry that are unique to the West stem from the music composed and sung by the western cowboys and Native Americans. Although the audience

is small, the interest in these types of music grew in the late 1990s and early 2000s, due to more exposure from traveling tourists and the media.

Foreign Influences on Western Leisure Lifestyles

Many of the leisure activities of holidays and calendar celebrations found in the West are not so different than those celebrated in other regions of America, save the ones that commemorate special events unique to particular areas of the West. But there are events that are unique to the West because of the influences of foreign immigrants settling there, particularly the influence of the Asian and the Hispanic immigrants. The Chinese New Year, the Mexican piñata at Christmas, and the Japanese boys' day and girls' day have become a part of the special days of leisure in the West, although not necessarily celebrated by all. These foreign cultural influences are another example of the people who came to the West to fit in with the rest of those searching for that life they dreamed about.

Concerns for the Future

Leisure in the West has had a major impact on the use of western lands and the culture of the people who live there. The pursuit of leisure activities has altered lifestyles and the economy and raised concerns for the future, including protecting the natural environment, and preserving the very culture that gave rise to western leisure in the first place.

Environmental Preservation User conflicts have developed in leisure pursuits throughout the United States, but these conflicts have been very pronounced in the West. Battles between conservationists and developers, consumptive users and nonconsumptive users of natural resources, and purists and high-tech enthusiasts are ongoing because the West has an abundance of untouched land still available for a variety of uses. The decisions on how the land will be used generate a dialogue among the different groups, and these discussions create awareness of the value of the land and the potentials it has for development and leisure resources. This awareness has been an education to people that the western region of the United States is unique and that before it is all lost, there needs to be a conservative approach to the use of the land.

Due to user conflicts and the general concern for preserving what is recognized as the source of many leisure pursuits in the west, many areas whose unique attractions have been popular are now protected by the local, state, and federal governments. Along with the intimate use of the land is the stewardship to protect it and use it wisely.

Losing the Culture. The leisure lifestyles of the West owe much to the land and culture of the region, but, in an ironic twist, these can be the very reasons for major changes to the land and culture that molded these lifestyles. The community and environment that originally supported, developed, and, in some cases, initiated the leisure lifestyle can find themselves being overwhelmed by outsiders wanting a piece of the pie and the control that goes along with that piece. The community's interest and culture can and has, in some western communities, shifted to what the visitors want, even if it means forsaking the heritage and culture that built the community in the first place. The quaint little mining town of Moab, Utah, or the farming and ranching community of Steamboat Springs, Colorado, are examples of a transformation that hardly resembles the original culture or the community control that once built them.

The western leisure lifestyle is diverse and various. Yet, the western leisure lifestyle has a common thread that runs through all the different activities and culture: the fact that the leisure pursuits that are closely connected to the West are also intimately connected to its land. Western leisure pursuits are the interactions with the land that is uniquely part of the West and that makes western leisure lifestyles unique in themselves.

See also: Backpacking and Hiking; Bicycling; Camping; Fishing, Freshwater; Hunting; Mountain Climbing; Native American Leisure Lifestyles; Recreational Vehicles; Rock Climbing; Rodeos; Scuba Diving/Snorkeling; Snowboarding; Skiing, Alpine; Surfing; Whitewater Sports; Windsurfing

BIBLIOGRAPHY

Edginton, Christopher R., Debra J. Jordan, Donald G. De-Graaf, and Susan R. Edginton. *Leisure and Life Satisfaction: Foundational Perspectives.* 3d edition. New York: McGraw-Hill, 2002.

Goodale, Thomas L., and Geoffrey C. Godbey. *The Evolution of Leisure: Historical and Philosophical Perspectives.* State College, Pa.: Venture Publishing, 1988.

Kelly, John R., and Rodney B. Warnick. *Recreation Trends and Markets: The 21st Century.* Champaign, Ill.: Sagamore Publishing, 1999.

Kraus, Richard. *Leisure in a Changing America: Multicultural Perspectives.* New York: Macmillan College Publishing Company, 1994.

Rothman, Hal K. *Devil's Bargains: Tourism in the Twentieth-Century American West.* Lawrence: University Press of Kansas, 1998.

Shaffer, Marguerite S. *See America First: Tourism and National Identity, 1880–1940.* Washington: Smithsonian Institution Press, 2001.

Shivers, Jay S., and Lee J. deLisle. *The Story of Leisure.* Champaign, Ill.: Human Kinetics, 1997.

White, Randy. "The Role of Culture in Location-Based Leisure Design." White Hutchinson Leisure and Learning Group. Available from http://www.whitehutchinson.com/leisure.

Wrobel, David M. *Promised Lands: Promotion, Memory, and the Creation of the American West.* Lawrence: University Press of Kansas, 2002.

Wrobel, David M., and Michael C. Steiner. "Many Wests: Discovering a Dynamic Western Regionalism." In *Many Wests: Place, Culture, and Regional Identity.* Edited by D. M. Wrobel and M. C. Steiner. Lawrence: University Press of Kansas, 1997.

Stacy T. Taniguchi

WHITEWATER SPORTS

Whitewater sports represent a wide variety of river craft and activities. River craft include canoes, dories, inflatables, kayaks, rafts, and riverboards. The term "whitewater" describes the use of any river craft in a challenging and inherently risky activity involving moving water. The majority of rivers and rapids are rated using the International Scale of River Difficulty. This scale rates rapids on a scale of 1 (easy) to 6 (extreme risk of life). Some western rivers are rated on the "Grand Canyon System" or "Deseret Scale" of 1 to 10.

Modern whitewater sports began in Europe. Whitewater paddling started in France and Germany in the late 1800s. The eastern Alps provided many whitewater opportunities for this fledgling sport. Kayak clubs were established as early as 1907 in Linz, Austria. In 1927, on the Weissensee River, Hans Pawlata was the first recorded European to perform an Eskimo roll (the technique of righting a capsized kayak without leaving the cockpit).

Materials and Designs

The development of whitewater sports has been intricately linked to the evolution of the materials and designs used for whitewater craft.

Canoes The early Native Americans used birch-bark canoes. Birch-bark canoes were also the choice of the early European explorers, missionaries, traders, and trappers. Canoes evolved from birch-bark to wood-and-canvas

416

construction or cedar-strip in the 1800s. Fiberglass canoes were developed in the early 1950s.

In 1945, the Grumman Corporation revolutionized canoeing with the introduction of the first aluminum canoes. The use of Royalex in the early 1960s created a very strong and forgiving canoe hull. Then, in the mid-1970s, the Coleman Company introduced the first plastic canoe. The durability and resiliency of the new material acrylonatrile butadeine styrene (ABS), which is a lamination of cross-linked vinyl, ABS plastic, and ABS closed-cell foam, created the ideal whitewater boat for beginners and experts alike.

Kayaks Kayaking has changed from the original Inuit sealskin boats to the play boats used in 2004. The earliest kayaks used for whitewater or touring were made from wood and canvas, and designed by an Englishman named John MacGregor around 1845. The Klepper or "foldboat," also a wood-and-canvas craft, built by Hans Klepper in 1905, was the standard used for the next fifty years. In the 1950s, fiberglass was introduced in kayak construction. The availability of fiberglass kayaks led to an increase in kayaking participation.

In 1973, Hollowform designed the first polyethylene plastic kayak, called the "River Chaser," in its Los Angeles factory. In 1976, a new company called Perception used a radical new manufacturing process called rotomolding to produce the Quest and, later, the Dancer lines of kayaks. Also in 1976, the first whitewater rodeo was held on the Salmon River in Stanley, Idaho. Whitewater rodeos are competitive events that judge acrobatic kayaking techniques performed in whitewater rapids. Modern kayaks fall into four categories: whitewater, touring, recreational, and sit-on-top.

Unique Whitewater Boats Throughout the history of whitewater sports, many types of river craft were used, with a variety of designs and purposes.

Sweep boats were used on the Salmon River in Idaho in the mid-1800s. One of the country's first commercial guides was Harry Guleke, who took a group of paying passengers down the Salmon in 1896 in a sweep boat.

Dories and **keeled cutwater boats** were used around 1869, when Major John Wesley Powell first explored the uncharted canyon of the Colorado.

In the 1890s, a Utah trapper named Nathaniel Galloway designed **flat-bottomed** boats. These boats revolutionized whitewater craft of the time. Galloway also created a new rowing style by rowing upstream, against the current, to increase maneuverability of the boat.

Torkel Kaarhus designed **McKenzie-style dories** or **drift boats** in the 1920s. Later, Woodie Hindman modified this design to accommodate a motor. The McKenzie-style dory is still common on rivers throughout the Northwest.

Norman Nevills designed **cataract boats** in the late 1930s. He used these boats on the first commercial Grand Canyon trip, in 1938.

Inflatables Modern inflatables came from a design by Pierre Debroutelle in 1937 and were patented in 1943. This design used a U-shape, with two lateral buoyancy chambers connecting a wooden transom; it was the direct predecessor of modern whitewater inflatable craft.

Inflatables were not commonly available until after World War II when military-surplus pontoons and rafts became abundant. In 1954, Hatch River Expeditions ran the first motorized commercial raft trip through the Grand Canyon, using a craft made with twenty-eight-foot bridge pontoons and a ten-man life raft.

In the late 1960s, Avon, Rubber Fabricators, and Rubber Manufacturers built the first rafts designed specifically for whitewater use. Innovations in the 1980s included self-bailing floors and catarafts. One- and two-person inflatable kayaks became popular in the early 1990s.

Riverboards Riverboards are similar to surfboards, but without a skeg (the stabilizing/steering fin on the rear bottom of a surfboard). They were introduced in the late 1980s. Riverboards are used both for river rescue and river running. The riverboard paddler lies on top of the riverboard and uses flippers to maneuver.

The Growing Popularity of Whitewater Rafting

In addition to the improved technology, several other factors have led to a rapid growth of whitewater sports in the last half century. These include the passage of the U.S. Wild and Scenic Rivers Act, the opening of urban whitewater parks, the growth of whitewater sports in the Olympics, and even the release of movies featuring whitewater activities. The Wild and Scenic Rivers Act, passed into law in 1968, contributed to the popularization of whitewater sports. This landmark piece of legislation preserved rivers or sections of rivers for all time in their free-flowing condition. Currently, less than 1 percent of the river miles in the United States have been included in the Wild and Scenic Rivers Act.

The Wild and Scenic Rivers classifications include wild, scenic, or recreational and correspond to varying degrees of preexisting development.

The Canoe/Kayak Slalom event was a demonstration sport in the 1924 Olympic Games and became a full medal sport at the 1936 Olympic Games in Munich, Germany. In 1972, whitewater slalom racing was added to the Olympic Canoe/Kayak venue.

The movie *Deliverance,* with Burt Reynolds, was released in 1972 and resulted in an immediate explosion of interest in whitewater sports. *River Wild,* released in 1994 and starring Meryl Streep, also generated interest in whitewater sports.

As the popularity of whitewater sports continues to explode, so has the demand for more accessible whitewater recreational opportunities in urban areas. The answer has been the creation of artificial whitewater parks. Augsburg, Germany, built the world's first true "artificial slalom course" in order to host the 1972 Munich Olympics. The East Race Waterway in South Bend, Indiana, was the first artificial whitewater course in North America. Artificial whitewater parks are a growing trend due to tourism and the economic impact of these parks on surrounding urban areas.

River Issues and Organizations

Along with the growth in whitewater sports has been the increase in river fatalities. According to the American Canoe Association, fatalities have gone from one or two in the mid-1970s to between thirty and fifty in the late 1990s for all kayakers, canoeists, and rafters.

There is a long list of organizations founded to organize, promote, and educate the public and government agencies about whitewater sports. The American Canoe Association, founded in 1870, is the oldest national canoeing organization in the United States. Efforts by these organizations help to protect resources, educate participants, and work with public and private organizations to address critical issues facing the future of whitewater sports. These issues include:

Reform of navigation and flood projects

Reclaiming urban rivers

Dam removal

Hydropower dam reform

Fish and wildlife protection

Floodplain and wetlands protection

Water-quality protection

Protection of wild and scenic rivers

River-access issues

Whitewater sports offer many opportunities and experiences, from river running and Olympic and national competitions to whitewater rodeos. The continued growth of whitewater sports will impact the very rivers and resources that are their lifeblood. More efforts on local and national levels are needed to ensure adequate resources and more river protection and access.

See also: Boating, Power; Extreme Sports

BIBLIOGRAPHY

"American Rivers: River Issues." Available from http://www.amrivers.org/issues.

Bechdel, L., and S. Ray. *River Rescue.* Boston: Appalachian Mountain Club, 1985.

Belknap, Lee. "What Happened in 1997?" Available from http://americanwhitewater.org.

Bennett, Jeff. *Rafting: The Complete Guide to Whitewater Rafting Techniques and Equipment.* Portland, Oreg. Swiftwater Publishing, 1993.

Inflatable Marine Products Network. "History of Inflatables." Available from http://www.allinflatables.com/support.

O.A.R.S. "Grand Canyon Dories." Available from http://www.oars.com/htdocs.

Riviere, Bill. *The Open Canoe.* Boston: Little, Brown and Company, 1985.

Staveley, Gaylord. "A Brief History of Grand Canyon River Running." Available from http://www.gcroa.org.

Tejoda-Flores, Lito. *Wildwater: The Sierra Club Guide to Kayaking and Whitewater Boating.* San Francisco: Sierra Club Books, 1978.

"Urban Whitewater: Whitewater Parks Around the Globe." Available from http://www.swwparkalliance.com.

"Wild & Scenic Rivers." Available from http://www.nps.gov/rivers.

Charles Hammersley

WILD WEST SHOWS

In the 1830s and 1840s, the western artist George Catlin inaugurated Wild West shows by displaying Plains Indians in the United States, the British Isles, and France. However, this form of entertainment did not become a major cultural phenomenon until the late nineteenth century, when Americans and Europeans became intrigued with the rapidly disappearing Plains frontier. Westerners carved their niche in outdoor entertainment by designating the frontier movement as the most important accomplishment in American history, and by forming shows that celebrated this achievement with programs combining history, patriotism, and adventure. Authentic Plains people, animals, and depictions of events involved in the winning of the West enhanced the appeal of shows.

Spectators enjoyed the dash and color of the shows, and the portrayal of a simple, romantic world in which heroic people on horseback enjoyed untrammeled freedom, quickly eliminated evil, and ensured the success of the "American" way. Vocal audiences exerted considerable influence on the direction and content of the shows. By cheering most loudly for vignettes showcasing colorful characters, adventure, and conflict on the Plains, these audiences helped define the concept of the "Wild West," a collaboratively crafted vision where Westerners instructed Easterners and Europeans but developed acts with an eye to satisfying audience expectations. Many elements of the performances remained the same, but the shows evolved over time to satisfy the ever-changing expectations of viewers.

Buffalo Bill's Wild West Show and His Successors

William F. "Buffalo Bill" Cody dominated the genre, and accurately gauged the changing moods at home and in Europe. He entered the Wild West show business in 1883, and quickly established its Western format. These shows celebrated horses and those who rode them in acts featuring races and bucking broncos. Sharpshooting, from horseback and from the ground, was always a part of the programs. Spectacles combined shooting and horsemanship in acts, such as one in which Indians attacked a settler's cabin and a band of cowboys brandishing six-shooters arrived just in time to save the family. Another spectacle, the rescue of the Deadwood stagecoach, featured hard-riding, gun-wielding cowboys dispatching Indians or bandits.

An international phase in the show extended from 1887 to 1893, when Buffalo Bill's Wild West show visited Queen Victoria's Golden Jubilee in London, and then moved to France, Spain, Italy, Austria, and Germany, before returning to the Columbian Exposition in Chicago in 1893. During this time, Cody and the show's publicists polished the image of performers—cowboys, in particular—in a way that retained their American vigor but made them less violent, more knightly and gentlemanly, and thereby more acceptable to Europeans. By camping out-of-doors in Europe, these Americans self-consciously played the role of innocent children of nature rejuvenated by contact with nature.

Buffalo Bill's Wild West Show

- Acts in Buffalo Bill's Wild West Show sometimes featured athletes, including a high jumper who jumped over horses, sprinters who raced horses, and Arabians who demonstrated feats of strength and tumbling.

- Buck Taylor, a cowboy in Buffalo Bill's Wild West show, probably served as the model for the protagonist in Owen Wister's novel The Virginian (1902).

- Annie Oakley, who was with the show from 1884 until 1901, encouraged women to become physically fit with activities such as equestrianism, fencing, running, and working out with weights.

- The show sold itself as a re-creation of life on the frontier, and among the staged acts that made up the show were scenes known as the Bison Hunt, the Train Robbery, the Indian War Battle Reenactment, and the Grand Finale—The Attack on the Burning Cabin.

- In 1893, a new act was added to the show. Called the Congress of Rough Riders of the World, the military-style act featured marksmen from around the world, including future U.S. president Theodore Roosevelt.

This depiction elevated the image of all in the show, but the cowboy image benefited most; from that point forward, the cowboy became an American icon. At the Columbian Exposition, Buffalo Bill's Wild West show reassured Americans that the United States could move confidently into the future because of core values developed on the frontier. By this time, the show contained a "Congress of Rough Riders" that included military units from the great powers of the world and exotic equestrians, such as Cossacks and gauchos. After 1893, Buffalo Bill celebrated militarism and imperialism along with all things western. Before Cody died in 1917, he was encouraging "preparedness" for America's entry into World War I.

The success of Buffalo Bill's show inspired many imitators and competitors. A perusal of the 116 shows listed in Don B. Russell's "Checklist of Wild West Shows" in The Wild West (pp. 121–127) indicates that from 1883 to 1900 there were perhaps twenty other entertainments, often run by men with flamboyant names, such as Dr. W.

Annie Oakley. Annie Oakley, whose real name was Phoebe Ann Moses, joined Buffalo Bill's Wild West Show in 1884 as a trick shooter known as "Little Sure Shot." In this early illustration from the show, Oakley shoots a rifle while standing on a bareback horse. © *Corbis*

F. Carver, or "Evil Spirit of the Plains," Pawnee Bill (both partners of Buffalo Bill for a time), Buckskin Joe, and Mexican Joe. From 1900 to 1920 the shows proliferated to over fifty, although many were small, circuslike affairs, such as Buckskin Ben's Wild West and Dog and Pony Show, and Indian Bill's Wild West and Cole and Rogers Circus combined. The celebrated outlaws Cole Younger and Frank James tried the business in 1903 and 1908. The Miller Brothers 101 Ranch Show (the employer of Buffalo Bill, 1916–1917) was the largest show to emerge (1907), and continued, with an interruption for World War I, until the Great Depression. From 1920 to 1940, approximately twenty Wild West shows existed, sometimes headed by movie stars such as Tom Mix, Tim Mc-Coy, and Ken Maynard. After 1940, only a handful of

shows appeared, but some included luminaries, such as Gene Autry's Flying A Ranch Stampede. Women occasionally ran Wild West shows, as evidenced by such names as Luella Forepaugh-Fish Wild West and the Kemp Sisters Wild West.

Wild West shows employed thousands of performers, some whose names are recognizable today, such as Annie Oakley, Sitting Bull, Will Rogers, Tom Mix, Bill Pickett, and Jess Willard. During their lifetimes, most Americans knew the names Buck Taylor, Johnny Baker, Antonio Esquibel, Lillian Smith, and Bessie and Della Ferrell. Indians were always conspicuous in Wild West shows, and the entertainment established the popular image of Native Americans as mounted Plains warriors.

The Decline and Significance of Wild West Shows

Wild West shows declined because they fit most comfortably into the late nineteenth and early twentieth centuries, when crowds flocked to tented entertainments and the end of the frontier concerned Americans. But Wild West shows also failed because they had succeeded so well that other forms of entertainment appropriated aspects of their programs. Wild West show performers, such as Tom Mix, transferred the genre's action, horsemanship, and sharpshooting to movies. In addition, rodeos became popular, powwows showcased Native American customs, and dude ranches and trail rides made the Wild West lifestyle available to anyone willing to pay for the experience.

The legacy of Wild West shows remains firmly ensconced in American culture, and in its sport and leisure. *Wild West* still designates a mythical and uniquely American place populated with lean and hardened men and women engaged in vigorous outdoor activities. Wild West shows introduced rodeo as a spectator sport, and those who saw cowboys and cowgirls such as Lucille Mulhall and Lulu Parr ride bucking broncos saw them as superior athletes. Spectators who saw Annie Oakley and Johnnie Baker shoot regarded guns as "American." Wild West shows stressed that the transcendent inner qualities of westerners matched their physical accomplishments, and that contact with nature sustained them. This attitude exists in contemporary America, and helps popularize camping, hunting, and other outdoor activities.

Wild West shows helped define "American," and they established a national mythology that enriched the nation's leisure activities. As such, these shows are a vital component in studying America's leisure, social, and sports histories.

See also: Rodeos, Western America Leisure Lifestyles

BIBLIOGRAPHY

Moses, L. G. *Wild West Shows and the Images of American Indians, 1883–1933.* Albuquerque: University of New Mexico Press, 1996.

Reddin, Paul. *Wild West Shows.* Urbana: University of Illinois Press, 1999.

Russell, Don B. *The Wild West.* Fort Worth, Tex.: Amon Carter Museum of Western Art, 1970.

Paul Reddin

WILDING

Although for many Americans the term "wilding" was introduced into the national vernacular following the events of April 1989 when a woman jogging in New York's Central Park was brutally beaten and raped by a gang of teenage boys, the expression of this group behavior has occurred in many forms throughout the history of the United States.

Wilding refers to youth violence directed at complete strangers and spurred by a hubris mentality typically shared among a group of adolescent boys or young men. Within the media, the term has been identified with crimes such as sexual violence, assault and battery, vandalism, and robbery.

Documented cases of wilding within the media and police department reports across the country characterize it as aimless and random violence motivated by a need for excitement, social pressures associated with adolescents' need for belonging and acceptance, and a desire for material wealth and respect. Others suggest that "wolf packing," as it is also known, may be motivated more by a celebration of hedonism than for any extrinsic rewards.

The emergence of wilding in the United States as a form of social rebellion and expression among youth is believed by some to have preceded the most recent occurrences such as the incident in Central Park and has its roots in the behaviors of other, similarly disaffected generations of young Americans. These previous generations of youth—from the children of seventeenth-century Puritan America who engaged in gambling and pirating as a response to their parents' strict adherence to Church doctrine, to the post–World War II baby boomers who gathered in great numbers to protest the previous generation's material self-interest and civil indifference—illustrate the cyclic pattern of violence in youth culture.

Despite the preponderance of attention the media ascribes to the significance of race and class when reporting the high-profile incidences of wilding, some researchers have argued that these menacing and unruly forms of group behavior have, to some degree, a biological or sociological basis. Biological theories on criminal behavior purport that men possess universal human traits like impulsivity and aggression that historically served adaptive functions in protecting and defending their communities from external threats but are no longer appropriate or functional within the moral constraints of modern societies. From a sociological perspective, contemporary shifts in family structure, particularly the significant rise in single-parent families, are related to increases in violent crime among youth.

As a symbol of the violence and excess of contemporary youth culture, wilding resonates in the public imagination in much the same way as other illicit youth activities such as raving and the drug Ecstasy, the public's moral outrage and indictment of such youth movements, rather than functioning to identify and highlight the social antecedents of such behavior, may serve only to lend credibility to such actions in the eyes of today's youth.

See also: Raves/Raving, Teenage Leisure Trends

BIBLIOGRAPHY

Katz, Jack. *Seductions of Crime: Moral and Sensual Attractions in Doing Evil.* New York: Basic Books, 1988.

Welch, Michael, Eric Price, and Nana Yankey. "Moral Panic over Youth Violence: Wilding and the Manufacture of Menace in the Media." *Youth & Society* 34, no. 1 (2002): 3–29.

John R. Persing

WINDSURFING

Windsurfing, an aquatic sport born in the 1960s, combines sailing and surfing. Also known as sailboarding or boardsailing, windsurfing employs a board-and-sail device—basically sailing a small surfboard using a hand-held sail rig with the mast attached to the deck by a universal joint. Unlike sailing, no rudder is involved; instead, steering and control are done manually by moving or tilting the sail while the rider stands on the board gliding on the water's surface. Unlike surfing, there is no wait for waves. Wind and waves are harnessed by maneuvering a board eight to twelve feet in length and weighing fifteen to forty pounds with a mast connected by a universal joint, a single Marconi-type rig (a triangular sail attached directly to the mast), and a wishbone boom. The universal joint makes a windsurfer a unique sailing craft. This special piece of equipment allows the mast with its sail to rotate throughout all angles of the vertical relative to the board itself. Speeds over forty knots can be reached.

History of Windsurfing

S. Newman Darby first introduced the Free-Sail-System Sailboard to Americans in a 1965 *Popular Science* maga-zine article that informed readers how to build and sail a sailboard. Just outside of Wilkes-Barre, Pennsylvania, the evolution from small rudderless sailboat (less than three meters long) to sailboard took place over a twenty-year period. Early designs included aluminum catamarans with a stayed sloop rig sail arrangement and a small flat-bottom sailing scow. Darby and his brother Ken started building and selling the first sailboards with universal joints in 1964. Approximately eighty were sold in the first full year of production (1965–1966). The Darby Sailboard was featured at the Philadelphia Boat Show in 1965 and as a prize on the popular American game show *The Price Is Right*. However, Darby's system was aerodynamically inefficient and difficult to use. Sailboarding would not catch on until others perfected the design.

In 1968, the first patented windsurf board, the Windsurfer, was introduced by two good friends, Jim Drake and Hoyle Schweitzer. Both from southern California, Drake was an aeronautical engineer and a sailor, while Schweitzer was a businessman and a surfer. The sport spread rapidly from California, throughout the United States and North America, Europe, and Australia.

Olympic Status

In the early 2000s, windsurfing (called "boardsailing" in Olympic jargon) was one of the eleven yachting events recognized by the International Olympic Committee. Windsurfing was a demonstration sport at the 1984 Los Angeles Summer Games and an Olympic event at each Games since. In 1992, separate contests for men and women were included.

All competitors use the same supplied Olympic boards selected by the International Olympic Committee based on the sailing conditions at the competition site. However, sailors often find the chosen equipment frustrating and unable to meet the demand of the competition. Timing of the selection was another problem. Early on, Olympic boards were selected within one year of the competition, leaving little time to train specifically on the equipment. Since the 1992 Games in Barcelona, Spain, the Olympic choice has been announced four years in advance; this fact, along with the inclusion of women, spurred a significant growth in Olympic windsurfing globally, as evidenced by the 1996 Games in Atlanta, when medalists came from all corners of the world, not just sailing nations.

Formula Windsurfing

In an effort to be more representative of the sport of windsurfing, proposals are being made to change the equipment in the 2008 Games. Arguments are being offered for Formula Windsurfing, which would replace the one design class. Formula Windsurfing is supported by the Professional Windsurfers Association, the International Funboard Class Association, and the International Boardsailors Association, who would oversee the format. As of 2004, sailors were required to use the Mistral One Design board. Formula Windsurfing would give greater flexibility by allowing sailors to choose any one production board and three production sails. Formula racing allows sailors to adjust for wind speeds, body weight, and personal style. In addition, speeds would increase, pumping the sail due to low winds would be limited, and top windsurfing professionals would compete in the Olympic Regatta.

Under the one design class, top athletes have not been able to devote necessary time to train on the Olympic equipment. Proponents of Formula Windsurfing believe that the change would better promote windsurfing in several ways: the media would promote the faster and more exciting sport, design and equipment development would increase, and interest in the sport would rise. Also, the declining popularity of windsurfing offered another reason to make the switch. Other windsurfing advocates warned that staying close to their sailing roots in the yachting fraternity offered protection to an otherwise vulnerable Olympic event. If sports were to be eliminated, sailboarding might be putting itself too far out on the extreme limb if Formula Windsurfing was introduced to the Olympics.

According to the National Sporting Goods Association, windsurfing participation in the United States plummeted by 71.4 percent between 1995 and 2000. While more than a million people windsurfed during the height of the sport in the mid-eighties, in the early 2000s approximately 200,000 Americans windsurfed at least once each year. The United States was not seeing the resurgence of popularity that Europe was experiencing; instead kite surfing was gaining enthusiasts.

The Modern Professional Windsurfer

Several professional associations sanction competitions involving hundreds of thousands of dollars in prize monies. More than 500 professional sailors (men and women) compete in dozens of class competitions throughout the world. Major players in professional windsurfing include the Professional Windsurfers Association, National Windsurfing Association, International Funboard Class Association, International Boardsailing Association, and National Boardsailing Association. These groups work together to promote windsurfing and offer opportunities for their members to compete on the most elite level.

Professional competition in modern windsurfing includes course racing, slalom, freestyle, and wave sailing, with competitions held throughout the world. Racing is divided into two types: upwind (course racing) and downwind (slalom) competition. Racing includes an imaginary start line and a marked course where sharp tactics and tuned equipment are necessary to succeed. It is a nonjudged event where the winner is determined by the amount of time needed to complete the race. Freestyle competition is very open: during a five-minute heat sailors can perform tricks, jumps, and wave rides to earn points for style, diversity, technical skill, and overall impression. The wave competition is the most spectacular spectator sport. The eight-minute heats include a number of double and combination jumps, rotations, wave rides, back loops and push loops. A point system is in place on the professional level, and sailors earn world ranking.

See also: Beaches, Extreme Sports, Surfing, Swimming

BIBLIOGRAPHY

Minkin, T. "Windjammer." *Women's Sport and Fitness* 13, no. 2 (May/June 1991): 39.

Riordan, Teresa. "Patents." *New York Times* 148, no. 51294 (September 1998): C6.

Sterba, James P. "Windsurfing Wipes Out On Wave of Own Hot Air." *Wall Street Journal* 227, no. 117 (June 1996): B9.

Wertheim, L. Jon. "Where Have All the Windsurfers Gone?" *Sports Illustrated* 95, no. 9 (September 2001): A4.

"Windsurfing." In *The Columbia Encyclopedia.* 6th ed. Edited by Paul Lagasse, Lora Goldman, Archie Hobson, and Susan R. Norton. New York: Columbia University Press.

Yahoo! Internet Life 8, no. 5 (May 2002): 85.

Zeugin, Michael. "Wind Riders." *New York State Conservationist* 58, no. 1 (August 2003): 8.

Jill Vasquez Mills

WINE TASTING

The history of wine tasting is inextricably linked to the history of wine itself. The earliest vines, found in the Mesopotamian region in 6,000 to 4,000 B.C., produced the beverage esteemed by the ancient Babylonian and Egyptian royalty; wine's popularity spread among the elite of Greece, Rome, and, later, Europe in the millennia following. Once the merchant trade in wine was established,

Wine tasting. At the Robert Mondavi Winery, visitors stop to sniff and then taste the wine. Located in Napa Valley, California the family-run business was founded by Robert G. Mondavi and his eldest son R. Michael Mondavi in 1966. © *Corbis*

it was necessary for both sellers and buyers to develop skills in tasting and evaluating the products for sale.

In more recent times, wine tasting has become increasingly popular as a leisure activity. The 1970s to 1990s in America saw the explosive growth of wine bars and cafés, festivals, and tasting events. Once attended only by upper-class connoisseurs, modern wine-tasting events are enjoyed by a wide range of people of varying backgrounds, interests, and positions, though some perceptions of elitism still exist. Many tasting events are coupled with food and sponsored by either restaurants or vineyards. In fact, many feel that wine is at its best when served alongside a meal, not only emphasizing the quality of the wine, but also enhancing the dining experience itself.

Several books and classes on wine tasting are available across the globe, which usually have the purpose of demystifying what can be a daunting activity for many. Some novice tasters desire simply to understand better which wine to order or serve with a meal, while others strive to learn how to identify regional and varietal differences in wines. The general interest in wines—both selection and taste—is evident in the number of articles and recurring columns on the topic found in daily and weekly newspapers and magazines.

Wine-tasting events are held informally among friends, as fund-raising events for nonprofit agencies, as tourist attractions, and as sales and marketing tools employed by wine makers and retailers. The act of wine tasting itself can be highly scientific, involving the senses of smell, taste, and sight, and there are many professional wine tasters who judge or rate wines for a variety of purposes, such as magazine or newspaper reviews. However, wine tasting as a recreation and leisure activity is often less formally structured, though those in attendance might have some background in the art and science of tasting.

Wine Tasting as Leisure Education and Social Recreation

Whether sponsored informally by wine enthusiasts or formally by wine merchants, clubs, or societies, many wine tastings are held for the purpose of educating those in attendance about wine. Commercial sponsors, including wine makers, wine merchants, and wine bars, hold such tastings as a means to increase sales. Additionally, wine-tasting events are frequently held by nonprofit organizations (including those associated with leisure and recreation) for fund-raising purposes. Whether formal or informal, commercial or not-for-profit, tasting (and drinking) wine is, for most, an enjoyable and freely chosen activity. However, the vast array of types and prices of wines, as well as the "rules" many associate with wine selection, create a sometimes-intimidating aura surrounding wine.

These events serve as leisure education in that they enable tasters to learn better how to select wine, how to judge its quality, and how to differentiate between varieties, vineyards, regions, and countries, all of which lead to an improved quality of experience for those who enjoy wine. Additionally, because tastings are typically social activities, conducted in social settings, one of their positive by-products is the social interaction enjoyed by participants. Many tasting events are actually theme parties, based on vintage, type, price range, vintner, region, or country, for example. There are even games and wine-tasting party kits available for purchase by those wishing to host parties themselves.

In addition to tasting events and the vast array of wine-tasting information available on the Internet and in books, magazines, and newspapers, many colleges and universities offer continuing education courses in wine appreciation. Those wishing to hone their wine-tasting skills further can enroll in certification programs sponsored by organizations such as the Court of Master Sommeliers and the International Wine Guild.

Wine Tourism

As a result of improvements in technology and changes in growing techniques, there are now vineyards and wineries in every state in the United States and in most countries of the world. Long popular in regions such as the Napa Valley in California, the growing wine tourism industry merges leisure travel, education, cultural opportunities, tourism destination marketing, economic development, and quality-of-life issues, providing substantial benefits to rural communities in particular. Whether for day trips or longer excursions, wine enthusiasts the world over enjoy trips to vineyards to learn more about the wineries' offerings, to have the opportunity to purchase wine at attractive prices, and to enjoy the natural beauty of the vineyards themselves.

See also: Bars, Coffee Houses and Café Society, Dining Out, Drinking, Leisure Class

BIBLIOGRAPHY

Broadbent, Michael. *Michael Broadbent's Vintage Wine.* New York: Harcourt, 2002.

Charters, Steve, and Jane Ali-Knight. "Who Is the Wine Tourist?" *Tourism Management* 23 (2002): 311–319.

Hall, C. Michael, Gary Johnson, and Richard Mitchell. "Wine Tourism and Regional Development." In *Wine Tourism Around the World: Development, Management, and Markets.* Edited by C. Michael Hall, Liz Sharples, Brock Cambourne, and Niki Macionis. Oxford, U.K.: Butterworth-Heinemann, 2000.

Hall, C. Michael, Gary Johnson, Brock Cambourne, Niki Macionis, Richard Mitchell, and Liz Sharples. "Wine Tourism: An Introduction." In *Wine Tourism Around the World: Development, Management, and Markets.* Edited by C. Michael Hall, Liz Sharples, Brock Cambourne, and Niki Macionis. Oxford, U.K.: Butterworth-Heinemann, 2000.

Immer, Andrea. *Great Wine Made Simple: Straight Talk from a Master Sommelier.* New York: Broadway Books, 2000.

Prial, Frank. *Decantations: Reflections on Wine.* New York: St. Martin's Press, 2001.

Robinson, Jancis. *How to Taste: A Guide to Enjoying Wine.* New York: Simon and Schuster, 2001.

Robinson, Jancis, ed. *The Oxford Companion to Wine.* New York: Oxford University Press, 1994.

Telfer, David J. "Strategic Alliances Along the Niagara Wine Route." *Tourism Management* 22 (2001): 21–30.

L. Allison Stringer

WOMEN'S LEISURE LIFESTYLES

The word "leisure" conjures up different images for different people: warm breezes, iced tea, and a comfortable chair; an exhausting yet exhilarating game of basketball; a stiff drink at the pub; an afternoon at the park with children. Leisure indicates both the freedom to do something and the freedom to do nothing, and it is an aspect of life that Americans have fought to attain and still fight to defend. For women, however, leisure is complicated by their many roles and responsibilities, their lack of access to aspects of the public sphere, and their very sense of an inherent right to leisure time and leisure activities.

Americans have long considered leisure the complement to the paid workday. In the late nineteenth and early twentieth centuries, industrial workers countered employers' fears of working-class idleness and "Sunday neurosis" with demands for free time. The movement to secure an eight-hour day for workers offered, as its most compelling slogan, "Eight Hours for Work, Eight Hours for Rest, and Eight Hours for What We Will." Originally hyphenated as the "week-end," days free from work became institutionalized as the weekend, a portion of the week that stands on its own and stands for freedom from paid employment.

Employers eager to maintain a cooperative workforce were not alone in their fears of working-class leisure time and leisure activities. Social reformers of the late nineteenth and early twentieth centuries also considered too much unchecked free time on the part of workers a threat to the social order. Alarmed at the link between leisure time, alcohol consumption, prostitution, and other vices, social reformers sought to influence workers in this unregulated arena of daily life. In envisioning and creating alternatives, however, they faced cultural and economic resistance. The notion of time free to do "what we will" signified workers' objections to having that time and activity, or the funds they used to support their leisure, defined by outsiders. Class differences between workers and reformers meant that the groups approached leisure time differently: For workers leisure signified an opportunity to socialize, escape from the pressures of daily life, and diffuse tensions. Wishful reformers had the added expectation that leisure activities signified edification and, for immigrants, Americanization.

Women as a Complicated Category

From the start, women's participation in leisure proved problematic. If paid employment served as the counterpoint to leisure, women's lives did not readily fit into the discussion. Women's double day of paid work and unpaid work applied in the nineteenth century as it applies in the early 2000s. For those unmarried women who worked in industrial settings, leisure time was compromised by the expectation, for many, that they would turn their wages over to their families. For their married counterparts in factories, a second shift rather than free time awaited them at the end of the paid workday. The constraints on women's and girls' access to leisure included housework, an inequitable division of labor in the home, and fragmented days and tasks. For women outside the sphere of paid work, the varied demands of their days proved no less onerous. The demand for "eight hours for what we will," available to men at least in terms of public discourse, proved quite difficult for women.

In addition to the demands of the family, women historically have had less access than men to the public realm. The term "streetwalker," an antiquated but revealing description of a prostitute, illustrates the social difficulty of any woman claiming a place in the public realm in general, on the street in particular. Many leisure

activities developed among workers and by social reformers necessitated that access and, as a result, deliberately or inadvertently discouraged women's participation. Organized sporting events and clubs, in addition to many hobbies, developed largely as masculine activities. Socially constructed "women's space" encouraged women to form particular and gendered maps of access to public areas; the parallel geography of leisure steered women toward activities that held home-based leisure over public leisure. Home-based leisure, then as in the early 2000s, did not require funds for transportation, travel on the streets at night, or complete freedom from the demands of the home. It also kept intact socially acceptable but discriminatory definitions of womanhood.

Women's multiple responsibilities and limited access to the public sphere, along with other social and economic constraints, compromised women's very sense of their right to leisure time and leisure-based activities. Few women truly felt free to do something not related to meeting the needs of others; fewer still felt free simply to do nothing. Women's sense of entitlement in relation to leisure has been low and continues to serve as a significant deterrent to women's participation in organized and unorganized leisure activities. As a result, women often pursued leisure activities only in combination with other, family-based work. Historically they have talked with friends while watching children; in the early 2000s they might have ironed clothes while watching television. Additionally, leisure pursuits, like other elements of life, demonstrate power dynamics within families; witness the late-twentieth-century debate about who controls the television remote control. Other terms of contemporary usage, like "holiday," "vacation," and "retirement," prove equally problematic when considering women's lives and the around-the-clock demands placed on them, even in the seemingly leisure-producing arenas of life.

Women's Leisure Activities: A Historical Snapshot

Early social reformers concerned with leisure did not ignore girls and women altogether. They recognized, particularly at the turn of the twentieth century, that girls as well as boys needed recreation, and they attempted to carve out a public space for girls. The Playground Association, formed in 1906, built playgrounds to provide that leisure-time space. The reformers found, however, that other factors compounded the problem of access. Many girls, exhausted by their family responsibilities, had little interest in activities that required energy. Additionally, girls' clothing restrained rather than promoted the free

Yoga class. Yoga has gained in popularity as a form of exercise and is practiced in large majority by women, although men and even children have become increasingly involved. Many gyms and other exercise facilities hold yoga classes, such as this one. © *Jose Luis Pelaez, Inc./Corbis*

use of their bodies in play. Cultural fears about girls and competition, in addition to a growing awareness of and anxieties about female sexuality, led to the development of activities that relegated women to single-sex, more passive leisure pursuits. During the Great Depression, that emphasis changed again, as reformers feared that too much single-sex activity on the part of girls and women, like the depression itself, threatened to empower females and make males redundant.

Organized clubs became one of the most significant leisure developments for girls and women. The Girl Scouts, the most famous of these organizations, was founded in the early twentieth century to provide outdoor experiences, foster self-improvement, and encourage homemaking-related activities. The group followed the lead of the Boy Scouts, mixing domestic concerns with an outdoor, military-minded regimen of activities. The idea of strengthening girls' bodies and minds threatened some Americans, but the group earned the regard of the nation with its emphasis on patriotic duty during World War I. As Laureen Tedesco argues, the motto "Be Pre-

pared" suggested that girls had something for which to be prepared. Interestingly, the mixing of domestic and professional concerns, nature study and nurture preparedness, made the Scouts a source of empowerment for many girls.

At the same time as the Girl Scouts and other similar organizations recruited girls and women into club life, the commercial leisure pursuits of dance halls, amusement parks, and cinemas lured girls into other definitions of having fun. Kathy Peiss and others have demonstrated that for many girls and young women, leisure time meant time to learn the rules and responsibilities of heterosexuality. Working-class and middle-class women alike learned to solicit the male gaze and gain popularity through fashion sense, stylish hairdos, and the use of cosmetics. The flapper, popular through the 1920s, mediated her life and leisure through movie stars, dancing, and general media awareness. These commercialized leisure pursuits caused conflicts between youth and their parents. Vicki Ruiz's study of Mexican American women from 1920–1950 illustrates how one ethnic group attempted, by institutionalizing the use of chaperones for young women, to offer resistance to the highly American and rapidly commercial elements of leisure activity.

For some women in the early twentieth century, leisure activity held an added component: politics. A study of African American female tobacco workers in the southern United States reveals that they used their leisure time to build solidarity in their communities so they could resist oppression. Leisure, in fact, provided both evidence of their subordination and a site for resistance. Tobacco employers did not feel any obligation to provide black workers with leisure time or activities—although they did provide these spaces for white workers— to dissipate unrest and cultivate loyalty. African American women recognized the injustice and transformed their scant leisure time into activities for building unity and fomenting change.

The feminist movement of the 1970s and 1980s provided more leisure activities and an enhanced sense of entitlement to girls and women. Policy makers came to recognize the need to change recreation to reflect more adequately girls' and women's interests and needs, and issues like sexual harassment and public safety have come to be included in analyses of leisure. Title IX, which formalized an approach to creating equity in the world of sports, has had an enormous impact on girls' access to sports in school settings and, as a result, professional settings as well. Contemporary questions include the impact of technology on girls' and women's leisure activities, as girls compete with boys in and for cyberspace, and economic and other interests make the future of Title IX and other feminist initiatives less secure.

Different Women, Different Uses of Leisure

As the examples of Mexican American and African American women suggest, women access and experience leisure differently based on race, ethnicity, social class, age, family status, sexual orientation, and other elements of identity. Women with dependent children are the least likely to be involved in community-based leisure activities, for example, although women over forty, with or without children, are most likely to take part in voluntary organizations. The more roles women hold, the less likely they are to find or make the time to engage in leisure pursuits. Lesbians, even those in family roles, may provide models of leisure activity for heterosexuals; research reveals that they engage in fewer predetermined roles in relation to leisure, they believe leisure for all leads to better family interactions, and they respect the need for their partners' as well as their own separate leisure time and activities. Leisure activity among older women has been linked pos-

itively to mental health. Social class, of course, plays a role in leisure, as women with more disposable income may also have increased access to transportation, leisure-related clothing and accessories, and safe spaces in which to play, relax, and gather.

Conclusion

As we move into the twenty-first century, women are engaging in an enormous range of leisure activities, from the active to the passive, the expensive to the free, the individual to the group, the competitive to the cooperative, the ephemeral to the educational. Because of their many differences, women do not share life experiences in as many ways as once thought. They may, however, share unequal access to leisure across class, racial, ethnic, sexual orientation, parenting, and regional lines. Leisure activities that replicate negative social notions of womanhood can actually disempower women further. One study, for example, demonstrated that women who increased their involvement in aerobics experienced also an increased dissatisfaction with their bodies. The realities of violence and fear of violence in public space mean that women and men continue to navigate different maps of leisure. Women have not yet adequately countered the seeming contradiction between providing for others and taking care of themselves.

Recent research reveals, however, that leisure may serve as a source of improving women's lives by empowering them. One study of women with physical disabilities found that leisure was a means by which these women could come to terms with their differences and feel empowered. Another study suggests that sports affirm women's fantasies of power and empower them to act in beneficial ways in their lives. Yet another study suggests that women who spend leisure time with other women may engage in socially subversive talk or activity that opens up new spaces in women's sense of self and others. Among the most significant issues related to leisure is stress; women and men alike feel compelled to work more and engage in leisure time less. Activities previously considered leisure activities can come to feel like additional demands on precious time. New developments in technology, in addition to evolving definitions of womanhood, may open opportunities for women. In any case, leisure, like other elements of life, is likely to remain contested, socially constructed, and, not incidentally, gendered.

See also: Beauty Culture; Civic Clubs, Women; Fashion; Home Decoration; Men's Leisure Lifestyles

BIBLIOGRAPHY

Aitchinson, Cara. "New Cultural Geographies: The Spatiality of Leisure, Gender, and Sexuality." *Leisure Studies* 18 (1999): 19–40.

Bialeschki, M. Deborah, and Kathryn Lynn Walbert. "'You Have to Have Some Fun to Go Along with Your Work': The Interplay of Race, Class, Gender and Leisure in the Industrial New South." *Journal of Leisure Research* 30 (1998): 79–101.

Bialeschki, M. Deborah, and Kimberly D. Pearce. "'I Don't Want a Lifestyle—I Want a Life: The Effects of Role Negotiations in the Leisure of Lesbian Mothers." *Journal of Leisure Research* 29 (1997): 113–132.

Deem, Rosemary. *All Work and No Play? A Study of Women and Leisure.* Milton Keynes, England: Open University Press, 1986.

Green, Eileen. "'Women Doing Friendship': An Analysis of Women's Leisure as a Site of Identity Construction, Empowerment and Resistance." *Leisure Studies* 17 (1998): 341–356.

Henderson, Karla A. "A Feminist Analysis of Selected Professional Recreation Literature about Girls/Women from 1907–1990." *Journal of Leisure Research* 25 (1993): 165–181.

———. "One Size Doesn't Fit All: The Meanings of Women's Leisure." *Journal of Leisure Research* 28 (1996): 139–154.

James, Kandy. "'You Can Feel Them Looking at You': The Experiences of Adolescent Girls at Swimming Pools." *Journal of Leisure Research* 32 (2000): 262–281.

Peiss, Kathy. *Cheap Amusements: Working Women and Leisure in Turn-of-the-Century New York.* Philadelphia: Temple University Press, 1986.

Riddick, Carol Cutler, and Debra Gonder Stewart. "An Examination of the Life Satisfaction and Importance of Leisure in the Lives of Older Female Retirees: A Comparison of Blacks to Whites." *Journal of Leisure Research* 26 (1994): 75–88.

Ruiz, Vicki. "The Flapper and the Chaperone: Cultural Constructions of Identity and Heterosexual Politics Among Adolescent Mexican American Women, 1920–1950." In *Delinquents and Debutantes: Twentieth-Century American Girls' Cultures.* Edited by Sherrie Inness. New York: New York University Press, 1998.

Rybczynski, Witold. *Waiting for the Weekend.* New York: Penguin Books, 1992.

Tedesco, Laureen. "Making a Girl into a Scout: Americanizing Scouting for Girls." In *Delinquents and Debutantes: Twentieth-Century American Girls' Cultures.* Edited by Sherrie Inness. New York: New York University Press, 1998.

Jennifer Scanlon

WOODWORKING

Many people take great pleasure in making things by hand that will later become family heirlooms. Throughout history, wood has been used for this purpose. Regardless of the period, people not only pursued woodworking for utilitarian purposes but also as a leisure activity because it provided a sense of personal satisfaction and accomplishment.

In colonial America, most settlers were farmers, and wood was abundant. Although their homes were simple, these farmers used a variety of carved woodenware, including knife boxes and spoon racks, to help cooks organize their kitchens. Wallace Nutting stated that woodenware such as bowls, trenchers, and tankards were important home supplies, as well as other kitchen utensils, including ladles and baskets. These kitchen items combined form and function with regional flair. Mary Norwak suggested that homeowners made these utilitarian pieces to also serve as decorations, replacing pictures on the wall. According to Drew Langsner, creating utensils was an excellent way to train for the fundamentals of woodworking. Making wooden dough troughs, for example, would improve a person's carving and hatching ability.

In the southern Appalachians and Ozark Mountains baskets were crafted from white oak and were useful for storing yarn and fishing equipment, as well as carrying garden products and wood for the stove. Basketry combined many skills: harvesting timber, carving basket pegs, and tapering and weaving the oak splits. Unlike many wood projects that were crafted primarily by males, both males and females created basketry.

Carl Bridenbaugh suggested furniture such as tables, chairs, hutches, and dressers generally were made by hand. At the beginning of the eighteenth century, 40 percent of Americans worked either in small shops or in their homes to produce their own furniture.

Woodworking trades encompassed a range of skilled workers. Joiners specialized in making stools, peg boards, shelves, and other items that required wood to be connected. Turners worked on lathes, creating cylindrical objects such as legs for tables and chairs. Cabinetmakers made finer products, often requiring dovetail joints, veneers and inlayed wood (Wallace). Tradesmen produced many of the finer homes and furnishings belonging to wealthier Americans.

With the dawn of the industrial age, the use of power-driven machinery to produce wood products replaced the work of tradesmen because the tradesmen could not compete with the mass production brought on by the industries (Russell). Brooke Hindle suggested high-speed woodworking tools were modified and special attention was given to lubrication and blade balancing, thus reducing wood waste. The circular saw had to compete with the band saw, which cut larger pieces of wood more efficiently and provided a continuous rather intermittent cutting action. Planing, mortising, and tenoning machines were created as early as 1830. Each machine was specialized and developed in new directions to accommodate specific needs.

The Metabo Company in Germany created the first electric handheld tool in 1934. Later companies such as Sears and Roebuck, Dewalt, and Porter Cable became leaders in power tool production in the United States. The availability of precision power tools has enhanced the abilities of both the hobbyist and the professional trades person. Faster saw-blade revolutions remove wood more evenly, lighter tool-casing materials reduce fatigue, and ergonomic grips make woodworking more comfortable.

How-to-books from *Reader's Digest*, Sunset Publishers, *Popular Mechanics*, and Time Life have had a large impact on the number of people who engage in woodworking as a leisure pursuit. These books made woodworking easier to understand because they provided step-by step instructions, detailed explanations, photographs, shop drawings, and measurements, thus making projects almost foolproof. Projects outlined in these books range from simple birdhouses and footstools to complex storage buildings, patios, and decks. Later, television shows such as *This Old House* and *New Yankee Workshop* encouraged woodworkers and further increased their participation and spending. It is estimated that 14.5 million viewers watch these television shows each week.

Modern woodworkers are upscale, work in fine woods, and are eager to find quality tools. In 1997, woodworkers spent $315 million on hand tools and another $1.5 billion on power tools. In 1998, the *New York Times* reported woodworking purchases have created a $14 billion industry. The article also indicated approximately 19 million people participated in woodworking, with the average hobbyist being a forty-five-year-old male (84 percent) with sixteen years of experience and an average household income of $100,000.

See also: Hobbies and Crafts, Men's Leisure Lifestyles

BIBLIOGRPAHY

Bridenbaugh, Carl. *The Colonial Craftsman.* New York: Dover Publications, 1990.

Hindle, Brooke. *America's Wooden Age: Aspects of Its Early Technology.* Tarrytown, New York: Sleepy Hollow Restorations, 1975.

Langsner, Drew. *Country Woodcraft.* Emmaus, Pa.: Rodale Press, 1978.

Norwak, Mary. *Kitchen Antiques.* New York: Praeger Publishers, 1975.

Nutting, Wallace. *Furniture of the Pilgrim Century.* New York: Dover Publications, 1965.

Russell, Ruth. *Pastimes: The Context of Contemporary Leisure.* Dubuque, Iowa: Brown and Benchmark, 1996.

"Woodworking Unplugged." *New York Times,* 23 July 1998.

Kevin Riley

WORK AND LEISURE ETHICS

An examination of work and leisure ethics in the United States of America reveals some shared similarities with other countries, particularly Canada and Western Europe, and some peculiarities and differences unique to the American condition. While there is arguably a mass culture in the United States that has its own identifiable values and attitudes, there is no monolithic ethic toward work and leisure shared by all Americans. Instead, the attitudes and values of Americans regarding work and leisure are both evolutionary and elusive: they have and continue to change with time and place, mirroring the country and experiences that spawned them. Any examination of the current state of American attitudes toward work and leisure will necessarily be rooted in attempts to understand this evolution.

A Brief History of Work and Leisure Ethics

The ethics associated with work and leisure in the United States are derivative of a number of influences, including Old World traditions, emerging religious values, the constraints and barriers imposed by the need for labor, the appearance of new technologies, and the varied natural and cultural environments found on the North American continent. A good starting point for evaluating American attitudes toward work and leisure, and the inherent conflicts found in these attitudes, is to examine traditional folk wisdom found in common sayings popular in the United States. "The devil makes work for idle hands" and "the early bird gets the worm" both seem to encourage industriousness and caution against excess free time. In contrast, "all work and no play make Jack a dull boy," and "the family that plays together stays together" both appear to point out the developmental value and essential nature of leisure. Taken together, these aphorisms point out the dissonance that exists in the American psyche regarding these concepts. Further, many of the old popular American warnings against leisure and idleness have even older precedents such as the German maxim "Idleness is the beginning of all vice". Similar, and older, maxims are found in other European languages, and in Hebrew and Arabic, all revealing the Old World origins of many notions commonly assumed to be American.

As Professor Serena Arnold and others have pointed out, even the etymological origins of the words leisure and recreation may have something to do with the way Americans think of these concepts. Leisure comes from the Old French *leisir,* which comes from the Latin word *licere,* meaning "to be permitted." In contrast, recreation comes from the Latin root *creare,* meaning "to create or make;" adding a prefix renders *recreo,* inferring restoration or creating anew. Similarly, the root form of the word recreation is related to other modern English words with generally positive connotations, such as *"creative "* and "Creator."

Conversely, the term leisure continues to connote wastefulness and sloth. Thus, as inferred from American connotations, recreation has social value and is compatible with work, while leisure stands in contrast to work and creativity, and is perhaps even antagonistic toward it. This is reflected in the overwhelming trend in the United States to use the term recreation, almost to the exclusion of the term leisure, in the naming of valued institutions and agencies: park and recreation departments, recreational sports leagues, and military MWR (Morale, Welfare and Recreation) provide many examples of this preference in nomenclature.

These intertwined and sometimes inscrutable American attitudes are not new. While much has been said about the disdain early European-American colonists held for leisure, in fact leisure in the colonies was valued, and had social meanings which are often misunderstood outside of their historical context. While the Puritans of the Massachusetts Bay Colony are famously remembered as taciturn advocates of a work-centered lifestyle, the values they placed upon recreation and play are largely forgotten. Leisure that was synonymous with sloth was eschewed, however the same Psalm Book of 1640 that proffered famous sayings against idleness was also a source of popular songs, and while some physical activity, such as dance, may have been looked down upon, singing was promoted. In fact, leisure time was valued in the early New England colonies as an opportunity for rest, commonality, family and community bonding, and proper courting.

Nevertheless, the Puritans also remain the typical starting point for discussions on religion's role in shaping New World values toward work and leisure. Within

that discussion, no phrase has been bandied about more than "Protestant work ethic," Max Weber's term referring to the social sanctioning of hard work and material wealth, and the avoidance of immediate pleasures. In this work ethic, seen by Weber as descendant from Calvinist theology, labor was seen as an act of piety and discipline, a means to transform the world from wild to civilized, from the secular to the sacred.

Of course, Weber's observations about American work ethics are also complementary with wholly secular views embraced by the young country, such as John Locke's labor theory of private property, which was and is very influential in American social philosophy and law. In part, Locke's theory holds that one's labor is the one thing that is unequivocally one's own possession, and that "mixing" this labor with the material world, such as is done by tilling land, is a means of bringing the external world under one's ownership. The synergy created through the combination of these Lockean political notions and the spiritual zeitgeist Weber attempted to describe was undoubtedly one of the powerful determinants in the formulation of early American pro-work attitudes.

Further, these emerging attitudes toward work (and leisure) were very different depending on what part of the United States one was describing. Indeed, some contemporaries find it surprising that the southern colonies were more liberal than their northern counterparts when it came to leisure and social mores. Card games, horse racing, shooting contests, wrestling and liquor consumption all were widespread leisure activities in the old south, while these pursuits were more likely to be seen by their northern counterparts as corporeal pleasures to be avoided.

As Americans pushed westward, these regional distinctions moved with them and evolved as new conventions and distinctions in culture, speech, and leisure behavior emerged. Alexis de Toqueville noticed that these cultural differences were perpetuated in the newer northern and southern states "separated by the Ohio River." The famous student of early America claimed that he observed a distinct social predisposition to indolence and sloth on his left (in Kentucky) and to industry and ingenuity to his right (in Ohio) as he traveled downstream on the river that connected the original colonies to their burgeoning western frontier.

Work and leisure values continued to change as Americans settled the frontier West. In fact, the expansion itself helped define a national purpose to work toward what many believed to be their "manifest destiny" which was to expand the United States to the Pacific. When the frontier line disappeared in the 1890s, it resulted in a sort of "psychic crisis" as noted by Roderick Nash in his classic book *Wilderness and the American Mind*. Aside from the romantic west being important to Americans as a mythic symbol of individualism, this loss of new territories generated a kind of national ennui, as the motivating force for work and growth seemed to evaporate along with the availability of new lands to conquer and develop.

Long after the actual frontier disappeared though, life among the relatively large rural population continued to have a strong influence on a young America. It provided an environment for a type of leisure ethic that was grounded in natural time and the passing of seasons, as well as a setting where real work was strongly tied to domestic life and everyday concerns. The Jeffersonian ideal of the yeoman farmer, the quintessential American citizen, was predicated on this living arrangement. Discovery and exploration were built in to the experiences associated with traditional rural recreation choices, such as camping, fishing, swimming, walking, and hunting. Community life was often centered around work experiences and confronting the hardships of everyday living.

The increased urbanization of the industrial revolution changed these experiences, and attitudes changed with them. Migration to the cities brought with it alienated work and new social ills, and reformers such as Jacob Riis and Jane Addams helped propel a new vision for leisure time: recreation as an instrument of social welfare, and play as an essential developmental opportunity for young people. The creation of the modern city was, paradoxically, the cradle of the burgeoning modern park movement. A combination of poor conditions for children's play and the perceived loss of the American wilderness helped spawn the several social movements of the late nineteenth century that changed American attitudes toward leisure and public lands. These included the park and open space movement, the muscular Christianity movement, and the playground movement.

A twentieth century that saw two world wars and continued urbanization was also a time where a newer and stronger national identity emerged, gender roles and expectations changed, time became increasingly seen as a commodity, and work and leisure moved further toward separation and compartmentalization. With the increased presence of women in the workplace, women and men began to interact in new social milieus, and co-ed sports and recreational leagues became not only acceptable, but increasingly appropriate places to meet others.

One of the biggest influences on American life in the twentieth century was the explosion of automobile ownership. Automobiles, in addition to providing increased potential for long distance personal travel, helped to define new attitudes toward privacy, the everyday experience of time, and even the physical design and evolution of communities. The American car became a symbol of freedom and personal identity, and its acquisition and mastery a modern rite of passage so important that, in some communities, it became the gateway to continued adolescent development and economic independence. The internal environment of the car has only continued to evolve as mobile living space, replete with a full menu of entertainment options and personal comfort features.

Many scholars regard the post-World War II era, especially the late 1950s through the mid 1960s, as the golden age of recreation and leisure. During this era, recreation became widely institutionalized in communities and universities, favorable legislation was passed by the eighty-ninth Congress, federally sanctioned research was conducted by groups such as the Outdoor Recreation Resources Review Commission (ORRRC), the work week continued to shorten, and vacation time increased. Many futurists of the time believed that a utopia of less labor, readily available commodities, and unlimited leisure was on the near horizon. Such beliefs led to serious discussions about the possibility of the end of work, and of leisure as a critical social issue.

Work and Leisure in the Early 2000s

Contemporary American values toward recreation and leisure run the gamut. Americans in the beginning of the twenty-first century saw leisure from a multitude of perspectives that were both simultaneous and juxtaposed. Leisure is a reward for work, leisure is a symbol of social status, leisure is just free time, leisure is corrupting, leisure is the *summum bonum* (greatest good) of life: all were held as true by Americans in 2004. Fears concerning leisure continued to be recurring themes in American thought. The possibility of ennui and anomie associated with free time were still held out as things to guard against, while others feared that leisure was elusive and would never be theirs. Recreation, though a synonym for leisure to some, was seen as an antidote to it by others. Programs such as "midnight basketball," which, depending on which American one spoke with, had become either well-known or notorious as publicly subsidized activities.

American attitudes toward subsidy itself are complex. While not all Americans view leisure as a commodity, it is clear that many do, and that a large number do not see it as a commodity that deserves widespread support with the public's treasure. The sense that the public needs to "pay to play" has started to replace the late-nineteenth- and twentieth-century notions that leisure was a public good that deserved subsidy. In the 1990s into the early 2000s, municipal departments scaled back operations, state and federal recreation agencies were perennially underfunded, and public and private nonprofit providers routinely raised fees and charges, all being essentially tolerated by the majority of the politically active public.

Work and leisure in many ways remain highly segmented in American culture. It has been said that "work is work, and leisure is leisure, and never the twain shall meet." This is readily observable in the fixed intervals commonly set aside for leisure: the weekend, the yearly vacation, summer camp, and official holidays. And while Americans prize their vacation time, they have fewer total days and large blocks of vacation time available than do many of their peers in other highly developed nations. In lieu of long or frequent vacations, Americans look toward federal holidays, switched in 1971 to Monday celebrations, to transform a number of traditional weekly breaks into three-day blocks. These three-day weekends have become prized times that help to punctuate the regular calendar for many Americans.

While the compartmentalization of leisure and work is clear, and its availability in smaller blocks also seems self-evident, there is an ongoing debate over whether these are good or bad developments. Juliet Schor's book *The Overworked American* stormed the early 1990s with a dystopian vision of the triumph of work over leisure, despite the promise of a coming golden age and the widespread availability of both necessities and laborsaving devices. Other scholars, such as Robinson and Godbey, later suggested that Schor's thesis was flawed, and that instead of having less time, more time was actually available in the many smaller blocks created by modern lifestyles.

Indeed, it remains unclear whether phenomena such as "home officing" and other work-away strategies, coupled with a myriad of smaller blocks of time will help society realize more leisure time or less. And the profusion of electronic technologies that have made all of these things possible have also made isolation, quiet, solitude, and complete separation from work an unknown for many contemporary Americans. It may be that what was once a dream, the seamless fusion of work and leisure experiences, may be realized as a curse of the modern age for some.

And when Americans do get free time, and despite the centrality of leisure in many Americans' lives, the duty of work can still trump the autonomy of leisure. On one hand, an individual's choice to participate in leisure time pursuits can still limit one's potential in the workplace, while on the other, forced leisure (for example, mandatory attendance for business socials, and the need to play for the company softball team) is still an expectation associated

with some work environments. Corporate interests have even co-opted outdoor pursuits and exercise as they look toward recreation as a tool to build group cohesion and identity, reduce stress, and promote general wellness.

Amidst all this was an odd and emerging social trend in twenty-first century America: the radical anti-work movement. Not to be confused with right-to-work or livable wage movements, or advocacy for better, more meaningful work, this movement was highly antagonistic toward the entire prospect of traditional labor arrangements. Oftentimes tongue-in-cheek, occasionally serious, the movement was spearheaded by young adults who felt disenchanted with both their current jobs and their future prospects. The movie *Office Space* was both a cult favorite and rallying cry, while organizations such as the now-defunct Leisure Party and the West Coast group CLAWS (Creating Livable Alternatives to Wage Slavery) were formed, and slogans such as "F**K WORK" made it to print; all palpable elements of the movement's sentiments.

The pursuits Americans indulge in also reveal an amazing complexity of interests and values. While it is true that nonconsumptive outdoor pursuits, such as birding and backpacking, are on the rise, and while the number of nimrods is decreasing and anglers are encouraged to engage in "catch and release" practices, hunting and fishing are still staples of outdoor recreation, especially in regions such as the Midwest, the South, and the Mountain West. While not in the mainstream, real blood sports such as cock fighting persist into the new millennium in some parts of the country. And in the years after the American people were confronted with the dangers associated with poor diet, substance abuse, and unsafe sexual practices, so-called "purple" or taboo leisure remained popular across all social and economic classes.

The Puritans, who are so often seen as exemplars of America's early moralism, would also be gratified to see that recreation, religion, and spirituality are still very much intertwined. With more than 90 percent of Americans professing some type of religious belief or spiritual orientation, churches and other institutions remain powerful arbiters of what constitutes good and bad in terms of work and leisure for many citizens. Aside from attendance itself continuing to be a principal form of recreation for many Americans, modern church recreation has emerged as a youth-retention tool, and an alternative to more worldly temptations. The Church of Jesus Christ of Latter Day Saints is an example of one religious group that actively promotes family leisure time, outdoor recreation, and play, as contributors to personal and community wellness. Many large contemporary Protestant churches, notably Methodist and Baptist congregations in the south, offer very active recreation programs that rival the scope and scale of municipal agencies.

It could be said that there is a new and healthy skepticism toward perceived views of work and leisure. Post-9/11 America experienced something of a return to home-centered leisure and church attendance, paired with a new introspection about life and priorities. But, again paradoxically, alongside the new skepticism is a new antinomianism (the belief that moral laws are relative in meaning and application as opposed to fixed or universal). While the 1980s saw a fitness craze, the late 1990s and early 2000s saw a decrease in health club memberships coupled with an increase in obesity. Gluttony, substance abuse, and promiscuity all established themselves as continuing favorites on the American leisure menu.

But perhaps no area of contemporary leisure is as prominent, pervasive, and preeminent as sport in American society. At every level, sport is a social and economic powerhouse, with a nearly singular capacity to draw crowds and shift priorities. Called the new gladiators by some, there is a clear emphasis on watching, which was prefigured by several generations in Jay B. Nash's writings on "spectatoritis." While this emphasis is widely condemned, scholars such as Gibson, Willming, and Holdnak have observed that modern sport spectatorship provides for an important source of meaningful community and group identity that is not easily substituted for in the mass culture. Beyond all other leisure forms, sport does help to define American mass culture, a mass culture where community is transitory, fragile, and available for consumption.

The mass culture is not the only American culture however, and its values and priorities are not universal. The Amish are an example of an insular culture in which leisure and work are valued and not highly segmented, and where a pious mindfulness can be tolerant of adolescent experimentation. Work and leisure experiences have also been different for African Americans, Native Americans, Hispanic Americans, Appalachians, and many other subcultures. It is important to remember that the attitudes, values, and ethics that emerge from these experiences can be different, too.

It could also be said that the coexistence of so many different perspectives toward work and leisure define both America and the postmodern age. Tradition, innovation, controversy, and consensus coexist as Americans picnic, skydive, cock fight, and play sports. Americans participate together and separately, openly and alongside each other, and in privacy or even secrecy. There is, in a sense, a return to regionalism, both literally and metaphorically.

When one searched for early twenty-first century American attitudes toward work and leisure, what was found was a pastiche of moral, political, spiritual, and aesthetic orientations. Neo-puritanism coexisted with hedonism; there were still Americans promoting a leisure-centered society, just as there were still "workaholics." Many 1980s-style yuppies (a term that comes from the phrase "Young Upwardly-mobile Person") merely morphed into more hip and contemporary twenty-first century BOBOs (Bourgeois Bohemians). In short, when looking for definitive American attitudes, values, and ethics toward work and leisure, what one sees may depend on who is looking.

See also: Blood Sports; Leisure, Theory of; Puritans at Leisure; Southern America Leisure Lifestyles; Vacations

BIBLIOGRAPHY

Arnold, Serena. "The Dilemma of Meaning." In *Issues in an Era of Change.* Edited by Thomas Goodale and Peter Witt. State College, Pa: Venture Publishing, Inc., 1991.

Bammel, Gene, and Lei Lane Burrus-Bammel. *Leisure and Human Behavior.* 2nd ed. Dubuque, Iowa: Wm. C. Brown Publishers, 1992.

Batteau, Alan. *The Invention of Appalachia.* Tucson: The University of Arizona Press, 1990.

Brooks, David. *BOBOs in Paradise: The New Upper Class and How They Got There.* New York: Simon and Schuster, 2001.

CLAWS (Creating Livable Alternatives to Wage Slavery) Web Site. Home page at http://www.whywork.org.

Cross, Gary. *A Social History of Leisure Since 1600.* State College, Pa: Venture Publishing, Inc., 1988.

de Grazia, Sebastian. *Of Time, Work, and Leisure.* Garden City, N.Y.: The Twentieth Century Fund, Inc., 1962.

de Tocqueville, Alexis. *Democracy in America.* New York: P.F. Collier and Son, 1900 (1835).

Garner, Richard T., and Andrew Oldenquist. *Society and the Individual: Readings in Political and Social Philosophy.* Belmont, Calif.: Wadsworth Publishing Company, 1990.

Gibson, Heather, Cynthia Willming, and Andrew Holdnak. "We're Gators . . . Not Just Gator Fans: Serious Leisure and University of Florida Football." *Journal of Leisure Research* 34, no. 4 (2002): 397–425.

Godbey, Geoffrey. *Leisure in Your Life.* 4th ed. State College, Pa: Venture Publishing, 1994.

Goodale, Thomas, and Geoffrey Godbey. *The Evolution of Leisure.* State College, Pa: Venture Publishing, Inc., 1988.

Hemingway, J. L. "Leisure, Social Capital, and Democratic Citizenship." *Journal of Leisure Research* 31, no. 2 (1999): 150–165.

Jessup, Harvey M. *The Hopeful Traveler Jay Bryan Nash.* Waldorf, Md: AAHPERD Publications, 1980.

Kelly, John R., and Valeria J. Freysinger. *21st Century Leisure: Current Issues.* Boston: Allyn and Bacon, 2000.

Kraus, R. *Leisure in a Changing America: Multicultural Perspectives.* New York: Macmillan College Publishing Company, 1994.

MacCannell, Dean. *The Tourist: A New Theory of the Leisure Class.* New York: Schocken Books, 1976.

Nash, Roderick Frazier. *Wilderness and The American Mind.* New Haven, Conn: Yale University Press, 1967.

Paulson, Amanda. "Fun at the Firm: The Role of Play at Work." *Christian Science Monitor,* 94, Issue 17 (2001): p.16ff.

Roberts, Kristin, and Peter Rupert. "A The Myth of the Overworked American." *Economic Commentary.* (15 January 1995).

Robinson, John P., and Geoffrey Godbey. *Time for Life: The Surprising Ways Americans Use Their Time.* University Park: The Penn State University Press, 1997.

Rybczynski, Witold. *Waiting for the Weekend.* New York: Viking, 1991.

Sanford, John. "U.S. Culture's Focus on Work Leaves Americans in a Quandary Over Leisure Time." *Stanford Report.* (19 February 2002).

Sarnoff, Susan. "Central Appalachia: Still the Other America." Journal of Poverty 7, no. 2 (2003): 123–139.

Schor, Juliet B. *The Overworked American: The Unexpected Decline of Leisure.* New York: Basic Books, 1991.

Stormann, Wayne F. "The Death of the Olmstedian Vision of Public Space." *Journal of Leisure Research* 32, no. 1 (2000): 166–170.

Sylvester, Charles. "The Ethics of Play, Leisure, and Recreation in the Twentieth Century, 1900–1983." *Leisure Sciences* 9 (1987): 173–188.

———. "The Western Idea of Work and Leisure: Traditions, Transformations, and the Future." In *Leisure Studies: Prospects for the Twenty-First Century.* Edited by Edgar L. Jackson and Thomas L. Burton. State College, Pa: Venture Publishing, Inc., 1999.

Veblen, Thorstein. *The Theory of the Leisure Class.* New York: The Viking Press, 1945 (1899).

Ziegler, Earle F. *An Introduction to Sport and Physical Education Philosophy.* Carmel, Ind.: Benchmark Press, Inc., 1989.

Zuefle, David Matthew. "The Spirituality of Recreation." *Park and Recreation* (September 1999): 28ff.

David Matthew Zuefle

WORKING-CLASS LEISURE LIFESTYLES

Wage earning Americans have developed distinct patterns of leisure, reflecting the character and conditions of their work and their income. Between 1870 and 1920, the urban population of the nation increased from less than 10 million to 54 million people. Male and female, immigrant and native laborers, often worked long, arduous hours at their factory jobs. It was not uncommon for skilled craftsmen, factory operatives, and common unskilled laborers to work six days a week for ten or more hours per day. Despite the heavy drudgery of industrial wage labor, workers' per capita income and free time gradually increased. In their demands for "eight hours for what we will" and a living wage, working men and women were not only seeking a reasonable work week and commensurate pay, they were demanding some measure of control over their lives, which had increasingly been dominated by their employer's needs and demands. In a world that defined their worth by hours labored, the working poor wished for a time and space that belonged solely to them, a realm separate and distinct from their role as wage earners. They found this space in their leisure time and in their recreational activities. Inevitably, however, their working lives, and the industrial social order that surrounded them, had a tremendous impact upon the kinds of recreations they chose.

In the nineteenth century, middle class notions of respectability were based on the separation of public and private spheres. While men were encouraged to participate in the public sphere, women were expected to protect the sanctity of the private sphere or the home. Both men and women viewed the home as a sanctuary, where the turbulent forces of industrial life were kept at a safe distance. Unlike their middle-class counterparts who stressed the importance of the private sphere, working-class men and women chose to spend almost all of their free time in public spaces. Escaping the cramped, uncomfortable quarters of the tenements and boarding houses, they flocked to street corners, saloons, ethnic churches, and public parks to seek solace and amusement. In the early decades of industrialization, the laboring poor engaged in largely non-commercial activities which were homosocial or segregated by gender (as opposed to heterosocial interaction where men and women mingle). While young boys loitered on street corners and stoops, most working class men congregated in local bars and saloons reserved for men of a certain neighborhood or ethnicity. According to one cultural historian, by 1884 there were more than 3,500 saloons in Chicago alone. By the turn of the twentieth century, many urban working class districts had at least one saloon for every fifty adult males.

The Saloon

Dubbed the "poor man's club," saloons were local institutions celebrating neighborhood ties and common ethnic backgrounds in an economy well on its way to the homogenizing effects of mass production and consumption. For the price of a drink, working men could use the public toilet, enjoy a free lunch, read the newspaper, pick up mail, and cash a check. In addition to meeting such practical needs, local saloons served as the keepers of working-class and ethnic culture. Rather than aid immigrant groups to conform to middle class values, saloons tended to cater to the communal aspirations of their clientele, thus conserving and reinforcing ethnic and class ties. Men often joined in song, treated each other to drinks, and pooled their money to buy a round of beer. Commenting on the social role of saloons, historian Roy Rosenzweig has suggested that treating others to a drink "implied resistance to individualism as well as acquisitiveness, because the ritual placed fraternal and communal needs over personal ones" (Kingsdale, p. 472, 489). In his study of Worcester, Massachusetts, Rosenzweig found that even in the absence of union activity, working-class men managed to create an alternative culture centered on their leisure time.

In contrast, middle class men and women often viewed leisure with measured suspicion for they were heavily influenced by notions of Protestant piety, Victorian respectability and the industrial work ethic. Reciprocal modes of social interaction, such as treating, may not have been oppositional, but they were certainly contrary to middle class values and to patterns of market exchange, which emphasized among other things, productivity, frugality, sobriety, and personal material gain.

With a little help from the saloonkeeper, workers created an all-male sub-culture separate from the demands of industry and the constraints of family. Yet, just outside the swinging double doors of the saloon, electric lamps lit the once dim city streets, inviting workingmen and women out of their homes, saloons, and workplaces and into a myriad of commercial recreations such as dance halls, theaters, and amusement parks. As their wages and free time increased, workers spent less time on their front stoops, at ethnic picnics and saloons, and more time in recreational pursuits independent from their local communities and ethnic groups.

Women, Heterosocial Spaces

Single working women were an early exception to homosocial patterns of leisure. (They are not predecessors: married women co-existed with single working women, but their experiences were dramatically different.) Unlike their mothers and married sisters, whose work hours seemed never-ending and who were by necessity confined to the tenements, urban women workers had a fixed workday. This meant that they could define the rest of the day, after work, as their own. Factory work may have been taxing, but it gave women access to a host of previously unattainable freedoms. As wage earners they had some discretionary income, as well as access to the city and its public spheres. Perhaps more importantly, factory work gave immigrant women access to a peer community outside the context of family and ethnicity. When the factory bell rang, single women would escape from work with entertainments such as dancing and theater. Increasingly, young women pooled their resources to create cooperative, mutually beneficial living arrangements in the city, away from parental supervision. Many American-born daughters still living with their immigrant parents bartered their wages for the freedom to come and go as they pleased. Historian Kathy Peiss asserts that "it was in leisure that women played with identity, trying on new images and roles, appropriating the cultural forms around them—clothing, music, language—to push at the boundaries of immigrant, working-class life"(p. 8). Dress, or "putting on style," was a favorite way to play with notions of respectability, independence, class, and identity In places like New York City, clothing shops offered women inexpensive versions of high fashion designs. Young women often went without food to spend what little they had on a feathered hat or a chinchilla coat.

In many ways, working women were actively challenging middle class definitions of femininity or "true womanhood," which emphasized domesticity, moral guardianship and sexual purity. Although by the late nineteenth century some bourgeois women ventured into the public sphere through their reform work and philanthropy, most middle class women were still guided by Victorian values, emphasizing the virtues of chastity and the primacy of motherhood and domesticity. For working women and those who paid attention to them, putting on style, promenading in the streets, and dancing in dance halls all seemed to fly in the face of middle-class notions of femininity and domesticity.

Nickelodeons

Middle-class reformers bemoaned what they saw as the physical and moral depravity in dance halls, amusement parks, and penny arcades. They worked hard to mitigate the social impact of these new urban forms of recreation. Nothing could prepare them, however, for perhaps the most influential form of working-class leisure: the nickelodeon. A descendant of penny arcades and vaudeville, the nickelodeon, also known as "the workingman's college," was a cheap form of entertainment accessible to those who spoke little or no English. For a nickel, working-class men, women, and children could attend a moving picture show, trade local gossip, hiss at villains on the screen, and accompany the piano player in a song or two. Nickelodeons represented what one historian has described as "an exhilarating, slightly scandalous break from routine. . .an act of almost pure hedonism—in the middle of the workday, where [they] certainly did not belong" (Nasaw, p. 164).

By 1910 there were more than 200 nickelodeons in Manhattan alone. A study of recreation found that approximately 75 percent of movie-goers in that period were working-class. Small store-front theaters could be found in most tenement districts. Their presence in local neighborhoods soon turned dime theaters into community gathering places. Many nickelodeons rented their rooms to local ethnic lodges, youth groups, and churches for meetings and dances. Like the saloons before them, nickelodeons were commercial spaces that often doubled as community resources. These new, inclusive spaces broadened the very definition of community. Unlike most saloons and vaudeville theaters, which actively catered to the ethnic make-up of the audience, movie theaters and nickelodeons welcomed immigrant men and women from all ethnic backgrounds.

Democratization of Leisure

Nickelodeons, dance halls, and other urban amusements were democratic arenas that unified white pleasure seekers regardless of gender, class, and national origin. These increasingly public commercial amusements began to draw "respectable" crowds. White-collar workers joined the audience as movie palaces with lobbies and balconies replaced the poorly-ventilated store-front nickelodeons. Theater owners and amusement entrepreneurs carefully created public spaces that were exciting enough to appeal to the masses, but respectable enough to draw in white-collar and middle-class crowds. Movie theaters began to occupy a cultural space just above the nickelodeon, yet more affordable than the live theater frequented by the upper class. The new films featured theatrical narratives that simultaneously appealed to the middle-class need for respectable entertainment and the working-class need for sensuousness and emotional release.

African Americans were a significant exception to this new "democratization of leisure." Blacks were often ridiculed and demonized in the amusement itself and were segregated or excluded from the general audience. Relegating African Americans to the category of "other" allowed European immigrants from all sorts of ethnic and class backgrounds to consider themselves "white." Exaggerating racial distinctions on stage and in the audience

distracted attention from social distinctions between "white" pleasure seekers. The exclusion and segregation of African Americans, however, certainly did not prevent them from having an impact on the landscape of American leisure.

In the years after emancipation, southern, agrarian, working- and lower-class African Americans from the Mississippi Delta region began developing a musical style called the blues. Rural music that captured the suffering and hopes of former slaves, tenant farmers, and workers, the blues originated from the field holler whose "call and response" style developed into work songs. As large numbers of African Americans migrated to northern cities like New York and Chicago, blues music gradually became an urban phenomenon. The impact of blues and jazz was especially apparent in the streets and dance halls of Harlem, New York, where the African American community was experiencing a cultural renaissance. Between the end of World War I and the Great Depression, New York City's Harlem district became the center of black cultural expression. Blues and jazz clubs popped up all over the city. Talented African American writers produced a sizable body of literature in the four prominent literary genres of poetry, fiction, drama, and essay. Americans grew familiar with the poetry of Langston Hughes and the novels of Zora Neale Hurston, but it was the music that was most infectious. In 1920, a New York vaudeville singer named Mamie Smith released "Crazy Blues," which quickly sold more than 1 million copies and launched the "race recording" industry; an industry that directly targeted African American audiences. The blues proved popular among a larger public as well, and blues recordings by Bessie Smith, Gertrude "Ma" Rainey, Louis Armstrong, Duke Ellington, and others became important parts of the musical landscape. Thus, despite their exclusion from the city's commercial amusements, African American writers, poets, artists, and musicians from Harlem and elsewhere contributed to the emerging urban landscape of leisure.

Americanization and Commercialization

By the 1930s, in urban centers around the country, there arose a new expressive urban culture steeped with working-class values and tastes. The needs and desires of working men and women played an important part in shaping the emerging mass culture. Yet the influence was not one directional: mass culture increasingly affected change among the working classes. As more and more workers participated in commercialized culture, they were less inclined to define themselves strictly in terms of class or ethnicity. Commercial leisure allowed immigrant workers to learn about American society outside of the context of work, resulting in the increased homogenization of the United States' working class. Yet the same cultural factors that produced homogenization also removed opportunities for communal thinking, promoting an individualistic existence through the mass culture of consumption. American workers increasingly defined themselves and others through consumer goods. Consumer culture offered a dominant ideology of individualism, privatism, and materialism that was at odds with the kinds of collective, communal ethics that had once characterized working-class leisure and recreation.

Post-World War II Privatization of Leisure

In the years during and after World War II, consumer culture began to permeate almost every aspect of leisure and recreation. During post-war reconversion, government agencies, big businesses, and unions embraced the idea that mass consumption would give all Americans a higher standard of living. Consumerism, it was believed, would result in a more prosperous and equitable nation. Despite inequalities in wealth, democracy could be ensured through equal access to the market. Like their union officials, many American workers became less interested in reducing work time and more interested in increasing their purchasing power. They were encouraged by manufacturers and businessmen who developed new strategies for fueling consumer demand through advertising, the extension of credit, and a cornucopia of mass-produced inexpensive products. The increase in consumer credit and the proliferation of installment plans (paying for a product in regular installments, where previously people had to pay for a product in full at the time of purchase) only fueled the fires of consumption. Historian Liz Cohen estimates that "the value of total consumer credit grew almost eleven-fold between 1945 and 1960, and installment credit—the major component of the total by the post war era—jumped a stunning nineteen-fold" (p. 125).

By the late 1950s, many Americans were actively participating in the buying frenzy of consumer culture and much of the spending centered around the home. Historian Elaine Tyler May observes that "in the five years after WWII, consumer spending increased 60 percent, but the amount spent on household furnishings and appliances rose 240 percent"(p. 165). More and more, Americans were living in the suburbs, driving automobiles, and watching a great deal of television. Although these cultural trends are often described as middle-class, a great number of working-class families were engaging in similar consumer behaviors. Increasing numbers of working-

class families were moving to low-income suburban homes. In 1961, 45 percent of all residents in the suburb of Levittown were blue-collar workers. By 1970, 82 percent of American families owned at least one car. By 1960, almost 90 percent of American households had at least one television set, with the average person watching approximately five hours each day.

Whether they were buying or renting homes, listening to the radio or watching television, American workers were spending more time at home and less time in public places. Attendance at movie theaters, sports stadiums, and downtown markets dramatically decreased. Ultimately, suburbanization, the decline of public transit due to automobiles, and the convenience and popularity of television made it more difficult for working-class audiences to reach downtown areas and theaters. The focal point of popular culture shifted away from public spaces and toward the privacy of single family homes. Home-centered entertainment such as video recordings, television, and radio discouraged collective communal forms of recreation and contributed to the privatization of working-class leisure.

In the last decades of the twentieth century, elements of working-class tastes and experiences could be found in everything from national television shows to the lyrics of popular music. Yet, many distinctive working-class leisure habits and sites which had once reinforced class identity were appropriated by mass culture, stripped of their dissention, and sold for a profit. Undeniably, working-class culture acquired a certain amount of cultural desirability. To be familiar with working class slang, music, and style was (and is) to have a certain amount of cultural capital. Yet this rarely translated into any kind of real political power and was hardly a strong foundation for working-class consciousness.

The privatization of leisure and the dominance of commercial recreation has continued well into the first part of the twenty-first century. In 2003, the Harris Poll asked a nationwide survey of 1,017 adults about their favorite leisure time activities. The poll found that "as in previous years, the largest numbers of people mention reading (24 percent), watching TV (17 percent) and spending time with the family and kids (17 percent) as their favorite leisure time activities" (Taylor, *The Harris Poll #72*). They also found that the median number of available leisure hours ("to relax, watch TV, take part in sports or hobbies, go swimming or skiing, go to the movies, theater, concerts, or other forms of entertainment, get together with friends") was estimated at nineteen hours. People participating in a similar poll in 1973 reported having significantly more leisure time (twenty-six hours). Although controversial, economists Juliet Schor's study of the "overworked American" found that people spent increasing number of hours at work in the last twenty years of the twentieth century, thereby reducing leisure time and reversing a hundred-year downward trend of hours spent on the job. Schor found that profit was the primary motive for the American worker's long hours. These studies, and others, show that the quality and quantity of working-class leisure has changed significantly over the past 100 years. Whether or not the trend of privatization will continue remains to be seen. One thing is certain, however: leisure and recreation continue to be an essential part of the American worker's identity.

See also: Bars; Civic Clubs, Men; Civic Clubs, Women; Expansion of Leisure; Leisure Class; Slave Singing/Music; Television's Impact on Youth and Children's Leisure

BIBLIOGRAPHY

Cohen, Lizabeth. *A Consumer's Republic: The Politics of Mass Consumption in Postwar America.* New York: Knopf, 2003.

Cross, Gary. *An All-Consuming Century: Why Commercialism Won in Modern America.* New York: Columbia University Press, 2000.

Kingsdale, Jon M. "The 'Poor Man's Club': Social Functions of the Urban Working-Class Saloon." *American Quarterly* 25, no.4 (October 1973): 472–489.

Lipsitz, George. *Rainbow at Midnight: Labor and Culture in the 1940s.* Urbana: University of Illinois Press, 1994.

McBee, Randy D. *Dance Hall Days: Intimacy and Leisure among Working-Class Immigrants in the United States.* New York: New York University Press, 2000.

Nasaw, David. *Going Out: The Rise and Fall of Public Amusements.* Cambridge. Mass.: Harvard University Press, 1993.

Oliver, Paul. *The Story of the Blues.* London: Barrie and Rockcliff, the Cresset P., 1969.

Peiss, Kathy. *Cheap Amusements: Working Women and Leisure in Turn-of-the-Century New York.* Philadelphia: Temple University Press, 1986.

Rosenzweig, Roy. *Eight Hours for What We Will: Workers and Leisure in an Industrial City, 1870–1920.* New York: Cambridge University Press, 1983.

Spiegel, Lynn. *Make Room for TV: Television and the Family Ideal in Postwar America.* Chicago: University of Chicago Press, 1992.

Schor, Juliet. *The Overworked American: The Unexpected Decline of Leisure.* New York: Basic Books, 1991.

Taylor, Humphrey, *The Harris Poll #72,* December 1, 2003. Available from http://www.harrisinteractive.com/.

Tyler May, Elaine. *Homeward Bound: American Families in the Cold War Era.* New York: Basic Books, 1988.

Aline Ohanesian

WORLD'S FAIRS

From the mid-nineteenth to the mid-twentieth century, world's fairs, sometimes called international expositions or exhibitions, helped define and change the meaning of leisure and recreation in the United States. Drawing inspiration from London's 1851 Crystal Palace Exhibition and the European fairs that followed in its wake, American fairs blended entertainment with education, fun with high-minded civic engagement, and mass consumption with America's nationalism. After World War II, with the proliferation of theme and amusement parks and with the rise of electronically mediated forms of mass entertainment through movies, television, video games, and the Internet, world's fairs seemingly lost relevance to postmodern life. But if Americans lost their fascination with these spectacles at the beginning of the twenty-first century, it is worth noting that people in other nations had not and that major universal expositions were being planned in Japan (2005) and China (2010).

Fairs of the Victorian Period

Anyone with knowledge of Charles Dickens's *Christmas Carol* can readily imagine the historical context that produced the first world's fair, London's fabled Crystal Palace Exhibition. By the midpoint of the nineteenth century, the Industrial Revolution had transformed England into a nation with a far-flung empire. At the same time, industrialization spawned population displacement, gross inequities of wealth, and pressures for social and political change that threatened established power relations. With thoughts in mind of the 1848 political revolutions in Europe and the Chartist movement in England, Queen Victoria's husband, Prince Albert, endorsed the idea of holding an international exposition that would feature the exhibits of the industrialized nations and impress the British public with England's position at the apex of "civilization." Housed in a building that looked like an enormous greenhouse, these displays attracted more than 6 million visitors and helped inspire confidence among England's middle classes in the future of England and its empire.

The success of the Crystal Palace captured the attention of a group of New Yorkers who raised private capital to organize the New York Crystal Palace Exhibition of 1853. It tanked. With tensions between the North and South on the increase, New York's exposition backers, who included newspaperman Horace Greeley and showman P. T. Barnum, failed to win backing from the federal government. Whether a federally funded fair in New

York might have helped Americans mend their sectional differences is an interesting question to contemplate, but the fact is that the United States went to war with itself between 1861 and 1865, and more than 600,000 Americans lost their lives as a result.

How could and should the American nation be reconstructed? This question led a number of influential politicians, business leaders, and scientists to look overseas for answers. What they saw mushrooming across Europe, in the aftermath of the Crystal Palace Exhibition, was a series of universal expositions that were explicitly intended to inspire national confidence and pride. In the early 1870s, civic leaders in Philadelphia approached Congress for support for an international exposition to be held in that city in 1876 to commemorate the anniversary of the American Revolution. With backing from the White House, Congress agreed to invest federal dollars in the enterprise. The outcome was the largest world's fair organized to date both in terms of acreage and scale of buildings.

Because the backers of the 1876 Philadelphia Centennial Exhibition saw their enterprise as a nation-building effort that would impart lessons about America's progress, civilization, and morality to the millions of visitors who came to the fair, exposition authorities made no room for popular entertainments. Indeed, when popular urban amusements, including inexpensive restaurants and prostitution, began to proliferate outside the fairgrounds, exposition authorities, citing the danger of fire, persuaded the city to destroy many of the buildings that had been given over to popular entertainments. In Philadelphia, the line between "high" and "low" culture was carved in stone.

At the next major American world's fair, the 1893 Chicago World's Columbian Exposition, thinking about the relationship between "high" and "low" forms of culture underwent an important shift. At the 1893 fair, exposition authorities, instead of expressing overt hostility to popular shows, actually embraced them as part of the exposition's educational mission and organized them along a mile-long avenue called the Midway Plaisance, which ran at a right angle to the main exposition grounds and was where one could find displays dedicated to "civilization."

What led to this change in thinking were several interconnected developments. First, the United States economy was unstable. A major depression in 1873 had triggered nationwide strikes, and these continued through the 1880s and 1890s. By the mid-1880s, a growing number of Americans were wondering aloud if the Civil War had only been the opening volley in a longer war that now seemed to involve not regions, but social classes. If world's fairs were to succeed in continuing the process of America's national reconstruction after a devastating civil war, a way had to be found to increase attendance and to educate visitors about the reasons they should be hopeful about America's future. Popular amusements provided that possibility. Second, Europeans, especially the French, who had been confronting mounting class warfare (the Paris Commune took place in 1871), had created new ways of joining education and entertainment through the medium of the world's fair. Around the base of the Eiffel Tower, which had been constructed for the 1889 Paris Universal Exposition, French exposition organizers had arranged a series of outdoor exhibits from French colonies that featured indigenous people from Africa, Asia, and the Middle East. Presented as "authentic" representations by leading French anthropologists, these living ethnological villages proved enormously popular and seemingly validated the need for the "civilized" nations to control "savages."

This lesson struck home in Chicago. Chicago's world's fair authorities placed the Midway Plaisance under the charge of prominent Harvard ethnologist Frederic W. Putnam. Midway shows featured villages of Africans, Asians, and Middle Easterners living in "authentic" settings in the shadow of the midway's (indeed the fair's) central icon, the enormous revolving wheel designed by engineer George Ferris in response to the tower erected that Gustavus Eiffel had designed for the 1889 Paris fair. Stretched out along the midway, so-called ethnological villages became outdoor demonstration lessons for social Darwinian ideas about the "progress" of human societies as they evolved from "savagery" to "civilization." As one visitor remarked when she passed under the railroad bridge that divided the midway from the main exposition palaces located on the main exposition grounds, "in what seemed like one step, you've passed out o' darkness and into light" (Burnham, p. 201).

The breakthrough that occurred at the 1893 fair was the growing realization by the fair's political, economic, and intellectual underwriters that lofty educational goals (introducing millions of people to racialized, social Darwinian ideas about the meaning of progress) could be fun and profitable. Because exposition managers had to worry about the fair's profitability, they appointed entrepreneur Sol Bloom as Putnam's assistant to oversee the money-making side of the midway. Bloom parlayed his success with shows that included risqué belly dancers and various mechanical amusements into a career that led him to Broadway and to a career in the U.S. Congress, where he contributed to founding the United Nations. Because of his and Putnam's efforts, never again would it be possi-

1933 World's Fair of Chicago. "A Century of Progress" served as the theme for the 1933 World's Fair in Chicago, which commemorated the 100th anniversary of the city. The fair officially opened on 27 May 1933 and ran through 31 October 1934; hundreds of concessions and exhibition buildings occupied 427 acres of land just south of the downtown area. This view of the fair was taken from the top of The Sky Ride that took passengers in enclosed cars up 218 feet between two 628-foot steel towers. © *AP/Wide World Photos*

ble to imagine a world's fair without a midway. Nevertheless, it is important to bear in mind that the layout of the Chicago fair, with the midway shows segregated from the main exposition palaces, still reflected some ambivalence about the relationship between culture and entertainment.

That ambivalence rapidly disappeared. At the 1904 St. Louis Louisiana Purchase Exposition, midway amusements, including ethnological shows, became part of the main exposition grounds. When the last of the Victorian-era fairs was held in San Francisco in 1915 to 1916, midway pleasures, including a heroic painting of a scantily clad woman with a mechanically driven rotating navel, had helped undermine many of the more repressive values of the American Victorians. Indeed, the commercialized amusements of the midways inspired the creation of

amusement parks, many of which featured mechanical rides that had first been introduced at world's fairs.

America's Depression-Era Fairs

Significantly, after World War I, many pundits declared world's fairs to be hopelessly out of date, believing that motion pictures and theme parks had rendered international expositions cultural dinosaurs. But just as America's Victorian fairs had been organized in response to the economic and political upheavals of its era, so America's fairs of the 1930s represented cultural responses to economic collapse, political tumult, and despair about the future.

With their modernistic and streamlined designs, Chicago's Century of Progress Exposition (1933–1934),

San Diego's California Pacific International Exposition (1935–1936), Dallas's Texas Centennial Exposition (1936), Cleveland's Great Lakes Exposition (1936), San Francisco's Golden Gate International Exposition (1939–1940), and New York's World's Fair (1939–1940) emphasized science and technology and mass consumption as solutions to depression-plagued America. Entertainment at the fairs, especially Sally Rand's famous fan dance at the Chicago exposition and numerous striptease shows at subsequent fairs, placed a "modern" stamp on these expositions and made the Victorian era seem a distant memory.

Three points need to be made about the entertainment and recreational possibilities of these fairs. First, the main pavilions dedicated to science, technology, and productive industries tried to make their exhibits fun. For instance, the Westinghouse exhibit featured a talking robot, while the General Motors Futurama exhibit included moving chairs that transported visitors into scenes that depicted an imaginary America in 1960. Second, as the depression continued, the fairs gave greater attention to becoming tourist destinations that would attract visitors from far distances and encourage them to spend their money, thus stimulating economic recovery. Third, like their Victorian forbears, the modernistic fairs of the 1930s still featured entertainments that explicitly demeaned different ethnic groups, especially African Americans, and people with physical disabilities, who were exhibited as "freaks."

American Fairs of the Space Age

World War II catapulted the United States out of the depression and into a decade of economic prosperity. The postwar years, however, were not without their share of anxieties about nuclear war and ecological disaster. In 1962, in response to the Soviet Union's successes in the space race, the U.S. government lent its support to a world's fair in Seattle that featured a Space Needle, a new monorail system, abundant science exhibits, and an adult show called Planet Eve that showcased topless women seducing men dressed as astronauts.

In 1964 to 1965, New York held another world's fair that celebrated the triumph of mass consumption and the potential of American mass culture to dominate the world. Like earlier fairs, the New York World's Fair relied heavily on corporate exhibitors, but the heavy involvement of the Walt Disney Corporation in planning exhibits reflected the prominence of theme parks in American life and hinted at a major challenge to the world's fair medium, namely how world's fairs, if they were seen primarily as sources of entertainment and

leisure, could compete with Disney and Disney-esque theme parks. It is ironic, to say the least, that Walt Disney's father had worked as a laborer at the 1893 Chicago fair and that this same fair had fired the imaginations of the entrepreneurs who made Coney Island America's first modern theme and amusement park—the very institution that would, by the middle of the twentieth century, threaten to render the world's fair medium obsolete.

The 1964 to 1965 New York World's Fair was the last major world's fair held in the United States. Smaller fairs in Fairbanks, Alaska (1967), San Antonio, Texas (1968), and Spokane, Washington (1974) sometimes had profound impacts on local economies, but never reached the scale of previous world's fairs. In the 1980s, fairs in Knoxville, Tennessee(1982), and New Orleans, Louisiana (1984), encountered serious financial problems. Then, when Chicago abandoned plans to host a fair in 1992 to celebrate Columbus's quincentennial, it seemed the world's fair bubble had burst—at least in the United States.

Predictions about the demise of the world's fairs, however, are nothing new. And, if the United States seems ambivalent about the medium, other nations continue to tumble over one another in the effort to secure recognition from the Bureau of International Expositions to hold world-class expositions. In 2005, Japan is hosting a major international exposition, and China is planning a universal-class exposition for 2010 that may either leave Americans smug about having abandoned their tradition of fairs or leave them wondering how to get back in the game.

Legacies

World's fairs are remembered as architectural laboratories (Louis Sullivan's Transportation Building at the 1893 Chicago fair), as showcases for inventions (television was introduced at the 1939 fair), and as supply lines for major museums (many of the Smithsonian Institution's artifacts are derived from world's fairs). However, they were also engines of mass culture and mass entertainment that helped make both central to America's national identity.

See also: City Parks; National Parks; Park Movements; State Parks; Theme and Amusement Parks; Urbanization of Leisure

BIBLIOGRAPHY

Brown, Julie K. *Contesting Images: Photography at the World's Columbian Exposition.* Tucson: University of Arizona Press, 1994.

Burnham, Clara Louisa. *Sweet Clover.* Chicago: Laird and Lee, 1893.

Findling, John E., and Kimberley D. Pelle, eds. *Historical Dictionary of World's Fairs and Expositions, 1851–1988.* New York: Greenwood Press, 1990.

Gilbert, James. *Perfect Cities: Chicago's Utopias of 1893.* Chicago: University of Chicago Press, 1991.

Greenhalgh, Paul. *Ephemeral Vistas: The Expositions Universelles, Great Exhibitions and World's Fairs, 1851–1939.* Manchester, U.K.: Manchester University Press, 1988.

Haddow, Robert H. *Pavilions of Plenty. Exhibiting American Culture Abroad in the 1950s.* Washington, D.C.: Smithsonian Institution Press, 1997.

Hoffenberg, Peter H. *An Empire on Display: English, Indian, and Australia Exhibitions from the Crystal Palace to the Great War.* Berkeley: University of California Press, 2001.

Rydell, Robert W. *All the World's a Fair: America's International Expositions, 1876–1916.* Chicago: University of Chicago Press, 1984.

———. *World of Fairs: The Century of Progress Expositions.* Chicago: University of Chicago Press, 1993.

Rydell, Robert W., and John E. Findling. *Fair America: World's Fairs in the United States.* Washington, D.C.: Smithsonian Institution Press, 2000.

Robert W. Rydell

WRESTLING, PROFESSIONAL

Professional wrestling's American roots reach back to the frontier tradition of itinerant grapplers who would travel alone or accompany minstrel shows and fairs, challenging all comers. Mark Twain drew the prototype in *Life on the Mississippi* in the fighter named "Sudden Death and General Desolation," whose boasting was nearly as effective as his strength in defeating his opponents. After 1900, wrestling moved to northern cities and became a popular spectator sport. These truly competitive matches could be long affairs, dominated by slow, defensive maneuvering that failed to hold fan interest, or they could end quickly in defeat. After a number of notable matches, including a 1909 Gotch-Hackenschmidt rematch in Chicago, which attracted some 40,000 spectators, legitimate wrestling went into decline as a professional sport.

In its place rose the modern variety of wrestling, characterized by exaggerated violence, theatrical conflicts, and outrageous characters. Early professional wrestlers sought to appeal to the urban immigrant working class of northern cities that composed the sport's base. Leading wrestlers of the 1920s included Irish Dan Mahoney,

Turkish-born Ali Baba, and Stan Zbyszko. Jim Londos (Christos Theophilou), the Golden Greek, reigned as the leading wrestler of the 1930s. After World War II, Killer Kowalski, Bruno Sammartino, and Antonio "Argentine" Rocca, who billed himself as both Hispanic and Italian by virtue of his Italian-Argentine heritage, continued the tradition of ethnic wrestlers.

The spread of television after World War II broadened professional wrestling's appeal. Wrestling was a staple of early television broadcasts, especially for smaller stations seeking cheap programming that could appeal to family audiences. In the early 1950s, Chicago stood as the center of professional wrestling, hosting nationally broadcasted wrestling cards on Wednesday and Saturday nights over the ABC and the now defunct Du Mont television networks.

Wrestling's burlesque antics, invisible on radio, were well suited to the new visual medium, and television promoted the stylized violence and outrageous characters that came to dominate the sport. The 1950s saw masked wrestlers such as Zuma, Man from Mars, and the Hooded Phantom, super patriots such as Mr. America, the thinly disguised homoerotic antics of "Gorgeous George" Wagner, who bleached his hair and disinfected the ring with perfume, and "Nature Boy" Buddy Rogers, who inspired the 1980s and 1990s wrestler Ric Flair. German and Japanese wrestlers enraged a public still seething with resentments from World War II, while Soviet wrestlers provided the new Cold War villains.

As professional wrestling's popularity grew with the television boom in the early 1950s, it also moved south. The sport initially migrated below the Mason-Dixon line in the 1930s when wrestlers like the German-born Milo Steinborn toured the region's leading cities, becoming especially popular in the Southeast. In the 1950s, regional promotions such as Jim Crockett's Charlotte-based National Wrestling Alliance (NWA) attracted ever larger audiences and gave the "Mid-Atlantic" Carolinas-Virginia circuit the reputation as "the hotbed of professional wrestling." Gulf Coast Championship Wrestling, operated by Dick Steinborn, son of Milo Steinborn, promoted wrestling in Alabama and Florida. Other leading promotions centered in western Tennessee, especially Memphis, and Texas. By the early 1960s, professional wrestling's popularity had declined in the North as more respectable mainstream sports, notably professional football, gained larger followings. Conversely, wrestling's popularity increased in the South, which still lacked a base of major-league professional franchises.

Like other loosely organized itinerant entertainment industries such as circuses and carnivals, the wrestling

"Stone Cold" Steve Austin. One of the World Wrestling Federation's (name changed to World Wrestling Entertainment Inc. in 2002) most popular stars, "Stone Cold" Steve Austin, shows off his championship belt at Wrestlemania XV in Philadelphia, Pennsylvania, on 28 March 1999. He defeated Rocky "The Rock" Maivia (real name Dwayne Johnson), who has since gone on to star in such big-budget motion pictures as *The Scorpion King.* © *Duomo/Corbis*

business has been a close-knit, family-organized affair. A remarkable number of wrestlers and promoters are the second or third generation in the business. Edward Welch, a wrestler and promoter who died in 1996 at the age of seventy-one, was the son and nephew of pioneering southern wrestlers and promoters. Welch wrestled and later promoted in the South under the name Buddy Fuller. His sons, Robert and Ronald, continued the family business. Robert Welch was better known as Colonel Rob Parker, a manager who adopted the persona of a southern gentleman. Welch's nephew also wrestled under the name "Bunkhouse Buck." Father-son combinations have also abounded: Jerry and Jeff Jarrett, Dusty and Dustin Rhodes. Sibling combinations have been common, too: Jake "The Snake" Roberts and Sam Houston are brothers; their sister wrestled under the name Rockin'

Robin. Similarly, the brothers Lanny Poffo and "Macho Man" Randy Savage are the sons of wrestler Angelo Poffo.

The 1980s saw wrestling enjoy increasing national exposure for the first time since the early 1950s. Bolstered by the popularity of superstars such as Terry Bollea, an ex-bodybuilder and failed rock musician from Florida who wrestled as Hulk Hogan, professional wrestling rose to unprecedented levels of popularity. Hogan appeared in films and on television, and he even graced the cover of *Sports Illustrated.* Celebrities such as rock musician Cyndi Lauper and comedian Andy Kaufman embraced the sport for its seemingly naïve extravagance and stylized artifice. In 1985, professional wrestling returned to national network broadcast television for the first time since 1955, with the airing of *Saturday Night's Main Event* on NBC. The series of wrestling extravaganzas known as WrestleMania became national entertainment events.

The growth of new cable television outlets for the sport sparked a consolidation in the industry in the 1980s. Like the networks in the 1950s, cable TV programmers were attracted to wrestling as an inexpensive way to fill airtime. Seeing opportunities for growth in the sport on the new cable medium, wrestling impresario Vince McMahon, a second-generation wrestling promoter, expanded his World Wrestling Federation (WWF) out of its traditional base in the northeast. The WWF's roster of stars, including Hulk Hogan, along with its popular and profitable WrestleMania and TV pay-per-view programs, allowed McMahon to buy or drive out of business most of the smaller regional wrestling organizations. In 1984, McMahon moved his WWF into the South, purchasing a time slot on Ted Turner's Atlanta-based cable "superstation" WTBS. Personality conflicts between Turner and McMahon, as well as programming disagreements, prompted McMahon to sell his slot to Jim Crockett's NWA. The smaller NWA, however, was poorly prepared to compete with the WWF and was near bankruptcy by 1988. Turner, who needed programming to fill the airtime of his growing cable empire, purchased the NWA, renaming it World Championship Wrestling (WCW).

In the 1990s, Turner's Atlanta-based WCW and McMahon's WWF emerged as the reigning powers in wrestling, fueling an intense competition for ratings and fan dollars. In 1995, the WWF and WCW grossed $58.4 million and $48.1 million, respectively, on cable television pay-per-view programs alone. In 1999, retail sales of WWF merchandise alone exceeded $400 million. By 2001, with the WCW lagging behind the WWF in television ratings and ticket sales, McMahon purchased the WCW and, after losing a 2002 trademark lawsuit to the World

Wildlife Fund, shortly thereafter renamed the newly-combined enterprise World Wrestling Entertainment, or WWE.

Professional wrestling targets males, aged eighteen to fifty-four, although just over one-fifth of the sport's audience is under eighteen. While wrestling promoters are fond of pointing out that the sport appeals to a wide range of education and income groups, three-quarters of the sport's television viewers had only a high school education or less. While males are wrestling's target group, women have long composed a substantial portion of the sport's audience. The chief sponsors of early-televised wrestling were household appliance dealers who sought to reach an adult female audience. In 2004, 36 percent of wrestling's television audience was female.

Given the fickleness of its target audience and many competing entertainment alternatives, professional wrestling has consistently attempted to anticipate the next new thing, which has led—and undoubtedly will continue to lead—to ceaseless changes in personae (though not necessarily in personnel), and in marketing strategies and tactics.

See also: Boxing; Commercialization of Leisure; Crowds at Leisure

BIBLIOGRAPHY

Ball, Michael R. *Professional Wrestling as Ritual Drama in American Popular Culture.* Lewiston, New York: Edwin Mellen Press, 1990.

Kyriakoudes, Louis M. and Peter A. Coclanis, "'The Tennessee Test of Manhood': Professional Wrestling and Southern Cultural Stereotypes." In *The Sporting World of the Modern South.* Edited by Patrick B. Miller. Urbana: University of Illinois Press, 2002.

Leverette, Marc. *Professional Wrestling, the Myth, the Mat, and American Popular Culture.* Lewiston, New York: E. Mellen Press, 2003.

Mazer, Sharon. *Professional Wrestling: Sport and Spectacle.* Jackson: University Press of Mississippi, 1998.

Louis M. Kyriakoudes and Peter A. Coclanis

ZOOS

Though modern zoos are usually traced to Paris and London in the 1700s, it is difficult to determine exactly when the collecting and cataloging of "exotic" animals began. Certainly the ancient Egyptians, the Greeks, the Mesopotamians, the Indians, the Chinese, and the Romans all had animal collections that were displayed in various ways to selected persons. Some medieval kings had collections of animals, and these royal zoos continued through the 1700s. In the late 1700s, some animals were moved to Paris so scientists from the new Museum of Natural History could have access to living animals to study.

The Establishment of Modern Zoos

Nevertheless, the first modern zoo is generally recognized as that established in London's Regent's Park from the King's Royal Collection in about 1829. Shortly after that, other European cities began to establish zoos, and, in 1867, the first American zoo, in Philadelphia, was established. These zoos were interested only in displaying animals for the amusement of people. People then, as in the early 2000s, were most amused by animal behavior that resembled human behavior. Some zoos began with the establishment of zoological societies that had scientific and educational goals, but these lofty initial goals were almost always underfunded and less important than simple animal acquisition and display.

The Philadelphia Zoo was the inspiration of Dr. William Camac, a man active in Philadelphia's civic affairs and widely traveled in Europe, where he visited many zoos. In 1859, he founded a zoological society. In 1873, the zoo began acquiring animals for display, under the guidance of Frank Thompson. Herman Schwarzmann, an engineer, did the initial zoo design, heavily influenced by the London Zoo, in Fairmount Park, and the zoo opened in July 1874. It continued to add to its buildings and collection, focusing on being ready for the 1876 Centennial Exhibition Year. Special events like world's fairs and national exhibitions have often provided the impetus for building or expanding zoos or zoo collections.

The establishment of both the Washington, D.C. (National) Zoo and the Bronx Zoo was accomplished at the end of the nineteenth century. In Washington, the U.S. Congress in 1889 appointed a board to plan a zoological park. Sydney Langley, a member of that board and the secretary of the Smithsonian Institution, and William Hornaday, curator of Living Animals at the Smithsonian Museum, were instrumental in the development of the park in Rock Creek Park, a site about two miles from the White House. The Bronx Zoo was led in its establishment by well-known New Yorkers like Theodore Roosevelt and members of his sportsmen's club, Boone and Crockett. Madison Grant was instrumental in the initial creation of the buildings in South Bronx Park and in the raising of funds from some of the most prominent New Yorkers of the time, including John D. Rockefeller, Cornelius and William Vanderbilt, and William C. Whitney.

Other great American zoos were formed at about this time and into the 1900s, including the Lincoln Park Zoo in Chicago and the Saint Louis Zoo, both located in large

San Diego Zoo. Dr. Harry Wegeforth established the San Diego Zoo in 1916. Elephants have been part of the collection since 1923. © *Gerald French/Corbis*

parks in the middle of the city, a pattern later emulated by zoos in Boston, Pittsburgh, Denver, Los Angeles, San Francisco, and San Diego, among others.

Attracting Visitors and Generating Revenue

The attraction of zoos was initially the opportunity to see animals, but in order for zoos to thrive, people had to continue to visit. When the Philadelphia Zoo first opened, it drew 200,000 visitors per year, and that number spiked to nearly 700,000 during the Centennial Exhibition in 1876. It then began to fall and bottomed out at 152,000 during the Great Depression. The loss of visitors meant a loss of revenue (only two great American zoos charge no admission—the Washington National Zoo and the Lincoln Park Zoo in Chicago). The revenue was directly connected to operating expenses, so zoos needed to attract return visitors regularly. That meant that there had to be new, more modern displays and buildings on a regular basis, as well as events that attracted people. These events included greater educational programs, docent-led tours, after-hours events for members, outreach programs, and other special events.

Initially, animals were displayed in cages, most of which were too small to allow the animals room to take more than a few steps in any direction. The "advantage" was that the cages were close enough for people to observe the animals. Most of the times the animals were not lively; in fact, caged behavior can usually be characterized by one of two words—morose or neurotic. Animals were often lethargic or pacing back and forth. This behavior was unhealthy for them and uninteresting for viewers, so the next display advancement was the building of pits for animals. These pits allowed viewers better sight lines, provided more room for animals, and allowed the animals to be displayed outdoors. Of course, warm weather animals were back in their connected indoor cages during winter months. Two changes since the 1980s further improved the viewing as well as the health of the animals. First, some zoos in the early 2000s used very thin but strong metals to build cages for those animals that could not be contained in pits or were able to escape from other types of enclosures. The other display advancement was the creation of more natural settings, where a number of species of animals are displayed in a habitat, such as a grassland or a marshland. More realistic displays were the result, though predator and prey are not displayed together, for obvious reasons. Zoo designers needed a much greater amount of land to create these natural settings; thus, a number of zoos relocated to spaces outside their cities, where land was less expensive and more widely available. The Milwaukee, Minnesota, and Toronto Zoos are three good examples of this change. A drawback to natural-setting displays is that the animals have room to "hide" or be less visible because of the limited viewer sites around the large display areas. Still, natural-setting displays allow zoo visitors to view animals interacting with other species and having the opportunity to run and romp.

Moving zoos out of their center-city locations creates transportation concerns. In many cases, visitors must depend upon their automobile to reach the sites, but a few zoos provide public transportation. In one noted instance—the Audubon Zoo in New Orleans—the transportation is almost as interesting as the zoo. The zoo is located in Audubon Park on the banks of the Mississippi River, and a zoo boat travels back and forth on the river from the downtown area to the zoo. In addition, the old trolley line with its wooden cars travels down St. Charles Street to the edge of Audubon Park, providing visitors with another alternative to automobiles.

Deciding what exactly to display is another issue for zoos. Some large American zoos have tried to take a "comprehensive" approach in displaying most of the well-known animals in the world. Zoos like the Bronx, National, San Diego, and Brookfield (outside Chicago) see this approach as part of their mission in a large urban area. Thus, these zoos built new areas for animals of tropical Asia or Australian habitats. Other zoos created unique niches for themselves, making their displays unrivaled. Two good examples are the Arizona Sonora Desert Museum outside Tucson and the Audubon Zoo in New Orleans. The former has animals of the desert arranged by climate, including a hummingbird aviary unlike any other. The latter has a Louisiana Swamp exhibit that draws on the unique ecosystem of the region. The display includes white alligators found in a Louisiana swamp. Though not geographically unique, the Cincinnati Zoo created a niche through its insectarium, unique to the United States but modeled on similar exhibits in some Asian zoos and since copied by some other North American zoos.

As indicated earlier, only two of the large American zoos are free. The entry fees are another issue relating to both attracting visitors and generating revenues. With entry fees running from $6 to $12 per person, a visit to the zoo can quickly become expensive for a family. Some zoos have days with reduced fees, which allow people with lower incomes to enjoy the facility. The funding of zoos has become more and more difficult as their mission has become more complex and expensive. The upkeep of a zoo is enormous; there are costs for animal care, zoo maintenance, and salaries of personnel. Fees generate only a small part of necessary monies. Most zoos are under the aegis of zoological societies, which often are related to the government in some manner. The park is usually kept up by the respective government entity while the zoological society offers memberships and sponsors various fund-raising events to support the zoo's missions. Large donors to the zoo often will sponsor an exhibit or aid in the purchase of some animals from another zoo.

Acquiring and Breeding Animals

The acquisition of animals has changed greatly since zoos first began in the United States. In the early parts of the twentieth-century zoos would requisition hunters to acquire zoo animals. Their methods were often unscientific and cruel. With many animals threatened or endangered in 2004, almost all zoo animals were acquired in one of two ways—either from other zoos or through breeding. Much of the breeding or trading of animals was under the auspices of the American Association of Zoological Parks and Aquariums (AAZPA) and/or the International Union of Directors of Zoological Gardens. The International Zoo Yearbook, published annually since 1960 by the Zoological Society of London, provides information on animal husbandry and management and the best methods of displaying various species. Breeding books are kept of almost all animal species in order to provide for the greatest diversity in the gene pool and to ensure that there is no inbreeding, which can increase the likelihood of diseases and defects.

The concern about inbreeding is but one of the ethical questions surrounding the idea of zoos. The biggest question, perhaps, is: Should zoos exist at all? Some individuals believe that the capture and incarceration of other species is unethical. At one time this was more of an issue, but in 2004, with the loss of habitat of many species because of human encroachment, there were a number of species that might not exist if not for zoos and other managed "wild" habitats.

Still, the breeding of animals, to some, seems wholly manipulative and unethical, but once animals are in zoos, there are few, if any, other opportunities for species perpetuation. Breeding is stressful to animals; they must be transported to other locations, then become acclimated to their new environments and, finally, to their new prospective mates. Some of the other ethical questions surrounding the breeding of animals include whether animals should be bred if their numbers are very small and their natural habitats nonexistent; whether animals bred in zoos should be reintroduced to the wild, and, if so, how; and what should happen to animals that reproduce to such an extent in zoos that there are no places to situate them.

There are also ethical questions regarding the notion of "good stewardship." How does one define a "good zoo" and who develops that definition? What are acceptable standards for the maintenance and welfare of animals in captivity? To what extent, if any, should captive animals be subject to experimentation? How should zoos explain the plight of endangered animals without becoming overly political? What is a "humane" way to display animals? There are not simple answers for these questions, and they continue to drive the dynamic of zoo construction and renovation. Many of these issues also relate to the earlier issue of funding, especially when much of the funding is publicly supported or generated.

Zoological Parks and American Cities

American zoos in the early 2000s included more than fifty outstanding zoological parks. Many cities view having a renowned zoo as a reflection of civic pride and progress. Almost all zoos had to make choices about how they would distinguish themselves from their brethren. As noted, the biggest zoos in the biggest cities often chose to have comprehensive animal exhibits. These great zoos include the Bronx Zoo in New York City, the National Zoo in Washington, D.C., the San Diego Zoo in Balboa Park (and its larger, wild animal enclosure in Escondido, thirty miles north), the Brookfield Zoo in suburban Chicago, the Philadelphia Zoo, the St. Louis Zoo (made famous by its director, Marlin Perkins, and the first zoo television show, *Zoo Parade*), the Miami Zoo, the Denver Zoo, the Los Angeles Zoo, and the Atlanta Zoo (which was once on the brink of ruin but rebounded through civic efforts since the 1980s).

A number of smaller cities created large zoos, often in areas just outside the city, and had many of the "popular" wild animals, but they also created unique exhibits and displayed their animals in large, multispecies displays. These include the Milwaukee Zoo, the Minnesota Zoo in Apple Valley, outside the Twin Cities of Minneapolis, the Pittsburgh Zoo, the Phoenix Zoo, the

Tacoma Zoo, the Portland Zoo (known for its successful elephant breeding), and the New Orleans Zoo.

Zoos have become an important attraction for many cities, but they also have turned into the last bastions of a number of endangered species. Though zoos are ostensibly for animal welfare, they were designed initially for, and continue to function largely for, human pleasure. At one time, animals that exhibited humanlike behaviors were more popular as people anthropomorphized the animal actions, but at the turn of the century, the greater educational programs of zoos, their more informative display placards, and the greatest exposure of animal species through various media made many other species popular with human visitors. Most zoos provide small children's zoos within the larger environs, where children may pet farm animals or other, more docile animals. Picnic areas are available in the parks, and many zoos have some sort of people mover, which provides better access for those with mobility limitations, as well as provides a guided overview of the parks.

See also: Circuses, City Parks, Disneyland, National Parks, Park Movements, Walt Disney World

BIBLIOGRAPHY

Baratay, Eric, and Elisabeth Hardouin-Fugier. *Zoo: A History of Zoological Gardens in the West.* Translated by Oliver Welsh. London: Reaktion Books, 2002.

Hancock, David. *A Different Nature: The Paradoxical World of Zoos and Their Uncertain Future.* Berkeley: University of California Press, 2001.

Hanson, Elizabeth. *Animal Attractions: Nature on Display in American Zoos.* Princeton, N.J.: Princeton University Press, 2002.

Kisling, Vernon N., Jr., ed. *Zoo and Aquarium History: Ancient Animal Collections to Zoological Gardens.* Boca Raton, La.: CRC Press, 2000.

Norton, Bryan G., Michael Hutchins, Elizabeth Stevens, and Terry Maple, eds. *Ethics on the Ark: Zoos, Animal Welfare, and Wildlife Conservation.* Washington, D.C.: Smithsonian Institution Press, 1995.

Rothfels, Nigel. *Savages and Beasts: The Birth of the Modern Zoo.* Baltimore: Johns Hopkins University Press, 2002.

Zuckerman, Lord. *Great Zoos of the World: Their Origins and Significance.* Boulder, Colo.: Westview Press, 1980.

Murry R. Nelson

Systematic Outline of Contents

This outline shows the conceptual framework of the *Encyclopedia of Recreation and Leisure in America*. It directs readers to entries associated with broad areas of interest. Entries are grouped under seven major categories with twenty-six subcategories.

1. Social Development of Leisure in America
2. Processes: Impact of Technologies
    Means of Transportation
    Media Technologies
3. Trends
    Institutionalization of Leisure and Recreation
4. People—Identities, Interactions, and Institutions
    Age and Ethnic Leisure Styles
    Class-Based Leisure Lifestyles
    Disability
    Gendered Leisure Lifestyles
    Leisure and Civil Society
    Regional Leisure Lifestyles
5. Ceremonial Occasions
    Rites of Passage
    Civil, Social, and Religious Occasions
6. Leisure Sites
    Fairs
    Parks
    Social Sites
    Special Sites
7. Leisure Activities, Past and Present
    Arts, Primary and Secondary Participation

Contemporary Patterns of Participation
Controversial Personal Pastimes
Cooking, Cuisine, Dining, and Drinking
Courtship Activities
Crafts, Collecting, and Hobbies
Gaming and Gambling Activities
Miscellaneous Personal Pastimes
Outdoor Pursuits
Personal Pastimes
Primary and Secondary Sport Participation

Each entry appears only once in this outline. Use the cross-references that appear at the end of each article for a more complete view of its interrelationships.

I. SOCIAL DEVELOPMENT OF LEISURE IN AMERICA

Colonial-Era Leisure and Recreation
Contemporary Leisure Patterns
Early National Leisure and Recreation
Gilded Age Leisure and Recreation
Interwar Leisure and Recreation
Postwar to 1980 Leisure and Recreation
Progressive-Era Leisure and Recreation
Puritans at Leisure

2. PROCESSES: IMPACT OF TECHNOLOGIES

Means of Transportation
Air Travel and Leisure
Automobiles and Leisure
Railroads and Leisure
Recreational Vehicles
Sea Travel and Leisure

Media Technologies
Computer's Impact on Leisure
Media, Technology, and Leisure
Movies' Impact on Popular Leisure
Television's Impact on Popular Leisure
Television's Impact on Youth and Children's Play

3. TRENDS

Institutionalization of Leisure and Recreation
Body Culture and Physical Culture
Children's Museums
Commercialization of Children's Play
Commercialization of Leisure
Crowds and Leisure
Expansion of Leisure Time
Globalization of American Leisure
Impresarios of Leisure, Rise of
Leisure Education
Leisure, Theory of
Literary Societies and Middlebrow Reading

Honeymooning
Hook-ups

Crafts, Collecting, and Hobbies
Amateur Radio
Antiques
Books and Manuscripts
Clocks and Watches
Coin Collecting
Collecting
Comic Magazines
Crossword Puzzles
Gardening and Lawn Care
Historical Reenactment Societies
Hobbies and Crafts
Home Decoration
Home Improvement
Modeling (Airplanes, Trains, etc.)
Photography
Quilting Parties
Rockhounding
Sporting Memorabilia
Stamp Collecting
Woodworking

Gaming and Gambling Activities
Board Games
Card Games
Computer/Video Games
Drinking Games
Gambling

Miscellaneous Personal Pastimes
Auctions
Auto Shows
Barn Raising
Beauty Culture
Beauty Pageants
Cruising
Fads
Fans and Fan Clubs
Fantasy Sports

Fashions
Frolics
Garage and Yard Sales
Graphic Arts
Internet
Joking
Mumming
Pet Care
Plantation Entertaining
Reunions
Shopping

Outdoor Pursuits
Backpacking and Hiking
Bicycling
Bird Watching
Boating, Power
Camping
Caving
Fishing, Freshwater
Fishing, Saltwater/Deep Sea
Hunting
Kite Flying
Mountain Climbing
Orienteering
Rock Climbing
Scuba Diving/Snorkeling
Whitewater Sports

Primary and Secondary Sport Participation
Aerobic Exercise
Archery
Auto Racing
Baseball, Amateur
Baseball Crowds
Basketball
Billiards/Pool
Blood Sports
Bodybuilding
Bowling

Boxing
Darts
Drag Racing
Extreme Sports
Field Hockey
Football
Football, Collegiate
Golf
Gymnastics
Handball
Horse Racing
Ice Hockey
Little League
Marathons
Martial Arts
Olympics
Open Wheel Racing
Racquetball
Rodeos
Roller Skating and Blading
Running and Jogging
Sailing and Yachting
Skateboarding
Skiing, Alpine
Skiing, Nordic
Snowboarding
Soccer
Softball
Sports Car Racing
Stock Car Racing
Surfing
Swimming
Target Shooting
Tennis
Tobogganing
Triathlons
Ultimate Frisbee
Volleyball
Waterskiing
Windsurfing
Wrestling, Professional

Directory of Contributors

Vernon Lee Andrews
University of Canterbury
  African American Leisure Lifestyles

David L. Andrews
University of Maryland
  Soccer

Robert Arlt
  Darts

Cindy S. Aron
University of Virginia
  Summer Resorts

Martha Barnes
University of Waterloo
  Philanthropy

Robert K. Barney
University of Western Ontario
  Olympics

Rebecca E. Barry
Arizona State University
  Choral Singing

Becky Beal
University of the Pacific
  Skateboarding

Russell Belk
University of Utah
  Collecting

Megan Bentan
Pacific Lutheran University
  Books and Manuscripts

Kendall Blanchard
Fort Lewis College, Durango
  Native American Leisure Lifestyles

Nicholas Bloom
New York Institute of Technology
  Suburbanization of Leisure

Anne Bolin
Elon University
  Bodybuilding

Douglas Booth
University of Waikato
  Surfing

Charlene Boyer Lewis
Kalamazoo College
  Plantation Entertaining

Simon Bronner
Pennsylvania State University
  Barn Raising
  Traditional Folk Music Festivals

Steven C. Bullock
Worcester Polytechnic Institute>
  Civic Clubs, Men

John Burnham
Ohio State University
  Gambling

Robert C. Burns
University of Florida
  Open Wheel Racing
  Sports Car Racing

Richard Butsch
Rider University
  Crowds at Leisure

Jennifer D. Carson
Clemson University
  Disability and Leisure Lifestyles

Daniel Cavicchi
Rhode Island School of Design
  Fans and Fan Clubs

Kelly Chandler
Kent State University
  Computer's Impact on Leisure
  Tennis

Ariel Chernin
University of Pennsylvania
  Television's Impact on Youth and
    Children's Play

I-Tsun Chiang
*National Pingtung University of Science
and Technology*
  Martial Arts

Garry Chick
Pennsylvania State University
  Billiards/Pool
  Leisure and Civil Society
  Modeling (Airplanes, Trains, Etc.)
  Rites of Passage

Peter A. Coclanis
University of North Carolina
  Wrestling, Professional

Kenneth Cohen
University of Delaware
Frolics

Carrie J. Cole
University of Maryland
Amateur Theatrics

John J. Confer
University of Florida
State Parks

Daniel Thomas Cook
University of Illinois
Commercialization of Leisure

Lila Corwin Berman
Yale University
Jewish-American Leisure Lifestyles

David R. Counts
Professor Emeritus, McMaster University
Recreational Vehicles

Dorothy Ayers Counts
Professor Emeritus, University of Waterloo
Recreational Vehicles

Diana Crane
University of Pennsylvania
Fashions

Scott A.G.M. Crawford
Eastern Illinois University
Skiing, Alpine
Skiing, Nordic

Gary Cross
Pennsylvania State University
Atlantic City
Home Improvement
Privatization of Leisure
Walt Disney World

Bruce C. Daniels
Texas Tech University
Blood Sports
Puritans at Leisure

Elissa David
George Washington University
Clocks and Watches
Drag Racing
Hot Rodding

Dennis K. Davis
Pennsylvania State University
Television's Impact on Popular
Leisure

Janet Davis
University of Texas
Circuses

T. Jason Davis
East Tennessee State University
Stock Car Racing

Jim Denison
University of Exeter
Running and Jogging

Matthew Dennis
University of Oregon
Parades

Gregory Dimitriadis
State University of New York, Buffalo
Rap Music Audiences

Jon Griffin Donlon
Center for Cultural Resources
Brothels
Fads
Prostitution

Peter Donnelly
University of Toronto
Mountain Climbing
Rock Climbing

Perry R. Duis
University of Illinois at Chicago
Tourism

Jill Dupont
University of North Texas
Boxing

Mark Dyreson
Pennsylvania State University
Patriotism and Leisure

Herbert B. Ershkowitz
Temple University
Shopping

Paula S. Fass
University of California at Berkeley
Dating

Philip F. Xie
Bowling Green State University
Childhood and Play
Field Hockey
Kite Flying

Eric Frauman
Middle Tennessee State University
Ultimate Frisbee

Jessica Freame
University of Melbourne
Botanical Gardens

Patti A. Freeman
Brigham Young University
Rodeos

Michael Friedman
University of Maryland
Baseball, Amateur

Joe L. Frost
Professor Emeritus, University of Texas
Playgrounds

Gerald R. Gems
North Central College
Football

Troy D. Glover
University of Illinois
Raves/Raving

George Gmelch
Union College
Baseball Crowds

Geof Godbey
Pennsylvania State University
Contemporary Leisure Patterns

Marni Goldenberg
California Polytechnic State University
Snowboarding

Douglas Gomery
University of Maryland
Media, Technology, and Leisure

Edwin Gómez
Old Dominion University
Latinos Leisure Lifestyles

Mark Gottdiener
State University of New York, Buffalo
Air Travel and Leisure
Las Vegas

Andrew Grainger
University of Maryland
Ice Hockey

Jane Granskog
California State University
Triathlons

Harvey Green
Northeastern University
Body Culture and Physical Culture

Katherine C. Grier
University of South Carolina
Home Decoration
Pet Care

Ann Marie Guilmette
Brock University
Joking

Jawaid Haider
Pennsylvania State University
Children's Museums

456

W. Scott Haine
University of Maryland
Coffee Houses and Café Society

Charles Hammersley
Northern Arizona University
Whitewater Sports

Judith Lynne Hanna
University of Maryland
Dance Classes
Performing Arts Audiences
Social Dancing

Sarah E. Hardin
Southeast Missouri State University
Bowling

James Harding
Union College
Cruising

Kristen Haring
Max Planck Institute for the History of Science
Amateur Radio

Laurlyn K. Harmon
Pennsylvania State University
Tailgating

Caitlin Haskell
Auctions

Danny Hedrick
East Tennessee State University
Stock Car Racing

John L. Hemingway
Western Illinois University
Leisure, Theory of

Rob Hess
Victoria University
Bicycling

Linda A. Heyne
Ithaca College
Central Park

Matthew Hilton
University of Birmingham
Smoking

Louis Hodges
Texas A&M University
Card Games
Coin Collecting
National Parks

Benjamin T. Hoffiz
Lawrence Technological University
Muslim-American Leisure Lifestyles

David Gerard Hogan
Heidelberg College
Fast Food

Richard Hummel
Eastern Illinois University
Hunting

Benjamin Kline Hunnicutt
University of Iowa
Expansion of Leisure Time
Interwar Leisure and Recreation
Shortage of Leisure
Vacations

Amy R. Hurd
Illinois State University
Board Games

Andrew Hurley
University of Missouri–St. Louis
Diners

Patricia Iamon
SUNY College at Brockport
Historical Reenactment Societies

Alan Ingham
Miami University
Professionalization of Sport

David Ingle
Recreational Fighting

William Irwin
Author, The New Niagara
Niagara Falls

Lisa Jacobson
University of California, Santa Barbara
Teenage Leisure Trends

Katherine Jellison
Ohio University
Weddings

Virginia Scott Jenkins
Author, The Lawn: A History of an American Obsession
Gardening and Lawn Care

Philip Jenkins
Pennsylvania State University
Pornography

Per Jorgensen
University of Southern Denmark
Volleyball

Valerie M. Joyce
University of Maryland
Mumming

Annemarie Jutel
Otago Polytechnic
Beauty Culture

Alexander Kahn
University at California, Berkeley
Band Playing

M. Alison Kibler
Franklin and Marshall College
Progressive-Era Leisure and Recreation

Margaret J. King
The Center for Cultural Studies and Analysis
Theme and Amusement Parks

Erik K.M. Kjeldsen
University of Massachusetts
Gymnastics

Stephen Kline
Simon Fraser University
Commercialization of Children's Play
Computer/Video Games

Sandra Wolf Klitzing
Illinois State University
Antiques

Anne Meis Knupfer
Purdue University
Civic Clubs, Women

Gerard Kyle
Clemson University
Agricultural Fairs

Louis M. Kyriakoudes
University of Southern Mississippi
Wrestling, Professional

Stephen Jay Langsner
University of Arkansas
Home Brewing

Katherine Lehman
University of New Mexico
Cyber Dating
Honeymooning
Hook-Ups
Reunions

Deborah Linebarger
University of Pennsylvania
Television's Impact on Youth and Children's Play

Ellen Litwicki
State University of New York, Fredonia
Fourth of July
Labor Day
Memorial Day

Jan Logemann
Pennsylvania State University
Home Improvement
Roller Skating and Blading
Sea World

Richard Longstreth
George Washington University
Shopping Malls

John W. Loy
Dean Emeritus, School of Physical Education, University of Otago
Sporting Memorabilia
Leisure and Civil Society
Leisure Class

Randy D. McBee
Texas Tech University
Dance Halls

Bryan P. McCormick
Indiana University
Adapted Leisure Formats

Alexis McCrossen
Southern Methodist University
Sabbatarianism

Marsha MacDowell
Michigan State University Museum
Quilting Parties

Philip McGowan
University of London
Carnivals

William D. McIntosh
Georgia Southern University
Comic Magazines

Margaret Mackey
University of Alberta
Children's Reading

David I. Macleod
Central Michigan University
"Muscular Christianity" and the
YM(W)CA Movements

William K. McNeil
Ozark Folk Center
Slave Singing/Music Making

Barry D. McPherson
Wilfrid Laurier University
Senior Leisure Lifestyles

John McWilliams
Pennsylvania State University, Dubois
Recreational Drug Use

Pirkko Markula
University of Exeter
Aerobic Exercise

William Marling
Case Western Reserve University
Globalization of American Leisure

Scott C. Martin
Bowling Green State University
Early National Leisure and Recreation

Kevin Mattson
Ohio University
Rock Concert Audiences

Mike Mayo
Host. Movie Show on Radio
Movies' Impact on Popular Leisure

Jay Mechling
University of California, Davis
Disneyland
Scouting Movements

Jill Vasquez Mills
Mount Olive College
Windsurfing

Glenn Moore
University of Melbourne
Botanical Gardens

Andrew J. Mowen
Pennsylvania State University
Auto Shows

David Myers
Loyola University
Fantasy Sports
Internet

Fred R. Nadis
Doshisha University
Gilded Age Leisure and Recreation

Heather S. Nathans
University of Maryland
Colonial-Era Leisure and Recreation
Theater, Live

Murry R. Nelson
Pennsylvania State University
Basketball
Zoos

Kevin A. Nelson
Western State College of Colorado
Square Dancing

James A. Newman
SUNY College at Brockport
Historical Reenactment Societies

Joshua I. Newman
University of Maryland
Football, Collegiate

Sarah Nicholls
Michigan State University
Home Movies

Aline Ohanesian
University of California, Irvine
Working-Class Leisure Lifestyles

Ray Oldenburg
Professor Emeritus, University of West Florida
Dining Out

Cele Otnes
University of Illinois
Birthdays
Christmas

Ted Ownby
University of Mississippi
Southern America Leisure
Lifestyles

Richard Panchyk
Cooking for Fun

Leslie Paris
University of British Columbia
Camping

Katharine A. Pawelko
Western Illinois University
Tobogganing

Diana Pecknold
University of Illinois at Chicago
Country Music Audiences

John R. Persing
Pennsylvania State University
Backpacking and Hiking
Wilding

Elizabeth H. Pleck
University of Illinois
Thanksgiving

Madelon Powers
University of New Orleans
Bars

Robert Proctor
Pennsylvania State University
Rockhounding

Caren Prommersberger
Cooking for Fun

Matthew Pustz
Kirkwood Community College
Comic Book Reading

Henry J. Rademacher
Pennsylvania State University
Railroads and Leisure

Paul Reddin
Mesa State College
Wild West Shows

Gerald Redmond
Professor Emeritus, University of Alberta
Golf
Sporting Halls of Fame

Woody Register
University of the South
Beaches
Coney Island

Kaitlyn Richards
Union College
Baseball Crowds

Steven A. Riess
Northeastern Illinois University
Men's Leisure Lifestyles
Stadiums

Kevin Riley
Appalachian State University
Graphic Arts
Woodworking

Robert E. Rinehart
Washington State University
Extreme Sports
Swimming

John P. Robinson
University of Maryland
Television's Impact on Popular
Leisure

Craig H. Roell
Georgia Southern University
Piano Playing

Nancy Brattain Rogers
Indiana State University
Adult Education (Earlier)

Don Romesburg
University of California, Berkeley
Gay Men's Leisure Lifestyles

W. J. Rorabaugh
University of Washington
Drinking

Kenneth D. Rose
California State University, Chico
Prohibition and Temperance

Ruth V. Russell
Indiana Universty
Boating, Power
Spring Breaks

Alexander Russo
Brown University
Radio Listening, Car and Home

Robert W. Rydell
Montana State University
World's Fairs

Daniel Sack
Associated Colleges of the Midwest
Church Socials

Diane M. Samdahl
University of Georgia
Lesbian Leisure Lifestyles

Kellen Sams
Green Mountain College
Snowboarding

Jack Santino
Bowling Green State University
Halloween
New Year's

Vinod Sasidharan
San Diego State University
Asian American Leisure Lifestyles

Jennifer Scanlon
Bowdoin College
Magazines, Women's
Women's Leisure Lifestyles

Abby Schlatter
Garage and Yard Sales
Softball

Barbara Elwood Schlatter
Illinois State University
Auto Racing

William R. Scott
University of California, Berkeley
Magazines, Men's

David Scott
Texas A&M University
Bird Watching

Kimberley J. Shinew
University of Illinois
Racial Diversity and Leisure
Lifestyles

Joshua A. Shuart
Sacred Heart University
Record, CD, Tape Collecting and
Listening

Kim L. Siegenthaler
Appalachian State University
Scuba Diving/Snorkeling
Waterskiing

Clare Simpson
Lincoln University
Bicycling

Erin A. Smith
University of Texas at Dallas
Genre Reading

J. Mark Souther
Cleveland State University
Urbanization of Leisure

John Springhall
University of Ulster at Coleraine
Impresarios of Leisure, Rise of

Peter N. Stearns
George Mason University
Regulation and Social Control of
Leisure

Robert A. Stebbins
University of Calgary
Hobbies and Crafts
Rational Recreation and Self-Im-
provement
Stamp Collecting

Tammie L. Stenger
Southeast Missouri State University
Bowling

Robert S. Stiefvater
North Carolina Central University
Drinking Games

Monika Stodolska
University of Illinois
Target Shooting

L. Allison Stringer
University of Northern Iowa
Wine Tasting

Hubert B. Stroud
Arkansas State University
Sun City

Anne-Marie Sullivan
Memorial University of Newfoundland
Leisure Education

Stacy Taniguchi
Brigham Young University
Western America Leisure Lifestyles

Dorceta E. Taylor
University of Michigan
Park Movements

James A. Therrell
Concordia University
Handball
Racquetball

Patricia M. Tice
Rochester Institute of Technology
Museum Movements

Cecelia Tichi
Vanderbilt University
    Postwar to 1980 Leisure and Recreation

Rachelle H. Toupence
University of Wisconsin–La Crosse
    Card Games
    Coin Collecting
    National Parks

Catherine Turner
College Misericordia
    Literary Societies and Middlebrow
    Reading

Edward Udd
Radford University
    City Parks

Lee Vander Velden
University of Maryland
    Horse Racing

Turgut Var
Texas A&M University
    Caving

Judith E. Voelkl
Clemson University
    Disability and Leisure Lifestyles

Rudi Volti
Pitzer College
    Automobiles and Leisure

John J. Weber
Eastern Illinois University
    Archery

James Weeks
    Easter
    Heritage Sites
    Marathons

Nancy Martha West
University of Missouri-Columbia
    Photography

Ryan E. White
University of Maryland
    Little League

Richard R. Wilk
Indiana University
    Beauty Pageants

Thomas Woodall
Professor Emeritus, Eastern Illinois University
    Barbershop Quartets

Sérgio Barcellos Ximenes
    Crossword Puzzles

Heewon Yang
Kent State University
    Computer's Impact on Leisure
    Tennis

Careen Yarnal
Pennsylvania State University
    Sailing and Yachting
    Sea Travel and Leisure

Daniel G. Yoder
Western Illinois University
    Fishing, Freshwater
    Fishing, Saltwater/Deep Sea
    Mardi Gras

David Matthew Zuefle
University of Mississippi
    Orienteering
    Work and Leisure Ethics

Index

Beach volleyball, 2:400, 402
Beaches, 1:**85–89,** 86
   Atlantic City, 1:33, 88
   bathing suits, 1:87, 88
   beauty pageants, 1:95
   California, 1:88
   "Christian retreats", 1:87
   Coney Island, 1:34, 87, 148,
      239–242, 240
   environmental issues, 1:88–89
   Florida, 1:86, 89
   Hawaii, 1:88
   spring break, 2:303–305
   suntan, 1:88
   windsurfing, 2:414, 422–423
Beadle, Irwin P., 1:399
Beadle and Adams, 1:397
Beadle's Dime Baseball Player, 1:399
Beanie Babies, 1:193
Bearbaiting, 1:106
Beard, Daniel Carter, 2:239
Beard, George, 1:117
Beard, James, 1:249
Beat generation, coffee houses, 1:188
Beatles, 2:223
Beauchamp, Johnny, 2:316
Beauty culture, 1:**89–93,** 90, 92
   See also Body culture and physical
      culture
Beauty magazines, 2:6
The Beauty Myth (Wolf), 1:90–91
Beauty pageants, 1:**93–95,** 94
Beck, Charles, 2:117
Beck, Martin, 1:398
Becker, Ernest, 1:197
Becker, Howard, 1:439
Becky Sharp (movie), 2:39
Bedford Springs (PA), 1:307
Beecher, Catherine E., 1:116, 445
Beecher, Henry Ward, 1:116
Beecher, Lyman, 1:116
Beer, 1:294, 443
Beer-making. See Home brewing
The Beggar's Opera (Gay), 1:203
Beisser, Arnold, 1:80
Belaying techniques, 2:218
Belk, Russell, 1:439
Belkaoui, Ahmed, 2:7
Belkaoui, Janice, 2:7
Bell, Phillip, 1:409
Bell, Roger, 1:409
Bell and Howell, 2:113
Bellagio (Las Vegas), 1:500
Bellamy, Edward, 2:124, 265
Belle Isle (MI), 1:155
Bellocq, Ernest J., 2:158
Belmont, Alva Vanderbilt, 1:512
Belmont Park, 1:453, 456
Belsnickling, 2:45, 88
Ben Hur, 1:396
Bend It Like Beckham (movie), 1:404
Benevolent and Protective Order of
   Elks, 1:181
Benjamin, Walter, 1:197
Bennett, Bruce, 2:331

Bennett, Garrett, 1:158
Bennett, James Gordon, Jr., 1:512;
   2:235, 236–237
Bennett, Lerone, Jr., 1:9
Bentley, William, 1:194
Berenson, Senda, 1:83
Berg, Patty, 1:411
Berger, Peter, 1:506
Bergoust, Eric, 2:273
Bergson, Henri Louis, 1:489
Berkeley Community Chorus,
   1:167–168
Berlin, Irving, 1:64
Berlin work, 1:445
Berners-Lee, Tim, 1:472
Berry, Chuck, 2:21
Berryman, Doris, 1:28, 30
Bertarelli, Ernesto, 1:513
Berto, Frank, 1:98
Bethel Historical and Literary
   Association, 1:530
Better Homes and Gardens (magazine),
   2:6
Betting, 1:373, 374
   See also Gambling
BFA. See Bicycle Federation of
   America
Bicycle Federation of America (BFA),
   1:99
Bicycle motocross machines. See BMX
   bikes
Bicycle touring, 1:96
Bicycling, 1:**95–100,** 96–100
   BMX bikes, 1:98, 100, 319
   cycle racing, 1:97
   cyclo-cross, 1:100
   organizations, 1:98–100
   Victorian mores and, 1:118
   by women, 1:96, 97
Big Boy Restaurants, 1:341
"Big-n-littles", 1:458
Big Six Conference (football), 1:363
The Big Sleep (Chandler), 2:121–122
Bill James Baseball Abstract, 1:331
Billfish (game fish), 1:349, 350
Billiard tables, 1:101, 102
Billiards/pool, 1:**101–102,** 102; 2:26
Binder, Paul, 1:177
Bingo, 1:379
Binion's (Las Vegas), 1:498
Biograph studio, 2:35, 36
Bird hunting, 1:463
Bird watching (birding), 1:**103**
The Birth of a Nation (movie), 1:402;
   2:37
Birth rites, 2:212
Birthday cards, 1:105
Birthday parties, 1:105
Birthdays, 1:**103–105,** 104
Bishop, Hazel, 1:90
Bishop, Jeff, 1:437–438
Bitter End Cafe, 1:188
The Bizarre (coffee house), 1:188
Black bottom (dance), 1:266
Black Cat Café, 1:390

Black church, recreation and, 1:10
Black-Connery Bill, 1:482
The Black Crook (musical), 1:397
Black Crook (show), 2:359
Black Entertainment Television, 2:19,
   21
Black Hat Cafe, 1:188
Black leisure lifestyles. See African
   American leisure lifestyles
Black Mask, 1:393
Blackboard Jungle (movie), 2:130, 222
Blackface, 2:277, 359, 387
   See also Minstrel shows
Blackheath, 1:344
Blacking Up: The Minstrel Show in
   Nineteenth-Century America (Toll),
   1:398
Blackjack (card game), 1:145
Blackpool Pleasure Beach, 1:407
"Blind pigs", 1:71
Blizzard Beach (water park), 2:408
Blood sports, 1:**105–108,** 106
Bloom, Sol, 2:440
Bloomer, Amelia, 1:97, 100
Bloomers, 1:97, 100
Bloomingdale's, 1:395
Blue jeans, history of, 1:333–334, 337
Blue Ribband, 2:245
Blue shark (game fish), 1:350
Bluefin tuna (game fish), 1:350
"Blues" (music), 2:437
"Blues notes", 1:137
Bly, Nellie, 1:396
BMX bikes, 1:98, 100, 319
B'nai Brith, 1:181, 485–486
Board games, 1:**108–112,** 109; 2:126,
   215
Boardsailing, 2:422
   See also Windsurfing
Boardwalk
   Atlantic City, 1:33
   Coney Island, 1:242
Boating, power, 1:**112–113**
Boats, freshwater fishing, 1:347
The Bobbsey Twins, 1:165, 166
Bobsled (bobsleigh), 2:368
Bodgan, Robert, 1:148
Body culture and physical culture,
   1:**113–120,** 114, 119
   athletic revival, 1:116–117
   counterculture and, 1:118–120
   history of, 1:113–118
   medical theory and, 1:114
   neurasthenia, 1:117–118
   obesity, 1:119
   religious and cultural context of,
      1:115
   sport and competition and,
      1:113–114
   warfare and, 1:113
   xenophobia, 1:117
   See also Beauty culture; Bodybuilding
Bodybuilding, 1:92, **120–123,** 121
   See also Body culture and physical
      culture

R